PENGUIN REFERENCE BOOKS

THE PENGUIN DICTIONARY OF QUOTATIONS

J. M. Cohen, born in London in 1903 and a Cambridge graduate, was the author of many Penguin translations, including versions of Cervantes, Rabelais and Montaigne. For some years he assisted E. V. Rieu in editing the Penguin Classics. He collected the three books of *Comic and Curious Verse* and anthologies of Latin American and Cuban writing. He frequently visited Spain and made several visits to Mexico, Cuba and other Spanish American countries. Towards the end of his life, though his vision was impaired, he continued to work and keep up with his favourite interests.

J. M. Cohen died in 1989. *The Times'* obituary described him as 'one of the last great English men of letters', while the *Independent* wrote that 'his influence will be felt for generations to come'.

His third son, M. J. Cohen, is an educational publisher who is married and has three daughters. He worked on the dictionary during most of his Cambridge vacations, in particular contributing quotations from drama and some seventeenth-century and modern writers. Both authors also collaborated on *The Penguin Dictionary of Modern Quotations*, the companion to this volume.

J. M. AND M. J. COHEN

THE PENGUIN DICTIONARY OF QUOTATIONS

*To fill up a work with these scraps may indeed,
be considered as a downright cheat on the learned world,
who are by such means imposed upon to buy a second
time in fragments and by retail, what they
have already in gross, if not in their
memories, upon their shelves.*

FIELDING: *Tom Jones*
Bk 12, Ch.1

Bloomsbury Books
London

PENGUIN BOOKS

Published by the Penguin Group
Penguin Books Ltd, 27 Wrights Lane, London W8 5TZ, England
Penguin Books USA Inc., 375 Hudson Street, New York, New York 10014, USA
Penguin Books Australia Ltd, Ringwood, Victoria, Australia
Penguin Books Canada Ltd, 10 Alcorn Avenue, Toronto, Ontario, Canada M4V 3B2
Penguin Books (NZ) Ltd, 182-190 Wairau Road, Auckland 10, New Zealand
Penguin Books Ltd, Registered Offices: Harmondsworth, Middlesex, England

First published in Great Britain by Penguin Books 1960
This edition published by Bloomsbury Books,
an imprint of Godfrey Cave Associates Ltd, 42 Bloomsbury Street, London WC1B 3QJ,
under licence from the Penguin Group, 1991
1 3 5 7 9 10 8 6 4 2

Printed in England by
BPCC Hazell Books
Aylesbury, Bucks, England
Member of BPCC Ltd

Set in Monotype Times

ISBN 1 85471 070 2

FOREWORD

A DICTIONARY OF QUOTATIONS MUST SERVE AT LEAST THREE PURPOSES. Its owner must be able to find, with the aid of the index, the speaker or writer responsible for a phrase that has stuck – or half-stuck – in his head, or for a reference found during his reading. His dictionary must guide him to the context, giving him, where possible, line and page references to some easily available edition. By use of the index too, he must be able to see what has been said on a particular subject by a variety of men; to turn up such key-words as *God, life, love, money, peace, war, word*, and *world* is to discover a babel of opinions, with one or more of which he may care to embellish his own writing or conversation at the proper moment. Direct use of the first section, moreover, arranged under alphabetical order of authors, will give him some of the outstanding statements made by the great, or by the not-so-great who have for some reason been remembered.

It is remarkable that it is not always those who are most read or respected who have left the greatest number of sayings in the popular memory. Samuel Butler the elder, for example, can have few readers today, yet his once universally quoted political satire *Hudibras* has enriched the language with a great number of almost proverbial maxims, many of which are included in the present book. Wilde and Shaw coined ready-made quotations as they wrote; Henry James and D. H. Lawrence, though at present even more

widely read, have left few phrases that are remembered. Single observations of theirs can seldom be detached from their context.

A large proportion of the quotations to be found here are necessary inclusions in any dictionary of quotations. The Bible, Shakespeare, *Paradise Lost*, and Boswell's *Life of Johnson* inevitably contribute a great number of pages. The compilers' free choice is limited to modern authors; and here they have to decide what will be read and quoted during the lifetime of their book. What to take from W. H. Auden, Christopher Fry, John Osborne, and Dylan Thomas; which, if any, of our present-day politicians will be remembered for anything at all; what newspaper, broadcasting, or advertising catchwords will last longer than the customary few months: these are problems which force them to take risks, at the price of possibly proving bad prophets.

Not only in the choice of modern authors, but also in the selection from writings in foreign languages, the present compilers have taken their own line. With the decline in the study of the Classics, it has seemed sensible to dispense with all quotations in the original Greek, and severely to limit the representation of Latin authors. On the other hand French is more adequately covered in this book than in most other dictionaries, and quite a few entries have been admitted in German. All foreign quotations are followed by a prose translation; and often, where the original does not stick in the English memory, the translation only is given. It would be pedantic, for instance, to print the very well-known sayings from *Don Quixote* in Spanish, since the book is invariably read in English.

Quotations are taken from the most readily available source; those from the Bible are, except when otherwise described taken from the Authorized Version; those from Shakespeare from the one-volume Oxford edition edited by W. J. Craig; those from the English poets from the Oxford Editions of Standard Authors; and those from the Latin from the Oxford Classical Texts. Line numbering invariably differs from edition to edition, particularly in Shakespeare, on account of the interpolated prose passages. Those possessing other editions therefore must be prepared to glance up and down the page.

The compilers hope that the book will prove easy to use. The index acts as a guide not only to the page on which the quotation is given, but to the number of that quotation on the page; and the indexing is, we hope, so thorough that the user will find the saying he wants by turning up any of the more striking words in it, that stick in his mind. Finally we hope that, in addition to its use as a reader's and writer's companion – and occasional aid in the solution of crossword puzzles – *The Penguin Dictionary of Quotations* will give some pleasure to those who browse in it.

J.M.C.   M.J.C.

In order to save space, lines of verse are run on and the divisions between lines are indicated by oblique strokes.

LUCIUS ACCIUS 170–c. 85 B.C.

1 *Oderint, dum metuant.* – Let them hate so long as they fear. [Quoted in Cicero's *Philippic*, I. 14]

LORD ACTON 1834–1902

2 Power tends to corrupt, and absolute power corrupts absolutely. Great men are almost always bad men. [*Historical Essays and Studies*, Appendix]

CHARLES FOLLEN ADAMS 1842–1918

3 I haf von funny leedle poy / Vot gomes schust to mine knee: / Der queerest schap, der createst rogue / As efer you dit see. [*Yawcob Strauss*]

F. P. ADAMS 1881–1960

4 The rich man has his motor car, / His country and his town estate. / He smokes a fifty-cent cigar / And jeers at Fate. [*The Rich Man*]

5 Yet though my lamp burns low and dim, / Though I must slave for livelihood – / Think you that I would change with him? / You bet I would! [*Ib.*]

JOHN QUINCY ADAMS 1767–1848

6 Think of your forefathers! Think of your posterity! [Speech, 22 Dec. 1802]

SAMUEL ADAMS 1722–1803

7 A nation of shopkeepers are very seldom so disinterested. [Speech said to have been made at Philadelphia, 1776]

SARAH FLOWER ADAMS 1805–1848

8 Nearer, my God, to Thee. [Hymn title]

JOSEPH ADDISON 1672–1719

9 And, pleased the Almighty's orders to perform, / Rides in the whirlwind, and directs the storm. [*The Campaign*, 291]

10 'Tis not in mortals to command success, / But we'll do more, Sempronius; we'll deserve it. [*Cato*, I. ii. 43]

11 And. if, the following day, he chance to find / A new repast, or an untasted spring, / Blesses his stars, and thinks it luxury. [*Ib.* I. iv. 68]

12 When love once pleads admission to our hearts, / In spite of all the virtue we can boast, / The woman that deliberates is lost. [*Ib.* IV. i. 29]

13 It must be so – Plato, thou reasonest well! – / Else whence this pleasing hope, this fond desire, / This longing after immortality? [*Ib.* V. i. 1]

14 'Tis heaven itself, that points out an hereafter, / And intimates eternity to man. / Eternity! thou pleasing, dreadful thought! [*Ib.* V. i. 8]

15 From hence, let fierce contending nations know / What dire effects from civil discord flow. [*Ib.* V. iv. 111]

16 For wheresoe'er I turn my ravished eyes, / Gay gilded scenes and shining prospects rise, / Poetic fields encompass me around, / And still I seem to tread on classic ground. [*Letter from Italy*]

17 Music, the greatest good that mortals know, / And all of heaven we have below. [*Song for St Cecilia's Day*]

18 Pray consider what a figure a man would make in the republic of letters. [*Ancient Medals*, i]

19 Thus I live in the world rather as a spectator of mankind than as one of the species. [*The Spectator*, 1]

20 Nothing is capable of being well set to music that is not nonsense. [*Ib.* 18]

21 A perfect tragedy is the noblest production of human nature. [*Ib.* 39]

1

1 In all thy humours, whether grave or mellow, / Thou'rt such a touchy, testy, pleasant fellow; / Hast so much wit, and mirth, and spleen about thee, / There is no living with thee nor without thee. [*The Spectator*, 68, adapted from Martial, xii. 47]

2 The infusion of a China plant sweetened with the pith of an Indian cane. [*Ib.* 69]

3 Sunday clears away the rust of the whole week. [*Ib.* 112]

4 Sir Roger told them, with the air of a man who would not give his judgement rashly, that much might be said on both sides. [*Ib.* 122]

5 I have often thought, says Sir Roger, it happens very well that Christmas should fall out in the middle of winter. [*Ib.* 269]

6 These widows, sir, are the most perverse creatures in the world. [*Ib.* 335]

7 This Mr Dryden calls 'the fairy way of writing'. [*Ib.* 419]

8 Through all Eternity to Thee / A joyful song I'll raise, / For oh! Eternity's too short / To utter all Thy praise. [*Ib.* 453]

9 We have in England a particular bashfulness in everything that regards religion. [*Ib.* 458]

10 The spacious firmament on high, / And all the blue ethereal sky, / And spangled heavens, a shining frame, / Their great Original proclaim. [*Ib.* 465, Ode]

11 Soon as the evening shades prevail, / The moon takes up the wondrous tale, / And nightly to the listening earth / Repeats the story of her birth:

Whilst all the stars that round her burn, / And all the planets, in their turn, / Confirm the tidings as they roll, / And spread the truth from pole to pole. [*Ib.*]

12 The Hand that made us is divine. [*Ib.*]

13 A woman seldom asks advice before she has bought her wedding clothes. [*Ib.* 475]

14 Our disputants put me in mind of the skuttle fish, that when he is unable to extricate himself, blackens all the water about him, till he becomes invisible. [*Ib.* 476]

15 I value my garden more for being full of blackbirds than of cherries, and very frankly give them fruit for their songs. [*Ib.* 477]

16 'We are always doing', says he, 'something for Posterity, but I would fain see Posterity doing something for us.' [*The Spectator*, 583]

17 I remember when our whole island was shaken with an earthquake some years ago, there was an impudent mountebank who sold pills which (as he told the country people) were very good against an earthquake. [*The Tatler*, 240]

18 I have but ninepence in ready money, but I can draw for a thousand pounds. [(Contrasting his powers of conversation and writing.) Quoted in Boswell's *Life of Johnson*, 7 May 1773]

19 See in what peace a Christian can die. [Dying words]

MAX ADELER   1847–1915

20 We have lost our little Hanner in a very painful manner. [*Little Hanner*]

21 Willie had a purple monkey climbing on a yellow stick, / And when he sucked the paint all off, it made him deathly sick. [*The Purple Monkey*]

THOMAS ADY   17 Cent.

22 Matthew, Mark, Luke, and John, / The bed be blest that I lie on. / Four angels to my bed, / Four angels round my head, / One to watch, and one to pray, / And two to bear my soul away. [*A Candle in the Dark* (1655)]

AESOP   *fl. c.* 550 B.C.

23 Beware that you do not lose the substance by grasping at the shadow. [*Fables*, 'The Dog and the Shadow']

24 I am sure the grapes are sour. [*Ib.* 'The Fox and the Grapes']

25 Thinking to get at once all the gold that the goose could give, he killed it, and opened it only to find – nothing. [*Ib.* 'The Goose with the Golden Eggs']

26 The gods help them that help themselves. [*Ib.* 'Hercules and the Waggoner']

27 It is not only fine feathers that make fine birds. [*Ib.* 'The Jay and the Peacock']

28 While I see many hoof-marks going in, I see none coming out. [*Ib.* 'The Lion, the Fox, and the Beasts']

29 I will have nothing to do with a man who can blow hot and cold with the same breath. [*Ib.* 'The Man and the Satyr']

1 Don't count your chickens before they are hatched. [*Fables*, 'The Milkmaid and her Pail']

2 The boy cried 'Wolf, wolf!' and the villagers came out to help him. [*Ib.* 'The Shepherd's Boy']

3 Only cowards insult dying majesty. [*Ib.* 'The Sick Lion']

4 The lamb that belonged to the sheep whose skin the wolf was wearing began to follow the wolf in the sheep's clothing. [*Ib.* 'The Wolf in Sheep's Clothing']

AGATHON   447?–401 B.C.

5 Even God cannot change the past. [Quoted in Aristotle's *Nicomachaean Ethics*, 6]

A. C. AINGER   1841–1919

6 God is working His purpose out as year succeeds to year, / God is working His purpose out and the time is drawing near; / Nearer and nearer draws the time, the time that shall surely be, / When the earth shall be filled with the glory of God as the waters cover the sea. [Hymn]

THOMAS À KEMPIS *see under* KEMPIS

MARK AKENSIDE   1721–1770

7 Such and so various are the tastes of men. [*The Pleasures of the Imagination*, iii. 567]

ALCUIN   735–804

8 *Nec audiendi sunt qui solent docere, 'Vox populi, vox dei'; cum tumultuositas vulgi semper insaniae proxima est.* – Nor should we listen to those who say, 'The voice of the people is the voice of God', for the turbulence of the mob is always close to insanity. [*Epistolae*, 166. §9]

HENRY ALDRICH   1647–1710

9 If all be true that I do think, / There are five reasons we should drink; / Good wine, a friend, or being dry, / Or lest we

should be by and by; / Or any other reason why. [*A Catch*]

ALEXANDER THE GREAT
     356–323 B.C.

10 I am dying with the help of too many physicians. [Quoted in *Treasury of Humorous Quotations*]

MRS C. F. ALEXANDER 1818–1895

11 All things bright and beautiful, / All creatures great and small, / All things wise and wonderful, / The Lord God made them all. [Hymn]

12 The rich man in his castle, / The poor man at his gate, / God made them, high or lowly, / And ordered their estate. [*Ib.*]

13 Jesus calls us; o'er the tumult / Of our life's wild, restless sea. [Hymn]

14 Once in royal David's city / Stood a lowly cattle shed, / Where a Mother laid her Baby / In a manger for His bed: / Mary was that Mother mild, / Jesus Christ her little Child. [Hymn]

15 There is a green hill far away, / Without a city wall, / Where the dear Lord was crucified, / Who died to save us all. [Hymn]

WILLIAM ALEXANDER, EARL OF STIRLING   1567?–1640

16 The weaker sex, to piety more prone. [*Doomsday*, Hour V. lv]

ALFONSO THE WISE, KING OF CASTILE   1221–1284

17 If I had been present at the creation, I would have given some useful hints for the better arrangement of the Universe. [Attr.]

RICHARD ALISON   *fl. c.* 1606

18 There is a garden in her face, / Where roses and white lilies grow. [*An Hour's Recreation in Music*]

19 There cherries grow, that none can buy / Till cherry-ripe themselves do cry. [*Ib.*]

ABBÉ D'ALLAINVAL   1700–1753

1 *L'embarras des richesse.* – Too much to choose from. [Title of play]

GRANT ALLEN   1848–1899

2 The Woman who Did. [Title of novel]

WILLIAM ALLINGHAM   1828–1889

3 Up the airy mountain, / Down the rushy glen, / We daren't go a-hunting, / For fear of little men. [*The Fairies*]

4 Four ducks on a pond, / A grass-bank beyond, / A blue sky of spring, / White clouds on the wing: / What a little thing / To remember for years – / To remember with tears! [*A Memory*]

ST AMBROSE   337–397

5 *Si fueris Romae, Romano vivito more: / Si fueris alibi, vivito sicut ibi.* – When in Rome, live as the Romans do; when elsewhere, live as they live elsewhere. [Advice to St Augustine, quoted by Jeremy Taylor]

HENRI-FRÉDERIC AMIEL   1821–1881

6 *Un paysage quelconque est un état de l'âme.* – Any landscape is a condition of the spirit. [*Fragments d'un journal intime*]

KINGSLEY AMIS   1922–

7 Lucky Jim. [Title of novel]
8 Feeling a tremendous rakehell, and not liking myself much for it, and feeling rather a good chap for not liking myself much for it, and not liking myself at all for feeling rather a good chap. [*That Uncertain Feeling*, Ch. 7]

HANS CHRISTIAN ANDERSEN   1805–1875

9 'But the Emperor has nothing at all on!' said a little child. [*The Emperor's New Clothes*]
10 The Ugly Duckling. [Title of story]

LANCELOT ANDREWES   1555–1626

11 The nearer the Church the further from God [*Sermon on the Nativity* (1622)]

NORMAN ANGELL   1874–1967

12 The Great Illusion [Title of book which proved that war could not pay]

ANONYMOUS

Advertisements

13 Dr Williams' pink pills for pale people.
14 He won't be happy till he gets it. [For Pears' Soap]
15 Is your journey really necessary? [Railway poster of 1939–45 War]
16 That schoolgirl complexion. [For Palmolive soap]
17 They come as a boon and a blessing to men, / The Pickwick, the Owl, and the Waverley pen.
18 What did you do in the Great War, daddy? [Recruiting poster, 1914–18 War]
19 Worth a guinea a box. [For Beecham's Pills]
20 You press the button, and we'll do the rest. [Kodak advertisement, *c.* 1888]

Play

21 Everyman, I will go with thee and be thy guide, / In thy most need to go by thy side. [*Everyman* (morality play)]

Poems

22 From alle wymmen my love is lent, / And lyht on Alysoun. [*Alysoun.* 13 Cent.]
23 Lenten ys come with love to toune, with blosmen and with briddes roune. [*Lenten is Come with Love to Town.* 13 Cent.]
24 Nou sprinkes the sprai, / al for love icche am to seeke / that slepen i ne mai. [*Now Springs the Spray.* 13 Cent.]
25 Sumer is icumen in. / Lhude sing cuccu! / Groweth sed and bloweth med / And springth the wude nu. [*Sumer is Icumen In.* 13 Cent.]
26 Maiden in the mor lay – / in the mor lay – / sevenyst fulle, sevenist fulle. [*Maiden of the Moor.* 14 Cent.]

1 Adam lay I-bowndyn, bowndyn in a bond, / Fowre thowsand wynter thowt he not to long; / And al was for an appil, an appil that he tok, / As clerkis fyndin wretyn in here book. [*Bless the Time the Apple was Taken!* 15 Cent.]

2 Western Wind, when wilt thou blow, / The small rain down can rain? / Christ if my love were in my arms / And I in my bed again! [16 Cent.]

3 From the hag and hungry goblin / That into rage would rend ye, / And the spirit that stands by the naked man / In the book of Moons defend ye! [*Tom o' Bedlam.* 17 Cent.]

4 The Gipsy snap and Pedro / Are none of Tom's comradoes. / The punk I scorn and the cut-purse sworn / And the roaring boys' bravado. [*Ib.*]

5 With an host of furious fancies / Whereof I am commande₁, / With a burning spear, and a horse of air, / To the wilderness I wander. / By a knight of ghosts and shadows / I summoned am to tourney / Ten leagues beyond the wide world's end, / Methinks it is no journey. [*Ib.*]

6 If all the world were paper, / And all the sea were ink, / And all the trees were bread and cheese, / What should we do for drink? [*If All the World were Paper.* 17 Cent.]

7 And when with envy Time, transported, / Shall think to rob us of our joys; / You'll in your girls again be courted, / And I'll go wooing in my boys. ['Winifreda'. D. Lewis, *Miscellaneous Poems* (1726)]

8 In his chamber, weak and dying, / While the Norman Baron lay, / Loud, without, his men were crying, / 'Shorter hours and better pay'. [*A Strike among the Poets.* 19 Cent.]

9 When he kill the Mudjokivis, / Of the skin he made him mittens, / Made them with the fur side inside, / Made them with the skin side outside. [*The Modern Hiawatha.* 19 Cent.]

Rhymes, Catches, and Epigrams

10 An Austrian army, awfully arrayed, / Boldly by battery besieged Belgrade. ['Siege of Belgrade', *The Trifler* (1817)]

11 The common cormorant or shag / Lays eggs inside a paper bag / The reason you will see no doubt / It is to keep the lightning out / But what these unobservant birds / Have never noticed is that herds / Of wandering bears may come with buns / And steal the bags to hold the crumbs. [W. H. Auden and John Garrett *The Poet's Tongue*]

12 Great Chatham with his sabre drawn / Stood waiting for Sir Richard Strachan; / Sir Richard, longing to be at 'em, / Stood waiting for the Earl of Chatham. [*At Walcheren* (1809)]

13 He that fights and runs away / May live to fight another day. [*Musarum Deliciae.* 17 Cent.]

14 Here lies Fred, / Who was alive and is dead: / Had it been his father, / I had much rather; / Had it been his brother, / Still better than another; / Had it been his sister, / No one would have missed her; / Had it been the whole generation, / Still better for the nation: / But since 'tis only Fred, / Who was alive and is dead, – / There's no more to be said. [Horace Walpole, *Memoirs of George II*]

15 Here we come gathering nuts in May, / Nuts in May, On a cold and frosty morning. [*Here We Come Gathering Nuts in May*]

16 I know two things about the horse, / And one of them is rather coarse. [*The Week-End Book*]

17 I slept and dreamed that life was beauty; / I woke and found that life was duty. [*Duty.* 19 Cent. Some sources ascribe to Ellen Sturgis Hooper]

18 King Charles the First walked and talked / Half an hour after his head was cut off. [Peter Puzzlewell, *A Choice Collection of Riddles, Charades, and Rebuses.* 18 Cent.]

19 The law doth punish man or woman / That steals the goose from off the common, / But lets the greater felon loose, / That steals the common from the goose. [On enclosures, 18 Cent.]

20 Little Willie from his mirror / Licked the mercury right off, / Thinking in his childish error, / It would cure the whooping cough. / At the funeral his mother / Smartly said to Mrs Brown: / "Twas a chilly day for Willie / When the mercury went down'. [*Willie's Epitaph*]

1 Lizzie Borden took an axe / And gave her mother forty whacks; / When she saw what she had done, / She gave her father forty-one! [On an American trial of the 1890s]

2 Miss Buss and Miss Beale / Cupid's darts do not feel. / How different from us, / Miss Beale and Miss Buss. [On two Victorian headmistresses]

3 Multiplication is vexation, / Division is as bad; / The Rule of three doth puzzle me, / And Practice drives me mad. [Elizabethan MS. (1570)]

4 The noble Duke of York, / He had ten thousand men, / He marched them up to the top of the hill, / And he marched them down again. / And when they were up, they were up, / And when they were down, they were down, / And when they were only half way up, / They were neither up nor down. [*The Noble Duke of York*. 18 Cent.]

5 Now I lay me down to sleep; / I pray the Lord my soul to keep. / If I should die before I wake, / I pray the Lord my soul to take. [Prayer. 18 Cent.]

6 Please to remember the Fifth of November, / Gunpowder Treason and Plot. [Traditional]

7 There was a young lady of Riga, / Who rode with a smile on a tiger; / They returned from the ride / With the lady inside, / And the smile on the face of the tiger. [Limerick]

8 There was an old man of Boulogne, / Who sang a most topical song, / It wasn't the words / Which frightened the birds, / But the horrible double-entendre. [Limerick]

9 Thirty days hath September, / April, June, and November; / All the rest have thirty-one, / Excepting February alone, / And that has twenty-eight days clear / And twenty-nine in each leap-year. [*Stevens MS.* (c. 1555)]

Sayings

10 A beast, but a just beast. [Of Dr Temple, Headmaster of Rugby]

11 Earned a precarious living by taking in one another's washing. [Quoted in *The Commonweal*, 6 Aug. 1887. Attr. by William Morris to Mark Twain]

12 The eternal triangle. [Book review, *Daily Chronicle*, 5 Dec. 1907]

13 From ghoulies and ghosties and long-leggety beasties / And things that go bump in the night, / Good Lord, deliver us! [Scottish prayer]

14 How different, how very different from the home life of our own dear Queen! [Irvin S. Cobb, *A Laugh a Day*. The alleged remark of a British matron during a performance of *Antony and Cleopatra*]

15 An intelligent Russian once remarked to us, 'Every country has its own constitution; ours is absolutism moderated by assassination'. [Count Münster, *Political Sketches of the State of Europe* (1868)]

16 The King over the water. [Jacobite toast]

17 Muscular Christianity. [Description of Kingsley's doctrine. *Edinburgh Review*, Jan. 1858]

18 A place within the meaning of the Act. [*The Betting Act*]

Songs

19 Absence makes the heart grow fonder. [From *Davison's Poetical Rhapsody* (1602)]

20 The animals went in one by one, / There's one more river to cross. [*One More River*]

21 As I sat on a sunny bank, / On Christmas Day in the morning, / I spied three ships come sailing by. [Carol: *As I sat on a Sunny Bank*]

22 Begone, dull care! I prithee begone from me! / Begone, dull care, you and I shall never agree. [*Begone Dull Care*]

23 The bells of hell go ting-a-ling-a-ling / For you but not for me. [Song of the 1914–18 War]

24 Bring us in no browne bred, for that is made of brane, / Nor bring us in no white bred, for therein is no gane, / But bring us in good ale! [*Bring us in Good Ale*]

25 But such a woe, believe me, as wins more hearts, / Than Mirth can do with her enticing parts. [*I saw my Lady weep*, set by John Dowland]

26 The Campbells are comin', oho, oho. [*The Campbells are Comin'* (c. 1715)]

27 Casey Jones, he mounted to the cabin, / Casey Jones, with his orders in his hand!

/ Casey Jones, he mounted to the cabin, / Took his farewell trip into the promised land. [*Casey Jones*]

1 Come lasses and lads, get leave of your dads, / And away to the Maypole hie, / For every he has got him a she, / And the fiddler's standing by. [*Come Lasses and Lads*]

2 Early one morning, just as the sun was rising, / I heard a maid singing in the valley below: / 'Oh, don't deceive me; Oh, never leave me! / How could you use a poor maiden so?' [*Early One Morning*]

3 Farewell and adieu to you, / Fair Spanish Ladies, / Farewell and adieu to you, Ladies of Spain. [*Spanish Ladies*]

4 For there was a man, sold lily-vite sand, / In Cupid's net had caught her; / And right over head and ears in love / Vent the putty little ratcatcher's daughter. [*The Ratcatcher's Daughter*]

5 For they're hangin' men and women there for the wearin' o' the Green. [*The Wearin' o' the Green*. Irish street ballad]

6 Frankie and Johnny were lovers, my gawd, how they could love, / Swore to be true to each other, true as the stars above; / He was her man, but he done her wrong. [*Frankie and Johnny*]

7 God rest you merry, gentlemen, / Let nothing you dismay; / Remember Christ our Saviour, / Who was born on Christmas Day. [Carol: *God Rest you*]

8 Greensleeves was all my joy. / Greensleeves was my delight, / Greensleeves was my heart of gold, / And who but Lady Greensleeves? [*Greensleeves*]

9 Alas my love! ye do me wrong / To cast me off discourteously. [*Ib.*]

10 Ha-ha-ha, you and me, / Little brown jug, don't I love thee! [*The Little Brown Jug*]

11 He was a wight of high renown, / And thou's but of low degree. / It's pride that puts this country down: / Man, put thy old cloak about thee! [*The Old Cloak*, sung in *Othello*, II, i]

12 Here we come a-wassailing. [Carol]

13 Hierusalem, my happie home / When shall I come to thee? [*Song*, 'made by F.D.P.']

14 The holly and the ivy, / When they are both full grown / Of all the trees that are in the wood, / The holly bears the crown: / The rising of the sun / And the running of the deer, / The playing of the merry organ, / Sweet singing in the choir. [Carol: *The Holly and the Ivy*]

15 I feel no pain, dear mother, now / But oh! I am so dry! / Oh, take me to a brewery / And leave me there to die. [Shanty]

16 In Dublin's fair city, where girls are so pretty, / I first set my eyes on sweet Molly Malone, / As she wheeled her wheelbarrow through streets broad and narrow, / Crying, Cockles and mussels! alive, alive, oh! [*Cockles and Mussels*]

17 In good King Charles's golden days, / When loyalty no harm meant; / A furious High-Churchman I was, / And so I gained preferment. [*The Vicar of Bray*]

18 And damned are those who dare resist, / Or touch the Lord's Anointed. / And this is law, I will maintain, / Unto my dying day, Sir, / That whatsoever King shall reign, / I will be the Vicar of Bray, Sir! [*Ib.*]

19 When George in pudding time came o'er, / And moderate men looked big, Sir. [*Ib.*]

20 Is that Mr Reilly, can anyone tell? / Is that Mr Reilly who owns the hotel? / Well, if that's Mr Reilly they speak of so highly, / Upon me soul, Reilly, you're doin' quite well. [*Is that Mr Reilly*, Chorus (1882)]

21 It is good to be merry and wise, / It is good to be honest and true, / It is best to be off with the old love, / Before you are on with the new. [*Songs of England and Scotland* (1835)]

22 It's love that makes the world go round. [Translation of French song]

23 King Stephen was a worthy peer; / His breeches cost him but a crown; / He held them sixpence all too dear, / Therefore he called the tailor lown. / Like a fine old English gentleman, / All of the olden time. [*The Fine Old English Gentleman*]

24 O, No, John! No, John! No, John! No! [*O No, John*]

25 Oh, Shenandoah, I long to hear you. / Away, you rolling river. [Shanty: *Oh, Shenandoah*]

26 Oh, 'tis my delight on a shining night, in the season of the year. [*The Lincolnshire Poacher*]

7

1 Oh! where is my wandering boy to-night? / The boy who was bravest of all. [*Oh! Where is my Boy To-night?*]

2 O ye'll tak' the high road, and I'll tak' the low road, / And I'll be in Scotland afore ye, / But me and my true love will never meet again, / On the bonnie, bonnie banks o' Loch Lomon'. [*The Bonnie Banks o' Loch Lomon'*]

3 An old Soldier of the Queen's, / And the Queen's old Soldier. [*An Old Soldier of the Queen's*]

4 Old soldiers never die; / They only fade away! [Song of the 1914–18 War]

5 She was poor but she was honest, / Victim of the squire's whim: / First he loved her, then he left her, / And she lost her honest name. [Song of the 1914–18 War, of which there are many versions]

6 See the little old-world village / Where her aged parents live, / Drinking the champagne she sends them; / But they never can forgive. [*Ib.*]

7 Standing on the bridge at midnight, / She says: 'Farewell, blighted Love.' / There's a scream, a splash – Good Heavens! / What is she a-doing of? [*Ib.*]

8 It's the same the whole world over, / It's the poor what gets the blame, / It's the rich what gets the pleasure, / Isn't it a blooming shame? [*Ib.*]

9 Some talk of Alexander, and some of Hercules; / Of Hector and Lysander, and such great names as these; / But of all the world's brave heroes, there's none that can compare / With the tow, row, row, row, row, row, for the British Grenadier. [*The British Grenadier*]

10 Swing low sweet chariot, / Comin' for to carry me home ; / I looked over Jordan, an' what did I see? / A band of Angels coming after me, / Comin' for to carry me home. [Negro spiritual]

11 There is a tavern in the town, / And there my true love sits him down. [*There is a Tavern in the Town*]

12 Fare thee well, for I must leave thee, / Do not let this parting grieve thee, / And remember that the best of friends must part. [*Ib.*]

13 Adieu, adieu, kind friends, adieu, adieu, adieu, / I can no longer stay with you, stay with you. / I'll hang my harp on a weeping willow-tree. / And may the world go well with thee. [*Ib.*]

14 Tom Pearse, Tom Pearse, lend me your grey mare, / All along, down along, out along lee. / For I want for to go to Widdicombe Fair, / Wi' Bill Brewer, Jan Stewer, Peter Gurney, Peter Davey, Dan'l Whiddon, Harry Hawk, / Old Uncle Tom Cobbleigh and all. [*Widdicombe Fair*]

15 Until he came to a mer-ma-id / At the bottom of the deep blue sea, / Singing, Rule Britannia, Britannia, rule the waves! / Britons never, never, never shall be marr-i-ed to a mer-ma-id / At the bottom of the deep blue sea. [*Oh! 'Twas in the Broad Atlantic*]

16 Wash me in the water / Where you wash your dirty daughter / And I shall be whiter / Than the whitewash on the wall. [*The Top of the Dixie Lid*. Song of the 1914–18 War]

17 We're here because we're here because we're here because we're here. [American song of the 1914–18 War]

18 Weep you no more, sad fountains; / What need you flow so fast? / Look how the snowy mountains / Heaven's sun doth gently waste. [*Weep you no more*, set by John Dowland]

19 What is our life? a play of passion, / Our mirth the music of derision, / Our mothers' wombs the tiring houses be, / Where we are dressed for this short comedy. [*On the Life of Man*, from Orlando Gibbons, *First Set of Madrigals and Motets*]

20 Only we die in earnest, that's no jest. [*Ib.*]

21 What shall we do with the drunken sailor? / Early in the morning? [Shanty]

Greek

22 Know thyself. [Written up in the temple at Delphi]

23 Nothing to excess. [Written up in the temple at Delphi, according to Plato's *Protagoras*]

Latin

24 *Adeste fideles, / Laete triumphantes; / Venite, venite in Bethlehem.* [Hymn, 18 Cent. See F. Oakely for translation]

25 *Ave Caesar, morituri te salutant.* – Hail Caesar, those about to die salute you. [Gladiators' salute on entering the arena]

1 *Cras amet qui nunquam amavit quique amavit cras amet.* – Tomorrow may he love who never loved before, and may he who has loved love too. [*Pervigilium Veneris*]

2 *Et in Arcadia ego.* – I too am in Arcadia. [Inscription on a tomb, the subject of paintings by Poussin and others]

3 *Gaudeamus igitur, / Iuvenes dum sumus.* – Let us live then and be glad / While young life's before us. [Medieval students' song]

4 *Quidquid agas, prudenter agas, et respice finem.* – Whatever you do, do cautiously, and look to the end. [*Gesta Romanorum*, cap. 103]

5 *Tempora mutantur, et nos mutamur in illis.* – Times change, and we change with them. [Quoted in Harrison, *Description of Britain* (1577), Pt III. Ch. iii]

French

6 *Ah! ça ira, ça ira, ça ira, ça ira, / Les aristocrates à la lanterne.* – Oh, it'll be, it'll be, it'll be, it'll be, / The aristocrats will hang. [Refrain of the French Revolution. The phrase '*ça ira*' is pre-revolutionary]

7 *Cet animal est très méchant, Quand on l'attaque il se défend.* – This creature is very wicked. He defends himself when attacked. [*La Ménagerie*, by Théodore P. K., identity unknown (1868)]

8 *Il ne faut pas être plus royaliste que le roi.* – You must not be more royalist than the king. [A phrase current in the reign of Louis XVI; see Chateaubriand, *La Monarchie selon la Charte*]

9 *Ils ne passeront pas.* – They shall not pass. [Watchword during defence of Verdun, 1916. The phrase was again used during the defence of Madrid by the Government 1936–8 in the Spanish form of *¡no pasarán!*]\

10 *Liberté! Égalité! Fraternité!* – Liberty Equality! Fraternity! [Phrase used in the French Revolution, but actually earlier in origin]

11 *Revenons à ces moutons.* – Let us return to those sheep: i.e. to the subject. [*La Farce de Maître Pathelin*, III. iv]

12 *Le roi est mort, vive le roi.* – The king is dead, long live the king. [Phrase used by the heralds to proclaim the death of one French king and the coming to the throne of his successor. First used in 1461]

Italian

13 *Se non è vero, è molto ben trovato.* – If it is not true, it is a very happy invention. [Common saying, quoted by Giordano Bruno, 1585]

APPIUS CAECUS 4 Cent. B.C.

14 *Fabrum esse suae quemque fortunae.* – Each man the architect of his own fate. [Quoted by Sallust, *De Civitate*, I. 2]

THOMAS APPLETON 1812–1884

15 Good Americans, when they die, go to Paris. [Quoted in O. W. Holmes, *Autocrat of the Breakfast Table*, Ch. 6]

ARABIAN NIGHTS

16 Who will change old lamps for new?... new lamps for old? [*The History of Aladdin*]

17 Open Sesame! [*The History of Ali Baba*]

ARCHIMEDES 287–212 B.C.

18 *Eureka!* – I have found it! [On making a discovery]

19 Give me a firm spot on which to stand, and I will move the earth. [On the lever]

COMTE D'ARGENSON 1652–1721

20 ABBÉ GUYOT DESFONTAINES (excusing himself for having written a libellous pamphlet): *Il faut que je vive.* – But I must live.
D'ARGENSON: *Je n'en vois pas la nécessité.* – I do not see the necessity.

LUDOVICO ARIOSTO 1474–1533

21 *Natura il fece, e poi ruppe la stampa.* – Nature made him, and then broke the mould. [*Orlando furioso*, X. 84]

ARISTOTLE 384–322 B.C.

22 A tragedy is the imitation of an action that is serious, and also, as having magnitude, complete in itself ... with incidents arousing pity and terror, with which to accomplish its purgation of these emotions. [*Poetics*, 6]

9

1 Tragedy is an imitation of a whole and complete action of some amplitude. . . . Now a whole is that which has a beginning, a middle, and an end. [*Poetics*, 7]

2 Poetry is more philosophical and of higher value than history. [*Ib.* 9]

3 A plausible impossibility is always preferable to an unconvincing possibility. [*Ib.* 24]

4 Man is by nature a political animal. [*Politics*, I. 2]

5 Either a beast or a god. [*Ib.* I. 14]

6 Plato is dear to me, but dearer still is truth. [*Attr.*]

JOHN ARMSTRONG   1709–1779

7 Th' athletic fool, to whom what Heaven denied / Of soul, is well compensated in limbs. [*The Art of Preserving Health*, III. 206]

8 Distrust yourself, and sleep before you fight. / 'Tis not too late tomorrow to be brave. [*Ib.* IV. 457]

SIR EDWIN ARNOLD   1832–1904

9 Veil after veil will lift – but there must be / Veil upon veil behind. [*The Light of Asia*, VIII]

10 Nor ever be ashamed / So we be named / Press-men; Slaves of the Lamp; Servants of Light. [*The Tenth Muse*]

GEORGE ARNOLD   1834–1865

11 The living need charity more than the dead. [*The Jolly Old Pedagogue*]

MATTHEW ARNOLD   1822–1888

12 And we forget because we must / And not because we will. [*Absence*]

13 And then he thinks he knows / The hills where his life rose, / And the sea where it goes. [*The Buried Life*]

14 The Sea of Faith / Was once, too, at the full and round earth's shore / Lay like the folds of a bright girdle furled. / But now I only hear / Its melancholy, long, withdrawing roar, / Retreating, to the breath / Of the night-wind, down the vast edges drear / And naked shingles of the world. [*Dover Beach*]

15 And we are here as on a darkling plain / Swept with confused alarms of struggle and flight, / Where ignorant armies clash by night. [*Dover Beach*]

16 Is it so small a thing / To have enjoyed the sun, / To have lived light in the spring,/ To have loved, to have thought, to have done? [*Empedocles on Etna*, l. ii. 397]

17 Not here, O Apollo! / Are haunts meet for thee. / But, where Helicon breaks down / In cliff to the sea. [*Ib.* II. 421]

18 'Tis Apollo comes leading / His choir, the Nine. / The leader is fairest, / But all are divine. [*Ib.* II. 445]

19 Eyes too expressive to be blue, / Too lovely to be grey. [*Faded Leaves*, 4]

20 Come, dear children, let us away; / Down and away below. [*The Forsaken Merman*, 1]

21 Now the great winds shoreward blow, / Now the salt tides seaward flow; / Now the wild white horses play, / Champ and chafe and toss in the spray. [*Ib.* 4]

22 Where the great whales come sailing by, / Sail and sail, with unshut eye. [*Ib.* 43]

23 Children dear, was it yesterday / (Call yet once) that she went away? [*Ib.* 48]

24 A wanderer is man from his birth. / He was born in a ship / On the breast of the river of Time. [*The Future*]

25 Wandering between two worlds, one dead, / The other powerless to be born. [*The Grande Chartreuse*, 85]

26 Years hence, perhaps, may dawn an age, / More fortunate, alas! than we, / Which without hardness will be sage, / And gay without frivolity. [*Ib.* 157]

27 Creep into thy narrow bed, / Creep, and let no more be said! [*The Last Word*]

28 Let the long contention cease! / Geese are swans, and swans are geese. [*Ib.*]

29 Let the victors, when they come, / When the forts of folly fall, / Find thy body by the wall. [*Ib.*]

30 He bears the seed of ruin in himself. [*Merope*, 856]

31 We cannot kindle when we will / The fire which in the heart resides, / The spirit bloweth and is still, / In mystery our soul abides. [*Morality*]

10

1 Now he is dead! Far hence he lies / In the lorn Syrian town; / And on his grave, with shining eyes, / The Syrian stars look down. [*Obermann Once More*, 173]

2 Strew on her roses, roses, / And never a spray of yew. / In quiet she reposes: / Ah! would that I did too! [*Requiescat*]

3 To-night it doth inherit / The vasty hall of death. [*Ib.*]

4 Not deep the poet sees, but wide. [*Resignation*, 214]

5 Friends who set forth at our side, / Falter, are lost in the storm. / We, we only, are left! [*Rugby Chapel*, 102]

6 Go, for they call you, shepherd, from the hill. [*The Scholar-Gypsy*, 1]

7 All the live murmur of a summer's day. [*Ib.* 20]

8 Tired of knocking at Preferment's door. [*Ib.* 35]

9 Crossing the stripling Thames at Bablock-hithe, / Trailing in the cool stream thy fingers wet, / As the slow punt swings round. [*Ib.* 74]

10 Waiting for the spark from heaven to fall. [*Ib.* 120]

11 Sad Patience, too near neighbour to despair. [*Ib.* 195]

12 This strange disease of modern life. [*Ib.* 203]

13 Still nursing the unconquerable hope, / Still clutching the inviolable shade. [*Ib.* 211]

14 The young light-hearted masters of the waves. [*Ib.* 241]

15 Shy traffickers, the dark Iberians come: / And on the beach undid his corded bales. [*Ib.* 249]

16 Others abide our question. Thou art free. / We ask and ask: Thou smilest and art still, / Out-topping knowledge. [*Shakespeare*]

17 And thou, who didst the stars and sunbeams know, / Self-schooled, self-scanned, self-honoured, self-secure / Didst tread on earth unguessed at. Better so! [*Ib.*]

18 Truth sits upon the lips of dying men. [*Sohrab and Rustum*, 656]

19 But the majestic river floated on, / Out of the mist and hum of that low land, / Into the frosty starlight, and there moved, / Rejoicing, through the hushed Chorasmian waste, / Under the solitary moon. [*Sohrab and Rustum*, 875]

20 The shorn and parcelled Oxus strains along / Through beds of sand and matted rushy isles – / Oxus, forgetting the bright speed he had / In his high mountain cradle in Pamere, / A foiled circuitous wanderer – till at last / The longed-for dash of waves is heard. [*Ib.* 884]

21 From whose floor the new-bathed stars / Emerge, and shine upon the Aral Sea. [*Ib.* 891]

22 And see all sights from pole to pole, / And glance, and nod, and bustle by; / And never once possess our soul / Before we die. [*A Southern Night*, 69]

23 The signal-elm, that looks on Ilsley downs. [*Thyrsis*, 14]

24 That sweet city with her dreaming spires. [(Oxford) *Ib.* 19]

25 He went; his piping took a troubled sound / Of storms that rage outside our happy ground. [*Ib.* 48]

26 The bloom is gone, and with the bloom go I. [*Ib.* 60]

27 Too quick despairer, wherefore wilt thou go? / Soon will the high midsummer pomps come on. [*Ib.* 61]

28 The heart less bounding at emotion new, / The hope, once crushed, less quick to spring again. [*Ib.* 139]

29 Roam on! The light we sought is shining still. / Dost thou ask proof? Our tree yet crowns the hill, / Our Scholar travels yet the loved hillside. [*Ib.* 238]

30 Who saw life steadily, and saw it whole: / The mellow glory of the Attic stage. [(Sophocles) *To a Friend*]

31 Dotting the shoreless watery wild, / We mortal millions live *alone*. [*To Marguerite, Isolation*]

32 The unplumbed, salt, estranging sea. [*Ib.*]

33 France, famed in all great arts, in none supreme. [*To a Republican Friend*]

34 Culture being a pursuit of our total perfection by means of getting to know, on all the matters which most concern us, the best which has been thought and said in the world. [*Culture and Anarchy*, Preface]

1 Our society distributes itself into Barbarians, Philistines, and Populace. [*Culture and Anarchy*, Preface]

2 The pursuit of perfection, then, is the pursuit of sweetness and light. [*Ib*. Ch. 1]

3 *Philistine* gives the notion of something particularly stiff-necked and perverse in the resistance to light and its children; and therein it specially suits our middle-class. [*Ib*. 3]

4 The governing idea of Hellenism is spontaneity of consciousness; that of Hebraism, strictness of conscience. [*Ib*. 4]

5 No man, who knows nothing else, knows even his Bible. [*Ib*. 5]

6 The magnificent roaring of the young lions of the *Daily Telegraph*. [*Essays in Criticism, 1st Series*, Preface]

7 [Oxford] whispering from her towers the last enchantments of the Middle Age. . . . Home of lost causes, and forsaken beliefs, and unpopular names, and impossible loyalties! [*Ib*.]

8 I am bound by my own definition of criticism: a disinterested endeavour to learn and propagate the best that is known and thought in the world. [*Ib*. 'The Function of Criticism at the Present Time']

9 Philistine must have originally meant, in the mind of those who invented the nickname, a strong, dogged, unenlightened opponent of the chosen people, of the children of light. [*Ib*. 'Heinrich Heine']

10 Philistinism! – We have not the expression in English. Perhaps we have not the word because we have so much of the thing. [*Ib*.]

11 [Shelley] a beautiful and ineffectual angel' beating in the void his luminous wings in vain. [*Essays in Criticism, 2nd Series*, 'Byron']

12 He never spoke out. [(Quoting letter from Gray's friend, James Brown) *Ib*. 'Gray']

13 Gray, a born poet, fell upon an age of reason. [*Ib*.]

14 The difference between genuine poetry and the poetry of Dryden, Pope, and all their school, is briefly this: their poetry is conceived in their wits, genuine poetry is conceived and composed in the soul. [*Ib*.]

15 [Poetry] a criticism of life under the conditions fixed for such a criticism by the laws of poetic truth and poetic beauty. [*Essays in Criticism, 2nd Series*, 'The Study of Poetry']

16 He [Chaucer] lacks the high seriousness of the great classics, and therewith an important part of their virtue. [*Ib*.]

17 His expression may often be called bald . . . but it is bald as the bare mountain tops are bald, with a baldness full of grandeur. [*Ib*. 'Wordsworth']

18 Culture, the acquainting ourselves with the best that has been known and said in the world, and thus with the history of the human spirit. [*Literature and Dogma*, Preface to edition of 1873]

19 Culture is the passion for sweetness and light, and (what is more) the passion for making them prevail. [*Ib*.]

20 Miracles do not happen. [*Ib*. Preface to edition of 1883]

21 The true meaning of religion is thus not simply morality, but morality touched by emotion. [*Ib*. Ch. i. §2]

22 Conduct is three-fourths of our life and its largest concern. [*Ib*. i. 3]

23 The eternal *not ourselves* that makes for righteousness. [*Ib*. viii. 1]

24 But there remains the question: what righteousness really is. The method and secret and sweet reasonableness of Jesus. [*Ib*. xii. 2]

25 He will find one English book and one only, where, as in the *Iliad* itself, perfect plainness of speech is allied with perfect nobleness; and that book is the Bible. [*On Translating Homer*, 3]

26 I think it will be found that the grand style arises in poetry, when a noble nature, poetically gifted, treats with simplicity or with severity a serious subject. [*Ib*. Last words]

SAMUEL J. ARNOLD 1774–1852

27 For England, home, and beauty. [*The Death of Nelson*]
See also under SARGENT, EPES

THOMAS ARNOLD 1795–1842

28 What we must look for here is, first, religious and moral principles; secondly, gentlemanly conduct; thirdly, intellectual ability. [Address to his scholars at Rugby]

GEORGE ASAF [GEORGE H. POWELL] 1880–1951

1 What's the use of worrying? / It never was worth while, / So, pack up your troubles in your old kit-bag, / And smile, smile, smile. [*Pack up Your Troubles in Your Old Kit-bag*]

LORD ASHBURTON 1731–1783

2 The power of the Crown has increased, is increasing, and ought to be diminished. [Motion in the House of Commons, 1780]

'DAISY ASHFORD' 1881–1972

3 Mr Salteena was an elderly man of 42 and was fond of asking peaple to stay with him. [*The Young Visiters*, Ch. 1]

4 I am parshial to ladies if they are nice I suppose it is my nature. I am not quite a gentleman but you would hardly notice it but cant be helped anyhow. [*Ib.*]

5 I am very pale owing to the drains in this house. [*Ib.* 2]

6 Bernard always had a few prayers in the hall and some whiskey afterwards as he was rarther pious but Mr Salteena was not very adicted to prayers so he marched up to bed. [*Ib.* 3]

7 It was a sumpshous spot all done up in gold with plenty of looking glasses. [*Ib.* 5]

8 What I say is what dose it matter we cant all be of the Blood royal can we. [*Ib.*]

9 My own idear is that these things are as piffle before the wind. [*Ib.*]

10 I am very fond of fresh air and royalties. [*Ib.*]

11 Here I am tied down to this life he said ... being royal has many painfull drawbacks. [*Ib.* 6]

12 Kindly drive us to the Gaierty Hotel he cried in a firm tone. The cabman waved his whip and off they dashed. [*Ib.* 7]

13 My life will be sour grapes and ashes without you. [*Ib.* 8]

14 She had very nice feet and plenty of money. [*Ib.* 12]

H. H. ASQUITH, EARL OF OXFORD 1852–1928

15 Wait and see. [Phrase used in speeches in 1910]

E. L. ATKINSON 1882–1929 and APSLEY CHERRY GARRARD 1886–1959

16 A very gallant gentleman. [Inscription on the burial-place of Captain Oates, in the Antarctic, 1912]

JOHN AUBREY 1626–1697

17 He was so fair that they called him *the lady of* Christ's College. [*Brief Lives*, 'John Milton']

ALEXANDER BOSWELL, LORD AUCHINLECK 1706–1782

18 He [Cromwell] gart kings ken they had a lith [joint] in their neck. [Quoted in Boswell's *Tour of the Hebrides*, note, 6 Nov. 1773]

W. H. AUDEN 1907–1973

19 August for the people and their favourite islands. / Daily the steamers sidle up to meet / The effusive welcome of the pier. [*August for the people*]

20 Alone, alone, about the dreadful wood / Of conscious evil runs a lost mankind, / Dreading to find its Father. [*For the Time Being*, 'Chorus']

21 When the Sex War ended with the slaughter of the Grandmothers, / They found a bachelor's baby suffocating under them; / Somebody called him George and that was the end of it: / They hitched him up to the Army. [*Ib.* 'Soldiers']

22 It is time for the destruction of error. / The chairs are being brought in from the garden, / The summer talk stopped on that savage coast / Before the storms. [*It is time*]

23 Lay your sleeping head, my love, / Human on my faithless arm. [*Lay your sleeping head*]

24 Far-sighted as falcons, they looked down another future; / For the seed in their

loins were hostile. [*Look, Stranger*, 'Prologue']

1 Some possible dream, long coiled in the ammonite's slumber / Is uncurling, prepared to lay on our talk and kindness / Its military silence, its surgeon's idea of pain. [*Ib.*]

2 Look, stranger, at this island now / The leaping light for your delight discovers. [*Look, Stranger*]

3 O Unicorn among the Cedars / To whom no magic charm can lead us, / White childhood moving like a sigh / Through the green woods. [*New Year Letter*]

4 My Dear One is mine as mirrors are lonely. [*The Sea and the Mirror*]

5 There is no such thing as the State / And no one exists alone; / Hunger allows no choice / To the citizen or the police; / We must love one another or die. [*September 1, 1939*]

6 Their fate must always be the same as yours, / To suffer the loss they were afraid of, yes, / Holders of one position, wrong for years. [*Since you are going to begin today*]

7 A shilling life will give you all the facts. [Sonnet: *A Shilling Life*]

8 Harrow the house of the dead; look shining at / New styles of architecture, a change of heart. [Sonnet: *Sir, no man's enemy*]

9 The stars are dead; the animals will not look: / We are left alone with our day, and the time is short and / History to the defeated / May say Alas but cannot help or pardon [*Spain 1937*]

10 A professor is one who talks in someone else's sleep. [Quoted in *Treasury of Humorous Quotations*]

ÉMILE AUGIER   1820–1889

11 *La nostalgie de la boue.* – A yearning for the gutter. [*Le Mariage d'Olympe*, I. i]

ST AUGUSTINE   354–430

12 Thou hast created us for Thyself, and our heart is not quiet until it rests in Thee. [*Confessions*, I. i]

13 To Carthage I came, where there sang all around my ears a cauldron of unholy loves. [*Ib.* III. 1]

14 It is impossible that the son of these tears should perish. [*Confessions*, III. 12]

15 Give me chastity and continency, but not yet. [*Ib.* VIII. 7]

16 The verdict of the world is final. [*Contra Epistolam Parmeniani*, III. 24]

17 There is no salvation outside the Church. [*De Bapt.* IV. 17]

18 Hear the other side. [*De Duabus Animabus*, XIV. 2]

19 Love, and do what you will. [*In Ioann.* VIII. 7]

20 Rome has spoken; the case is concluded. [*Sermons*, Bk I]

MARCUS AURELIUS
ANTONINUS   121–180

21 Whatever this is that I am, it is a little flesh and breath, and the ruling part. [*Meditations*, II. 2]

22 And thou wilt give thyself relief, if thou doest every act of thy life as if it were the last. [*Ib.* II. 5]

23 Remember that no man loses any other life than this which he now lives, nor lives any other than this which he now loses. [*Ib.* II. 14]

24 All things from eternity are of like forms and come round in a circle. [*Ib.*]

25 The universe is transformation; our life is what our thoughts make it. [*Ib.* IV. 3]

26 Everything that happens happens as it should, and if you observe carefully, you will find this to be so. [*Ib.* IV. 10]

27 Remember this, that there is a proper value and proportion to be observed in the performance of every act. [*Ib.* IV. 32]

28 Everything is only for a day, both that which remembers and that which is remembered. [*Ib.* IV. 35]

29 Time is like a river made up of the events which happen, and its current is strong; no sooner does anything appear than it is swept away, and another comes in its place, and will be swept away too. [*Ib.* IV. 43]

30 Nothing happens to any man that he is not formed by nature to bear. [*Ib.* V. 18]

31 Live with the gods. And he does so who constantly shows them that his soul is

satisfied with what is assigned to him. [*Meditations*, V. 27]

1 Remember that to change your mind and follow him who sets you right is to be none the less free than you were before. [*Ib*. VIII. 16]

2 Whatever may happen to you was prepared for you from all eternity; and the implication of causes was from eternity spinning the thread of your being. [*Ib*. X. 5]

JANE AUSTEN   1775–1817

3 An egg boiled very soft is not unwholesome. [(Mr Woodhouse) *Emma*, Ch. 3]

4 One half of the world cannot understand the pleasures of the other. [(Emma) *Ib*. 9]

5 A basin of nice smooth gruel, thin, but not too thin. [*Ib*. 12]

6 Drinking too much of Mr Weston's good wine. [*Ib*. 15]

7 Human nature is so well disposed towards those who are in interesting situations, that a young person, who either marries or dies, is sure to be kindly spoken of. [*Ib*. 22]

8 The sooner every party breaks up the better. [(Mr Woodhouse) *Ib*. 25]

9 But, surely, Mr Churchill, nobody would think of opening the windows at Randalls. Nobody could be so imprudent. [(Mr Woodhouse) *Ib*. 29]

10 Business, you know, may bring money, but friendship hardly ever does. [(John Knightley) *Ib*. 34]

11 One has no great hopes from Birmingham. I always say there is something direful in the sound. [(Mrs Elton) *Ib*. 36]

12 'And what are you reading, Miss —?' 'Oh! it is only a novel!' . . . or, in short, only some work in which the most thorough knowledge of human nature, the happiest delineation of its varieties, the liveliest effusions of wit and humour are conveyed to the world in the best chosen language. [*Northanger Abbey*, Ch. 5]

13 I have heard that something very shocking indeed will soon come out in London. [(Catherine) *Ib*. 14]

14 My sore throats are always worse than anyone's. [(Mary Musgrove) *Persuasion*, Ch. 18]

15 All the privilege I claim for my own sex ... is that of loving longest, when existence or when hope is gone. [(Anne) *Ib*. 23]

16 It is a truth universally acknowledged, that a single man in possession of a good fortune, must be in want of a wife. [*Pride and Prejudice*, Ch. 1]

17 She was a woman of mean understanding, little information, and uncertain temper. [(Mrs Bennet) *Ib*.]

18 A lady's imagination is very rapid; it jumps from admiration to love, from love to matrimony in a moment. [(Darcy) *Ib*. 6]

19 How can you contrive to write so even? [(Miss Bingley) *Ib*. 10]

20 It is happy for you that you possess the talent of flattering with delicacy. May I ask whether these pleasing attentions proceed from the impulse of the moment, or are the result of previous study? [(Mr Bennet) *Ib*. 14]

21 You have delighted us long enough. [(Mr Bennet) *Ib*. 18]

22 It does not appear to me that my hand is unworthy your acceptance, or that the establishment I can offer would be any other than highly desirable. [(Mr Collins) *Ib*. 19]

23 From this day you must be a stranger to one of your parents. – Your mother will never see you again if you do *not* marry Mr Collins, and I will never see you again if you *do*. [(Mr Bennet) *Ib*. 20]

24 Nobody is on my side, nobody takes part with me: I am cruelly used, nobody feels for my poor nerves. [(Mrs Bennet) *Ib*.]

25 'If it was not for the entail I should not mind it.'
'What should not you mind?'
'I should not mind anything at all.'
'Let us be thankful that you are preserved from a state of such insensibility.' [(Mrs and Mr Bennet) *Ib*. 23]

26 Next to being married, a girl likes to be crossed in love a little now and then. [(Mr Bennet) *Ib*. 24]

27 One cannot be always laughing at a man without now and then stumbling on something witty. [(Elizabeth) *Ib*. 40]

1 You ought certainly to forgive them as a Christian, but never to admit them in your sight, or allow their names to be mentioned in your hearing. [(Mr Collins) *Pride and Prejudice*, 57]

2 An annuity is a very serious business. [(Mrs Dashwood) *Sense and Sensibility*, Ch. 2]

3 The pleasantness of an employment does not always evince its propriety. [(Elinor) *Ib*. 13]

4 What dreadful hot weather we have! It keeps me in a continual state of inelegance. [*Letters*, 18 Sept. 1796]

5 Mrs Hall of Sherbourne was brought to bed yesterday of a dead child, some weeks before she expected, owing to a fright. I suppose she happened unawares to look at her husband. [*Ib*. 27 Oct. 1798]

6 I do not want people to be very agreeable, as it saves me the trouble of liking them a great deal. [*Ib*. 24 Dec. 1798]

7 The little bit (two inches wide) of ivory on which I work with so fine a brush, as produces little effect after much labour. [*Ib*. 16 Dec. 1816]

ALFRED AUSTIN   1835–1913

8 Across the wires the electric message came: / 'He is no better, he is much the same.' [*On the Illness of the Prince of Wales*, attr. to Austin, but probably not his]

W. E. AYTOUN   1813–1865

9 Take away the star and garter – / Hide them from my aching sight! / Neither king nor prince shall tempt me / From my lonely room this night. [*Charles Edward at Versailles on the Anniversary of Culloden*]

10 Fhairshon swore a feud / Against the clan M'Tavish; / Marched into their land / To murder and to rafish; / For he did resolve / To extirpate the vipers, / With four-and-twenty men / And five-and-thirty pipers. [*The Massacre of the Macpherson*]

FRANCIS BACON   1561–1626

11 If a man will begin with certainties, he shall end in doubts; but if he will be content to begin with doubts, he shall end in certainties. [*The Advancement of Learning*, I. v. 8]

12 [Knowledge is] a rich storehouse for the glory of the Creator, and the relief of man's estate. [*Ib*. I. v. 11]

13 They are ill discoverers that think there is no land, when they can see nothing but sea. [*Ib*. I. vii. 5]

14 But men must know, that in this theatre of man's life it is reserved only for God and angels to be lookers-on. [*Ib*. II. xx. 8]

15 We are much beholden to Machiavel and others, that write what men do, and not what they ought to do. [*Ib*. II. xxi. 9]

16 All good moral philosophy is but the handmaid to religion. [*Ib*. II. xxii. 14]

17 Fortunes . . . come tumbling into some men's laps. [*Ib*. II. xxiii. 43]

18 That other principle of Lysander, 'That children are to be deceived with comfits, and men with oaths'. [*Ib*. II. xxiii. 45]

19 Anger makes dull men witty, but it keeps them poor. [*Apothegms*, 5. Attr. by Bacon to Queen Elizabeth I]

20 Hope is a good breakfast, but it is a bad supper. [*Ib*. 36]

21 Like strawberry wives, that laid two or three great strawberries at the mouth of their pot, and all the rest were little ones. [*Ib*. 54. Attr. to Queen Elizabeth I]

22 One of the Seven was wont to say: 'That laws were like cobwebs; where the small flies were caught, and the great brake through.' [*Ib*. 181]

23 Riches are a good handmaiden, but the worst mistress. [*De dignitate et augmentis scientiarium*, Pt I. vi. 3. 6]

24 I have often thought upon death, and I find it the least of all evils. [*An Essay on Death*]

25 My essays . . . come home, to men's business, and bosoms. [*Essays*, Dedication (1625)]

26 What is truth? said jesting Pilate; and would not stay for an answer. [*Ib*. 1, 'Of Truth']

27 A mixture of a lie doth ever add pleasure. [*Ib*.]

28 It is not the lie that passeth through the mind, but the lie that sinketh in and settleth in it, that doth the hurt. [*Ib*.]

1 Certainly it is a heaven upon earth, to
have a man's mind to move in charity,
rest in providence, and turn upon the
poles of truth. [*Essays*, 1, 'Of Truth']

2 Men fear death, as children fear to go in
the dark; and as that natural fear in
children is increased with tales, so is the
other. [*Ib.* 2, 'Of Death']

3 Revenge triumphs over death; love
slights it; honour aspireth to it; grief
flieth to it. [*Ib.*]

4 It is as natural to die as to be born; and
to a little infant, perhaps, the one is as
painful as the other. [*Ib.*]

5 All colours will agree in the dark. [*Ib.* 3,
'Of Unity in Religion']

6 Revenge is a kind of wild justice. [*Ib.* 4,
'Of Revenge']

7 A man that studieth revenge keeps his
own wounds green. [*Ib.*]

8 Prosperity is the blessing of the Old
Testament, adversity is the blessing of the
New. [*Ib.* 5, 'Of Adversity']

9 Prosperity is not without many fears and
distastes; and adversity is not without
comforts and hopes. [*Ib.*]

10 Prosperity doth best discover vice, but
adversity doth best discover virtue. [*Ib.*]

11 Nakedness is uncomely as well in mind,
as body. [*Ib.* 6, 'Of Simulation and Dissimulation']

12 The joys of parents are secret, and so are
their griefs and fears. [*Ib.* 7, 'Of Parents
and Children']

13 Children sweeten labours; but they make
misfortunes more bitter. [*Ib.*]

14 The noblest works and foundations have
proceeded from childless men. [*Ib.*]

15 He that hath wife and children, hath given
hostages to fortune; for they are impediments to great enterprises, either of
virtue, or mischief. [*Ib.* 8, 'Of Marriage
and Single Life']

16 There are some other that account wife
and children but as bills of charges. [*Ib.*]

17 Wives are young men's mistresses; companions for middle age; and old men's
nurses. [*Ib.*]

18 He was reputed one of the wise men that
made answer to the question, when a man
should marry? 'A young man not yet,
an elder man not at all.' [*Ib.*]

19 The speaking in a perpetual hyperbole is
comely in nothing but in love. [*Essays*, 10,
'Of Love']

20 The arch-flatterer, with whom all the
petty flatterers have intelligence, is a
man's self. [*Ib.*]

21 Nuptial love maketh mankind; friendly
love perfecteth it; but wanton love
corrupteth and embaseth it. [*Ib.*]

22 Men in great place are thrice servants:
servants of the sovereign or state; servants
of fame; and servants of business. [*Ib.* 11,
'Of Great Place']

23 It is a strange desire to seek power and to
lose liberty. [*Ib.*]

24 Set it down to thyself, as well to create
good precedents as to follow them. [*Ib.*]

25 Severity breedeth fear, but roughness
breedeth hate. Even reproofs from
authority ought to be grave and not
taunting. [*Ib.*]

26 As in nature things move violently to
their place and calmly in their place, so
virtue in ambition is violent, in authority
settled and calm. [*Ib.*]

27 He said it, that knew it best. [*Ib.* 12, 'Of
Boldness']

28 There is in human nature generally more
of the fool than of the wise. [*Ib.*]

29 In civil business; what first? Boldness;
what second, and third? Boldness. And
yet boldness is a child of ignorance and
baseness. [*Ib.*]

30 Boldness is an ill-keeper of promise. [*Ib.*]

31 If the hill will not come to Mahomet,
Mahomet will go to the hill. [*Ib.*]

32 In charity there is no excess. [*Ib.* 13, 'Of
Goodness and Goodness of Nature']

33 If a man be gracious and courteous to
strangers, it shows he is a citizen of the
world. [*Ib.*]

34 New nobility is but the act of power, but
ancient nobility is the act of time. [*Ib.* 14,
'Of Nobility']

35 Nobility of birth commonly abateth industry. [*Ib.*]

36 The four pillars of government ... (which
are religion, justice, counsel, and treasure). [*Ib.* 15, 'Of Seditions and Troubles']

37 The surest way to prevent seditions (if
the times do bear it) is to take away the
matter of them. [*Ib.*]

1 Money is like muck, not good except it be spread. [*Essays*, 15, 'Of Seditions and Troubles']

2 The remedy is worse than the disease. [*Ib.*]

3 God never wrought miracle to convince atheism, because his ordinary works convince it. [*Ib.* 16, 'Of Atheism']

4 A little philosophy inclineth man's mind to atheism; but depth in philosophy bringeth men's minds about to religion. [*Ib.*]

5 For none deny there is a God, but those for whom it maketh that there were no God. [*Ib.*]

6 It were better to have no opinion of God at all, than such an opinion as is unworthy of him. [*Ib.* 17, 'Of Superstition']

7 There is a superstition in avoiding superstition. [*Ib.*]

8 Travel, in the younger sort, is a part of education; in the elder, a part of experience. [*Ib.* 18, 'Of Travel']

9 Let diaries, therefore, be brought in use. [*Ib.*]

10 Books will speak plain when counsellors blanch. [*Ib.* 20, 'Of Counsel']

11 There be that can pack the cards, and yet cannot play well. [*Ib.* 22, 'Of Cunning']

12 When he wrote a letter, he would put that which was most material in the postscript, as if it had been a by-matter. [*Ib.*]

13 Nothing doth more hurt in a state than that cunning men pass for wise. [*Ib.*]

14 Be so true to thyself, as thou be not false to others. [*Ib.* 23, 'Of Wisdom for a Man's Self']

15 Certainly it is the nature of extreme self-lovers, as they will set an house on fire, and it were but to roast their eggs. [*Ib.*]

16 It is the wisdom of the crocodiles, that shed tears when they would devour. [*Ib.*]

17 He that will not apply new remedies must expect new evils; for time is the greatest innovator. [*Ib.* 24, 'Of Innovations']

18 A wise man that had it for a by-word, when he saw men hasten to a conclusion, 'Stay a little, that we may make an end the sooner'. [*Ib.* 25, 'Of Dispatch']

19 To choose time is to save time. [*Ib.*]

20 The French are wiser than they seem, and the Spaniards seem wiser than they are. [*Essays*, 26, 'Of Seeming Wise']

21 It had been hard for him that spake it to have put more truth and untruth together, in few words, than in that speech: 'Whosoever is delighted in solitude is either a wild beast, or a god'. [*Ib.* 27, 'Of Friendship']

22 A crowd is not company, and faces are but a gallery of pictures. [*Ib.*]

23 Cure the disease and kill the patient. [*Ib.*]

24 Riches are for spending. [*Ib.* 28, 'Of Expense']

25 Neither is money the sinews of war (as it is trivially said). [*Ib.* 29, 'Of the True Greatness of Kingdoms']

26 He that commands the sea is at great liberty, and may take as much and as little of the war as he will. [*Ib.*]

27 Age will not be defied. [*Ib.* 30, 'Of Regimen of Health']

28 Suspicions amongst thoughts are like bats amongst birds, they ever fly by twilight. [*Ib.* 31, 'Of Suspicion']

29 There is nothing makes a man suspect much, more than to know little. [*Ib.*]

30 Intermingle . . . jest with earnest. [*Ib.* 32, 'Of Discourse']

31 [Dreams and predictions] ought to serve but for winter talk by the fireside. [*Ib.* 35, 'Of Prophecies']

32 Nature is often hidden; sometimes overcome; seldom extinguished. [*Ib.* 38, 'Of Nature in Men']

33 A man's nature runs either to herbs, or to weeds; therefore let him seasonably water the one, and destroy the other. [*Ib.*]

34 Virtue is like a rich stone, best plain set. [*Ib.* 43, 'Of Beauty']

35 Houses are built to live in and not to look on. [*Ib.* 45, 'Of Building']

36 God Almighty first planted a garden; and, indeed, it is the purest of human pleasures. [*Ib.* 46, 'Of Gardens']

37 There is little friendship in the world, and least of all between equals. [*Ib.* 48, 'Of Followers']

38 Studies serve for delight, for ornament, and for ability. [*Ib.* 50, 'Of Studies']

39 To spend too much time in studies is sloth. [*Ib.*]

1 Read not to contradict and confute, nor to believe and take for granted, nor to find talk and discourse, but to weigh and consider. [*Essays*, 50, 'Of Studies']

2 Some books are to be tasted, others to be swallowed, and some few to be chewed and digested. [*Ib.*]

3 Reading maketh a full man; conference a ready man; and writing an exact man. [*Ib.*]

4 Histories make men wise; poets, witty; the mathematics, subtle; natural philosophy, deep; moral, grave; logic and rhetoric, able to contend. [*Ib.*]

5 A wise man will make more opportunities than he finds. [*Ib.* 52, 'Of Ceremonies and Respects']

6 Fame is like a river, that beareth up things light and swollen, and drowns things weighty and solid. [*Ib.* 53, 'Of Praise']

7 It was prettily devised of Aesop, 'The fly sat upon the axle-tree of the chariot-wheel and said, What a dust do I raise'. [*Ib.* 54, 'Of Vain-glory']

8 The place of justice is a hallowed place. [*Ib.* 56, 'Of Judicature']

9 Lucid intervals and happy pauses. [*The History of King Henry VII*, § 3]

10 I would live to study and not study to live. [*Memorial of Access*]

11 For knowledge itself is power. [*Religious Meditations*, 'Of Heresies']

12 The world's a bubble; and the life of man, / Less than a span. [*The World*]

13 Who then to frail mortality shall trust, / But limns the water, or but writes in dust. [*Ib.*]

14 What is it then to have or have no wife, / But single thraldom, or a double strife? [*Ib.*]

15 What then remains, but that we still should cry, / Not to be born, or being born, to die? [*Ib.*]

16 I have taken all knowledge to be my province. [Letter to Lord Burleigh, 1592]

WALTER BAGEHOT   1826–1877

17 The best reason why Monarchy is a strong government is that it is an intelligible government. The mass of mankind understand it, and they hardly anywhere in the world understand any other. [*The English Constitution*, Ch. 2]

18 Of all nations in the world the English are perhaps the least a nation of pure philosophers. [*Ib.*]

P. J. BAILEY   1816–1902

19 We live in deeds, not years; in thoughts, not breaths; / In feelings, not in figures on a dial. / We should count time by heart-throbs. He most lives / Who thinks most – feels the noblest – acts the best. [*Festus*, 5]

BRUCE BAIRNSFATHER   1887–1959

20 Well, if you knows of a better 'ole, go to it. [*Fragments from France*, 1]

SIR H. W. BAKER   1821–1877

21 The King of love my Shepherd is, / Whose goodness faileth never; / I nothing lack if I am His, / And He is mine for ever. [Hymn]

STANLEY, EARL BALDWIN   1867–1947

22 When you think about the defence of England, you no longer think of the chalk cliffs of Dover. You think of the Rhine. That is where our frontier lies today. [Speech in House of Commons, 30 July 1934]

A. J. BALFOUR   1848–1930

23 Defence of philosophic doubt. [Article in *Mind*, 1878]

24 The energies of our system will decay, the glory of the sun will be dimmed, and the earth, tideless and inert, will no longer tolerate the race which has for a moment disturbed its solitude. Man will go down into the pit, and all his thoughts will perish. [*The Foundations of Belief*, Pt I. Ch. 1]

25 It is unfortunate, considering that enthusiasm moves the world, that so few enthusiasts can be trusted to speak the truth. [Letter to Mrs Drew, 1918]

JOHN BALL   ?–1381

1 When Adam delved and Eve span, / Who was then the gentleman? [Text for sermon at outbreak of Peasants' Revolt. Adapted from poem by Richard Rolle of Hampole]

BALLADS

2 'I prithee, sweetheart, canst thou tell me / Whether thou dost know / The bailiff's daughter of Islington?' / 'She's dead, sir, long ago.' [*The Bailiff's Daughter of Islington*]

3 But I hae dreamed a dreary dream, / Beyond the Isle of Skye; / I saw a dead man win a fight, / And I think that man was I. [*The Battle of Otterbourne*]

4 It fell about the Lammas tide / When husbands win their hay, / The doughty Douglas bound him to ride, / In England to take a prey. [*The Battle of Otterburn*]

5 There were twa sisters sat in a bour; / *Binnorie, O Binnorie!* / There came a knight to be their wooer, / *By the bonnie milldams o' Binnorie.* [*Binnorie*]

6 Ye Highlands and ye Lawlands, / Oh where have you been? / They have slain the Earl of Murray, / And they laid him on the green. [*The Bonny Earl of Murray*]

7 He was a braw gallant, / And he played at the glove; / And the bonny Earl of Murray, / Oh he was the Queen's love! [*Ib.*]

8 O then bespoke our Saviour, / All in his mother's womb; / 'Bow down, good cherry-tree, / To my mother's hand.' [*The Cherry-Tree Carol*]

9 The Percy out of Northumberland, / An avow to God made he / That he would hunt in the mountains / Of Cheviot within days three, / In the maugre of doughty Douglas, / And all that e'er with him be. [*Chevy Chase*]

10 Clerk Saunders and May Margaret / Walked o'er yon gravelled green, / And sad and heavy was the love, / I wot, it fell these twa between. [*Clerk Saunders*]

11 She had not sailed a league, a league, / A league but barely three, / When dismal grew his countenance, / And drumlie grew his ee. [*The Daemon Lover*]

12 'O what hills are yon, yon pleasant hills, / That the sun shines sweetly on?' / 'O yon are the hills of heaven,' he said, / 'Where you will never won.' [*The Daemon Lover*]

13 He strack the top-mast wi' his hand, / The fore-mast wi' his knee, / And he brake the gallant ship in twain, / And sank her in the sea. [*Ib.*]

14 'And what will ye leave to your ain mither dear, Edward, Edward? / And what will ye leave to your ain mither dear, / Me dear son, now tell me, O?' / 'The curse of hell frae me sall ye bear, Mither, Mither: / The curse of hell frae me sall ye bear: / Sic counsels ye gave to me, O.' [*Edward*]

15 'O where are ye gaun?' / Quo' the false knight upon the road: / 'I'm gaun to the school,' / Quo' the wee boy and still he stood. [*The False Knight Upon the Road*]

16 But ne'er a word wad ane o' them speak, / For barring of the door. [*Get up and Bar the Door*]

17 Goodman, you've spoken the foremost word, / Get up and bar the door. [*Ib.*]

18 A ship I have got in the North Country / And she goes by the name of the *Golden Vanity*. / O I fear she'll be taken by a Spanish Ga-la-lee, / As she sails by the Low-lands low. [*The Golden Vanity*]

19 He bored with his auger, he bored once and twice, / And some were playing cards and some were playing dice. [*Ib.*]

20 I wish I were where Helen lies, / Night and day on me she cries; / O that I were where Helen lies, / On fair Kirkconnell lea! [*Helen of Kirkconnell*]

21 Cursed be the heart that thought the thought, / And cursed be the hand that fired the shot, / When in my arms burd Helen dropped, / And died to succour me! [*Ib.*]

22 Gae hame, gae hame, my mither dear, / Prepare my winding sheet, / And at the back o' merry Lincoln / The morn I will you meet. [*Hugh of Lincoln*]

23 O he's gart build a bonny ship, / To sail on the salt sea; / The mast was o' the beaten gold, / The sails o' cramoisie. [*The Lass of Lochroyan*]

24 'O where ha you been, Lord Randal, my son? / And where ha you been, my handsome young man?' / 'I ha been at the

greenwood; mother, make my bed soon, / For I'm wearied wi' hunting, and fain would lie down.' [*Lord Randal*]

1 This ae nighte, this ae nighte, / *Every nighte and alle*, / Fire and fleet and candle-lighte, / *And Christ receive thy saule.* [*A Lyke-Wake Dirge*]

2 When captains courageous, whom death could not daunt, / Did march to the siege of the city of Gaunt. [*Mary Ambree*]

3 For, in my mind, of all mankind / I love but you alone. [*The Nut Brown Maid*]

4 For I must to the green-wood go / Alone, a banished man. [*Ib.*]

5 Yestreen the Queen had four Maries, / The night she'll hae but three; / There was Marie Seaton, and Marie Beaton, / And Marie Carmichael, and me. [*The Queen's Maries*]

6 But the merriest month in all the year / Is the merry month of May. [*Robin Hood and the Three Squires*]

7 Let me have length and breadth enough, / With a green sod under my head; / That they may say when I am dead, / Here lies bold Robin Hood. [*Robin Hood's Death*]

8 The king sits in Dunfermline town / Drinking the blude-red wine. [*Sir Patrick Spens*]

9 The king has written a braid letter, / And signed it wi' his hand, / And sent it to Sir Patrick Spens / Was walking on the strand. [*Ib.*]

10 To Noroway, to Noroway, / To Noroway o'er the faem; / The king's daughter o' Noroway, / 'Tis thou must bring her hame. [*Ib.*]

11 Late, late yestreen I saw the new moon, / Wi' the auld moon in her arm. [*Ib.*]

12 O lang, lang may the ladies stand, / Wi' their gold kems in their hair, / Waiting for their ain dear lords, / For they'll see them na mair. [*Ib.*]

13 Half owre, half owre to Aberdour, / 'Tis fifty fathom deep, / And there lies guid Sir Patrick Spens / Wi' the Scots lords at his feet. [*Ib.*]

14 Janet has kilted her green kirtle / A little aboon her knee, / And she has braided her yellow hair / A little aboon her bree. [*Tam Lin*]

15 She turned about her milk-white steed, / And took true Thomas up behind. [*Thomas Rhymer*]

16 It was mirk, mirk night, there was nae starlight. / They waded thro' red blude to the knee; / For all the blude that's shed on the earth / Runs through the springs o' that country. [*Ib.*]

17 And see not ye that braid, braid road, / That lies across yon lilly leven ? / That is the path of wickedness, / Tho' some call it the road to heaven. [*Ib.*]

18 There were three ravens sat on a tree, / They were as black as black might be. / The one of them said to his mate, / 'Where shall we our breakfast take?' [*The Three Ravens*]

19 As I was walking all alane, / I heard twa corbies making a mane; / The tane unto the tither did say, / 'Where sall we gang and dine to-day?'

'In behint yon auld fail dyke, / I wot there lies a new-slain knight; / And naebody kens that he lies there, / But his hawk, his hound, and lady fair.

'His hound is to the hunting gane, / His hawk to fetch the wild-fowl hame, / His lady's ta'en anither mate, / So we may mak our dinner sweet.' [*The Twa Corbies*]

20 O'er his white banes, when they are bare, / The wind sall blaw for evermair. [*Ib.*]

21 The wind doth blow today, my love, / And a few small drops of rain; / I never had but one true-love, / In cold grave she was lain. [*The Unquiet Grave*]

22 'Tis I, my love, sits on your grave, / And will not let you sleep; / For I crave one kiss of your clay-cold lips, / And that is all I seek. [*Ib.*]

23 O waly, waly, up the bank, / And waly, waly, down the brae, / And waly, waly, yon burn-side, / Where I and my love wont to gae. [*Waly, Waly*]

24 But had I wist, before I kissed, / That love had been sae ill to win, / I had locked my heart in a case o' gowd, / And pinned it wi' a siller pin. [*Ib.*]

HONORÉ DE BALZAC 1799–1850

25 *Elles doivent avoir les défauts de leurs qualités.* – They must have the defects of their qualities. [*Le Lys dans la vallée*]

21

J. C. BAMPFYLDE   1754–1796

1 Rugged the breast that beauty cannot tame. [*Sonnet in Praise of Delia*]

EDWARD BANGS   *fl.* 1775

2 Yankee Doodle came to town, / Riding on a pony; / Stuck a feather in his cap / And called it Macaroni. [*Yankee Doodle*]

THÉODORE DE BANVILLE
    1823–1891

3 *Nous n'irons plus aux bois, les lauriers sont coupés.* – We will go to the woods no more, the laurels are cut down. [*Les Cariatides*]

ANNA LETITIA BARBAULD
    1743–1825

4 Life! we've been long together, / Through pleasant and through cloudy weather; / 'Tis hard to part when friends are dear, / Perhaps 'twill cost a sigh, a tear; / Then steal away, give little warning; / Choose thine own time; / Say not 'Good-night'; but in some brighter clime / Bid me 'Good-morning'. [*Ode to Life*]

W. N. P. BARBELLION
[B. F. CUMMINGS]   1889–1919

5 Am writing an essay on the life-history of insects and have abandoned the idea of writing on 'How Cats Spend their Time'. [*The Journal of a Disappointed Man*, 3 Jan. 1903]

JOHN BARBOUR   1316?–1395

6 A! fredome is a noble thing! / Fredome mayse man to haiff liking. / Fredome al solace to man giffis; / He levys at eas that frely levys. [*The Bruce*, 225]

REV. R. H. BARHAM   1788–1845

7 'Pooh!' says his pal, 'you great dunce! / You've pouched the good gentleman's money, / So out with your whinger at once, / And scrag Jane, while I spifflicate Johnny!' [*The Babes in the Wood*]

8 Why, Captain! – my Lord! – Here's the devil to pay! / The fellow's been cut down and taken away! / What's to be done? / We've missed all the fun! – / Why, they'll laugh at and quiz us all over the town, / We are all of us done so uncommonly brown! [*Hon. Mr Sucklethumbkin's Story*]

9 The Jackdaw sat in the Cardinal's chair! / Bishop and abbot and prior were there; / Many a monk, and many a friar, / Many a knight, and many a squire, / With a great many more of lesser degree. / In sooth a goodly company; / And they served the Lord Primate on bended knee. / Never, I ween, / Was a prouder seen, / Read of in books, or dreamt of in dreams, / Than the Cardinal Lord Archbishop of Rheims. [*The Jackdaw of Rheims*]

10 And six little singing-boys, – dear little souls! / In nice clean faces, and nice white stoles. [*Ib.*]

11 And a nice little boy had a nice cake of soap, / Worthy of washing the hands of the Pope. [*Ib.*]

12 In holy anger, and pious grief, / He solemnly cursed that rascally thief! / He cursed him at board, he cursed him in bed; / From the sole of his foot to the crown of his head; / He cursed him in sleeping, that every night / He should dream of the devil, and wake in a fright. [*Ib.*]

13 Never was heard such a terrible curse!! / But what gave rise / To no little surprise, / Nobody seemed one penny the worse! [*Ib.*]

14 His head was as bald as the palm of your hand; / His eye so dim, / So wasted each limb, / That, heedless of grammar, they all cried, 'THAT'S HIM!' [*Ib.*]

15 The Lady Jane was tall and slim, / The Lady Jane was fair. [*The Knight and the Lady*]

16 He would pore by the hour, o'er a weed or a flower, / Or the slugs that come crawling out after a shower. [*Ib.*]

17 Ah, ha! my good friend! – Don't you wish you may get it? [*The Lay of St Aloys*]

18 A Franklyn's Dogge leped over a style, / And hys name was littel Byngo. [*A Lay of St Gengulphus*]

1 He had no little handkerchief to wipe his little nose. [*Misadventures at Margate*]

2 And now I'm here, from this here pier it is my fixed intent / To jump, as Mr Levi did from off the Monu-ment! [*Ib.*]

3 But when the Crier cried, 'O Yes!' the people cried, 'O No!' [*Ib.*]

4 And then he hitched his trousers up, as is, I'm told, their use, / – It's very odd that Sailor-men should wear those things so loose. [*Ib.*]

5 He smiled and said, 'Sir, does your mother know that you are out?' [*Ib.*]

6 They were a little less than 'kin', and rather more than 'kind'. [*Nell Cook*]

7 She drank prussic acid without any water, / And died like a Duke-and-a-Duchess's daughter! [*The Tragedy*]

S. BARING-GOULD   1834–1924

8 Now the day is over, / Night is drawing nigh, / Shadows of the evening / Steal across the sky. [Hymn]

9 Birds and beasts and flowers / Soon will be asleep. [*Ib.*]

10 Onward, Christian soldiers, / Marching as to war, / With the Cross of Jesus / Going on before. [Hymn]

11 Hell's foundations quiver / At the shout of praise; / Brothers, lift your voices, / Loud your anthems raise. [*Ib.*]

12 Through the night of doubt and sorrow / Onward goes the pilgrim band, / Singing songs of expectation, / Marching to the Promised Land. [Hymn]

GEORGE BARKER   1913–

13 My tall dead wives with knives in their breasts / Gaze at me, I am guilty, as they roll / Like derelicts in my tempest. [*My tall dead Wives*]

14 Seismic with laughter, / Gin and chicken helpless in her Irish hand, / Irresistible as Rabelais, but most tender for / The lame dogs and hurt birds. [Sonnet: *To my Mother*]

LADY ANNE BARNARD
1750–1825

15 My father argued sair – my mother didna speak, / But she looked in my face till

my heart was like to break; / They gied him my hand but my heart was in the sea; / And so auld Robin Gray, he was gudeman to me. [*Auld Robin Gray*]

WILLIAM BARNES   1801–1886

16 My love is the maïd ov all maïdens, / Though all mid be comely. [*In the Spring*]

17 Since I noo mwore do zee your feäce / Up steäirs or down below. [*The Wife A-Lost*]

18 When sycamore leaves wer a spreadèn, / Green-ruddy, in hedges, / Bezide the red doust o' the ridges, / A-dried at Woak Hill. [*Woak Hill*]

RICHARD BARNFIELD 1574–1627

19 As it fell upon a day, / In the merry month of May. [*Ode*]

20 King Pandion he is dead, / All thy friends are lapped in lead. [*Ib.*]

21 My flocks feed not, / My ewes breed not, / My rams speed not, / All is amiss. / Love is dying, / Faith's defying, / Heart's denying, / Causer of this. [*A Shepherd's Complaint*]

22 Nothing more certain than incertainties; / Fortune is full of fresh variety: / Constant in nothing but inconstancy. [*The Shepherd's Content*, xi]

PHINEAS T. BARNUM 1810–1891

23 There's a sucker born every minute. [Attr.]

SIR JAMES BARRIE   1860–1937

24 His lordship may compel us to be equal upstairs, but there will never be equality in the servants' hall. [*The Admirable Crichton*, I]

25 If it's heaven for climate, it's hell for company. [*The Little Minister*, Ch. 3]

26 It's grand, and ye canna expect to be baith grand and comfortable. [*Ib.* 10]

27 I do loathe explanations. [*My Lady Nicotine*, Ch. 14]

28 When the first baby laughed for the first time, the laugh broke into a thousand

pieces and they all went skipping about, and that was the beginning of fairies. [*Peter Pan*, I]

1 Every time a child says 'I don't believe in fairies,' there's a little fairy somewhere that falls down dead. [*Ib.*]

2 To die will be an awfully big adventure. [*Ib.* III]

3 But the gladness of her gladness / And the sadness of her sadness / Are as nothing, Charles, / To the badness of her badness when she's bad. [*Rosalind*]

4 One's religion is whatever he is most interested in, and yours is Success. [*The Twelve-Pound Look*]

5 It's a sort of bloom on a woman. If you have it [charm], you don't need to have anything else; and if you don't have it, it doesn't much matter what else you have. [*What Every Woman Knows*, I]

6 A young Scotsman of your ability let loose upon the world with £300, what could he not do? It's almost appalling to think of; especially if he went among the English. [*Ib.*]

7 You've forgotten the greatest moral attribute of a Scotsman, Maggie, that he'll do nothing which might damage his career. [*Ib.* II]

8 There are few more impressive sights in the world than a Scotsman on the make. [*Ib.*]

GEORGE BARRINGTON
1755–c. 1835

9 True patriots we; for be it understood, / We left our country for our country's good. [*Prologue for the opening of the Playhouse, Sydney, N.S.W.*, 1796 (the company being composed of convicts). Also attr. to Henry Carter]

WILLIAM BASSE   ?–1653?

10 Renownèd Spenser, lie a thought more nigh / To learned Chaucer, and rare Beaumont lie / A little nearer Spenser, to make room / For Shakespeare, in your threefold, fourfold tomb. [*On Shakespeare*]

EDGAR BATEMAN   19 Cent.

11 Wiv a ladder and some glasses, / You could see to 'Ackney Marshes, / If it wasn't for the 'ouses in between. [*If it wasn't for the 'ouses in between*]

CHARLES BAUDELAIRE
1821–1867

12 *Le Poète est semblable au prince des nuées / Qui hante la tempête et se rit de l'archer; / Exilé sur le sol, au milieu des huées, / Ses ailes de géant l'empêchent de marcher.* – The poet is like the prince of the clouds, who rides the tempest and scorns the archer. Exiled on the ground, amidst boos and insults, his giant's wings prevent his walking. [*L'Albatros*]

13 *Hypocrite lecteur! mon semblable, mon frère!* – Hypocritical reader, my double, my brother! [*Au Lecteur*]

14 *La nature est un temple où de vivants piliers / Laissent parfois sortir de confuses paroles; / L'homme y passe à travers des forêts de symboles / Qui l'observent avec des regards familiers.* – Nature is a temple in which living columns sometimes emit confused words. Man approaches it through forests of symbols, which observe him with familiar glances. [*Correspondances*]

15 *Voici le soir charmant, ami du criminel; / Il vient comme un complice, à pas de loup.* – Here is the charming evening, the criminal's friend. It comes like an accomplice, with stealthy tread. [*Le Crépuscule du soir*]

16 *Entends, ma chère, entends la douce Nuit qui marche.* – Listen, my darling, listen to soft night approaching. [*Recueillement*]

17 *Fourmillante cité, cité pleine de rêves, / Où le spectre en plein jour raccroche le passant! / Les mystères partout coulent comme des sèves / Dans les canaux étroits du colosse puissant.* – Swarming city, city full of dreams, where a ghost in daylight clutches a passer-by! Mysteries everywhere flow like sap in the narrow channels of the great giant. [*Les Sept Vieillards*]

18 *J'ai plus de souvenirs que si j'avais mille ans.* – I have more memories than if I were a thousand years old. [*Spleen*]

19 *Ô Mort, vieux capitaine, il est temps! levons l'ancre!* – Death, old captain, it is time, let us raise anchor! [*Le Voyage*]

24

1 *Quelle est cette île triste et noir? – C'est Cythère, / Nous dit-on, un pays fameux dans les chansons, / Eldorado banal de tous les vieux garçons. / Regardez! après tout, c'est une pauvre terre.* – What is that sad, dark island? It is Cythera, they tell us, a country famous in song, banal Eldorado of every elderly bachelor. Look, after all, it is a poor land! [*Un Voyage à Cythère*]

RICHARD BAXTER   1615–1691

2 I preached as never sure to preach again, / And as a dying man to dying men! [*Love Breathing Thanks and Praise*, 2]

SEIGNEUR DE BAYARD
                          1476–1524

3 *Le chevalier sans peur et sans reproche.* – Knight without fear and without reproach. [Description of him]

T. H. BAYLY   1797–1839

4 I'd be a butterfly; living a rover, / Dying when fair things are fading away. [*I'd be a Butterfly*]

5 Absence makes the heart grow fonder, / Isle of Beauty, fare thee well! [*Isle of Beauty*]

6 It was a dream of perfect bliss, / Too beautiful to last. [*It was a Dream*]

7 The mistletoe hung in the castle hall, / The holly branch shone on the old oak wall. [*The Mistletoe Bough*]

8 Oh! no! we never mention her, / Her name is never heard; / My lips are now forbid to speak / That once familiar word. [*Oh! No! We Never Mention Her*]

9 Oh, pilot! 'tis a fearful night, / There's danger on the deep. [*The Pilot*]

10 She wore a wreath of roses, / The night that first we met. [*She Wore a Wreath of Roses*]

11 We met, 'twas in a crowd, and I thought he would shun me. [*We Met, 'twas in a Crowd*]

12 Gaily the Troubadour / Touched his guitar. [*Welcome Me Home*]

13 Why don't the men propose, mamma, / Why don't the men propose? [*Why Don't the Men Propose?*]

PIERRE-AUGUSTIN DE
BEAUMARCHAIS   1732–1799

14 *Aujourd'hui, ce qui ne vaut pas la peine d'être dit, on le chante.* – Today when something is not worth saying, they sing it. [*Le Barbier de Séville*, I. ii]

15 *Je me presse de rire de tout, de peur d'être obligé d'en pleurer.* – I force myself to laugh at everything, for fear of being compelled to weep. [*Ib.*]

16 *Boire sans soif et faire l'amour en tout temps, madame; il n'y a que ça qui nous distingue des autres bêtes.* – Drinking when we are not thirsty and making love at all seasons, madam: that is all there is to distinguish us from the other animals. [*Le Mariage de Figaro*, II. xxi]

17 *On pense à moi pour une place, mais par malheur j'y étais propre: il fallait un calculateur, ce fut un danseur qui l'obtint.* – They thought of me for a place, but unfortunately I was suitable for it; they needed a calculator, it was a dancer that got it. [*Ib.* V. iii]

18 *Parce que vous êtes un grand seigneur, vous vous croyez un grand génie! . . . Vous vous êtes donné la peine de naître, et rien de plus.* – Because you are a great lord, you think you are a great genius! . . . You took the trouble to be born, and that is all. [*Ib.*]

FRANCIS BEAUMONT   1584–1616

19 What things have we seen, / Done at the Mermaid! heard words that have been / So nimble, and so full of subtle flame, / As if that every one from whence they came / Had meant to put his whole wit in a jest, / And had resolved to live a fool, the rest / Of his dull life. [*Letter to Ben Jonson*]

20 Mortality, behold and fear! / What a change of flesh is here! [*On the Tombs in Westminster Abbey*]

FRANCIS BEAUMONT and
JOHN FLETCHER   1579–1625

21 Bad's the best of us. [*The Bloody Brother*, IV. ii]

22 You are no better than you should be. [*The Coxcomb*, IV. iii]

25

1 But what is past my help is past my care. [*The Double Marriage*, I. i]

2 Nose, nose, jolly red nose, / And who gave thee this jolly red nose? . . . / Nutmegs and ginger, cinnamon and cloves, / And they gave me this jolly red nose. [*The Knight of the Burning Pestle*, I. iii]

3 This is a pretty flim-flam. [*Ib.* II. iii]

4 Thou wilt scarce be a man before thy mother. [*Love's Cure*, II. ii]

5 Upon my buried body lie / Lightly, gentle earth. [*The Maid's Tragedy*, II. i]

6 Nothing's so dainty sweet as lovely melancholy. [*The Nice Valour*, III. iii, Song]

7 As men / Do walk a mile, women should talk an hour, / After supper. 'Tis their exercise. [*Philaster*, II. iv]

8 All your better deeds / Shall be in water writ, but this in marble. [*Ib.* V. iii]

9 Oh, love will make a dog howl in rhyme. [*The Queen of Corinth*, IV. i]

10 Kiss till the cow come home. [*The Scornful Lady*, II. ii]

11 There is no other purgatory but a woman. [*Ib.* III. i]

12 Daisies smell-less, yet most quaint, / And sweet thyme true, / Primrose, first born child of Ver, / Merry Spring-time's harbinger. [*Two Noble Kinsmen*, I. i]

13 Care-charming Sleep, thou easer of all woes, / Brother to Death. [*Valentinian*, V. ii]

14 Come sing now, sing; for I know ye sing well, / I see ye have a singing face. [*The Wild Goose Chase*, II. ii]

SAMUEL BECKETT   1906–

15 We could have saved sixpence. We have saved fivepence. (*Pause*) But at what cost? [*All That Fall*]

16 VLADIMIR: That passed the time.
ESTRAGON: It would have passed in any case.
VLADIMIR: Yes, but not so rapidly. [*Waiting for Godot*, I]

WILLIAM BECKFORD   1759–1844

17 He did not think . . . that it was necessary to make a hell of this world to enjoy paradise in the next. [*Vathek*]

18 I am not over-fond of resisting temptation. [*Ib.*]

THOMAS BECON   1512–1567

19 For when the wine is in, the wit is out. [*Catechism*, 375]

T. L. BEDDOES   1798–1851

20 If thou wilt ease thine heart / Of love and all its smart, / Then sleep, dear, sleep. [*Death's Jest Book*, II. ii]

21 Old Adam, the carrion crow. [*Ib.* V. iv]

22 If there were dreams to sell, / What would you buy? / Some cost a passing bell; / Some a light sigh, / That shakes from Life's fresh crown / Only a roseleaf down. [*Dream-Pedlary*]

THE VENERABLE BEDE 673–735

23 When we compare the present life of man with that time of which we have no knowledge, it seems to me like the swift flight of a lone sparrow through the banqueting-hall where you sit in the winter months. . . . This sparrow flies swiftly in through one door of the hall, and out through another. . . . Similarly, man appears on earth for a little while, but we know nothing of what went on before this life, and what follows. [*History of the English Church and People*, 2. Ch. 13, transl. L. Sherley-Price]

BERNARD BEE   1823–1861

24 There is Jackson standing like a stone wall. [At first battle of Bull Run, 1861]

MAX BEERBOHM   1872–1956

25 I believe the twenty-four hour day has come to stay. [*A Christmas Garland*, 'Perkins and Mankind']

26 Most women are not so young as they are painted. [*A Defence of Cosmetics*]

27 A swear-word in a rustic slum / A simple swear-word is to some, / To Masefield something more. [*Fifty Caricatures*, caption]

1 Undergraduates owe their happiness chiefly to the consciousness that they are no longer at school. The nonsense which was knocked out of them at school is all put gently back at Oxford or Cambridge. [*Going Back to School*]

2 None, it is said, of all who revelled with the Regent, was half so wicked as Lord George Hell. [*The Happy Hypocrite*, Ch.1]

3 No Roman ever was able to say, 'I dined last night with the Borgias'. [*Hosts and Guests*]

4 Fate wrote her [Queen Caroline] a most tremendous tragedy, and she played it in tights. [*King George the Fourth*]

5 'After all,' as a pretty girl once said to me, 'women are a sex by themselves, so to speak.' [*The Pervasion of Rouge*]

6 Love-sick? He, love-sick? 'Tis a goodly jest! / The confirmed misogyn a ladies' man! [*Savonarola Brown*]

7 Hush, Sir! 'Tis my little sister / The poisoner, right well-beloved by all / Whom she as yet hath spared. [*Ib.*]

8 O the disgrace of it! – / The scandal, the incredible come-down! [*Ib.*]

9 A pretty sort of prison I have come to, / In which a self-respecting lady's cell / Is treated as a lounge. [*Ib.*]

10 At the door of the first-class waiting-room, aloof and venerable, stood the Warden of Judas. [*Zuleika Dobson*, Ch. 1]

11 Zuleika, on a desert island, would have spent most of her time in looking for a man's footprint. [*Ib.* 2]

12 The dullard's envy of brilliant men is always assuaged by the suspicion that they will come to a bad end. [*Ib.* 6]

13 'Ah, say that again', she murmured. 'Your voice is music.'
He repeated his question.
'Music,' she said dreamily; and such is the force of habit that 'I don't,' she added, 'know anything about music, really. But I know what I like.' [*Ib.* 16]

APHRA BEHN   1640–1689

14 Love ceases to be a pleasure, when it ceases to be a secret. [*The Lover's Watch*, 'Four o'Clock']

15 Faith, sir, we are here today, and gone tomorrow. [*The Lucky Chance*, IV]

16 Variety is the soul of pleasure. [*The Rover*, Pt 2. I]

17 Come away; poverty's catching. [*Ib.*]

18 Money speaks sense in a language all nations understand. [*Ib.* 2. III. i]

W. H. BELLAMY   19 Cent.

19 Old Simon the Cellarer keeps a rare store / Of malmsey and malvoisie. [*Simon the Cellarer*]

BELLAY *see under* DU BELLAY

HILAIRE BELLOC   1870–1953

20 I shoot the Hippopotamus / With bullets made of platinum, / Because if I use leaden ones / His hide is sure to flatten 'em. [*Bad Child's Book of Beasts*, 'The Hippopotamus']

21 The nicest child I ever knew / Was Charles Augustus Fortescue. [*Cautionary Tales*, 'Charles Augustus Fortescue']

22 He thus became immensely rich, / And built the splendid mansion which / Is called 'The Cedars, Muswell Hill'. [*Ib.*]

23 Alas! That such affected tricks / Should flourish in a child of six! [*Ib.* 'Godolphin Horne']

24 The chief defect of Henry King / Was chewing little bits of string. [*Ib.* 'Henry King']

25 They answered, as they took their fees, / 'There is no cure for this disease'. [*Ib.*]

26 There was a boy whose name was Jim; / His friends were very good to him. [*Ib.* 'Jim']

27 'Ponto!' he cried, with angry frown, / 'Let go, Sir! Down, Sir! Put it down!' [*Ib.*]

28 And always keep a hold of Nurse / For fear of finding something worse. [*Ib.*]

29 Lord Lundy from his earliest years / Was far too freely moved to tears. [*Ib.* 'Lord Lundy']

30 In my opinion butlers ought / To know their place, and not to play / The Old Retainer night and day. [*Ib.*]

31 We had intended you to be / The next Prime Minister but three. [*Ib.*]

1 My language fails! / Go out and govern New South Wales! [*Cautionary Tales,* 'Lord Lundy']

2 Matilda told such dreadful lies, / It made one gasp and stretch one's eyes; / Her aunt, who, from her earliest youth, / Had kept a strict regard for truth, / Attempted to believe Matilda: / The effort very nearly killed her. [*Ib.* 'Matilda']

3 And summoned the immediate aid / Of London's noble Fire Brigade. [*Ib.*]

4 For every time she shouted 'Fire!' / They only answered 'Little liar!' [*Ib.*]

5 Her aunt went off to the theatre / To see that interesting play / *The Second Mrs Tanqueray.* [*Ib.*]

6 A trick that everyone abhors / In little girls is slamming doors. [*Ib.* 'Rebecca']

7 From quiet homes and first beginning, / Out to the undiscovered ends, / There's nothing worth the wear of winning, / But laughter and the love of friends. [*Dedicatory Ode*]

8 They died to save their country and they only saved the world. [*The English Graves*]

9 I said to Heart, 'How goes it?' Heart replied: / 'Right as a Ribstone Pippin!' But it lied. [*Epigrams,* 'The False Heart']

10 Of this bad world the loveliest and best / Has smiled and said 'Good Night', and gone to rest. [*Ib.* 'On a Dead Hostess']

11 The accursed power which stands on Privilege / (And goes with Women, and Champagne, and Bridge) / Broke – and Democracy resumed her reign: / (Which goes with Bridge, and Women, and Champagne). [*Ib.* 'On a General Election']

12 When I am dead, I hope it may be said: / 'His sins were scarlet, but his books were read'. [*Ib.* 'On His Books']

13 The Devil, having nothing else to do, / Went off to tempt my Lady Poltagrue. / My Lady, tempted by a private whim, / To his extreme annoyance, tempted him. [*Ib.* 'On Lady Poltagrue']

14 Sally is gone that was so kindly, / Sally is gone from Ha'nacker Hill. [*Ha'nacker Mill*]

15 The most degraded of them all / Mediterranean we call. / His hair is crisp, and even curls, / And he is saucy with the girls. [*Ladies and Gentlemen,* 'The Three Races']

16 Remote and ineffectual Don / That dared attack my Chesterton. [*Lines to a Don*]

17 Dons admirable! Dons of might! / Uprising on my inward sight / Compact of ancient tales, and port, / And sleep – and learning of a sort. [*Ib.*]

18 Oh! let us never, never doubt / What nobody is sure about! [*More Beasts for Worse Children,* 'The Microbe']

19 I had an aunt in Yucatan / Who bought a python from a man / And kept it for a pet. / She died, because she never knew / These simple little rules and few: – / The snake is living yet. [*Ib.* 'The Python']

20 When I am living in the Midlands / That are sodden and unkind. [*The South Country*]

21 I will hold my house in the high wood / Within a walk of the sea, / And the men that were boys when I was a boy / Shall sit and drink with me. [*Ib.*]

22 Do you remember an inn, / Miranda? [*Tarantella*]

23 The fleas that tease in the high Pyrenees. [*Ib.*]

24 It is the best of all trades, to make songs, and the second best to sing them. [*On Everything,* 'On Song']

25 When you have lost your inns drown your empty selves, for you will have lost the last of England. [*This and That,* 'On Inns']

P.-L. DE BELLOY 1727–1775

26 *Plus je vis d'étrangers, plus j'aimai ma patrie.* – The more foreigners I saw, the more I loved my native land. [*Le Siège de Calais,* ii. 2]

ROBERT BENCHLEY 1889–1945

27 I do most of my work sitting down; that's where I shine. [Quoted in *Treasury of Humorous Quotations*]

JULIEN BENDA 1867–1952

28 *La Trahison des clercs.* – The treason of the intellectuals. [Title of book, 1927]

ARNOLD BENNETT 1867–1931

1 'Ye can call it influenza if ye like,' said Mrs Machin. 'There was no influenza in my young days. We called a cold a cold.' [*The Card*, Ch. 8]

2 Pessimism, when you get used to it, is just as agreeable as optimism. [*Things that have Interested Me*, 'The Slump in Pessimism']

3 Well, my deliberate opinion is – it's a jolly strange world. [*The Title*, I]

4 Being a husband is a whole-time job. That is why so many husbands fail. They cannot give their entire attention to it. [*Ib.*]

5 Journalists say a thing that they know isn't true, in the hope that if they keep on saying it long enough it *will* be true. [*Ib.* II]

A. C. BENSON 1862–1925

6 Land of Hope and Glory, Mother of the Free, / How shall we extol thee, who are born of thee? / Wider still and wider shall thy bounds be set; / God who made thee mighty, make thee mightier yet. [Song from *Pomp and Circumstance*, set by Sir Edward Elgar]

JEREMY BENTHAM 1748–1832

7 The greatest happiness of the greatest number is the foundation of morals and legislation. [*The Commonplace Book*]

8 All punishment is mischief: all punishment in itself is evil. [*Principles of Morals and Legislation*, Ch. 13]

E. C. BENTLEY 1875–1956

9 I cannot think of any repartee, / I simply wag my great, long, furry ears. [*Ballade of Plain Common Sense*]

10 Geography is about maps, / But Biography is about chaps. [*Biography for Beginners*]

11 What I like about Clive / Is that he is no longer alive. / There is a great deal to be said / For being dead. [*Ib.* 'Clive']

12 George the Third / Ought never to have occurred. / One can only wonder / At so grotesque a blunder. [*Ib.* 'George III']

13 Sir Christopher Wren / Said, 'I am going to dine with some men, / If anybody calls / Say I am designing St Paul's.' [*Biography for Beginners*. 'Sir Christopher Wren']

RICHARD BENTLEY 1662–1742

14 It is a pretty poem, Mr Pope, but you must not call it Homer. [Of Pope's *Iliad*. Quoted in Johnson's *Life of Pope*]

15 It is a maxim with me that no man was ever written out of reputation but by himself. [Quoted in Monk's *Life of Bentley*]

PIERRE-JEAN DE BÉRANGER 1780–1857

16 *Nos amis, les ennemis.* – Our friends, the enemy. [*L'Opinion de ces demoiselles*]

BISHOP GEORGE BERKELEY 1685–1753

17 Westward the course of empire takes its way; / The four first acts already past, / A fifth shall close the drama with the day: / Time's noblest offspring is the last. [*On the Prospects of Planting Arts and Learning in America*]

W. B. BERNARD 1807–1875

18 A Storm in a Teacup. [Title of a farce]

THEOBALD VON BETHMANN HOLLWEG 1856–1921

19 Just for a word – 'neutrality', a word which in wartime has so often been disregarded, just for a scrap of paper – Great Britain is going to make war. [To Sir Edward Goschen, 4 Aug. 1914]

JOHN BETJEMAN 1906–

20 Phone for the fish knives, Norman, / As Cook is a little unnerved. [*How to Get on in Society*]

21 The Church's Restoration / In eighteen-eighty-three / Has left for contemplation / Not what there used to be. [*Hymn*]

29

1 Sing art and crafty praise! / He gave the brass for burnishing, / He gave the thick red baize. [*Hymn*]

2 Conifer county of Surrey approached / Through remarkable wrought-iron gates. [*Pot Pourri from a Surrey Garden*]

UGO BETTI 1892–1953

3 Everyone has, inside himself ... what shall I call it? A piece of good news! Everyone is ... a very great, very important character! [*The Burnt Flower-Bed*, II]

JACOB BEULER 19 Cent.

4 If I had a donkey wot wouldn't go / D'ye think I'd wollop him? no, no, no. [*Song* (*c.* 1822)]

WILLIAM, LORD BEVERIDGE 1879–1963

5 The object of government in peace and in war is not the glory of rulers or of races, but the happiness of the common man. [*Social Insurance*]

BHAGAVAD-GITA

6 It is not that I have never existed before, nor thou, nor all these kings. Nor is it that all shall cease to exist hereafter.
As in this body the embodied soul passes through childhood, youth and old age, in the same manner it goes from one body to another; therefore the wise are never deluded regarding it. [Ch. II. 12]

7 He who considers this [Self] as a slayer or he who thinks that this [Self] is slain, neither of these knows the Truth. For it does not slay, nor is it slain. [*Ib.* II. 19]

8 For that which is born death is certain, and for the dead birth is certain. Therefore grieve not over that which is unavoidable. [*Ib.* II. 27]

THE BIBLE
Old Testament

Genesis

9 In the beginning God created the heaven and the earth.
And the earth was without form, and void; and darkness was upon the face of the deep. [1:1]

10 And God said, Let there be light: and there was light. [1:3]

11 *Fiat lux.* [*Ib. Vulgate* version]

12 So God created man in his own image, in the image of God created he him; male and female created he them. [1:27]

13 Be fruitful, and multiply, and replenish the earth. [1:28]

14 And God saw everything that he had made, and, behold, it was very good. [1:31]

15 And the Lord God formed man of the dust of the ground, and breathed into his nostrils the breath of life; and man became a living soul. [2:7]

16 And the Lord God said, It is not good that the man should be alone. [2:18]

17 This is now bone of my bones, and flesh of my flesh. [2:23]

18 Therefore shall a man leave his father and his mother, and shall cleave unto his wife: and they shall be one flesh. [2:24]

19 Now the serpent was more subtil than any beast of the field. [3:1]

20 Ye shall be as gods, knowing good and evil. [3:5]

21 And they sewed fig-leaves together, and made themselves aprons. [('breeches' for 'aprons' in *Genevan Bible*, 1560) 3:7]

22 And they heard the voice of the Lord God walking in the garden in the cool of the day. [3:8]

23 I was afraid, because I was naked; and I hid myself. [3:10]

24 Upon thy belly shalt thou go, and dust shalt thou eat all the days of thy life. [3:14]

25 In sorrow thou shalt bring forth children. [3:16]

26 In the sweat of thy face shalt thou eat bread. [3:19]

27 For dust thou art, and unto dust shalt thou return. [*Ib.*]

28 The mother of all living. [3:20]

29 Am I my brother's keeper? [4:9]

30 The voice of thy brother's blood crieth unto me from the ground. [4:10]

31 My punishment is greater than I can bear. [4:13]

1 And the Lord set a mark upon Cain. [4:15]

2 Dwelt in the land of Nod, on the east of Eden. [4:16]

3 The sons of God saw the daughters of men, that they were fair. [6:2]

4 There were giants in the earth in those days. [6:4]

5 Mighty men which were of old, men of renown. [Ib.]

6 The same day were all the fountains of the great deep broken up, and the windows of heaven were opened. [7:11]

7 But the dove found no rest for the sole of her foot. [8:9]

8 In her mouth was an olive-leaf pluckt off. [8:11]

9 Whoso sheddeth man's blood, by man shall his blood be shed. [9:6]

10 I do set my bow in the cloud, and it shall be for a token of a covenant between me and the earth. [9:13]

11 Nimrod the mighty hunter before the Lord. [10:9]

12 Thou shalt be buried in a good old age. [15:15]

13 His hand will be against every man, and every man's hand against him. [16:12]

14 Shall not the Judge of all the earth do right? [18:25]

15 Behold behind him a ram caught in the thicket by his horns. [22:13]

16 Esau selleth his birthright for a mess of pottage. [25. Chapter heading in *Genevan Bible*]

17 The voice is Jacob's voice, but the hands are the hands of Esau. [27:22]

18 And Mizpah; for he said, The Lord watch between thee and me, when we are absent one from another. [31:49]

19 I will not let thee go, except thou bless me. [32:26]

20 He made him a coat of many colours. [37:3]

21 Behold, this dreamer cometh. [37:19]

22 And the lean and the ill favoured kine did eat up the first seven fat kine. [41:20]

23 Jacob saw that there was corn in Egypt. [42:1]

24 Ye are spies; to see the nakedness of the land ye are come. [42:9]

25 Then shall ye bring down my grey hairs with sorrow to the grave. [42:38]

26 Ye shall eat the fat of the land. [45:18]

27 See that ye fall not out by the way. [45:24]

28 Few and evil have the days of the years of my life been. [47:9]

29 Unstable as water, thou shalt not excel. [49:4]

Exodus

30 Now there arose up a new king over Egypt, which knew not Joseph. [1:8]

31 I have been a stranger in a strange land. [2:22]

32 Behold, the bush burned with fire, and the bush was not consumed. [3:2]

33 A land flowing with milk and honey. [3:8]

34 And God said unto Moses, I AM THAT I AM. [3:14]

35 But I am slow of speech, and of a slow tongue. [4:10]

36 Ye shall no more give the people straw to make brick. [5:7]

37 Multiply my signs and my wonders in the land of Egypt. [7:3]

38 Even darkness which may be felt. [10:21]

39 With your loins girded, your shoes on your feet, and your staff in your hand. [12:11]

40 They spoiled the Egyptians. [12:36]

41 In the land of Egypt, when we sat by the flesh pots, and when we did eat bread to the full. [16:3]

42 Eye for eye, tooth for tooth, hand for hand foot for foot. [21:24; also *Deuteronomy* 19:21]

43 Thou shalt not seethe a kid in his mother's milk. [23:19]

44 Thou art a stiff-necked people. [33:3]

45 There shall no man see me, and live. [33:20]

Leviticus

46 Let him go for a scapegoat into the wilderness. [16:10]

1 Thou shalt love thy neighbour as thyself. [19:18; also *St Matthew*, 19:19]

Numbers

2 The Lord bless thee, and keep thee.
The Lord make his face shine upon thee, and be gracious unto thee. [6:24]

3 Sent to spy out the land. [13:16]

4 Smote him with the edge of the sword. [21:24]

5 Let me die the death of the righteous, and let my last end be like his! [23:10]

6 Be sure your sin will find you out. [32:23]

Deuteronomy

7 Man doth not live by bread only, but by every word that proceedeth out of the mouth of the Lord doth man live. [8:3; also *St Matthew*, 4:4 and *St Luke*, 4:4 (with 'alone' for 'only')]

8 If there arise among you a prophet, or a dreamer of dreams. [13:1]

9 The wife of thy bosom. [13:6]

10 Thou shalt not muzzle the ox when he treadeth out the corn. [25:4]

11 In the morning thou shalt say, Would God it were even! and at even thou shalt say, Would God it were morning! [28:67]

12 He kept him as the apple of his eye. [32:10]

13 Jeshurun waxed fat, and kicked. [32:15]

14 As thy days, so shall thy strength be. [33:25]

15 The eternal God is thy refuge, and underneath are the everlasting arms. [33:27]

Joshua

16 This line of scarlet thread. [2:18]

17 Hewers of wood and drawers of water. [9:21]

18 I am going the way of all the earth. [23:14]

Judges

19 I arose a mother in Israel. [5:7]

20 The stars in their courses fought against Sisera. [5:20]

21 She brought forth butter in a lordly dish. [5:25]

22 At her feet he bowed, he fell, he lay down. [5:27]

23 Why tarry the wheels of his chariots? [5:28]

24 Have they not divided the prey; to every man a damsel or two? [5:30]

25 Faint, yet pursuing. [8:4]

26 Out of the eater came forth meat, and out of the strong came forth sweetness. [14:14]

27 If ye had not plowed with my heifer, ye had not found out my riddle. [14:18]

28 He smote them hip and thigh [15:8]

29 The Philistines be upon thee. [16:9]

30 He wist not that the Lord was departed from him. [16:20]

31 From Dan even to Beer-sheba. [20:1]

32 The people arose as one man. [20:8]

Ruth

33 Whither thou goest, I will go; and where thou lodgest, I will lodge: thy people shall be my people, and thy God my God. [1:16]

34 The Lord do so to me, and more also, if ought but death part thee and me. [1:17]

1 Samuel

35 Speak, Lord; for thy servant heareth. [3:9]

36 Be strong, and quit yourselves like men. [4:9]

37 I-chabod, saying, The glory is departed from Israel. [4:21]

38 Is Saul also among the prophets? [10:11]

39 The Lord hath sought him a man after his own heart. [13:14]

40 Agag came unto him delicately. And Agag said, Surely the bitterness of death is past. [15:32]

41 Saul hath slain his thousands, and David his ten thousands. [18:7]

2 Samuel

42 Tell it not in Gath, publish it not in the streets of Askelon; lest the daughters of

the Philistines rejoice, lest the daughters of the uncircumcised triumph. [1:20]

1 Saul and Jonathan were lovely and pleasant in their lives, and in their death they were not divided. [1:23]

2 How are the mighty fallen in the midst of the battle! [1:25]

3 Thy love to me was wonderful, passing the love of women. [1:26]

4 Abner with the hinder end of the spear smote him under the fifth rib. [2:23]

5 Tarry at Jericho until your beards be grown. [10:5]

6 The poor man had nothing, save one little ewe lamb. [12:3]

7 And Nathan said to David, Thou art the the man. [12:7]

8 Come out, come out, thou bloody man, and thou man of Belial. [16:7]

9 Would God I had died for thee, O Absalom, my son, my son! [18:33]

1 Kings

10 A proverb and a byword among all people. [9:7]

11 Behold, the half was not told me. [10:7]

12 My father hath chastised you with whips, but I will chastise you with scorpions. [12:11]

13 To your tents, O Israel. [12:16]

14 He slept with his fathers. [14:20]

15 How long halt ye between two opinions? [18:21]

16 He is talking, or he is pursuing, or he is in a journey, or peradventure he sleepeth, and must be awaked. [18:27]

17 There ariseth a little cloud out of the sea, like a man's hand. [18:44]

18 And after the fire a still small voice. [19:12]

19 Elijah passed by him, and cast his mantle upon him. [19:19]

20 Hast thou found me, O mine enemy? [21:20]

21 I saw all Israel scattered upon the hills, as sheep that have not a shepherd. [22:17]

22 And a certain man drew a bow at a ven-

ture, and smote the king of Israel between the joints of the harness. [22:34]

2 Kings

23 Go up, thou bald head. [2:23]

24 Is it well with the child? And she answered, It is well. [4:26]

25 There is death in the pot. [4:40]

26 He shall know that there is a prophet in Israel. [5:8]

27 Is thy servant a dog, that he should do this great thing? [8:13]

28 The driving is like the driving of Jehu, the son of Nimshi; for he driveth furiously. [9:20]

29 Had Zimri peace, who slew his master? [9:31]

Esther

30 Let it be written among the laws of the Persians and the Medes, that it be not altered. [1:19]

31 Thus shall it be done to the man whom the king delighteth to honour. [6:9]

Job

32 One that feared God, and eschewed evil. [1:1]

33 And the Lord said unto Satan, Whence comest thou? Then Satan answered the Lord, and said, From going to and fro in the earth, and from walking up and down in it. [1:7]

34 Naked came I out of my mother's womb, and naked shall I return thither: the Lord gave, and the Lord hath taken away; blessed be the name of the Lord. [1:21]

35 Skin for skin, yea, all that a man hath will he give for his life. [2:4]

36 Curse God, and die. [2:9]

37 There the wicked cease from troubling; and there the weary be at rest. [3:17]

38 The hair of my flesh stood up. [4:15]

39 Shall mortal man be more just than God? shall a man be more pure than his maker? [4:17]

40 Man is born unto trouble, as the sparks fly upward. [5:7]

41 My days are swifter than a weaver's shuttle, and are spent without hope. [7:6]

1 He shall return no more to his house, neither shall his place know him any more. [7:10]

2 Canst thou by searching find out God? [11:7]

3 No doubt but ye are the people, and wisdom shall die with you. [12:2]

4 Man that is born of a woman is of few days, and full of trouble. [14:1]

5 Miserable comforters are ye all. [16:2]

6 I am escaped with the skin of my teeth. [19:20]

7 I know that my redeemer liveth, and that he shall stand at the latter day upon the earth. [19:25]

8 Seeing the root of the matter is found in me. [19:28]

9 The price of wisdom is above rubies. [28:18]

10 I was eyes to the blind, and feet was I to the lame.
   I was a father to the poor: and the cause which I knew not I searched out. [29:15]

11 That mine adversary had written a book. [31:35]

12 Who is this that darkeneth counsel by words without knowledge? [38:2]

13 Gird up now thy loins like a man. [38:3]

14 When the morning stars sang together, and all the sons of God shouted for joy. [38:7]

15 Canst thou bind the sweet influences of the Pleiades, or loose the bands of Orion? [38:31]

16 He saith among the trumpets, Ha, ha; and he smelleth the battle afar off, the thunder of the captains, and the shouting. [39:25]

17 Canst thou draw out leviathan with an hook? [41:1]

18 He maketh the deep to boil like a pot. [41:31]

19 I have heard of thee by the hearing of the ear: but now mine eye seeth thee. [42:5]

20 So the Lord blessed the latter end of Job more than his beginning. [42:12]

Psalms

21 Nor sitteth in the seat of the scornful. [1:1]

22 Why do the heathen rage, and the people imagine a vain thing? [2:1]

23 Thou shalt break them with a rod of iron; thou shalt dash them in pieces like a potter's vessel. [2:9]

24 Stand in awe, and sin not: commune with your heart upon your bed, and be still. [4:4]

25 Lord, lift thou up the light of thy countenance upon us. [4:6]

26 Let them perish through their own imaginations. [5:11, *Book of Common Prayer* version]

27 God is a righteous Judge, strong and patient: and God is provoked every day. [7:12, *Book of Common Prayer* version]

28 Out of the mouth of babes and sucklings hast thou ordained strength. [8:2]

29 Thou hast made him a little lower than the angels. [8:5]

30 The fowl of the air, and the fish of the sea, and whatsoever passeth through the paths of the seas. [8:8]

31 Their memorial is perished with them. [9:6]

32 Up, Lord, and let not man have the upper hand. [9:19, *Book of Common Prayer* version]

33 They do but flatter with their lips, and dissemble in their double heart. [12:2, *Book of Common Prayer* version]

34 The fool hath said in his heart, There is no God. [14:1 and 53:1]

35 He that sweareth to his own hurt, and changeth not. [15:4]

36 The lines are fallen unto me in pleasant places; yea, I have a goodly heritage. [16:6]

37 Keep me as the apple of the eye; hide me under the shadow of thy wings. [17:8]

38 Yea, he did fly upon the wings of the wind. [18:10]

39 The heavens declare the glory of God; and the firmament sheweth his handiwork.
   Day unto day uttereth speech, and

night unto night sheweth knowledge. [19:1]

1 More to be desired are they than gold, yea, than much fine gold: sweeter also than honey and the honeycomb. [19:10]

2 Let the words of my mouth, and the meditation of my heart, be acceptable in thy sight, O Lord. [19:14]

3 Some trust in chariots, and some in horses: but we will remember the name of the Lord our God. [20:7]

4 My God, my God, why hast thou forsaken me? [22:1; also St Matthew, 27:46 and St Mark, 15:34]

5 O my God, I cry in the daytime, but thou hearest not; and in the night season, and am not silent. [22:2]

6 But I am a worm, and no man; a reproach of men, and despised of the people. [22:6]

7 Strong bulls of Bashan have beset me round. [22:12]

8 They pierced my hands and my feet.
I may tell all my bones: they look and stare upon me.
They part my garments among them, and cast lots upon my vesture. [22:16]

9 The Lord is my shepherd; I shall not want.
He maketh me to lie down in green pastures: he leadeth me beside the still waters. [23:3]

10 Yea, though I walk through the valley of the shadow of death, I will fear no evil: for thou art with me; thy rod and thy staff they comfort me. [23:4]

11 The earth is the Lord's, and the fulness thereof; the world, and they that dwell therein. [24:1]

12 Lift up your heads, O ye gates; and be ye lift up, ye everlasting doors; and the King of glory shall come in.
Who is this King of glory? The Lord strong and mighty, the Lord mighty in battle. [24:7]

13 Remember not the sins of my youth, nor my transgressions. [25:7]

14 I should utterly have fainted: but that I believe verily to see the goodness of the Lord in the land of the living. [27:15, Book of Common Prayer version]

15 Weeping may endure for a night, but joy cometh in the morning. [30:5]

16 Into thy hands I commend my spirit. [31:6, Book of Common Prayer version]

17 I am clean forgotten, as a dead man out of mind. [31:14, Book of Common Prayer version]

18 Thou shalt keep them secretly in a pavilion from the strife of tongues. [31:20]

19 Sing unto him a new song; play skilfully with a loud noise, [33:3]

20 The Lord bringeth the counsel of the heathen to nought. [33:10]

21 Eschew evil, and do good: seek peace, and ensue it. [34:14, Book of Common Prayer version]

22 I have been young, and now am old; yet have I not seen the righteous forsaken, nor his seed begging bread. [37:25]

23 I myself have seen the ungodly in great power: and flourishing like a green bay tree. [37:36, Book of Common Prayer version]

24 He heapeth up riches, and knoweth not who shall gather them. [39:6]

25 Thou makest his beauty to consume away, like as it were a moth fretting a garment: every man therefore is but vanity. [39:12, Book of Common Prayer version]

26 Blessed is he that considereth the poor: the Lord will deliver him in time of trouble. [41:1]

27 Yea, mine own familiar friend, in whom I trusted, which did eat of my bread, hath lifted up his heel against me. 41:9]

28 As the hart panteth after the water brooks, so panteth my soul after thee, O God. [42:1]

29 Deep calleth unto deep. [42:7]

30 My heart is inditing a great matter: I speak of the things which I have made touching the king: my tongue is the pen of a ready writer. [45:1]

31 God is our refuge and strength, a very present help in trouble. [46:1]

32 He maketh wars to cease unto the end of the earth; he breaketh the bow, and cutteth the spear in sunder; he burneth the chariot in the fire.

Be still, and know that I am God. [46:9]

1 He shall subdue the people under us, and the nations under our feet. [47:3]

2 God is gone up with a merry noise: and the Lord with the sound of the trump. [47:5, *Book of Common Prayer* version]

3 Their inward thought is, that their houses shall continue for ever, and their dwelling-places to all generations; they call their lands after their own names.

Nevertheless, man being in honour abideth not: he is like the beasts that perish. [49:11]

4 For every beast of the forest is mine, and the cattle upon a thousand hills. [50:10]

5 Purge me with hyssop, and I shall be clean: wash me, and I shall be whiter than snow. [51:7]

6 The sacrifices of God are a broken spirit; a broken and a contrite heart, O God, thou wilt not despise. [51:17]

7 O that I had wings like a dove! for then would I fly away, and be at rest. [55:6]

8 We took sweet counsel together, and walked unto the house of God in company. [55:14]

9 The words of his mouth were smoother than butter, but war was in his heart: his words were softer than oil, yet were they drawn swords. [55:21]

10 They have digged a pit before me, into the midst whereof they are fallen themselves. [57:6]

11 They are like the deaf adder that stoppeth her ear;

Which will not hearken to the voice of charmers, charm he never so wisely. [58:4]

12 They grin like a dog, and run about through the city. [59:6, *Book of Common Prayer* version]

13 Moab is my wash-pot; over Edom will I cast out my shoe. [60:8]

14 Give us help from trouble: for vain is the help of man. [60:11 and 108:12]

15 He only is my rock and my salvation: he is my defence; I shall not be moved. [62:6]

16 If riches increase, set not your heart upon them.

God hath spoken once; twice have I heard this; that power belongeth unto God. [62:10]

17 When I remember thee upon my bed, and meditate on thee in the night watches. [63:6]

18 They shall fall by the sword: they shall be a portion for foxes. [63:10]

19 O thou that hearest prayer, unto thee shall all flesh come. [65:2]

20 Thou crownest the year with thy goodness; and thy paths drop fatness.

They drop upon the pastures of the wilderness: and the little hills rejoice on every side. [65:11]

21 God be merciful unto us, and bless us: and shew us the light of his countenance, and be merciful unto us. [67:1, *Book of Common Prayer* version]

22 Let God arise, let his enemies be scattered: let them also that hate him flee before him.

As smoke is driven away, so drive them away: as wax melteth before the fire, so let the wicked perish at the presence of God. [68:1]

23 A father of the fatherless, and a judge of the widows, is God in his holy habitation. [68:5]

24 Why leap ye, ye high hills? [68:16]

25 Thou hast ascended on high, thou hast led captivity captive. [68:18]

26 The singers went before, the players on instruments followed after; amongst them were the damsels playing with timbrels. [68:25]

27 They gave me also gall for my meat; and in my thirst they gave me vinegar to drink. [69:21]

28 His enemies shall lick the dust. [72:9]

29 God is the judge: he putteth down one, and setteth up another. [75:7]

30 In the hand of the Lord, there is a cup, and the wine is red. [75:8]

31 A stubborn and rebellious generation. [78:8]

32 Man did eat angels' food. [78:25]

33 Then the Lord awaked as one out of sleep, and like a mighty man that shouteth by reason of wine.

And he smote his enemies in the hinder parts. [78:65]

1 Thou feedest them with the bread of tears. [80:5]

2 They go from strength to strength. [84:7]

3 For a day in thy courts is better than a thousand. I had rather be a doorkeeper in the house of my God, than to dwell in the tents of wickedness. [84:10]

4 Mercy and truth are met together; righteousness and peace have kissed each other. [85:10]

5 Before the mountains were brought forth, or ever thou hadst formed the earth and the world, even from everlasting to everlasting, thou art God. [90:2]

6 Thou art God from everlasting, and world without end. [Ib. Book of Common Prayer version]

7 For a thousand years in thy sight are but as yesterday when it is past, and as a watch in the night. [90:4]

8 In the morning they are like grass which groweth up.
In the morning it flourisheth, and groweth up; in the evening it is cut down, and withereth. [90:5]

9 We spend our years as a tale that is told.
The days of our years are threescore years and ten; and if by reason of strength they be fourscore years, yet is their strength labour and sorrow; for it is soon cut off, and we fly away. [90:9]

10 So teach us to number our days, that we may apply our hearts unto wisdom. [90:12]

11 Surely he shall deliver thee from the snare of the fowler, and from the noisome pestilence. [91:3]

12 Thou shalt not be afraid for the terror by night; nor for the arrow that flieth by day.
Nor for the pestilence that walketh in darkness; nor for the destruction that wasteth at noonday.
A thousand shall fall at thy side, and ten thousand at thy right hand; but it shall not come nigh thee. [91:5]

13 For he shall give his angels charge over thee, to keep thee in all thy ways.
They shall bear thee up in their hands, lest thou dash thy foot against a stone. [91:11]

14 But my horn shalt thou exalt like the horn of an unicorn: I shall be anointed with fresh oil. [92:10]

15 The righteous shall flourish like the palm-tree: he shall grow like a cedar in Lebanon. [92:12]

16 They shall bring forth fruit in old age; they shall be fat and flourishing. [92:14]

17 He that planted the ear, shall he not hear? he that formed the eye, shall he not see? [94:9]

18 O sing unto the Lord a new song. [96:1 and 98:1]

19 Let the floods clap their hands: let the hills be joyful together. [98:8]

20 I am like a pelican of the wilderness: I am like an owl of the desert.
I watch, and am as a sparrow alone upon the house-top. [102:6]

21 As for man, his days are as grass: as a flower of the field, so he flourisheth.
For the wind passeth over it, and it is gone; and the place thereof shall know it no more [103:15]

22 And wine that maketh glad the heart of man, and oil to make his face to shine, and bread which strengtheneth man's heart. [104:15]

23 The young lions roar after their prey, and seek their meat from God. [104:21]

24 Man goeth forth to his work, and to his labour until the evening. [104:23]

25 Thus were they defiled with their own works, and went a whoring with their own inventions. [106:39]

26 He brought them out of darkness and the shadow of death, and brake their bands in sunder. [107:14]

27 They were even hard at death's door. [107:18, Book of Common Prayer version]

28 They that go down to the sea in ships, that do business in great waters.
These see the works of the Lord, and his wonders in the deep. [107:23]

29 They reel to and fro, and stagger like a drunken man, and are at their wit's end. [107:27]

30 Sit thou at my right hand, until I make thine enemies thy footstool. [110:1]

31 The fear of the Lord is the beginning of wisdom. [111:10]

1 He raiseth up the poor out of the dust, and lifteth the needy out of the dunghill. [113:7]

2 The mountains skipped like rams, and the little hills like lambs. [114:4]

3 They have mouths, but they speak not: eyes have they, but they see not.

They have ears, but they hear not; noses have they, but they smell not. [115:5]

4 I said in my haste, All men are liars. [116:11]

5 Precious in the sight of the Lord is the death of his saints. [116:15]

6 The stone which the builders refused is become the head stone of the corner. [118:22]

7 Thy word is a lamp unto my feet, and a light unto my path [119:105]

8 Woe is me, that I sojourn in Mesech, that I dwell in the tents of Kedar. [120: 5]

9 I am for peace: but when I speak, they are for war. [120:7]

10 I will lift up mine eyes unto the hills from whence cometh my help. [121:1]

11 He will not suffer thy foot to be moved: he that keepeth thee will not slumber. [121:3]

12 The Lord is thy keeper: the Lord is the shade upon thy right hand.

The sun shall not smite thee by day, nor the moon by night. [121:5]

13 The Lord shall preserve thy going out, and thy coming in, from this time forth, and even for evermore. [121:8]

14 Peace be within thy walls, and prosperity within thy palaces. [122:7]

15 The Lord hath done great things for us; whereof we are glad.

Turn again our captivity, O Lord, as the streams in the south.

They that sow in tears, shall reap in joy. [126:3]

16 Except the Lord build the house, they labour in vain that build it. [127:1]

17 It is vain for you to rise up early, to sit up late, to eat the bread of sorrows: for so he giveth his beloved sleep. [127:2]

18 Happy is the man that hath his quiver full of them [children]. [127:5]

19 Thy children like the olive-branches round about thy table. [128:3, *Book of Common Prayer* version]

20 Out of the depths have I cried unto thee, O Lord. [130:1]

21 If thou, Lord, shouldst mark iniquities, O Lord, who shall stand? [130:3]

22 Behold, how good and how pleasant it is for brethren to dwell together in unity!

It is like the precious ointment upon the head that ran down upon the beard, even Aaron's beard, that went down to the skirts of his garments. [133:1]

23 His mercy endureth for ever. [136:1]

24 By the rivers of Babylon, there we sat down, yea, we wept when we remembered Zion.

We hanged our harps upon the willows in the midst thereof. [137:1]

25 Sing us one of the songs of Zion.

How shall we sing the Lord's song in a strange land?

If I forget thee, O Jerusalem, let my right hand forget her cunning. [137:3]

26 If I take the wings of the morning, and dwell in the uttermost parts of the sea;

Even there shall thy hand lead me, and thy right hand shall hold me. [139:9]

27 I am fearfully and wonderfully made. [139:14]

28 Set a watch, O Lord, before my mouth, keep the door of my lips. [141:3]

29 Let the wicked fall into their own nets, whilst that I withal escape. [141:10]

30 Put not your trust in princes, nor in the son of man, in whom there is no help. [146:3]

31 He gathereth together the outcasts of Israel.

He healeth the broken in heart, and bindeth up their wounds. [147:2]

32 He delighteth not in the strength of the horse: he taketh not pleasure in the legs of a man. [147:10]

33 Let the saints be joyful in glory: let them sing aloud upon their beds.

Let the high praises of God be in their mouth, and a two-edged sword in their hand;

To execute vengeance upon the heathen and punishments upon the people;

To bind their kings with chains, and their nobles with fetters of iron. [149:5]

1 Praise him upon the loud cymbals; praise him upon the high-sounding cymbals. [150:5]

Proverbs

2 The fear of the Lord is the beginning of knowledge. [1:7]

3 Surely in vain the net is spread in the sight of the bird. [1:17]

4 Wisdom crieth without; she uttereth her voice in the streets. [1:20]

5 Her ways are ways of pleasantness, and all her paths are peace. [3:17]

6 Wisdom is the principal thing; therefore get wisdom: and with all thy getting get understanding. [4:7]

7 The path of the just is as the shining light, that shineth more and more unto the perfect day. [4:18]

8 Go to the ant, thou sluggard, consider her ways, and be wise. [6:6]

9 Yet a little sleep, a little slumber, a little folding of the hands to sleep. [6:10]

10 Can a man take fire in his bosom, and his clothes not be burned? [6:27]

11 He goeth after her, straightway, as an ox goeth to the slaughter, or as a fool to the correction of the stocks. [7:22]

12 Wisdom is better than rubies. [8:11]

13 Stolen waters are sweet, and bread eaten in secret is pleasant. [9:17]

14 A wise son maketh a glad father: but a foolish son is the heaviness of his mother. [10:1]

15 The rich man's wealth is his strong city: the destruction of the poor is their poverty. [10:15]

16 Where no counsel is, the people fall: but in the multitude of counsellors there is safety. [11:14]

17 He that is surety for a stranger shall smart for it. [11:15]

18 As a jewel of gold in a swine's snout, so is a fair woman which is without discretion. [11:22]

19 A virtuous woman is a crown to her husband: but she that maketh ashamed is as rottenness in his bones. [12:4]

20 A righteous man regardeth the life of his beast. [12:10]

21 Hope deferred maketh the heart sick. [13:12]

22 The way of transgressors is hard. [13:15]

23 The desire accomplished is sweet to the soul. [13:19]

24 He that spareth his rod hateth his son. [13:24]

25 Fools make a mock at sin. [14:9]

26 In all labour there is profit: but the talk of the lips tendeth only to penury. [14:23]

27 Righteousness exalteth a nation. [14:34]

28 A soft answer turneth away wrath: but grievous words stir up anger. [15:1]

29 A merry heart maketh a cheerful countenance. [15:13]

30 Better is a dinner of herbs where love is, than a stalled ox and hatred therewith. [15:17]

31 A word spoken in due season, how good is it! [15:23]

32 Pride goeth before destruction, and an haughty spirit before a fall. [16:18]

33 The hoary head is a crown of glory, if it be found in the way of righteousness. [16:31]

34 He that repeateth a matter separateth very friends. [17:9]

35 Let a bear robbed of her whelps meet a man, rather than a fool in his folly. [17:12]

36 He that begetteth a fool doeth it to his sorrow. [17:21]

37 He that hath knowledge spareth his words. [17:27]

38 A wounded spirit who can bear? [18:14]

39 There is a friend that sticketh closer than a brother. [18:24]

40 Wine is a mocker, strong drink is raging. [20:1]

41 Every fool will be meddling. [20:3]

42 Even a child is known by his doings. [20:11]

43 It is naught, it is naught, saith the buyer: but when he is gone his way, then he boasteth. [20:14]

39

1 It is better to dwell in a corner of the house-top, than with a brawling woman in a wide house. [21:9]

2 A good name is rather to be chosen than great riches. [22:1]

3 The rich and poor meet together: the Lord is the maker of them all. [22:2]

4 Train up a child in the way he should go: and when he is old, he will not depart from it. [22:6]

5 Remove not the ancient landmark, which thy fathers have set. [22:28]

6 Riches certainly make themselves wings. [23:5]

7 Look not upon the wine when it is red. [23:31]

8 The heart of kings is unsearchable. [25:3]

9 Heap coals of fire upon his head. [25:22]

10 As cold waters to a thirsty soul, so is good news from a far country. [25:25]

11 A whip for the horse, a bridle for the ass, and a rod for the fool's back. [26:3]

12 Answer not a fool according to his folly, lest thou also be like unto him. [26:4]

13 Answer a fool according to his folly, lest he be wise in his own conceit. [26:5]

14 As a dog returneth to his vomit, so a fool returneth to his folly. [26:11]

15 Seest thou a man wise in his own conceit? there is more hope of a fool than of him. [26:12]

16 The slothful man saith, There is a lion in the way; a lion is in the streets. [26:13]

17 The sluggard is wiser in his own conceit than seven men that can render a reason. [26:16]

18 Whoso diggeth a pit shall fall therein: and he that rolleth a stone, it will return upon him. [26:27]

19 Boast not thyself of to-morrow; for thou knowest not what a day may bring forth. [27:1]

20 Faithful are the wounds of a friend. [27:6]

21 A continual dropping in a very rainy day and a contentious woman are alike. [27:15]

22 Iron sharpeneth iron; so a man sharpeneth the countenance of his friend. [27:17]

23 Though thou shouldst bray a fool in a mortar among wheat with a pestle, yet will not his foolishness depart from him. [27:22]

24 The wicked flee when no man pursueth: but the righteous are bold as a lion. [28:1]

25 He that maketh haste to be rich shall not be innocent. [28:20]

26 A fool uttereth all his mind. [29:11]

27 Where there is no vision, the people perish. [29:18]

28 Give me neither poverty nor riches; feed me with food convenient for me. [30:8]

29 The horseleach hath two daughters, crying, Give, give. [30:15]

30 The way of an eagle in the air; the way of a serpent upon a rock; the way of a ship in the midst of the sea; and the way of a man with a maid. [30:19]

31 The spider taketh hold with her hands, and is in kings' palaces. [30:28]

32 Who can find a virtuous woman? for her price is far above rubies. [31:10]

33 Her children arise up, and call her blessed. [31:28]

Ecclesiastes

34 Vanity of vanities, saith the Preacher, vanity of vanities; all is vanity.
What profit hath a man of all his labour which he taketh under the sun?
One generation passeth away, and another generation cometh. [1:2]

35 All the rivers run into the sea; yet the sea is not full. [1:7]

36 All things are full of labour; man cannot utter it: the eye is not satisfied with seeing, nor the ear filled with hearing.
The thing that hath been, it is that which shall be; and that which is done is that which shall be done: and there is no new thing under the sun. [1:8]

37 All is vanity and vexation of spirit. [1:14]

38 In much wisdom is much grief: and he that increaseth knowledge increaseth sorrow. [1:18]

1 Wisdom excelleth folly, as far as light excelleth darkness. [2:13]

2 One event happeneth to them all. [2:14]

3 To every thing there is a season, and a time to every purpose under the heaven.
   A time to be born, and a time to die; a time to plant, and a time to pluck up that which is planted. [3:1]

4 I praised the dead which are already dead more than the living which are yet alive. [4:2]

5 Woe to him that is alone when he falleth, for he hath not another to help him up. [4:10]

6 A threefold cord is not quickly broken. [4:12]

7 God is in heaven, and thou upon earth: therefore let thy words be few. [5:2]

8 Better is it that thou shouldst not vow, than that thou shouldst vow and not pay. [5:5]

9 The sleep of a labouring man is sweet. [5:12]

10 A good name is better than precious ointment; and the day of death than the day of one's birth.
   It is better to go to the house of mourning, than to go to the house of feasting. [7:1]

11 As the crackling of thorns under a pot, so is the laughter of the fool. [7:6]

12 Better is the end of a thing than the beginning thereof. [7:8]

13 Say not thou, What is the cause that the former days were better than these? for thou dost not enquire wisely concerning this. [7:10]

14 In the day of prosperity be joyful, but in the day of adversity consider. [7:14]

15 Be not righteous over much; neither make thyself over wise. [7:16]

16 One man among a thousand have I found; but a woman among all those have I not found. [7:28]

17 God hath made man upright; but they have sought out many inventions. [7:29]

18 There is no discharge in that war. [8:8]

19 A man hath no better thing under the sun than to eat, and to drink, and to be merry. [8:15]

20 A living dog is better than a dead lion. [9:4]

21 Whatsoever thy hand findeth to do, do it with thy might; for there is no work, nor device, nor knowledge, nor wisdom, in the grave whither thou goest. [9:10]

22 The race is not to the swift, nor the battle to the strong. [9:11]

23 Dead flies cause the ointment of the apothecary to send forth a stinking savour. [10:1]

24 He that diggeth a pit shall fall into it. [10:8]

25 Wine maketh merry: but money answereth all things. [10:19]

26 Curse not the king, no not in thy thought; and curse not the rich in thy bedchamber: for a bird of the air shall carry the voice, and that which hath wings shall tell the matter. [10:20]

27 Cast thy bread upon the waters: for thou shalt find it after many days. [11:1]

28 In the place where the tree falleth, there it shall be. [11:3]

29 He that observeth the wind shall not sow; and he that regardeth the clouds shall not reap. [11:4]

30 Truly the light is sweet, and a pleasant thing it is for the eyes to behold the sun. [11:7]

31 Rejoice, O young man, in thy youth. [11:9]

32 Remember now thy Creator in the days of thy youth, while the evil days come not, nor the years draw nigh, when thou shalt say, I have no pleasure in them. [12:1]

33 The strong men shall bow themselves, and the grinders cease because they are few. [12:3]

34 The almond-tree shall flourish, and the grasshopper shall be a burden, and desire shall fail: because man goeth to his long home. [12:5]

35 Or ever the silver cord be loosed, or the golden bowl be broken, or the pitcher be broken at the fountain, or the wheel broken at the cistern.
   Then shall the dust return to the earth

as it was: and the spirit shall return unto God who gave it. [12:6]

1 The words of the wise are as goads. [12:11]

2 Of making many books there is no end; and much study is a weariness of the flesh. [12:12]

3 Fear God, and keep his commandments: for this is the whole duty of man. [12:13]

Song of Solomon

4 Let him kiss me with the kisses of his mouth: for thy love is better than wine. [1:2]

5 I am black, but comely, O ye daughters of Jerusalem. [1:5]

6 As the lily among thorns, so is my love among the daughters. [2:2]

7 Stay me with flagons, comfort me with apples: for I am sick of love. [2:5]

8 Rise up, my love, my fair one, and come away.
For, lo, the winter is past, the rain is over and gone;
The flowers appear on the earth; the time of the singing of birds is come, and the voice of the turtle is heard in our land. [2:10]

9 Take us the foxes, the little foxes, that spoil the vines. [2:15]

10 Until the day break, and the shadows flee away. [2:17]

11 A fountain of gardens, a well of living waters, and streams from Lebanon. [4:15]

12 I sleep, but my heart waketh. [5:2]

13 Fair as the moon, clear as the sun, and terrible as an army with banners. [6:10]

14 Thy belly is like an heap of wheat set about with lilies.
Thy two breasts are like two young roes that are twins. [7:2]

15 Set me as a seal upon thine heart, as a seal upon thine arm; for love is strong as death; jealousy is cruel as the grave. [8:6]

16 Many waters cannot quench love, neither can the floods drown it. [8:7]

17 We have a little sister, and she hath no breasts. [8:8]

Isaiah

18 The ox knoweth his owner, and the ass his master's crib. [1:3]

19 Bring no more vain oblations; incense is an abomination unto me; the new moons and sabbaths, the calling of assemblies, I cannot away with. [1:13]

20 Though your sins be as scarlet, they shall be as white as snow. [1:18]

21 They shall beat their swords into plowshares, and their spears into pruninghooks: nation shall not lift up sword against nation, neither shall they learn war any more. [2:4; also Micah, 4:3 ('a sword' for 'sword')]

22 What mean ye that ye beat my people to pieces, and grind the faces of the poor? [3:15]

23 Woe unto them that join house to house, that lay field to field, till there be no place, that they may be placed alone in the midst of the earth! [5:8]

24 Woe unto them that call evil good, and good evil. [5:20]

25 Woe unto them that are wise in their own eyes, and prudent in their own sight! [5:21]

26 Above it stood the seraphims: each one had six wings; with twain he covered his face, and with twain he covered his feet, and with twain he did fly. [6:2]

27 Then said I, Lord, how long? [6:11]

28 Behold, a virgin shall conceive, and bear a son, and shall call his name Immanuel. [7:14]

29 For a stone of stumbling and for a rock of offence. [8:14]

30 Wizards that peep, and that mutter. [8:19]

31 The people that walked in darkness have seen a great light: they that dwell in the land of the shadow of death, upon them hath the light shined. [9:2]

32 For unto us a child is born, unto us a son is given: and the government shall be upon his shoulder: and his name shall be called Wonderful, Counsellor, The mighty God, The everlasting Father, The Prince of Peace. [9:6]

33 And there shall come forth a rod out of the stem of Jesse, and a Branch shall grow out of his roots. [11:1]

1 The wolf also shall dwell with the lamb, and the leopard shall lie down with the kid; and the calf and the young lion and the fatling together; and a little child shall lead them. [11:6]

2 Hell from beneath is moved for thee to meet thee at thy coming. [14:9]

3 How art thou fallen from heaven, O Lucifer, son of the morning! [14:12]

4 Watchman, what of the night?
The watchman said, The morning cometh, and also the night. [21:11]

5 Tyre, the crowning city, whose merchants are princes. [23:8]

6 For precept must be upon precept, precept upon precept; line upon line, line upon line; here a little, and there a little. [28:10]

7 They are drunken, but not with wine. [29:9, cf. 51:21]

8 Their strength is to sit still. [30:7]

9 Speak unto us smooth things, prophesy deceits. [30:10]

10 In quietness and in confidence shall be your strength. [30:15]

11 One thousand shall flee at the rebuke of one. [30:17]

12 Though the Lord give you the bread of adversity. [30:20]

13 This is the way, walk ye in it. [30:21]

14 An habitation of dragons, and a court for owls. [34:13]

15 The desert shall rejoice, and blossom as the rose. [35:1]

16 Sorrow and sighing shall flee away. [35:10]

17 Lo, thou trustest in the staff of this broken reed, on Egypt; whereon, if a man lean, it will go into his hand and pierce it. [36:6, cf. 2 Kings, 18:21]

18 Set thine house in order: for thou shalt die. [38:1]

19 I shall go softly all my years in the bitterness of my soul. [38:15]

20 Comfort ye, comfort ye my people, saith your God. [40:1]

21 The voice of him that crieth in the wilderness, Prepare ye the way of the Lord. [40:3]

22 Every valley shall be exalted, and every mountain and hill shall be made low: and the crooked shall be made straight, and the rough places plain. [40:4]

23 All flesh is grass, and all the goodliness thereof is as the flower of the field. [40:6, cf. 1 Peter, 1:24]

24 The grass withereth, the flower fadeth: because the spirit of the Lord bloweth upon it: surely the people is grass. [40:7]

25 He shall feed his flock like a shepherd: he shall gather the lambs with his arm, and carry them in his bosom, and shall gently lead those that are with young. [40:11]

26 Behold, the nations are as a drop of a bucket, and are counted as the small dust of the balance. [40:15]

27 Have ye not known? have ye not heard? hath it not been told you from the beginning? [40:21]

28 They that wait upon the Lord shall renew their strength; they shall mount up with wings as eagles. [40:31]

29 A bruised reed shall he not break, and the smoking flax shall he not quench. [42:3]

30 Seeing many things, but thou observest not. [42:20]

31 He warmeth himself, and saith, Aha, I am warm, I have seen the fire. [44:16]

32 Shall the clay say to him that fashioneth it, What makest thou? [45:9]

33 I have chosen thee in the furnace of affliction. [48:10]

34 There is no peace, saith the Lord, unto the wicked. [48:22]

35 How beautiful upon the mountains are the feet of him that bringeth good tidings, that publisheth peace. [52:7]

36 They shall see eye to eye, when the Lord shall bring again Zion. [52:8]

37 The Lord hath comforted his people, he hath redeemed Jerusalem. [52:9]

38 He is despised and rejected of men; a man of sorrows, and acquainted with grief. [53:3]

39 All we like sheep have gone astray. [53:6]

40 He was oppressed, and he was afflicted, yet he opened not his mouth: he is brought

43

as a lamb to the slaughter, and as a sheep before her shearers is dumb, so he openeth not his mouth. [53:7]

1 He was cut off out of the land of the living. [53:8]

2 He was numbered with the transgressors; and he bare the sin of many. [53:12]

3 Seek ye the Lord while he may be found, call ye upon him while he is near. [55:6]

4 For my thoughts are not your thoughts, neither are your ways my ways, saith the Lord. [55:8]

5 I will give them an everlasting name, that shall not be cut off. [56:5]

6 They are all dumb dogs, they cannot bark. [56:10]

7 Their feet run to evil, and they make haste to shed innocent blood. [59:7]

8 Arise, shine, for thy light is come. [60:1]

9 He hath sent me to bind up the broken-hearted, to proclaim liberty to the captives, and the opening of the prison to them that are bound;
To proclaim the acceptable year of the Lord, and the day of vengeance of our God; to comfort all that mourn. [61:1]

10 To give unto them beauty for ashes. [61:3]

11 I have trodden the winepress alone. [63:3]

12 All our righteousnesses are as filthy rags; and we all do fade as a leaf. [64:6]

13 For, behold, I create new heavens and a new earth. [65:17]

14 As one whom his mother comforteth, so will I comfort you. [66:13]

Jeremiah

15 They were as fed horses in the morning: every one neighed after his neighbour's wife. [5:8]

16 Saying, Peace, peace; when there is no peace. [6:14]

17 The harvest is past, the summer is ended, and we are not saved. [8:20]

18 Is there no balm in Gilead; is there no physician there? [8:22]

19 I was like a lamb or an ox that is brought to the slaughter. [11:19]

20 Can the Ethiopian change his skin, or the leopard his spots? [13:23]

21 The heart is deceitful above all things, and desperately wicked. [17:9]

Lamentations

22 Is it nothing to you, all ye that pass by? behold, and see if there be any sorrow like unto my sorrow. [1:12]

Ezekiel

23 They four had one likeness, as if a wheel had been in the midst of a wheel. [10:10]

24 The fathers have eaten sour grapes, and the children's teeth are set on edge. [18:2]

25 The king of Babylon stood at the parting of the way [21:21]

26 She doted upon the Assyrians her neighbours, captains and rulers clothed most gorgeously, horsemen riding upon horses, all of them desirable young men. [23:12]

27 Set me down in the midst of the valley which was full of bones. [37:1]

28 And he said unto me, Son of man, can these bones live? [37:3]

29 Prophesy unto the wind. [37:9]

30 Son of man, set thy face against Gog, the land of Magog. [38:2]

Daniel

31 This image's head was of fine gold, his breast and his arms of silver, his belly and his thighs of brass,
His legs of iron, his feet part of iron and part of clay. [2:32]

32 The sound of the cornet, flute, harp, sackbut, psaltery, dulcimer, and all kinds of music. [3:5]

33 Cast into the midst of a burning fiery furnace. [3:11]

34 MENE, MENE, TEKEL, UPHARSIN. [5:25]

35 Thou art weighed in the balances, and art found wanting. [5:27]

36 Thy kingdom is divided, and given to the Medes and Persians. [5:28]

37 The Ancient of days did sit, whose garment was white as snow. [7:9]

Hosea

38 They have sown the wind, and they shall reap the whirlwind. [8:7]

44

1 Ye have plowed wickedness, ye have reaped iniquity. [10:13]

2 I drew them with cords of a man, with bands of love. [11:4]

3 I have multiplied visions, and used similitudes. [12:10]

Joel

4 That which the palmerworm hath left hath the locust eaten. [1:4]

5 Your sons and your daughters shall prophesy, your old men shall dream dreams, your young men shall see visions. [2:28]

6 Multitudes in the valley of decision. [3:14]

Amos

7 Can two walk together, except they be agreed? [3:3]

8 As a firebrand plucked out of the burning. [4:11]

Jonah

9 So they cast lots, and the lot fell upon Jonah. [1:7]

10 And also much cattle. [4:11]

Micah

11 They shall sit every man under his vine and under his fig-tree. [4:4]

12 What doth the Lord require of thee, but to do justly, and to love mercy, and to walk humbly with thy God? [6:8]

Habakkuk

13 Write the vision, and make it plain upon tables, that he may run that readeth it. [2:2]

Zechariah

14 For who hath despised the day of small things? [4:10]

15 Turn you to the stronghold, ye prisoners of hope. [9:12]

16 Woe to the idle shepherd that leaveth the flock! [11:17]

17 I was wounded in the house of my friends. [13:6]

Malachi

18 Have we not all one father? hath not one God created us? [2:10]

19 Those that oppress the hireling in his wages. [3:5]

20 Unto you that fear my name shall the Sun of righteousness arise with healing in his wings. [4:2]

Apocrypha

I Esdras

21 Women are strongest: but above all things Truth beareth away the victory. [13:12]

22 Great is truth, and mighty above all things. [4:41]

23 *Magna est veritas et praevalet.* [*Ib. Vulgate* version]

2 Esdras

24 If he went not through the narrow, how could he come into the broad? [7:5]

25 I shall light a candle of understanding in thine heart, which shall not be put out. [14:25]

Tobit

26 So they went forth both, and the young man's dog with them. [5:16]

Wisdom of Solomon

27 Love righteousness, ye that be judges of the earth. [1:1]

28 The ear of jealousy heareth all things. [1:10]

29 Let us crown ourselves with rosebuds, before they be withered. [2:8]

30 Through envy of the devil came death into the world. [2:24]

31 The souls of the righteous are in the hand of God, and there shall no torment touch them. [3:1]

32 Having been a little chastised, they shall be greatly rewarded. [3:5]

Ecclesiasticus

33 My son, if thou come to serve the Lord, prepare thy soul for temptation. [2:1]

34 Be not curious in unnecessary matters: for more things are shewed unto thee than men understand. [3:23]

35 There is a shame that bringeth sin, and there is a shame which is glory and grace. [4:21]

1 A faithful friend is the medicine of life. [6:16]

2 Miss not the discourse of the elders. [8:9]

3 Open not thine heart to every man, lest he requite thee with a shrewd turn. [8:19]

4 Forsake not an old friend; for the new is not comparable to him; a new friend is as new wine; when it is old, thou shalt drink it with pleasure. [9:10]

5 Many kings have sat upon the ground; and one that was never thought of hath worn the crown. [11:5]

6 Judge none blessed before his death. [11:28]

7 He that toucheth pitch shall be defiled therewith. [13:1]

8 How agree the kettle and the earthen pot together? for if the one be smitten against the other, it shall be broken. [13:2]

9 Be not made a beggar by banqueting upon borrowing. [18:33]

10 He that contemneth small things shall fall by little and little. [19:1]

11 Make little weeping for the dead, for he is at rest: but the life of the fool is worse than death. [22:11]

12 All wickedness is but little to the wickedness of a woman. [25:19]

13 The stroke of the whip maketh marks in the flesh; but the stroke of the tongue breaketh bones. [28:17]

14 Envy and wrath shorten the life. [30:24]

15 Leave off first for manners' sake. [31:17]

16 Let thy speech be short, comprehending much in few words. [32:8]

17 Leave not a stain in thine honour. [33:22]

18 There is a friend, which is only a friend in name. [37:1]

19 Honour a physician with the honour due unto him for the uses which you may have of him: for the Lord hath created him. [38:1]

20 Take no heaviness to heart: drive it away, and remember the last end. [38:20]

21 How can he get wisdom ... whose talk is of bullocks? [38:25]

22 They will maintain the state of the world, and all their desire is in the work of their craft. [38:34]

23 Better it is to die than to beg. [40:28]

24 Let us now praise famous men, and our fathers that begat us. [44:1]

25 All these were honoured in their generations. [44:7]

26 There be of them that have left a name behind them. [44:8]

27 Their bodies are buried in peace; but their name liveth for evermore. [44:14]

2 Maccabees

28 It is a foolish thing to make a long prologue, and to be short in the story itself. [2:32]

29 When he was at the last gasp. [7:9]

30 Nicanor lay dead in his harness. [15:28]

New Testament

St Matthew

31 Rachel weeping for her children, and would not be comforted, because they are not. [2:18]

32 The voice of one crying in the wilderness. [3:3]

33 His meat was locusts and wild honey. [3:4]

34 O generation of vipers, who hath warned you to flee from the wrath to come? [3:7]

35 And now also the axe is laid unto the root of the trees. [3:10]

36 Man shall not live by bread alone. [4:4]

37 I will make you fishers of men. [4:19]

38 Blessed are the poor in spirit: for theirs is the kingdom of heaven. [5:3]

39 Blessed are the pure in heart: for they shall see God.
Blessed are the peacemakers: for they shall be called the children of God. [5:8]

40 Ye are the salt of the earth: but if the salt hath lost his savour, wherewith shall it be salted? [5:13]

1 Neither do men light a candle, and put it under a bushel. [5:15]

2 Whoever shall say, Thou fool, shall be in danger of hell fire. [5:22]

3 Agree with thine adversary quickly, whiles thou art in the way with him. [5:25]

4 Till thou hast paid the uttermost farthing. [5:26]

5 Resist not evil: but whosoever shall smite thee on thy right cheek, turn to him the other also. [5:39]

6 Love your enemies. [5:44]

7 He maketh his sun rise on the evil and on the good, and sendeth rain on the just and on the unjust. [5:45]

8 Let not thy left hand know what thy right hand doeth. [6:3]

9 Give us this day our daily bread. [6:11]

10 Forgive us our debts, as we forgive our debtors. [6:12]

11 Lead us not into temptation, but deliver us from evil. [6:13]

12 Where moth and rust doth corrupt, and where thieves break through and steal. [6:19]

13 Where your treasure is, there will your heart be also. [6:21]

14 No man can serve two masters. [6:24]

15 Ye cannot serve God and mammon. [Ib.]

16 Which of you by taking thought can add one cubit unto his stature? [6:27]

17 Consider the lilies of the field, how they grow; they toil not, neither do they spin:
And yet I say unto you, that even Solomon in all his glory was not arrayed like one of these. [6:28]

18 Seek ye first the kingdom of God, and his righteousness; and all these things shall be added unto you. [6:33]

19 Take therefore no thought for the morrow: for the morrow shall take thought for the things of itself. Sufficient unto the day is the evil thereof. [6:34]

20 Judge not, that ye be not judged. [7:1]

21 Why beholdest thou the mote that is in thy brother's eye, but considerest not the beam that is in thine own eye? [7:3]

22 Neither cast ye your pearls before swine. [7:6]

23 Ask, and it shall be given you; seek, and ye shall find; knock, and it shall be opened unto you. [7:7]

24 What man is there of you, whom if his son ask bread, will he give him a stone? [7:9]

25 Therefore all things whatsoever ye would that men should do to you, do ye even so to them: for this is the law and the prophets. [7:12]

26 Wide is the gate, and broad is the way, that leadeth to destruction. [7:13]

27 Strait is the gate, and narrow is the way, which leadeth unto life, and few there be that find it. [7:14]

28 Beware of false prophets, which come to you in sheep's clothing, but inwardly they are ravening wolves. [7:15]

29 By their fruits ye shall know them. [7:20]

30 I have not found so great faith, no, not in Israel. [8:10]

31 But the children of the kingdom shall be cast out into outer darkness: there shall be weeping and gnashing of teeth. [8:12]

32 The foxes have holes, and the birds of the air have nests; but the Son of man hath not where to lay his head. [8:20]

33 Let the dead bury their dead. [8:22]

34 They that be whole need not a physician, but they that are sick. [9:12]

35 Neither do men put new wine into old bottles. [9:17]

36 The maid is not dead, but sleepeth. [9:24]

37 The harvest truly is plenteous, but the labourers are few. [9:37]

38 Freely ye have received, freely give. [10:8]

39 When ye depart out of that house or city, shake off the dust of your feet. [10:14]

40 Be ye therefore wise as serpents, and harmless as doves. [10:16]

41 He that endureth to the end shall be saved. [10:22]

42 Are not two sparrows sold for a farthing? and one of them shall not fall on the ground without your Father. [10:29]

1 The very hairs of your head are all numbered. [10:30]

2 I came not to send peace, but a sword. [10:34]

3 He that findeth his life shall lose it: and he that loseth his life for my sake shall find it. [10:39]

4 What went ye out into the wilderness to see? A reed shaken with the wind? [11:7]

5 The kingdom of heaven suffereth violence, and the violent take it by force. [11:12]

6 Wisdom is justified of her children. [11:19]

7 Come unto me, all ye that labour and are heavy laden, and I will give you rest. [11:28]

8 He that is not with me is against me. [12:30]

9 The blasphemy against the Holy Ghost shall not be forgiven unto men. [12:31]

10 Every idle word that men shall speak, they shall give account thereof in the day of judgement. [12:36]

11 An evil and adulterous generation seeketh after a sign. [12:39]

12 He findeth it empty, swept, and garnished. [12:44]

13 The last state of that man is worse than the first. [12:45]

14 Some seeds fell by the way side. [13:4]

15 An enemy hath done this. [13:28]

16 Found one pearl of great price. [13:46]

17 A prophet is not without honour, save in his own country. [13:57]

18 Be of good cheer; it is I; be not afraid. [14:27]

19 O thou of little faith, wherefore didst thou doubt? [14:31]

20 Besought him that they might only touch the hem of his garment. [14:36]

21 Not that which goeth into the mouth defileth a man; but that which cometh out of the mouth, this defileth a man. [15:11]

22 If the blind lead the blind, both shall fall into the ditch. [15:14]

23 It is not meet to take the children's bread, and to cast it to dogs. [15:26]

24 The dogs eat of the crumbs which fall from their masters' table. [15:27]

25 Can ye not discern the signs of the times? [16:3]

26 Thou art Peter, and upon this rock I will build my church; and the gates of hell shall not prevail against it. [16:18]

27 Get thee behind me, Satan. [16:23]

28 Let him deny himself, and take up his cross, and follow me. [16:24]

29 What is a man profited, if he shall gain the whole world, and lose his own soul? [16:26]

30 If ye have faith as a grain of mustard seed, ye shall say unto this mountain, Remove hence to yonder place; and it shall remove. [17:20]

31 Except ye be converted, and become as little children, ye shall not enter into the kingdom of heaven. [18:3]

32 Whoso shall offend one of these little ones which believe in me, it were better that a millstone were hanged about his neck, and that he were drowned in the depth of the sea. [18:6]

33 It must needs be that offences come; but woe to that man by whom the offence cometh! [18:7]

34 If thine eye offend thee, pluck it out. [18:9]

35 Until seventy times seven. [18:22]

36 For this cause shall a man leave father and mother, and shall cleave to his wife: and they twain shall be one flesh. [19:5]

37 What therefore God hath joined together, let not man put asunder. [19:6]

38 Thou shalt love thy neighbour as thyself. [19:19]

39 Thou shalt have treasure in heaven. [19:21]

40 He went away sorrowful: for he had great possessions. [19:22]

41 It is easier for a camel to go through the eye of a needle, than for a rich man to enter into the kingdom of God. [19:24]

42 With God all things are possible. [19:26]

1 But many that are first shall be last; and the last shall be first. [19:30]

2 Borne the burden and heat of the day. [20:12]

3 Is it not lawful for me to do what I will with mine own? Is thine eye evil, because I am good? [20:15]

4 Whosoever will be chief among you, let him be your servant. [20:27]

5 My house shall be called the house of prayer; but ye have made it a den of thieves. [21:13]

6 Out of the mouths of babes and sucklings thou hast perfected praise. [21:16]

7 The stone which the builders rejected, the same is become the head of the corner. [21:42]

8 A man which had not on a wedding garment. [22:11]

9 Cast him into outer darkness; there shall be weeping and gnashing of teeth. [22:13]

10 Many are called, but few are chosen. [22:14]

11 Render therefore unto Caesar the things which are Caesar's; and unto God the things that are God's. [22:21]

12 For in the resurrection they neither marry, nor are given in marriage. [22:30]

13 All their works they do for to be seen of men. [23:5]

14 Whosoever shall exalt himself shall be abased; and he that shall humble himself shall be exalted. [23:12]

15 Ye blind guides, which strain at a gnat, and swallow a camel. [23:24]

16 Ye are like unto whited sepulchres, which indeed appear beautiful outward, but are within full of dead men's bones, and of all uncleanness. [23:27]

17 Ye shall hear of wars and rumours of wars. [24:6]

18 The end is not yet. [Ib.]

19 The abomination of desolation. [24:15]

20 Wheresoever the carcase is, there will the eagles be gathered together. [24:28]

21 Eating and drinking, marrying and giving in marriage. [24:38]

22 Well done, good and faithful servant. [25:23]

23 Unto every one that hath shall be given, and he shall have abundance: but from him that hath not shall be taken away even that which he hath. [25:29]

24 He shall separate them one from another, as a shepherd divideth his sheep from the goats. [25:32]

25 I was an hungred, and ye gave me meat: I was thirsty, and ye gave me drink: I was a stranger, and ye took me in. [25:35]

26 They covenanted with him for thirty pieces of silver. [26:15]

27 It had been good for that man if he had not been born. [26:24]

28 Before the cock crow, thou shalt deny me thrice. [26:34]

29 Let this cup pass from me. [26:39]

30 Watch and pray, that ye enter not into temptation: the spirit indeed is willing, but the flesh is weak. [26:41]

31 All they that take the sword shall perish with the sword. [26:52]

32 He took water, and washed his hands before the multitude, saying, I am innocent of the blood of this just person. [27:24]

33 His blood be on us, and on our children. [27:25]

34 He saved others, himself he cannot save. [27:42]

35 My God, my God, why hast thou forsaken me? [27:46]

St Mark

36 The sabbath was made for man, and not man for the sabbath. [2:27]

37 And if a house be divided against itself, that house cannot stand. [3:25]

38 He that hath ears to hear, let him hear. [4:9]

39 With what measure ye mete, it shall be measured to you. [4:24]

40 My name is Legion: for we are many. [5:9]

41 Sitting, and clothed, and in his right mind. [5:15]

42 Knowing in himself that virtue had gone out of him. [5:30]

49

1 I see men as trees, walking. [8:24]

2 What shall it profit a man, if he shall gain the whole world, and lose his own soul? [8:36]

3 Lord, I believe; help thou mine unbelief. [9:24]

4 Where their worm dieth not, and the fire is not quenched. [9:44]

5 Suffer the little children to come unto me, and forbid them not: for of such is the kingdom of heaven. [10:14]

6 Which devour widows' houses, and for a pretence make long prayers. [12:40]

7 And there came a certain poor widow, and she threw in two mites. [12:42]

St Luke

8 My soul doth magnify the Lord,
And my spirit hath rejoiced in God my Saviour. [1:46]

9 To give light to them that sit in darkness and in the shadow of death, to guide our feet into the way of peace. [1:79]

10 Because there was no room for them in the inn. [2:7]

11 And lo, the angel of the Lord came upon them, and the glory of the Lord shone round about them: and they were sore afraid. [2:9]

12 Glory to God in the highest, and on earth peace, good will toward men. [2:14]

13 Lord, now lettest thou thy servant depart in peace, according to thy word. [2:29]

14 Wist ye not that I must be about my Father's business? [2:49]

15 Shewed unto him all the kingdoms of the world in a moment of time. [4:5]

16 Physician, heal thyself. [4:23]

17 Woe unto you, when all men shall speak well of you! [6:26]

18 The only son of his mother, and she was a widow. [7:12]

19 The labourer is worthy of his hire. [10:7]

20 Fell among thieves. [10:30]

21 He passed by on the other side. [10:31]

22 Go, and do thou likewise. [10:37]

23 Mary hath chosen that good part, which shall not be taken away from her. [10:42]

24 When a strong man armed keepeth his palace, his goods are in peace. [11:21]

25 His armour wherein he trusted. [11:22]

26 He that is not with me is against me. [11:23]

27 Thou fool, this night thy soul shall be required of thee. [12:20]

28 Let your loins be girded about, and your lights burning. [12:35]

29 Go and sit down in the lowest room; that when he that bade thee cometh, he may say to thee, Friend, go up higher. [14:10]

30 I have married a wife, and therefore I cannot come. [14:20]

31 The poor, and the maimed, and the halt, and the blind. [14:21]

32 Go out into the highways and hedges, and compel them to come in. [14:23]

33 Rejoice with me; for I have found my sheep which was lost. [15:6]

34 Joy shall be in heaven over one sinner that repenteth, more than over ninety and nine just persons, which need no repentance. [15:7]

35 Took his journey into a far country, and there wasted his substance with riotous living. [15:13]

36 He would fain have filled his belly with the husks that the swine did eat. [15:16]

37 Bring hither the fatted calf, and kill it. [15:23]

38 I cannot dig; to beg I am ashamed. [16:3]

39 The children of this world are in their generation wiser than the children of light. [16:8]

40 Make to yourselves friends of the mammon of unrighteousness. [16:9]

41 Clothed in purple and fine linen. [16:19]

42 The crumbs which fell from the rich man's table. [16:21]

43 Between us and you there is a great gulf fixed. [16:26]

1 We are unprofitable servants: we have done that which was our duty to do. [17:10]

2 The kingdom of God is within you. [17:21]

3 Remember Lot's wife. [17:32]

4 God, I thank thee, that I am not as other men are. [18:11]

5 God, be merciful to me a sinner. [18:13]

6 Out of thine own mouth will I judge thee. [19:22]

7 If these should hold their peace, the stones would immediately cry out. [19:40]

8 And when they heard it, they said, God forbid. [20:16]

9 In your patience possess ye your souls. [21:19]

10 Nevertheless, not my will, but thine, be done. [22:42]

11 If they do these things in a green tree, what shall be done in the dry? [23:31]

12 Father, forgive them; for they know not what they do. [23:34]

13 Why seek ye the living among the dead? [24:5]

14 And their words seemed to them as idle tales. [24:11]

St John

15 In the beginning was the Word, and the Word was with God, and the Word was God. [1:1]

16 The light shineth in darkness; and the darkness comprehended it not. [1:5]

17 There was a man sent from God, whose name was John. [1:6]

18 He was not that Light, but was sent to bear witness of that Light. [1:8]

19 He came unto his own, and his own received him not. [1:11]

20 And the Word was made flesh, and dwelt among us. [1:14]

21 Whose shoe's latchet I am not worthy to unloose. [1:27]

22 Can there any good thing come out of Nazareth? [1:46]

23 Woman, what have I to do with thee? mine hour is not yet come. [2:4]

24 The wind bloweth where it listeth, and thou hearest the sound thereof, but canst not tell whence it cometh, and whither it goeth. [3:8]

25 How can these things be? [3:9]

26 God so loved the world, that he gave his only begotten Son, that whosoever believeth in him should not perish, but have everlasting life. [3:16]

27 Men loved darkness rather than light, because their deeds were evil. [3:19]

28 God is a Spirit; and they that worship him must worship him in spirit and in truth. [4:24]

29 They are white already to harvest. [4:35]

30 Rise, take up thy bed, and walk. [5:8]

31 He was a burning and a shining light. [5:35]

32 Search the scriptures. [5:39]

33 It is the spirit that quickeneth. [6:63]

34 Judge not according to the appearance. [7:24]

35 He that is without sin among you, let him first cast a stone at her. [8:7]

36 The truth shall make you free. [8:32]

37 He was a murderer from the beginning, and abode not in the truth, because there is no truth in him. [8:44]

38 He is a liar, and the father of it. [Ib.]

39 The night cometh, when no man can work. [9:4]

40 The good shepherd giveth his life for the sheep. [10:11]

41 I am the resurrection, and the life. [11:25]

42 Jesus wept. [11:35]

43 For the poor always ye have with you. [12:8]

44 A new commandment I give unto you, That ye love one another. [13:34]

45 In my Father's house are many mansions. [14:2]

46 I am the way, the truth, and the life: no man cometh unto the Father, but by me. [14:6]

47 Greater love hath no man than this, that a man lay down his life for his friends. [15:13]

1 Whither goest thou? [16:5]

2 *Quo vadis?* [*Ib. Vulgate* version]

3 Pilate saith unto him, What is truth? [18:38]

4 Now Barabbas was a robber. [18:40]

5 Behold the man! [19:5]

6 *Ecce homo!* [*Ib. Vulgate* version]

7 What I have written, I have written. [19:22]

8 It is finished. [19:30]

9 *Consummatum est.* [*Ib. Vulgate* version]

10 Touch me not. [20:17]

11 *Noli me tangere.* [*Ib. Vulgate* version]

12 Feed my sheep. [21:16]

Acts of the Apostles

13 Cloven tongues like as of fire. [2:3]

14 Silver and gold have I none; but such as I have give I thee. [3:6]

15 Thy money perish with thee. [8:20]

16 Breathing out threatenings and slaughter. [9:1]

17 It is hard for thee to kick against the pricks. [9:5]

18 The street which is called Straight. [9:11]

19 This woman was full of good works. [9:36]

20 God is no respecter of persons. [10:34]

21 We also are men of like passions with you. [14:15]

22 Come over into Macedonia, and help us. [16:9]

23 Certain lewd fellows of the baser sort. [17:5]

24 For all the Athenians and strangers which were there spent their time in nothing else, but either to tell, or to hear some new thing. [17:21]

25 An altar with its inscription, TO THE UNKNOWN GOD. [17:23]

26 For in him we live, and move, and have our being. [17:28]

27 As certain also of your own poets have said. [*Ib.*]

28 Gallio cared for none of these things. [18:17]

29 Great is Diana of the Ephesians. [19:34]

30 It is more blessed to give than to receive. [20:35]

31 A citizen of no mean city. [21:39]

32 Brought up in this city at the feet of Gamaliel. [22:3]

33 A conscience void of offence toward God, and toward men. [24:16]

34 I appeal unto Caesar. [25:11]

35 Hast thou appealed unto Caesar? unto Caesar shalt thou go. [25:12]

36 Paul, thou art beside thyself; much learning doth make thee mad. [26:24]

37 For, this thing was not done in a corner. [26:26]

38 Almost thou persuadest me to be a Christian. [26:28]

Romans

39 Without ceasing I make mention of you always in my prayers. [1:9]

40 The just shall live by faith. [1:17]

41 Served the creature more than the Creator. [1:25]

42 These, having not the law, are a law unto themselves. [2:14]

43 Let God be true, but every man a liar. [3:4]

44 (Some affirm that we say,) Let us do evil, that good may come. [3:8]

45 Where no law is, there is no transgression. [4:15]

46 Who against hope believed in hope. [4:18]

47 Hope maketh not ashamed. [5:5]

48 Where sin abounded, grace did much more abound. [5:20]

49 Death hath no more dominion over him. [6:9]

50 The wages of sin is death. [6:23]

51 For the good that I would I do not: but the evil which I would not, that I do. [7:19]

52 Who shall deliver me from the body of this death? [7:24]

53 To be carnally minded is death. [8:6]

54 We know that the whole creation groaneth, and travaileth in pain together until now. [8:22]

1 All things work together for good to them that love God. [8:28]

2 If God be for us, who can be against us? [8:31]

3 Neither death, nor life, nor angels, nor principalities, nor powers, nor things present, nor things to come,
   Nor height, nor depth, nor any other creature, shall be able to separate us from the love of God. [8:38]

4 My kinsmen according to the flesh. [9:3]

5 Hath not the potter power over the clay, of the same lump to make one vessel unto honour, and another unto dishonour? [9:21]

6 A zeal of God, but not according to knowledge. [10:2]

7 Let love be without dissimulation. [12:9]

8 Rejoice with them that do rejoice, and weep with them that weep. [12:15]

9 Be not wise in your own conceits. [12:16]

10 Vengeance is mine; I will repay, saith the Lord. [12:19]

11 Be not overcome of evil, but overcome evil with good. [12:21]

12 Let every soul be subject unto the higher powers. [13:1]

13 The powers that be are ordained of God. [Ib.]

14 Render therefore to all their dues: tribute to whom tribute is due; custom to whom custom; fear to whom fear; honour to whom honour. [13:7]

15 Love is the fulfilling of the law. [13:10]

16 The night is far spent, the day is at hand. [13:12]

17 Him that is weak in the faith receive ye, but not to doubtful disputations. [14:1]

18 Let every man be fully persuaded in his own mind. [14:5]

19 None of us liveth to himself. [14:7]

20 That no man put a stumbling-block or an occasion to fall in his brother's way. [14:13]

21 We then that are strong ought to bear the infirmities of the weak. [15:1]

1 Corinthians

22 God hath chosen the foolish things of the world to confound the wise. [1:27]

23 I have planted, Apollos watered; but God gave the increase. [3:6]

24 Every man's work shall be made manifest. [3:13]

25 The wisdom of this world is foolishness with God. [3:19]

26 A spectacle unto the world, and to angels, and to men. [4:9]

27 Absent in body, but present in spirit. [5:3]

28 Know ye not that a little leaven leaveneth the whole lump? [5:6]

29 Your body is the temple of the Holy Ghost. [6:19]

30 It is better to marry than to burn. [7:9]

31 The fashion of this world passeth away. [7:31]

32 Knowledge puffeth up, but charity edifieth. [8:1]

33 I am made all things to all men. [9:22]

34 They do it to obtain a corruptible crown; but we an incorruptible. [9:25]

35 So fight I, not as one that beateth the air. [9:26]

36 But I keep under my body, and bring it into subjection. [9:27]

37 Let him that thinketh he standeth take heed lest he fall. [10:12]

38 God is faithful, who will not suffer you to be tempted above that ye are able. [10:13]

39 All things are lawful for me, but all things are not expedient. [10:23]

40 For the earth is the Lord's, and the fulness thereof. [10:26]

41 Whether therefore ye eat, or drink, or whatsoever ye do, do all to the glory of God. [10:31]

42 If a woman have long hair, it is a glory to her. [11:15]

43 Now there are diversities of gifts, but the same Spirit. [12:4]

1 Though I speak with the tongues of men and of angels, and have not charity, I am become as sounding brass, or a tinkling cymbal. [13:1]

2 Charity suffereth long, and is kind. [13:4]

3 Charity never faileth: but whether there be prophecies, they shall fail. [13:8]

4 For we know in part, and we prophesy in part. [13:9]

5 When I was a child, I spake as a child, I understood as a child, I thought as a child: but when I became a man, I put away childish things.
For now we see through a glass, darkly; but then face to face. [13:11]

6 And now abideth faith, hope, charity, these three; but the greatest of these is charity. [13:13]

7 Let your women keep silence in the churches. [14:34]

8 Let all things be done decently and in order. [14:40]

9 One born out of due time. [15:8]

10 I laboured more abundantly than they all: yet not I, but the grace of God which was with me. [15:10]

11 We are of all men most miserable. [15:19]

12 As in Adam all die, even so in Christ shall all be made alive. [15:22]

13 The last enemy that shall be destroyed is death. [15:26]

14 Let us eat and drink; for to morrow we die. [15:32, cf. *Isaiah*, 22:13]

15 Evil communications corrupt good manners. [15:33]

16 One star differeth from another star in glory. [15:41]

17 It is sown in corruption; it is raised in incorruption. [15:42]

18 The first man is of the earth, earthy. [15:47]

19 In a moment, in the twinkling of an eye, at the last trump. [15:52]

20 O death, where is thy sting? O grave, where is thy victory? [15:55]

21 Quit you like men, be strong. [16:13]

22 Let him be Anathema, Maran-atha. [16:22]

2 Corinthians

23 Not in tables of stone, but in fleshy tables of the heart. [3:3]

24 The letter killeth, but the spirit giveth life. [3:6]

25 An house not made with hands. [5:1]

26 We walk by faith, not by sight. [5:7]

27 We are ambassadors for Christ. [5:20]

28 Behold, now is the accepted time; behold, now is the day of salvation. [6:2]

29 As having nothing, and yet possessing all things. [6:10]

30 God loveth a cheerful giver. [9:7]

31 For ye suffer fools gladly, seeing ye yourselves are wise. [11:19]

32 Whether in the body, I cannot tell; or whether out of the body, I cannot tell: God knoweth. [12:2]

33 There was given to me a thorn in the flesh. [12:7]

34 My strength is made perfect in weakness. [12:9]

Galatians

35 The right hands of fellowship. [2:9]

36 Weak and beggarly elements. [4:9]

37 I have bestowed upon you labour in vain. [4:11]

38 Which things are an allegory. [4:24]

39 Ye are fallen from grace. [5:4]

40 Be not deceived; God is not mocked: for whatsoever a man soweth, that shall he also reap. [6:7]

41 Let us not be weary in well doing. [6:9]

Ephesians

42 The unsearchable riches of Christ. [3:8]

43 To be strengthened with might by his Spirit in the inner man. [3:16]

44 Carried about with every wind of doctrine. [4:14]

45 We are members one of another. [4:25]

46 Be ye angry and sin not: let not the sun go down upon your wrath. [4:26]

47 Let no man deceive you with vain words: for because of these things cometh the wrath of God upon the children of disobedience. [5:6]

1 Redeeming the time, because the days are evil. [5:16]

2 Put on the whole armour of God. [6:11]

3 For we wrestle not against flesh and blood, but against principalities, against powers, against the rulers of the darkness of this world, against spiritual wickedness in high places. [6:12]

Philippians

4 For to me to live is Christ, and to die is gain. [1:21]

5 Work out your own salvation with fear and trembling. [2:12]

6 But what things were gain for me, those I counted loss for Christ. [3:7]

7 Whose God is their belly, and whose glory is in their shame. [3:19]

8 Rejoice in the Lord alway: and again I say, Rejoice. [4:4]

9 The peace of God, which passeth all understanding. [4:7]

10 Whatsoever things are true, whatsoever things are honest, whatsoever things are just, whatsoever things are pure, whatsoever things are lovely, whatsoever things are of good report; if there be any virtue, and if there be any praise, think on these things. [4:8]

11 I have learned, in whatsoever state I am, therewith to be content. [4:11]

Colossians

12 Touch not; taste not; handle not. [2:21]

13 Husbands, love your wives, and be not bitter against them. [3:19]

14 Let your speech be alway with grace, seasoned with salt. [4:6]

1 Thessalonians

15 Remembering without ceasing your work of faith, and labour of love. [1:3]

16 Study to be quiet, and to do your own business. [4:11]

17 Pray without ceasing. [5:17]

18 Prove all things; hold fast that which is good. [5:21]

2 Thessalonians

19 If any would not work, neither should he eat. [3:10]

1 Timothy

20 Neither give heed to fables and endless genealogies. [1:4]

21 I did it ignorantly in unbelief. [1:13]

22 Not greedy of filthy lucre. [3:3]

23 Every creature of God is good. [4:4]

24 But refuse profane and old wives' fables. [4:7]

25 Worse than an infidel. [5:8]

26 Drink no longer water, but use a little wine for thy stomach's sake and thine often infirmities. [5:23]

27 For we brought nothing into this world, and it is certain we can carry nothing out. [6:7]

28 The love of money is the root of all evil. [6:10]

29 Fight the good fight of faith. [6:12]

30 Rich in good works. [6:18]

31 Oppositions of science falsely so called. [6:20]

2 Timothy

32 Be instant in season, out of season. [4:2]

33 I have fought a good fight, I have finished my course, I have kept the faith. [4:7]

34 The Lord reward him according to his works. [4:14]

Titus

35 Unto the pure all things are pure. [1:15]

Hebrews

36 For the word of God is quick, and powerful, and sharper than any two-edged sword, piercing even to the dividing asunder of soul and spirit. [4:12]

37 It is a fearful thing to fall into the hands of the living God. [10:31]

38 Faith is the substance of things hoped for, the evidence of things not seen. [11:1]

39 Confessed that they were strangers and pilgrims on the earth. [11:13]

40 Seeing we also are compassed about with so great a cloud of witnesses. [12:1]

41 Whom the Lord loveth he chasteneth. [12 : 6]

1 The spirits of just men made perfect. [12:23]

2 Let brotherly love continue.
Be not forgetful to entertain strangers: for thereby some have entertained angels unawares. [13:1]

3 Jesus Christ the same yesterday, and to day, and for ever. [13:8]

4 For here we have no continuing city, but we seek one to come. [13:14]

James

5 Every good gift and every perfect gift is from above, and cometh down from the Father of lights, with whom is no variableness, neither shadow of turning. [1:17]

6 Let every man be swift to hear, slow to speak, slow to wrath. [1:19]

7 Pure religion and undefiled before God and the Father is this, To visit the fatherless and widows in their affliction, and to keep himself unspotted from the world. [1:27]

8 Faith without works is dead. [2:20]

9 How great a matter a little fire kindleth! [3:5]

10 The tongue can no man tame; it is an unruly evil. [(Commonly misquoted as ' The tongue is an unruly member ') [3:8]

11 Resist the devil, and he will flee from you. [4:7]

12 Ye have heard of the patience of Job. [5:11]

13 Let your yea be yea; and your nay, nay. [5:12]

1 Peter

14 Be sober, and hope to the end. [1:13]

15 As newborn babes, desire the sincere milk of the word. [2:2]

16 But ye are a chosen generation, a royal priesthood, an holy nation, a peculiar people. [2:9]

17 Honour all men. Love the brotherhood. Fear God. Honour the king. [2:17]

18 Even the ornament of a meek and quiet spirit. [3:4]

19 Giving honour unto the wife, as unto the weaker vessel. [3:7]

20 Charity shall cover the multitude of sins. [4:8]

21 Be sober, be vigilant; because your adversary the devil, as a roaring lion, walketh about, seeking whom he may devour. [5:8]

2 Peter

22 The dog is turned to his own vomit again; and the sow that was washed to her wallowing in the mire. [2:22]

1 John

23 If we say that we have no sin, we deceive ourselves, and the truth is not in us. [1:8]

24 Shutteth up his bowels of compassion. [3:17]

25 He that loveth not knoweth not God; for God is love. [4:8]

26 There is no fear in love; but perfect love casteth out fear. [4:18]

27 He that loveth not his brother whom he hath seen, how can he love God whom he hath not seen? [4:20]

Jude

28 Wandering stars, to whom is reserved the blackness of darkness for ever. [13]

Revelation of St John

29 His head and his hairs were white like wool, as white as snow; and his eyes were as a flame of fire. [1:14]

30 His voice as the sound of many waters. [1:15]

31 I am he that liveth, and was dead. [1:18]

32 I have somewhat against thee, because thou hast left thy first love. [2:4]

33 Be thou faithful unto death, and I will give thee a crown of life. [2:10]

34 He shall rule them with a rod of iron. [2:27]

35 I will not blot out his name out of the book of life. [3:5]

36 Because thou art lukewarm, and neither cold nor hot, I will spue thee out of my mouth. [3:16]

37 Behold, I stand at the door, and knock. [3:20]

38 Four beasts full of eyes before and behind. [4:6]

39 He went forth conquering, and to conquer. [6:2]

1 Behold, a pale horse: and his name that sat on him was Death. [6:8]

2 A great multitude, which no man could number, of all nations, and kindreds, and people, and tongues. [7:9]

3 These are they which came out of great tribulation, and have washed their robes, and made them white in the blood of the Lamb. [7:14]

4 When he had opened the seventh seal, there was silence in heaven about the space of half an hour. [8:1]

5 Those men which have not the seal of God in their foreheads. [9:4]

6 And there were stings in their tails. [9:10]

7 A woman clothed with the sun, and the moon under her feet, and upon her head a crown of twelve stars. [12:1]

8 The devil is come down unto you, having great wrath, because he knoweth that he hath but a short time. [12:12]

9 Let him that hath understanding count the number of the beast: for it is the number of a man; and his number is Six hundred threescore and six. [13:18]

10 Babylon is fallen, is fallen, that great city. [14:8]

11 Blessed are the dead which die in the Lord from henceforth: Yea, saith the Spirit, that they may rest from their labours; and their works do follow them. [14:13]

12 Behold, I come as a thief. [16:15]

13 A place called in the Hebrew tongue Armageddon. [16:16]

14 I will shew unto thee the judgement of the great whore that sitteth upon many waters. [17:1]

15 The woman was arrayed in purple and scarlet colour. [17:4]

16 And he laid hold on the dragon, that old serpent, which is the Devil, and Satan, and bound him a thousand years. [20:2]

17 The sea gave up the dead which were in it. [Ib. 20:13]

18 And I saw a new heaven and a new earth: for the first heaven and the first earth were passed away; and there was no more sea. [Ib. 21:1]

19 The holy city, new Jerusalem, coming down from God out of heaven, prepared as a bride adorned for her husband. [21:2]

20 And God shall wipe away all tears from their eyes; and there shall be no more death, neither sorrow, nor crying, neither shall there be any more pain: for the former things are passed away. [21:4]

21 Behold, I make all things new. [21:5]

22 I will give unto him that is athirst of the fountain of the water of life freely. [21:6]

23 The street of the city was pure gold. [21:21]

24 And the leaves of the tree were for the healing of the nations. [22:2]

25 I am Alpha and Omega, the beginning and the end, the first and the last. [22:13]

26 Whosoever loveth and maketh a lie. [22:15]

ISAAC BICKERSTAFFE
1735?–1812?

27 There was a jolly miller once, / Lived on the river Dee; / He worked and sang from morn till night; / No lark more blithe than he. [Love in a Village, I. v]

28 And this the burden of his song / For ever used to be, / I care for nobody, not I, / If no one cares for me. [Ib.]

29 We all love a pretty girl – under the rose. [Ib. II. ii]

JOSH BILLINGS see
SHAW, HENRY WHEELER

LAURENCE BINYON   1869–1943

30 Now is the time for the burning of the leaves. [The Burning of the Leaves]

31 With proud thanksgiving, a mother for her children, / England mourns for her dead across the sea. [For the Fallen]

32 They shall grow not old, as we that are left grow old: / Age shall not weary them, nor the years condemn. / At the going down of the sun and in the morning / We will remember them. [Ib.]

AUGUSTINE BIRRELL 1850–1933

1 That great dust-heap called 'history'. [*Obiter Dicta*, 'Carlyle']

OTTO VON BISMARCK
1815–1898

2 Politics is no exact science. [Speech in Prussian Chamber, 18 Dec. 1863]

3 An honest broker. [Speech in the Reichstag, 19 Feb. 1878]

4 Blood and iron. [Speech in Prussian Chamber, 28 Jan. 1886]

VALENTINE BLACKER 1778–1823

5 Put your trust in God, my boys, and keep your powder dry. [*Oliver Cromwell's Advice*]

SIR WILLIAM BLACKSTONE
1723–1780

6 Man was formed for society. [*Commentary on the Laws of England*, Introduction]

7 The king never dies. [*Ib.* Bk I. 7]

8 Time whereof the memory of man runneth not to the contrary. [*Ib.* I. 18]

9 That the king can do no wrong is a necessary and fundamental principle of the English constitution. [*Ib.* III. 17]

10 It is better that ten guilty persons escape than one innocent suffer. [*Ib.* IV. 27]

HELEN BLACKWOOD, LADY DUFFERIN 1807–1867

11 I'm sitting on the stile, Mary, / Where we sat, side by side. [*Lament of the Irish Emigrant*]

12 And the red was on your lip, Mary, / The love-light in your eye. [*Ib.*]

13 They say there's bread and work for all, / And the sun shines always there: / But I'll not forget old Ireland, / Were it fifty times as fair. [*Ib.*]

ROBERT BLAIR 1699–1746

14 The schoolboy, with his satchel in his hand, / Whistling aloud to bear his courage up. [*The Grave*, 58]

15 Its visits, / Like those of angels, short, and far between. [*The Grave*, 588]

CHARLES DUPEE BLAKE
1846–1903

16 Rock-a-bye baby on the tree top, / When the wind blows the cradle will rock, / When the bough bends the cradle will fall, / Down comes the baby, cradle and all. [Attr.]

WILLIAM BLAKE 1757–1827

17 For everything that lives is holy, life delights in life. [*America*, 71]

18 To see a World in a grain of sand, / And a Heaven in a wild flower, / Hold Infinity in the palm of your hand, / And Eternity in an hour. [*Auguries of Innocence*]

19 A robin redbreast in a cage / Puts all Heaven in a rage. [*Ib.*]

20 A dog starved at his master's gate / Predicts the ruin of the State. [*Ib.*]

21 A skylark wounded in the wing, / A cherubim does cease to sing. [*Ib.*]

22 Every wolf's and lion's howl / Raises from Hell a human soul. [*Ib.*]

23 He who shall hurt the little wren / Shall never be beloved by men. [*Ib.*]

24 The caterpillar on the leaf / Repeats to thee thy mother's grief. [*Ib.*]

25 A truth that's told with bad intent / Beats all the lies you can invent. [*Ib.*]

26 Every tear from every eye / Becomes a babe in Eternity. [*Ib.*]

27 He who shall teach the child to doubt / The rotting grave shall ne'er get out. [*Ib.*]

28 The strongest poison ever known / Came from Caesar's laurel crown. [*Ib.*]

29 If the Sun and Moon should doubt, / They'd immediately go out. [*Ib.*]

30 The harlot's cry from street to street / Shall weave old England's winding-sheet. [*Ib.*]

31 Does the Eagle know what is in the pit / Or wilt thou go ask the Mole? / Can Wisdom be put in a silver rod, / Or Love in a golden bowl? [*The Book of Thel*, Thel's motto]

1 The Vision of Christ that thou dost see /
Is my vision's greatest enemy. [*The Everlasting Gospel*, α]

2 Both read the Bible day and night, / But
thou read'st black where I read white.
[*Ib.*]

3 Humility is only doubt, / And does the
sun and moon blot out. [*Ib.* γ]

4 This life's five windows of the soul /
Distorts the Heavens from pole to pole,/
And leads you to believe a lie / When
you see with, not thro', the eye. [*Ib.*]

5 I am sure this Jesus will not do, /Either
for Englishman or Jew. [*Ib.* 'Epilogue']

6 Mutual Forgiveness of each vice, / Such
are the Gates of Paradise. [*The Gates of
Paradise*, Prologue]

7 Truly, my Satan, thou art but a dunce, /
And dost not know the garment from the
man; / Every harlot was a virgin once, /
Nor canst thou ever change Kate into
Nan.

Tho' thou art worshipped by the
names divine / Of Jesus and Jehovah,
thou art still / The Son of Morn in weary
Night's decline, / The lost traveller's
dream under the hill. [*Ib.* Epilogue]

8 Great things are done when men and
mountains meet; / This is not done by
jostling in the street. [*Gnomic Verses*]

9 The Angel that presided o'er my birth /
Said 'Little creature, formed of joy and
mirth, / Go, love without the help of
anything on earth.' [*Ib.* 'Riches']

10 He who bends to himself a Joy / Doth
the wingèd life destroy; / But he who
kisses the Joy as it flies / Lives in Eternity's sunrise. [*Ib.* 'Several Questions
Answered']

11 I must Create a System, or be enslaved
by another Man's; / I will not Reason
and Compare; my business is to Create.
[*Jerusalem*, f. 10. 20]

12 I see the Fourfold Man; the Humanity in
deadly sleep, / And its fallen Emanation,
the Spectre and its cruel Shadow. / I see
the Past, Present, and Future existing all
at once / Before me. [*Ib.* f. 15. 6]

13 The fields from Islington to Marybone, /
To Primrose Hill and Saint John's
Wood, / Were builded over with pillars
of gold; / And there Jerusalem's pillars
stood. [*Ib.* f. 27]

14 For a tear is an intellectual thing; / And
a sigh is the sword of an angel king; /
And the bitter groan of a martyr's woe /
Is an arrow from the Almighty's bow.
[*Jerusalem*, f. 52]

15 I give you the end of a golden string; /
Only wind it into a ball, / It will lead you
in at Heaven's gate, / Built in Jerusalem's
wall. [*Ib.* f. 77]

16 England! awake! awake! awake! / Jerusalem thy sister calls! / Why wilt thou
sleep the sleep of death, / And close her
from thy ancient walls? [*Ib.*]

17 And now the time returns again: / Our
souls exult, and London's towers /
Receive the Lamb of God to dwell / In
England's green and pleasant bowers.
[*Ib.*]

18 I care not whether a man is good or evil;
all that I care / Is whether he is a wise
man or a fool. Go! put off holiness, / And
put on intellect. [*Ib.* f. 91 : 54]

19 'Father, O father! what do we here / In
this land of unbelief and fear? / The Land
of Dreams is better far, / Above the light
of the morning star.' [*The Land of Dreams*]

20 And did those feet in ancient time /
Walk upon England's mountains green? /
And was the holy Lamb of God / On
England's pleasant pastures seen?

And did the Countenance Divine /
Shine forth upon our clouded hills? /
And was Jerusalem builded here /
Among these dark Satanic mills?

Bring me my bow of burning gold! /
Bring me my arrows of desire! / Bring
me my spear! O clouds, unfold! / Bring
me my chariot of fire!

I will not cease from mental fight, /
Nor shall my sword sleep in my hand, /
Till we have built Jerusalem / In Eng-
land's green and pleasant land. [*Milton*,
Preface]

21 When a man has married a wife, he finds
out whether / Her knees and elbows are
only glued together. [*Miscellaneous Epigrams*]

22 Mock on, mock on, Voltaire, Rousseau;
/ Mock on, mock on; 'tis all in vain! /
You throw the sand against the wind, /
And the wind blows it back again.
[*Mock on, mock on, Voltaire, Rousseau*]

1 My Spectre around me night and day /
Like a wild beast guards my way; / My
Emanation far within / Weeps incessantly
for my sin. [*My Spectre around me night
and day*]

2 Never seek to tell thy love, / Love that
never told can be; / For the gentle wind
does move / Silently, invisibly. [*Never
seek to tell thy Love*]

3 Soon as she was gone from me, / A
traveller came by, / Silently, invisibly: /
He took her with a sigh. [*Ib.*]

4 When Sir Joshua Reynolds died / All
Nature was degraded; / The King dropped
a tear in the Queen's ear, / And all his
pictures faded. [*On Art and Artists*]

5 A petty sneaking thief I knew – / O! Mr
Cr—, how do you do? [*On Cromek*]

6 Hear the voice of the Bard! / Who
present, past, and future sees; / Whose
ears have heard / The Holy Word / That
walked among the ancient trees. [*Songs of
Experience*, Introduction]

7 Ah, Sun-flower! weary of time, / Who
countest the steps of the sun; / Seeking
after that sweet golden clime, / Where
the traveller's journey is done;

Where the Youth pined away with
desire, / And the pale Virgin shrouded in
snow, / Arise from their graves, and
aspire / Where my Sun-flower wishes
to go. [*Ib.* 'Ah! Sun-Flower']

8 Love seeketh not itself to please, / Nor
for itself hath any care, / But for another
gives its ease, / And builds a Heaven in
Hell's despair. [*Ib.* 'The Clod and the
Pebble']

9 And the gates of this Chapel were shut, /
And 'Thou shalt not' writ over the door.
[*Ib.* 'The Garden of Love']

10 And priests in black gowns were walking
their rounds, / And binding with briars
my joys and desires. [*Ib.*]

11 Pity would be no more / If we did not
make somebody poor; / And Mercy no
more could be / If all were as happy as
we. [*Ib.* 'The Human Abstract']

12 My mother groaned, my father wept, /
Into the dangerous world I leapt; /
Helpless, naked, piping loud, / Like a
fiend hid in a cloud. [*Ib.* 'Infant Sorrow']

13 But if at the Church they would give us
some ale, / And a pleasant fire our souls
to regale, / We'd sing and we'd pray all
the livelong day, / Nor ever once wish
from the Church to stray. [*Songs of
Experience*, 'The Little Vagabond']

14 I was angry with my friend: / I told my
wrath, my wrath did end. / I was angry
with my foe: / I told it not, my wrath did
grow. [*Ib.* 'A Poison Tree']

15 O Rose, thou art sick! / The invisible
worm, / That flies in the night, / In the
howling storm,

Has found out thy bed / Of crimson
joy; / And his dark secret love / Does
thy life destroy. [*Ib.* 'The Sick Rose']

16 Tiger! Tiger! burning bright / In the
forests of the night, / What immortal
hand or eye / Could frame thy fearful
symmetry? [*Ib.* 'The Tiger']

17 When the stars threw down their spears, /
And watered heaven with their tears, /
Did he smile his work to see? / Did he
who made the Lamb make thee? [*Ib.*]

18 Piping down the valleys wild, / Piping
songs of pleasant glee, / On a cloud I saw
a child. [*Songs of Innocence*, Introduction]

19 'Pipe a song about a Lamb!' / So I piped
with merry cheer. [*Ib.*]

20 And I made a rural pen, / And I stained
the water clear, / And I wrote my happy
songs / Every child may joy to hear. [*Ib.*]

21 When my mother died, I was very young,
/ And my father sold me while yet my
tongue / Could scarcely cry "weep!
'weep! 'weep! 'weep!' / So your chim-
neys I sweep, and in soot I sleep. [*Ib.*
'The Chimney Sweeper']

22 To Mercy, Pity, Peace, and Love / All
pray in their distress. [*Ib.* 'The Divine
Image']

23 For Mercy has a human heart, / Pity a
human face, / And Love, the human
form divine, / And Peace, the human
dress. [*Ib.*]

24 'Twas on a Holy Thursday, their innocent faces clean, / The children walking
two and two, in red and blue and green.
[*Ib.* 'Holy Thursday']

25 Then cherish pity, lest you drive an angel
from your door. [*Ib.*]

26 'I have no name: / I am but two days
old.' / What shall I call thee? / 'I happy
am, / Joy is my name.' / Sweet joy befall
thee! [*Ib.* 'Infant Joy']

1 Little Lamb, who made thee? / Dost thou know who made thee? / Gave thee life, and bid thee feed, / By the stream and o'er the mead; / Gave thee clothing of delight, / Softest clothing, woolly, bright; / Gave thee such a tender voice, Making all the vales rejoice? [*Songs of Innocence,* 'The Lamb']

2 He is meek, and He is mild; / He became a little child. / I a child, and thou a lamb, / We are callèd by His name. / Little Lamb, God bless thee! [*Ib.*]

3 When the green woods laugh with the voice of joy. [*Ib.* 'Laughing Song']

4 My mother bore me in the southern wild, / And I am black, but O! my soul is white. [*Ib.* 'The Little Black Boy']

5 Father! father! where are you going? / O do not walk so fast. / Speak, father, speak to your little boy, / Or else I shall be lost. [*Ib.* 'The Little Boy Lost']

6 Farewell, green fields and happy groves, / Where flocks have took delight, / Where lambs have nibbled, silent moves / The feet of angels bright; / Unseen they pour blessing, / And joy without ceasing, / On each bud and blossom, / And each sleeping bosom. [*Ib.* 'Night']

7 When the voices of children are heard on the green, / And laughing is heard on the hill, / My heart is at rest within my breast, / And everything else is still. [*Ib.* 'Nurse's Song']

8 Can I see another's woe, / And not be in sorrow too? [*Ib.* 'On Another's Sorrow']

9 Cruelty has a human heart, / And Jealousy a human face; / Terror the human form divine, / And Secrecy the human dress. [*Appendix to the Songs of Innocence and of Experience,* 'A Divine Image']

10 I mock thee not, though I by thee am mockèd; / Thou call'st me madman, but I call thee blockhead. [*To Flaxman*]

11 Thy friendship oft has made my heart to ache: / Do be my enemy – for friendship's sake. [*To Hayley*]

12 Whether on Ida's shady brow, / Or in the chambers of the East, / The chambers of the sun, that now / From ancient melody have ceased;

Whether in Heaven ye wander fair, / Or the green corners of the earth, / Or the blue regions of the air / Where the melodious winds have birth. [*To the Muses*]

13 Wandering in many a coral grove, / Fair Nine, forsaking Poetry! [*Ib.*]

14 The sound is forced, the notes are few! [*Ib.*]

15 O! why was I born with a different face? / Why was I not born like the rest of my race? [*To Thomas Butts*]

16 Without contraries is no progression. [*The Marriage of Heaven and Hell,* 'The Argument']

17 Man has no Body distinct from his Soul; for that called Body is a portion of Soul discerned by the five Senses, the chief inlets of Soul in this age. [*Ib.* 'The Voice of the Devil']

18 Energy is eternal delight! [*Ib.*]

19 Those who restrain Desire, do so because theirs is weak enough to be restrained. [*Ib.* 'Those who restrain Desire . . .']

20 The reason Milton wrote in fetters when he wrote of Angels and God, and at liberty when of Devils and Hell, is because he was a true poet, and of the Devil's party without knowing it. [*Ib.* note]

21 In seed time learn, in harvest teach, in winter enjoy. [*Ib.* 'Proverbs of Hell']

22 The road of excess leads to the palace of wisdom. [*Ib.*]

23 He who desires but acts not breeds pestilence. [*Ib.*]

24 The cut worm forgives the plough. [*Ib.*]

25 A fool sees not the same tree that a wise man sees. [*Ib.*]

26 Eternity is in love with the productions of time. [*Ib.*]

27 If the fool would persist in his folly he would become wise. [*Ib.*]

28 Prisons are built with stones of Law, brothels with bricks of Religion. [*Ib.*]

29 The pride of the peacock is the glory of God. / The lust of the goat is the bounty of God. / The wrath of the lion is the wisdom of God. / The nakedness of woman is the work of God. [*Ib.*]

30 What is now proved was once only imagined. [*Ib.*]

31 The tigers of wrath are wiser than the horses of instruction. [*Ib.*]

1 Damn braces. Bless relaxes. [*The Marriage of Heaven and Hell*, 'Proverbs of Hell']

2 Truth can never be told so as to be understood, and not be believed. [*Ib.*]

3 Then I asked: 'Does a firm persuasion that a thing is so, make it so?'
He replied: 'All Poets believe that it does, and in ages of imagination this firm persuasion removed mountains; but many are not capable of a firm persuasion of anything.' [*Ib.* 'A Memorable Fancy: "The Prophets Isaiah and Ezekiel . . ."']

4 If the doors of perception were cleansed, everything would appear to man as it is, infinite. [*Ib.* 'The ancient tradition . . .']

5 I was in a Printing-house in Hell, and saw the method in which knowledge is transmitted from generation to generation. [*Ib.* 'A Memorable Fancy: "I was in a Printing-house . . ."']

6 Man's Desires are limited by his Perceptions; none can desire what he has not perceived. [*There is no Natural Religion*]

7 The Desire of Man being Infinite, the possession is Infinite, and himself Infinite. [*Ib.*]

8 To generalize is to be an idiot. [Quoted in Gilchrist's *Life of Blake*]

PHILIP BLISS   1838–1876

9 Hold the fort, for I am coming. [*Ho, my Comrades, see the Signal*]

ROBERT BLOOMFIELD   1766–1823

10 Strange to the world, he wore a bashful look, / The fields his study, Nature was his book. [*Farmer's Boy*, 'Spring', 31]

MARSHAL BLÜCHER   1742–1814

11 What a place to plunder! [On seeing London in 1814]

EDMUND BLUNDEN   1896–1974

12 I am for the woods against the world, / But are the woods for me? [*The Kiss*]

13 Dance on this ball-floor thin and wan, / Use him as though you love him; / Court him, elude him, reel and pass, / And let him hate you through the glass. [*The Midnight Skaters*]

14 I have been young, and now am not too old; / And I have seen the righteous forsaken, / His health, his honour and his quality taken, / This is not what we were formerly told. [*Report on Experience*]

W. SCAWEN BLUNT   1840–1922

15 He who has once been happy is for aye / Out of destruction's reach. [*Esther*, 1]

16 I like the hunting of the hare / Better than that of the fox. [*The Old Squire*]

BOETHIUS   480?–524

17 For in all adversity of fortune the worst sort of misery is to have been happy. [*Consolation of Philosophy*, Bk II. Prose 4]

JAKOB BÖHME   1575–1624

18 THE SCHOLAR: Whither goes the soul when the body dies?
THE MASTER: There is no necessity for it to go anywhere. [*Of Heaven and Hell, A Dialogue*]

NICOLAS BOILEAU   1636–1711

19 *Quelque sujet qu'on traite, ou plaisant, ou sublime, / Que toujours le bon sens s'accorde avec la rime.* Whether one is treating a light or an exalted subject, let the sense and the rhyme always agree. [*L'Art poétique*, I. 27]

20 *Qui ne sait se borner ne sut jamais écrire.* – No one who cannot limit himself has ever been able to write. [*Ib.* I. 63]

21 *Souvent la peur d'un mal nous conduit dans un pire.* – Often the fear of one evil leads us into a worse. [*Ib.* I. 64]

22 *Enfin Malherbe vint, et, le premier en France, / Fit sentir dans les vers une juste cadence.* – At last came Malherbe, and made verse run smoothly the first in France to do so. [*Ib.* I. 131]

23 *Vingt fois sur le métier remettez votre ouvrage; / Polissez-le sans cesse et le repolissez.* – Bring your work back to the workshop twenty times. Polish it continuously, and polish it again. [*Ib.* I. 172]

1 *Un sot trouve toujours un plus sot qui l'admire.* – A fool always finds a greater fool to admire him. [*L'Art poétique*, I. 232]

2 *Qu'en un lieu, qu'en un jour, un seul fait accompli, / Tienne jusqu'à la fin le théâtre rempli.* – Let a single complete action, in one place and one day, keep the theatre packed to the last. [*Ib*. III. 45]

3 *Chaque âge a ses plaisirs, son esprit et ses mœurs.* – Every age has its own pleasures, its own wit and customs. [*Ib*. III. 374]

4 *Soyez plutôt maçon, si c'est votre talent.* – Be a mason instead, if you have a talent for that. [*Ib*. IV. 26]

5 *Ma pensée au grand jour partout s'offre et s'expose, / Et mon vers, bien ou mal, dit toujours quelque chose.* – Everywhere my thought offers and exposes itself to the light of day, and my verse, whether good or bad, always says something. [*Épitres*, IX. 59]

6 *Le pénible fardeau de n'avoir rien à faire.* – The dreadful burden of having nothing to do. [*Ib*. XI. 86]

7 *Reprenez vos esprits et souvenez-vous bien / Qu'un dîner réchauffé ne valut jamais rien.* – Take fresh heart and never forget that a warmed-up dinner is worth nothing at all. [*Le Lutrin*, 103]

L'or, même à la laideur, donne un teint de beauté. – Gold gives even to plainness the colour of beauty. [*Satires*, I. 205]

9 *Grand roi, cesse de vaincre, ou je cesse d'écrire.* – Great king, cease winning victories, or I shall give up writing. [*Ib*. VIII. 1]

HENRY ST JOHN, VISCOUNT BOLINGBROKE   1678–1751

10 Truth lies within a little and certain compass, but error is immense. [*Reflections upon Exile*]

11 They make truth serve as a stalking-horse to error. [*On the Study of History*, Letter 1]

12 Nations, like men, have their infancy. [*Ib*. 4]

13 They [Thucydides and Xenophon] maintained the dignity of history. [*Ib*. 5]

HORATIUS BONAR   1808–1889

14 A few more years shall roll, / A few more seasons come; / And we shall be with those that rest, / Asleep within the tomb. [Hymn]

JAMES BONE   1872–1962

15 He made righteousness readable. [Of C. P. Scott of the *Manchester Guardian*]

BARTON BOOTH   1681–1733

16 True as the needle to the pole, / Or as the dial to the sun. [*Song*]

GENERAL WILLIAM BOOTH   1829–1912

17 This Submerged Tenth – is it, then, beyond the reach of the nine-tenths in the midst of whom they live? [*In Darkest England*, I. ii. 23]

LUDWIG BÖRNE   1786–1837

18 Let us have no care, but be glad of the approaching springtime of the peoples. Let us have no fear of the movement into the open. [*Gesammelte Schriften*, III. (1829) 135]

GEORGE BORROW   1803–1881

19 The author of 'Amelia', the most singular genius which their island ever produced, whose works it has long been the fashion to abuse in public and to read in secret. [*The Bible in Spain*, Ch. 1]

20 The genuine spirit of localism. [*Ib*. 31]

21 There are no countries in the world less known by the British than these selfsame British Islands. [*Lavengro*, Preface]

22 Translation is at best an echo. [*Ib*. Ch. 25]

23 There's night and day, brother, both sweet things; sun, moon, and stars, brother, all sweet things; there's likewise a wind on the heath. Life is very sweet, brother; who would wish to die? [*Ib*.]

24 A losing trade, I assure you, sir: literature is a drug. [*Ib*. 30]

25 Youth will be served, every dog has his day, and mine has been a fine one. [*Ib*. 92]

MARÉCHAL BOSQUET   1810–1861

26 *C'est magnifique, mais ce n'est pas la guerre.* – It is magnificent, but it is not

war. [Comment on the Charge of the Light Brigade]

J. C. BOSSIDY   1860–1928

1 And this is good old Boston, / The home of the bean and the cod, / Where the Lowells talk to the Cabots, / And the Cabots talk only to God. [Toast proposed at Harvard dinner, 1910]

JACQUES BÉNIGNE BOSSUET
1627–1704

2 *L'Angleterre, ah! la perfide Angleterre.* – England, oh, perfidious England! [*Sermon sur la Circoncision.* (By the time of the French Revolution this had become *Albion perfide*)]

GORDON BOTTOMLEY
1874–1948

3 Poetry is founded on the hearts of men: / Though in Nirvana or the Heavenly courts / The principle of beauty shall persist, / Its body of poetry, as the body of man, / Is but a terrene form, a terrene use, / That swifter being will not loiter with; / And, when mankind is dead and the world cold, / Poetry's immortality will pass. [*Atlantis*]

4 The snow had fallen many nights and days; / The sky was come upon the world at last, / Sifting thinly down as endlessly / As though within the system of blind planets / Something had been forgot or overdriven. [*The End of the World*]

BOULAY DE LA MEURTHE
1761–1840

5 *C'est pire qu'un crime, c'est une faute.* – It is worse than a crime, it is a blunder. [Comment on the execution of the Duc d'Enghien]

SIR H. E. BOULTON   1859–1935

6 Speed, bonny boat, like a bird on the wing; / 'Onward', the sailors cry; / Carry the lad that's born to be king / Over the sea to Skye. [*Skye Boat Song*]

F. W. BOURDILLON   1852–1921

7 The night has a thousand eyes, / And the day but one; / Yet the light of the bright world dies / With the dying sun. [*Light*]

LORD BOWEN   1835–1894

8 The rain it raineth on the just / And also on the unjust fella: / But chiefly on the just, because / The unjust steals the just's umbrella. [Quoted in Walter Sichel, *Sands of Time*]

9 *On a metaphysician:* A blind man in a dark room, looking for a black hat – which is not there. [Attr.]

W. L. BOWLES   1762–1850

10 The Cause of Freedom is the cause of God! [*Edmund Burke*, 78]

JOHN BRADFORD   1510?–1555

11 But for the grace of God, there goes John Bradford. [On seeing some criminals led to execution]

F. H. BRADLEY   1846–1924

12 Metaphysics is the finding of bad reasons for what we believe upon instinct; but to find these reasons is no less an instinct. [*Appearance and Reality*, Preface]

13 A ballet dance of bloodless categories. [*Logic*]

14 His mind is open; yes, it is so open that nothing is retained; ideas simply pass through him. [Quoted in *Treasury of Humorous Quotations*]

JOHN BRAHAM   1774?–1856

15 England, home and beauty. [*The Americans*, Song]

HARRY BRAISTED   19 Cent.

16 If you want to win her hand, / Let the maiden understand / That she's not the only pebble on the beach. [*You're not the only Pebble on the Beach*]

ERNEST BRAMAH
[E. B. SMITH]   1868–1942

1 My low-class appellation is Wan, that of my mentally defective father being Ah-shoo. [*Kai Lung Unrolls His Mat*, 'The Protecting Ancestors']

2 It is a mark of insincerity of purpose to spend one's time in looking for the sacred Emperor in the low-class tea-shops. [*The Wallet of Kai Lung*, 'Transmutation of Ling']

3 An expression of no-encouragement. [*Ib.* 'Confession of Kai Lung']

4 The whole narrative is permeated with the odour of joss-sticks and honourable high-mindedness. [*Ib.* 'Kin Yen']

SEBASTIAN BRANT   1458–1521

5 *Die Welt die will betrogen sein.* – The world, which wishes to be deceived. [*Das Narrenschiff*]

RICHARD BRATHWAITE
1588?–1673

6 I saw a Puritan-one / Hanging of his cat on Monday, / For killing of a mouse on Sunday. [*Barnabee's Journal*, Pt 1]

JANE BRERETON   1685–1740

7 The picture, placed the busts between, / Adds to the thought much strength; / Wisdom and Wit are little seen, / But Folly's at full length. [*On Mr Nash's Picture at Full Length between the Busts of Sir Isaac Newton and Mr Pope.* Also attr. to Lord Chesterfield]

NICHOLAS BRETON 1545?–1626?

8 I wish my deadly foe no worse / Than want of friends, and empty purse. [*A Farewell to Town*]

9 A Mad World, My Masters. [Title of dialogue.]

10 Much ado there was, God wot, / He would love, and she would not. [*Phillida and Corydon*]

ROBERT BRIDGES   1844–1930

11 Awake, my heart, to be loved, awake,
awake! / The darkness silvers away, the morn doth break, / It leaps in the sky: unrisen lustres slake / The o'ertaken moon. Awake, O heart, awake! [*Awake, my heart, to be loved*]

12 Wherefore to-night so full of care, / My soul, revolving hopeless strife? [*Dejection*]

13 For beauty being the best of all we know / Sums up the unsearchable and secret aims / Of nature. [*The Growth of Love*, 8]

14 Beauty sat with me all the summer day, / Awaiting the sure triumph of her eye; / Nor mark'd I till we parted, how, hard by, / Love in her train stood ready for his prey. [*Ib.* 56]

15 The hill pines were sighing, / O'ercast and chill was the day: / A mist in the valley lying / Blotted the pleasant May. [*The Hill Pines were Sighing*]

16 I heard a linnet courting / His lady in the spring. [*I heard a linnet*]

17 I will not let thee go. / Had not the great sun seen, I might; / Or were he reckoned slow / To bring the false to light, / Then might I let thee go. [*I will not let thee go*]

18 When men were all asleep the snow came flying, / In large white flakes falling on the city brown, / Stealthily and perpetually settling and loosely lying, / Hushing the latest traffic of the drowsy town. [*London Snow*]

19 'O look at the trees!' they cried, 'O look at the trees!' [*Ib.*]

20 The south-wind strengthens to a gale, / Across the moon the clouds fly fast, / The house is smitten as with a flail, / The chimney shudders to the blast. [*Low Barometer*]

21 And Reason kens he herits in / A haunted house. Tenants unknown / Assert their squalid lease of sin / With earlier title than his own. [*Ib.*]

22 My delight and thy delight / Walking, like two angels white, / In the gardens of the night. [*My Delight and thy Delight*]

23 Beautiful must be the mountains whence ye come, / And bright in the fruitful valleys the streams, wherefrom / Ye learn your song. [*Nightingales*]

24 Perfect little body, without fault or stain on thee. [*On a dead Child*]

1 Whither, O splendid ship, thy white sails crowding, / Leaning across the bosom of the urgent West. [*A Passer-by*]

2 Spring goeth all in white, / Crowned with milk-white may: / In fleecy flocks of light / O'er heaven the white clouds stray. [*Spring goeth all in White*]

3 Thus ever at every season in every hour and place / visions await the soul on wide ocean or shore / mountain forest or garden in wind and floating cloud / in busy murmur of bees or blithe carol of birds. [*The Tapestry*, 34]

4 How was November's melancholy endear'd to me / in the effigy of plowteams following and recrossing / patiently the delicat landscape from dawn to dusk, / as the slow-creeping ripple of their single furrow / submerged the sodden litter of summer's festival! [*The Testament of Beauty*, III. 354]

5 When death to either shall come, – / I pray it be first to me. [*When Death to either shall come*]

6 The day begins to droop, – / Its course is done: / But nothing tells the place / Of the setting sun. [*Winter Nightfall*]

JOHN BRIGHT   1811–1889

7 My opinion is that the Northern States will manage somehow to muddle through. [Said during the American Civil War]

8 The knowledge of the ancient languages is mainly a luxury. [Letter in the *Pall Mall Gazette*, 1886]

9 The angel of death has been abroad throughout the land; you may almost hear the beating of his wings. [Speech in House of Commons, 23 Feb. 1855]

10 I am for 'Peace, retrenchment and reform', the watchword of the great Liberal party thirty years ago. [Speech at Birmingham, 28 April 1859]

11 England is the mother of Parliaments. [*Ib.* 18 Jan. 1865]

12 The right honourable gentleman ... has retired into what may be called his political Cave of Adullam – and he has called about him everyone that was in distress and everyone that was discontented. [Speech in House of Commons, 13 Mar. 1866]

13 A free breakfast table. [Address to Edinburgh Chamber of Commerce in favour of repeal of food duties, 1868]

14 Force is not a remedy. [Speech at Birmingham, 16 Nov. 1880]

15 And he adores his maker. [Attr. (When told that he should give Disraeli credit for being a self-made man)]

ANTHELME BRILLAT-
SAVARIN   1755–1826

16 *Dis-moi ce que tu manges, et je te dirai ce que tu es.* – Tell me what you eat, and I will tell you what you are. [*Physiologie du goût*]

RICHARD BROME   ?– 1652?

17 I am a gentleman, though spoiled i' the breeding. / The Buzzards are all gentlemen. We came in with the Conqueror. [*The English Moor*, III. ii]

CHARLOTTE BRONTË 1816–1855

18 Reader, I married him. [*Jane Eyre*, Ch. 38]

EMILY BRONTË   1818–1848

19 No coward soul is mine, / No trembler in the world's storm-troubled sphere: / I see Heaven's glories shine, / And faith shines equal, arming me from fear. [*Last Lines*]

20 Vain are the thousand creeds / That move men's hearts: unutterably vain. [*Ib.*]

21 Though earth and man were gone, / And suns and universes ceased to be, / And Thou wert left alone, / Every existence would exist in Thee. [*Ib.*]

22 Oh! dreadful is the check – intense the agony – / When the ear begins to hear, and the eye begins to see; / When the pulse begins to throb, the brain to think again; / The soul to feel the flesh, and the flesh to feel the chain. [*The Prisoner*]

23 Cold in the earth – and the deep snow piled above thee, / Far, far, removed, cold in the dreary grave! [*Remembrance*]

24 Once drinking deep of that divinest anguish, / How could I seek the empty world again? [*Ib.*]

1 I lingered round them, under that benign sky: watched the moths fluttering among the heath and harebells; listened to the soft wind breathing through the grass; and wondered how anyone could ever imagine unquiet slumbers for the sleepers in that quiet earth. [*Wuthering Heights*, conclusion]

RUPERT BROOKE   1887–1915

2 Blow out, you bugles, over the rich Dead! / There's none of these so lonely and poor of old, / But, dying, has made us rarer gifts than gold. / These laid the world away; poured out the red / Sweet wine of youth; gave up the years to be / Of work and joy, and that unhoped serene, / That men call age; and those who would have been, / Their sons, they gave, their immortality. [*The Dead*]

3 Honour has come back, as a king, to earth, / And paid his subjects with a royal wage; / And Nobleness walks in our ways again; / And we have come into our heritage. [*Ib.*]

4 Unfading moths, immortal flies, / And the worm that never dies. / And in that heaven of all their wish, / There shall be no more land, say fish. [*Heaven*]

5 Breathless, we flung us on the windy hill, / Laughed in the sun, and kissed the lovely grass. [*The Hill*]

6 And then you suddenly cried and turned away. [*Ib.*]

7 Here tulips bloom as they are told; / Unkempt about those hedges blows / An English unofficial rose; / And there the unregulated sun / Slopes down to rest when day is done, / And wakes a vague unpunctual star, / A slippered Hesper. [*The Old Vicarage, Grantchester*]

8 And spectral dance, before the dawn, / A hundred Vicars down the lawn; / Curates, long dust, will come and go / On lissom, clerical, printless toe; / And oft between the boughs is seen / The sly shade of a Rural Dean. [*Ib.*]

9 For England's the one land, I know, / Where men with Splendid Hearts may go; / And Cambridgeshire, of all England, / The shire for Men who Understand. [*Ib.*]

10 For Cambridge people rarely smile, / Being urban, squat, and packed with guile. [*The Old Vicarage, Grantchester*]

11 They love the Good; they worship Truth; / They laugh uproariously in youth; / (And when they get to feeling old, / They up and shoot themselves, I'm told). [*Ib.*]

12 Stands the Church clock at ten to three? / And is there honey still for tea? [*Ib.*]

13 Now, God be thanked who has matched us with His hour, / And caught our youth, and wakened us from sleeping. [*Peace*]

14 And the worst friend and enemy is but Death. [*Ib.*]

15 War knows no power. Safe shall be my going, / Secretly armed against all death's endeavour; / Safe though all safety's lost; safe where men fall; / And if these poor limbs die, safest of all. [*Safety*]

16 If I should die, think only this of me: / That there's some corner of a foreign field / That is for ever England. There shall be / In that rich earth a richer dust concealed. [*The Soldier*]

17 And think, this heart, all evil shed away, / A pulse in the eternal mind, no less / Gives somewhere back the thoughts by England given. [*Ib.*]

18 In hearts at peace, under an English heaven. [*Ib.*]

19 Spend in pure converse our eternal day; / Think each in each, immediately wise; / Learn all we lacked before; hear, know, and say / What this tumultuous body now denies; / And feel, who have laid our groping hands away; / And see, no longer blinded by our eyes. [Sonnet: *Not with vain Tears*]

20 Oh! Death will find me long before I tire / Of watching you; and swing me suddenly / Into the shade and loneliness and mire / Of the last land! [Sonnet: *Oh! Death will find me*]

PHILLIPS BROOKS   1835–1893

21 O little town of Bethlehem, / How still we see thee lie; / Above thy deep and dreamless sleep / The silent stars go by. [*Hymn*]

SHIRLEY BROOKS 1816–1874

1 I takes and paints, / Hears no complaints, / And sells before I'm dry; / Till savage Ruskin / He sticks his tusk in, / Then nobody will buy. [*Poem by a Perfectly Furious Academician*]

2 Says Hyam to Moses, / 'Let's cut off our noses.' / Says Moses to Hyam, / 'Ma tear, who vould buy 'em?' [*A Practical Answer*]

R. B. BROUGH 1828–1860

3 My Lord Tomnoddy is thirty-four; / The Earl can last but a few years more. / My Lord in the Peers will take his place: / Her Majesty's councils his words will grace. / Office he'll hold and patronage sway; / Fortunes and lives he will vote away; / And what are his qualifications? ONE / He's the Earl of Fitzdotterel's eldest son. [*My Lord Tomnoddy*]

LORD BROUGHAM 1778–1868

4 The schoolmaster is abroad, and I trust more to him, armed with his primer, than I do to the soldier in full military array, for upholding and extending the liberties of his country. [Speech in House of Commons, 29 Jan. 1828]

5 Education makes a people easy to lead, but difficult to drive easy to govern but impossible to enslave. [Attr.]

6 The great Unwashed. [Attr.]

THOMAS BROWN 1663–1704

7 I do not love thee, Doctor Fell, / The reason why I cannot tell; / But this alone I know full well, / I do not love thee, Doctor Fell. [Transl. of Martial, i. 32]

T. E. BROWN 1830–1897

8 O blackbird, what a boy you are! / How you do go it! [*The Blackbird*]

9 A rich man's joke is always funny. [*The Doctor*]

10 A garden is a lovesome thing, God wot! [*My Garden*]

SIR THOMAS BROWNE 1605–1682

They do most by Books, who could do much without them, and he that chiefly owes himself unto himself, is the substantial Man. [*Christian Morals*, II. 11]

12 Life is itself but the shadow of death, and souls departed but the shadows of the living. All things fall under this name. The sun itself is but the dark *simulacrum*, and light but the shadow of God. [*Garden of Cyrus*, Ch. 4]

13 But the quincunx of heaven runs low, and 'tis time to close the five ports of knowledge. [*Ib.* 5]

14 And though in the bed of Cleopatra, can hardly with any delight raise up the ghost of a rose. [*Ib.*]

15 The huntsmen are up in America, and they are already past their first sleep in Persia. [*Ib.*]

16 Dreams out of the ivory gate, and visions before midnight. [*On Dreams*]

17 I dare, without usurpation, assume the honourable style of a Christian. [*Religio Medici*, Pt I. 1]

18 Yet at my devotion I love to use the civility of my knee, my hat, and hand. [*Ib.* I. 3]

19 As for those wingy mysteries in divinity, and airy subtleties in religion, which have unhinged the brains of better heads, they never stretched the *pia mater* of mine. [*Ib.* I. 9]

20 Methinks there be not impossibilities enough in religion for an active faith. [*Ib.*]

21 I love to lose myself in a mystery; to pursue my reason to an *O altitudo!* [*Ib.*]

22 We carry with us the wonders we seek without us: there is all Africa and her prodigies in us. [*Ib.* I. 15]

23 All things are artificial; for nature is the art of God. [*Ib.* I. 16]

24 Thus the devil played at chess with me, and yielding a pawn, thought to gain a queen of me, taking advantage of my honest endeavours. [*Ib.* I. 18]

25 For my part, I have ever believed, and do now know, that there are witches. [*Ib.* I. 30]

26 Thus we are men and we know not how:

there is something in us that can be without us, and will be after us. [*Religio Medici*, I. 35]

1 Certainly there is no happiness within this circle of flesh, nor is it in the optics of these eyes to behold felicity. The first day of our jubilee is death. [*Ib.* I. 43]

2 To believe only possibilities is not faith, but mere philosophy. [*Ib.* I. 47]

3 There is no road or ready way to virtue. [*Ib.* I. 54]

4 The multitude: that numerous piece of monstrosity, which, taken asunder, seem men, and the reasonable creatures of God; but, confused together, make but one great beast, and a monstrosity more hideous than Hydra. [*Ib.* II. 1]

5 It is the common wonder of all men, how among so many millions of faces, there should be none alike. [*Ib.* II. 2]

6 No man can justly censure or condemn another, because indeed no man truly knows another. [*Ib.* II. 4]

7 *Charity begins at home*, is the voice of the world. [*Ib.*]

8 The whole world was made for man; but the twelfth part of man for woman: man is the whole world, and the breath of God; woman the rib and crooked piece of man. I could be content that we might procreate like trees, without conjunction, or that there were any way to perpetuate the world without this trivial and vulgar way of union. [*Ib.* II. 9]

9 Sure there is music even in the beauty, and the silent note which Cupid strikes, far sweeter than the sound of an instrument. For there is music where ever there is a harmony, order, or proportion: and thus far we may maintain the music of the spheres. [*Ib.*]

10 We all labour against our own cure; for death is the cure of all diseases. [*Ib.*]

11 For the world, I count it not an inn, but an hospital; and a place not to live but to die in. [*Ib.* II. 11]

12 There is surely a piece of divinity in us, something that was before the elements, and owes no homage unto the sun. [*Ib.*]

13 Sleep is a death; O make me try, / By sleeping, what it is to die; / And as gently lay my head / On my grave, as now my bed. [*Ib.* II. 12]

14 Old mortality, the ruins of forgotten times. [*Urn Burial*, Preface]

15 What song the Syrens sang, or what name Achilles assumed when he hid himself among women, though puzzling questions, are not beyond all conjecture. [*Ib.* Ch. 5]

16 But the iniquity of oblivion blindly scattereth her poppy, and deals with the memory of men without distinction to merit of perpetuity. [*Ib.*]

17 The night of time far surpasseth the day, and who knows when was the equinox? [*Ib.*]

18 Man is a noble animal, splendid in ashes, and pompous in the grave. [*Ib.*]

WILLIAM BROWNE 1590?–1645?

19 Underneath this sable hearse / Lies the subject of all verse: / Sidney's sister, Pembroke's mother: / Death, ere thou hast slain another, / Fair, and learned, and good as she, / Time shall throw a dart at thee. [*Epitaph on the Dowager Countess of Pembroke*]

20 Steer hither, steer, your winged pines, / All beaten mariners, / Here lie love's undiscovered mines, / A prey to passengers. ['Song of the Sirens', from the *Inner Temple Masque*]

SIR WILLIAM BROWNE 1692–1774

21 The King to Oxford sent a troop of horse, / For Tories own no argument but force: / With equal skill to Cambridge books he sent, / For Whigs admit no force but argument. [Reply to epigram by Joseph Trapp, q.v.]

ELIZABETH BARRETT BROWNING 1806–1861

22 Since when was genius found respectable? [*Aurora Leigh*, Bk VI]

23 And kings crept out again to feel the sun. [*Crowned and Buried*]

24 Do you hear the children weeping, O my brothers, / Ere the sorrow comes with years? [*The Cry of the Children*]

25 In the pleasant orchard closes, / 'God

bless all our gains', say we; / But 'May God bless all our losses' / Better suits with our degree. [*The Lost Bower*]

1 What was he doing, the great god Pan, / Down in the reeds by the river? / Spreading ruin and scattering ban, / Splashing and paddling with hoofs of a goat, / And breaking the golden lilies afloat / With the dragon-fly on the river. [*A Musical Instrument*]

2 O earth, so full of dreary noises! / O men, with wailing in your voices! / O delvèd gold, the wailers heap! / O strife, O curse, that o'er it fall! / God strikes a silence through you all, / And giveth his beloved, sleep. [*The Sleep*]

3 I tell you, hopeless grief is passionless. [*Sonnet: Grief*]

4 'Guess now who holds thee?' – 'Death', I said, but there / The silver answer rang, ... 'Not Death, but Love.' [*Sonnets from the Portuguese*, vii]

5 If thou must love me, let it be for naught / Except for love's sake only. [*Ib*. xiv]

6 God's gifts put man's best gifts to shame. [*Ib*. xxvi]

7 How do I love thee? Let me count the ways. / I love thee to the depth and breadth and height / My soul can reach, when feeling out of sight / For the ends of Being and ideal Grace. [*Ib*. xliii]

8 I love thee with a love I seemed to lose / With my lost saints – I love thee with the breath, / Smiles, tears, of all my life! – and, if God choose, / I shall but love thee better after death. [*Ib*.]

9 Thou large-brained woman and large-hearted man. [*To George Sand, A Desire*]

10 Life treads on life, and heart on heart: / We press too close in church and mart / To keep a dream or grave apart. [*A Vision of Poets*, conclusion]

11 Our Euripides, the human, / With his droppings of warm tears, / And his touches of things common / Till they rose to touch the spheres. [*Wine of Cyprus*, xii]

ROBERT BROWNING 1812–1889

12 The high that proved too high, the heroic for earth too hard, / The passion that left the ground to lose itself in the sky, / Are music sent up to God by the lover and the bard; / Enough that he heard it once; we shall hear it by-and-by. [*Abt Vogler*, x]

13 The rest may reason and welcome; 'tis we musicians know. [*Ib*. xi]

14 Well, it is earth with me; silence resumes her reign: / I will be patient and proud, and soberly acquiesce. [*Ib*. xii]

15 I have dared and done, for my resting-place is found, / The C major of this life: so, now I will try to sleep. [*Ib*.]

16 How he lies in his rights of a man! / Death has done all death can. [*After*]

17 Love, we are in God's hand. / How strange now looks the life he makes us lead. / So free we seem, so fettered fast we are! [*Andrea del Sarto*, 49]

18 Ah, but a man's reach should exceed his grasp, / Or what's a heaven for? [*Ib*. 98]

19 Four great walls in the New Jerusalem, / Meted on each side by the angel's reed, / For Leonard, Rafael, Agnolo and me / To cover. [*Ib*. 263]

20 Again the Cousin's whistle! Go, my Love. [*Ib*. 269]

21 Why need the other women know so much? [*Any Wife to any Husband*]

22 It's wiser being good than bad; / It's safer being meek than fierce: / It's fitter being sane than mad. / My own hope is, a sun will pierce / The thickest cloud earth ever stretched; / That, after Last, returns the First, / Though a wide compass round be fetched; / That what began best can't end worst, / Nor what God blessed once, prove accurst. [*Apparent Failure*]

23 Hatred and cark and care, what place have they / In yon blue liberality of heaven? [*Aristophanes' Apology*, 52]

24 My sun sets to rise again. [*At the 'Mermaid'*]

25 Lo, life again knocked laughing at the door! / The world goes on, goes ever, in and through, / And out again o' the cloud. [*Balaustion's Adventure*, John Murray's edition, Vol. i. p. 650, l. 2]

26 So, you despise me, Mr Gigadibs. [*Bishop Blougram's Apology*, John Murray's edition, Vol. i. p. 528, l. 13]

27 Truth that peeps / Over the glasses' edge when dinner's done, / And body gets its

sop and holds its noise / And leaves soul
free a little. [*Bishop Blougram's Apology*,
i. 528. 16]

1 Best be yourself, imperial, plain and true!
[*Ib*. i. 529. 55]

2 We mortals cross the ocean of this world
/ Each in his average cabin of a life. [*Ib*.
i. 530. 8]

3 Just when we are safest, there's a sunset-
touch, / A fancy from a flower-bell,
someone's death, / A chorus-ending
from Euripides, – / And that's enough
for fifty hopes and fears / As old and new
at once as nature's self, / To rap and
knock and enter in our soul. [*Ib*. i. 531.
17]

4 The grand Perhaps! [*Ib*. i. 531. 25]

5 All we have gained then by our unbelief /
Is a life of doubt diversified by faith, /
For one of faith diversified by doubt: /
We called the chess-board white, – we
call it black. [*Ib*. i. 531. 45]

6 You, for example, clever to a fault, / The
rough and ready man that write apace, /
Read somewhat seldomer, think perhaps
even less. [*Ib*. i. 534. 25]

7 And that's what all the blessed evil's for.
[*Ib*. i. 537. 26]

8 No, when the fight begins within himself,
/ A man's worth something. [*Ib*. i. 537.
65]

9 Gigadibs the literary man, / Who played
with spoons, explored his plate's design, /
And ranged the olive stones about its
edge. [*lb*. i. 541. 40]

10 He said true things, but called them by
wrong names. [*Ib*. i. 541. 61]

11 By this time he has tested his first plough,
/ And studied his last chapter of St John.
[*Ib*. i. 542. 5]

12 Saint Praxed's ever was the church for
peace. [*The Bishop orders his Tomb*]

13 Saint Praxed in a glory, and one Pan /
Ready to twitch the Nymph's last gar-
ment off, / And Moses with the tables.
[*Ib*.]

14 Horses for ye, and brown Greek manu-
scripts, / And mistresses with great
smooth marbly limbs. [*Ib*.]

15 I shall lie through centuries, / And hear
the blessed mutter of the mass, / And see
God made and eaten all day long. [*Ib*.]

16 There's a woman like a dew-drop, she's
so purer than the purest. [*A Blot in the
'Scutcheon*, I. iii]

17 How well I know what I mean to do /
When the long, dark autumn-evenings
come. [*By the Fire-side*, i]

18 Not verse now, only prose! [*Ib*. ii]

19 That great brow / And the spirit-small
hand propping it. [*Ib*. xxiii]

20 When earth breaks up and heaven ex-
pands, / How will the change strike me
and you / In the house not made with
hands? [*Ib*. xxvii]

21 We two stood there with never a third.
[*Ib*. xxxviii]

22 Oh, the little more, and how much it is! /
And the little less, and what worlds
away! [*Ib*. xxxix]

23 If two lives join, there is oft a scar, / They
are one and one, with a shadowy third; /
One near one is too far. [*Ib*. xlvi]

24 Setebos, Setebos, and Setebos! / 'Thinketh, He dwelleth i' the cold o' the moon. /
'Thinketh He made it, with the sun to
match, / But not the stars; the stars came
otherwise. [*Caliban upon Setebos*, 24]

25 'Let twenty pass, and stone the twenty-
first, / Loving not, hating not, just choosing so. [*Ib*. 103]

26 This Quiet, all it hath a mind to do, doth.
[*Ib*. 138]

27 'Tis the Last Judgment's fire must cure
this place, / Calcine its clods and set my
prisoners free. ['*Childe Roland to the
Dark Tower Came*', xi]

28 As for the grass, it grew as scant as hair
/ In leprosy. [*Ib*. xiii]

29 One stiff blind horse, his every bone
a-stare, / Stood stupefied, however he
came there: / Thrust out past service
from the devil's stud! [*Ib*.]

30 I never saw a brute I hated so; / He must
be wicked to deserve such pain. [*Ib*. xiv]

31 The hills, like giants at a hunting, lay, /
Chin upon hand, to see the game at bay.
[*Ib*. xxxii]

32 Dauntless the slug-horn to my lips I set,
/ And blew. '*Childe Roland to the Dark
Tower Came*.' [*Ib*. xxxiv]

33 Though Rome's gross yoke / Drops off,
no more to be endured, / Her teaching is

not so obscured / By errors and perversities, / That no truth shines athwart the lies. [*Christmas Eve*, xi]

1 I watched my foolish heart expand / In the lazy glow of benevolence, / O'er the various modes of man's belief. [*Ib.* xx]

2 I have written three books on the soul, / Proving absurd all written hitherto, / And putting us to ignorance again. [*Cleon*, 57]

3 What survives myself? / The brazen statue to o'erlook my grave, / Set on the promontory which I named. [*Ib.* 175]

4 Certain slaves / Who touched on this same isle, preached him and Christ; / And (as I gather from a bystander) / Their doctrine could be held by no sane man. [*Ib.* 250]

5 It is a lie – their Priests, their Pope, / Their Saints. [*The Confessional*]

6 What is he buzzing in my ears? / 'Now that I come to die, / Do I view the world as a vale of tears?' / Ah, reverend sir, not I! [*Confessions*]

7 How sad and bad and mad it was – / But then, how it was sweet! [*Ib.*]

8 Ages past the soul existed, / Here an age 'tis resting merely. [*Cristina*]

9 Your ghost will walk, you lover of trees / (If our loves remain) / In an English lane, / By a cornfield-side a-flutter with poppies. ['*De Gustibus –*']

10 And let them pass, as they will too soon, / With the bean-flowers' boon, / And the blackbird's tune, / And May, and June! [*Ib.*]

11 Open my heart and you will see / Graved inside of it, 'Italy'. [*Ib.*]

12 Such 'ever was love's way; to rise, it stoops. [*A Death in the Desert*, 134]

13 For life, with all its yields of joy and woe, / And hope and fear, – believe the aged friend – / Is just a chance o' the prize of learning love. [*Ib.* 245]

14 For I say, this is death, and the sole death, / When a man's loss comes to him from his gain, / Darkness from light, from knowledge ignorance, / And lack of love from love made manifest. [*Ib.* 482]

15 Man partly is and wholly hopes to be. [*Ib.* 588]

16 Reads verse and thinks she understands. [*Dis aliter visum*, iv]

17 Schumann's our music-maker now; / Has his march-movement youth and mouth? / Ingres's the modern man that paints; / Which will lean on me, of his saints? / Heine for songs; for kisses, how? [*Ib.* viii]

18 How very hard it is / To be a Christian! [*Easter-Day*, i]

19 At last awake / From life, that insane dream we take / For waking now. [*Ib.* xiv]

20 A fierce vindictive scribble of red. [*Ib.* xv]

21 At the midnight in the silence of the sleep-time, / When you set your fancies free. [*Epilogue to Asolando*]

22 Oh to love so, be so loved, yet so mistaken! [*Ib.*]

23 One who never turned his back but marched breast forward, / Never doubted clouds would break, / Never dreamed, though right were worsted, wrong would triumph, / Held we fall to rise, are baffled to fight better, / Sleep to wake. [*Ib.*]

24 No, at noonday in the bustle of man's worktime / Greet the unseen with a cheer! [*Ib.*]

25 Karshish, the picker-up of learning's crumbs, / The not-incurious in God's handiwork. [*An Epistle . . . of Karshish, the Arab Physician*, 1]

26 – That he was dead and then restored to life / By a Nazarene physician of his tribe. [*Ib.* 98]

27 'But love I gave thee, with myself to love. / And thou must love me who have died for thee!' / The madman saith He said so: it is strange. [*Ib.* last lines]

28 There, that is our secret: go to sleep! / You will wake, and remember, and understand. [*Evelyn Hope*]

29 I am poor brother Lippo, by your leave! [*Fra Lippo Lippi*, 1]

30 Where sportive ladies leave their doors ajar. [*Ib.* 6]

31 He's Judas to a tittle, that man is! / Just such a face! [*Ib.* 25]

32 Flower o' the broom, / Take away love, and our earth is a tomb! [*Ib.* 53]

33 All the Latin I construe is, 'amo' I love! [*Ib.* 111]

1 If you get simple beauty and nought else, / You get about the best thing God invents. [*Fra Lippo Lippi*, 217]

2 You should not take a fellow eight years old / And make him swear to never kiss the girls. [*Ib.* 224]

3 I always see the garden and God there / A-making man's wife. [*Ib.* 265]

4 This is our master, famous calm and dead, / Borne on our shoulders. [*A Grammarian's Funeral*, 27]

5 He said, 'What's time? Leave Now for dogs and apes! / Man has Forever.' [*Ib.* 83]

6 *Calculus* racked him: / Leaden before, his eyes grew dross of lead: / *Tussis* attacked him. [*Ib.* 86]

7 He settled *Hoti's* business – let it be! – / Properly based *Oun* – / Gave us the doctrine of the enclitic *De*, / Dead from the waist down. [*Ib.* 129]

8 Here – here's his place, where meteors shoot, clouds form, / Lightnings are loosened, / Stars come and go. [*Ib.* 141]

9 Give both the infinitudes their due – / Infinite mercy, but, I wis, / As infinite a justice too. [*The Heretic's Tragedy*]

10 I liken his Grace to an acorned hog. [*Holy-Cross Day*]

11 The Lord will have mercy on Jacob yet, / And again in his border see Israel set. [*Ib.*]

12 Oh, to be in England, / Now that April's there. [*Home Thoughts from Abroad*]

13 While the chaffinch sings on the orchard bough / In England – now! [*Ib.*]

14 And after April, when May follows, / And the whitethroat builds, and all the swallows! [*Ib.*]

15 That's the wise thrush; he sings each song twice over, / Lest you should think he never could recapture / The first fine careless rapture! [*Ib.*]

16 Nobly, nobly Cape Saint Vincent to the North-west died away; / Sunset ran, one glorious blood-red, reeking into Cadiz bay. [*Home Thoughts from the Sea*]

17 'Here and here did England help me: how can I help England?' – say, / Whoso turns as I, this evening, turn to God to praise and pray, / While Jove's planet rises yonder, silent over Africa. [*Ib.*]

18 '*With this same key / Shakespeare unlocked his heart*', once more! / Did Shakespeare? If so, the less Shakespeare he! [*House*]

19 I sprang to the stirrup, and Joris, and he; / I galloped, Dirck galloped, we galloped all three. ['*How they brought the Good News from Ghent to Aix*']

20 At Aershot, up leaped of a sudden the sun. [*Ib.*]

21 I count life just a stuff / To try the soul's strength on. [*In a Balcony*, 651]

22 The moth's kiss, first! / Kiss me as if you made believe / You were not sure, this eve, / How my face, your flower, had pursed / Its petals up. [*In a Gondola*]

23 The bee's kiss, now! / Kiss me as if you entered gay / My heart at some noonday. [*Ib.*]

24 Still ailing, Wind? Wilt be appeased or no? [*James Lee's Wife*, VI]

25 Oh, good gigantic smile o' the brown old earth. [*Ib.* VII]

26 There's heaven above, and night by night / I look right through its gorgeous roof. [*Johannes Agricola in Meditation*]

27 So, one day more I am deified. / Who knows but the world may end tonight? [*The Last Ride Together*, ii]

28 Where had I been now if the worst befell? / And here we are riding, she and I. [*Ib.* iv]

29 And you, great sculptor – so, you gave / A score of years to Art, her slave, / And that's your Venus, whence we turn / To yonder girl that fords the burn! [*Ib.* viii]

30 What if we still ride on, we two / With life forever old yet new, / Changed not in kind but in degree, / The instant made eternity – / And heaven just prove that I and she / Ride, ride together, for ever ride? [*Ib.* x]

31 Escape me? / Never – / Beloved! / While I am I, and you are you, / So long as the world contains us both, / Me the loving and you the loth, / While the one eludes, must the other pursue. [*Life in a Love*]

32 To dry one's eyes and laugh at a fall, / And, baffled, get up and begin again. [*Ib.*]

33 And, Robert Browning, you writer of plays, / Here's a subject made to your hand! [*A Light Woman*, xiv]

1 Just for a handful of silver he left us, / Just for a riband to stick in his coat. [*The Lost Leader*]

2 Shakespeare was with us, Milton was for us / Burns, Shelley, were with us, – they watch from their graves. [*Ib.*]

3 Blot out his name, then, record one lost soul more, / One task more declined, one more footpath untrod, / One more devils'-triumph and sorrow for angels, / One wrong more to man, one more insult to God! [*Ib.*]

4 Then let him receive the new knowledge and wait us, / Pardoned in heaven, the first by the throne! [*Ib.*]

5 All's over, then; does truth sound bitter / As one at first believes? / Hark, 'tis the sparrows' good-night twitter / About your cottage eaves! [*The Lost Mistress*]

6 Mere friends are we, – well, friends the merest / Keep much that I resign. [*Ib.*]

7 I will hold your hand but as long as all may, / Or so very little longer! [*Ib.*]

8 Where the quiet-coloured end of evening smiles, / Miles and miles. [*Love among the Ruins*, i]

9 Love is best. [*Ib.* vii]

10 The only fault's with time; / All men become good creatures: but so slow! [*Luria*, V]

11 Backward and forward each throwing his shuttle, / Death ending all with a knife. [*Master Hugues of Saxe-Gotha*, xxii]

12 What, you want, do you, to come unawares, / Sweeping the church up for first morning-prayers, / And find a poor devil has ended his cares / At the foot of your rotten-runged rat-riddled stairs? / Do I carry the moon in my pocket? [*Ib.* xxix]

13 A tap at the pane, the quick sharp scratch / And blue spurt of a lighted match, / And a voice less loud, thro' its joys and fears, / Than the two hearts beating each to each. [*Meeting at Night*]

14 Ah, did you once see Shelley plain, / And did he stop and speak to you / And did he speak to you again? / How strange it seems and new! [*Memorabilia*]

15 A moulted feather, an eagle-feather! / Well, I forget the rest. [*Ib.*]

16 This is a spray the Bird clung to. [*Misconceptions*]

17 This is a heart the Queen leant on. [*Misconceptions*]

18 If such as came for wool, sir, went home shorn, / Where is the wrong I did them? [*Mr Sludge, 'The Medium'*, 630]

19 There's a real love of a lie, / Liars find ready-made for lies they make, / As hand for glove, or tongue for sugar-plum. [*Ib.* 689]

20 There's a more hateful form of foolery – / The social sage's, Solomon of saloons / And philosophic diner-out, the fribble / Who wants a doctrine for a chopping-block / To try the edge of his faculty upon. [*Ib.* 772]

21 My care is for myself; / Myself am whole and sole reality. [*Ib.* 908]

22 Why should I set so fine a gloss on things? [*Ib.* 1354]

23 Boston's a hole, the herring-pond is wide. [*Ib.* two lines from end]

24 She had / A heart – how shall I say? – too soon made glad, / Too easily impressed. [*My Last Duchess*]

25 Give me of Nelson only a touch. [*Nationality in Drinks*]

26 Never the time and the place / And the loved one all together! [*Never the Time and the Place*]

27 What's come to perfection perishes. / Things learned on earth, we shall practise in heaven. / Works done least rapidly, Art most cherishes. [*Old Pictures in Florence*, xvii]

28 There remaineth a rest for the people of God: / And I have had troubles enough, for one. [*Ib.*]

29 Suddenly, as rare things will, it vanished. [*One Word More*, iv]

30 Dante, who loved well because he hated, / Hated wickedness that hinders loving. [*Ib.* v]

31 God be thanked, the meanest of his creatures / Boasts two soul-sides, one to face the world with, / One to show a woman when he loves her! [*Ib.* xvii]

32 Oh, their Rafael of the dead Madonnas, / Oh, their Dante of the dread Inferno, / Wrote one song – and in my brain I sing it, / Drew one angel – borne, see, on my bosom! [*Ib.* xix]

33 Unless God send his hail / Or blinding fire balls, sleet or stifling snow, / In some

time, his good time, I shall arrive. [*Paracelsus*, Pt I]

1 PARACELSUS: I am he that aspired to *know*: and thou? APRILE: I would *love* infinitely, and be loved! [*Ib.* II]

2 God is the perfect poet, / Who in his person acts his own creations. [*Ib.*]

3 Heap cassia, sandal-buds and stripes / Of labdanum, and aloe-balls, / Smeared with dull nard an Indian wipes / From out her hair. [*Ib.* IV]

4 Progress is / The law of life, man is not man as yet. [*Ib.* V]

5 Round the cape of a sudden came the sea, / And the sun looked over the mountain's rim: / And straight was a path of gold for him, / And the need of a world of men for me. [*Parting at Morning*]

6 It was roses, roses, all the way, / With myrtle mixed in my path like mad. [*The Patriot*]

7 Alack, it was I who leaped at the sun / To give it my loving friends to keep! / Nought man could do, have I left undone: / And you see my harvest, what I reap / This very day, now a year is run. [*Ib.*]

8 Sun-treader, I believe in God and truth / And love. [(Shelley) *Pauline*]

9 Hamelin Town's in Brunswick, / By famous Hanover city; / The river Weser, deep and wide, / Washes its wall on the southern side; / A pleasanter spot you never spied. [*The Pied Piper of Hamelin*, i]

10 Rats! / They fought the dogs and killed the cats, / And bit the babies in the cradles, / And ate the cheeses out of the vats. [*Ib.* ii]

11 With shrieking and squeaking / In fifty different sharps and flats. [*Ib.*]

12 Save when at noon his paunch grew mutinous / For a plate of turtle green and glutinous. [*Ib.* iv]

13 And the muttering grew to a grumbling; / And the grumbling grew to a mighty rumbling; / And out of the houses the rats came tumbling. [*Ib.* vii]

14 I heard a sound as of scraping tripe, / And putting apples wondrous ripe, / Into a cider-press's gripe. [*Ib.*]

15 So munch on, crunch on, take your nuncheon, / Breakfast, supper, dinner, luncheon! [*The Pied Piper of Hamelin*, vii]

16 The year's at the spring / And day's at the morn; / Morning's at seven; / The hillside's dew-pearled; / The lark's on the wing; / The snail's on the thorn: / God's in his heaven – / All's right with the world! [*Pippa Passes*, Pt I]

17 God must be glad one loves His world so much. [*Ib.* III]

18 A king lived long ago, / In the morning of the world, / When earth was nigher heaven than now. [*Ib.*]

19 Such grace had kings when the world begun! [*Ib.*]

20 All service ranks the same with God – / With God, whose puppets, best and worst, / Are we: there is no last or first. [*Ib.*]

21 Stand still, true poet that you are! / I know you; let me try and draw you. / Some night you'll fail us: when afar / You rise, remember one man saw you, / Knew you and named a star! [*Popularity*]

22 Who fished the murex up? / What porridge had John Keats? [*Ib.*]

23 The rain set early in to-night, / The sullen wind was soon awake. / It tore the elm-tops down for spite, / And did its worst to vex the lake. [*Porphyria's Lover*]

24 No pain felt she; / I am quite sure she felt no pain. [*Ib.*]

25 And thus we sit together now, / And all night long we have not stirred, / And yet God has not said a word! [*Ib.*]

26 Fear death? – to feel the fog in my throat, / The mist in my face. [*Prospice*]

27 Where he stands, the Arch Fear in a visible form, / Yet the strong man must go. [*Ib.*]

28 I was ever a fighter, so – one fight more, / The best and the last! [*Ib.*]

29 No! let me taste the whole of it, fare like my peers / The heroes of old, / Bear the brunt, in a minute pay glad life's arrears / Of pain, darkness and cold. [*Ib.*]

30 O thou soul of my soul! I shall clasp thee again, / And with God be the rest! [*Ib.*]

31 Grow old along with me! / The best is yet to be, / The last of life, for which the first was made: / Our times are in His

hand / Who saith, 'A whole I planned, / Youth shows but half; trust God: see all noı be afraid!' [*Rabbi ben Ezra*, i]

1 Irks care the crop-full bird? Frets doubt the maw-crammed beast? [*Ib.* iv]

2 Then, welcome each rebuff / That turns earth's smoothness rough, / Each sting that bids nor sit nor stand but go! [*Ib.* vi]

3 For thence – a paradox / Which comforts while it mocks, – / Shall life succeed in that it seems to fail: / What I aspired to be, / And was not, comforts me: / A brute I might have been, but would not sink i' the scale. [*Ib.* vii]

4 I see the whole design, / I, who saw power, see now love perfect too. [*Ib.* x]

5 Let us not always say / 'Spite of this flesh today / I strove, made head, gained ground upon the whole!' / As the bird wings and sings, / Let us cry 'All good things / Are ours, nor soul helps flesh more, now, than flesh helps soul.' [*Ib.* xii]

6 Therefore I summon age / To grant youth's heritage. [*Ib.* xiii]

7 Leave the fiıe ashes, what survives is gold. [*Ib.* xv]

8 For note, when evening shuts, / A certain moment cuts / The deed off, calls the glory from the grey. [*Ib.* xvi]

9 Now, who shall arbitrate? / Ten men love what I hate, / Shun what I follow, slight what I receive; / Ten who in ears and eyes / Match me: we all surmise, / They this thing, and I that: whom shall my soul believe? [*Ib.* xxii]

10 But all, the world's coarse thumb / And finger failed to plumb, / So passed in making up the main account. [*Ib.* xxiv]

11 Thoughts hardly to be packed / Into a narrow act, / Fancies that broke through language and escaped. [*Ib.* xxv]

12 Let age approve of youth, and death complete the same. [*Ib.* xxxii]

13 Do you see this square old yellow Book, I toss / I' the air, and catch again. [*Ring and the Book*, I. 33]

14 The Life, Death, Miracles of Saint Somebody, / Saint Somebody Else, his Miracles, Death and Life, – / With this, one glance at the lettered back of which, / And 'Stall!' cried I: a *lira* made it mine. [*Ib.* I. 80]

15 Well, British Public, ye who like me not, / (God love you!) and will have your proper laugh / At the dark question, laugh it! I laugh first. [*Ring and the Book*, I. 410]

16 Whom but a dusk misfeatured messenger, / No other than the angel of this life, / Whose care is lest men see too much at once. [*Ib.* I. 593]

17 Our murder has been done three days ago, / The frost is over and done, the south wind laughs, / And, to the very tiles of each red roof / A-smoke i' the sunshine, Rome lies gold and glad. [*Ib.* I. 904]

18 Vows can't change nature, priests are only men, / And love likes stratagem and subterfuge. [*Ib.* I. 1057]

19 O lyric Love, half angel and half bird / And all a wonder and a wild desire. [*Ib.* I. 1391]

20 Never may I commence my song, my due / To God who best taught song by gift of thee, / Except with bent head and beseeching hand – / That still, despite the distance and the dark, / What was, again may be. [*Ib.* I. 1403]

21 A personage came by the private door / At noon to have his look: I name no names. [*Ib.* II. 152]

22 Everyone soon or late comes round by Rome. [*Ib.* V. 296]

23 Creation purged o' the miscreate, man redeemed, / A spittle wiped off from the face of God! [*Ib.* VI. 1478]

24 But I, not privileged to see a saint / Of old when such walked earth with crown and palm, / If I call 'saint' what saints call something else – / The saints must bear with me. [*Ib.* VII. 1512]

25 O lover of my life, O soldier-saint. [*Ib.* VII. 1786]

26 Through such souls alone / God stooping shows sufficient of His light / For us i' the dark to rise by. And I rise. [*Ib.* VII. 1843]

27 On our Pompilia, faultless to a fault. [*Ib.* IX. 1177]

28 Just the one prize vouchsafed unworthy me, / Seven years a gardener of the untoward ground. [*Ib.* X. 1030]

29 Thou at first prompting of what I call God, / And fools call Nature, didst hear,

comprehend, / Accept the obligation laid on thee. [*Ring and the Book*, X. 1073]

1 Why comes temptation but for man to meet / And master and make crouch beneath his foot, / And so be pedestaled in triumph? [*Ib.* X. 1185]

2 White shall not neutralize the black, nor good / Compensate bad in man, absolve him so: / Life's business being just the terrible choice. [*Ib.* X. 1236]

3 There's a new tribunal now, / Higher than God's – the educated man's! [*Ib.* X. 1976]

4 Abate, – Cardinal, – Christ, – Maria, – God, ... / Pompilia, will you let them murder me? [*Ib.* XI. 2424]

5 It is the glory and the good of Art, / That Art remains the one way possible / Of speaking truth, to minds like mine at least. [*Ib.* XII. 842]

6 Oh, the wild joys of living! the leaping from rock up to rock, / The strong rending of boughs from the fir-tree, the cool silver shock / Of the plunge in a pool's living water. [*Saul*, ix]

7 How good is man's life, the mere living! how fit to employ / All the heart and the soul and the senses for ever in joy! [*Ib.*]

8 Leave the flesh to the fate it was fit for! the spirit be thine! [*Ib.* xiii]

9 I have gone the whole round of creation: I saw and I spoke: / I, a work of God's hand for that purpose, received in my brain / And pronounced on the rest of his handwork – returned him again / His creation's approval or censure: I spoke as I saw: / I report, as a man may of God's work – all's love, yet all's law. [*Ib.* xvii]

10 In the first is the last, in thy will is my power to believe. [*Ib.* xviii]

11 He who did most, shall bear most; the strongest shall stand the most weak. [*Ib.*]

12 The iron gate / Ground its teeth to let me pass! [*A Serenade at the Villa*]

13 Because a man has shop to mind / In time and place, since flesh must live, / Needs spirit lack all life behind, / All stray thoughts, fancies fugitive, / All loves except what trade can give?

I want to know a butcher paints, / A baker rhymes for his pursuit, / Candlestick-maker much acquaints / His soul

with song, or, haply mute, / Blows out his brains upon the flute! [*Shop*, xx]

14 Gr-r-r – there go, my heart's abhorrence! / Water your damned flower-pots, do! / If hate killed men, Brother Lawrence, / God's blood, would not mine kill you! [*Soliloquy of the Spanish Cloister*]

15 What's the Greek name for Swine's Snout? [*Ib.*]

16 There's a great text in Galatians, / Once you trip on it, entails / Twenty-nine distinct damnations, / One sure if another fails. [*Ib.*]

17 Or, my scrofulous French novel / On grey paper with blunt type! / Simply glance at it, you grovel / Hand and foot in Belial's gripe. [*Ib.*]

18 'St, there's Vespers! *Plena gratiâ / Ave, Virgo!* Gr-r-r – you swine! [*Ib.*]

19 Nay but you, who do not love her, / Is she not pure gold, my mistress? [*Song*]

20 Who will, may hear Sordello's story told. [*Sordello*, i]

21 Sidney's self, the starry paladin. [*Ib.*]

22 Still more labyrinthine buds the rose. [*Ib.*]

23 A touch divine – / And the scaled eyeball owns the mystic rod; / Visibly through his garden walketh God. [*Ib.*]

24 Who would has heard Sordello's story told. [*Ib.* vi]

25 I have known *Four*-and-twenty leaders of revolts. [*A Soul's Tragedy*, last words]

26 She looked at him, as one who awakes: / The past was a sleep, and her life began. [*The Statue and the Bust*, 10]

27 The world and its way have a certain worth. [*Ib.* 46]

28 The glory dropped from their youth and love, / And both perceived they had dreamed a dream. [*Ib.* 51]

29 And the sin I impute to each frustrate ghost / Is – the unlit lamp and the ungirt loin. [*Ib.* 82]

30 There may be heaven; there must be hell; / Meantime, there is our earth here – well! [*Time's Revenges*]

31 What of soul was left, I wonder, when the kissing had to stop? [*A Toccata of Galuppi's*, xiv]

32 Dear dead women, with such hair, too – what's become of all the gold / Used to

hang and brush their bosoms? I feel chilly and grow old. [*A Toccata of Galuppi's*, xv]

1 Another Boehme with a tougher book / And subtler meanings of what roses say. ['*Transcendentalism*']

2 Where is the thread now? Off again! / The old trick! only I discern – / Infinite passion, and the pain / Of finite hearts that yearn. [*Two in the Campagna*, xii]

3 Had I but plenty of money, money enough and to spare, / The house for me, no doubt, were a house in the city-square. [*Up at a Villa – Down in the City*, i]

4 *Bang-whang-whang* goes the drum, *tootle-te-tootle* the fife; / No keeping one's haunches still: it's the greatest pleasure in life. [*Ib.*]

5 What's become of Waring / Since he gave us all the slip? [*Waring*, I. i]

6 Oh, never star / Was lost here but it rose afar! / Look East, where whole new thousands are! / In Vishnu-land what Avatar? [*Ib.* II. iii]

7 Let's contend no more, Love, / Strive nor weep: / All be as before, Love, / – Only sleep! [*A Woman's Last Word*]

8 Where the apple reddens / Never pry – / Lest we lose our Edens, / Eve and I. [*Ib.*]

9 I knew you once: but in Paradise, / If we meet, I will pass nor turn my face. [*The Worst of It*, xix]

10 For spring bade the sparrows pair, / And the boys and girls gave guesses, / And stalls in our street looked rare / With bulrush and watercresses. [*Youth and Art*, ix]

11 And nobody calls you a dunce, / And people suppose me clever: / This could but have happened once, / And we missed it, lost it for ever. [*Ib.* xvii]

MICHAEL BRUCE   1746–1767

12 Thou hast no sorrow in thy song, / No winter in thy year! [*To the Cuckoo*. Also attr. to John Logan]

'BEAU' BRUMMELL   1778–1840

13 Who's your fat friend? [Of George, Prince of Wales. Quoted in Gronow, *Reminiscences*]

W. J. BRYAN   1860–1925

14 You shall not press down upon the brow of labour this crown of thorns, you shall not crucify mankind upon a cross of gold. [Speech at the National Democratic Convention, 1896]

R. W. BUCHANAN   1841–1901

15 The Fleshly School of Poetry. [Title of article in the *Contemporary Review*, Oct. 1871]

16 She just wore / Enough for modesty – no more. [*White Rose and Red*, I. v. 60]

GEORGE VILLIERS, SECOND DUKE OF BUCKINGHAM
1628–1687

17 The world is made up for the most part of fools and knaves. [To Mr Clifford, on his *Humane Reason*]

18 What the devil does the plot signify, except to bring in fine things? [*The Rehearsal*, III. i]

19 Ay, now the plot thickens very much upon us. [*Ib.* III. ii]

JOHN SHEFFIELD, FIRST DUKE OF BUCKINGHAM AND NORMANBY   1648–1721

20 Read Homer once, and you can read no more, / For all books else appear so mean, so poor, / Verse will seem prose; but still persist to read, / And Homer will be all the books you need. [*An Essay on Poetry*]

21 A faultless monster which the world ne'er saw. [*Ib.*]

H. J. BUCKOLL   1803–1871

22 Lord, dismiss us with Thy blessing, / Thanks for mercies past received. [Hymn]

J. B. BUCKSTONE   1802–1879

23 On such an occasion as this, / All time and nonsense scorning, / Nothing shall come amiss, / And we won't go home till morning. [*Billy Taylor*, I. ii]

BUDDHA   5 Cent. B.C.

1 This Ariyan Eightfold Path, that is to say: Right view, right aim, right speech, right action, right living, right effort, right mindfulness, right contemplation. [F. L. Woodward, *Some Sayings of the Buddha*, p. 8]

2 Ye must leave righteous ways behind, not to speak of unrighteous ways. [*Ib.* 317]

3 All things, oh priests, are on fire. . . . The eye is on fire; forms are on fire; eye-consciousness is on fire; impressions received by the eye are on fire. [*The Fire Sermon*]

GEORGE-LOUIS DE BUFFON
1707–1788

4 *Le style est l'homme même.* – Style is the man himself. [*Discours sur le style*]

5 *Le génie n'est qu'une grande aptitude à la patience.* – Genius is nothing but a great aptitude for patience. [Attr.]

ARTHUR BULLER   1874–1944

6 There was a young lady named Bright, / Whose speed was far faster than light; / She set out one day / In a relative way, / And returned home the previous night. [Limerick in *Punch*, 19 Dec. 1923]

ALFRED BUNN   1796?–1860

7 Alice, where art thou? [Title of song]

8 I dreamt that I dwelt in marble halls, / With vassals and serfs at my side. [*The Bohemian Girl*, II]

JOHN BUNYAN   1628–1688

9 Some said, 'John, print it'; others said, 'Not so.' / Some said, 'It might do good'; others said, 'No'. [*Pilgrim's Progress*, Apology for his Book]

10 As I walked through the wilderness of this world. [*Ib.* Pt I]

11 Do you see yonder wicket-gate? [*Ib.*]

12 The name of the slough was Despond. [*Ib.*]

13 The gentleman's name was Mr Worldly-Wise-Man. [*Ib.*]

14 I come from the city of Destruction. [*Pilgrim's Progress*, I]

15 Set down my name, Sir. [*Ib.*]

16 A very stately palace before him, the name of which was Beautiful. [*Ib.*]

17 The valley of Humiliation. [*Ib.*]

18 Then Apollyon straddled quite over the whole breadth of the way. [*Ib.*]

19 It beareth the name of Vanity Fair, because the town where 'tis kept is lighter than vanity. [*Ib.*]

20 So soon as the man overtook me, he was but a word and a blow. [*Ib.*]

21 Hanging is too good for him. [*Ib.*]

22 My great grandfather was but a waterman, looking one way, and rowing another. [(Mr By-Ends) *Ib.*]

23 They are for religion when in rags and contempt, but I am for him when he walks in his golden slippers in the sunshine, and with applause. [(Mr By-Ends) *Ib.*]

24 A castle, called Doubting Castle, the owner whereof was Giant Despair. [*Ib.*]

25 They came to the Delectable Mountains. [*Ib.*]

26 Then I saw that there was a way to hell, even from the gates of heaven. [*Ib.*]

27 So I awoke, and behold it was a dream. [*Ib.*]

28 One Great-heart. [*Ib.* II]

29 He that is down needs fear no fall, / He that is low no pride. [*Ib.* Shepherd Boy's Song]

30 Come wind, come weather. [*Ib.*]

31 He who would valiant be / 'Gainst all disaster / Let him in constancy / Follow the Master. / There's no discouragement / Shall make him once relent, / His first avowed intent / To be a pilgrim. [*Ib.* (*English Hymnal* version)]

32 Who so beset him round / With dismal stories, / Do but themselves confound; / His strength the more is. [*Ib.*]

33 Then fancies flee away! / I'll fear not what men say. / I'll labour night and day / To be a pilgrim. [*Ib.*]

34 Mr Standfast. [*Ib.*]

35 So he passed over, and all the trumpets sounded for him on the other side. [*Ib.*]

GOTTFRIED AUGUST BURGER
1708–1775

1 *O Mutter, Mutter! Hin ist hin! / Verloren ist verloren!* – Oh mother, mother! Gone is gone! Lost is lost! [*Lenore*]

F. G. BURGESS
1866–1951

2 I never saw a Purple Cow, / I never hope to see one; / But I can tell you, anyhow, / I'd rather see than be one! [*Burgess Nonsense Book*, 'The Purple Cow']

3 Ah, yes! I wrote the 'Purple Cow' – / I'm sorry, now, I wrote it! / But I can tell you anyhow, / I'll kill you if you quote it! [*Ib. 'Cinq Ans après'*]

J. W. BURGON
1813–1888

4 Match me such marvel save in Eastern clime, / A rose-red city – 'half as old as time'! [*Petra*, 132]

JOHN BURGOYNE
1722–1792

5 You have only, when before your glass, to keep pronouncing to yourself nimini-pimini – the lips cannot fail of taking their plie. [*The Heiress*, III. ii]

EDMUND BURKE
1729–1797

6 I have in general no very exalted opinion of the virtue of paper government. [Speech on conciliation with America, 22 Mar. 1775]

7 The concessions of the weak are the concessions of fear. [*Ib.*]

8 Through a wise and salutary neglect, a generous nature has been suffered to take her own way to perfection. [*Ib.*]

9 The use of force alone is but *temporary*. It may subdue for a moment; but it does not remove the necessity of subduing again: and a nation is not governed, which is perpetually to be conquered. [*Ib.*]

10 Abstract liberty, like other mere abstractions, is not to be found. [*Ib.*]

11 The mysterious virtue of wax and parchment. [*Ib.*]

12 I do not know the method of drawing up an indictment against a whole people. [*Ib.*]

13 The march of the human mind is slow. [Speech on conciliation with America, 22 Mar. 1775]

14 All government, indeed every human benefit and enjoyment, every virtue, and every prudent act, is founded on compromise and barter. [*Ib.*]

15 Slavery they can have anywhere. It is a weed that grows in every soil. [*Ib.*]

16 Magnanimity in politics is not seldom the truest wisdom; and a great empire and little minds go ill together. [*Ib.*]

17 Your representative owes you, not his industry only, but his judgement; and he betrays instead of serving you if he sacrifices it to your opinion. [Speech to the electors of Bristol, 3 Nov. 1774]

18 A rapacious and licentious soldiery. [Speech on Fox's East India Bill, 1 Dec. 1783]

19 What the greatest inquest of the nation has begun, its highest Tribunal [the House of Commons] will accomplish. [Impeachment of Warren Hastings, 15 Feb. 1788]

20 Religious persecution may shield itself under the guise of a mistaken and over-zealous piety. [*Ib.* 17 Feb. 1788]

21 A thing may look specious in theory, and yet be ruinous in practice; a thing may look evil in theory, and yet be in practice excellent. [*Ib.* 19 Feb. 1788]

22 An event has happened, upon which it is difficult to speak, and impossible to be silent. [*Ib.* 5 May 1789]

23 There is but one law for all, namely, that law which governs all law, the law of our Creator, the law of humanity, justice, equity – the law of nature, and of nations. [*Ib.* 28 May 1794]

24 The greater the power, the more dangerous the abuse. [Speech on the Middlesex Election, 1771]

25 Dangers by being despised grow great. [Speech on the Petition of the Unitarians, 1792]

26 There is, however, a limit at which forbearance ceases to be a virtue. [*Observations on 'The Present State of the Nation'*]

27 It is a general popular error to imagine the loudest complainers for the public to be the most anxious for its welfare. [*Ib.*]

1 I am convinced that we have a degree of delight, and that no small one, in the real misfortunes and pains of others. [*On the Sublime and Beautiful*, I. xiv]

2 No passion so effectually robs the mind of all its powers of acting and reasoning as fear. [*Ib.* II. ii]

3 Beauty in distress is much the most affecting beauty. [*Ib.* III. ix]

4 Custom reconciles us to everything. [*Ib.* IV. xviii]

5 Whenever our neighbour's house is on fire, it cannot be amiss for the engines to play a little on our own. [*Reflections on the Revolution in France*]

6 A state without the means of some change is without the means of its conservation. [*Ib.*]

7 Government is a contrivance of human wisdom to provide for human *wants*. Men have a right that these wants should be provided for by this wisdom. [*Ib.*]

8 But the age of chivalry is gone. That of sophisters, economists, and calculators, has succeeded; and the glory of Europe is extinguished for ever. [*Ib.*]

9 That chastity of honour, that felt a stain like a wound. [*Ib.*]

10 Vice itself lost half its evil, by losing all its grossness. [*Ib.*]

11 Kings will be tyrants from policy, when subjects are rebels from principle. [*Ib.*]

12 Because half a dozen grasshoppers under a fern make the field ring with their importunate chink ... do not imagine that those who make the noise are the only inhabitants of the field. [*Ib.*]

13 The little, meagre, shrivelled, hopping, though loud and troublesome *insects* of the hour. [*Ib.*]

14 Man is by his constitution a religious animal. [*Ib.*]

15 A perfect democracy is therefore the most shameless thing in the world. [*Ib.*]

16 The men of England, the men, I mean, of light and leading in England. [*Ib.*]

17 Superstition is the religion of feeble minds. [*Ib.*]

18 He that wrestles with us strengthens our nerves, and sharpens our skill. Our antagonist is our helper. [*Ib.*]

19 Our patience will achieve more than our force. [*Reflections on the Revolution in France*]

20 Good order is the foundation of all things. [*Ib.*]

21 Having first looked to government for bread, on the very first scarcity they will turn and bite the hand that fed them. [*Thoughts and Details on Scarcity*]

22 The wisdom of our ancestors. [*Thoughts on the Cause of the Present Discontents*]

23 When bad men combine, the good must associate; else they will fall, one by one, an unpitied sacrifice in a contemptible struggle. [*Ib.*]

24 'Not men but measures': a sort of charm by which many people get loose from every honourable engagement. [*Ib.*]

25 So to be patriots as not to forget that we are gentlemen. [*Ib.*]

26 The only infallible criterion of wisdom to vulgar minds – success. [*Letter to a Member of the National Assembly*]

27 You can never plan the future by the past. [*Ib.*]

28 To innovate is not to reform. [*A Letter to a Noble Lord*, 1796]

29 These gentle historians, on the contrary, dip their pens in nothing but the milk of human kindness. [*Ib.*]

30 I know that many have been taught to think that moderation, in a case like this, is a sort of treason. [*Letter to the Sheriffs of Bristol*]

31 If any ask me what a free government is, I answer, that for any practical purpose, it is what the people think so. [*Ib.*]

32 Liberty, too, must be limited in order to be possessed. [*Ib.*]

33 Nothing is so fatal to religion as indifference, which is, at least, half infidelity. [Letter to Wm Smith, 29 Jan. 1795]

34 Somebody has said, that a king may make a nobleman, but he cannot make a gentleman. [*Ib.*]

35 If we command our wealth, we shall be rich and free; if our wealth commands us, we are poor indeed. [*Letters on a Regicide Peace*, 1]

36 Example is the school of mankind, and they will learn at no other. [*Ib.*]

1 Not merely a chip of the old 'block', but the old block itself. [On Pitt's first speech, 1781]

WILLIAM CECIL, LORD BURLEIGH   1520–1598

2 What! all this for a song? [To Queen Elizabeth when ordered to pay Spenser £100. Birch, *Life of Spenser*]

BISHOP GILBERT BURNET
1643–1715

3 There was a sure way never to see it lost, and that was to die in the last ditch. [*History of his own Times*, I, speech attr. to William III]

4 He [Halifax] had said that he had known many kicked downstairs, but he never knew any kicked upstairs before. [*Original Memoirs*]

FANNY BURNEY [MME D'ARBLAY]   1752–1840

5 In the bosom of her respectable family resided Camilla. [*Camilla*, I. Ch. 1]

6 Travelling is the ruin of all happiness! There's no looking at a building here after seeing Italy. [*Cecilia*, IV. Ch. 2]

7 'True, very true, ma'am,' said he, yawning, 'one really lives nowhere; one does but vegetate, and wish it all at an end.' [*Ib.* VII. 5]

8 'Why, what the D—l,' cried the Captain, 'do you come to the play, without knowing what it is?'
'O yes, Sir, yes, very frequently; I have no time to read play-bills; one merely comes to meet one's friends, and show that one's alive.' [*Evelina*, Letter 20]

9 Now I am ashamed of confessing that I have nothing to confess. [*Ib.* 59]

10 Indeed, the freedom with which Dr Johnson condemns whatever he disapproves is astonishing. [*Diary*, 23 Aug. 1778]

JOHN BURNS   1858–1943

11 Every drop of the Thames is liquid 'istory. [Saying to Transatlantic visitors, attr. by Sir Frederick Whyte]

J. D. BURNS   1823–1864

12 Hushed was the evening hymn, – The temple courts were dark; / The lamp was burning dim / Before the sacred Ark, / When suddenly a voice divine / Rang through the silence of the shrine. [Hymn: *The Child Samuel*]

ROBERT BURNS   1759–1796

13 O thou! whatever title suit thee, / Auld Hornie, Satan, Nick, or Clootie. [*Address to the Deil*, 1]

14 But faith! he'll turn a corner jinkin' / An' cheat you yet. [*Ib.* 119]

15 But fare you weel, auld Nickie-ben! / O wad ye tak a thought an' men'! / Ye aiblins might – I dinna ken – / Still hae a stake: / I'm wae to think upo' yon den, / Ev'n for your sake! [*Ib.* 121]

16 Then gently scan your brother man, / Still gentler sister woman; / Tho' they may gang a kennin wrang, / To step aside is human. [*Address to the Unco Guid*, 49]

17 What's done we partly may compute, / But know not what's resisted. [*Ib.* 63]

18 Ae fond kiss, and then we sever! [*Ae Fond Kiss*]

19 But to see her was to love her, / Love but her, and love for ever. [*Ib.*]

20 Had we never lov'd sae kindly, / Had we never lov'd sae blindly, / Never met – or never parted, / We had ne'er been broken-hearted. [*Ib.*]

21 Should auld acquaintance be forgot, / And never brought to min'? [*Auld Lang Syne*]

22 We'll tak a cup o' kindness yet, / For auld lang syne. [*Ib.*]

23 And there's a hand, my trusty fiere, / And gie's a hand o' thine. [*Ib.*]

24 Freedom and Whisky gang thegither! [*The Author's Earnest Cry and Prayer*, 185]

25 O saw ye bonnie Lesley / As she gaed o'er the border? / She's gane, like Alexander, / To spread her conquests farther.
To see her is to love her, / And love but her for ever: / For Nature made her

what she is, / And never made anither!
[*Bonnie Lesley*]

1 Gin a body meet a body / Coming
through the rye; / Gin a body kiss a body,
/ Need a body cry? [*Coming through the
Rye*]

2 Contented wi' little, and cantie wi' mair.
[*Contented wi' Little*]

3 The mother, wi' her needle and her
shears, / Gars auld claes look amaist as
weel's the new. [*The Cotter's Saturday
Night*, 43]

4 The halesome parritch, chief of Scotia's
food. [*Ib*. 92]

5 He wales a portion with judicious care, /
And 'Let us worship God!' he says with
solemn air. [*Ib*. 107]

6 From scenes like these old Scotia's
grandeur springs, / That makes her loved
at home, revered abroad: / Princes and
lords are but the breath of kings, / 'An
honest man's the noblest work of God.'
[*Ib*. 163]

7 I wasna fou, but just had plenty. [*Death
and Dr Hornbook*, 14]

8 On ev'ry hand it will allow'd be, / He's
just – nae better than he should be. [*A
Dedication to Gavin Hamilton*, 25]

9 There's threesome reels, and foursome
reels, / There's hornpipes and strath-
speys, man; / But the ae best dance e'er
cam to our lan', / Was – the De'il's awa'
wi' the Exciseman. [*The De'il's awa' wi'
the Exciseman*]

10 But Facts are chiels that winna ding, /
An' downa be disputed. [*A Dream*, 30]

11 If honest nature made you fools, / What
sairs your grammars? [*Epistle to John
Lapraik*, 63]

12 Gie me ae spark o' Nature's fire, / That's
a' the learning I desire. [*Ib*. 73]

13 The social, friendly, honest man, /
Whate'er he be, / 'Tis he fulfils great
Nature's plan, / And none but he!
[*Epistle to Lapraik*, No. 2, 87]

14 Perhaps it may turn out a sang, / Perhaps turn out a sermon. [*Epistle to a
Young Friend*, 7]

15 But still keep something to yoursel / Ye
scarcely tell to ony. [*Ib*. 35]

16 I waive the quantum o' the sin, / The
hazard of concealing; / But oh! it hardens

a' within, / And petrifies the feeling!
[*Epistle to a Young Friend*, 45]

17 Here lie Willie Michie's banes; / O Satan,
when ye tak him, / Gie him the schoolin'
of your weans, / For clever deils he'll
mak them! [*Epitaph on a Schoolmaster*]

18 A man's a man for a' that! [*For a' that
and a' that*]

19 Go fetch to me a pint o' wine, / An' fill it
in a silver tassie. [*Go Fetch to me a Pint o'
Wine*]

20 Green grow the rashes O; / The sweetest
hours that e'er I spend, / Are spent
among the lasses O! [*Green grow the
Rashes*]

21 What signifies the life o' man, / An'
'twere na for the lasses O. [*Ib*.]

22 Auld nature swears, the lovely dears /
Her noblest work she classes O; / Her
prentice han' she tried on man, / An'
then she made the lasses O. [*Ib*.]

23 O, gie me the lass that has acres o' charms,
/ O, gie me the lass wi' the weel-stockit
farms. [*Hey for a Lass wi' a Tocher*]

24 The golden hours on angel wings / Flew
o'er me and my dearie; / For dear to me
as light and life / Was my sweet Highland Mary. [*Highland Mary*]

25 Here some are thinkin' on their sins, /
An' some upo' their claes. [*The Holy Fair*,
82]

26 There's some are fou o' love divine, /
There's some are fou o' brandy. [*Ib*. 239]

27 There's death in the cup – sae beware!
[*Inscription on a Goblet*]

28 It was a' for our rightfu' King, / We left
fair Scotland's strand. [*It was a' for our
Rightfu' King*]

29 He turn'd him right and round about /
Upon the Irish shore; / And gae his
bridle-reins a shake, / With adieu for
evermore, / My dear, / Adieu for evermore. [*Ib*.]

30 John Anderson my jo, John, / When we
were first acquent, / Your locks were like
the raven, / Your bonnie brow was brent.
[*John Anderson my Jo*]

31 There was three Kings into the east, /
Three Kings both great and high, / And
they hae sworn a solemn oath / John
Barleycorn should die. [*John Barleycorn*]

32 Let them cant about decorum / Who have
characters to lose. [*The Jolly Beggars*, 310]

1 Nature's law, / That man was made to mourn. [*Man was made to Mourn*, 31]

2 Man's inhumanity to man / Makes countless thousand mourn! [*Ib.* 55]

3 My heart's in the Highlands, my heart is not here; / My heart's in the Highlands a-chasing the deer. [*My Heart's in the Highlands*]

4 O, my Luve's like a red red rose / That's newly sprung in June: / O, my Luve's like the melodie / That's sweetly play'd in tune. [*My Love is like a Red Red Rose*]

5 O, wert thou in the cauld blast, / On yonder lea, on yonder lea, / My plaidie to the angry airt, / I'd shelter thee, I'd shelter thee. [*O, Wert Thou in the Cauld Blast*]

6 The desert were a paradise, / If thou wert there, if thou wert there. [*Ib.*]

7 Of a' the airts the wind can blaw, / I dearly like the west. [*Of a' the Airts*]

8 Hear, Land o' Cakes, and brither Scots. [*On the Late Capt. Grose's Peregrinations*]

9 The mair they talk I'm kent the better, / E'en let them clash. [*The Poet's Welcome to his Love-begotten Daughter*]

10 Scots, wha hae wi' Wallace bled, / Scots, wham Bruce has aften led, / Welcome to your gory bed, / Or to victorie. [*Scots, Wha Hae*]

11 Liberty's in every blow! / Let us do or die! [*Ib.*]

12 Some hae meat, and canna eat, / And some wad eat that want it, / But we hae meat and we can eat, / And sae the Lord be thankit. [*The Selkirk Grace*]

13 Where sits our sulky sullen dame, / Gathering her brows like gathering storm, / Nursing her wrath to keep it warm. [*Tam o' Shanter*, 10]

14 Auld Ayr, wham ne'er a town surpasses / For honest men and bonnie lasses. [*Ib.* 15]

15 Ah, gentle dames! It gars me greet / To think how mony counsels sweet, / How mony lengthen'd sage advices, / The husband frae the wife despises! [*Ib.* 33]

16 His ancient, trusty, drouthy crony; / Tam lo'ed him like a vera brither; / They had been fou for weeks thegither. [*Ib.* 42]

17 Kings may be blest, but Tam was glorious, / O'er a' the ills o' life victorious! [*Ib.* 57]

18 But pleasures are like poppies spread – / You seize the flow'r, its bloom is shed; / Or like the snow falls in the river – A moment white, then melts for ever. [*Tam o' Shanter*, 59]

19 That hour, o' night's black arch the key-stane. [*Ib.* 69]

20 Inspiring bold John Barleycorn! / What dangers thou canst make us scorn! / Wi' tippenny, we fear nae evil; / Wi' usquebae, we'll face the devil. [*Ib.* 105]

21 As Tammie glowr'd, amaz'd, and curious, / The mirth and fun grew fast and furious. [*Ib.* 143]

22 Ah, Tam! ah, Tam! thou'll get thy fairin'! / In hell they'll roast thee like a herrin'! [*Ib.* 201]

23 He'll hae misfortunes great and sma', / But aye a heart aboon them a'. [*There was a Lad*]

24 Fair fa' your honest sonsie face, / Great chieftain o' the puddin'-race! / Aboon them a' ye tak your place, / Painch, tripe, or thairm: / Weel are ye worthy o' a grace / As lang's my arm. [*To a Haggis*]

25 O wad some Pow'r the giftie gie us / To see oursels as others see us! / It wad frae mony a blunder free us, / And foolish notion. [*To a Louse*]

26 Wee modest crimson-tippèd flow'r. [*To a Mountain Daisy*]

27 Wee, sleekit, cow'rin', tim'rous beastie, / O what a panic's in thy breastie! / Thou need na start awa sae hasty, / Wi' bickering brattle! [*To a Mouse*]

28 The best laid schemes o' mice an' men / Gang aft a-gley. [*Ib.*]

29 To make a happy fire-side clime / To weans and wife, / That's the true pathos and sublime / Of human life. [*To Dr Blacklock*]

30 We labour soon, we labour late, / To feed the titled knave, man; / And a' the comfort we're to get / Is that ayont the grave, man. [*The Tree of Liberty*, attributed to Burns]

31 His lockèd, letter'd, braw brass collar, / Shew'd him the gentleman and scholar. [*The Twa Dogs*, 13]

32 But human bodies are sic fools, / For a' their colleges and schools, / That when nae real ills perplex them, / They make enow themselves to vex them. [*Ib.* 195]

1 But yet the light that led astray / Was light from Heaven. [*The Vision*, 239]

2 O whistle, and I'll come to you, my lad. [*Whistle, and I'll Come to you, my Lad*]

3 Ye banks and braes o' bonnie Doon, / How can ye bloom sae fresh and fair? / How can ye chant, ye little birds, / And I sae weary fu' o' care? [*Ye Banks and Braes*]

4 And my fause lover stole my rose, / But ah! he left the thorn wi' me. [*Ib.*]

5 Don't let the awkward squad fire over me. [A. Cunningham's *Life*, Vol. i. p. 344]

B. H. BURT   19 Cent.

6 When you're all dressed up and no place to go. [Title of song]

ROBERT BURTON   1577–1640

7 All my joys to this are folly, / Naught so sweet as melancholy. [*Anatomy of Melancholy*, 'The Author's Abstract']

8 They lard their lean books with the fat of others' works. [*Ib.* 'Democritus to the Reader']

9 We can say nothing but what hath been said.... Our poets steal from Homer ... he that comes last is commonly best. [*Ib.*]

10 Like watermen, that row one way and look another. [*Ib.*]

11 All poets are mad. [*Ib.*]

12 Were it not that they are loath to lay out money on a rope, they would be hanged forthwith, and sometimes die to save charges. [*Ib.* Pt I. §2. memb. 3. 12]

13 One was never married, and that's his hell; another is, and that's his plague. [*Ib.* I. §2. memb. 4. 7]

14 If there is a hell upon earth, it is to be found in a melancholy man's heart. [*Ib.* I. §4. memb. 1. 3]

15 [Fabricius] finds certain spots and clouds in the sun. [*Ib.* II. §2. memb. 3]

16 Who cannot give good counsel? 'Tis cheap, it costs them nothing. [*Ib.* II. §3. memb. 3]

17 What is a ship but a prison? [*Ib.* II. §3. memb. 4]

18 All places are distant from heaven alike. [*Ib.*]

19 Tobacco, divine, rare, superexcellent tobacco, which goes far beyond all their panaceas, potable gold, and philosopher's stones, a sovereign remedy to all diseases ... But, as it is commonly abused by most men, which take it as tinkers do ale, 'tis a plague, a mischief, a violent purger of goods, lands, health, hellish, devilish, and damned tobacco, the ruin and overthrow of body and soul. [*Anatomy of Melancholy*, II. §4. memb. 2. 1]

20 'Let me not live', said Aretine's Antonia, 'if I had not rather hear thy discourse than see a play.' [*Ib.* III. §1. memb. 1. 1]

21 To enlarge and illustrate this – is to set a candle in the sun. [*Ib.* III. §2. memb. 1. 2]

22 Cornelia kept her in talk till her children came from school, and these, said she, are my jewels. [*Ib.* III. §2. memb. 2. 3]

23 England is a paradise for women, and hell for horses: Italy a paradise for horses, hell for women, as the diverb goes. [*Ib.* III. §3. memb. 1. 2]

24 The miller sees not all the water that goes by his mill. [*Ib.* III. §3. memb. 4. 1]

25 The fear of some divine and supreme powers keeps men in obedience. [*Ib.* III §4. memb. 1. 2]

26 One religion is as true as another. [*Ib.* III. §4. memb. 2. 1]

WILHELM BUSCH   1832–1908

27 *Max und Moritz ihrerseits / Fanden darin keinen Reiz.* – Max and Moritz for their part found no attraction in it. [*Max und Moritz*]

BISHOP JOSEPH BUTLER
1692–1752

28 That which is the foundation of all our hopes and of all our fears; all our hopes and fears which are of any consideration: I mean a Future Life. [*The Analogy of Religion*, Introduction]

29 But to *us*, probability is the very guide of life. [*Ib.*]

30 Sir, the pretending to extraordinary revelations and gifts of the Holy Ghost is a horrid thing, a very horrid thing. [To John Wesley. Quoted in Wesley, *Works*, xiii]

1 Things and actions are what they are, and the consequences of them will be what they will be: why then should we desire to be deceived? [*Fifteen Sermons*, 7. 16]

NICHOLAS MURRAY BUTLER
1862–1947

2 An expert is one who knows more and more about less and less. [Commencement Address, Columbia University]

SAMUEL BUTLER   1612–1680

3 When civil dudgeon first grew high, / And men fell out they knew not why. [*Hudibras*, I. i. 1]

4 Besides 'tis known he could speak Greek, / As naturally as pigs squeak. [*Ib.* I. i. 51]

5 He could distinguish, and divide / A hair 'twixt south and south-west side. / On either which he would dispute, / Confute, change hands, and still confute. [*Ib.* I. i. 63]

6 For he by geometric scale / Could take the size of pots of ale. [*Ib.* I. i. 121]

7 For every why he had a wherefore. [*Ib.* I. i. 132]

8 He knew what's what, and that's as high / As metaphysic wit can fly. [*Ib.* I. i. 149]

9 'Twas Presbyterian true blue. [*Ib.* I. i. 189]

10 Such as do build their faith upon / The holy text of pike and gun. [*Ib.* I. i. 193]

11 And prove their doctrine orthodox / By apostolic blows and knocks. [*Ib.* I. i. 197]

12 Compound for sins, they are inclined to / By damning those they have no mind to. [*Ib.* I. i. 213]

13 He ne'er considered it, as loath / To look a gift-horse in the mouth. [*Ib.* I. i. 483]

14 Quoth Hudibras, I smell a rat; / Ralpho, thou dost prevaricate. [*Ib.* I. i. 815]

15 Through perils both of wind and limb, / Through thick and thin she followed him. [*Ib.* I. ii. 369]

16 Ay me! what perils do environ / The man that meddles with cold iron! [*Ib.* I. iii. 1]

17 I'll make the fur / Fly round the ears of the old cur. [*Ib.* I. iii. 277]

18 Cleric before, and Lay behind; / A lawless linsy-woolsy brother, / Half of one order, half another. [*Hudibras*, I. iii. 1226]

19 Quoth Hudibras, Friend Ralph, thou hast / Outrun the constable at last. [*Ib.* I. iii. 1367]

20 Love is a boy, by poets styled, / Then spare the rod, and spoil the child. [*Ib.* II. i. 844]

21 And like a lobster boiled, the morn / From black to red began to turn. [*Ib.* II. ii. 31]

22 Have always been at daggers-drawing, / And one another clapper-clawing. [*Ib.* II. ii. 79]

23 Oaths are but words, and words but wind. [*Ib.* II. ii. 107]

24 He made an instrument to know / If the moon shine at full or no. [*Ib.* II. iii. 261]

25 To swallow gudgeons ere they're catched, And count their chickens ere they're hatched. [*Ib.* II. iii. 923]

26 Still amorous, and fond, and billing, / Like Philip and Mary on a shilling. [*Ib.* III. i. 687]

27 Neither have the hearts to stay, / Nor wit enough to run away. [*Ib.* III. ii. 569]

28 For, those that fly, may fight again, / Which he can never do that's slain. [*Ib.* III. iii. 243]

29 He that complies against his will, / Is of his own opinion still. [*Ib.* III. iii. 547]

30 The souls of women are so small, / That some believe they've none at all. [*Miscellaneous Thoughts*]

SAMUEL BUTLER   1835–1902

31 Some who had received a liberal education at the Colleges of Unreason, and taken the highest degrees in hypothetics, which are their principal study. [*Erewhon*, Ch. 9]

32 Straighteners, managers and cashiers of the Musical Banks. [*Ib.*]

33 While to deny the existence of an unseen kingdom is bad, to pretend that we know more about it than its bare existence is no better. [*Ib.* 15]

34 The wish to spread those opinions that we hold conducive to our own welfare is so deeply rooted in the English character that few of us can escape its influence. [*Ib.* 20]

1 An art can only be learned in the workshop of those who are winning their bread by it. [*Erewhon*, 20]

2 It has been said that the love of money is the root of all evil. The want of money is so quite as truly. [*Ib.*]

3 Spontaneity is only a term for man's ignorance of the gods. [*Ib.* 25]

4 I keep my books at the British Museum and at Mudie's. [*Humour of Homer*, 'Ramblings in Cheapside']

5 Life is one long process of getting tired. [*Notebooks*, 'Life', 7]

6 Life is the art of drawing sufficient conclusions from insufficient premises. [*Ib.* 9]

7 All progress is based upon a universal innate desire on the part of every organism to live beyond its income. [*Ib.* 16]

8 The healthy stomach is nothing if not conservative. Few radicals have good digestions. [*Ib.* 'Mind and Matter: Indigestion']

9 Though analogy is often misleading, it is the least misleading thing we have. [*Ib.* 'Music, Pictures and Books: Thought and Word', 2]

10 When a man is in doubt about this or that in his writing, it will often guide him if he asks himself how it will tell a hundred years hence. [*Ib.* final note]

11 If Bach wriggles, Wagner writhes. [*Ib.* 'Handel and Music: Musical Criticism']

12 The history of art is the history of revivals. [*Ib.* 'Handel and Music: Anachronism']

13 The phrase 'unconscious humour' is the one contribution I have made to the current literature of the day. [*Ib.* 'Homo Unius Libri': Myself and "Unconscious Humour"']

14 I am the *enfant terrible* of literature and science. [*Ib.* 'Enfant Terrible: Myself']

15 Virgil was no good because Tennyson ran him, and as for Tennyson – well, Tennyson goes without saying. [*Ib.* 'Enfant Terrible: Blake, Dante, etc.']

16 An apology for the Devil – it must be remembered that we have only heard one side of the case. God has written all the books. [*Ib.* 'Higgledy-Piggledy: An Apology for the Devil']

17 God is Love – I dare say. But what a mischievous devil Love is! [*Notebooks*, 'Higgledy-Piggledy: God is Love']

18 To live is like to love – all reason is against it, and all healthy instinct for it. [*Ib.* 'Higgledy-Piggledy: Life and Love']

19 The public buys its opinions as it buys its meat, or takes in its milk, on the principle that it is cheaper to do this than to keep a cow. So it is, but the milk is more likely to be watered. [*Ib.* 'Material for a Proposed Sequel: Public Opinion']

20 To be at all is to be religious more or less. [*Ib.* 'Reconciliation: Religion']

21 An honest God's the noblest work of man. [*Further Extracts*, Vol. 1, 'An Honest God']

22 Taking numbers into account, I should think more mental suffering had been undergone in the streets leading from St George's, Hanover Square, than in the condemned cells of Newgate. [*Way of All Flesh*, Ch. 13]

23 Every man's work, whether it be literature or music or pictures or architecture or anything else, is always a portrait of himself. [*Ib.* 14]

24 That vice pays homage to virtue is notorious; we call it hypocrisy. [*Ib.* 19]

25 Pleasure after all is a safer guide than either right or duty. [*Ib.*]

26 The advantage of doing one's praising for oneself is that one can lay it on so thick and exactly in the right places. [*Ib.* 34]

27 There's many a good tune played on an old fiddle. [*Ib.* 61]

28 'Tis better to have loved and lost than never to have lost at all. [*Ib.* 77]

29 Brigands demand your money or your life; women require both. [Quoted in *Treasury of Humorous Quotations*]

30 Stowed away in a Montreal lumber room / The Discobolus standeth and turneth his face to the wall; / Dusty, cobweb-covered, maimed and set at naught, / Beauty crieth in an attic and no man regardeth: / O God! O Montreal! [*Psalm of Montreal*]

WILLIAM BUTLER   1535–1618

31 Doubtless God could have made a better berry [than the strawberry] but doubtless God never did. [Walton, *Compleat Angler*, Pt 1. Ch. 3]

JOHN BYROM   1692–1763

1 Some say, that Signor Bononcini, / Compared to Handel's a mere ninny; / Others aver, to him, that Handel / Is scarcely fit to hold a candle. / Strange! that such high dispute should be / 'Twixt Tweedledum and Tweedledee. [*Epigram on the Feuds between Handel and Bononcini*]

2 Bone and Skin, two millers thin, / Would starve us all, or near it; / But be it known to Skin and Bone / That Flesh and Blood can't bear it. [*Epigram on Two Monopolists*]

3 I shall prove it – as clear as a whistle. [*Epistle to Lloyd*, I. xii]

4 Christians awake, salute the happy morn, / Whereon the Saviour of the world was born. [*Hymn for Christmas Day*]

5 God bless the King, I mean the Faith's Defender; / God bless – no harm in blessing – the Pretender; / But who Pretender is, or who is King, / God bless us all – that's quite another thing. [*To an Officer in the Army*]

GEORGE GORDON, LORD BYRON   1788–1824

6 The 'good old times' – all times when old are good – / Are gone. [*The Age of Bronze*, i]

7 For what were all these country patriots born? / To hunt, and vote, and raise the price of corn? [*Ib.* xiv]

8 The land self-interest groans from shore to shore, / For fear that plenty should attain the poor. [*Ib.*]

9 In short, he was a perfect cavaliero, / And to his very valet seemed a hero. [*Beppo*, xxxiii]

10 His heart was one of those which most enamour us, / Wax to receive, and marble to retain. [*Ib.* xxxiv]

11 The nursery still lisps out in all they utter – / Besides, they always smell of bread and butter. [*Ib.* xxxix]

12 Know ye the land where the cypress and myrtle / Are emblems of deeds that are done in their clime? / Where the rage of the vulture, the love of the turtle, / Now melt into sorrow, now madden to crime! [*The Bride of Abydos*, I. i]

13 Where the virgins are soft as the roses they twine, / And all, save the spirit of man, is divine. [*The Bride of Abydos*, I. i]

14 Mark! where his carnage and his conquests cease! / He makes a solitude, and calls it – peace! [*Ib.* II. xx]

15 Hark! to the hurried question of Despair: / 'Where is my child?' – an Echo answers – 'Where?' [*Ib.* II. xxvii]

16 Maidens, like moths, are ever caught by glare, / And Mammon wins his way where Seraphs might despair. [*Childe Harold's Pilgrimage*, I. ix]

17 Adieu, adieu! my native shore / Fades o'er the waters blue. [*Ib.* I. xiii]

18 My native Land – Good Night! [*Ib.*]

19 War, war is still the cry, 'War even to the knife!' [*Ib.* I. lxxxvi]

20 Well didst thou speak, Athena's wisest son! / 'All that we know is, nothing can be known.' [*Ib.* II. vii]

21 Ah! happy years! once more who would not be a boy? [*Ib.* II. xxiii]

22 Foul Superstition! howsoe'er disguised, / Idol, saint, virgin, prophet, crescent, cross, / For whatsoever symbol thou art prized, / Thou sacerdotal gain, but general loss! / Who from true worship's gold can separate thy dross? [*Ib.* II. xliv]

23 Hereditary bondsmen! know ye not / Who would be free themselves must strike the blow? [*Ib.* II. lxxvi]

24 Where'er we tread 'tis haunted, holy ground. [*Ib.* II. lxxxviii]

25 What is the worst of woes that wait on age? / What stamps the wrinkle deeper on the brow? / To view each loved one blotted from life's page, / And be alone on earth, as I am now. [*Ib.* II. xcviii]

26 There was a sound of revelry by night, / And Belgium's capital had gathered then / Her Beauty and her Chivalry, and bright / The lamps shone o'er fair women and brave men; / A thousand hearts beat happily; and when / Music arose with its voluptuous swell, / Soft eyes looked love to eyes that spake again, / And all went merry as a marriage bell; / But hush! hark! a deep sound strikes like a rising knell! [*Ib.* III. xxi]

27 Did ye not hear it? – No; 'twas but the wind, / Or the car rattling o'er the stony street; / On with the dance! let joy be

unconfined; / No sleep till morn, when Youth and Pleasure meet / To chase the glowing Hours with flying feet. [*Childe Harold's Pilgrimage*, III. xxii]

1 Arm! Arm! it is – it is – the cannon's opening roar! [*Ib.*]

2 Or whispering, with white lips – 'The foe! they come! they come!' [*Ib.* III. xxv]

3 Rider and horse, – friend, foe, – in one red burial blent! [*Ib.* III. xxviii]

4 But Life will suit / Itself to Sorrow's most detested fruit, / Like to the apples on the Dead Sea's shore, / All ashes to the taste. [*Ib.* III. xxxiv]

5 The castle crag of Drachenfels / Frowns o'er the wide and winding Rhine. [*Ib.* III. lv]

6 To fly from, need not be to hate, mankind: / All are not fit with them to stir and toil, / Nor is it discontent to keep the mind / Deep in its fountain. [*Ib.* III. lxix]

7 I live not in myself, but I become / Portion of that around me; and to me / High mountains are a feeling, but the hum / Of human cities torture. [*Ib.* III. lxxii]

8 Ye stars! which are the poetry of heaven! [*Ib.* III. lxxxviii]

9 Then stirs the feeling infinite, so felt / In solitude, where we are *least* alone. [*Ib.* III. xc]

10 I have not loved the world, nor the world me; / I have not flattered its rank breath, nor bowed / To its idolatries a patient knee, / Nor coined my cheek to smiles, nor cried aloud / In worship of an echo. [*Ib.* III. cxiii]

11 I stood / Among them, but not of them; in a shroud / Of thoughts which were not their thoughts. [*Ib.*]

12 I stood in Venice, on the Bridge of Sighs; / A palace and a prison on each hand. [*Ib.* IV. i]

13 Where Venice sat in state, throned on her hundred isles! [*Ib.*]

14 The Ariosto of the North. [(Walter Scott) *Ib.* IV. xl]

15 Let these describe the indescribable. [*Ib.* IV. liii]

16 Then farewell, Horace; whom I hated so, / Not for thy thoughts, but mine. [*Ib.* IV. lxxvii]

17 Yet, Freedom! yet thy banner, torn, but flying, / Streams like the thunder-storm *against* the wind. [*Childe Harold's Pilgrimage*, IV. xcviii]

18 Alas! our young affections run to waste, / Or water but the desert. [*Ib.* IV. cxx]

19 Of its own beauty is the mind diseased, / And fevers into false creation. [*Ib.* IV. cxxii]

20 Time, the avenger! unto thee I lift / My hands, and eyes, and heart, and crave of thee a gift. [*Ib.* IV. cxxx]

21 I see before me the Gladiator lie: / He leans upon his hand – his manly brow / Consents to death, but conquers agony. [*Ib.* IV. cxl]

22 The arena swims around him – he is gone, / Ere ceased the inhuman shout which hailed the wretch who won. [*Ib.*]

23 He heard it, but he heeded not – his eyes / Were with his heart, and that was far away; / He recked not of the life he lost nor prize, / But where his rude hut by the Danube lay, / *There* were his young barbarians all at play, / *There* was their Dacian mother – he, their sire, / Butchered to make a Roman holiday. [*Ib.* IV. cxli]

24 While stands the Coliseum, Rome shall stand; / When falls the Coliseum, Rome shall fall; / And when Rome falls – the World. [*Ib.* IV. cxlv]

25 Oh! that the Desert were my dwelling place, / With one fair Spirit for my minister, / That I might all forget the human race, / And, hating no one, love but only her! [*Ib.* IV. clxxvii]

26 There is a pleasure in the pathless woods, / There is a rapture on the lonely shore, / There is society, where none intrudes, / By the deep sea, and music in its roar: / I love not man the less, but Nature more. [*Ib.* IV. clxxviii]

27 Roll on, thou deep and dark blue Ocean – roll! / Ten thousand fleets sweep over thee in vain; / Man marks the earth with ruin – his control / Stops with the shore. [*Ib.* IV. clxxix]

28 He sinks into thy depths with bubbling groan, / Without a grave, unknelled, uncoffined, and unknown. [*Ib.*]

29 Time writes no wrinkle on thine azure brow: / Such as creation's dawn beheld, thou rollest now. [*Ib.* IV. clxxxii]

1 Thou glorious mirror, where the Almighty's form / Glasses itself in tem-
pests. [*Childe Harold's Pilgrimage*, IV.
clxxxiii]

2 Dark-heaving – boundless, endless, and
sublime, / The image of eternity, the
throne / Of the Invisible. [*Ib.*]

3 And I have loved thee, Ocean! and my
joy / Of youthful sports was on thy
breast to be / Borne, like thy bubbles,
onward: from a boy / I wantoned with
thy breakers. [*Ib.* IV. clxxxiv]

4 The fatal facility of the octosyllabic
verse. [*The Corsair*, Introduction]

5 Such hath it been – shall be – beneath the
sun / The many still must labour for the
one! [*Ib.* I. viii]

6 The spirit burning but unbent, / May
writhe, rebel – the weak alone repent!
[*Ib.* II. x]

7 She for him had given / Her all on earth,
and more than all in heaven! [*Ib.* III.
xvii]

8 He left a Corsair's name to other times, /
Linked with one virtue, and a thousand
crimes. [*Ib.* III. xxiv]

9 I tell thee, be not rash; a golden bridge /
Is for a flying enemy. [*The Deformed
Transformed*, II. ii]

10 Explaining metaphysics to the nation – /
I wish he would explain his explanation.
[(Of Coleridge) *Don Juan*, Dedication,
ii]

11 In virtues nothing earthly could surpass
her, / Save thine 'incomparable oil',
Macassar! [*Ib.* I. xvii]

12 But – Oh! ye lords of ladies intellectual, /
Inform us truly, have they not hen-
pecked you all? [*Ib.* I. xxii]

13 She / Was married, charming, chaste,
and twenty-three. [*Ib.* I. lix]

14 Her stature tall – I hate a dumpy woman.
[*Ib.* I. lxi]

15 What men call gallantry, and gods adultery, / Is much more common where the
climate's sultry. [*Ib.* I. lxiii]

16 Christians have burnt each other, quite
persuaded / That all the Apostles would
have done as they did. [*Ib.* I. lxxxiii]

17 A little still she strove, and much re-
pented, / And whispering 'I will ne'er
consent' – consented. [*Ib.* I. cxvii]

18 'Tis sweet to hear the watch-dog's honest
bark / Bay deep-mouthed welcome as we
draw near home; / 'Tis sweet to know
there is an eye will mark / Our coming,
and look brighter when we come. [*Don
Juan*, I. cxxiii]

19 Sweet is revenge – especially to women.
[*Ib.* I. cxxiv]

20 Pleasure's a sin, and sometimes sin's a
pleasure. [*Ib.* I. cxxxiii]

21 Man's love is of man's life a thing apart,
/ 'Tis woman's whole existence. [*Ib.* I.
cxciv]

22 So for a good old-gentlemanly vice, / I
think I must take up with avarice. [*Ib.*
I. ccxvi]

23 There's nought, no doubt, so much the
spirit calms / As rum and true religion.
[*Ib.* II. xxxiv]

24 But he, poor fellow, had a wife and
children, / Two things for dying people
quite bewildering. [*Ib.* II. xliii]

25 If this be true, indeed, / Some Christians
have a comfortable creed. [*Ib.* II. lxxxvi]

26 He could, perhaps, have passed the
Hellespont, / As once (a feat on which
ourselves we prided) / Leander, Mr
Ekenhead, and I did. [*Ib.* II. cv]

27 Let us have wine and women, mirth and
laughter, / Sermons and soda-water the
day after. [*Ib.* II. clxxviii]

28 Man, being reasonable, must get drunk; /
The best of life is but intoxication. [*Ib.* II.
clxxix]

29 Alas! the love of women! it is known / To
be a lovely and a fearful thing. [*Ib.* II.
cxcix]

30 In her first passion woman loves her lover,
/ In all the others all she loves is love. [*Ib.*
III. iii]

31 For no one cares for matrimonial coo-
ings, / There's nothing wrong in a connubial kiss: / Think you, if Laura had
been Petrarch's wife, / He would have
written sonnets all his life? [*Ib.* III. viii]

32 All tragedies are finished by a death, /
All comedies are ended by a marriage.
[*Ib.* III. ix]

33 Dreading that climax of all human ills, /
The inflammation of his weekly bills. [*Ib.*
III. xxxv]

1 He was the mildest mannered man / That ever scuttled ship or cut a throat. [*Don Juan*, III. xli]

2 Cost his enemies a long repentance, / And made him a good friend, but bad acquaintance. [*Ib*. III. liv]

3 Though sages may pour out their wisdom's treasure, / There is no sterner moralist than Pleasure. [*Ib*. III. lxv]

4 But Shakespeare also says, 'tis very silly / 'To gild refinèd gold, or paint the lily'. [*Ib*. III. lxxvi]

5 Agree to a short armistice with truth. [*Ib*. III. lxxxiii]

6 The isles of Greece, the isles of Greece! / Where burning Sappho loved and sung, / Where grew the arts of war and peace, / Where Delos rose, and Phoebus sprung! / Eternal summer gilds them yet, / But all, except their sun, is set. [*Ib*. III. lxxxvi. 1]

7 The mountains look on Marathon – / And Marathon looks on the sea; / And musing there an hour alone, / I dreamed that Greece might yet be free. [*Ib*. III. lxxxvi. 3]

8 He counted them at break of day – / And when the sun set where were they? [*Ib*. III. lxxxvi. 4]

9 Of the three hundred grant but three, / To make a new Thermopylae! [*Ib*. III. lxxxvi. 7]

10 Fill high the cup with Samian wine! [*Ib*. III. lxxxvi. 9]

11 To think such breasts must suckle slaves. [*Ib*. III. lxxxvi. 15]

12 Milton's prince of poets – so we say; / A little heavy, but no less divine. [*Ib*. III. xci]

13 Nothing so difficult as a beginning / In poesy, unless perhaps the end. [*Ib*. IV. i]

14 Imagination droops her pinion. [*Ib*. IV. iii]

15 And if I laugh at any mortal thing, / 'Tis that I may not weep. [*Ib*. IV. iv]

16 'Whom the gods love die young' was said of yore. [*Ib*. IV. xii]

17 'Arcades ambo', *id est* – blackguards both. [*Ib*. IV. xciii]

18 I've stood upon Achilles' tomb, / And heard Troy doubted; time will doubt of Rome. [*Ib*. IV. ci]

19 Oh! 'darkly, deeply, beautifully blue', / As someone somewhere sings about the sky. [*Don Juan*, IV. cx]

20 The negroes more philosophy displayed, – / Used to it, no doubt, as eels are to be flayed. [*Ib*. V. vii]

21 I thought it would appear / That there had been a lady in the case. [*Ib*. V. xix]

22 And put himself upon his good behaviour. [*Ib*. V. xlvii]

23 That all-softening, overpowering knell, / The tocsin of the soul – the dinner-bell. [*Ib*. V. xlix]

24 A moral (like all morals) melancholy. [*Ib*. V. lxiii]

25 Not to admire is all the art I know. [*Ib*. V. ci]

26 The women pardoned all except her face. [*Ib*. V. cxiii]

27 Why don't they knead two virtuous souls for life / Into that moral centaur, man and wife? [*Ib*. V. clviii]

28 There is a tide in the affairs of women, / Which, taken at the flood, leads – God knows where. [*Ib*. VI. ii]

29 Dudù said nothing, as / Her talents were of the more silent class. [*Ib*. VI. xlix]

30 A lady of a 'certain age', which means / Certainly aged. [*Ib*. VI. lxix]

31 A 'strange coincidence', to use a phrase / By which such things are settled nowadays. [*Ib*. VI. lxxviii]

32 He said / Little, but to the purpose. [*Ib*. IX. lxxxiii]

33 When Bishop Berkeley said 'there was no matter', / And proved it – 'twas no matter what he said. [*Ib*. XI. i]

34 But Tom's no more – and so no more of Tom. [*Ib*. XI. xx]

35 And, after all, what is a lie? 'Tis but / The truth in masquerade. [*Ib*. XI. xxxvii]

36 'Tis strange the mind, that very fiery particle, / Should let itself be snuffed out by an article. [(John Keats) *Ib*. XI. lx]

37 And hold up to the sun my little taper. [*Ib*. XII. xxi]

38 A finished gentleman from top to toe. [*Ib*. XII. lxxxiv]

39 Now hatred is by far the longest pleasure; / Men love in haste, but they detest at leisure. [*Ib*. XIII. vi]

1 Cool, and quite English, imperturbable. [*Don Juan*, XIII. xiv]

2 The English winter – ending in July, / To recommence in August. [*Ib*. XIII. xlii]

3 Society is now one polished horde, / Formed of two mighty tribes, the *Bores* and *Bored*. [*Ib*. XIII. xcv]

4 I for one venerate a petticoat. [*Ib*. XIV. xxvi]

5 Of all the horrid, hideous notes of woe, / Sadder than owl-songs or the midnight blast, / Is that portentous phrase, 'I told you so'. [*Ib*. XIV. l]

6 She had consented to create again / That Adam, called 'the happiest of men'. [*Ib*. XIV. lv]

7 'Tis strange – but true; for truth is always strange; / Stranger than fiction. [*Ib*. XIV. ci]

8 Not so her gracious, graceful, graceless Grace. [*Ib*. XVI. xlix]

9 The loudest wit I e'er was deafened with. [*Ib*. XVI. lxxxi]

10 And both were young, and one was beautiful. [*The Dream*, ii]

11 Still must I hear? – shall hoarse Fitzgerald bawl / His creaking couplets in a tavern hall, / And I not sing? [*English Bards and Scottish Reviewers*, 1]

12 I'll publish, right or wrong: / Fools are my theme, let satire be my song. [*Ib*. 5]

13 'Tis pleasant, sure, to see one's name in print; / A book's a book, although there's nothing in't. [*Ib*. 51]

14 A man must serve his time to every trade / Save censure – critics all are ready made. / Take hackneyed jokes from Miller, got by rote, / With just enough of learning to misquote. [*Ib*. 63]

15 As soon / Seek roses in December – ice in June; / Hope constancy in wind, or corn in chaff; / Believe a woman or an epitaph, / Or any other thing that's false, before / You trust in critics. [*Ib*. 75]

16 Better to err with Pope, than shine with Pye. [*Ib*. 102]

17 The simple Wordsworth ... / Who, both by precept and example, shows / That prose is verse, and verse is merely prose. [*Ib*. 237 and 241]

18 Be warm, but pure; be amorous, but be chaste. [*Ib*. 306]

19 Comus all allows; / Champaign, dice, music, or your neighbour's spouse. [*English Bards and Scottish Reviewers*, 650]

20 To live like Clodius, and like Falkland fall. [*Ib*. 686]

21 But who forgives the senior's ceaseless verse, / Whose hairs grow hoary as his rhymes grow worse? [*Ib*. 729]

22 That mighty master of unmeaning rhyme. [(Darwin) *Ib*. 894]

23 Let simple Wordsworth chime his childish verse, / And brother Coleridge lull the babe at nurse. [*Ib*. 917]

24 Nay more, though all my rival rhymesters frown, / I too can hunt a poetaster down. [*Ib*. 7 lines from end]

25 The world is a bundle of hay, / Mankind are the asses who pull; / Each tugs it a different way, / And the greatest of all is John Bull. [*Epigram*]

26 Dear Doctor, I have read your play, / Which is a good one in its way, / Purges the eyes and moves the bowels, / And drenches handkerchiefs like towels. [*Epistle from Mr Murray to Dr Polidori*]

27 With death doomed to grapple, / Beneath this cold slab, he / Who lied in the chapel / Now lies in the Abbey. [*Epitaph for William Pitt*]

28 And know, whatever thou hast been, / 'Tis something better not to be. [*Euthanasia*]

29 Fare thee well! and if for ever, / Still for ever, fare thee well. [*Fare thee well*]

30 Clime of the unforgotten brave! / Whose land from plain to mountain-cave / Was Freedom's home or Glory's grave! [*The Giaour*, 103]

31 For Freedom's battle once begun, / Bequeathed by bleeding Sire to Son, / Though baffled oft is ever won. [*Ib*. 123]

32 And lovelier things have mercy shown / To every failing but their own, / And every woe a tear can claim / Except an erring sister's shame. [*Ib*. 418]

33 I die, – but first I have possessed, / And come what may, I *have been* blessed. [*Ib*. 1127]

34 The Assyrian came down like the wolf on the fold, / And his cohorts were gleaming in purple and gold; / And the sheen of their spears was like stars on the sea, /

When the blue wave rolls nightly on deep Galilee. [*Hebrew Melodies*, 'The Destruction of Sennacherib']

1 For the Angel of Death spread his wings on the blast. [*Ib.*]

2 And the might of the Gentile, unsmote by the sword, / Hath melted like snow in the glance of the Lord! [*Ib.*]

3 Oh! snatched away in beauty's bloom, / On thee shall press no ponderous tomb. [*Ib.* 'Oh! Snatched away']

4 She walks in beauty, like the night / Of cloudless climes and starry skies; / And all that's best of dark and bright / Meet in her aspect and her eyes. [*Ib.* 'She walks in Beauty']

5 A mind at peace with all below, / A heart whose love is innocent! [*Ib.*]

6 Friendship is Love without his wings! [*Hours of Idleness*, 'L'Amitié']

7 Though women are angels, yet wedlock's the devil. [*Ib.* 'To Eliza']

8 Who killed John Keats? / 'I', says the Quarterly, / So savage and Tartarly; / 'Twas one of my feats.' [*John Keats*]

9 Maid of Athens, ere we part, / Give, oh give me back my heart! [*Maid of Athens*]

10 When the moon is on the wave, / And the glow-worm in the grass, / And the meteor on the grave, / And the wisp on the morass; / When the falling stars are shooting, / And the answered owls are hooting, / And the silent leaves are still / In the shadow of the hill. [*Manfred*, I. i]

11 In truth, he was a noble steed. [*Mazeppa*, ix]

12 The Cincinnatus of the West, / Whom envy dared not hate, / Bequeathed the name of Washington, / To make man blush there was but one! [*Ode to Napoleon Buonaparte*, xix]

13 My hair is grey, but not with years, / Nor grew it white / In a single night, / As men's have grown from sudden fears. [*The Prisoner of Chillon*, i]

14 A light broke in upon my brain, – / It was the carol of a bird; / It ceased, and then it came again, / The sweetest song ear ever heard. [*Ib.* x]

15 Even I / Regained my freedom with a sigh. [*Ib.* xiv]

16 I am the very slave of circumstance / And impulse – borne away with every breath! [*Sardanapalus*, IV. i]

17 So, we'll go no more a roving / So late into the night, / Though the heart be still as loving, / And the moon be still as bright.

For the sword outwears its sheath, / And the soul wears out the breast, / And the heart must pause to breathe, / And love itself have rest.

Though the night was made for loving, / And the day returns too soon, / Yet we'll go no more a roving / By the light of the moon. [*So, we'll go no more a roving*]

18 Eternal Spirit of the chainless Mind! / Brightest in dungeons, Liberty! thou art. [*Sonnet on Chillon*]

19 Chillon! thy prison is a holy place, / And thy sad floor an altar. [*Ib.*]

20 May none these marks efface! / For they appeal from tyranny to God. [*Ib.*]

21 There be none of Beauty's daughters / With a magic like thee. [*Stanzas for Music*, 'There be none of Beauty's daughters']

22 There's not a joy the world can give like that it takes away. [*Ib.* 'There's not a joy']

23 Nor be, what man should ever be, / The friend of Beauty in distress? [*To Florence*]

24 Saint Peter sat by the celestial gate: / His keys were rusty, and the lock was dull. [*The Vision of Judgment*, i]

25 The angels all were singing out of tune, / And hoarse with having little else to do, / Excepting to wind up the sun and moon, / Or curb a runaway young star or two. [*Ib.* ii]

26 A better farmer ne'er brushed dew from lawn, / A worse king never left a realm undone! [(George III) *Ib.* viii]

27 That household virtue, most uncommon, / Of constancy to a bad, ugly woman. [*Ib.* xii]

28 But he, with first a start and then a wink, / Said, 'There's another star gone out, I think!' [*Ib.* xvi]

29 An old man / With an old soul, and both extremely blind. [*Ib.* xxiii]

30 He pattered with his keys at a great rate, / And sweated through his apostolic skin: /

Of course his perspiration was but ichor, / Or some such other spiritual liquor. [*The Vision of Judgment*, xxv]

1 By many stories, / And true, we learn the angels are all Tories. [*Ib.* xxvi]

2 Though they did not kiss, / Yet still between his Darkness and his Brightness / There passed a mutual glance of great politeness. [*Ib.* xxxv]

3 Satan met his ancient friend / With more hauteur, as might an old Castilian / Poor noble meet a mushroom rich civilian. [*Ib.* xxxvi]

4 He had written much blank verse, and blanker prose. [(Southey) *Ib.* xcviii]

5 All I saw farther, in the last confusion, / Was, that King George slipped into heaven for one; / And when the tumult dwindled to a calm, / I left him practising the hundredth psalm. [*Ib.* cvi]

6 When we two parted / In silence and tears, / Half broken-hearted / To sever for years, / Pale grew thy cheek and cold, / Colder thy kiss; / Truly that hour foretold / Sorrow to this. [*When we Two Parted*]

7 The dew of the morning / Sunk chill on my brow – / It felt like a warning / Of what I feel now. [*Ib.*]

8 If I should meet thee / After long years, / How should I greet thee? / With silence and tears. [*Ib.*]

9 By headless Charles see heartless Henry lies. [*Windsor Poetics*]

10 The Princess of Parallelograms. [Description of Annabella Milebanke to Lady Melbourne]

11 Friendship may, and often does, grow into love, but love never subsides into friendship. [Attr.]

12 I awoke one morning and found myself famous. [On instantaneous success of *Childe Harold*]

HENRY J. BYRON   1834–1884

13 I'm going to 'go it' a bit before *I* settle down. [*Our Boys*, a comedy, I]

14 Life's too short for chess. [*Ib.*]

15 He's up to these grand games, but one of these days I'll loore him on to skittles – and astonish him. [*Ib.* II]

JAMES BRANCH CABELL
1879–1958

16 I am willing to taste any drink once. [*Jurgen*, Ch. 1]

17 Why is the King of Hearts the only one that hasn't a moustache? [*The Rivet in Grandfather's Neck*]

18 The optimist proclaims that we live in the best of all possible worlds; and the pessimist fears this is so. [*The Silver Stallion*, Bk iv. Ch. 2]

AUGUSTUS CAESAR
63 B.C.–A.D. 14

19 *Quintili Vari, legiones redde.* – Quintilius Varus, give me back my legions. [Suetonius, *Divus Augustus*, 23]

20 *Ad kalendas Graecas soluturos.* – To be paid at the Greek Kalends. [*Ib.* 87]

JULIUS CAESAR   102?–44 B.C.

21 *Gallia est omnis divisa in partes tres.* – The whole of Gaul is divided into three parts. [*De Bello Gallico*, I. i]

22 *Et tu, Brute?* – You also, Brutus? [Alleged dying words, for which there is no authority]

23 *Iacta alea est.* – The die is cast. [(At the crossing of the Rubicon) Suetonius, *Divus Julius*, 32]

24 *Veni, vidi, vici.* – I came, I saw, I conquered. [*Ib.* 37. 2]

25 Caesar's wife must be above suspicion. [Traditional, based on Plutarch's *Life of Julius Caesar*, x. 6]

PEDRO CALDERÓN DE LA
BARCA   1601–1681

26 *Pues el delito mayor / del hombre es haber nacido.* – For man's greatest crime is to have been born. [*La Vida es Sueño*, I]

27 *Pues veo estando dormido / que sueñe estando despierto.* – For I see now that I am asleep that I dream when I am awake. [*Ib.* II]

28 *Que aun en sueños / no se pierde el hacer bien.* – For even in dreams a good deed is not lost. [*Ib.*]

CALIGULA 12–41

1 *Utinam populus Romanus unam cervicem haberet!* – I wish the Roman people had only one neck! [Suetonius, *Caligula*, 30]

C. S. CALVERLEY 1831–1884

2 The auld wife sat at her ivied door, / (*Butter and eggs and a pound of cheese*) / A thing she had frequently done before; / And her spectacles lay on her aproned knees. [*Ballad*]

3 And this song is considered a perfect gem, / And as to the meaning, it's what you please. [*Ib.*]

4 O Beer! O Hodgson, Guinness, Allsop, Bass! / Names that should be on every infant's tongue! [*Beer*]

5 The heart which grief hath cankered / Hath one unfailing remedy – the Tankard. [*Ib.*]

6 He that would shine, and petrify his tutor, / Should drink draught Allsop in its 'native pewter'. [*Ib.*]

7 I cannot sing the old songs now! / It is not that I deem them low; / 'Tis that I can't remember how / They go. [*Changed*]

8 I'll drink my arrowroot, and go / To bed. [*Ib.*]

9 You see this pebble-stone? It's a thing I bought / Of a bit of a chit of a boy i' the mid o' the day – / I like to dock the smaller parts-o'-speech, / As we curtail the already cur-tail'd cur. [*The Cock and the Bull*]

10 Complete with hat and gloves, / One on and one a-dangle i' my hand, / And ombrifuge (Lord love you!), case o' rain, / I flopp'd forth, 'sbuddikins! on my own ten toes. [*Ib.*]

11 The boy, a bare-legg'd beggarly son of a gun. [*Ib.*]

12 Get out, you blazing ass! / Gabble o' the goose. Don't bugaboo-baby me! [*Ib.*]

13 You observed / The dative? Pretty i' the Mantuan! [*Ib.*]

14 Might, odds-bobs, sir! in judicious hands, / Extend from here to Mesopotamy. [*Ib.*]

15 Life is with such all beer and skittles; / They are not difficult to please / About their victuals. [*Contentment*]

16 Grinder, who serenely grindest / At my door the Hundredth Psalm. [*Lines on hearing the Organ*]

17 Meaning, however, is no great matter. [*Lovers, and a Reflection*]

18 I must mention again it was gorgeous weather, / Rhymes are so scarce in this world of ours. [*Ib.*]

19 Thou who, when fears attack, / Bidst them avaunt, and Black / Care, at the horseman's back / Perching, unseatest; / Sweet, when the morn is gray; / Sweet, when they've cleared away / Lunch, and at close of day / Possibly sweetest. [*Ode to Tobacco*]

20 Manifold / Stories, I know, are told, / Not to thy credit. [*Ib.*]

21 How they who use fusees / All grow by slow degrees / Brainless as chimpanzees, / Meagre as lizards; / Go mad, and beat their wives; / Plunge (after shocking lives) / Razors and carving knives / Into their gizzards. [*Ib.*]

22 Jones – (who, I'm glad to say, / Asked leave of Mrs J. –) / Daily absorbs a clay / After his labours. [*Ib.*]

23 Cats may have had their goose / Cooked by tobacco-juice; / Still why deny its use / Thoughtfully taken? [*Ib.*]

24 Dashed the bold fork through pies of pork; / O'er hard-boiled eggs the salt-spoon shook. [*The Palace*]

25 Yet it is better to drop thy friends, O my daughter, than to drop thy 'H's'. [*Proverbial Philosophy*, 'Of Friendship']

26 Study first Propriety: for she is indeed the Pole-star. [*Ib.* 'Of Propriety']

27 Read not Milton, for he is dry; nor Shakespeare, for he wrote of common life. [*Ib.* 'Of Reading']

28 Eugene Aram, though a thief, a liar, and a murderer, / Yet, being intellectual, was amongst the noblest of mankind. [*Ib.*]

BARON DE CAMBRONNE 1770–1842

29 *Le Garde meurt, mais ne se rend pas.* – The Guards die, but do not surrender. [When called on to surrender at Waterloo. Cambronne denied having said it.]

WILLIAM CAMDEN   1551–1623

1 Betwixt the stirrup and the ground /
Mercy I asked, mercy I found. [*Epitaph
for a Man killed by falling from his Horse*]

JANE MONTGOMERY
CAMPBELL   1817–1878

2 We plough the fields, and scatter / The
good seed on the land, / But it is fed and
watered / By God's Almighty Hand.

He sends the snow in winter, / The
warmth to swell the grain, / The breezes
and the sunshine, / And soft refreshing
rain. [*Hymn*]

3 He paints the wayside flower, / He lights
the evening star. [*Ib.*]

ROY CAMPBELL   1902–1957

4 You praise the firm restraint with which
they write – / I'm with you there, of
course : / They use the snaffle and the bit
all right, / But where's the bloody horse?
[*On Some South African Novelists*]

THOMAS CAMPBELL   1777–1844

5 Of Nelson and the North / Sing the
glorious day's renown, / When to battle
fierce came forth / All the might of
Denmark's crown, / And her arms along
the deep proudly shone. [*Battle of the
Baltic*]

6 There was silence deep as death, / And
the boldest held his breath / For a time.
[*Ib.*]

7 Ye are brothers, ye are men, / And we
conquer but to save. [*Ib.*]

8 Spare, woodman, spare the beechen tree.
[*The Beech-Tree's Petition*]

9 And wherever I went was my poor dog
Tray. [*The Harper*]

10 On Linden, when the sun was low, / All
bloodless lay the untrodden snow, / And
dark as winter was the flow / Of Iser,
rolling rapidly. [*Hohenlinden*]

11 The combat deepens. On, ye brave, /
Who rush to glory, or the grave! / Wave,
Munich! all thy banners wave, / And
charge with all thy chivalry! [*Ib.*]

12 Lochiel, Lochiel! beware of the day /
When the Lowlands shall meet thee in
battle array! [*Lochiel's Warning*]

13 A chieftain to the Highlands bound /
Cries, 'Boatman, do not tarry! / And I'll
give thee a silver pound / To row us o'er
the ferry'. [*Lord Ullin's Daughter*]

14 O, I'm the chief of Ulva's isle, / And this
Lord Ullin's daughter. [*Ib.*]

15 I'll meet the raging of the skies, / But not
an angry father. [*Ib.*]

16 The waters wild went o'er his child, /
And he was left lamenting. [*Ib.*]

17 'Tis distance lends enchantment to the
view, / And robes the mountain in its
azure hue. [*Pleasures of Hope*, I. 7]

18 The proud, the cold untroubled heart of
stone, / That never mused on sorrow but
its own. [*Ib.* I. 185]

19 Hope, for a season, bade the world farewell, / And Freedom shrieked – as
Kosciusko fell! [*Ib.* I. 381]

20 And muse on Nature with a poet's eye.
[*Ib.* II. 98]

21 What though my wingèd hours of bliss
have been, / Like angel-visits, few and
far between? [*Ib.* II. 377]

22 Our bugles sang truce – for the night-
cloud had lowered, / And the sentinel
stars set their watch in the sky. [*The
Soldier's Dream*]

23 Star that bringest home the bee, / And
settest the weary labourer free! [*Song to
the Evening Star*]

24 Ye Mariners of England / That guard
our native seas, / Whose flag has braved,
a thousand years, / The battle and the
breeze. [*Ye Mariners of England*]

25 While the battle rages loud and long, /
And the stormy winds do blow. [*Ib.*]

26 Britannia needs no bulwarks, / No towers
along the steep; / Her march is o'er the
mountain waves, / Her home is on the
deep. [*Ib.*]

27 The meteor flag of England / Shall yet
terrific burn, / Till danger's troubled
night depart / And the star of peace
return. [*Ib.*]

28 Now Barabbas was a publisher. [Attr.]

THOMAS CAMPION   1567–1620

29 Follow thy fair sun, unhappy shadow.
[*Follow Thy Fair Sun*]

1 Follow your saint, follow with accents sweet; / Haste you, sad notes, fall at her flying feet. [*Follow Your Saint*]

2 Rose-cheeked Laura, come; / Sing thou smoothly with thy beauty's / Silent music, either other / Sweetly gracing. [*Laura*]

3 The man of life upright, / Whose guiltless heart is free / From all dishonest deeds / Or thought of vanity. [*The Man of Life Upright*]

4 Good thoughts his only friends, / His wealth a well-spent age, / The earth his sober inn / And quiet pilgrimage. [*Ib.*]

5 Never weather-beaten sail more willing bent to shore, / Never tired pilgrim's limbs affected slumber more. [*Never Weather-beaten Sail*]

6 The Summer hath his joys, / And Winter his delights. / Though Love and all his pleasures are but toys, / They shorten tedious nights. [*Now Winter Nights Enlarge*]

7 There is a garden in her face, / Where roses and white lilies grow; / A heavenly paradise is that place, / Wherein all pleasant fruits do flow. / There cherries grow which none may buy, / Till 'Cherry-ripe' themselves do cry. [*There is a Garden in her Face*]

8 When thou must home to shades of underground, / And there arrived, a new admired guest, / The beauteous spirits do engirt thee round, / White Iope, blithe Helen, and the rest. [*When Thou Must Home*]

GEORGE CANNING   1770–1827

9 In matters of commerce the fault of the Dutch / Is offering too little and asking too much. / The French are with equal advantage content, / So we clap on Dutch bottoms just twenty per cent. [Dispatch to Ambassador at The Hague, 31 Jan. 1826]

10 Needy Knife-grinder! whither are you going? / Rough is the road, your wheel is out of order – / Bleak blows the blast; – your hat has got a hole in't. / So have your breeches. [*The Friend of Humanity and the Knife-Grinder*]

11 Story! God bless you! I have none to tell, Sir. [*Ib.*]

12 *I* give thee sixpence! I will see thee damned first – / Wretch! whom no sense of wrongs can rouse to vengeance; / Sordid, unfeeling, reprobate, degraded, / Spiritless outcast! [*The Friend of Humanity and the Knife-Grinder*]

13 A steady patriot of the world alone, / The friend of every country but his own. [*New Morality*, 113]

14 And finds, with keen discriminating sight, / Black's not so black; – nor white so very white. [*Ib.* 199]

15 But of all plagues, good Heaven, thy wrath can send, / Save me, oh, save me, from the candid friend! [*Ib.* 209]

16 Pitt is to Addington / As London is to Paddington. [*The Oracle*]

17 Whene'er with haggard eyes I view / This Dungeon, that I'm rotting in, / I think of those Companions true / Who studied with me in the U– –NIVERSITY OF GOTTINGEN, – / –NIVERSITY OF GOTTINGEN. [*Song*]

18 Here's to the Pilot that weathered the storm. [Song for the inauguration of the Pitt Club, 1802]

19 I called the New World into existence, to redress the balance of the Old. [Speech, 12 Dec. 1826]

FRANCESCO CARACCIOLI
1752–1799

20 There are in England sixty different religious sects, but only one sauce. [Attr.]

THOMAS CAREW   1595?–1639

21 He that loves a rosy cheek, / Or a coral lip admires, / Or, from star-like eyes, doth seek / Fuel to maintain his fires; / As old Time makes these decay, / So his flames must waste away. [*Disdain Returned*]

22 Here lies a King that ruled, as he thought fit, / The universal monarchy of wit. [*Elegy on the Death of Dr Donne*]

23 Good to the poor, to kindred dear, / To servants kind, to friendship clear, / To nothing but herself severe. [Inscription on the Tomb of Lady Mary Wentworth]

24 Give me more love or more disdain; / The torrid or the frozen zone. [*Mediocrity in Love Rejected*]

97

1 Ask me no more where Jove bestows, / When June is past, the fading rose; / For in your beauty's orient deep / These flowers, as in their causes, sleep. [Song: *Ask me no more*]

2 Then fly betimes, for only they / Conquer Love that run away. [Song: *Conquest by Flight*]

HENRY CAREY   1693?–1743

3 Go call a coach, and let a coach be call'd; / And let the man who calls it be the caller; / And in his calling let him nothing call, / But Coach, Coach, Coach! O for a Coach, Ye Gods! [*Chrononhotonthologos*, II. iv]

4 Ha! Dead! Impossible! It cannot be! / I'd not believe it though himself should swear it. [*Ib.*]

5 God save our gracious king! / Long live our noble king! / God save the king! [*God save the King*]

6 Confound their politics, / Frustrate their knavish tricks. [*Ib.*]

7 Of all the girls that are so smart / There's none like pretty Sally, / She is the darling of my heart, / And she lives in our alley. [*Sally in our Alley*]

8 Of all the days that's in the week / I dearly love but one day – / And that's the day that comes betwixt / A Saturday and Monday. [*Ib.*]

JANE WELSH CARLYLE
     1801–1866

9 When one has been threatened with a great injustice, one accepts a smaller as a favour. [*Journal*, 21 Nov. 1855]

10 Some new neighbours, that came a month or two ago, brought with them an accumulation of all the things to be guarded against in a London neighbourhood, viz., a pianoforte, a lap-dog, and a parrot. [Letter to Mrs Carlyle, 6 May 1839]

THOMAS CARLYLE   1795–1881

11 A poet without love were a physical and metaphysical impossibility. [*Critical and Miscellaneous Essays*, 'Burns']

12 A witty statesman said, you might prove anything by figures. [*Critical and Miscellaneous Essays*, 'Chartism', Ch. 2]

13 In epochs when cash payment has become the sole nexus of man to man. [*Ib.* 6]

14 All reform except a moral one will prove unavailing. [*Ib.* 'Corn Law Rhymes']

15 The foul sluggard's comfort: 'It will last my time'. [*Ib.* 'Count Cagliostro. Flight Last']

16 Thou wretched fraction, wilt thou be the ninth part even of a tailor? [*Ib.* 'Doctor Francia']

17 This Mirabeau's work, then, is done. He sleeps with the primeval giants. He has gone over to the majority: *Abiit ad plures*. [*Ib.* 'Mirabeau']

18 History is the essence of innumerable biographies. [*Ib.* 'On History']

19 A well-written Life is almost as rare as a well-spent one. [*Ib.* 'Richter']

20 Poetry and Religion (and it is really worth knowing) are 'a product of the smaller intestines'. [*Ib.* 'Signs of the Times']

21 Silence is deep as Eternity; speech is shallow as Time. [*Ib.* 'Sir Walter Scott']

22 To the very last, he [Napoleon] had a kind of idea; that, namely, of *La carrière ouverte aux talents*, The tools to him that can handle them. [*Ib.*]

23 The three great elements of modern civilization, Gunpowder, Printing, and the Protestant Religion. [*Ib.* 'The State of German Literature']

24 Literary men are ... a perpetual priesthood. [*Ib.*]

25 Genius (which means transcendent capacity of taking trouble, first of all). [*Frederick the Great*, Bk iv. Ch. 3]

26 Happy the people whose annals are blank in history books! [*Ib.* xvi. 1]

27 France was long a despotism tempered by epigrams. [*French Revolution*, Pt I. Bk i. Ch. 1]

28 To a shower of gold most things are penetrable. [*Ib.* I. iii. 7]

29 A whiff of grapeshot. [*Ib.* I. v. 3]

30 The gospel according to Jean Jacques. [(Rousseau) *Ib.* II. i. 6]

31 The seagreen Incorruptible. [(Robespierre) *Ib.* II. iv. 4]

1 Worship is transcendent wonder. [*Heroes and Hero-Worship*, i, 'The Hero as Divinity']

2 No great man lives in vain. The history of the world is but the biography of great men. [*Ib.*]

3 The true University of these days is a collection of books. [*Ib.* v, 'The Hero as Man of Letters']

4 Burke said that there were Three Estates in Parliament; but, in the Reporters' Gallery yonder, there sat a *Fourth Estate*, more important far than they all. [*Ib.*]

5 For one man that can stand prosperity, there are a hundred that will stand adversity. [*Ib.*]

6 Respectable Professors of the Dismal Science. [(Political Economy) *Latter Day Pamphlets*, 1, 'The Present Time']

7 A Parliament speaking through reporters to Buncombe and the twenty-seven millions mostly fools. [*Ib.* 6, 'Parliaments']

8 A healthy hatred of scoundrels. [*Ib.* 12]

9 Transcendental moonshine. [*Life of John Sterling*, Pt i. Ch. 15]

10 Brothers, I am sorry I have got no Morrison's Pill for curing the maladies of Society. [*Past and Present*, Bk i. Ch. 4]

11 Blessed is he who has found his work; let him ask no other blessedness. [*Ib.* iii. 11]

12 Captains of Industry. [*Ib.* iv. 4, title]

13 Work is the grand cure of all the maladies and miseries that ever beset mankind. [Rectorial Address at Edinburgh, 2 Apr. 1886]

14 I never heard tell of any clever man that came of entirely stupid people. [*Ib.*]

15 No man who has once heartily and wholly laughed can be altogether irreclaimably bad. [*Sartor Resartus*, Bk i. Ch. 4]

16 Man is a tool-using animal. . . . Without tools he is nothing, with tools he is all. [*Ib.* i. 5]

17 Be not the slave of Words. [*Ib.* i. 8]

18 Lives there the man that can figure a naked Duke of Windlestraw addressing a naked House of Lords? [*Ib.* i. 9]

19 Sarcasm I now see to be, in general, the language of the devil. [*Sartor Resartus*, ii. 4]

20 The everlasting No. [*Ib.* ii. 7, title]

21 The everlasting Yea. [*Ib.* ii. 9, title]

22 Man's unhappiness, as I construe, comes of his greatness; it is because there is an Infinite in him, which with all his cunning he cannot quite bury under the Finite. [*Ib.*]

23 Close thy Byron; open thy Goethe. [*Ib.*]

24 'Do the duty that lies nearest thee', which thou knowest to be a duty! Thy second duty will already have become clearer. [*Ib.*]

25 Produce! Produce! Were it but the pitifullest infinitesimal fraction of a product, produce it in God's name! 'Tis the utmost thou hast in thee: out with it, then. [*Ib.*]

26 The Public is an old woman. Let her maunder and mumble. [*Journal*, 1835]

27 The crash of the whole solar and stellar systems could only kill you once. [Letter to John Carlyle, 1831]

28 It were better to perish than to continue schoolmastering. [Remark, quoted in D. A. Wilson's *Carlyle till Marriage*]

29 If Jesus Christ were to come to-day, people wouldn't even crucify him. They would ask him to dinner, and hear what he had to say, and make fun of it. [Remark, quoted in D. A. Wilson's *Carlyle at his Zenith*]

30 I don't pretend to understand the Universe – it's a great deal bigger than I am. . . . People ought to be modester. [Remark to Wm Allingham, quoted in D. A. Wilson's and D. Wilson McArthur's *Carlyle in Old Age*]

31 Macaulay is well for a while, but one wouldn't *live* under Niagara. [Remark, quoted in R. M. Milnes's *Notebook*]

32 There is only one post fit for you, and that is the office of perpetual president of the Heaven and Hell Amalgamation Society. [Remark to Lord Houghton, quoted in T. E. Wemyss Reid's *Life of Lord Houghton*]

33 Thirty millions, mostly fools. [(When asked the population of England) Attr.]

34 MARGARET FULLER: I accept the universe. CARLYLE: Gad! she'd better! [Attr.]

DALE CARNEGIE   1888–1955

1 How to Win Friends and Influence People. [Title of book]

JULIA CARNEY   1823–1908

2 Little drops of water, little grains of sand, / Make the mighty ocean, and the pleasant land. / So the little minutes, humble though they be, / Make the mighty ages of eternity. [*Little Things.* Wrongly attr. to various other writers]

3 Little deeds of kindness, little words of love, / Help to make earth happy, like the heaven above. / [(Later reading of second line: 'Make this earth an Eden') *Ib.*]

J. E. CARPENTER   1813–1885

4 What are the wild waves saying / Sister, the whole day long. / That ever amid our playing, / I hear but their low lone song? [*What are the Wild Waves Saying?*]

LEWIS CARROLL [CHARLES DODGSON]   1832–1898

5 'What is the use of a book,' thought Alice, 'without pictures or conversations?' [*Alice in Wonderland*, Ch. 1]

6 Do cats eat bats?–Do bats eat cats? [*Ib.*]

7 Curiouser and curiouser! [*Ib.* 2]

8 How doth the little crocodile / Improve his shining tail, / And pour the waters of the Nile, / On every golden scale! [*Ib.*]

9 'I'll be judge, I'll be jury,' said cunning old Fury: / 'I'll try the whole cause, and condemn you to death.' [*Ib.* 3]

10 The Duchess! The Duchess! Oh my dear paws! Oh my fur and whiskers! [*Ib.* 4]

11 'You are old, Father William,' the young man said, / 'And your hair has become very white; / And yet you incessantly stand on your head – / Do you think, at your age, it is right?'

'In my youth,' Father William replied to his son, / 'I feared it might injure the brain; / But now that I'm perfectly sure I have none, / Why, I do it again and again.' [*Ib.* 5]

12 Do you think I can listen all day to such stuff? / Be off, or I'll kick you downstairs! [*Alice in Wonderland*, 5]

13 'If everybody minded their own business,' the Duchess said in a hoarse growl, 'the world would go round a deal faster than it does.' [*Ib.* 6]

14 Speak roughly to your little boy, / And beat him when he sneezes: / He only does it to annoy, / Because he knows it teases. [*Ib.*]

15 It [the Cheshire Cat] vanished quite slowly, beginning with the end of the tail, and ending with the grin, which remained some time after the rest of it had gone. [*Ib.*]

16 'Then you should say what you mean,' the March Hare went on.
'I do,' Alice hastily replied; 'at least – at least I mean what I say – that's the same thing, you know.' [*Ib.* 7]

17 It was the *best* butter. [*Ib.*]

18 Twinkle, twinkle, little bat! / How I wonder what you're at! / Up above the world you fly, / Like a tea-tray in the sky. [*Ib.*]

19 They lived at the bottom of a well – ... They lived on treacle. [*Ib.*]

20 Off with her head! [*Ib.* 8]

21 Everything's got a moral, if only you can find it. [*Ib.* 9]

22 Take care of the sense, and the sounds will take care of themselves. [*Ib.*]

23 That's nothing to what I could say if I chose. [*Ib.*]

24 We called him Tortoise because he taught us. [*Ib.*]

25 'Reeling and Writhing, of course, to begin with,' the Mock Turtle replied; 'and then the different branches of Arithmetic – Ambition, Distraction, Uglification, and Derision.' [*Ib.*]

26 *He* taught us Drawling, Stretching and Fainting in Coils. [*Ib.*]

27 'That's the reason they're called lessons,' the Gryphon remarked: 'because they lessen from day to day.' [*Ib.*]

28 'Will you walk a little faster?' said a whiting to a snail, / 'There's a porpoise close behind us, and he's treading on my tail.' [*Ib.* 10]

1 Will you, won't you, will you, won't you, will you join the dance? [*Alice in Wonderland*, 10]

2 The further off from England, the nearer is to France – / Then turn not pale, beloved snail, but come and join the dance. [*Ib.*]

3 Soup of the evening, beautiful Soup! [*Ib.*]

4 'Begin at the beginning,' the King said, gravely, 'and go on till you come to the end; then stop.' [*Ib.* 12]

5 They told me you had been to her, / And mentioned me to him: / She gave me a good character, / But said I could not swim. [*Ib.*]

6 Sentence first – verdict afterwards. [*Ib.*]

7 'Twas brillig, and the slithy toves / Did gyre and gimble in the wabe; / All mimsy were the borogoves, / And the mome raths outgrabe. [*Through the Looking Glass*, Ch. 1]

8 Beware the Jabberwock, my son! / The jaws that bite, the claws that catch! / Beware the Jubjub bird, and shun / The frumious Bandersnatch! [*Ib.*]

9 One, two! One, two! and through and through / The vorpal blade went snickersnack! / He left it dead, and with its head / He went galumphing back. [*Ib.*]

10 'And hast thou slain the Jabberwock? / Come to my arms, my beamish boy! / O frabjous day! Callooh! Callay!' / He chortled in his joy. [*Ib.*]

11 Curtsey while you're thinking what to say. It saves time. [*Ib.* 2]

12 Now, *here*, you see, it takes all the running *you* can do, to stay in the same place. If you want to get somewhere else, you must run at least twice as fast as that! [*Ib.*]

13 'If you think we're wax-works,' he said, 'you ought to pay, you know. Wax-works weren't made to be looked at for nothing. Nohow!' [*Ib.* 4]

14 Tweedledum and Tweedledee / Agreed to have a battle; / For Tweedledum said Tweedledee / Had spoiled his nice new rattle. [*Ib.*]

15 'Contrariwise,' continued Tweedledee, 'if it was so, it might be; and if it were so, it would be: but as it isn't, it ain't. That's logic.' [*Ib.*]

16 The sun was shining on the sea, / Shining with all his might: / He did his very best to make / The billows smooth and

bright – / And this was odd because it was / The middle of the night. [*Through the Looking Glass*, 4]

17 'It's very rude of him,' she said, / 'To come and spoil the fun!' [*Ib.*]

18 You could not see a cloud, because / No cloud was in the sky: / No birds were flying overhead – / There were no birds to fly. [*Ib.*]

19 The Walrus and the Carpenter / Were walking close at hand; / They wept like anything to see / Such quantities of sand: / 'If this were only cleared away,' / They said, 'it *would* be grand!'

'If seven maids with seven mops / Swept it for half a year, / Do you suppose,' the Walrus said, / 'That they could get it clear?' / 'I doubt it,' said the Carpenter, / And shed a bitter tear. [*Ib.*]

20 And thick and fast they came at last, / And more, and more, and more. [*Ib.*]

21 'The time has come,' the Walrus said, / 'To talk of many things: / Of shoes – and ships – and sealing-wax – / Of cabbages – and kings – / Of why the sea is boiling hot – / And whether pigs have wings.' [*Ib.*]

22 'The night is fine,' the Walrus said. / 'Do you admire the view?' [*Ib.*]

23 The Carpenter said nothing but, / 'The butter's spread too thick!' [*Ib.*]

24 'I weep for you,' the Walrus said: / 'I deeply sympathize.' / With sobs and tears he sorted out / Those of the largest size, / Holding his pocket-handkerchief / Before his streaming eyes. [*Ib.*]

25 But answer came there none – / And this was scarcely odd because / They'd eaten every one. [*Ib.*]

26 The rule is, jam to-morrow and jam yesterday – but never jam to-day. [*Ib.* 5]

27 They gave it me ... for an un-birthday present. [*Ib.* 6]

28 The little fishes of the sea, / They sent an answer back to me. / The little fishes' answer was / 'We cannot do it, Sir, because –' [*Ib.*]

29 I said it very loud and clear; / I went and shouted in his ear. [*Ib.*]

30 He's an Anglo-Saxon Messenger – and those are Anglo-Saxon attitudes. [*Ib.* 7]

31 The other Messenger's called Hatta. I must have *two*, you know – to come and go. One to come, and one to go. [*Ib.*]

1 It's as large as life, and twice as natural!
[*Through the Looking Glass*, 7]

2 It's my own invention. [*Ib.* 8]

3 But I was thinking of a plan / To dye one's
whiskers green. [*Ib.*]

4 Or madly squeeze a right-hand foot /
Into a left-hand shoe. [*Ib.*]

5 No admittance till the week after next.
[*Ib.* 9]

6 What I tell you three times is true.
[*Hunting of the Snark*, Fit 1]

7 He would answer to 'Hi!' or to any loud
cry, / Such as 'Fry me!' or 'Fritter my
wig!' / To 'What-you-may-call-um!' or
'What-was-his-name!' / But especially
'Thing-um-a-jig!' [*Ib.*]

8 His intimate friends called him 'Candle-
ends', / And his enemies 'Toasted-
cheese'. [*Ib.*]

9 Then the bowsprit got mixed with the
rudder sometimes. [*Ib.* 2]

10 You may seek it with thimbles – and seek
it with care; / You may hunt it with forks
and hope; / You may threaten its life
with a railway-share; / You may charm
it with smiles and soap. [*Ib.* 3]

11 I said it in Hebrew – I said it in Dutch – /
I said it in German and Greek; / But I
wholly forgot (and it vexes me much) /
That English is what you speak! [*Ib.* 4]

12 In the midst of the word he was trying to
say / In the midst of his laughter and
glee, / He had softly and suddenly
vanished away – / For the Snark *was* a
Boojum, you see. [*Ib.* 8]

13 He thought he saw an Elephant, / That
practised on a fife: / He looked again,
and found it was / A letter from his wife.
/ 'At length I realize,' he said, / 'The
bitterness of life!' [*Sylvie and Bruno*,
Ch. 5]

14 He thought he saw a Banker's Clerk /
Descending from the 'bus: / He looked
again, and found it was / A Hippopotamus. / 'If this should stay to dine,' he said,
/ 'There won't be much for us!' [*Ib.* 7]

WILLIAM LORENZO CARTER
1813–1860

15 'O daughter, dear,' her mother said, 'this
blanket round you fold, / 'Tis such a
dreadful night abroad, you will catch
your death of cold.' [*Young* (or *Fair*)
Charlotte]

16 Young ladies, think of this fair girl and
always dress aright, / And never venture
thinly clad on such a wintry night. [*Ib.*]

PHOEBE CARY   1824–1871

17 And though hard be the task, / 'Keep a
stiff upper lip'. [*Keep a Stiff Upper Lip*]

PHILA HENRIETTA CASE
fl. 1864

18 Oh! why does the wind blow upon me so
wild? – Is it because I'm nobody's child?
[*Nobody's Child*]

HARRY CASTLING   19 Cent.

19 Let's all go down the Strand. [Title of
song]

20 What-Ho! She bumps! [Title of song]

EDWARD CASWALL   1814–1878

21 Days and moments quickly flying, /
Blend the living with the dead; / Soon
will you and I be lying / Each within our
narrow bed. [Hymn]

22 My God, I love Thee; not because / I
hope for heaven thereby. [Hymn]

23 Sleep, Holy Babe, / Upon thy mother's
breast! [Hymn]

CATO, THE ELDER   234–149 B.C.

24 *Delenda est Carthago.* – Carthage must
be destroyed. [Plutarch, *Life of Cato*]

CATULLUS   87–54? B.C.

25 *Lugete, o Veneres Cupidinesque, / Et
quantum est hominum venustiorum. /
Passer mortuus est meae puellae, / Passer
deliciae meae puellae, / Quem plus illa
oculis suis amabat.* – Mourn, O Graces
and Loves, and all men whom the Graces
love. My mistress's sparrow is dead, my
mistress's pet which she loved more than
her very eyes. [*Carmina*, iii]

1 *Qui nunc it per iter tenebricosum* / *Illuc,*
unde negant redire quemquam. – Now he is
treading that dark road to the place from
which they say no one has ever returned.
[*Carmina*, iii]

2 *Vivamus, mea Lesbia, atque amemus,* /
Rumoresque senum severiorum / *Omnes*
unius aestimemus assis. / *Soles occidere*
et redire possunt: / *Nobis cum semel*
occidit brevis lux, / *Nox est perpetua una*
dormienda. – Let us live, my Lesbia, and
love, and not give a farthing for the talk
of censorious old men. Suns may set and
rise again. As for us, when the brief light
has once set, we must sleep one endless
night. [*Ib.* v]

3 *Da mi basia mille, deinde centum,* / *Dein*
mille altera. – Give me a thousand kisses,
then a hundred, then a thousand more.
[*Ib.*]

4 *Miser Catulle, desinas ineptire,* / *Et quot*
vides perisse perditum ducas. – Poor
Catullus, cease your folly and give up for
lost what you see is lost. [*Ib.* viii]

5 *Nam castum esse decet pium poetam* /
Ipsum, versiculos nihil necesse est. – For
the godly poet must be chaste himself,
but there is no need for his verses to be
so. [*Ib.* xvi]

6 *Paene insularum, Sirmio, insularumque*
ocelle. – Sirmio, little eye of peninsulas
and islands. [*Ib.* xxxi]

7 *O quid solutis est beatius curis?* / *Cum*
mens onus reponit, ac peregrino / *Labore*
fessi venimus larem ad nostrum, / *Desi-*
deratoque acquiescimus lecto. / *Hoc est,*
quod unum est pro laboribus tantis. – O what
is more blessed than to throw cares aside,
as the mind puts down its burden and,
weary with the labour of far journeys, we
return home and rest on the couch that
we longed for? This alone is worth all
that labour. [*Ib.*]

8 *Nam risu inepto res ineptior nulla est.* –
There is nothing sillier than a silly laugh.
[*Ib.* xxxix]

9 *Iam ver egelidos refert tepores,* / *Iam*
caeli furor aequinoctialis / *Iucundis*
Zephyri silescit auris. – Now Spring
restores the balmy heat, now Zephyr's
sweet breezes calm the rage of the
equinoctial sky. [*Ib.* xlvi]

10 *Gratias tibi maximas Catullus* / *Agit*
pessimus omnium poeta / *Tanto pessimus*
omnium poeta / *Quanto tu optimus*
omnium's patronum. – Catullus, the
worst of all poets, gives you his warmest
thanks; he being as much the worst of
all poets as you are the best of all
patrons. [*Carmina*, xlix]

11 *Vesper adest, iuvenes, consurgite: Vesper*
Olympo / *Exspectata diu vix tandem*
lumina tollit. – Rise up, lads, the evening
is coming. The evening star is just raising
his long-awaited light in heaven. [*Ib.* lxii]

12 *Ut flos in saeptis secretus nascitur hortis,* /
Ignotus pecori, nullo contusus aratro, /
Quem mulcent aurae, firmat sol, educat
imber; / *Multi illum pueri, multae opta-*
vere puellae. – As a flower springs up
secretly in a fenced garden, known to no
cattle, bruised by no plough, caressed by
the winds, strengthened by the sun, and
drawn up by the shower, so many a boy
and many a girl desire it. [*Ib.*]

13 *Sed mulier cupido quod dicit amanti* / *In*
vento et rapida scribere oportet aqua. –
But what a woman says to her desirous
lover should be written in wind and swift-
flowing water. [*Ib.* lxx]

14 *Siqua recordanti benefacta priora voluptas*
/ *Est homini.* – If a man can take pleasure
in recalling the kindnesses he has done.
[*Ib.* lxxvi]

15 *Difficile est longum subito deponere*
amorem. / *Difficile est, verum hoc qua*
lubet efficias. – It is difficult suddenly to
put aside a long-standing love; it is
difficult, but somehow you must do it.
[*Ib.*]

16 *O di, reddite mi hoc pro pietate mea.* – O
gods, grant me this in return for my piety.
[*Ib.*]

17 *Odi et amo: quare id faciam, fortasse*
requiris, / *Nescio, sed fieri sentio et*
excrucior. – I hate and love. You may
ask why I do so. I do not know, but I feel
it and am in torment. [*Ib.* lxxxv]

18 *Nunc tamen interea haec prisco quae more*
parentum / *Tradita sunt tristi munere ad*
inferias, / *Accipe fraterno multum man-*
antia fletu. / *Atque in perpetuum, frater,*
ave atque vale. – But now meanwhile take
these offerings, according to the old
custom of our fathers, the tribute of
sorrow, for a funeral sacrifice. Take them,
wet with many a tear of your brother's.
And for ever, Brother, hail and farewell.
[*Ib.* ci]

EDITH CAVELL   1865–1915

1 I realize that patriotism is not enough. I must have no hatred or bitterness towards anyone. [Last words, 12 Oct. 1915]

MADISON JULIUS CAWEIN
1865–1914

2 An old Spanish saying is that 'a kiss without a moustache is like an egg without salt'. [Nature-Notes]

THOMAS OF CELANO   c. 1250

3 Dies irae, dies illa / Solvet saeclum in favilla, / Teste David cum Sibylla. – Day of wrath and doom impending, / David's word with Sibyl's blending, / Heaven and earth in ashes ending. [Analecta Hymnica (transl. Dr W. J. Irons in The English Hymnal)]

SUSANNAH CENTLIVRE
1667?–1723

4 The real Simon Pure. [A Bold Stroke for a Wife, V. i]

MIGUEL CERVANTES 1547–1616

5 I swear by all the orders of chivalry in the world to pay you every single real, and perfumed into the bargain. [Don Quixote, Pt I. Ch. 4]

6 I know who I am, and I know too that I am capable of being not only the characters I have named, but all the Twelve Peers of France, and all the Nine Worthies as well. [Ib. I. 5]

7 Wouldn't it be better to stay peacefully at home, and not roam about the world seeking better bread than is made of wheat, never considering that many go for wool and come back shorn? [Ib. I. 7]

8 Take care, your worship, those things over there are not giants but windmills. [Ib. I. 8]

9 I hate to keep things long in case they go mouldy from over-keeping. [Ib. I. 17]

10 Didn't I tell you, Don Quixote, sir, to turn back, for they were not armies you were going to attack, but flocks of sheep? [Ib. I. 18]

11 Wasn't it my father's son who got tossed in the blanket yesterday? [Don Quixote, I. 18]

12 The Knight of the Sad Countenance. [Ib. I. 19]

13 Fear has many eyes and can see things underground. [Ib. I. 20]

14 A leap over the hedge is better than good men's prayers. [Ib. I. 21]

15 I have always heard, Sancho, that doing good to base fellows is like throwing water into the sea. [Ib. I. 23]

16 Let them eat the lie and swallow it with their bread. Whether the two were lovers or no, they'll have accounted to God for it by now. I have my own fish to fry. I know nothing. I'm not one to pry into other people's lives. It's no good lying about the price; your purse always knows better. What's more, I was born naked and naked I am now: I neither lose nor win. Suppose they were lovers, what's that to me? Plenty of people expect to find bacon where there's not so much as a hook to hang it on. Who can hedge in the cuckoo? [Ib. I. 25]

17 A knight errant who turns mad for a reason deserves neither merit nor thanks. The thing is to do it without cause. [Ib.]

18 One shouldn't talk of halters in the hanged man's house. [Ib.]

19 She isn't a bad bit of goods, the Queen! I wish all the fleas in my bed were as good. [Ib. I. 30]

20 In me the need to talk is a primary impulse, and I can't help saying right off what comes to my tongue. [Ib.]

21 If you don't believe me, you'll see it when the eggs are fried [Ib. I. 37]

22 Oh, sir, sir, there are more tricks done in the village than make a noise – saving her ladyship's presence. [Ib. I. 46]

23 Every man's the son of his own deeds; and since I am a man I can become pope. [Ib. I. 47]

24 Have you no mind to do what nobody can do for you? [Ib. I. 48]

25 I've as large a soul as the next man, and as stout a body as the best of them, and I'd be as good a king of my estate as any other King. [Ib. I. 50]

26 The sage left nothing in his ink-horn. [Ib. II. 3]

1 Without a governorship you came out of your mother's womb, without a governorship you've lived to this day, and without a governorship you'll go – or they'll take you – to the grave. [*Don Quixote*, II. 5]

2 Hunger is the best sauce in the world. [*Ib.*]

3 An honest woman and a broken leg are best at home, and for an honest girl a job of work's her holiday. [*Ib.*]

4 We cannot all be friars, and many are the ways by which God bears his chosen to heaven. [*Ib.* II. 8]

5 Well, now, there's a remedy for everything except death. [*Ib.* II. 10]

6 Never meddle with play-actors, for they're a favoured race. [*Ib.* II. 11]

7 All the physicians and authors in the world could not give a clear account of his madness. He is mad in patches, full of lucid intervals. [*Ib.* II. 18]

8 There are only two families in the world, my old grandmother used to say, the *Haves* and the *Have-nots*. [*Ib.* II. 20]

9 If that should not be, cousin, I say: patience and shuffle the cards. [*Ib.* II. 23]

10 'If I had a water thirst', replied Sancho, 'there are wells on the road where I could have quenched it.' [*Ib.* II. 24]

11 God bless the inventor of sleep, the cloak that covers all men's thoughts, the food that cures all hunger . . . the balancing weight that levels the shepherd with the king and the simple with the wise. [*Ib.* II. 68]

JOSEPH CHAMBERLAIN
1836–1914

12 Provided that the City of London remains as it is at present, the clearing-house of the world. [Speech in London, 19 Jan. 1904]

13 Learn to think Imperially. [*Ib.*]

14 The day of small nations has long passed away. The day of Empires has come. [Speech at Birmingham, 12 May 1904]

NEVILLE CHAMBERLAIN
1869–1940

15 In war, whichever side may call itself the victor, there are no winners, but all are losers. [Speech at Kettering, 3 July 1938]

16 I believe it is peace for our time . . . peace with honour. [Wireless speech after Munich Agreement, 1 Oct. 1938]

17 Hitler has missed the bus. [Public speech in anticipation of German landing in Norway]

CHARLES HADDON CHAMBERS
1860–1921

18 The long arm of coincidence. [*Captain Swift*, II]

NICOLAS CHAMFORT 1741–1794

19 *Quelqu'un disait d'un homme très personnel: il brûlerait votre maison pour se faire cuire deux œufs.* – Someone said of a very great egotist: 'He would burn your house down to cook himself a couple of eggs.' [*Caractères et anecdotes*]

20 *La plus perdue de toutes les journées est celle où l'on n'a pas ri.* – The most wasted of all days is that on which one has not laughed. [*Maximes et pensées*]

21 *L'amour, tel qu'il existe dans la société, n'est que l'échange de deux fantaisies et le contact de deux épidermes.* – Love, in present-day society, is just the exchange of two imaginary pictures, and the contact of one epidermis with another. [*Ib.*]

JOHN CHANDLER
1806–1876

22 Conquering kings their titles take / From the foes they captive make: / Jesu, by a nobler deed, / From the thousands He hath freed. [Hymn]

GEORGE CHAPMAN 1559?–1634

23 An Englishman, / Being flattered, is a lamb; threatened, a lion. [*Alphonsus*, I. ii]

24 Give me a spirit that on this life's rough sea / Loves t'have his sails filled with a lusty wind, / Even till his sail-yards tremble, his masts crack, / And his rapt ship run on her side so low / That she drinks water, and her keel ploughs air. [*Byron's Conspiracy*, III. i]

1 We have watered our horses in Helicon. [*May-Day*, III. iii]

2 His naked Ulysses clad in eternal fiction. [*Odysseys of Homer*, Epistle Dedicatory]

3 And let a scholar all Earth's volumes carry, / He will be but a walking dictionary. [*Tears of Peace*, 266]

CHARLES I   1600–1649

4 Never make a defence of apology before you be accused. [Letter to Lord Wentworth, 3 Sept. 1636]

5 And therefore I tell you (and I pray God it be not laid to your charge) that I am the Martyr of the People. [Speech on the scaffold]

CHARLES II   1630–1685

6 Better than a play! [On the Lords' debate on Lord Ross's Divorce Bill, 1670]

7 This is very true: for my words are my own, and my actions are my ministers'. [Reply to Lord Rochester's premature epitaph on him, q.v.]

8 Not a religion for gentlemen. [(Presbyterianism) Burnet, *History of My Own Times*, Vol. I. Bk ii. Ch. 2]

9 Let not poor Nelly starve. [(Of Nell Gwynn, on his deathbed) *Ib.* I. ii. 17]

10 Brother, I am too old to go again to my travels. [Hume, *History of Great Britain*, Vol. ii. Ch. 7]

11 He had been, he said, an unconscionable time dying; but he hoped that they would excuse it. [Macaulay, *History of England*, Vol. i. Ch. 4]

EMPEROR CHARLES V   1500–1558

12 I speak Spanish to God, Italian to women, French to men, and German to my horse. [Attr.]

SALMON PORTLAND CHASE   1808–1873

13 The only way to resumption is to resume. [Letter to Horace Greely, 1866]

FRANÇOIS-RENÉ DE CHATEAUBRIAND   1768–1848

14 An original writer is not one who imitates nobody, but one whom nobody can imitate. [*Génie du Christianisme*]

EARL OF CHATHAM *see under* PITT, WILLIAM

THOMAS CHATTERTON   1752–1770

15 O! synge untoe mie roundelaie, / O! droppe the brynie teare wythe mee, / Daunce ne moe atte hallie daie, / Lycke a reynynge ryver bee; / Mie love ys dedde, / Gon to hys death-bedde, / Al under the wyllowe-tree [*Mynstrelles Songe*]

GEOFFREY CHAUCER   1340?–1400

16 Flee fro the prees, and dwelle with sothfastnesse ... / Forth, pilgrim, forth! Forth, beste, out of thy stal! / Know thy contree, look up, thank God of al! / Hold the hye wey, and lat thy gost thee lede; / And trouthe shal delivere, hit is no drede. [*Balade de Bon Conseyl*]

17 Whan that Aprille with his shoures sote / The droghte of Marche hath perced to the rote. [*Canterbury Tales*, 'Prologue', 1]

18 And smale fowles maken melodye, / That slepen al the night with open yë / (So priketh hem nature in hir corages): / Than longen folk to goon on pilgrimages. [*Ib.* 9]

19 And of his port as meke as is a mayde. [*Ib.* 69]

20 He was a verray parfit gentil knight. [*Ib.* 72]

21 He was as fresh as is the month of May. [*Ib.* 92]

22 Ful wel she song the service divyne, / Entuned in hir nose ful semely; / And Frensh she spak ful faire and fetisly, / After the scole of Stratford atte Bowe, / For Frensh of Paris was to hir unknowe. [*Ib.* 122]

23 Ther was first write a crowned A, / And after, '*Amor vincit omnia*'. [*Ib.* 161]

1 He yaf not of that text a pulled hen, / That seith, that hunters been nat holy men. [*Canterbury Tales*, 'Prologue', 177]

2 His palfrey was as broun as is a berye. [*Ib*. 207]

3 He knew the tavernes wel in every toun. [*Ib*. 240]

4 A Clerk ther was of Oxenford also. [*Ib*. 285]

5 As lene was his hors as is a rake. [*Ib*. 287]

6 For him was lever have at his beddes heed / Twenty bokes, clad in blak or reed, / Of Aristotle and his philosophye, / Than robes riche, or fithele, or gay sautrye. / But al be that he was a philosophre, / Yet hadde he but litel gold in cofre. [*Ib*. 293]

7 And gladly wolde he lerne, and gladly teche. [*Ib*. 308]

8 No-wher so bisy a man as he ther nas, / And yet he semed bisier than he was. [*Ib*. 321]

9 It snewed in his hous of mete and drinke. [*Ib*. 345]

10 And, certeinly, he was a good felawe. [*Ib*. 395]

11 His studie was but litel on the bible. [*Ib*. 438]

12 She was a worthy womman al hir lyve, / Housbondes at chirche-dore she hadde fyve, / Withouten other companye in youthe. [*Ib*. 459]

13 This noble ensample to his sheep he yaf, / That first he wroghte, and afterward he taughte. [*Ib*. 496]

14 If gold ruste, what shal iren do? [*Ib*. 500]

15 But Cristes lore, and his apostles twelve, / He taughte, and first he folwed it himselve. [*Ib*. 527]

16 That hadde a fyr-reed cherubinnes face. [*Ib*. 624]

17 His walet lay biforn him in his lappe, / Bret-ful of pardoun come from Rome al hoot. [*Ib*. 686]

18 Love wol nat ben constreyned by maistrye; / Whan maistrie comth, the god of love anon / Beteth hise winges, and farewel! he is gon! [*Ib*. 'The Frankeleyns Tale', 36]

19 Trouthe is the hyeste thing that man may kepe. [*Ib*. 751]

20 The carl spak oo thing, but he thoghte another. [*Canterbury Tales*, 'The Freres Tale', 270]

21 And therfore, at the kinges court, my brother, / Ech man for him-self, ther is non other. [*Ib*. 'The Knightes Tale', 323]

22 The bisy larke, messager of day. [*Ib*. 633]

23 The smyler with the knyf under the cloke. [*Ib*. 1141]

24 Up roos the sonne, and up roos Emelye. [*Ib*. 1415]

25 What is this world? what asketh men to have? / Now with his love, now in his colde grave, / Allone, with-outen any companye. [*Ib*. 1919]

26 This world nis but a thurghfare ful of wo, / And we ben pilgrimes, passinge to and fro; / Deeth is an ende of every worldly sore. [*Ib*. 1989]

27 'Tehee!' quod she, and clapte the window to. [*Ib*. 'The Miller's Tale', 554]

28 Tragedie is to seyn a certeyn storie, / As olde bokes maken us memorie, / Of him that stood in greet prosperitee / And is y-fallen out of heigh degree / Into miserie, and endeth wrecchedly. [*Ib*. 'The Monk's Prologue', 85]

29 Mordre wol out, that see we day by day. [*Ib*. 'The Nonne Preestes Tale', 232]

30 For dronkenesse is verray sepulture / Of mannes wit and his discrecioun. [*Ib*. 'The Pardoner's Tale', 230]

31 She was as digne as water in a dich. [*Ib*. 'The Reve's Tale', 44]

32 The gretteste clerkes been noght the wysest men. [*Ib*. 134]

33 So was hir joly whistle wel y-wet. [*Ib*. 235]

34 Thou lokest as thou woldest finde an hare, / For ever up-on the ground I see thee stare. [*Ib*. 'Prologue to Sir Thopas', 6]

35 That in his owene grece I made him frye. [*Ib*. 'The Prologue of the Wyves Tale of Bathe', 487]

36 And for to see, and eke for to be seye. [*Ib*. 552]

37 A womman cast hir shame away, / Whan she cast of hir smok. [*Ib*. 782]

38 As thikke as motes in the sonne-beem. [*Ib*. 'The Tale of the Wyf of Bathe', 12]

1 Wommen desyren to have sovereyntee /
As wel over hir housbond as hir love.
[*Canterbury Tales*, 'The Tale of the Wyf
of Bathe', 182]

2 Whan that the month of May / Is comen,
and that I here the foules singe, / And
that the floures ginnen for to springe, /
Farwel my book and my devocioun!
[*The Legend of Good Women*, Prologue, 36
(2nd version)]

3 Of alle the floures in the mede, / Than
love I most these floures whyte and rede, /
Swiche as men callen daysies in our toun.
[*Ib.* 41]

4 And she was fair as is the rose in May.
[*Ib.* 'Legend of Cleopatra', 34]

5 The lyf so short, the craft so long to
lerne, / Th' assay so hard, so sharp the
conquering. [*The Parlement of Foules*, 1]

6 Unknowe, unkist, and lost that is unsought. [*Troilus and Criseyde*, i. 809]

7 For I have seyn, of a ful misty morwe /
Folwen ful ofte a mery someres day. [*Ib.*
iii. 1060]

8 Right as an aspes leef she gan to quake.
[*Ib.* iii. 1200]

9 For of fortunes sharp adversitee / The
worst kinde of infortune is this, / A man
to have ben in prosperitee, / And it
remembren, whan it passed is. [*Ib.* iii.
1625]

10 Oon ere it herde, at the other out it
wente. [*Ib.* iv. 434]

11 Paradys stood formed in hir yën. [*Ib.* v.
817]

12 Ye, fare-wel al the snow of ferne yere!
[*Ib.* v. 1176]

13 Th' entente is al, and nought the lettres
space. [*Ib.* v. 1630]

14 Go, litel book, go litel myn tragedie. [*Ib.*
v. 1786]

15 O moral Gower, this book I directe / To
thee. [*Ib.* v. 1856]

ANTON CHEKHOV   1860–1904

16 LIUBOV ANDREEVNA: Are you still a
student?
TROFIMOV: I expect I shall be a student to
the end of my days. [*The Cherry Orchard*,
I]

17 I cannon off the cushion! I pot into the
middle pocket. [*Ib.* II *et passim*]

18 Before the cherry orchard was sold
everybody was worried and upset, but as
soon as it was all settled finally and once
for all, everybody calmed down, and felt
quite cheerful. [*The Cherry Orchard*, IV]

19 It seemed that the next minute they would
discover a solution. Yet it was clear to
both of them that the end was still far,
far off, and that the hardest and most
complicated part was only just beginning.
[*The Lady with the Dog*]

20 MEDVIENKO: Why do you always wear
black?
MASHA: I am in mourning for my life. I
am unhappy. [*The Seagull*, I]

21 The time's come: there's a terrific
thunder-cloud advancing upon us, a
mighty storm is coming to freshen us up.
... It's going to blow away all this idleness and indifference, and prejudice
against work. ... I'm going to work, and
in twenty-five or thirty years' time every
man and woman will be working. [*Three
Sisters*, I]

22 If only we could go back to Moscow!
Sell the house, finish with our life here,
and go back to Moscow. [*Ib.*]

ANDREW CHERRY   1762–1812

23 The next day, / There she lay, / In the
Bay of Biscay, O! [*The Bay of Biscay*]

EARL OF CHESTERFIELD
1694–1773

24 Be wiser than other people if you can,
but do not tell them so. [Letter to his
son, 19 Nov. 1745]

25 An injury is much sooner forgotten than
an insult. [*Ib.* 9 Oct. 1746]

26 Courts and camps are the only places to
learn the world in. [*Ib.* 2 Oct. 1747]

27 Take the tone of the company you are in.
[*Ib.* 9 Oct. 1747]

28 I knew once a very covetous, sordid
fellow [perhaps William Lowndes], who
used to say, 'Take care of the pence, for
the pounds will take care of themselves.'
[*Ib.* 6 Nov. 1747]

29 Advice is seldom welcome; and those
who want it the most always want it the
least. [*Ib.* 29 Jan. 1748]

1 Sacrifice to the Graces. [Letter to his son 9 Mar. 1748]

2 In my mind, there is nothing so illiberal and so ill-bred, as audible laughter. [*Ib.*]

3 I am sure that since I have had the full use of my reason, nobody has ever heard me laugh. [*Ib.*]

4 A man of sense only trifles with them [women], plays with them, humours and flatters them, as he does with a sprightly and forward child; but he neither consults them about, nor trusts them with, serious matters. [*Ib.* 5 Sept. 1748]

5 Due attention to the inside of books, and due contempt for the outside, is the proper relation between a man of sense and his books. [*Ib.* 10 Jan. 1749]

6 Idleness is only the refuge of weak minds. [*Ib.* 20 July 1749]

7 Women are much more like each other than men: they have, in truth, but two passions, vanity and love; these are their universal characteristics. [*Ib.* 19 Dec. 1749]

8 Is it possible to love such a man? No. The utmost I can do for him is to consider him as a respectable Hottentot. [(Dr Johnson, or Lord Lyttelton) *Ib.* 28 Feb. 1751]

9 Every woman is infallibly to be gained by every sort of flattery, and every man by one sort or other. [*Ib.* 16 Mar. 1752]

10 A chapter of accidents. [*Ib.* 16 Feb. 1753]

11 Religion is by no means a proper subject of conversation in a mixed company. [Letter to his godson No. 112 (undated)]

12 Tyrawley and I have been dead these two years; but we don't choose to have it known. [Quoted in Boswell's *Life of Johnson*, 3 Apr. 1773]

13 He once exclaimed to Anstis, Garter King at Arms, 'You foolish man, you do not even know your own foolish business'. [Quoted in Jesse's *Memoirs of the Court of England*, Vol. ii]

14 Unlike my subject will I frame my song, / It shall be witty and it shan't be long. [*Epigram on ('Long') Sir Thomas Robinson*]

15 Give Dayrolles a chair. [Last words]

G. K. CHESTERTON 1874–1936

16 Are they clinging to their crosses, / F. E. Smith? [*Antichrist*]

17 But the souls of Christian peoples. .... / Chuck it, Smith! [*Antichrist*]

18 Before the gods that made the gods / Had seen their sunrise pass, / The White Horse of the White Horse Vale / Was cut out of the grass. [*Ballad of the White Horse*, i]

19 I tell you naught for your comfort. [*Ib.*]

20 For the great Gaels of Ireland / Are the men that God made mad, / For all their wars are merry, / And all their songs are sad. [*Ib.* ii]

21 Heaven shall forgive you Bridge at dawn, / The clothes you wear – or do not wear. [*Ballade d'une grande dame*]

22 I rose politely in the club / And said, 'I feel a little bored; / Will someone take me to a pub?' [*Ballade of an Anti-Puritan*]

23 The gallows in my garden, people say, / Is new and neat and adequately tall. [*Ballade of Suicide*]

24 After all / I think I will not hang myself today. [*Ib.*]

25 With monstrous head and sickening cry / And ears like errant wings, / The devil's walking parody / On all four-footed things. [*The Donkey*]

26 Fools! for I also had my hour; / One far fierce hour and sweet: / There was a shout about my ears, / And palms before my feet. [*Ib.*]

27 White founts falling in the courts of the sun, / And the Soldan of Byzantium is smiling as they run. [*Lepanto*]

28 Strong gongs groaning as the guns boom far, / Don John of Austria is going to the war. [*Ib.*]

29 The folk that live in Liverpool, their heart is in their boots; / They go to hell like lambs, they do, because the hooter hoots. [*Me Heart*]

30 Before the Roman came to Rye or out to Severn strode, / The rolling English drunkard made the rolling English road. [*The Rolling English Road*]

31 That night we went to Birmingham by way of Beachy Head. [*Ib.*]

32 For there is good news yet to hear and fine things to be seen, / Before we go to Paradise by way of Kensal Green. [*Ib.*]

1 Smile at us, pay us, pass us; but do not quite forget. / For we are the people of England, that never have spoken yet. [*The Secret People*]

2 God made the wicked Grocer / For a mystery and a sign, / That men might shun the awful shop / And go to inns to dine. [*Song against Grocers*]

3 He crams with cans of poisoned meat / The subjects of the King, / And when they die by thousands / Why, he laughs like anything. [*Ib.*]

4 And we were angry and poor and happy, / And proud of seeing our names in print. [*A Song of Defeat*]

5 They haven't got no noses, / The fallen sons of Eve. [*The Song of Quoodle*]

6 And goodness only knowses / The Nose-lessness of Man. [*Ib.*]

7 If an angel out of heaven / Brings you other things to drink, / Thank him for his kind attentions, / Go and pour them down the sink. [*The Song of Right and Wrong*]

8 Tea, although an Oriental, / Is a gentle-man at least; / Cocoa is a cad and coward, / Cocoa is a vulgar beast. [*Ib.*]

9 And Noah he often said to his wife when he sat down to dine, / 'I don't care where the water goes if it doesn't get into the wine'. [*Wine and Water*]

10 The human race, to which so many of my readers belong. [*The Napoleon of Notting Hill*, Ch. 1]

11 Hardy went down to botanize in the swamp, while Meredith climbed towards the sun. Meredith became, at his best, a sort of daintily dressed Walt Whitman: Hardy became a sort of village atheist brooding and blaspheming over the village idiot. [*The Victorian Age in Literature*, Ch. 2]

12 If a thing is worth doing it is worth doing badly. [*What's Wrong with the World*, 'Folly and Female Education']

13 'The Christian ideal', it is said, 'has not been tried and found wanting; it has been found difficult and left untried.' [*Ib.* 'The Unfinished Temple']

HENRY CHETTLE   c. 1560–1607

14 Diaphenia, like the daffadowndilly, / White as the sun, fair as the lily, / Heigh ho, how I do love thee! [*Diaphenia*. (Also attr. to Henry Constable)]

ALBERT CHEVALIER   1861–1923

15 Wot's the good of Hanyfink? – Why – Nuffink! [Music-hall refrain]

16 There ain't a lady livin' in the land / As I'd swop for my dear old Dutch! [*My Old Dutch*]

17 Laugh! I thought I should 'ave died, / Knocked 'em in the Old Kent Road. [*Wot Cher* or *Knocked 'em in the Old Kent Road*]

H. F. CHORLEY   1808–1872

18 God the All-terrible! King, who ordainest / Great winds Thy clarions, the lightnings Thy sword. [Hymn]

CHARLES CHURCHILL
                 1731–1764

19 Though by whim, envy, or resentment led, / They damn those authors whom they never read. [*The Candidate*, 57]

20 Be England what she will, / With all her faults, she is my country still. [*The Farewell*, 27]

21 Just to the windward of the law. [*The Ghost*, III. 56]

22 Who often, but without success, have prayed / For apt Alliteration's artful aid. [*The Prophecy of Famine*, 85]

23 Genius is of no country; her pure ray / Spreads all abroad, as general as the day. [*The Rosciad*, 207]

24 Statesman all over, in plots famous grown, / He mouths a sentence, as curs mouth a bone. [*Ib.* 321]

25 So loud each tongue, so empty was each head, / So much they talked, so very little said. [*Ib.* 549]

26 With various readings stored his empty skull, / Learn'd without sense, and venerably dull. [*Ib.* 591]

27 Those who would make us feel, must feel themselves. [*Ib.* 962]

28 Where he falls short, 'tis Nature's fault alone; / Where he succeeds, the merit's all his own. [*Ib.* 1025]

1 The best things carried to excess are wrong. [*The Rosciad*, 1039]

LORD RANDOLPH CHURCHILL
1849–1894

2 The old gang. [(Members of the Conservative Government) Speech in House of Commons, 7 Mar. 1878]

3 Ulster will fight; Ulster will be right. [Letter, 7 May 1886]

4 I never could make out what those damn dots meant. [(Of the decimal point) Quoted by Winston Churchill]

WINSTON CHURCHILL
1874–1965

5 It cannot in the opinion of His Majesty's Government be classified as slavery in the extreme acceptance of the word without some risk of terminological inexactitude. [Speech in House of Commons, 22 Feb. 1906]

6 The maxim of the British people is 'Business as usual'. [Speech at Guildhall, 9 Nov. 1914]

7 I would say to the House, as I said to those who have joined this Government, 'I have nothing to offer but blood, toil, tears and sweat'. [Speech in House of Commons, 13 May 1940]

8 We shall defend our island, whatever the cost may be, we shall fight on the beaches, we shall fight on the landing grounds, we shall fight in the fields and in the streets, we shall fight in the hills; we shall never surrender. [*Ib.* 4 June 1940]

9 Let us therefore brace ourselves to our duties, and so bear ourselves that, if the British Empire and its Commonwealth last for a thousand years, men will still say: 'This was their finest hour.' [*Ib.* 18 June 1940]

10 Never in the field of human conflict was so much owed by so many to so few. [(The Battle of Britain) *Ib.* 20 Aug. 1940]

11 We are waiting for the long-promised invasion. So are the fishes. [Broadcast to the French people, 21 Oct. 1940]

12 Give us the tools, and we will finish the job. [Broadcast, addressed to President Roosevelt, 9 Feb. 1941]

13 It becomes still more difficult to reconcile Japanese action with prudence or even with sanity. What kind of a people do they think we are? [Speech to U.S. Congress, 24 Dec. 1941]

14 'In three weeks England will have her neck wrung like a chicken.' Some chicken; some neck! [Speech to Canadian Senate, 30 Dec. 1941]

15 This is not the end. It is not even the beginning of the end. But it is, perhaps, the end of the beginning. [(Of the victory in Egypt) Speech at the Mansion House, 10 Nov. 1942]

16 There is no finer investment for any community than putting milk into babies. [Broadcast, 21 Mar. 1943]

17 An iron curtain has descended across the Continent. [Address at Westminster College, Fulton, U.S.A., 5 Mar. 1946]

18 No one can guarantee success in war, but only deserve it. [*The Second World War*, Vol. ii, *Their Finest Hour*]

19 Dictators ride to and fro upon tigers which they dare not dismount. And the tigers are getting hungry. [*While England Slept*]

20 This is the sort of English up with which I will not put. [Marginal comment on state document, quoted in Sir Ernest Gowers, *Plain Words*]

COLLEY CIBBER   1671–1757

21 Whilst thus I sing, I am a King, / Altho' a poor blind boy. [*The Blind Boy*]

22 Dumb's a sly dog. [*Love makes the Man*, IV. i]

23 One had as good be out of the world, as out of the fashion. [*Love's Last Shift*, II]

24 Off with his head – so much for Buckingham. [*Richard III* (altered), IV. iii]

25 Conscience avaunt, Richard's himself again. [*Ib.* V. iii]

26 Perish the thought! [*Ib.* V. v]

MARCUS TULLIUS CICERO
106–43 B.C.

27 *Nihil tam absurde dici potest, quod non dicatur ab aliquo philosophorum.* – Nothing so absurd can be said, that some philosopher has not said it. [*De Divinatione*, ii. 58]

1 *Salus populi suprema est lex.* – The good of the people is the chief law. [*De Legibus*, III. iii]

2 *'Ipse dixit.' 'Ipse' autem erat Pythagoras.* – 'He himself said it', and this *self* was Pythagoras. [*De Natura Deorum*, I. v. 10]

3 *Summum bonum.* – The highest good. [*De Officiis*, I. ii]

4 *Cedant arma togae, concedant laurea laudi.* – Let arms give place to civic robes, laurels to paeans. [*Ib.* I. xxii]

5 *O tempora, O mores!* – What times! What habits! [*In Catilinam*, I. i]

6 *Abiit, excessit, evasit, erupit.* – He departed, withdrew, rushed off, broke away. [*Ib.* II. i]

7 *Civis Romanus sum.* – I am a Roman citizen. [*In Verrem*, V. lvii]

8 *Quod di omen avertant.* – May the gods avert the omen. [*Philippic*, III. xiv]

9 *Silent enim leges inter arma.* – Laws are dumb in time of war. [*Pro Milone*, IV. xi]

10 *Cui bono?* – To whose profit? [*Ib.* XII, xxxii]

11 *Errare, mehercule, malo cum Platone ... quam cum istis vera sentire.* – I swear I would rather be wrong with Plato than see the truth with men like these. [(The Pythagoreans) *Tusculanae Disp.* I. 17]

12 *O fortunatam natam me consule Romam!* – O happy Rome, born when I was consul! [Quoted in *Juvenal*, X. 122]

JOHN CLARE   1793–1864

13 He could not die when trees were green, / For he loved the time too well. [*The Dying Child*]

14 I am: yet what I am none cares, or knows. [*I am*]

15 I long for scenes where man has never trod; / A place where woman never smiled or wept; / There to abide with my Creator, God, / And sleep as I in childhood sweetly slept: / Untroubling and untroubled where I lie; – The grass below – above the vaulted sky [*Ib.*]

16 Love lies beyond / The tomb, the earth, which fades like dew! / I love the fond, / The faithful, and the true. ['*Love lies beyond the Tomb*']

17 If life had a second edition, how I would correct the proofs. [Letter to a friend]

EDWARD HYDE, EARL OF CLARENDON   1609–1674

18 He [Hampden] had a head to contrive, a tongue to persuade, and a hand to execute any mischief. [*History of the Rebellion*]

19 So enamoured on peace that he [Falkland] would have been glad the King should have bought it at any price. [*Ib.*]

KARL VON CLAUSEWITZ   1780–1831

20 *Der Krieg ist nichts anderes als die Fortsetzung der Politik mit anderen Mitteln.* – War is nothing more than the continuation of politics by other means. [*Vom Kriege*]

HENRY CLAY   1777–1852

21 I had rather be right than be President. [Speech, 1850]

SAMUEL LANGHORNE CLEMENS *see* **TWAIN, MARK**

JOHN CLEVELAND   1613–1658

22 Strafford who was hurried hence / 'Twixt treason and convenience. [*Epitaph on the Earl of Strafford*]

23 Had Cain been Scot, God would have changed his doom / Not forced him wander, but confined him home. [*The Rebel Scot*]

ROBERT, LORD CLIVE   1725–1774

24 By God, Mr Chairman, at this moment I stand astonished at my own moderation! [Reply during Parliamentary inquiry, 1773]

THE CLOUD OF UNKNOWING   14 Cent.

25 And smite upon that thick cloud of unknowing with a sharp dart of longing

love; and go not thence for thing that befalleth. [Ch. 6]

ARTHUR HUGH CLOUGH
1819–1861

1 Well, I know, after all, it is only juxtaposition, – / Juxtaposition, in short; and what is juxtaposition? [*Amours de voyage*, I. xi]

2 I am in love, you say; I do not think so, exactly. [*Ib*. II. x]

3 *Action will furnish belief*, – but will that belief be the true one? / This is the point, you know. [*Ib*. V. ii]

4 Whither depart the souls of the brave that die in the battle, / Die in the lost, lost fight, for the cause that perishes with them? [*Ib*. V. vi]

5 Still more plain the Tutor, the grave man, nicknamed Adam, / White-tied, clerical, silent, with antique square-cut waistcoat / Formal, unchanged, of black cloth, but with sense and feeling beneath it. [*The Bothie of Tober-na-Vuolich*, I. 20]

6 *Shady* in Latin, said Lindsay, but *topping* in Plays and Aldrich. [*Ib*. I. 25]

7 Good are the Ethics, I wis; good absolute, not for me, though; / Good, too, Logic, of course; in itself, but not in fine weather. [*Ib*. II. 255]

8 Gay in the mazy, / Moving, imbibing the rosy, and pointing a gun at the horny! [*Ib*. III. 97]

9 Grace is given of God, but knowledge is born in the market. [*Ib*. IV. 81]

10 A world where nothing is had for nothing. [*Ib*. VIII. 5]

11 How pleasant it is to have money, heigh-ho! / How pleasant it is to have money. [*Dipsychus*, I. ii]

12 And almost every one when age, / Disease, or sorrows strike him, / Inclines to think there is a God, / Or something very like Him. [*Ib*. I. v]

13 This world is very odd we see, / We do not comprehend it; / But in one fact we all agree, / God won't, and we can't mend it. [*Ib*. II. ii]

14 Trust me, I've read your German sage / To far more purpose than e'er you did; / You find it in his wisest page, / Whom God deludes is well deluded. [*Ib*.]

15 Thou shalt have one God only; who / Would be at the expense of two? [*The Latest Decalogue*]

16 Thou shalt not kill; but needst not strive / Officiously to keep alive. [*Ib*.]

17 Thou shalt not covet, but tradition / Approves all forms of competition. [*Ib*.]

18 'Tis better to have fought and lost, / Than never to have fought at all. [*Peschiera*]

19 Say not the struggle naught availeth, / The labour and the wounds are vain, / The enemy faints not, nor faileth, / And as things have been, things remain. [*Say not the Struggle Naught Availeth*]

20 And not by eastern windows only, / When daylight comes, comes in the light, / In front the sun climbs slow, how slowly, / But westward, look, the land is bright. [*Ib*.]

21 Where lies the land to which the ship would go? / Far, far ahead, is all her seamen know, / And where the land she travels from? Away, / Far, far behind, is all that they can say. [*Where lies the Land*]

WILLIAM COBBETT   1762–1835

22 The slavery of the tea and coffee and other slop-kettle. [*Advice to Young Men*, Letter 1]

23 The great wen of all. [(London) *Rural Rides* (1821)]

CHARLES COBORN   1852–1945

24 Two lovely black eyes, / Oh, what a surprise! / Only for telling a man he was wrong. / Two lovely black eyes! [*Two Lovely Black Eyes*]

ALISON COCKBURN   1713–1794

25 For the flowers of the forest are withered away. [*The Flowers of the Forest*]

JEAN COCTEAU   1891–1963

26 Tact consists in knowing how far we may go too far. [Quoted in *Treasury of Humorous Quotations*]

CODE NAPOLÉON   1804

1 *La recherche de la paternité est interdite.* – Investigations into paternity are forbidden. [Article 340]

SIR EDWARD COKE   1552–1634

2 How long soever it hath continued, if it be against reason, it is of no force in law. [*Institutes*, 'Commentary upon Littleton', I. 80]

3 The gladsome light of Jurisprudence. [*Ib.* I, Epilogue]

4 For a man's house is his castle. [*Ib.* III. 73]

5 Magna Charta is such a fellow, that he will have no sovereign. [On the Lords' Amendment to the Petition of Right, 17 May 1628]

6 They [corporations] cannot commit treason, nor be outlawed, nor excommunicate, for they have no souls. [*Sutton's Hospital Case*]

7 Six hours in sleep, in law's grave study six, / Four spend in prayer, the rest on Nature fix. [Epigram]

FRANK COLBY   1865–1925

8 Men will confess to treason, murder, arson, false teeth, or a wig. How many of them will own up to a lack of humour? [*Essays*, I]

9 I have found some of the best reasons I ever had for remaining at the bottom simply by looking at the men at the top. [*Ib.* II]

HARTLEY COLERIDGE
                     1796–1849

10 She is not fair to outward view / As many maidens be; / Her loveliness I never knew / Until she smiled on me. [Song: *She is not Fair*]

11 Her very frowns are fairer far, / Than smiles of other maidens are. [*Ib.*]

MARY COLERIDGE   1861–1907

12 We were young, we were merry, we were very, very wise, / And the door stood open at our feast, / When there passed us a woman with the West in her eyes, / And a man with his back to the East. [*Unwelcome*]

S. T. COLERIDGE   1772–1834

13 It is an ancient mariner, / And he stoppeth one of three. [*Ancient Mariner*, Pt i]

14 The guests are met, the feast is set. / May'st hear the merry din. [*Ib.*]

15 He holds him with his glittering eye. [*Ib.*]

16 The ship was cheered, the harbour cleared, / Merrily did we drop. [*Ib.*]

17 The sun came up upon the left, / Out of the sea came he! / And he shone bright, and on the right / Went down into the sea. [*Ib.*]

18 The bride hath paced into the hall, / Red as a rose is she. [*Ib.*]

19 And ice, mast-high, came floating by, / As green as emerald. [*Ib.*]

20 The ice was here, the ice was there, / The ice was all around; / It cracked and growled, and roared and howled, / Like noises in a swound! [*Ib.*]

21 The fair breeze blew, the white foam flew, / The furrow followed free; / We were the first that ever burst / Into that silent sea. [*Ib.* ii.]

22 As idle as a painted ship / Upon a painted ocean. [*Ib.*]

23 Water, water, everywhere, / Nor any drop to drink. [*Ib.*]

24 Yea, slimy things did crawl with legs / Upon the slimy sea. [*Ib.*]

25 The Nightmare Life-in-Death was she, / Who thicks man's blood with cold. [*Ib.* iii]

26 'The game is done! I've won, I've won!' / Quoth she, and whistles thrice. [*Ib.*]

27 The sun's rim dips; the stars rush out: / At one stride comes the dark. [*Ib.*]

28 Till clomb above the eastern bar / The hornèd moon, with one bright star / Within the nether tip. [*Ib.*]

29 I fear thee, ancient Mariner! / I fear thy skinny hand! [*Ib.* iv]

30 Alone, alone, all, all alone, / Alone on a wide, wide sea! [*Ib.*]

1 The moving moon went up the sky, / And nowhere did abide: / Softly she was going up, / And a star or two beside. [*Ancient Mariner*, iv]

2 A spring of love gushed from my heart, / And I blessed them unaware. [*Ib.*]

3 Oh sleep! it is a gentle thing, / Beloved from pole to pole! [*Ib.* v]

4 We were a ghastly crew. [*Ib.*]

5 A noise like of a hidden brook. / In the leafy month of June, / That to the sleeping woods all night / Singeth a quiet tune. [*Ib.*]

6 Like one that on a lonesome road / Doth walk in fear and dread. / And having once turned round walks on, / And turns no more his head; / Because he knows, a frightful fiend / Doth close behind him tread. [*Ib.* vi]

7 No voice; but oh! the silence sank / Like music on my heart. [*Ib.*]

8 When the ivy-tod is heavy with snow, / And the owlet whoops to the wolf below. [*Ib.* vii]

9 'Ha! ha!' quoth he, 'full plain I see, / The Devil knows how to row.' [*Ib.*]

10 I pass, like night, from land to land; / I have strange power of speech. [*Ib.*]

11 O Wedding-Guest! this soul hath been / Alone on a wide wide sea; / So lonely 'twas that God himself / Scarce seemèd there to be. [*Ib.*]

12 He prayeth well, who loveth well / Both man and bird and beast. [*Ib.*]

13 He prayeth best, who loveth best / All things both great and small; / For the dear God who loveth us, / He made and loveth all. [*Ib.*]

14 A sadder and a wiser man, / He rose the morrow morn. [*Ib.*]

15 And the spring comes slowly up this way. [*Christabel*, Pt i. 22]

16 The one red leaf, the last of its clan, / That dances as often as dance it can, / Hanging so light, and hanging so high, / On the topmost twig that looks up at the sky. [*Ib.* i. 49]

17 And what can ail the mastiff bitch? [*Ib.* i. 149]

18 A sight to dream of, not to tell! [*Ib.* i. 253]

19 Saints will aid if men will call: / For the blue sky bends over all! [*Ib.* i. 330]

20 Life is thorny; and youth is vain; / And to be wroth with one we love / Doth work like madness in the brain. [*Christabel*, ii. 413]

21 I counted two and seventy stenches, / All well defined, and several stinks! [*Cologne*]

22 Well! If the Bard was weather-wise, who made / The grand old ballad of Sir Patrick Spence. [*Dejection: an Ode*, 1]

23 I see them all so excellently fair, / I see, not feel, how beautiful they are! [*Ib.* 37]

24 I may not hope from outward forms to win / The passion and the life, whose fountains are within. [*Ib.* 45]

25 O Lady! we receive but what we give, / And in our life alone does Nature live. [*Ib.* 47]

26 Swans sing before they die – 'twere no bad thing / Did certain persons die before they sing. [*Epigram on a Volunteer Singer*]

27 The Frost performs its secret ministry, / Unhelped by any wind. [*Frost at Midnight*, 1]

28 Therefore all seasons shall be sweet to thee, / Whether the summer clothe the general earth / With greenness, or the redbreast sit and sing / Betwixt the tufts of snow on the bare branch / Of mossy apple tree. [*Ib.* 65]

29 Whether the eave-drops fall / Heard only in the trances of the blast, / Or if the secret ministry of frost / Shall hang them up in silent icicles, / Quietly shining to the quiet moon. [*Ib.* 70]

30 The Knight's bones are dust, / And his good sword rust; – / His soul is with the saints, I trust. [*The Knight's Tomb*]

31 In Xanadu did Kubla Khan / A stately pleasure-dome decree; / Where Alph, the sacred river, ran / Through caverns measureless to man / Down to a sunless sea.

So twice five miles of fertile ground / With walls and towers was girdled round: / And there were gardens bright with sinuous rills, / Where blossomed many an incense-bearing tree; / And here were forests ancient as the hills, / Enfolding sunny spots of greenery. [*Kubla Khan*]

32 A savage place! as holy and enchanted / As e'er beneath a waning moon was

haunted / By woman wailing for her demon lover! [*Kubla Khan*]

1 As if this earth in fast thick pants were breathing. [*Ib.*]

2 Five miles meandering with a mazy motion. [*Ib.*]

3 Ancestral voices prophesying war! [*Ib.*]

4 It was a miracle of rare device, / A sunny pleasure-dome with caves of ice! [*Ib.*]

5 A damsel with a dulcimer / In a vision once I saw: / It was an Abyssinian maid, / And on her dulcimer she played, / Singing of Mount Abora. [*Ib.*]

6 And all should cry, Beware! Beware! / His flashing eyes, his floating hair! / Weave a circle round him thrice, / And close your eyes with holy dread, / For he on honey-dew hath fed, / And drunk the milk of Paradise. [*Ib.*]

7 All thoughts, all passions, all delights, / Whatever stirs this mortal frame, / All are but ministers of Love, / And feed his sacred flame. [*Love*]

8 With Donne whose muse on dromedary trots, / Wreathe iron pokers into true-love knots. [*On Donne's Poetry*]

9 In the hexameter rises the fountain's silvery column; / In the pentameter aye falling in melody back. [*Ovidian Elegiac Metre*]

10 Something Childish, but very Natural. [Title of poem]

11 So for the mother's sake the child was dear, / And dearer was the mother for the child. [*Sonnet to a Friend . . .*]

12 And this reft house is that the which he built, / Lamented Jack! [*Sonnets Attempted in the Manner of Contemporary Writers*, 3]

13 This lime-tree bower my prison! [*This Lime-tree Bower my Prison*]

14 Life went a-maying / With Nature, Hope, and Poesy, / When I was young! [*Youth and Age*]

15 He who begins by loving Christianity better than Truth will proceed by loving his own sect or church better than Christianity, and end by loving himself better than all. [*Aids to Reflection, Moral and Religious Aphorisms*, xxv]

16 If a man could pass through Paradise in a dream, and have a flower presented to him as a pledge that his soul had really been there, and if he found that flower in his hand when he awoke – Aye, and what then? [*Anima Poetae* (1816)]

17 The primary imagination I hold to be the living power and prime agent of all human perception, and as a repetition in the finite mind of the eternal act of creation in the infinite I AM. [*Biographia Literaria*, Ch. 13]

18 The Fancy is indeed no other than a mode of memory emancipated from the order of time and space. [*Ib.*]

19 That willing suspension of disbelief for the moment, which constitutes poetic faith. [*Ib.* 14]

20 Nothing can permanently please, which does not contain in itself the reason why it is so, and not otherwise. [*Ib.*]

21 Our *myriad-minded* Shakespeare. [*Ib.* 15]

22 No man was ever yet a great poet, without being at the same time a profound philosopher. [*Ib.*]

23 The dwarf sees farther than the giant, when he has the giant's shoulder to mount on. [*The Friend*, I. 8]

24 Poetry is not the proper antithesis to prose, but to science. Poetry is opposed to science, and prose to metre. [*Lectures and Notes of 1818*, Section I]

25 To read Dryden, Pope, etc., you need only count syllables; but to read Donne you must measure *time*, and discover the time of each word by the sense of passion. [*Ib.*]

26 Reviewers are usually people who would have been poets, historians, biographers, etc., if they ould; they have tried their talents at one or at the other, and have failed; therefore they turn critics. [*Lectures on Shakespeare and Milton*, I]

27 The faults of great authors are generally excellences carried to an excess. [*Miscellanies*, 149]

28 Summer has set in with its usual severity. [Remark quoted in Lamb's letter to V. Novello, 9 May 1826]

29 Schiller has the material sublime. [*Table Talk*, 29 Dec. 1822]

30 You abuse snuff! Perhaps it is the final cause of the human nose. [*Ib.* 4 Jan. 1823]

1 Prose = words in their best order; poetry = the *best* words in the best order. [*Table Talk*, 12 July 1827]

2 The man's desire is for the woman; but the woman's desire is rarely other than for the desire of the man. [*Ib.* 23 July 1827]

3 My mind is in a state of philosophical doubt. [*Ib.* 30 Apr. 1830]

4 Poetry is certainly something more than good sense, but it must be good sense at all events; just as a palace is more than a house, but it must be a house, at least. [*Ib.* 9 May 1830]

5 I believe the souls of five hundred Sir Isaac Newtons would go to the making up of a Shakespeare or a Milton. [Letter to Thomas Poole, 23 Mar. 1801]

JESSE COLLINGS   1831–1920

6 Three acres and a cow. [Slogan for Land Reform]

MORTIMER COLLINS   1827–1876

7 A man is as old as he's feeling, / A woman as old as she looks. [*The Unknown Quantity*]

WILKIE COLLINS   1824–1889

8 I am not against hasty marriages, where a mutual flame is fanned by an adequate income. [*No Name*, Sc. IV. Ch. 8]

WILLIAM COLLINS   1721–1759

9 To fair Fidele's grassy tomb / Soft maids and village hinds shall bring / Each opening sweet, of earliest bloom, / And rifle all the breathing Spring. [*Dirge in Cymbeline*]

10 Beloved, till life can charm no more; / And mourned, till Pity's self be dead. [*Ib.*]

11 If aught of oaten stop, or pastoral song, / May hope, chaste Eve, to soothe thy modest ear. [*Ode to Evening*]

12 While now the bright-haired sun / Sits in yon western tent, whose cloudy skirts, / With brede ethereal wove, / O'erhang his wavy bed: / Now air is hushed, save where the weak-eyed bat, / With short

shrill shriek flits by on leathern wing, / Or where the beetle winds / His small but sullen horn. [*Ode to Evening*]

13 Hamlets brown, and dim-discovered spires. [*Ib.*]

14 Bathe thy breathing tresses, meekest Eve! [*Ib.*]

15 Faints the cold work till thou inspire the whole. [*Ode to Simplicity*]

16 How sleep the brave, who sink to rest, / By all their country's wishes blest! [*Ode written in the Year 1746*]

17 By fairy hands their knell is rung; / By forms unseen their dirge is sung; / There Honour comes, a pilgrim gray, / To bless the turf that wraps their clay; / And Freedom shall awhile repair, / To dwell a weeping hermit there! [*Ib.*]

18 When Music, heav'nly maid, was young. [*The Passions, An Ode for Music*, 1]

19 With eyes upraised, as one inspired, / Pale Melancholy sat retired; / And from her wild sequestered seat, / In notes by distance made more sweet, / Poured through the mellow horn her pensive soul. [*Ib.* 57]

20 In hollow murmurs died away. [*Ib.* 68]

21 O Music! sphere-descended maid, / Friend of Pleasure, Wisdom's aid! [*Ib.* 95]

GEORGE COLMAN, THE ELDER   1732–1794

22 Love and a cottage! Eh, Fanny! Ah, give me indifference and a coach and six! [*The Clandestine Marriage*, I. ii]

GEORGE COLMAN, THE YOUNGER   1762–1836

23 Mum's the word. [*The Battle of Hexham*, II. i]

24 Lord help you! Tell 'em Queen Anne's dead. [*The Heir-at-Law*, I. i]

25 Not to be sneezed at. [*Ib.* II. i]

26 His heart runs away with his head. [*Who Wants a Guinea?* I. i]

27 Like two single gentlemen rolled into one. [*Lodgings for Single Gentlemen*]

28 When taken, / To be well shaken. [*The Newcastle Apothecary*]

1 Says he, 'I am a handsome man, but I'm a gay deceiver.' [*Unfortunate Miss Bailey*]

2 Crying, 'Bless you, Wicked Captain Smith, remember poor Miss Bailey.' [*Ib.*]

CHARLES COLTON 1780?–1832

3 Men will wrangle for religion; write for it; fight for it; anything but – live for it. [*Lacon*, I. 25]

4 When you have nothing to say, say nothing. [*Ib.* I. 183]

5 Examinations are formidable even to the best prepared, for the greatest fool may ask more than the wisest man can answer. [*Ib.* I. 322]

6 The debt which cancels all others. [*Ib.* II. 66]

WILLIAM CONGREVE 1670–1729

7 There is nothing more unbecoming a man of quality than to laugh; 'tis such a vulgar expression of the passion! [*The Double Dealer*, I. iv]

8 See how love and murder will out. [*Ib.* IV. vi]

9 Thou liar of the first magnitude. [*Love for Love*, II. v]

10 I came upstairs into the world; for I was born in a cellar. [*Ib.* II. vii]

11 O fie miss, you must not kiss and tell. [*Ib.* II. x]

12 I know that's a secret, for it's whispered everywhere. [*Ib.* III. iii]

13 If I marry, Sir Sampson, I'm for a good estate with any man, and for any man with a good estate. [*Ib.* III. v]

14 He that first cries out stop thief, is often he that has stolen the treasure. [*Ib.* III. xiv]

15 A branch of one of your antediluvian families, fellows that the flood could not wash away. [*Ib.* V. ii]

16 'Tis well enough for a servant to be bred at an university: but the education is a little too pedantic for a gentleman. [*Ib.* V. iii]

17 Music hath charms to soothe a savage breast, / To soften rocks, or bend a knotted oak. [*The Mourning Bride*, I. i]

18 Heaven has no rage like love to hatred turned, / Nor hell a fury, like a woman scorned. [*The Mourning Bride*, III. viii]

19 Is he then dead? / What, dead at last, quite, quite for ever dead! [*Ib.* V. xi]

20 In my conscience I believe the baggage loves me: for she never speaks well of me herself, nor suffers anybody else to rail at me. [*The Old Bachelor*, I. iii]

21 One of love's April-fools. [*Ib.* I. iv]

22 Well, Sir Joseph, you have such a winning way with you. [*Ib.* V. vii]

23 I could find it in my heart to marry thee, purely to be rid of thee. [*Ib.* V. x]

24 Courtship to marriage, as a very witty prologue to a very dull play. [*Ib.*]

25 They come together like the coroner's inquest, to sit upon the murdered reputations of the week. [*The Way of the World*, I. i]

26 She once used me with that insolence, that in revenge I took her to pieces; sifted her, and separated her failings; I studied 'em, and got 'em by rote. The catalogue was so large, that I was not without hopes, one day or other to hate her heartily. [*Ib.* I. iii]

27 Nay, I'll do him justice. I'm his friend, I won't wrong him. – And if he had any judgement in the world, – he would not be altogether contemptible. Come, come, don't detract from the merits of my friend. [*Ib.* I. vi]

28 O the pious friendships of the female sex! [*Ib.* II. iii]

29 Here she comes i' faith full sail, with her fan spread and streamers out, and a shoal of fools for tenders. [*Ib.* II. iv]

30 O ay, letters – I had letters – I am persecuted with letters – I hate letters – nobody knows how to write letters; and yet one has 'em, one does not know why – they serve one to pin up one's hair [*Ib.*]

31 Only with those in verse, Mrs Witwoud. I never pin up my hair with prose. [*Ib.*]

32 MILLAMANT: I believe I gave you some pain.
MIRABEL: Does that please you?
MILLAMANT: Infinitely; I love to give pain. [*Ib.*]

33 Lord, what is a lover that it can give? Why one makes lovers as fast as one pleases,

and they live as long as one pleases, and they die as soon as one pleases: and then if one pleases one makes more. [*The Way of the World*, II. iv]

1 If I have not fretted myself till I am pale again, there's no veracity in me. [*Ib*. III. i]

2 Yes, but tenderness becomes me best – a sort of dyingness – you see that picture has a sort of a – ha, Foible? A swimmingness in the eyes. [*Ib*. III. v]

3 Love's but the frailty of the mind, – When 'tis not with ambition joined. [*Ib*. III. xii]

4 No, I'm no enemy to learning; it hurts not me. [*Ib*. III. xiii]

5 Rise to meet him in a pretty disorder – yes – O, nothing is more alluring than a levee from a couch in some confusion. [*Ib*. IV. i]

6 I nauseate walking; 'tis a country diversion, I loathe the country. [*Ib*. IV. iv]

7 Wife, spouse, my dear, joy, jewel, love, sweet-heart and the rest of that nauseous cant, in which men and their wives are so fulsomely familiar. [*Ib*. IV. v]

8 Let us be very strange and well-bred: Let us be as strange as if we had been married a great while; and as well-bred as if we were not married at all. [*Ib*.]

9 These articles subscribed, if I continue to endure you a little longer, I may by degrees dwindle into a wife. [*Ib*.]

10 O horrid provisoes! [*Ib*.]

11 I hope you do not think me prone to an iteration of nuptials. [*Ib*. IV. xii]

12 You are all camphire and frankincense, all chastity and odour. [*Ib*.]

13 O, she is the antidote to desire. [*Ib*. IV. xiv]

14 I chiefly made it my own care to initiate her very infancy in the rudiments of virtue, and to impress upon her tender years a young odium and aversion to the very sight of men. [*Ib*. V. v]

15 Careless she is with artful care, / Affecting to seem unaffected. [*Amoret*]

16 The good received, the giver is forgot. [*Epistle to Lord Halifax*, 40]

17 Whom she refuses, she treats still / With so much sweet behaviour, / That her refusal, through her skill, / Looks almost like a favour. [Song: *Doris*]

18 Would she could make of me a saint, / Or I of her a sinner. [Song: *Pious Selinda goes to Prayers*]

JAMES CONNELL 1852–1929

19 Then raise the scarlet standard high! / Beneath its shade we'll live and die! / Though cowards flinch, and traitors jeer, / We'll keep the Red Flag flying here! [*The Red Flag*]

T. W. CONNOR 19 Cent.

20 She was one of the early birds, / And I was one of the worms. [*She was a Dear Little Dickie-Bird*]

JOSEPH CONRAD 1857–1924

21 Mistah Kurtz – he dead. [*The Heart of Darkness*]

22 A work that aspires, however humbly, to the condition of art should carry its justification in every line. [*The Nigger of the Narcissus*, Preface]

23 This could have occurred nowhere but in England, where men and sea interpenetrate, so to speak. [*Youth*]

BENJAMIN CONSTANT 1767–1830

24 *Je ne suis pas la rose, mais j'ai vécu avec elle*. – I am not the rose, but I have lived with her. [Attr.]

CONSTANTINE 288?–337

25 *In hoc signo vinces*. – Beneath this sign thou shalt conquer. [Words heard in a vision]

J. GORDON COOGLER 1869–?

26 Alas! for the South, her books have grown fewer – / She was never much given to literature. [*Purely Original Verse*]

ELIZA COOK 1818–1889

27 I love it, I love it; and who shall dare / To chide me for loving that old arm-chair? [*The Old Arm-Chair*]

119

CALVIN COOLIDGE   1872–1933

1 He said he was against it. [On being asked what a clergyman had said in a sermon on sin]
2 They hired the money, didn't they? [Of the Allies' war-debt, 1925]

JAMES FENIMORE COOPER
1789–1851

3 The Last of the Mohicans. [Title of novel]

RICHARD CORBET   1582–1635

4 Farewell rewards and fairies, / Good housewives now may say, / But now foul sluts in dairies / Do fare as well as they, / And though they sweep their hearths no less / Than maids were wont to do, / Yet who of late for cleanliness, / Finds six-pence in her shoe? [*The Fairies' Farewell*]
5 By which we note the fairies / Were of the old profession; / Their songs were Ave Maries, / Their dances were procession. [*Ib.*]

TRISTAN CORBIÈRE   1845–1875

6 *Mélange adultère de tout.* – Adulterous mixture of everything. [*Épitaphe*]

PIERRE CORNEILLE   1606–1684

7 *Cette obscure clarté qui tombe des étoiles.* – This dark brightness that falls from the stars. [*Le Cid*, IV. iii]
8 *Et le combat cessa, faute de combattants.* – And the battle ended through lack of combatants. [*Ib.*]
9 *Je suis maître de moi comme de l'univers / Je le suis, je veux l'être.* – I am master of myself, as of the Universe; I am, and I wish to be so. [*Cinna*, V. iii]
10 *Faites votre devoir, et laissez faire aux dieux.* – Do your duty, and leave the rest to the gods. [*Horace*, II. viii]
11 *Hélas! je sors d'un mal pour tomber dans un pire.* – Alas, I emerge from one disaster to fall into a worse. [*Le Menteur*, III. ii]
12 *À raconter ses maux, souvent on les soulage.* – One often calms one's grief by recounting it. [*Polyeucte*, I. iii]

FRANCES CORNFORD 1886–1960

13 Magnificently unprepared / For the long littleness of life. [*Rupert Brooke*]
14 O why do you walk through the fields in gloves, / Missing so much and so much? / O fat white woman whom nobody loves. [*To a Fat Lady seen from a Train*]

ANNE BIGOT DE CORNUEL
1605–1694

15 *Il n'y a pas de heros pour son valet de chambre.* – No man is a hero to his valet. [*Lettres de Mlle Aissé*, 13 Aug. 1728]

W. J. CORY   1823–1892

16 They told me, Heraclitus, they told me you were dead, / They brought me bitter news to hear, and bitter tears to shed. [*Heraclitus*]
17 How often you and I / Had tired the sun with talking and sent him down the sky. [*Ib.*]
18 A handful of grey ashes, long, long ago at rest. [*Ib.*]
19 Still are thy pleasant voices, thy nightingales, awake; / For Death, he taketh all away, but them he cannot take. [*Ib.*]
20 But oh, the very reason why / I clasp them, is because they die. [*Mimnermus in Church*]

NATHANIEL COTTON 1705–1788

21 Yet still we hug the dear deceit. [*Visions*, 'Content']

ÉMILE COUÉ   1857–1926

22 *Tous les jours, à tous points de vue, je vais de mieux en mieux.* – Every day, in every way, I'm getting better and better. [Formula of his faith-cures]

VICTOR COUSIN   1792–1867

23 *Il faut de la religion pour la religion, de la morale pour la morale, de l'art pour l'art.* – We need religion for religion's sake, morality for morality's sake and art for art's sake. [*Cours de philosophie*]

THOMAS, BARON COVENTRY
1578–1640

1 The wooden walls are the best walls of this kingdom. [Speech to the Judges, 17 June 1635]

NOEL COWARD   1899–1973

2 We're Regency Rakes / And each of us makes / A personal issue of adipose tissue. [*Conversation Piece*, I. iv]

3 There's always something fishy about the French. [*Ib.* I. vi]

4 And though the Van Dycks have to go / And we pawn the Bechstein grand, / We'll stand by the Stately Homes of England. [*Operette*, I. vii]

5 Mad dogs and Englishmen go out in the midday sun. [*Words and Music*]

6 Don't let's be beastly to the Germans. [Lyric: *Don't Let's be Beastly to the Germans*]

7 Don't put your daughter on the stage, Mrs Worthington. [Lyric: *Don't Put your Daughter on the Stage*]

8 Poor Little Rich Girl [Title of song]

ABRAHAM COWLEY   1618–1667

9 The thirsty earth soaks up the rain, / And drinks, and gapes for drink again. / The plants suck in the earth, and are / With constant drinking fresh and fair. [*Anacreontic: Drinking*]

10 For why / Should every creature drink but I, / Why, man of morals, tell me why? [*Ib.*]

11 Love in her sunny eyes does basking play; / Love walks the pleasant mazes of her hair; / Love does on both her lips for ever stray; / And sews and reaps a thousand kisses there. / In all her outward parts Love's always seen; / But, oh, he never went within. [*The Change*]

12 God the first garden made, and the first city Cain. [*The Garden*]

13 The world's a scene of changes, and to be / Constant, in Nature were inconstancy. [*Inconstancy*]

14 This only grant me, that my means may lie / Too low for envy, for contempt too high. [*Of Myself*]

15 But boldly say each night, / To-morrow let my sun his beams display, / Or in clouds hide them; I have lived to-day. [*Of Myself*]

16 Hail, old patrician trees, so great and good! [*Of Solitude*]

17 Thou needst not make new songs, but say the old. [*On the Death of Mr Crashaw*]

18 His faith perhaps in some nice tenets might / Be wrong; his life, I'm sure, was always in the right. [*Ib.*]

19 And I myself a Catholic will be, / So far at least, great saint, to pray to thee. / Hail, Bard triumphant! and some care bestow / On us, the Poets militant below. [*Ib.*]

20 Though you be absent here, I needs must say / The trees as beauteous are, and flowers as gay, / As ever they were wont to be. [*The Spring*]

21 Life is an incurable disease. [*To Dr Scarborough*]

22 Well then; I now do plainly see, / This busy world and I shall ne'er agree. [*The Wish*]

23 Ah, yet, e'er I descend to th' grave / May I a small house, and large garden have! / And a few friends, and many books, both true, / Both wise, and both delightful too! / And since Love ne'er will from me flee, / A mistress moderately fair, / And good as guardian-angels are, / Only beloved, and loving me! [*Ib.*]

HANNAH COWLEY   1743–1809

24 I have been five minutes too late all my life-time! [*The Belle's Stratagem*, I. i]

25 But what is woman? – only one of Nature's agreeable blunders. [*Who's the Dupe?* II. ii]

WILLIAM COWPER   1731–1800

26 When the British warrior queen, / Bleeding from the Roman rods, / Sought, with an indignant mien, / Counsel of her country's gods. [*Boadicea*]

27 Rome shall perish – write that word / In the blood that she has spilt. [*Ib.*]

28 Hark! the Gaul is at her gates! [*Ib.*]

29 Regions Caesar never knew / Thy posterity shall sway. [*Ib.*]

1 Obscurest night involved the sky, / Th'
Atlantic billows roared, / When such a
destined wretch as I, / Washed headlong
from on board, / Of friends, of hope, of
all bereft, / His floating home for ever
left. [*The Castaway*]

2 But misery still delights to trace / Its
semblance in another's case. [*Ib.*]

3 We perished, each alone: / But I beneath
a rougher sea, / And whelmed in deeper
gulfs than he. [*Ib.*]

4 Grief is itself a med'cine. [*Charity*, 159]

5 He found it inconvenient to be poor. [*Ib.*
189]

6 Heaven held his hand, the likeness must
be true. [*Ib.* 434]

7 With outstretched hoe I slew him at the
door, / And taught him NEVER TO COME
THERE NO MORE. [(A viper that attacked
three kittens) *The Colubriad*]

8 A fool must now and then be right, by
chance. [*Conversation*, 96]

9 Contradiction for its own dear sake. [*Ib.*
106]

10 A noisy man is always in the right. [*Ib.*
114]

11 Pernicious weed! whose scent the fair
annoys, / Unfriendly to society's chief
joys, / Thy worst effect is banishing for
hours / The sex whose presence civilizes
ours. [*Ib.* 251]

12 I cannot talk with civet in the room, / A
fine puss-gentleman that's all perfume.
[*Ib.* 283]

13 A fool with judges, amongst fools a
judge: / He says but little, and that little
said / Owes all its weight, like loaded
dice, to lead. / His wit invites you by his
looks to come, / But when you knock, it
never is at home. [*Ib.* 300]

14 Some farrier should prescribe his proper
course, / Whose only fit companion is his
horse. [*Ib.* 411]

15 An honest man, close-buttoned to the
chin, / Broadcloth without, and a warm
heart within. [*Epistle to Joseph Hill*]

16 The busy trifler dreams himself alone, /
Frames many a purpose, and God works
his own. [*Expostulation*, 322]

17 Thousands, careless of the damning sin, /
Kiss the book's outside who ne'er look
within. [*Ib.* 388]

18 'Twas April, as the bumpkins say, / The
legislature called it May. [*A Fable*]

19 The man that hails you Tom or Jack, /
And proves by thumps upon your back /
How he esteems your merit, / Is such a
friend, that one had need / Be very much
his friend indeed / To pardon or to bear
it. [*Friendship*, 163]

20 And diff'ring judgements serve but to
declare, / That truth lies somewhere, if
we knew but where. [*Hope*, 423]

21 Absence from whom we love is worse
than death. ['*Hope, like the Short-lived
Ray*']

22 John Gilpin was a citizen / Of credit and
renown, / A train-band captain eke was
he / Of famous London town. [*John
Gilpin*, i]

23 To-morrow is our wedding-day, / And
we will then repair / Unto the Bell at
Edmonton, / All in a chaise and pair.
[*Ib.* iii]

24 So you must ride / On horseback after
we. [*Ib.* iv]

25 O'erjoyed was he to find / That, though
on pleasure she was bent, / She had a
frugal mind. [*Ib.* viii]

26 Smack went the whip, round went the
wheels, / Were never folk so glad; / The
stones did rattle underneath, / As if
Cheapside were mad. [*Ib.* xi]

27 And up he got, in haste to ride, / But soon
came down again. [*Ib.* xii]

28 For loss of time, / Although it grieved
him sore, / Yet loss of pence, full well he
knew, / Would trouble him much more.
[*Ib.* xiv]

29 So, Fair and softly, John he cried, / But
John he cried in vain. [*Ib.* xxii]

30 Away went Gilpin, neck or naught, /
Away went hat and wig! [*Ib.* xxv]

31 The dogs did bark, the children screamed,
/ Up flew the windows all; / And every
soul bawled out, Well done! / As loud as
he could bawl. [*Ib.* xxviii]

32 Away went Gilpin – who but he? / His
fame soon spread around – He carries
weight! he rides a race! / 'Tis for a
thousand pound! [*Ib.* xxix]

33 The dinner waits, and we are tired: /
Said Gilpin – So am I! [*Ib.* xxxvii]

34 Which brings me to / The middle of my
song. [*Ib.* xxxix]

1 My hat and wig will soon be here, / They are upon the road. [*John Gilpin*, xliv]

2 Right glad to find / His friend in merry pin. [*Ib.* xlv]

3 My head is twice as big as yours, / They therefore needs must fit. [*Ib.* xlvii]

4 Says John, It is my wedding-day, / And all the world would stare, / If wife should dine at Edmonton, / And I should dine at Ware. [*Ib.* xlix]

5 So turning to his horse, he said, / I am in haste to dine; / 'Twas for your pleasure you came here, / You shall go back for mine. [*Ib.* l]

6 Now let us sing, Long live the king, / And Gilpin, long live he; / And when he next doth ride abroad, / May I be there to see! [*Ib.* lxiii]

7 No dancing bear was so genteel, / Or half so *dégagé*. [*Of Himself*]

8 Oh for a closer walk with God, / A calm and heavenly frame; / A light to shine upon the road / That leads to me to the Lamb! [*Olney Hymns*, 1]

9 What peaceful hours I once enjoyed! / How sweet their memory still! / But they have left an aching void / The world can never fill. [*Ib.*]

10 Nor sword nor spear the stripling took, / But chose a pebble from the brook. [*Ib.* 4]

11 My God, till I received thy stroke, / How like a beast was I! / So unaccustomed to the yoke, / So backward to comply. [*Ib.* 12]

12 There is a fountain filled with blood / Drawn from Emmanuel's veins; / And sinners, plunged beneath that flood, / Lose all their guilty stains. [*Ib.* 15]

13 When this poor, lisping, stammering tongue / Lies silent in the grave. [*Ib.*]

14 Can a woman's tender care / Cease towards the child she bare? / Yes, she may forgetful be, / Yet will I remember thee. [*Ib.* 18]

15 Prayer makes the Christian's armour bright; / And Satan trembles when he sees / The weakest saint upon his knees. [*Ib.* 29]

16 I seem forsaken and alone, / I hear the lion roar; / And every door is shut but one, / And that is Mercy's door. [*Ib.* 33]

17 God moves in a mysterious way, / His wonders to perform; / He plants his footsteps in the sea, / And rides upon the storm.

Deep in unfathomable mines / Of never-failing skill, / He treasures up his bright designs, / And works his sovereign will. [*Olney Hymns*, 35]

18 Behind a frowning providence / He hides a smiling face. [*Ib.*]

19 The bud may have a bitter taste, / But sweet will be the flower. [*Ib.*]

20 Toll for the brave – / The brave! that are no more: / All sunk beneath the wave, / Fast by their native shore. [*On the Loss of the Royal George*]

21 A land-breeze shook the shrouds, / And she was overset; / Down went the Royal George, / With all her crew complete. [*Ib.*]

22 It was not in the battle, / No tempest gave the shock, / She sprang no fatal leak, / She ran upon no rock; / His sword was in the sheath, / His fingers held the pen, / When Kempenfelt went down / With twice four hundred men. [*Ib.*]

23 He and his eight hundred / Must plough the wave no more. [*Ib.*]

24 There goes the parson, oh! illustrious spark, / And there, scarce less illustrious, goes the clerk! [*On observing some Names of Little Note recorded in the 'Biographica Britannica'*]

25 Oh that those lips had language! Life has passed / With me but roughly since I heard thee last. [*On the Receipt of My Mother's Picture*, 1]

26 Blest be the art that can immortalize. [*Ib.* 8]

27 Wretch even then, life's journey just begun. [*Ib.* 24]

28 May I but meet thee on that peaceful shore, / The parting word shall pass my lips no more! [*Ib.* 34]

29 Dupe of to-morrow even from a child. [*Ib.* 41]

30 Where once we dwelt our name is heard no more, / Children not thine have trod my nursery floor; / And where the gardener Robin, day by day, / Drew me to school along the public way, / Delighted with my bauble coach, and wrapped / In scarlet mantle warm, and

velvet capped, / 'Tis now become a history little known, / That once we called the pastoral house our own. [*On the Receipt of My Mother's Picture*, 46]

1 Thy morning bounties ere I left my home, / The biscuit or confectionary plum. [*Ib.* 60]

2 Not scorned in Heaven, though little noticed here. [*Ib.* 73]

3 Me howling blasts drive devious, tempest-tossed, / Sails ripped, seams opening wide, and compass lost. [*Ib.* 102]

4 I shall not ask Jean Jacques Rousseau / If birds confabulate or no. [*Pairing Time Anticipated*]

5 The poplars are felled, farewell to the shade, / And the whispering sound of the cool colonnade! [*The Poplar Field*]

6 Unmissed but by his dogs and by his groom. [*The Progress of Error*, 95]

7 Oh, laugh or mourn with me the rueful jest, / A cassocked huntsman and a fiddling priest! [*Ib.* 110]

8 He takes the field, the master of the pack / Cries, 'Well done, Saint!' and claps him on the back. [*Ib.* 114]

9 Himself a wanderer from the narrow way, / His silly sheep, what wonder if they stray? [*Ib.* 118]

10 Remorse, the fatal egg by Pleasure laid / In every bosom where her nest is made. [*Ib.* 239]

11 Mortals, whose pleasures are their only care, / First wish to be imposed on, and then are. [*Ib.* 289]

12 Thou god of our idolatry, the Press. [*Ib.* 461]

13 Then, shifting his side (as a lawyer knows how). [*The Report of an Adjudged Case*]

14 For 'tis a truth well known to most, / That whatsoever thing is lost – / We seek it, ere it come to light, / In every cranny but the right. [*The Retired Cat*, 95]

15 Always, he mounted, kissed his horse. [*Retirement*, 578]

16 Absence of occupation is not rest, / A mind quite vacant is a mind distressed. [*Ib.* 623]

17 Built God a church, and laughed his Word to scorn. [(Voltaire) *Ib.* 688]

18 Philologists who chase / A panting syllable through time and space, / Start it

at home, and hunt it in the dark, / To Gaul, to Greece, and into Noah's ark. [*Retirement*, 691]

19 Beggars invention and makes fancy lame. [*Ib.* 710]

20 Mary! I want a lyre with other strings. [*Sonnet to Mrs Unwin*]

21 And, of all lies (be that one poet's boast) / The lie that flatters I abhor the most. [*Table Talk*, 87]

22 As if the world and they were hand and glove. [*Ib.* 173]

23 Stop, while ye may; suspend your mad career! [*Ib.* 435]

24 Made poetry a mere mechanic art; / And every warbler has his tune by heart. [(Pope) *Ib.* 656]

25 I sing the Sofa. [*The Task*, Bk I, 'The Sofa', 1]

26 The nurse sleeps sweetly, hired to watch the sick, / Whom, snoring, she disturbs. [*Ib.* I. 89]

27 He [the mole], not unlike the great ones of mankind, / Disfigures earth; and, plotting in the dark, / Toils much to earn a monumental pile, / That may record the mischiefs he has done. [*Ib.* I. 274]

28 A tawny skin, / The vellum of the pedigree they [gipsies] claim. [*Ib.* I. 568]

29 God made the country, and man made the town. [*Ib.* I. 749]

30 Oh for a lodge in some vast wilderness, / Some boundless contiguity of shade, / Where rumour of oppression and deceit, / Of unsuccessful or successful war, / Might never reach me more! [*Ib.* II, 'The Timepiece', 1]

31 Mountains interposed / Make enemies of nations, who had else, / Like kindred drops, been mingled into one. [*Ib.* II. 17]

32 Slaves cannot breathe in England; if their lungs / Receive our air, that moment they are free; / They touch our country, and their shackles fall. [*Ib.* II. 40]

33 England, with all thy faults, I love thee still – / My country! [*Ib.* II. 206]

34 There is a pleasure in poetic pains / Which only poets know. [*Ib.* II. 285]

35 Variety's the very spice of life, / That gives it all its flavour. [*Ib.* II. 606]

1 Let her pass, and charioted along / In guilty splendour, shake the public ways! [*The Task*, III, 'The Garden'. 69]

2 I was a stricken deer, that left the herd / Long since. [*Ib*. III. 108]

3 Charge / His mind with meanings that he never had. [*Ib*. III. 148]

4 Great contest follows, and much learned dust / Involves the combatants. [*Ib*. III. 161]

5 From reveries so airy, from the toil / Of dropping buckets into empty wells, / And growing old in drawing nothing up. [*Ib*. III. 188]

6 Riches have wings, and grandeur is a dream. [*Ib*. III. 263]

7 Detested sport, / That owes its pleasures to another's pain. [*Ib*. III. 326]

8 How various his employments, whom the world / Calls idle; and who justly, in return, / Esteems that busy world an idler too! [*Ib*. III. 352]

9 Who loves a garden loves a greenhouse too. [*Ib*. III. 566]

10 He comes, the herald of a noisy world, / With spattered boots, strapped waist, and frozen locks; / News from all nations lumbering at his back. [*Ib*. IV, 'The Winter Evening', 5]

11 Now stir the fire, and close the shutters fast, / Let fall the curtains, wheel the sofa round, / And, while the bubbling and loud-hissing urn / Throws up a steamy column, and the cups, / That cheer but not inebriate, wait on each, / So let us welcome peaceful evening in. [*Ib*. IV. 36]

12 'Tis pleasant, through the loopholes of retreat, / To peep at such a world; to see the stir / Of the great Babel, and not feel the crowd. [*Ib*. IV. 88]

13 O Winter, ruler of th' inverted year. [*Ib*. IV. 120]

14 Spare feast! a radish and an egg. [*Ib*. IV. 173]

15 With spots quadrangular of diamond form, / Ensanguined hearts, clubs typical of strife, / And spades, the emblem of untimely graves. [*Ib*. IV. 217]

16 In indolent vacuity of thought. [*Ib*. IV. 297]

17 It seems the part of wisdom. [*Ib*. IV. 336]

18 All learned, and all drunk! [*The Task*, IV. 478]

19 'Tis your country bids! / Gloriously drunk, obey th' important call! [*Ib*. IV. 509]

20 Preposterous sight! the legs without the man. [*Ib*. V, 'The Winter Morning Walk', 20]

21 Shaggy, and lean, and shrewd, with pointed ears, / And tail cropped short, half lurcher and half cur. [*Ib*. V. 45]

22 Silently as a dream the fabric rose; – / No sound of hammer or of saw was there. [*Ib*. V. 144]

23 Great princes have great playthings. [*Ib*. V. 177]

24 But war's a game, which, were their subjects wise, / Kings would not play at. [*Ib*. V. 187]

25 And the first smith was the first murderer's son. [*Ib*. V. 219]

26 All constraint, / Except what wisdom lays on evil men, / Is evil. [*Ib*. V. 448]

27 There is in souls a sympathy with sounds; / And, as the mind is pitched the ear is pleased / With melting airs, or martial, brisk, or grave; / Some chord in unison with what we hear / Is touched within us, and the heart replies. [*Ib*. VI, 'The Winter Walk at Noon', 1]

28 Meditation here / May think down hours to moments. Here the heart / May give a useful lesson to the head, / And Learning wiser grow without his books. [*Ib*. VI. 84]

29 Nature is but a name for an effect, / Whose cause is God. [*Ib*. VI. 223]

30 A cheap but wholesome salad from the brook. [*Ib*. VI. 304]

31 I would not enter on my list of friends / (Though graced with polished manners and fine sense, / Yet wanting sensibility) thé man / Who needlessly sets foot upon a worm. [*Ib*. VI. 560]

32 Shine by the side of every path we tread / With such a lustre, he who runs may read. [*Tirocinium*, 79]

33 The parson knows enough who knows a duke. [*Ib*. 403]

34 As a priest, / A piece of mere church furniture at best. [*Ib*. 425]

35 Thy lot thy brethren of the slimy fin / Would envy, could they know that thou

wast doomed / To feed a bard, and to be praised in verse. [*To the Immortal Memory of the Halibut on which I Dined*]

1 Greece, sound thy Homer's, Rome thy Virgil's name, / But England's Milton equals both in fame. [*To John Milton*]

2 The twentieth year is well-nigh past, / Since first our sky was overcast; / Ah would that this might be the last! / My Mary! [*To Mary*]

3 Al' thy threads with magic art / Have wound themselves about this heart. [*Ib.*]

4 Just knows, and knows no more, her Bible true – / A truth the brilliant Frenchman [Voltaire] never knew. [*Truth*, 327]

5 I am monarch of all I survey, / My right there is none to dispute; / From the centre all round to the sea / I am lord of the fowl and the brute. / Oh, solitude, where are the charms / That sages have seen in thy face? / Better dwell in the midst of alarms, / Than reign in this horrible place. [*Verses supposed to be written by Alexander Selkirk*]

6 Society, friendship, and love, / Divinely bestowed upon man, / Oh, had I the wings of a dove, / How soon would I taste you again! [*Ib.*]

7 But the sound of the church-going bell / These valleys and rocks never heard, / Ne'er sighed at the sound of a knell, / Or smiled when a Sabbath appeared. [*Ib.*]

8 But the sea-fowl has gone to her nest, / The beast is laid down in his lair. [*Ib.*]

9 He kissed likewise the maid in the kitchen, and seemed upon the whole a most loving, kissing, kind-hearted gentleman. [Letter to the Rev. J. Newton, 29 Mar. 1784]

GEORGE CRABBE   1754–1832

10 What is a church? – Our honest sexton tells, / 'Tis a tall building, with a tower and bells. [*The Borough*, Letter ii. 'The Church', 11]

11 Habit with him was all the test of truth, / 'It must be right: I've done it from my youth.' [*Ib.* iii, 'The Vicar', 138]

12 Books cannot always please, however good; / Minds are not ever craving for their food. [*Ib.* xxiv, 'Schools', 402]

13 The ring so worn, as you behold, / So thin, so pale, is yet of gold. [*His Mother's Wedding Ring*]

14 A master-passion is the love of news. [*The Newspaper*, 279]

15 Oh! rather give me commentators plain, / Who with no deep researches vex the brain; / Who from the dark and doubtful love to run, / And hold their glimmering tapers to the sun. [*The Parish Register*, 'Baptisms', 89]

16 When the coarse cloth she saw, with many a stain, / Soiled by rude hinds, who cut and came again. [*Tales*, vii, 'The Widow's Tale', 25]

17 But 'twas a maxim he had often tried, / That right was right, and there he would abide. [*Ib.* xv, 'The Squire and the Priest', 365]

18 He tried the luxury of doing good. [*Tales of the Hall*, iii, 'Boys at School', 139]

19 'The game', said he, 'is never lost till won.' [*Ib.* xv, 'Gretna Green', 334]

DINAH MARIA CRAIK
[*née* MULOCK]   1826–1887

20 Douglas, Douglas, tender and true. [*Songs of our Youth*, 'Douglas, Douglas']

THOMAS CRANMER   1489–1556

21 This hand hath offended. [Said at his burning, of the hand that had signed a recantation]

RICHARD CRASHAW   1613?–1649

22 O thou undaunted daughter of desires! / By all thy dower of lights and fires; / By all the eagle in thee, all the dove; / By all thy lives and deaths of love; / By thy large draughts of intellectual day. [*The Flaming Heart upon the Book of Saint Teresa*, 93]

23 By the full kingdom of that final kiss / That seized thy parting soul, and sealed thee His; / By all the Heavens thou hast in Him – / Fair sister of the Seraphim! [*Ib.* 101]

24 It was Thy day, sweet! and did rise / Not from the East, but from Thine eyes. [*Hymn of the Nativity*, 21]

1 Love, thou art absolute sole Lord / Of life and death. [*Hymn to Saint Teresa*, 1]

2 Farewell house, and farewell home! / She's for the Moors, and martyrdom. [*Ib.* 63]

3 I would be married, but I'd have no wife, / I would be married to a single life. [*On Marriage*]

4 *Nympha pudica Deum vidit, et erubuit.* – The conscious water saw its God, and blushed. [*Sacred Epigram*, in Latin and English]

5 Two walking baths; two weeping motions; / Portable, and compendious oceans. [*Saint Mary Magdalene, or The Weeper*, xix]

6 Does the day-star rise? / Still thy stars do fall and fall. / Does day close his eyes? / Still the fountain weeps for all. / Let night or day do what they will, / Thou hast thy task; thou weepest still. [*Ib.* xxiii]

7 Whoe'er she be, / That not impossible she / That shall command my heart and me;

Where e'er she lie, / Lockt up from mortal eye, / In shady leaves of destiny. [*Wishes to his Supposed Mistress*, 1]

8 A face made up, / Out of no other shop / Than what nature's white hand sets ope. [*Ib.* 28]

9 Life, that dares send / A challenge to his end, / And when it comes say, 'Welcome, friend!' [*Ib.* 85]

MRS EDMUND CRASTER
? – 1874

10 The Centipede was happy quite, / Until the Toad in fun / Said, 'Pray which leg goes after which?' / And worked her mind to such a pitch, / She lay distracted in the ditch / Considering how to run. [Attr.]

JULIA CRAWFORD   19 Cent.

11 Kathleen Mavourneen! the grey dawn is breaking, / The horn of the hunter is heard on the hill. [*Kathleen Mavourneen*]

12 It may be for years, and it may be for ever, / Oh! why art thou silent, thou voice of my heart? [*Ib.*]

JOHN WILSON CROKER
1780–1857

13 We now are, as we always have been, decidedly and conscientiously attached to what is called the Tory, and which might with more propriety be called the Conservative, party. [*Quarterly Review*, Jan. 1830]

14 A game which a sharper once played with a dupe, entitled, 'Heads I win, tails you lose.' [*Croker Papers*]

OLIVER CROMWELL   1599–1658

15 A few honest men are better than numbers. [Letter to Sir W. Spring, Sept. 1643]

16 Such men as had the fear of God before them ... the plain russet-coated captain that knows what he fights for and loves what he knows. [Letter, Sept. 1643]

17 The State, in choosing men to serve it, takes no notice of their opinions. If they be willing faithfully to serve it, that satisfies. [Before Marston Moor, 2 July 1644]

18 I beseech you, in the bowels of Christ, think it possible you may be mistaken. [Letter to the Church of Scotland, 3 Aug. 1650]

19 It [the Battle of Worcester] is for aught I know a crowning mercy. [Letter, 4 Sept. 1651]

20 Remark all these roughnesses, pimples, warts, and everything as you see me, otherwise I will never pay a farthing for it. [Instructions to Lely, on the painting of his portrait]

21 What shall we do with this bauble? There, take it way. [(The mace) When dismissing Parliament, 20 Apr. 1653]

22 It is not fit that you should sit here any longer! ... you shall now give place to better men. [Speech to the Rump Parliament, 22 Jan. 1654]

23 Necessity hath no law. Feigned necessities, imaginary necessities ... are the greatest cozenage that men can put upon the Providence of God, and make pretences to break known rules by. [Speech to Parliament, 12 Sept. 1654]

24 It is not my design to drink or to sleep, but my design is to make what haste I can to be gone. [Dying words]

127

T. W. H. CROSLAND   1868–1924

1 The Unspeakable Scot. [Title of an essay]

**BISHOP RICHARD CUMBER-
LAND**   1631–1718

2 It is better to wear out than to rust out.
[Quoted in Horne, *The Duty of Contending for the Faith*]

E. E. CUMMINGS   1894–1962

3 next to of course god america i / love you
land of the pilgrims and so forth oh
[*Next to of Course God*]

4 (and down went / my Uncle / Sol / and
started a worm farm) [*Nobody Loses all
the Time*]

5 a politician is an arse upon which everyone has sat except a man [*A Politician*]

ALLAN CUNNINGHAM   1784–1842

6 It's hame and it's hame, hame fain wad I
be, / O, hame, hame, hame to my ain
countree! [*It's Hame and It's Hame*]

7 Wha the deil hae we got for a king, / But
a wee, wee German lairdie! [*The Wee,
Wee German Lairdie*]

8 A wet sheet and a flowing sea, / A wind
that follows fast / And fills the white and
rustling sail / And bends the gallant mast.
[*A Wet Sheet and a Flowing Sea*]

**ROBERT CUNNINGHAME-
GRAHAM**   1735–1797

9 If doughty deeds my lady please, / Right
soon I'll mount my steed. [*If Doughty
Deeds My Lady Please*]

WILL CUPPY   1884–1949

10 The Dodo never had a chance. He seems
to have been invented for the sole purpose
of becoming extinct and that was all he
was good for. [*How to Become Extinct*]

JOHN PHILPOT CURRAN   1750–1817

11 The condition upon which God hath given

liberty to man is eternal vigilance.
[Speech on the right of election of Lord
Mayor of Dublin, 10 July 1790]

'COLIN CURZON'   20 Cent.

12 I'll tell you in a phrase, my sweet, exactly
what I mean: / ... Not tonight, Josephine. [*Not tonight, Josephine*]

CYRANO DE BERGERAC
1620–1655

13 *Périsse l'Univers, pourvu que je me venge.*
– Perish the Universe, provided I have
my revenge. [*Agrippine*, IV. iii]

HARRY DACRE   End of 19 Cent.

14 Daisy, Daisy, give me your answer, do! /
I'm half crazy, all for the love of you! /
It won't be a stylish marriage, / I can't
afford a carriage, / But you'll look sweet
upon the seat / Of a bicycle made for
two! [*Daisy Bell*]

CHARLES A. DANA   1819–1897

15 When a dog bites a man that is not news,
but when a man bites a dog that is news.
['What is News?' *New York Sun*, 1882]

SAMUEL DANIEL   1562–1619

16 Princes in this case / Do hate the traitor,
though they love the treason. [*Tragedy of
Cleopatra*, IV. i]

17 Love is a sickness full of woes, / All
remedies refusing; / A plant that with
most cutting grows, / Most barren with
best using. / Why so? / More we enjoy
it, more it dies; / If not enjoyed, it sighing
cries, / Hey ho. [*Hymen's Triumph*, I. v]

18 How dost thou wear and weary out thy
days, / Restless Ambition, never at an
end! [*Philotas*, chorus]

19 Fair is my love, and cruel as she's fair, /
Her brow shades frowns, although her
eyes are sunny. [*Sonnets to Delia*, 6]

20 Care-charmer Sleep, son of the sable
Night, / Brother to Death, in silent
darkness born, / Relieve my languish,
and restore the light, / With dark forgetting of my cares return. / And let the

day be time enough to mourn / The ship-wreck of my ill-adventured youth. [*Sonnets to Delia*, 44]

1 Let others sing of knights and paladins / In aged accents and untimely words; / Paint shadows in imaginary lines, / Which well the reach of their high wits records. [*Ib.* 46]

2 Unless above himself he can / Erect himself, how poor a thing is man. [*To the Lady Margaret, Countess of Cumberland*, 12]

3 Come, worthy Greek! Ulysses, come; / Possess these shores with me! / The winds and seas are troublesome / And here we may be free. [*Ulysses and the Siren*, 1]

4 Custom, that is before all law; Nature, that is above all art. [*A Defence of Rhyme*]

DANTE ALIGHIERI   1265–1321

5 *Nel mezzo del cammin di nostra vita.* – In the mid-course of our life. [*Divina Commedia*, 'Inferno', i. 1]

6 *Lasciate ogni speranza voi ch'entrate.* – All hope abandon, ye who enter here. [*Ib.* iii. 9]

7 *Il gran rifiuto.* – The great refusal. [*Ib.* iii. 60]

8 *Nessun maggior dolore / Che ricordarsi del tempo felice / Nella miseria.* – There is no greater grief than to recall a time of happiness when in misery. [*Ib.* V. 121]

9 *E'n la sua volontade è nostra pace.* – In His will is our peace. [*Ib.* 'Paradiso', iii. 85]

10 *L'amor che move il sole e l'altre stelle.* – Love that moves the sun and the other stars. [*Ib.* xxxiii. 145]

GEORGES JACQUES DANTON
1759–1794

11 *De l'audace, encore de l'audace, et tou-jours de l'audace!* – Boldness, more boldness, and perpetual boldness! [Speech in the Legislative Assembly, 2 Sept. 1792]

RICHARD DARRÉ   1895–1953

12 *Blut und Boden.* – Blood and soil. [*Law for the Establishment of Hereditary Farms*, 29 Sept. 1933]

CHARLES DARWIN   1809–1882

13 The highest possible stage in moral culture is when we recognize that we ought to control our thoughts. [*The Descent of Man*, Ch. 4]

14 Man with all his noble qualities, with sympathy that feels for the most debased, with benevolence which extends not only to other men but to the humblest living creature, with his god-like intellect which has penetrated into the movements and constitution of the solar system – with all these exalted powers -- still bears in his bodily frame the indelible stamp of his lowly origin. [*Ib.* conclusion]

15 I have called this principle, by which each slight variation, if useful, is preserved, by the term of Natural Selection. [*The Origin of Species*, Ch. 3]

16 We will now discuss in a little more detail the struggle for existence. [*Ib.*]

17 The expression often used by Mr Herbert Spencer of the Survival of the Fittest is more accurate, and is sometimes equally convenient. [*Ib.*]

ERASMUS DARWIN   1731–1802

18 Soon shall thy arm, unconquered steam! afar / Drag the slow barge, or drive the rapid car; / Or on wide-waving wings expanded bear / The flying chariot through the field of air. [*The Botanic Garden*, I. i. 289]

CHARLES DAVENANT 1656–1714

19 Custom, that unwritten law, / By which the people keep even kings in awe. [*Circe*, II. iii]

SIR WILLIAM DAVENANT
1606–1668

20 The lark now leaves his watery nest / And climbing, shakes his dewy wings; / He takes this window for the east; / And to implore your light, he sings; / Awake, awake the morn will never rise, / Till she can dress her beauty at your eyes. [*Song*]

JOHN DAVIDSON   1857–1909

21 When the pods went pop on the broom, green broom. [*A Runnable Stag*]

22 As I went down to Dymchurch Wall,

heard the South sing o'er the land. [*In Romney Marsh*]

1 I step into my heart and there I meet / A god-almighty devil singing small, / Who would like to shout and whistle in the street, / And squelch the passers flat against the wall. [*Thirty Bob a Week*, 43]

2 With thirty bob a week to keep a bride / He fell in love and married in his teens: / At thirty bob he stuck; but he knows it isn't luck: / He knows the seas are deeper than tureens. [*Ib.* 50]

SIR JOHN DAVIES   1569–1626

3 Wedlock, indeed, hath oft comparèd been / To public feasts, where meet a public rout; / Where they that are without would fain go in. / And they that are within would fain go out. [*Contention betwixt a Wife, A Widow and a Maid*, 196]

4 Judge not the play before the play be done. [*Respice Finem*]

W. H. DAVIES   1870–1940

5 A rainbow and a cuckoo's song / May never come together again; / May never come / This side the tomb. [*A Great Time*]

6 What is this life if, full of care, / We have no time to stand and stare? [*Leisure*]

7 Sweet Stay-at-Home, sweet Well-content. [*Sweet Stay-at-Home*]

JEFFERSON DAVIS   1808–1889

8 All we ask is to be let alone. [Inaugural Address as President of the Confederate States of America, 1861. Attr.]

T. O. DAVIS   1814–1845

9 Come in the evening, or come in the morning, / Come when you're looked for, or come without warning. [*The Welcome*]

C. DAY LEWIS   1904–1972

10 I sang as one / Who on a tilting deck sings / To keep men's courage up, though the wave hangs / That shall cut off their sun. [*The Conflict*]

11 Now the peak of summer's past, the sky is overcast / And the love we swore would last for an age seems deceit. [*Hornpipe*]

12 Suppose that we, to-morrow or the next day, / Came to an end – in storm the shafting broken, / Or a mistaken signal, the flange lifting – / Would that be premature, a text for sorrow? [*Suppose that we*]

STEPHEN DECATUR   1779–1820

13 Our country! In her intercourse with foreign nations, may she always be in the right; but our country, right or wrong. [Toast given at Norfolk, Virginia, Apr. 1816]

MARQUISE DU DEFFAND   1697–1780

14 *La distance n'y fait rien; il n'y a que le premier pas qui coûte.* – The distance doesn't matter; it is only the first step that is difficult. [(On the legend that St Denis walked six miles, carrying his head in his hand) Letter to d'Alembert, 7 July 1763]

DANIEL DEFOE   1661 ?–1731

15 He bade me observe it, and I should always find, that the calamities of life were shared among the upper and lower part of mankind; but that the middle station had the fewest disasters. [*Robinson Crusoe*, Pt 1]

16 One day, about noon, going towards my boat, I was exceedingly surprised with the print of a man's naked foot on the shore, which was very plain to be seen in the sand. [*Ib.*]

17 I takes my man Friday with me. [*Ib.*]

18 The best of men cannot suspend their fate: / The good die early, and the bad die late. [*Character of the late Dr S. Annesley*]

19 All men would be tyrants if they could. [*The Kentish Petition*, addenda, 11]

20 Wherever God erects a house of prayer, / The Devil always builds a chapel there; / And 'twill be found, upon examination, / The latter has the largest congregation. [*The True-Born Englishman*, Pt i. 1]

THOMAS DEKKER   1572 ?–1632

21 The best of men / That e'er wore earth about him, was a sufferer, / A soft, meek,

patient, humble, tranquil spirit, / The
first true gentleman that ever breathed.
[*The Honest Whore*, Pt 1. V. ii]

1 Art thou poor, yet hast thou golden
slumbers? / O sweet content! / Art thou
rich, yet is thy mind perplexed? / O
punishment! [*Patient Grissill*, I]

2 To add to golden numbers, golden numbers. [*Ib.*]

3 Honest labour bears a lovely face. [*Ib.*]

4 Golden slumbers kiss your eyes, / Smiles
awake you when you rise. / Sleep, pretty
wantons, do not cry, / And I will sing a
lullaby. [*Ib.* IV. ii]

5 Brave shoemakers, all gentlemen of the
gentle craft. [*Shoemaker's Holiday*, III. i]

6 Troll the bowl, the jolly nut-brown bowl,
/ And here, kind mate, to thee! / Let's
sing a dirge for Saint Hugh's soul, / And
down it merrily. [*Ib.* V. iv]

WALTER DE LA MARE
1873–1956

7 Ann, Ann! / Come! quick as you can! /
There's a fish that *talks* / In the frying
pan. [*Alas, Alack*]

8 Oh, no man knows / Through what wild
centuries / Roves back the rose. [*All
That's Past*]

9 Very old are we men; / Our dreams are
tales / Told in dim Eden / By Eve's
nightingales. [*Ib.*]

10 Silence and sleep like fields / Of amaranth
lie. [*Ib.*]

11 Far are the shades of Arabia, / Where
the Princes ride at noon. [*Arabia*]

12 He is crazed with the spell of far Arabia, /
They have stolen his wits away. [*Ib.*]

13 Here lies a most beautiful lady, / Light
of step and heart was she; / I think she
was the most beautiful lady / That ever
was in the West Country. [*An Epitaph*]

14 When I lie where shades of darkness /
Shall no more assail mine eyes. [*Fare
Well*]

15 Look thy last on all things lovely, /
Every hour. [*Ib.*]

16 Since that all things thou wouldst praise
/ Beauty took from those who loved
them / In other days. [*Ib.*]

17 Nought but vast sorrow was there – /
The sweet cheat gone. [*The Ghost*]

18 Three jolly gentlemen, / In coats of red, /
Rode their horses / Up to bed. [*The
Huntsmen*]

19 Do diddle di do, / Poor Jim Jay / Got
stuck fast / In Yesterday. [*Jim Jay*]

20 'Is there anybody there?' said the Traveller, / Knocking on the moonlit door.
[*The Listeners*]

21 'Tell them I came, and no-one answered,
That I kept my word', he said. [*Ib.*]

22 And how the silence surged softly backward, / When the plunging hoofs were
gone. [*Ib.*]

23 It's a very odd thing – / As odd as can
be – / That whatever Miss T. eats / Turns
into Miss T. [*Miss T.*]

24 Softly along the road of evening, / In a
twilight dim with rose, / Wrinkled with
age, and drenched with dew, / Old Nod,
the shepherd, goes. [*Nod*]

25 Three jolly Farmers / Once bet a pound /
Each dance the other would / Off the
ground. [*Off the Ground*]

26 Old Sallie Worm from her hole doth
peep; / 'Come!' said Old Shellover, /
'Ay!' said Creep. [*Old Shellover*]

27 Slowly, silently, now the moon / Walks
the night in her silver shoon. [*Silver*]

28 Who said, 'Peacock Pie'? / The old king
to the sparrow: / Who said, 'Crops are
ripe'? / Rust to the harrow. [*The Song of
the Mad Prince*]

29 Who said, 'Where sleeps she now? /
Where rests she now her head, / Bathed
in eve's loveliness'? / That's what I said.
[*Ib.*]

30 Who said, 'Ay, mum's the word'? /
Sexton to willow. [*Ib.*]

31 Life's troubled bubble broken. [*Ib.*]

ABBÉ JACQUES DELILLE
1738–1813

32 *Le sort fait les parents, la choix fait les
amis.* – Fate chooses your relations, you
choose your friends. [*Malheur et pitié*, I]

SIR JOHN DENHAM   1615–1669

33 O could I flow like thee, and make my
stream / My great example, as it is my

131

theme! / Though deep, yet clear, though gentle, yet not dull, / Strong without rage, without o'er-flowing full. [*Cooper's Hill*, 189]

THOMAS, LORD DENMAN
1779–1854

1 Trial by jury itself . . . will be a delusion, a mockery, and a snare. [Judgement in O'Connell *v.* the Queen, 4 Sept. 1844]

C. J. DENNIS   1876–1938

2 Me name is Mud. [*The Sentimental Bloke*]

JOHN DENNIS   1657–1734

3 A man who could make so vile a pun would not scruple to pick a pocket. [Attr.]

4 Damn them! they will not let my play run, but they steal my thunder! [Attr. (on hearing his stage effects used by another dramatist)]

NIGEL DENNIS   1912–

5 This man, she reasons, as she looks at her husband, is a poor fish. But he is the nearest I can get to the big one that got away. [*Cards of Identity*, p. 176]

6 But then one is always excited by descriptions of money changing hands. It's much more fundamental than sex. [*Ib.* 179]

THOMAS DE QUINCEY
1785–1859

7 So then, Oxford Street, stony-hearted stepmother, thou that listenest to the sighs of orphans, and drinkest the tears of children, at length I was dismissed from thee. [*Confessions of an English Opium Eater*, Pt i]

8 Everlasting farewells! and again, and yet again reverberated – everlasting farewells! [*Ib.* ii]

9 Murder Considered as One of the Fine Arts. [Title of essay]

10 If once a man indulges himself in murder, very soon he comes to think little of robbing; and from robbing he comes

next to drinking and sabbath-breaking, and from that to incivility and procrastination. [*On Murder*]

EDWARD, EARL OF DERBY
1799–1869

11 A great Whig authority used always to say that the duty of an Opposition was very simple – it was, to oppose everything, and propose nothing. [Speech in House of Commons, 4 June 1841]

12 Don't you see that we have dished the Whigs? [In reference to the Reform Bill of 1867]

LORD DESART   1845–1898

13 Mother Hubbard, you see, was old: there being no mention of others, we may presume she was alone; a widow – a friendless, old, solitary widow. Yet did she despair? Did she sit down and weep, ·or read a novel, or wring her hands? No! She went to the cupboard. [*Mock Sermon: Old Mother Hubbard*]

RENÉ DESCARTES   1596–1650

14 *Le bon sens est la chose du monde la mieux partagée: car chacun pense en être si bien pourvu, que ceux même qui sont les plus difficiles à contenter en toute autre chose n'ont point coutume d'en désirer plus qu'ils en ont.* – Common sense is the most widely distributed commodity in the world, for everyone thinks himself so well endowed with it that those who are hardest to please in any other respect generally have no desire to possess more of it than they have. [*Le Discours de la méthode*, I]

15 *La lecture de tous les bons livres est comme une conversation avec les plus honnêtes gens des siècles passés.* – The reading of all good books is like a conversation with the finest men of past centuries. [*Ib.*]

16 *C'est quasi le même de converser avec ceux des autres siècles que de voyager.* – Travelling is almost like talking with men of other centuries. [*Ib.*]

17 *Cogito, ergo sum.* – I think, therefore I am. [*Ib.* IV]

EUSTACHE DESCHAMPS
1345–1406

1 *Qui pendra la sonnette au chat? –* Who will bell the cat? [*Ballade: Le Chat et les souris*]

PHILIPPE DESTOUCHES
1680–1754

2 *Les absents ont toujours tort. –* The absent are always in the wrong. [*L'Obstacle imprévu*, I. vi]

EDWARD DE VERE see under
OXFORD, EARL OF

PORFIRIO DIAZ   1830–1915

3 Poor Mexico, so far from God and so near to the United States! [Attr.]

CHARLES DIBDIN   1745–1814

4 Did you ever hear of Captain Wattle? / He was all for love and a little for the bottle. [*Captain Wattle and Miss Roe*]

5 What argufies pride and ambition? / Soon or late death will take us in tow: / Each bullet has got its commission, / And when our time's come we must go. [*Each Bullet has its Commission*]

6 In every mess I find a friend, / In every port a wife. [*Jack in his Element*]

7 Then trust me, there's nothing like drinking / So pleasant on this side the grave; / It keeps the unhappy from thinking, / And makes e'en the valiant more brave. [*Nothing like Grog*]

8 For they say there's a Providence sits up aloft, / To keep watch for the life of poor Jack! [*Poor Jack*]

9 The lass that loves a sailor. [*The Round Robin*]

10 Here, a sheer hulk, lies poor Tom Bowling, / The darling of our crew. [*Tom Bowling*]

11 Faithful, below, he did his duty; / But now he's gone aloft. [*Ib.*]

12 As he rowed along, thinking of nothing at all. [*The Waterman*]

THOMAS DIBDIN   1771–1841

13 Oh! it's a snug little island, / A right little, tight little island! [*The Snug Little Island*]

CHARLES DICKENS   1812–1870

14 Rather a tough customer in argeyment, Joe, if anybody was to try and tackle him. [(Parkes) *Barnaby Rudge*, Ch. 1]

15 Something will come of this. I hope it mayn't be human gore. [(Simon Tappertit) *Ib.* 4]

16 'There are strings', said Mr Tappertit, '... in the human heart that had better not be wibrated.' [*Ib.* 22]

17 Oh gracious, why wasn't I born old and ugly? [(Miss Miggs) *Ib.* 70]

18 This is a London particular.... A fog, miss. [*Bleak House*, Ch. 3]

19 I expect a judgement. Shortly. [(Miss Flite) *Ib.*]

20 Educating the natives of Borrioboola-Gha, on the left bank of the Niger. [(Mrs Jellyby) *Ib.* 4]

21 I am always conscious of an uncomfortable sensation now and then when the wind is blowing in the east. [(Mr Jarndyce) *Ib.* 6]

22 I only ask to be free. The butterflies are free. [(Harold Skimpole) *Ib.*]

23 Think! I've got enough to do, and little enough to get for it, without thinking. [(Coavinses) *Ib.*]

24 Not to put too fine a point upon it. [(Mr Snagsby) *Ib.* 11]

25 He wos very good to me, he wos! [(Jo) *Ib.*]

26 He [Mr Turveydrop] is celebrated almost everywhere, for his Deportment. [(Caddy) *Ib.* 14]

27 What is peace? Is it war? No. Is it strife? No. Is it lovely, and gentle, and beautiful, and pleasant, and serene, and joyful? O yes! [(Mr Chadband) *Ib.* 19]

28 Jobling, there *are* chords in the human mind. [(Guppy) *Ib.* 20]

29 Mrs Jellyby was looking far away into Africa. [*Ib.* 23]

1 'It is', says Chadband, 'the ray of rays, the sun of suns, the moon of moons, the star of stars. It is the light of Terewth.' [*Bleak House*, 25]

2 It's my old girl that advises. She has the head. But I never own to it before her. Discipline must be maintained. [(Mr Bagnet) *Ib.* 27]

3 'Old girl,' says Mr Bagnet, 'give him my opinion. You know it.' [*Ib.*]

4 It is a melancholy truth that even great men have their poor relations. [*Ib.* 28]

5 She's Colour-Serjeant of the Nonpareil battalion. [(Mr Bagnet) *Ib.* 52]

6 Far better hang wrong fler than no fler. [(The debilitated cousin) *Ib.* 53]

7 Oh let us love our occupations, / Bless the squire and his relations, / Live upon our daily rations, / And always know our proper stations. [*The Chimes*, 2nd Quarter]

8 In came a fiddler – and tuned like fifty stomach-aches. / In came Mrs Fezziwig, one vast substantial smile. [*A Christmas Carol*, Stave 2]

9 'God bless us every one!' said Tiny Tim, the last of all. [*Ib.* 3]

10 'Somebody's sharp.' 'Who is?' asked the gentleman, laughing. . . 'Only Brooks of Sheffield,' said Mr Murdstone. [*David Copperfield*, Ch. 2]

11 'I am a lone lorn creetur',' were Mrs Gummidge's words . . . 'and everythink goes contrairy with me.' [*Ib.* 3]

12 'I feel it more than other people,' said Mrs Gummidge. [*Ib.*]

13 She's been thinking of the old 'un! [(Mr Peggotty of Mrs Gummidge) *Ib.*]

14 Barkis is willin'. [*Ib.* 5]

15 I live on broken wittles – and I sleep on the coals. [(The Waiter) *Ib.*]

16 Experientia does it – as papa used to say. [(Mrs Micawber) *Ib.* 11]

17 'In case anything turned up', which was his favourite expression. [(Mr Micawber) *Ib.*]

18 I never will desert Mr Micawber. [(Mrs Micawber) *Ib.* 12]

19 Annual income twenty pounds, annual expenditure nineteen nineteen six, result happiness. Annual income twenty pounds, annual expenditure twenty pounds ought and six, result misery. [(Mr Micawber) *David Copperfield*, 12]

20 The mistake was made of putting some of the trouble out of King Charles's head into my head. [(Mr Dick) *Ib.* 17]

21 We are so very 'umble. [(Uriah Heep) *Ib.*]

22 Uriah, with his long hands slowly twining over one another, made a ghastly writhe from the waist upwards. [*Ib.*]

23 'Orses and dorgs is some men's fancy. They're wittles and drink to me. [(The Gentleman on the Coach) *Ib.* 19]

24 I only ask for information. [(Rosa Dartle) *Ib.* 20]

25 'It was as true', said Mr Barkis, '. . . as taxes is. And nothing's truer than them.' [*Ib.* 21]

26 What a world of gammon and spinnage it is, though, ain't it! [(Miss Mowcher) *Ib.* 22]

27 Ain't I volatile? [(Miss Mowcher) *Ib.*]

28 I should be happy, myself, to propose two months. . . . but I have a partner, Mr Jorkins. [(Mr Spenlow) *Ib.* 23]

29 I assure you she's the dearest girl. [(Traddles) *Ib.* 27]

30 Accidents will occur in the best-regulated families. [(Mr Micawber) *Ib.* 28; similar phase occurs in *Pickwick Papers*, Ch. 2]

31 He's a going out with the tide. [(Mr Peggotty) (*Ib.* 30]

32 You know, Trotwood, I don't want to swing a cat. I never do swing a cat. [(Mr Dick) *Ib.* 35]

33 Only my child-wife. [(Dora) *Ib.* 44]

34 Circumstances beyond my individual control. [(Mr Micawber) *Ib.* 49]

35 I'm Gormed – and I can't say no fairer than that! [(Mr Peggotty) *Ib.* 63]

36 He's tough, ma'am, tough, is J.B. Tough and devilish sly! [(Major Bagstock) *Dombey and Son*, Ch. 7]

37 I want to know what it says. . . . The sea, Floy, what it is that it keeps on saying. [(Paul Dombey) *Ib.* 8]

38 'Wal'r, my boy,' replied the Captain, 'in the Proverbs of Solomon you will find the following words, "May we never want a friend in need, nor a bottle to give him!" When found, make a note of' [(Captain Cuttle) *Ib.* 15]

1 Train up a fig-tree in the way it should go, and when you are old sit under the shade of it. [(Captain Cuttle) *Dombey and Son*, 19]

2 Cows are my passion. What I have ever sighed for has been to retreat to a Swiss farm, and live entirely surrounded by cows – and china. [(Mrs Skewton) *Ib.* 21]

3 The bearings of this observation lays in the application on it. [(Bunsby) *Ib.* 23]

4 Say, like those wicked Turks, there is no What's-his-name but Thingummy, and What-you-may-call-it is his prophet! [(Mrs Skewton) *Ib.* 27]

5 I positively adore Miss Dombey; – I–I am perfectly sore with loving her. [(Mr Toots) *Ib.* 30]

6 If you could see my legs when I take my boots off, you'd form some idea of what unrequited affection is. [(Mr Toots) *Ib.* 48]

7 Stranger, pause and ask thyself the question, Canst thou do likewise? If not, with a blush retire. [(Mrs Sapsea's epitaph) *Edwin Drood*, Ch. 4]

8 'Dear me,' said Mr Grewgious, peeping in, 'it's like looking down the throat of Old Time.' [*Ib.* 9]

9 There's a young man hid with me, in comparison with which young man I am a Angel. That young man hears the words I speak. That young man has a secret way pecooliar to himself, of getting at a boy, and at his heart, and at his liver. [(Magwitch) *Great Expectations*, Ch. 1]

10 He calls the knaves, Jacks, this boy! ... And what coarse hands he has! And what thick boots! [(Estella) *Ib.* 8]

11 I've a pretty large experience of boys, and you're a bad set of fellows. Now mind ... you behave yourself! [(Mr Jaggers) *Ib.* 11]

12 On the Rampage, Pip, and off the Rampage, Pip; such is Life! [(Joe Gargery) *Ib.* 15]

13 You don't object to an aged parent, I hope? [(Wemmick) *Ib.* 25]

14 We didn't find that it [London] come up to its likeness in the red bills – it is there drawd too architectooralooral. [(Joe Gargery) *Ib.* 27]

15 Halloa! Here's a church! ... Let's go in! ... Here's Miss Skiffins! Let's have a wedding. [(Wemmick) *Ib.* 55]

16 Now, what I want is Facts. ... Facts alone are wanted in life. [(Mr Gradgrind) *Hard Times*, Bk I. Ch. 1]

17 It couldn't exist without allonging and marshonging to something or other. [(Mr Meagles) *Little Dorrit*, Bk I. Ch. 2]

18 Whatever was required to be done, the Circumlocution Office was beforehand with all the public departments in the art of perceiving – HOW NOT TO DO IT. [*Ib.* I. 10]

19 Look here. Upon my soul you mustn't come into the place saying you want to know, you know. [(Barnacle Junior) *Ib.*]

20 I hate a fool! [(Mr F.'s Aunt) *Ib.* I. 13]

21 Take a little time – count five-and-twenty, Tattycoram. [(Mr Meagles) *Ib.* I. 16]

22 In company with several other old ladies of both sexes. [*Ib.* I. 17]

23 It was not a bosom to repose upon, but it was a capital bosom to hang jewels upon. [(Mrs Merdle's) *Ib.* I. 21]

24 There's milestones on the Dover Road! [(Mr F.'s Aunt) *Ib.* I. 23]

25 It came like magic in a pint bottle; it was not ecstasy but it was comfort. [(Flora Finching) *Ib.* I. 24]

26 Papa, potatoes, poultry, prunes and prism, are all very good words for the lips; especially prunes and prism. [(Mrs General) *Ib.* II. 5]

27 Once a gentleman, and always a gentleman. [(Rigaud) *Ib.* II. 28]

28 The Lord No Zoo. [(Toby Chuzzlewit) *Martin Chuzzlewit*, Ch. 1]

29 Any man may be in good spirits and good temper when he's well dressed. There an't much credit in that. [(Mark Tapley) *Ib.* 5]

30 There might be some credit in being jolly. [(Mark Tapley) *Ib.*]

31 A highly geological home-made cake. [*Ib.*]

32 With affection beaming in one eye, and calculation out of the other. [(Mrs Todgers) *Ib.* 8]

33 'Do not repine, my friends,' said Mr Pecksniff, tenderly. 'Do not weep for me. It is chronic.' [*Ib.* 9]

34 Let us be moral, Let us contemplate existence. [(Mr Pecksniff) *Ib.*]

1 Here's the rule for bargains: 'Do other men, for they would do you.' That's the true business precept. [(Jonas Chuzzlewit) *Martin Chuzzlewit* 11]

2 Buy an annuity cheap, and make your life interesting to yourself and everybody else that watches the speculation. [*Ib.* 18]

3 'Mrs Harris,' I says, 'leave the bottle on the chimley-piece, and don't ask me to take none, but let me put my lips to it when I am so dispoged.' [(Mrs Gamp) *Ib.* 19]

4 Some people ... may be Rooshans, and others may be Prooshans; they are born so, and will please themselves. Them which is of other naturs thinks different. [(Mrs Gamp) *Ib.*]

5 Therefore I *do* require it, which I makes confession, to be brought reg'lar and draw'd mild. [(Mrs Gamp) *Ib.* 25]

6 'She's the sort of woman now', said Mould ... 'one would almost feel disposed to bury for nothing: and do it neatly too!' [*Ib.*]

7 He'd make a lovely corpse. [(Mrs Gamp) *Ib.*]

8 'Sairey,' says Mrs Harris, 'sech is life. Vich likeways is the hend of all things!' [(Mrs Gamp) *Ib.* 29]

9 Our backs is easy ris. We must be cracked-up, or they rises, and we snarls. We shows our teeth, I tell you, fierce. You'd better crack us up, you had! [(Chollop) *Ib.* 33]

10 Oh Sairey, Sairey, little do we know wot lays afore us! [(Mrs Gamp) *Ib.* 40]

11 'Bother Mrs Harris!' said Betsey Prig ... 'I don't believe there's no sich a person!' [*Ib.* 49]

12 But the words she spoke of Mrs Harris, lambs could not forgive ... nor worms forget. [(Mrs Gamp) *Ib.*]

13 Which fiddle-strings is weakness to expredge my nerves this night! [(Mrs Gamp) *Ib.* 51]

14 United Metropolitan Improved Hot Muffin and Crumpet and Punctual Delivery Company. [*Nicholas Nickleby*, Ch. 2]

15 At Mr Wackford Squeers's Academy, Dotheboys Hall ... Youth are boarded, clothed, booked, furnished with pocket-money, provided with all necessaries, instructed in all languages living and dead. [*Nicholas Nickleby*, 3]

16 He had but one eye and the popular prejudice runs in favour of two. [(Mr Squeers) *Ib.* 4]

17 Subdue your appetites, my dears, and you've conquered human natur. [(Mr Squeers) *Ib.* 5]

18 Here's richness! [(Mr Squeers) *Ib.*]

19 C-l-e-a-n, clean, verb active, to make bright, to scour. W-i-n, win, d-e-r, der, winder, a casement. When the boy knows this out of the book, he goes and does it. [(Mr Squeers) *Ib.* 8]

20 When he has learnt that bottinney means a knowledge of plants, he goes and knows 'em. That's our system, Nickleby; what do you think of it? [(Mr Squeers) *Ib.*]

21 As she frequently remarked when she made any such mistake, it would be all the same a hundred years hence. [(Mrs Squeers) *Ib.* 9]

22 There are two styles of portrait painting; the serious and the smirk. [(Miss La Creevy) *Ib.* 10]

23 One mask of brooses both blue and green. [(Fanny Squeers) *Ib.* 15]

24 I pity his ignorance and despise him. [(Fanny Squeers) *Ib.*]

25 We've got a private master comes to teach us at home, but we ain't proud, because ma says it's sinful. [(Mrs Kenwigs) *Ib.* 16]

26 'What's the water in French, sir?' '*L'eau*,' replied Nicholas. 'Ah!' said Mr Lillywick, shaking his head mournfully. 'I thought as much. Lo, eh? I don't think anything of that language – nothing at all.' [*Ib.*]

27 Language was not powerful enough to describe the infant phenomenon. [*Ib.* 23]

28 She's the only sylph *I* ever saw, who could stand upon one leg, and play the tambourine on her other knee, *like* a sylph. [(Mr Crummles) *Ib.* 25]

29 I am a demd villain! ... I will fill my pockets with change for a sovereign in half-pence and drown myself in the Thames ... who for her sake will become a demd, damp, moist, unpleasant body! [(Mr Mantalini) *Ib.* 34]

1 In the absence of the planet Venus, who has gone on business to the Horse Guards. [(The Gentleman in the Small-clothes) *Nicholas Nickleby*, 41]

2 She is come at last – at last – and all is gas and gaiters! [(The Gentleman in the Small-clothes) *Ib*. 49]

3 My life is one demd horrid grind! [(Mr Mantalini) *Ib*. 64]

4 He has gone to the demnition bow-wows. [(Mr Mantalini) *Ib*.]

5 Is the old min agreeable? [(Dick Swiveller) *Old Curiosity Shop*, Ch. 2]

6 What is the odds so long as the fire of soul is kindled at the taper of conwiviality, and the wing of friendship never moults a feather! [(Dick Swiveller) *Ib*.]

7 Pass the rosy wine. [(Dick Swiveller) *Ib*. 7]

8 Codlin's the friend, not Short. [(Codlin) *Ib*. 19]

9 It's calm and – what's that word again – critical! – no – classical, that's it – it is calm and classical. [(Mrs Jarley) *Ib*. 27]

10 We cannot have single gentlemen to come into this establishment and sleep like double gentlemen without paying extra for it ... an equal quantity of slumber was never got out of one bed and bedstead, and if you want to sleep in that way, you must pay for a double-bedded room. [(Dick Swiveller) *Ib*. 35]

11 It was a maxim with Foxey – our revered father, gentlemen – 'Always suspect everybody'. [(Sampson Brass) *Ib*. 66]

12 Oliver Twist has asked for more! [(Bumble) *Oliver Twist*, Ch. 2]

13 Known by the *sobriquet* of 'The artful Dodger'. [*Ib*. 8]

14 'Hard,' replied the Dodger. 'As nails,' added Charley Bates. [*Ib*. 9]

15 There is a passion for hunting something deeply implanted in the human breast. [*Ib*. 10]

16 I only know two sorts of boys. Mealy boys, and beef-faced boys. [(Mr Grimwig) *Ib*. 14]

17 A beadle! A parish beadle, or I'll eat my head! [(Mr Grimwig) *Ib*. 17]

18 There's light enough for what I've got to do. [(Bill Sikes) *Ib*. 47]

19 'If the law supposes that,' said Mr Bumble, ... 'the law is a ass – a idiot.' [*Oliver Twist*, 51]

20 A literary man – *with* a wooden leg. [(Mr Boffin on Silas Wegg) *Our Mutual Friend*, Bk I. Ch. 5]

21 Professionally he declines and falls, and as a friend he drops into poetry. [(Mr Boffin on Silas Wegg) *Ib*.]

22 Decline-and-Fall-Off-the-Rooshan-Empire. [(Mr Boffin) *Ib*.]

23 'Mrs Boffin, Wegg,' said Boffin, 'is a highflyer at Fashion.' [*Ib*.]

24 Meaty jelly, too, especially when a little salt, which is the case when there's ham, is mellering to the organ. [(Silas Wegg) *Ib*.]

25 Mr Podsnap settled that whatever he put behind him he put out of existence. ... Mr Podsnap had even acquired a peculiar flourish of his right arm in often clearing the world of its most difficult problems, by sweeping them behind him. [*Ib*. I. 11]

26 The question [with Mr Podsnap] was, would it bring a blush into the cheek of the young person? [*Ib*.]

27 Oh! *I* know their tricks and their manners. [(Fanny Cleaver) *Ib*. II. 1]

28 I think ... that it is the best club in London. [(Mr Twemlow, on the House of Commons) *Ib*. II. 3]

29 Queer Street is full of lodgers just at present. [(Fledgeby) *Ib*. III. 1]

30 O Mrs Higden, Mrs Higden, you was a woman and a mother, and a mangler in a million million. [(Sloppy) *Ib*. III. 9]

31 T'other governor. [(Mr Riderhood) *Ib*. IV. 1]

32 The dodgerest of the dodgers. [(Mr Fledgeby) *Ib*. IV. 8]

33 The Golden Dustman. [(Mr Boffin) *Ib*. IV. 11]

34 He had used the word in its Pickwickian sense. [(Mr Blotton) *Pickwick Papers*, Ch. 1]

35 'An observer of human nature, sir,' said Mr Pickwick. [*Ib*. 2]

36 Half a crown in the bill, if you look at the waiter. [(Jingle) *Ib*.]

37 Not presume to dictate, but broiled fowl and mushrooms – capital thing! [(Jingle) *Ib*.]

1 Kent, sir – everybody knows Kent – apples, cherries, hops and women. [(Jingle) *Pickwick Papers.* 2]

2 I wants to make your flesh creep. [(The Fat Boy) *Ib.* 8]

3 'It's always best on these occasions to do what the mob do.' 'But suppose there are two mobs?' suggested Mr Snodgrass. 'Shout with the largest,' replied Mr Pickwick. [*Ib.* 13]

4 Can I unmoved see the dying / On a log, / Expiring frog! [(Mrs Leo Hunter) *Ib.* 15]

5 Tongue; well, that's a wery good thing when it an't a woman's. [(Mr Weller) *Ib.* 19]

6 Battledore and shuttlecock's a wery good game, ven you an't the shuttlecock and two lawyers the battledores, in which case it gets too excitin' to be pleasant. [(Mr Weller) *Ib.* 20]

7 Mr Weller's knowledge of London was extensive and peculiar. [*Ib.*]

8 Take example by your father, my boy, and be wery careful o' vidders all your life, specially if they've kept a public house, Sammy. [(Mr Weller) *Ib.*]

9 The wictim o' connubiality, as Blue Beard's domestic chaplain said, with a tear of pity, ven he buried him. [(Mr Weller) *Ib.*]

10 Poverty and oysters always seem to go together. [(Sam Weller) *Ib.* 22]

11 Wery good power o' suction, Sammy ... You'd ha' made an uncommon fine oyster, Sammy, if you'd been born in that station o' life. [(Mr Weller) *Ib.* 23]

12 It's over, and can't be helped, and that's one consolation, as they always say in Turkey, ven they cuts the wrong man's head off. [(Sam Weller) *Ib.*]

13 Dumb as a drum vith a hole in it, sir. [(Sam Weller) *Ib.* 25]

14 Wery glad to see you, indeed, and hope our acquaintance may be a long 'un, as the gen'l'm'n said to the fi' pun' note. [(Sam Weller) *Ib.*]

15 Subscribe to our noble society for providing the infant negroes in the West Indies with flannel waistcoats and moral pocket handkerchiefs. [(Mr Stiggins) *Ib.* 27]

16 Vether it's worth goin' through so much, to learn so little, as the charity-boy said ven he got to the end of the alphabet, is a matter o' taste. [(Mr Weller) *Pickwick Papers*, 27]

17 Eccentricities of genius. [*Ib.* 30]

18 A double glass o' the inwariable. [(Mr Weller) *Ib.* 33]

19 Poetry's unnat'ral; no man ever talked poetry 'cept a beadle on boxin' day. [(Mr Weller) *Ib.*]

20 I am afeerd that werges on the poetical, Sammy. [(Mr Weller) *Ib.*]

21 'That's rather a sudden pull up, ain't it, Sammy?' inquired Mr Weller.
'Not a bit on it,' said Sam; 'she'll vish there wos more, and that's the great art o' letter writin'.' [*Ib.*]

22 Never sign a walentine with your own name. [(Sam Weller) *Ib.*]

23 If your governor don't prove a alleybi, he'll be what the Italians call reg'larly flummoxed. [(Mr Weller) *Ib.*]

24 She's a swellin' wisibly before my wery eyes. [(Mr Weller) *Ib.*]

25 It's my opinion, sir, that this meeting is drunk. [(Mr Stiggins) *Ib.*]

26 A Being, erect upon two legs, and bearing all the outward semblance of a man, and not of a monster. [(Sergeant Buzfuz) *Ib.* 34]

27 'Do you spell it with a "V" or a "W"?' inquired the judge.
'That depends upon the taste and fancy of the speller, my Lord,' replied Sam. [*Ib.*]

28 'Oh, quite enough to get, sir, as the soldier said ven they ordered him three hundred and fifty lashes,' replied Sam.
'You must not tell us what the soldier, or any other man, said, sir,' interposed the judge; 'it's not evidence.' [*Ib.*]

29 'Yes I have a pair of eyes,' replied Sam, 'and that's just it. If they wos a pair o' patent double million magnifyin' gas microscopes of hextra power, p'raps I might be able to see through a flight o' stairs and a deal door; but bein' only eyes, you see, my wision's limited.' [*Ib.*]

30 Oh Sammy, Sammy, vy worn't there a alleybi! [(Mr Weller) *Ib.*]

31 A friendly swarry, consisting of a boiled leg of mutton with the usual trimmings. [*Ib.* 37]

32 'You disliked the killibeate taste, perhaps?'

'I don't know much about that 'ere,' said Sam. 'I thought they'd a wery strong flavour o' warm flat-irons.'

'That *is* the killibeate, Mr Weller,' observed Mr John Smauker, contemptuously. [*Pickwick Papers*, 37]

1 'That 'ere young lady,' replied Sam. 'She knows wot's wot, she does.' [*Ib.*]

2 *We* know, Mr Weller – we, who are men of the world – that a good uniform must work its way with the women, sooner or later. [(The Gentleman in Blue) *Ib.*]

3 Anythin' for a quiet life, as the man said wen he took the sitivation at the light-house. [(Sam Weller) *Ib.* 43]

4 Wich is your partickler wanity? Wich wanity do you like the flavour on best, sir? [(Sam Weller) *Ib.* 45]

5 I'm wery much mistaken if that 'ere Jingle worn't a doin' somethin' in the water-cart way. [(Sam Weller) *Ib.*]

6 'Never ... see a dead postboy, did you?' inquired Sam. ... 'No,' rejoined Bob, 'I never did.' 'No,' rejoined Sam triumphantly. 'Nor never vill; and there's another thing that no man never see, and that's a dead donkey.' [*Ib.* 51]

7 'There's a Providence in it all,' said Sam. 'O' course there is,' replied his father with a nod of grave approval. 'Wot 'ud become o' the undertakers without it, Sammy?' [*Ib.* 52]

8 Grief never mended no broken bones, and as good people's wery scarce, what I says is, make the most on 'em. [*Sketches by Boz*, 'Scenes', Ch. 22, 'Gin-Shops']

9 A smattering of everything, and a knowledge of nothing. [(Minerva House) *Ib.* 'Tales', Ch. 3, 'Sentiment']

10 I pass my whole life, miss, in turning an immense pecuniary Mangle. [(Mr Lorry) *A Tale of Two Cities*, Bk I. Ch. 4]

11 Although it's a long time on the road, it is on the road and coming. I tell thee it never retreats, and never stops. [(Mme Defarge) *Ib.* II. 16]

12 'It is possible that it may not come, during our lives. We shall not see the triumph.' [Defarge] 'We shall have helped it,' returned madame. [*Ib.*]

13 'It is a far, far better thing that I do, than I have ever done; it is a far, far better rest, that I go to, than I have ever known.' [(Sidney Carton) *A Tale of Two Cities*, III. 15]

EMILY DICKINSON 1830–1886

14 Ample make this bed. / Make this bed with awe; / In it wait till judgement break / Excellent and fair. [*Ample make this Bed*]

15 Because I could not stop for Death, / He kindly stopped for me; / The carriage held but just ourselves / And Immortality. [*The Chariot*]

16 It was not death, for I stood up, / And all the dead lie down; / It was not night, for all the bells / Put out their tongues, for noon. [*It was not Death, for I stood up*]

17 How dreary to be somebody! / How public, like a frog / To tell your name the livelong day / To an admiring bog! [*Life*]

18 Our journey had advanced; / Our feet were almost come / To that odd fork in Being's road, / Eternity by term. [*Our Journey had Advanced*]

19 My life closed twice before its close; / It yet remains to see / If Immortality unveil / A third event to me. [*Parting*]

20 Parting is all we know of heaven, / And all we need of hell. [*Ib.*]

21 There came a wind like a bugle; / It quivered through the grass. [*There came a Wind*]

22 How much can come / And much can go, / And yet abide the world! [*Ib.*]

23 There's a certain slant of light, / On winter afternoons, / That oppresses, like the weight / Of cathedral tunes. [*There's a certain Slant of Light*]

24 I never saw a moor, / I never saw the sea; / Yet know I how the heather looks, / And what a wave must be. [*Time and Eternity*]

DENIS DIDEROT 1713–1784

25 *Faire son devoir tellement quellement, toujours dire du bien de M. le prieur et laisser aller le monde à sa fantaisie.* – To do his duty somehow, always to speak well of the Prior, and let the world go its own way. [*Le Neveu de Rameau*]

1 *L'esprit de l'escalier.* – Staircase wit (i.e. the good retort thought of after the conversation is finished). [*Paradoxe sur le comédien*]

2 *On a dit que l'amour qui ôtait l'esprit à ceux qui en avaient en donnait à ceux qui n'en avaient pas.* – It has been said that love robs those who have it of their wit, and gives it to those who have none. [*Ib.*]

DIODORUS SICULUS
2nd half of 1 Cent. B.C.

3 Medicine for the soul. [Inscription quoted, I. 49. 3]

DIOGENES
fl. c. 380 B.C.

4 Stand a little less between me and the sun. [(When asked by Alexander if he lacked anything) Plutarch's *Life of Alexander*, 14]

DIONYSIUS OF HALICAR-
NASSUS
c. 40–8 B.C.

5 History is philosophy drawn from examples. [*Ars rhetorica*, 11. 2]

BENJAMIN DISRAELI 1804–1881

6 Though I sit down now, the time will come when you will hear me. [Maiden speech in House of Commons, 7 Dec. 1837]

7 The Continent will not suffer England to be the workshop of the world. [Speech in House of Commons, 15 Mar. 1838]

8 The noble Lord [Lord Stanley] is the Rupert of parliamentary discussion. [*Ib.* 24 Apr. 1844]

9 The right honourable gentleman [Sir Robert Peel] caught the Whigs bathing and walked away with their clothes. [*Ib.* 28 Feb. 1845]

10 A Conservative government is an organized hypocrisy. [*Ib.* 17 Mar. 1845]

11 A precedent embalms a principle. [*Ib.* 22 Feb. 1848]

12 England does not love coalitions. [*Ib.* 16 Dec. 1852]

13 Finality is not the language of politics. [*Ib.* 28 Feb. 1859]

14 I am myself a gentleman of the Press, and I bear no other scutcheon. [Speech in House of Commons, 18 Feb. 1863]

15 The characteristic of the present age is a craving credulity. [Speech at Oxford Diocesan Conference, 25 Nov. 1864]

16 Man . . . is a being born to believe. [*Ib.*]

17 Is man an ape or an angel? Now I am on the side of the angels. [*Ib.*]

18 I had to prepare the mind of the country [for Reform], and . . . to educate our party. [Speech at Edinburgh, 29 Oct. 1867]

19 You behold a range of exhausted volcanoes. [(Referring to ministers on the Government Bench) Speech at Manchester, 3 Apr. 1872]

20 A University should be a place of light, of liberty, and of learning. [Speech in House of Commons, 11 Mar. 1873]

21 An author who speaks about his own books is almost as bad as a mother who talks about her own children. [Speech at banquet in Glasgow, 19 Nov. 1873]

22 Lord Salisbury and myself have brought you back peace – but a peace I hope with honour. [Speech in House of Commons, 16 July 1878]

23 A sophistical rhetorician inebriated with the exuberance of his own verbosity. [(Gladstone) Speech at banquet, 27 July 1878]

24 No Government can be long secure without a formidable Opposition. [*Coningsby*, Bk II. Ch. 1]

25 The Arch-Mediocrity who presided, rather than ruled, over this Cabinet of Mediocrities. [*Ib.*]

26 A sound Conservative government . . . Tory men and Whig measures. [*Ib.* II. 6]

27 Youth is a blunder; Manhood a struggle; Old Age a regret. [*Ib.* III. 1]

28 Read no history: nothing but biography, for that is life without theory. [*Contarini Fleming*, Pt I. Ch. 23]

29 'Sensible men are all of the same religion.' 'And pray, what is that?' inquired the prince. 'Sensible men never tell.' [*Endymion*, Bk I. Ch. 81]

30 Time is the great physician. [*Ib.* VI. 9]

31 They [the Furies] mean well; their feelings are strong, but their hearts are in

the right place. [*The Infernal Marriage,* Pt I. 1]

1 The blue ribbon of the turf. [(The Derby) *Life of Lord George Bentinck*, Ch. 26]

2 The gondola of London. [(A hansom-cab) *Lothair*, Ch. 27]

3 When a man fell into his anecdotage it was a sign for him to retire from the world. [*Ib.* 28]

4 Every woman should marry – and no man. [*Ib.* 30]

5 Little things affect little minds. [*Sybil*, Bk III. Ch. 2]

6 Mr Kremlin himself was distinguished for ignorance, for he had only one idea, – and that was wrong. [*Ib.* IV. 5]

7 I was told that the Privileged and the People formed Two Nations. [*Ib.* IV. 8]

8 London is a modern Babylon. [*Tancred*, Bk V. Ch. 5]

9 I repeat . . . that all power is a trust – that we are accountable for its exercise – that, from the people, and for the people, all springs, and all must exist. [*Vivian Grey*, Bk VI. Ch. 7]

10 All Paradise opens! Let me die eating ortolans to the sound of soft music! [*The Young Duke*, Bk I. Ch. 10]

11 A *dark* horse, which had never been thought of . . . rushed past the grand stand to sweeping triumph. [*Ib.* II. 5]

12 A man may speak very well in the House of Commons, and fail very completely in the House of Lords. There are two distinct styles requisite: I intend, in the course of my career, if I have time, to give a specimen of both. [*Ib.* V. 6]

13 Everyone likes flattery; and when you come to Royalty you should lay it on with a trowel. [Attr. remark to Matthew Arnold]

14 I am dead: dead, but in the Elysian fields. [(When translated to the House of Lords) Attr.]

15 If a traveller were informed that such a man [Lord John Russell] was leader of the House of Commons, he may well begin to comprehend how the Egyptians worshipped an insect. [Attr.]

16 Pray remember, Mr Dean, no dogma, no Dean. [Attr.]

17 We authors, Ma'am. [Attr. remark to Queen Victoria]

18 When I want to read a novel I write one. [Attr.]

19 Your dexterity seems a happy compound of the smartness of an attorney's clerk and the intrigue of a Greek of the lower empire. [Attr. remark to Lord Palmerston]

SYDNEY DOBELL   1824–1874

20 The murmur of the mourning ghost / That keeps the shadowy kine, / 'O Keith of Ravelston, / The sorrows of thy line!' [*A Nuptial Eve*]

AUSTIN DOBSON   1840–1921

21 And I wove the thing to a random rhyme, / For the Rose is Beauty, the Gardener, Time. [*A Fancy from Fontenelle*]

22 The ladies of St James's! / They're painted to the eyes, / Their white it stays for ever, / Their red it never dies: / But Phyllida, my Phyllida! / Her colour comes and goes; / It trembles to a lily, – / It wavers to a rose. [*The Ladies of St James's*]

23 I intended an Ode, / And it turned to a Sonnet. [*Rose Leaves*]

24 For I respectfully decline / To dignify the Serpentine, / And make *hors-d'œuvres* for fishes. [*To 'Lydia Languish'*]

PHILIP DODDRIDGE   1702–1751

25 Behold the bleeding Lamb of God, / Our spotless sacrifice! [Hymn]

26 O God of Bethel, by whose hand / Thy people still are fed. [(Later altered to 'O God of Jacob') Hymn]

27 Return, my roving heart, return. [Hymn]

28 See the old Dragon from his throne / Sink with enormous ruin down! [Hymn]

CHARLES FLETCHER DOLE   1845–1927

29 Democracy is on trial in the world, on a more colossal scale than ever before. [*The Spirit of Democracy*]

AELIUS DONATUS   4 Cent.

1 *Pereant qui ante nos nostra dixerunt.* —
Confound the men who have made our
remarks before us. [St Jerome, *Commentary on Ecclesiastes*, Ch. 1]

JOHN DONNE   1571?–1631

2 Twice or thrice had I loved thee / Before
I knew thy face or name, / So in a voice,
so in a shapeless flame, / Angels affect us
oft, and worshipped be. [*Air and Angels*]

3 Only our love hath no decay; / This, no
tomorrow hath, nor yesterday, / Running it never runs from us away, / But
truly keeps his first, last, everlasting day.
[*The Anniversary*]

4 Come live with me, and be my love, / And
we will some new pleasures prove / Of
golden sands and crystal brooks / With
silken lines, and silver hooks. [*The Bait*]

5 The day breaks not, it is my heart. [*Break
of Day*. Also attributed to John Dowland]

6 For God's sake hold your tongue, and
let me love. [*The Canonization*]

7 Dear love, for nothing less than thee /
Would I have broke this happy dream, /
It was a theme / For reason, much too
strong for fantasy, / Therefore tnou
waked'st me wisely; yet / My dream thou
brok'st not, but continued'st it. [*The
Dream*]

8 She, and comparisons are odious. [*Elegies*,
VIII, 'The Comparison', 54]

9 No spring, nor summer beauty hath such
grace, / As I have seen in one autumnal
face. [*Ib.* IX, 'The Autumnal'. 1]

10 So, if I dream I have you, I have you, /
For all our joys are but fantastical. [*Ib.*
X, 'The Dream', 13]

11 By our first strange and fatal interview.
[*Ib.* XVI, 'On His Mistress', 1]

12 Nurse, O my love is slain, I saw him go /
O'er the white Alps alone. [*Ib.* 52]

13 Whoever loves, if he do not propose /
The right true end of love, he's one that
goes / To sea for nothing but to make
him sick. [*Ib.* XVIII, 'Love's Progress', 1]

14 O my America! my new-found-land. [*Ib.*
XIX, 'To His Mistress Going to Bed', 27]

15 The household bird, with the red stomacher. [*Epithalamions*, 'On the Lady
Elizabeth and Count Palatine', 8]

16 So, so, break off this last lamenting kiss, /
Which sucks two souls, and vapours both
away, / Turn thou ghost that way, and
let me turn this, / And let our selves
benight our happiest day. [*The Expiration*]

17 Where, like a pillow on a bed, / A pregnant bank swelled up, to rest / The
violet's reclining head, / Sat we two, one
another's best. [*The Extasie*, 1]

18 Pictures in our eyes to get / Was all our
propagation. [*Ib.* 11]

19 All day, the same our postures were, /
And we said nothing all the day. [*Ib.* 19]

20 But O alas, so long, so far / Our bodies
why do we forbear? / They're ours,
though they're not we, we are / The
intelligences, they the sphere. [*Ib.* 49]

21 So must pure lovers' souls descend /
T'affections, and to faculties, / Which
sense may reach and apprehend, / Else a
great Prince in prison lies. [*Ib.* 65]

22 Who ever comes to shroud me, do not
harm / Nor question much / That subtle
wreath of hair, which crowns my arm.
[*The Funeral*]

23 Since you would save none of me, I bury
some of you. [*Ib.*]

24 I wonder by my troth, what thou, and I /
Did, till we loved? were we not weaned
till then, / But sucked on country pleasures, childishly / Or snorted we in the
seven sleepers' den? [*The Good-Morrow*]

25 And now good morrow to our waking
souls, / Which watch not one another
out of fear. [*Ib.*]

26 For love, all love of other sights controls,
/ And makes one little room, an everywhere [*Ib.*]

27 Where can we find two better hemispheres / Without sharp North, without
declining West? [*Ib.*]

28 Thou hast made me, and shall thy work
decay? [*Holy Sonnets*, I]

29 I am a little world made cunningly / Of
elements, and an angelic spright. [*Ib.* V]

30 This is my play's last scene, here heavens
appoint / My pilgrimage's last mile. [*Ib.*
VI]

1 At the round earth's imagined corners, blow / Your trumpets, Angels, and arise, arise / From death, you numberless infinities / Of souls. [*Holy Sonnets*, VII]

2 All whom the flood did, and fire shall o'erthrow, / All whom war, dearth, age, agues, tyrannies, / Despair, law, chance, hath slain. [*Ib.*]

3 But let them sleep, Lord, and me mourn a space. [*Ib.*]

4 Death be not proud, though some have called thee / Mighty and dreadful, for, thou art not so, / For, those whom thou think'st, thou dost overthrow / Die not, poor death. [*Ib.* X]

5 One short sleep past, we wake eternally, / And death shall be no more; death, thou shalt die. [*Ib.*]

6 Spit in my face you Jews, and pierce my side. [*Ib.* XI]

7 What if this present were the world's last night? [*Ib.* XIII]

8 Batter my heart, three personed God; for you / As yet but knock, breathe, shine and seek to mend. [*Ib.* XIV]

9 I, like an usurpt town, to another due, / Labour to admit you, but Oh, to no end. [*Ib.*]

10 For I / Except you enthrall me, never shall be free, / Nor ever chaste, except you ravish me. [*Ib.*]

11 Show me, dear Christ, thy spouse, so bright and clear. [*Ib.* XVIII]

12 Wilt thou forgive that sin, where I begun, / Which is my sin, though it were done before? / Wilt thou forgive those sins through which I run / And do them still, though still I do deplore? / When thou hast done, thou hast not done, / For I have more. [*Hymn to God the Father*]

13 Since I am coming to that holy room, / Where, with thy quire of Saints for evermore, / I shall be made thy Music; As I come / I tune the instrument here at the door, / And what I must do then, think here before. [*Hymn to God in My Sickness*]

14 When I died last, and, Dear, I die / As often as from thee I go, / Though it be but an hour ago, / And lovers' hours be full eternity. [*The Legacy*]

15 If yet I have not all thy love, / Dear, I shall never have it all. [*Lovers' Infiniteness*]

16 I long to talk with some old lover's ghost, / Who died before the god of love was born. [*Love's Deity*]

17 Rebel and Atheist too, why murmur I, / As though I felt the worst that love could do? [*Ib.*]

18 Send home my long strayed eyes to me, / Which, Oh, too long have dwelt on thee. [*The Message*]

19 'Tis the year's midnight, and it is the day's. [*Nocturnal upon St Lucy's Day*]

20 The world's whole sap is sunk: / The general balm th' hydroptic earth hath drunk. [*Ib.*]

21 Nature's great masterpiece, an elephant / The only harmless great thing. [*The Progress of the Soul*, 381]

22 When my grave is broke up again / Some second guest to entertain. [*The Relique*]

23 A bracelet of bright hair about the bone. [*Ib.*]

24 Her pure and eloquent blood / Spoke in her cheeks, and so distinctly wrought, / That one might almost say, her body thought. [*The Second Anniversary*, 244]

25 Sweetest love, I do not go, / For weariness of thee, / Nor in hope the world can show / A fitter Love for me; / But since that I / Must die at last, 'tis best / To use myself in jest, / Thus by feigned deaths to die. [Song: '*Sweetest love . . .*']

26 Go, and catch a falling star, / Get with child a mandrake root, / Tell me, where all past years are, / Or who cleft the Devil's foot. [Song: '*Go and Catch . . .*']

27 Ride ten thousand days and nights, / Till age snow white hairs on thee. [*Ib.*]

28 Though she were true, when you met her, / And last, till you write your letter, / Yet she / Will be / False, ere I come, to two, or three. [*Ib.*]

29 Busy old fool, unruly Sun, / Why dost thou thus, / Through windows, and through curtains call on us? / Must to thy motions lovers' seasons run? [*The Sun Rising*]

30 Love all alike, no season knows, nor clime, / Nor hours, days, months, which are the rags of time. [*Ib.*]

31 She is all States, and all Princes, I, / Nothing else is. / Princes do but play us. [*Ib.*]

1 Shine here to us, and thou art everywhere, / This bed thy centre is, these walls, thy sphere. [*The Sun Rising*]

2 I am two fools, I know, / For loving, and for saying so, / In whining Poetry. [*The Triple Fool*]

3 I have done one braver thing / Than all the Worthies did, / And yet a braver thence doth spring, / Which is to keep that hid. [*The Undertaking*]

4 As virtuous men pass mildly away, / And whisper to their souls to go, / Whilst some of their sad friends do say, / The breath goes now, and some say no. [*Valediction: Forbidding Mourning*]

5 If they be two, they are two so / As stiff twin compasses are two, / Thy soul the fixt foot makes no show / To move, but doth, if the other do.

And though it in the centre sit, / Yet when the other far doth roam, / It leans, and hearkens after it, / And grows erect, as that comes home. [*Ib.*]

6 On a round ball / A workman that hath copies by, can lay / An Europe, Afrique and an Asia, / And quickly make that, which was nothing, All. [*Valediction: Of Weeping*]

7 But I do nothing upon myself, and yet I am mine own Executioner. [*Devotions*, XII]

8 No man is an Island, entire of itself; every man is a piece of the Continent, a part of the main. [*Ib.* XVII]

9 Any man's death diminishes me, because I am involved in Mankind; And therefore never send to know for whom the bell tolls; it tolls for thee. [*Ib.*]

10 I neglect God and his Angels, for the noise of a fly, for the rattling of a coach, for the whining of a door. [*Sermons*, I. lxxx]

THOMAS SACKVILLE, EARL OF DORSET   1536–1608

11 His drink, the running stream; his cup, the bare / Of his palm closed; his bed, the hard, cold ground. [*Mirour for Magistrates*, Induction, 264]

12 His withered fist still knocking at Death's door. [*Ib.* 334]

13 So, in this way of writing without thinking, / Thou hast a strange alacrity in sinking. [*Satire on Edward Howard*]

FËDOR DOSTOYEVSKY   1821–1881

14 If you were to destroy in mankind the belief in immortality, not only love but every living force maintaining the life of the world would at once be dried up. Moreover, nothing then would be immoral, everything would be permissible, even cannibalism. [*Brothers Karamazov*, Pt 1. Bk i. Ch. 6]

15 I think if the devil doesn't exist, but man has created him, he has created him in his own image and likeness. [*Ib.* II. v. 4]

16 It's not God that I don't accept, Alyosha, only I most respectfully return Him the ticket. [*Ib.*]

SARAH DOUDNEY   1843–1926

17 But the waiting time, my brothers, / Is the hardest time of all. [*Psalm of Life*, 'The Hardest Time of All']

ARCHIBALD DOUGLAS, FIFTH EARL OF ANGUS   1449–1514

18 I'll bell the cat. [Said at a meeting of Scottish nobles, 1482]

NORMAN DOUGLAS   1868–1952

19 The fountain of Saint Elias, sulphurous and saponaceous, was renowned for its calming influence on all who suffered from abuse of lechery or alcohol, or from ingrowing toe-nails. [*South Wind*, Ch. 16]

20 Many a man who thinks to found a home discovers that he has merely opened a tavern for his friends. [*Ib.* 24]

WILLIAM DOUGLAS   1672–1748

21 And for bonnie Annie Laurie / I'll lay me doun and dee. [*Annie Laurie*]

LORENZO DOW   1777–1834

22 You will be damned if you do – And you will be damned if you don't. [Definition

of Calvinism from *Reflections on the Love of God*]

ERNEST DOWSON   1867–1900

1 And I was desolate and sick of an old passion. [*Non Sum Qualis Eram*]

2 I have been faithful to thee, Cynara! in my fashion. [*Ib.*]

3 They are not long, the weeping and the laughter, / Love and desire and hate: / I think they have no portion in us after/ We pass the gate. [*Vitae Summa Brevis*]

SIR ARTHUR CONAN DOYLE
1859–1930

4 Singularity is almost invariably a clue. The more featureless and commonplace a crime is, the more difficult is it to bring it home. [*The Adventures of Sherlock Holmes*, 'The Boscombe Valley Mystery']

5 A little monograph on the ashes of one hundred and forty different varieties of pipe, cigar, and cigarette tobacco. [*Ib.*]

6 It has long been an axiom of mine that the little things are infinitely the most important. [*Ib.* 'A Case of Identity']

7 It is my belief, Watson, founded upon my experience, that the lowest and vilest alleys of London do not present a more dreadful record of sin than does the smiling and beautiful countryside. [*Ib.* 'The Copper Beeches']

8 It is quite a three-pipe problem. [*Ib.* 'The Red-Headed League']

9 I have nothing to do today. My practice is never very absorbing. [*Ib.*]

10 All other men are specialists, but his specialism is omniscience. [*His Last Bow*, 'The Bruce-Partington Plans']

11 But here, unless I am mistaken, is our client. [*Ib.* 'Wisteria Lodge']

12 You know my methods, Watson. [*The Memoirs of Sherlock Holmes*, 'The Crooked Man']

13 'Excellent!' I cried. 'Elementary,' said he. [*Ib.*]

14 He [Professor Moriarty] is the Napoleon of crime. [*Ib.* 'The Final Problem']

15 You mentioned your name as if I should recognize it, but beyond the obvious facts that you are a bachelor, a solicitor, a Freemason, and an asthmatic, I know nothing whatever about you. [*The Memoirs of Sherlock Holmes*, 'The Norwood Builder']

16 A long shot, Watson; a very long shot! [*Ib.* 'Silver Blaze']

17 'Is there any point to which you would wish to draw my attention?'
'To the curious incident of the dog in the night-time.'
'The dog did nothing in the night-time.'
'That was the curious incident,' remarked Sherlock Holmes. [*Ib.*]

18 The Baker Street irregulars. [*The Sign of Four*]

19 The vocabulary of 'Bradshaw' is nervous and terse, but limited. [*Valley of Fear*, Ch. 1]

SIR FRANCIS DOYLE   1810–1888

20 Last night among his fellow roughs, / He jested, quaffed, and swore; / A drunken private of the Buffs, / Who never looked before. [*The Private of the Buffs*]

SIR FRANCIS DRAKE 1540?–1596

21 There is plenty of time to win this game, and to thrash the Spaniards too. [Attr. saying, when the Armada was sighted 20 July 1588]

22 I remember Drake ... would call the Enterprise [of Cadiz, 1587] the singeing of the King of Spain's beard. [Bacon, *Considerations touching a War with Spain*]

MICHAEL DRAYTON   1563–1631

23 Fair stood the wind for France, / When we our sails advance, / Nor now to prove our chance, / Longer will tarry. [*Ballad of Agincourt*]

24 Upon Saint Crispin's Day / Fought was this noble fray, / Which fame did not delay, / To England to carry. / O when shall English men / With such acts fill a pen, / Or England breed again / Such a King Harry? [*Ib.*]

25 Had in him those brave translunary things / That the first poets had. [(Marlowe) *To Henry Reynolds, of Poets and Poesy*, 106]

1 For that fine madness still he did retain /
Which rightly should possess a poet's
brain. [*To Henry Reynolds, of Poets and
Poesy*, 109]

2 Next these, learn'd Jonson, in this list I
bring, / Who had drunk deep of the
Pierian spring. [*Ib.* 129]

3 I pray thee leave, love me no more, /
Call home the heart you gave me, / I but
in vain the saint adore, / That can, but
will not, save me. [*To His Coy Love*]

4 And Queens hereafter shall be glad to
live / Upon the alms of thy superfluous
praise. [*Sonnets*, 'Idea', vi]

5 Since there's no help, come let us kiss and
part. [*Ib.* lxi]

6 Shake hands for ever, cancel all our
vows, / And when we meet at any time
again, / Be it not seen in either of our
brows, / That we one jot of former love
retain. [*Ib.*]

7 When faith is kneeling by his bed of
death, / And innocence is closing up his
eyes, / Now if thou would'st, when all
have given him over, / From death to
life, thou might'st him yet recover. [*Ib.*]

WILLIAM DRENNAN   1754–1820

8 The men of the Emerald Isle. [*Erin*]

JOHN DRINKWATER   1882–1937

9 Moon-washed apples of wonder. [*Moonlit Apples*]

THOMAS DRUMMOND
1797–1840

10 Property has its duties as well as its
rights. [Letter to Earl of Donoughmore,
22 May 1838]

WILLIAM DRUMMOND
1585–1649

11 The last and greatest herald of Heaven's
King, / Girt with rough skins, hies to the
deserts wild. [*For the Baptist*]

12 Phoebus arise, / And paint the sable skies
/ With azure, white, and red. [Song:
Phoebus Arise]

13 Of this fair volume which we world do
name / If we the sheets and leaves could
turn with care. [*The World*]

JOHN DRYDEN   1631–1700

14 In pious times, ere priestcraft did begin, /
Before polygamy was made a sin.
[*Absalom and Achitophel*, Pt I. 1]

15 And, wide as his command, / Scattered
his Maker's image through the land. [*Ib.*
I. 9]

16 Whate'er he did was done with so much
ease, / In him alone 'twas natural to
please. [*Ib.* I. 27]

17 God's pampered people whom, de-
bauched with ease, / No king could
govern, nor no God could please. [*Ib.* I.
47]

18 Plots, true or false, are necessary things, /
To raise up commonwealths, and ruin
kings. [*Ib.* I. 83]

19 Of these the false Achitophel was first: /
A name to all succeeding ages curst. [*Ib.*
I. 150]

20 A fiery soul, which working out its way, /
Fretted the pigmy-body to decay: / And
o'er-informed the tenement of clay. / A
daring pilot in extremity; / Pleased with
the danger, when the waves went high, /
He sought the storms; but for a calm
unfit, / Would steer too nigh the sands to
boast his wit. / Great wits are sure to
madness near allied, / And thin partitions
do their bounds divide. [*Ib.* I. 156]

21 Bankrupt of life, yet prodigal of ease. [*Ib.*
I. 168]

22 And all to leave, what with his toil he
won, / To that unfeathered, two-legged
thing, a son. [*Ib.* I. 169]

23 Born a shapeless lump, like Anarchy. [*Ib.*
I. 172]

24 Resolved to ruin or to rule the state. [*Ib.*
I. 174]

25 For politicians neither love nor hate. [*Ib.*
I. 223]

26 The people's prayer, the glad diviner's
theme, / The young men's vision, and the
old men's dream! [*Ib.* I. 238]

27 Than a successive title, long, and dark, /
Drawn from the mouldy rolls of Noah's
ark. [*Ib.* I. 301]

28 All empire is no more than power in
trust. [*Ib.* I. 411]

29 But far more numerous was the herd of
such, / Who think too little, and who
talk too much. [*Ib.* I. 533]

1 A man so various that he seemed to be / Not one, but all mankind's epitome. / Stiff in opinions, always in the wrong; / Was everything by starts and nothing long: / But, in the course of one revolving moon, / Was chemist, fiddler, statesman, and buffoon. [*Absalom and Achitophel*, I. 545]

2 So over-violent, or over-civil, / That every man, with him, was God or Devil. [*Ib.* I. 557]

3 In squandering wealth was his peculiar art: / Nothing went unrewarded but desert. / Beggared by fools, whom still he found too late: / He had his jest, and they had his estate. [*Ib.* I. 559]

4 Did wisely from expensive sins refrain, / And never broke the Sabbath, but for gain. [*Ib.* I. 587]

5 During his office, treason was no crime. / The sons of Belial had a glorious time. [*Ib.* I. 597]

6 His tribe were God Almighty's gentlemen. [*Ib.* I. 645]

7 Youth, beauty, graceful action, seldom fail: / But common interest always will prevail. [*Ib.* I. 723]

8 Nor is the people's judgement always true; / The most may err as grossly as the few. [*Ib.* I. 781]

9 Beware the fury of a patient man [*Ib.* I. 1005]

10 Doeg, though without knowing how or why, / Made still a blundering kind of melody; / Spurred boldly on, and dashed through thick and thin, / Through sense and nonsense, never out nor in; / Free from all meaning, whether good or bad, / And in one word, heroically mad. [*Ib.* II. 412]

11 For every inch that is not fool is rogue. [*Ib.* II. 463]

12 To die for faction is a common evil, / But to be hanged for nonsense is the Devil. [*Ib.* II. 498]

13 The lovely Thais by his side, / Sat like a blooming Eastern bride. [*Alexander's Feast*, 9]

14 None but the brave deserves the fair. [*Ib.* 15]

15 With ravished ears / The monarch hears, / Assumes the god, / Affects to nod, / And seems to shake the spheres. [*Ib.* 37]

16 Bacchus ever fair, and ever young. [*Alexander's Feast*, 44]

17 Drinking is the soldier's pleasure. [*Ib.* 57]

18 Rich the treasure, / Sweet the pleasure; / Sweet is pleasure after pain. [*Ib.* 58]

19 Fought all his battles o'er again; / And thrice he routed all his foes; and thrice he slew the slain. [*Ib.* 67]

20 Fallen from his high estate / And welt'ring in his blood. [*Ib.* 78]

21 War, he sung, is toil and trouble; / Honour but an empty bubble; / Never ending, still beginning, / Fighting still, and still destroying. / If all the world be worth thy winning, / Think, oh think, it worth enjoying. [*Ib.* 99]

22 Sighed and looked, and sighed again. [*Ib.* 120]

23 Revenge, revenge, Timotheus cries, / See the Furies arise! [*Ib.* 131]

24 And, like another Helen, fired another Troy. [*Ib.* 154]

25 Could swell the soul to rage, or kindle soft desire. [*Ib.* 160]

26 He raised a mortal to the skies; / She drew an angel down. [*Ib.* 179]

27 So sicken waning moons too near the sun, / And blunt their crescents on the edge of day. [*Annus Mirabilis*, 125]

28 By viewing Nature, Nature's handmaid, art, / Makes mighty things from small beginnings grow. [*Ib.* 155]

29 An horrid stillness first invades the ear, / And in that stillness we the tempest fear. [*Astraea Redux*, 7]

30 Of seeming arms to make a short essay, / Then hasten to be drunk, the business of the day. [*Cymon and Iphigenia*, 407]

31 Better to hunt in fields, for health unbought, / Than fee the doctor for a nauseous draught. / The wise, for cure, on exercise depend; / God never made his work for man to mend. [*Epistle to John Driden of Chesterton*, 92]

32 Theirs was the giant race, before the flood. [*Epistle to Mr Congreve*, 5]

33 Here lies my wife: here let her lie! / Now she's at rest, and so am I. [*Epitaph intended for his Wife*]

34 She feared no danger for she knew no sin. [*The Hind and the Panther*, I. 4]

1 For truth has such a face and such a mien / As to be loved needs only to be seen. [*The Hind and the Panther*, I. 33]

2 My thoughtless youth was winged with vain desires, / My manhood, long misled by wandering fires, / Followed false lights; and when their glimpse was gone, / My pride struck out new sparkles of her own. / Such was I, such by nature still I am. / Be thine the glory, and be mine the shame. [*Ib.* I. 72]

3 Reason to rule but mercy to forgive: / The first is law, the last prerogative. [*Ib.* I. 261]

4 Too black for heav'n, and yet too white for hell. [*Ib.* I. 343]

5 Much malice mingled with a little wit. [*Ib.* III. 1]

6 They found the new Messiah by the star. [*Ib.* III. 176]

7 By education most have been misled; / So they believe, because they so were bred. / The priest continues what the nurse began, / And thus the child imposes on the man. [*Ib.* III. 389]

8 T' abhor the makers, and their laws approve, / Is to hate traitors, and the treason love. [*Ib.* III. 706]

9 Three poets, in three distant ages born, / Greece, Italy, and England, did adorn. / The first in loftiness of thought surpassed; / The next in majesty, in both the last. / The force of nature could no further go; / To make a third she joined the former two. [*Lines under Portrait of Milton*]

10 All human things are subject to decay, / And when fate summons, monarchs must obey. [*Mac Flecknoe*, 1]

11 The rest to some faint meaning make pretence, / But Shadwell never deviates into sense. / Some beams of wit on other souls may fall, / Strike through and make a lucid interval. / But Shadwell's genuine night admits no ray, / His rising fogs prevail upon the day. [*Ib.* 19]

12 And torture one poor word ten thousand ways. [*Ib.* 208]

13 To live at ease, and not be bound to think. [*The Medal*, 236]

14 So poetry, which is in Oxford made / An art, in London only is a trade. [*Prologue to the University of Oxford*]

15 And this unpolished rugged verse I chose / As fittest for discourse and nearest prose. [*Religio Laici*, 453]

16 From harmony, from heavenly harmony / This universal frame began: / From harmony to harmony / Through all the compass of the notes it ran, / The diapason closing full in Man. [*Song for St Cecilia's Day*, i]

17 What passion cannot music raise and quell! [*Ib.* ii]

18 The trumpet's loud clangour / Excites us to arms. [*Ib.* iii]

19 The soft complaining flute. [*Ib.* iv]

20 The trumpet shall be heard on high, / The dead shall live, the living die, / And music shall untune the sky. [*Ib.* viii]

21 Farewell, too little and too lately known, / Whom I began to think and call my own. [*To the Memory of Mr Oldham*]

22 Wit will shine / Through the harsh cadence of a rugged line. [*Ib.*]

23 While yet a young probationer, / And candidate of heaven. [*To the Memory of Mrs Killigrew*, 21]

24 When rattling bones together fly, / From the four corners of the sky. [*Ib.* 184]

25 Happy the man, and happy he alone, / He, who can call to-day his own: / He who, secure within, can say, / To-morrow do thy worst, for I have lived to-day. [*Transl. of Horace*, Bk III. xxix]

26 Look round the habitable world! how few / Know their own good; or knowing it, pursue. [*Transl. of Juvenal*, X]

27 To see and to be seen, in heaps they run; / Some to undo, and some to be undone. [*Transl. of Ovid, Ars amatoria*, I. 109]

28 Who, for false quantities, was whipped at school. [*Transl. of Persius, Satires*, I. 135]

29 She knows her man, and when you rant or swear, / Can draw you to her with a single hair. [*Ib.* V. 246]

30 Errors, like straws, upon the surface flow; / He who would search for pearls must dive below. [*All for Love*, Prologue, 25]

31 She deserves / More worlds than I can lose. [*Ib.* I. i]

32 Fool that I was, upon my eagle's wings / I bore this wren till I was tired with soaring, / And now he mounts above me. [*Ib.* II. i]

1 Witness ye days and nights, and all your hours, / That danced away with down upon your feet. [*All for Love*, II. i]

2 Men are but children of a larger growth. [*Ib*. IV. i]

3 Your Cleopatra; Dolabella's Cleopatra; every man's Cleopatra. [*Ib*.]

4 Whistling to keep myself from being afraid. [*Amphitryon*, III. i]

5 I am as free as nature first made man, / Ere the base laws of servitude began, / When wild in woods the noble savage ran. [*The Conquest of Granada*, Pt 1. I. i]

6 Forgiveness to the injured does belong; / For they ne'er pardon, who have done the wrong. [*Ib*. 2. I. ii]

7 This is the porcelain clay of humankind. [*Don Sebastian*, I. i]

8 And love's the noblest frailty of the mind. [*The Indian Emperor*, II. ii]

9 All heiresses are beautiful. [*King Arthur*, I. i]

10 I am to be married within these three days; married past redemption. [*Marriage à la Mode*, I. i]

11 For, Heaven be thanked, we live in such an age, / When no man dies for love, but on the stage. [*Mithridates*, Epilogue]

12 All, all of a piece throughout; / Thy chase had a beast in view; / Thy wars brought nothing about; / Thy lovers were all untrue. / 'Tis well an old age is out, / And time to begin a new. [*The Secular Masque*]

13 There is a pleasure sure / In being mad, which none but madmen know! [*The Spanish Friar*, II. i]

14 Dying bless the hand that gave the blow. [*Ib*.]

15 Looks as he were Lord of humankind. [*Ib*. II. ii]

16 A thing well said will be wit in all languages. [*Essay of Dramatic Poesy*]

17 He [Shakespeare] was the man who of all modern, and perhaps ancient poets, had the largest and most comprehensive soul. ... He was naturally learned; he needed not the spectacles of books to read nature; he looked inwards, and found her there. [*Ib*.]

18 'Tis sufficient to say [of Chaucer], according to the proverb, that here is God's plenty. [Preface to *Fables*]

19 He [Chaucer] is a perpetual fountain of good sense. [*Ib*.]

20 A man is to be cheated into passion, but to be reasoned into truth. [Preface to *Religio Laici*]

21 Cousin Swift, you will never be a poet. [Quoted in Johnson's *Lives of the Poets*, 'Swift']

JOACHIM DU BELLAY
1515–1560

22 *France, mère des arts, des armes et des lois.* – France, mother of the arts, of arms and of law. [*Les Regrets*, ix]

23 *Heureux qui, comme Ulysse, a fait un beau voyage.* – Happy is he who, like Ulysses, has made a fine voyage. [*Ib*. xxxi]

GEORGE DUFFIELD   1818–1888

24 Stand up! stand up for Jesus! [Hymn]

ALEXANDRE DUMAS   1803–1870

25 *Il y a une femme dans toutes les affaires; aussitôt qu'on me fait un rapport, je dis: 'Cherchez la femme'.* – There is a woman in every case; as soon as they bring me a report, I say, 'Look for the woman'. [*Les Mohicans de Paris*, II. iii]

26 *Tous pour un, un pour tous.* – All for one, one for all. [Motto, *Les Trois Mousquetaires*]

ALEXANDRE DUMAS fils
1824–1895

27 All generalizations are dangerous, even this one. [Quoted in *Treasury of Humorous Quotations*]

MARÉCHAL DUMOURIEZ
1739–1823

28 *Les courtisans qui l'entourent* [Louis XVIII] *n'ont rien oublié et n'ont rien appris.* – The courtiers who surround him have forgotten nothing and learnt nothing. [*Examen*]

WILLIAM DUNBAR 1460?–1520?

1 Our plesance heir is all vane glory, / This fals warld is bot transitory, / The flesche is brukle, the Fend is sle; / *Timor mortis conturbat me.* [*Lament for the Makaris*]

2 London, thou art the flour of cities all! [*London*]

3 Done is a battell on the dragon blak, / Our campioun Christ confountet hes his force; / The yettis of hell ar brokin with a crak, / The signe triumphall rasit is of the croce. [*On the Resurrection of Christ*]

FINLEY PETER DUNNE
1867–1936

4 Th' dead ar-re always pop'lar. I knowed a society wanst to vote a monyment to a man an' refuse to help his fam'ly, all in wan night. [*Mr Dooley in Peace and War*, 'On Charity']

5 'Th' American nation in th' Sixth Ward is a fine people,' he says. 'They love th' eagle', he says, 'on th' back iv a dollar.' [*Ib.* 'Oratory on Politics']

THOMAS D'URFEY 1653–1723

6 Neighbours o'er the Herring Pond. [*Pills to Purge Melancholy*, Vol. ii, 'Fable of the Lady, the Lurcher and the Marrow-Puddings']

LAWRENCE DURRELL 1911–

7 The Good Lord Nelson had a swollen gland, / Little of the scripture did he understand / Till a woman led him to the promised land / Aboard the Victory, Victory O. [*A Ballad of the Good Lord Nelson*]

SIR EDWARD DYER 1540?–1607

8 My mind to me a kingdom is, / Such present joys therein I find, / That it excels all other bliss / That earth affords or grows by kind. [*My Mind to me a Kingdom is*]

JOHN DYER Early 18 Cent.

9 And he that will this health deny, / Down among the dead men let him lie. [Toast: *Here's a Health to the King*]

150

JOHN DYER 1700?–1758

10 Ever charming, ever new, / When will the landscape tire the view? [*Grongar Hill*, 5]

11 A little rule, a little sway, / A sunbeam in a winter's day, / Is all the proud and mighty have / Between the cradle and the grave. [*Ib.* 89]

MARIA EDGEWORTH 1767–1849

12 Well, some people talk of morality, and some of religion, but give me a little snug property. [*The Absentee*, Ch. 2]

13 And all the young ladies said that a love-match was the only thing for happiness, where the parties could anyway afford it. [*Castle Rackrent*, 'Continuation of Memoirs']

14 I've a great fancy to see my own funeral afore I die. [*Ib.*]

15 Come when you're called, / And do as you're bid; / Shut the door after you, / And you'll never be chid. [*The Contrast*, Ch. 1]

16 Business was his pleasure; pleasure was his business. [*Ib.* 2]

THOMAS ALVA EDISON
1847–1931

17 Genius is one per cent inspiration and ninty-nine per cent perspiration. [Newspaper interview]

EDWARD III OF ENGLAND
1312–1377

18 Let the boy win his spurs. [Of the Black Prince at Crécy]

EDWARD VII 1841–1910

19 We are all Socialists nowadays. [Speech at Mansion House, 5 Nov. 1895]

RICHARD EDWARDES
1523?–1566

20 The falling out of faithful friends, renewing is of love. [*Amantium Irae*]

OLIVER EDWARDS 1711–1791

1 You are a philosopher, Dr Johnson. I have tried too in my time to be a philosopher; but I don't know how, cheerfulness was always breaking in. [Quoted in Boswell's *Life of Johnson*, 17 Apr. 1778]

GEORGE ELIOT [MARY ANN CROSS] 1819–1880

2 It's but little good you'll do a-watering the last year's crop. [*Adam Bede*, Ch. 18]

3 It was a pity he couldna be hatched o'er again, an' hatched different. [*Ib.*]

4 It's them that take advantage that get advantage i' this world. *Ib.* 32]

5 He was 'ike a cock who 'hought the sun had risen to hear him crow. [*Ib.* 33]

6 We hand folks over to God's mercy, and show none ourselves. [*Ib.* 42]

7 I'm not denyin' the women are foolish: God Almighty made 'em to match the men. [*Ib.* 53]

8 Men's men: gentle or simple, they're much of a muchness. [*Daniel Deronda*, Bk IV. Ch. 21]

9 The law's made to take care o' raskills. [*The Mill on the Floss*, Bk III. Ch. 4

10 I've never any pity for conceited people, because I think they carry their comfort about with them. [*Ib.* V. 4]

11 The happiest women, like the happiest nations, have no history. [*Ib.* VI. 3]

12 'Character', says Novalis, in one of his questionable aphorisms – 'character is destiny'. [*Ib.* VI. 6]

13 In every parting there is an image of death. [*Scenes of Clerical Life*, 'Amos Barton', Ch. 10]

14 Animals are such agreeable friends – they ask no questions, they pass no criticisms. [*Ib.* 'Mr Gilfil's Love-Story', Ch. 7]

15 Debasing the moral currency. [*Theophrastus Such*: title of essay]

16 Oh may I join the choir invisible / Of those immortal dead who live again / In minds made better by their presence. [*Poems*, 'Oh May I Join the Choir Invisible']

T. S. ELIOT 1888–1965

17 Pray for us now and at the hour of our birth. [*Animula*]

18 Because I do not hope to turn again / Because I do not hope / Because I do not hope to turn. [*Ash Wednesday*, I]

19 Teach us to care and not to care / Teach us to sit still. [*Ib.*]

20 Lady, three white leopards sat under a juniper tree / In the cool of the day. [*Ib.* II]

21 At the first turning of the second stair / I turned and saw below / The same shape twisted on the banister. [*Ib.* III]

22 Redeem / The time. Redeem / The unread vision in the higher dream. [*Ib.* IV]

23 Will the veiled sister pray / For children at the gate / Who will not go away and cannot pray. [*Ib.* V]

24 Time present and time past / Are both perhaps present in time future, / And time future contained in time past. [*Four Quartets*, 'Burnt Norton', I]

25 Footfalls echo in the memory / Down the passage which we did not take / Towards the door we never opened / Into the rose-garden. [*Ib.*]

26 Human kind / Cannot bear very much reality. [*Ib.*]

27 At the still point of the turning world. [*Ib.* II]

28 In my beginning is my end. [*Ib.* 'East Coker', I]

29 The intolerable wrestle / With words and meanings. [*Ib.* II]

30 The houses are all gone under the sea. / The dancers are all gone under the hill. [*Ib.*]

31 The wounded surgeon plies the steel / That questions the distempered part. [*Ib.* IV]

32 So here I am, in the middle way, having had twenty years – / Twenty years largely wasted, the years of *l'entre deux guerres*. [*Ib.* V]

33 Undisciplined squads of emotion. [*Ib.*]

34 In my end is my beginning. [*Ib.*]

35 I do not know much about gods; but I think that the river / Is a strong brown god. [*Ib.* 'Dry Salvages', I]

1 The river is within us, the sea is all about us. [*Four Quartets*, 'Dry Salvages', I]

2 You are not the same people who left that station / Or who will arrive at any terminus, / While the narrowing rails slide together behind you. [*Ib*. III]

3 Not fare well, / But fare forward, voyagers. [*Ib*.]

4 Ash on an old man's sleeve / Is all the ash the burnt roses leave. / Dust in the air suspended / Marks the place where a story ended. [*Ib*. 'Little Gidding', II]

5 The dove descending breaks the air / With flame of incandescent terror. [*Ib*. IV]

6 We are the hollow men / We are the stuffed men / Leaning together. [*The Hollow Men*, I]

7 Here we go round the prickly pear / At five o'clock in the morning. [*Ib*. V]

8 Between the idea / And the reality / Between the motion / And the act / Falls the Shadow. [*Ib*.]

9 This is the way the world ends / Not with a bang but a whimper. [*Ib*.]

10 A cold coming we had of it, / Just the worst time of the year / For a journey. [*Journey of the Magi*]

11 When the evening is spread out against the sky / Like a patient etherised upon a table. [*Love Song of J. Alfred Prufrock*]

12 In the room the women come and go / Talking of Michelangelo [*Ib*.]

13 The yellow fog that rubs its back upon the windowpanes. [*Ib*.]

14 I have measured out my life with coffee spoons. [*Ib*.]

15 I should have been a pair of ragged claws / Scuttling across the floors of silent seas. [*Ib*.]

16 And I have seen the eternal Footman hold my coat, and snicker, / And in short, I was afraid. [*Ib*.]

17 No! I am not Prince Hamlet, nor was meant to be; / Am an attendant lord. [*Ib*.]

18 I grow old ... I grow old ... / I shall wear the bottoms of my trousers rolled. [*Ib*.]

19 He always has an alibi, and one or two to spare: / At whatever time the deed took place – Macavity wasn't there! [*Macavity: The Mystery Cat*]

20 I am aware of the damp souls of housemaids / Sprouting despondently at area gates. [*Morning at the Window*]

21 The winter evening settles down / With smell of steaks in passage ways. [*Preludes*, I]

22 Birth, and copulation, and death. / That's all the facts when you come to brass tacks. [*Sweeney Agonistes*, 'Fragment of an Agon']

23 April is the cruellest month, breeding / Lilacs out of the dead land. [*The Waste Land*, 1]

24 I read, much of the night, and go south in the winter. [*Ib*. 18]

25 What are the roots that clutch, what branches grow / Out of this stony rubbish? [*Ib*. 19]

26 And I will show you something different from either / Your shadow at morning striding behind you / Or your shadow at evening rising to meet you; / I will show you fear in a handful of dust [*Ib*. 27]

27 Madame Sosostris, famous clairvoyante, / Had a bad cold, nevertheless / Is known to be the wisest woman in Europe, / With a wicked pack of cards. [*Ib*. 43]

28 Here, said she, / Is your card, the drowned Phoenician Sailor. [*Ib*. 46]

29 Unreal City, / Under the brown fog of a winter dawn, / A crowd flowed over London Bridge, so many, / I had not thought death had undone so many. [*Ib*. 60]

30 That corpse you planted last year in your garden, / Has it begun to sprout? Will it bloom this year? [*Ib*. 71]

31 The Chair she sat in, like a burnished throne, / Glowed on the marble. [*Ib*. 77]

32 The change of Philomel, by the barbarous king / So rudely forced. [*Ib*. 99]

33 'Jug jug' to dirty ears. [*Ib*. 103]

34 My nerves are bad to-night. Yes, bad. [*Ib*. 111]

35 When Lil's husband got demobbed, I said – / I didn't mince my words, I said to her myself, / Hurry up please, it's time. [*Ib*. 139]

1 Musing upon the king my brother's wreck / And on the king my father's death before him. [*The Waste Land*, 191]

2 O the moon shone bright on Mrs Porter / And on her daughter / They wash their feet in soda water. [*Ib*. 199]

3 One of the low on whom assurance sits / As a silk hat on a Bradford millionaire. [*Ib*. 233]

4 When lovely woman stoops to folly and / Paces about her room again, alone, / She smoothes her hair with automatic hand, / And puts a record on the gramophone. [*Ib*. 253]

5 After the frosty silence in the gardens / After the agony in stony places. [*Ib*. 323]

6 Who is the third who walks always beside you? / When I count, there are only you and I together. [*Ib*. 359]

7 A woman drew her long black hair out tight / And fiddled whisper music on those strings / And bats with baby faces in the violet light / Whistled. [*Ib*. 377]

8 Webster was much possessed by death / And saw the skull beneath the skin. [*Whispers of Immortality*]

9 Donne, I suppose, was such another / Who found no substitute for sense. / To seize and clutch and penetrate; / Expert beyond experience. [*Ib*.]

10 You've missed the point completely, Julia: / There *were* no tigers. *That* was the point. [*Cocktail Party*, I. i]

11 As I was drinkin' gin and water, / And me bein' the One Eyed Riley. [*Ib*.]

12 Hell is oneself; / Hell is alone, the other figures in it / Merely projections. There is nothing to escape from / And nothing to escape to. One is always alone. [*Ib*. I. iii]

13 Why do we feel embarrassed, impatient, fretful, ill at ease, / Assembled like amateur actors who have not been assigned their parts? [*The Family Reunion*, I. i]

14 There is nothing at all to be done about it, / There is nothing to do about anything, / And now it is nearly time for the news. [*Ib*. II. i]

15 The clock has stopped in the dark. [*Ib*. II. iii]

16 Round and round the circle / Completing the charm / So the knot be unknotted / The cross be uncrossed / The crooked be made straight / And the curse be ended. [*The Family Reunion*, II. iii]

17 Since golden October declined into sombre November / And the apples were gathered and stored, and the land became brown sharp points of death in a waste of water and mud. [*Murder in the Cathedral*, I]

18 The last temptation is the greatest treason: / To do the right deed for the wrong reason. [*Ib*.]

19 After the erection of the Chinese Wall of Milton, blank verse has suffered not only arrest but retrogression. [*Selected Essays*, 'Christopher Marlowe']

20 Tennyson and Browning are poets, and they think; but they do not feel their thought as immediately as the odour of a rose. A thought to Donne was an experience; it modified his sensibility. [*Ib*. 'Metaphysical Poets']

21 In the seventeenth century a dissociation of sensibility set in. [*Ib*.]

22 The only way of expressing emotion in the form of art is by finding an 'objective correlative'; in other words, a set of objects, a situation, a chain of events which shall be the formula of that particular emotion. [*Tradition and the Individual Talent*, p. 124]

QUEEN ELIZABETH I 1533–1603

23 I will make you shorter by a head. [Chamberlin, *Sayings of Queen Elizabeth*]

24 Madam, I may not call you; mistress I am ashamed to call you; and so I know not what to call you; but howsoever, I thank you. [(To the wife of the Archbishop of Canterbury) Harington, *Brief View of the State of the Church*]

25 God forgive you, but I never can. [(To the Countess of Nottingham) Hume, *History of England under the House of Tudor*]

26 I know I have the body of a weak and feeble woman, but I have the heart and stomach of a king, and of a king of England too. [Speech at Tilbury, on the approach of the Spanish Armada]

27 All my possessions for a moment of time. [Last words]

JOHN ELLERTON   1826–1893

1 Now the labourer's task is o'er; / Now the battle-day is past; / Now upon the further shore / Lands the voyager at last. [Hymn]

CHARLOTTE ELLIOTT
1789–1871

2 Christian, seek not yet repose, / Hear thy guardian angel say, / 'Thou art in the midst of foes: /Watch and pray'. [Hymn]

EBENEZER ELLIOTT   1781–1849

3 What is a communist? One who hath yearnings / For equal division of unequal earnings. [Epigram]

JANE ELLIOTT   1727–1805

4 I've heard them lilting, at our ewe milking, / Lasses a' lilting, before dawn of day: / But now they are moaning on ilka green loaning; / The flowers o' the forest are a' wede away. [The Flowers of the Forest]

GEORGE ELLIS [SIR GEORGE GANDER]   1753–1815

5 Snowy, Flowy, Blowy, / Showery, Flowery, Bowery, / Hoppy, Croppy, Droppy, / Breezy, Sneezy, Freezy. [The Twelve Months]

HENRY HAVELOCK ELLIS
1859–1939

6 Every artist writes his own autobiography. [The New Spirit, 'Tolstoi', II]

ELSTOW   Early 16 Cent.

7 We know the way to heaven to be as ready by water as by land. [(When threatened with drowning by Henry VIII) Stow's Annals]

RALPH WALDO EMERSON
1803–1882

8 If the red slayer thinks he slays, / Or if the slain think he is slain, / They know not well the subtle ways / I keep, and pass, and turn again. [Brahma]

9 I am the doubter and the doubt, / And I the hymn the Brahmin sings. [Brahma]

10 Heartily know, / When half-gods go, / The gods arrive. [Give All to Love]

11 Here once the embattled farmers stood, / And fired the shot heard round the world. [Hymn sung at the Completion of the Concord Monument]

12 Things are in the saddle, / And ride mankind. [Ode, inscribed to W. H. Channing]

13 He builded better than he knew; – / The conscious stone to beauty grew. [The Problem]

14 Some of your hurts you have cured, / And the sharpest you still have survived, / But what torments of grief you endured / From evils which never arrived! [Quatrains, 'Borrowing' (from the French)]

15 So nigh is grandeur to our dust, / So near is God to man, / When Duty whispers low, Thou must, / The youth replies, I can. [Voluntaries, iii]

16 Art is a jealous mistress. [Conduct of Life, 'Power']

17 The louder he talked of his honour, the faster we counted our spoons. [Ib. 'Worship']

18 Though we travel the world over to find the beautiful, we must carry it with us or we find it not. [Essays, 'Art']

19 Beware when the great God lets loose a thinker on this planet. [Ib. 'Circles']

20 Nothing great was ever achieved without enthusiasm. [Ib.]

21 The wise through excess of wisdom is made a fool. [Ib. 'Experience']

22 Thou art to me a delicious torment. [Ib. 'Friendship']

23 A friend is a person with whom I may be sincere. Before him I may think aloud. [Ib.]

24 The only reward of virtue is virtue; the only way to have a friend is to be one. [Ib.]

25 There is properly no history; only biography. [Ib. 'History']

26 All mankind love a lover. [Ib. 'Love']

27 Men are conservatives when they are least vigorous, or when they are most luxurious. They are conservatives after dinner. [Ib. 'New England Reformers']

154

1 We are wiser than we know. [*Essays*, 'The Over-Soul']

2 The faith that stands on authority is not faith. [*Ib.*]

3 Language is fossil poetry. [*Ib.* 'The Poet']

4 Whoso would be a man must be a nonconformist. [*Ib.* 'Self-Reliance']

5 A foolish consistency is the hobgoblin of little minds, adored by little statesmen and philosophers and divines. [*Ib.*]

6 To be great is to be misunderstood. [*Ib.*]

7 I like the silent church before the service begins better than any preaching. [*Ib.*]

8 An institution is the lengthened shadow of one man. [*Ib.*]

9 What is a weed? A plant whose virtues have not yet been discovered. [*Fortune of the Republic*]

10 Talent alone cannot make a writer. There must be a man behind the book. [*Representative Men*, 'Goethe']

11 Every hero becomes a bore at last. [*Ib.* 'Uses of Great Men']

12 I have heard with admiring submission the experience of the lady who declared that the sense of being well-dressed gives a feeling of inward tranquillity which religion is powerless to bestow. [*Social Aims*]

13 Never read any book that is not a year old. [*Society and Solitude*, 'Books']

14 Hitch your wagon to a star. [*Ib.* 'Civilization']

15 We boil at different degrees. [*Ib.* 'Eloquence']

16 America is a country of young men. [*Ib.* 'Old Age']

17 Every man is a borrower and a mimic, life is theatrical and literature a quotation. [*Ib.* 'Success']

18 If a man write a better book, preach a better sermon, or make a better mousetrap than his neighbour, though he build his house in the woods, the world will make a beaten path to his door. [Lecture, noted down by Mrs Sarah Yule]

19 We are always getting ready to live, but never living. [*Journals*, 13 Apr. 1834]

EMPEDOCLES 5 Cent. B.C.

20 God is a circle whose centre is everywhere and whose circumference is nowhere.

WILLIAM EMPSON 1906–

21 It seemed the best thing to be up and go. [*Aubade*]

22 The heart of standing is you cannot fly. [*Ib.*]

23 Waiting for the end, boys, waiting for the end. [*Just a Smack at Auden*]

24 Seven Types of Ambiguity. [Title of book]

PÈRE ENFANTIN 1796–1864

25 Exploitation without work of man by man. [*Œuvres de Saint Simon et Enfantin*]

HENRY ERSKINE 1746–1817

26 The rule of the road is a paradox quite, / Both in riding and driving along; / If you keep to the left, you are sure to be right, / If you keep to the right you are wrong. [*The Rule of the Road*]

LORD ERSKINE 1750–1823

27 The uncontrolled licentiousness of a brutal and insolent soldiery. [*In defence of William Stone*]

HENRI ESTIENNE 1531–1598

28 *Si jeunesse savait; si vieillesse pouvait.* – If youth knew, if age could. [*Les Prémices*, cxci]

SIR GEORGE ETHEREDGE 1635–1691

29 Whate'er you say, I know all beyond High-Park's a desart to you. [*The Man of Mode*, V. ii]

EUCLID *fl. c.* 300 B.C.

30 *Quod erat demonstrandum.* – Which was to be proved. [Transl. from Greek]

EURIPIDES 480–406 B.C.

1 Whom God wishes to destroy, he first makes mad. [*Fragments* (Exists in many forms; the Latin version '*Quos deus vult perdere, prius dementat*' is quoted in Boswell's *Johnson*)]

ANTHONY EUWER 1877–1955

2 As a beauty I'm not a great star. / Others are handsomer far; / But my face – I don't mind it / Because I'm behind it; / It's the folk out in front that I jar. [Limerick]

ABEL EVANS 1679–1737

3 When Tadlow walks the streets, the paviours cry, / 'God bless you, Sir!' and lay their rammers by. [Epigram: *On Dr Tadlow*]

4 Under this stone, reader, survey / Dead Sir John Vanbrugh's house of clay. / Lie heavy on him, Earth! For he / Laid many heavy loads on thee! [*Epitaph*]

JOHN EVELYN 1620–1706

5 A studious decliner of honours and titles. [*Diary*, Introduction]

6 I saw Hamlet Prince of Denmark played; but now the old plays begin to disgust this refined age. [*Ib.* 26 Nov. 1661]

DAVID EVERETT 1770–1813

7 Large streams from little fountains flow, / Tall oaks from little acorns grow. [*Lines written for a School Declamation*]

W. N. EWER 1885–1976

8 How odd / Of God / To choose / The Jews. [*How Odd*]

FREDERICK WILLIAM FABER 1814–1863

9 Have mercy on us worms of earth. [Hymn]

10 My God, how wonderful Thou art, / Thy majesty how bright, / How beautiful Thy mercy-seat / In depths of burning light! [Hymn]

11 The music of the Gospel leads us home. [Hymn: *The Pilgrims of the Night*]

ROBERT FABYAN ?–1513

12 Finally he paid the deot of nature. [*Chronicles*, Pt II. xli]

HANS FALLADA 1893–194?

13 *Kleiner Mann, was nun?* – Little Man, What Now? [Title of novel]

CATHERINE MARIA FAN-SHAWE 1765–1834

14 'Twas whispered in heaven, 'twas muttered in hell, / And echo caught faintly the sound as it fell; / On the confines of earth 'twas permitted to rest, / And the depths of the ocean its presence confessed. [*Enigma, The Letter H*]

EDWARD FARMER 1809?–1876

15 I have no pain, dear mother, now; but oh! I am so dry: / Just moisten poor Jim's lips once more; and, mother, do not cry! [*The Collier's Dying Child*]

GEORGE FARQUHAR 1678–17(7

16 Sir, you shall taste my *Anno Domini*. [*The Beaux' Stratagem*, I. i]

17 I have fed purely upon ale; I have eat my ale, drank my ale, and I always sleep upon ale. [*Ib.*]

18 My Lady Bountiful. [*Ib.*]

19 Says little, thinks less, and does – nothing at all, faith. [*Ib.*]

20 There's no scandal like rags, nor any crime so shameful as poverty. [*Ib.*]

21 I believe they talked of me, for they laughed consumedly. [*Ib.* III. i]

22 'Twas for the good of my country that I should be abroad. Anything for the good of one's country – I'm a Roman for that. [*Ib.* III. ii]

23 Captain is a good travelling name and so I take it. [*Ib.*]

24 How a little love and good company improves a woman! [*Ib.* IV. i]

1 Spare all I have, and take my life. [*The Beaux' Stratagem*, V. ii]

2 Poetry's a mere drug, Sir. [*Love and a Bottle*, III. ii]

3 Hanging and marriage, you know, go by Destiny. [*The Recruiting Officer*, III. ii]

FREDERICK WILLIAM FARRAR   1831–1903

4 Russell, let me always call you Edwin, and call me Eric. [*Eric, or Little by Little*, Ch. 4]

5 'What a surly devil that is,' said Eric . . . 'A surly – ? Oh, Eric, that's the first time I ever heard you swear.' [*Ib.* 8]

GUY FAWKES   1570–1606

6 Desperate diseases require desperate remedies. [(Gunpowder Plot) *Dic. of Nat. Biog.*]

FRANÇOIS DE FÉNELON   1651–1715

7 Nothing is more despicable than a professional talker who uses his words as a quack uses his remedies. [Letter to M. Dacier]

8 A good historian is timeless; although he is a patriot, he will never flatter his country in any respect. [*Ib.*]

EMPEROR FERDINAND I   1506–1564

9 *Fiat iusticia, et pereat mundus.* – Let justice be done, though the world perish. [Saying]

JOHN FERRIAR   1761–1815

10 Now cheaply bought for thrice their weight in gold. [*Illustrations of Sterne*, 'Bibliomania']

LUDWIG FEUERBACH   1804–1872

11 *Der Mensch ist, was er isst.* – A man is what he eats. [*Blätter für Literarische Unterhaltung*, 12 Nov. 1850]

EUGENE FIELD   1850–1895

12 A little peach in the orchard grew. [*The Little Peach*]

13 Listen to my tale of woe. [*Ib.*]

14 Wynken, Blynken and Nod one night / Sailed off in a wooden shoe – / Sailed on a river of crystal light, / Into a sea of dew. [*Wynken, Blynken and Nod*]

HENRY FIELDING   1707–1754

15 'Tace, madam,' answered Murphy, 'is Latin for a candle.' [*Amelia*, Bk I. Ch. 10]

16 When widows exclaim loudly against second marriage, I would always lay a wager that the man, if not the wedding-day, is absolutely fixed on. [*Ib.* VI. 8]

17 One of my illustrious predecessors. [*Covent Garden Journal*, No. 3, 11 Jan. 1752]

18 I am as sober as a judge. [*Don Quixote in England*, III. xiv]

19 Oh! The roast beef of England, / And old England's roast beef. [*Grub Street Opera*, III. iii]

20 Never trust the man who hath reason to suspect that you know he hath injured you. [*Jonathan Wild*, Bk III. Ch. 4]

21 He in a few minutes ravished this fair creature, or at least would have ravished her, if she had not, by a timely compliance, prevented him. [*Ib.* III. 7]

22 But pray, Mr Wild, why bitch? [*Ib.* III. 8]

23 For clergy are men as well as other folks. [*Joseph Andrews*, Bk II. Ch. 6]

24 To whom nothing is given, of him can nothing be required. [*Ib.* II. 8]

25 I describe not men, but manners; not an individual, but a species. [*Ib.* III. 1]

26 Public schools are the nurseries of all vice and immorality. [*Ib.* III. 5]

27 Some folks rail against other folks, because other folks have what some folks would be glad of. [*Ib.* IV. 6]

28 Love and scandal are the best sweeteners of tea. [*Love in Several Masques*, IV. xi]

29 Every physician almost hath his favourite disease. [*Tom Jones*, Bk II. Ch. 9]

1 Thwackum was for doing justice, and leaving mercy to heaven. [*Tom Jones*, III. 10]

2 O! more than Gothic ignorance. [*Ib*. VII. 3]

3 An amiable weakness. [*Ib*. X. 8]

4 His designs were strictly honourable, as the saying is; that is, to rob a lady of her fortune by way of marriage. [*Ib*. XI. 4]

5 Composed that monstrous animal a husband and wife. [*Ib*. XV. 9]

6 All Nature wears one universal grin. [*Tom Thumb the Great*, I. i]

7 To sun myself in Huncamunca's eyes. [*Ib*. I. iii]

8 When I'm not thanked at all, I'm thanked enough, / I've done my duty, and I've done no more. [*Ib*.]

9 The hounds all join in glorious cry, / The huntsman winds his horn: / And a-hunting we will go. [*A-Hunting We Will Go*]

J. T. FIELDS   1816–1881

10 'I'm an owl; you're another. Sir Critic, good day!' / And the barber kept on shaving. [*The Owl-Critic*]

JOHN ARBUTHNOT, LORD FISHER   1841–1920

11 You will always be fools! We shall never be gentlemen. [Quoted as the saying of a German Naval officer to his British confrère]

12 Sack the lot! [Letter to *The Times*, 2 Sept. 1919]

EDWARD FITZGERALD   1809–1883

13 Awake! for Morning in the Bowl of Night / Has flung the Stone that puts the Stars to Flight: / And Lo! the Hunter of the East has caught / The Sultan's Turret in a Noose of Light. [*The Rubá'iyát of Omar Khayyám*, Ed. 1. i]

14 Dreaming when Dawn's Left Hand was in the sky / I heard a Voice within the Tavern cry: / 'Awake, my Little ones, and fill the Cup / Before Life's Liquor in its Cup be dry.' [*Ib*. Ed. 1. ii]

15 Now the New Year reviving old Desires, / The thoughtful Soul to Solitude retires, / Where the White Hand of Moses on the Bough / Puts out, and Jesus from the Ground suspires. [*The Rubá'iyát of Omar Khayyám*, Ed. 1. iv]

16 But still the Vine her ancient Ruby yields, / And still a Garden by the Water blows. [*Ib*. Ed. 1. v]

17 Come, fill the Cup, and in the Fire of Spring / The Winter Garment of Repentance fling: / The Bird of Time has but a little way / To fly – and Lo! the Bird is on the Wing. [*Ib*. Ed. 1. vii]

18 The Wine of Life keeps oozing drop by drop, / The Leaves of Life keep falling one by one. [*Ib*. Ed. 4. viii]

19 Each Morn a thousand Roses brings, you say: / Yes, but where leaves the Rose of Yesterday? [*Ib*. Ed. 4. ix]

20 Here with a Loaf of Bread beneath the Bough, / A Flask of Wine, a Book of Verse – and Thou / Beside me singing in the Wilderness – / And Wilderness is Paradise enow. [*Ib*. Ed. 1. xi]

21 A Book of Verses underneath the Bough / A Jug of Wine, a Loaf of Bread – and Thou. [*Ib*. Ed. 4. xii]

22 Ah, take the Cash, and let the Credit go, / Nor heed the rumble of a distant Drum! [*Ib*. Ed. 4. xiii]

23 The Worldly Hope men set their Hearts upon / Turns Ashes – or it prospers; and anon, / Like Snow upon the Desert's dusty face, / Lighting a little Hour or two – is gone. [*Ib*. Ed. 1. xiv]

24 This battered Caravanserai / Whose Portals are alternate Night and Day. [*Ib*. Ed. 4. xvii]

25 They say the Lion and the Lizard keep / The Courts where Jamshýd gloried and drank deep: / And Bahrám, that great Hunter – the Wild Ass / Stamps o'er his Head, and he lies fast asleep. [*Ib*. Ed. 1. xvii]

26 I sometimes think that never blows so red / The Rose as where some buried Caesar bled; / That every Hyacinth the Garden wears / Dropt in her Lap from some once lovely Head. [*Ib*. Ed. 1. xviii]

27 *To-morrow?* – Why, To-morrow I may be / Myself with Yesterday's Sev'n Thousand Years. [*Ib*. Ed. 1. xx]

28 One by one crept silently to Rest. [*Ib*. Ed. 1. xxi]

1 One thing is certain, that Life flies; / One thing is certain, and the Rest is Lies; / The Flower that once has blown for ever dies. [*The Rubá'iyát of Omar Khayyám*, Ed. 1. xxvi]

2 Myself when young did eagerly frequent / Doctor and Saint, and heard great Argument / About it and about: but evermore / Came out by the same Door as in I went. [*Ib.* Ed. 1. xxvii]

3 I came like Water, and like Wind I go. [*Ib.* Ed. 1. xxviii]

4 Into this Universe, and *Why* not knowing / Nor *Whence*, like Water willy-nilly flowing: / And out of it, as Wind along the Waste, / I know not *Whither*, willy-nilly blowing. [*Ib.* Ed. 1. xxix]

5 There was a Door to which I found no Key: / There was a Veil past which I could not see. [*Ib.* Ed. 1. xxxii]

6 Ah, fill the Cup: – what boots it to repeat / How Time is slipping underneath our Feet. [*Ib.* Ed. 1. xxxvii]

7 One Moment in Annihilation's Waste, / One Moment, of the Well of Life to taste – / The Stars are setting and the Caravan / Starts for the Dawn of Nothing – Oh, make haste! [*Ib.* Ed. 1. xxxviii]

8 The Grape that can with Logic absolute / The Two-and-Seventy jarring Sects confute. [*Ib.* Ed. 1. xliii]

9 'Tis all a Chequer-board of Nights and Days / Where Destiny with Men for Pieces plays: / Hither and thither moves, and mates, and slays, / And one by one back in the Closet lays. [*Ib.* Ed. 1. xlix]

10 The Ball no question makes of Ayes and Noes, / But Here or There as strikes the Player goes. [*Ib.* Ed. 4. lxx]

11 The Moving Finger writes; and, having writ, / Moves on: nor all thy Piety nor Wit / Shall lure it back to cancel half a Line, / Nor all thy Tears wash out a Word of it. [*Ib.* Ed. 1. li]

12 And that inverted Bowl we call The Sky, / Whereunder crawling coop't we live and die, / Lift not thy hands to *It* for help – for It / Rolls impotently on as Thou or I. [*Ib.* Ed. 1. lii]

13 One Flash of It within the Tavern caught / Better than in the Temple lost outright. [*Ib.* Ed. 4. lxxvii]

14 O Thou who didst with Pitfall and with Gin / Beset the Road I was to wander in, / Thou wilt not with Predestination round / Enmesh me, and impute my Fall to Sin? [*The Rubá'iyát of Omar Khayyám*, Ed. 1. lvii]

15 Oh, Thou, who Man of baser Earth didst make, / And who with Eden didst devise the Snake; / For all the Sin wherewith the Face of Man / Is blackened, Man's Forgiveness give – and take! [*Ib.* Ed. 1. lviii]

16 Who *is* the Potter, pray, and who the Pot? [*Ib.* Ed. 1. lx]

17 Said one: 'Folks of a surly Tapster tell, / And daub his Visage with the Smoke of Hell; / They talk of some strict Testing of us – Pish! / He's a Good Fellow, and 'twill all be well.' [*Ib.* Ed. I. lxiv]

18 Indeed the Idols I have loved so long / Have done my credit in this World much wrong: / Have drowned my Honour in a Shallow Cup / And sold my Reputation for a Song. [*Ib.* Ed. 1. lxix]

19 I often wonder what the Vintners buy / One half so precious as the Goods they sell. [*Ib.* Ed. 1. lxxi]

20 Alas, that Spring should vanish with the Rose! / That Youth's sweet-scented Manuscript should close! [*Ib.* Ed. 1. lxxii]

21 Ah Love! Could thou and I with Fate conspire / To grasp this sorry Scheme of Things entire, / Would not we shatter it to bits – and then / Re-mould it nearer to the Heart's Desire! [*Ib.* Ed. 1. lxxiii]

22 Ah, Moon of my Delight who know'st no wane, / The Moon of Heav'n is rising once again: / How oft hereafter rising shall she look; / Through this same Garden after me – in vain! [*Ib.* Ed. 1. lxxiv]

23 And when Thyself with shining Foot shall pass / Among the Guests Star-scattered on the Grass, / And in thy joyous Errand reach the Spot / Where I made one – turn down an empty Glass! [*Ib.* Ed. 1. lxxv]

24 And when like her, O Saki, you shall pass. [*Ib.* Ed. 4. ci]

25 A Mr Wilkinson, a clergyman. [Parody of Wordsworth, quoted in Hallam Tennyson's *Tennyson*]

GUSTAVE FLAUBERT 1821–1880

26 I maintain that ideas are events. It is more difficult to make them interesting I know,

but if you fail the style is at fault. [Letter to Louise Colet, 15 Jan. 1853]

1 All one's inventions are true, you can be sure of that. Poetry is as exact a science as geometry. [*Ib.* 14 Aug. 1853]

2 Do not read, as children do, to amuse yourself, or like the ambitious, for the purpose of instruction. No, read in order to live. [Letter to Mlle de Chantepie, June 1857]

J. E. FLECKER   1884–1915

3 For pines are gossip pines the wide world through. [*Brumana*]

4 West of these out to seas colder than the Hebrides I must go, / Where the fleet of stars is anchored and the young star-captains glow. [*The Dying Patriot*]

5 The dragon-green, the luminous, the dark, the serpent-haunted sea. [*The Gates of Damascus*, 'West Gate']

6 We who with songs beguile your pilgrim-age / And swear that Beauty lives though lilies die, / We poets of the proud old lineage / Who sing to find your hearts, we know not why, – / What shall we tell you? Tales, marvellous tales / Of ships and stars and isles where good men rest. [*The Golden Journey to Samarkand*, Prologue]

7 When the great markets by the sea shut fast / All that calm Sunday that goes on and on: / When even lovers find their peace at last, / And Earth is but a star, that once had shone. [*Ib.*]

8 And some to Mecca turn to pray, and I toward thy bed, Yasmin. [*Hassan*, I. ii.]

9 For one night or the other night / Will come the Gardener in white, and gathered flowers are dead, Yasmin. [*Ib.*]

10 For lust of knowing what should not be known, / We take the Golden Road to Samarkand. [*Ib.* V. ii]

11 I have seen old ships sail like swans asleep / Beyond the village which men still call Tyre. [*The Old Ships*]

12 And with great lies about his wooden horse / Set the crew laughing and forgot his course. [*Ib.*]

13 It was so old a ship – who knows, who knows? / And yet so beautiful, I watched in vain / To see the mast burst open with

a rose / And the whole deck put on its leaves again. [*The Old Ships*]

14 A ship, an isle, a sickle moon – / With few but with how splendid stars / The mirrors of the sea are strewn / Between their silver bars. [*A Ship, an Isle, a Sickle Moon*]

15 And old Maeonides the blind / Said it three thousand years ago. [*To a Poet a Thousand Years Hence*]

MARJORIE FLEMING   1803–1811

16 A direful death indeed they had / That would put any parent mad / But she was more than usual calm / She did not give a singel dam. [*Journal*]

17 Today I pronounced a word which should never come out of a lady's lips it was that I called John a Impudent Bitch. [*Ib.*]

18 Sentiment is what I am not acquainted with. [*Ib.*]

ANDREW FLETCHER OF SALTOUN   1655–1716

19 I knew a very wise man so much of Sir Christopher's sentiment, that he believed if a man were permitted to make all the ballads, he need not care who should make the laws of a nation. [*Letter to the Marquis of Montrose and others*]

PHINEAS FLETCHER   1582–1650

20 Drop, drop, slow tears, / And bathe those beauteous feet, / Which brought from Heaven / The news and Prince of Peace. [*An Hymn*]

21 Love is like linen often changed, the sweeter. [*Sicelides*, III. v]

22 The coward's weapon, poison. [*Ib.* V. iii]

23 Love's tongue is in his eyes. [*Piscatory Eclogues*, V. xiii]

JOHN FLORIO   1553?–1625

24 England is the paradise of women, the purgatory of men, and the hell of horses. [*Second Frutes*]

MARSHAL FOCH 1851–1929

1 My centre is giving way, my right is in retreat; situation excellent. I shall attack. [Message to Joffre, Sept. 1914]

SAMUEL FOOTE 1720–1777

2 Born in a cellar . . . and living in a garret. [*The Author*, II]

3 So she went into the garden to cut a cabbage-leaf, to make an apple-pie; and at the same time a great she-bear, coming up the street, pops its head into the shop. 'What! no soap?' So he died, and she very imprudently married the barber. [Nonsense, quoted by Maria Edgeworth in *Harry and Lucy Concluded*]

4 The great Panjandrum himself. [*Ib.*]

5 They all fell to playing the game of catch as catch can, till the gun powder ran out at the heels of their boots. [*Ib.*]

6 When house and land are gone and spent, / Then learning is most excellent. [*Taste*, I. i]

7 He is not only dull in himself, but the cause of dullness in others. [Remark quoted in Boswell's *Life of Johnson*]

HENRY FORD 1863–1947

8 History is bunk. [In the witness-box, when suing the *Chicago Tribune*, July 1919]

JOHN FORD 1586–1639?

9 I am . . . a mushroom / On whom the dew of heaven drops now and then. [*The Broken Heart*, I. iii]

10 Revenge proves its own executioner. [*Ib.* IV. i]

11 He hath shook hands with time. [*Ib.* V. ii]

12 They are the silent griefs which cut the heart-strings. [*Ib.* V. iii]

13 We can drink till all look blue. [*The Lady's Trial*, IV. ii]

14 Why, I hold fate / Clasped in my fist, and could command the course / Of time's eternal motion, hadst thou been / One thought more steady than an ebbing sea. [*'Tis Pity She's a Whore*. V. v.]

LENA FORD ?–1916?

15 Keep the home fires burning while your hearts are yearning, / Though your lads are far away, they dream of home. / There's a silver lining through the dark cloud shining: / Turn the dark cloud inside out, till the boys come home. [*Keep the Home Fires Burning*]

THOMAS FORD 1580?–1648

16 There is a lady sweet and kind, / Was never face so pleased my mind; / I did but see her passing by, / And yet I love her till I die. [*There is a Lady*]

LIEUTENANT-COMMANDER FORGY 1908–

17 Praise the Lord and pass the ammunition. [Said at Pearl Harbor 7 Dec. 1941]

E. M. FORSTER 1879–1970

18 Beethoven's Fifth Symphony is the most sublime noise that has ever penetrated into the ear of man. [*Howards End*, Ch. 5]

19 *Ulysses* is a dogged attempt to cover the universe with mud. [*Aspects of the Novel*, Ch. 6]

CHARLES FOSTER 1828–1904

20 Isn't this a billion dollar country? [Retorting to a gibe about 'a million dollar Congress']

SIR GEORGE FOSTER 1847–1931

21 In these somewhat troublesome days when the great Mother Empire stands splendidly isolated in Europe. [Speech in Canadian House of Commons, 16 Jan. 1896]

S. C. FOSTER 1826–1864

22 I come down dah wid my hat caved in, / Doodah! doodah! / I go back home wid a pocket full of tin, / Oh! doodah day! / Gwine to run all night! / Gwine to run all day! / I bet my money on the bob-tail nag. / Somebody bet on the bay. [*Camptown Races*]

161

1 Weep no more, my lady, / Oh! weep no
more today! / We will sing one song for
the old Kentucky Home, / For the old
Kentucky Home far away. [*My Old
Kentucky Home*]

2 O, Susanna! O, don't you cry for me, /
I've come from Alabama, wid my banjo
on my knee. [*O, Susanna*]

3 'Way down upon de Swanee Ribber, /
Far, far away, / Dere's where my heart is
turning ebber: / Dere's where de old
folks stay. / All up and down de whole
creation / Sadly I roam, / Still longing
for de old plantation, / And for de old
folks at home. [*Old Folks at Home*]

4 I'm coming, I'm coming, / For my head
is bending low / I hear their gentle
voices calling, 'Poor old Joe'. [*Poor Old
Joe*]

5 He had no wool on de top of his head. /
In de place where de wool ought to grow.
[*Uncle Ned*]

6 Dere's no more work for poor old Ned, /
He's gone whar de good niggers go. [*Ib.*]

CHARLES JAMES FOX
1749–1806

7 How much the greatest event it is that
ever happened in the world! and how
much the best! [Letter to Fitzpatrick,
30 July 1789, on the Fall of the Bastille]

GEORGE FOX   1624–1690

8 I heard a voice which said, 'There is one,
even Christ Jesus, that can speak to thy
condition', and when I heard it, my
heart did leap for joy. [*Journal*]

9 When the Lord sent me forth into the
world, He forbade me to put off my hat
to any, high or low. [*Ib.*]

ANATOLE FRANCE   1844–1924

10 *Le bon critique est celui qui raconte les
aventures de son âme au milieu des chefs-
d'œuvre.* – A good critic is one who
narrates the adventures of his mind
among masterpieces. [*La Vie littéraire*, I,
Preface]

FRANCIS I, KING OF FRANCE
1494–1547

11 *Tout est perdu fors l'honneur.*– All is lost
save honour. [Traditional comment on
the loss of the battle of Pavia]

BENJAMIN FRANKLIN
1706–1790

12 Remember that time is money. [*Advice
to Young Tradesmen*]

13 Here Skugg lies snug / As a bug in a rug.
[Letter to Miss G. Shipley, 26 Sept. 1772]

14 There never was a good war or a bad
peace. [Letter to Quincy, 11 Sept. 1783]

15 In this world nothing can be said to be
certain, except death and taxes. [Letter
to Jean-Baptiste Le Roy, 13 Nov. 1789]

16 A little neglect may breed mischief ...
for want of a nail the shoe was lost; for
want of a shoe the horse was lost; and for
want of a horse the rider was lost. [*Maxims* ... prefixed to *Poor Richard's Almanac*]

17 Some are weather-wise, some are otherwise. [*Poor Richard's Almanac*, Feb. 1735]

18 He that lives upon hope will die fasting.
[*Ib.* Preface 1758]

19 Poor man, said I, you pay too much for
your whistle. [*The Whistle*, 10 Nov. 1779]

20 Yes, we must, indeed, all hang together
or, most assuredly, we shall all hang
separately. [Remark at signing of Declaration of Independence]

21 Man is a tool-making animal. [Quoted
in Boswell's *Life of Johnson*, 7 Apr. 1778]

KARL EMIL FRANZOS 1848–1904

22 *Jedes Land hat die Juden, die es verdient.* –
Every country has the Jews that it deserves. [*Schlüssel zur neueren Geschichte
der Juden*]

FREDERICK THE GREAT OF
PRUSSIA   1712–1786

23 *Lorsque Auguste buvait, la Pologne était
ivre.* – When Augustus drank, Poland
became drunk. [*Les Trois Sultanes*, iii. 3]

1 You rogues, do you want to live for ever? [When the Guards hesitated at Kolin, 1757]

2 A German singer! I should as soon expect to get pleasure from the neighing of my horse. [Quoted in *Treasury of Humorous Quotations*]

JOHN FREEMAN 1880–1929

3 It was the lovely moon – she lifted / Slowly her white brow among / Bronze cloud-waves that ebbed and drifted / Faintly, faintlier afar. [*It was the lovely moon*]

4 Than these November skies / Is no sky lovelier. The clouds are deep; / Into their grey the subtle spies / Of colour creep, / Changing their high austerity to delight, / Till ev'n the leaden interfolds are bright. [*November Skies*]

5 Last night a sword-light in the sky / Flashed a swift terror on the dark. / In that sharp light the fields did lie / Naked and stone-like; each tree stood / Like a tranced woman, bound and stark, / Far off the wood / With darkness ridged the riven dark. [*Stone Trees*]

JOHN HOOKHAM FRERE 1769–1846

6 The feathered race with pinions skim the air – / Not so the mackerel, and still less the bear. [*Progress of Man*, 34]

7 A Conservative is only a Tory who is ashamed of himself. [Attr.]

CHARLES FROHMAN 1860–1915

8 Why fear death? It is the most beautiful adventure in life. [Last words before going down in the *Lusitania*]

ROBERT FROST 1874–1963

9 Some say the world will end in fire, / Some say in ice. / From what I've tasted of desire / I hold with those who favour fire, / But if I had to perish twice, / I think I know enough of hate / To say that for destruction ice / Is also great / And would suffice. [*Fire and Ice*]

10 Something there is that doesn't love a wall. [*Mending a Wall*]

11 My apple trees will never get across / And eat the cones under his pines, I tell him. / He only says, 'Good fences make good neighbours'. [*Mending a Wall*]

12 I shall be telling this with a sigh / Somewhere ages and ages hence: / Two roads diverged in a wood, and I – / I took the one less travelled by, / And that has made all the difference. [*The Road not Taken*]

13 The woods are lovely, dark and deep. / But I have promises to keep, / And miles to go before I sleep. [*Stopping by Woods on a Snowy Evening*]

14 A diplomat is a man who always remembers a woman's birthday but never remembers her age. [Quoted in *Treasury of Humorous Quotations*]

JAMES ANTHONY FROUDE 1818–1894

15 Wild animals never kill for sport. Man is the only one to whom the torture and death of his fellow-creatures is amusing in itself. [*Oceana*, Ch. 5]

CHRISTOPHER FRY 1907–

16 Why so shy, my pretty Thomasina? / Thomasin, O Thomasin, / Once you were so promisin'. [*The Dark Is Light Enough*, II]

17 I know your cause is lost, but in the heart / Of all right causes is a cause that cannot lose. [*Ib.* III]

18 Damnation's a good girl. She loves me. [*The Lady's not for Burning*, I]

19 I travel light; as light, / That is, as a man can travel who will / Still carry his body around because / Of its sentimental value. [*Ib.*]

20 It's quite inadequate / To pray for my sons. Praying only acts / As an obbligato to their inclinations. [*Ib.*]

21 You slawzy poodle, you tike, / You crapulous puddering pipsqueak! Do I have to kill you / A second time? [*Ib.*]

22 Religion / Has made an honest woman of the supernatural, / And we won't have it kicking over the traces again. [*Ib.* II]

23 Where in this small-talking world can I find / A longitude with no platitude? [*Ib.* III]

1 The moon is nothing / But a circumambulatory aphrodisiac / Divinely subsidized to provoke the world / Into a rising birth-rate. [*The Lady's not for Burning*, III]

2 That was the pickaxe voice of a cock, beginning / To break up the night. [*Ib.*]

3 Try thinking of love, or something. / *Amor vincit insomnia.* [*A Sleep of Prisoners*]

THOMAS FULLER   1608–1661

4 There is a great difference between painting a face and not washing it. [*Church History*, Bk VII. Sect. i. 32]

5 He knows little, who tells his wife all he knows. [*Holy State*, Bk I. Ch. 3]

6 A little skill in antiquity inclines a man to Popery; but depth in that study brings him about again to our religion. [*Ib.* II. 6]

7 Light, God's eldest daughter, is a principal beauty in a building. [*Ib.* II. 7]

8 Anger is one of the sinews of the soul; he that wants it hath a maimed mind. [*Ib.* III. 8]

9 The pyramids themselves, doting with age, have forgotten the names of their founders. [*Ib.* III. 14]

10 Learning hath gained most by those books by which the printers have lost. [*Ib.* III. 18]

11 They that marry ancient people merely in expectation to bury them, hang themselves, in hope that one will come and cut the halter. [*Ib.* III. 22]

12 Men have a touchstone whereby to try gold, but gold is the touchstone whereby to try men. [*Ib.* IV. 7]

13 Security is the mother of danger and the grandmother of destruction. [*Ib.* V. 18, 1]

14 Often the cockloft is empty in those which nature hath built many stories high. [*Ib.* V. 18. 9]

15 Much matter decocted into a few words. [(Definition of a proverb) *The Worthies of England*, Ch. 2]

16 Many were the wit-combats betwixt him and Ben Jonson, which two I behold like a Spanish great galleon, and an English man of war; Master Jonson (like the former) was built far higher in learning; solid but slow in his performances. Shakespeare with the English man of war, lesser in bulk, but lighter in sailing, could turn with all tides, tack about and take advantage of all winds, by the quickness of his wit and invention. [*The Worthies of England*, *Warwickshire*, 'Shakespeare']

ALFRED FUNKE   1869–?

17 *Gott strafe England!* – God punish England! [*Schwert und Myrte*]

HENRY FUSELI   1741–1825

18 Blake is damned good to steal from. [Quoted in Gilchrist's *Life of Blake*, Ch. 7]

19 Nature puts me out. [*Ib.* 39]

ROSE FYLEMAN   1877–1957

20 There are fairies at the bottom of our garden. [*Fairies*]

GAIUS   2 Cent.

21 *Damnosa hereditas.* – Ruinous inheritance. [*Inst.* ii. 163]

GALILEO GALILEI   1564–1642

22 *E pur si muove.* – Yet it does move. [Attributed saying, after being forced to recant his doctrine that the earth moves round the sun]

JOHN GALSWORTHY   1867–1933

23 Nobody tells me anything. [*The Man of Property*, Pt I. Ch. 1]

24 Oh, your precious 'lame ducks'! [*Ib.* II. 12]

25 The French cook; we open tins. [Quoted in *Treasury of Humorous Quotations*]

LÉON GAMBETTA   1838–1882

26 *Il n'y a pas de question sociale.* – There is no social question. [Favourite saying]

27 *Les temps héroïques sont passés.* – The heroic times have passed away. [Saying]

DAVID GARRICK 1717–1779

1 Come cheer up, my lads! 'tis to glory we steer, / To add something more to this wonderful year; / To honour we call you, not press you like slaves, / For who are so free as the sons of the waves? / Heart of oak are our ships, / Heart of oak are our men: / We always are ready; / Steady, boys, steady; / We'll fight and we'll conquer again and again. [*Heart of Oak*]

2 Here lies Nolly Goldsmith, for shortness called Noll, / Who wrote like an angel, but talked like poor Poll. [*Impromptu Epitaph*]

3 A fellow-feeling makes one wondrous kind. [*Occasional Prologue on Quitting the Theatre*]

4 That blessed word Mesopotamia. [Which in the mouth of George Whitfield was said to have had the power of making men laugh or cry]

WILLIAM LLOYD GARRISON 1805–1879

5 I am in earnest – I will not equivocate – I will not excuse – I will not retreat a single inch – and I will be heard! [*Salutatory Address of the Liberator*, 1 Jan. 1832]

SIR SAMUEL GARTH 1661–1719

6 Hard was their lodging, homely was their food, / For all their luxury was doing good. [*Claremont*, 148]

7 A barren superfluity of words. [*The Dispensary*, II. 95]

8 Some fell by laudanum, and some by steel, / And death in ambush lay in every pill. [*Ib.* IV. 62]

ELIZABETH GASKELL 1810–1865

9 A man ... is *so* in the way in the house! [*Cranford*, Ch. 1]

10 We were none of us musical, though Miss Jenkyns beat time, out of time, by way of appearing to be so. [*Ib.*]

11 Bombazine would have shown a deeper sense of her loss. [*Ib.* 7]

THÉOPHILE GAUTIER 1811–1872

12 *Ce que j'écris n'est pas pour les petites filles.* – What I write is not for little girls. [*Albertus*, 98]

13 *Oui, l'œuvre sort plus belle / D'une forme au travail / Rebelle, / Vers, marbre, onyx, émail.* – Yes, the work comes out more beautiful from a material that resists the process, verse, marble, onyx, or enamel. [*L'Art*]

14 *Je suis un homme pour qui le monde extérieur existe.* – I am a man for whom the outside world exists. [Quoted in *Journal des Goncourt*, 1 May 1857]

GAVARNI [S. G. CHEVALIER] 1804–1866

15 *Les enfants terribles.* – The embarrassing young. [Title of a series of prints]

JOHN GAY 1685–1732

16 I rage, I melt, I burn, / The feeble God has stabbed me to the heart. [*Acis and Galatea*, II]

17 Bring me a hundred reeds of decent growth, / To make a pipe for my capacious mouth. [*Ib.*]

18 O ruddier than the cherry, / O sweeter than the berry, / O nymph more bright / Than moonshine night, / Like kidlings blithe and merry. [*Ib.*]

19 'Tis woman that seduces all mankind, / By her we first were taught the wheedling arts. [*The Beggar's Opera*, I. ii]

20 How, like a moth, the simple maid / Still plays about the flame! [*Ib.* I. iv]

21 Our Polly is a sad slut! nor heeds what we have taught her. / I wonder any man alive will ever rear a daughter! [*Ib.* I. viii]

22 O Polly, you might have toyed and kissed. / By keeping men off, you keep them on. [*Ib.* I. ix]

23 A fox may steal your hens, sir, / ... If lawyer's hand is fee'd, sir / He steals your whole estate. [*Ib.* I. x]

24 For on the rope that hangs my dear / Depends poor Polly's life. [*Ib.* I. xii]

25 I sipped each flower, / I changed ev'ry hour, / But here ev'ry flower is united. [*Ib.* I. xiii]

1 If with me you'll fondly stray, / Over the hills and far away. [*The Beggar's Opera*, I. xiii]

2 Fill ev'ry glass, for wine inspires us, / And fires us / With courage, love and joy. / Women and wine should life employ. / Is there aught else on earth desirous? [*Ib*. II. i]

3 If the heart of a man is depressed with cares, / The mist is dispelled when a woman appears. [*Ib*. II. iii]

4 Youth's the season made for joys, / Love is then our duty. [*Ib*. II. iv]

5 Man may escape from rope and gun; / Nay, some have out-lived the doctor's pill; / Who takes a woman must be undone, / That basilisk is sure to kill. [*Ib*. II. viii]

6 The fly that sips treacle is lost in the sweets. [*Ib*.]

7 Do like other widows – buy yourself weeds, and be cheerful. [*Ib*. II. xi]

8 How happy could I be with either, / Were t'other dear charmer away! / But while ye thus tease me together, / To neither a word will I say. [*Ib*. II. xiii]

9 One wife is too much for most husbands to hear, / But two at a time there's no mortal can bear. [*Ib*. III. xi]

10 The charge is prepared; the lawyers are met, / The judges all ranged (a terrible show!). [*Ib*.]

11 She who has never loved has never lived. [*Captives*, II. i]

12 Where yet was ever found a mother, / Who'd give her booby for another? [*Fables*, Pt I. iii. 33]

13 In every age and clime we see, / Two of a trade can ne'er agree. [*Ib*. I. xxi. 43]

14 'While there is life, there's hope,' he cried; / 'Then why such haste?' so groaned and died. [*Ib*. I. xxvii. 49]

15 Those who in quarrels interpose, / Must often wipe a bloody nose. [*Ib*. I. xxxiv. 1]

16 And when a lady's in the case, / You know, all other things give place. [*Ib*. I. l. 41]

17 'Tis a gross error, held in schools, / That Fortune always favours fools. [*Ib*. II. xii. 119]

18 Life is a jest; and all things show it. / I thought so once; but now I know it. [*My own Epitaph*]

19 All in the Downs the fleet was moored, / The streamers waving in the wind, / When black-eyed Susan came aboard. [*Sweet William's Farewell*]

20 We only part to meet again. / Change, as ye list, ye winds; my heart shall be / The faithful compass that still points to thee. [*Ib*.]

21 Adieu! she cries; and waved her lily hand. [*Ib*.]

22 'Twas when the seas were roaring / With hollow blasts of wind; / A damsel lay deploring, / All on a rock reclined. [*The What D'Ye Call It*, II. viii]

SIR ERIC GEDDES   1875–1937

23 We will get everything out of her [Germany] that you can squeeze out of a lemon, and a bit more. . . . I will squeeze her until you can hear the pips squeak. [Speech at Cambridge, 9 Dec. 1918]

GEORGE I   1660–1727

24 I hate all Boets and Bainters. [Quotation in Campbell, *Lives of the Chief Justices*, Ch. 30]

GEORGE II   1683–1760

25 KING (replying to Queen Caroline's death-bed injunctions to marry again): *Non, j'aurai des maîtresses.* – No, I will take mistresses.
QUEEN CHARLOTTE: *Ah! mon Dieu! Cela n'empêche pas.* – But, Goodness me, that won't prevent you! [Hervey, *Memoirs of George II*]

26 Oh! he [General Wolfe] is mad, is he? Then I wish he would *bite* some other of my generals. [F. Thackeray, *History of William Pitt*]

GEORGE III   1738–1820

27 Born and educated in this country, I glory in the name of Briton. [First speech in Parliament, 1760]

28 'Was there ever', cried he, 'such stuff as great part of Shakespeare? Only one mustn't say so!' [Fanny Burney's *Diary*, 19 Dec. 1785]

GEORGE V 1865–1936

1 Wake up, England. [Title of reprinted speech, 1911]

2 How is the Empire? [Last words]

EDWARD GIBBON 1737–1794

3 The romance of *Tom Jones*, that exquisite picture of human manners, will outlive the palace of the Escurial and the imperial eagle of the house of Austria. [*Autobiography*]

4 To the University of Oxford I acknowledge no obligation; and she will as willingly renounce me for a son, as I am willing to disclaim her for a mother. I spent fourteen months at Magdalen College; they proved the fourteen months the most idle and unprofitable of my whole life. [*Ib.*]

5 Decent easy men, who supinely enjoyed the gifts of the founder. [*Ib.*]

6 I sighed as a lover, I obeyed as a son. [*Ib.*]

7 Crowds without company, and dissipation without pleasure [(Of London) *Ib.*]

8 My English text is chaste, and all licentious passages are left in the decent obscurity of a learned language. [*Ib.*]

9 The various modes of worship, which prevailed in the Roman world, were all considered by the people as equally true; by the philosopher, as equally false; and by the magistrate, as equally useful. [*Decline and Fall of the Roman Empire*, Ch. 2]

10 The principles of a free constitution are irrevocably lost when the legislative power is nominated by the executive. [*Ib.* 3]

11 His reign is marked by the rare advantage of furnishing very few materials for history; which is, indeed, little more than the register of the crimes, follies and misfortunes of mankind. [*Ib.*]

12 It has been calculated by the ablest politicians that no State, without becoming soon exhausted, can maintain above the hundredth part of its members in arms and idleness. [*Ib.* 5]

13 Twenty-two acknowledged concubines, and a library of sixty-two thousand volumes, attested the variety of his inclinations; and from the productions which he left behind him, it appears that the former as well as the latter were designed for use rather than ostentation. [*Decline and Fall of the Roman Empire*, 7]

14 All taxes must, at last, fall upon agriculture. [*Ib.* 8]

15 Corruption, the most infallible symptom of constitutional liberty. [*Ib.* 21]

16 The ecclesiastical writers, who, in the heat of religious faction, are apt to despise the profane virtues of sincerity and moderation. [*Ib.* 26]

17 In every deed of mischief he [Comenus] had a heart to resolve, a head to contrive, and a hand to execute. [*Ib.* 48]

18 Our sympathy is cold to the relation of distant misery. [*Ib.* 49]

19 All that is human must be retrograde if it does not advance. [*Ib.* 71]

STELLA GIBBONS 1902–

20 Something nasty in the woodshed. [*Cold Comfort Farm, passim*]

21 Graceless, Pointless, Feckless and Aimless waited their turn to be milked. [*Ib.* Ch. 3]

ANDRÉ GIDE 1869–1951

22 *L'acte gratuite.* – The unmotivated action. [*Les Caves du Vatican, passim*]

RICHARD GIFFORD 1725–1807

23 Revolves the sad vicissitude of things. [*Contemplation*]

WILLIAM GIFFORD 1756–1826

24 The insatiate itch of scribbling. [Transl. of Juvenal, vii. 79]

25 His namby-pamby madrigals of love. [*The Baviad*, 176]

FRED GILBERT 1850–1903

26 At Trinity Church I met my doom. [Title of song]

27 As I walk along the Bois Bou-long, / With an independent air, / You can hear

the girls declare, / 'He must be a millionaire'; / You can hear them sigh and wish to die, / You can see them wink the other eye / At the man who broke the Bank at Monte Carlo. [*The Man who Broke the Bank at Monte Carlo*]

SIR HUMPHREY GILBERT
1539?–1583

1 We are as near to heaven by sea as by land. [Hakluyt's *Voyages*]

SIR W. S. GILBERT   1836–1911

2 Among them was a Bishop, who / Had lately been appointed to / The balmy isle of Rum-ti-Foo, / And Peter was his name. [*Bab Ballads*, 'Bishop of Rum-ti-Foo']

3 But they couldn't chat together – they had not been introduced. [*Ib.* 'Etiquette']

4 There were captains by the hundred, there were baronets by dozens. [*Ib.* 'Ferdinando and Elvira']

5 The padre said, 'Whatever have you been and gone and done?' [*Ib.* 'Gentle Alice Brown']

6 The mildest curate going. [*Ib.* 'The Rival Curates']

7 Then they began to sing / That extremely lovely thing, / 'Scherzando! ma non troppo, ppp.' [*Ib.* 'The Story of Prince Agib']

8 Oh, I am a cook and a captain bold, / And the mate of the *Nancy* brig, / And a bo'sun tight, and a midshipmite, / And the crew of the captain's gig. [*Ib.* 'The Yarn of the Nancy Bell']

9 He led his regiment from behind – / He found it less exciting. [*The Gondoliers*, I]

10 That celebrated, / Cultivated, / Underrated / Nobleman, / The Duke of Plaza-Toro! [*Ib.*]

11 Of that there is no manner of doubt – / No probable, possible shadow of doubt – / No possible doubt whatever. [*Ib.*]

12 A taste for drink, combined with gout, / Had doubled him up for ever. [*Ib.*]

13 Try we life-long, we can never / Straighten out life's tangled skein. [*Ib.*]

14 Life's a pudding full of plums. [*Ib.*]

15 Oh, 'tis a glorious thing, I ween, / To be a regular Royal Queen! / No half-and-half-affair, I mean, / But a right-down regular Royal Queen! [*The Gondoliers*, I]

16 Take a pair of sparkling eyes. [*Ib.* II]

17 Take my counsel, happy man; / Act upon it, if you can! [*Ib.*]

18 Dukes were three a penny. [*Ib.*]

19 When everyone is somebodee, / Then no one's anybody. [*Ib.*]

20 I am a courtier grave and serious / Who is about to kiss your hand: / Try to combine a pose imperious / With a demeanour nobly bland. [*Ib.*]

21 I'm called Little Buttercup – dear Little Buttercup, / Though I could never tell why. [*H.M.S. Pinafore*, I]

22 Though 'Bother it' I may / Occasionally say, / I never use a big, big D. –
ALL: What never?
CAPT: No, never!
ALL: What, *never*?
CAPT: Hardly ever! [*Ib.*]

23 And so do his sisters, and his cousins, and his aunts! [*Ib.*]

24 When I was a lad I served a term / As office-boy to an Attorney's firm; / I cleaned the windows and I swept the floor, / And I polished up the handle of the big front door. / I polished up that handle so successfullee, / That now I am the Ruler of the Queen's Navee! [*Ib.*]

25 And I copied all the letters in a big round hand. [*Ib.*]

26 And I always voted at my party's call, / And I never thought of thinking for myself at all. [*Ib.*]

27 Things are seldom what they seem, / Skim milk masquerades as cream. [*Ib.* II]

28 Never mind the why and wherefore. [*Ib.*]

29 He is an Englishman! / For he himself has said it, / And it's greatly to his credit, / That he is an Englishman! [*Ib.*]

30 For he might have been a Roosian, / A French, or Turk, or Proosian, / Or perhaps Ital-ian! / But in spite of all temptations / To belong to other nations, / He remains an Englishman! [*Ib.*]

31 Bow, bow, ye lower middle classes! / Bow, bow, ye tradesmen, bow, ye masses. [*Iolanthe*, I]

32 The Law is the true embodiment / Of everything that's excellent. / It has no kind of fault or flaw, / And I, my lords, embody the Law. [*Ib.*]

1 The constitutional guardian I, / Of pretty young Wards in Chancery. [*Iolanthe*, I]

2 A pleasant occupation for / A rather susceptible Chancellor! [*Ib.*]

3 Hearts just as pure and fair / May beat in Belgrave Square / As in the lowly air / Of Seven Dials. [*Ib.*]

4 When I went to the Bar as a very young man, / (Said I to myself, said I). [*Ib.*]

5 I often think it's comical / How Nature always does contrive / That every boy and ever gal, / That's born into the world alive, / Is either a little Liberal, / Or else a little Conservative! [*Ib.* II]

6 The House of Peers, throughout the war, / Did nothing in particular, / And did it very well. [*Ib.*]

7 When you're lying awake with a dismal headache, and repose is tabooed by anxiety, / I conceive you may use any language you choose to indulge in without impropriety. [*Ib.*]

8 For you dream you are crossing the Channel, and tossing about in a steamer from Harwich, / Which is something between a large bathing-machine and a very small second-class carriage. [*Ib.*]

9 Pooh-Bah (Lord High Everything Else). [*Mikado*, Dramatis Personae]

10 A wandering minstrel I – / A thing of shreds and patches. [*Ib.* I]

11 And I am right, / And you are right, / And all is right as right can be! [*Ib.*]

12 I can trace my ancestry back to a protoplasmal primordial atomic globule. Consequently, my family pride is something inconceivable. I can't help it. I was born sneering. [*Ib.*]

13 It revolts me, but I do it! [*Ib.*]

14 As some day it may happen that a victim must be found, / I've got a little list – I've got a little list / Of society offenders who might well be underground, / And who never would be missed – who never would be missed! [*Ib.*]

15 Three little maids from school are we, / Pert as a schoolgirl well can be / Filled to the brim with girlish glee! [*Ib.*]

16 Life is a joke that's just begun. [*Ib.*]

17 Three little maids who, all unwary, / Come from a ladies' seminary. [*Ib.*]

18 Modified rapture! [*Ib.*]

19 We are not shy; / We're very wide awake, / The moon and I! [*Mikado*, I]

20 My object all sublime / I shall achieve in time – / To let the punishment fit the crime. [*Ib.* II]

21 A source of innocent merriment. [*Ib.*]

22 On a cloth untrue / With a twisted cue, / And elliptical billiard balls. [*Ib.*]

23 I drew my snickersnee! [*Ib.*]

24 Something lingering with boiling oil in it, I fancy. [*Ib.*]

25 Merely corroborative detail, intended to give artistic verisimilitude to an otherwise bald and unconvincing narrative. [*Ib.*]

26 The flowers that bloom in the spring, / Tra la, / Have nothing to do with the case. [*Ib.*]

27 I've got to take under my wing, / Tra la, / A most unattractive old thing, / Tra la, / With a caricature of a face. [*Ib.*]

28 On a tree by a river a little tomtit / Sang 'Willow, titwillow, titwillow.' [*Ib.*]

29 Twenty love-sick maidens we, / Love-sick all against our will. [*Patience*, I]

30 When I first put this uniform on. [*Ib.*]

31 If you're anxious for to shine in the high aesthetic line, as a man of culture rare. [*Ib.*]

32 The meaning doesn't matter if it's only idle chatter of a transcendental kind. [*Ib.*]

33 Why, what a very singularly deep young man, this deep young man must be! [*Ib.*]

34 An attachment à la Plato for a bashful young potato, or a not-too-French French bean. [*Ib.*]

35 By no endeavour, / Can magnet ever / Attract a silver churn! [*Ib.* II]

36 Sing 'Hey to you – good day to you' – / Sing 'Bah to you – ha! ha! to you.' [*Ib.*]

37 Francesca di Rimini, miminy, piminy, / 'Je-ne-sais-quoi' young man! [*Ib.*]

38 A very delectable, highly respectable, / Threepenny-bus young man. [*Ib.*]

39 I'm a greenery-yallery, Grosvenor Gallery, / Foot-in-the-grave young man! [*Ib.*]

40 I am the very model of a modern Major-General. [*Pirates of Penzance*, I]

1 When the foeman bares his steel, / Tarantara, tarantara! / We uncomfortable feel. [*Pirates of Penzance*, II]

2 When constabulary duty's to be done, / The policeman's lot is not a happy one. [*Ib.*]

3 When the enterprising burglar's not a-burgling. [*Ib.*]

4 Politics we bar, / They are not our bent: / On the whole we are / Not intelligent. [*Princess Ida*, I]

5 We will hang you, never fear, / Most politely, most politely! [*Ib.*]

6 Man's a ribald – Man's a rake, / Man is Nature's sole mistake. [*Ib.* II]

7 All baronets are bad. [*Ruddigore*, I]

8 He uses language that would make your hair curl. [*Ib.*]

9 Such a bright little, tight little, / Slight little, light little, / Trim little, prim little craft! [*Ib.* II]

10 Some word that teems with hidden meaning – like 'Basingstoke'. [*Ib.*]

11 Time was when Love and I were well acquainted. [*The Sorcerer*, I]

12 I was a pale young curate then. [*Ib.*]

13 So I fell in love with a rich attorney's / Elderly ugly daughter. [*Trial by Jury*]

14 She may very well pass for forty-three / In the dusk with a light behind her! [*Ib.*]

15 And many a burglar I've restored / To his friends and his relations. [*Ib.*]

16 For now I am a Judge, / And a good Judge too. [*Ib.*]

17 Is life a boon? / If so, it must befall / That death, whene'er he call, / Must call too soon. [*The Yeomen of the Guard*, I]

18 HE: I have a song to sing O! SHE: Sing me your song O! [*Ib.*]

19 It's the song of a merryman, moping mum, / Whose soul was sad, and whose glance was glum, / Who supped no sup, and who craved no crumb, / As he sighed for the love of a ladye. [*Ib.*]

JAMES GILLRAY   1757–1815

20 Political Ravishment, or The Old Lady of Threadneedle Street in Danger. [Caption of a caricature, 1797]

MME DE GIRARDIN   1804–1855

21 Business is other people's money. [*Marguerites*, Vol. ii. p. 104]

W. E. GLADSTONE   1809–1898

22 You cannot fight against the future. Time is on our side. [Speech on the Reform Bill, 1866]

23 [The Turks] one and all, bag and baggage, shall, I hope, clear out from the province they have desolated and profaned. [Speech in House of Commons, 7 May 1877]

24 Out of the range of practical politics. [Speech at Dalkeith, 26 Nov. 1879]

25 The resources of civilization are not yet exhausted. [Speech at Leeds, 7 Oct. 1881]

26 I would tell them of my own intention to keep my own counsel ... and I will venture to recommend them, as an old Parliamentary hand, to do the same. [Speech in House of Commons, 21 Jan. 1886]

27 All the world over, I will back the masses against the classes. [Speech at Liverpool, 28 June 1886]

28 This is the negation of God erected into a system of government. [Letter to the Earl of Aberdeen on the state of Naples, 1851]

WILLIAM HENRY, DUKE OF GLOUCESTER   1743–1805

29 Another damned, thick, square book! Always scribble, scribble, scribble! Eh! Mr Gibbon? [Quoted in note to Boswell's *Life of Johnson*]

JOHN A. GLOVER-KIND   Late 19 Cent.

30 I do Like to be Beside the Seaside. [Title of song]

A. D. GODLEY   1856–1925

31 What is this that roareth thus? / Can it be a Motor Bus? / Yes, the smell and hideous hum / Indicat Motorem Bum. [*The Motor Bus*]

HERMANN GOERING 1893–1946

1 Guns will make us powerful; butter will only make us fat. [Broadcast, 1936]

2 When I hear anyone talk of Culture, I reach for my revolver. [Attr.]

JOHANN WOLFGANG VON GOETHE 1749–1832

3 *Es irrt der Mensch, so lang er strebt.* – Man errs so long as he strives. [*Faust, I, Prolog im Himmel*]

4 *Da steh' ich nun, ich armer Tor! / Und bin so klug als wie zuvor.* – There I am, a poor fool, and am no wiser than I was before. [*Ib. I. Nacht*]

5 *Der Geist, der stets verneint!* – The spirit that always denies. [*Ib. I. Studierzimmer*]

6 *Entbehren sollst du, sollst entbehren! / Das ist der ewige Gesang.* – You shall abstain, shall abstain. That is the eternal song. [*Ib.*]

7 *Werd ich zum Augenblicke sagen: / Verweile doch! Du bist so schön!* – If I say to the moment: 'Stay now! You are so beautiful!' [*Ib.*]

8 *Denn eben, wo Begriffe fehlen, / Da stellt ein Wort zur rechten Zeit sich ein.* – For just when ideas fail, a word comes in to save the situation. [*Ib.*]

9 *Meine Ruh' ist hin, / Mein Herz ist schwer.* – My peace is gone, my heart is heavy. [*Ib. I. Gretchens Stube*]

10 *Wer immer strebend sich bemüht, / Den können wir erlösen.* – If a man makes continuous efforts, we can save him. [*Ib. II, Bergschluchten, Wald, Fels und Einöde*]

11 *Alles Vergängliche / Ist nur ein Gleichnis.* – All that is transitory is only an image. [*Ib.*]

12 *Das Ewig-Weibliche, / Zieht uns hinan.* – The eternal in woman draws us on. [*Ib.*]

13 *Du musst herrschen und gewinnen, / Oder dienen und verlieren, / Leiden oder triumphieren, / Amboss oder Hammer sein.* – You must either conquer and rule or serve and lose, suffer or triumph, be the anvil or the hammer. [*Der Gross-Cophta, II*]

14 *Ein unnütz Leben ist ein früher Tod.* – A useless life is an early death. [*Iphigenie, I. ii*]

15 *Es bildet ein Talent sich in der Stille, / Sich ein Charakter in dem Strom der Welt.* – Genius is formed in quiet, character in the stream of human life. [*Tasso, I. ii*]

16 *Und so lang du das nicht hast, / Dieses: Stirb und werde! / Bist du nur ein trüber Gast / Auf der dunklen Erde.* – And until you have grasped this: 'Die and be transformed!' you will be nothing but a sombre guest on the sorry earth. [*Selige Sehnsucht*]

17 *In der Beschränkung zeigt sich erst der Meister.* – It is in self-limitation that a master first shows himself. [*Sonett: Natur und Kunst*]

18 *Über allen Gipfeln / Ist Ruh'.* – On all the peaks lies peace. [*Wanderers Nachtlied*]

19 *In der Kunst ist das Beste gut genug.* – In art the best is good enough. [*Italienische Reise*]

20 *Wer nie sein Brot mit Tränen ass, / Wer nie die kummervollen Nächte / Auf seinem Bette weinend sass, / Der kennt euch nicht, ihr himmlischen Mächte.* – Who never ate his bread with tears, who never sat through the sorrowful night, weeping upon his bed, does not know you, O heavenly powers. [*Wilhelm Meister, 'Harfenspielerslied'*]

21 *Denn alle Schuld rächt sich auf Erden.* – For all guilt is punished on earth. [*Ib.*]

22 *Kennst du das Land wo die Zitronen blühn?* – Do you know the land where the lemon-trees flower? [*Ib. 'Mignonslied'*]

23 *Was hat man dir, du armes Kind, getan?* – What have they done to you, my poor child? [*Ib.*]

24 *Lord Byron is nur gross, wenn er dichtet; so bald er reflektiert ist er ein Kind.* – Lord Byron is only great as a poet; as soon as he reflects he is a child. [*Gespräche mit Eckermann, 18 Jan. 1825*]

25 *Nationalliteratur will jetzt nicht viel sagen, die Epoche der Weltliteratur ist an der Zeit.* – National literature no longer means very much, the age of world literature is due. [*Ib. 31 Jan. 1827*]

26 *Ich habe unter meinen Papieren ein Blatt gefunden . . . wo ich die Baukunst eine erstarrte Musik nenne.* – I have found among my papers a sheet . . . in which I call architecture frozen music. [*Ib. 23 Mar. 1829*]

171

1 *Mehr Licht!* – More light! [Reported dying words. Actually he asked for the second shutter of his window to be opened, so that more light could come in]

OLIVER GOLDSMITH 1728–1774

2 Sweet Auburn! loveliest village of the plain. [*The Deserted Village*, 1]

3 The bashful virgin's side-long looks of love, / The matron's glance that would those looks reprove. [*Ib.* 29]

4 Ill fares the land, to hastening ills a prey, / Where wealth accumulates, and men decay; / Princes and lords may flourish, or may fade; / A breath can make them, as a breath has made; / But a bold peasantry, their country's pride, / When once destroyed, can never be supplied. [*Ib.* 51]

5 For him light labour spread her wholesome store, / Just gave what life required, but gave no more: / His best companions, innocence and health; / And his best riches, ignorance of wealth. [*Ib.* 59]

6 How happy he who crowns in shades like these, / A youth of labour with an age of ease. [*Ib.* 99]

7 And, all his prospects brightening to the last, / His heaven commences ere the world be past! [*Ib.* 111]

8 The watch-dog's voice that bayed the whispering wind, / And the loud laugh that spoke the vacant mind. [*Ib.* 121]

9 A man he was, to all the country dear, / And passing rich with forty pounds a year; / Remote from towns he ran his godly race, / Nor e'er had changed, nor wished to change his place. [*Ib.* 141]

10 Far other aims his heart had learned to prize, / More skilled to raise the wretched than to rise. / His house was known to all the vagrant train, / He chid their wanderings, but relieved their pain. [*Ib.* 147]

11 Shouldered his crutch, and shewed how fields were won. [*Ib.* 158]

12 And e'en his failings leaned to Virtue's side. [*Ib.* 164]

13 He tried each art, reproved each dull delay, / Allured to brighter worlds, and led the way. [*Ib.* 169]

14 And fools, who came to scoff, remained to pray. [*Ib.* 180]

15 Even children followed with endearing wile, / And plucked his gown, to share the good man's smile. [*The Deserted Village*, 183]

16 Beside yon straggling fence that skirts the way, / With blossomed furze unprofitably gay. [*Ib.* 193]

17 A man severe he was, and stern to view, / I knew him well, and every truant knew; / Well had the boding tremblers learned to trace / The day's disasters in his morning face; / Full well they laughed with counterfeited glee, / At all his jokes, for many a joke had he; / Full well the busy whisper, circling round, / Conveyed the dismal tidings when he frowned; / Yet he was kind, or if severe in aught, / The love he bore to learning was in fault. [*Ib.* 197]

18 In arguing too, the parson owned his skill, / For e'en though vanquished, he could argue still; / While words of learned length, and thundering sound, / Amazed the gazing rustics ranged around; / And still they gazed, and still the wonder grew, / That one small head could carry all he knew. [*Ib.* 211]

19 Where village statesmen talked with looks profound, / And news much older than their ale went round. [*Ib.* 223]

20 The white-washed wall, the nicely sanded floor, / The varnished clock that clicked behind the door; / The chest contrived a double debt to pay, / A bed by night, a chest of drawers by day. [*Ib.* 227]

21 The twelve good rules, the royal game of goose. [*Ib.* 232]

22 And, e'en while fashion's brightest arts decoy, / The heart distrusting asks, if this be joy. [*Ib.* 263]

23 How wide the limits stand / Between a splendid and an happy land. [*Ib.* 267]

24 Sweet as the primrose peeps beneath the thorn. [*Ib.* 330]

25 In all the silent manliness of grief. [*Ib.* 384]

26 Thou source of all my bliss, and all my woe, / That foundst me poor at first, and keepst me so. [*Ib.* 413]

27 The king himself has followed her, – / When she has walked before. [*Elegy on Mrs Mary Blaize*]

28 The fat was so white, and the lean was so ruddy. [*The Haunch of Venison*, 4]

1 Too nice for a statesman, too proud for a wit. [(Edmund Burke) *Retaliation*, 38]

2 Too fond of the *right* to pursue the *expedient*. [(Edmund Burke) *Ib.* 40]

3 An abridgement of all that was pleasant in man. [(David Garrick) *Ib.* 94]

4 As a wit, if not first, in the very first line. [(Garrick) *Ib.* 96]

5 On the stage he was natural, simple, affecting, / 'Twas only that, when he was off, he was acting. [(Garrick) *Ib.* 101]

6 When they talked of their Raphaels, Correggios and stuff, / He shifted his trumpet, and only took snuff. [(Reynolds) *Ib.* 145]

7 The best-humoured man with the worst-humoured muse. [(Whitefoord) *Ib.* 174]

8 O Memory! thou fond deceiver, / Still importunate and vain, / To former joys recurring ever, / And turning all the past to pain! [Song: *O Memory*]

9 Where'er I roam, whatever realms to see, / My heart untravelled fondly turns to thee. [*The Traveller*, 7]

10 And learn the luxury of doing good. [*Ib.* 22]

11 These little things are great to little man. [*Ib.* 42]

12 Creation's heir, the world, the world is mine. [*Ib.* 50]

13 Such is the patriot's boast, where'er we roam, / His first, best country ever is at home. [*Ib.* 73]

14 The land of scholars, and the nurse of arms. [*Ib.* 356]

15 Laws grind the poor, and rich men rule the law. [*Ib.* 386]

16 How small, of all that human hearts endure, / That part which laws or kings can cause or cure. [*Ib.* 429]

17 Still to ourselves in every place consigned, / Our own felicity we make or find. [*Ib.* 431]

18 You may all go to pot. [*Verses in Reply to an Invitation to Dinner at Dr Baker's*]

19 As writers become more numerous, it is natural for readers to become more indolent. [*The Bee*, No. 175, 'Upon Unfortunate Merit']

20 'The Republic of Letters' is a very common expression among the Europeans. [*Citizen of the World*, 20]

21 A night-cap decked his brows instead of bay, / A cap by night – a stocking all the day! [*Citizen of the World*, 30]

22 'Did I say so?' replied he coolly; 'to be sure, if I said so, it was so.' [*Ib.* 54]

23 I hate the French because they are all slaves, and wear wooden shoes. [*Essays*, 24, 'Distresses of a Common Soldier']

24 Hope, like the gleaming taper's light, / Adorns and cheers our way; / And still, as darker grows the night, / Emits a brighter ray. [*The Captivity*, II]

25 This same philosophy is a good horse in the stable, but an arrant jade on a journey. [*The Good-Natured Man*, I]

26 I'm now no more than a mere lodger in my own house. [*Ib.*]

27 Friendship is a disinterested commerce between equals; love, an abject intercourse between tyrants and slaves. [*Ib.*]

28 Don't let's make imaginary evils, when you know we have so many real ones to encounter. [*Ib.*]

29 LEONTINE: An only son, sir, might expect more indulgence.
CROAKER: An only father, sir, might expect more obedience. [*Ib.*]

30 I am told he makes a very handsome corpse, and becomes his coffin prodigiously. [*Ib.*]

31 Silence is become his mother tongue. [*Ib.* II]

32 In my time, the follies of the town crept slowly among us, but now they travel faster than a stage-coach. [*She Stoops to Conquer*, I]

33 I love everything that's old: old friends, old times, old manners, old books, old wines. [*Ib.*]

34 As for disappointing them, I should not so much mind ; but I can't abide to disappoint myself. [*Ib.*]

35 The very pink of perfection. [*Ib.*]

36 Let schoolmasters puzzle their brain, / With grammar, and nonsense, and learning, / Good liquor, I stoutly maintain, / Gives genius a better discerning. [*Ib.* song]

37 It's a damned long, dark, boggy, dirty, dangerous way. [*Ib.*]

38 This is Liberty-Hall, gentlemen. [*Ib.* II]

39 The first blow is half the battle. [*Ib.*]

1 We are the boys / That fear no noise / Where the thundering cannons roar. [*She Stoops to Conquer*, II]

2 Was there ever such a cross-grained brute? [*Ib.* III]

3 As for murmurs, mother, we grumble a little now and then, to be sure. But there's no love lost between us. [*ib.* IV]

4 A book may be amusing with numerous errors, or it may be very dull without a single absurdity. [*The Vicar of Wakefield*, Preface]

5 I was ever of the opinion, that the honest man who married and brought up a large family, did more service than he who continued single, and only talked of population. [*Ib.* Ch. 1]

6 I... chose my wife, as she did her wedding gown, not for a fine glossy surface, but such qualities as would wear well. [*Ib.*]

7 I was never much displeased with those harmless delusions that tend to make us more happy. [*Ib.* 3]

8 I find you want me to furnish you with argument and intellects too. [*Ib.* 7]

9 That's a good girl. I find you are perfectly qualified for making converts, and so go help your mother to make the gooseberry-pie. [*Ib.*]

10 Man wants but little here below, / Nor wants that little long. [*Ib.* 8, *A Ballad*, 30]

11 By the living jingo, she was all of a muck of sweat. [*Ib.* 9]

12 With other fashionable topics, such as pictures, taste, Shakespeare, and the musical glasses. [*Ib.*]

13 It seemed to me pretty plain, that they had more of love than matrimony in them. [*Ib.* 16]

14 Good people all, of every sort, / Give ear unto my song; / And if you find it wondrous short, / It cannot hold you long. [*Ib.* 17, *An Elegy on the Death of a Mad Dog*]

15 That still a godly race he ran, / Whene'er he went to pray. [*Ib.*]

16 The naked every day he clad, / When he put on his clothes. [*Ib.*]

17 The dog, to gain some private ends, / Went mad and bit the man. [*Ib.*]

18 The man recovered of the bite, / The dog it was that died. [*Ib.*

19 When lovely woman stoops to folly, / And finds too late that men betray, / What charm can soothe her melancholy, / What art can wash her guilt away? [*The Vicar of Wakefield*, 29]

20 There is no arguing with Johnson; for when his pistol misses fire, he knocks you down with the butt end of it. [Boswell's *Life of Johnson*, 26 Oct. 1769]

21 As I take my shoes from the shoemaker, and my coat from the tailor, so I take my religion from the priest. [*Ib.* 9 Apr. 1773]

22 If you were to make little fishes talk, they would talk like whales. [(Said to Johnson) *Ib.* 27 Apr. 1773]

23 Is he like Burke, who winds into a subject like a serpent? [(To Boswell, of Johnson) *Ib.* 10 May 1773]

24 A pampered menial. [Alteration of a phrase in T. Moss, *Beggar's Petition*]

SAMUEL GOLDWYN   1882–1974

25 In two words: im-possible. [Quoted in Alva Johnson, *The Great Goldwyn*]

26 For years I have been known for saying 'include me out'; but today I am giving it up for ever. [Address at Balliol, Oxford, 1 Mar. 1945]

EDMOND and JULES DE GONCOURT
1822–1896 and 1830–1870

27 *Les historiens sont des raconteurs du passé, les romanciers des raconteurs du présent.* – Historians tell the story of the past, novelists the story of the present. [*Journal*]

ADAM LINDSAY GORDON
1833–1870

28 Life is mostly froth and bubble, / Two things stand like stone, / Kindness in another's trouble, / Courage in your own. [*Ye Wearie Wayfarer*, Fytte 8]

LORD GOSCHEN   1831–1907

29 I have not the temerity to give a political blank cheque to Lord Salisbury. [Speech in House of Commons, 19 Feb. 1884]

1 We have stood alone in that which is called isolation – our splendid isolation, as one of our colonial friends was good enough to call it. [(See under Sir George Foster) Speech at Lewes, 26 Feb. 1896]

VINCENT DE GOURNAY
1712–1759

2 *Laissez faire, laissez passer.* – Liberty of action, liberty of movement. [Speech, Sept. 1758. Also attributed to Marquis d'Argenson and François Quesnay]

RICHARD GRAFTON ?–1572?

3 Thirty days hath November, / April, June and September, / February hath twenty-eight alone, / And all the rest have thirty-one. [*Abridgement of the Chronicles of England*, Introduction (1570)]

HARRY GRAHAM 1874–1936

4 'There's been an accident!' they said, / 'Your servant's cut in half; he's dead!' / 'Indeed!' said Mr Jones, 'and please / Send me the half that's got my keys.' [*Ruthless Rhymes*, 'Mr Jones']

5 Billy, in one of his nice new sashes, / Fell in the fire and was burnt to ashes; / Now, although the room grows chilly, / I haven't the heart to poke poor Billy. [*Ib.* 'Tender Heartedness']

JAMES GRAHAME 1765–1811

6 Hail, Sabbath, thee I hail, the poor man's day. [*The Sabbath*, 29]

KENNETH GRAHAME 1859–1932

7 'O Mr Hodgitts!' I heard her cry, 'you are brave! for my sake do not be rash!' He was not rash. [*The Golden Age*, 'The Burglars']

8 Monkeys, who very sensibly refrain from speech, lest they should be set to earn their livings. [*Ib.* 'The Magic Ring']

9 There is nothing – absolutely nothing – half so much worth doing as simply messing about in boats. [*The Wind in the Willows*, Ch. 1]

10 The clever men at Oxford / Know all that there is to be knowed. / But they none of them know one half as much / As intelligent Mr Toad. [*The Wind in the Willows*, 10, Song]

JAMES GRAINGER 1721?–1766

11 What is fame? an empty bubble; / Gold? a transient, shining trouble. [*Solitude*, 96]

SIR ROBERT GRANT 1779–1838

12 O worship the King, all glorious above! / O gratefully sing his power and his love! / Our Shield and Defender – the Ancient of Days, / Pavilioned in splendour, and girded with praise. [Hymn]

13 The earth with its store of wonders untold, / Almighty! thy power hath founded of old; / Hath 'stablished it fast by a changeless decree, / And round it hath cast like a mantle the sea. [*Ib.*]

14 Thy mercies how tender, how firm to the end, / Our Maker, Defender, Redeemer and Friend! [*Ib.*]

GENERAL GRANT 1822–1885

15 I purpose to fight it out on this line, if it takes all summer. [Dispatch to Washington, 11 May 1864]

16 No terms except unconditional and immediate surrender can be accepted. [To General Buckner at Fort Donelson, 16 Feb. 1862]

GEORGE GRANVILLE, BARON LANSDOWNE
1667–1735

17 Of all the plagues with which the world is cursed, / Of every ill, a woman is the worst. [*The British Enchanters*, II. i]

LORD GRANVILLE 1815–1891

18 Spheres of action. [Letter, 29 Apr. 1885]

A. P. GRAVES 1846–1931

19 Och! Father O'Flynn, you've the wonderful way wid you. [*Father O'Flynn*]

1 Checkin' the crazy ones, coaxin' onaisy ones, / Liftin' the lazy ones on wid the stick. [*Father O'Flynn*]

J. W. GRAVES   1795–1886

2 D'ye ken John Peel with his coat so gray? /D'ye ken John Peel at the break of the day? / D'ye ken John Peel when he's far far away / With his hounds and his horn in the morning?

'Twas the sound of his horn called me from my bed, / And the cry of his hounds has me oft-times led; / For Peel's view-hollo would waken the dead, / Or a fox from his lair in the morning. [*John Peel*]

ROBERT GRAVES   1895–

3 No escape, / No such thing; to dream of new dimensions, / Cheating checkmate by painting the king's robe / So that he slides like a queen. [*The Castle*]

4 Christ of his gentleness, / Thirsting and hungering / Walked in the wilderness; / Soft words of grace he spoke / Unto lost desert-folk / That listened wondering. [*In the Wilderness*]

5 Across two counties he can hear / And catch your words before you speak. / The woodlouse or the maggot's weak / Clamour rings in his sad ear, / And noise so slight it would surpass / Credence. [*Lost Love*]

6 Those famous men of old, the Ogres – / They had long beards and stinking armpits, / They were wide-mouthed, long-yarded and great-bellied / Yet of no taller stature, Sirs, than you. [*Ogres and Pygmies*]

7 The Philatelist Royal / Was always too loyal / To say what he honestly / Thought of Philately. [*Philatelist Royal*]

8 You reading over my shoulder, peering beneath / My writing arm. [*The Reader Over my Shoulder* (also title of a book of criticism)]

9 Let me tell you the story of how I began: / I began as the knife-boy and ended as the boot-man, / With nothing in my pockets but a jack-knife and a button, / With nothing in my pockets. [Song: *Lift-boy*]

10 'How is your trade, Aquarius, / This frosty night?' / 'Complaints is many and various / And my feet are cold,' says Aquarius. [*Star-talk*]

11 'What did the mayor do?' / 'I was coming to that.' [*Welsh Incident*]

THOMAS GRAY   1716–1771

12 Ruin seize thee, ruthless King! / Confusion on thy banners wait; / Though fanned by Conquest's crimson wing, / They mock the air with idle state. [*The Bard*, I. i]

13 Vocal no more, since Cambria's fatal day, / To high-born Hoel's harp, or soft Llewellyn's lay. [*Ib.* I. ii]

14 Dear as the light that visits these sad eyes; / Dear as the ruddy drops that warm my heart. [*Ib.* I. iii]

15 Weave the warp, and weave the woof, / The winding-sheet of Edward's race. / Give ample room, and verge enough / The characters of hell to trace. [*Ib.* II. i]

16 The swarm that in thy noontide beam were born, / Gone to salute the rising morn. [*Ib.* II. ii]

17 In gallant trim the gilded vessel goes, / Youth on the prow, and Pleasure at the helm; / Regardless of the sweeping whirlwind's sway, / That, hushed in grim repose, expects his evening prey. [*Ib.*]

18 Ye towers of Julius, London's lasting shame, / With many a foul and midnight murther fed. [*Ib.* II. iii]

19 Visions of glory, spare my aching sight, / Ye unborn ages, crowd not on my soul! [*Ib.* III. i]

20 And Truth severe, by fairy Fiction dressed. [*Ib.* III. iii]

21 The curfew tolls the knell of parting day, / The lowing herd winds slowly o'er the lea, / The ploughman homeward plods his weary way, / And leaves the world to darkness and to me. [*Elegy Written in a Country Churchyard*, i]

22 Now fades the glimmering landscape on the sight, / And all the air a solemn stillness holds, / Save where the beetle wheels his droning flight, / And drowsy tinklings lull the distant fold. [*Ib.* ii]

1 Save that from yonder ivy-mantled tower, / The moping owl does to the moon complain. [*Elegy Written in a Country Churchyard*, iii]

2 Each in his narrow cell for ever laid, / The rude forefathers of the hamlet sleep. [*Ib.* iv]

3 The breezy call of incense-breathing Morn, / The swallow twittering from the straw-built shed, / The cock's shrill clarion, or the echoing horn, / No more shall rouse them from their lowly bed. [*Ib.* v]

4 Let not ambition mock their useful toil, / Their homely joys, and destiny obscure; / Nor grandeur hear with a disdainful smile / The short and simple annals of the poor. [*Ib.* viii]

5 The boast of heraldry, the pomp of power, / And all that beauty, all that wealth e'er gave, / Awaits alike th'inevitable hour, / The paths of glory lead but to the grave. [*Ib.* ix]

6 Where through the long-drawn aisle and fretted vault / The pealing anthem swells the note of praise. [*Ib.* x]

7 Can storied urn or animated bust / Back to its mansion call the fleeting breath? / Can honour's voice provoke the silent dust, / Or flattery soothe the dull cold ear of death? [*Ib.* xi]

8 Hands, that the rod of empire might have swayed, / Or waked to ecstasy the living lyre. [*Ib.* xii]

9 Chill penury repressed their noble rage, / And froze the genial current of the soul. [*Ib.* xiii]

10 Full many a gem of purest ray serene / The dark unfathomed caves of ocean bear: / Full many a flower is born to blush unseen, / And waste its sweetness on the desert air. [*Ib.* xiv]

11 Some village Hampden, that with dauntless breast / The little tyrant of his fields withstood; / Some mute inglorious Milton here may rest, / Some Cromwell guiltless of his country's blood. [*Ib.* xv]

12 Th' applause of listening senates to command, / The threats of pain and ruin to despise, / To scatter plenty o'er a smiling land, / And read their history in a nation's eyes. [*Ib.* xvi]

13 Forbade to wade through slaughter to a throne, / And shut the gates of mercy on mankind. [*Ib.* xvii]

14 Far from the madding crowd's ignoble strife, / Their sober wishes never learned to stray; / Along the cool sequestered vale of life / They kept the noiseless tenor of their way. [*Elegy Written in a Country Churchyard*, xix]

15 Implores the passing tribute of a sigh. [*Ib.* xx]

16 For who to dumb Forgetfulness a prey, / This pleasing anxious being e'er resigned, / Left the warm precincts of the cheerful day / Nor cast one longing ling'ring look behind? [*Ib.* xxii]

17 On some fond breast the parting soul relies, / Some pious drops the closing eye requires; / E'en from the tomb the voice of Nature cries, / E'en in our ashes live their wonted fires. [*Ib.* xxiii]

18 Brushing with hasty steps the dews away / To meet the sun upon the upland lawn. [*Ib.* xxv]

19 Here rests the head upon the lap of Earth / A youth to fortune and to fame unknown. / Fair Science frowned not on his humble birth, / And Melancholy marked him for her own.

Large was his bounty, and his soul sincere, / Heav'n did a recompense as largely send: / He gave to Mis'ry all he had, a tear, / He gained from Heav'n ('twas all he wished) a friend.

No farther seek his merits to disclose, / Or draw his frailties from their dread abode, / (There they alike in trembling hope repose), / The bosom of his Father and his God. [*Ib.* xxx]

20 Daughter of Jove, relentless power, / Thou tamer of the human breast, / Whose iron scourge and tort'ring hour / The bad affright, afflict the best. [*Hymn to Adversity*]

21 And leave us leisure to be good. [*Ib.*]

22 Owls would have hooted in St Peter's choir, / And foxes stunk and littered in St Paul's. [*Impromptu on Lord Holland's Seat*]

23 Hence, avaunt! ('tis holy ground). [*Ode for Music*]

24 Servitude that hugs her chain. [*Ib.*]

25 There sit the sainted sage, the bard divine, / The few, whom genius gave to shine / Through every unborn age, and undiscovered clime. [*Ib.*]

1 Their tears, their little triumphs o'er, / Their human passions now no more. [*Ode for Music*]

2 Demurest of the tabby kind, / The pensive Selima, reclined. [*Ode on the Death of a Favourite Cat*]

3 What female heart can gold despise? / What cat's averse to fish? [*Ib.*]

4 A fav'rite has no friend. [*Ib.*]

5 Not all that tempts your wand'ring eyes / And heedless hearts, is lawful prize; / Nor all that glisters, gold. [*Ib.*]

6 Ye distant spires! ye antique towers. [*Ode on a Distant Prospect of Eton College*, i]

7 Where once my careless childhood strayed, / A stranger yet to pain. [*Ib.* ii]

8 Who foremost now delight to cleave / With pliant arm thy glassy wave? [*Ib.* iii]

9 Urge the flying ball. [*Ib.*]

10 They hear a voice in every wind, / And snatch a fearful joy. [*Ib.* iv]

11 Alas, regardless of their doom, / The little victims play! / No sense have they of ills to come, / Nor care beyond to-day. [*Ib.* vi]

12 To each his suff'rings: all are men, / Condemned alike to groan; / The tender for another's pain, / Th' unfeeling for his own. / Yet ah! why should they know their fate? / Since sorrow never comes too late, / And happiness too swiftly flies. / Thought would destroy their paradise. / No more; where ignorance is bliss, / 'Tis folly to be wise. [*Ib.* x]

13 The meanest flowret of the vale, / The simplest note that swells the gale, / The common sun, the air, and skies, / To him are opening paradise. [*Ode on the Pleasure arising from Vicissitude*]

14 The Attic warbler pours her throat, / Responsive to the cuckoo's note. [*Ode on the Spring*]

15 How vain the ardour of the crowd,/ How low, how little are the proud, / How indigent the great! [*Ib.*]

16 To Contemplation's sober eye. / Such is the race of Man. [*Ib.*]

17 The sun is set, the spring is gone – / We frolic while 'tis May. [*Ib.*]

18 Woods that wave o'er Delphi's steep, / Isles that crown th' Aegean deep. [*The Progress of Poesy*, II. iii]

19 Far from the sun and summer-gale, / In thy green lap was Nature's darling laid. [(Shakespeare) *The Progress of Poesy*, III. i]

20 Or ope the sacred source of sympathetic tears. [*Ib.*]

21 He passed the flaming bounds of space and time: / The living throne, the sapphire-blaze, / Where angels tremble while they gaze, / He saw; but blasted with excess of light, / Closed his eyes in endless night. [(Milton) *Ib.* III. ii]

22 Beyond the limits of a vulgar fate, / Beneath the good how far – but far above the great. [(Dryden) *Ib.* III. iii]

23 Too poor for a bribe, and too proud to importune, / He had not the method of making a fortune. [*Sketch of His own Character*]

24 And weep the more, because I weep in vain. [*Sonnet on the Death of Richard West*]

25 The language of the age is never the language of poetry, except among the French, whose verse, where the thought or image does not support it, differs in nothing from prose. [Letter to West, 8 Apr. 1742]

26 I shall be but a shrimp of an author. [Letter to Walpole, 25 Feb. 1768 (long after the publication of his Elegy)]

HORACE GREELEY   1811–1872

27 Go West, young man, and grow up with the country. [*Hints towards Reform*]

MATTHEW GREEN   1696–1737

28 They politics like ours profess, / The greater prey upon the less. [*The Grotto*, 69]

29 To cure the mind's wrong bias, Spleen, / Some recommend the bowling-green; / Some, hilly walks; all, exercise; / Fling but a stone, the giant dies. / Laugh and be well. [*The Spleen*, 89]

GRAHAM GREENE   1904–

30 That whisky priest, I wish we had never had him in the house. [*The Power and the Glory*, Pt I. ii and *passim*]

31 Of course, before we *know* he is a saint, there will have to be miracles. [*Ib.* IV]

ROBERT GREENE   1560?–1592

1 Weep not, my wanton, smile upon my knee; / When thou art old there's grief enough for thee. / Mother's wag, pretty boy, / Father's sorrow, father's joy. [*Sephestia's Song*]

2 The wanton smiled, father wept; / Mother cried, baby lept. [*Ib.*]

3 If country loves such sweet desires gain, / What lady would not love a shepherd swain? [*Shepherd's Wife's Song*]

4 For there is an upstart crow, beautified with our feathers, that with his tiger's heart wrapped in a player's hide, supposes he is as well able to bumbast out a blank verse as the best of you; and being an absolute *Iohannes fac totum*, is in his own conceit the only Shake-scene in a country. [*Groatsworth of Wit*]

GREGORY I   540–604

5 *Responsum est, quod Angli vocarentur. At ille: 'Bene,' inquit; 'nam et angelicam habent faciem, et tales angelorum in caelis decet esse coherides.'* – The reply was that they were Angles. 'It is well,' said he, 'for they have the faces of angels, and such should be the co-heirs of the angels in heaven.' [(Traditionally quoted as '*Non Angli sed Angeli*' – 'Not Angles but angels') Bede, *Ecclesiastical History*, II. i]

GREGORY VII   1020–1085

6 I have loved justice and hated iniquity; therefore I die in exile. [Attr.]

ÉTIENNE DE GRELLET
[STEPHEN GRELLET] 1773–1855

7 I shall pass through this world but once. If, therefore, there be any kindness I can show, or any good thing I can do, let me do it now; let me not defer it or neglect it, for I shall not pass this way again. [Attr. to Grellet, and to others]

FULKE GREVILLE, LORD
BROOKE   1554–1628

8 If in my heart all saints else be defaced, / Honour the shrine where you alone are placed. [*Caelica*, Sonnet 3]

9 Silence augmenteth grief, writing increaseth rage, / Staled are my thoughts, which loved and lost the wonder of our age: / Yet quickened now with fire, though dead with frost ere now, / Enraged I write I know not what; dead, quick, I know not how. [*Epitaph on Sir Philip Sidney*]

10 Vast Superstition! Glorious style of weakness! / Sprung from the deep disquiet of Man's passion, / To desolation, and despair of Nature. [*Mustapha*, Chorus 5]

11 Oh wearisome condition of humanity! / Born under one law, to another bound: / Vainly begot, and yet forbidden vanity; / Created sick, commanded to be sound. [*Ib.* V. iv]

VISCOUNT GREY OF
FALLODEN   1862–1933

12 The lamps are going out all over Europe; we shall not see them lit again in our lifetime. [On the eve of war, 3 Aug. 1914]

GEORGE and WEEDON
GROSSMITH
    1847–1912 and 1854–1919

13 What's the good of a home if you are never in it? [*The Diary of a Nobody*, Ch. 1]

14 I left the room with silent dignity, but caught my foot in the mat. [*Ib.* 12]

15 I am a poor man, but I would gladly give ten shillings to find out who sent me the insulting Christmas card I received this morning. [*Ib.* 13]

GEORGE GROSSMITH THE
YOUNGER   1874–1935
and FRED THOMPSON
    1884–1949

16 Another little drink wouldn't do us any harm. [*The Bing Boys*, 'Another Little Drink']

17 If you were the only girl in the world, / And I were the only boy. [*Ib.* 'If you were the Only Girl']

PHILIP GUEDALLA   1889–1944

18 The work of Henry James has always seemed divisible by a simple dynastic

arrangement into three reigns: James I, James II, and the Old Pretender. [*Collected Essays*, 'Mr Henry James']

1 Any stigma will do to beat a dogma. [Quoted in *Treasury of Humorous Quotations*]

TEXAS GUINAN   1884–1933

2 Fifty million Frenchmen can't be wrong. [Attr.]

ARTHUR GUITERMAN 1871–1943

3 The Prophet's Cam-u-el, that primal Desert Ship. [*The Legend of the First Cam-u-el*]

4 Lightly we follow our cue, / 'Exit, pursued by a bear'. [*The Shakesperean Bear*]

FRANÇOIS GUIZOT   1787–1874

5 *Enrichissez-vous!* – Enrich yourselves! [Speech, 1 Mar. 1843]

DOROTHY GURNEY   1858–1932

6 The kiss of the sun for pardon, / The song of the birds for mirth, / One is nearer God's Heart in a garden / Than anywhere else on earth. [*God's Garden*]

JOHN HABBERTON   1842–1921

7 Want to shee the wheels go wound. [*Helen's Babies*, 1]

EMPEROR HADRIAN   76–138

8 *Animula vagula blandula, / Hospes comesque corporis, / Qui nunc abibis in loca / Pallidula rigida nudula, / Nec ut soles dabis iocos!* – Little soul, wandering and pleasant guest and companion of the body, into what places will you now depart, pale, stiff, and naked; and you will sport no longer as you did! [Poem]

H. RIDER HAGGARD   1856–1925

9 She-who-must-be-obeyed. [*She, passim*]

EARL HAIG   1861–1928

10 Every position must be held to the last man: there must be no retirement. With our backs to the wall, and believing in the justice of our cause, each one of us must fight on to the end. [Order to the British troops, 12 Apr. 1918]

SARAH HALE   1788–1879

11 Mary had a little lamb, / Its fleece was white as snow, / And everywhere that Mary went / The lamb was sure to go. [*Mary's Little Lamb*]

THOMAS CHANDLER
HALIBURTON   1796–1865

12 I want you to see Peel, Stanley, Graham, Shiel, Russell, Macaulay, Old Joe, and so on. These men are all upper crust here. [*Sam Slick in England*, Ch. 24]

MARQUIS OF HALIFAX
1633–1695

13 The innocent word 'Trimmer' signifies no more than this, that if men are together in a boat, and one part of the company would weigh it down on one side, another would make it lean as much to the contrary. [*Character of a Trimmer*, Preface]

14 Popularity is a crime from the moment it is sought; it is only a virtue where men have it whether they will or no. [*Moral Thoughts and Reflections*]

15 Men are not hanged for stealing horses, but that horses may not be stolen. [*Political Thoughts and Reflections*, 'Of Punishment']

CHARLES SPRAGUE HALL
fl. 1860

16 John Brown's body lies a-mouldering in the grave, / His soul is marching on! [*John Brown's Body*]

JOSEPH HALL   1574–1656

17 Death borders upon our birth, and our cradle stands in the grave. [*Epistles*, 2]

18 I first adventure, follow me who list / And be the second English satirist. [*Virgidemiae*, Prologue]

OWEN HALL [JAMES DAVIS]
1854–1907

1 Tell me, pretty maiden, are there any more at home like you? [*Florodora*, II]

ROBERT HALL   1764–1831

2 Glass of brandy and water! That is the current but not the appropriate name: ask for a glass of liquid fire and distilled damnation. [Gregory's *Life*]

GAIL HAMILTON [MARY ABIGAIL DODGE]   1838–1896

3 The total depravity of inanimate things. [*Epigram*]

WILLIAM HAMILTON 1704–1754

4 Busk ye, busk ye, my bonny bonny bride, / Busk ye, busk ye, my winsome marrow. [*The Braes of Yarrow*]

SIR WILLIAM HAMILTON
1788–1856

5 On earth there is nothing great but man; in man there is nothing great but mind. [*Lectures on Metaphysics*]

WILLIAM GERARD HAMILTON   1729–1796

6 Johnson is dead. – Let us go to the next best: – There is nobody; no man can be said to put you in mind of Johnson. [Boswell's *Life of Johnson*, 1784]

OSCAR HAMMERSTEIN
1895–1960

7 The last time I saw Paris, her heart was warm and gay, / I heard the laughter of her heart in every street café. [*The Last Time I Saw Paris*]

MINNY MAUD HANFF   *fl.* 1900

8 Since then they called him Sunny Jim. [Advertisement for Force, a breakfast food]

KATHERINE HANKEY 1834–1911

9 Tell me the old, old story. [Hymn]

ERNST AUGUST, ELECTOR OF HANOVER   1629–1698

10 *Les chevaux du roi de France sont mieux logés que moi.* – The king of France's horses are better housed than I. [On seeing Louis XIV's stables at Versailles]

EARL OF HARDWICKE
1690–1764

11 His doubts are better than most people's certainties. [Reference to Dirleton's *Doubts*, quoted in Boswell's *Life of Johnson*]

REV. E. J. HARDY   20 Cent.

12 How To Be Happy Though Married. [Title of book, 1910]

THOMAS HARDY   1840–1928

13 When the Present has latched its postern behind my tremulous stay, / And the May month flaps its glad green leaves like wings, / Delicate-filmed as new-spun silk, will the neighbours say, / 'He was a man who used to notice such things'? [*Afterwards*]

14 The bower we shrined to Tennyson, / Gentlemen, / Is roof-wrecked; damps there drip upon / Sagged seats, the creeper-nails are rust, / The spider is sole denizen. [*An Ancient to Ancients*]

15 Any little old song / Will do for me. [*Any little old song*]

16 So zestfully canst thou sing? / And all this indignity, / With God's consent, on thee! / Blinded ere yet a-wing. [*The Blinded Bird*]

17 The Immanent Will that stirs and urges everything. [*The Convergence of the Twain*]

18 So little cause for carolings / Of such ecstatic sound / Was written on terrestrial things / Afar or nigh around, / That I could think there trembled through / His happy good-night air / Some blessed Hope, whereof he knew / And I was unaware. [*The Darkling Thrush*]

1 His landmark is a kopje-crest / That breaks the veldt around; / And foreign constellations west / Each night above his mound. [*Drummer Hodge*]

2 We two kept house, the Past and I. [*The Ghost of the Past*]

3 O man-projected Figure, of late / Imaged as we, thy knell who shall survive? / Whence came it we were tempted to create / One whom we can no longer keep alive? [*God's Funeral*]

4 Crass Casualty obstructs the sun and rain, / And dicing Time for gladness casts a moan ... / These purblind Doomsters had as readily strown / Blisses about my pilgrimage as pain. [*Hap*]

5 Well, World, you have kept faith with me, / Kept faith with me; / Upon the whole you have proved to be / Much as you said you were. [*He never expected much*]

6 I am the family face; / Flesh perishes, I live on, / Projecting trait and trace / Through time to times anon, / And leaping from place to place / Over oblivion. [*Heredity*]

7 I need not go / Through sleet and snow / To where I know / She waits for me: / She will tarry there / Till I find it fair, / And have time to spare / From company. [*I need not go*]

8 Who holds that if way to the Better there be, it exacts a full look at the Worst. [*In Tenebris*, II]

9 Only a man harrowing clods / In a slow silent walk / With an old horse that stumbles and nods / Half asleep as they stalk. [*In the Time of 'The Breaking of Nations'*]

10 Yonder a maid and her wight / Come whispering by: / War's annals will cloud into night / Ere their story die. [*Ib.*]

11 Let me enjoy the earth no less / Because the all-enacting Might / That fashioned forth its loveliness / Had other aims than my delight. [*Let me enjoy*]

12 What of the faith and fire within us / Men who march away / Ere the barn-cocks say / Night is growing gray, / Leaving all that here can win us? [*Men who march away*]

13 In the third-class seat sat the journeying boy, / And the roof-lamp's oily flame / Played down on his listless form and face, / Bewrapt past knowing to what he was going, / Or whence he came. [*Midnight on the Great Western*]

14 And both of us, scorning parochial ways, / Had lived like the wives in the patriarchs' days. [*Over the Coffin*]

15 Christmas Eve, and twelve of the clock. / 'Now they are all on their knees.' [*Oxen*]

16 A pinch of unseen, unguarded dust. [*Shelley's Skylark*]

17 'What do you think of it, Moon, / As you go? / Is life much or no?' / 'O, I think of it, often think of it / As a show / God ought surely to shut up soon, / As I go.' [*To the Moon*]

18 A star looks down at me, / And says: 'Here I and you / Stand, each in our degree: / What do you mean to do?' [*Waiting Both*]

19 This is the weather the cuckoo likes, / And so do I. [*Weathers*]

20 When I set out for Lyonnesse, / A hundred miles away, / The rime was on the spray. [*When I set out for Lyonnesse*]

21 Who's in the next room? – who? / I seemed to see / Somebody in the dawning passing through, / Unknown to me. [*Who's in the next room?*]

22 A local cult, called Christianity. [*Dynasts*, I. vi]

23 To persons standing alone on a hill during a clear midnight such as this, the roll of the world eastward is almost a palpable movement. [*Far From the Madding Crowd*, Ch. 2]

24 A nice unparticular man. [*Ib.* 8]

25 Ethelberta breathed a sort of exclamation, not right out, but stealthily, like a parson's damn. [*The Hand of Ethelberta*]

26 Done because we are too menny. [*Jude the Obscure*, Pt VI. Ch. 2]

27 Life's Little Ironies. [Title of volume of stories]

28 All her shining keys will be took from her, and her cupboards opened, and things a' didn't wish seen, anybody will see; and her little wishes and ways will all be as nothing. [*The Mayor of Casterbridge*, Ch. 18]

29 ... The long, laborious road, dry, empty, and white. It was quite open to the heath

on each side, and bisected that vast dark surface like the parting-line on a head of black hair, diminishing and bending away on the furthest horizon. [*The Return of the Native*, Ch. 2]

1 A little one-eyed, blinking sort o' place. [*Tess of the D'Urbervilles*, Ch. 1]

2 'Justice' was done, and the President of the Immortals, in Aeschylean phrase, had ended his sport with Tess. [*Ib.* 59]

3 Good, but not religious-good. [*Under the Greenwood Tree*, I. Ch. 2]

4 I like a story with a bad moral . . . all good stories have a coarse touch or a bad moral, depend on't. If the story-tellers could ha' got decency and good morals from true stories, who'd have troubled to invent parables? [*Ib.* I. 8]

5 Silent? ah, he is silent! He can keep silence well. That man's silence is wonderful to listen to. [*Ib.* II. 5]

6 You was a good man, and did good things. [*The Woodlanders*, Ch. 48]

JULIUS and AUGUSTUS HARE 1795–1855 and 1792–1834

7 Half the failures in life arise from pulling in one's horse as he is leaping. [*Guesses at Truth*, I]

8 Purity is the feminine, Truth the masculine, of Honour. [*Ib.*]

MAURICE E. HARE 1886–1967

9 There once was a man who said, 'Damn! / It is borne in upon me I am / An engine that moves / In predestinate grooves, / I'm not even a bus, I'm a tram.' [Limerick]

W. F. HARGREAVES 1846–1919

10 I'm Burlington Bertie: / I rise at ten-thirty. [*Burlington Bertie*]

11 I walk down the Strand / With my gloves on my hand, / And I walk down again / With them off. [*Ib.*]

SIR JOHN HARINGTON 1561–1612

12 Treason doth never prosper: what's the reason? / For if it prosper, none dare call it treason. [*Epigrams*, 'Of Treason']

CHARLES K. HARRIS 1865–1930

13 Many a heart is aching, if you could read them all, / Many the hopes that have vanished, after the ball. [*After the Ball*]

CLIFFORD HARRIS 20 Cent.

14 You called me Baby Doll a year ago. [*A Broken Doll*]

JOEL CHANDLER HARRIS 1848–1908

15 'Law, Brer Tarrypin!' sez Brer Fox, sezee, 'you ain't see no trouble yit. Ef you wanter see sho' nuff trouble, you des oughter go 'longer me; I'm de man w'at kin show you trouble', sezee. [*Nights with Uncle Remus*, Ch. 17]

16 Hit look lak sparrer-grass, hit feel lak sparrer-grass, hit tas'e lak sparrer-grass, en I bless ef 'taint sparrer-grass. [(Asparagus) *Ib.* 27]

17 A contrapshun what he call a Tar-Baby. [*Uncle Remus*, Ch. 2]

18 Tar-Baby ain't sayin' nuthin', en Brer Fox, he lay low. [*Ib.*]

19 Ez soshubble ez a baskit er kittens. [*Ib.* 3]

20 Bred en bawn in a brier-patch, Brer Fox. [*Ib.* 4]

21 Lounjun' 'roun' en suffer'n. [*Ib.* 12]

22 I'm de'f in one year, en I can't hear out'n de udder. [*Ib.* 19]

23 Ole man Know-All died las' year. [*Ib.* 34]

24 Lazy fokes' stummucks don't git tired. [*Ib.*]

25 Licker talks mighty loud w'en it git loose from de jug. [*Ib.*]

26 Oh, war shill we go w'en de great day comes, / Wid de blowin' er de trumpits en de bangin' er de drums? / How many po' sinners'll be kotched out late / En find no latch ter de golden gate? [*Ib. Ht. Songs*, I]

FRANCIS BRETT [BRET] HARTE 1836–1902

27 Thar ain't no sense / In gittin' riled! [*Jim*]

1 Which I wish to remark, / And my language is plain, / That for ways that are dark / And for tricks that are vain, / The heathen Chinee is peculiar, / Which the same I would rise to explain. [*Plain Language from Truthful James*]

2 But he smiled as he sat by the table, / With the smile that was childlike and bland. [*Ib.*]

3 And the same with intent to deceive. [*Ib.*]

4 We are ruined by Chinese cheap labour. [*Ib.*]

5 I reside at Table Mountain, and my name is Truthful James. [*The Society upon the Stanislaus*]

6 And he smiled a kind of sickly smile, and curled up on the floor, / And the subsequent proceedings interested him no more. [*Ib.*]

H. DE CRONIN HASTINGS
1902–

7 Worm's eye view. [Caption to photograph in the *Architectural Review*, *c.* 1932 and *passim*]

STEPHEN HAWES
c. 1475–before 1530

8 For though the day be never so longe, / At last the belles ringeth to evensonge. [*Passetyme of Pleasure*, 42]

R. S. HAWKER
1803–1875

9 And have they fixed the where and when? / And shall Trelawny die? / Here's twenty thousand Cornish men / Will know the reason why! [*Song of the Western Men*. (The last three lines are traditional)]

NATHANIEL HAWTHORNE
1804–1864

10 Life is made up of marble and mud. [*The House of the Seven Gables*, Ch. 2]

11 What other dungeon is so dark as one's own heart! What jailer so inexorable as one's self! [*Ib.* 11]

12 She named the infant 'Pearl', as being of great price – purchased with all she had. [*The Scarlet Letter*, Ch. 6]

13 Dr Johnson's morality was as English an article as a beefsteak. [*Our Old Home*, 'Lichfield and Uttoxeter']

LORD CHARLES HAY ?–1760

14 Gentlemen of the French Guard, fire first! [At Battle of Fontenoy, 1745]

IAN HAY [JOHN HAY BEITH]
1876–1952

15 Funny peculiar, or funny ha-ha? [*The Housemaster*, III]

WILLIAM HAZLITT 1778–1830

16 The least pain in our little finger gives us more concern and uneasiness than the destruction of millions of our fellow-beings. [*American Literature*, 'Dr Channing']

17 If the world were good for nothing else, it is a fine subject for speculation. [*Characteristics*, 302]

18 His sayings are generally like women's letters; all the pith is in the postscript. [(Charles Lamb) *Conversations of Northcote*, 'Boswell Redivivus']

19 His worst is better than any other person's best. [(Scott) *English Literature*, Ch. 14]

20 His works (taken together) are almost like a new edition of human nature. [(Scott) *Ib.*]

21 When a person dies who does any one thing better than anyone else in the world, which so many others are trying to do well, it leaves a gap in society. [(On the death of John Cavanagh, the fives-player) *The Indian Jugglers*]

22 He [Coleridge] talked on for ever; and you wished him to talk on for ever. [*Lectures on the English Poets*, 8]

23 So have I loitered my life away, reading books, looking at pictures, going to plays, hearing, thinking, writing on what pleased me best. I have wanted only one thing to make me happy, but wanting that have wanted everything. [*My first Acquaintance with Poets*]

24 There is nothing good to be had in the country, or, if there is, they will not let you have it. [*Observations on Mr Wordsworth's* Excursion]

1 Those who make their dress a principal part of themselves, will, in general, become of no more value than their dress. [*On the Clerical Character*]

2 I do not think there is anything deserving the name of society to be found out of London. [*On Coffee-House Politicians*]

3 The English (it must be owned) are rather a foul-mouthed nation. [*On Criticism*]

4 There is an unseemly exposure of the mind, as well as of the body. [*On Disagreeable People*]

5 No young man believes he shall ever die. [*On the Feeling of Immortality in Youth*]

6 One of the pleasantest things in the world is going a journey; but I like to go by myself. [*On Going a Journey*]

7 When I am in the country I wish to vegetate like the country. [*Ib.*]

8 Give me the clear blue sky above my head, and the green turf beneath my feet, a winding road before me, and a three hours' march to dinner – and then to thinking! It is hard if I cannot start some game on these lone heaths. [*Ib.*]

9 The *incognito* of an inn is one of its striking privileges. [*Ib.*]

10 It is great to shake off the trammels of the world and of public opinion . . . and become the creature of the moment . . . known by no other title than *The Gentleman in the Parlour*! [*Ib.*]

11 It is better to be able neither to read nor write than to be able to do nothing else. [*On the Ignorance of the Learned*]

12 You will hear more good things on the outside of a stagecoach from London to Oxford than if you were to pass a twelvemonth with the undergraduates, or heads of colleges, of that famous university. [*Ib.*]

13 There is not a more mean, stupid, dastardly, pitiful, selfish, spiteful, envious, ungrateful animal than the Public. It is the greatest of cowards, for it is afraid of itself. [*On Living to One's Self*]

14 The art of pleasing consists in being pleased. [*On Manner*]

15 A nickname is the heaviest stone that the devil can throw at a man. [*On Nicknames*]

16 Venerate art as art. [*On Patronage*]

17 We never do anything well till we cease to think about the manner of doing it. [*On Prejudice*]

18 Violent antipathies are always suspicious, and betray a secret affinity. [*On Vulgarity and Affectation*]

19 Ignorance alone makes monsters or bugbears: our actual acquaintances are all very common-place people. [*Why Distant Objects Please*]

20 We can scarcely hate anyone that we know. [*Ib.*]

21 Well, I've had a happy life. [Last words]

BISHOP HEBER 1782–1826

22 Brightest and best of the sons of the morning, / Dawn on our darkness, and lend us Thine aid! [Hymn]

23 By cool Siloam's shady rill / How sweet the lily grows! / How sweet the breath beneath the hill / Of Sharon's dewy rose! [Hymn]

24 From Greenland's icy mountains, / From India's coral strand, / Where Afric's sunny fountains / Roll down their golden sand. [Hymn]

25 What though the spicy breezes / Blow soft o'er Ceylon's isle, / Though every prospect pleases, / And only man is vile.

In vain with lavish kindness / The gifts of God are strown, / The heathen in his blindness / Bows down to wood and stone. [*Ib.*]

26 Waft waft, ye winds, His story. [*Ib.*]

27 Holy, holy, holy, Lord God Almighty! / Early in the morning our song shall rise to thee. [Hymn]

28 Holy, holy, holy! all the saints adore Thee, / Casting down their golden crowns around the glassy sea; / Cherubim and seraphim falling down before Thee, / Which wert, and art, and evermore shalt be. [*Ib.*]

GEORG WILHELM HEGEL 1770–1831

29 What experience and history teach is this – that people and governments never have learnt anything from history, or acted on principles deduced from it. [Quoted in G. B. Shaw's *The Revolutionist's Handbook*]

HEINRICH HEINE   1797–1856

1 *Auf Flügeln des Gesanges.* – On wings of song. [Title of a song]

2 *Ich weiss nicht, was soll es bedeuten, / Dass ich so traurig bin; / Ein Märchen aus alten Zeiten, / Das kommt mir nicht aus dem Sinn.* – I do not know why it should be, but I am so sad; there is an old-time story which I cannot get out of my head. [*Die Lorelei*]

3 *Du bist wie eine Blume.* – You are like a flower. [*Du Bist wie eine Blume*]

4 *Ich grolle nicht, und wenn das Herz auch bricht.* – I do not complain, even if my heart breaks. [Title of a song]

5 *Gut ist der Schlaf, der Tod ist besser – freilich / Das beste wäre, nie geboren sein.* – Sleep is good, death is better; but of course, the best thing would be never to have been born at all. [*Morphine*]

6 It is extremely difficult for a Jew to be converted, for how can he bring himself to believe in the divinity of – another Jew? [Attr.]

7 *Dieu me pardonnera, c'est son métier.* – God will pardon me, it is His trade. [Last words]

SIR ARTHUR HELPS   1813–1875

8 Reading is sometimes an ingenious device for avoiding thought. [*Friends in Council*, Bk II. Ch. 1]

FELICIA HEMANS   1793–1835

9 Not there, not there, my child! [*The Better Land*]

10 The boy stood on the burning deck – / Whence all but he had fled. [*Casabianca*]

11 There came a burst of thunder sound – / The boy – oh! where was he? [*Ib.*]

12 They grew in beauty, side by side, / They filled one home with glee; – / Their graves are severed, far and wide, / By mount, and stream, and sea. [*The Graves of a Household*]

13 He Never Smiled Again. [(Henry I) Title of poem]

14 The stately homes of England, / How beautiful they stand! [*The Homes of England*]

15 The cottage homes of England! / By thousands on her plains. [*The Homes of England*]

W. E. HENLEY   1849–1903

16 What have I done for you, / England, my England? / What is there I would not do, / England, my own? [*For England's Sake*, iii]

17 Out of the night that covers me, / Black as the pit from pole to pole, / I thank whatever gods may be / For my unconquerable soul. [*Invictus*]

18 Under the bludgeonings of chance / My head is bloody, but unbowed. [*Ib.*]

19 It matters not how strait the gate, / How charged with punishments the scroll, / I am the master of my fate: / I am the captain of my soul. [*Ib.*]

20 Night with her train of stars / And her great gift of sleep. [*Margaritae Sororis*]

21 Or ever the knightly years were gone / With the old world to the grave, / I was a King in Babylon / And you were a Christian slave. [*To W.A.*]

HENRI IV, OF FRANCE
    1553–1610

22 I want there to be no peasant in my kingdom so poor that he cannot have a chicken in his pot every Sunday. [Attr.]

23 Paris is well worth a mass. [Attr. also to Sully]

24 The wisest fool in Christendom. [(James I) Attr. also to Sully]

HENRY II   1133–1189

25 Who will rid me of this turbulent priest? [(Becket) Attr.]

HENRY VIII   1491–1547

26 This man [Cranmer] hath the right sow by the ear. [Attr.]

MATTHEW HENRY   1662–1714

27 Many a dangerous temptation comes to us in gay, fine colours, that are but skin-deep. [*Commentaries, Genesis,* 3:1]

1 To their own second and sober thoughts. [*Commentaries, Job*, 6:29]

2 He rolls it under his tongue as a sweet morsel. [*Ib. Psalms*, 36:2]

3 Men of polite learning and a liberal education. [*Ib. Acts*, 10:1]

4 All this and heaven too. [*Life of Philip Henry*]

O. HENRY [W. S. PORTER] 1862–1910

5 It couldn't have happened anywhere but in little old New York. [*A Little Local Colour*]

6 If men knew how women pass the time when they are alone, they'd never marry. [*Memoirs of a Yellow Dog*]

7 It was beautiful and simple as all truly great swindles are. [*The Octopus Marooned*]

8 Take it from me – he's got the goods. [*The Unprofitable Servant*]

9 Turn up the lights, I don't want to go home in the dark. [Last words, quoting popular song]

HERACLEITUS 6 Cent. B.C.

10 All is flux, nothing stays still. [Diels, *Fragments of the Pre-Socratics*]

11 The way up is the way down. [*Ib.*]

SIR A. P. HERBERT 1890–1971

12 Don't tell my mother I'm living in sin. [*Don't Tell my Mother*]

13 Not huffy or stuffy, nor tiny or tall, / But fluffy, just fluffy, with no brains at all. [*I Like them Fluffy*]

14 It may be life, but ain't it slow? [*It May Be Life*]

15 As my poor father used to say / In 1863, / Once people start on all this Art / Goodbye, moralitee! / And what my father used to say / Is good enough for me. [*Lines for a Worthy Person*]

16 Holy Deadlock. [Title of novel]

17 People must not do things for fun. We are not here for fun. There is no reference to fun in any Act of Parliament. [*Uncommon Law*]

GEORGE HERBERT 1593–1633

18 Let all the world in every corner sing / My God and King. [*Temple*, 'Antiphon']

19 A verse may find him who a sermon flies, / And turn delight into a sacrifice. [*Ib.* 'Church Porch', i]

20 Drink not the third glass which thou canst not tame / When once it is within thee. [*Ib.* v]

21 Dare to be true: nothing can need a lie; / A fault, which needs it most, grows two thereby. [*Ib.* xiii]

22 Do all things like a man, not sneakingly: / Think the king sees thee still; for his King does. [*Ib.* xxi]

23 I struck the board, and cried, 'No more; / I will abroad.' / What, shall I ever sigh and pine? / My lines and life are free; free as the road, / Loose as the wind, as large as store. [*Ib.* 'The Collar']

24 But as I raved and grew more fierce and wild / At every word, / Methought I heard one calling, 'Child'; / And I replied, 'My Lord'. [*Ib.*]

25 Throw away thy rod, / Throw away thy wrath: / O my God, / Take the gentle path. [*Ib.* 'Discipline']

26 Love is swift of foot; / Love's a man of war, / And can shoot, / And can hit from far. [*Ib.*]

27 I got Thee flowers to strew Thy way, / I got me boughs off many a tree; / But Thou wast up by break of day, / And brought'st Thy sweets along with Thee. [*Ib.* 'Easter']

28 Teach me, my God and King, / In all things Thee to see, / And what I do in anything / To do it as for Thee. [*Ib.* 'The Elixir']

29 Who sweeps a room, as for thy laws, / Makes that and th' action fine. [*Ib.*]

30 He that is weary, let him sit. / My soul would stir / And trade in courtesies and wit. [*Ib.* 'Employment']

31 Death is still working like a mole, / And digs my grave at each remove. [*Ib.* 'Grace']

32 Who says that fictions only and false hair / Become a verse? Is there in truth no beauty? / Is all good structure in a winding stair? [*Ib.* 'Jordan']

1 I envy no man's nightingale or spring; /
Nor let them punish me with loss of
rhyme, / Who plainly say, 'My God my
King'. [*Temple*, 'Jordan']

2 Love bade me welcome; yet my soul
drew back / Guilty of dust and sin. [*Ib.*
'Love']

3 'You must sit down,' says Love, 'and
taste my meat.' / So I did sit and eat. [*Ib.*]

4 When God at first made man, / Having
a glass of blessings standing by, / Let us
(said he) pour on him all we can: / Let
the world's riches, which dispersed lie, /
Contract into a span. [*Ib.* 'The Pulley']

5 Let him be rich and weary, that at least, /
If goodness lead him not, yet weariness /
May toss him to my breast. [*Ib.*]

6 At length I heard a ragged noise and
mirth / Of thieves and murderers: there
I him espied, / Who straight, 'Your suit
is granted,' said, and died. [*Ib.* 'Redemption']

7 But who does hawk at eagles with a
dove? [*Ib.* 'The Sacrifice', xxiii]

8 Bibles laid open, millions of surprises.
[*Ib.* 'Sin']

9 Sweet day, so cool, so calm, so bright, /
The bridal of the earth and sky, / The
dew shall weep thy fall to-night; / For
thou must die. [*Ib.* 'Virtue']

10 Sweet spring, full of sweet days and
roses, / A box where sweets compacted
lie. [*Ib.*]

11 Only a sweet and virtuous soul, / Like
seasoned timber, never gives; / But
though the whole world turn to coal, /
Then chiefly lives. [*Ib.*]

12 Lord, how can man preach thy eternal
word? / He is a brittle crazy glass: / Yet
in thy Temple thou dost him afford /
This glorious and transcendent place, /
To be a window, through thy grace. [*Ib.*
'Windows']

13 Do well and right, and let the world sink.
[*Priest to the Temple*, Ch. 29]

J.-M. DE HERÉDIA   1842–1905

14 *Et sur elle courbé, l'ardent Imperator, /
Vit dans ses larges yeux étoilés de points
d'or / Toute une mer immense où fuyaient
des galères.* – And bending over her, the
ardent Emperor saw in her great eyes,

flecked with golden points, a whole great
sea, with galleys fleeing across it. [*Antoine et Cléopatre*]

15 *Où penchés à l'avant des blanches cara-
velles, / Ils regardaient monter en un ciel
ignoré / Du fond de l'Océan des étoiles
nouvelles.* – Where leaning over the prow
of white four-masters, they saw new stars
climb from the depths of the ocean into
an unknown sky. [*Les Conquérants*]

ROBERT HERRICK   1591–1674

16 I sing of brooks, of blossoms, birds, and
bowers: / Of April, May, of June, and
July-flowers. / I sing of maypoles, hock-
carts, wassails, wakes, / Of bridegrooms,
brides, and of their bridal cakes. [*Hesperides*, The Argument]

17 Fair pledges of a fruitful tree, / Why do
ye fall so fast? [*Ib.* 'Blossoms']

18 Cherry ripe, ripe, ripe, I cry / Full and
fair ones; come and buy; / If so be, you
ask me where / They do grow? I answer
there, / Where my Julia's lips do smile; /
There's the land, or cherry-isle. [*Ib.*
'Cherry Ripe']

19 What needs complaints, / When she a
place / Has with the race / Of Saints?
[*Ib.* 'Comfort to a Youth who had Lost
his Love']

20 A sweet disorder in the dress / Kindles
in clothes a wantonness. [*Ib.* 'Delight in
Disorder']

21 A winning wave (deserving note) / In the
tempestuous petticoat: / A careless shoe-
string, in whose tie / I see a wild civility: /
Do more bewitch me than when art / Is
too precise in every part. [*Ib.*]

22 Only a little more / I have to write, /
Then I'll give o'er, / And bid the world
good-night. [*Ib.* 'His Poetry his Pillar']

23 You say, to me-wards your affection's
strong; / Pray love me little, so you love
me long. [*Ib.* 'Love me Little, Love me
Long']

24 Her eyes the glow-worm lend thee, / The
shooting-stars attend thee; / And the
elves also, / Whose little eyes glow, /
Like the sparks of fire, befriend thee. [*Ib.*
'The Night-Piece, to Julia']

25 Night makes no difference 'twixt the
priest and clerk; / Joan as my Lady is as
good i' th' dark. [*Ib.* 'No Difference i' th'
Dark']

1 Fain would I kiss my Julia's dainty leg, /
Which is as white and hairless as an egg.
[*Hesperides*, 'On Julia's Legs']

2 A little saint best fits a little shrine, / A
little prop best fits a little vine, / As my
small cruse best fits my little wine. [*Ib.*
'A Ternary of Littles']

3 Bid me to live, and I will live / Thy
Protestant to be: / Or bid me love, and I
will give / A loving heart to thee. [*Ib.*
'To Anthea, Who May Command Him
Anything']

4 Bid me to weep, and I will weep, / While
I have eyes to see. [*Ib.*]

5 Fair daffodils, we weep to see / You
haste away so soon: / As yet the early-
rising sun / Has not attained his noon.
[*Ib.* 'To Daffodils']

6 I dare not ask a kiss; / I dare not beg a
smile; / Lest having that, or this, / I
might grow proud the while. [*Ib.* 'To
Electra']

7 Only to kiss that air, / That lately kissèd
thee. [*Ib.*]

8 Welcome maids of honour, / You do
bring / In the Spring; / And wait upon
her. [*Ib.* 'To Violets']

9 Gather ye rosebuds while ye may, / Old
Time is still a-flying: / And this same
flower that smiles to-day, / To-morrow
will be dying. [*Ib.* 'To Virgins, to Make
Much of time']

10 Her pretty feet / Like snails did creep /
A little out, and then, / As if they started
at bo-peep, / Did soon draw in agen.
[*Ib.* 'Upon her Feet']

11 Whenas in silks my Julia goes, / Then,
then (methinks) how sweetly flows /
That liquefaction of her clothes. [*Ib.*
'Upon Julia's Clothes']

12 Here a little child I stand, / Heaving up
my either hand; / Cold as paddocks
though they be, / Here I lift them up to
Thee, / For a benison to fall / On our
meat, and on us all. Amen. [*Noble
Numbers*, 'Another Grace for a Child']

JAMES HERVEY   1714–1758

13 E'en crosses from his sov'reign hand /
Are blessings in disguise. [*Reflections on
a Flower-Garden*]

JOHN HEYWOOD   1497?–1580?

14 Let the world slide, let the world go: / A
fig for care, and a fig for woe! / If I can't
pay, why I can owe, / And death makes
equal the high and the low. [*Be Merry,
Friends*]

15 All a green willow is my garland. [*The
Green Willow*]

THOMAS HEYWOOD 1572?–1641

16 Seven cities warred for Homer, being
dead, / Who, living, had no roof to
shroud his head. [*Hierarchy of the
Blessed Angels*]

17 A Woman Killed with Kindness. [Title
of play]

WILLIAM EDWARD HICKSON
1803–1870

18 'Tis a lesson you should heed, / Try, try
again. / If at first you don't succeed, /
Try, try again. [*Try and Try Again*]

'DR BREWSTER HIGLEY' 19 Cent.

19 Oh give me a home where the buffalo
roam, / Where the deer and the antelope
play, / Where seldom is heard a discouraging word / And the skies are not
cloudy all day. [*Home on the Range*]

AARON HILL   1685–1750

20 Tender-handed stroke a nettle, / And it
stings you for your pains; / Grasp it like
a man of mettle, / And it soft as silk
remains. [*Verses written on a Window*]

ROWLAND HILL   1744–1833

21 He did not see any reason why the devil
should have all the good tunes. [E. W.
Roome, *Rev. Rowland Hill*]

JAMES HILTON   1900–1954

22 Anno domini – that's the most fatal
complaint of all in the end. [*Good-bye,
Mr Chips*, Ch. 1]

189

1 When the High Lama asked him whether Shangri-la was not unique in his experience, and if the Western world could offer anything in the least like it, he answered with a smile: 'Well, yes – to be quite frank, it reminds me very slightly of Oxford.' [*Lost Horizon*, Ch. 9]

HIPPOCRATES   c. 460–357 B.C.

2 The life so short, the craft so long to learn. [*Aphorisms*, I. i (transl. Chaucer). Often quoted in Latin: *Ars longa, vita brevis*]

3 Extreme remedies are most appropriate for extreme diseases. [*Ib*. vi]

ADOLF HITLER   1889–1945

4 The great masses of the people ... will more easily fall victims to a great lie than to a small one. [*Mein Kampf*, Ch. 10]

5 It [the Sudetenland] is the last territorial claim that I have to make in Europe. [Speech, 26 Sept. 1938]

PRINCE HOARE   1755–1834

6 The saucy Arethusa. [Song: *The Arethusa*]

THOMAS HOBBES   1588–1679

7 The condition of man ... is a condition of war of everyone against everyone. [*Leviathan*, Pt i. Ch. 4]

8 Words are wise men's counters, they do but reckon with them, but they are the money of fools. [*Ib*.]

9 Sudden glory is the passion which maketh those grimaces called laughter. [*Ib*. i. 6]

10 No arts; no letters; no society; and which is worst of all, continual fear and danger of violent death; and the life of man, solitary, poor, nasty, brutish, and short. [*Ib*. i. 13]

11 The Papacy is not other than the Ghost of the deceased Roman Empire, sitting crowned upon the grave thereof. [*Ib*. iv. 47]

12 I am about to take my last voyage, a great leap in the dark. [Last words]

JOHN CAM HOBHOUSE, BARON BROUGHTON
1786–1869

13 When I invented the phrase 'His Majesty's Opposition' [Canning] paid me a compliment on the fortunate hit. [*Recollections of a Long Life*]

EDWARD WALLIS HOCH
1849–1925

14 There is so much good in the worst of us, / And so much bad in the best of us, / That it hardly becomes any of us / To talk about the rest of us. [*Good and Bad*. Authorship not absolutely certain]

RALPH HODGSON   1871–1962

15 'Twould ring the bells of Heaven / The wildest peal for years, / If Parson lost his senses / And people came to theirs. [*The Bells of Heaven*]

16 See an old unhappy bull, / Sick in soul and body both. [*The Bull*]

17 Reason has moons, but moons not hers / Lie mirror'd on her sea, / Confounding her astronomers, / But, O! delighting me. [*Reason Has Moons*]

18 I climbed a hill as light fell short, / And rooks came home in scramble sort, / And filled the trees and flapped and fought / And sang themselves to sleep. [*The Song of Honour*]

19 I heard the hymn of being sound / From every well of honour found / In human sense and soul. [*Ib*.]

20 The song of men divinely wise / Who look and see in starry skies / Not stars so much as robins' eyes, / And when these pale away / Hear flocks of shiny pleiades/ Among the plums and apple trees / Sing in the summer day. [*Ib*.]

21 When stately ships are twirled and spun / Like whipping tops and help there's none / And mighty ships ten thousand ton / Go down like lumps of lead. [*Ib*.]

22 I heard it all, I heard the whole / Harmonious hymn of being roll / Up through the chapel of my soul / And at the altar die, / And in the awful quiet then / Myself I heard, Amen, Amen, / Amen I heard me cry. [*Ib*.]

1 Without a wish, without a will, / I stood upon that silent hill / And stared into the sky until / My eyes were blind with stars and still / I stared into the sky. [*The Song of Honour*]

2 Time, you old gipsy man, / Will you not stay, / Put up your caravan / Just for one day? [*Time, You Old Gipsy Man*]

ELISHA B. HOFFMANN
1839–?

3 Have you been to Jesus for the cleansing power? / Are you washed in the blood of the Lamb? [Hymn]

E. T. A. HOFFMANN   1776–1822

4 He's a wicked man that comes after children when they won't go to bed and throws handfuls of sand in their eyes. [*The Sandman*]

HEINRICH HOFFMAN 1809–1874

5 Augustus was a chubby lad; / Fat ruddy cheeks Augustus had; / And everybody saw with joy / The plump and hearty healthy boy. [*Struwwelpeter*, 'Augustus']

6 Take the soup away! / O take the nasty soup away! / I won't have any soup to-day. [*Ib.*]

7 Here is cruel Frederick, see! / A horrid wicked boy was he. [*Ib.* 'Cruel Frederick']

8 The trough was full and faithful Tray / Came out to drink one sultry day. [*Ib.*]

9 At this good Tray grew very red, / And growled and bit him till he bled. [*Ib.*]

10 Let me see if Philip can / Be a little gentleman. [*Ib.* 'Fidgety Phil']

11 But Fidgety Phil / He won't sit still; / He wriggles / And giggles / And then, I declare, / Swings backwards and forwards, / And tilts up his chair. [*Ib.*]

12 'Me-ow,' they said, 'me-ow, me-o, / You'll burn to death, if you do so.' [*Ib.* 'Harriet and the Matches']

13 Now tall Agrippa lived close by, – /So tall he almost touched the sky; / He had a mighty inkstand too, / In which a great goose-feather grew. [*Ib.* 'The Inky Boys']

14 Boys, leave the black-a-moor alone! / For if he tries with all his might, / He cannot change from black to white. [*Ib.*]

15 Look at little Johnny there, / Little Johnny Head-In-Air. [*Struwwelpeter*, 'Johnny Head-In-Air']

16 The door flew open, in he ran, / The great, long, red-legged scissor-man. [*Ib.* 'The Little-Suck-a-Thumb']

17 Snip! Snap! Snip! They go so fast. / That both his thumbs are off at last [*Ib.*]

18 'Ah!' said Mamma, 'I knew he'd come / To naughty little Suck-a-Thumb.' [*Ib.*]

19 The hare sits snug in leaves and grass, / And laughs to see the green man pass. [*Ib.* 'The Man that went out Shooting']

20 And while he slept like any top, / The little hare came, hop, hop, hop. [*Ib.*]

21 Such fun I do not understand. [*Ib.*]

22 Anything to me is sweeter / Than to see Shock-headed Peter. [*Ib.* 'Shock-headed Peter']

HEINRICH HOFFMANN VON
FALLERSLEBEN   1798–1876

23 *Deutschland, Deutschland über alles. –* Germany, Germany before all else. [*Lied*]

JAMES HOGG   1770–1835

24 Come weel, come wo, we'll gather and go, / And live or die wi' Charlie. [*Jacobite Relics of Scotland*, 76, 'O'er the Water to Charlie']

25 There grows a bonny brier bush in our kail yard. [*Ib.* 78, 'An You Be He']

26 Will you no come back again? / Better lo'ed you'll never be, / And will ye no come back again? [*Ib.* 195, 'Will Ye No Come Back Again?']

27 Where the pools are bright and deep, / Where the grey trout lies asleep, / Up the river and o'er the lea, / That's the way for Billy and me. [*A Boy's Song*]

28 Late, late in the gloamin' Kilmeny came hame! [*Kilmeny*]

29 My love she's but a lassie yet. [Title of song]

SIR RICHARD HOLLAND
mid 15 Cent.

30 O Dowglas, O Dowglas, tendir and trewe! [*Buke of the Howlat*, xxxi]

191

J. H. HOLMES   1879–1964

1 The universe is not hostile, nor yet is it friendly. It is simply indifferent. [*Sensible Man's View of Religion*]

OLIVER WENDELL HOLMES
1809–1894

2 It was a tall young oysterman lived by the riverside. [*The Ballad of the Oysterman*]

3 I read it in the story-book, that, for to kiss his dear, / Leander swam the Hellespont – and I will swim this here. [*Ib.*]

4 And now they keep an oyster shop for mermaids down below. [*Ib.*]

5 Have you heard of the wonderful one-hoss shay, / That was built in such a logical way / It ran a hundred years to a day? [*The Deacon's Masterpiece*]

6 Day has put on his jacket, and around / His burning bosom buttoned it with stars. [*Evening*]

7 And since, I never dare to write / As funny as I can. [*The Height of the Ridiculous*]

8 When the last reader reads no more. [*The Last Reader*]

9 And silence, like a poultice, comes / To heal the blows of sound. [*The Music Grinders*]

10 For him in vain the envious seasons roll / Who bears eternal summer in his soul. [*The Old Player*]

11 We love the precepts for the teacher's sake. [*A Rhymed Lesson*]

12 And when you stick on conversation's burrs, / Don't strew your pathway with those dreadful *urs*. [*Ib.*]

13 Man wants but little drink below, / But wants that little strong. [*A Song of Other Days* (parody of Goldsmith)]

14 Man has his will – but woman has her way. [*The Autocrat of the Breakfast Table*, Ch. 1]

15 Build thee more stately mansions, O my soul, / As the swift seasons roll! [*Ib.* 4, 'The Chambered Nautilus']

16 The axis of the earth sticks out visibly through the centre of each and every town or city. [*Ib.* 6]

17 The world's great men have not commonly been scholars, nor its great scholars great men. [*The Autocrat of the Breakfast Table*, 6]

18 Depart, – be off, – excede, – evade, – erump! [*Ib.* 11]

19 A moment's insight is sometimes worth a life's experience. [*The Professor at the Breakfast Table*, Ch. 10]

20 To be seventy years young is sometimes far more hopeful than to be forty years old. [*On the Seventieth Birthday of Julia Ward Howe*]

JOHN HOME   1722–1808

21 My name is Norval; on the Grampian hills / My father feeds his flocks; a frugal swain, / Whose constant cares were to increase his store. [*Douglas*, II. i]

22 He seldom errs / Who thinks the worst he can of womankind. [*Ib.* III. iii]

23 Like Douglas conquer, or like Douglas die. [*Ib.* III. v]

HOMER   c. 900 B.C.

24 He went off without a word along the shore of the sounding sea. [*Iliad*, I. 34, transl. E. V. Rieu]

25 Winged words. [*Ib.* I. 201]

26 Over the wine-dark sea. [*Ib.* I. 350]

27 Men in their generations are like the leaves of the trees. The wind blows and one year's leaves are scattered on the ground; but the trees burst into bud and put on fresh ones when the spring comes round. [*Ib.* VI. 146]

28 She [Andromache] was smiling through her tears. [*Ib.* VI. 484]

29 He saw the cities of many peoples and learnt their ways. He suffered many hardships on the high seas in his struggles to preserve his life and bring his comrades home. [*Odyssey*, I. 4, transl. E. V. Rieu]

30 As soon as Dawn with her rose-tinted hands had lit the East. [*Ib.* II. 1]

31 Put me on earth again, and I would rather be a serf in the house of some landless man ... than king of all these dead men that have done with life. [*Ib.* XI. 489]

32 Bear, O my heart; thou hast borne a yet harder thing. [*Ib.* XX. 18]

WILLIAM HONE   1780–1842

1 A good lather is half the shave. [*Every-Day Book*, I. 1269]

2 John Jones may be described as 'one of the *has* beens'. [*Ib*. II. 820]

THOMAS HOOD   1799–1845

3 It was not in the winter / Our loving lot was cast! / It was the time of roses, / We plucked them as we passed! [Ballad: *It was not in the Winter*]

4 One more Unfortunate, / Weary of breath, / Rashly importunate, / Gone to her death.

Take her up tenderly, / Lift her with care; / Fashioned so slenderly, / Young, and so fair! [*The Bridge of Sighs*]

5 Our very hopes belied our fears, / Our fears our hopes belied – / We thought her dying when she slept, / And sleeping when she died! [*The Death Bed*]

6 Ben Battle was a soldier bold, / And used to war's alarms: / But a cannon-ball took off his legs, / So he laid down his arms. [*Faithless Nelly Gray*]

7 For here I leave my second leg, / And the Forty-second Foot. [*Ib*.]

8 The love that loves a scarlet coat / Should be more uniform. [*Ib*.]

9 His death, which happened in his berth, / At forty odd befell: / They went and told the sexton, and / The sexton toll'd the bell. [*Faithless Sally Brown*]

10 A hollow voice is all I have / But this I tell you plain, / Marry come up! – you marry, Ma'am, / And I'll come up again. [*The Ghost*]

11 I remember, I remember, / The house where I was born, / The little window where the sun / Came peeping in at morn. [*I Remember*]

12 Alas! my everlasting peace / Is broken into pieces. [*Mary's Ghost*]

13 And then, in the fullness of joy and hope, / Seem'd washing his hands with invisible soap, / In imperceptible water. [*Miss Kilmansegg*, 'Her Christening']

14 There's Bardus, a six-foot column of fop, / A lighthouse without any light atop. [*Ib*. 'Her First Step']

15 For one of the pleasures of having a rout, / Is the pleasure of having it over. [*Miss Kilmansegg*, 'Her Dream']

16 No sun – no moon! / No morn – no noon – / No dawn – no dusk – no proper time of day – [*No!*]

17 No shade, no shine, no butterflies, no bees, / No fruits, no flowers, no leaves, no birds, – November! [*Ib*.]

18 I saw old Autumn in the misty morn / Stand shadowless like Silence, listening / To silence. [Ode: *Autumn*]

19 She stood breast high amid the corn. [*Ruth*]

20 With fingers weary and worn, / With eyelids heavy and red, / A woman sat in unwomanly rags, / Plying her needle and thread – / Stitch! stitch! stitch! [*The Song of the Shirt*]

21 'Extremes meet,' as the whiting said with its tail in its mouth. [*The Doves and the Crows*]

TOM HOOD THE YOUNGER

1834–1874

22 If you were queen of bloaters / And I were king of soles, / The sea we'd wag our fins in. / Nor heed the crooked pins in / The water, dropped by boaters / To catch our heedless joles. [*A Catch*]

23 I never nursed a dear gazelle, / To glad me with its dappled hide, / But when it came to know me well / It fell upon the buttered side. [*Muddled Metaphors*]

RICHARD HOOKER   1554?–1600

24 He that goeth about to persuade a multitude that they are not so well governed as they ought to be, shall never want attentive and favourable hearers. [*Ecclesiastical Polity*, Bk I. §i]

25 Change is not made without inconvenience, even from worse to better. [Quoted by Johnson in the Preface to the *English Dictionary*]

ELLEN STURGIS HOOPER

1816–1841

26 I slept, and dreamed that life was Beauty; / I woke, and found that life was Duty. [*Life a Duty*]

HERBERT HOOVER   1874–1964

1 The American system of rugged individualism. [Campaign speech in New York, 22 Oct. 1928]

ANTHONY HOPE [SIR ANTHONY HOPE HAWKINS] 1863–1933

2 Economy is going without something you do want in case you should, some day, want something you probably won't want. [*The Dolly Dialogues*, 12]

3 Unless one is a genius, it is best to aim at being intelligible. [*Ib.* 15]

4 'Boys will be boys – '
'And even that wouldn't matter if we could only prevent girls from being girls.' [*Ib.* 16]

5 '*Bourgeois*', I observed, 'is an epithet which the riff-raff apply to what is respectable, and the aristocracy to what is decent.' [*Ib.* 17]

6 He is very fond of making things which he does not want, and then giving them to people who have no use for them. [*Ib.*]

7 Good families are generally worse than any others. [*The Prisoner of Zenda*, Ch. 1]

8 His foe was folly and his weapon wit. [Inscription on tablet to Sir W. S. Gilbert.]

LAURENCE HOPE [ADELA FLORENCE NICOLSON] 1865–1904

9 Less than the dust beneath thy chariot wheel, / Less than the weed that grows beside thy door. [*Indian Love Lyrics*, 'Less than the Dust']

10 Pale hands I loved beside the Shalimar, / Where are you now? Who lies beneath your spell? [*Ib.* 'Pale Hands I Loved']

GERARD MANLEY HOPKINS 1844–1889

11 As kingfishers catch fire, dragonflies dráw fláme; / As tumbled over rim in roundy wells / Stones ring. [*As Kingfishers catch Fire*]

12 Just for lack / Of answer the eagerer a-wanting Jessy or Jack / There God to aggrándise, God to glorify. [*The Candle Indoors*]

13 Not, I'll not, carrion comfort, Despair, not feast on thee; / Not untwist – slack they may be – these last strands of man / In me ór, most weary, cry *I can no more.* I can; / Can something, hope, wish day come, not choose not to be. [*Carrion Comfort*]

14 That night, that year / Of now done darkness I wretch lay wrestling with (my God!) my God. [*Ib.*]

15 Felix Randal the farrier, O he is dead then? [*Felix Randal*]

16 Didst fettle for the great grey drayhorse his bright and battering sandal! [*Ib.*]

17 The world is charged with the grandeur of God. [*God's Grandeur*]

18 Elected Silence, sing to me / And beat upon my whorlèd ear. [*Habit of Perfection*]

19 Hard as hurdle arms, with a broth of goldish flue / Breathed round. [*Harry Ploughman*]

20 I have desired to go / Where springs not fail, / To fields where flies no sharp and sided hail / And a few lilies blow. [*Heaven-Haven*]

21 Where no storms come, / Where the green swell is in the havens dumb, / And out of the swing of the sea. [*Ib.*]

22 I wake and feel the fell of dark, not day. / What hours, O what black hoùrs we have spent / This night! [*I wake and feel the fell*]

23 And my lament / Is cries countless, cries like dead letters sent / To dearest him that lives alas! away. [*Ib.*]

24 I am gall, I am heartburn. [*Ib.*]

25 I see / The lost are like this, and their scourge to be / As I am mine, their sweating selves; but worse. [*Ib.*]

26 What would the world be, once bereft / Of wet and of wildness? Let them be left, / O let them be left, wildness and wet; / Long live the weeds and the wilderness yet. [*Inversnaid*]

27 No worst, there is none. Pitched past pitch of grief, / More pangs will, schooled

at forepangs, wilder wring. / Comforter, where, where is your comforting? [*No worst, there is none*]

1 O the mind, mind has mountains; cliffs of fall / Frightful, sheer, no-man-fathomed. Hold them cheap / May who ne'er hung there. [*Ib.*]

2 All / Life death does.end and each day dies with sleep. [*Ib.*]

3 Glory be to God for dappled things – / For skies of couple-colour as a brinded cow; / For rose-moles all in stipple upon trout that swim. [*Pied Beauty*]

4 All trádes, their gear and tackle and trim. [*Ib.*]

5 All things counter, original, spare, strange; / Whatever is fickle, freckled (who knows how?) / With swift, slow; sweet, sour; adazzle, dim; / He fathers-forth whose beauty is past change. / Praise him. [*Ib.*]

6 Honour is flashed off exploit, so we say. [*St Alphonsus Rodriguez*]

7 Look at the stars! look, look up at the skies! / O look at all the fire-folk sitting in the air! / The bright boroughs, the circle-citadels there! [*The Starlight Night*]

8 This piece-bright paling shuts the spouse / Christ home, Christ and his mother and all his hallows. [*Ib.*]

9 Thou art indeed just, Lord, if I contend / With thee; but, sir, so what I plead is just. / Why do sinners' ways prosper? and why must / Disappointment all I endeavour end? [*Thou art indeed just, Lord*]

10 Birds build – but not I build; no, but strain, / Time's eunuch, and not breed one work that wakes. / Mine, O thou lord of life, send my roots rain. [*Ib.*]

11 The fine delight that fathers thought; the strong / Spur, live and lancing like the blowpipe flame, / Breathes once and, quenchèd faster than it came, / Leaves yet the mind a mother of immortal song. [*To R.B.*]

12 O then if in my lagging lines you miss / The roll, the rise, the carol, the creation. [*Ib.*]

13 I caught this morning morning's minion, kingdom of daylight's dauphin, dapple-dawn-drawn Falcon. [*The Windhover*]

14 The achieve of, the mastery of the thing! [*Ib.*]

15 A few other little things; some in sprung rhythm, with various other experiments. [Letter to R. W. Dixon, 5 Oct. 1878]

16 Now it is the virtue of design, pattern, or inscape to be distinctive and it is the vice of distinctiveness to become queer. [Letter to Robert Bridges, 15 Feb. 1879]

17 The poetical language of an age should be the current language heightened. [*Ib.* 14 Aug. 1879]

HORACE   65–8 B.C.

18 '*Pictoribus atque poetis* / *Quidlibet audendi semper fuit aequa potestas.*' / *Scimus, et hanc veniam petimusque damusque vicissim.* – 'Painters and poets', you say, 'have always had an equal licence for bold invention.' We know this; we claim the liberty for ourselves and we give it to others. [*Ars Poetica*, 9]

19 *Inceptis gravibus plerumque et magna professis* / *Purpureus, late qui splendeat, unus et alter* / *Adsuitur pannus.* – Often a purple patch or two is tacked on to a serious work of high promise, to give an effect of colour. [*Ib.* 14]

20 *Brevis esse laboro,* / *Obscurus fio.* – It is when I struggle to be brief that I become obscure. [*Ib.* 25]

21 *Grammatici certant et adhuc sub iudice lis est.* – Grammarians dispute, and the case is still before the courts. [*Ib.* 78]

22 *Proicit ampullas et sesquipedalia verba.* – He tosses aside his paint-pots and his words a foot and a half long. [*Ib.* 97]

23 *Parturient montes, nascetur ridiculus mus.* – Mountains will be in labour, and the birth will be an absurd little mouse. [*Ib.* 139]

24 *Semper ad eventum festinat et in medias res* / *Non secus ac notas auditorem rapit.* / He always hurries to the issue, rushing his readers into the middle of the story as if they knew it already. [*Ib.* 148]

25 *Difficilis, querulus, laudator temporis acti* / *Se puero.* – Testy, querulous and given to praising the way things were when he was a boy. [*Ib.* 173]

26 *Vos exemplaria Graeca* / *Nocturna versate manu, versate diurna.* – As for you, turn over the pages of the Greeks by night and by day. [*Ib.* 268]

1 *Grais ingenium, Grais dedit ore rotundo /
Musa loqui.* – The Muse gave the Greeks
genius and the art of the well-turned
phrase. [*Ars Poetica*, 323]

2 *Omne tulit punctum qui miscuit utile dulci,
/ Lectorem delectando pariterque monendo.*
– He has won every vote who mingles
profit with pleasure, by delighting and
instructing the reader at the same time.
[*Ib.* 343]

3 *Indignor quandoque bonus dormitat Homerus.* – But if Homer, who is good, nods for
a moment, I think it a shame. [*Ib.* 359]

4 *Ut pictura poesis.* – As in painting, so in
poetry. [*Ib.* 361]

5 *Mediocribus esse poetis / Non homines,
non di, non concessere columnae.* –
Neither men nor gods nor bookstalls
have ever allowed poets to be mediocre.
[*Ib.* 372]

6 *Nonumque prematur in annum.* – Let it
not be published until the ninth year. [*Ib.*
388]

7 *Virtus est vitium fugere, et sapientia
prima / Stultitia caruisse.* – To flee vice is
a virtue, and the beginning of wisdom is
to be done with folly. [*Epistles*, I. i. 41]

8 *Si possis recte, si non, quocumque modo
rem.* – By right means, if you can, but by
any means make money. [*Ib.* I. i. 66]

9 *Olim quod vulpes aegroto cauta leoni /
Respondit referam: 'quia me vestigia ter-
rent, / Omnia te adversum spectantia,
nulla retrorsum.'* – The wary fox in the
fable answered the sick lion: 'Because I
am frightened by the footprints. I see
them all pointing towards your den. None
of them point away.' [*Ib.* I. i. 73]

10 *Quidquid delirant reges, plectuntur Achivi.*
– For every folly of their princes, the
Greeks feel the lash. [*Ib.* I. ii. 14]

11 *Dimidium facti qui coepit habet: sapere
aude.* – He who has begun has half done.
Have the courage to be wise. [*Ib.* I. ii. 40]

12 *Ira furor brevis est.* – Anger is a brief
madness. [*Ib.* I. ii. 62]

13 *Omnem crede diem tibi diluxisse supre-
mum. / Grata superveniet quae non
sperabitur hora. / Me pinguem et nitidum
bene curata cute vises / Cum ridere voles
Epicuri de grege porcum.* – Think to
yourself that every day is your last; the
hour to which you do not look forward
will come as a welcome surprise. As for
me, when you want a good laugh, you
will find me, in a fine state, fat and sleek,
a true hog of Epicurus' sty. [*Epistles*, I. iv.
13]

14 *Naturam expellas furca, tamen usque
recurret.* – Though you drive Nature out
with a pitchfork, she will still find her
way back. [*Ib.* I. x. 24]

15 *Caelum non animum mutant qui trans mare
currunt.* – They change their skies but not
their souls who run across the sea. [*Ib.*
I. xi. 27]

16 *Quod petis hic est, / Est Ulubris, animus
si te non deficit aequus.* – What you seek is
here, at Ulubrae, if you have but equa-
nimity. [*Ib.* I. xi. 29]

17 *Concordia discors.* – Harmony in discord.
[*Ib.* I. xii. 19]

18 *Principibus placuisse viris non ultima laus
est. / Non cuivis homini contingit adire
Corinthum.* – It is no mean glory to have
found favour with the leaders of men. It
is not everyone that can get to Corinth.
[*Ib.* I. xvii. 35]

19 *Et semel emissum volat irrevocabile verbum.* – Once a word has been allowed to
escape, it cannot be recalled. [*Ib.* I.
xviii. 71]

20 *Nam tua res agitur, paries cum proximus
ardet.* – When your neighbour's wall is on
fire, it becomes your business. [*Ib.* I.
xviii. 84]

21 *Nulla placere diu nec vivere carmina
possunt / Quae scribuntur aquae potoribus.*
– No poems can please for long or live
that are written by water-drinkers. [*Ib.* I.
xix. 2]

22 *Atque inter silvas Academi quaerere
verum.* – And seek the truth in the groves
of Academus. [*Ib.* II. ii. 45]

23 *Singula de nobis anni praedantur euntes.* –
The years as they pass plunder one thing
after another. [*Ib.* II. ii. 55]

24 *Multa fero, ut placem genus irritabile
vatum.* – I put up with a great deal to
pacify the touchy tribe of poets. [*Ib.* II.
ii. 102]

25 *Lusisti satis, edisti satis atque bibisti:
Tempus abire tibi est.* – You have played
enough; you have eaten and drunk
enough. Now it is time for you to depart.
[*Ib.* II. ii. 214]

1 *Beatus ille, qui procul negotiis, / Ut prisca gens mortalium, / Paterna rura bubus exercet suis, / Solutus omni faenore.* – Happy the man who, far from business schemes, like the early race of mortals, ploughs and reploughs his ancestral land, with oxen of his own breeding, and no slavish yoke round his neck. [*Epodes*, II. 1]

2 *Quodsi me lyricis vatibus inseres, / Sublimi feriam sidera vertice.* – But if you place me among the lyric bards, I shall touch the stars with my exalted head. [*Odes*, I. i. 35]

3 *Illi robur et aes triplex / Circa pectus erat, qui fragilem truci / Commisit pelago ratem / Primus.* – His heart was mailed with oak and triple brass who first committed a frail ship to the wild seas. [*Ib.* I. iii. 9]

4 *Pallida Mors aequo pulsat pede pauperum tabernas / Regumque turris.* – Pale Death knocks with impartial foot at poor men's hovels and kings' palaces. [*Ib.* I. iv. 13]

5 *Vitae summa brevis spem nos vetat incohare longam.* – Life's short span forbids our embarking on far-reaching hopes. [*Ib.* I. iv. 15]

6 *Nil desperandum Teucro duce et auspice Teucro.* – With Teucer as leader and under Teucer's star, never despair. [*Ib.* I. vii. 27]

7 *Cras ingens iterabimus aequor.* – To-morrow we take our course once more over the mighty seas. [*Ib.* I. vii. 32]

8 *Permitte divis cetera.* – Leave the rest to the gods. [*Ib.* I. ix. 9]

9 *Tu ne quaesieris, scire nefas.* – Do not ask. Such knowledge is not for us. [*Ib.* I. xi. 1]

10 *Carpe diem, quam minimum credula postero.* – Seize today, and put as little trust as you can in the morrow. [*Ib.* I. xi. 8]

11 *O matre pulchra filia pulchrior.* – O fairer daughter of a fair mother. [*Ib.* I. xvi. 1]

12 *Integer vitae scelerisque purus.* – The man of upright life, unstained by guilt. [*Ib.* I. xxii. 1]

13 *Dulce ridentem Lalagen amabo, / Dulce loquentem.* – I will love the sweetly laughing, sweetly chattering Lalage. [*Ib.* I. xxii. 23]

14 *Nunc est bibendum, nunc pede libero / Pulsanda tellus.* – Now is the time for drinking, now the time to beat the earth with unfettered foot. [*Odes*, I. xxxvii. 1]

15 *Persicos odi, puer, apparatus.* – Boy, I loathe Persian luxury. [*Ib.* I. xxxviii. 1]

16 *Aequam memento rebus in arduis / Servare mentem.* – Remember, when life's path is steep, to keep an even mind. [*Ib.* II. iii. 1]

17 *Omnes eodem cogimur.* – We are all driven into the same fold. [*Ib.* II. iii. 25]

18 *Auream quisquis mediocritatem / Diligit.* – Whoever prizes the golden mean. [*Ib.* II. x. 5]

19 *Neque semper arcum / Tendit Apollo.* – Apollo does not always keep his bow strung. [*Ib.* II. x. 19]

20 *Eheu fugaces, Postume, Postume, / Labuntur anni.* – Alas, Postumus, Postumus, the fleeting years are slipping by. [*Ib.* II. xiv. 1]

21 *Nihil est ab omni / Parte beatum.* – No lot is in all respects happy. [*Ib.* II. xvi. 27]

22 *Odi profanum vulgus et arceo; / Favete linguis; carmina non prius / Audita Musarum sacerdos / Virginibus puerisque canto.* – I hate the uninitiated crowd and keep them away. Observe silence! I, the Muses' priest, sing for girls and boys songs never heard before. [*Ib.* III. i. 1]

23 *Post equitem sedet atra Cura.* – Black Care takes her seat behind the horseman. [*Ib.* III. i. 40]

24 *Dulce et decorum est pro patria mori.* – It is a sweet and seemly thing to die for one's country. [*Ib.* III. ii. 13]

25 *Iustum et tenacem propositi virum / Non civium ardor prava iubentium, / Non vultus instantis tyranni / Mente quatit solida.* – The man who is tenacious of purpose in a rightful cause is not shaken from his firm resolve by the frenzy of his fellow citizens clamouring for what is wrong, or by the tyrant's threatening face. [*Ib.* III. iii. 1]

26 *Si fractus illabitur orbis / Impavidum ferient ruinae.* – If the vault of heaven crack, the ruins will strike him fearless still. [*Ib.* III. iii. 7]

27 *Auditis an me ludit amabilis / Insania?* – Do you hear, or does some fond illusion mock me? [*Ib.* III. iv. 5]

1 *Fratesque tendentes opaco / Pelion imposuisse Olympo.* – The brothers who strove to pile Pelion on shady Olympus. [*Odes*, III. iv. 51]

2 *Vis consili expers mole ruit sua.* – Brute force without wisdom falls by its own weight. [*Ib.* III. iv. 65]

3 *Delicta maiorum immeritus lues.* – Though guiltless, you must expiate your fathers' sins. [*Ib.* III. vi. 1]

4 *Splendide mendax et in omne virgo / Nobilis aevum.* – Gloriously false, a maid famous for all time. [*Ib.* III. xi. 35]

5 *O fons Bandusiae splendidior vitro.* – O spring of Bandusia, brighter than glass. [*Ib.* III. xiii. 1]

6 *Magnas inter opes inops.* – A pauper in the midst of wealth. [*Ib.* III. xvi. 28]

7 *Vixi puellis nuper idoneus / Et militavi non sine gloria; / Nunc arma defunctumque bello / Barbiton hic paries habebit.* – Till lately I was still fit for the maidens, and served in battle not without renown. Now my armour and my lute, whose campaigns are over, will hang on yonder wall. [*Ib.* III. xxvi. 1]

8 *Exegi monumentum aere perennius.* – I have completed a monument more lasting than brass. [*Ib.* III. xxx. 1]

9 *Non omnis moriar.* – I shall not altogether die. [*Ib.* III. xxx. 6]

10 *Non sum qualis eram bonae / Sub regno Cinarae. Desine, dulcium / Mater saeva Cupidinum.* – I am not what I was when kindly Cinara was queen. Strive no more, cruel mother of sweet loves. [*Ib.* IV. i. 3 (Last line repeats *Odes*, I. xix. 1)]

11 *Merses profundo: pulchrior evenit.* – Plunge it in the depths; it comes up fairer. [*Ib.* IV. iv. 65]

12 *Diffugere nives, redeunt iam gramina campis / Arboribusque comae.* – The snows have fled; already the grass is returning to the fields and the leaves to the trees. [*Ib.* IV. vii. 1]

13 *Misce stultitiam consiliis brevem: / Dulce est desipere in loco.* – Mingle some brief folly with your wisdom. To forget it in due place is sweet. [*Ib.* IV. xii. 27]

14 *Mutato nomine de te / Fabula narratur.* – Change the name, and the tale is about you. [*Satires*, I. i. 69]

15 *Hoc genus omne.* – All that tribe. [*Satires*, I. ii. 2]

16 *Tempora certa modosque, et quod prius ordine verbum est / Posterius facias, praeponens ultima primis ... / Invenias etiam disiecti membra poetae.* – Take away the rhythm and the metre, and put the first word last and the last first; still the dispersed limbs are those of a poet. [*Ib.* I. iv. 58–9 and 62]

17 *Ad unguem / Factus homo.* – A man finished to the last hair. [*Ib.* I. v. 32]

18 *Credat Iudaeus Apella, / Non ego.* – Let Apella the Jew believe that, not I. [*Ib.* I. v. 100]

19 *Par nobile fratrum.* – A noble pair of brothers. [*Ib.* II. iii. 243]

20 *Hoc erat in votis: modus agri non ita magnus, / Hortus ubi et tecto vicinus iugis aquae fons / Et paulum silvae super his foret.* – This was what I prayed for: a plot of land not too large, containing a garden, and near the house a fresh spring of water, and a bit of forest to complete it. [*Ib.* II. vi. 1]

21 *O noctes cenaeque deum!* – O nights and feasts of the gods! [*Ib.* II. vi. 65]

RICHARD HENRY [HENGIST] HORNE   1803–1884

22 'Tis always morning somewhere in the world. [*Orion*, Bk iii. Ch. 2]

BARON HOUGHTON see under
MILNES, R. MONCKTON

A. E. HOUSMAN   1859–1936

23 The Grizzly Bear is huge and wild; / He has devoured the infant child. / The infant child is not aware / He has been eaten by the bear. [*Infant Innocence*]

24 Pass me the can, lad; there's an end of May. [*Last Poems*, ix]

25 May will be fine next year as like as not: / Oh ay, but then we shall be twenty-four. [*Ib.*]

26 We for a certainty are not the first / Have sat in taverns while the tempest hurled / Their hopeful plans to emptiness, and cursed / Whatever brute and blackguard made the world. [*Ib.*]

1 The troubles of our proud and angry dust / Are from eternity, and shall not fail. / Bear them we can, and if we can we must. / Shoulder the sky, my lad, and drink your ale. [*Last Poems*, ix]

2 But men at whiles are sober / And think by fits and starts, / And if they think, they fasten / Their hands upon their hearts. [*Ib.* x]

3 I, a stranger and afraid / In a world I never made. [*Ib.* xii]

4 And then the clock collected in the tower / Its strength and struck. [*Ib.* xv, 'Eight O'Clock']

5 Made of earth and sea / His overcoat for ever, / And wears the turning globe. [*Ib.* xx]

6 The fairies break their dances / And leave the printed lawn. [*Ib.* xxi]

7 The young man feels his pockets / And wonders what's to pay. [*Ib.*]

8 These, in the day when heaven was falling, / The hour when earth's foundations fled, / Followed their mercenary calling / And took their wages and are dead.

Their shoulders held the skies suspended; / They stood, and earth's foundations stay; / What God abandoned, these defended, / And saved the sum of things for pay. [*Ib.* xxxvii, 'Epitaph on an Army of Mercenaries']

9 To air the ditty / And to earth I. [*Ib.* xli, 'Fancy's Knell']

10 The rainy Pleiads wester, / Orion plunges prone, / The stroke of midnight ceases, / And I lie down alone. [*More Poems*, xi]

11 Loveliest of trees, the cherry now / Is hung with bloom along the bough. [*A Shropshire Lad*, ii]

12 Now, of my threescore years and ten, / Twenty will not come again. [*Ib.*]

13 Clay lies still, but blood's a rover; / Breath's a ware that will not keep. / Up, lad; when the journey's over / There'll be time enough for sleep. [*Ib.* iv, 'Reveille']

14 A neck God made for other use / Than strangling in a string. [*Ib.* ix]

15 Lovers lying two by two / Ask not whom they sleep beside, / And the bridegroom all night through / Never turns him to the bride. [*Ib.* xii]

16 When I was one-and-twenty / I heard a wise man say, / 'Give crowns and pounds and guineas / But not your heart away.' [*A Shropshire Lad*, xiii]

17 Oh, when I was in love with you, / Then I was clean and brave. [*Ib.* xviii]

18 And silence sounds no worse than cheers / After death has stopped the ears. [*Ib.* xix, 'To an Athlete Dying Young']

19 In summertime on Bredon / The bells they sound so clear; / Round both the shires they ring them / In steeples far and near, / A happy noise to hear.

Here of a Sunday morning / My love and I would lie, / And see the coloured counties, / And hear the larks so high / About us in the sky. [*Ib.* xxi]

20 'Come all to church, good people,' – / Oh, noisy bells, be dumb; / I hear you, I will come. [*Ib.*]

21 They carry back bright to the coiner the mintage of man, / The lads that will die in their glory and never be old. [*Ib.* xxiii]

22 Is my team ploughing, / That I was used to drive? [*Ib.* xxvii]

23 No change, though you lie under / The land you used to plough. [*Ib.*]

24 The goal stands up, the keeper / Stands up to keep the goal. [*Ib.*]

25 The flag of morn in conqueror's state / Enters at the English gate: / The vanquished eve, as night prevails, / Bleeds upon the road to Wales. [*Ib.* xxviii, 'The Welsh Marches']

26 Today the Roman and his trouble / Are ashes under Uricon. [*Ib.* xxxi]

27 From far, from eve and morning / And yon twelve-winded sky, / The stuff of life to knit me / Blew hither: here am I. [*Ib.* xxxii]

28 That is the land of lost content, / I see it shining plain, / The happy highways where I went / And cannot come again. [*Ib.* xl]

29 And the feather pate of folly / Bears the falling of the sky. [*Ib.* xlix]

30 Think no more; 'tis only thinking / Lays lads underground. [*Ib.*]

31 With rue my heart is laden / For golden friends I had, / For many a rose-lipt maiden / And many a lightfoot lad. [*Ib.* liv]

1 Malt does more than Milton can / To justify God's ways to man. [*A Shropshire Lad*, lxii]

2 Ale, man, ale's the stuff to drink / For fellows whom it hurts to think. [*Ib.*]

3 Mithridates, he died old. [*Ib.*]

4 Good religious poetry ... is likely to be most justly appreciated and most discriminately relished by the undevout. [*The Name and Nature of Poetry*]

5 Even when poetry has a meaning, as it usually has, it may be inadvisable to draw it out. ... Perfect understanding will sometimes almost extinguish pleasure. [*Ib.*]

6 If a line of poetry strays into my memory, my skin bristles so that the razor ceases to act. [*Ib.*]

BISHOP HOW　　　　1823–1897

7 For all the Saints who from their labours rest, / Who Thee by faith before the world confessed, / Thy name, O Jesu, be for ever blest. / Alleluia! [Hymn]

SAMUEL HOWARD　　　1710–1782

8 Gentle Shepherd, tell me where. [*Song*]

JULIA WARD HOWE　　1819–1910

9 Mine eyes have seen the glory of the coming of the Lord: / He is trampling out the vintage where the grapes of wrath are stored. [*Battle Hymn of the American Republic*]

10 Oh! be swift, my soul, to answer Him! be jubilant, my feet! / Our God is marching on. [*Ib.*]

11 In the beauty of the lilies Christ was born across the sea, / With a glory in his bosom that transfigures you and me: / As he died to make men holy, let us die to make men free, / While God is marching on. [*Ib.*]

JAMES HOWELL　　　1594?–1666

12 Some hold translations not unlike to be / The wrong side of a Turkish tapestry. [*Familiar Letters*, Bk I. 6]

13 This life at best is but an inn, / And we the passengers. [*Ib.* I. 73]

W. D. HOWELLS　　　1837–1920

14 Some people can stay longer in an hour than others can in a week. [Quoted in *Treasury of Humorous Quotations*]

MARY HOWITT　　　1799–1888

15 Buttercups and daisies, / Oh, the pretty flowers; / Coming ere the Springtime, / To tell of sunny hours. [*Buttercups and Daisies*]

16 'Will you walk into my parlour?' said a spider to a fly: / ''Tis the prettiest little parlour that ever you did spy.' [*The Spider and the Fly*]

EDMOND HOYLE　　　1672–1769

17 When in doubt, win the trick. [*Hoyle's Games, Whist*, 'Twenty-four Short Rules for Learners']

ELBERT HUBBARD　　　1859–1915

18 Life is just one damned thing after another. [*Thousand and One Epigrams*]

THOMAS HUGHES　　　1822–1896

19 He never wants anything but what's right and fair; only when you come to settle what's right and fair, it's everything that he wants and nothing that you want. [*Tom Brown's Schooldays*, Pt II. Ch. 2]

20 It's more than a game. It's an institution. [(Cricket) *Ib.* II. 7]

VICTOR HUGO　　　1802–1885

21 *Car le mot, c'est le Verbe, et le Verbe c'est Dieu.* – For words are the Word, and the Word is God. [*Les Contemplations*, I. i. 8]

22 *Waterloo! Waterloo! Waterloo! Morne plaine! / Comme une onde qui bout dans une urne trop pleine, / Dans ton cirque de bois, de coteaux, de vallons, / La pâle mort mêlait les sombres bataillons.* – Waterloo! Waterloo! Waterloo! Sad plain! Like a wave breaking into an overfilled cup, pale death mingled the dark battalions in your arena of woods, hills, and valleys. [*L'Expiation*, ii. 1]

1 *Lorsque l'enfant paraît, le cercle de famille / Applaudit à grands cris.* – When the child appears, the family greet it with loud cries. [*Les Feuilles d'automne*, xix. 1]

2 *Oh! combien de marins, combien de capitaines / Qui sont partis joyeux pour des courses lointaines, / Dans ce morne horizon se sont évanouis.* – Oh! how many sailors, how many captains who have gaily set out for long voyages have vanished behind that sad horizon! [*Oceano Nox*]

3 *Les champs n'étaient point noirs, les cieux n'étaient pas mornes.* – The fields were not dark, the skies were not dull. [*Tristesse d'Olympio*]

4 *La popularité? c'est la gloire en gros sous.* – Popularity? It's glory's small change. [*Ruy Blas*, iii. 4]

5 *Vous créez un frisson nouveau.* – You create a new shiver of horror. [Letter to Charles Baudelaire, 6 Oct. 1859]

T. E. HULME 1883–1917

6 I walked abroad, / And saw the ruddy moon lean over a hedge / Like a red-faced farmer. / I did not stop to speak, but nodded / And round about were the wistful stars / With white faces like town children. [*Autumn*]

DAVID HUME 1711–1776

7 Avarice, the spur of industry. [*Essays*, 'Of Civil Liberty']

8 Beauty in things exists in the mind which contemplates them. [*Ib.* 'Of Tragedy']

9 Custom, then, is the great guide of human life. [*Inquiry concerning Human Understanding*, Sec. 5. Pt 1]

10 Never literary attempt was more unfortunate than my Treatise of Human Nature. It fell *dead-born from the press*. [*My Own Life*, Ch. 1]

MARGARET HUNGERFORD 1855?–1897

11 Beauty is in the eye of the beholder. [Quoted in *Molly Bawn*]

G. W. HUNT 1825–1904

12 We don't want to fight; but, by Jingo, if we do, / We've got the ships, we've got the men, we've got the money too. [Music-hall song, 1878]

J. H. LEIGH HUNT 1784–1859

13 Abou Ben Adhem (may his tribe increase!) / Awoke one night from a deep dream of peace. [*Abou Ben Adhem and the Angel*]

14 Write me as one that loves his fellow-men. [*Ib.*]

15 And lo! Ben Adhem's name led all the rest. [*Ib.*]

16 A Venus grown fat! [*Blue-stocking Revels*]

17 The laughing queen that caught the world's great hands. [*The Nile*]

18 If you become a nun, dear, / A friar I will be. [*The Nun*]

19 Jenny kissed me when we met, / Jumping from the chair she sat in; / Time, you thief, who love to get / Sweets into your list, put that in. [*Rondeau*]

20 This Adonis in loveliness was a corpulent man of fifty. [(The Prince Regent) *The Examiner*, 22 Mar. 1812]

21 The Earl of Liverpool, whom Madame de Stael is said to have described as having 'a talent for silence'. [*Autobiography*, Ch. 11]

ANNE HUNTER 1742–1821

22 My mother bids me bind my hair / With bands of rosy hue. [*My Mother Bids Me Bind My Hair*]

JOHN HUSS 1373–1415

23 *O sancta simplicitas!* – O holy simplicity! [On seeing a peasant bringing a faggot to throw on the pile on which Huss was to be burnt]

FRANCIS HUTCHESON 1694–1746

24 Wisdom denotes the pursuing of the best ends by the best means. [*Inquiry into the Original of Our Ideas of Beauty and Virtue*, I. v]

201

1 That action is best which procures the greatest happiness for the greatest numbers. [*Inquiry into the Original of Our Ideas of Beauty and Virtue*, II. iii]

ALDOUS HUXLEY　　1894–1963

2 Gumbril's Patent Small-Clothes protect the lumbar ganglia. [*Antic Hay*, Ch. 11]

3 'Tomorrow', Mrs Viveash interrupted him, 'will be as awful as today.' [*Ib.* 22]

4 'Going to the Feelies this evening, Henry?' enquired the Assistant Predestinator. 'I hear the new one at the Alhambra is first-rate. There's a love scene on a bearskin rug; they say it's marvellous. Every hair of the bear reproduced.' [*Brave New World*, Ch. 3]

5 Our Ford . . . had been the first to reveal the appalling dangers of family life. [*Ib.*]

6 Oh, she's a splendid girl. Wonderfully pneumatic. [*Ib.*]

7 The sexophones wailed like melodious cats under the moon. [*Ib.* 5]

8 I can sympathize with people's pains, but not with their pleasures. There is something curiously boring about somebody else's happiness. [*Limbo*, 'Cynthia']

9 'What are you thinking about, Teddy Bear?'
    'Nothing.' [*Mortal Coils*, 'The Gioconda Smile']

10 Parodies and caricatures are the most penetrating of criticisms. [*Point Counter Point*, Ch. 28]

11. Burlap walked home. He was feeling pleased with himself and the world at large. 'I accept the Universe', was how, only an hour before, he had concluded his next week's leader. [*Ib.* 37]

12 And what a romp they had! The bathroom was drenched with their splashings. Of such is the kingdom of heaven. [*Ib.*]

13 But when the wearied Band / Swoons to a waltz, I take her hand, / And there we sit in peaceful calm, / Quietly sweating palm to palm. [*Frascati's*]

14 A million million spermatozoa, / All of them alive: / Out of their cataclysm but one poor Noah / Dare hope to survive. / And among that billion minus one / Might have chanced to be / Shakespeare, another Newton, a new Donne – / But the One was Me. [*The Fifth Philosopher's Song*]

15 Beauty for some provides escape, / Who gain a happiness in eyeing / The gorgeous buttocks of the ape / Or Autumn sunsets exquisitely dying. [*The Ninth Philosopher's Song*]

T. H. HUXLEY　　1825–1895

16 Science is nothing but trained and organized common sense. [*Collected Essays*, iv, 'The Method of Zadig']

17 Irrationally held truths may be more harmful than reasoned errors. [*Ib.* xii, 'The Coming of Age of the Origin of Species']

18 It is the customary fate of new truths to begin as heresies and to end as superstitions. [*Ib.*]

19 I took thought, and invented what I conceived to be the appropriate title of 'agnostic'. [*Science and Christian Tradition*, Ch. 7]

HENRIK IBSEN　　1828–1906

20 When did the squirrel get home? [*A Doll's House*, I]

21 Home life ceases to be free and beautiful as soon as it is founded on borrowing and debt. [*Ib.*]

22 I don't wish you anything but just what you are – my own sweet little song-bird. [*Ib.*]

23 In that moment it burst upon me that I had been living here these eight years with a strange man, and had borne him three children. [*Ib.* III]

24 The minority is always right. [*An Enemy of the People*, IV]

25 One should never put on one's best trousers to go out to battle for freedom and truth. [*Ib.* V]

26 The strongest man upon earth is he who stands most alone. [*Ib.*]

27 Mother, give me the sun. [*Ghosts*, III]

28 I can see him. With vine leaves in his hair. [*Hedda Gabler*, II]

29 But, merciful God! One doesn't *do* that kind of thing. [*Ib.* IV]

30 The younger generation will come knocking at my door. [*The Master Builder*, I]

1 Go round about, Peer! [*Peer Gynt*, II. vii]

2 What's a man's first duty? / The answer's brief: To be himself. [*Ib*. IV. i]

3 You're not an emperor, you're an onion! / Now my dear Peer, I'm going to peel you, / However little you may enjoy it. [*Ib*. V. v]

4 I am a button-moulder; and you / Must be popped into my casting ladle. [*Ib*. V. vii]

5 Sleep, my boy, my dearest boy! / I will rock you to sleep and guard you. [*Ib*. V. xi, Solveig's song]

6 They may soon expect the white horse at Rosmersholm now. [*Rosmersholm*, II]

7 It was love for me – *her* kind of love – that drove her into the mill-race. [*Ib*. III]

8 Always do that, wild duck. Stick at the bottom. Deep as they can get. ... And so they never come up again. [*The Wild Duck*, II]

9 Take the saving lie from the average man and you take his happiness away, too. [*Ib*. V]

10 Oh, life would be tolerable enough, even so, if we could only get·rid of these infernal duns who come to us poor people's doors with their claim of the ideal [*Ib*.]

11 BELLING: May I ask – what *is* your destiny?
GREGERS: To be thirteenth at table. [*Ib*.]

REV. CHARLES INGE   20 Cent.

12 This very remarkable man / Commends a most practical plan: / You can do what you want / If you don't think you can't, / So don't think you can't if you can. [*On M. Coué*]

W. R. INGE, DEAN OF ST PAUL'S   1860–1954

13 Literature flourishes best when it is half a trade and half an art. [*The Victorian Age*]

14 A man may build himself a throne of bayonets, but he cannot sit on it. [Marchant, *Wit and Wisdom of Dean Inge*]

JEAN INGELOW   1820–1897

15 Play uppe 'The Brides of Enderby'. [*The High Tide on the Coast of Lincolnshire*]

16 'Cusha! Cusha! Cusha!' calling. / Ere the early dews were falling. [*Ib*.]

17 A sweeter woman ne'er drew breath / Than my sonne's wife Elizabeth. [*Ib*.]

R. G. INGERSOLL   1833–1899

18 An honest God is the noblest work of man. [*Gods*, Pt 1]

19 In nature there are neither rewards nor punishments – there are consequences. [*Lectures and Essays, 3rd Series*, 'Some Reasons Why']

20 Few rich men own their own property. The property owns them. [Address to the McKinley League, New York, 29 Oct. 1896]

WASHINGTON IRVING   1783–1859

21 A woman's whole life is a history of the affections. [*The Sketch Book*, 'The Broken Heart']

22 A sharp tongue is the only edged tool that grows keener with constant use. [*Ib*. 'Rip Van Winkle']

23 The almighty dollar, that great object of universal devotion throughout our land, seems to have no genuine devotees in these peculiar villages. [*Wolfert's Roost*, 'The Creole Village']

W. W. JACOBS   1863–1943

24 'Sailor men 'ave their faults,' said the night-watchman, frankly. 'I'm not denying it. I used to 'ave myself when I was at sea.' [*The Lady of the Barge*, 'Bill's Paper Chase']

JAMES I OF ENGLAND AND VI OF SCOTLAND   1566–1625

25 A branch of the sin of drunkenness, which is the root of all sins. [*A Counterblast to Tobacco*]

1 Herein is not only a great vanity, but a great contempt of God's good gifts, that the sweetness of man's breath, being a good gift of God, should be wilfully corrupted by this stinking smoke. [*A Counterblast to Tobacco*]

2 He was a bold man who first swallowed an oyster. [Quoted in Swift's *Polite Conversation*, Dialogue II]

3 Dr Donne's verses are like the peace of God; they pass all understanding. [Attr.]

4 No bishop, no king. [Attr.]

HENRY JAMES   1843–1916

5 The deep well of unconscious cerebration. [Preface to *The American*]

6 Cats and monkeys, monkeys and cats – all human life is there. [*The Madonna of the Future*]

7 The Real Right Thing. [Title of story]

8 We must grant the artist his subject, his idea, his *donné*: our criticism is applied only to what he makes of it. [*The Art of Fiction*, 'Partial Portraits']

9 The time-honoured bread-sauce of the happy ending. [*Theatricals, 2nd Series*]

WILLIAM JAMES   1842–1910

10 There is no more miserable human being than one in whom nothing is habitual but indecision. [*Psychology*, Ch. 10]

11 The whole drift of my education goes to persuade me that the world of our present consciousness is only one out of many worlds of consciousness that exist. [*The Varieties of Religious Experience*, Lecture XX]

THOMAS JEFFERSON   1743–1826

12 We hold these truths to be sacred and undeniable; that all men are created equal and independent, that from that equal creation they derive rights inherent and inalienable, among which are the preservation of life, and liberty, and the pursuit of happiness. [Original draft for the American Declaration of Independence]

13 Error of opinion may be tolerated where reason is left free to combat it. [First inaugural address, 4 Mar. 1801]

14 Peace, commerce, and honest friendship with all nations – entangling alliances with none. [First inaugural address, 4 Mar. 1801]

15 A little rebellion now and then is a good thing. [Letter to James Madison, 30 Jan. 1787]

16 The tree of liberty must be refreshed from time to time with the blood of patriots and tyrants. It is its natural manure. [Letter to W. S. Smith, 13 Nov. 1787]

17 Indeed I tremble for my country when I reflect that God is just. [*Notes on Virginia*, Query 18, 'Manners']

FRANCIS, LORD JEFFERY   1773–1850

18 This will never do. [(On Wordsworth's *Excursion*) *Edinburgh Review*, Nov. 1814]

PAUL JENNINGS   1918–

19 Resistentialism is concerned with what Things think about men. [*Even Oddlier*, 'Developments in Resistentialism']

20 When numbered pieces of toast and marmalade were dropped on various samples of carpet arranged in quality, from coir matting to the finest Kirman rugs, the marmalade-downwards-incidence ($\mu\delta I$) varied indirectly with the quality of the carpet (Qc) – the Principle of the Graduated Hostility of Things. [*Ib.*]

21 Ventre's stark dictum that *les choses sont contre nous*. [*Ib.*]

JEROME K. JEROME   1859–1927

22 It is impossible to enjoy idling thoroughly unless one has plenty of work to do. [*Idle Thoughts of an Idle Fellow*, 'On Being Idle']

23 Love is like the measles; we all have to go through it. [*Ib.* 'On Being in Love']

24 The only malady I could conclude I had not got was housemaid's knee. [*Three Men in a Boat*, Ch. 1]

25 I like work: it fascinates me. I can sit and look at it for hours. I love to keep it by me: the idea of getting rid of it nearly breaks my heart. [*Ib.* 15]

1 The Passing of the Third Floor Back. [Title of play]

DOUGLAS JERROLD 1803–1857

2 Mrs Caudle's Curtain Lectures. [Title of book]

3 That fellow would vulgarize the day of judgement. [*Wit and Opinions*, 'A Comic Author']

4 Earth is here so kind [Australia], that just tickle her with a hoe and she laughs with a harvest. [*Ib.* 'A Land of Plenty']

5 We love peace, as we abhor pusillanimity; / But not peace at any price. [*Ib.* 'Peace']

6 Love's like the measles – all the worse when it comes late in life. [*Ib.* 'A Philanthropist']

7 The only athletic sport I ever mastered was backgammon. [Quoted in W. Jerrold, *Douglas Jerrold*]

LIONEL JOHNSON 1867–1902

8 The saddest of all Kings / Crowned, and again discrowned. [*By the Statue of King Charles I at Charing Cross*]

9 Speak after sentence? Yea: / And to the end of time. [*Ib.*]

10 Some players upon plaintive strings / Publish their wistfulness abroad; / I have not spoken of these things, / Save to one man, and unto God. [*The Precept of Silence*]

PHILANDER JOHNSON
1866–1939

11 Cheer up, the worst is yet to come. [*Shooting Stars*]

DR SAMUEL JOHNSON
1709–1784

12 Here falling houses thunder on your head, / And here a female atheist talks you dead. [*London*, 17]

13 Of all the griefs that harass the distressed, / Sure the most bitter is a scornful jest. [*Ib.* 166]

14 This mournful truth is ev'rywhere confessed, / Slow rises worth by poverty depressed. [*Ib.* 176]

15 Long-expected one and twenty, / Lingering year at length is flown. [*One and Twenty*]

16 I put my hat upon my head, / I walked into the Strand, / And there I met another man / Whose hat was in his hand. [*Parodies of the Hermit of Warkworth*]

17 When learning's triumph o'er her barb'rous foes / First reared the stage, immortal Shakespeare rose; / Each change of many-coloured life he drew, / Exhausted worlds, and then imagined new: / Existence saw him spurn her bounded reign, / And panting Time toiled after him in vain. [*Prologue at the Opening of Theatre in Drury Lane*]

18 The drama's laws, the drama's patrons give, / For we that live to please, must please to live. [*Ib.*]

19 Let observation, with extensive view, / Survey mankind from China to Peru. [*Vanity of Human Wishes*, 1]

20 Deign on the passing world to turn thine eyes, / And pause awhile from letters, to be wise; / There mark what ills the scholar's life assail, / Toil, envy, want, the patron, and the jail. [*Ib.* 157]

21 Around his tomb let Art and Genius weep / But hear his death, ye blockheads! hear and sleep. [*Ib.* 173]

22 His fall was destined to a barren strand, / A petty fortress, and a dubious hand; / He left the name, at which the world grew pale, / To point a moral, or adorn a tale. [*Ib.* 219]

23 Hides from himself his state, and shuns to know / That life protracted is protracted woe. [*Ib.* 257]

24 In life's last scene what prodigies surprise, / Fears of the brave, and follies of the wise! / From Marlborough's eyes the streams of dotage flow, / And Swift expires a driv'ller and a show. [*Ib.* 315]

25 Must helpless man, in ignorance sedate, / Roll darkling down the torrent of his fate? [*Ib.* 345]

26 Still raise for good the supplicating voice, / But leave to Heaven the measure and the choice. [*Ib.* 351]

27 With these celestial Wisdom calms the mind, / And makes the happiness she does not find. [*Ib.* 367]

1 *Lexicographer*. A writer of dictionaries, a harmless drudge. [*Dictionary of the English Language*]

2 *Oats*. A grain, which in England is generally given to horses, but in Scotland supports the people. [*Ib.*]

3 *Patron*. Commonly a wretch who supports with insolence, and is paid with flattery. [*Ib.*]

4 When two Englishmen meet, their first talk is of the weather. [*The Idler*, 11]

5 Whatever withdraws us from the power of our senses; whatever makes the past, the distant, or the future, predominate over the present, advances us in the dignity of thinking beings. [*Journey to the Western Islands*, 'Inch Kenneth']

6 About things on which the public thinks long it commonly attains to think right. [*Lives of the English Poets*, 'Addison']

7 The true genius is a mind of large general powers, accidentally determined to some particular direction. [*Ib.* 'Cowley']

8 About the beginning of the seventeenth century appeared a race of writers that may be termed the *metaphysical poets*. [*Ib.*]

9 Their thoughts are often new, but seldom natural. [*Ib.*]

10 The most heterogeneous ideas are yoked by violence together. [*Ib.*]

11 The father of English criticism. [*Ib.* 'Dryden']

12 The *Churchyard* abounds with images which find a mirror in every mind, and with sentiments to which every bosom returns an echo. [*Ib.* 'Gray']

13 New things are made familiar, and familiar things are made new. [*Ib.* 'Pope']

14 If Pope be not a poet, where is poetry to be found? [*Ib.*]

15 Preserve me from unseasonable and immoderate sleep. [*Prayers and Meditations* (1767)]

16 This world, where much is to be done and little to be known. [*Ib.* 'Against Inquisitive and Perplexing Thoughts']

17 Nothing can please many, and please long, but just representations of general nature. Particular manners can be known to few, and, therefore, few only can judge how nearly they are copied. [*Preface to Shakespeare*]

18 In his tragic scenes there is always something wanting. [*Ib.*]

19 I have always suspected that the reading is right which requires many words to prove it wrong, and the emendation wrong which cannot without so much labour appear to be right. [*Ib.*]

20 Notes are often necessary, but they are necessary evils. [*Ib.*]

21 Particulars are not to be examined till the whole has been surveyed. [*Ib.*]

22 I shall long to see the miseries of the world, since the sight of them is necessary to happiness. [*Rasselas*, Ch. 3]

23 To a poet nothing can be useless. [*Ib.* 10]

24 The business of a poet, said Imlac, is to examine, not the individual but the species; to remark general properties and large appearances. He does not number the streaks of the tulip. [*Ib.*]

25 Human life is everywhere a state in which much is to be endured and little to be enjoyed. [*Ib.* 11]

26 Marriage has many pains, but celibacy has no pleasures. [*Ib.* 26]

27 Example is always more efficacious than precept. [*Ib.* 29]

28 The endearing elegance of female friendship. [*Ib.* 45]

29 The rod produces an effect which terminates in itself. A child is afraid of being whipped, and gets his task, and there's an end on't; whereas by exciting emulation and comparisons of superiority, you lay the foundation of lasting mischief; you make brothers and sisters hate each other. [(On Mr Hunter, his headmaster) Boswell's *Life of Johnson*, Introductory]

30 BOSWELL: That, Sir, was great fortitude of mind.
JOHNSON: No, Sir, stark insensibility. [*Ib.* 1728]

31 Sir, we are a nest of singing birds. [(Of Pembroke College) *Ib.* 1730]

32 If you call a dog *Hervey*, I shall love him. [*Ib.* 1737]

33 Tom Birch is as brisk as a bee in conversation; but no sooner does he take a pen

in his hand, than it becomes a torpedo to him, and benumbs all his faculties. [Boswell's *Life of Johnson*, 1743]

1 When asked how he felt upon the ill-success of his tragedy, he replied, 'Like the Monument'; meaning that he continued firm and unmoved as that column. [*Ib.* 1749]

2 I'll come no more behind your scenes, David; for the silk stockings and white bosoms of your actresses excite my amorous propensities. [*Ib.* 1750]

3 A man may write at any time, if he will set himself doggedly to it. [*Ib.* Mar. 1750]

4 Sir, he lived in London, and hung loose upon society. [(F. Lewis) *Ib.* 1750]

5 Wretched *un-idea'd* girls. [*Ib.* 1753]

6 No man is well pleased to have his all neglected, be it ever so little. [*Ib.* Letter to Lord Chesterfield, 7 Feb. 1754]

7 Is not a patron, my lord, one who looks with unconcern on a man struggling for life in the water, and when he has reached ground, encumbers him with help? [*Ib.*]

8 The notice which you have been pleased to take of my labours, had it been early, had been kind; but it has been delayed till I am indifferent, and cannot enjoy it; till I am solitary, and cannot impart it; till I am known, and do not want it. [*Ib.*]

9 A fly, Sir, may sting a stately horse, and make him wince; but one is but an insect, and the other is a horse still. [*Ib.* Footnote on Warburton, 1754]

10 This man, I thought, had been a Lord among wits; but, I find, he is only a wit among Lords! [(Lord Chesterfield) *Ib.* 1754]

11 They teach the morals of a whore, and the manners of a dancing-master. [(Lord Chesterfield's Letters) *Ib.*]

12 Sir, he [Lord Bolingbroke] was a scoundrel and a coward: a scoundrel for charging a blunderbuss against religion and morality; a coward, because he had not resolution to fire it off himself, but left half a crown to a beggarly Scotchman [David Mallet], to draw the trigger after his death! [*Ib.* 6 Mar. 1754]

13 When the messenger who carried the last sheet [of Johnson's *Dictionary*] to Millar returned, Johnson asked him, 'Well, what did he say?' – 'Sir (answered the mes-

senger), he said, thank God I have done with him.' – 'I am glad (replied Johnson, with a smile,) that he thanks God for anything.' [Boswell's *Life of Johnson*, Apr. 1755]

14 I respect Millar; he has raised the price of literature. [*Ib.*]

15 Ignorance, Madam, pure ignorance. [(On being asked how, in his *Dictionary*, he came to define *Pastern* as the knee of a horse) *Ib.* 1755]

16 If a man does not make new acquaintance as he advances through life, he will soon find himself alone. A man, Sir, should keep his friendship *in constant repair*. [*Ib.*]

17 No man will be a sailor who has contrivance enough to get himself into a jail; for being in a ship is being in a jail, with the chance of being drowned. . . . A man in a jail has more room, better food, and commonly better company. [*Ib.* Mar. 1759]

18 BOSWELL: I do indeed come from Scotland, but I cannot help it . . . JOHNSON: That, Sir, I find, is what a very great many of your countrymen cannot help. [*Ib.* 16 May 1763]

19 When a butcher tells you his heart bleeds for his country, he has, in fact, no uneasy feeling. [*Ib.*]

20 Dr Blair . . . asked . . . whether he thought any man of a modern age could have written such poems [*Ossian*]. . . . 'Yes, Sir, many men, many women, and many children.' [*Ib.* 24 May 1763]

21 He insisted on people praying with him; and I'd as lief pray with Kit Smart as anyone else. [*Ib.*]

22 Another charge was, that he [Smart] did not love clean linen; and I have no passion for it. [*Ib.*]

23 You may scold a carpenter who has made you a bad table, though you cannot make a table. It is not your trade to make tables. [*Ib.* 25 June 1763]

24 Campbell is a good man, a pious man. I am afraid he has not been in the inside of a church for many years; but he never passes a church without pulling off his hat. This shews that he has good principles. [*Ib.* 1 July 1763]

25 A man ought to read just as inclination leads him; for what he reads as a task will do him little good. [*Ib.* 9 July 1763]

1 If he does really think there is no distinction between virtue and vice, why, Sir, when he leaves our houses let us count our spoons. [Boswell's *Life of Johnson*, 9 July 1763]

2 Subordination tends greatly to human happiness. Were we all upon an equality, we should have no other enjoyment than mere animal pleasure. [*Ib.* 20 July 1763]

3 Truth, Sir, is a cow, which will yield such people [sceptics] no more milk, and so they are gone to milk the bull. [*Ib.* 21 July 1763]

4 Your levellers wish to level *down* as far as themselves; but they cannot bear levelling *up* to themselves. [*Ib.*]

5 Why, Sir, Sherry [Thomas Sheridan] is dull, naturally dull; but it must have taken a great deal of pains to become what we now see him. Such an excess of stupidity, Sir, is not in Nature. [*Ib.* 28 July 1763]

6 Sir, it is burning a farthing candle at Dover, to shew a light at Calais. [(On Sheridan's influence upon the English language) *Ib.*]

7 Sir, a woman's preaching is like a dog's walking on his hind legs. It is not done well; but you are surprised to find it done at all. [*Ib.* 31 July 1763]

8 I look upon it, that he who does not mind his belly, will hardly mind anything else. [*Ib.* 5 Aug. 1763]

9 This was a good dinner enough, to be sure; but it was not a dinner to *ask* a man to. [*Ib.*]

10 BOSWELL: It is impossible to refute it. . . . Johnson, striking his foot with mighty force against a large stone, till he rebounded from it, answered, 'I refute it *thus*.' [(On Bishop Berkeley's proof of the non-existence of matter) *Ib.* 6 Aug. 1763]

11 A very unclubbable man. [(Sir John Hawkins) *Ib.* 1764]

12 I would consent to have a limb amputated to recover my spirits. [*Ib.*]

13 It was not for me to bandy civilities with my Sovereign. [*Ib.* Feb. 1767]

14 Well, (said he), we had a good talk. BOSWELL: Yes, Sir, you tossed and gored several persons. [*Ib.* 1768]

15 We *know* our will is free, and *there's* an end on't. [*Ib.* 10 Oct. 1769]

16 In the description of night in *Macbeth*, the beetle and the bat detract from the general idea of darkness – inspissated gloom. [Boswell's *Life of Johnson*, 16 Oct. 1769]

17 Shakespeare never has six lines together without a fault. [*Ib.* 19 Oct. 1769]

18 Most schemes of political improvement are very laughable things. [*Ib.* 26 Oct. 1769]

19 It matters not how a man dies, but how he lives. The act of dying is not of importance, it lasts so short a time. [*Ib.*]

20 His [a player's] conversation usually threatened and announced more than it performed; that he fed you with a continual renovation of hope, to end in a constant succession of disappointment. [*Ib.* 1770]

21 That man [Lord Lyttelton] sat down to write a book, to tell the world what the world had all his life been telling him. [*Ib.*]

22 That fellow seems to me to possess but one idea, and that is a wrong one. [(Of a dull fellow) *Ib.*]

23 A gentleman who had been very unhappy in marriage, married immediately after his wife died: Johnson said, it was the triumph of hope over experience. [*Ib.*]

24 He said that few people had intellectual resources sufficient to forgo the pleasures of wine. They could not otherwise contrive how to fill the interval between dinner and supper. [*Ib.* 1772]

25 Sir, it is so far from being natural for a man and a woman to live in a state of marriage, that we find all the motives that they have for remaining in that connection, and the restraints which civilised society imposes to prevent separation, are hardly sufficient to keep them together. [*Ib.* 31 Mar. 1772]

26 There is more knowledge of the heart in one letter of Richardson's, than in all *Tom Jones*. [*Ib.* 6 Apr. 1772]

27 Much . . . may be made of a Scotchman, if he be *caught* young. [(On Lord Mansfield) *Ib.* 1772]

28 'What (said Elphinston), have you read it through?' . . . 'No, Sir, do *you* read books *through*?' [*Ib.* 19 Apr. 1773]

29 Read over your compositions, and where ever you meet with a passage which you

think is particularly fine, strike it out. [(Quoting a college tutor) Boswell's *Life of Johnson*, 30 Apr. 1773]

1 The woman's a whore, and there's an end on't. [(Lady Diana Beauclerk) *Ib.* 7 May 1773]

2 I hope I shall never be deterred from detecting what I think a cheat, by the menaces of a ruffian. [*Ib.* Letter to James Macpherson, Feb. 1775]

3 There are few ways in which a man can be more innocently employed than in getting money. [(To William Strahan) *Ib.* 27 Mar. 1775]

4 A man will turn over half a library to make one book. [*Ib.* 6 Apr. 1775]

5 Patriotism is the last refuge of a scoundrel. [*Ib.* 7 Apr. 1775]

6 Knowledge is of two kinds. We know a subject ourselves, or we know where we can find information upon it. [*Ib.* 18 Apr. 1775]

7 In lapidary inscriptions a man is not upon oath. [*Ib.* 1775]

8 Nothing odd will do long. *Tristram Shandy* did not last. [*Ib.* 20 Mar. 1776]

9 There is nothing which has yet been contrived by man, by which so much happiness is produced as by a good tavern or inn. [*Ib.* 21 Mar. 1776]

10 BOSWELL: Sir, you observed one day ... that a man is never happy for the present, but when he is drunk. Will you not add,— or when driving rapidly in a post-chaise? JOHNSON: No, Sir, you are driving rapidly *from* something, or *to* something. [*Ib.* 29 Mar. 1776]

11 If a madman were to come into this room with a stick in his hand, no doubt we should pity the state of his mind; but our primary consideration would be to take care of ourselves. We should knock him down first, and pity him afterwards. [*Ib.* 3 Apr. 1776]

12 No man but a blockhead ever wrote, except for money. [*Ib.* 5 Apr. 1776]

13 A man who has not been in Italy, is always conscious of an inferiority. [*Ib.* 11 Apr. 1776]

14 BOSWELL: Then, Sir, what is poetry? JOHNSON: Why, Sir, it is much easier to say what it is not. We all *know* what light is; but it is not easy to *tell* what it is. [*Ib.*]

15 *Olivarii Goldsmith, Poetae, Physici, Historici, qui nullum fere scribendi genus non tetigit, nullum quod tetigit non ornavit.* – To Oliver Goldsmith, poet, naturalist, and historian, who left hardly any style of writing untouched, and touched nothing that he did not adorn. [Boswell's *Life of Johnson*, Goldsmith's epitaph, May 1776]

16 If ... I had no duties, and no reference to futurity, I would spend my life in driving briskly in a post-chaise with a pretty woman. [*Ib.* 19 Sept. 1777]

17 Depend upon it, Sir, when a man knows he is to be hanged in a fortnight, it concentrates his mind wonderfully. [*Ib.*]

18 When a man is tired of London he is tired of life; for there is in London all that life can afford. [*Ib.* 20 Sept. 1777]

19 It is wonderful that five thousand years have now elapsed since the creation of the world, and still it is undecided whether or not there has ever been an instance of the spirit of any person appearing after death. All argument is against it; but all belief is for it. [*Ib.* 31 Mar. 1778]

20 Every man thinks meanly of himself for not having been a soldier, or not having been at sea. [*Ib.* 10 Apr. 1778]

21 I am willing to love all mankind, *except an American*. [*Ib.* 15 Apr. 1778]

22 All censure of a man's self is oblique praise. It is in order to show how much he can spare. [*Ib.* 25 Apr. 1778]

23 I have always said, the first Whig was the Devil. [*Ib.* 28 Apr. 1778]

24 If it rained knowledge, I'd hold out my hand; but I would not give myself the trouble to go in quest of it. [*Ib.* 12 May 1778]

25 Claret is the liquor for boys; port for men; but he who aspires to be a hero ... must drink brandy. [*Ib.* 7 Apr. 1779]

26 BOSWELL: Is not the Giant's Causeway worth seeing? JOHNSON: Worth seeing? yes; but not worth going to see. [*Ib.* 12 Oct. 1779]

27 If you are idle, be not solitary; if you are solitary, be not idle. [*Ib.* Letter to Boswell, 27 Oct. 1779]

28 Greek, Sir, ... is like lace; every man gets as much of it as he can. [*Ib.* 1780]

1 Sir, your wife, *under pretence of keeping a bawdy-house*, is a receiver of stolen goods. [Boswell's *Life of Johnson*, 1780]

2 There are people whom one should like very well to drop, but would not wish to be dropped by. [*Ib.* Mar. 1781]

3 He fills a chair. [(Lord North) *Ib.* 1 Apr. 1781]

4 Sir, I have two cogent reasons for not printing any list of subscribers; – one, that I have lost all the names, – the other, that I have spent all the money. [*Ib.* May 1781]

5 My dear friend, clear your *mind* of cant. [*Ib.* 15 May 1783]

6 As I know more of mankind I expect less of them, and am ready now to call a man *a good man*, upon easier terms than I was formerly. [*Ib.* Sept. 1783]

7 I should as soon think of contradicting a bishop. [(Of George Psalmanazar) *Ib.* 15 May 1784]

8 Milton . . . was a genius that could cut a Colossus from a rock, but could not carve heads upon cherry-stones. [*Ib.* 13 June 1784]

9 Who drives fat oxen should himself be fat. [(Line composed in parody of a line in a tragedy) *Ib.* June 1784]

10 Sir, I have found you an argument; but I am not obliged to find you an understanding. [*Ib.*]

11 Sir, . . . there is not a sapling upon Parnassus more severely blown about by every wind of criticism. [(Of a vain author) *Ib.*]

12 A lawyer has no business with the justice or injustice of the cause which he undertakes, unless his client asks his opinion, and then he is bound to give it honestly. The justice or injustice of the cause is to be decided by the judge. [Boswell, *Tour of the Hebrides*, 15 Aug. 1773]

13 True, Sir; but sensation is sensation. [(On the 'kindness' of a tedious visit) *Ib.* 23 Aug.]

14 I have, all my life long, been lying till noon; yet I tell all young men, and tell them with great sincerity, that nobody who does not rise early will ever do any good. [*Ib.* 14 Sept.]

15 I inherited a vile melancholy from my father, which has made me mad all my life, at least not sober. [*Ib.* 16 Sept.]

16 Wickedness is always easier than virtue; for it takes the short cut to everything. [Boswell, *Tour of the Hebrides*, 17 Sept.]

17 I am always sorry when any language is lost, because languages are the pedigree of nations. [*Ib.* 18 Sept.]

18 I do not like much to see a Whig in any dress; but I hate to see a Whig in a parson's gown. [*Ib.* 24 Sept.]

19 A fellow who makes no figure in company, and has a mind as narrow as the neck of a vinegar cruet. [*Ib.* 30 Sept.]

20 A cucumber should be well sliced, and dressed with pepper and vinegar, and then thrown out, as good for nothing. [*Ib.* 5 Oct.]

21 By seeing London, I have seen as much of life as the world can show. [*Ib.* 11 Oct.]

22 It is ridiculous for a Whig to pretend to be honest. He cannot hold it out. [*Ib.* 21 Oct.]

23 A man may be very sincere in good principles, without having good practice. [*Ib.* 25 Oct.]

24 Sir, the noblest prospect that a Scotchman ever sees, is the high road that leads him to London. [*Ib.* 10 Nov.]

25 I am sorry I have not learnt to play at cards. It is very useful in life: it generates kindness, and consolidates society. [*Ib.* 11 Nov.]

26 Wheresoe'er I turn my view, / All is strange, yet nothing new; / Endless labour all along, / Endless labour to be wrong. [*Anecdotes of Johnson*, by Mrs Piozzi]

27 Hermit hoar, in solemn cell, / Wearing out life's evening gray; / Strike thy bosom, sage! and tell / What is bliss, and which the way? / Thus I spoke, and speaking sighed, / Scarce repressed the starting tear, / When the hoary sage replied, / 'Come, my lad, and drink some beer.' [*Ib.*]

28 If a man who turnips cries, / Cry not when his father dies, / 'Tis a proof that he had rather / Have a turnip than a father. [*Ib.* 'Burlesque of lines by Lope de Vega']

29 Dear Bathurst . . . was a man to my very heart's content: he hated a fool, and he hated a rogue, and he hated a Whig; he was a very good hater. [*Ib.*]

1 Life is a pill which none of us can bear to swallow without gilding. [*Anecdotes of Johnson*, by Mrs. Piozzi]

2 He will not, whither he is now gone, find much difference, I believe, either in the climate or the company. [(Of a gentleman from Jamaica, recently dead) *Ib.*]

3 I would advise no man to marry, Sir, . . . who is not likely to propagate understanding. [*Ib.*]

4 You could not stand five minutes with that man [Edmund Burke] beneath a shed while it rained, but you must be convinced you had been standing with the greatest man you had ever yet seen. [(Also quoted by Boswell) *Ib.*]

5 Was there ever yet anything written by mere man that was wished longer by its readers, excepting *Don Quixote, Robinson Crusoe*, and the *Pilgrim's Progress*? [*Ib.*]

6 It is all cant; the dog knows he is miserable all the time. [(On being told that anyone was happy) *Ib.*]

7 I have heard him assert, that a tavern chair was the throne of human felicity. [Hawkins' *Life of Johnson*]

8 Difficult do you call it, Sir? I wish it were impossible. [(Of a violinist's playing) *Anecdotes by William Seward*]

9 Love is the wisdom of the fool and the folly of the wise. [William Cooke's *Life of Samuel Foote*]

10 No two men can be half an hour together, but one shall acquire an evident superiority over the other. [Attr.]

JOHN BENN JOHNSTONE

1803–1891

11 I want you to assist me in forcing her on board the lugger; once there, I'll frighten her into marriage. [(Commonly quoted as: 'Once aboard the lugger and the girl is mine.') *The Gipsy Farmer*]

AL JOLSON   1886–1950

12 You ain't heard nothin' yet, folks. [Remark in the first talking film, *The Jazz Singer*, 1927]

SIR WILLIAM JONES 1746–1794

13 Seven hours to law, to soothing slumber seven, / Ten to the world allot, and all to heaven. [*Lines in Substitution for those of Sir Edward Coke, q.v.*]

BEN JONSON   1573–1637

14 Fortune, that favours fools. [*The Alchemist*, Prologue]

15 I have a humour, / I would not willingly be gulled. [*Ib.* II. i]

16 Bells are profane, a tune may be religious. [*Ib.* III. ii]

17 I will eat exceedingly, and prophesy. [*Bartholomew Fair*, I. vi]

18 This is the very womb and bed of enormity. [*Ib.* II. i]

19 Neither do thou lust after that tawny weed tobacco. [*Ib.* II. vi]

20 Slow, slow, fresh fount, keep time with my salt tears; / Yet slower yet, O faintly, gentle springs. [*Cynthia's Revels*, I. i]

21 Queen and huntress, chaste and fair, / Now the sun is laid to sleep, / Seated in thy silver chair, / State in wonted manner keep: / Hesperus entreats thy light, / Goddess, excellently bright. [*Ib.* V. iii]

22 If he were / To be made honest by an act of parliament, / I should not alter in my faith of him. [*The Devil is an Ass*, IV. i]

23 Still to be neat, still to be drest, / As you were going to a feast. [*Epicœne*, I. i]

24 Lady, it is to be presumed, / Though art's hid causes are not found, / All is not sweet, all is not sound. [*Ib.*]

25 Such sweet neglect more taketh me, / Than all the adulteries of art; / They strike mine eyes, but not my heart. [*Ib.*]

26 Have you a stool there to be melancholy upon? [*Every Man in His Humour*, III. i]

27 I do hold it, and will affirm it before any prince in Europe, to be the most sovereign and precious weed that ever the earth rendered to the use of man. [*Ib.* III. ii]

28 I do honour the very flea of his dog. [*Ib.* IV. ii]

29 Apes are apes, though clothed in scarlet. [*The Poetasters* V]

1 'Twas only fear first in the world made gods. [*Sejanus*, II. ii]

2 Good morning to the day: and next, my gold! – / Open the shrine that I may see my saint. [*Volpone*, I. i]

3 Come, my Celia, let us prove, / While we can, the sports of love. [*Ib.* III. vi]

4 Suns that set may rise again, / But if once we lose this light, / 'Tis with us perpetual night. [*Ib.*]

5 Have you seen but a bright lily grow, / Before rude hands have touched it? / Have you marked but the fall o' the snow / Before the soil hath smutched it? ... / O so white! O so soft! O so sweet is she! [*Celebration of Charis*, IV (Her Triumph)]

6 She is Venus when she smiles; / But she's Juno when she walks, / And Minerva when she talks. [*Ib.* V]

7 Underneath this stone doth lie / As much beauty as could die. [*Epitaph on Elizabeth L. H.*]

8 It is not growing like a tree / In bulk, doth make men better be. [*Ode on the Death of Sir H. Morison*]

9 Wherein the graver had a strife / With Nature to out-do the life. [*On the Portrait of Shakespeare*]

10 Reader, look / Not on his picture, but his book. [*Ib.*]

11 Follow a shadow, it still flies you, / Seem to fly it, it will pursue. / So court a mistress, she denies you; / Let her alone, she will court you. / Say, are not women truly, then, / Styled but the shadows of us men? [Song: *That Women are but Men's Shadows*]

12 Drink to me only with thine eyes, / And I will pledge with mine; / Or leave a kiss but in the cup, / And I'll not look for wine. [*To Celia*]

13 Soul of the Age! / The applause! delight! the wonder of our stage! / My Shakespeare, rise; I will not lodge thee by / Chaucer, or Spenser, or bid Beaumont lie / A little further, to make thee a room; / Thou art a monument without a tomb. [*To the Memory of Shakespeare*]

14 Sporting Kyd, or Marlowe's mighty line. [*Ib.*]

15 And though thou hadst small Latin, and less Greek. [*Ib.*]

16 He was not of an age, but for all time! [*To the Memory of Shakespeare*]

17 For a good poet's made as well as born. [*Ib.*]

18 Sweet swan of Avon! [*Ib.*]

19 I remember the players have often mentioned it as an honour to Shakespeare that in his writing (whatsoever he penned) he never blotted out a line. My answer hath been, 'Would he had blotted a thousand.' [*Timber, or Discoveries*, 64]

20 For I loved the man, and do honour his memory, on this side idolatry, as much as any. [(Shakespeare) *Ib.*]

21 There was ever more in him to be praised than to be pardoned. [(Shakespeare) *Ib.*]

22 The fear of every man that heard him was, lest he should make an end. [(Bacon) *Ib.* 78]

23 In his adversity I ever prayed, that God would give him strength; for greatness he could not want. [(Bacon) *Ib.* 80]

24 O rare Ben Jonson. [Epitaph on his tombstone]

DOROTHEA JORDAN 1762–1816

25 'Oh where, and Oh where is your Highland laddie gone?' / 'He's gone to fight the French, for King George upon the throne, / And it's Oh! in my heart, how I wish him safe at home!' [*The Blue Bells of Scotland*]

BENJAMIN JOWETT 1817–1893

26 The lie in the Soul is a true lie. [From the Introduction to his translation of Plato's *Republic*]

JAMES JOYCE 1882–1941

27 A Portrait of the Artist as a Young Man. [Title of book]

28 I go to encounter for the millionth time the reality of experience, and to forge in the smithy of my soul the uncreated conscience of my race. Old father, old artificer, stand me now and ever in good stead. [*Ib.* Final words of Stephen Daedalus]

29 History, Stephen said, is a nightmare from which I am trying to awake. [*Ulysses*, p. 31]

1 Gold by bronze heard iron steel [*Ulysses*, 256]

2 I shall call rebutting evidence to prove up to the hilt that the hidden hand is again at its old game. When in doubt persecute Bloom. [*Ib.* 442]

3 I regard him as the whitest man I know. He is down on his luck at present owing to the mortgaging of his extensive property at Agendath Netaim in faraway Asia Minor, slides of which will now be shown. [*Ib.*]

JULIAN   *c.* 331–363

4 *Vicisti, Galilaee.* – Thou hast conquered, O Galilean. [Latin translation of alleged dying words]

JULIANA OF NORWICH
                                          14 Cent.

5 Sin is behovely, but all shall be well, and all shall be well, and all manner of thing shall be well. [*Revelations of Divine Love*, Ch. xxvii]

C. G. JUNG   1875–1961

6 Religion, it might be said, is the term that designates the attitude peculiar to a consciousness which has been altered by the experience of the *numinosum*. [*Psychology and Religion*, Ch. 1]

JUNIUS [identity unknown]   18 Cent.

7 The liberty of the Press is the *Palladium* of all the civil, political, and religious rights of an Englishman. [*Letters*, Dedication]

8 In all the mazes of metaphorical confusion. [*Ib.* 7]

9 It is not that you do wrong by design, but that you should never do right by mistake. [*Ib.* 12]

10 There is a holy mistaken zeal in politics as well as in religion. By persuading others, we convince ourselves. [*Ib.* 35]

11 Whether it be the heart to conceive, the understanding to direct, or the hand to execute. [*Ib.* 37]

12 The injustice done to an individual is sometimes of service to the public. [*Ib.* 41]

GENERAL JUNOT   1771–1813

13 I am my own ancestor. [On being created duke]

JUVENAL   60–*c.* 130

14 *Probitas laudatur et alget.* – Honesty is praised and starves. [*Satires*, i. 74]

15 *Quidquid agunt homines, votum timor ira voluptas / Gaudia discursus nostri farrago libelli est.* – All men's activities – their wishes, fears, anger, pleasures, joys, and miscellaneous pursuits – is the hodge-podge of my book. [*Ib.* i. 85]

16 *Dat veniam corvis, vexat censura columbas.* – Censure acquits the raven, but pursues the dove. [*Ib.* ii. 63]

17 *Nemo repente fuit turpissimus.* – No one ever reached the depths of wickedness all at once. [*Ib.* ii. 83]

18 *Grammaticus rhetor geometres pictor aliptes / Augur schoenobates medicus magus, omnia novit / Graeculus esuriens; in caelum miseris, ibit.* – Grammarian, rhetorician, geometer, painter, ringmaster, soothsayer, rope-dancer, physician, magician – he knows everything. Tell the hungry little Greek to go to heaven, and he will go. [*Ib.* iii. 76]

19 *Nil habet infelix paupertas durius in se / Quam quod ridiculos homines facit.* – Poverty is bitter, but it has no harder pang than that it makes men ridiculous. [*Ib.* iii. 152]

20 *Haud facile emergunt quorum virtutibus opstat / Res angusta domi.* – It is not easy for men to emerge from obscurity if their qualities are thwarted by narrow means at home. [*Ib.* iii. 164]

21 *Hic vivimus ambitiosa / Paupertate omnes.* – Here we all live in a state of ambitious poverty. [*Ib.* iii. 182]

22 *Omnia Romae / Cum pretio.* – At Rome, all things can be had at a price. [*Ib.* iii. 183]

23 *Rara avis in terris nigroque simillima cycno.* – A rare bird on earth, and very like a black swan. [*Ib.* vi. 165]

24 *Hoc volo, sic iubeo, sit pro ratione voluntas.* – I wish it, I command it. Let my will take the place of a reason. [*Ib.* vi. 223]

1 *Nulla fere causa est, in qua non femina litem moverit.* – There is hardly a case in which the dispute was not caused by a woman. [*Satires*, vi. 242]

2 *Quis custodiet ipsos / Custodes?* – Who is to guard the guards themselves? [*Ib.* vi. 347]

3 *Tenet insanabile multos / Scribendi cacoethes et aegro in corde senescit.* – An inveterate and incurable itch for writing besets many and grows old with their sick hearts. [*Ib.* vii. 51]

4 *Occidit miseros crambe repetita magistros.* – Warmed up cabbage wears out the poor master's life. [*Ib.* vii. 154]

5 *Nobilitas sola est atque unica virtus.* – Virtue is the one and only nobility. [*Ib.* viii. 20]

6 *Cantabit vacuus coram latrone viator.* – The traveller with empty pockets will sing in the thief's face. [*Ib.* x. 22]

7 *Duas tantum res anxius optat, / Panem et circenses.* – Limits the Romans' anxieties to two things – bread and games. [*Ib.* x. 80]

8 *Orandum est ut sit mens sana in corpore sano.* – Your prayer must be for a sound mind in a sound body. [*Ib.* x. 356]

9 *Prima est haec ultio quod se / Iudice nemo nocens absolvitur.* – This is his first punishment, that by the verdict of his own heart no guilty man is acquitted. [*Ib.* xiii. 2]

FRANZ KAFKA   1883–1924

10 You may object that it is not a trial at all; you are quite right, for it is only a trial if I recognize it as such. [*The Trial*, II, 'First Interrogation']

11 'But I am not guilty,' said K.; 'it's a misunderstanding. And if it comes to that, how can any man be called guilty?' [*Ib.* IX, 'In the Cathedral']

IMMANUEL KANT   1724–1804

12 Two things fill my mind with ever-increasing wonder and awe, the more often and the more intensely the reflection dwells on them: the starry heavens above me and the moral law within me. [*Critique of Pure Reason*, conclusion]

13 A categorical imperative would be one which represented an action as objectively necessary in itself, without reference to any other purpose. [*Fundamental Principles of Morals*]

ALPHONSE KARR   1808–1890

14 *Plus ça change, plus c'est la même chose.* – The more things change, the more they are the same. [*Les Guêpes*, Jan. 1849]

15 *Si l'on veut abolir la peine de mort en ce cas, que MM. les assassins commencent.* – If we are to abolish the death penalty, let our friends the murderers make the first move. [*Ib.*]

TED KAVANAGH   1892–1958

16 Can I do you now, sir? [(Mrs Mop) *Itma* programmes]

17 Don't forget the diver. [*Ib.*]

18 Foonf speaking. [*Ib.*]

19 I don't mind if I do. [(Colonel Chinstrap) *Ib.*]

20 It's that man again. [*Ib.*]

21 Wot, me? In my state of health! [(Charles Atlas) *Ib.*]

DENIS KEARNEY   1847–1907

22 Horny-handed sons of toil. [Speech in San Francisco, *c.* 1878]

JOHN KEATS   1795–1821

23 Bards of Passion and of Mirth, / Ye have left your souls on earth! / Have ye souls in heaven too? [*Bards of Passion and of Mirth*]

24 The imagination of a boy is healthy, and the mature imagination of a man is healthy; but there is a space of life between, in which the soul is in a ferment, the character undecided, the way of life uncertain, the ambition thick-sighted: thence proceeds mawkishness. [*Endymion*, Preface]

25 A thing of beauty is a joy for ever: / Its loveliness increases; it will never / Pass into nothingness. [*Ib.* Bk I. 1]

26 Solitary thinkings; such as dodge / Conception to the very bourne of heaven, / Then leave the naked brain. [*Ib.* I. 294]

1 Pleasure is oft a visitant; but pain / Clings cruelly to us. [*Endymion*, I. 906]

2 O Sorrow, / Why dost borrow / Heart's lightness from the merriment of May? [*Ib*. IV. 164]

3 To Sorrow / I bade good-morrow, / And thought to leave her far away behind; / But cheerly, cheerly, / She loves me dearly; / She is so constant to me, and so kind. [*Ib*. IV. 173]

4 Their smiles, / Wan as primroses gathered at midnight / By chilly fingered Spring. [*Ib*. IV. 969]

5 It is a flaw / In happiness to see beyond our bourn, – / It forces us in summer skies to mourn, / It spoils the singing of the nightingale. [*Epistle to J. H. Reynolds*, 82]

6 St Agnes' Eve – Ah, bitter chill it was! / The owl, for all his feathers, was a-cold; / The hare limped trembling through the frozen grass, / And silent was the flock in woolly fold. [*The Eve of St Agnes*, i]

7 Soon, up aloft, / The silver, snarling trumpets 'gan to chide. [*Ib*. iv]

8 Upon the honeyed middle of the night. [*Ib*. vi]

9 Out went the taper as she hurried in; / Its little smoke, in pallid moonshine, died. [*Ib*. xxiii]

10 Full on this casement shone the wintry moon, / And threw warm gules on Madeline's fair breast. [*Ib*. xxv]

11 A heap / Of candied apple, quince, and plum, and gourd; / With jellies soother than the creamy curd, / And lucent syrops tinct with cinnamon. [*Ib*. xxx]

12 He played an ancient ditty, long since mute, / In Provence called 'La belle dame sans merci'. [*Ib*. xxxiii]

13 The arras, rich with horseman, hawk, and hound, / Fluttered in the besieging wind's uproar; / And the long carpets rose along the dusty floor. [*Ib*. xl]

14 Fanatics have their dreams, wherewith they weave / A paradise for a sect. [*The Fall of Hyperion*, Bk I. 1]

15 Ever let the fancy roam, / Pleasure never is at home. [*Fancy*, 1]

16 Where's the cheek that doth not fade, / Too much gazed at? [*Ib*. 69]

17 Where's the face / One would meet in every place? / Where's the voice, however soft, / One would hear so very oft? [*Fancy*, 73]

18 God of the golden bow, / And of the golden lyre, / And of the golden hair, / And of the golden fire, / Charioteer / Of the patient year, / Where – where slept thine ire? [*Hymn to Apollo*]

19 Deep in the shady sadness of a vale / Far sunken from the healthy breath of morn, / Far from the fiery noon, and eve's one star, / Sat gray-haired Saturn, quiet as a stone. [*Hyperion*, Bk I. 1]

20 No stir of air was there, / Not so much life as on a summer's day / Robs not one light seed from the feathered grass, / But where the dead leaf fell, there did it rest. [*Ib*. I. 7]

21 O how frail / To that large utterance of the early Gods! [*Ib*. I. 50]

22 As when, upon a trancèd summer-night, / Those green-robed senators of mighty woods, / Tall oaks, branch-charmèd by the earnest stars, / Dream, and so dream all night without a stir. [*Ib*. I. 72]

23 A solitary sorrow best befits / Thy lips, and antheming a lonely grief. [*Ib*. III. 5]

24 Point me out the way / To any one particular beauteous star. [*Ib*. III. 99]

25 I stood tip-toe upon a little hill. ['*I stood tip-toe*', 1]

26 Here are sweet-peas, on tip-toe for a flight: / With wings of gentle flush o'er delicate white, / And taper fingers catching at all things, / To bind them all about with tiny rings. [*Ib*. 57]

27 Lorenzo, a young palmer in Love's eye. [*Isabella*, i]

28 Parting they seemed to tread upon the air, / Twin roses by the zephyr blown apart / Only to meet again more close. [*Ib*. x]

29 Why were they proud? again we ask aloud, / Why in the name of Glory were they proud? [*Ib*. xvi]

30 So the two brothers and their murdered man / Rode past fair Florence. [*Ib*. xxvii]

31 O cruelty, / To steal my Basil-pot away from me! [*Ib*. lxiii]

1 Oh what can ail thee, wretched wight, / Alone and palely loitering; / The sedge is withered from the lake, / And no birds sing. [*La Belle Dame sans Merci*, i]

2 I see a lilly on thy brow, / With anguish moist and fever dew; / And on thy cheek a fading rose / Fast withereth too.

I met a lady in the meads / Full beautiful, a faery's child; / Her hair was long, her foot was light, / And her eyes were wild. [*Ib.* iii]

3 She looked at me as she did love, / And made sweet moan. [*Ib.* vi]

4 And sure in language strange she said, / I love thee true. [*Ib.* vii]

5 And there I shut her wild, wild eyes / With kisses four. [*Ib.* viii (Lord Houghton's version)]

6 The latest dream I ever dreamed / On the cold hill side. [*Ib.* ix]

7 I saw pale kings and princes too, / Pale warriors, death-pale were they all; / Who cry'd – 'La belle Dame sans merci / Hath thee in thrall!'

I saw their starved lips in the gloam / With horrid warning gapèd wide, / And I awoke, and found me here / On the cold hill side. [*Ib.* x]

8 Real are the dreams of Gods, and smoothly pass / Their pleasures in a long immortal dream. [*Lamia*, I. 127]

9 Love in a hut, with water and a crust, / Is – Love forgive us! – cinders, ashes, dust. [*Ib.* II. 1]

10 Philosophy will clip an angel's wings. [*Ib.* II. 234]

11 Souls of poets dead and gone, / What Elysium have ye known, / Happy field or mossy cavern, / Choicer than the Mermaid Tavern? / Have ye tippled drink more fine / Than mine host's Canary wine? [*Lines on the Mermaid Tavern*]

12 Thou still unravished bride of quietness, / Thou foster-child of silence and slow time. [*Ode on a Grecian Urn*, i]

13 Heard melodies are sweet, but those unheard / Are sweeter; therefore, ye soft pipes, play on; / Not to the sensual ear, but, more endeared, / Pipe to the spirit ditties of no tone. [*Ib.* ii]

14 She cannot fade, though thou hast not thy bliss, / For ever wilt thou love and she be fair. [*Ib.*]

15 For ever piping songs for ever new. [*Ode on a Grecian Urn*, iii]

16 All breathing human passion far above, / That leaves a heart high-sorrowful and cloyed, / A burning forehead and a parching tongue. [*Ib.*]

17 To what green altar, O mysterious priest, / Lead'st thou that heifer lowing at the skies, / And all her silken flanks with garlands drest? / What little town by river or sea shore, / Or mountain-built with peaceful citadel, / Is emptied of this folk, this pious morn? [*Ib.* iv]

18 Thou, silent form, dost tease us out of thought / As doth eternity: Cold Pastoral! [*Ib.* v]

19 'Beauty is truth, truth beauty,' – that is all / Ye know on earth, and all ye need to know. [*Ib.*]

20 Leaving great verse unto a little clan. [*Ode to Maia*]

21 No, no, go not to Lethe, neither twist / Wolf's-bane, tight-rooted, for its poisonous wine. [*Ode on Melancholy*, i]

22 But when the melancholy fit shall fall / Sudden from heaven like a weeping cloud, / That fosters the droop-headed flowers all, / And hides the green hill in an April shroud; / Then glut thy sorrow on a morning rose. [*Ib.* ii]

23 She dwells with Beauty – Beauty that must die; / And Joy, whose hand is ever at his lips / Bidding adieu; and aching pleasure nigh, / Turning to Poison while the bee-mouth sips: / Ay, in the very temple of delight / Veiled Melancholy has her sovran shrine, / Though seen of none save him whose strenuous tongue / Can burst Joy's grape against his palate fine; / His soul shall taste the sadness of her might, / And be among her cloudy trophies hung. [*Ib.* iii]

24 My heart aches, and a drowsy numbness pains / My sense, as though of hemlock I had drunk. [*Ode to a Nightingale*, i]

25 Thou, light-winged Dryad of the trees, / In some melodious plot / Of beechen green, and shadows numberless, / Singest of summer in full-throated ease. [*Ib.*]

26 O for a draught of vintage! that hath been / Cooled a long age in the deep delvèd earth, / Tasting of Flora and the country green, / Dance, and Provençal song, and sunburnt mirth! / O for a

beaker full of the warm South, / Full of
the true, the blushful Hippocrene, / With
beaded bubbles winking at the brim, /
And purple-stainèd mouth; / That I
might drink, and leave the world unseen,
/ And with thee fade away into the forest
dim.

Fade far away, dissolve, and quite forget / What thou among the leaves hast
never known, / The weariness, the fever,
and the fret / Here, where men sit and
hear each other groan. [*Ode to a Nightingale*, ii]

1 Where youth grows pale and spectre-
thin, and dies; / Where but to think is to
be full of sorrow / And leaden-eyed
despairs. [*Ib.* iii]

2 Away! away! for I will fly to thee, / Not
charioted by Bacchus and his pards, /
But on the viewless wings of Poesy. [*Ib.*
iv]

3 I cannot see what flowers are at my feet, /
Nor what soft incense hangs upon the
boughs. [*Ib.* v]

4 Mid-May's eldest child, / The coming
musk-rose, full of dewy wine, / The
murmurous haunt of flies on summer
eves. [*Ib.*]

5 Darkling I listen; and, for many a time /
I have been half in love with easeful
death, / Called him soft names in many a
musèd rhyme, / To take into the air my
quiet breath; / Now more than ever it
seems rich to die, / To cease upon the
midnight with no pain, / While thou art
pouring forth thy soul abroad / In such
an ecstasy! / Still wouldst thou sing, and I
have ears in vain – / To thy high requiem
become a sod.

Thou wast not born for death, immortal Bird! / No hungry generations
tread thee down; / The voice I hear this
passing night was heard / In ancient days
by emperor and clown; / Perhaps the
self-same song that found a path /
Through the sad heart of Ruth, when,
sick for home, / She stood in tears amid
the alien corn; / The same that oft-times
hath / Charmed magic casements, opening on the foam / Of perilous seas, in
faery lands forlorn.

Forlorn! the very word is like a bell / To
toll me back from thee to my sole self!
[*Ib.* vi]

6 Thy plaintive anthem fades / Past the
near meadows, over the still stream, /

Up the hill-side; and now 'tis buried deep
/ In the next valley-glades: / Was it a
vision or a waking dream? / Fled is that
music: – Do I wake or sleep? [*Ode to a
Nightingale*, viii]

7 O latest born and loveliest vision far / Of
all Olympus' faded hierarchy. [*Ode to
Psyche*, 24]

8 Virgin-choir to make delicious moan /
Upon the midnight hours. [*Ib.* 30]

9 All the gardener Fancy e'er could feign, /
Who breeding flowers, will never breed
the same. [*Ib.* 62]

10 A bright torch, and a casement ope at
night, / To let the warm Love in. [*Ib.* 66]

11 Stop and consider! life is but a day; / A
fragile dew-drop on its perilous way /
From a tree's summit; a poor Indian's
sleep / While his boat hastens to the
monstrous steep / Of Montmorenci.
[*Sleep and Poetry*, 85]

12 O for ten years, that I may overwhelm /
Myself in poesy; so I may do the deed /
That my own soul has to itself decreed.
[*Ib.* 96]

13 A drainless shower / Of light is poesy;
'tis the supreme power; / 'Tis might half
slumbering on his own right arm. [*Ib.*
235]

14 They shall be accounted poet kings /
Who simply tell the most heart-easing
things. [*Ib.* 267]

15 There was a naughty Boy, / And a
naughty boy was he, / He ran away to
Scotland / The people for to see – / Then
he found / That the ground / Was as
hard, / That a yard / Was as long, / That
a song / Was as merry, / That a cherry /
Was as red – / That lead / Was as
weighty, / That fourscore / Was as
eighty, / That a door / Was as wooden /
As in England – / So he stood in his
shoes / And he wondered. [*A Song about
myself*]

16 Bright star, would I were steadfast as
thou art – / Not in lone splendour hung
aloft the night / And watching, with
eternal lids apart, / Like Nature's
patient, sleepless Eremite, / The moving
waters at their priestlike task / Of pure
ablution round earth's human shores.
[Sonnet: *Bright Star*]

17 Still, still to hear her tender-taken breath,
/ And so live ever – or else swoon to
death. [*Ib.*]

1 Happy is England, sweet her artless daughters; / Enough their simple loveliness for me. [Sonnet: *Happy is England*]

2 Four seasons fill the measure of the year; / There are four seasons in the mind of man. [*Ib. The Human Seasons*]

3 Much have I travelled in the realms of gold, / And many goodly states and kingdoms seen; / Round many western islands have I been / Which bards in fealty to Apollo hold. [*Ib. On First Looking into Chapman's Homer*]

4 Then felt I like some watcher of the skies / When a new planet swims into his ken; / Or like stout Cortez, when with eagle eyes / He stared at the Pacific – and all his men / Looked at each other with a wild surmise – / Silent, upon a peak in Darien. [*Ib.*]

5 It keeps eternal whispering around / Desolate shores. [*Ib. On the Sea*]

6 Mortality / Weighs heavily on me like unwilling sleep. [*Ib. On seeing the Elgin Marbles*]

7 There is a budding morrow in midnight, / There is a triple sight in blindness keen. [*Ib. To Homer*]

8 To one who has been long in city pent, / 'Tis very sweet to look into the fair / And open face of heaven. [*Ib. To one who has been long in City pent*]

9 O soft embalmer of the still midnight, / Shutting, with careful fingers and benign / Our gloom-pleased eyes. [*Ib. To Sleep*]

10 Turn the key deftly in the oilèd wards, / And seal the hushèd Casket of my Soul. [*Ib.*]

11 When I have fears that I may cease to be / Before my pen has gleaned my teeming brain. [*Ib. When I have fears*]

12 When I behold, upon the night's starred face, / Huge cloudy symbols of a high romance. [*Ib.*]

13 Then on the shore / Of the wide world I stand alone, and think / Till love and fame to nothingness do sink. [*Ib.*]

14 Verse, Fame and Beauty are intense indeed, / But Death intenser – Death is Life's high meed. [*Ib. Why did I laugh to-night?*]

15 In a drear-nighted December, / Too happy, happy tree, / Thy branches ne'er

remember / Their green felicity. [*Stanzas In a Drear-nighted December*]

16 But were there ever any / Writhed not at passed joy? [*Ib.*]

17 Season of mists and mellow fruitfulness, / Close bosom-friend of the maturing sun; / Conspiring with him how to load and bless / With fruit the vines that round the thatch-eaves run. [*To Autumn*, i]

18 To set budding more, / And still more, later flowers for the bees, / Until they think warm days will never cease, / For Summer has o'erbrimmed their clammy cells. [*Ib.*]

19 On a half-reapèd furrow sound asleep, / Drowsed with the fume of poppies, while thy hook / Spares the next swath and all its twinèd flowers. [*Ib.* ii]

20 Where are the songs of Spring? Ay, where are they? / Think not of them, thou hast thy music too. [*Ib.* iii]

21 Then in a wailful choir the small gnats mourn. [*Ib.*]

22 The red-breast whistles from a garden-croft; / And gathering swallows twitter in the skies. [*Ib.*]

23 A man should have the fine point of his soul taken off to become fit for this world. [Letter to J. H. Reynolds, 22 Nov. 1817]

24 I am certain of nothing but the holiness of the heart's affections and the truth of the imagination. – What the imagination seizes as beauty must be truth. [Letter to Benjamin Bailey, 22 Nov. 1817]

25 I have never yet been able to perceive how anything can be known for truth by consecutive reasoning – and yet it must be. [*Ib.*]

26 O for a life of sensations rather than of thoughts! [*Ib.*]

27 Negative Capability, that is, when a man is capable of being in uncertainties, mysteries, doubts, without any irritable reaching after fact and reason. [Letter to G. and T. Keats, 21 Dec. 1817]

28 There is nothing stable in the world; uproar's your only music. [Letter to G. and T. Keats, 13 Jan. 1818]

29 We hate poetry that has a palpable design upon us – and if we do not agree, seems to put its hand in its breeches pocket. Poetry should be great and un-

obtrusive, a thing which enters into one's soul, and does not startle or amaze it with itself, but with its subject. [Letter to J. H. Reynolds, 3 Feb. 1818]

1 Poetry should surprise by a fine excess, and not by singularity; it should strike the reader as a wording of his own highest thoughts, and appear almost a remembrance. [Letter to John Taylor, 27 Feb. 1818]

2 If poetry comes not as naturally as the leaves to a tree it had better not come at all. [*Ib.*]

3 Scenery is fine – but human nature is finer. [Letter to Benjamin Bailey, 13 Mar. 1818]

4 We read fine things but never feel them to the full until we have gone the same steps as the author. [Letter to J. H. Reynolds, 3 May 1818]

5 I compare human life to a large mansion of many apartments, two of which I can only describe, the doors of the rest being as yet shut upon me. [*Ib.*]

6 Were it in my choice I would reject a petrarchal coronation – on account of my dying day, and because women have cancers. [Letter to Benjamin Bailey, 10 June 1818]

7 I wish I could say Tom was any better. His identity presses upon me so all day that I am obliged to go out. [Letter to C. W. Dilke, 21 Sept. 1818]

8 I would sooner fail than not be among the greatest. [Letter to J. A. Hessey, 9 Oct. 1818]

9 I think I shall be among the English poets after my death. [Letter to G. and G. Keats, 14 Oct. 1818]

10 The roaring of the wind is my wife and the stars through the window pane are my children. [*Ib.*]

11 A poet is the most unpoetical of anything in existence, because he has no identity – he is continually informing and filling some other body. [Letter to R. Woodhouse, 27 Oct. 1818]

12 It is true that in the height of enthusiasm I have been cheated into some fine passages; but that is not the thing. [Letter to B. R. Haydon, 8 Mar. 1819]

13 A man's life of any worth is a continual allegory – and very few eyes can see the mystery of his life – a life like the scriptures – figurative. [Letter to G. and G. Keats, 14 Feb.–3 May 1819]

14 Shakespeare led a life of allegory; his works are the comments on it. [*Ib.*]

15 Call the world if you please 'The Vale of Soul-making'. [*Ib.*]

16 I have two luxuries to brood over in my walks, your loveliness and the hour of my death. O that I could have possession of them both in the same minute. [Letter to Fanny Brawne, 25 July 1819]

17 The only means of strengthening one's intellect is to make up one's mind about nothing – to let the mind be a thoroughfare for all thoughts. [Letter to G. and G. Keats, 17–27 Sept. 1819]

18 'If I should die', said I to myself, 'I have left no immortal work behind me – nothing to make my friends proud of my memory – but I have loved the principle of beauty in all things, and if I had had time I would have made myself remembered.' [Letter to Fanny Brawne, Feb. 1820(?)]

19 You might curb your magnanimity, and be more of an artist, and load every rift of your subject with ore. [Letter to P. B. Shelley, Aug. 1820]

20 Here lies one whose name was writ in water. [Epitaph, written by himself]

JOHN KEBLE   1792–1866

21 New every morning is the love / Our wakening and uprising prove. [*The Christian Year*, 'Morning']

22 We need not bid, for cloistered cell, / Our neighbour and our work farewell. / Nor strive to wind ourselves too high / For sinful man beneath the sky. [*Ib.*]

23 The trivial round, the common task, / Would furnish all we ought to ask; / Room to deny ourselves, a road / To bring us, daily, nearer God. [*Ib.*]

24 And help us, this and every day, / To live more nearly as we pray. [*Ib.*]

25 Sun of my soul! Thou Saviour dear, / It is not night if thou be near. [*Ib.* 'Evening']

1 Abide with me from morn to eve, / For without Thee I cannot live: / Abide with me when night is nigh, / For without Thee I dare not die. [*The Christian Year*, 'Evening']

2 Be every mourner's sleep tonight / Like infant's slumbers. pure and light. [*Ib.*]

3 The voice that breathed o'er Eden, / That earliest wedding day. [*Poems*, 'Holy Matrimony']

THOMAS KELLY   1769–1854

4 The Head that once was crowned with thorns / Is crowned with glory now. [Hymn]

J. P. KEMBLE   1757–1823

5 When late I attempted your pity to move, / Why seemed you so deaf to my prayers? / Perhaps it was right to dissemble your love, / But – why did you kick me downstairs? [*The Panel*, I. i (an adaptation of Isaac Bickerstaffe's comedy '*Tis Well 'tis no Worse*)]

THOMAS À KEMPIS   1380–1471

6 *Sic transit gloria mundi.* – Oh, how swiftly the glory of the world passes away! [*Imitation of Christ*, I. vi]

7 It is much safer to obey than to rule. [*Ib.* I. ix]

8 If you cannot mould yourself as you would wish, how can you expect other people to be entirely to your liking? [*Ib.* I. xvi]

9 Man proposes but God disposes. [*Ib.* I. xix]

10 Would to God that we might spend a single day really well! [*Ib.* I. xxiii]

JOHN KEMPTHORNE 1775–1838

11 Praise the Lord! ye heavens adore Him, / Praise Him, Angels in the height! [Hymn]

BISHOP THOMAS KEN
          1637–1711

12 Awake, my soul, and with the sun / Thy daily stage of duty run; / Shake off dull sloth, and joyful rise, / To pay thy morning sacrifice. [*A Morning Hymn*]

13 Redeem thy mis-spent time that's past; / Live this day, as if 'twere thy last. [*A Morning Hymn*]

14 Teach me to live, that I may dread / The grave as little as my bed. [*An Evening Hymn*]

15 Praise God from whom all blessings flow, / Praise him all creatures here below. [*A Midnight Hymn*]

WILLIAM KENDRICK   ?–1777

16 In durance vile. [*Falstaff's Wedding*, I. ii]

LADY CAROLINE KEPPEL
          1735–?

17 O! they're all fled with thee, / Robin Adair. [*Robin Adair*]

JOSEPH KESSELRING 1902–

18 Arsenic and Old Lace. [Title of play]

WILLIAM KETHE   ?–1608

19 All people that on earth do dwell, / Sing to the Lord with cheerful voice. [Hymn]

20 Praise, laud and bless his name always, / For it is seemly so to do. [*Ib.*]

21 His mercy is for ever sure. [*Ib.*]

FRANCIS SCOTT KEY 1779–1843

22 'Tis the star-spangled banner, O! long may it wave / O'er the land of the free and the home of the brave! [*The Star-Spangled Banner*]

SIDNEY KEYES   1922–1943

23 He never loved the frenzy of the sun / Nor the clear seas. / He came with hero's arms and bullock's eyes / Afraid of nothing but his nagging gods. [*Dido's Lament for Aeneas*]

24 There is no virtue now in blind reliance / On place or person or the forms of love. / The storm bears down the pivotal tree, the cloud / Turns to the net of an inhuman fowler / And drags us from the air. [*The Kestrels*]

SØREN KIERKEGAARD
1813–1855

1 *The Two Ways:* One is to suffer; the other is to become a professor of the fact that another suffered. [Auden, *Kierkegaard Anthology*, p. 20]

2 That is the road we all have to take – over the Bridge of Sighs into eternity. [*Ib.* 23]

3 Dread is a sympathetic antipathy and an antipathetic sympathy. [*Ib.* 134]

JOYCE KILMER
1888–1918

4 I think that I shall never see / A poem lovely as a tree. [*Trees*]

5 Poems are made by fools like me, / But only God can make a tree. [*Ib.*]

BENJAMIN KING
1857–1894

6 Nothing to do but work, / Nothing to eat but food, / Nothing to wear but clothes / To keep one from going nude. [*The Pessimist*]

7 Nowhere to fall but off, / Nowhere to stand but on! [*Ib.*]

HARRY KING
19 Cent.

8 Young men taken in and done for. [Title of song]

BISHOP HENRY KING
1592–1669

9 Stay for me there; I will not fail / To meet thee in that hollow vale. / And think not much of my delay; / I am already on the way. [*The Exequy*, 79]

10 But hark! My pulse like a soft drum / Beats my approach, tells thee I come. [*Ib.* 101]

STODDARD KING
1889–1933

11 There's a long, long trail a-winding / Into the land of my dreams. [*The Long, Long Trail*]

CHARLES KINGSLEY
1819–1875

12 Airly Beacon, Airly Beacon; / Oh the pleasant sight to see / Shires and towns from Airly Beacon, / While my love climbed up to me! [*Airly Beacon*]

13 Be good, sweet maid, and let who will be clever; / Do noble things, not dream them, all day long; / And so make Life, and Death, and that For Ever, / One grand sweet song. [*A Farewell. To C.E.G.*]

14 Do the work that's nearest, / Though it's dull at whiles, / Helping, when we meet them, / Lame dogs over stiles. [*Letter to Thomas Hughes*]

15 Oh! that we two were Maying. [*The Saint's Tragedy*, II. ix]

16 O Mary, go and call the cattle home / And call the cattle home, / And call the cattle home, / Across the sands of Dee. [*The Sands of Dee*]

17 I once had a sweet little doll, dears, / The prettiest doll in the world. [*Songs from The Water Babies*, 'My Little Doll']

18 When all the world is young, lad, / And all the trees are green; / And every goose a swan, lad / And every lass a queen; / Then hey for boot and horse, lad, / And round the world away: / Young blood must have its course, lad, / And every dog his day. [*Ib.* 'Young and Old']

19 Three fishers went sailing away to the west, / Away to the west as the sun went down. [*The Three Fishers*]

20 For men must work and women must weep, / And the sooner it's over, the sooner to sleep. [*Ib.*]

21 To be discontented with the divine discontent, and to be ashamed with the noble shame, is the very germ of the first upgrowth of all virtue. [*Health and Education*, 'The Science of Health']

22 Truth, for its own sake, had never been a virtue with the Romish clergy. Father Newman informs us that it need not, and on the whole ought not to be; that cunning is the weapon which Heaven has given to the saints wherewith to withstand the brute male force of the wicked world which marries and is given in marriage. Whether his notion be doctrinally correct or not, it is at least historically so. [Review of Froude's *History of England*]

23 He did not know that a keeper is only a poacher turned outside in, and a poacher a keeper turned inside out. [*The Water Babies*, Ch. 1]

221

1 As thorough an Englishman as ever coveted his neighbour's goods. [*The Water Babies*, 4]

2 Mrs Bedonebyasyoudid is coming. [*Ib.* 5]

3 The loveliest fairy in the world; and her name is Mrs Doasyouwouldbedoneby. [*Ib.*]

4 All the butterflies and cockyolybirds would fly past me. [*Ib.* 8]

5 More ways of killing a cat than choking her with cream. [*Westward Ho*, Ch. 20]

6 Some say that the age of chivalry is past, that the spirit of romance is dead. The age of chivalry is never past, so long as there is a wrong left unredressed on earth. [Attr.]

RUDYARD KIPLING   1865–1936

7 When you've shouted 'Rule Britannia', when you've sung 'God save the Queen', / When you've finished killing Kruger with your mouth. [*The Absent-Minded Beggar*]

8 He's an absent-minded beggar, and his weaknesses are great – / But we and Paul must take him as we find him. / He's out on active service, wiping something off a slate – / And he's left a lot of little things behind him! [*Ib.*]

9 Duke's son – cook's son – son of a hundred kings – / (Fifty thousand horse and foot going to Table Bay!). [*Ib.*]

10 Pass the hat for your credit's sake, and pay – pay – pay! [*Ib.*]

11 Back to the army again, sergeant, / Back to the army again, / Out o' the cold an' the rain. [*Back to the Army Again*]

12 Oh, East is East, and West is West, and never the twain shall meet, / Till Earth and Sky stand presently at God's great Judgment Seat; / But there is neither East nor West, Border, nor Breed, nor Birth, / When two strong men stand face to face, though they come from the ends of the earth! [*The Ballad of East and West*]

13 Four things greater than all things are, – / Women and Horses and Power and War. [*The Ballad of the King's Jest*]

14 And a woman is only a woman, but a good cigar is a smoke. [*The Betrothed*]

15 Oh, where are you going to, all you Big Steamers, / With England's own coal, up and down the salt seas? [*Big Steamers*]

16 (Boots – boots – boots – boots – movin' up and down again!) / There's no discharge in the war! [*Boots*]

17 I've a head like a concertina, I've a tongue like a button-stick, / I've a mouth like an old potato, and I'm more than a little sick. [*Cells*]

18 Teach us delight in simple things, / And mirth that has no bitter springs. [*The Children's Song*]

19 The coastwise lights of England watch the ships of England go! [*The Coastwise Lights*]

20 They know the worthy General as 'that most immoral man'. [*A Code of Morals*]

21 We know that the tail must wag the dog, for the horse is drawn by the cart; / But the Devil whoops, as he whooped of old: 'It's clever, but is it Art?' [*The Conundrum of the Workshops*]

22 Till the Devil whispered behind the leaves, / 'It's pretty, but is it Art?' [*Ib.*]

23 If once you have paid him the Dane-geld / You never get rid of the Dane. [*Danegeld*]

24 The 'eathen in 'is blindness bows down to wood and stone; / 'E don't obey no orders unless they is 'is own. [*The 'Eathen*]

25 Winds of the World, give answer! They are whimpering to and fro – / And what should they know of England who only England know? [*The English Flag*]

26 Something lost behind the Ranges. Lost and waiting for you. Go! [*The Explorer*]

27 For the female of the species is more deadly than the male. [*The Female of the Species*]

28 The Hun is at the gate! [*For All We Have and Are*]

29 What stands if Freedom fall? / Who dies if England live? [*Ib.*]

30 So 'ere's to you, Fuzzy-Wuzzy, at your 'ome in the Soudan; / You're a pore benighted 'eathen but a first-class fightin' man. [*Fuzzy-Wuzzy*]

31 'E's all 'ot sand an' ginger when alive, / An' 'e's generally shammin' when 'e's dead. [*Ib.*]

1 To the legion of the lost ones, to the cohort of the damned. [*Gentlemen-Rankers*]

2 Gentlemen-Rankers out on the spree, / Damned from here to Eternity. [*Ib.*]

3 The uniform 'e wore / Was nothin' much before, / An' rather less than 'arf o' that be'ind. [*Gunga Din*]

4 An' for all 'is dirty 'ide / 'E was white, clear white inside / When 'e went to tend the wounded under fire. [*Ib.*]

5 You're a better man than I am, Gunga Din! [*Ib.*]

6 If you can keep your head when all about you / Are losing theirs and blaming it on you. [*If –*]

7 If you can meet with Triumph and Disaster / And treat those two impostors just the same. [*Ib.*]

8 If you can talk with crowds and keep your virtue, / Or walk with kings – nor lose the common touch. [*Ib.*]

9 If you can fill the unforgiving minute / With sixty seconds' worth of distance run, / Yours is the Earth and everything that's in it, / And – which is more – you'll be a Man, my son! [*Ib.*]

10 There are nine and sixty ways of constructing tribal lays, / And – every – single – one – of – them – is – right! [*In the Neolithic Age*]

11 Then ye returned to your trinkets; then ye contented your souls / With the flannelled fools at the wicket or the muddied oafs at the goals. [*The Islanders*]

12 And I'd like to roll to Rio / Some day before I'm old! [*Just-So Stories*, 'The Beginning of the Armadilloes']

13 I keep six honest serving-men / (They taught me all I knew); / Their names are What and Why and When / And How and Where and Who. [*Ib.* follows 'The Elephant's Child']

14 We get the Hump – / Cameelious Hump – / The Hump that is black and blue! [*Ib.* 'How the Camel Got His Hump']

15 'Confound Romance!' ... And all unseen / Romance brought up the nine-fifteen. [*The King*]

16 For Allah created the English mad – the maddest of all mankind! [*Kitchener's School*]

17 An' I learned about women from 'er! [*The Ladies*]

18 For the Colonel's Lady an' Judy O'Grady / Are sisters under their skins! [*Ib.*]

19 Now this is the Law of the Jungle – as old and as true as the sky. [*The Law of the Jungle*]

20 We have had an Imperial lesson; it may make us an Empire yet! [*The Lesson*]

21 The Liner she's a lady, an' she never looks nor 'eeds. [*The Liner She's a Lady*]

22 There's a whisper down the field where the year has shot her yield, / And the ricks stand grey to the sun, / Singing:– 'Over then, come over, for the bee has quit the clover, / And your English summer's done'. [*The Long Trail*]

23 You have heard the beat of the off-shore wind, / And the thresh of the deep-sea rain; / You have heard the song – how long? how long? / Pull out on the trail again! [*Ib.*]

24 Pull out, pull out on the Long Trail – the trail that is always new! [*Ib.*]

25 There's a Legion that never was 'listed, / That carries no colours or crest. [*The Lost Legion*]

26 Predestination in the stride o' yon connectin'-rod. [*McAndrew's Hymn*]

27 Ye thought? Ye are not paid to think. [*Ib.*]

28 On the road to Mandalay, / Where the flyin'-fishes play, / An' the dawn comes up like thunder outer China 'crost the Bay! [*Mandalay*]

29 A-wastin' Christian kisses on an 'eathen idol's foot. [*Ib.*]

30 An' there ain' no buses runnin' from the Bank to Mandalay [*Ib.*]

31 Tho' I walks with fifty 'ousemaids outer Chelsea to the Strand, / An' they talks a lot o' lovin', but wot do they understand? [*Ib.*]

32 Ship me somewhere east of Suez, where the best is like the worst, / Where there aren't no Ten Commandments, an' a man can raise a thirst: / For the temple-bells are callin', an' it's there that I would be – / By the old Moulmein Pagoda, looking lazy at the sea. [*Ib.*]

33 And your rooms at college was beastly – more like a whore's than a man's. [*The 'Mary Gloster'*]

223

KIPLING

1 I've seen your carriages blocking the half o' the Cromwell Road, / But never the doctor's brougham to help the missus unload. [*The 'Mary Gloster'*]

2 Stiff-necked Glasgow beggar! I've heard he's prayed for my soul, / But he couldn't lie if you paid him, and he'd starve before he stole. [*Ib.*]

3 My new-cut ashlar takes the light / Where crimson-blank the windows flare. [*My New-cut Ashlar*]

4 And the end of the fight is a tombstone white with the name of the late deceased, / And the epitaph drear: 'A fool lies here who tried to hustle the East'. [*Naulahka*, heading to Ch. 5]

5 Daughter am I in my mother's house, / But mistress in my own. [*Our Lady of the Snows*]

6 The toad beneath the harrow knows / Exactly where each tooth-point goes; / The butterfly upon the road / Preaches contentment to that toad. [*Pagett M.P.*]

7 Brothers and Sisters, I bid you beware / Of giving your heart to a dog to tear. [*The Power of the Dog*]

8 Little Tin Gods on Wheels. [*Public Waste*]

9 God of our fathers, known of old, / Lord of our far-flung battle-line. [*Recessional*]

10 The tumult and the shouting dies; / The Captains and the Kings depart: / Still stands thine ancient sacrifice, / An humble and a contrite heart. / Lord God of Hosts, be with us yet, / Lest we forget – lest we forget! [*Ib.*]

11 Such boastings as the Gentiles use, / Or lesser breeds without the Law. [*Ib.*]

12 Brandy for the Parson, / 'Baccy for the Clerk; / Laces for a lady, letters for a spy, / Watch the wall, my darling, while the Gentlemen go by! [*A Smuggler's Song*]

13 'E's a kind of a giddy harumfrodite – soldier an' sailor too! [*Soldier an' Sailor too!*]

14 If blood be the price of admiralty, / Lord God, we ha' paid in full! [*The Song o' the Dead*]

15 'Let us now praise famous men' – / Men of little showing – / For their work continueth, / And their work continueth, / Broad and deep continueth, / Greater than their knowing! [*Stalky and Co.* 'School Song']

16 You may carve it on his tombstone, you may cut it on his card, / That a young man married is a young man marred. [*The Story of the Gadsbys*]

17 God gives all men all earth to love, / But, since man's heart is small, / Ordains for each one spot shall prove / Belovèd over all. / Each to his choice, and I rejoice / The lot has fallen to me / In a fair ground – in a fair ground – / Yea, Sussex by the sea! [*Sussex*]

18 For the sin ye do by two and two ye must pay for one by one! [*Tomlinson*]

19 Oh, it's Tommy this, an' Tommy that, an' 'Tommy, go away'; / But it's 'Thank you, Mr Atkins', when the band begins to play. [*Tommy*]

20 We aren't no thin red 'eroes, nor we aren't no blackguards too. / But single men in barracks, most remarkable like you; / And if sometimes our conduck isn't all your fancy paints, / Why, single men in barracks don't grow into plaster saints. [*Ib.*]

21 Of all the trees that grow so fair, / Old England to adorn, / Greater are none beneath the Sun, / Than Oak and Ash and Thorn. [*A Tree Song*]

22 How very little, since things were made, / Things have altered in the building trade. [*A Truthful Song*]

23 But a fool must follow his natural bent / (Even as you and I!). [*The Vampire*]

24 They shut the road through the woods / Seventy years ago. [*The Way Through the Woods*]

25 All the people like us are We, / And every one else is They. [*We and They*]

26 When the Earth's last picture is painted and the tubes are twisted and dried. [*When Earth's Last Picture*]

27 And, each in his separate star, / Shall draw the Thing as he sees it for the God of things as they are! [*Ib.*]

28 Your new-caught, sullen peoples / Half devil and half child. [*The White Man's Burden*]

29 Take up the White Man's burden – / And reap his old reward: / The blame of those ye better, / The hate of those ye guard. [*Ib.*]

1 'Ave you 'eard o' the Widow at Windsor / With a hairy gold crown on 'er 'ead? [*The Widow at Windsor*]

2 But you won't get away from the tune that they play / To the bloomin' old rag over 'ead. [*Ib.*]

3 He travels the fastest who travels alone. [*The Winners*]

4 Good hunting! [*The Jungle Book*, 'Kaa's Hunting']

5 The Cat. He walked by himself, and all places were alike to him. [*Just So Stories*, 'The Cat That Walked by Himself']

6 An Elephant's Child – who was full of 'satiable curtiosity. [*Ib.* 'The Elephant's Child']

7 You haf too much Ego in your Cosmos. [*Life's Handicap*, 'Bertran and Bimi']

8 What's the good of argifying? [*Ib.* 'On Greenhow Hill']

9 The Light that Failed. [Title of a novel]

10 Never praise a sister to a sister, in the hope of your compliments reaching the proper ears. [*Plain Tales from the Hills*, 'False Dawn']

11 The silliest woman can manage a clever man; but it needs a very clever woman to manage a fool. [*Ib.* 'Three and – an Extra']

12 But that is another story. [*Ib.*]

13 She was as immutable as the hills. But not quite so green. [*Ib.* 'Venus Annodomini']

14 Being kissed by a man who didn't wax his moustache was – like eating an egg without salt. [*Soldiers Three*, 'The Gadsbys, Poor Dear Mamma']

15 Steady the Buffs. [*Ib.*]

16 A member of the most ancient profession in the world. [*Ib.* 'On the City Wall']

17 I gloat! Hear me gloat! [*Stalky and Co.* Ch. 1]

18 Your Uncle Stalky. [*Ib.*]

19 'This man', said M'Turk, with conviction, 'is the Gadarene Swine.' [*Ib.* 'The Flag of Their Country']

20 'Tisn't beauty, so to speak, nor good talk necessarily. It's just IT. [*Traffics and Discoveries*, 'Mrs Bathurst']

21 Words are, of course, the most powerful drug used by mankind. [Speech, 14 Feb. 1923]

FRIEDRICH VON KLINGER 1752–1831

22 *Sturm und Drang.* – Storm and stress. [Title of a play]

FRIEDRICH KLOPSTOCK 1724–1803

23 God and I both knew what it [a passage in one of his poems] meant once; now God alone knows. [Attr. by Cesare Lombroso. Also ascribed to Browning]

CHARLES KNIGHT 20 Cent.

24 Here we are! here we are!! here we are again!!! / There's Pat and Mac and Tommy and Jack and Joe. / When there's trouble brewing, / When there's something doing, / Are we downhearted? / No! Let 'em all come! [*Here we are! Here we are again!!*]

MARY KNOWLES 1733–1807

25 He [Dr Johnson] gets at the substance of a book directly; he tears the heart out of it. [Boswell's *Life of Johnson*, 15 Apr. 1778]

JOHN KNOX 1505–1572

26 The First Blast of the Trumpet Against the Monstrous Regiment of Women. [Title of pamphlet]

RONALD KNOX 1888–1957

27 There once was a man who said, 'God / Must find it exceedingly odd / If he finds that this tree / Continues to be / When there's no one about in the quad'. [Limerick]

ARTHUR KOESTLER 1905–1983

28 The Yogi and the Commissar. [Title of book]

THOMAS KYD 1557–1595?

29 In time the savage bull sustains the yoke, / In time all haggard hawks will stoop to

lure, / In time small wedges cleave the hardest oak, / In time the flint is pierced with softest shower. [*The Spanish Tragedy*, I. vi]

1 Oh eyes, no eyes, but fountains fraught with tears; / O life, no life, but lively form of death; / Oh world, no world, but mass of public wrongs. [*Ib*. III. ii]

2 Why then, I'll fit you. [*Ib*. IV. i. 69. Quoted in T. S. Eliot's *Waste Land*, 431; followed by 'Hieronymo's mad againe']

3 My son – and what's a son? A thing begot / Within a pair of minutes, thereabouts, / A lump bred up in darkness. [*Ib*. III. xi. Anonymous additions]

HENRY LABOUCHERE
1831–1912

4 He [Labouchere] did not object, he once said, to Gladstone's always having the ace of trumps up his sleeve, but only to his pretence that God put it there. [Quoted in *Dictionary of National Biography*]

JEAN DE LA BRUYÈRE
1645–1696

5 Liberality lies less in giving liberally than in the timeliness of the gift. [*Les Caractères*, 'Du cœur', 47]

6 One must laugh before one is happy, or one may die without ever laughing at all. [*Ib*. 63]

7 Women run to extremes; they are either better or worse than men. [*Ib*. 'Des femmes', 53]

8 There are only three events in a man's life; birth, life, and death; he is not conscious of being born, he dies in pain, and he forgets to live. [*Ib*. 'De l'homme', 48]

9 The majority of men devote the greater part of their lives to making their remaining years unhappy. [*Ib*. 102]

10 A strict observer is one who would be an atheist under an atheistic king. [*Ib*. 'De la mode', 21]

11 Everything has been said, and we come too late after more than seven thousand years in which Man has existed and thought. [*Ib*. 'Des ouvrages de l'esprit' 1]

12 Making books is a skilled trade, like making clocks. [*Ib*. 3]

13 The pleasure of criticizing robs us of the pleasure of being moved by some very fine things. [*Les Caractères*, 'Des ouvrages de l'esprit', 20]

14 The former [Corneille] paints men as they should be, the latter [Racine] paints them as they are. [*Ib*. 54]

15 The punishment of a criminal is an example to the rabble; but every decent man is concerned if an innocent person is condemned. [*Ib*. 'De quelques usages', 52]

16 There are some who speak one moment before they think. [*Ib*. 'De la société et la conversation', 15]

JEAN DE LA FONTAINE
1621–1695

17 *Elle alla crier famine / Chez la fourmi sa voisine.* – She went to cry famine at her neighbour's the ant's. [*Fables*, I. 1, 'La Cigale et la Fourmi']

18 *La fourmi n'est pas prêteuse: / C'est là son moindre défaut.* – The ant is no lender; that is the least of her faults. [*Ib*.]

19 *Vous chantiez? j'en suis fort aise: / Eh bien, dansez maintenant.* – You sang? I am delighted. Well, dance now. [*Ib*.]

20 *Apprenez que tout flatteur / Vit aux dépens de celui qui l'écoute.* – Be advised that all flatterers live at the expense of those who listen to them. [*Ib*. I. 2, 'Le Corbeau et le Renard']

21 *Cette leçon vaut bien un fromage sans doute.* – That lesson is undoubtedly well worth a cheese. [*Ib*.]

22 *Mais quelqu'un troubla la fête.* – But someone disturbed the feast. [*Ib*. I. 9, 'Le Rat de Ville et le Rat des Champs']

23 *La raison du plus fort est toujours la meilleure.* – The stronger man's argument is always the best. [*Ib*. I. 10, 'Le Loup et l'Agneau']

24 *Plutôt souffrir que mourir, / C'est la devise des hommes.* – Rather suffer than die is man's motto. [*Ib*. I. 16, 'La Mort et le Bûcheron']

25 *Hé! mon ami, tire-moi de danger: / Tu feras après ta harangue.* – Well, my friend, get me out of danger. You can make your speech afterwards. [*Ib*. I. 19, 'L'Enfant et le Maître d'École']

26 *Je plie et ne romps pas.* – I bend but do not break. [*Ib*. I. 22, 'Le Chêne et le Roseau']

1 *Il faut, autant qu'on peut, obliger tout le monde: / On a souvent besoin d'un plus petit que soi.* – One should oblige everyone to the extent of one's ability. One often needs someone smaller than oneself. [*Fables*, II. 11, 'Le Lion et le Rat']

2 *Patience et longueur de temps / Font plus que force ni que rage.* – Patience and passage of time do more than strength and fury. [*Ib.*]

3 *C'est double plaisir de tromper le trompeur.* – It's a double pleasure to trick the trickster. [*Ib.* II. 15, 'The Coq et le Renard']

4 *Le plus âne des trois n'est pas celui qu'on pense.* – The greatest ass of the three is not the one you would think. [*Ib.* III. 1, 'Le Meunier, son Fils et l'Ane']

5 *Celui-ci ne voyait pas plus loin que son nez.* – This fellow did not see further than his own nose. [*Ib.* III. 5, 'Le Renard et le Bouc']

6 *En toute chose il faut considérer la fin.* – In all matters one must consider the end. [*Ib.*]

7 *Ils sont trop verts, dit-il, et bon pour des goujats.* – They are too green, he said, and only good for boobies. [*Ib.* III. 11, 'Le Renard et les Raisins']

8 *Chacun se dit ami: mais fou qui s'y repose; / Rien n'est plus commun que le nom, / Rien n'est plus rare que la chose.* – Everyone calls himself a friend, but only a fool relies on it; nothing is commoner than the name, nothing rarer than the thing. [*Ib.* IV. 17, 'Parole de Socrate']

9 *Ne t'attends qu'à toi seul; c'est un commun proverbe.* – Rely only on yourself; it is a common proverb. [*Ib.* IV. 22, 'L'Alouette et ses Petits avec le Maître d'un Champ']

10 *Une montagne en mal d'enfant / Jetait une clameur si haute / Que chacun, au bruit accourant, / Crut qu'elle accoucherait sans faute / D'une cité plus grosse que Paris: / Elle accoucha d'une souris.* – A mountain in labour shouted so loud that everyone, summoned by the noise, ran up expecting that she would be delivered of a city bigger than Paris; she brought forth a mouse. [*Ib.* V. 10, 'La Montagne qui accouche']

11 *Il m'a dit qu'il ne faut jamais / Vendre la peau de l'ours qu'on ne l'ait mis par terre.* – He told me never to sell the bear's skin before one has killed the beast. [*Fables*, V. 20. 'L'Ours et les deux Compagnons']

12 *Aide-toi, le ciel t'aidera.* – Help yourself, and heaven will help you. [*Ib.* VI. 18, 'Le Chartier embourbé']

13 *Ne soyons pas si difficiles: / Les plus accommodants, ce sont les plus habiles.* – Let us not be so difficult; the most accommodating are the cleverest. [*Ib.* VII. 4, 'Le Héron']

14 *Le lait tombe: adieu veau, vache, cochon, couvée.* – The milk falls, farewell calf, cow, pig, and clutch of eggs. [*Ib.* VII. 9, 'La Laitière et le Pot au Lait']

15 *Il faut s'entr'aider: c'est la loi de nature.* – People must help one another; it is nature's law. [*Ib.* VIII. 17, 'L'Âne et le Chien']

16 *Mais un fripon d'enfant (cet âge est sans pitié).* – But a rascally child – that is a pitiless age. [*Ib.* IX. 2, 'Les Deux Pigeons']

17 *Dieu fait bien ce qu'il fait.* – What God does, He does well. [*Ib.* IX. 4, 'Le Gland et la Citrouille']

18 *Ventre affamé n'a point d'oreilles.* – A hungry stomach has no ears. [*Ib.* IX. 18, 'Le Milan et le Rossignol']

19 *Mais les ouvrages les plus courts / Sont toujours les meilleurs.* – But the shortest works are always the best. [*Ib.* X. 14, 'Les Lapins']

ALPHONSE DE LAMARTINE
1790–1869

20 *Ô temps! suspends ton vol; et vous, heures propices! / Suspendez votre cours: / Laissez-nous savourer les rapides délices / Des plus beaux de nos jours!* – O time, suspend your flight, and you, happy hours, stay your feet! Let us savour the swift delights of our life's loveliest days! [*Le Lac*, 21]

21 *J'aimais les voix du soir dans les airs répandues, / Le bruit lointain des chars gémissant sous leur poids, / Et le sourd tintement des cloches suspendues / Au cou des chevreaux dans les bois.* – I loved voices drifting down the breeze at evening, the distant sound of carts creaking beneath their loads, and the dull jangling of bells hung on the goats' necks in the woods. [*Les Préludes*, 328]

A. J. LAMB 1870–1928

1 She's a bird in gilded cage. [Title of song]

LADY CAROLINE LAMB
1785–1828

2 Mad, bad, and dangerous to know. [(Byron) *Journal*]

CHARLES LAMB 1775–1834

3 For thy sake, Tobacco, I / Would do anything but die. [*A Farewell to Tobacco*, 122]

4 Gone before / To that unknown and silent shore. [*Hester*]

5 Angel-duck, angel-duck, winged and silly, / Pouring a watering-pot over a lily. [*Nonsense Verses*]

6 I have had playmates, I have had companions, / In my days of childhood, in my joyful school-days, – / All, all are gone, the old familiar faces. [*The Old Familiar Faces*]

7 Riddle of destiny, who can show / What thy short visit meant, or know / What thy errand here below? [*On an Infant Dying as soon as Born*]

8 Who first invented work and bound the free / And holiday-rejoicing spirit down? [*Work*]

9 Truths, which transcend the searching School-men's vein, / And half had staggered that stout Stagirite. [*Written at Cambridge*]

10 Good Master Raymund Lully, you look wise. Pray correct that error. [*Essays of Elia*, 'All Fools' Day']

11 Nothing is to me more distasteful than that entire complacency and satisfaction which beam in the countenances of a new-married couple. [*Ib.* 'A Bachelor's Complaint of Married People']

12 I have no ear. [*Ib.* 'A Chapter on Ears']

13 I even think that sentimentally I am disposed to harmony. But organically I am incapable of a tune. [*Ib.*]

14 'Presents', I often say, 'endear absents.' [*Ib.* 'A Dissertation upon Roast Pig']

15 We are nothing; less than nothing, and dreams. We are only what might have been, and must wait upon the tedious shores of Lethe millions of ages before we have existence, and a name. [*Essays of Elia*, 'Dream Children']

16 I hate a man who swallows it [his food], affecting not to know what he is eating. I suspect his taste in higher matters. [*Ib.* 'Grace before Meat']

17 C— [Coleridge] holds that a man cannot have a pure mind who refuses apple-dumplings. [*Ib.*]

18 I am, in plainer words, a bundle of prejudices – made up of likings and dislikings. [*Ib.* 'Imperfect Sympathies']

19 I have been trying all my life to like Scotchmen, and am obliged to desist from the experiment in despair. [*Ib.*]

20 You must beware of indirect expressions before a Caledonian. Clap an extinguisher on your irony, if you are unhappily blessed with a vein of it. [*Ib.*]

21 'A clear fire, a clean hearth, and the rigour of the game.' This was the celebrated wish of old Sarah Battle (now with God), who, next to her devotions, loved a good game at whist. [*Ib.* 'Mrs Battle's Opinions on Whist']

22 They do not play at cards, but only play at playing at them. [*Ib.*]

23 All people have their blind side – their superstitions; and I have heard her declare, under the rose, that hearts were her favourite suit. [*Ib.*]

24 She unbent her mind afterwards – over a book. [*Ib.*]

25 Man is a gaming animal. He must always be trying to get the better in something or other. [*Ib.*]

26 Boys are capital fellows in their own way, among their mates; but they are unwholesome companions for grown people. [*Ib.* 'The Old and the New Schoolmaster']

27 The human species, according to the best theory I can form of it, is composed of two distinct races, *the men who borrow* and *the men who lend*. [*Ib.* 'The Two Races of Men']

28 What a liberal confounding of those pedantic distinctions of *meum* and *tuum*! or rather what a noble simplification of language! [*Ib.*]

1 Your *borrowers of books* – those mutilators of collections – spoilers of the symmetry of shelves, and creators of odd volumes. [*Essays of Elia*, 'The Two Races of Men']

2 Not many sounds in life, and I include all urban and rural sounds, exceed in interest a knock at the door. [*Ib.* 'Valentine's Day']

3 Credulity is the man's weakness, but the child's strength. [*Ib.* 'Witches and other Night Fears']

4 How sickness enlarges the dimensions of a man's self to himself. [*Last Essays of Elia*, 'The Convalescent']

5 I love to lose myself in other men's minds. When I am not walking, I am reading; I cannot sit and think. Books think for me. [*Ib.* 'Detached Thoughts on Books and Reading']

6 Newspapers always excite curiosity. No one ever lays one down without a feeling of disappointment. [*Ib.*]

7 A poor relation – is the most irrelevant thing in nature. [*Ib.* 'Poor Relations']

8 It [a pun] is a pistol let off at the ear; not a feather to tickle the intellect. [*Ib.* 'Popular Fallacies', 9]

9 I would not call that man my friend who should be offended with 'the divine chitchat of Cowper'. [Letter to Coleridge, 5 Dec. 1796]

10 I came home ... hungry as a hunter. [Letter to Coleridge, Apr. 1800]

11 Separate from the pleasure of your company, I don't much care if I never see another mountain in my life. [Letter to Wordsworth, 30 Jan. 1801]

12 The man must have a rare recipe for melancholy, who can be dull in Fleet Street. [Letter to T. Manning, 15 Feb. 1802]

13 A little thin, flowery border round, neat, not gaudy. [Letter to Wordsworth, June 1806]

14 Nothing puzzles me more than time and space; and yet nothing troubles me less, as I never think about them. [Letter to T. Manning, 2 Jan. 1810]

15 Anything awful makes me laugh. I misbehaved once at a funeral. [Letter to Southey, 9 Aug. 1815]

16 His face when he repeats his verses hath its ancient glory, an Archangel a little damaged. [(Coleridge) Letter to Wordsworth, 26 Apr. 1816]

17 How I like to be liked, and what I do to be liked! [Letter to Dorothy Wordsworth, 8 Jan. 1821]

18 When my sonnet was rejected, I exclaimed, 'Damn the age; I will write for Antiquity!' [Letter to B. W. Proctor, 22 Jan. 1829]

19 What a lass that were to go a-gipsying through the world with. ['The Jovial Crew', *The Examiner*, July 1819]

20 The greatest pleasure I know is to do a good action by stealth, and to have it found out by accident. ['Table Talk by the late Elia', *The Athenaeum*, 4 Jan. 1834]

MARY LAMB   1764–1847

21 A child's a plaything for an hour. [*Parental Recollections*]

JOHN LAMBTON, EARL OF DURHAM   1792–1840

22 He said he considered £40,000 a year a moderate income – such a one as a man *might jog on with*. [Quoted in *Creevey Papers*]

WILLIAM JAMES LAMPTON   1859–1917

23 Same old slippers, / Same old rice, / Same old glimpse of / Paradise. [*June Weddings*]

LETITIA LANDON   1802–1838

24 As beautiful as woman's blush, – / As evanescent too. [*Apple Blossoms*]

WALTER SAVAGE LANDOR   1775–1864

25 Child of a day, thou knowest not / The tears that overflow thy urn. [*Child of a Day*]

26 Stand close around, ye Stygian set, / With Dirce in one boat conveyed! / Or Charon, seeing, may forget / That he is old and she a shade. [*Dirce*]

1 George the First was always reckoned /
Vile, but viler George the Second; / And
what mortal ever heard / Any good of
George the Third? / When from earth
the Fourth descended / God be praised,
the Georges ended! [*Epigram*]

2 I strove with none; for none was worth
my strife; / Nature I loved, and, next to
Nature, Art; / I warmed both hands
before the fire of life; / It sinks, and I am
ready to depart. [*I Strove with None*]

3 I loved him not; and yet now he is gone /
I feel I am alone. [*Maid's Lament*]

4 Mother, I cannot mind my wheel.
[*Mother, I cannot Mind my Wheel*]

5 Proud word you never spoke, but you
will speak / Four not exempt from pride
some future day. / Resting on one white
hand a warm wet cheek / Over my open
volume you will say, / 'This man loved
me!' then rise and trip away. [*Proud
Word You Never Spoke*]

6 Ah, what avails the sceptred race! / Ah,
what the form divine! [*Rose Aylmer*]

7 There is delight in singing, tho' none hear
/ Beside the singer. [*To Robert Browning*]

8 Browning! Since Chaucer was alive and
hale, / No man hath walked along our
roads with step / So active, so inquiring
eye, or tongue / So varied in discourse.
[*Ib.*]

9 The Siren waits thee, singing song for
song. [*Ib.*]

10 Laodameia died; Helen died; Leda, the
beloved of Jupiter, went before. [*Imaginary Conversations*, 'Aesop and Rhodope']

11 There are no fields of amaranth on this
side of the grave: there are no voices, O
Rhodope! that are not soon mute, however tuneful: there is no name, with
whatever emphasis of passionate love
repeated, of which the echo is not faint
at last. [*Ib.*]

GEORGE MARTIN LANE
1823–1897

12 The waiter roars it through the hall: /
'We don't give bread with one fish-ball!'
[*One Fish-Ball*]

ANDREW LANG   1844–1912

13 *I* am the batsman and the bat, / *I* am the
bowler and the ball, / The umpire, the
pavilion cat, / The roller, pitch, and
stumps, and all. [*Brahma* (imitation of
Emerson)]

14 The surge and thunder of the Odyssey.
[*The Odyssey*]

15 He uses statistics as a drunken man uses
lamp-posts – for support rather than
illumination. [Quoted in *Treasury of
Humorous Quotations*]

FREDERICK LANGBRIDGE
1849–1923

16 Two men look out through the same
bars: / One sees the mud, and one the
stars. [*Cluster of Quiet Thoughts*]

WILLIAM LANGLAND
1330?–1400?

17 In a somer seson whan soft was the
sonne. [*Piers Plowman*, B Text, Prologue,
1]

18 A faire felde ful of folke fonde I there
bitwene, / Of alle manner of men, the
mene and the riche, / Worching and
wandring as the worlde asketh. [*Ib.* 17]

19 Dowel, Dobet and Dobest. [*Ib.* B Text,
Passus 8]

20 'After sharpest shoures,' quath Pees,
'most sheene is the sonne; / Is no weder
warmer than after watery cloudes. [*Ib.*
C Text, Passus 21. 456]

ARCHBISHOP STEPHEN
LANGTON   ?–1228

21 *Veni, Sancte Spiritus, / Et emitte coelitus
/ Lucis tuae radium.* – Come, thou holy
Paraclete, / And from thy celestial seat /
Send thy light and brilliancy. [Transl.
J. M. Neale]

LAO-TZŬ   3 Cent. B.C.

22 The Way is like an empty vessel that yet
may be drawn from. [*Tao-tê-ching*, 4]

23 Heaven and earth are not ruthful; to
them the ten thousand things are but as
straw dogs. [*Ib.* 5]

BISHOP HUGH LATIMER
1485?–1555

1 Be of good comfort, Master Ridley, and play the man. We shall this day light such a candle by God's grace in England, as (I trust) shall never be put out. [Said when he and Ridley were about to be burned]

SIR HARRY LAUDER 1870–1950

2 I love a lassie. [Song]

3 Just a wee deoch-an-duoris / Before we gang awa' ... / If y' can say / It's a braw brecht moonlecht necht, / Yer a' recht, that's a'. [Song]

4 Keep right on to the end of the road. [Song]

5 O! it's nice to get up in the mornin', / But it's nicer to stay in bed. [Song]

6 Roamin' in the gloamin', / By the bonny banks of Clyde. [Song]

WILLIAM L. LAURENCE
1888–1977

7 At first it [the first atomic explosion] was a giant column that soon took the shape of a supramundane mushroom. [*New York Times*, 26 Sept. 1945]

D. H. LAWRENCE 1885–1930

8 Along the avenue of cypresses, / All in their scarlet cloaks and surplices / Of linen, go the chanting choristers / The priests in gold and black, the villagers. [*Giorno dei Morti*]

9 How beastly the bourgeois is especially the male of the species. [*How Beastly the Bourgeois Is*]

10 Too much of the humble Willy wet-leg / And the holy can't-help-it touch. [*Now It's Happened*]

11 A snake came to my water-trough / On a hot, hot day, and I in pyjamas for the heat, / To drink there. [*Snake*]

12 Not I, not I, but the wind that blows through me! / A fine wind is blowing the new direction of Time. [*Song of a Man Who Has Come Through*]

13 The English people on the whole are surely the *nicest* people in the world, and everyone makes everything so easy for everybody else, that there is almost nothing to resist at all. [*Dull London*]

14 It is as if the life had retreated eastwards. As if the Germanic life were slowly ebbing away from contact with western Europe, ebbing to the deserts of the east. [*A Letter from Germany*, 1924]

15 The autumn always gets me badly, as it breaks into colours. I want to go south, where there is no autumn, where the cold doesn't crouch over one like a snow-leopard waiting to pounce. The heart of the North is dead, and the fingers are corpse fingers. [Letter to J. M. Murry, 3 Oct. 1924]

T. E. LAWRENCE 1888–1935

16 I loved you, so I drew these tides of men into my hands and wrote my will across the sky in stars. [*Seven Pillars of Wisdom*, Dedication]

SIR AUSTEN HENRY LAYARD
1817–1894

17 ... If we sent the right man to fill the right place. [Speech in House of Commons, 15 Jan. 1855]

STEPHEN LEACOCK 1869–1944

18 It [the medicine] stood at the head of the bed on a bracket, and the nurse accidentally removed it from the bracket without changing the sign. [*Literary Lapses*, 'A, B, and C']

19 'A,' whispered C, 'I think I'm going fast.' 'How fast do you think you'll go, old man?' murmured A. 'I don't know,' said C, 'but I'm going at any rate.' [*Ib.*]

20 The landlady of a boarding-house is a parallelogram – that is, an oblong angular figure, which cannot be described, but which is equal to anything. [*Ib.* 'Boarding-House Geometry']

21 On the same bill and on the same side of it there should not be two charges for the same thing. [*Ib.*]

22 Electricity is of two kinds, positive and negative. The difference is, I presume,

231

that one comes a little more expensive, but is more durable; the other is a cheaper thing, but the moths get into it. [*Literary Lapses*, 'A Manual of Education']

1 He flung himself from the room, flung himself upon his horse and rode madly off in all directions. [*Nonsense Novels*, 'Gertrude the Governess']

2 The general idea, of course, in any first-class laundry is to see that no shirt or collar ever comes back twice. [*Winnowed Wisdom*, Ch. 6]

EDWARD LEAR   1812–1888

3 There was an Old Man in a tree, / Who was horribly bored by a bee; / When they said, 'Does it buzz?' / He replied, 'Yes, it does! / It's a regular brute of a bee!' [*Book of Nonsense*]

4 There was an Old Man who said, 'Hush! / I perceive a young bird in this bush!' / When they said, 'Is it small?' / He replied, 'Not at all! / It is four times as big as the bush!' [*Ib.*]

5 There was an Old Man with a beard, / Who said, 'It is just as I feared! – / Two owls and a hen, / Four larks and a wren, / Have all built their nests in my beard!' [*Ib.*]

6 'How pleasant to know Mr Lear!' / Who has written such volumes of stuff! / Some think him ill-tempered and queer, / But a few think him pleasant enough. [*Nonsense Songs*, Preface]

7 Who or why, or which or *what*, / Is the Akond of Swat? [*Ib.* 'The Akond of Swat']

8 On the coast of Coromandel / Where the early pumpkins blow, / In the middle of the woods / Lived the Yonghy-Bonghy-Bò. / Two old chairs, and half a candle, – / One old jug without a handle, – / These were all his worldly goods. [*Ib.* 'The Courtship of the Yonghy-Bonghy-Bò']

9 When awful darkness and silence reign / Over the great Gromboolian plain. [*Ib.* 'The Dong with a Luminous Nose']

10 When Storm-clouds brood on the towering heights / Of the Hills of the Chankly Bore. [*Ib.*]

11 The Dong! – the Dong! / The wandering Dong through the forest goes! / The Dong! – the Dong! / The Dong with a luminous Nose! [*Nonsense Songs*, 'The Dong with a luminous nose']

12 And who so happy, – O who, / As the Duck and the Kangaroo? [*Ib.* 'The Duck and the Kangaroo']

13 In spite of all their friends could say, / On a winter's morn, on a stormy day, / In a sieve they went to sea! [*Ib.* 'The Jumblies']

14 Far and few, far and few, / Are the lands where the Jumblies live; / Their heads are green, and their hands are blue, / And they went to sea in a sieve. [*Ib.*]

15 And they bought an Owl, and a useful Cart, / And a pound of Rice, and a Cranberry Tart. [*Ib.*]

16 The Owl and the Pussy-Cat went to sea / In a beautiful pea-green boat, / They took some honey, and plenty of money, / Wrapped up in a five-pound note. / The Owl looked up to the stars above, / And sang to a small guitar, / 'O lovely Pussy! O Pussy, my love, / What a beautiful Pussy you are!' [*Ib.* 'The Owl and the Pussy-Cat']

17 Pussy said to the Owl, 'You elegant fowl! / How charmingly sweet you sing! / O let us be married! too long we have tarried: / But what shall we do for a ring?' / They sailed away for a year and a day, / To the land where the Bong-Tree grows, / And there in a wood a Piggy-wig stood, / With a ring at the end of his nose. [*Ib.*]

18 'Dear Pig, are you willing to sell for one shilling / Your ring?' Said the Piggy, 'I will.' [*Ib.*]

19 They dined on mince, and slices of quince, / Which they ate with a runcible spoon; / And hand in hand, on the edge of the sand, / They danced by the light of the moon. [*Ib.*]

20 Ploffskin, Pluffskin, Pelican jee! / We think no Birds so happy as we! / Plumpskin, Ploshskin, Pelican jill! / We think so then and we thought so still. [*Ib.* 'The Pelican Chorus']

21 The Pobble who has no toes / Had once as many as we; / When they said, 'Some day you may lose them all'; / He replied – 'Fish fiddle de-dee!' [*Ib.* 'The Pobble who has no Toes']

1 He has gone to fish for his Aunt Jobis- ka's / Runcible Cat with crimson whiskers! [*Nonsense Songs*, 'The Pobble who has no Toes']

2 It's a fact the whole world knows, / That Pobbles are happier without their toes. [*Ib.*]

3 Two old Bachelors were living in one house; / One caught a Muffin, the other caught a Mouse. [*Ib.* 'The Two Old Bachelors']

4 There was an old man of Thermopylae, / Who never did anything properly; / But they said, 'If you choose / To boil eggs in your shoes, / You shall never remain in Thermopylae.' [*One Hundred Nonsense Pictures*]

5 Serve up in a clean dish, and throw the whole out of the window as fast as pos- sible. [*To make an Amblongus Pie*]

MARY LEASE   1853–1933

6 Kansas had better stop raising corn and begin raising hell. [Attr.]

LE CORBUSIER   1887–1965

7 *Une maison est une machine-à-habiter.* – A house is a machine for living in. [*Vers une architecture*]

HENRY LEE   1756–1818

8 First in war, first in peace, first in the hearts of his fellow countrymen. [(Wash- ington) Speech in House of Representa- tives, 1799]

NATHANIEL LEE   1655–1692

9 Then he will talk, – good gods, how he will talk! [*The Rival Queens*, I. iii]

10 When Greeks joined Greeks, then was the tug of war! [*Ib.* IV. ii]

11 Man, false man, smiling, destructive man. [*Theodosius*, III. ii]

RICHARD LE GALLIENNE
                                1866–1947

12 The cry of the Little Peoples goes up to God in vain, / For the world is given over to the cruel sons of Cain. [*The Cry of the Little Peoples*]

13 She's somewhere in the sunlight strong, / Her tears are in the falling rain, / She calls me in the wind's soft song, / And with the flowers she comes again. [*Song*]

14 What of the Darkness? Is it very fair? [*What of the Darkness?*]

H. S. LEIGH   1837–1883

15 That loathsome centipede, Remorse, / Invaded with a stealthy tread / My nasal organ. [*An Allegory, written in Deep Dejection*]

16 I wondered hugely what she meant, / And said, 'I'm bad at riddles; / But I know where little girls are sent / For telling taradiddles.' [*Only Seven*]

17 In form and feature, face and limb, / I grew so like my brother / That folks got taking me for him / And each for one another. [*The Twins*]

18 For one of us was born a twin / And not a soul knew which. [*Ib.*]

C. G. LELAND   1824–1903

19 I tont dink mooch of beoplesh / Dat goes mit demselfs alone. [*Breitmann Ballads*, 'Ballad']

20 She drawed him oonder der wasser, / De maiden mit nodings on. [*Ib.*]

21 Hans Breitmann gife a barty; / Dey had biano-blayin', / I felled in lofe mit a Merican frau, / Her name vas Madilda Yane. [*Ib.* 'Hans Breitmann's Barty']

22 Und efery dime she gife a shoomp / She make de vindows sound. [*Ib.*]

23 Dey rolled in more ash sefen kecks / Of foost-rate lager beer. [*Ib.*]

24 Hans Breitmann gife a barty – / Vhere ish dat barty now? / Vhere ish de lofely golden cloud / Dat float on de moun- dain's prow? [*Ib.*]

25 All goned afay mit de lager beer – / Afay in de ewigkeit! [*Ib.*]

NINON DE LENCLOS   1620–1705

26 *La vieillesse est l'enfer des femmes.* – Old age is woman's hell. [Attr.]

N. LENIN   1870–1924

1 It is true that liberty is precious – so precious that it must be rationed. [Attr.]

LUIS DE LÉON   1528?–1591

2 As I was saying the other day. [Resuming a lecture interrupted by five years' imprisonment]

ALAIN RENÉ LESAGE   1668–1747

3 Justice is such a fine thing that we cannot pay too dearly for it. [*Crispin rival de son maître*, IX]

4 They made peace between us; we embraced, and we have been mortal enemies ever since. [*Le Diable boiteux*, Ch. 3]

GOTTHOLD EPHRAIM LESSING   1729–1781

5 A man who does not lose his reason over certain things has none to lose. [*Emilia Galotti*, IV. vii]

6 Mocking laughter from Hell. [*Ib.* V. ii]

7 A single grateful thought raised to heaven is the most perfect prayer. [*Minna von Barnhelm*, II. vii]

8 Absolute truth belongs to Thee alone. [*Wolfenbüttler Fragmente*]

SIR ROGER L'ESTRANGE   1616–1704

9 It is with our passions as it is with fire and water, they are good servants, but bad masters. [*Aesop's Fables*, 38]

10 Though this may be play to you, 'tis death to us. [*Ib.* 398]

DUC DE LÉVIS   1764–1830

11 *Noblesse oblige.* – Nobility carries its obligations. [*Maximes et réflexions*]

G. H. LEWES   1817–1878

12 Murder, like talent, seems occasionally to run in families. [*Physiology of Common Life*, Ch. 12]

C. S. LEWIS   1898–1963

13 There must be several young women who would render the Christian life intensely difficult to him if only you could persuade him to marry one of them. [*Screwtape Letters, XIX*]

ROBERT LEY   1890–1945

14 *Kraft durch Freude.* – Strength through joy. [German Labour Front slogan]

GEORGE LEYBOURNE   ?– 1884

15 O, he flies through the air with the greatest of ease, / This daring young man on the flying trapeze. [*The Man on the Flying Trapeze*]

PRINCE DE LIGNE   1735–1814

16 *Le congrès ne marche pas, il danse.* – The Congress makes no progress, but it dances. [Remark on the Congress of Vienna]

GEORGE LILLO   1693–1739

17 There's sure no passion in the human soul, / But finds its food in music. [*Fatal Curiosity*, I. ii]

ABRAHAM LINCOLN   1809–1865

18 I intend no modification of my oft-expressed personal wish that all men everywhere could be free. [Letter, 22 Aug. 1862]

19 I claim not to have controlled events, but confess plainly that events have controlled me. [Letter, 4 Apr. 1864]

20 People who like this sort of thing will find this the sort of thing they like. [Of a book]

21 The ballot is stronger than the bullet. [Speech, 19 May 1856]

22 What is conservatism? Is it not adherence to the old and tried, against the new and untried? [*Ib.* 27 Feb. 1860]

23 In giving freedom to the slave, we assure freedom to the free, – honourable alike in what we give and what we preserve. [*Ib.* 1 Dec. 1862]

1 That this nation, under God, shall have a new birth of freedom; and that government of the people, by the people, and for the people, shall not perish from the earth. [Speech, 19 Nov. 1863]

2 An old Dutch farmer, who remarked to a companion once that it was not best to swap horses when crossing a stream. [*Ib.* 9 June 1864]

3 With malice toward none; with charity for all; with firmness in the right, as God gives us to see the right, let us strive on to finish the work we are in. [*Ib.* 4 Mar. 1865]

4 You can fool all the people some of the time, and some of the people all the time, but you cannot fool all the people all the time. [Attr. words in speech, 8 Sept. 1858]

5 The Lord prefers common-looking people. That is the reason he makes so many of them. [Attr. by J. Morgan]

N. VACHEL LINDSAY   1879–1931

6 Then I saw the Congo, creeping through the black, / Cutting through the jungle with a golden track. [*The Congo*, 1]

7 Mumbo-Jumbo is dead in the jungle. [*Ib.* 3]

GEORGE LINLEY   1798–1865

8 Oh, let the prayer re-echo: / 'God bless the Prince of Wales!' [*God Bless the Prince of Wales*]

9 Tho' lost to sight, to mem'ry dear / Thou ever wilt remain. [Attr. song]

W. J. LINTON   1812–1898

10 For he's one of Nature's Gentlemen, the best of every time. [*Nature's Gentleman*]

MAXIM LITVINOV   1876–1951

11 Peace is indivisible. [Said at Geneva]

LIVY   59 B.C.–A.D. 17

12 *Vae victis.* – Woe to the vanquished. [*History*, V. 48]

MARIE LLOYD   1870–1922

13 A little of what you fancy does you good. [Song]

14 I'm one of the ruins that Cromwell knocked about a bit. [Song]

15 Oh, mister porter, what shall I do? I / wanted to go to Birmingham, but they've carried me on to Crewe. [Song, words by Le Brunn]

ROBERT LLOYD   1733–1764

16 Slow and steady wins the race. [*The Hare and the Tortoise*]

D. LLOYD GEORGE   1863–1945

17 What is our task? To make Britain a fit country for heroes to live in. [Speech, 24 Nov. 1918]

JOHN LOCKE   1632–1704

18 New opinions are always suspected, and usually opposed, without any other reason but because they are not already common. [*Essay on the Human Understanding*, Dedication]

19 All men are liable to error; and most men are, in many points, by passion or interest, under temptation to it. [*Ib.* Ch. 20. 17]

FREDERICK LOCKER-LAMPSON   1821–1895

20 The world's as ugly, ay, as sin, / And almost as delightful. [*The Jester's Plea*]

21 And many are afraid of God – / And more of Mrs Grundy. [*Ib.*]

J. G. LOCKHART   1794–1854

22 Here lies that peerless peer Lord Peter, / Who broke the laws of God and man and metre. [*Epitaph for Lord Robertson*. Also attr. in slightly different form to Sir Walter Scott and Francis, Lord Jeffery]

THOMAS LODGE   1558?–1625

23 Love, in my bosom, like a bee, / Doth suck his sweet. [*Love, in my Bosom*. Also attr. to Robert Greene]

1 Devils are not so black as they are painted. [*Margarite of America*]

2 Heigh ho, would she were mine! [*Rosalind's Description*]

JOHN LOGAN   1748–1788

3 Thou hast no sorrow in thy song, / No winter in thy year. [*To the Cuckoo*, attr.]

CESARE LOMBROSO   1836–1909

4 The ignorant man always adores what he cannot understand. [*The Man of Genius*, Pt III. Ch. 3]

H. W. LONGFELLOW   1807–1882

5 I shot an arrow into the air, / It fell to earth, I know not where. [*The Arrow and the Song*]

6 And the song, from beginning to end, / I found again in the heart of a friend. [*Ib.*]

7 I know a maiden fair to see, / Take care! / She can both false and friendly be, / Beware! Beware! [*Beware!*]

8 I stood on the bridge at midnight, / As the clocks were striking the hour. [*The Bridge*]

9 Build me straight, O worthy Master! / Staunch and strong, a goodly vessel, / That shall laugh at all disaster, / And with wave and whirlwind wrestle! [*The Building of the Ship*]

10 Thou, too, sail on, O Ship of State! / Sail on, O Union, strong and great! / Humanity with all its fears, / With all the hopes of future years, / Is hanging breathless on thy fate! [*Ib.*]

11 Between the dark and the daylight, / When the night is beginning to lower, / Comes a pause in the day's occupations, / That is known as the Children's Hour. [*The Children's Hour*]

12 Singing the Hundredth Psalm, the grand old Puritan anthem. [*The Courtship of Miles Standish*, 3]

13 Archly the maiden smiled, with eyes overrunning with laughter, / Said, in a tremulous voice, 'Why don't you speak for yourself, John?' [*Ib.*]

14 The bards sublime, / Whose distant footsteps echo / Through the corridors of Time. [*The Day is Done*]

15 The cares that infest the day / Shall fold their tents, like the Arabs, / And as silently steal away. [*The Day is Done*]

16 This is the forest primeval. [*Evangeline*, 'Prelude']

17 Silently one by one, in the infinite meadows of heaven / Blossomed the lovely stars, the forget-me-nots of the angels. [*Ib.* I. iii]

18 Sorrow and silence are strong, and patient endurance is godlike. [*Ib.* II. i]

19 The shades of night were falling fast, / As through an Alpine village passed / A youth, who bore, 'mid snow and ice, / A banner with the strange device, / Excelsior! [*Excelsior*]

20 'Try not the pass!' the old man said; / 'Dark lowers the tempest overhead.' [*Ib.*]

21 Beware the pine-tree's withered branch! / Beware the awful avalanche! [*Ib.*]

22 A traveller, by the faithful hound, / Half-buried in the snow was found. [*Ib.*]

23 Giotto's tower, / The lily of Florence blossoming in stone. [*Giotto's Tower*]

24 Saint Augustine! well hast thou said, / That of our vices we can frame / A ladder, if we will but tread / Beneath our feet each deed of shame! [*The Ladder of St Augustine*]

25 The heights by great men reached and kept / Were not attained by sudden flight, / But they, while their companions slept, / Were toiling upward in the night. [*Ib.*]

26 Know how sublime a thing it is / To suffer and be strong. [*The Light of Stars*]

27 You would attain to the divine perfection, / And yet not turn your back upon the world. [*Michael Angelo*, I. v]

28 A boy's will is the wind's will, / And the thoughts of youth are long, long thoughts. [*My Lost Youth*]

29 Not in the clamour of the crowded street, / Not in the shouts and plaudits of the throng, / But in ourselves, are triumph and defeat. [*The Poets*]

30 Tell me not in mournful numbers, / Life is but an empty dream! / For the soul is dead that slumbers, / And things are not what they seem.

Life is real! Life is earnest! / And the grave is not its goal. / Dust thou art, to dust returnest, / Was not spoken of the soul. [*A Psalm of Life*]

1 Art is long, and Time is fleeting. [*Ib.*]

2 Trust no Future, howe'er pleasant / Let the dead Past bury its dead! / Act, – act in the living Present! / Heart within, and God o'erhead! [*Ib.*]

3 Lives of great men all remind us / We can make our lives sublime, / And, departing, leave behind us / Footprints on the sands of time. [*Ib.*]

4 Let us, then, be up and doing. / With a heart for any fate; / Still achieving, still pursuing, / Learn to labour and to wait. [*Ib.*]

5 There is a Reaper whose name is Death, / And, with his sickle keen, / He reaps the bearded grain at a breath, / And the flowers that grow between. [*The Reaper and the Flowers*]

6 Though the mills of God grind slowly, yet they grind exceeding small; / Though with patience He stands waiting, with exactness grinds He all. [*Retribution* (transl. of von Logau)]

7 A Lady with a Lamp shall stand / In the great history of the land. / A noble type of good, / Heroic womanhood. [*Santa Filomena*]

8 'Wouldst thou' – so the helmsman answered. – / 'Learn the secret of the sea? / Only those who brave its dangers / Comprehend its mystery!' [*The Secret of the Sea*]

9 Beside the ungathered rice he lay. / His sickle in his hand. [*The Slave's Dream*]

10 By the shining Big-Sea-Water. [*The Song of Hiawatha*, iii]

11 From the waterfall he named her, / Minnehaha, Laughing Water. [*Ib.* iv]

12 As unto the bow the cord is, / So unto the man is woman; / Though she bends him, she obeys him, / Though she draws him, yet she follows; / Useless each without the other! [*Ib.* x]

13 He seemed the incarnate 'Well, I told you so!' [*Tales of A Wayside Inn*, Pt 1, 'The Poet's Tale']

14 Our ingress into the world / Was naked and bare; / Our progress through the world / Is trouble and care. [*Ib.* 2, 'The Student's Tale']

15 Ships that pass in the night, and speak each other in passing; / Only a signal shown and a distant voice in the darkness; / So on the ocean of life we pass and speak one another, / Only a look and a voice; then darkness again and a silence. [*Tales of a Wayside Inn*, 3 'The Theologian's Tale']

16 There was a little girl / Who had a little curl / Right in the middle of her forehead; / And when she was good / She was very, very good, / But when she was bad she was horrid. [*There was a Little Girl*]

17 Under the spreading chestnut tree / The village smithy stands; / The smith, a mighty man is he, / With large and sinewy hands; / And the muscles of his brawny arms / Are strong as iron bands. [*The Village Blacksmith*]

18 Looks the whole world in the face, / For he owes not any man. [*Ib.*]

19 Something attempted, something done, / Has earned a night's repose. [*Ib.*]

20 It was the schooner Hesperus, / That sailed the wintry sea; / And the skipper had taken his little daughter, / To bear him company. [*The Wreck of the Hesperus*]

21 But the father answered never a word, / A frozen corpse was he. [*Ib.*]

ANITA LOOS   1893–1981

22 Kissing your hand may make you feel very, very good but a diamond and safire bracelet lasts for ever. [*Gentlemen Prefer Blondes*, Ch. 4]

FEDERICO GARCÍA LORCA
1899–1936

23 *A las cinco de la tarde. / Eran las cinco en punto de la tarde. / Un niño trajo la blanca sábana / a las cinco de la tarde.* – At five in the afternoon. It was exactly five in the afternoon. A boy brought the white sheet at five in the afternoon. [*Llanto por Ignacio Sánchez Mejías*]

LORD LOTHIAN   1882–1940

24 A limitation of armaments by political appeasement. [Letter to *The Times*, May 1934]

237

LOUIS XIV   1638–1715

1 *Ah! si je n'étais pas roi, je me mettrais en colère.* – Ah, if I were not king, I should lose my temper. [Attr.]

2 *Dieu, a-t-il donc oublié ce que j'ai fait pour lui?* – Has God then forgotten what I have done for him? [Attr., after the battle of Malplaquet]

3 *L'État c'est moi.* – I am the state. [Attr. to speech, 13 Apr. 1655]

4 *Il n'y a plus de Pyrénées.* – The Pyrenees are no more. [Attr. by Voltaire]

5 *J'ai failli attendre!* – I very nearly had to wait! [Attr.]

6 *Les premiers sentiments sont toujours les plus naturels.* – First feelings are always the most natural. [Reported by Mme de Sévigné]

LOUIS XVIII   1755–1824

7 *L'exactitude est la politesse des rois.* – Punctuality is the politeness of kings. [Attr.]

LOUIS-PHILIPPE   1773–1850

8 *La cordiale entente qui existe entre mon gouvernement et le sien* [Great Britain]. – The cordial understanding that exists between our two countries. [Speech, 27 Dec. 1843]

RICHARD LOVELACE   1618–1658

9 And when she ceased, we sighing saw / The floor lay paved with broken hearts. [*Gratiana Dancing and Singing*]

10 Lady, it is already morn, / And 'twas last night I swore to thee / That fond impossibility. [*The Scrutiny*]

11 Fishes, that tipple in the deep, / Know no such liberty. [*To Althea, From Prison*]

12 Stone walls do not a prison make / Nor iron bars a cage; / Minds innocent and quiet take / That for an hermitage. [*Ib.*]

13 Tell me not, Sweet, I am unkind, / That from the nunnery / Of thy chaste breast, and quiet mind, / To war and arms I fly. [*To Lucasta, Going to the Wars*]

14 Yet this inconstancy is such, / As you too shall adore; / I could not love thee, Dear, so much, / Loved I not honour more. [*Ib.*]

MARIA LOVELL   1803–1877

15 Two souls with but a single thought, / Two hearts that beat as one. [*Ingomar the Barbarian*, II (transl. of Friedrich Halm)]

ROBERT LOVEMAN   1864–1923

16 It is not raining rain to me, / It's raining violets. [*April Rain*]

SAMUEL LOVER   1797–1868

17 'There's luck in odd numbers,' says Rory O'More. [*Rory O'More*]

18 'Now women are mostly troublesome cattle to deal with mostly,' said Goggins. [*Handy Andy*, Ch. 36]

JAMES RUSSELL LOWELL   1819–1891

19 An' you've gut to git up airly / Ef you want to take in God. [*The Biglow Papers, First Series*, 1]

20 He's been true to *one* party – an' thet is himself. [*Ib.* 2]

21 A marciful Providence fashioned us holler, / O' purpose thet we might our principles swaller. [*Ib.* 4]

22 But libbaty's a kind o' thing / That don't agree with niggers. [*Ib.* 6]

23 An' in convartin' public trusts / To very privit uses. [*Ib.*]

24 I *don't* believe in princerple, / But oh, I *du* in interest. [*Ib.*]

25 I scent wich pays the best, an' then / Go into it baldheaded. [*Ib.*]

26 God makes sech nights, all white and still, / Fur'z you can look or listen. [*Ib. Second Series*, Introduction]

27 All kin' o' smily round the lips, / An' teary round the lashes. [*Ib.*]

28 My gran'ther's rule was safer 'n 't is to crow: / Don't never prophesy – onless ye know. [*Ib.* 2]

29 Of all the sarse that I can call to mind, / England doos make the most onpleasant kind: / It's you're the sinner 'ollers, she's the saint; / Wut's good's all English, all thet isn't ain't. [*Ib.*]

1 There comes Emerson first, whose rich words, every one, / Are like gold nails in temples to hang trophies on; / Whose prose is grand verse, while his verse, the Lord knows, / Is some of it pr – No, 'tis not even prose. [*A Fable for Critics*]

2 There comes Poe, with his raven, like Barnaby Rudge, / Three fifths of him genius and two fifths sheer fudge. [*Ib.*]

3 A wise scepticism is the first attribute of a good critic. [*Among My Books*, 'Shakespeare Once More']

4 There is no good in arguing with the inevitable. The only argument available with an east wind is to put on your overcoat. [*Democracy and Addresses*, 'Democracy']

5 The misfortunes hardest to bear are those which never come. [*Ib.*]

SAINT IGNATIUS LOYOLA
1491–1556

6 To give and not to count the cost; / To fight and not to heed the wounds; / To toil and not to seek for rest; / To labour and not ask for any reward / Save that of knowing that we do Thy will. [*Prayer for Generosity*]

LUCAN
39–65

7 *Victrix causa deis placuit, sed victa Catoni.* – The victorious cause pleased the Gods, but the conquered one pleased Cato. [*Pharsalia*, I. 128]

8 *Stat magni nominis umbra.* – There stands the shadow of a glorious name. [*Ib.* I. 135]

9 *Vivit post proelia Magnus, sed fortuna perit.* – Pompey lives after his battles, but his fortune has perished. [*Ib.* VIII. 84]

10 *Clarum et venerabile nomen / Gentibus.* – An illustrious name, revered by the nations. [*Ib.* IX. 203]

11 *Estne Dei sedes nisi terra, et pontus, et aer, / Et coelum, et virtus? Superos quid quaerimus ultra? Iupiter est quodcumque vides, quocumque moveris.* – Is the abode of God anywhere but in the earth, and sea, and sky, and air, and virtue? Why do we seek the heavenly ones beyond? Whatever you see, and whatever you touch, that is Jupiter. [*Ib.* IX. 578]

LUCRETIUS
99–55 B.C.

12 *Ergo vivida vis animi pervicit, et extra / Processit longe flammantia moenia mundi / Atque omne immensum peragravit, mente animoque.* – So the lively force of his mind has broken down all barriers, and he has passed far beyond the fiery walls of the world, and in mind and spirit has traversed the boundless universe. [*De Rerum Natura*, I. 72]

13 *Tantum religio potuit suadere malorum.* – Such are the heights of wickedness to which men are driven by religion. [*Ib.* I. 101]

14 *Nil posse creari / De nilo.* – Nothing can be created out of nothing. [*Ib.* I. 155]

15 *Stilicidi casus lapidem cavat.* – Constant dripping hollows out a stone. [*Ib.* I. 313]

16 *Suave, mari magno turbantibus aequora ventis, / E terra magnum alterius spectare laborem.* – Sweet it is, when on the high seas the winds are lashing the waters, to gaze from the land on another's struggles. [*Ib.* II. 1]

17 *Inque brevi spatio mutantur saecla animantum / Et quasi cursores vitai lampada tradunt.* – The generations of living things pass in a short time, and like runners hand on the torch of life. [*Ib.* II. 78]

18 *Ut quod ali cibus est aliis fuat acre venenum.* – What is food to one man is bitter poison to others. [*Ib.* IV. 637]

19 *Medio de fonte leporum / Surgit amari aliquid quod in ipsis floribus angat.* – From the heart of the fountain of delight rises a jet of bitterness that tortures us among the very flowers. [*Ib.* IV. 1133]

MARTIN LUTHER
1483–1546

20 *Esto peccator et pecca fortiter, sed fortius fide et guade in Christo.* – Be a sinner and strong in your sins, but be stronger in your faith and rejoice in Christ. [Letter to Melanchthon]

21 *Hier stehe ich, ich kann nicht anders.* – Here I stand, I cannot do otherwise. [Speech at the Diet of Worms, 1521]

22 *Ein' feste Burg ist unser Gott, / Ein gute Wehr und Waffen.* – A safe stronghold our God is still, / A trusty shield and weapon. [*Ein' feste Burg*, transl. T. Carlyle]

1 *Gedanken sind zollfrei.* – Thoughts pay no duty. [Motto of *Von weltlicher Obrigkeit*]

2 *Wer nicht liebt Wein, Weib und Gesang, / Der bleibt ein Narr sein Lebelang.* – Who loves not wine, woman and song, / Remains a fool his whole life long. [Attr.]

JOHN LYDGATE   1370?–1451?

3 Sithe of our language he was the lodesterre. [(Chaucer) *The Falls of Princes*, Prologue, 252]

JOHN LYLY   1554?–1606

4 Cupid and my Campaspe played / At cards for kisses, Cupid paid. [*Campaspe*, III. v]

5 What bird so sings, yet so does wail? / O 'tis the ravished nightingale. / Jug, jug, jug, jug, tereu, she cries. [*Ib.* V. i]

6 None but the lark so shrill and clear; / How at heaven's gates she claps her wings, / The morn not waking till she sings. [*Ib.*]

7 It seems to me (said she) that you are in some brown study. [*Euphues* (Arber Ed. p. 80)]

H. F. LYTE   1793–1847

8 Abide with me! Fast falls the eventide; / The darkness deepens: Lord, with me abide! / When other helpers fail, and comforts flee, / Help of the helpless, O abide with me! [Hymn]

9 Change and decay in all around I see; / O Thou, who changest not, abide with me! [*Ib.*]

GEORGE LYTTELTON 1709–1773

10 What is your sex's earliest, latest care, / Your heart's supreme ambition? – To be fair. [*Advice to a Lady*]

11 Where none admire, 'tis useless to excel;/ Where none are beaux, 'tis vain to be a belle. [*Soliloquy of a Beauty*]

EDWARD BULWER-LYTTON
1803–1873

12 Revolutions are not made with rosewater. [*The Parisians*, Bk V. Ch. vii]

13 Beneath the rule of men entirely great, / The pen is mightier than the sword. [*Richelieu*, II. ii]

14 In the lexicon of youth, which fate reserves / For a bright manhood, there is no such word / As – *fail*. [*Ib.*]

15 Life would be tolerably agreeable if it were not for its amusements. [Quoted in *Treasury of Humorous Quotations*]

EARL OF LYTTON *see under*
MEREDITH, OWEN

THE MABINOGION

16 He could see a tall tree on the river bank, and the one half of it was burning from its root to its tip, and the other half with green leaves on it. [*Peredur Son of Efrawg*]

ROSE MACAULAY   1889–1958

17 'Take my camel, dear', said my aunt Dot, as she climbed down from this animal on her return from High Mass. [*The Towers of Trebizond*, Ch. 1]

18 It was a book to kill time for those who like it better dead. [Quoted in *Treasury of Humorous Quotations*]

THOMAS BABINGTON
MACAULAY   1800–1859

19 Attend, all ye who list to hear our noble England's praise! / I tell of the thrice-noble deeds she wrought in ancient days. [*The Armada*]

20 The sentinel on Whitehall gate looked forth into the night. [*Ib.*]

21 Obadiah Bind-their-kings-in-chains-and-their-nobles-with-links-of-iron. [*The Battle of Naseby*]

22 Oh, wherefore come ye forth in triumph from the north, / With your hands, and your feet, and your raiment all red? / And wherefore doth your rout send forth a joyous shout? / And whence be the grapes of the wine-press which ye tread? [*Ib.*]

23 Press where ye see my white plume shine, amidst the ranks of war, / And be your oriflamme to-day the helmet of Navarre. [*Ivry*]

240

1 By those white cliffs I never more must see, / By that dear language which I spake like thee, / Forget all feuds, and shed one English tear / O'er English dust. A broken heart lies here. [*A Jacobite's Epitaph*]

2 One of us two, Herminius, / Shall never more go home. / I will lay on for Tusculum, / And lay thou on for Rome! [*Lays of Ancient Rome*, 'The Battle of Lake Regillus', xxvii]

3 These be the great Twin Brethren / To whom the Dorians pray. [*Ib.* xl]

4 Lars Porsena of Clusium / By the nine gods he swore / That the great house of Tarquin / Should suffer wrong no more. / By the Nine Gods he swore it, / And named a trysting day, / And bade his messengers ride forth, / East and west and south and north, / To summon his array. [*Ib.* 'Horatius', i]

5 Then out spake brave Horatius, / The Captain of the Gate: / 'To every man upon this earth / Death cometh soon or late. / And how can man die better / Than facing fearful odds, / For the ashes of his fathers, / And the temples of his Gods?' [*Ib.* xxvii]

6 Now who will stand on either hand, / And keep the bridge with me? [*Ib.* xxix]

7 Then none was for a party; / Then all were for the state; / Then the great man helped the poor, / And the poor man loved the great. [*Ib.* xxxii]

8 The Romans were like brothers / In the brave days of old. [*Ib.*]

9 Oh Tiber! father Tiber! / To whom the Romans pray, / A Roman's life, a Roman's arms, / Take thou in charge this day! [*Ib.* lix]

10 And even the ranks of Tuscany / Could scarce forbear to cheer. [*Ib.* lx]

11 Ye diners-out from whom we guard our spoons. [*Political Georgics* (letter to Hannah Macaulay, 29 June 1831)]

12 The object of oratory alone is not truth but persuasion. [*Essay on Athenian Orators*]

13 In order that he might rob a neighbour whom he had promised to defend, black men fought on the coast of Coromandel, and red men scalped each other by the Great Lakes of North America. [*Historical Essays*, 'Frederic the Great']

14 The business of everybody is the business of nobody. [*Historical Essays*, 'Hallam's Constitutional History']

15 The gallery in which the reporters sit has become a fourth estate of the realm. [*Ib.*]

16 Every schoolboy knows who imprisoned Montezuma, and who strangled Atahualpa. [*Ib.* 'Lord Clive']

17 They [the Nabobs] raised the price of everything in their neighbourhood, from fresh eggs to rotten boroughs. [*Ib.*]

18 The reluctant obedience of distant provinces generally costs more than it is worth. [*Ib.* 'Lord Mahon's War of the Succession']

19 The history of England is emphatically the history of progress. [*Ib.* 'Sir J. Mackintosh's History of the Revolution']

20 When some traveller from New Zealand shall, in the midst of a vast solitude, take his stand on a broken arch of London Bridge to sketch the ruins of St Paul's. [*Ib.* 'Von Ranke']

21 She [the Roman Church] thoroughly understands what no other Church has ever understood, how to deal with enthusiasts. [*Ib.*]

22 The Chief Justice was rich, quiet, and infamous [*Ib.* 'Warren Hastings']

23 The great Proconsul. [*Ib.*]

24 Thus our democracy was, from an early period, the most aristocratic, and our aristocracy the most democratic in the world. [*History of England*, I. Ch. 1]

25 He . . . felt towards those whom he had deserted that peculiar malignity which has, in all ages, been characteristic of apostates. [*Ib.*]

26 The Puritan hated bear-baiting, not because it gave pain to the bear, but because it gave pleasure to the spectators. [*Ib.* I. 2]

27 There were gentlemen and there were seamen in the navy of Charles the Second. But the seamen were not gentlemen; and the gentlemen were not seamen. [*Ib.* I. 3]

28 He [Rumbold] never would believe that Providence had sent a few men into the world ready booted and spurred to ride, and millions ready saddled and bridled to be ridden. [*Ib.* I. 5]

29 In every age the vilest specimens of human nature are to be found among demagogues. [*Ib.*]

1 Boswell is the first of biographers. [*Literary Essays*, 'Boswell's Life of Johnson']

2 The conformation of his mind was such that whatever was little seemed to him great, and whatever was great seemed to him little. [*Ib.* 'Horace Walpole']

3 An acre in Middlesex is better than a principality in Utopia. [*Ib.* 'Lord Bacon']

4 A sort of broken Johnsonese. [*Ib.* 'Madame d'Arblay']

5 The dust and silence of the upper shelf. [*Ib.* 'Milton']

6 As civilisation advances, poetry almost necessarily declines. [*Ib.*]

7 Perhaps no person can be a poet, or can even enjoy poetry, without a certain unsoundness of mind. [*Ib.*]

8 Nobles by the right of an earlier creation, and priests by the imposition of a mightier hand. [*Ib.*]

9 A propensity which, for want of a better name, we will venture to christen Boswellism. [*Ib.*]

10 We know no spectacle so ridiculous as the British public in one of its periodical fits of morality. [*Ib.* 'Moore's Life of Byron']

11 From the poetry of Lord Byron they drew a system of ethics, compounded of misanthropy and voluptuousness, in which the two great commandments were, to hate your neighbour, and to love your neighbour's wife. [*Ib.*]

12 We have heard it said that five per cent is the natural interest of money. [*Ib.* 'Southey's Colloquies']

13 The English Bible, a book which, if everything else in our language should perish, would alone suffice to show the whole extent of its beauty and power. [*On John Dryden*]

14 I shall not be satisfied unless I produce something that shall for a few days supersede the last fashionable novel on the tables of young ladies. [Letter to Macvey Napier, 5 Nov. 1841]

JOSEPH McCARTHY   20 Cent.

15 You made me love you, / I didn't want to do it. [Song]

242

GEORGE McCLELLAN 1826–1885

16 All quiet along the Potomac. [Attr., in the American Civil War]

JOHN MACRAE   1872–1918

17 In Flanders fields the poppies blow / Between the crosses, row on row. [*In Flanders Fields*]

GEORGE MACDONALD
1824–1905

18 Where did you come from, baby dear? / Out of the everywhere into here. [*At the Back of the North Wind*, Ch. 33, Song]

19 Where did you get your eyes so blue? / Out of the sky as I came through. [*Ib.*]

20 Here lie I, Martin Elginbrodde: / Hae mercy o' my soul, Lord God; / As I wod do, were I Lord God, / And ye were Martin Elginbrodde. [*David Elginbrod*, Bk I. Ch. 13]

CHARLES MACKAY   1814–1889

21 There's a good time coming, boys. [*The Good Time Coming*]

22 Cheer! Boys, cheer! [Title of song]

HENRY MACKENZIE   1745–1831

23 The Man of Feeling. [Title of novel]

SIR JAMES MACKINTOSH
1765–1831

24 Disciplined inaction. [*The Causes of the Revolution*, Ch. 7]

25 The Commons, faithful to their system, remained in a wise and masterly inactivity. [*Vindiciae Gallicae*]

FIONA MACLEOD
[WILLIAM SHARP]   1856–1905

26 How beautiful they are, / The lordly ones, / Who dwell in the hills, / In the hollow hills. [*The Immortal Hour*, ii]

27 My heart is a lonely hunter that hunts on a lonely hill. [*The Lonely Hunter*, vi]

NORMAN MACLEOD 1812–1872

1 Courage, brother! do not stumble, /
Though thy path be dark as night; /
There's a star to guide the humble: /
'Trust in God, and do the Right'. [Hymn:
Trust in God]

MARSHAL McMAHON 1808–1893

2 *J'y suis, j'y reste.* – Here I am and here I
stay. [Attr., at taking of Malakoff, 1855]

LEONARD McNALLY 1752–1820

3 On Richmond Hill there lives a lass, /
More sweet than May day morn, / Whose
charms all other maids surpass, / A rose
without a thorn. [*The Lass of Richmond
Hill*]

LOUIS MACNEICE 1907–1963

4 It's no go the merrygoround, it's no go
the rickshaw, / All we want is a limousine
and a ticket for the peepshow. / Their
knickers are made of crêpe-de-chine, their
shoes are made of python, / Their halls
are lined with tiger rugs and their walls
with heads of bison. [*Bagpipe Music*]

5 It's no go, my honey love, it's no go, my
poppet; / Work your hands from day to
day, the winds will blow the profit. / The
glass is falling hour by hour, the glass will
fall for ever, / But if you break the bloody
glass you won't hold up the weather. [*Ib.*]

6 Between the enormous fluted Ionic
columns / There seeps from heavily
jowled or hawk-like foreign faces / The
guttural sorrow of the refugees. [*The
British Museum Reading Room*]

7 When our brother Fire was having his
dog's day / Jumping the London streets
with millions of tin cans / Clanking at his
tail, we heard some shadow say / 'Give
the dog a bone'. [*Brother Fire*]

8 Crumbling between the fingers, under the
feet, / Crumbling behind the eyes, /
Their world gives way and dies / And
something twangs and breaks at the end
of the street. [*Débâcle*]

JAMES MACPHERSON
1736–1796

9 They came forth to war, but they always
fell. [*Ossian*, 'Cath-Loda', 2]

MAURICE DE MAETERLINCK
1862–1949

10 *Il n'y a pas de morts.* – There are no dead.
[*L'Oiseau bleu*, IV. ii]

MAGNA CHARTA 1215

11 *Nisi per legale iudicium parium suorum vel
per legem terrae.* – Except by the legal
judgement of his equals or the law of the
land. [Clause 39]

F. S. MAHONY *see*
PROUT, FATHER

JOSEPH DE MAISTRE 1754–1821

12 Every nation has the government that it
deserves. [Letter on the subject of
Russia, Aug. 1811]

13 Scratch the Russian and you will find the
Tartar. [Attr. also to Napoleon and
Prince de Ligne]

FRANÇOIS DE MALHERBE
1555–1628

14 *Mais elle était du monde où les plus
belles choses / Ont le pire destin; / Et
rose, elle a vécu ce que vivent les roses, /
L'espace d'un matin.* – But she was of the
world where the fairest things have the
worst fate, Like a rose, she has lived as
long as roses live, the space of one
morning. [*Consolation à M. du Périer*]

STÉPHANE MALLARMÉ
1842–1898

15 *La chair est triste, hélas! et j'ai lu tous les
livres.* – The flesh, alas, is sad, and I have
read all the books. [*Brise marine*]

16 *Mais ô mon cœur, entends le chant des
matelots.* – But, oh my soul, hear the
song of the sailors. [*Ib.*]

17 *Donner un sens plus pur aux mots de la
tribu.* – To give a purer sense to the
language of the tribe. [*Le Tombeau
d'Edgar Poe*]

SIR THOMAS MALORY ?–1471

18 Whoso pulleth out this sword of this
stone and anvil is rightwise king born of

all England. [*Morte d'Arthur*, Bk I. Ch. 4]

1 This beast went to the well and drank, and the noise was in the beast's belly like unto the questing of thirty couple hounds, but all the while the beast drank there was no noise in the beast's belly. [*Ib.* I. 19]

2 King Pellinore that time followed the questing beast. [*Ib.*]

3 So they rode till they came to a lake that was a fair water and broad. And in the midst Arthur was ware of an arm clothed in white samite, that held a fair sword in that hand. [*Ib.* I. 25]

4 What, nephew, said the king, is the wind in that door? [*Ib.* VII. 34]

5 And anon there came in a dove at a window, and in her mouth there seemed a little censer of gold, and therewithal there was such a savour as all the spicery of the world had been there. [*Ib.* XI. 2]

6 For, as I suppose, no man in this world hath lived better than I have done, to achieve that I have done. [*Ib.* XVII. 16]

7 The month of May was come, when every lusty heart beginneth to blossom, and to bring forth fruit. [*Ib.* XVIII. 25]

8 For love that time was not as love is nowadays. [*Ib.* XX. 3]

9 And much more am I sorrier for my good knights' loss than for the loss of my fair queen; for queens I might have enough, but such a fellowship of good knights shall never be together in no company. [*Ib.* XX. 9]

10 I saw nothing but waters wap [lap] and waves wanne [come]. [*Ib.* XXI. 5]

11 Through this same man and me hath all this war been wrought, and the death of the most noblest knights of the world; for through our love that we have loved together is my most noble lord slain. [*Ib.* XXI. 9]

12 For as well as I have loved thee heretofore, mine heart will not serve now to see thee; for through thee and me is the flower of kings and knights destroyed. [*Ib.*]

13 Then Sir Launcelot saw her visage, but he wept not greatly, but sighed! [*Ib.* XXI. 11]

14 Thou wert never matched of earthly knight's hand. ... And thou wert the

truest friend to thy lover that ever bestrad horse, and thou wert the truest lover of a sinful man that ever loved woman; and thou wert the kindest man that ever struck with sword. And thou wert the goodliest person that ever came among press of knights; and thou wert the meekest man and the gentlest that ever ate in hall among ladies, and thou wert the sternest knight to thy mortal foe that ever put spear in the rest. [*Morte d'Arthur*, XXI. 13]

T. R. MALTHUS 1766–1834

15 The perpetual struggle for room and food. [*On Population*, Ch. 3]

W. R. MANDALE 19 Cent.

16 Up and down the City Road, / In and out the Eagle, / That's the way the money goes – / Pop goes the weasel! [*Pop Goes the Weasel*]

J. C. MANGAN 1803–1849

17 My Dark Rosaleen! [Title of poem]

LORD JOHN MANNERS 1818–1906

18 Let wealth and commerce, laws and learning die, / But leave us still our old nobility. [*England's Trust*, Pt III. 227]

WALTER MAP c. 1140–c. 1209

19 If die I must, let me die drinking in an inn. [*De Nugis Curialium*]

MARCUS AURELIUS ANTONINUS *see under* **AURELIUS**

WILLIAM MARCY 1786–1857

20 They see nothing wrong in the rule that to the victors belong the spoils of the enemy. [Speech in U.S. Senate, Jan. 1832]

QUEEN MARIE-ANTOINETTE 1755–1793

21 *Qu'ils mangent de la brioche.* – Let them eat cake. [Attr. (on being told that the people could not afford bread) In fact a remark found earlier]

CHRISTOPHER MARLOWE
1564–1593

1 Live and die in Aristotle's works. [*Doctor Faustus*, 33]

2 I'll have them fly to India for gold, / Ransack the ocean for orient pearl. [*Ib.* 110]

3 Unhappy spirits that fell with Lucifer, / Conspired against our God with Lucifer, / And are for ever damned with Lucifer. [*Ib.* 310]

4 Hell hath no limits, nor is circumscribed / In one self place; for where we are is hell, / And where hell is, must we ever be. [*Ib.* 560]

5 When all the world dissolves, / And every creature shall be purified, / All place shall be hell that is not heaven. [*Ib.* 563]

6 Was this the face that launched a thousand ships, / And burnt the topless towers of Ilium? / Sweet Helen, make me immortal with a kiss! / Her lips suck forth my soul: see, where it flies! – / Come, Helen, come give me my soul again. / Here will I dwell, for heaven be in these lips, / And all is dross that is not Helena. [*Ib.* 1354]

7 Oh, thou art fairer than the evening air / Clad in the beauty of a thousand stars. [*Ib.* 1367]

8 Now hast thou but one bare hour to live / And then thou must be damned perpetually! / Stand still, you ever-moving spheres of heaven, / That time may cease and midnight never come. [*Ib.* 1450]

9 *O lente, lente currite noctis equi!* / The stars move still, time runs, the clock will strike, / The devil will come, and Faustus must be damned. / Oh, I'll leap up to my God! Who pulls me down? / See, see, where Christ's blood streams in the firmament! / One drop would save my soul, half a drop: ah, my Christ! [*Ib.* 1458]

10 You stars that reigned at my nativity, / Whose influence hath allotted death and hell, / Now draw up Faustus, like a foggy mist, / Into the entrails of yon labouring cloud. [*Ib.* 1473]

11 O soul, be changed into little waterdrops, / And fall into the ocean, ne'er be found! [*Ib.* 1502]

12 Ugly hell, gape not! come not, Lucifer! / I'll burn my books! [*Doctor Faustus*, 1506]

13 Cut is the branch that might have grown full straight, / And burnèd is Apollo's laurel-bough, / That sometime grew within this learnèd man. [*Ib.* 1508]

14 My men like satyrs grazing on the lawns, / Shall with their goat-feet dance an antic hay. [*Edward II*, I. i. 59]

15 I count religion but a childish toy, / And hold there is no sin but ignorance. [*The Jew of Malta*, Prologue, 14]

16 As their wealth increaseth, so enclose / Infinite riches in a little room. [*Ib.* I. 36]

17 I'm arm'd with more than complete steel – / The justice of my quarrel. [*Lust's Dominion*, IV. iii. Authorship of play doubtful]

18 Jigging veins of rhyming mother wits. [*Tamburlaine the Great*, Prologue]

19 Our swords shall play the orators for us. [*Ib.* Pt 1. I. ii. 132]

20 Accursed be he that first invented war. [*Ib.* 1. II. iv. 1]

21 Is it not passing brave to be a king, / And ride in triumph through Persepolis? [*Ib.* 1. II. v. 53]

22 Ah, fair Zenocrate! – divine Zenocrate! / Fair is too foul an epithet for thee. [*Ib.* 1. V. i. 135]

23 Yet should there hover in their restless heads / One thought, one grace, one wonder, at the least, / Which into words no virtue can digest. [*Ib.* 1. V. i. 171]

24 Now walk the angels on the walls of heaven, / As sentinels to warn th' immortal souls / To entertain divine Zenocrate. [*Ib.* 2. II. iv. 15]

25 Yet let me kiss my lord before I die, / And let me die with kissing of my lord. [*Ib.* 2. II. iv. 69]

26 Holla, ye pampered jades of Asia! / What, can ye draw but twenty miles a day? [*Ib.* 2. IV. iii. 1]

27 For Tamburlaine, the scourge of God, must die. [*Ib.* 2. V. iii. 249]

28 Who ever loved, that loved not at first sight? [*Hero and Leander*, I. 176]

1 Come live with me and be my love, / And we will all the pleasures prove / That hills and valleys, dales and fields, / Woods, or steepy mountain yields. [*The Passionate Shepherd to his Love*]

2 By shallow rivers to whose falls / Melodious birds sing madrigals. [*Ib.*]

3 And I will make thee beds of roses / And a thousand fragrant posies. [*Ib.*]

CLÉMENT MAROT 1495–1544

4 *Pipeur, larron, jureur, blasphémateur, / Sentant la hart de cent pas à la ronde, / Au demeurant le meilleur fils du monde.* – A cheat, a thief, a swearer and blasphemer, who smelt of the rope from a hundred yards away, but for the rest the best lad in the world. [*Épitres*, XXIX]

DON MARQUIS 1878–1937

5 now and then / there is a person born / who is so unlucky / that he runs into accidents / which started out to happen / to somebody else [*archy's life of mehitabel*, 'archy the cockroach says']

6 toujours gai, archy, toujours gai [*Ib.* 'the life of mehitabel the cat']

7 Ours is a world where people don't know what they want and are willing to go through hell to get it. [Quoted in *Treasury of Humorous Quotations*]

CAPTAIN FREDERICK MARRYAT 1792–1848

8 As savage as a bear with a sore head. [*The King's Own*, Ch. 26]

9 If you please, ma'am, it was a very little one. [(Excusing an illegitimate baby) *Midshipman Easy*, Ch. 3]

10 All zeal, Mr Easy. [*Ib.* 9]

11 It's just six of one and half-a-dozen of the other. [*The Pirate*, Ch. 4]

12 Every man paddle his own canoe. [*Settlers in Canada*, Ch. 8]

T. R. MARSHALL 1854–1925

13 What this country needs is a good five-cent cigar. [Said to John Crockett]

MARTIAL c. 40–c. 104

14 *Laudant illa sed ista legunt.* – Those they praise, but they read the others. [*Epigrammata*, IV. 49]

15 *Non est vivere, sed valere vita est.* – Life is not living, but being in health. [*Ib.* VI. 70]

16 *Rus in urbe.* – The country in town. [*Ib.* XII. 57]

ANDREW MARVELL 1621–1678

17 Where the remote Bermudas ride, / In the ocean's bosom unespied. [*Bermudas*, 1]

18 He hangs in shades the orange bright, / Like golden lamps in a green night. [*Ib.* 17]

19 Echo beyond the Mexique Bay. [*Ib.* 36]

20 My love is of a birth as rare / As 'tis, for object, strange and high; / It was begotten by despair, / Upon impossibility. [*The Definition of Love*]

21 As lines, so loves oblique, may well / Themselves in every angle greet : / But ours so truly parallel, / Though infinite, can never meet.

Therefore the love which us doth bind, / But Fate so enviously debars, / Is the conjunction of the mind, / And opposition of the stars. [*Ib.*]

22 Earth cannot show so brave a sight, / As when a single soul does fence / The batteries of alluring sense / And Heaven views it with delight. [*A Dialogue between the Resolved Soul and Created Pleasure*, 45]

23 How vainly men themselves amaze, / To win the palm, the oak, or bays; / And their incessant labours see / Crowned from some single herb or tree. [*The Garden*, 1]

24 Fair quiet, have I found thee here / And innocence thy sister dear ? [*Ib.* 9]

25 The nectarine, and curious peach, / Into my hands themselves do reach; / Stumbling on melons, as I pass, / Ensnared with flowers, I fall on grass. [*Ib.* 37]

26 The mind, that ocean where each kind / Does straight its own resemblance find; / Yet it creates, transcending these, / Far

other worlds, and other seas, / Annihilating all that's made / To a green thought in a green shade. [*The Garden*, 41]

1 Here at the fountain's sliding foot, / Or at some fruit tree's mossy root, / Casting the body's vest aside, / My soul into the boughs does glide. [*Ib.* 49]

2 But 'twas beyond a mortal's share / To wander solitary there: / Two paradises 'twere in one, / To live in paradise alone. [*Ib.* 61]

3 The inglorious arts of peace. [*Horatian Ode upon Cromwell's Return from Ireland*, 10]

4 He nothing common did, or mean, / Upon that memorable scene, / But with his keener eye / The axe's edge did try. [*Ib.* 57]

5 So much one man can do / That does both act and know. [*Ib.* 75]

6 Ye country comets, that portend / No war nor prince's funeral, / Shining unto no higher end / Than to presage the grass's fall. [*The Mower to the Glow Worms*]

7 Had it lived long, it would have been / Lilies without, roses within. [*The Nymph Complaining for the Death of her Fawn*, 91]

8 Who can foretell for what high cause / This darling of the Gods was born? [*The Picture of Little T.C. in a Prospect of Flowers*]

9 Gather the flowers, but spare the buds. [*Ib.*]

10 Had we but world enough, and time, / This coyness, lady, were no crime. [*To His Coy Mistress*]

11 I would / Love you ten years before the flood, / And you should if you please refuse / Till the conversion of the Jews; / My vegetable love should grow / Vaster than empires and more slow. [*Ib.*]

12 But at my back I always hear / Time's wingèd chariot hurrying near, / And yonder all before us lie / Deserts of vast eternity. / Thy beauty shall no more be found, / Nor, in thy marble vaults, shall sound / My echoing song; then worms shall try / That long-preserved virginity, / And your quaint honour turn to dust, / And into ashes all my lust: / The grave's a fine and private place, / But none, I think, do there embrace. [*Ib.*]

13 Thus, though we cannot make our sun / Stand still, yet we will make him run. [*To His Coy Mistress*]

14 The tawny mowers enter next, / Who seem like Israelites to be / Walking on foot through a green sea. [*Upon Appleton House*, 388]

15 And now the salmon-fishers moist / Their leathern boats begin to hoist; / And like Antipodes in shoes, / Have shod their heads in their canoes. [*Ib.* 769]

KARL MARX 1818–1883

16 The workers have nothing to lose but their chains. They have a world to gain. Workers of the world, unite. [*The Communist Manifesto*]

17 From each according to his abilities, to each according to his needs. [*Criticism of the Gotha Programme*]

18 Religion ... is the opium of the people. [*Criticism of Hegel's Philosophy of Right*, Introduction]

19 The dictatorship of the proletariat. [Quoted by the Webbs]

MARY TUDOR 1516–1558

20 When I am dead and opened, you shall find 'Calais' lying in my heart. [Holinshed's *Chronicles*]

THEOPHILE MARZIALS 1850–1920

21 And 'tis but a penny to Twickenham Town. [*Twickenham Ferry*]

JOHN MASEFIELD 1878–1967

22 Coming in solemn beauty like slow old tunes of Spain. [*Beauty*]

23 But the loveliest things of beauty God ever showed to me, / Are her voice, and her hair, and eyes, and the dear red curve of her lips. [*Ib.*]

24 Oh some are fond of Spanish wine, and some are fond of French. [*Captain Stratton's Fancy*]

25 Quinquireme of Nineveh from distant Ophir / Rowing home to haven in sunny Palestine, / With a cargo of ivory, / And apes and peacocks, / Sandalwood, cedarwood and sweet white wine. [*Cargoes*]

1 Dirty British coaster with a salt-caked smoke stack, / Butting through the Channel in the mad March days, / With a cargo of Tyne coal, / Road-rail, pig-lead, / Firewood, iron-ware, and cheap tin-trays. [*Cargoes*]

2 Laugh and be merry, remember, better the world with a song. / Better the world with a blow in the teeth of a wrong. [*Laugh and Be Merry*]

3 Death opens unknown doors. It is most grand to die. [*Pompey the Great*, i]

4 One road leads to London, / One road runs to Wales, / My road leads me seawards / To the white dipping sails. [*Roadways*]

5 I must down to the seas again, to the lonely sea and the sky, / And all I ask is a tall ship and a star to steer her by, / And the wheel's kick and the wind's song and the white sail's shaking, / And a grey mist on the sea's face and a grey dawn breaking. [*Sea Fever*]

6 I must down to the seas again, for the call of the running tide / Is a wild call and a clear call that may not be denied. [*Ib.*]

7 I must down to the seas again, to the vagrant gypsy life, / To the gull's way and the whale's way where the wind's like a whetted knife; / And all I ask is a merry yarn from a laughing fellow-rover, / And quiet sleep and a sweet dream when the long trick's over. [*Ib.*]

8 It's a warm wind, the west wind, full of birds' cries. [*The West Wind*]

WALT MASON   1862–1939

9 He's the Man Who Delivers the Goods. [*The Man Who Delivers the Goods*]

WILLIAM MASON   1724–1797

10 The fattest hog in Epicurus' sty. [*An Heroic Epistle*, 24]

PHILIP MASSINGER   1583–1640

11 He that would govern others, first should be / The master of himself. [*The Bondman*, I. iii]

12 Now speak, / Or be for ever silent. [*The Duke of Milan*, IV. iii]

13 I am driven / Into a desperate strait and cannot steer / A middle course. [*The Great Duke of Florence*, III. i]

14 The devil turned precisian! [*A New Way to Pay Old Debts*, I. i]

15 Death hath a thousand doors to let out life: / I shall find one. [*A Very Woman*, V. iv]

W. SOMERSET MAUGHAM
1874–1965

16 You know, of course, that the Tasmanians, who never committed adultery, are now extinct. [*The Bread-Winner*, iii]

17 A woman will always sacrifice herself if you give her the opportunity. It is her favourite form of self-indulgence. [*The Circle*, III]

18 When married people don't get on they can separate, but if they're not married it's impossible. It's a tie that only death can sever. [*Ib.*]

19 It's only if a man's a gentleman that he won't hesitate to do an ungentlemanly thing. Mortimer is on the boundary line and it makes him careful. [*The Constant Wife*, II]

20 The degree of a nation's civilization is marked by its disregard for the necessities of existence. [*Our Betters*, I]

21 Impropriety is the soul of wit. [*The Moon and Sixpence*, Ch. 4]

22 People ask you for criticism, but they only want praise. [*Of Human Bondage*, Ch. 50]

23 I would sooner read a time-table or a catalogue than nothing at all. ... They are much more entertaining than half the novels that are written. [*The Summing Up*, 25]

24 Music-hall songs provide the dull with wit, just as proverbs provide them with wisdom. [*A Writer's Notebook*, 1892]

25 Men have an extraordinarily erroneous opinion of their position in nature; and the error is ineradicable. [*Ib.* 1896]

26 There are times when I look over the various parts of my character with perplexity. I recognize that I am made up of several persons and that the person that at the moment has the upper hand will

inevitably give place to another. But which is the real one? All of them or none? [*A Writer's Notebook*, 1896]

1 The highest activities of consciousness have their origins in physical occurrences of the brain just as the loveliest melodies are not too sublime to be expressed by notes. [*Ib.* 1902]

2 I can't think of a single Russian novel in which one of the characters goes to a picture gallery. [*Ib.* 1917]

3 Sentimentality is only sentiment that rubs you up the wrong way. [*Ib.* 1941]

SIR WILLIAM MAULE 1788–1858

4 My lords, we are vertebrate animals, we are mammalia! My learned friend's manner would be intolerable in Almighty God to a black beetle. [In court]

HUGHES MEARNS 1875–1965

5 As I was going up the stair / I met a man who wasn't there. / He wasn't there again today. / I wish, I wish he'd go away. [*The Psychoed*]

WILLIAM MEE 1788–1862

6 She's all my fancy painted her; / She's lovely, she's divine. [*Alice Gray*]

VISCOUNT MELBOURNE 1779–1848

7 I wish that I was as cocksure of anything as Tom Macaulay is of everything. [Attr. by Earl Cowper]

8 Things have come to a pretty pass when religion is allowed to invade the sphere of private life. [Attr. by G. W. E. Russell]

THOMAS MELLOR 1880–1926

9 I Wouldn't Leave My Little Wooden Hut for You. [Title of song]

HERMAN MELVILLE 1819–1891

10 Better sleep with a sober cannibal than a drunken Christian. [*Moby Dick*, Ch. 3]

11 This, shipmates, this is that other lesson; and woe to that pilot of the living God who slights it. [*Moby Dick*, 9]

12 A whale ship was my Yale College and my Harvard. [*Ib.* 24]

H. L. MENCKEN 1880–1956

13 I've made it a rule never to drink by daylight and never to refuse a drink after dark. [Quoted in *New York Post*]

LOUIS-SÉBASTIEN MERCIER 1740–1814

14 *Les extrèmes se touchent.* – Extremes meet. [*Tableau de Paris*, Vol. IV. Ch. 348, heading]

GEORGE MEREDITH 1828–1909

15 Under yonder beech-tree single on the greensward, / Couched with her arms behind her golden head, / Knees and tresses folded to slip and ripple idly, / Lies my young love sleeping in the shade. [*Love in the Valley*, i]

16 She whom I love is hard to catch and conquer, / Hard, but O the glory of the winning were she won! [*Ib.* ii]

17 Lovely are the curves of the white owl sweeping / Wavy in the dusk lit by one large star. / Lone on the fir-branch, his rattle-note unvaried. / Brooding o'er the gloom, spins the brown eve-jar. / Darker grows the valley, more and more forgetting: / So were it with me if forgetting could be willed. [*Ib.* v]

18 Love that so desires would fain keep her changeless; / Fain would fling the net, and fain have her free. [*Ib.* vi]

19 On a starred night Prince Lucifer uprose. / Tired of his dark dominion swung the fiend. [*Lucifer in Starlight*]

20 Around the ancient track marched, rank on rank, / The army of unalterable law. [*Ib.*]

21 Not till the fire is dying in the grate, / Look we for any kinship with the stars. [*Modern Love*, iv]

22 And if I drink oblivion of a day, / So shorten I the stature of my soul. [*Ib.* xii]

23 That rarest gift / To Beauty, Common Sense. [*Ib.* xxxii]

1 In tragic life, God wot, / No villain need be! Passions spin the plot: / We are betrayed by what is false within. [*Modern Love*, xliii]

2 We saw the swallows gathering in the sky. [*Ib.* xlvii]

3 Ah, what a dusty answer gets the soul / When hot for certainties in this our life. [*Ib.* l]

4 Into the breast that gives the rose, / Shall I with shuddering fall? [*Ode to the Spirit of Earth in Autumn*]

5 Bring the army of the faithful through. [*To J(ohn) M(orley)*]

6 Sweet as Eden is the air, / And Eden-sweet the ray. [*Woodland Peace*]

7 Enter these enchanted woods, / You who dare. [*The Woods of Westermain*]

8 Men may have rounded Seraglio Point: they have not yet doubled Cape Turk. [*Diana of the Crossways*, Ch. 1]

9 'Tis Ireland gives England her soldiers, her generals too. [*Ib.* 2]

10 'Hog's my feed,' said Andrew Hedger.... 'Ah could eat hog a solid hower.' [*Ib.* 8]

11 'But how divine is utterance,' she said. 'As we to the brutes, poets are to us.' [*Ib.* 16]

12 You see he has a leg. [*The Egoist*, Ch. 2]

13 A Phoebus Apollo turned fasting friar. [*Ib.*]

14 A dainty rogue in porcelain. [*Ib.* 5]

15 Cynicism is intellectual dandyism. [*Ib.* 7]

16 An aged and a great wine. [*Ib.* 20]

17 None of your dam punctilio. [*One of Our Conquerors*, Ch. 1]

18 I expect that Woman will be the last thing civilized by Man. [*The Ordeal of Richard Feverel*, Ch. 1]

19 Who rises from prayer a better man, his prayer is answered. [*Ib.* 12]

20 Kissing don't last: cookery do! [*Ib.* 28]

21 Speech is the small change of silence. [*Ib.* 34]

OWEN MEREDITH [EARL OF LYTTON] 1831–1891

22 Genius does what it must, and Talent does what it can. [*Last Words of a Sensitive Second-Rate Poet*]

DIXON MERRITT 1879–1954

23 A wonderful bird is the pelican, / His bill will hold more than his belican. / He can take in his beak / Enough food for a week, / But I'm darned if I know how the helican. [*The Pelican*]

PRINCE METTERNICH 1773–1859

24 Italy is a geographical expression. [Letter, 19 Nov. 1849]

ALICE MEYNELL 1847–1922

25 Flocks of the memories of the day draw near / The dovecot doors of sleep. [*At Night*]

26 I must not think of thee; and, tired yet strong, / I shun the thought that lurks in all delight – / The thought of thee – and in the blue heaven's height, / And in the sweetest passage of a song. [*Renouncement*]

27 She walks – the lady of my delight – / A shepherdess of sheep. [*The Shepherdess*]

JULES MICHELET 1798–1874

28 You are one of the forces of nature. [Letter to Alexandre Dumas, quoted in Dumas' *Memoirs*, Vol. 6, Ch. 138]

WILLIAM MICKLE 1735–1788

29 The dews of summer night did fall, / The moon, sweet regent of the sky, / Silvered the walls of Cumnor Hall, / And many an oak that grew thereby. [*Cumnor Hall*]

THOMAS MIDDLETON 1570?–1627

30 A wondrous necessary man. [*The Changeling*, V. i]

31 Beneath the stars, upon yon meteor / Ever hung my fate, 'mongst things corruptible. [*Ib.* V. iii]

32 By many a happy accident. [*No Wit, No Help, Like a Woman's*, IV. i]

33 Though I be poor, I'm honest. [*The Witch*, III. ii]

1 There's no hate lost between us. [*The Witch*, IV. ii]

2 Black spirits and white, red spirits and gray, / Mingle, mingle, mingle, you that mingle may! [*Ib.* V. ii]

A. MIDLANE 1825–1909

3 There's a Friend for little children / Above the bright blue sky, / A Friend who never changes, / Whose love will never die. [Hymn]

GEORGE MIKES 1912–

4 Continental people have sex life; the English have hot-water bottles. [*How to be an Alien*]

JOHN STUART MILL 1806–1873

5 Ask yourself whether you are happy, and you cease to be so. [*Autobiography*, Ch. 5]

6 Unearned increment. [*Dissertations and Discussions*, IV]

7 He who knows only his own side of the case knows little of that. [*On Liberty*, Ch. 2]

8 The liberty of the individual must be thus far limited; he must not make himself a nuisance to other people. [*Ib.* 3]

9 All good things which exist are the fruits of originality. [*Ib.*]

10 Liberty consists in doing what one desires. [*Ib.* 5]

11 The worth of a State, in the long run, is the worth of the individuals composing it. [*Ib.*]

EMMA MILLARD 1787–1870

12 Rocked in the cradle of the deep. [Song]

EDNA ST VINCENT MILLAY 1892–1950

13 My candle burns at both ends; / It will not last the night; / But, ah, my foes, and oh, my friends – / It gives a lovely light. [*Figs from Thistles*, 'First Fig']

14 And if I loved you Wednesday, / Well what is that to you? / I do not love you Thursday – / So much is true. [*Thursday*]

MRS E. MILLER 1833–1913

15 I love to hear the story / Which angel voices tell. [Hymn]

WILLIAM MILLER 1810–1872

16 Wee Willie Winkie rins through the town, / Upstairs and downstairs in his nicht-gown. [*Willie Winkie*]

SPIKE MILLIGAN 1918–

17 'Do you come here often?'
'Only in the mating season.' [The Goon Show (exchange between any two characters)]

A. J. MILLS 19 Cent.

18 Just like the Ivy I'll cling to you. [Title of song]

HENRY MILMAN 1791–1868

19 And the cold marble leapt to life a god. [*The Belvedere Apollo*]

20 Ride on! ride on in majesty! / In lowly pomp ride on to die. [*Ride On*]

A. A. MILNE 1882–1956

21 They're changing guard at Buckingham Palace – / Christopher Robin went down with Alice. [*When We Were Very Young*, 'Buckingham Palace']

22 James James / Morrison Morrison / Weatherby George Dupree / Took great / Care of his Mother / Though he was only three. [*Ib.* 'Disobedience']

23 You must never go down to the end of the town if you don't go down with me. [*Ib.*]

24 The King asked / The Queen, and / The Queen asked / The Dairymaid: / 'Could we have some butter for / The Royal slice of bread?' [*Ib.* 'The King's Breakfast']

25 Nobody, my darling, could call me / A fussy man – / BUT / I do like a little bit of butter to my bread! [*Ib.*]

1 Hush! Hush! Whisper who dares! / Christopher Robin is saying his prayers. [*When We Were Very Young*, 'Vespers']

2 And nobody knows / (Tiddely pom), / How cold my toes / (Tiddely pom), / How cold my toes / (Tiddely pom), / Are growing. [*House at Pooh Corner*, Ch. 1]

3 Tiggers don't like honey. [*Ib.* 2]

4 Isn't it funny / How a bear likes honey? / Buzz! Buzz! Buzz! / I wonder why he does? [*Winnie-the-Pooh*, Ch. 1]

5 How sweet to be a Cloud / Floating in the Blue! [*Ib.*]

6 I am a Bear of Very Little Brain and long words Bother Me. [*Ib.* 4]

7 I have decided to catch a Heffalump. [*Ib.* 5]

8 'Pathetic,' he said. 'That's what it is. Pathetic.' [*Ib.* 6]

9 Time for a little something. [*Ib.*]

10 Kanga and Baby Roo. [*Ib.* 7]

11 On Monday, when the sun is hot, / I wonder to myself a lot: / 'Now is it true, or is it not, / That what is which and which is what?' [*Ib.*]

12 An Expotition to the North Pole. [*Ib.* 8, heading]

LORD MILNER　　　　1854–1925

13 Damn the consequences. [Speech, 26 Nov. 1909]

R. MONCKTON MILNES, BARON HOUGHTON 1809–1885

14 But the beating of my own heart / Was all the sound I heard. [Song: *The Brookside*]

JOHN MILTON　　　　1608–1674

15 Such sweet compulsion doth in music lie. [*Arcades*, 68]

16 Blest pair of Sirens, pledges of Heav'n's joy, / Sphere-born harmonious sisters, voice and verse. [*At a Solemn Music*, 1]

17 Before the starry threshold of Jove's Court / My mansion is. [*Comus*, 1]

18 Above the smoke and stir of this dim spot, / Which men call earth. [*Ib.* 5]

19 An old, and haughty nation proud in arms. [*Comus*, 33]

20 Bacchus, that first from out the purple grape, / Crushed the sweet poison of misusèd wine. [*Ib.* 46]

21 What hath night to do with sleep? [*Ib.* 122]

22 Ere the blabbing Eastern scout, / The nice Morn on th' Indian steep / From her cabined loop-hole peep. [*Ib.* 138]

23 Come, knit hands, and beat the ground, / In a light fantastic round. [*Ib.* 143]

24 When the grey-hooded Ev'n / Like a sad votarist in palmer's weed, / Rose from the hindmost wheels of Phoebus' wain. [*Ib.* 188]

25 The stars, / That nature hung in heaven, and filled their lamps / With everlasting oil, to give due light / To the misled and lonely traveller. [*Ib.* 197]

26 O welcome pure-eyed Faith, white-handed Hope, / Thou hovering angel girt with golden wings. [*Ib.* 213]

27 Was I deceived, or did a sable cloud / Turn forth her silver lining on the night? [*Ib.* 221]

28 By slow Meander's margent green, / And in the violet-embroidered vale. [*Ib.* 232]

29 Dingle, or bushy dell of this wild wood, / And every bosky bourn from side to side. [*Ib.* 313]

30 With thy long levelled rule of streaming light. [*Ib.* 340]

31 Virtue could see to do what Virtue would / By her own radiant light, though sun and moon / Were in the flat sea sunk. [*Ib.* 373]

32 He that has light within his own clear breast / May sit i' th' centre, and enjoy bright day, / But he that hides a dark soul, and foul thoughts / Benighted walks under the midday sun. [*Ib.* 381]

33 The unsunned heaps / Of miser's treasure. [*Ib.* 398]

34 'Tis Chastity, my brother, Chastity: / She that has that is clad in complete steel. [*Ib.* 420]

35 How charming is divine philosophy! / Not harsh, and crabbèd as dull fools suppose, / But musical as is Apollo's lute,

/ And a perpetual feast of nectared sweets, / Where no crude surfeit reigns. [*Comus*, 476]

1 Storied of old in high immortal verse / Of dire chimeras and enchanted isles, / And rifted rocks whose entrance leads to Hell. [*Ib.* 516]

2 Wrapt in a pleasing fit of melancholy. [*Ib.* 546]

3 And filled the air with barbarous dissonance. [*Ib.* 550]

4 I was all ear / And took in strains that might create a soul / Under the ribs of Death. [*Ib.* 560]

5 That power / Which erring men call Chance. [*Ib.* 587]

6 Virtue may be assailed, but never hurt, / Surprised by unjust force, but not enthralled. [*Ib.* 589]

7 If this fail, / The pillared firmament is rottenness, / And earth's base built on stubble. [*Ib.* 597]

8 Those budge doctors of the Stoic fur. [*Ib.* 707]

9 Praising the lean and sallow abstinence. [*Ib.* 709]

10 Beauty is Nature's coin, must not be hoarded, / But must be current. [*Ib.* 739]

11 Beauty is Nature's brag, and must be shown / In courts, at feasts, and high solemnities. [*Ib.* 745]

12 It is for homely features to keep home, / They had their name thence; coarse complexions / And cheeks of sorry grain will serve to ply / The sampler, and to tease the housewife's wool. / What need a vermeil-tinctured lip for that, / Love-darting eyes, or tresses like the morn? [*Ib.* 748]

13 Sabrina fair, / Listen where thou art sitting / Under the glassy, cool, translucent wave, / In twisted braids of lilies knitting / The loose train of thy amber-dropping hair. [*Ib.* 859]

14 Mortals, that would follow me, / Love virtue, she alone is free, / She can teach ye how to climb / Higher than the sphery chime; / Or if virtue feeble were, / Heav'n itself would stoop to her. [*Ib.* 1018]

15 Hence, vain deluding joys, / The brood of Folly without father bred. [*Il Penseroso*, 1]

16 The gay motes that people the sunbeams. [*Il Penseroso*, 8]

17 Hail divinest melancholy. [*Ib.* 12]

18 Sober, steadfast, and demure. [*Ib.* 32]

19 And looks commercing with the skies, / Thy rapt soul sitting in thine eyes. [*Ib.* 39]

20 Him that yon soars on golden wing, / Guiding the fiery-wheelèd throne, / The Cherub Contemplation. [*Ib.* 52]

21 Sweet bird, that shunn'st the noise of folly, / Most musical, most melancholy! [*Ib.* 61]

22 To behold the wandering moon, / Riding near her highest noon, / Like one that had been led astray / Through the heav'n's wide pathless way; / And oft, as if her head she bowed, / Stooping through a fleecy cloud. [*Ib.* 67]

23 I hear the far-off curfew sound, / Over some wide-watered shore, / Swinging slow with sullen roar. [*Ib.* 74]

24 Far from all resort of mirth, / Save the cricket on the hearth! [*Ib.* 81]

25 Sometime let gorgeous Tragedy / In sceptred pall come sweeping by, / Presenting Thebes, or Pelops' line, / Or the tale of Troy divine. [*Ib.* 97]

26 Or bid the soul of Orpheus sing / Such notes as, warbled to the string, / Drew iron tears down Pluto's cheek. [*Ib.* 105]

27 Or call up him that left half told / The story of Cambuscan bold. [*Ib.* 109]

28 Where more is meant than meets the ear. [*Ib.* 120]

29 Hide me from day's garish eye / While the bee with honied thigh / That at her flowery work doth sing. [*Ib.* 141]

30 With antique pillars massy proof, / And storied windows richly dight, / Casting a dim religious light. / There let the pealing organ blow, / To the full-voiced quire below. [*Ib.* 158]

31 Till old experience do attain / To something like prophetic strain. [*Ib.* 173]

32 Hence loathèd Melancholy, / Of Cerberus and blackest Midnight born. [*L'Allegro*, 1]

33 So buxom, blithe, and debonair. [*Ib.* 24]

34 Haste thee, nymph, and bring with thee / Jest and youthful jollity, / Quips and cranks, and wanton wiles, / Nods, and becks, and wreathèd smiles. [*Ib.* 25]

1 Sport that wrinkled Care derides, / And Laughter holding both his sides. / Come and trip it as ye go / On the light fantastic toe. [*L'Allegro*, 31]

2 The mountain nymph, sweet Liberty. [*Ib.* 36]

3 To hear the lark begin his flight, / And singing startle the dull night, / From his watch-tower in the skies, / Till the dappled dawn doth rise. [*Ib.* 41]

4 While the cock with lively din, / Scatters the rear of darkness thin, / And to the stack, or the barn door, / Stoutly struts his dames before. [*Ib.* 49]

5 Right against the eastern gate, / Where the great sun begins his state. [*Ib.* 59]

6 And every shepherd tells his tale / Under the hawthorn in the dale. [*Ib.* 67]

7 Meadows trim with daisies pied, / Shallow brooks and rivers wide. / Towers, and battlements it sees / Bosomed high in tufted trees, / Where perhaps some beauty lies, / The cynosure of neighbouring eyes. [*Ib.* 75]

8 Of herbs and other country messes, / Which the neat-handed Phyllis dresses. [*Ib.* 85]

9 To many a youth and many a maid, / Dancing in the chequered shade. [*Ib.* 95]

10 Then to the spicy nut-brown ale. [*Ib.* 100]

11 Towered cities please us then, / And the busy hum of men. [*Ib.* 117]

12 Store of ladies, whose bright eyes / Rain influence, and judge the prize. [*Ib.* 121]

13 Then to the well-trod stage anon, / If Jonson's learned sock be on, / Or sweetest Shakespeare, Fancy's child, / Warble his native wood-notes wild. [*Ib.* 131]

14 And ever, against eating cares, / Lap me in soft Lydian airs, / Married to immortal verse / Such as the meeting soul may pierce / In notes, with many a winding bout / Of linkèd sweetness long drawn out. [*Ib.* 135]

15 The melting voice through mazes running; / Untwisting all the chains that tie / The hidden soul of harmony. [*Ib.* 142]

16 Such strains as would have won the ear / Of Pluto, to have quite set free / His half-regained Eurydice. [*Ib.* 148]

17 Yet once more, O ye laurels, and once more / Ye myrtles brown, with ivy never sere, / I come to pluck your berries harsh and crude, / And with forced fingers rude, / Shatter your leaves before the mellowing year. [*Lycidas*, 1]

18 He knew / Himself to sing, and build the lofty rhyme. [*Ib.* 10]

19 Without the meed of some melodious tear. [*Ib.* 14]

20 Under the opening eye-lids of the morn. [*Ib.* 26]

21 But O the heavy change, now thou art gone, / Now thou art gone, and never must return! [*Ib.* 37]

22 Gadding vine. [*Ib.* 40]

23 As killing as the canker to the rose. [*Ib.* 45]

24 And strictly meditate the thankless Muse. [*Ib.* 66]

25 To sport with Amaryllis in the shade, / Or with tangles of Neaera's hair. [*Ib.* 68]

26 Fame is the spur that the clear spirit doth raise / (That last infirmity of noble mind) / To scorn delights, and live laborious days; / But the fair guerdon when we hope to find, / And think to burst out into sudden blaze, / Comes the blind Fury with th' abhorrèd shears, / And slits the thin-spun life. [*Ib.* 70]

27 Fame is no plant that grows on mortal soil. [*Ib.* 78]

28 It was that fatal and perfidious bark / Built in th' eclipse, and rigged with curses dark. [*Ib.* 100]

29 Last came, and last did go, / The Pilot of the Galilean lake, / Two massy keys he bore, of metals twain, / (The golden opes, the iron shuts amain). [*Ib.* 108]

30 Blind mouths! that scarce themselves know how to hold / A sheep-hook. [*Ib.* 119]

31 And when they list, their lean and flashy songs / Grate on their scrannel pipes of wretched straw, / The hungry sheep look up, and are not fed, / But swoln with wind, and the rank mist they draw, / Rot inwardly, and foul contagion spread. [*Ib.* 123]

32 But that two-handed engine at the door, / Stands ready to smite once, and smite no more. [*Ib.* 130]

33 Throw hither all your quaint enamelled eyes / That on the green turf suck the

honied showers, / And purple all the ground with vernal flowers. / Bring the rathe primrose that forsaken dies, / The tufted crow-toe and pale jessamine, / The white pink, and the pansy freaked with jet, / The glowing violet, / The musk-rose and the well-attired woodbine, / With cowslips wan that hang the pensive head, / And every flower that sad embroidery wears: / Bid amaranthus all his beauty shed, / And daffadillies fill their cups with tears, / To strew the laureate hearse where Lycid lies. [*Lycidas*, 139]

1 So sinks the day-star in the ocean bed, / And yet anon repairs his drooping head, / And tricks his beams, and with new-spangled ore, / Flames in the forehead of the morning sky. [*Ib.* 168]

2 At last he rose, and twitched his mantle blue; / Tomorrow to fresh woods, and pastures new. [*Ib.* 192]

3 O fairest flower, no sooner blown but blasted, / Soft silken primrose fading timelessly. [*On the Death of a Fair Infant*, 1]

4 This is the month and this the happy morn. [*On the Morning of Christ's Nativity*, 1]

5 Forsook the courts of everlasting day. [*Ib.* 13]

6 It was the winter wild, / While the Heaven-born child, / All meanly wrapt in the rude manger lies. [*Ib.* 29]

7 Nor war, or battle's sound / Was heard the world around. [*Ib.* 53]

8 Time will run back, and fetch the age of gold. [*Ib.* 135]

9 The oracles are dumb. [*Ib.* 173]

10 No nightly trance or breathèd spell, / Inspires the pale-eyed priest from the prophetic cell. [*Ib.* 179]

11 So when the sun in bed, / Curtained with cloudy red, / Pillows his chin upon an orient wave. [*Ib.* 229]

12 What needs my Shakespeare, for his honoured bones, / The labour of an age in pilèd stones? [*On Shakespeare*]

13 Dear son of memory, great heir of fame, / What need'st thou such weak witness of thy name? [*Ib.*]

14 Rhyme being no necessary adjunct or true ornament of poem or good verse, in

longer works especially, but the invention of a barbarous age, to set off wretched matter with lame metre. [*Paradise Lost*, Preface: The Verse]

15 The troublesome and modern bondage of rhyming. [*Ib.*]

16 Of Man's first disobedience, and the fruit / Of that forbidden tree, whose mortal taste / Brought death into the world, and all our woe, / With loss of Eden. [*Ib.* Bk I. 1]

17 Things unattempted yet in prose or rhyme. [*Ib.* I. 16]

18 What in me is dark / Illumine, what is low raise and support; / That to the height of this great argument / I may assert eternal Providence, / And justify the ways of God to men. [*Ib.* I. 22]

19 To bottomless perdition, there to dwell / In adamantine chains and penal fire. [*Ib.* I. 47]

20 As far as angels' ken. [*Ib.* I. 59]

21 Yet from those flames / No light, but rather darkness visible / Served only to discover sights of woe, / Regions of sorrow, doleful shades where peace / And rest can never dwell, hope never comes / That comes to all. [*Ib.* I. 62]

22 Sense of injured merit. [*Ib.* I. 98]

23 What though the field be lost? / All is not lost; th' unconquerable will, / And study of revenge, immortal hate, / And courage never to submit or yield: / And what is else not to be overcome? [*Ib.* I. 105]

24 To be weak is miserable / Doing or suffering. [*Ib.* I. 157]

25 And out of good still to find means of evil. [*Ib.* I. 165]

26 Farewell happy fields / Where joy for ever dwells: Hail horrors, hail! [*Ib.* I. 249]

27 A mind not to be changed by place or time. / The mind is its own place, and in itself / Can make a heav'n of hell, a hell of heav'n. [*Ib.* I. 253]

28 Better to reign in hell than serve in heav'n. [*Ib.* I. 263]

29 Thick as autumnal leaves that strow the brooks / In Vallombrosa, where th' Etrurian shades / High overarched imbower. [*Ib.* I. 302]

30 Awake, arise, or be for ever fall'n! [*Ib.* I. 330]

1 Execute their aery purposes. [*Paradise Lost*, I. 430]

2 When night / Darkens the streets, then wander forth the sons / Of Belial, flown with insolence and wine. [*Ib*. I. 500]

3 The imperial ensign, which, full high advanced, / Shone like a meteor, streaming to the wind. [*Ib*. I. 536]

4 A shout that tore hell's concave, and beyond / Frightened the reign of Chaos and old Night. [*Ib*. I. 542]

5 In perfect phalanx to the Dorian mood / Of flutes and soft recorders. [*Ib*. I. 550]

6 His form had yet not lost / All her original brightness, nor appeared / Less than archangel ruined, and th' excess / Of glory obscured. [*Ib*. I. 591]

7 In dim eclipse disastrous twilight sheds / On half the nations, and with fear of change / Perplexes monarchs. [*Ib*. I. 597]

8 Care / Sat on his faded cheek. [*Ib*. I. 601]

9 Tears such as angels weep, burst forth. [*Ib*. I. 620]

10 Who overcomes / By force, hath overcome but half his foe. [*Ib*. I. 648]

11 Let none admire / That riches grow in hell; that soil may best / Deserve the precious bane. [*Ib*. I. 690]

12 Anon out of the earth a fabric huge / Rose like an exhalation. [*Ib*. I. 710]

13 From morn / To noon he fell, from noon to dewy eve, / A summer's day; and with the setting sun / Dropt from the zenith like a falling star. [*Ib*. I. 742]

14 Pandemonium, the high capital / Of Satan and his peers. [*Ib*. I. 756]

15 Fairy elves, / Whose midnight revels, by a forest side / Or fountain, some belated peasant sees, / Or dreams he sees, while overhead the moon / Sits arbitress. [*Ib*. I. 781]

16 Satan exalted sat, by merit raised / To that bad eminence. [*Ib*. II. 5]

17 Rather than be less / Cared not to be at all. [*Ib*. II. 47]

18 My sentence is for open war; of wiles, / More unexpert, I boast not. [*Ib*. II. 51]

19 Though his tongue / Dropt manna, and could make the worse appear / The better reason. [*Ib*. II. 112]

20 For who would lose, / Though full of pain, this intellectual being, / Those thoughts that wander through eternity, / To perish rather, swallowed up and lost / In the wide womb of uncreated night, / Devoid of sense and motion? [*Paradise Lost*, II. 146]

21 His red right hand. [*Ib*. II. 174]

22 Unrespited, unpitied, unreprieved, / Ages of hopeless end. [*Ib*. II. 185]

23 Thus Belial, with words clothed in reason's garb, / Counselled ignoble ease, and peaceful sloth, / Not peace. [*Ib*. II. 226]

24 With grave / Aspect he rose, and in his rising seemed / A pillar of state; deep on his front engraven / Deliberation sat and public care; / And princely counsel in his face yet shone, / Majestic though in ruin. [*Ib*. II. 300]

25 Through the palpable obscure find out / His uncouth way. [*Ib*. II. 406]

26 Long is the way / And hard, that out of hell leads up to light. [*Ib*. II. 432]

27 Vain wisdom all, and false philosophy. [*Ib*. II. 565]

28 O'er many a frozen, many a fiery Alp, / Rocks, caves, lakes, fens, bogs, dens, and shades of death. [*Ib*. II. 620]

29 The other shape, / If shape it might be called that shape had none. [*Ib*. II. 666]

30 Black it stood as night, / Fierce as ten furies, terrible as hell, / And shook a dreadful dart. [*Ib*. II. 670]

31 Whence and what art thou, execrable shape? [*Ib*. II. 681]

32 Sable-vested Night, eldest of things. [*Ib*. II. 962]

33 With ruin upon ruin, rout on rout, / Confusion worse confounded. [*Ib*. II. 995]

34 Hail holy light, offspring of heav'n firstborn, / Or of th' Eternal co-eternal beam. [*Ib*. III. 1]

35 The rising world of waters dark and deep. [*Ib*. III. 11]

36 Then feed on thoughts, that voluntary move / Harmonious numbers. [*Ib*. III. 37]

37 Thus with the year / Seasons return, but not to me returns / Day, or the sweet approach of ev'n or morn, / Or sight of vernal bloom, or summer's rose, / Or flocks, or herds, or human face divine. [*Ib*. III. 40]

1 From the cheerful ways of men / Cut off, and for the book of knowledge fair / Presented with a universal blank / Of nature's works to me expunged and razed, / And wisdom at one entrance quite shut out. [*Paradise Lost*, III. 46]

2 Dark with excessive bright. [*Ib.* III. 380]

3 Embryos and idiots, eremites and friars / White, black, and grey, with all their trumpery. [*Ib.* III. 474]

4 Into a Limbo large and broad, since called / The paradise of fools, to few unknown. [*Ib.* III. 495]

5 At whose sight all the stars / Hide their diminished heads. [*Ib.* IV. 34]

6 Me miserable! which way shall I fly / Infinite wrath, and infinite despair? / Which way I fly is hell; myself am hell; / And in th.. lowest deep a lower deep / Still threatening to devour me opens wide, / To which the hell I suffer seems a heav'n. [*Ib.* IV. 73]

7 So farewell hope, and with hope farewell fear, / Farewell remorse: all good to me is lost; / Evil be thou my Good. [*Ib.* IV. 108]

8 Sabean odours from the spicy shore / Of Araby the blest. [*Ib.* IV. 162]

9 Thence up he flew, and on the Tree of Life, / The middle tree and highest there that grew, / Sat like a cormorant. [*Ib.* IV. 194]

10 A heav'n on earth. [*Ib.* IV. 208]

11 Flowers of all hue, and without thorn the rose. [*Ib.* IV. 256]

12 The mantling vine. [*Ib.* IV. 258]

13 For contemplation he and valour formed; / For softness she and sweet attractive grace, / He for God only, she for God in him: / His fair large front and eye sublime declared / Absolute rule. [*Ib.* IV. 297]

14 Implied / Subjection, but required with gentle sway / And by her yielded, by him best received; / Yielded with coy submission, modest pride, / And sweet reluctant amorous delay. [*Ib.* IV. 307]

15 Adam the goodliest man of men since born / His sons, the fairest of her daughters Eve. [*Ib.* IV. 323]

16 With necessity, / The tyrant's plea, excused his devilish deeds. [*Ib.* IV. 393]

17 Imparadised in one another's arms. [*Paradise Lost*, IV. 506

18 All but the wakeful nightingale; / She all night long her amorous descant sung. [*Ib.* IV. 602]

19 God is thy law, thou mine: to know no more / Is woman's happiest knowledge, and her praise. [*Ib.* IV. 637]

20 With thee conversing I forget all time. [*Ib.* IV. 639]

21 Sweet the coming on / Of grateful evening mild then silent night / With this her solemn bird and this fair moon, / And these the gems of heaven, her starry train. [*Ib.* IV. 646]

22 Hail wedded love, mysterious law, true source / Of human offspring, sole propriety / In Paradise of all things common else. [*Ib.* IV. 750]

23 Blest pair; and O yet happiest if ye seek / No happier state, and know to know no more. [*Ib.* IV. 774]

24 Squat like a toad, close at the ear of Eve. [*Ib.* IV. 800]

25 Not to know me argues yourselves unknown. [*Ib.* IV. 830]

26 Abashed the devil stood, / And felt how awful goodness is. [*Ib.* IV. 846]

27 Wherefore with thee / Came not all hell broke loose? [*Ib.* IV. 917]

28 The starry cope of heaven. [*Ib.* IV. 992]

29 Fled / Murmuring, and with him fled the shades of night. [*Ib.* IV. 1014]

30 Now morn her rosy steps in th' eastern clime / Advancing, sowed the earth with orient pearl. [*Ib.* V. 1]

31 My fairest, my espoused, my latest found, / Heaven's last best gift, my ever new delight. [*Ib.* V. 18]

32 Best image of myself and dearer half. [*Ib.* V. 95]

33 These are thy glorious works, Parent of good! [*Ib.* V. 153]

34 Him first, him last, him midst, and without end. [*Ib.* V. 165]

35 A wilderness of sweets. [*Ib.* V. 294]

36 Freely we serve / Because we freely love, as in our will / To love or not; in this we stand or fall. [*Ib.* V. 538]

37 Thrones, dominations, princedoms, virtues, powers. [*Ib.* V. 601]

1 All seemed well pleased, all seemed but were not all. [*Paradise Lost*, V. 617]

2 The seraph Abdiel, faithful found, / Among the faithless, faithful only he. [*Ib.* V. 893]

3 Servant of God, well done, well hast thou fought / The better fight, who singly hast maintained / Against revolted multitudes the cause / Oft ruth, in word mightier than they in arms. [*Ib.* VI. 29]

4 He onward came, far off his coming shone. [*Ib.* VI. 768]

5 More safe I sing with mortal voice, unchanged / To hoarse or mute though fall'n on evil days, / On evil days though fall'n, and evil tongues; / In darkness, and with dangers compassed round, / And solitude. [*Ib.* VII. 24]

6 Still govern thou my song, / Urania, and fit audience find, though few. [*Ib.* VII. 30]

7 Endued / With sanctity of reason. [*Ib.* VII. 507]

8 Liquid lapse of murmuring streams. [*Ib.* VIII. 263]

9 And feel that I am happier than I know. [*Ib.* VIII. 282]

10 Grace was in all her steps, heaven in her eye, / In every gesture dignity and love. [*Ib.* VIII. 488]

11 Her virtue and the conscience of her worth, / That would be wooed, and not unsought be won. [*Ib.* VIII. 502]

12 The sum of earthly bliss. [*Ib.* VIII. 522]

13 So absolute she seems / And in herself complete, so well to know / Her own, that what she wills to do or say, / Seems wisest, virtuousest, discreetest, best. [*Ib.* VIII. 547]

14 Accuse not Nature, she hath done her part; / Do thou but thine. [*Ib.* VIII. 561]

15 A smile that glowed / Celestial rosy red, love's proper hue. [*Ib.* VIII. 618]

16 My unpremeditated verse. [*Ib.* IX. 24]

17 Since first this subject for heroic song / Pleased me long choosing, and beginning late. [*Ib.* IX. 25]

18 The serpent subtlest beast of all the field. [*Ib.* IX. 86]

19 For solitude sometimes is best society, / And short retirement urges sweet return. [*Ib.* IX. 249]

20 She fair, divinely fair, fit love for Gods. [*Paradise Lost*, IX. 489]

21 God so commanded, and left that command / Sole daughter of his voice; the rest we live / Law to ourselves, our reason is our law. [*Ib.* IX. 652]

22 Earth felt the wound, and Nature from her seat / Sighing through all her works gave signs of woe, / That all was lost. [*Ib.* IX. 782]

23 O fairest of creation! last and best / Of all God's works! Creature in whom excelled / Whatever can to sight or thought be formed, / Holy, divine, good, amiable, or sweet! [*Ib.* IX. 896]

24 A pillared shade / High overarched, and echoing walks between. [*Ib.* IX. 1106]

25 Yet shall I temper so / Justice with mercy. [*Ib.* X. 77]

26 Demoniac frenzy, moping melancholy, / And moon-struck madness. [*Ib.* XI. 485]

27 Nor love thy life, nor hate; but what thou liv'st, / Live well, how long or short permit to heav'n. [*Ib.* XI. 553]

28 The evening star, / Love's harbinger. [*Ib.* XI. 588]

29 The brazen throat of war had ceased to roar, / All now was turned to jollity and game, / To luxury and riot, feast and dance. [*Ib.* XI. 713]

30 Now I see / Peace to corrupt no less than war to waste. [*Ib.* XI. 783]

31 Some natural tears they dropped, but wiped them soon; / The world was all before them, where to choose / Their place of rest, and Providence their guide: / They hand in hand with wandering steps and slow / Through Eden took their solitary way. [*Ib.* XII. 645]

32 Most men admire / Virtue, who follow not her lore. [*Paradise Regained*, Bk I. 482]

33 Beauty stands / In the admiration only of weak minds / Led captive. [*Ib.* II. 220]

34 Fairy damsels met in forest wide / By knights of Logres, or of Lyones, / Lancelot or Pelleas, or Pellenore. [*Ib.* II. 359]

35 Of whom to be dispraised were no small praise. [*Ib.* III. 56]

36 The childhood shows the man, / As morning shows the day. Be famous then / By wisdom; as thy empire must extend, / So let extend thy mind o'er all the world. [*Ib.* IV. 220]

1 Athens, the eye of Greece, mother of arts / And eloquence. [*Paradise Regained*, IV. 240]

2 The olive-grove of Academe, / Plato's retirement, where the Attic bird / Trills her thick-warbled notes the summer long. [*Ib*. IV. 244]

3 The first and wisest of them all professed / To know this only, that he nothing knew. [*Ib*. IV. 293]

4 Deep versed in books and shallow in himself. [*Ib*. IV. 327]

5 Till morning fair / Came forth with pilgrim steps in amice grey. [*Ib*. IV. 426]

6 He unobserved / Home to his mother's house private returned. [*Ib*. IV. 638]

7 Let us with a gladsome mind / Praise the Lord, for he is kind, / For his mercies ay endure, / Ever faithful, ever sure. [*Psalm 136*]

8 A little onward lend thy guiding hand / To these dark steps, a little further on. [*Samson Agonistes*, 1]

9 Eyeless in Gaza at the mill with slaves. [*Ib*. 41]

10 O dark, dark, dark, amid the blaze of noon, / Irrecoverably dark, total eclipse / Without all hope of day! [*Ib*. 80]

11 The sun to me is dark / And silent as the moon, / When she deserts the night / Hid in her vacant, interlunar cave. [*Ib*. 86]

12 To live a life half-dead, a living death. [*Ib*. 100]

13 This, this is he; softly awhile, / Let us not break in upon him; / O change beyond report, thought, or belief! [*Ib*. 115]

14 Ran on embattled armies clad in iron, / And weaponless himself, / Made arms ridiculous. [*Ib*. 129]

15 Wisest men / Have erred, and by bad women been deceived; / And shall again, pretend they ne'er so wise. [*Ib*. 210]

16 Just are the ways of God, / And justifiable to men; / Unless there be who think not God at all. [*Ib*. 293]

17 What boots it at one gate to make defence, / And at another to let in the foe? [*Ib*. 560]

18 My race of glory run, and race of shame, / And I shall shortly be with them that rest. [*Ib*. 597]

19 But who is this, what thing of sea or land? / Female of sex it seems, / That so bedecked, ornate, and gay, / Comes this way sailing / Like a stately ship / Of Tarsus, bound for th' isles / Of Javan or Gadier / With all her bravery on, and tackle trim, / Sails filled, and streamers waving, / Courted by all the winds that hold them play, / An amber scent of odorous perfume / Her harbinger. [*Samson Agonistes*, 710]

20 Yet beauty, though injurious, hath strange power, / After offence returning, to regain / Love once possessed. [*Ib*. 1003]

21 He's gone and who knows how he may report / Thy words by adding fuel to the flame? [*Ib*. 1350]

22 For evil news rides post, while good news baits. [*Ib*. 1538]

23 Like that self-begotten bird / In the Arabian woods embost, / That no second knows nor third, / And lay ere while a holocaust. [*Ib*. 1699]

24 Nothing is here for tears, nothing to wail / Or knock the breast, no weakness, no contempt, / Dispraise, or blame; nothing but well and fair, / And what may quiet us in a death so noble. [*Ib*. 1721]

25 All is best, though we oft doubt, / What the unsearchable dispose. [*Ib*. 1745]

26 Oft he seems to hide his face, / But unexpectedly returns / And to his faithful champion hath in place / Bore witness gloriously. [*Ib*. 1749]

27 He with new acquist / Of true experience from this great event / With peace and consolation hath dismissed, / And calm of mind, all passion spent. [*Ib*. 1755]

28 The bright morning star, day's harbinger. [Song: *On May Morning*]

29 How soon hath Time, the subtle thief of youth, / Stoln on his wing my three and twentieth year! [Sonnet: *On being arrived at the age of twenty-three*]

30 All is, if I have grace to use it so, / As ever in my great Task-Master's eye. [*Ib*.]

31 Licence they mean when they cry liberty. [*Ib*. *On the detraction . . .*]

32 When I consider how my light is spent / Ere half my days in this dark world and wide, / And that one talent which is death to hide, / Lodged with me useless. [*Ib*. *On his blindness*]

259

1 Doth God exact day-labour, light denied, / I fondly ask; but patience, to prevent / That murmur, soon replies, God doth not need / Either man's work or his own gifts; who best / Bear his mild yoke, they serve him best; his state / Is kingly; thousands at his bidding speed, / And post o'er land and ocean without rest, / They also serve who only stand and wait. [Sonnet: *On his blindness*]

2 Methought I saw my late espousèd saint / Brought to me like Alcestis, from the grave. [*Ib. On his deceased wife*]

3 But O as to embrace me she inclined, / I waked, she fled, and day brought back my night. [*Ib.*]

4 Avenge, O Lord, thy slaughtered saints, whose bones / Lie scattered on the Alpine mountains cold; / Even them who kept thy truth so pure of old / When all our fathers worshipped stocks and stones. [*Ib. On the late massacre in Piedmont*]

5 The bloody Piedmontese that rolled / Mother with infant down the rocks. [*Ib.*]

6 New Presbyter is but old Priest writ large. [*Ib. On the new forcers of conscience*]

7 Peace hath her victories / No less renowned than war. [*Ib. To Cromwell*]

8 For what can war, but endless war still breed? [*Ib. To Fairfax*]

9 O nightingale, that on yon bloomy spray / Warblest at eve, when all the woods are still. [*Ib. To the nightingale*]

10 Captain, or colonel, or knight in arms. [*Ib. When the assault was intended to the city*]

11 He who would not be frustrate of his hope to write well hereafter in laudable things ought himself to be a true poem. [*Apology for Smectymnuus*]

12 Books are not absolutely dead things, but do contain a potency of life in them to be as active as that soul was whose progeny they are; nay they do preserve as in a vial the purest efficacy and extraction of that living intellect that bred them. [*Areopagitica*]

13 As good almost kill a man as kill a good book; who kills a man kills a reasonable creature, God's image; but he who destroys a good book, kills reason itself, kills the image of God, as it were in the eye. [*Ib.*]

14 A good book is the precious life-blood of a master spirit, embalmed and treasured up on purpose to a life beyond life. [*Areopagitica*]

15 I cannot praise a fugitive and cloistered virtue, unexercised and unbreathed, that never sallies out and sees her adversary, but slinks out of the race, where that immortal garland is to be run for, not without dust and heat. [*Ib.*]

16 Our sage and serious poet Spenser. [*Ib.*]

17 God is decreeing to begin some new and great period in His Church, even to the reforming of the Reformation itself. What does He then but reveal Himself to His servants, and as His manner is, first to His Englishmen? [*Ib.*]

18 Methinks I see in my mind a noble and puissant nation rousing herself like a strong man after sleep, and shaking her invincible locks. Methinks I see her as an eagle mewing her mighty youth, and kindling her undazzled eyes at the full midday beam. [*Ib.*]

19 To chronicle the wars of kites and crows, fighting in the air. [*History of Britain*, Bk IV]

20 Rhetoric ... To which poetry would be made subsequent, or indeed rather precedent, as being less subtle and fine, but more simple, sensuous and passionate. [*Of Education*]

21 A poet soaring in the high region of his fancies with his garland and singing robes about him. [*Reason of Church Government*, Bk II, Introduction]

22 None can love freedom heartily, but good men; the rest love not freedom, but licence. [*Tenure of Kings and Magistrates*]

23 One tongue is sufficient for a woman. [Attr., when asked whether he would instruct his daughters in foreign languages]

COMTE DE MIRABEAU
1749/1791

24 War is Prussia's national industry. [Attributed to Mirabeau by Albert Sorel, but probably a misquotation of a longer passage in his *Monarchie prussienne*]

MISSAL

25 *O felix culpa, quae talem ac tantum meruit habere Redemptorem.* – O happy

fault, which has earned the possession of such and so great a Redeemer. [*Exsultet* on Holy Saturday]

MARY RUSSELL MITFORD
1787–1855

1 She [Jane Austen] was then the prettiest, silliest, most affected, husband-hunting butterfly she ever remembers. [Letter, 3 Apr. 1815]

2 Perpendicular, precise and taciturn. [(Jane Austen) Quoted in *Life and Letters of Mary R. Mitford*, I. p. 306]

NANCY MITFORD   1904–1973

3 All the heat there was seemed to concentrate in the Hons' cupboard, which was always stifling. Here we would sit, huddled up on the slatted shelves, and talk for hours about life and death. [*The Pursuit of Love*, Ch. 2]

GENERAL EMILIO MOLA
?–1936

4 The fifth column. [Radio speech during Spanish Civil War]

J. B. POQUELIN,
called MOLIÈRE   1622–1673

5 M. JOURDAIN: *Quoi? quand je dis: 'Nicole, apportez moi mes pantoufles, et me donnez mon bonnet de nuit', c'est de la prose?* – What? When I say, 'Nicole, bring me my slippers and give me my nightcap', that's prose? LE MAÎTRE DE PHILOSOPHIE: *Oui, monsieur.* – Yes, sir. M. JOURDAIN: *Par ma foi! il y a plus de quarante ans que je dis de la prose sans que j'en susse rien.* – Gracious me! I've been talking prose for the last forty years and have never known it. [*Le Bourgeois Gentilhomme*, II. iv]

6 *Ah, la belle chose que de savoir quelque-chose.* – Oh, how fine it is to know a thing or two. [*Ib.* II. vi]

7 *On ne meurt qu'une fois, et c'est pour si longtemps!* – One only dies once – but one is dead so long! [*Le Dépit amoureux*, V. iii]

8 *Il n'est rien d'égal au tabac; c'est la passion des honnêtes gens, et qui vit sans tabac n'est pas digne de vivre.* – There's nothing like tobacco; it is the passion of all decent men; a man who lives without tobacco does not deserve to live. [*Don Juan*, I. i]

9 *Je consens qu'une femme ait des clartés de tout, / Mais je ne lui veux point la passion choquante / De se rendre savante afin d'être savante / Et j'aime que souvent, aux questions qu'on fait, / Elle sache ignorer les choses qu'elle sait.* – I am quite agreeable that a woman shall be informed about everything, but I cannot allow her the shocking passion for acquiring learning in order to be learned. When she is asked questions, I like her often to know how not to know the thing she does know. [*Les Femmes savantes*, I. iii]

10 *La grammaire qui sait régenter jusqu'aux rois.* – Grammar, which can govern even kings. [*Ib.* II. vi]

11 *Je vis de bonne soupe, et non de beau langage.* – I live on good soup, not on fine words. [*Ib.* II. vii]

12 *Guenille, si l'on veut: ma guenille m'est chère.* – Rags they may be, but I love my rags. [*Ib.*]

13 *Et je vous suis garant / Qu'un sot savant est sot plus qu'un sot ignorant.* – I assure you that a learned fool is more foolish than an ignorant fool. [*Ib.* IV. iii]

14 *Que diable allait-il faire dans cette galère?* – What the devil was he up to in that galley? [*Les Fourberies de Scapin*, II. vii]

15 *Vous l'avez voulu, George Dandin, vous l'avez voulu.* – You asked for it, George Dandin, you asked for it. [*George Dandin*, I. ix]

16 *Il faut qu'il ait tué bien des gens pour s'être fait si riche.* – He must have killed a lot of men to have made so much money. [*Le Malade imaginaire*, I. v]

17 *Je veux qu'il me batte, moi. . . . Il me plait d'être battue.* – I want him to beat me. . . . I like being beaten. [*Le Medicin malgré lui*, I. ii]

18 GÉRONTE: *Il me semble que vous les placez autrement qu'ils ne sont; que le cœur est du côté gauche, et le foie du côté droit.* – I think you are putting them in their wrong places. The heart is on the left and the liver on the right.

261

SGANARELLE: *Oui, cela était autrefois ainsi, mais nous avons changé tout cela.* – Yes, that was so in the old days. But we have changed all that. [*Le Medicin malgré lui*, II. iv]

1 *Je veux qu'on me distingue; et pour le trancher net, / L'ami du genre humain n'est pas du tout mon trait.* – I want to be understood; to be quite frank, the friend of the human race is not in the least my role. [*Le Misanthrope*, I. i]

2 *Ces haines vigoureuses / Que doit donner le vice aux âmes vertueuses.* – Those strong dislikes that vice should inspire in virtuous souls. [*Ib.*]

3 *Il faut, parmi le monde, une vertu traitable.* – Virtue in this world should be malleable. [*Ib.*]

4 *La parfaite raison fuit tout extrémité, / Et veut que l'on soit sage avec sobriété.* – Pure reason avoids extremes, and requires one to be wise in moderation. [*Ib.*]

5 *C'est une folie à nulle autre seconde, / De vouloir se mêler à corriger le monde.* – It is a stupidity second to none, to busy oneself with the correction of the world. [*Ib.*]

6 *Si le roi m'avait donné / Paris, sa grand' ville, / Et qu'il me fallût quitter / L'amour de ma mie, / Je dirais au roi Henri: / Reprenez votre Paris.* – If the king gave me Paris, his great city, and I had to give up my darling's love, I should say to King Henry, Take your Paris back. [(Old song) *Ib.* I. ii]

7 *Et les deux bras croisés, du haut de son esprit, / Il regarde en pitié tout ce que chacun dit.* – And with his arms crossed he looks pityingly down from his spiritual height on everything that anyone says. [*Ib.* II. ii]

8 *On doit se regarder soi-même un fort long temps, / Avant que de songer à condamner les gens.* – One should examine oneself for a very long time before thinking of condemning others. [*Ib.* III. iv]

9 *L'âge amènera tout, et ce n'est pas le temps, / Madame, comme on sait, d'être prude à vingt ans.* – Age will bring all things, and everyone knows, Madame, that twenty is no age to be a prude. [*Ib.*]

10 *Oui, je vous l'ai déjà dit, ils commencent ici* [Paris] *par faire pendre un homme et puis ils lui font son procès.* – Yes, as I have already told you, here they hang a man first and try him afterwards. [*Monsieur de Pourceaugnac*, III. i]

11 *Les gens de qualité savent tout sans avoir rien appris.* – People of quality know everything without learning anything. [*Les Précieuses ridicules*, ix]

12 *Le pauvre homme!* – Poor man! [*Tartuffe*, I. iv, *passim*]

13 *Couvrez ce sein que je ne saurais voir: / Par de pareils objets les âmes sont blessées, / Et cela fait venir de coupables pensées.* – Cover that bosom. I must not see it. Souls are wounded by such things, and they arouse wicked thoughts. [*Ib.* III. ii]

14 *Ah! pour être dévot, je n'en suis pas moins homme!* – Oh, I may be devout, but I am human all the same. [*Ib.* III. iii]

15 *Le ciel défend, de vrai, certains contentements: / Mais on trouve avec lui des accommodements.* – Of course heaven forbids certain pleasures, but one finds means of compromise. [*Ib.* IV. v]

16 *La scandale du monde est ce qui fait l'offense, / Et ce n'est pas pécher que pécher en silence.* – It is a public scandal that offends; to sin in secret is no sin at all. [*Ib.*]

17 *L'homme est, je vous l'avoue, un méchant animal.* – Man is, I confess, a wicked creature. [*Ib.* V. vi]

COSMO MONKHOUSE 1840–1901

18 There was an old party of Lyme, / Who married three wives at one time, / When asked, 'Why the third?' / He replied, 'One's absurd, / And bigamy, sir, is a crime!' [Limerick]

DUKE OF MONMOUTH 1649–1685

19 Do not hack me as you did my Lord Russell. [Words to his executioner]

HAROLD MONRO 1879–1932

20 When the tea is brought at five o'clock, / And all the neat curtains are drawn with care, / The little black cat with bright green eyes / Is suddenly purring there. [*Milk for the Cat*]

1 The white saucer like some full moon descends / At last from the clouds of the table above. [*Milk for the Cat*]

JOHN MONSELL   1811–1875

2 Fight the good fight with all thy might, / Christ is thy strength and Christ thy right. / Lay hold on life, and it shall be / Thy joy and crown eternally. [Hymn]

LADY MARY WORTLEY MONTAGU   1689–1762

3 Be plain in dress, and sober in your diet; / In short, my deary! kiss me, and be quiet. [*Summary of Lord Lyttelton's Advice*]

4 Satire should, like a polished razor keen, / Wound with a touch that's scarcely felt or seen. [*To the Imitator of the First Satire of Horace*, Bk II]

5 This world consists of men, women, and Herveys. [*Letters and Works*, 'Introductory Anecdotes']

C. E. MONTAGUE   1867–1928

6 I was born below par to th' extent of two whiskies. [*Fiery Particles*]

MICHEL DE MONTAIGNE   1533–1592

7 Unless a man feels he has a good enough memory, he should never venture to lie. [*Essays*, I. ix]

8 The continuous labour of your life is to build the house of death. [*Ib.* I. xx]

9 One must always have one's boots on and be ready to go. [*Ib.*]

10 The value of life lies, not in the length of days, but in the use we make of them; a man may live long, yet live very little. Satisfaction in life depends not on the number of your years, but on your will. [*Ib.*]

11 The daughter-in-law of Pythagoras said that a woman who goes to bed with a man ought to lay aside her modesty with her skirt, and put it on again with her petticoat. [*Ib.* I. xxi]

12 A little of everything and nothing thoroughly, after the French fashion. [*Ib.* I. xxvi]

13 If I were pressed to say why I loved him, I feel that my only reply could be: 'Because it was he, because it was I'. [*Essays*, I. xxviii]

14 The greatest thing in the world is to know how to be self-sufficient. [*Ib.* I. xxxix]

15 To know how to live is my trade and my art. [*Ib.* II. vi]

16 Virtue will have nothing to do with ease ... It demands a steep and thorny road. [*Ib.* II. xi]

17 When I play with my cat, who knows whether she is not amusing herself with me more than I with her. [*Ib.* II. xii]

18 Life is a dream; when we sleep we are awake, and when awake we sleep. [*Ib.*]

19 *Que sais-je?* – What do I know? [*Ib.* Also inscribed on Montaigne's medal]

20 There is, in public affairs, no state so bad, provided it has age and stability on its side, that it is not preferable to change and disturbance. [*Ib.* II. xvii]

21 Many a man has been a wonder to the world, whose wife and valet have seen nothing in him that was even remarkable. Few men have been admired by their servants. [*Ib.* III. ii]

22 It [marriage] is like a cage; one sees the birds outside desperate to get in, and those inside equally desperate to get out. [*Ib.* III. v]

23 The world is but a school of inquiry. [*Ib.* III. viii]

24 Poverty of goods is easily cured; poverty of soul, impossible. [*Ib.* III. x]

25 It might well be said of me that here I have merely made up a bunch of other men's flowers, and provided nothing of my own but the string to bind them. [*Ib.* III. xii]

26 A man who fears suffering is already suffering from what he fears. [*Ib.* III. xiii]

LÉON MONTENAEKEN   1859–?

27 *La vie est vaine: / Un peu d'amour, / Un peu de haine. .... / Et puis – bonjour!*

    La vie est brève: / Un peu d'espoir, / Un peu de rêve / Et puis – bon soir!

    Life is fruitless: a little love, a little hate ... and then – good morning.

Life is brief: a little hope, a little dream and then – good night! [*Peu de chose*]

CHARLES, BARON DE MONTESQUIEU 1689–1755

1 An empire founded by war has to maintain itself by war. [*Considérations sur les causes de la grandeur des Romains et de leur décadence*, Ch. 8]

2 Liberty is the right to do everything which the laws allow. [*L'Esprit des lois*, XI. 3]

3 There is a very good saying that if triangles invented a god, they would make him three-sided. [*Lettres persanes*, 59]

4 I suffer from the disease of writing books and being ashamed of them when they are finished. [*Pensées diverses*, 'Portrait de Montesquieu par lui-même']

JAMES MONTGOMERY 1771–1854

5 Here in the body pent, / Absent from Him I roam, / Yet nightly pitch my moving tent / A day's march nearer home. [Hymn: *For Ever with the Lord*]

ROBERT MONTGOMERY 1807–1855

6 The solitary monk who shook the world. [*Luther, Man's Need and God's Supply*, 68]

MARQUIS OF MONTROSE 1612–1650

7 My dear and only love, I pray / This noble world of thee, / Be governed by no other sway / But purest monarchy. [*My dear and only Love*]

8 He either fears his fate too much, / Or his deserts are small, / That puts it not unto the touch / To win or lose it all. [*Ib.*]

9 But if thou wilt be constant then, / And faithful of thy word, / I'll make thee glorious by my pen, / And famous by my sword. [*Ib.*]

PERCY MONTROSE 19 Cent.

10 In a cavern, in a canyon, / Excavating for a mine. / Dwelt a miner, Forty-niner, / And his daughter, Clementine. / Oh, my darling, Oh, my darling, Oh, my darling Clementine! / Thou art lost and gone for ever, dreadful sorry, Clementine. [*Clementine*]

11 Light she was and like a fairy, / And her shoes were number nine; / Herring boxes without topses, / Sandals were for Clementine. [*Ib.*]

12 But I kissed her little sister, / And forgot my Clementine. [*Ib.*]

EDWARD MOORE 1712–1757

13 This is adding insult to injuries. [*The Foundling*, V. ii]

GEORGE MOORE 1852–1933

14 All reformers are bachelors. [*The Bending of the Bough*, I]

15 A man travels the world over in search of what he needs and returns home to find it. [*The Brook Kerith*, Ch. 11]

16 Acting is therefore the lowest of the arts, if it is an art at all. [*Mummer-Worship*]

THOMAS MOORE 1779–1852

17 Row, brothers, row, the stream runs fast, / The Rapids are near and the daylight's past. [*A Canadian Boat Song*]

18 Believe me, if all those endearing young charms, / Which I gaze on so fondly to-day. [*Irish Melodies*, 'Believe me, if all . . .']

19 As the sun-flower turns on her god, when he sets, / The same look which she turned, when he rose. [*Ib.*]

20 Eyes of most unholy blue! [*Ib.* 'By that Lake']

21 You may break, you may shatter the vase, if you will, / But the scent of the roses will hang round it still. [*Ib.* 'Farewell! But Whenever']

22 The harp that once through Tara's halls / The soul of music shed, / Now hangs as mute as Tara's walls / As if that soul were fled. [*Ib.* 'The Harp that Once']

23 No, there's nothing half so sweet in life / As love's young dream. [*Ib.* 'Love's Young Dream']

1 The Minstrel Boy to the war is gone, / In the ranks of death you'll find him; / His father's sword he has girded on, / And his wild harp slung behind him. [*Irish Melodies*, 'The Minstrel Boy']

2 Oh! blame not the bard. [*Ib.* 'Oh! Blame Not']

3 Oh! breathe not his name, let it sleep in the shade, / Where cold and unhonoured his relics are laid. [*Ib.* 'Oh! Breathe Not']

4 Rich and rare were the gems she wore, / And a bright gold ring on her hand she bore. [*Ib.* 'Rich and Rare']

5 She is far from the land where her young hero sleeps, / And lovers are round her, sighing: / But coldly she turns from their gaze, and weeps, / For her heart in his grave is lying. [*Ib.* 'She is Far']

6 The light, that lies / In woman's eyes, / Has been my heart's undoing. [*Ib.* 'The Time I've Lost']

7 'Tis the last rose of summer / Left blooming alone; / All her lovely companions / Are faded and gone. [*Ib* ''Tis the Last Rose']

8 Then awake! the heavens look bright, my dear; / 'Tis never too late for delight, my dear; / And the best of all ways / To lengthen our days / Is to steal a few hours from the night, my dear! [*Ib.* 'The Young May Moon']

9 'Come, come,' said Tom's father, 'at your time of life, / There's no longer excuse for thus playing the rake – / It is time you should think, boy, of taking a wife' – / 'Why, so it is, father – whose wife shall I take?' [*A Joke Versified*]

10 I never nursed a dear gazelle, / To glad me with its soft black eye, / But when it came to know me well, / And love me, it was sure to die! [*Lalla-Rookh*, 'Fire-Worshippers', i. 279]

11 Like Dead Sea fruits, that tempt the eye, / But turn to ashes on the lips! [*Ib.* i. 484]

12 Some flow'rets of Eden ye still inherit, / But the trail of the serpent is over them all! [*Ib.* 'Paradise and the Peri', 206]

13 Oft in the stilly night, / Ere Slumber's chain has bound me, / Fond Memory brings the light / Of other days around me; / The smiles, the tears, / Of boyhood's years, / The words of love then spoken; / The eyes that shone, / Now

dimmed and gone, / The cheerful hearts now broken! [*National Airs*, 'Oft in the Stilly Night']

14 I feel like one / Who treads alone / Some banquet-hall deserted, / Whose lights are fled, / Whose garlands dead / And all but he departed! [*Ib.*]

15 Disguise our bondage as we will, / 'Tis woman, woman, rules us still. [*Sovereign Woman*]

THOMAS MORDAUNT 1730–1809

16 Sound, sound the clarion, fill the fife, / Throughout the sensual world proclaim, / One crowded hour of glorious life / Is worth an age without a name. [*Verses written during the War 1756–63*]

SIR THOMAS MORE 1478–1535

17 Your sheep, that were wont to be so meek and tame and so small eaters, now, as I hear say, be become so great devourers, and so wild, that they eat up and swallow down the very men themselves. [*Utopia*, Bk I]

18 This hath not offended the king. [(As he pushed his beard aside at his execution) Bacon, *Apophthegms*, 22]

19 Yea, marry, now it is somewhat, for now it is rhyme; before, it was neither rhyme nor reason. [(To a friend who had versified an indifferent book) *Ib.* 287]

20 Is not this house [the Tower of London] as nigh heaven as my own? [Roper, *Life of Sir T. More*]

21 I pray you, Master Lieutenant, see me safe up, and for my coming down let me shift for myself. [(On mounting the scaffold) *Ib.*]

J. M. MOREHEAD 1796–1866

22 It's a long time between drinks. [Said to the Governor of South Carolina, when Morehead was Governor of North Carolina]

THOMAS MORELL 1703–1784

23 See, the conquering hero comes! / Sound the trumpets, beat the drums! [*Joshua*, Pt 3]

AUGUSTUS DE MORGAN
1806–1871

1 Great fleas have little fleas upon their backs to bite 'em, / And little fleas have lesser fleas, and so *ad infinitum*. [*A Budget of Paradoxes*, p. 377]

CHARLES MORRIS   1745–1838

2 If one must have a villa in summer to dwell, / Oh give me the sweet shady side of Pall Mall! [*The Contrast*, last lines]

G. P. MORRIS   1802–1864

3 Woodman, spare that tree! / Touch not a single bough! / In youth it sheltered me, / And I'll protect it now. [*Woodman, spare that Tree*]

WILLIAM MORRIS   1834–1896

4 The idle singer of an empty day. [*The Earthly Paradise*, 'An Apology']

5 Dreamer of dreams, born out of my due time, / Why should I strive to set the crooked straight? / Let it suffice me that my murmuring rhyme / Beats with light wing against the ivory gate, / Telling a tale not too importunate. [*Ib.*]

6 Forget six counties overhung with smoke, / Forget the snorting steam and piston stroke, / Forget the spreading of the hideous town; / Think rather of the packhorse on the down, / And dream of London, small and white and clean, / The clear Thames bordered by its gardens green. [*Ib.* Prologue, 'The Wanderers']

7 Had she come all the way for this, / To part at last without a kiss? [*The Haystack in the Floods*]

8 Swerve to the left, son Roger, he said, / When you catch his eyes through the helmet-slit, / Swerve to the left, then out at his head, / And the Lord God give you the joy of it! [*The Judgment of God*]

9 I know a little garden close / Set thick with lily and red rose, / Where I would wander if I might / From dewy dawn to dewy night, / And have one with me wandering. [*The Life and Death of Jason*, IV. 577]

10 Love is enough: though the world be a-waning, / And the woods have no voice but the voice of complaining. [*Love is Enough*]

11 You must be very old, Sir Giles, / I said; he said: Yea, very old! [*Old Love*]

12 There were four of us about that bed; / The mass-priest knelt at the side, / I and his mother stood at the head, / Over his feet lay the bride. [*Shameful Death*]

13 He did not die in the night, / He did not die in the day, / But in the morning twilight / His spirit passed away. [*Ib.*]

14 Pray but one prayer for me 'twixt thy closed lips. [*Summer Dawn*]

15 Speak but one word to me over the corn, / Over the tender, bowed locks of the corn. [*Ib.*]

16 There was a knight came riding by / In early spring, when the roads were dry; / And he heard that lady sing at the noon, / *Two red roses across the moon*. [*Two Red Roses across the Moon*]

17 Wind, wind! thou art sad, art thou kind? / Wind, wind, unhappy! thou art blind, / Yet still thou wanderest the lily-seed to find. [*The Wind*]

18 Fellowship is heaven, and lack of fellowship is hell; fellowship is life, and lack of fellowship is death; and the deeds that ye do upon the earth, it is for fellowship's sake that ye do them. [*The Dream of John Ball*, Ch. 4]

THOMAS MORTON   1764–1838

19 Push on – keep moving. [*A Cure for the Heartache*, II. i]

20 Approbation from Sir Hubert Stanley is praise indeed. [*Ib.* V. ii]

21 Always ding, dinging Dame Grundy into my ears – What will Mrs Grundy say? What will Mrs Grundy think? [*Speed the Plough*, I. i]

WILLIAM MOTHERWELL
1797–1835

22 I've wandered east, I've wandered west, / Through mony a weary way; / But never, never can forget / The love o' life's young day. [*Jeannie Morrison*]

J. L. MOTLEY   1814–1877

1 As long as he lived, he was the guiding-star of a whole brave nation, and when he died the little children cried in the streets. [(William the Silent) *The Rise of the Dutch Republic*, Pt VI. Ch. 7]

2 Give us the luxuries of life, and we will dispense with its necessities. [O. W. Holmes, *Autocrat of the Breakfast Table*, Ch. 6]

PETER MOTTEUX   1660–1718

3 The devil was sick, the devil a monk wou'd be: / The devil was well, and the devil a monk he'd be. [Translation of Rabelais, Bk IV. Ch. 24]

EDWIN MUIR   1887–1959

4 We have seen / Good men made evil wrangling with the evil, / Straight minds grown crooked fighting crooked minds. / Our peace betrayed us; we betrayed our peace. / Look at it well. This was the good town once. [*The Good Town*]

5 Oh these deceits are strong almost as life. /Last night I dreamt I was in the labyrinth, / And woke far on. I did not know the place. [*The Labyrinth*]

6 There is a road that turning always / Cuts off the country of Again. / Archers stand there on every side / And as it runs Time's deer is slain, / And lies where it has lain. [*The Road*]

7 See him, the gentle Bible beast, / With lacquered hoofs and curling mane, / His wondering journey from the East / Half done, between the rock and plain. [*The Toy Horse*]

DINAH MULOCK *see* **CRAIK, DINAH**

ANTHONY MUNDAY   1553–1633

8 Beauty sat bathing by a spring. [*To Colin Clout*]

H. H. MUNRO *see* **SAKI**

ERNST MÜNSTER   1766–1839

9 Absolutism tempered by assassination. [(Describing the Russian Constitution) Letter]

ARTHUR MURPHY   1727–1805

10 Above the vulgar flight of common souls. [*Zenobia*, V. i]

C. W. MURPHY   19 Cent.

11 Has anybody here seen Kelly? / Kelly from the Isle of Man? [*Has Anybody Here seen Kelly?*]

12 We all go the Same Way Home. [Title of song]

FRED MURRAY   ?–1922

13 Our Lodger's such a nice young Man. [Title of song]

ALFRED DE MUSSET   1810–1857

14 *Je ne puis; – malgré moi l'infini me tourmente.* – I cannot help it; – in spite of myself, infinity torments me. [*L'Espoir en Dieu*, 9]

15 *Les grands artistes n'ont pas de patrie.* – Great artists have no country. [*Lorenzaccio*, I. v]

16 *Les plus désespérés sont les chants les plus beaux* / *Et j'en sais d'immortels qui sont de purs sanglots.* – The most despairing songs are the most beautiful, and I know some immortal ones that are pure tears. [*La Nuit de mai*]

17 *Il faut qu'une porte soit ouverte ou fermée.* – A Door must be either Open or Shut. [Title of comedy]

18 *On ne badine pas avec l'amour.* – One Must not Trifle with Love. [Title of comedy]

IAN NAIRN   1930–1983

19 Subtopia. [Title of article in *Architectural Review*, June 1955]

LADY NAIRNE   1766–1845

20 Better lo'ed ye canna be, / Will ye no come back again? [*Bonnie Charlie's now awa!*]

21 Wha'll buy my caller herrin'? / They're bonnie fish and halesome farin'. [*Caller Herring*]

1 Charlie is my darling, my darling, my darling, / Charlie is my darling, the young Chevalier. [*Charlie is my Darling*]

2 Wi' a hundred pipers an' a', an' a'. [*The Hundred Pipers*]

3 I was daft to refuse the Laird o' Cockpen. [*The Laird o' Cockpen*]

4 I'm wearin' awa'. / To the land o' the leal. [*The Land o' the Leal*]

SIR CHARLES NAPIER 1782–1853

5 *Peccavi.* [(I have Scinde) Dispatch after victory of Hyderabad in Scinde, 1843]

NAPOLEON BONAPARTE 1769–1821

6 Soldiers, consider that from the summit of these pyramids, forty centuries look down upon you. [Speech before the Battle of the Pyramids, 1798]

7 In war, moral considerations account for three-quarters, the balance of actual forces only for the other quarter. [Letter, 27 Aug. 1808]

8 There rises the sun of Austerlitz. [Before Moscow, 1812]

9 From the sublime to the ridiculous there is only one step. [After the retreat from Moscow, 1812]

10 The bullet that is to kill me has not yet been moulded. [Said in 1814, when the Spanish king asked whether he had ever been hit by a cannon-ball]

11 Every French soldier carries in his cartridge-pouch the baton of a marshal of France. [Quoted in E. Blaze, *La Vie militaire sous l'empire*]

12 *Le courage de l'improviste.* – Spontaneous courage. [Quoted in Las Cases, *Mémorial de Ste Hélène*]

13 England is a nation of shopkeepers. [(Quoting Adam Smith) O'Meara, *Napoleon at St Helena*]

14 *La carrière ouverte aux talents.* – The career open to talents. [Quoted in O'Meara, *Napoleon in Exile*]

15 An army marches on its stomach. [Attr.]

16 *Tête d'Armée.* – Chief of the Army. [Last words]

17 Love then, and even later, was the whole concern of everyone's life. That is always the fate of leisured societies. [Quoted by F. L. Lucas in *Tragedy*]

OGDEN NASH 1902–1971

18 Ask Daddy, He Won't Know. [Title of poem]

19 The song of canaries / Never varies, / And when they're moulting / They're pretty revolting. [*The Canary*]

20 May I join you in the doghouse, Rover? / I wish to retire till the party's over. [*Children's Party*]

21 To be an Englishman is to belong to the most exclusive club there is. [*England Expects*]

22 Children aren't happy with nothing to ignore, / And that's what parents were created for. [*The Parent*]

23 Middle-aged life is merry, and I love to lead it. [*Peekaboo, I almost See You*]

24 A bit of talcum / Is always walcum [*Reflection on Babies*]

25 Candy is dandy, / But liquor is quicker. [*Reflection on Ice-Breaking*]

26 When Ah itchez, Ah scratchez. [*Requiem*]

27 What chills the finger not a bit / Is so frigid upon the fundament. [*Samson Agonistes*]

28 I think that I shall never see / A billboard lovely as a tree. / Perhaps unless the billboards fall, / I'll never see a tree at all. [*Song of the Open Road*]

THOMAS NASHE 1567–1601

29 Adieu, farewell earth's bliss, / This world uncertain is. [*In Plague Time*]

30 Beauty is but a flower / Which wrinkles will devour; / Brightness falls from the air, / Queens have died young and fair, / Dust hath closed Helen's eye, / I am sick, I must die. / Lord, have mercy on us! [*Ib.*]

31 Spring, the sweet spring, is the year's pleasant king; / Then blooms each thing, then maids dance in a ring, / Cold doth not sting, the pretty birds do sing: / Cuckoo, jug-jug, pu-we, to-witta-woo! [*Spring*]

JAMES NAYLOR   1860–1945

1 King David and King Solomon / Led merry, merry lives. [*Ancient Authors*]

JOHN MASON NEALE 1818–1866

2 Around the throne of God, a band / Of glorious angels ever stand. [Hymn]

3 Art thou weary, art thou languid, / Art thou sore distressed? [Hymn]

4 Brief life is here our portion; / Brief sorrow, short-lived care. [Hymn]

5 Christian! dost thou see them / On the holy ground, / How the troops of Midian / Prowl and prowl around? / Christian! up and smite them. / Counting gain but loss: / Smite them by the merit / Of the Holy Cross! [Hymn]

6 Ever Three and ever One; / Consubstantial, co-eternal, / While unending ages run. [Hymn: *Come ye Faithful*]

7 Good King Wenceslas looked out, / On the Feast of Stephen; / When the snow lay round about, / Deep and crisp and even. [Carol]

8 Hither, page, and stand by me, / If thou know'st it, telling, / Yonder peasant, who is he? / Where and what his dwelling? [*Ib.*]

9 In his master's steps he trod, / Where the snow lay dinted. [*Ib.*]

10 Jerusalem the golden, / With milk and honey blest, / Beneath thy contemplation / Sink heart and voice opprest. [Hymn]

HORATIO, VISCOUNT NELSON   1758–1805

11 The Nelson touch. [Private diary, 9 Oct. 1805]

12 You must hate a Frenchman as you hate the devil. [Southey's *Life of Nelson*, Ch. 3]

13 Westminster Abbey or victory! [(At Battle of Cape St Vincent) *Ib.* 4]

14 Before this time tomorrow I shall have gained a peerage, or Westminster Abbey. [(Battle of Nile) *Ib.* 5]

15 It is warm work; and this day may be the last to any of us at a moment. But mark you! I would not be elsewhere for thousands. [(Battle of Copenhagen) *Ib.* 7]

16 I have a right to be blind sometimes . . . I really do not see the signal! [(Putting the telescope to his blind eye at the Battle of Copenhagen) Southey's *Life of Nelson*, 7]

17 England expects every man will do his duty. [(Battle of Trafalgar) *Ib.* 9]

18 Thank God, I have done my duty. [*Ib.*]

19 Kiss me, Hardy. [*Ib.*]

EMPEROR NERO   37–68

20 *Qualis artifex pereo!* – What an artist dies in me! [Dying words, quoted by Suetonius, *Nero*, 49]

GÉRARD DE NERVAL 1808–1855

21 *Je suis le ténébreux, – le veuf, – l'inconsolé, / Le prince d'Aquitaine à la tour abolie.* – I am the shadowy one – the widower – the unconsoled – the prince of Aquitaine whose tower has been destroyed. [*El Desdichado*]

E. NESBIT   1858–1924

22 Oh! little brown brother, / Are you awake in the dark? [*Baby Seed Song*]

ALLAN NEVINS   1890–1971

23 Offering Germany too little, and offering even that too late. [*Current History*, May 1935]

SIR HENRY NEWBOLT 1862–1938

24 Here's to the bold and free! [*Admirals All*]

25 Admirals all, for England's sake. [*Ib.*]

26 To set the cause above renown, / To love the game beyond the prize, / To honour, while you strike him down, / The foe that comes with fearless eyes. [*Clifton Chapel*]

27 'Qui procul hinc', the legend's writ, – / The frontier-grave is far away – / 'Qui ante diem periit: / Sed miles, sed pro patria.' [(Who died far from here, before his time, but as a soldier, and for his country) *Ib.*]

28 Take my drum to England, hang et by the shore. / Strike et when your powder's runnin' low; / If the Dons sight Devon,

I'll quit the port o' Heaven, / An' drum them up the Channel as we drummed them long ago. [*Drake's Drum*]

1 Drake he's in his hammock till the great Armadas come. (Capten, art tha sleepin' there below?) [*Ib.*]

2 Where the old trade's plyin', an' the old flag flyin'. [*Ib.*]

3 She's the Fighting Téméraire. [*The Fighting Téméraire*]

4 'Ye have robbed,' said he, 'ye have slaughtered and made an end, / Take your ill-got plunder, and bury the dead.' [*He Fell Among Thieves*]

5 There's a breathless hush in the Close tonight – / Ten to make and the match to win – / A bumping pitch and a blinding light, / An hour to play and the last man in. / And it's not for the sake of a ribboned coat, / Or the selfish hope of a season's fame, / But his Captain's hand on his shoulder smote – / 'Play up! play up! and play the game!' [*Vitae Lampada*]

6 The sand of the desert is sodden red, – Red with the wreck of a square that broke; – / The gatling's jammed and the colonel dead, / And the regiment blind with the dust and smoke. / The river of death has brimmed its banks / And England's far and honour a name, / But the voice of a schoolboy rallies the ranks: / 'Play up! play up! and play the game!' [*Ib.*]

MARGARET, DUCHESS OF NEWCASTLE   1624?–1673

7 For all the Brothers were valiant, and all the Sisters virtuous. [Her epitaph in Westminster Abbey]

CARDINAL NEWMAN   1801–1890

8 He has attempted (as I may call it) to *poison the wells*. [*Apologia Pro Vita Sua*, 'Mr Kingsley's Method of Disputation']

9 I recollect an acquaintance saying to me that 'the Oriel Common Room stank of Logic.' [*History of My Religious Opinions*]

10 It is almost a definition of a gentleman to say that he is one who never inflicts pain. [*The Idea of a University*, 'Knowledge and Religious Duty']

11 Lead, Kindly Light, amid the encircling gloom, / Lead Thou me on! / The night is dark, and I am far from home – / Lead Thou me on! [Hymn]

12 I loved the garish day, and, spite of fears, / Pride ruled my will: remember not past years. [*Ib.*]

13 And with the morn those angel faces smile / Which I have loved long since, and lost awhile. [*Ib.*]

SIR ISAAC NEWTON   1642–1727

14 I do not know what I may appear to the world, but to myself I seem to have been only like a boy playing on the sea-shore, and diverting myself in now and then finding a smoother pebble or a prettier shell than ordinary, whilst the great ocean of truth lay all undiscovered before me. [Brewster's *Memoirs of Newton*, II. Ch. 27]

15 O Diamond! Diamond! thou little knowest the mischief done! [Attr. remark to a dog that 'destroyed the almost finished labours of some years']

JOHN NEWTON   1725–1807

16 Glorious things of thee are spoken, / Zion, city of our God. [*Olney Hymns*, 'Glorious Things']

17 How sweet the name of Jesus sounds / In a believer's ear! [*Ib.* 'The Name of Jesus']

NICHOLAS I OF RUSSIA   1796–1855

18 We have a sick man – a seriously sick man on our hands. [(Turkey) Quoted in a letter by Sir G. H. Seymour, 1853]

19 Russia has two generals in whom she can trust – Generals Janvier and Février. [*Punch*, 10 Mar. 1853]

ADELA NICOLSON *see* HOPE, LAURENCE

FRIEDRICH NIETZSCHE   1844–1900

20 I teach you the superman. Man is something that is to be surpassed. [*Also sprach Zarathustra*, Prologue, Ch. 3]

1 As an artist, a man has no home in Europe save in Paris. [*Ecce Homo*]

2 My time has not yet come either; some are born posthumously. [*Ib.*]

3 The masters have been abolished; the morality of the common man has triumphed. [*Genealogie der Moral*, Aphorism 9]

4 Morality in Europe today is herd-morality. [*Jenseits von Gut und Böse*]

5 Is not life a hundred times too short for us to bore ourselves? [*Ib.*]

FLORENCE NIGHTINGALE
1820–1910

6 Too kind – too kind. [When handed the insignia of the Order of Merit on her deathbed]

NIMROD [CHARLES APPERLEY] 1779–1843

7 'But he'll be drowned,' exclaims Lord Kinnaird.
  'I shouldn't wonder,' observes Mr William Coke. 'But the pace is too good to inquire.' [*The Chase*]

8 Quite the cream of the thing. [*Ib.*]

MILTON NOBLES 1847–1924

9 The villain still pursued her. [*Phoenix*, I. iii]

A. J. NOCK 1873–1945

10 It is an economic axiom as old as the hills that goods and services can be paid for only with goods and services. [*Memoirs of a Superfluous Man*, III. Ch. 3]

THOMAS NOEL 1799–1861

11 Rattle his bones over the stones; / He's only a pauper, whom nobody owns! [*The Pauper's Drive*]

REV. JOHN NORRIS 1657–1711

12 Like Angels' visits, short and bright; / Mortality's too weak to bear them long. [*The Parting*]

CHRISTOPHER NORTH [JOHN WILSON] 1785–1854

13 His Majesty's dominions, on which the sun never sets. [*Noctes Ambrosianae*, 20]

14 Laws were made to be broken. [*Ib.* 24]

SIR STAFFORD NORTHCOTE 1818–1887

15 That grand old man, the Prime Minister. [(Gladstone) Speech, 12 Apr. 1882]

CAROLINE NORTON 1808–1877

16 The Arab's Farewell to his Steed. [Title of poem]

17 I do not love thee! – no! I do not love thee! / And yet when thou art absent I am sad. [*I do Not Love Thee*]

18 All our calm is in that balm – / Not lost but gone before. [*Not Lost But Gone Before*]

NOVALIS [FRIEDRICH VON HARDENBERG] 1772–1801

19 *Ein Gott-betrunkener Mensch.* – A God-intoxicated man. [Description of Spinoza]

ALFRED NOYES 1880–1958

20 Go down to Kew in lilac-time, in lilac-time, in lilac-time. [*The Barrel Organ*]

NURSERY RHYMES

For sources, see Oxford Dictionary of Nursery Rhymes

21 A was an apple-pie; / B bit it; / C cut it.

22 As I was going to St Ives, / I met a man with seven wives.

23 Baa, baa, black sheep, / Have you any wool? / Yes, sir, yes, sir, / Three bags full.

24 Bobby Shaftoe's gone to sea, / Silver buckles at his knee; / He'll come back and marry me, / Bonny Bobby Shaftoe.

25 Boys and girls come out to play, / The moon doth shine as bright as day.

1 Bye, baby bunting, / Daddy's gone a-hunting, / Gone to get a rabbit skin / To wrap the baby bunting in.

2 Cock a doodle doo! / My dame has lost her shoe, / My master's lost his fiddling stick, / And knows not what to do.

3 Come, let's to bed, / Says Sleepy-head; / Tarry a while, says Slow; / Put on the pot, says Greedy-gut, / We'll sup before we go.

4 Cross-patch, / Draw the latch, / Sit by the fire and spin.

5 Curly locks. Curly locks, / Wilt thou be mine? / Thou shalt not wash dishes / Nor yet feed the swine; / But sit on a cushion / And sew a fine seam, / And feed upon strawberries, / Sugar and cream.

6 Daffy-down-dilly is new come to town, / With a yellow petticoat, and a green gown.

7 Ding, dong, bell, / Pussy's in the well. / Who put her in? / Little Johnny Green.

8 Fee, fi, fo, fum, / I smell the blood of an Englishman; / Be he alive or be he dead, / I'll grind his bones to make my bread.

9 A frog he would a wooing go. / 'Heigh ho!' says Rowley.

10 Georgie Porgie, pudding and pie, / Kissed the girls and made them cry; / When the boys came out to play, / Georgie Porgie ran away.

11 Goosey goosey gander, / Whither shall I wander? / Upstairs and downstairs, / And in my lady's chamber. / There I met an old man / Who would not say his prayers; / I took him by the left leg, / And threw him down the stairs.

12 Here is the church, and here is the steeple; / Open the door and here are the people.

13 Hey diddle, diddle, / The cat and the fiddle, / The cow jumped over the moon; / The little dog laughed / To see such sport, / And the dish ran away with the spoon.

14 Hickory, dickory, dock, / The mouse ran up the clock. / The clock struck one, / The mouse ran down, / Hickory, dickory, dock.

15 Hot cross buns! Hot cross buns! / One a penny, two a penny, / Hot cross buns!

16 How many miles to Babylon? / Three-score and ten. / Can I get there by candle-light? / Yes, and back again.

17 Humpty Dumpty sat on a wall, / Humpty Dumpty had a great fall; / All the King's horses, and all the King's men, / Couldn't put Humpty together again.

18 Hush-a-bye, baby, on the tree top, / When the wind blows the cradle will rock; / When the bough breaks the cradle will fall, / Down will come baby, cradle, and all.

19 I had a little nut tree, / Nothing would it bear / But a silver nutmeg / And a golden pear; / The King of Spain's daughter / Came to visit me, / And all for the sake / Of my little nut tree.

20 I love little pussy, / Her coat is so warm, / And if I don't hurt her, / She'll do me no harm.

21 I love sixpence. jolly little sixpence, / I love sixpence better than my life.

22 I'm the king of the castle, / Get down you dirty rascal.

23 Jack and Jill / Went up the hill, / To fetch a pail of water; / Jack fell down, / And broke his crown, / And Jill came tumbling after.

24 Jack Sprat could eat no fat, / His wife could eat no lean; / And so between them both, you see, / They licked the platter clean.

25 Ladybird, ladybird, / Fly away home, / Your house is on fire, / And your children all gone.

26 The lion and the unicorn / Were fighting for the crown; / The lion beat the unicorn / All around the town.
Some gave them white bread, / And some gave them brown; / Some gave them plum cake / And drummed them out of town.

27 Little Bo-Peep has lost her sheep, / And doesn't know where to find them; / Leave them alone, and they'll come home, / Bringing their tails behind them.

28 Little boy blue, / Come blow up your horn, / The sheep's in the meadow, / The cow's in the corn. / Where is the boy / Who looks after the sheep? / He's under a haycock / Fast asleep.

29 Little Jack Horner / Sat in the corner, / Eating a Christmas pie; / He put in his thumb, and pulled out a plum, / And said, 'What a good boy am I!'

30 Little Miss Muffet / Sat on a tuffet, / Eating her curds and whey; / There came

a big spider, / Who sat down beside her / And frightened Miss Muffet away.

1 Little Polly Flinders / Sat among the cinders.

2 Little Tommy Tucker, / Sings for his supper. / What shall we give him? / White bread and butter.

3 London bridge is broken down, / My fair lady.

4 Mary had a little lamb, / His fleece was white as snow; / And everywhere that Mary went / The lamb was sure to go.

5 Mary, Mary, quite contrary, / How does your garden grow? / With silver bells, and cockle shells, / And pretty maids all in a row.

6 Monday's child is fair of face, / Tuesday's child is full of grace.

7 The north wind doth blow, / And we shall have snow, / And what will poor Robin do then? / Poor thing.
He'll sit in a barn, / And keep himself warm, / And hide his head under his wing, / Poor thing.

8 O dear, what can the matter be? / Johnny's so long at the fair.

9 He promised he'd bring me a bunch of blue ribbons / To tie up my bonny brown hair [Ib.]

10 Old King Cole / Was a merry old soul, / And a merry old soul was he; / He called for his pipe, / And he called for his bowl, / And he called for his fiddlers three.

11 Old Mother Hubbard / Went to the cupboard, / To get her poor dog a bone; / But when she got there, / The cupboard was bare, / And so the poor dog had none.

12 One, two, / Buckle my shoe; / Three, four, / Knock at the door.

13 Oranges and lemons, / Say the bells of St Clement's.

14 You owe me five farthings, / Say the bells of St Martin's. / When will you pay me? / Say the bells at Old Bailey. / When I grow rich, / Say the bells at Shoreditch. [Ib.]

15 Here comes a candle to light you to bed, / Here comes a chopper to chop off your head. [Ib.]

16 Pat-a-cake, pat-a-cake, baker's man, / Bake me a cake as fast as you can.

17 Pease porridge hot / Pease porridge cold, / Pease porridge in the pot / Nine days old.

18 Peter Piper picked a peck of pickled pepper.

19 Pussy cat, pussy cat, / Where have you been? / I've been up to London / To look at the Queen. / Pussy cat, pussy cat, / What did you there? / I frightened a little mouse / Under her chair.

20 The Queen of Hearts / She made some tarts, / All on a summer's day; / The Knave of Hearts / He stole the tarts, / And took them clean away.

21 Rain, rain, go away, / Come again another day.

22 Ride a cock-horse to Banbury Cross, / To see a fine lady upon a white horse; / Rings on her fingers and bells on her toes, / And she shall have music wherever she goes.

23 Ring-a-ring o' roses, / A pocket full of posies, / A-tishoo! A-tishoo! / We all fall down.

24 Round and round the rugged rock / The ragged rascal ran.

25 See-saw, Margery Daw, / Jacky shall have a new master; / Jacky shall have but a penny a day, / Because he can't work any faster.

26 Simple Simon met a pieman / Going to the fair.

27 Sing a song of sixpence, / A pocket full of rye; / Four and twenty blackbirds, / Baked in a pie.
When the pie was opened, / The birds began to sing; / Was not that a dainty dish, / To set before the king?
The king was in his counting-house, / Counting out his money; / The queen was in the parlour, / Eating bread and honey.
The maid was in the garden, / Hanging out the clothes, / When down came a blackbird / And pecked off her nose.

28 Solomon Grundy, / Born on a Monday.

29 Taffy was a Welshman, / Taffy was a thief; / Taffy came to my house / And stole a piece of beef.

30 Tell tale, tit! / Your tongue shall be split, / And all the dogs in the town / Shall have a little bit.

273

1 There was a crooked man, / And he walked a crooked mile, / He found a crooked sixpence / Against a crooked stile.

2 There was an old woman who lived in a shoe, / She had so many children she didn't know what to do.

3 This is the farmer sowing his corn, / That kept the cock that crowed in the morn, / That waked the priest all shaven and shorn, / That married the man all tattered and torn, / That kissed the maiden all forlorn, / That milked the cow with the crumpled horn, / That tossed the dog, / That worried the cat, / That killed the rat, / That ate the malt, / That lay in the house that Jack built. [*The House that Jack Built*]

4 This little pig went to market; / This little pig stayed at home.

5 Three blind mice, see how they run! / They all ran after the farmer's wife, / Who cut off their tails with a carving knife, / Did ever you see such a thing in your life, / As three blind mice?

6 Three wise men of Gotham / Went to sea in a bowl; / And if the bowl had been stronger, / My song would have been longer.

7 Tom, he was a piper's son, / He learned to play when he was young, / But all the tune that he could play / Was, 'Over the hills and far away.'

8 Tom, Tom, the piper's son, / Stole a pig and away he run; / The pig was eat, and Tom was beat, / And Tom went howling down the street. [*Ib.*]

9 We are all in the dumps, / For diamonds are trumps; / The kittens are gone to St Paul's. / The babies are bit, / The Moon's in a fit, / And the houses are built without walls.

10 Wee Willie Winkie runs through the town, / Upstairs and downstairs in his nightgown.

11 What are little boys made of? / What are little boys made of? / Frogs and snails / And puppy-dogs' tails, / That's what little boys are made of.

What are little girls made of? / What are little girls made of? / Sugar and spice / And all things nice, / That's what little girls are made of.

12 Where are you going to, my pretty maid? / I'm going a-milking, sir, she said.

13 My face is my fortune, sir, she said. [*Where are you going to . . . ?*]

14 Then I can't marry you, my pretty maid. / Nobody asked you, sir she said. [*Ib.*]

15 Who killed Cock Robin? / I, said the Sparrow, / With my bow and arrow, / I killed Cock Robin.

16 Who saw him die? / I, said the Fly, / With my little eye, / I saw him die. [*Ib.*]

FREDERICK OAKELEY 1802–1880

17 O come all ye faithful, / Joyful and triumphant, / O come ye, O come ye to Bethlehem. [Hymn, transl. from Latin, *Adeste Fideles*]

SEAN O'CASEY   1880–1964

18 The whole world is in a state of chassis. [*Juno and the Paycock*, I. i]

ADOLPH OCHS   1858–1935

19 All the news that's fit to print. [Motto of the *New York Times*]

PATRICK O'KEEFE   1872–1934

20 Say it with flowers. [Slogan for Society of American Florists]

JOHN O'KEEFFE   1747–1833

21 Amo, amas, I love a lass, / As a cedar tall and slender; / Sweet cowslip's grace / Is her nominative case, / And she's of the feminine gender. [*The Agreeable Surprise*, II. ii]

22 Fat, fair and forty. [*Irish Minnie*, ii]

23 You shall always except the present company. [*The London Hermit*, I. ii]

DENNIS O'KELLY   1720?–1787

24 It will be Eclipse first, the rest nowhere. [At Epsom, 3 May 1769]

JOHN OLDHAM   1653–1683

25 Racks, gibbets, halters, were their arguments. [*Satires upon the Jesuits*, 'Garnet's Ghost', 176]

WILLIAM OLDYS   1696–1761

1 Busy, curious, thirsty fly / Drink with me, and drink as I. [*Busy, Curious, Thirsty Fly*]

JOHN OPIE   1761–1806

2 I mix them with brains, sir. [(When asked how he mixed his colours) Quoted in Samuel Smiles, *Self-Help*, Ch. 4]

BARONESS ORCZY   1865 1947

3 We seek him here, we seek him there, / Those Frenchies seek him everywhere. / Is he in heaven? – Is he in hell? / That demmed, elusive Pimpernel? [*The Scarlet Pimpernel*, Ch. 12]

J. B. O'REILLY   1844–1890

4 The organized charity, scrimped and iced, / In the name of a cautious, statistical Christ. [*In Bohemia*]

META ORRED   19 Cent.

5 In the gloaming, O, my darling! / When the lights are dim and low, / And the quiet shadows falling / Softly come and softly go. [*In the Gloaming*]

GEORGE ORWELL   1903–1950

6 Man is the only creature that consumes without producing. [*Animal Farm*, Ch. 1]

7 Four legs good, two legs bad. [*Ib.* 3]

8 All animals are equal, but some animals are more equal than others. [*Ib.* 10]

9 The creatures outside looked from pig to man, and from man to pig, and from pig to man again; but already it was impossible to say which was which. [*Ib.*]

10 Big Brother is watching you. [*1984*, Pt I. Ch. 1]

11 Only the Thought Police mattered. [*Ib.*]

12 War is Peace / Freedom is Slavery / Ignorance is Strength. [*Ib.*]

13 Newspeak was the official language of Oceania. [*Ib.* (footnote)]

14 His mind ... fetched up with a bump against the Newspeak word *doublethink*. [*Ib.*]

15 The Two Minutes Hate. [*1984*, I. 1]

16 The proles are not human beings. [*Ib.* I. 5]

17 Hate Week. [*Ib.*]

JOHN OSBORNE   1929–

18 But I have a go, lady, don't I? / I 'ave a go. I do. [*The Entertainer*, vii]

19 Don't clap too hard – it's a very old building. [*Ib.*]

20 Thank God we're normal, normal, normal, / Thank God we're normal, / Yes, this is our finest shower! [*Ib.*]

21 Well, there are only two posh papers on a Sunday – the one you're reading and this one. [*Look Back in Anger*, I]

22 He really deserves some sort of decoration ... a medal inscribed 'For Vaguery in the Field'. [*Ib.*]

23 I'm not mentioned at all because my name is a dirty word. [*Ib.*]

24 I don't think one 'comes down' from Jimmy's university. According to him, it's not even red brick, but white tile. [*Ib.* II. i]

25 They spend their time mostly looking forward to the past. [*Ib.*]

26 Poor old Daddy – just one of those sturdy old plants left over from the Edwardian Wilderness, that can't understand why the sun isn't shining any more. [*Ib.* II. ii]

27 There aren't any good brave causes left. If the big bang does come, and we all get killed off, it won't be in aid of the old-fashioned, grand design. It'll just be the Brave New-nothing-very-much-thank-you. [*Ib.* III. i]

ARTHUR O'SHAUGHNESSY
1844–1881

28 We are the music-makers / And we are the dreamers of dreams, / Wandering by lone sea-breakers, / And sitting by desolate streams; / World-losers and world-forsakers, / On whom the pale moon gleams: / Yet we are the movers and shakers / Of the world forever, it seems. [*Ode*]

29 One man with a dream, at pleasure, / Shall go forth and conquer a crown; /

And three with a new song's measure / Can trample a kingdom down. [*Ode*]

1 For each age is a dream that is dying, / Or one that is coming to birth. [*Ib.*]

JAMES OTIS   1725–1783

2 Taxation without representation is tyranny. [Watchword of the American Revolution. Attr.]

THOMAS OTWAY   1652–1685

3 Destructive, damnable, deceitful woman! [*The Orphan*, III. i]

4 O woman! lovely woman! Nature made thee / To temper man: we had been brutes without you; / Angels are painted fair, to look like you. [*Venice Preserved*, I, i]

SIR THOMAS OVERBURY
                               1581–1613

5 In part to blame is she, / Which hath without consent been only tried: / He comes too near that comes to be denied. [*A Wife*, 26]

OVID   43 B.C.–A.D. 17

6 *Procul hinc, procul este, severae!* – Stay far hence, far hence, forbidding ones! [*Amores*, II, i, 3]

7 *Forsitan et nostrum nomen miscebitur istis.* – Perhaps too our name will be joined with these. [*Ars Amatoria*, iii. 339]

8 *Gutta cavat lapidem, consumitur anulus usu.* – The dropping of rain hollows out a stone, a ring is worn by use. [*Epistulae Ex Ponto*, IV. x. 5]

9 *Iam seges est ubi Troia fuit.* – Now there are fields where Troy once was. [*Heroides*, I. i. 53]

10 *Medio tutissimus ibis.* – You will go most safely in the middle. [*Metamorphoses*, II. 137]

11 *Inopem me copia fecit.* – Plenty makes me poor. [*Ib.* III. 466]

12 *Video meliora, proboque; / Deteriora sequor.* – I see better things and approve; I follow the worse. [*Ib.* VII. 20]

13 *Tempus edax rerum.* – Time the devourer of things. [*Metamorphoses*, XXV. 234]

14 *Tu quoque.* – Thou also. [*Tristia*, ii. 39]

ROBERT OWEN   1771–1858

15 All the world is queer save thee and me, and even thou art a little queer. [When ending his partnership with William Allen]

WILFRED OWEN   1893–1918

16 What passing-bells for these who die as cattle? / Only the monstrous anger of the guns. / Only the stuttering rifles' rapid rattle / Can patter out their hasty orisons. [*Anthem for doomed Youth*]

17 And bugles calling for them from sad shires. [*Ib.*]

18 And each slow dusk a drawing-down of blinds. [*Ib.*]

19 Move him into the sun – / Gently its touch awoke him once / At home. [*Futility*]

20 Red lips are not so red / As the stained stones kissed by the English dead. / Kindness of wooed and wooer / Seems shame to their love pure. [*Greater Love*]

21 One sprang up, and stared / With piteous recognition in fixed eyes, / Lifting distressful hands, as if to bless. [*Strange Meeting*]

22 'Strange friend,' I said, 'here is no cause to mourn.' / 'None,' said the other, 'save the undone years, / The hopelessness. Whatever hope is yours / Was my life also; I went hunting wild / After the wildest beauty in the world.' [*Ib.*]

23 Courage was mine, and I had mystery, / Wisdom was mine, and I had mastery; / To miss the march of the retreating world / Into vain citadels that are not walled. [*Ib.*]

24 My subject is War, and the pity of War. The Poetry is in the pity. [Preface to *Poems*]

EDWARD OXENFORD 1847–1929

25 I fear no foe in shining armour. [Song]

AXEL COUNT OXENSTIERNA
1583–1654

1 Do you not know, my son, with how little wisdom the world is governed? [Letter to his son, 1648]

EDWARD DE VERE, EARL OF OXFORD   1550–1604

2 If women could be fair and yet not fond. [*Women's Changeableness*]

THOMAS PAINE   1737–1809

3 The sublime and the ridiculous are often so nearly related that it is difficult to class them separately. One step above the sublime makes the ridiculous; and one step above the ridiculous makes the sublime again. [*The Age of Reason*, ii, note]

4 These are the times that try men's souls. ['The American Crisis', in the *Pennsylvania Journal*, 1776]

5 The summer soldier and the sunshine patriot will, in this crisis, shrink from the service of their country. [*Ib.* 1785]

6 Government, even in its best state, is but a necessary evil; in its worst state, an intolerable one. [*Common Sense*, Ch. 1]

7 The final event to himself [Mr Burke] has been, that as he rose like a rocket, he fell like the stick. [*Letter to the Addressers on the late Proclamation*]

8 My country is the world, and my religion is to do good. [*The Rights of Man*, Pt ii, Ch. 5]

9 The religion of humanity. [Attr.]

JOSÉ DE PALAFOX   1780–1847

10 War to the knife. [When summoned to surrender Saragossa, 1808]

REV. WILLIAM PALEY
1743–1805

11 Who can refute a sneer? [*Moral Philosophy*, V. Ch. 9]

SAMUEL PALMER   1805–1881

12 A picture has been said to be something between a thing and a thought. [Quoted in Arthur Symons' *Life of Blake*]

VISCOUNT PALMERSTON
1784–1865

13 Accidental and fortuitous concurrence of atoms. [Speech in House of Commons, 1857]

14 Die, my dear Doctor, that's the last thing I shall do! [Attr. last words]

EDWARD PARAMORE   1895–1956

15 Hard-boiled as a picnic egg. [*The Ballad of Yukon Jake*]

DOROTHY PARKER   1893–1967

16 Men seldom make passes / At girls who wear glasses [*News Item*]

17 Guns aren't lawful; / Nooses give; / Gas smells. awful; / You might as well live. [*Résumé*]

18 Where's the man could ease a heart, / Like a satin gown? [*The Satin Dress*]

19 Excuse my dust. [*Her own Epitaph*]

20 She ran the whole gamut of her emotions from A to B. [Quoted in *Treasury of Humorous Quotations*]

MARTIN PARKER   ?–1656

21 You gentlemen of England / Who live at home at ease, / How little do you think / On the dangers of the seas. [*The Valiant Sailors*]

22 The Man in the Moon may wear out his shoon, / By running after Charles-his-Wain, / But all's to no end; for the times will not mend / Till the King enjoys his own again. [*When the King enjoys his Own again*]

CLARKE ROSS PARKER 1914–1974 and HUGHIE CHARLES 1907–

23 There'll always be an England / While there's a country lane, / Wherever there's a cottage small / Beside a field of grain [*There'll Always Be an England*]

CHARLES STEWART PARNELL 1846–1891

1 No man has a right to fix the boundary of the march of a nation; no man has a right to say to his country – thus far shalt thou go and no further. [Speech, 1885]

THOMAS PARNELL 1679–1717

2 We call it only pretty Fanny's way. [*An Elegy to an old Beauty*]

3 Remote from man, with God he passed the days, / Prayer all his business, all his pleasure praise. [*The Hermit*, 5]

4 Still an angel appear to each lover beside, / But still be a woman to you. [Song: *When thy Beauty Appears*]

SAMUEL PARR 1747–1825

5 Now that the old lion is dead, every ass thinks he may kick at him. [(Dr Johnson) Quoted in Boswell's *Life of Johnson*, 1784]

BLAISE PASCAL 1623–1662

6 Not to care for philosophy is to be a true philosopher [*Pensées*, I. 4]

7 The more intelligence one has the more people one finds original. Commonplace people see no difference between men. [*Ib.* I. 7]

8 The last thing one discovers in writing a book is what to put first. [*Ib.* I. 19]

9 When one finds a natural style, one is amazed and delighted, for where one expected to see an author, one discovers a man. [*Ib.* I. 29]

10 If you want people to think well of you, do not speak well of yourself. [*Ib.* I. 44]

11 Man of wit, bad character. [*Ib.* I. 46]

12 I cannot forgive Descartes; in all his philosophy he did his best to dispense with God. But he could not avoid making Him set the world in motion with a flip of His thumb; after that he had no more use for God. [*Ib.* II. 77]

13 If Cleopatra's nose had been shorter, the whole face of the earth would have changed. [*Ib.* II. 162]

14 The heart has its reasons, which are quite unknown to the head. [*Pensées*, IV. 277]

15 Man is no more than a reed, the weakest in nature. But he is a thinking reed. [*Ib.* VI. 347]

16 The I is hateful. [*Ib.* VII. 434]

17 Be comforted. You would not be seeking Me if you had not found Me. [*Ib.* VII. 552]

WALTER PATER 1839–1894

18 All art constantly aspires towards the condition of music. [*The Renaissance*, 'Giorgione']

19 She is older than the rocks among which she sits; like the vampire, she has been dead many times, and learned the secrets of the grave; and has been a diver in deep seas, and keeps their fallen day about her; and trafficked for strange webs with Eastern merchants: and, as Leda, was the mother of Helen of Troy, and, as Saint Anne, the mother of Mary; and all this has been to her but as the sound of lyres and flutes, and lives only in the delicacy with which it has moulded the changing lineaments, and tinged the eyelids and the hands. [(Mona Lisa) *Ib.* 'Leonardo da Vinci']

20 Art comes to you proposing frankly to give nothing but the highest quality to your moments as they pass, and simply for those moments' sake. [*Ib.* Conclusion]

21 To burn always with this hard, gem-like flame, to maintain this ecstasy, is success in life. [*Ib.*]

ANDREW PATERSON 1864–1941

22 Once a jolly swagman camped by a billy-bong, / Under the shade of a coolibah tree, / And he sang as he sat and waited for his billy-boil, / 'You'll come a-waltzing, Matilda, with me.' [*Waltzing Matilda*]

COVENTRY PATMORE 1823–1896

23 Ah, wasteful woman, she who may / On her sweet self set her own price, / Knowing man cannot choose but pay, / How has she cheapened paradise; / How given for nought her priceless gift, / How spoiled the bread and spilled the wine, /

Which, spent with due respective thrift, / Had made brutes men and men divine. [*The Angel in the House*, Bk I. iii, Prelude 3]

1 Love's perfect blossom only blows / Where noble manners veil defect. / Angels may be familiar; those / Who err each other must respect. [*Ib.* I. xi, Prelude 2]

2 'I saw you take his kiss!' ''Tis true.' / 'Oh, modesty!' ''Twas strictly kept: / He thought me asleep; at least, I knew / He thought I thought he thought I slept.' [*Ib.* II. viii, Prelude 3]

3 A woman is a foreign land, / Of which, though there he settle young, / A man will ne'er quite understand / The customs, politics, and tongue. [*Ib.* II. ix, Prelude 2]

4 Why, having won her, do I woo? / Because her spirit's vestal grace / Provokes me always to pursue, / But, spirit-like, eludes embrace. [*Ib.* II. xii, Prelude 1]

5 Because, in short, / She's not and never can be mine. [*Ib.*]

6 I, singularly moved / To love the lovely that are not beloved, / Of all the seasons, most / Love winter. [*The Unknown Eros*, Bk I. iii, 'Winter']

7 It was not like your great and gracious ways! / Do you, that have nought other to lament, / Never, my Love, repent / Of how, that July afternoon, / You went, / With sudden, unintelligible phrase, – And frightened eye, / Upon your journey of so many days, / Without a single kiss or a good-bye? [*Ib.* I. viii, 'Departure']

8 And the only loveless look the look with which you passed. [*Ib.*]

9 My little son, who looked from thoughtful eyes / And moved and spoke in quiet grown-up wise, / Having my law the seventh time disobeyed, / I struck him, and dismissed / With hard words and unkissed, / His mother, who was patient, being dead. [*Ib.* I. x, 'The Toys']

10 Here, in this little bay, / Full of tumultuous life and great repose, / Where, twice a day, / The purposeless, glad ocean comes and goes. [*Ib.* I. xii, 'Magna est Veritas']

11 For want of me the world's course will not fail: / When all its work is done, the lie shall rot; / The truth is great, and shall prevail, / When none cares whether it prevail or not. [*The Unknown Eros*, I. xii, 'Magna est Veritas']

12 If I were dead, you'd sometimes say, Poor Child! [*Ib.* I. xiv, 'If I were Dead']

13 With all my will, but much against my heart, / We two now part, / My Very Dear, / Our solace is, the sad road lies so clear. [*Ib.* I. xvi, 'A Farewell']

14 Shall I, the gnat that dances in thy ray, / Dare to be reverent? [*Ib.* II. xiv, 'Psyche's Discontent']

15 This is to say, my dear Augusta, / We've had another awful buster: / Ten thousand Frenchmen sent below! / Thank God from whom all blessings flow. [*Epigram on King William's dispatch to Queen Augusta, Aug. 1870.* From B. Champneys, *Coventry Patmore*]

JEAN PAUL [J. P. RICHTER] 1763–1825

16 *Diesen Weltschmerz kann er, so zu sagen, nur aushalten durch den Anblick der Seligkeit.* – He can, so to speak, only bear the sorrow of this world by gazing on blessedness. [*Selina*]

LESLIE PAUL 1905–

17 Angry Young Man. [Title of book, 1951]

JAMES PAYN 1830–1898

18 I never had a piece of toast / Particularly long and wide / But fell upon the sandy floor / And always on the buttered side. ['Parody', *Chambers' Journal*, 1884]

J. H. PAYNE 1792–1852

19 'Mid pleasures and palaces though we may roam, / Be it ever so humble, there's no place like home. [*Clari, the Maid of Milan*, 'Home, Sweet Home']

SIR EUSTACE PEACHTREE 17 Cent.

20 When men heard thunder on the left the gods had somewhat of special advertisement to impart. [*The Dangers of this Mortal Life*]

T. L. PEACOCK   1785–1866

1 A book that furnishes no quotations is, *me judice*, no book – it is a plaything. [*Crotchet Castle*, Ch. 9]

2 My house has been broken open on the most scientific principles. [*Ib.* 17]

3 Not drunk is he who from the floor / Can rise alone and still drink more; / But drunk is he, who prostrate lies, / Without the power to drink or rise. [*The Misfortunes of Elphin*, Ch. 3, heading]

4 The mountain sheep are sweeter, / But the valley sheep are fatter; / We therefore deemed it meeter / To carry off the latter. [*Ib.* 11]

5 He was sent, as usual, to a public school, where a little learning was painfully beaten into him, and from thence to the university, where it was carefully taken out of him. [*Nightmare Abbey*, Ch. 1]

6 Laughter is pleasant, but the exertion is too much for me. [(Hon. Mr Listless) *Ib.* 5]

7 Seamen three! what men be ye? / Gotham's three Wise Men we be. / Whither in your bowl so free? / To rake the moon from out the sea. / The bowl goes trim. The moon doth shine, / And our ballast is old wine. [*Ib.* 11, 'Three Men of Gotham']

COMMANDER R. PEARY   1856–1920

8 The Eskimo had his own explanation. Said he: 'The devil is asleep or having trouble with his wife, or we should never have come back so easily.' [*The North Pole*]

GEORGE PEELE   1558?–1597?

9 God in the whizzing of a pleasant wind / Shall march upon the tops of mulberry trees. [*David and Bethsabe*, XII]

10 Whenas the rye reach to the chin, / And chopcherry, chopcherry ripe within, / Strawberries swimming in the cream, / And schoolboys playing in the stream, / Then O, then O, then O, my true love said, / Till that time come again / She could not live a maid. [*The Old Wives' Tale*]

11 His golden locks time hath to silver turned; / O time too swift, O swiftness never ceasing! [*Polyhymnia*, Sonnet]

12 His helmet now shall make a hive for bees; / And lovers' sonnets turned to holy psalms, / A man-at-arms must now serve on his knees, / And feed on prayers, which are age's alms. [*Polyhymnia*, Sonnet]

13 Goddess, allow this aged man his right, / To be your beadsman now, that was your knight. [*Ib.*]

EARL OF PEMBROKE   1734–1794

14 Dr Johnson's sayings would not appear so extraordinary were it not for his *bow-wow-way*. [Boswell's *Life of Johnson*, 27 Mar. 1775, note]

WILLIAM PENN   1644–1718

15 No pain, no palm; no thorns, no throne; no gall, no glory; no cross, no crown. [*No Cross, No Crown*]

16 Men are more careful of the breed of their horses and dogs than of their children. [*Reflexions and Maxims*, i. 85]

SAMUEL PEPYS   1633–1703

17 And so to bed. [*Diary*, 20 Apr. 1660 and *passim*]

18 A silk suit, which cost me much money, and I pray God to make me able to pay for it. [*Ib.* 1 July 1660]

19 A good honest and painful sermon. [*Ib.* 17 Mar. 1661]

20 But Lord! to see the absurd nature of Englishmen that cannot forbear laughing and jeering at everything that looks strange. [*Ib.* 27 Nov. 1662]

21 My wife, who, poor wretch, is troubled with her lonely life. [*Ib.* 19 Dec. 1662]

22 No high-flyer. [*Ib.* 27 May 1663]

23 Most of their discourse was about hunting, in a dialect I understand very little. [*Ib.* 22 Nov. 1663]

24 Several poor creatures carried by, by constables, for being at a conventicle. . . . I would to God they would either conform, or be more wise, and not be catched! [*Ib.* 7 Aug. 1664]

25 Pretty witty Nell. [(Gwynne) *Ib.* 3 Apr. 1665]

1 But Lord! what a sad time it is to see no boats upon the River; and grass grows all up and down White Hall Court. [*Diary,* 20 Sept. 1665]

2 Strange to say what delight we married people have to see these poor fools decoyed into our condition. [*Ib.* 25 Dec. 1665]

3 Music and women I cannot but give way to, whatever my business is. [*Ib.* 9 Mar. 1666]

4 Home, and, being washing-day, dined upon cold meat. [*Ib.* 4 Apr. 1666]

5 And mighty proud I am (and ought to be thankful to God Almighty) that I am able to have a spare bed for my friends. [*Ib.* 8 Aug. 1666]

6 But it is pretty to see what money will do. [*Ib.* 21 Mar. 1667]

7 To church; and with my mourning, very handsome, and new periwig, make a great show. [*Ib.* 31 Mar. 1667]

8 My wife hath something in her gizzard, that only waits an opportunity of being provoked to bring up. [*Ib.* 17 June 1668]

9 A good dinner, and company that pleased me mightily, being all eminent men in their way. [*Ib.* 19 July 1668]

10 And so I betake myself to that course, which is almost as much as to see myself go into my grave; for which, and all the discomforts that will accompany my being blind, the good God prepare me. [*Ib.* final entry]

JOHN PERCY 19 Cent.

11 Your Molly has never been false, she declares, / Since last time we parted at Wapping Old Stairs. [Song: *Wapping Old Stairs*]

CHARLES PERRAULT 1628–1703

12 'Sister Anne, Sister Anne, can you see nothing coming?' And her sister Anne answered her, 'I see nothing but the sun which raises a dust, and the grass growing green.' [*Fairy Tales*]

EDWARD PERRONET 1726–1792

13 All hail, the power of Jesus' name! / Let angels prostrate fall. [Hymn]

PERSIUS 34–62

14 *Virtutem videant, intabescantque relicta.* – Let them look upon virtue and pine because they have lost her. [*Satires*, III. 38]

15 *Venienti occurrite morbo.* – Meet the disease on its first appearance. [*Ib.* III. 64]

PETRONIUS ?–c. 66

16 *Abiit ad plures.* – He has joined the great majority. [*Cena Trimalchionis*, 42.5]

17 *Horatii curiosa felicitas.* – The studied felicity of Horace. [*Satyricon*, 118]

E. J. PHELPS 1822–1900

18 The man who makes no mistakes does not usually make anything. [Speech at Mansion House, 24 Jan. 1899]

J. W. PHILIP 1840–1900

19 Don't cheer, boys; those poor devils are dying. [At the Battle of Santiago, 1898]

AMBROSE PHILIPS c. 1674–1749

20 The flowers anew, returning seasons bring! / But beauty faded has no second spring. [*The First Pastoral*, 55]

JOHN PHILIPS 1676–1709

21 Happy the man, who, void of cares and strife, / In silken or in leathern purse retains / A Splendid Shilling. [*The Splendid Shilling*, 1]

STEPHEN PHILLIPS 1864–1915

22 A man not old, but mellow, like good wine. [*Ulysses*, III. ii]

WENDELL PHILLIPS 1811–1884

23 We live under a government of men and morning newspapers. [*Address, the Press*]

24 One, on God's side, is a majority. [Speech at Brooklyn, 1 Nov. 1859]

25 Every man meets his Waterloo at last. [*Ib.*]

EDEN PHILLPOTTS   1862–1961

1 His father's sister had bats in the belfry and was put away. [*Peacock House*, 'My First Murder']

PINDAR   518–*c.* 438 B.C.

2 Water is best. [(Inscription over the Pump Room, Bath) *Olympian Odes*, I]

PETER PINDAR [JOHN WOLCOT]   1738–1819

3 Care to our coffin adds a nail no doubt; / And ev'ry grin, so merry, draws one out. [*Expostulatory Odes*, 15]

4 A fellow in a market town, / Most musical, cried razors up and down. [*Some More Lyric Odes*, 3]

5 What rage for fame attends both great and small! / Better be damned than mentioned not at all! [*To the Royal Academicians*, 8]

SIR ARTHUR PINERO   1855–1934

6 From forty to fifty a man is at heart either a stoic or a satyr. [*Second Mrs Tanqueray*, I]

7 I love fruit, when it is expensive. [*Ib.*]

WILLIAM PITT, EARL OF CHATHAM   1708–1778

8 The atrocious crime of being a young man . . . I shall attempt neither to palliate nor to deny. [Speech in reply to Walpole, 27 Jan. 1741]

9 Where laws end, tyranny begins. [Speech on the Wilkes case, 9 Jan. 1770]

10 We have a Calvinistic creed, a Popish liturgy, and an Arminian clergy. [Speech in House of Lords, 19 May 1772]

11 If I were an American, as I am an Englishman, while a foreign troop was landed in my country, I never would lay down my arms – never – never – never! [*Ib.* 18 Nov. 1777]

12 It was a saying of Lord Chatham, that the parks were the lungs of London. [W. Windham in speech in House of Commons, 30 June 1808]

WILLIAM PITT   1759–1806

13 Necessity is the plea for every infringement of human freedom. It is the argument of tyrants; it is the creed of slaves. [Speech, 18 Nov. 1783]

14 England has saved herself by her exertions; and will, as I trust, save Europe by her example. [*Ib.* 9 Nov. 1805]

15 Roll up that map [of Europe]; it will not be wanted these ten years. [Said in Jan. 1806, after Napoleon's victory at Austerlitz]

16 O my country! how I leave my country. [(Or 'love' for 'leave') Attr. last words]

17 I think I could eat one of Bellamy's veal pies. [Attr. last words]

J. R. PLANCHÉ   1796–1880

18 It would have made a cat laugh. [*The Queen of the Frogs*, I. iv]

PLATO   *c.* 428–347 B.C.

19 Socrates is guilty of corrupting the minds of the young, and of believing in deities of his own invention instead of the gods recognized by the State. [*Apology*, 24B]

20 I wonder if we could contrive . . . some magnificent myth* that would in itself carry conviction to our whole community. [(*Also translated as 'the noble lie') *Republic*, Bk 3. 414]

21 There will be no end to the troubles of states, or indeed, my dear Glaucon, of humanity itself, till philosophers become kings in this world, or till those we now call kings and rulers really and truly become philosophers. [*Ib.* 5. 473]

22 Democracy passes into despotism. [*Ib.* 8. 562]

PLAUTUS   254–184 B.C.

23 *Quem di diligunt / Adulescens moritur.* – He whom the gods favour dies young. [*Bacchides* IV. 816]

24 *Miles Gloriosus.* – Vainglorious Soldier. [Title of play]

PLINY, THE ELDER   23–79

25 *Brutum fulmen.* – A harmless thunderbolt. [*Natural History*, Bk II. Ch. 43]

1 *Ut non sit satis aestimare, parens melior homini an tristior noveca fuerit* — It is far from easy to determine whether she [Nature] has proved a kind parent to man or a merciless step-mother. [*Natural History*, VII. 1]

2 *Ex Africa semper aliquid novi.* – There is always something new out of Africa. [Proverbial adaptation of *Ib.* VIII. 17]

3 *In vino veritas.* – Truth comes out in wine. [Proverbial adaptation of *Ib.* XIV. 28]

4 *Sal Atticum.* – Attic salt. [*Ib.* XXXI. 41]

5 *Nulla dies sine linea.* – Not a day without a line. [Proverbial adaptation of *Ib.* XXXV. 36. 84]

PLOTINUS   205–270

6 And here we have, incidentally, lighted upon the cause of the Circuit of the All; it is a movement which seeks perpetuity by way of futurity. [*Enneads*, III. 7]

JOSEPH PLUNKETT   1887–1916

7 I see His blood upon the rose / And in the stars the glory of His eyes. [*I see His Blood*]

EDGAR ALLAN POE   1809–1849

8 I was a child and she was a child, / In this kingdom by the sea; / But we loved with a love that was more than love – / I and my Annabel Lee. [*Annabel Lee*]

9 Keeping time, time, time, / In a sort of Runic rhyme, / To the tintinabulation that so musically wells / From the bells, bells, bells, bells. [*The Bells*, 9]

10 The viol, the violet, and the vine. [*The City in the Sea*]

11 That the play is the tragedy 'Man', / And its hero the Conqueror Worm. [*The Conqueror Worm*, 39]

12 All that we see or seem / Is but a dream within a dream. [*A Dream within a Dream*]

13 The fever called 'Living' / Is conquered at last. [*For Annie*]

14 This – all this – was in the olden Time long ago. [*The Haunted Palace*]

15 A dirge for her, the doubly dead, / In that she died so young. [*Lenore*]

16 Once upon a midnight dreary, while I pondered, weak and weary, / Over many a quaint and curious volume of forgotten lore, / While I nodded nearly napping, suddenly there came a tapping, / As of someone gently rapping. [*The Raven*, i]

17 Deep into the darkness peering, long I stood there, wondering, fearing, / Doubting, dreaming dreams no mortal ever dared to dream before. [*Ib.* v]

18 'Prophet!' said I, 'thing of evil – prophet still, if bird or devil! / By that heaven that bends above us – by that God we both adore.' [*Ib.* xvi]

19 Take thy beak from out my heart and take thy form from off my door! / Quoth the Raven, 'Nevermore'. [*Ib.* xvii]

20 Helen, thy beauty is to me / Like those Nicean barks of yore. [*To Helen*]

21 Thy Naiad airs have brought me home / To the glory that was Greece, / And the grandeur that was Rome. [*Ib.*]

22 The skies they were ashen and sober; / The leaves they were crispèd and sere – / The leaves they were withering and sere; / It was night in the lonesome October / Of my most immemorial year. [*Ulalume*]

MME DE POMPADOUR
1721–1764

23 *Après nous le déluge.* – After us the deluge. [After Battle of Rossbach, 1757]

JOHN POOLE   1786?–1872

24 I hope I don't intrude. [*Paul Pry*, I. ii]

ALEXANDER POPE   1688–1744

25 Ye gods! annihilate but space and time, / And make two lovers happy. [*The Art of Sinking in Poetry*, 11]

26 And thou Dalhousy, the great God of War, / Lieutenant-Colonel to the Earl of Mar. [*Ib.*]

27 Whether you choose Cervantes' serious air, / Or laugh and shake in Rabelais' armchair. [*The Dunciad*, Bk I. 21]

28 Poetic Justice, with her lifted scale, / Where, in nice balance, truth with gold she weighs, / And solid pudding against empty praise. [*Ib.* I. 52]

1 Now night descending, the proud scene was o'er, / But lived in Settle's numbers one day more. [*The Dunciad*, I. 89]

2 While pensive poets painful vigils keep / Sleepless themselves to give their readers sleep. [*Ib.* I. 93]

3 How here he sipped, how there he plundered snug, / And sucked all o'er, like an industrious bug. [*Ib.* I. 129]

4 Or where the pictures for the page atone, / And Quarles is saved for beauties not his own. [*Ib.* I. 139]

5 Some daemon stole my pen (forgive th' offence) / And once betrayed me into common sense. / Else all my prose and verse were much the same. [*Ib.* I. 187]

6 A vast, vamped future, old, revived new piece. [*Ib.* I. 284]

7 Loud thunder to its bottom shook the bog, / And the hoarse nation croaked, 'God save King Log!' [*Ib.* I. 329]

8 And gentle dullness ever loves a joke. [*Ib.* II. 34]

9 A brain of feathers and a heart of lead. [*Ib.* II. 44]

10 Peeled, patched, and piebald, linsey-wolsey brothers, / Grave mummers! sleeveless some, and shirtless others. [*Ib.* III. 115]

11 All crowd, who foremost shall be damned to fame. [*Ib.* III. 158]

12 So sweetly mawkish and so smoothly dull. [*Ib.* III. 171]

13 Right well mine eyes arede the myster wight, / On parchment scraps y-fed and Wormius hight. [*Ib.* III. 187]

14 And Alma Mater all dissolved in port. [*Ib.* III. 338]

15 A wit with dunces, and a dunce with wits. [*Ib.* IV. 90]

16 Let standard-authors, thus, like trophies borne, / Appear more glorious as more hacked and torn. [*Ib.* IV. 123]

17 The right divine of kings to govern wrong. [*Ib.* IV. 188]

18 When man's whole frame is obvious to a flea. [*Ib.* IV. 238]

19 We bring to one dead level ev'ry mind. [*Ib.* IV. 268]

20 To happy convents, bosomed deep in vines, / Where slumber abbots, purple as their wines. [*Ib.* IV. 301]

21 Stretched on the rack of a too easy chair. [*The Dunciad*, IV. 342]

22 Religion blushing veils her sacred fires, / And unawares morality expires. / Nor public flame, nor private, dares to shine; / Nor human spark is left nor glimpse divine! / Lo! thy dread empire, Chaos! is restored; / Light dies before thy uncreating word; / Thy hand, great Anarch! lets the curtain fall / And universal darkness buries all. [*Ib.* IV. 649]

23 Vital spark of heav'nly flame! / Quit, oh quit this mortal frame: / Trembling, hoping, ling'ring, flying, / Oh the pain, the bliss of dying. [*The Dying Christian to his Soul*]

24 I mount! I fly! / O grave! where is thy victory? / O death! where is thy sting? [*Ib.*]

25 What beck'ning ghost, along the moon-light shade / Invites my steps, and points to yonder glade? [*Elegy to the Memory of an Unfortunate Lady*, 1]

26 Is it, in heav'n, a crime to love too well? [*Ib.* 6]

27 Is there no bright reversion in the sky, / For those who greatly think, or bravely die? [*Ib.* 9]

28 Ambition first sprung from your bless'd abodes; / The glorious fault of angels and of gods. [*Ib.* 13]

29 By foreign hands thy dying eyes were closed, / By foreign hands thy decent limbs composed, / By foreign hands thy humble grave adorned / By strangers honoured, and by strangers mourned! [*Ib.* 51]

30 Yet shall thy grave with rising flow'rs be dressed, / And the green turf lie lightly on thy breast. [*Ib.* 63]

31 A heap of dust alone remains of thee; / 'Tis all thou art, and all the proud shall be! [*Ib.* 73]

32 Line after line my gushing eyes o'erflow, / Led through a sad variety of woe. [*Eloisa to Abelard*, 35]

33 Speed the soft intercourse from soul to soul, / And waft a sigh from Indus to the Pole. [*Ib.* 57]

34 And love th' offender, yet detest th' offence. [*Ib.* 192]

35 How happy is the blameless vestal's lot! / The world forgetting, by the world forgot. [*Ib.* 207]

1 One thought of thee puts all the pomp to flight, / Priests, tapers, temples, swim before my sight. [*Eloisa to Abelard*, 273]

2 See my lips tremble, and my eye-balls roll, / Suck my last breath, and catch my flying soul! [*Ib.* 323]

3 You beat your pate, and fancy wit will come: / Knock as you please, there's nobody at home. [Epigram: *An Empty House*]

4 Shut, shut the door, good John! fatigued I said. / Tie up the knocker, say I'm sick, I'm dead. / The dog-star rages! [*Epistle to Dr Arbuthnot*, 1]

5 Is there a parson, much bemused in beer, / A maudlin poetess, a rhyming peer, / A clerk foredoomed his father's soul to cross / Who pens a stanza, when he should engross? [*Ib.* 15]

6 Fired that the house reject him, "Sdeath I'll print it, / And shame the fools.' [*Ib.* 61]

7 No creature smarts so little as a fool. [*Ib.* 84]

8 Destroy his fib or sophistry, in vain, / The creature's at his dirty work again. [*Ib.* 91]

9 As yet a child, nor yet a fool to fame, I lisped in numbers, for the numbers came. [*Ib.* 127]

10 This long disease, my life. [*Ib.* 132]

11 And he whose fustian's so sublimely bad / It is not poetry, but prose run mad. [*Ib.* 187]

12 Were there one whose fires / True genius kindles, and fair fame inspires; / Blest with each talent and each art to please, / And born to write, converse, and live with ease; / Should such a man, too fond to rule alone, / Bear, like the Turk, no brother near the throne, / View him with scornful, yet with jealous eyes, / And hate for arts that caused himself to rise; / Damn with faint praise, assent with civil leer, / And, without sneering, teach the rest to sneer; / Willing to wound, and yet afraid to strike, / Just hint a fault, and hesitate dislike; / Alike reserved to blame, or to commend, / A tim'rous foe, and a suspicious friend; / Dreading e'en fools, by flatterers besieged, / And so obliging that he ne'er obliged; / Like Cato, give his little senate laws, / And sit attentive to his own applause; / ... Who but must laugh, if such a man there be? / Who would not weep, if Atticus were he? [*Epistle to Dr Arbuthnot*, 193]

13 Curst be the verse, how well soe'er it flow, / That tends to make one worthy man my foe. [*Ib.* 283]

14 Let Sporus tremble. – A. What? that thing of silk, / Sporus, that mere white curd of ass's milk? / Satire or sense, alas! can Sporus feel? / Who breaks a butterfly upon a wheel?
P. Yet let me flap this bug with gilded wings – / This painted child of dirt, that stinks and stings. [*Ib.* 305]

15 Eternal smiles his emptiness betray, / As shallow streams run dimpling all the way. [*Ib.* 315]

16 He himself one vile antithesis. [*Ib.* 325]

17 Wit that can creep, and pride that licks the dust. [*Ib.* 333]

18 Unlearn'd, he knew no schoolman's subtle art, / No language, but the language of the heart. [*Ib.* 398]

19 Nature and Nature's laws lay hid in night: / God said 'Let Newton be!' and all was light. [*Epitaph intended for Sir Isaac Newton*]

20 In wit a man; simplicity a child. [*Epitaph on Gay*]

21 Heav'n, as its purest gold, by tortures tried; / The saint sustained it, but the woman died. [*Epitaph on Mrs Corbet*]

22 'Tis with our judgements as our watches, none / Go just alike, yet each believes his own. [*An Essay on Criticism*, 9]

23 Pride, the never failing vice of fools. [*Ib.* 204]

24 A little learning is a dang'rous thing; / Drink deep, or taste not the Pierian spring: / There shallow draughts intoxicate the brain, / And drinking largely sobers us again. [*Ib.* 215]

25 Hills peep o'er hills, and Alps on Alps arise! [*Ib.* 232]

26 Whoever thinks a faultless piece to see, / Thinks what ne'er was, nor is, nor e'er shall be. [*Ib.* 253]

27 True wit is nature to advantage dressed, / What oft was thought but ne'er so well expressed. [*Ib.* 297]

1 Words are like leaves; and where they most abound, / Much fruit of sense beneath is rarely found. [*An Essay on Criticism*, 309]

2 Such laboured nothings, in so strange a style, / Amaze th' unlearn'd, and make the learned smile. [*Ib*. 326]

3 Be not the first by whom the new are tried, / Nor yet the last to lay the old aside. [*Ib*. 335]

4 As some to church repair, / Not for the doctrine, but the music there. [*Ib*. 342]

5 While expletives their feeble aid do join, / And ten low words oft creep in one dull line. [*Ib*. 346]

6 Where'er you find 'the cooling western breeze', / In the next line, it 'whispers through the trees': / If crystal streams 'with pleasing murmurs creep', / The reader's threatened, not in vain, with 'sleep'. / Then, at the last and only couplet fraught / With some unmeaning thing they call a thought, / A needless Alexandrine ends the song, / That, like a wounded snake, drags its slow length along. [*Ib*. 350]

7 True ease in writing comes from art, not chance, / As those move easiest who have learned to dance. / 'Tis not enough no harshness gives offence, / The sound must seem an echo to the sense. [*Ib*. 362]

8 For fools admire, but men of sense approve. [*Ib*. 391]

9 But let a lord once own the happy lines, / How the wit brightens! how the style refines! [*Ib*. 420]

10 Some praise at morning what they blame at night; / But always think the last opinion right. [*Ib*. 430]

11 Nor in the critic let the man be lost. [*Ib*. 523]

12 To err is human, to forgive, divine. [*Ib*. 525]

13 Then unbelieving priests reformed the nation, / And taught more pleasant methods of salvation. [*Ib*. 546]

14 All seems infected that th' infected spy, / As all looks yellow to the jaundiced eye. [*Ib*. 558]

15 Men must be taught as if you taught them not / And things unknown proposed as things forgot. [*Ib*. 574]

16 The bookful blockhead, ignorantly read, / With loads of learned lumber in his head. [*An Essay on Criticism*, 612]

17 For fools rush in where angels fear to tread. [*Ib*. 625]

18 Awake my St John! Leave all meaner things / To low ambition, and the pride of kings. / Let us, since life can little more supply / Than just to look about us and to die, / Expatiate free o'er all this scene of man; / A mighty maze! but not without a plan. [*An Essay on Man*, I. 1]

19 Eye Nature's walks, shoot folly as it flies, / And catch the manners living as they rise; / Laugh where we must, be candid where we can; / But vindicate the ways of God to man. [*Ib*. I. 13]

20 Who sees with equal eye, as God of all, / A hero perish, or a sparrow fall, / Atoms or systems into ruin hurled, / And now a bubble burst and now a world. [*Ib*. I. 87]

21 Hope springs eternal in the human breast: / Man never is, but always to be blessed. [*Ib*. I. 95]

22 Lo, the poor Indian! whose untutored mind / Sees God in clouds, or hears him in the wind; / His soul proud science never taught to stray / Far as the solar walk or milky way. [*Ib*. I. 99]

23 Why has not man a microscopic eye? / For this plain reason, man is not a fly. [*Ib*. I. 193]

24 Die of a rose in aromatic pain? [*Ib*. I. 200]

25 The spider's touch, how exquisitely fine! / Feels at each thread, and lives along the line. [*Ib*. I. 217]

26 All are but parts of one stupendous whole, / Whose body nature is, and God the soul. [*Ib*. I. 267]

27 All nature is but art, unknown to thee; / All chance, direction which thou canst not see; / All discord, harmony not understood; / All partial evil, universal good; / And, spite of pride, in erring reason's spite, / One truth is clear, Whatever is, is right. [*Ib*. I. 289]

28 Know then thyself, presume not God to scan; / The proper study of mankind is man. [*Ib*. II. 1]

29 Chaos of thought and passion, all confused; / Still by himself abused, or disabused; / Created half to rise, and half

to fall; / Great Lord of all things, yet a prey to all; / Sole judge of truth, in endless error hurled: / The glory, jest, and riddle of the world! [*An Essay on Man*. II. 13]

1 And hence one master-passion in the breast, / Like Aaron's serpent, swallows up the rest. [*Ib.* II. 131]

2 Vice is a monster of so frightful mien, / As to be hated needs but to be seen; / Yet seen too oft, familiar with her face, / We first endure, then pity, then embrace. [*Ib.* II. 217]

3 Behold the child, by nature's kindly law / Pleased with a rattle, tickled with a straw: / Some livelier plaything gives his youth delight, / A little louder, but as empty quite: / Scarfs, garters, gold, amuse his riper stage, / And beads and prayerbooks are the toys of age: / Pleased with this bauble still, as that before; / Till tired he sleeps, and life's poor play is o'er. [*Ib.* II. 275]

4 For forms of government let fools contest, / Whate'er is best administered is best: / For modes of faith let graceless zealots fight; / His can't be wrong whose life is in the right. / In faith and hope the world will disagree, / But all mankind's concern is charity. [*Ib.* III. 303]

5 O happiness! our being's end and aim! / Good, pleasure, ease, content! whate'er thy name: / That something still which prompts th' eternal sigh, / For which we bear to live, or dare to die. [*Ib.* IV. 1]

6 Order is heaven's first law. [*Ib.* IV. 49]

7 An honest man's the noblest work of God. [*Ib.* IV. 248]

8 If parts allure thee, think how Bacon shined, / The wisest, brightest, meanest of mankind: / Or, ravished with the whistling of a name, / See Cromwell, damned to everlasting fame! [*Ib.* IV. 281]

9 Slave to no sect, who takes no private road, / But looks through nature up to nature's God. [*Ib.* IV. 331]

10 Formed by thy converse happily to steer / From grave to gay, from lively to severe. [*Ib.* IV. 379]

11 Thou wert my guide, philosopher, and friend. [*Ib.* IV. 390]

12 That true self-love and social are the same. [*Ib.* IV. 396]

13 To observations which ourselves we make, / We grow more partial for th' observer's sake. [*Moral Essays*, Epistle I. 11]

14 Grant but as many sorts of mind as moss. [*Ib.* I. 18]

15 Like following life through creatures you dissect, / You lose it in the moment you detect. [*Ib.* I. 29]

16 'Tis education forms the common mind, / Just as the twig is bent, the tree's inclined. [*Ib.* I. 149]

17 'Odious! in woollen! 'twould a saint provoke' / (Were the last words that poor Narcissa spoke). [*Ib.* I. 246]

18 One would not, sure, be frightful when one's dead – / And, Betty, give this cheek a little red. [*Ib.* I. 250]

19 And you, brave Cobham! to the latest breath / Shall feel your ruling passion strong in death. [*Ib.* I. 262]

20 Most women have no characters at all. [*Ib.* II. 2]

21 Fine by defect and delicately weak. [*Ib.* II. 43]

22 With too much quickness ever to be taught; / With too much thinking to have common thought. [*Ib.* II. 97]

23 'With every pleasing, every prudent part, / Say, what can Chloe want?' – She wants a heart. [*Ib.* II. 159]

24 Men, some to business, some to pleasure take; / But every woman is at heart a rake. [*Ib.* II. 215]

25 See how the world its veterans rewards! / A youth of frolics, an old age of cards. [*Ib.* II. 243]

26 She who ne'er answers till a husband cools, / Or if she rules him, never shows she rules; / Charms by accepting, by submitting sways, / Yet has her humour most when she obeys. [*Ib.* II. 261]

27 And mistress of herself though China fall. [*Ib.* II. 268]

28 Woman's at best a contradiction still. [*Ib.* II. 270]

29 Who shall decide when doctors disagree? [*Ib.* III. 1]

30 But thousands die, without or this or that, / Die, and endow a college, or a cat. [*Ib.* III. 95]

1 The ruling passion, be it what it will, / The ruling passion conquers reason still. [*Moral Essays*, III. 153]

2 Rise, honest Muse! and sing the Man of Ross. [*Ib*. III. 250]

3 In the worst inn's worst room, with mat half-hung, / The floors of plaster and the walls of dung, / On once a flock-bed, but repaired with straw, / With tape-tied curtains, never meant to draw, / The George and Garter dangling from that bed / Where tawdry yellow strove with dirty red, / Great Villiers lies. [*Ib*. III. 299]

4 To rest, the cushion and soft dean invite, / Who never mentions hell to ears polite. [*Ib*. IV. 149]

5 Statesman, yet friend to truth! of soul sincere / In action faithful, and in honour clear, / Who broke no promise, served no private end, / Who gained no title, and who lost no friend. [*Ib*. V. 67]

6 Happy the man whose wish and care / A few paternal acres bound, / Content to breathe his native air, / In his own ground. [*Ode on Solitude*]

7 Has she no faults then (Envy says), Sir? / Yes she has one, I must aver; / When all the world conspires to praise her, / The woman's deaf and does not hear. [*On a Certain Lady at Court*]

8 I am his Highness' dog at Kew; / Pray tell me, sir, whose dog are you? [*On the Collar of a Dog which I gave to his Royal Highness*]

9 Where'er you walk, cool gales shall fan the glade, / Trees where you sit shall crowd into a shade: / Where'er you tread, the blushing flowers shall rise, / And all things flourish where you turn your eyes. [*Pastorals*, 'Summer', 73]

10 To make mankind in conscious virtue bold, / Live o'er each scene, and be what they behold. [*Prologue to Mr Addison's 'Cato'*, 3]

11 What dire offence from am'rous causes springs, / What mighty contests rise from trivial things. [*The Rape of the Lock*, I. 1]

12 Now lap-dogs give themselves the rousing shake, / And sleepless lovers, just at twelve, awake. [*Ib*. I. 15]

13 They shift the moving toyshop of their heart. [*Ib*. I. 100]

14 Where wigs with wigs, with sword-knots sword-knots strive. / Beaux banish beaux, and coaches coaches drive. [*The Rape of the Lock*, I. 101]

15 And all Arabia breathes from yonder box. [*Ib*. I. 134]

16 Here files of pins extend their shining rows, / Puffs, powders, patches, bibles, billet-doux. [*Ib*. I. 137]

17 On her white breast a sparkling cross she wore, / Which Jews might kiss, and infidels adore. [*Ib*. II. 7]

18 If to her share some female errors fall, / Look on her face, and you'll forget 'em all. [*Ib*. II. 17]

19 Fair tresses man's imperial race ensnare, / And beauty draws us with a single hair. [*Ib*. II. 27]

20 To love an altar built, / Of twelve vast French romances, neatly gilt. [*Ib*. II. 37]

21 Whether the nymph shall break Diana's law, / Or some frail china jar receive a flaw; / Or stain her honour, or her new brocade; / Forget her prayers, or miss a masquerade; / Or lose her heart, or necklace, at a ball. [*Ib*. II. 105]

22 Here thou, great Anna! whom three realms obey, / Dost sometimes counsel take – and sometimes tea. [*Ib*. III. 7]

23 At ev'ry word a reputation dies. [*Ib*. III. 16]

24 The hungry judges soon the sentence sign, / And wretches hang that jurymen may dine. [*Ib*. III. 21]

25 'Let Spades be trumps!' she said, and trumps they were. [*Ib*. III. 46]

26 Gained but one trump and one plebeian card. [*Ib*. III. 54]

27 Coffee, which makes the politician wise, / And see through all things with his half-shut eyes. [*Ib*. III. 117]

28 Fate urged the shears, and cut the sylph in twain; / (But airy substance soon unites again) / The meeting points the sacred hair dissever / From the fair head, for ever and for ever! [*Ib*. III. 151]

29 Not louder shrieks to pitying heav'n are cast, / When husbands, or when lap-dogs breathe their last. [*Ib*. III. 157]

30 She sighs for ever on her pensive bed, / Pain at her side, and Megrim at her head. [*Ib*. IV. 23]

1 Sooner let earth, air, sea, to chaos fall, / Men, monkeys, lap-dogs, parrots, perish all! [*The Rape of the Lock*, IV. 119]

2 Sir Plume, of amber snuff-box justly vain, / And the nice conduct of a clouded cane. [*Ib.* IV. 123]

3 Charms strike the sight, but merit wins the soul. [*Ib.* V. 34]

4 There St John mingles with my friendly bowl / The feast of reason and the flow of soul. [*Satires and Epistles of Horace Imitated*, Bk II. Sat. i. 127]

5 Shakespeare ... / For gain not glory, winged his roving flight, / And grew immortal in his own despite. [*Ib.* Bk II. Ep. i. 69]

6 The people's voice is odd, / It is, and it is not, the voice of God. [*Ib.* II. Ep. i. 89]

7 In quibbles angel and archangel join, / And God the Father turns a school-divine. [*Ib.* II. Ep. i. 101, on *Paradise Lost*]

8 The mob of gentlemen who wrote with ease. [*Ib.* II. Ep. i. 108]

9 One simile, that solitary shines / In a dry desert of a thousand lines. [*Ib.* II. Ep. i. 111]

10 Waller was smooth; but Dryden taught to join / The varying verse, the full-resounding line, / The long majestic march, and energy divine. [*Ib.* II. Ep. i. 267]

11 Ev'n copious Dryden wanted, or forgot, / The last and greatest art, the art to blot. [*Ib.* II. Ep. i. 280]

12 The many-headed monster of the pit. [*Ib.* II. Ep. i. 305]

13 The vulgar boil, the learned roast an egg. [*Ib.* II. Ep. ii. 85]

14 Do good by stealth, and blush to find it fame. [*Epilogue to the Satires*, Dialogue I. 136]

15 Ask you what provocation I have had? / The strong antipathy of good to bad. [*Ib.* II. 197]

16 Yes; I am proud, I must be proud to see / Men not afraid of God, afraid of me. [*Ib.* II. 208]

17 Nor fame I slight, nor for her favours call; / She comes unlooked for, if she comes at all. [*The Temple of Fame*, 513]

18 Teach me to feel another's woe, / To hide the fault I see; / That mercy I to others show, / That mercy show to me. [*The Universal Prayer*]

19 Not chaos-like, together crushed and bruised, / But, as the world harmoniously confused: / Where order in variety we see, / And where, though all things differ, all agree. [*Windsor Forest*, 13]

20 Achilles' wrath, to Greece the direful spring / Of woes unnumbered, heavenly goddess sing! [*Homer's Iliad*, I. 1]

21 She moves a goddess, and she looks a queen. [*Ib.* III. 1]

22 Tell me, Muse, of the man of many wiles. [(Odysseus) *Homer's Odyssey*, I. 1]

23 So perish all who do the like again. [*Ib.* I. 47]

24 True friendship's laws are by this rule expressed, / Welcome the coming, speed the parting guest. [*Ib.* XV. 83]

25 Not to admire, is all the art I know / To make men happy, and to keep them so. [*Transl. of Horace*, Ep. I. vi]

26 I never knew any man in my life who could not bear another's misfortunes perfectly like a Christian. [*Thoughts on Various Subjects*]

27 When men grow virtuous in their old age, they only make a sacrifice to God of the devil's leavings. [*Ib.*]

28 'Blessed is the man who expects nothing, for he shall never be disappointed' was the ninth beatitude. [Letter to Fortescue, 23 Sept. 1725]

RICHARD PORSON   1759–1808

29 When Dido found Aeneas would not come, / She mourned in silence, and was Di-do-dum. [*Epigram on Latin Gerunds*]

30 I went to Frankfort, and got drunk / With that most learn'd professor, Brunck, / I went to Wortz, and got more drunken, / With that more learn'd professor, Ruhnken. [*Facetiae Cantabrigienses*]

31 The Germans in Greek / Are sadly to seek; / Not five in five score, / But ninety-five more; / All, save only Hermann, / And Hermann's a German. [Quoted in Clarke's *Richard Porson*]

FRANCIS POTT   1832–1909

32 The strife is o'er, the battle done; / Now is the Victor's triumph won; / O let the song of praise be sung. Alleluia! [Hymn]

STEPHEN POTTER   1900–1971

1 Gamesmanship or, The Art of Winning Games without actually Cheating. [Title of book]

2 Could not this simple gambit of Joad's be extended to include other aspects of the game   to include all games? For me it was the birth of gamesmanship. [*Gamesmanship*, I, Introductory]

3 *How to be one up* · how to make the other man feel that something has gone wrong, however slightly. [*Lifemanship*]

4 There was one ploy of Gattling's which I found particularly effective, and I believe it must have been about this time that I first murmured to myself the word 'Lifemanship'. [*Ib.*]

5 Just as there are O.K.-words in conversationship so there are O.K.-*people to mention* in Newstatesmanship. [*Ib.*]

6 This gambit is called 'Rilking'. [*Ib.*]

EZRA POUND   1885–1972

7 Winter is icumen in, / Lhude sing Goddamm. / Raineth drop and staineth slop, / And how the wind doth ramm! / Sing: Goddamm. [*Ancient Music*]

8 Hang it all, Robert Browning, / There can be but one 'Sordello'. [*Cantos*, II]

9 And even I can remember / A day when the historians left blanks in their writings, / I mean for things they didn't know. [*Ib.* XIII]

10 Bah! I have sung women in three cities, / But it is all the same; / And I will sing of the sun. [*Cino*]

11 The apparition of these faces in the crowd; / Petals on a wet black bough. [*In a Station of the Metro*]

12 For three years, out of key with his time, / He strove to resuscitate the dead art / Of poetry to maintain 'the sublime' / In the old sense. Wrong from the start. [*Pour l'élection de son sépulcre*]

W. M. PRAED   1802–1839

13 I think that nought is worth a thought, / And I'm a fool for thinking. [*The Chant of the Brazen Head*]

14 The ice of her Ladyship's manners, / The ice of his Lordship's champagne. [*Good-night to the Season*]

15 My own Araminta, say 'No!' [*A Letter of Advice*]

16 For all who understood admired, / And some who did not understand them. [*The Vicar*]

THE BOOK OF COMMON PRAYER

17 A Table of the Moveable Feasts. [*Ib.* introductory pages]

18 Dearly beloved brethren, the Scripture moveth us in sundry places to acknowledge and confess our manifold sins and wickedness. [*Morning Prayer*, 'The Invitation to Confession']

19 We have erred and strayed from thy ways like lost sheep. [*Ib.* 'General Confession']

20 We have left undone those things which we ought to have done; And we have done those things which we ought not to have done; And there is no health in us. [*Ib.*]

21 A godly, righteous, and sober life. [*Ib.*]

22 And forgive us our trespasses, As we forgive them that trespass against us. [*Ib.* 'Lord's Prayer']

23 PRIEST: O Lord, open thou our lips. ANSWER: And our mouth shall shew forth thy praise. PRIEST: O God, make speed to save us. ANSWER: O Lord, make haste to help us. [*Ib.* 'Versicles and Responses']

24 As it was in the beginning, is now, and ever shall be: world without end. Amen. [*Ib.* 'Gloria']

25 Lord God of Sabaoth. [*Ib.* 'Te Deum']

26 The noble army of Martyrs. [*Ib.*]

27 Of an infinite Majesty. [*Ib.*]

28 O all ye Works of the Lord, bless ye the Lord: praise him and magnify him for ever. [*Ib.* 'Benedicite']

29 O ye Whales, and all that move in the Waters. [*Ib.*]

30 Give peace in our time, O Lord. [*Ib.* 'Versicles']

31 Jesus Christ his only Son our Lord. Who was conceived by the Holy Ghost, Born

of the Virgin Mary, Suffered under Pontius Pilate, Was crucified, dead, and buried. [*Morning Prayer*, 'Apostles' Creed']

1 The holy Catholic Church, the Communion of Saints; the Forgiveness of sins; the Resurrection of the body, And the life everlasting. [*Ib.*]

2 Lord have mercy upon us. [Response] Christ have mercy upon us. [*Ib.* 'Responses']

3 Whose service is perfect freedom. [*Ib.* 'Second Collect, for Peace']

4 Neither run into any kind of danger. [*Ib.* 'Third Collect, for Grace']

5 In choirs and places where they sing, here followeth the anthem. [*Ib.* rubric]

6 The fountain of all goodness. [*Ib.* 'Prayer for the Royal Family']

7 The continual dew of thy blessing. [*Ib.* 'Prayer for the Clergy and People']

8 Lighten our darkness, we beseech thee, O Lord. [*Evening Prayer*, 'Third Collect']

9 Neither confounding the Persons: nor dividing the Substance. [*Athanasian Creed*]

10 Not three Gods: but one God. [*Ib.*]

11 Have mercy upon us miserable sinners. [*Litany*]

12 Envy, hatred, and malice, and all uncharitableness. [*Ib.*]

13 The world, the flesh, and the devil. [*Ib.*]

14 From battle and murder, and from sudden death. [*Ib.*]

15 In the hour of death, and in the day of judgement. [*Ib.*]

16 Unity, peace, and concord. [*Ib.*]

17 The kindly fruits of the earth. [*Ib.*]

18 PRIEST: O Lord, deal not with us after our sins.
ANSWER: Neither reward us after our iniquities. [*Ib.*]

19 All sorts and conditions of men. [*Prayer for All Conditions of Men*]

20 Our creation, preservation, and all the blessings of this life. [*A General Thanksgiving*]

21 For the means of grace, and for the hope of glory. [*Ib.*]

22 Put upon us the armour of light, now in the time of this mortal life. [*Collect, 1st Sunday in Advent*]

23 Read, mark, learn, and inwardly digest. [*Collect, 2nd Sunday in Advent*]

24 That most excellent gift of charity. [*Collect. Quinquagesima Sunday*]

25 Jews, Turks, Infidels, and Heretics. [*Third Collect for Good Friday*]

26 The author and giver of all good things. [*Collect, 7th Sunday after Trinity*]

27 Serve thee with a quiet mind. [*Collect, 21st Sunday after Trinity*]

28 Whom truly to know is everlasting life. [*Collect, St Philip and St James's Day*]

29 Unto whom all hearts be open, all desires known, and from whom no secrets are hid. [*Holy Communion. Collect*]

30 Ye that do truly and earnestly repent you of your sins, and are in love and charity with your neighbours. [*Ib.* 'Invitation']

31 Very God of Very God, Begotten not made. [*Ib.* 'The Nicene Creed']

32 Hear what comfortable words. [*Ib.* 'Priest's Exhortation']

33 Be amongst you and remain with you always. [*Ib.* 'Blessing']

34 All our works, begun, continued, and ended in thee. [*Ib.* 'Collect after the Offertory']

35 The old Adam in this Child may be so buried, that the new man may be raised up in him. [*Public Baptism of Infants*, 'Blessing']

36 Renounce the devil and all his works. [*Ib. passim*]

37 Such as are of Riper Years. [*Public Baptism . . .*]

38 The pomps and vanity of this wicked world. [*Catechism*]

39 Governors, teachers, spiritual pastors and masters. [*Ib.*]

40 To keep my hands from picking and stealing. [*Ib.*]

41 To do my duty in that state of life unto which it shall please God to call me. [*Ib.*]

42 An outward and visible sign of an inward and spiritual grace. [*Ib.*]

43 In their Mother Tongue. [*Ib.* rubric]

44 Laying on of Hands. [*Confirmation*, section heading]

45 Being now come to years of discretion. [*Ib.* Preface]

1 If any of you know cause, or just impediment. [*Solemnization of Matrimony*, 'Banns']

2 This is the first time of asking. [*Ib.*]

3 Brute beasts that have no understanding. [*Ib.* 'Exhortation']

4 First, it was ordained for the procreation of children. [*Ib.*]

5 Let him now speak, or else hereafter for ever hold his peace. [*Ib.*]

6 Wilt thou have this woman to thy wedded wife? [*Ib.* 'Betrothal']

7 To have and to hold from this day forward, for better for worse, for richer for poorer, in sickness and in health, to love and to cherish, till death us do part. [*Ib.*]

8 To love, cherish and to obey. [*Ib.*]

9 With this ring I thee wed, with my body I thee worship, and with all my worldly goods I thee endow. [*Ib.*]

10 Those whom God hath joined together let no man put asunder. [*Ib.* prayer]

11 Holy wedlock. [*Ib.* 'Priest's Address']

12 Peace be to this house. [*The Visitation of the Sick*]

13 The inner man. [*Ib.* 'Prayer . . . when there appeareth small hope of recovery']

14 Against the hour of death. [*Ib.*]

15 Laid violent hands upon themselves. [*The Burial of the Dead*, opening rubric]

16 Man that is born of a woman hath but a short time to live, and is full of misery. [*Ib.* Anthem]

17 In the midst of life we are in death [*Ib.*]

18 We therefore commit his body to the ground; earth to earth, ashes to ashes, dust to dust; in sure and certain hope of the Resurrection to eternal life. [*Ib.* 'Committal']

19 We therefore commit his body to the deep, to be turned into corruption, looking for the resurrection of the body, (when the Sea shall give up her dead). [*At the Burial of their Dead at Sea*]

20 Of Works of Supererogation. [*Articles of Religion*, XIV, heading]

21 Fond thing vainly invented. [*Ib.* XXII 'Of Purgatory']

22 The Bishop of *Rome* hath no jurisdiction in this Realm of *England*. [*Ib.* XXXVII]

23 A Man may not marry his Grandmother. [*Table of Kindred*]

MATTHEW PRIOR   1664–1721

24 Dear Cloe, how blubbered is that pretty face! [*A Better Answer*]

25 Odds life! must one swear to the truth of a song? [*Ib.*]

26 I court others in verse: but I love thee in prose; / And they have my whimsies, but thou hast my heart. [*Ib.*]

27 Be to her virtues very kind; / Be to her faults a little blind; / Let all her ways be unconfined; / And clap your padlock – on her mind. [*An English Padlock*]

28 To John I owed great obligation; / But John, unhappily, thought fit / To publish it to all the nation: / Sure John and I are more than quit. [*Epigram*]

29 Nobles and heralds, by your leave, / Here lies what once was Matthew Prior; / The son of Adam and of Eve, / Can Bourbon or Nassau go higher? [*Epitaph on Himself*]

30 He bought her sermons. psalms, and graces, / And doubled down the useful places. [*Hans Carvel*, 51]

31 Her religion so well with her learning did suit / That in practice sincere, and in controverse mute, / She shewed she knew better to live than dispute. [*Jinny the Just*]

32 The merchant, to secure his treasure, / Conveys it in a borrowed name: / Euphelia serves to grace my measure; / But Cloe is my real flame. [*An Ode, 'The Merchant to Secure his Treasure'*]

33 She chuckled when a bawd was carted: / And thought the nation ne'er would thrive, / Till all the whores were burnt alive. [*Paolo Purganti and his Wife*, 44]

34 The doctor understood the call; / But had not always wherewithal. [*Ib.* 81]

35 Cured yesterday of my disease, / I died last night of my physician. [*The Remedy Worse than the Disease*]

36 Abra was ready ere I called her name; / And, though I called another, Abra came. [*Solomon*, II. 362]

37 For hope is but the dream of those that wake. [*Ib.* III. 102]

1 Now fitted the halter, now traversed the cart; / And often took leave, but was loath to depart. [*The Thief and the Cordelier*]

2 For, as our different ages move, / 'Tis so ordained (would fate but mend it!) / That I shall be past making love / When she begins to comprehend it. [*To a Child of Quality, five years old*]

3 They never taste who always drink; / They always talk, who never think. [*Upon this Passage in the Scaligeriana*]

ADELAIDE PROCTER   1825–1864

4 Seated one day at the organ, / I was weary and ill at ease, / And my fingers wandered idly / Over the noisy keys. [*A Lost Chord*]

5 But I struck one chord of music, / Like the sound of a great Amen. [*Ib.*]

PROTAGORAS   *c.* 485–415 B.C.

6 Man is the measure of all things. [Quoted by Plato in *Theaetetus*, 160D]

PIERRE-JOSEPH PROUDHON   1809–1865

7 *La propriété c'est le vol.* – Property is theft. [*Qu'est-ce que la propriété?*]

FATHER PROUT [F. S. MAHONY]   1804–1866

8 'Tis the bells of Shandon, / That sound so grand on / The pleasant waters / Of the River Lee. [*The Bells of Shandon*]

W. J. PROWSE   1836–1870

9 Though the latitude's rather uncertain, / And the longitude also is vague, / The persons I pity who know not the city, / The beautiful city of Prague. [*The City of Prague*]

WILLIAM PULTENEY, EARL OF BATH   1684–1764

10 Since twelve honest men have decided the cause, / And were judges of fact, tho' not judges of laws. [*The Honest Jury*, iii]

PUNCH

11 Advice to persons about to marry. – Don't. [Vol. viii. p. 1. 1845]

12 You pays your money and you takes your choice. [x. 17. 1846]

13 Never do to-day what you can put off till to-morrow. [xvii. 241. 1849]

14 Who's 'im, Bill? – A stranger! 'Eave 'arf a brick at 'im. [xxvi. 82. 1854]

15 It's the 'ammer, 'ammer, 'ammer along the 'ard 'igh road. [xxx. 218. 1856]

16 Mun, a had na' been the-erre abune twa hoours when – *bang* – went *saxpence*!! [lv. 235. 1868]

17 Nothink for nothink 'ere, and precious little for sixpence! [lvii. 152, 1869]

18 It appears the Americans have taken umbrage – The deuce they have! Whereabouts is that? [lxiii. 189. 1872]

19 Go directly, – see what she's doing, and tell her she mustn't! [lxiii. 202. 1872]

20 There was *one* poor tiger that *hadn't got* a Christian! [lxviii. 143. 1875]

21 What did *you* take out of the bag, Mamma? *I* only got sixpence. [lxx. 139. 1876]

22 I never read books – I *write* them. [lxxiv. 210. 1878]

23 I used your soap two years ago; since then I have used no other. [lxxxvi. 197. 1884]

24 Don't look at me, Sir, with – ah – in that tone of voice, Sir! [lxxxvii. 38. 1884]

25 Nearly all our best men are dead! Carlyle, Tennyson, Browning, George Eliot! – I'm not feeling very well myself! [civ. 210. 1893]

26 I'm afraid you've got a bad egg, Mr Jones! Oh no, my Lord, I assure you! Parts of it are excellent! [cix. 222. 1895]

27 Look here, Steward, if this is coffee, I want tea; but if this is tea, then I wish for coffee. [cxxiii. 44. 1902]

ISRAEL PUTNAM   1715–1790

28 Don't one of you fire until you see the whites of their eyes. [At Bunker Hill, 1775. Also attr. to W. Prescott]

FRANCIS QUARLES   1592–1644

1 Be wisely worldly, be not worldly wise. [*Emblems*, Bk ii. 2. 46]

2 My soul, sit thou a patient looker-on; / Judge not the play before the play is done; / Her plot hath many changes; every day / Speaks a new scene; the last act crowns the play. [Epigram: *Respice Finem*]

3 We'll cry both arts and learning down, / And hey! then up go we! [*The Shepherd's Oracles*, 'Song of Anarchus', 4]

SIR ARTHUR QUILLER-
COUCH   1863–1944

4 Know you her secret none can utter? / – Hers of the Book, the tripled Crown? [*Alma Mater*]

JOSIAH QUINCY   1772–1864

5 As it will be the right of all, so it will be the duty of some, definitely to prepare for a separation, amicably if they can, violently if they must. [*Abridged Congressional Debates*, 14 Jan. 1811]

FRANÇOIS RABELAIS
c. 1492–1553

6 I drink for the thirst to come. [*Gargantua*, Ch. 5]

7 *L'appétit vient en mangeant.* – Appetite comes with eating. [*Ib.*]

8 Hope to catch larks if the heavens fell. [*Ib.* 11]

9 The strength of a war waged without monetary reserves is as fleeting as a breath. Money is the sinews of battle. [*Ib.* 46]

10 *À la venue des cocquecigrues.* – About the coming of the cocklicranes. [*Ib.* 49]

11 *En leur reigle n'estoit que ceste clause: Fais ce que voudras.* – In their rules there was only one clause: Do what you will. [*Ib.* 57]

12 I was born and brought up as a child in Touraine, which is the garden of France. [*Pantagruel*, Ch. 9]

13 So Anarch became a good crier of green sauce. [*Ib.* 31]

14 Man never found the deities so kindly / As to assure him that he'd live tomorrow. [*Pantagruel*, III. 2]

15 Not everyone is a debtor who wishes to be; not everyone who wishes makes creditors. [(Panurge) *Ib.* III. 3]

16 This is a great year for cuckolds. [*Ib.* III. 9]

17 This flea that I have in my ear has been tickling me. [(Panurge) *Ib.* III. 31]

18 The dice of judgement ... the same dice as you gentlemen use in this supreme court of yours. [(Bridlegoose) *Ib.* III. 39]

19 Few and signally blest are those whom Jupiter has destined to be cabbage-planters. For they've always one foot on the ground, and the other not far from it. [(Panurge) *Ib.* IV. 18]

20 'Devil take me,' began Friar John. 'I'll go halves with him,' interrupted Panurge. [*Ib.* IV. 23]

21 *Vogue la galère.* – Let her go. [*Ib.*]

22 You can keep your litter and your hay and your oats. Long live the thistles of the field, for there you can play the stallion to your heart's content. [*Ib.* V. 7]

23 On the other square, to the left, was elegantly engraved in capital letters this sentence: ALL THINGS MOVE TO THEIR END. [*Ib.* V. 37]

24 Then this one word was heard: *Trink*. [*Ib.* V. 45]

25 *Trink* is a panomphaean word. It speaks oracles, that is to say, in all languages. [*Ib.* V. 46]

26 *Tirez le rideau, la farce est jouée.* – Ring down the curtain, the farce is over. [Attr. last words]

27 *Je m'en vais chercher un grand peut-être.* – I am going in search of a great perhaps. [Attr. last words]

JEAN RACINE   1639–1699

28 *Ah! je l'ai trop aimé pour ne le point haïr!* – Oh, I have loved him too much to feel no hate for him. [*Andromaque*, II. i. 416]

29 *Mon innocence enfin commence à me peser.* – Now my innocence begins to weigh me down. [*Ib.* III. i. 772]

30 *Je t'aimais inconstant, qu'aurais-je fait fidèle?* – I loved you when you were

294

inconstant. What should I have done if you had been faithful? [*Andromaque*, IV. v. 1365]

1 *C'était pendant l'horreur d'une profonde nuit.* – It was during the horror of an intensely dark night. [*Athalie*, II. v. 490]

2 *Elle flotte, elle hésite; en un mot, elle est femme.* – She wavers, she hesitates; in one word, she is a woman. [*Ib.* III. iii. 876]

3 *Ce n'est plus une ardeur dans mes veines cachée: / C'est Vénus toute entière à sa proie attachée.* – It is no longer a heat concealed in my blood, it is Venus herself grasping her prey. [*Phèdre*, II. v. 304]

4 *Ainsi que la vertu le crime a ses degrés.* – Crime, like virtue, has its degrees. [*Ib.* IV. ii. 1096]

5 *Le jour n'est pas plus pur que le fond de mon cœur.* – Day is not purer than the depths of my heart. [*Ib.* IV. ii. 1112]

6 *On apprend à hurler, dit l'autre, avec les loups.* – One learns, said the other, to howl with the wolves. [*Les Plaideurs*, I. i. 6]

THOMAS RAINBOROWE ?–1648

7 The poorest he that is in England hath a life to live as the greatest he. [*Army Debates at Putney*, 29 Oct. 1647]

SIR WALTER RALEGH
c. 1552–1618

8 As you came from the holy land / Of Walsinghame, / Met you not with my true love / By the way as you came?

How shall I know your true love, / That have met many one / As I went to the holy land, / That have come, that have gone? [*As you Came*]

9 Go, Soul, the body's guest, / Upon a thankless arrant: / Fear not to touch the best; / The truth shall be thy warrant: / Go, since I needs must die, / And give the world the lie. [*The Lie*]

10 Give me my scallop-shell of quiet, / My staff of faith to walk upon, / My scrip of joy, immortal diet, / My bottle of salvation, / My gown of glory, hope's true gage, / And thus I'll take my pilgrimage. [*The Passionate Man's Pilgrimage*]

11 O eloquent, just, and mighty Death! whom none could advise, thou hast persuaded; what none hath dared, thou hast done; and whom all the world hath flattered, thou only hast cast out of the world and despised: thou hast drawn together all the far-stretched greatness, all the pride, cruelty, and ambition of man, and covered it all over with these two narrow words, *Hic Jacet*. [*A History of the World*, Bk V, Ch. 6]

12 The world itself is but a large prison, out of which some are daily led to execution. [When returning to prison from his trial]

13 Fain would I climb, yet fear I to fall. [Line written on a window-pane. Queen Elizabeth is said to have written under it, 'If the heart fails thee, climb not at all'.]

14 'Tis a sharp remedy [the executioner's axe], but a sure one for all ills. [Attr. by Hume]

15 So the heart be right, it is no matter which way the head lieth. [When laying his head on the block]

SIR WALTER A. RALEIGH
1861–1922

16 I wish I loved the Human Race; / I wish I loved its silly face; / I wish I liked the way it walks; / I wish I liked the way it talks; / And when I'm introduced to one / I wish I thought *What Jolly Fun!* [*Laughter from a Cloud*, 'Wishes of an Elderly Man']

JULIAN RALPH   1853–1903

17 News value. [Lecture at Columbia, 1892]

ALLAN RAMSAY   1685–1758

18 Farewell to Lochaber, and farewell my Jean. [*Lochaber No More*]

J. R. RANDALL   1839–1908

19 The despot's heel is on thy shore, Maryland! [*Maryland, My Maryland*]

J. E. RANKIN   1828–1904

20 God be with you till we meet again; / By His counsels guide, uphold you, / With His sheep securely fold you. [Hymn]

JOHN CROWE RANSOM
1888–1974

1 Two evils, monstrous either one apart, / Possessed me, and were long and loath at going; / A cry of Absence, Absence, in the heart, / And in the wood the furious winter blowing. [*Winter Remembered*]

THOMAS RAVENSCROFT
1592?–1635?

2 We be three poor mariners / Newly come from the seas. [*Deuteromelia*]

CHARLES READE
1814–1884

3 *Courage, l'ami, le diable est mort.* – Courage, my friend, the devil is dead. [*The Cloister and the Hearth*, Ch. 24]

4 Make 'em laugh; make 'em cry; make 'em wait. [Recipe for novel-writing in serial form

ERICH MARIA REMARQUE
1898–1970

5 *Im Westen nichts Neues.* – All Quiet on the Western Front. [Title of novel]

WALTER REUTHER
1907–1970

6 Mr John Foster Dulles – the world's longest range misguided missile. [*Observer* 'Sayings of the Week', 1 July 1956]

EBEN REXFORD
1848–1916

7 Darling, I am growing old, / Silver threads among the gold. [*Silver Threads among the Gold*]

FREDERIC REYNOLDS
1764–1841

8 How goes the enemy? [(Said by Mr Ennui, 'the time-killer') *The Dramatist*, I. i]

SIR JOSHUA REYNOLDS
1723–1792

9 If you have great talents, industry will improve them: if you have but moderate abilities, industry will supply their deficiency. [*Discourses*, 2]

10 A mere copier of nature can never produce anything great. [*Discourses*, 3]

CECIL RHODES
1853–1902

11 So little done, so much to do. [Last words]

WILLIAM BARNES RHODES
1772–1826

12 'Who dares this pair of boots displace, / Must meet Bombastes face to face.' / Thus do I challenge all the human race. [*Bombastes Furioso*, iv]

GRANTLAND RICE
1880–1954

13 For when the One Great Scorer comes / To write against your name, / He marks – not that you won or lost – / But how you played the game. [*Alumnus Football*]

SIR STEPHEN RICE
1637–1715

14 'I will drive,' he used to say, 'a coach and six through the Act of Settlement.' [Macaulay's *History*, Ch. 12]

CARDINAL RICHELIEU
1585–1642

15 If you give me six lines written by the most honest man, I will find something in them to hang him. [Attr. in various forms]

JEAN PAUL RICHTER 1763–1825

16 Providence has given to the French the empire of the land, to the English that of the sea, and to the Germans that of the air. [Quoted by Carlyle]

J. W. RILEY
1852–1916

17 An' the gobble-uns 'll git you / Ef you don't watch out! [*Little Orphant Annie*]

RAINER MARIA RILKE
1875–1926

18 It was the sinister, princely death which the chamberlain had carried with him

and had himself nourished during his whole life. [*Notebooks of Malte Laurids Brigge*, Pt I]

1 It is good to say it aloud: 'Nothing has happened'. Once again: 'Nothing has happened'. Does that help? [*Ib.*]

J.-A. RIMBAUD   1854–1891

2 *A noir, E blanc, I rouge, U vert. O bleu, voyelles.* – A black, E white, I red, U green, O blue, vowels. [*Voyelles*]

R. L. RIPLEY   1893–1949

3 Believe it or not. [Title of newspaper feature]

ANTOINE DE RIVAROL
1753–1801

4 *Ce qui n'est pas clair n'est pas français.* – What is not clear is not French. [*De l'universalité de la langue française*]

GEORGE ROBEY   1869–1954

5 They knew her by the pimple, / The pimple on her nose. [Song: *The Simple Pimple*]

SIR BOYLE ROCHE   1743–1807

6 What has posterity done for us? [Speech in Irish Parliament, 1780]

7 Mr Speaker I smell a rat; I see him forming in the air and darkening the sky; but I'll nip him in the bud. [Attr.]

DUC DE LA ROCHEFOUCAULD   1613–1680

8 We have all enough strength to bear other people's troubles. [*Les Maximes*, 19]

9 We need greater virtues to bear good fortune than bad. [*Ib.* 25]

10 If we had no faults we should not take so much pleasure in noticing them in others. [*Ib.* 31]

11 One is never as fortunate or as unfortunate as one imagines. [*Ib.* 49]

12 To establish oneself in the world one has to do all one can to appear established. [*Ib.* 56]

13 If one judges love by the majority of its effects, it is more like hatred than like friendship. [*Les Maximes*, 72]

14 Love of justice in most men is no more than the fear of suffering injustice. [*Ib.* 78]

15 It is more shameful to distrust one's friends than to be deceived by them. [*Ib.* 84]

16 Everyone complains of his memory, but no one complains of his judgement. [*Ib.* 89]

17 The intellect is always fooled by the heart. [*Ib.* 102]

18 One gives nothing so freely as advice. [*Ib.* 110]

19 One had rather malign oneself than not speak of oneself at all. [*Ib.* 138]

20 To refuse praise reveals a desire to be praised twice over. [*Ib.* 149]

21 Flattery is false coin that is only current thanks to our vanity. [*Ib.* 158]

22 Hypocrisy is the homage paid by vice to virtue. [*Ib.* 218]

23 One's over-great haste to repay an obligation is a kind of ingratitude. [*Ib.* 226]

24 It takes great cleverness to be able to conceal one's cleverness. [*Ib.* 245]

25 We only confess our little faults to persuade people that we have no large ones. [*Ib.* 327]

26 We seldom attribute common sense except to those who agree with us. [*Ib.* 347]

27 We may give advice, but we can never prompt behaviour. [*Ib.* 378]

28 Nothing prevents us from being natural so much as the desire to appear so. [*Ib.* 431]

29 Quarrels would not last so long if the fault were on only one side. [*Ib.* 496]

30 In the misfortunes of our best friends, we find something that is not unpleasing. [*Maximes supprimés*, 583]

31 Most usually our virtues are only vices in disguise. [Added to the 4th edition of *Les Maximes*]

32 Anything may happen in France. [Attr. remark to Mazarin, quoted by Sainte-Beuve, *Portraits de femmes*]

DUC DE LA ROCHEFOU-CAULD-LIANCOURT 1747–1827

1 LOUIS XVI: *C'est une révolte? –* Is it a revolt?

THE DUKE: *Non, Sire, c'est une révolution.–* No, Sire, it's a revolution. [On hearing of the Fall of the Bastille, 1789]

JOHN WILMOT, EARL OF ROCHESTER 1647–1680

2 The best good man, with the worst-natured muse. [(Lord Buckhurst) *An Allusion to Horace*]

3 Here lies our sovereign lord the king / Whose promise none relies on; / He never said a foolish thing, / Nor ever did a wise one. [*Epitaph on Charles II.* Various forms exist]

4 If I, by miracle, can be / This live-long minute true to thee, / 'Tis all that heaven allows. *Love and Life, A Song*]

5 I'd be a dog, a monkey, or a bear, / Or anything but that vain animal, / Who is so proud of being rational. [*A Satire against Mankind*, 5]

6 Reason, an *ignis fatuus* of the mind. [*Ib.* 12]

7 Then old age, and experience, hand in hand, / Lead him to death, and make him understand, / After a search so painful, and so long, / That all his life he has been in the wrong. [*Ib.* 25]

8 Most men are cowards, all men should be knaves. [*Ib.* 158]

9 A merry monarch, scandalous and poor. [*A Satire on King Charles II*]

10 Nothing, thou elder brother ev'n to shade, / Thou hadst a being ere the world was made. [*Upon Nothing*]

LUDWIG VON ROENNE 1804–1891

11 If anything can give us a claim to the title of his Majesty's loyal opposition, it is, I think, our present debate, and our present resolution. [Speech in Prussian House, 1863]

E. W. ROGERS 1864–1913

12 Ev'ry member of the force / Has a watch and chain, of course; / If you want to know the time, / Ask a P'liceman! [*Ask a P'liceman*]

13 Hi-tiddley-hi-ti. [Title of song]

J. E. T. ROGERS 1823–1900

14 While ladling butter from alternate tubs / Stubbs butters Freeman, Freeman butters Stubbs. [Attr. by Hutton]

R. C. ROGERS 1862–1912

15 The hours I spent with thee, dear heart, / Are as a string of pearls to me; / I count them over, every one apart, / My rosary. [*My Rosary*]

SAMUEL ROGERS 1763–1855

16 Ward has no heart, they say; but I deny it: / He has a heart, and gets his speeches by it. [*Epigram upon Lord Dudley*]

17 Think nothing done while aught remains to do. [*Human Life*, 49]

18 Never less alone than when alone, / Those whom he loved so long and sees no more, / Loved and still loves – not dead – but gone before, / He gathers round him. [*Ib.* 755]

19 Oh! she was good as she was fair. / None – none on earth above her! / As pure in thought as angels are, / To know her was to love her. [*Jacqueline*, l. 68]

20 Sheridan was listened to with such attention that you might have heard a pin drop. [*Table Talk*]

21 It doesn't much signify whom one marries, for one is sure to find next morning that it was someone else. [*Ib.*]

22 When a new book is published, read an old one. [Attr.]

23 A man who attempts to read all the new productions must do as the fleas do – skip. [Attr.]

MME ROLAND 1754–1793

24 *Ô Liberté! Ô Liberté! que de crimes on commet en ton nom. –* O liberty, liberty, what crimes are committed in your name! [On passing the statue of Liberty, on her way to the scaffold]

JAMES ROLMAZ   19 Cent.

1 Where did you get that hat? / Where did you get that tile? [*Where Did You Get That Hat?*]

PIERRE DE RONSARD
1524 or 1525–1585

2 *Mignonne, allons voir si la rose / Qui ce matin avait déclose / Sa robe de pourpre au soleil / A point perdu cette vesprée / Les plis de sa robe pourprée, / Et son teint au vôtre pareil.* – Darling, let us go to see if the rose, which this morning had spread her purple robe to the sun, has not this evening lost the folds of her purple robe and her colour, that is like yours. [*Odes, À Cassandre*, xvii]

3 *Quand vous serez bien vieille, au soir à la chandelle, / Assise auprès du feu, dévidant et filant, / Direz, chantant mes vers, en vous émerveillant, / Ronsard me célébrait du temps que j'étais belle.* – When you are very old and sit at evening beside the fire, by candlelight, carding and spinning, you will say with wonder, as you recite my verses: 'Ronsard sang of me in the time when I was fair.' [*Sonnets à Hélène*, II. 43]

FRANKLIN D. ROOSEVELT
1882–1945

4 The forgotten man at the bottom of the economic pyramid. [Broadcast speech, 7 Apr. 1932]

5 I pledge you – I pledge myself – to a new deal for the American people. [Speech at Convention, Chicago, 2 July 1932]

6 Let me assert my firm belief that the only thing we have to fear is fear itself. [First Inaugural Address, 4 Mar. 1933]

7 In the field of world policy I would dedicate this nation to the policy of the good neighbour. [*Ib.*]

8 I see one-third of a nation ill-housed, ill-clad, ill-nourished. [Second Inaugural Address, 20 Jan. 1937]

9 We must be the great arsenal of democracy. [*Fireside Chat*, 29 Dec. 1940]

10 A world founded upon four essential freedoms. The first is freedom of speech and expression–everywhere in the world. The second is freedom of every person to worship God in his own way – everywhere in the world. The third is freedom from want . . . everywhere in the world. The fourth is freedom from fear . . . anywhere in the world. [Speech, 6 Jan. 1941]

11 A radical is a man with both feet firmly planted in the air. [Quoted in *Treasury of Humorous Quotations*]

THEODORE ROOSEVELT
1858–1919

12 I wish to preach, not the doctrine of ignoble ease, but the doctrine of the strenuous life. [Speech in Chicago, 10 Apr. 1899]

13 Speak softly and carry a big stick; you will go far. [Speech at Minnesota, 2 Sept. 1901]

14 A man who is good enough to shed his blood for his country is good enough to be given a square deal afterwards. More than that no man is entitled to, and less than that no man shall have. [Speech at Springfield, Illinois, 4 June 1903]

15 The men with the muck-rakes are often indispensable to the well-being of society; but only if they know when to stop raking the muck. [At laying of corner-stone, House of Representatives 14 Apr. 1906]

16 The lunatic fringe in all reform movements. [*Autobiography*, Ch. 7]

17 No man is justified in doing evil on the ground of expediency. [*The Strenuous Life*, 'Latitude and Longitude among Reformers']

18 Hyphenated Americans. [*Metropolitan Magazine*, Oct. 1915]

19 The most successful politician is he who says what everybody is thinking most often and in the loudest voice. [Quoted in *Treasury of Humorous Quotations*]

EARL OF ROSCOMMON
1637–1685

20 Choose an author as you choose a friend. [*Essay on Translated Verse*, 96]

21 Immodest words admit of no defence, / For want of decency is want of sense. [*Ib*, 113]

22 The multitude is always in the wrong. [*Ib.* 183]

EARL OF ROSEBERY 1847–1929

1 The Empire is a Commonwealth of Nations. [Speech at Adelaide, 18 Jan. 1884]

2 It is beginning to be hinted that we are a nation of amateurs. [Rectorial Address, Glasgow, 16 Nov. 1900]

3 I must plough my furrow alone. [Speech, 19 July 1901]

4 You have to clean your plate. [(Advice to the Liberal Party) Speech at Chesterfield, 16 Dec. 1901]

ALAN S. C. ROSS 1907–1980

5 U and Non-U, An Essay in Sociological Linguistics. [Title of essay, included in *Noblesse Oblige*]

ALEXANDER ROSS 1699–1784

6 Married, and wooed, and a'! / And was she nae very weel off / That was wooed, and married, and a'? [*Wooed, and Married, and A'*]

CHRISTINA ROSSETTI
1830–1894

7 My heart is like a singing bird / Whose nest is in a watered shoot; / My heart is like an apple-tree / Whose boughs are bent with thickset fruit; / My heart is like a rainbow shell / That paddles in a halcyon sea; / My heart is gladder than all these / Because my love is come to me. [*A Birthday*]

8 Because the birthday of my life / Is come, my love is come to me. [*Ib.*]

9 For there is no friend like a sister / In calm or stormy weather. [*Goblin Market*, towards the end]

10 Snow had fallen, snow on snow, / Snow on snow, / In the bleak mid-winter, / Long ago. [*Mid-Winter*]

11 Remember me when I am gone away, / Gone far away into the silent land. [*Remember*]

12 Better by far you should forget and smile / Than that you should remember and be sad. [*Ib.*]

13 Darkness more clear than noonday holdeth her, / Silence more musical than any song. [*Rest*]

14 Who has seen the wind? / Neither you nor I: / But when the trees bow down their heads / The wind is passing by. [*Sing-Song*]

15 But pluck an ivy branch for me / Grown old before my time. [Song: *Oh Roses for the Flush*]

16 When I am dead, my dearest, / Sing no sad songs for me; / Plant thou no roses at my head, / Nor shady cypress tree: / Be the green grass above me / With showers and dewdrops wet; / And if thou wilt, remember, / And if thou wilt, forget. [Song: *When I am Dead, my Dearest*]

17 'Does the road wind up-hill all the way?' / 'Yes, to the very end.' / 'Will the day's journey take the whole long day?' / 'From morn to night, my friend.' [*Up-Hill*]

18 'May not the darkness hide it from my face?' / 'You cannot miss that inn.' [*Ib.*]

19 'Will there be beds for me and all who seek?' / 'Yea, beds for all who come.' [*Ib.*]

DANTE GABRIEL ROSSETTI
1828–1882

20 The blessed damozel leaned out / From the gold bar of heaven; / Her eyes were deeper than the depth / Of waters stilled at even; / She had three lilies in her hand, / And the stars in her hair were seven. [*The Blessed Damozel*, i]

21 Her hair that lay along her back / Was yellow like ripe corn. [*Ib.* ii]

22 As low as where this earth / Spins like a fretful midge. [*Ib.* vi]

23 And the souls mounting up to God / Went by her like thin flames. [*Ib.* vii]

24 'Was it a friend or foe that spread these lies?' / 'Nay, who but infants question in such wise? / 'Twas one of my most intimate enemies.' [*Fragment*]

25 A sonnet is a moment's monument, – / Memorial from the Soul's eternity / To one dead deathless hour. [*The House of Life*, 1, Introduction]

1 'Tis visible silence, still as the hour-glass. / Deep in the sun-searched growths the dragon-fly / Hangs like a blue thread loosened from the sky: – / So this winged hour is dropped to us from above. [*The House of Life*, 19, 'Silent Noon']

2 And though thy soul sail leagues and leagues beyond, – / Still, leagues beyond those leagues, there is more sea. [*Ib.* 73, 'The Choice']

3 This is that Lady Beauty, in whose praise / Thy voice and hand shake still, – long known to thee / By flying hair and fluttering hem, – the beat / Following her daily of thy heart and feet, / How passionately and irretrievably, / In what fond flight, how many ways and days! [*Ib.* 77, 'Soul's Beauty']

4 I do not see them here; but after death / God knows I know the faces I shall see, / Each one a murdered self, with low last breath. / 'I am thyself, – what hast thou done to me?' / 'And I – and I – thyself' (lo! each one saith,) / 'And thou thyself to all eternity!' [*Ib.* 86, 'Lost Days']

5 My name is Might-have-been; / I am also called No-more, Too-late, Farewell. [*Ib.* 97, 'A Superscription']

6 O Mother, Mary Mother, / Three days today, between Hell and Heaven. [*Sister Helen*]

7 I have been here before, / But when or how I cannot tell: / I know the grass beyond the door, / The sweet keen smell, / The sighing sound, the lights around the shore. [*Sudden Light*]

8 Conception, my boy, *fundamental brainwork*, is what makes the difference in all art. [Letter to Hall Caine, quoted in Caine's *Recollections of Rossetti*]

9 The Stealthy School of Criticism. [Title of a letter to the *Athenaeum*, 1871]

GIOACCHINO ROSSINI
1792–1868

10 Give me a laundry-list and I'll set it to music. [Quoted in *Treasury of Humorous Quotations*]

EDMOND ROSTAND   1868–1918

11 *Énorme, mon nez! / – Vil camus, sot camard, tête plate, apprenez / Que je m'enorgueillis d'un pareil appendice, / Attendu qu'un grand nez est proprement l'indice / D'un homme affable, bon, courtois, spirituel, / Libéral, courageux, tel que je suis.* – My nose is huge! Vile snub-nose, flat-nosed ass, flat-head, let me inform you that I am proud of such an appendage, since a big nose is the proper sign of a friendly, good, courteous, witty, liberal, and brave man, such as I am. [*Cyrano de Bergerac*, I. i]

12 *À la fin de l'envoi, je touche.* – At the end of the envoy, I shall strike. [*Ib.* I. iv]

ROUGET DE LISLE   1760–1836

13 *Allons, enfants de la patrie, / Le jour de gloire est arrivé.* – Come, children of our native land, / The day of glory has arrived. [*La Marseillaise*]

14 *Aux armes, citoyens!* [*Ib.*]

JEAN-JACQUES ROUSSEAU
1712–1778

15 *L'homme est né libre, et partout il est dans les fers.* – Man was born free, and everywhere he is in chains. [*Du contrat social*, Ch. 1]

16 Everything is good when it leaves the Creator's hands; everything degenerates in the hands of man. [*Émile*, I. i]

17 Happiness: a good bank account, a good cook, and a good digestion. [Quoted in *Treasury of Humorous Quotations*]

MARTIN ROUTH   1755–1854

18 You will find it a very good practice always to verify your references, sir. [Attr. by Burgon]

NICHOLAS ROWE   1674–1718

19 At length the morn and cold indifference came. [*The Fair Penitent*, I. i]

20 Is this that haughty, gallant, gay Lothario? [*Ib.* V. i]

'RED ROWLEY'   20 Cent.

21 Mademoiselle from Armenteers, / Hasn't been kissed for forty years, / Hinky pinky, parley-voo. [*Mademoiselle from Armentières*]

JEAN DE ROYE 1425–?

1 *Chronique scandaleuse.* – Scandalous Chronicle. [Title given to his Journal in the edition of 1611]

JOHN RUSKIN 1819–1900

2 You hear of me, among others, as a respectable architectural man-milliner; and you send for me that I may tell you the leading fashion. [*The Crown of Wild Olive*, 'Traffic', §3]

3 I have seen, and heard, much of cockney impudence before now; but never expected to hear a coxcomb ask two hundred guineas for flinging a pot of paint in the public's face. [(Of Whistler's *Nocturne in Black and Gold*) *Fors Clavigera*, Letter 79]

4 A falseness in all our impressions of external things, which I would generally characterize as the 'pathetic fallacy'. [*Modern Painters* Vol. 3. Pt iv. Ch. 12]

5 Mountains are the beginning and the end of all natural scenery. [*Ib.* 4. v. 20, beginning]

6 Be sure that you go to the author to get at *his* meaning, not to find yours. [*Sesame and Lilies*, 1. §13]

7 Which of us ... is to do the hard and dirty work for the rest – and for what pay? Who is to do the pleasant and clean work, and for what pay? [*Ib.* 1. §30, note]

8 When we build, let us think that we build for ever. [*The Seven Lamps of Architecture*, Ch. 5. §10]

9 Remember that the most beautiful things in the world are the most useless; peacocks and lilies for instance. [*The Stones of Venice*, I. Ch. 2. §17]

10 The purest and most thoughtful minds are those which love colour the most. [*Ib.* I. 5. §30]

11 Fine art is that in which the hand, the head, and the heart of man go together. [*The Two Paths*, Lecture 2]

12 Not only is there but one way of *doing* things rightly, but there is only one way of *seeing* them, and that is seeing the whole of them. [*Ib.*]

13 There is no wealth but Life. [*Unto this Last*, IV. §77]

14 Trust thou thy Love: if she be proud, is she not sweet? / Trust thou thy Love: if she be mute, is she not pure? / Lay thou thy soul full in her hands, low at her feet; – / Fail, sun and breath! – Yet for thy peace, she shall endure. [*Trust Thou Thy Love*]

BERTRAND, LORD RUSSELL 1872–1970

15 Brief and powerless is Man's life; on him and all his race the slow, sure doom falls pitiless and dark. [*Mysticism and Logic*, 'A Free Man's Worship']

16 Mathematics possesses not only truth, but supreme beauty – a beauty cold and austere, like that of sculpture. [*Ib.* 'The Study of Mathematics']

LORD JOHN RUSSELL 1792–1878

17 Among the defects of the Bill, which were numerous, one provision was conspicuous by its presence and another by its absence. [Speech to his constituents, Apr. 1859]

18 A proverb is one man's wit and all men's wisdom. [Attr.]

SIR WILLIAM RUSSELL 1820–1907

19 [The Russians] dash on towards the thin red line tipped with steel. [*The British Expedition to the Crimea*]

JOHN L. ST JOHN 20 Cent.

20 Archibald – certainly not! [Title of song]

MARQUIS DE SAINT-LAMBERT 1716–1803

21 *Souvent j'écoute encor quand le chant a cessé.* – Often I am still listening when the song is over. [*Les Saisons*, 'Le Printemps']

W. ST LEGER *fl.* 1890

22 There is a fine stuffed chavender, / A chavender, or chub, / That decks the

rural pavender, / The pavender, or pub, / Wherein I eat my gravender, / My gravender or grub. [*A False Gallop of Analogies*]

CHARLES-AUGUSTIN SAINTE-BEUVE   1804–1869

1 *Et Vigny, plus secret, / Comme en son tour d'ivoire, avant midi, rentrait.* – And Vigny, more discreet, as if in his ivory tower, returned before noon. [*À M. Villemain*]

2 Every additional man who learns to read is another reader for Molière. [*Portraits littéraires*, Vol. 2]

SAKI [H. H. MUNRO]   1870–1916

3 You can't expect a boy to be depraved until he has been to a good school. [*A Baker's Dozen*]

4 'The man is a common murderer.'
'A common murderer, possibly, but a very uncommon cook.' [*The Blind Spot*]

5 Addresses are given to us to conceal our whereabouts. [*Cross Currents*]

6 'I believe I take precedence,' he said coldly; 'you are merely the club Bore: I am the club Liar.' [*A Defensive Diamond*]

7 Children with Hyacinth's temperament don't know better as they grow older; they merely know more. [*Hyacinth*]

8 In baiting a mouse-trap with cheese, always leave room for the mouse. [*The Infernal Parliament*]

9 I might have been a gold-fish in a glass bowl for all the privacy I got. [*The Innocence of Reginald*]

10 He's simply got the instinct for being unhappy highly developed. [*The Match-Maker*]

11 The cook was a good cook, as cooks go; and as cooks go she went. [*Reginald on Besetting Sins*]

12 His 'Noontide Peace', a study of two dun cows under a walnut tree, was followed by 'A Mid-day Sanctuary', a study of a walnut tree with two dun cows under it. [*The Stalled Ox*]

13 This story has no moral. If it points out an evil, at any rate it suggests no remedy.

[*The Unbearable Bassington*, author's note]

14 A woman whose dresses are made in Paris and whose marriage has been made in Heaven might be equally biased for and against free imports. [*Ib.* Ch. 9]

15 Sherard Blaw, the dramatist who had discovered himself, and who had given so ungrudgingly of his discovery to the world. [*Ib.* 13]

LORD SALISBURY   1830–1903

16 By office boys for office boys. [Description of the *Daily Mail*]

SALLUST   86–34 B.C.

17 Coveting other men's property, and squandering his own. [*Catiline*, 5]

18 To like and dislike the same things, that is indeed true friendship. [*Ib.* 20]

COMTE DE SALVANDY   1795–1856

19 We are dancing on a volcano. [Said just before the revolution of 1830]

CARL SANDBURG   1878–1967

20 When Abraham Lincoln was shovelled into the tombs, / he forgot the copperheads and the assassin. . . . / in the dust, in the cool tombs. [*Cool Tombs*]

21 The fog comes / on little cat feet. [*Fog*]

22 Pile the bodies high at Austerlitz and Waterloo, / Shovel them under and let me work – / I am the grass; I cover all. [*Grass*]

IRA D. SANKEY   1840–1908

23 Gather with the saints at the river, / That flows by the throne of God. [*Sacred Songs*, 'Shall We Gather']

24 In the sweet by-and-by, / We shall meet on that beautiful shore. [*Ib.* 'Sweet By-and-by']

GEORGE SANTAYANA   1863–1952

25 The Bible is literature, not dogma. [*Introduction to the Ethics of Spinoza*]

1 England is the paradise of individuality, eccentricity, heresy, anomalies, hobbies, and humours. [*Soliloquies in England*, 'The British Character']

2 There is no cure for birth and death save to enjoy the interval. [*Ib.* 'War Shrines']

3 It is a great advantage for a system of philosophy to be substantially true. [*The Unknowable*]

EPES SARGENT   1813–1880

4 A life on the ocean wave, / A home on the rolling deep. [*A Life on the Ocean Wave*. These lines were taken from a song by Samuel J. Arnold]

JOHN SINGER SARGENT
1856–1925

5 Every time I paint a portrait I lose a friend. [Quoted in *Treasury of Humorous Quotations*]

SIEGFRIED SASSOON 1886–1967

6 Soldiers are citizens of death's grey land, / Drawing no dividend from time's to-morrows. [*Dreamers*]

7 Everyone suddenly burst out singing. [*Everyone Sang*]

8 The song was wordless; / The singing will never be done. [*Ib.*]

RICHARD SAVAGE   1698–1743

9 No tenth transmitter of a foolish face. [*The Bastard*, 8]

HENRY SAYERS   1855–1932

10 Ta-ra-ra-boom-de-ay! [Title of song]

FRIEDRICH VON SCHILLER
1759–1805

11 *Freude, schöner Götterfunken, / Tochter aus Elysium.* – Joy, lovely radiance of the God, thou daughter of Elysium. [*An die Freude*]

12 *Alle Menschen werden Brüder.* – All men become brothers. [*Ib.*]

13 *Seid umschlungen, Millionen!* – Embrace one another, ye millions! [*An die Freude*]

14 *Sieh da! sieh da, Timotheus, / Die Kraniche des Ibykus!* – See there, see there, Timotheus, the cranes of Ibykus! [*Die Kraniche des Ibykus*]

15 *Die Weltgeschichte ist das Weltgericht.* – World history is the world's court of judgement. [*Resignation*]

16 *Die Sonne geht in meinem Staat nicht unter.* – The sun does not set in my dominions. [(Philip II) *Don Carlos*, I. vi]

17 *Mit der Dummheit kämpfen Götter selbst vergebens.* – Against stupidity the gods themselves struggle in vain. [*Die Jungfrau von Orleans*, III. vi]

18 *Ein ruheloser Marsch war unser Leben / Und wie des Windes Sausen, heimatlos, / Durchstürmten wir die kriegbewegte Erde.* – Our life was but a battle and a march / And like the wind's blast, never-resting, homeless, – We stormed across the war-convulsèd heath. [*Wallensteins Tod*, III. 15 (transl. Coleridge)]

FRIEDRICH VON SCHLEGEL
1772–1829

19 A historian is a prophet in reverse. [*Athenäum*, I, 'Fragmente']

20 Revolution from above. [*Concordia*, 38]

F. E. D. SCHLEIERMACHER
1768–1834

21 To be silent in seven languages. [(Of the philologist, Immanuel Becker) Attr.]

MAX SCHNECKENBURGER
1819–1849

22 *Die Wacht am Rhein.* – The Watch on the Rhine. [Title of song]

LOUIS SCHNEIDER   1805–1878

23 *O Tannenbaum, O Tannenbaum, / Wie grün sind deine Blätter* – O pine-tree, O pine-tree, / How green are your leaves! [*Der Kurmärker und die Picarde*. Modernization of lines from a folk-song, previously rendered by August Zarnack (1777–1827): '*Wie treu sind deine Blätter*']

ARTHUR SCHOPENHAUER
1788–1860

1 To be alone is the fate of all great minds – a fate deplored at times, but still always chosen as the less grievous of two evils. [*Aphorismen zur Lebensweisheit*, '*Von dem was Einer ist*']

2 Intellect is invisible to the man who has none. [*Ib.* '*Von dem was Einer vorstellt*']

3 Every parting gives a foretaste of death; every coming together again a foretaste of the resurrection. [*Gedanken über vielerlei Gegenstände*, XXVI, '*Psychologische Bemerkungen*']

4 The fundamental fault of the female character is that it has no sense of justice. [*Ib.* XXVII, '*Über die Weiber*']

SCIPIO AFRICANUS 236–184?B.C.

5 Never less idle than when unoccupied, nor less alone than when without company. [Quoted by Cicero, *De Officiis*, III. i]

C. P. SCOTT 1846–1932

6 Comment is free but facts are sacred. [*Manchester Guardian*, 6 May 1926]

CAPTAIN R. F. SCOTT 1868–1912

7 For God's sake look after our people. [*Journal*, 25 Mar. 1912]

SIR WALTER SCOTT 1771–1832

8 To the Lords of Convention 'twas Claver'se who spoke. ['Bonny Dundee', *The Doom of Devorgoil*, II. ii]

9 Come fill up my cup, come fill up my can, / Come saddle your horses, and call up your men; / Come open the West Port, and let me gang free, / And it's room for the bonnets of Bonny Dundee. [*Ib.*]

10 Look back, and smile at perils past. [*The Bridal of Triermain*, Introduction, ii]

11 But answer came there none. [*Ib.* III. x]

12 The stag at eve had drunk his fill, / When danced the moon on Monan's rill. [*The Lady of the Lake*, I. i]

13 In listening mood, she seemed to stand, / The guardian Naiad of the strand. [*The Lady of the Lake*, I, xvii]

14 Forward and frolic glee was there, / The will to do, the soul to dare. [*Ib.* I. xxi]

15 Yet seemed that tone, and gesture bland, / Less used to sue than to command. [*Ib.*]

16 Soldier, rest! thy warfare o'er, / Dream of fighting fields no more: / Sleep the sleep that knows not breaking, / Morn of toil, nor night of waking. [*Ib.* I. xxxi]

17 Hail to the chief who in triumph advances! [*Ib.* II. xix]

18 Like the dew on the mountain, / Like the foam on the river, / Like the bubble on the fountain, / Thou art gone, and for ever. [*Ib.* III. xvi]

19 And the stern joy which warriors feel / In foemen worthy of their steel. [*Ib.* V. x]

20 The way was long, the wind was cold, / The Minstrel was infirm and old; / His withered cheek and tresses grey / Seemed to have known a better day. [*The Lay of the Last Minstrel*, Introduction]

21 The unpremeditated lay. [*Ib.*]

22 To her bidding she could bow / The viewless forms of air. [*Ib.* I. xii]

23 If thou wouldst view fair Melrose aright, / Go visit it by the pale moonlight. [*Ib.* II. i]

24 Love rules the court, the camp, the grove, / And men below, and saints above; / For love is heaven, and heaven is love. [*Ib.* III. ii]

25 For ne'er / Was flattery lost on poet's ear: / A simple race! they waste their toil / For the vain tribute of a smile. [*Ib.* IV, Conclusion]

26 Call it not vain; they do not err, / Who say, that when the Poet dies, / Mute Nature mourns her worshipper, / And celebrates his obsequies. [*Ib.* V. i]

27 True love's the gift which God has given / To man alone beneath the heaven. [*Ib.* V. xiii]

28 Breathes there the man, with soul so dead, / Who never to himself hath said, / This is my own, my native land! [*Ib.* VI. i]

29 The wretch, concentred all in self, / Living, shall forfeit fair renown, / And, doubly dying, shall go down / To the vile

305

dust. from whence he sprung, / Unwept, unhonoured, and unsung. [*The Lay of the Last Minstrel*]

1 O Caledonia! stern and wild, / Meet nurse for a poetic child! / Land of brown heath and shaggy wood, / Land of the mountain and the flood, / Land of my sires! [*Ib.* VI. ii]

2 That day of wrath, that dreadful day, / When heaven and earth shall pass away. [*Ib.* VI. xxxi]

3 His bright and brief career is o'er. [*The Lord of the Isles.* IV. xi]

4 O! many a shaft, at random sent / Finds mark the archer little meant! / And many a word, at random spoken, / May soothe or wound a heart that's broken! [*Ib.* V. xviii]

5 To that dark inn, the grave! [*Ib.* VI. xxvi]

6 O hush thee. my babie, thy sire was a knight, / Thy mother a lady, both lovely and bright. [*Lullaby of an Infant Chief*]

7 November's sky is chill and drear, / November's leaf is red and sear. [*Marmion*, I, Introduction]

8 But search the land of living men, / Where wilt thou find their like agen? [*Ib.* I. xi]

9 And come he slow, or come he fast, / It is but Death who comes at last. [*Ib.* II. xxx]

10 O, young Lochinvar is come out of the west, / Through all the wide Border his steed was the best. [*Ib.* V. xii]

11 So faithful in love, and so dauntless in war, / There never was knight like the young Lochinvar. [*Ib.*]

12 With a smile on her lips, and a tear in her eye. [*Ib.*]

13 Heap on more wood! the wind is chill; / But let it whistle as it will. / We'll keep our Christmas merry still. [*Ib.* VI, Introduction]

14 England was merry England, when / Old Christmas brought his sports again. [*Ib.*]

15 And dar'st thou then / To beard the lion in his den, / The Douglas in his hall? [*Ib.* VI. xiv]

16 What, warder, ho! / Let the portcullis fall. [*Ib.*]

17 O, what a tangled web we weave, / When first we practise to deceive! [*Ib.* VI. xvii]

18 O Woman! in our hours of ease, / Uncertain, coy, and hard to please, / And variable as the shade / By the light quivering aspen made; / When pain and anguish wring the brow, / A ministering angel thou! [*Marmion*, VI. xxx]

19 'Charge, Chester, charge! On, Stanley, on!' / Were the last words of Marmion. [*Ib.* VI. xxxii]

20 The stubborn spear-men still made good / Their dark impenetrable wood, / Each stepping where his comrade stood, / The instant that he fell. [*Ib.* VI. xxxiv]

21 Come as the winds come, when / Forests are rended; / Come as the waves come, when / Navies are stranded! [*Pibroch of Donuil Dhu*]

22 Still are the thoughts to memory dear. [*Rokeby*, I. xxxiii]

23 A weary lot is thine, fair maid. / A weary lot is thine. [*Ib.* III. xxviii]

24 Whirled them to the back o' beyont. [*The Antiquary*, Ch. 2]

25 Look not thou on beauty's charming, – / Sit thou still while kings are arming, – / Taste not when the wine-cup glistens, – / Speak not when the people listens, – / Stop thine ear against the singer, – / From the red gold keep thy finger; – / Vacant heart and hand, and eye, – / Easy live and quiet die. [*The Bride of Lammermoor*, Ch. 3]

26 It's ill taking the breeks aff a wild Highlandman. [*The Fair Maid of Perth*, Ch. 5]

27 For a con-si-de-ra-tion. [*Ib.* 22]

28 Ever after designated as a 'stickit minister'. [*Guy Mannering*, Ch. 2]

29 MRS BERTRAM: That sounds like nonsense, my dear.
MR BERTRAM: May be so, my dear; but it may be very good law for all that. [*Ib.* 9]

30 'Pro-di-gi-ous!' exclaimed Dominie Sampson. [*Ib.* 14]

31 The ancient and now forgotten pastime of high jinks. [*Ib.* 36]

32 The hour is come, but not the man. [*The Heart of Midlothian*, Ch. 4, heading]

33 Proud Maisie is in the wood, / Walking so early, / Sweet Robin sits in the bush, / Singing so rarely. [*Ib.* 40]

1 There is a Southern proverb, – fine words butter no parsnips. [*The Legend of Montrose*, Ch. 3]

2 And it's ill speaking between a fou man and a fasting. [*Redgauntlet*, Letter 11. 'Wandering Willie's Tale']

3 Come weal, come woe, we'll gather and go, / And live or die with Charlie. [*Ib.* Ch. 11]

4 Among the sea of upturned faces which bent their eyes on the pulpit as a common centre. [*Rob Roy*, Ch. 20]

5 If your honour disna ken when ye hae a gude servant, I ken when I hae a gude master. [*Ib.* 24]

6 There's a gude time coming. [*Ib.* 32]

7 My foot is on my native heath, and my name is MacGregor! [*Ib.* 34]

8 The play-bill, which is said to have announced the tragedy of Hamlet, the character of the Prince of Denmark being left out. [*The Talisman*, Introduction]

9 My heart's in the Highlands, my heart is not here, / My heart's in the Highlands a-chasing the deer. [*Waverley*, Ch. 28]

10 But I must say to the Muse of fiction, as the Earl of Pembroke said to the ejected nun of Wilton, 'Go spin, you jade, go spin!' [*Journal*, 9 Feb. 1826]

11 The Big Bow-Wow strain I can do myself like anyone now going; but the exquisite touch, which renders ordinary commonplace things and characters interesting, from the truth of the description and the sentiment, is denied to me. [(Of Jane Austen) *Ib.* 14 Mar. 1826]

12 I would like to be there, were it but to see how the cat jumps. [*Ib.* 7 Oct. 1826]

13 From the lone shieling of the misty island / Mountains divide us and the waste of seas – / Yet still the blood is strong, the heart is Highland, / And we in dreams behold the Hebrides! [*Canadian Boat Song* (authorship disputed)]

WILLIAM SCOTT, LORD STOWELL   1745–1836

14 The elegant simplicity of the three per cents. [Campbell's *Chancellors*, Vol. X. Ch. 212]

15 A dinner lubricates business. [Boswell's *Life of Johnson*, 1781]

16 A precedent embalms a principle. [Attr. opinion, while Advocate-General]

RONALD SEARLE   1920–

17 The Terror of St Trinian's. [Title of book by D. B. Wyndham Lewis (Timothy Shy) and illustrated by Searle]

E. H. SEARS   1810–1876

18 It came upon the midnight clear, / That glorious song of old, / From Angels bending near the earth / To touch their harps of gold; / 'Peace on the earth; good will to man / From Heaven's all gracious King.' / The world in solemn stillness lay / To hear the angels sing. [*That Glorious Song of Old*]

GENERAL SEBASTIANI   1772–1851

19 At the moment of writing, calm [or 'order'] reigned in Warsaw. [After brutal suppression of the Polish rising, 1831]

SIR CHARLES SEDLEY   1639?–1701

20 Love still has something of the sea / From whence his mother rose. [*Love still has Something*]

21 Not, Celia, that I juster am / Or better than the rest. [*Not, Celia, that I juster am*]

22 When change itself can give no more, / 'Tis easy to be true. [*Ib.*]

23 Phyllis is my only joy, / Faithless as the winds or seas; / Sometimes coming, sometimes coy, / Yet she never fails to please. [*Phyllis is my only Joy*]

24 Phyllis, without frown or smile, / Sat and knotted all the while. [*Phyllis Knotting*]

ALAN SEEGER   1888–1916

25 I have a rendezvous with Death / At some disputed barricade. [*I Have a Rendezvous with Death*]

SIR J. R. SEELEY   1834–1895

26 We seem, as it were, to have conquered and peopled half the world in a fit of

absence of mind. [*The Expansion of England*, Lecture I]

JOHN SELDEN   1584–1654

1 Old friends are best. King James used to call for his old shoes; they were easiest for his feet. [*Table Talk*, XLVII]

2 'Tis not the eating, nor 'tis not the drinking that is to be blamed, but the excess. [*Ib.* LIV]

3 Commonly we say a judgement falls on a man for something in him we cannot abide. [*Ib.* LXVI]

4 A king is a thing men have made for their own sakes, for quietness' sake. Just as if in a family one man is appointed to buy the meat. [*Ib.* LXXI]

5 Ignorance of the law excuses no man: not that all men know the law, but because 'tis an excuse every man will plead, and no man can tell how to refute him. [*Ib.* LXXVII]

6 Take a straw and throw it up into the air, you shall see by that which way the wind is. [*Ib.* LXXXI]

7 Marriage is nothing but a civil contract. [*Ib.* LXXXV]

8 There never was a merry world since the fairies left off dancing, and the parson left conjuring. [*Ib.* XCIX]

9 Pleasure is nothing else but the intermission of pain [*Ib.* CIV]

10 Pleasures are all alike simply considered in themselves. . . . He that takes pleasure to hear sermons enjoys himself as much as he that hears plays. [*Ib.*]

11 Preachers say, Do as I say, not as I do. [*Ib.* CXI]

W. C. SELLAR   1898–1951
and R. J. YEATMAN   1897–1968

12 1066 and All That. [Title of book]

13 The Roman Conquest was, however, a *Good Thing*. [*Ib.* Ch. 1]

14 The Venomous Bead (author of *The Rosary*). [*Ib.* 3]

15 The Memorable Round Table made to have the Conferences at, so that it was impossible to say who was top knight. [*Ib.* 6]

16 Whenever he returned to England he always set out again immediately for the Mediterranean and was therefore known as Richard Gare de Lyon. [1066 *and All That*, 17]

17 '*Honi soie qui mal y pense*' (Honey, your silk stocking's hanging down'). [*Ib.* 24]

18 Finding, however, that he was not memorable, he very patriotically abdicated in favour of Henry IV, part II. [*Ib.* 26]

19 Lumbago and the Laxative Islands. [*Ib.* 41]

20 Napoleon's armies always used to march on their stomachs, shouting: 'Vive l'Intérieur!' [*Ib.* 48]

ROBERT W. SERVICE   1874–1958

21 This is the Law of the Yukon, that only the Strong shall thrive; / That surely the Weak shall perish, and only the Fit survive. [*The Law of the Yukon*]

22 Back of the bar, in a solo game, sat Dangerous Dan McGrew, / And watching his luck was his light o' love, the lady that's known as Lou. [*The Shooting of Dan McGrew*]

MME DE SÉVIGNÉ   1626–1692

23 The more I see of men, the more I admire dogs. [Attr.]

W. H. SEWARD   1801–1872

24 But there is a higher law than the Constitution. [Speech in U.S. Senate, 11 Mar. 1850]

EDWARD SEXBY   ?–1658

25 Killing no murder Briefly Discourst in Three Questions. [Title of pamphlet, 1657]

THOMAS SHADWELL   1642?–1692

26 Words may be false and full of art; / Sighs are the natural language of the heart. [*Pysche*, III]

27 And wit's the noblest frailty of the mind. [*A True Widow*, II. i]

28 Instantly, in the twinkling of a bed-staff. [*Virtuoso*, I. i]

ANTHONY ASHLEY COOPER, EARL OF SHAFTESBURY

1621–1683

1 Men of sense are really but of one religion. . . . 'Pray, my lord, what religion is that which men of sense agree in?' 'Madam,' says the earl immediately, 'men of sense never tell it.' [Onslow's note to Burnet's *History*]

WILLIAM SHAKESPEARE

1564–1616

References are to the Oxford single volume edition, ed. Craig.

Line references in scenes containing prose are in brackets.

All's Well that Ends Well

2 It were all one / That I should love a bright particular star / And think to wed it, he is so above me. [I. i. (97)]

3 The hind that would be mated by the lion / Must die for love. [I. i. (103)]

4 Your old virginity is like one of our French withered pears; it looks ill, it eats drily. [I. i. (176)]

5 Our remedies oft in ourselves do lie, / Which we ascribe to heaven. [I. i. (235)]

6 My friends were poor but honest. [I. iii. (203)]

7 They say miracles are past. [II. iii. (1)]

8 A young man married is a man that's marred. [II. iii. (315)]

9 The web of our life is of a mingled yarn, good and ill together. [IV. iii. (83)]

10 There's place and means for every man alive. [IV. iii. (379)]

11 Praising what is lost / Makes the remembrance dear. [V. iii. 19]

12 Mine eyes smell onions; I shall weep anon. [V. iii. (325)]

Antony and Cleopatra

13 The triple pillar of the world transformed / Into a strumpet's fool. [I. i. 12]

14 There's beggary in the love that can be reckoned. [I. i. 15]

15 Let Rome in Tiber melt, and the wide arch / Of the ranged empire fall! Here is my space. / Kingdoms are clay. [I. i. 33]

16 In Nature's infinite book of secrecy / A little I can read. [I. ii. (11)]

17 I love long life better than figs. [I. ii. (34)]

18 Mine, and most of our fortunes, to-night, shall be, – drunk to bed. [I. ii. (47)]

19 Eternity was in our lips and eyes, / Bliss in our brows. [I. iii. 135]

20 Though age from folly could not give me freedom, / It does from childishness. [I. iii. 57]

21 Give me to drink mandragora. [I. v. 4]

22 That I might sleep out this great gap of time / My Antony is away. [I. v. 5]

23 Where's my serpent of Old Nile? [I. v. 25]

24 A morsel for a monarch. [I. v. 31]

25 My salad days, / When I was green in judgement. [I. v. 73]

26 No worse a husband than the best of men. [II. ii. 135]

27 The barge she sat in, like a burnished throne, / Burned on the water; the poop was beaten gold, / Purple the sails, and so perfumed, that / The winds were love-sick with them, the oars were silver / Which to the tune of flutes kept stroke, and made / The water which they beat to follow faster, / As amorous of their strokes. For her own person, / It beggared all description. [II. ii. (199)]

28 The air; which, but for vacancy, / Had gone to gaze on Cleopatra too / And made a gap in nature. [II. ii. (224)]

29 Age cannot wither her, nor custom stale / Her infinite variety; other women cloy / The appetites they feed. [II. ii. (243)]

30 Music, moody food / Of us that trade in love. [II. v. 1]

31 Let's to billiards. [II. v. 3]

32 Though it be honest, it is never good / To bring bad news. [II. v. 85]

33 What manner o' thing is your crocodile? [II. vii. (47)]

34 Ambition, / The soldier's virtue. [III. i. 22]

35 Celerity is never more admired / Than by the negligent. [III. vii. 24]

36 We have kissed away / Kingdoms and provinces. [III. viii. 17]

37 I found you as a morsel, cold upon / Dead Caesar's trencher. [III. xi. 116]

1 Let's have one other gaudy night. [III. xi. 182]

2 Unarm, Eros; the long day's task is done / And we must sleep. [IV. xii. 35]

3 But I will be / A bridegroom in my death, and run into 't / As to a lover's bed. [IV. xii. 99]

4 I am dying, Egypt, dying. [IV. xiii. 18]

5 O! withered is the garland of the war, / The soldier's pole is fallen; young boys and girls / Are level now with men; the odds is gone, / And there is nothing left remarkable / Beneath the visiting moon. [IV. xiii. 64]

6 Let's do it after the high Roman fashion, / And make death proud to take us. [IV. xiii. 87]

7 For his bounty, / There was no winter in't; an autumn 'twas / That grew the more by reaping ... [V. ii. 86]

8 The bright day is done, / And we are for the dark. [V. ii. 192]

9 I shall see / Some squeaking Cleopatra boy my greatness. [V. ii. 218]

10 His biting is immortal; those that do die of it do seldom or never recover. [V. ii. (246)]

11 I wish you joy o' the worm. [V. ii. (281)]

12 Give me my robe, put on my crown; I have / Immortal longings in me. [V. ii. (282)]

13 Dost thou not see my baby at my breast, / That sucks the nurse asleep? [V. ii. (302)]

14 Now boast thee, death, in thy possession lies / A lass unparalleled. [V. ii. (317)]

As You Like It

15 Fleet the time carelessly, as they did in the golden world. [I. i. (126)]

16 Let us sit and mock the good housewife Fortune from her wheel, that her gifts may henceforth be bestowed equally. [I. ii. (35)]

17 How now, wit! whither wander you? [I. ii. (60)]

18 Well said: that was laid on with a trowel. [I. ii. (113)]

19 Your heart's desires be with you! [I. ii. (214)]

20 One out of suits with fortune. [I. ii. (263)]

21 My pride fell with my fortunes. [I. ii. (269)]

22 Hereafter in a better world than this, / I shall desire more love and knowledge of you. [I. ii. (301)]

23 O, how full of briers is this working-day world! [I. iii. (12)]

24 Beauty provoketh thieves sooner than gold. [I. iii. (113)]

25 We'll have a swashing and a martial outside, / As many other mannish cowards have / That do outface it with their semblances. [I. iii. (123)]

26 Sweet are the uses of adversity, / Which, like the toad, ugly and venomous, / Wears yet a precious jewel in his head; / And this our life, exempt from public haunt, / Finds tongues in trees, books in the running brooks, / Sermons in stones, and good in everything. [II. i. 12]

27 The big round tears / Coursed one another down his innocent nose, / In piteous chase. [II. i. 38]

28 'Poor deer,' quoth he, 'thou makest a testament / As worldlings do, giving thy sum of more. / To that which had too much.' [II. i. 47]

29 Sweep on, you fat and greasy citizens! [II. i. 55]

30 For in my youth I never did apply / Hot and rebellious liquors to the blood. [II. iii. 48]

31 Therefore my age is as the lusty winter, / Frosty, but kindly. [II. iii. 52]

32 O good old man! how well in thee appears / The constant service of the antique world, / When service sweat for duty, not for meed! / Thou art not for the fashion of these times, / Where none will sweat but for promotion. [II. iii. 56]

33 Ay, now am I in Arden; the more fool I: when I was at home, I was in a better place: but travellers must be content. [II. iv. (16)]

34 If thou remember'st not the slightest folly / That ever love did make thee run into, / Thou hast not loved. [II. iv. (34)]

35 We that are true lovers run into strange capers. [II. iv. (53)]

36 Thou speakest wiser than thou art ware of. [II. iv. (57)]

37 I shall ne'er be ware of mine own wit till I break my shins against it. [II. iv. (59)]

38 Under the greenwood tree / Who loves to lie with me, / And turn his merry note /

Unto the sweet bird's throat, / Come hither, come hither, come hither: / Here shall he see / No enemy / But winter and rough weather. [II. v. 1]

1 I can suck melancholy out of a song, as a weasel sucks eggs. [II. v. (12)]

2 Who doth ambition shun, / And loves to live i' the sun, / Seeking the food he eats, / And pleased with what he gets. [II. v. (38)]

3 I'll rail against all the first-born of Egypt. [II. v. (60)]

4 A fool, a fool! I met a fool i' the forest. / A motley fool. [II. vii. 12]

5 And railed on Lady Fortune in good terms, / In good set terms. [II. vii. 16]

6 And then he drew a dial from his poke, / And looking on it with lack-lustre eye, / Says, very wisely, 'It is ten o'clock; / Thus may we see,' quoth he, 'how the world wags.' [II. vii. 20]

7 And so, from hour to hour we ripe and ripe, / And then from hour to hour we rot and rot, / And thereby hangs a tale. [II. vii. 26]

8 My lungs began to crow like chanticleer, / That fools should be so deep-contemplative, / And I did laugh sans intermission / An hour by his dial. [II. vii. 30]

9 Motley's the only wear. [II. vii. 34]

10 And says, if ladies be but young and fair, / They have the gift to know it; and in his brain, – / Which is as dry as the remainder biscuit / After a voyage, – he hath strange places crammed / With observation, the which he vents / In mangled forms. [II. vii. 37]

11 I must have liberty / Withal, as large a charter as the wind, / To blow on whom I please. [II. vii. 47]

12 The 'why' is plain as way to parish church. [II. vii. 52]

13 Whate'er you are / That in this desert inaccessible, / Under the shade of melancholy boughs, / Lose and neglect the creeping hours of time; / If ever you have looked on better days. [II. vii. 109]

14 All the world's a stage, / And all the men and women merely players: / They have their exits and their entrances; / And one man in his time plays many parts, / His acts being seven ages. At first the infant, / Mewing and puking in the nurse's arms. / And then the whining school-boy, with his satchel / And shining morning face, creeping like snail / Unwillingly to school. And then the lover / Sighing like furnace, with a woeful ballad / Made to his mistress' eyebrow. Then a soldier, / Full of strange oaths, and bearded like the pard, / Jealous in honour, sudden and quick in quarrel, / Seeking the bubble reputation / Even in the cannon's mouth. And then the justice, / In fair round belly with good capon lined, / With eyes severe, and beard of formal cut, / Full of wise saws and modern instances, / And so he plays his part. The sixth age shifts / Into the lean and slippered pantaloon / With spectacles on nose and pouch on side, / His youthful hose well saved a world too wide / For his shrunk shank; and his big manly voice, / Turning again toward childish treble, pipes / And whistles in his sound. Last scene of all, / That ends this strange eventful history, / Is second childishness and mere oblivion, / Sans teeth, sans eyes, sans taste, sans everything. [II. vii. 139]

15 Blow, blow, thou winter wind, / Thou art not so unkind / As man's ingratitude: / Thy tooth is not so keen, / Because thou art not seen, / Although thy breath be rude. [II. vii. 174]

16 Most friendship is feigning, most loving mere folly. / Then heigh-ho! the holly! / This life is most jolly. [II. vii. 181]

17 The fair, the chaste and unexpressive she. [III. ii. 10]

18 Hast any philosophy in thee, shepherd? [III. ii. (22)]

19 He that wants money, means, and content is without three good things. [III. ii. (25)]

20 Truly, thou art damned like an ill-roasted egg, all on one side. [III. ii. (39)]

21 Thou art in a parlous state. [III. ii. (46)]

22 This is the very false gallop of verses. [III. ii. (120)]

23 Let us make honourable retreat; though not with bag and baggage, yet with scrip and scrippage. [III. ii. (170)]

24 O wonderful, wonderful, and most wonderful! and yet again wonderful, and after that, out of all whooping! [III. ii. (202)]

1 Do you not know I am a woman? When I think, I must speak. [III. ii. (265)]

2 I do desire we may be better strangers. [III. ii. (276)]

3 Time travels in divers paces with divers persons. I'll tell you who Time ambles withal, who Time trots withal, who Time gallops withal, and who he stands still withal. [III. ii. (328)]

4 Every one fault seeming monstrous till his fellow-fault came to match it. [III. ii. (377)]

5 Truly, I would the gods had made thee poetical. [III. iii. (16)]

6 I am not a slut, though I thank the gods I am foul. [III. iii. (40)]

7 Down on your knees, / And thank heaven, fasting, for a good man's love. [III. v. 57]

8 It is a melancholy of mine own, compounded of many simples, extracted from many objects, and indeed the sundry contemplation of my travels, which, by often rumination, wraps me in a most humorous sadness. [IV. i. (16)]

9 I had rather have a fool to make me merry than experience to make me sad. [IV. i. (28)]

10 Men have died from time to time, and worms have eaten them, but not for love. [IV. i. (110)]

11 Men are April when they woo, December when they wed: maids are May when they are maids, but the sky changes when they are wives. [IV. i. (153)]

12 The horn, the horn, the lusty horn / Is not a thing to laugh to scorn. [IV. ii. (17)]

13 Chewing the food of sweet and bitter fancy. [IV. iii. (103)]

14 It is meat and drink to me to see a clown. [V. i. (11)]

15 No sooner met but they looked; no sooner looked but they loved; no sooner loved but they sighed; no sooner sighed but they asked one another the reason; no sooner knew the reason but they sought the remedy. [V. ii. (37)]

16 Oh! how bitter a thing it is to look into happiness through another man's eyes. [V. ii. (48)]

17 It is to be all made of sighs and tears: / And so am I for Phebe. [V. ii. (91)]

18 It is to be all made of faith and service / ... It is to be all made of fantasy, / All made of passion and all made of wishes, / All adoration, duty, and observance, / All humbleness, all patience and impatience, / All purity, all trial, all obeisance. [V. ii. (96)]

19 It was a lover and his lass, / With a hey, and a ho, and a hey nonino, / That o'er the green corn-field did pass, / In the spring time, the only pretty ring time, / When birds do sing, hey ding a ding, ding; / Sweet lovers love the spring. [V. iii. (18)]

20 An ill-favoured thing, sir, but mine own. [V. iv. (60)]

21 The first, 'the retort courteous'; the second, 'the quip modest'; the third, 'the reply churlish'; the fourth, 'the reproof valiant'; the fifth, 'the countercheck quarrelsome'; the sixth, 'the lie with circumstance'; the seventh, 'the lie direct'. [V. iv. (96)]

22 Your 'if' is the only peace-maker; much virtue in 'if'. [V. iv. (108)]

23 He uses his folly like a stalking-horse, and under the presentation of that he shoots his wit. [V. iv. (112)]

24 If it be true that 'good wine needs no bush', 'tis true that a good play needs no epilogue. [Epilogue, (3)]

The Comedy of Errors

25 The pleasing punishment that women bear. [I. i. 46]

26 They brought one Pinch, a hungry lean-faced villain, / A mere anatomy, a mountebank, / A threadbare juggler, and a fortune-teller, / A needy, hollow-eyed, sharp-looking wretch, / A living-dead man. [V. i. 238]

Coriolanus

27 Rubbing the poor itch of your opinion, / Make yourself scabs. [I. i. (171)]

28 They threw their caps / As they would hang them on the horns o' the moon, / Shouting their emulation. [I. i. (218)]

29 My gracious silence, hail! [II. i. (194)]

30 He himself stuck not to call us the many-headed multitude. [II. iii. 18]

31 Bid them wash their faces, / And keep their teeth clean. [II. iii. (65)]

1 I thank you for your voices, thank you, / Your most sweet voices. [II. iii. (179)]

2 The mutable, rank-scented many. [III. i. 65]

3 Hear you this Triton of the minnows? mark you / His absolute 'shall'? [III. i. 88]

4 His nature is too noble for the world: / He would not flatter Neptune for his trident, / Or Jove for's power to thunder. [III. i. 254]

5 You common cry of curs! whose breath I hate / As reek o' the rotten fens, whose loves I prize / As the dead carcasses of unburied men / That do corrupt my air, I banish you. [III. iii. 118]

6 The beast / With many heads butts me away. [IV. i. 1]

7 THIRD SERV.: Where dwell'st thou?
CORIOL.: Under the canopy. [IV. v. (40)]

8 O, a kiss / Long as my exile, sweet as my revenge! [V. iii. 44]

9 Chaste as the icicle / That's curdied by the frost from purest snow, / And hangs on Dian's temple. [V. iii. 65]

10 He wants nothing of a god but eternity and a heaven to throne in. [V. iv. (25)]

11 If you have writ your annals true, 'tis there, / That, like an eagle in a dove-cote, I / Fluttered your Volscians in Corioli: / Alone I did it. [V. v. 114]

12 Thou hast done a deed whereat valour will weep. [V. v. 134]

Cymbeline

13 She is alone the Arabian bird. [I. vi. 17]

14 Boldness be my friend! [I. vi. 18]

15 On her left breast / A mole cinque-spotted, like the crimson drops / I' the bottom of a cowslip. [II. ii. 37]

16 Hark! hark! the lark at heaven's gate sings, / And Phoebus 'gins arise, / His steeds to water at those springs / On chaliced flowers that lies; / And winking Mary-buds begin / To ope their golden eyes: / With everything that pretty is, / My lady sweet, arise. [II. iii. (22)]

17 Is there no way for men to be, but women / Must be half-workers? [II. v. 1]

18 There be many Caesars / Ere such another Julius. Britain is / A world by

itself, and we will nothing pay / For wearing our own noses. [III. i. 11]

19 O! for a horse with wings! [III. ii. (49)]

20 Some jay of Italy. [III. iv. (51)]

21 I have not slept one wink. [III. iv. (103)]

22 Weariness / Can snore upon the flint, when resty sloth / Finds the down pillow hard. [III. vi. 33]

23 Thou shalt not lack / The flower that's like thy face, pale primrose, nor / The azured harebell, like thy veins. [IV. ii. 220]

24 Thersites' body is as good as Ajax' / When neither are alive. [IV. ii. 252]

25 Fear no more the heat o' the sun, / Nor the furious winter's rages; / Thou thy worldly task hast done, / Home art gone and ta'en thy wages: / Golden lads and girls all must, / As chimney-sweepers, come to dust.

Fear no more the frown o' the great, / Thou art past the tyrant's stroke. / Care no more to clothe and eat; / To thee the reed is as the oak: / The sceptre, learning, physic must. / All follow this, and come to dust. [IV. ii. 258]

26 O! the charity of a penny cord. [V. iv. (169)]

27 He that sleeps feels not the toothache. [V. iv. (176)]

28 Hang there like fruit, my soul, / Till the tree die! [V. v. 264]

Hamlet

29 For this relief much thanks, 'tis bitter cold, / And I am sick at heart. [I. i. 8]

30 Not a mouse stirring. [I. i. 10]

31 But in the gross and scope of my opinion, / This bodes some strange eruption to our state. [I. i. 68]

32 Whose sore task / Does not divide the Sunday from the week. [I. i. 75]

33 This sweaty haste / Doth make the night joint-labourer with the day. [I. i. 77]

34 In the most high and palmy state of Rome / A little ere the mightiest Julius fell, / The graves stood tenantless and the sheeted dead / Did squeak and gibber in the Roman streets. [I. i. 113]

35 The moist star / Upon whose influence Neptune's empire stands / Was sick almost to doomsday with eclipse. [I. i. 118]

1 Then it started like a guilty thing / Upon a fearful summons. [I. i. 148]

2 But look, the morn, in russet mantle clad, / Walks o'er the dew of yon high eastern hill. [I. i. 166]

3 The memory be green. [I. ii. 2]

4 With one auspicious and one dropping eye, / With mirth in funeral and with dirge in marriage, / In equal scale weighing delight and dole. [I. ii. 11]

5 The head is not more native to the heart. [I. ii. 47]

6 A little more than kin, and less than kind. [I. ii. 65]

7 Not so, my lord; I am too much i' the sun. [I. ii. 67]

8 All that live must die, / Passing through nature to eternity. [I. ii. 72]

9 Seems, madam! Nay, it is; I know not 'seems'. / 'Tis not alone my inky cloak, good mother, / Nor customary suits of solemn black. [I. ii. 76]

10 But I have that within which passeth show; / These but the trappings and the suits of woe. [I. ii. 85]

11 O! that this too too solid flesh would melt, / Thaw, and resolve itself into a dew; / Or that the Everlasting had not fixed / His canon 'gainst self-slaughter! O God! O God! / How weary, stale, flat, and unprofitable / Seem to me all the uses of this world. / Fie on't! O fie! 'tis an unweeded garden, / That grows to seed; things rank and gross in nature / Possess it merely. [I. ii. 129]

12 So excellent a king; that was, to this, / Hyperion to a satyr: so loving to my mother, / That he might not beteem the winds of heaven / Visit her face too roughly. [I. ii. 139]

13 Why, she would hang on him, / As if increase of appetite had grown / By what it fed on. [I. ii. 143]

14 Frailty, thy name is woman! [I. ii. 146]

15 Like Niobe, all tears. [I. ii. 149]

16 A beast that wants discourse of reason. [I. ii. 150]

17 It is not nor it cannot come to good. [I. ii. 158]

18 A truant disposition, good my lord. [I. ii. 169]

19 Thrift, thrift, Horatio! the funeral baked meats / Did coldly furnish forth the marriage tables. [I. ii. 180]

20 In my mind's eye, Horatio. [I. ii. 185]

21 He was a man, take him for all in all, / I shall not look upon his like again. [I. ii. 187]

22 Season your admiration for a while. [I. ii. 192]

23 In the dead vast and middle of the night. [I. ii. 198]

24 Armed at points exactly, cap-a-pe. [I. ii. 200]

25 A countenance more in sorrow than in anger. [I. ii. 231]

26 HAMLET: His beard was grizzled, no? HORATIO: It was, as I have seen it in his life, / A sable silvered. [I. ii. 239]

27 Give it an understanding but no tongue. [I. ii. 249]

28 All is not well; / I doubt some foul play. [I. ii. 254]

29 But you must fear, / His greatness weighed, his will is not his own, / For he himself is subject to his birth. [I. iii. 16]

30 The chariest maid is prodigal enough / If she unmask her beauty to the moon. [I. iii. 36]

31 Do not, as some ungracious pastors do, / Show me the steep and thorny way to heaven, / Whiles, like a puffed and reckless libertine, / Himself the primrose path of dalliance treads, / And recks not his own rede. [I. iii. 47]

32 Give thy thoughts no tongue, / Nor any unproportioned thought his act. / Be thou familiar, but by no means vulgar. / Those friends thou hast, and their adoption tried, / Grapple them to thy soul with hoops of steel. [I. iii. 59]

33 Beware / Of entrance to a quarrel, but, being in, / Bear 't that the opposed may beware of thee, / Give every man thine ear, but few thy voice; / Take each man's censure, but reserve thy judgement. / Costly thy habit as thy purse can buy, / But not expressed in fancy; rich, not gaudy; / For the apparel oft proclaims the man. [I. iii. 65]

34 Neither a borrower nor a lender be; / For loan oft loses both itself and friend, / And borrowing dulls the edge of hus-

bandry. / This above all: to thine own self be true, / And it must follow, as the night the day, / Thou canst not then be false to any man. [I. iii. 75]

1 You speak like a green girl, / Unsifted in such perilous circumstance. [I. iii. 101]

2 Ay springes to catch woodcocks. [I. iii. 115]

3 Be somewhat scanter of your maiden presence. [I. iii. 121]

4 HAMLET: The air bites shrewdly; it is very cold.
HORATIO: It is a nipping and an eager air. [I. iv. 1]

5 But to my mind, – though I am native here, / And to the manner born, – it is a custom / More honoured in the breach than the observance. [I. iv. 14]

6 Angels and ministers of grace defend us! / Be thou a spirit of health or goblin damned, / Bring with thee airs from heaven or blasts from hell, / Be thy intents wicked or charitable, / Thou com'st in such a questionable shape / That I will speak to thee. [I. iv. 39]

7 Hath oped his ponderous and marble jaws. [I. iv. 50]

8 What may this mean, / That thou, dead corse, again in complete steel, / Revisit'st thus the glimpses of the moon, / Making night hideous? [I. iv. 51]

9 I do not set my life at a pin's fee; / And for my soul, what can it do to that, / Being a thing immortal as itself? [I. iv. 65]

10 Unhand me, gentlemen, / By heaven! I'll make a ghost of him that lets me. [I. iv. 84]

11 Something is rotten in the state of Denmark. [I. iv. 90]

12 But that I am forbid / To tell the secrets of my prison-house, / I could a tale unfold whose lightest word / Would harrow up thy soul, freeze thy young blood, / Make thy two eyes, like stars, start from their spheres, / Thy knotted and combinèd locks to part, / And each particular hair to stand on end, / Like quills upon the fretful porpentine: / But this eternal blazon must not be / To ears of flesh and blood. [I. v. 13]

13 Murder most foul, as in the best it is; / But this most foul, strange, and unnatural. [I. v. 27]

14 With wings as swift / As meditation or the thoughts of love. [I. v. 29]

15 And duller shouldst thou be than the fat weed / That rots itself in ease on Lethe wharf. [I. v. 32]

16 O my prophetic soul! / My uncle! [I. v. 40]

17 What a falling-off was there. [I. v. 47]

18 But, soft! methinks I scent the morning air. [I. v. 58]

19 In the porches of mine ears. [I. v. 63]

20 Cut off even in the blossoms of my sin, / Unhouseled, disappointed, unaneled. / No reckoning made, but sent to my account / With all my imperfections on my head. [I. v. 76]

21 Leave her to heaven, / And to those thorns that in her bosom lodge, / To prick and sting her. [I. v. 86]

22 The glow-worm shows the matin to be near, / And 'gins to pale his uneffectual fire. [I. v. 89]

23 While memory holds a seat / In this distracted globe. Remember thee! / Yea from the table of my memory / I'll wipe away all trivial fond records. [I. v. 96]

24 O villain, villain, smiling, damned villain! / My tables, – meet it is I set it down, / That one may smile, and smile, and be a villain, / At least I'm sure it may be so in Denmark. [I. v. 106]

25 There's ne'er a villain dwelling in all Denmark, / But he's an arrant knave. [I. v. 123]

26 These are but wild and whirling words. [I. v. 133]

27 There are more things in heaven and earth, Horatio, / Than are dreamt of in your philosophy. [I. v. 166]

28 To put an antic disposition on. [I. v. 172]

29 Rest, rest, perturbèd spirit! [I. v. 182]

30 The time is out of joint; O cursèd spite, / That ever I was born to set it right! [I. v. 188]

31 By indirections find directions out. [II. i. 66]

32 Brevity is the soul of wit. [II. ii. 90]

33 For, to define true madness, / What is't but to be nothing else but mad. [II. ii. 93]

34 More matter with less art. [II. ii. 95]

1 That he is mad, 'tis true; 'tis true 'tis pity; / And pity 'tis 'tis true. [II. ii. 97]

2 Doubt thou the stars are fire; / Doubt that the sun doth move; / Doubt truth to be a liar; / But never doubt I love. [II. ii. (115)]

3 POLONIUS: Do you know me, my lord? HAMLET: Excellent well; you are a fishmonger. [II. ii. (173)]

4 To be honest, as this world goes, / Is to be one man picked out of ten thousand. [II. ii. (179)]

5 Still harping on my daughter. [II. ii. (190)]

6 POLONIUS: What do you read, my lord? HAMLET: Words, words, words. [II. ii. (195)]

7 Though this be madness, yet there is method in't. [II. ii. (211)]

8 On Fortune's cap we are not the very button. [II. ii. (237)]

9 Faith, her privates we. [II. ii. (242)]

10 There is nothing either good or bad, but thinking makes it so. [II. ii. (259)]

11 I could be bounded in a nutshell, and count myself a king of infinite space, were it not that I have bad dreams. [II. ii. (264)]

12 Beggar that I am, I am even poor in thanks. [II. ii. (286)]

13 It goes so heavily with my disposition that this goodly frame, the earth, seems to me a sterile promontory; this most excellent canopy, the air, look you, this brave o'erhanging firmament, this majestic roof fretted with golden fire, why, it appears no other thing to me but a foul and pestilent congregation of vapours! What a piece of work is a man! How noble in reason! how infinite in faculty! in form, in moving, how express and admirable! in action how like an angel! in apprehension how like a god! the beauty of the world! the paragon of animals! And yet, to me, what is this quintessence of dust? man delights not me; no, nor woman neither. [II. ii. (316)]

14. What lenten entertainment the players shall receive from you. [II. ii. (337)]

15 He that plays the king. [II. ii. 341)]

16 I am but mad north-north-west: when the wind is southerly I know a hawk from a handsaw. [II. ii. (405)]

17 The best actors in the world, either for tragedy, comedy, history, pastoral, pastoral-comical, historical, tragical-historical, tragical-comical-historical-pastoral, scene individable or poem unlimited. [II. ii. (424)]

18 Come give us a taste of your quality. [II. ii. (460)]

19 The play, I remember, pleased not the million; 'twas caviare to the general. [II. ii. (465)]

20 The mobled queen. [II. ii. (533)]

21 They are the abstracts and brief chronicles of the time: after your death you were better have a bad epitaph than their ill report while you live. [II. ii. (555)]

22 Use every man after his desert and who would 'scape whipping? [II. ii. (561)]

23 O! what a rogue and peasant slave am I: Is it not monstrous that this player here, / But in a fiction, in a dream of passion, / Could force his soul so to his own conceit. [II. ii. (584)]

24 What's Hecuba to him or he to Hecuba / That he should weep for her? [II. ii. (593)]

25 A dull and muddy-metalled rascal. [II. ii. (602)]

26 I should have fatted all the region kites / With this slave's offal. Bloody, bawdy villain! / Remorseless, treacherous lecherous, kindless villain! [II. ii. (615)]

27 The play's the thing / Wherein I'll catch the conscience of the king. [II. ii. (641)]

28 With devotion's visage / And pious action we do sugar o'er / The devil himself. [III. i. 47]

29 To be or not to be: that is the question: / Whether 'tis nobler in the mind to suffer / The slings and arrows of outrageous fortune, / Or to take arms against a sea of troubles, / And by opposing end them? / To die: to sleep; / No more; and by a sleep to say we end / The heart-ache and the thousand natural shocks / That flesh is heir to, 'tis a consummation / Devoutly to be wished. To die, to sleep: / To sleep: perchance to dream: ay, there's the rub. / For in that sleep of death what dreams may come / When we have shuffled off this mortal coil, / Must give us pause. There's the respect / That makes calamity of so long life; / For who would bear the whips and scorns of time, / The

oppressor's wrong, the proud man's contumely, / The pangs of disprized love, the law's delay, / The insolence of office, and the spurns / That patient merit of the unworthy takes, / When he himself might his quietus make / With a bare bodkin? who would fardels bear, / To grunt and sweat under a weary life, / But that the dread of something after death, / The undiscovered country from whose bourn / No traveller returns, puzzles the will, / And makes us rather bear those ills we have / Than fly to others that we know not of? / Thus conscience does make cowards of us all; / And thus the native hue of resolution / Is sicklied o'er with the pale cast of thought, / And enterprises of great pith and moment / With this regard their currents turn awry, / And lose the name of action. [III. i. 56]

1 Nymph, in thy orisons / Be all my sins remembered. [III. i. 89]

2 For to the noble mind / Rich gifts wax poor when givers prove unkind. [III. i. 100]

3 Get thee to a nunnery. [III. i (124)]

4 Be thou as chaste as ice, as pure as snow, thou shalt not escape calumny. [III. i. (142)]

5 I have heard of your paintings too, well enough. God hath given you one face, and you make yourselves another. [III. i. (150)]

6 I say, we will have no more marriages. [III. i. (156)]

7 O, what a noble mind is here o'erthrown: / The courtier's, soldier's, scholar's eye, tongue, sword; / The expectancy and rose of the fair state, / The glass of fashion, and the mould of form, / The observed of all observers quite, quite down! [III. i. (159)]

8 That noble and most sovereign reason, / Like sweet bells jangled, out of tune and harsh; / That unmatched form and figure of blown youth / Blasted with ecstasy. [III. i. (166)]

9 Speak the speech, I pray you, as I pronounced it to you, trippingly on the tongue; but if you mouth it as many of your players do, I had as lief the towncrier spoke my lines. Nor do not saw the air too much with your hand, thus; but use all gently. [III. ii. 1]

10 Tear a passion to tatters, to very rags, to split the ears of the groundlings. [III. ii. (11)]

11 It out-herods Herod. [III. ii. (16)]

12 Suit the action to the word, the word to the action; with this special observance, that you o'erstep not the modesty of nature. [III. ii. (20)]

13 The purpose of playing, whose end, both at the first and now, was and is, to hold, as 'twere, the mirror up to nature. [III. ii. (24)]

14 I have thought some of nature's journeymen had made men, and not made them well, they imitated humanity so abominably. [III. ii. (38)]

15 A man that fortune's buffets and rewards / Hast ta'en with equal thanks; and blessed are those / Whose blood and judgement are so well co-mingled / That they are not a pipe for fortune's finger / To sound what stop she please. [III. ii. (72)]

16 Give me that man / That is not passion's slave, and I will wear him / In my heart's core, ay, in my heart of heart, / As I do thee. [III. ii. (76)]

17 My imaginations are as foul / As Vulcan's stithy. [III. ii. (88)]

18 The chameleon's dish: I eat the air promise-crammed. [III. ii. (98)]

19 Here's metal more attractive. [III. ii. (117)]

20 This is miching mallecho; it means mischief. [III. ii. (148)]

21 OPHELIA: 'Tis brief, my lord.
HAMLET: As woman's love. [III. ii. (165)]

22 The lady doth protest too much, methinks. [III. ii. (242)]

23 Let the galled jade wince, our withers are unwrung. [III. ii. (256)]

24 The story is extant, and writ in very choice Italian. [III. ii. (277)]

25 What! frighted with false fire? [III. ii. (282)]

26 Why, let the stricken deer go weep, / The hart ungalled play; / For some must watch, while some must sleep: / So runs the world away. [III. ii. (287)]

27 We shall obey, were she ten times our mother. [III. ii. (352)]

1 The proverb is something musty. [III. ii. (366)]

2 You would play upon me; you would seem to know my stops; you would pluck out the heart of my mystery; you would sound me from my lowest note to the top of my compass. [III. ii. (387)]

3 Do you see yonder cloud that's almost in shape of a camel? [III. ii. (400)]

4 They fool me to the top of my bent. [III. ii. (408)]

5 'Tis now the very witching time of night, / When churchyards yawn and hell itself breathes out / Contagion to this world. [III. ii. (413)]

6 Let me be cruel, not unnatural; / I will speak daggers to her but use none. [III. ii. (420)]

7 O! my offence is rank, it smells to heaven. [III. iii. 36]

8 Now might I do it pat, now he is praying. [III. iii. 73]

9 My words fly up, my thoughts remain below: / Words without thoughts never to heaven go. [III. iii. 97]

10 How now! a rat? Dead for a ducat, dead! [III. iv. 23]

11 As false as dicers' oaths. [III. iv. 45]

12 Look here upon this picture, and on this; / The counterfeit presentment of two brothers. / See what a grace was seated on this brow; / Hyperion's curls; the front of Jove himself, / An eye like Mars, to threaten and command, / A station like the herald Mercury / New-lighted on a heaven-kissing hill, / A combination and a form indeed, / Where every god did seem to set his seal, To give the world assurance of a man. [III. iv. 53]

13 Could you on this fair mountain leave to feed, / And batten on this moor? [III. iv. 66]

14 You cannot call it love; for at your age / The hey-day in the blood is tame, it's humble, / And waits upon the judgement. [III. iv. 68]

15 A cut-purse of the empire and the rule, / That from a shelf the precious diadem stole, / And put it in his pocket! [III. iv. 99]

16 A king of shreds and patches. [III. iv. 102]

17 This is the very coinage of your brain. [III. iv. 136]

18 Lay not that flattering unction to your soul. [III. iv. 145]

19 Assume a virtue, if you have it not. [III. iv. 160]

20 I must be cruel only to be kind. [III. iv. 178]

21 For 'tis the sport to have the enginer / Hoist with his own petar. [III. iv. 206]

22 I'll lug the guts into the neighbour room. [III. iv. 212]

23 Diseases desperate grown, / By desperate appliance are relieved, / Or not at all. [IV. iii. 9]

24 A certain convocation of politic worms are e'en at him. [IV. iii. (21)]

25 A man may fish with the worm that hath eat of a king, and eat of the fish that hath fed of that worm. [IV. iii. (29)]

26 How all occasions do inform against me, / And spur my dull revenge! What is a man, / If his chief good and market of his time / Be but to sleep and feed? a beast, no more. / Sure he that made us with such large discourse, / Looking before and after, gave us not / That capability and god-like reason / To fust in us unused. [IV. iv. 32]

27 Some craven scruple / Of thinking too precisely on the event. [IV. iv. 40]

28 Rightly to be great / Is not to stir without great argument, / But greatly to find quarrel in a straw / When honour's at the stake. [IV. iv. 53]

29 So full of artless jealousy is guilt, / I. spills itself in fearing to be spilt. [IV. v. 19]

30 How should I your true love know / From another one? / By his cockle hat and staff, / And his sandal shoon. [IV. v. (23)]

31 He is dead and gone, lady, / He is dead and gone; / At his head a grass-green turf, / At his heels a stone. [IV. v. (29)]

32 We know what we are, but know not what we may be. [IV. v. (43)]

33 I a maid at your window / To be your Valentine. [IV. v. (51)]

34 Come my coach! Good-night, ladies; good-night, sweet ladies; good-night good-night. [IV. v. (72)]

1 When sorrows come, they come not single spies, / But in battalions. [IV. v. (78)]

2 We have done but greenly, / In hugger-mugger to inter him. [IV. v. (83)]

3 There's such divinity doth hedge a king, / That treason can but peep to what it would. [IV. v. (123)]

4 To hell, allegiance! vows to the blackest devil! / Conscience and grace to the profoundest pit! / I dare damnation. [IV. v. (130)]

5 They bore him barefaced on the bier; / Hey non nonny, nonny, hey nonny; / And in his grave rained many a tear. [IV. v. (163)]

6 There's rosemary, that's for remembrance; pray, love, remember: and there is pansies, that's for thoughts. [IV. v. (174)]

7 You must wear your rue with a difference. [IV. v (181)]

8 They say he made a good end. [IV. v. (184)]

9 A very riband in the cap of youth. [IV. vii. (77)]

10 One woe doth tread upon another's heel, / So fast they follow. [IV. vii. (164)]

11 There is a willow grows aslant a brook, / That shows his hoar leaves in the glassy stream. [IV. vii. (167)]

12 Her clothes spread wide, / And, mermaid-like, awhile they bore her up; / Which time she chanted snatches of old tunes, / As one incapable of her own distress, / Or like a creature native and indued / Unto that element; but long it could not be / Till that her garments, heavy with their drink. / Pulled the poor wretch from her melodious lay / To muddy death. [IV. vii. (176)]

13 Cudgel thy brains no more about it. [V. i. (61)]

14 Has this fellow no feeling of his business. [V. i. (71)]

15 The hand of little employment hath the daintier sense. [V. i. (75)]

16 How absolute the knave is! we must speak by the card, or equivocation will undo us. [V. i. (147)]

17 Alas! poor Yorick. I knew him, Horatio; a fellow of infinite jest, of most excellent fancy; he hath borne me on his back a thousand times; and now, how abhorred in my imagination it is! my gorge rises at it. [V. i. (201)]

18 Where be your gibes now? your gambols? your songs? your flashes of merriment, that were wont to set the table in a roar? [V. l. (207)]

19 Now get you to my lady's chamber, and tell her, let her paint an inch thick, to this favour she must come. [V. i. (211)]

20 To what base uses we may return, Horatio! Why may not imagination trace the noble dust of Alexander, till he find it stopping a bung-hole? [V. i. (222)]

21 Imperious Caesar, dead and turned to clay, / Might stop a hole to keep the wind away. [V. i. (235)]

22 Lay her i' the earth; / And from her fair and unpolluted flesh / May violets spring! [V. i. (260)]

23 A ministering angel shall my sister be. [V. i. (263)]

24 Sweets to the sweet: farewell! [V. i. (265)]

25 I thought thy bride-bed to have decked, sweet maid, / And not have strewed thy grave. [V. i. (267)]

26 Forty thousand brothers / Could not, with all their quantity of love, / Make up my sum. [V. i. (291)]

27 Nay, an thou'lt mouth, / I'll rant as well as thou. [V. i. (305)]

28 Let Hercules himself do what he may, / The cat will mew and dog will have his day. [V. i. (313)]

29 There's a divinity that shapes our ends, / Rough-hew them how we will. [V. ii. 10]

30 It did me yeoman's service. [V. ii. 36]

31 Not shriving-time allowed. [V. ii. 47]

32 Into a towering passion. [V. ii. 80]

33 The phrase would be more german to the matter, if we could carry cannon by our sides. [V. ii. (165)]

34 Not a whit, we defy augury; there's a special providence in the fall of a sparrow. If it be now, 'tis not to come; if it be not to come, it will be now; if it be not now, yet it will come: the readiness is all. [V. ii. (232)]

35 A hit, a very palpable hit. [V. ii. (295)]

1 This fell sergeant, death, / Is strict in his arrest. [V. ii. (350)]

2 Report me and my cause aright. [V. ii. (353)]

3 If thou didst ever hold me in thy heart, / Absent thee from felicity awhile, / And in this harsh world draw thy breath in pain, / To tell my story. [V. ii. (360)]

4 The rest is silence. [V. ii. (372)]

5 Now cracks a noble heart. Good-night, sweet prince, / And flights of angels sing thee to thy rest! [V. ii. (373)]

Henry IV, Pt 1

6 So shaken as we are, so wan with care. [I. i. 1]

7 In those holy fields / Over whose acres walked those blessed feet / Which fourteen hundred years ago were nailed / For our advantage on the bitter cross. [I. i. 24]

8 Let us be Diana's foresters, gentlemen of the shade, minions of the moon. [I. ii. (28)]

9 FALSTAFF: And is not my hostess of the tavern a most sweet wench? / PRINCE: As the honey of Hybla, my old lad of the castle. [I. ii. (44)]

10 What, in thy quips and thy quiddities? [I. ii. (50)]

11 Old father antick the law. [I. ii. (69)]

12 O! thou hast damnable iteration, and art indeed able to corrupt a saint. [I. ii. (101)]

13 Now am I, if a man should speak truly, little better than one of the wicked. [I. ii. (105)]

14 'Tis my vocation, Hal; 'tis no sin for a man to labour in his vocation. [I. ii. (116)]

15 There's neither honesty, manhood, nor good fellowship in thee. [I. ii. (154)]

16 Farewell, thou latter spring! Farewell, All-hallown summer! [I. ii. (176)]

17 I know you all, and will awhile uphold / The unyoked humour of your idleness. [I. ii. (217)]

18 If all the year were playing holidays, / To sport would be as tedious as to work. [I. ii. (226)]

19 A certain lord, neat, and trimly dressed, / Fresh as a bridegroom; and his chin new-reaped, / Showed like a stubble-land at harvest-home. / He was perfumèd like a milliner, / And 'twixt his finger and his thumb he held / A pouncet-box, which ever and anon / He gave his nose and took't away again. [I. iii. 33]

20 And as the soldiers bore dead bodies by, / He called them untaught knaves, unmannerly, / To bring a slovenly unhandsome corpse / Betwixt the wind and his nobility. [I. iii. 42]

21 He made me mad / To see him shine so brisk and smell so sweet / And talk so like a waiting-gentlewoman / Of guns, and drums, and wounds, – God save the mark! – / And telling me the sovereign'st thing on earth / Was parmaceti for an inward bruise; / And that it was great pity, so it was, / This villainous salt-petre should be digged / Out of the bowels of the harmless earth, / Which many a good tall fellow had destroyed / So cowardly; and but for these vile guns, / He would himself have been a soldier. [I. iii. 53]

22 O! the blood more stirs / To rouse a lion than to start a hare. [I. iii. 197]

23 By heaven methinks it were an easy leap / To pluck bright honour from the pale-faced moon, / Or dive into the bottom of the deep, / Where fathom-line could never touch the ground, / And pluck up drownèd honour by the locks. [I. iii. 201]

24 Why what a candy deal of courtesy / This fawning greyhound then did proffer me! [I. iii. 251]

25 I know a trick worth two of that. [II. i. (40)]

26 I am bewitched with the rogue's company: / If the rascal have not given me medicines to make me love him, I'll be hanged. [II. ii. (19)]

27 It would be argument for a week, laughter for a month, and a good jest for ever. [II. ii. (104)]

28 Falstaff sweats to death, / And lards the lean earth as he walks along. [II. ii. (119)]

29 Out of this nettle, danger, we pluck this flower, safety. [II. iii. (11)]

30 Constant you are, / But yet a woman. [II. iii. (113)]

31 A Corinthian, a lad of mettle, a good boy. [II. iv. (13)]

32 He that kills me some six or seven dozen of Scots at a breakfast, washes his hands, and says to his wife, 'Fie upon this quiet life! I want work.' [II. iv. (117)]

1 A plague of all cowards, I say. [II. iv. (129)]

2 There live not three good men unhanged in England, and one of them is fat and grows old. [II. iv. (146)]

3 Call you that backing of your friends? A plague upon such backing! Give me them that will face me. [II. iv. (168)]

4 I am a Jew else; an Ebrew Jew. [II. iv. (201)]

5 I have peppered two of them; two I am sure I have paid, two rogues in buckram suits. I tell thee what, Hal, if I tell thee a lie, spit in my face, call me horse. Thou knowest my old ward; here I lay, and thus I bore my point. Four rogues in buckram let drive at me. [II. iv. (214)]

6 O monstrous! eleven buckram men grown out of two. [II. iv. (247)]

7 Three misbegotten knaves in Kendal Green. [II. iv. (249)]

8 Give you a reason on compulsion! If reasons were as plentiful as blackberries, I would give no man a reason upon compulsion, I. [II. iv. (267)]

9 Mark now, how a plain tale shall put you down. [II. iv. (285)]

10 Ah! No more of that, Hal, an thou lovest me. [II. iv. (316)]

11 A plague of sighing and grief! It blows a man up like a bladder. [II. iv. (370)]

12 I will do it in King Cambyses' vein. [II. iv. (430)]

13 That reverend vice, that grey iniquity, that father ruffian, that vanity in years. [II. iv. (505)]

14 Banish plump Jack and banish all the world. [II. iv. (534)]

15 O monstrous! but one half-pennyworth of bread to this intolerable deal of sack! [II. iv. (598)]

16 I am not in the roll of common men. [III. i. (43)]

17 GLENDOWER: I can call spirits from the vasty deep.
HOTSPUR: Why so can I, or so can any man; / But will they come when you do call for them? [III. i. (53)]

18 O! while you live, tell truth, and shame the devil! [III. i. (62)]

19 I had rather be a kitten and cry mew / Than one of these same metre ballad-mongers. [III. i. (128)]

20 Mincing poetry. [III. i. (133)]

21 And such a deal of skimble-skamble stuff. [III. i. (153)]

22 I understand thy kisses and thou mine, / And that's a feeling disputation. [III. i. (204)]

23 Swear me, Kate, like a lady as thou art, / A good mouth-filling oath. [III. i. (257)]

24 A fellow of no mark, nor likelihood. [III. ii. 45]

25 He was but as the cuckoo is in June, / Heard but not regarded. [III. ii. 75]

26 Do I not bate? do I not dwindle? Why, my skin hangs about me like an old lady's loose gown; I am withered like an old apple-john. [III. iii. (2)]

27 Company, villanous company, hath been the spoil of me. [III. iii. (10)]

28 Shall I not take mine ease at mine inn? [III. iii. (91)]

29 I have more flesh than another man, and therefore more frailty. [III. iii. (187)]

30 That daffed the world aside, / And bid it pass. [IV. i. 96]

31 I saw young Harry with his beaver on, / His cushes on his thighs, gallantly armed, / Rise from the ground like feathered Mercury, / And vaulted with such ease into his seat / As if an angel dropped down from the clouds, / To turn and wind a fiery Pegasus / And witch the world with noble horsemanship. [IV. i. 104]

32 Doomsday is near; die all, die merrily. [IV. i. 134]

33 The cankers of a calm world and a long peace. [IV. ii. (32)]

34 Food for powder; they'll fill a pit as well as better: tush, man, mortal men, mortal men. [IV. ii. (73)]

35 To the latter end of a fray and the beginning of a feast / Fits a dull fighter and a keen guest. [IV. ii. (86)]

36 Rebellion lay in his way, and he found it. [V. i. 28]

37 I would it were bed-time, Hal, and all well. [V. i. (125)]

1 Honour pricks me on. Yea, but how if honour prick me off when I come on? – how then? Can honour set-to a leg? No. Or an arm? No. Or take away the grief of a wound? No. Honour hath no skill in surgery, then? No. What is honour? A word. What is that word, honour? Air. A trim reckoning! Who hath it? He that died o' Wednesday. Doth he feel it? No. Doth he hear it? No. It is insensible then? Yea, to the dead. But will it not live with the living? No. Why? Detraction will not suffer it. Therefore I'll none of it: honour is a mere scutcheon: and so ends my catechism. [V. i. (131)]

2 The time of life is short; / To spend that shortness basely were too long. [V. ii. 81]

3 Two stars keep not their motion in one sphere. [V. iv. 65]

4 But thought's the slave of life, and life's time's fool; / And time, that makes survey of all the world, / Must have a stop. [V. iv. (81)]

5 Ill-weaved ambition, how much art thou shrunk! / When that this body did contain a spirit, / A kingdom for it was too small a bound; / But now, two paces of the vilest earth / Is room enough: this earth, that bears thee dead, / Bears not alive so stout a gentleman. [V. iv. (88)]

6 What! old acquaintance! could not all this flesh / Keep in a little life? Poor Jack, farewell! / I could have better spared a better man. [V. iv. (102)]

7 The better part of valour is discretion. [V. iv. (120)]

8 Full bravely hast thou fleshed / Thy maiden sword. [V. iv. (132)]

9 Lord, Lord, how this world is given to lying! [V. iv. (148)]

10 I'll purge, and leave sack, and live cleanly, as a nobleman should do. [V. iv. (168)]

Henry IV, Pt 2

11 Even such a man, so faint, so spiritless, / So dull, so dead in look, so woe-begone, / Drew Priam's curtain in the dead of night, / And would have told him half his Troy was burned. [I. i. 70]

12 Yet the first bringer of unwelcome news / Hath but a losing office, and his tongue / Sounds ever after as a sullen bell, / Remembered knolling a departed friend. [I. i. 100]

13 I am not only witty in myself, but the cause that wit is in other men. I do here walk before thee like a sow that hath overwhelmed all her litter but one. [I. ii. (10)]

14 A rascally yea-forsooth knave. [I. ii. (40)]

15 I am as poor as Job, my lord, but not so patient. [I. ii. (145)]

16 We that are in the vaward of our youth. [I. ii. (201)]

17 I was born about three of the clock in the afternoon, with a white head, and something a round belly. For my voice, I have lost it with hollaing, and singing of anthems. [I. ii. (213)]

18 It was always yet the trick of our English nation, if they have a good thing, to make it too common. [I. ii. (244)]

19 I can get no remedy against this consumption of the purse: / borrowing only lingers it out, but the disease is incurable. [I. ii. (268)]

20 Past and to come seems best; things present, worst. [I. iii. 108]

21 A poor lone woman. [II. i. (37)]

22 Away, you scullion! you rampallion! You fustilarian! I'll tickle your catastrophe. [II. 8. (67)]

23 He hath eaten me out of house and home. [II. i. (82)]

24 Thou didst swear to me upon a parcel-gilt goblet, sitting in my Dolphin-chamber, at the round table, by a sea-coal fire, upon Wednesday in Wheeson week. [II. i. (97)]

25 Let the end try the man. [II. ii. (52)]

26 He was indeed the glass / Wherein the noble youth did dress themselves. [II. iii. 21]

27 I beseek you now, aggravate your choler. [II. iv. (174)]

28 Hollow pampered jades of Asia. [II. iv. (177)]

29 Is it not strange that desire should so many years outlive performance. [II. iv. (283)]

30 O sleep! O gentle sleep! / Nature's soft nurse, how have I frighted thee, / That thou no more wilt weigh mine eyelids down / And steep my senses in forgetfulness? [III. i. 5]

1 Wilt thou upon the high and giddy mast /
Seal up the ship-boy's eyes, and rock his
brains / In cradle of the rude imperious
surge, / And in the visitation of the
winds, / Who take the ruffian billows by
the top, / Curling their monstrous heads,
and hanging them / With deafening
clamour in the slippery clouds, / That
with the hurly death itself awakes. [III. i.
18]

2 With all appliances and means to boot.
[III. i. 29]

3 Uneasy lies the head that wears a crown.
[III. i. 31]

4 There is a history in all men's lives. [III. i.
80]

5 Death, as the Psalmist saith, is certain to
all; all shall die. How a good yoke of
bullocks at Stamford Fair? [III. ii. (41)]

6 We have heard the chimes at midnight.
[III. ii. (231)]

7 A man can die but once; we owe God a
death. [III. ii. (253)]

8 Lord, Lord, how subject we old men are
to this vice of lying! [III. ii. (329)]

9 Against ill chances men are ever merry, /
But heaviness foreruns the good event.
[IV. ii. 81]

10 A peace is of the nature of a conquest; /
For then both parties nobly are subdued,
/ And neither party loser. [IV. ii. 89]

11 I may justly say with the hook-nosed
fellow of Rome, 'I came, saw and over-
came'. [IV. iii. (44)]

12 If I had a thousand sons, the first human
principle I would teach them should be,
to forswear thin potations and to addict
themselves to sack. [IV. iii. (133)]

13 O polished perturbation! golden care! /
That keep'st the ports of slumber open
wide / To many a watchful night! [IV. v.
22]

14 Thy wish was father, Harry, to that
thought. [IV. v. 91]

15 Commit / The oldest sins the newest kind
of ways. [IV. v. 124]

16 A joint of mutton, and any pretty little
tiny kickshaws, tell William cook. [V. i.
(28)]

17 Not Amurath an Amurath succeeds, /
But Harry, Harry. [V. ii. 48]

18 A foutra for the world and worldlings
base! / I speak of Africa and golden joys.
[V. iii. (100)]

19 Under which king, Bezonian? speak or
die. [V. iii. (114)]

20 I know thee not, old man: fall to thy
prayers; / How ill white hairs become a
fool and jester! [V. v. 52]

Henry V

21 O! for a Muse of fire, that would ascend
/ The brightest heaven of invention.
[Chorus, 1]

22 Can this cockpit hold / The vasty fields of
France? or may we cram / Within this
wooden O the very casques / That did
affright the air at Agincourt? [Ib. 11]

23 Consideration like an angel came, / And
whipped the offending Adam out of him.
[I. i. 28]

24 When he speaks, / The air, a chartered
libertine, is still. [I. i. 47]

25 And make your chronicle as rich with
praise / As is the ooze and bottom of the
sea / With sunken wreck and sumless
treasuries. [I. ii. 163]

26 For so work the honey-bees, / Creatures
that by a rule in nature teach / The act of
order to a peopled kingdom. / They have
a king and officers of sorts; / Where some,
like magistrates, correct at home, /
Others, like merchants, venture trade
abroad, / Others, like soldiers, armèd in
their stings, / Make boot upon the
summer's velvet buds; / Which pillage
they with merry march bring home / To
the tent-royal of their emperor: / Who,
busied in his majesty, surveys / The
singing masons building roofs of gold, /
The civil citizens kneading up the honey,
/ The poor mechanic porters crowding in
/ Their heavy burdens at his narrow gate,
/ The sad-eyed justice, with his surly
hum, / Delivering o'er to executors pale /
The lazy yawning drone. [I. ii. 187]

27 HENRY: What treasure, uncle?
EXETER: Tennis-balls, my liege. [I. ii. 258]

28 Now all the youth of England are on fire,
/ And silken dalliance in the wardrobe
lies; / Now thrive the armourers, and
honour's thought / Reigns solely in the
breast of every man: / They sell the
pasture now to buy the horse, / Following the mirror of all Christian kings, /

With wingèd heels, as English Mercuries. / For now sits Expectation in the air. [II, Chorus, 1]

1 I dare not fight; but I will wink and hold out mine iron. [II. i. (7)]

2 Though patience be a tired mare, yet she will plod. [II. i. (25)]

3 Base is the slave that pays. [II. i. (100)]

4 He's in Arthur's bosom, if ever man went to Arthur's bosom. [II. iii. (9)]

5 Even at the turning o' the tide. [II. iii. (13)]

6 His nose was as sharp as a pen, and a' babbled of green fields. [II. iii. (17)]

7 Now I, to comfort him, bid him a' should not think of God, I hoped there was no need to trouble himself with any such thoughts yet. [II. iii. (20)]

8 As cold as any stone. [II. iii. (25)]

9 Trust none; / For oaths are straws, men's faiths are wafer-cakes, / And hold-fast is the only dog, my duck. [II. iii. (53)]

10 Once more unto the breach, dear friends, once more; / Or close the wall up with our English dead. / In peace there's nothing so becomes a man / As modest stillness and humility: / But when the blast of war blows in our ears, / Then imitate the action of the tiger; / Stiffen the sinews, summon up the blood, / Disguise fair nature with hard-favoured rage. [III. i. 1]

11 On, on, you noblest English, / Whose blood is fet from fathers of war-proof! / Fathers that, like so many Alexanders, / Have in these parts from morn till even fought, / And sheathed their swords for lack of argument. [III. i. 17]

12 And you, good yeomen, / Whose limbs were made in England, show us here / The mettle of your pasture. [III. i. 25]

13 I see you stand like greyhounds in the slips, / Straining upon the start. The game's afoot: / Follow your spirit; and, upon this charge / Cry 'God for Harry! England and Saint George!' [III. i. 31]

14 Men of few words are the best men. [III. ii. (40)]

15 I know the disciplines of wars. [III. ii. (156)]

16 Now entertain conjecture of a time / When creeping murmur and the poring dark / Fills the wide vessel of the universe. / From camp to camp, through the foul womb of night, / The hum of either army stilly sounds. [IV, Chorus, 1]

17 How can they charitably dispose of anything when blood is their argument? [IV. i. (150)]

18 Every subject's duty is the king's; but every subject's soul is his own. [IV. i. (189)]

19 And what have kings that privates have not too, / Save ceremony, save general ceremony? [IV. i. (258)]

20 Sleep so soundly as the wretched slave / Who with a body filled and vacant mind / Gets him to rest, crammed with distressful bread. [IV. i. (288)]

21 O! that we now had here / But one ten thousand of those men in England / That do no work today. [IV. iii. 16]

22 If we are marked to die, we are enow / To do our country loss; and if to live, / The fewer men, the greater share of honour. [IV. iii. 20]

23 But if it be a sin to covet honour, / I am the most offending soul alive. [IV. iii. 28]

24 This day is called the feast of Crispian. / He that outlives this day, and comes safe home, / Will stand a tip-toe when this day is named, / And rouse him at the name of Crispian. [IV. iii. 40]

25 Old men forget: yet all shall be forgot, / But he'll remember with advantages / What feats he did that day. Then shall our names, / Familiar in his mouth as household words, / Harry the King, Bedford and Exeter, / Warwick and Talbot, Salisbury and Gloucester, / Be in their flowing cups freshly remembered. [IV. iii. 49]

26 We few, we happy few, we band of brothers; / For he today that sheds his blood with me / Shall be my brother; be he ne'er so vile / This day shall gentle his condition: / And gentlemen in England now a-bed / Shall think themselves accursed they were not here, / And hold their manhoods cheap whiles any speaks / That fought with us upon Saint Crispin's day. [IV. iii. 60]

27 Kill the poys and the luggage! [IV. vii. 1]

28 But now behold, / In the quick forge and working-house of thought. [V, Chorus, 22]

1 There is occasions and causes why and wherefore in all things. [V. i. (3)]

2 By this leek, I will most horribly revenge. I eat and eat, I swear. [V. i. (49)]

3 For these fellows of infinite tongue, that can rhyme themselves into ladies' favours, they do always reason themselves out again. [V. ii. (162)]

4 Nice customs curtsey to great kings. [V. ii. (291)]

Henry VI, Pt 1

5 Hung be the heavens with black, yield day to night! [I. i. 1]

6 Unbidden guests / Are often welcomest when they are gone. [II. ii. 55]

7 Delays have dangerous ends. [III. ii. 33]

8 I owe him little duty and less love. [IV. iv. 34]

9 She's beautiful and therefore to be wooed; / She is a woman, therefore to be won. [V. iii. 78]

Henry VI, Pt 2

10 Could I come near your beauty with my nails / I'd set my ten commandments in your face. [I. iii. (144)]

11 Smooth runs the water where the brook is deep. [III. i. 53]

12 What stronger breastplate than a heart untainted! / Thrice is he armed that hath his quarrel just, / And he but naked, though locked up in steel, / Whose conscience with injustice is corrupted. [III. ii. 232]

13 I will make it felony to drink small beer. [IV. ii. (76)]

14 The first thing we do, let's kill all the lawyers. [IV. ii. (86)]

15 Away with him! away with him! he speaks Latin. [IV. vii. (62)]

Henry VI, Pt 3

16 O tiger's heart wrapped in a woman's hide! [I. iv. 137]

17 O God! methinks it were a happy life, / To be no better than a homely swain; / To sit upon a hill, as I do now, / To carve out dials, quaintly, point by point, / Thereby to see the minutes how they run, / How many make the hour full complete; / How many hours bring about the day; /

How many days will finish up the year; / How many years a mortal man may live. [II. v. 21]

18 Gives not the hawthorn bush a sweeter shade / To shepherds, looking on their silly sheep, / Than doth a rich embroidered canopy / To kings that fear their subjects' treachery? [II. v. 42]

19 Warwick, peace; / Proud setter up and puller down of kings. [III. iii. 156]

20 A little fire is quickly trodden out, / Which being suffered, rivers cannot quench. [IV. viii. 7]

21 Down, down to hell; and say I sent thee thither. [V. vi. 67]

Henry VIII

22 Heat not a furnace for your foe so hot / That it do singe yourself. [I. i. 140]

23 If I chance to talk a little wild, forgive me; / I had it from my father. [I. iv. 26]

24 The mirror of all courtesy. [II. i. 53]

25 This bold bad man. [II. ii. (44)]

26 I swear 'tis better to be lowly born, / And range with humble livers in content, / Than to be perked up in a glistering grief, / And wear a golden sorrow. [II. iii. 19]

27 I would not be a queen / For all the world. [II. iii. 45]

28 Orpheus with his lute made trees, / And the mountain tops that freeze, / Bow themselves when he did sing. [III. i. 3]

29 In all you writ to Rome, or else / To foreign princes, 'Ego et Rex meus' / Was still inscribed. [III. i. 314]

30 I have touched the highest point of all my greatness; / And from that full meridian of my glory, / I haste now to my setting: I shall fall / Like a bright exhalation in the evening, / And no man see me more. [III. ii. 224]

31 Farewell! a long farewell, to all my greatness! / This is the state of man: today he puts forth / The tender leaves of hope; tomorrow blossoms, / And bears his blushing honours thick upon him; / The third day comes a frost, a killing frost, / And when he thinks, good easy man, full surely / His greatness is a-ripening, nips his root, / And then he falls, as I do. I have ventured, / Like little

wanton boys that swim on bladders, /
This many summers in a sea of glory, /
But far beyond my depth. [III. ii. 351]

1 Vain pomp and glory of this world, I
hate ye: / I feel my heart new opened.
O! how wretched / Is that poor man that
hangs on princes' favours! / There is,
betwixt that smile we would aspire to, /
That sweet aspect of princes, and their
ruin, / More pangs and fears than wars
or women have; / And when he falls, he
falls like Lucifer, / Never to hope again.
[III. ii. 365]

2 A peace above all earthly dignities, / A
still and quiet conscience. [III. ii. 380]

3 Cromwell, I charge thee, fling away
ambition: / By that sin fell the angels.
[III. ii. 441]

4 Love thyself last: cherish those hearts
that hate thee; / Corruption wins not
more than honesty. / Still in thy right
hand carry gentle peace, / To silence
envious tongues: be just, and fear not. /
Let all the ends thou aim'st at be thy
country's, / Thy God's and truth's. [III.
ii. 444]

5 Had I but served my God with half the
zeal / I served my king, he would not in
mine age / Have left me naked to mine
enemies. [III. ii. 456]

6 An old man, broken with the storms of
state, / Is come to lay his weary bones
among ye; / Give him a little earth for
charity. [IV. ii. 21]

7 He gave his honours to the world again, /
His blessed part to heaven, and slept in
peace. [IV. ii. 29]

8 So may he rest; his faults lie gently on
him! [IV. ii. 31]

9 He was a man / Of an unbounded stomach. [IV. ii. 33]

10 Men's evil manners live in brass; their
virtues / We write in water. [IV. ii. 45]

11 He was a scholar, and a ripe and good
one; / Exceeding wise, fair-spoken and
persuading: / Lofty and sour to them
that loved him not; / But to those men
that sought him sweet as summer. [IV. ii.
51]

12 Those twins of learning that he raised in
you, / Ipswich, and Oxford! [IV. ii. 58]

13 To dance attendance on their lordships'
pleasures. [V. ii. 30]

14 Nor shall this peace sleep with her; but
as when / The bird of wonder dies, the
maiden phoenix, / Her ashes new-create
another heir / As great in admiration as
herself. [V. v. 40]

15 Some come to take their ease / And sleep
an act or two. [Epilogue]

Julius Caesar

16 All that I live by is with the awl . . . I am,
indeed, sir, a surgeon to old shoes. [I. i.
(23)]

17 As proper men as ever trod upon neat's-
leather. [I. i. (27)]

18 You blocks, you stones, you worse than
senseless things! [I. i. (39)]

19 Beware the ides of March. [I. ii. 18]

20 Well, honour is the subject of my story. /
I cannot tell what you and other men /
Think of this life: but, for my single self, /
I had as lief not be as live to be / In awe
of such a thing as I myself. [I. ii. 92]

21 And this man / Is now become a god. [I.
ii. 115]

22 Ye gods, it doth amaze me, / A man of
such a feeble temper should / So get the
start of the majestic world, / And bear
the palm alone. [I. ii. 128]

23 Why, man, he doth bestride the narrow
world / Like a Colossus; and we petty
men / Walk under his huge legs, and peep
about / To find ourselves dishonourable
graves. / Men at some time are masters
of their fates; / The fault, dear Brutus, is
not in our stars, / But in ourselves, that
we are underlings. [I. ii. 134]

24 Upon what meat doth this our Caesar
feed, / That he is grown so great? [I. ii.
148]

25 Let me have men about me that are fat; /
Sleek-headed men and such as sleep o'
nights; / Yond Cassius has a lean and
hungry look; / He thinks too much: such
men are dangerous. [I. ii. 191]

26 He reads much; / He is a great observer,
and he looks / Quite through the deeds
of men. [I. ii. 200]

27 Seldom he smiles, and smiles in such a
sort / As if he mocked himself, and
scorned his spirit, / That could be moved
to smile at anything. [I. ii. 204]

28 'Tis very like: he hath the falling sickness.
[I. ii. (255)]

1 For my own part, it was Greek to me. [I. ii. (288)]

2 Yesterday the bird of night did sit. / Even at noon-day, upon the market-place, / Hooting and shrieking. [I. iii. 26]

3 So every bondman in his own hand bears / The power to cancel his captivity. [I. iii. 101]

4 It is the bright day that brings forth the adder; / And that craves wary walking. [II. i. 14]

5 That lowliness is young ambition's ladder, / Whereto the climber-upward turns his face; / But when he once attains the upmost round, / He then unto the ladder turns his back, / Looks in the clouds, scorning the base degrees / By which he did ascend. [II. i. 22]

6 Between the acting of a dreadful thing / And the first motion, all the interim is / Like a phantasma or a hideous dream: / The genius and the mortal instruments / Are then in council; and the state of man, / Like to a little kingdom, suffers then / The nature of an insurrection. [II. i. 63]

7 For he will never follow anything / That other men begin. [II. i. 151]

8 Let us be sacrificers, but not butchers. [II. i. 166]

9 Let's carve him as a dish fit for the gods. [II. i. 173]

10 But when I tell him he hates flatterers, / He says he does, being then most flattered. [II. i. 207]

11 Dwell I but in the suburbs / Of your good pleasure? If it be no more, / Portia is Brutus' harlot, not his wife. [II. i. 285]

12 A lioness hath whelped in the streets; / And graves have yawned and yielded up their dead. [II. ii. 17]

13 When beggars die, there are no comets seen; / The heavens themselves blaze forth the death of princes. [II. ii. 30]

14 Cowards die many times before their deaths; / The valiant never taste of death but once. [II. ii. 32]

15 How hard it is for women to keep counsel! [II. iv. 9]

16 But I am constant as the northern star, / Of whose true fixed and resting quality / There is no fellow in the firmament. [III. i. 60]

17 Et tu, Brute! [III. i. 77]

18 Why he that cuts off twenty years of life / Cuts off so many years of fearing death. [III. i. 101]

19 How many ages hence / Shall this our lofty scene be acted o'er / In states unborn and accents yet unknown! [III. i. 111]

20 O mighty Caesar! dost thou lie so low? / Are all thy conquests, glories, triumphs, spoils, / Shrunk to this little measure? [III. i. 148]

21 The choice and master spirits of this age. [III. i. 163]

22 Though last, not least in love. [III. i. 189]

23 O! pardon me, thou bleeding piece of earth, / That I am meek and gentle with these butchers; / Thou art the ruins of the noblest man / That ever lived in the tide of times. [III. i. 254]

24 Cry 'Havoc!' and let slip the dogs of war. [III. i. 273]

25 As Caesar loved me, I weep for him; as he was fortunate, I rejoice at it; as he was valiant, I honour him; but as he was ambitious, I slew him. . . . Who is there so base that would be a bondman? If any, speak; for him have I offended. [III. ii. (26)]

26 Friends, Romans, countrymen, lend me your ears; / I come to bury Caesar, not to praise him. / The evil that men do lives after them, / The good is oft interred with their bones. [III. ii. (79)]

27 For Brutus is an honourable man; / So are they all, all honourable men. [III. ii. (88)]

28 Ambition should be made of sterner stuff. [III. ii. (98)]

29 O judgment! thou art fled to brutish beasts, / And men have lost their reason. [III. ii. (110)]

30 But yesterday the word of Caesar might / Have stood against the world; now lies he there, / And none so poor to do him reverence. [III. ii. (124)]

31 If you have tears, prepare to shed them now. [III. ii. (174)]

32 See what a rent the envious Casca made. [III. ii. (180)]

33 This was the most unkindest cut of all. [III. ii. (188)]

1 O! what a fall was there, my countrymen; / Then I, and you, and all of us fell down, / Whilst bloody treason flourished over us. [III. ii. (195)]

2 I come not, friends, to steal away your hearts. / I am no orator, as Brutus is; / But, as you know me all, a plain, blunt man, / That love my friend. [III. ii. (220)]

3 Put a tongue / In every wound of Caesar, that should move / The stones of Rome to rise and mutiny. [III. ii. (232)]

4 He shall not live; look, with a spot I damn him. [IV. i. 6]

5 When love begins to sicken and decay, / It useth an enforcèd ceremony! / There are no tricks in plain and simple faith. [IV. ii. 20]

6 You yourself / Are much condemned to have an itching palm. [IV. iii. 9]

7 I had rather be a dog and bay the moon, / Than such a Roman. [IV. iii. 27]

8 Away, slight man! [IV. iii. 37]

9 There is no terror, Cassius, in your threats; / For I am armed so strong in honesty / That they pass by me as the idle wind, / Which I respect not. [IV. iii. 66]

10 A friend should bear his friend's infirmities, / But Brutus makes mine greater than they are. [IV. iii. 85]

11 All his faults observed, / Set in a note-book, learned, and conned by rote, / To cast into my teeth. [IV. iii. 96]

12 There is a tide in the affairs of men, / Which, taken at the flood, leads on to fortune; / Omitted, all the voyage of their life / Is bound in shallows and in miseries. [IV. iii. 217]

13 Never come such division 'tween our souls! [IV. iii. 234]

14 For ever, and for ever, farewell, Cassius! / If we do meet again, why we shall smile! / If not, why then, this parting was well made. [V. i. 117]

15 O! that a man might know / The end of this day's business ere it come. [V. i. 123]

16 O! Julius Caesar! thou art mighty yet! / Thy spirit walks abroad and turns our swords / In our own proper entrails. [V. iii. 94]

17 The last of all the Romans, fare thee well! [V. iii. 99]

18 Caesar, now be still; / I killed not thee with half so good a will. [V. v. 50]

19 This was the noblest Roman of them all. / All the conspirators save only he / Did that they did in envy of great Caesar. [V. v. 68]

20 His life was gentle, and the elements / So mixed in him that Nature might stand up, / And say to all the world, 'This was a man!' [V. v. 73]

King John

21 Lord of thy presence and no land beside. [I. i. 137]

22 For new-made honour doth forget men's names. [I. i. 187]

23 For courage mounteth with occasion. [II. i. 82]

24 Saint George, that swinged the dragon, and e'er since / Sits on his horse back at mine hostess' door. [II. i. 288]

25 Zounds! I was never so bethumped with words / Since I first called my brother's father dad. [II. i. 466]

26 Mad world! mad kings! mad composition! [II. i. 561]

27 That smooth-faced gentleman, tickling Commodity, / Commodity, the bias of the world. [II. i. 573]

28 Well, whiles I am a beggar, I will rail, / And say there is no sin but to be rich; / And, being rich, my virtue then shall be / To say there is no vice but beggary. [II. i. 593]

29 Here I and sorrows sit; / Here is my throne, bid kings come bow to it. [III. i. 73]

30 Thou wear a lion's hide! doff it for shame, / And hang a calf's-skin on those recreant limbs! [III. i. 128]

31 Bell, book and candle shall not drive me back / When gold and silver becks me to come on. [III. iii. 12]

32 Grief fills the room up of my absent child, / Lies in his bed, walks up and down with me, / Puts on his pretty looks, repeats his words, / Remembers me of all his gracious parts, / Stuffs out his vacant garments with his form. [III. iv. 93]

1 Life is as tedious as a twice-told tale, / Vexing the dull ear of a drowsy man. [III. iv. 108]

2 When Fortune means to men most good, / She looks upon them with a threatening eye. [III. iv. 119]

3 Heat me these irons hot. [IV. i. 1]

4 To gild refinèd gold, to paint the lily, / To throw a perfume on the violet, / To smooth the ice, or add another hue / Unto the rainbow, or with taper-light / To seek the beauteous eye of heaven to garnish, / Is wasteful and ridiculous excess. [IV. ii. 11]

5 And oftentimes excusing of a fault / Doth make the fault the worse by the excuse. [IV. ii. 30]

6 Another lean unwashed artificer. [IV. ii. 201]

7 How oft the sight of means to do ill deeds / Makes ill deeds done! [IV. ii. 219]

8 Heaven take my soul, and England keep my bones! [IV. iii. 10]

9 Unthread the bold eye of rebellion, / And welcome home again discarded faith. [V. iv. 11]

10 I beg cold comfort. [V. vii. 42]

11 This England never did, nor never shall, / Lie at the proud foot of a conqueror, / But when it first did help to wound itself: / Now these her princes are come home again, / Come the three corners of the world in arms, / And we shall shock them, Nought shall make us rue / If England to itself do rest but true. [V. vii. 112]

King Lear

12 Nothing will come of nothing: speak again. [I. i. (92)]

13 LEAR: So young and so untender? CORDELIA: So young, my lord, and true. [I. i. (108)]

14 A still-soliciting eye. [I. i. (234)]

15 Why brand they us / With base? with baseness? bastardy? base, base? / ... Edmund the base / Shall top the legitimate: – I grow, I prosper; / Now, gods stand up for bastards! [I. ii. 9 and 20]

16 These late eclipses in the sun and moon portend no good to us. [I. ii. (115)]

17 This is the excellent foppery of the world ... we make guilty of our disasters the sun, the moon and the stars, as if we were villains by necessity, fools by heavenly compulsion, knaves, thieves and treachers by spherical predominance, drunkards, liars and adulterers by an enforced obedience of planetary influence. [I. ii. (132)]

18 I should have been that I am had the maidenliest star in the firmament twinkled on my bastardizing. [I. ii. (147)]

19 Pat he comes, like the catastrophe of the old comedy: my cue is villanous melancholy, with a sigh like Tom o' Bedlam. [I. ii. (150)]

20 How sharper than a serpent's tooth it is / To have a thankless child! [I. iv. (312)]

21 Striving to better, oft we mar what's well. [I. iv. (370)]

22 O! Let me not be mad, not mad, sweet heaven; / Keep me in temper; I would not be mad. [I. v. (51)]

23 The son and heir of a mongrel bitch. [II. ii. (23)]

24 Thou whoreson zed! thou unnecessary letter! [II. ii. (68)]

25 I am too old to learn. [II. ii. (134)]

26 Fortune, good night, smile once more, turn thy wheel! [II. ii. (180)]

27 Hysterica passio! down, thou climbing sorrow! / Thy element's below. [II. iv. (57)]

28 You are old; / Nature in you stands on the very verge / Of her confine. [II. iv. (148)]

29 Necessity's sharp pinch. [II. iv. (214)]

30 No, I'll not weep: / I have full cause of weeping, but this heart / Shall break into a hundred thousand flaws / Or ere I'll weep. O fool! I shall go mad. [II. iv. (286)]

31 Blow, winds, and crack your cheeks! rage! blow! / You cataracts and hurricanoes spout / Till you have drenched our steeples, drowned the cocks! [III. ii. 1]

32 Rumble thy bellyful! Spit, fire! spout, rain! / Nor rain, wind, thunder, fire are my daughters / I tax you not, you elements, with unkindness. [III. ii. (14)]

33 Here I stand, your slave, / A poor, infirm, weak, and despised old man. [III. ii. (19)]

1 There was never yet fair woman but she made mouths in a glass. [III. ii. (35)]

2 I will be the pattern of all patience. [III. ii. (37)]

3 I am a man / More sinned against than sinning. [III. ii. (59)]

4 Take physic, pomp; / Exposed thyself to feel what wretches feel. [III. iv. 33]

5 Pillicock sat on Pillicock-hill. / Halloo, halloo, loo, loo! [III. iv. (75)]

6 Defy the foul fiend. [III. iv. (99)]

7 Unaccommodated man is no more but such a poor, bare, forked animal as thou art. [III. iv. (109)]

8 'Tis a naughty night to swim in. [III. iv. (113)]

9 Drinks the green mantle of the standing pool. [III. iv. (136)]

10 The prince of darkness is a gentleman. [III. iv. (148)]

11 Poor Tom's a-cold. [III. iv. (151)]

12 Child Rowland to the dark tower came, / His word was still, Fie, foh, and fum, / I smell the blood of a British man. [III. iv. (185)]

13 I am tied to the stake, and I must stand the course. [III. vii. (54)]

14 Out, vile jelly! / Where is thy lustre now? [III. vii. (83)]

15 The lowest and most dejected thing of fortune. [IV. i. 3]

16 The worst is not; / So long as we can say, 'This is the worst.' [IV. i. 27]

17 As flies to wanton boys, are we to the gods; / They kill us for their sport. [IV. i. 36]

18 Wisdom and goodness to the vile seem vile; / Filths savour but themselves. [IV. ii. 38]

19 It is the stars, / The stars above us, govern our conditions. [IV. iii. 34]

20 How fearful / And dizzy 'tis to cast one's eyes so low! / The crows and choughs that wing the midway air / Show scarce so gross as beetles; half-way down / Hangs one that gathers samphire, dreadful trade! / Methinks he seems no bigger than his head. / The fishermen that walk upon the beach / Appear like mice, and yon tall anchoring bark / Diminished to her cock, her cock a buoy / Almost too small for sight. The murmuring surge / That on the unnumbered idle pebbles chafes, / Cannot be heard so high. [IV. vi. 12]

21 Nature's above art in that respect. [IV. vi. (87)]

22 Ay, every inch a king. [IV. vi. (110)]

23 The wren goes to 't, and the small gilded fly / Does lecher in my sight. / Let copulation thrive. [IV. vi. (115)]

24 Give me an ounce of civet, good apothecary, to sweeten my imagination. [IV. vi. (133)]

25 GLOUC.: O! Let me kiss that hand!
LEAR: Let me wipe it first, it smells of mortality. [IV. vi. (136)]

26 See how yond justice rails upon yond simple thief. Hark in thine ear: change places; and handy-dandy, which is the justice, which is the thief? [IV. vi. (156)]

27 Through tattered clothes small vices do appear; / Robes and furred gowns hide all. [IV. vi. (169)]

28 Get thee glass eyes; / And, like a scurvy politician, seem / To see the things thou dost not. [IV. vi. (175)]

29 When we are born, we cry that we are come / To this great stage of fools. [IV. vi. (187)]

30 Mine enemy's dog, / Though he had bit me, should have stood that night / Against my fire. [IV. vii. 36]

31 Thou art a soul in bliss; but I am bound / Upon a wheel of fire. [IV. vii. 46]

32 I am a very foolish, fond old man, / Fourscore and upward, not an hour more or less; / And, to deal plainly, / I fear I am not in my perfect mind. [IV. vii. 60]

33 Pray you now, forget and forgive. [IV. vii. (85)]

34 Men must endure / Their going hence, even as their coming hither: / Ripeness is all. [V. ii. 9]

35 Come, let's away to prison; / We two alone will sing like birds i' the cage: / When thou dost ask me blessing, I'll kneel down, / And ask of thee forgiveness: so we'll live, / And pray, and sing, and tell old tales, and laugh / At gilded butterflies, and hear poor rogues / Talk of court news; and we'll talk with them too, / Who loses and who wins; who's in,

who's out; / And take upon 's the mystery of things, / As if we were God's spies; and we'll wear out, / In a walled prison, packs and sets of great ones / That ebb and flow by the moon. [V. iii. 8]

1 Upon such sacrifices, my Cordelia, / The gods themselves throw incense! [V. iii. 20]

2 The gods are just, and of our pleasant vices / Make instruments to plague us. [V. iii. (172)]

3 The wheel is come full circle. [V. iii. (176)]

4 Her voice was ever soft, / Gentle and low, an excellent thing in woman. [V. iii. (274)]

5 Never, never, never, never, never! / Pray you, undo this button. [V. iii. (310)]

6 Vex not his ghost: O! let him pass; he hates him / That would upon the rack of this tough world / Stretch him out longer. [V. iii. (314)]

7 The oldest hath borne most: we that are young / Shall never see so much, nor live so long. [V. iii. (327)]

Love's Labour's Lost

8 Spite of cormorant devouring Time. [I. i. 4]

9 Why, all delights are vain; but that most vain / Which, with pain purchased, doth inherit pain. [I. i. 72]

10 Study is like the heaven's glorious sun, / That will not be deep-searched with saucy looks; / Small have continuous plodders ever won, / Save base authority from others' books. [I. i. 84]

11 At Christmas I no more desire a rose / Than wish a snow in May's new-fangled mirth. [I. i. 105]

12 A child of our grandmother Eve, a female; or, for thy more sweet understanding, a woman. [I. i. (263)]

13 Affliction may one day smile again; and till then, sit thee down, sorrow! [I. i. (312)]

14 Devise, wit; write, pen; for I am for whole volumes in folio. [I. ii. (194)]

15 Warble, child; make passionate my sense of hearing. [III. i. 1]

16 Remuneration! O! that's the Latin word for three farthings. [III. i. (143)]

17 A very beadle to a humorous sigh. [III. i. (185)]

18 This wimpled, whining, purblind, wayward boy, / This senior-junior, giant-dwarf, Dan Cupid; / Regent of love rhymes, lord of folded arms, / The anointed sovereign of sighs and groans, / Liege of all loiterers and malcontents. [III. i. (189)]

19 He hath not fed of the dainties that are bred in a book; he hath not eat paper, as it were; he hath not drunk ink. [IV. ii. (25)]

20 For where is any author in the world / Teaches such beauty as a woman's eye? / Learning is but an adjunct to ourself. [IV. iii. (312)]

21 It adds a precious seeing to the eye; / A lover's eyes will gaze an eagle blind; / A lover's ear will hear the lowest sound. [IV. iii. (333)]

22 When Love speaks, the voice of all the gods / Makes heaven drowsy with the harmony. [IV. iii. (344)]

23 From women's eyes this doctrine I derive: / They sparkle still the right Promethean fire; / They are the books, the arts, the academes, / That show, contain, and nourish all the world. [IV. iii. (350)]

24 Priscian a little scratched; 'twill serve. [V. i. (31)]

25 They have been at a great feast of languages, and stolen the scraps. [V. i. (39)]

26 In the posteriors of this day; which the rude multitude call the afternoon. [V. i. (96)]

27 Taffeta phrases, silken terms precise, / Three-piled hyperboles, spruce affectation, / Figures pedantical. [V. ii. 407]

28 In russet yeas and honest kersey noes. [V. ii. 414]

29 A jest's prosperity lies in the ear / Of him that hears it, never in the tongue / Of him that makes it. [V. ii. (869)]

30 When daisies pied and violets blue / And lady-smocks all silver-white / And cuckoo-buds of yellow hue / Do paint the meadows with delight, / The cuckoo then, on every tree, / Mocks married men; for thus sings he, / Cuckoo, / Cuckoo, cuckoo: O word of fear, / Unpleasing to a married ear. [V. ii. (902)]

1 When icicles hang by the wall / And Dick the shepherd blows his nail, / And Tom bears logs into the hall / And milk comes frozen home in pail, / When blood is nipped, and ways be foul, / Then nightly sings the staring owl / Tu-who; / Tu-whit, tu-who – a merry note, / While greasy Joan doth keel the pot. [V. ii. (920)]

2 When all aloud the wind doth blow, / And coughing drowns the parson's saw, / And birds sit brooding in the snow, / And Marian's nose looks red and raw, / When roasted crabs hiss in the bowl. [V. ii. (929)]

3 The words of Mercury are harsh after the songs of Apollo. [V. ii. (938)]

Macbeth

4 1ST WITCH: When shall we three meet again / In thunder, lightning, or in rain? 2ND WITCH: When the hurly-burly's done, / When the battle's lost and won. [I. i. 1]

5 Fair is foul, and foul is fair. [I. i. 11]

6 What bloody man is that ? [I. ii. 1]

7 He unseamed him from the nave to the chaps. [I. ii. 22]

8 Sleep shall neither night nor day / Hang upon his pent-house lid; / He shall live a man forbid: / Weary se'nnights nine times nine / Shall he dwindle, peak and pine. [I. iii. 19]

9 So foul and fair a day I have not seen. [I. iii. 38]

10 If you can look into the seeds of time, / And say which grain will grow and which will not. [I. iii. 58]

11 And to be king / Stands not within the prospect of belief. [I. iii. 73]

12 The earth hath bubbles, as the water has, / And these are of them. [I. iii. 79]

13 Or have we eaten of the insane root / That takes the reason prisoner? [I. iii. 84]

14 And oftentimes, to win us to our harm, / The instruments of darkness tell us truths, / Win us with honest trifles, to betray's / In deepest consequence. [I. iii. 123]

15 Two truths are told, / As happy prologues to the swelling act / Of the imperial theme. [I. iii. 127]

16 This supernatural soliciting / Cannot be ill, cannot be good. [I. iii. 130]

17 Why do I yield to that suggestion / Whose horrid image doth unfix my hair / And make my seated heart knock at my ribs, / Against the use of nature? Present fears / Are less than horrible imaginings. [I. iii. 134]

18 Come what come may, / Time and the hour runs through the roughest day. [I. iii. 146]

19 Nothing in his life / Became him like the leaving it; he died / As one that had been studied in his death / To throw away the dearest thing he owed, / As 'twere a careless trifle. [I. iv. 7]

20 There's no art / To find the mind's construction in the face; / He was a gentleman on whom I built / An absolute trust. [I. iv. 11]

21 Yet do I fear thy nature; / It is too full o' the milk of human kindness / To catch the nearest way. [I. v. (17)]

22 What thou wouldst highly, / That wouldst thou holily; wouldst not play false, / And yet wouldst wrongly win. [I. v. (21)]

23 The golden round, / Which fate and metaphysical aid doth seem / To have thee crowned withal. [I. v. (29)]

24 The raven himself is hoarse / That croaks the fatal entrance of Duncan / Under my battlements. [I. v. (39)]

25 Unsex me here, / And fill me from the crown to the toe top full / Of direst cruelty! [I. v. (42)]

26 That no compunctious visitings of nature / Shake my fell purpose. [I. v. (46)]

27 Come to my woman's breasts / And take my milk for gall, you murdering ministers, / Wherever in your sightless substances, / You wait on nature's mischief. [I. v. (48)]

28 Your face, my thane, is as a book where men / May read strange matters. [I. v. (63)]

29 Look like the innocent flower, / But be the serpent under 't. [I. v. (66)]

30 This castle hath a pleasant seat; the air / Nimbly and sweetly recommends itself / Unto our gentle senses. [I. vi. 1]

1 This guest of summer, / The temple-haunting martlet, does approve / By his loved mansionry that the heaven's breath / Smells wooingly here: no jutty, frieze, / Buttress nor coign of vantage, but this bird / Hath made his pendent bed and procreant cradle: / Where they most breed and haunt, I have observed, / The air is delicate. [I. vi. 3]

2 If it were done when 'tis done, then 'twere well / It were done quickly: if the assassination / Could trammel up the consequence, and catch / With his surcease success; that but this blow / Might be the be-all and the end-all here, / But here, upon this bank and shoal of time, / We'd jump the life to come. [I. vii. 1]

3 This even-handed justice. [I. vii. 10]

4 Besides, this Duncan / Hath borne his faculties so meek, hath been / So clear in his great office, that his virtues / Will plead like angels trumpet-tongued against / The deep damnation of his taking-off; / And pity, like a naked new-born babe, / Striding the blast, or heaven's cherubim, horsed / Upon the sightless couriers of the air, / Shall blow the horrid deed in every eye. [I. vii. 16]

5 I have no spur / To prick the sides of my intent, but only / Vaulting ambition, which o'er-leaps itself / And falls on the other. [I. vii. 25]

6 I have bought / Golden opinions of all sorts of people. [I. vii. 32]

7 Letting 'I dare not' wait upon 'I would', / Like the poor cat i' the adage. [I. vii. 44]

8 I dare do all that may become a man; / Who dares do more is none. [I. vii. 46]

9 I have given suck and know / How tender 'tis to love the babe that milks me: / I would, while it was smiling in my face, / Have plucked my nipple from his boneless gums, / And dashed the brains out, had I so sworn as you / Have done to this. [I. vii. 54]

10 MACBETH: If we should fail –
LADY MACBETH: We fail! / But screw your courage to the sticking place, / And we'll not fail. [I. vii. 59]

11 That memory, the warder of the brain, / Shall be a fume. [I. vii. 65]

12 Bring forth men children only. [I. vii. 72]

13 There's husbandry in heaven; / Their candles are all out. [II. i. 4]

14 Merciful powers! / Restrain in me the cursed thoughts that nature / Gives way to in repose. [II. i. 7]

15 Shut up / In measureless content. [II. i. 16]

16 Is this a dagger which I see before me, / The handle toward my hand? Come, let me clutch thee: / I have thee not, and yet I see thee still, / Art thou not, fatal vision, sensible / To feeling as to sight? or art thou but / A dagger of the mind, a false creation, / Proceeding from the heat-oppressèd brain? [II. i. 33]

17 The bell invites me. / Hear it not, Duncan; for it is a knell / That summons thee to heaven or to hell. [II. i. 62]

18 It was the owl that shrieked, the fatal bellman, / Which gives the stern'st goodnight. [II. ii. 4]

19 The attempt and not the deed / Confounds us. [II. ii. 12]

20 As they had seen me with these hangman's hands. [II. ii. 29]

21 I had most need of blessing, and 'Amen' / Stuck in my throat. [II. ii. 33]

22 These deeds must not be thought / After these ways; so, it will make us mad. [II. ii. 34]

23 Methought I heard a voice cry, 'Sleep no more! / Macbeth does murder sleep', the innocent sleep, / Sleep that knits up the ravelled sleave of care, / The death of each day's life, sore labour's bath, / Balm of hurt minds, great nature's second course, / Chief nourisher in life's feast. [II. ii. 36]

24 Infirm of purpose! / Give me the daggers. The sleeping and the dead / Are but as pictures; 'tis the eye of childhood / That fears a painted devil. [II. ii. 53]

25 Will all great Neptune's ocean wash this blood / Clean from my hand? No, this my hand will rather / The multitudinous seas incarnadine, / Making the green one red. [II. ii. 61]

26 A little water clears us of this deed. [II. ii. 68]

27 The primrose way to the everlasting bonfire. [II. iii. (22)]

28 The labour we delight in physics pain. [II. iii. (56)]

29 Confusion now hath made his masterpiece! / Most sacrilegious murder hath

broke ope / The Lord's anointed temple, and stole thence / The life o' the building! [II. iii. (72)]

1 Shake off this downy sleep, death's counterfeit, / And look on death itself! [II. iii. (83)]

2 There's nothing serious in mortality. / All is but toys; renown and grace is dead, / The wine of life is drawn, and the mere lees / Is left this vault to brag of. [II. iii. (100)]

3 Who can be wise, amazed, temperate and furious, / Loyal and neutral, in a moment? No man. [II. iii. (115)]

4 Look to the lady. [II. iii. (126)]

5 A falcon, towering in her pride of place, / Was by a mousing owl hawked at and killed. [II. iv. 12]

6 I must become a borrower of the night / For a dark hour or twain. [III. i. 27]

7 To be thus is nothing; / But to be safely thus. [III. i. 48]

8 1ST MURDERER: We are men, my liege. MACBETH: Ay, in the catalogue ye go for men. [III. i. 91]

9 I am one, my liege, / Whom the vile blows and buffets of the world / Have so incensed that I am reckless what / I do to spite the world. [III. i. 108]

10 Things without all remedy / Should be without regard: what's done is done. [III. ii. 11]

11 We have scotched the snake, not killed it. [III. ii. 13]

12 Duncan is in his grave; / After life's fitful fever he sleeps well; / Treason has done his worst: not steel, nor poison, / Malice domestic, foreign levy, nothing / Can touch him further. [III. ii. 22]

13 But in them nature's copy's not eterne. [III. ii. 38]

14 The shard-borne beetle with his drowsy hums / Hath rung night's yawning peal. [III. ii. 42]

15 A deed of dreadful note. [III. ii. 44]

16 Come, seeling night, / Scarf up the tender eye of pitiful day. [III. ii. 46]

17 Light thickens; and the crow / Makes wing to the rooky wood: / Good things of day begin to droop and drowse, / Whiles night's black agents to their preys do rouse. [III. ii. 50]

18 Now spurs the lated traveller apace / To gain the timely inn. [III. iii. 6]

19 BANQUO: It will be rain tonight. 1ST MURDERER: Let it come down. [III. iii. 16]

20 But now I am cabined, cribbed, confined, bound in / To saucy doubts and fears. [III. iv. 24]

21 Now, good digestion wait on appetite, / And health on both! [III. iv. 38]

22 Thou canst not say I did it: never shake / Thy gory locks at me. [III. iv. 50]

23 The air-drawn dagger. [III. iv. 62]

24 The times have been, / That when the brains were out, the man would die, / And there an end; but now they rise again, / With twenty mortal murders on their crowns, / And push us from our stools. [III. iv. 78]

25 Thou hast no speculation in those eyes / Which thou dost glare with. [III. iv. 95]

26 What man dare, I dare. [III. iv. 99]

27 Hence, horrible shadow! / Unreal mockery, hence! [III. iv. 106]

28 Can such things be / And overcome us like a summer's cloud, / Without our special wonder? [III. iv. 110]

29 Stand not upon the order of your going, / But go at once. [III. iv. 119]

30 MACBETH: What is the night? LADY MACBETH: Almost at odds with morning, which is which. [III. iv. 126]

31 I am in blood / Stepped in so far that, should I wade no more, / Returning were as tedious as go o'er. [III. iv. 136]

32 Double, double, toil and trouble; / Fire burn and cauldron bubble. [IV. i. 10]

33 Eye of newt and toe of frog, / Wool of bat and tongue of dog. [IV. i. 14]

34 By the pricking of my thumbs, / Something wicked this way comes. / Open locks, / Whoever knocks. [IV. i. 44]

35 How now, you secret, black, and midnight hags! [IV. i. 48]

36 A deed without a name. [IV. i. 49]

37 Be bloody, bold, and resolute. [IV. i. 79]

38 But yet I'll make assurance double sure, / And take a bond of fate. [IV. i. 83]

39 Macbeth shall never vanquished be until / Great Birnam wood to high Dunsinane hill / Shall come against him. [IV. i. 92]

1 What! will the line stretch out to the crack of doom? [IV. i. 117]

2 The weird sisters. [IV. i. 136]

3 His flight was madness: when our actions do not, / Our fears do make us traitors. [IV. ii. 3]

4 He wants the natural touch. [IV. ii. 9]

5 Angels are bright still, though the brightest fell. [IV. iii. 22]

6 Stands Scotland where it did? [IV. iii. 164]

7 Give sorrow words: the grief that does not speak / Whispers the o'er-fraught heart, and bids it break. [IV. iii. 209]

8 What! all my pretty chickens and their dam, / At one fell swoop? [IV. iii. 218]

9 MALCOLM: Dispute it like a man. MACDUFF: I shall do so; / But I must also feel it like a man; / I cannot but remember such things were, / That were most precious to me. [IV. iii. 219]

10 Out, damned spot! out, I say! One; two: why then, 'tis time to do 't. Hell is murky! Fie, my lord, fie! a soldier, and afeard? [V. i. (38)]

11 Yet who would have thought the old man to have had so much blood in him? [V. i. (42)]

12 The Thane of Fife had a wife: where is she now? What! will these hands ne'er be clean? [V. i. (46)]

13 Here's the smell of the blood still: all the perfumes of Arabia will not sweeten this little hand. [V. i. (55)]

14 Now does he feel his title / Hang loose about him like a giant's robe / Upon a dwarfish thief. [V. ii. 20]

15 The devil damn thee black, thou cream-faced loon! / Where gott'st thou that goose look? [V. iii. 11]

16 Thou lily-livered boy. [V. iii. 15]

17 I have lived long enough: my way of life / Is fall'n into the sear, the yellow leaf; / And that which should accompany old age, / As honour, love, obedience, troops of friends, / I must not look to have; but, in their stead, / Curses, not loud but deep, mouth-honour, breath, / Which the poor heart would fain deny and dare not. [V. iii. 22]

18 Canst thou not minister to a mind diseased, / Pluck from the memory a rooted sorrow, / Raze out the written troubles of the brain, / And with some sweet oblivious antidote / Cleanse the stuffed bosom of that perilous stuff / Which weighs upon the heart? [V. iii. 40]

19 Throw physic to the dogs; I'll none of it. [V. iii. 47]

20 If thou couldst, doctor, cast / The water of my land, find her disease, / And purge it to a sound and pristine health, / I would applaud thee to the very echo, / That should applaud again. [V. iii. 50]

21 Hang out the banners on the outward walls: / The cry is still 'They come'; our castle's strength / Will laugh a siege to scorn. [V. v. 1]

22 The time has been my senses would have cooled / To hear a night-shriek, and my fell of hair / Would at a dismal treatise rouse and stir / As life were in't. I have supped full with horrors; / Direness, familiar to my slaughterous thoughts, / Cannot once start me. [V. v. 10]

23 She should have died hereafter; / There would have been a time for such a word. / To-morrow, and to-morrow, and to-morrow, / Creeps in this petty pace from day to day, / To the last syllable of recorded time; / And all our yesterdays have lighted fools / The way to dusty death. Out, out, brief candle! / Life's but a walking shadow, a poor player / That struts and frets his hour upon the stage, / And then is heard no more: it is a tale / Told by an idiot, full of sound and fury, / Signifying nothing. [V. v. 17]

24 I 'gin to grow aweary of the sun, / And wish the estate o' the world were now undone. [V. v. 49]

25 Blow, wind! Come, wrack! / At least we'll die with harness on our back. [V. v. 51]

26 They have tied me to a stake; I cannot fly, / But bear-like I must fight the course. [V. vii. 1]

27 Why should I play the Roman fool, and die / On mine own sword? [V. vii. 30]

28 I bear a charmèd life. [V. vii. 41]

29 Despair thy charm; / And let the angel whom thou still hast served / Tell thee, Macduff was from his mother's womb / Untimely ripped. [V. vii. 42]

1 And be these juggling fiends no more believed, / That palter with us in a double sense; / That keep the word of promise to our ear, / And break it to our hope. [V. vii. 48]

2 Live to be the show and gaze o' the time. [V. vii. 53]

3 Lay on, Macduff; / And damned be him that first cries, 'Hold, enough!' [V. vii. 62]

Measure for Measure

4 Spirits are not finely touched / But to fine issues [I. i. 35]

5 I hold you as a thing enskyed and sainted. [I. iv. 34]

6 A man whose blood / Is very snow-broth; one who never feels / The wanton stings and motions of the sense. [I. iv. 57]

7 Our doubts are traitors, / And make us lose the good we oft might win, / By fearing to attempt. [I. iv. 77]

8 'Tis one thing to be tempted, Escalus, / Another thing to fall. I do not deny, / The jury, passing on the prisoner's life, / May in the sworn twelve have a thief or two / Guiltier than him they try. [II. i. 17]

9 Some rise by sin, and some by virtue fall. [II. i. 38]

10 This will last out a night in Russia, / When nights are longest there. [II. i. 144]

11 Condemn the fault and not the actor of it? [II. ii. 37]

12 No ceremony that to great ones 'longs, / Not the king's crown, nor the deputed sword, / The marshal's truncheon nor the judge's robe, / Become them with one half so good a grace / As mercy does. [II. ii. 59]

13 How would you be, / If He, which is the top of judgement, should / But judge you as you are? [II. ii. 75]

14 The law hath not been dead, though it hath slept. [II. ii. 90]

15 O! it is excellent / To have a giant's strength, but it is tyrannous / To use it like a giant. [II. ii. 107]

16 But man, proud man, / Drest in a little brief authority, / Most ignorant of what he's most assured, / His glassy essence, like an angry ape, / Plays such fantastic tricks before high heaven / As make the angels weep. [II. ii. 117]

17 That in the captain's but a choleric word, / Which in the soldier is flat blasphemy. [II. ii. 130]

18 The miserable hath no other medicine / But only hope. [III. i. 2]

19 Be absolute for death; either death or life / Shall thereby be the sweeter. Reason thus with life: / If I do lose thee, I do lose a thing / That none but fools would keep: a breath thou art, / Servile to all the skyey influences. [III. i. 5]

20 Palsied eld. [III. i. 36]

21 The sense of death is most in apprehension, / And the poor beetle, that we tread upon, / In corporal sufferance finds a pang as great / As when a giant dies. [III. i. 75]

22 If I must die, / I will encounter darkness as a bride, / And hug it in my arms. [III. i. 81]

23 Ay, but to die, and go we know not where; / To lie in cold obstruction and to rot; / This sensible warm motion to become / A kneaded clod; and the delighted spirit / To bathe in fiery floods, or to reside. / In thrilling region of thick-ribbèd ice; / To be imprisoned in the viewless winds, / And blown with restless violence round about / The pendant world! [III. i. 116]

24 The weariest and most loathèd worldly life / That age, ache, penury and imprisonment / Can lay on nature is a paradise / To what we fear of death. [III. i. 127]

25 Virtue is bold, and goodness never fearful. [III. i. (214)]

26 There, at the moated grange, resides this dejected Mariana. [III. i. (279)]

27 Take, O take those lips away, / That so sweetly were forsworn / And those eyes, the break of day, / Lights that do mislead the morn: / But my kisses bring again, bring again; / Seals of love, but sealed in vain, sealed in vain. [IV. i. 1]

28 Every true man's apparel fits your thief. [IV. ii. (46)]

29 I am a kind of burr; I shall stick. [IV. iii. (193)]

30 A forted residence 'gainst the tooth of time, / And razure of oblivion. [V. i. 12]

31 Haste still pays haste, and leisure answers leisure; / Like doth quit like, and Measure still for Measure. [V. i. (411)]

1 They say best men are moulded out of faults, / And for the most, become much more the better / For being a little bad. [V. i. (440)]

2 What's mine is yours, and what is yours is mine. [V. i. (539)]

The Merchant of Venice

3 Nature hath framed strange fellows in her time: / Some that will evermore peep through their eyes / And laugh like parrots at a bag-piper: / And other of such vinegar aspect / That they'll not show their teeth in way of smile, / Though Nestor swear the jest be laughable. [I. i. 51]

4 I hold the world but as the world, Gratiano; / A stage where every man must play a part, / And mine a sad one. [I. i. 77]

5 Why should a man whose blood is warm within, / Sit like his grandsire cut in alabaster? [I. i. 83]

6 There are a sort of men whose visages / Do cream and mantle like a standing pond. [I. i. 88]

7 As who would say, 'I am Sir Oracle, / And when I ope my lips, let no dog bark!' [I. i. 93]

8 Gratiano speaks an infinite deal of nothing, more than any man in Venice. His reasons are as two gains of wheat, hid in two bushels of chaff: you shall seek all the day ere you find them; and, when you have them, they are not worth the search. [I. i. 114]

9 They are as sick that surfeit with too much, as they that starve with nothing. [I. ii. (5)]

10 Superfluity comes sooner by white hairs, but competency lives longer. [I. ii. (9)]

11 If to do were as easy as to know what were good to do, chapels had been churches, and poor men's cottages princes' palaces. [I. ii. (13)]

12 God made him, and therefore let him pass for a man. [I. ii. (59)]

13 I will do anything, Nerissa, ere I will be married to a sponge. [I. ii. (105)]

14 I dote on his very absence. [I. ii. (118)]

15 Ships are but boards, sailors but men; there be land-rats and water-rats, land-thieves and water-thieves. [I. iii. (22)]

16 How like a fawning publican he looks! / I hate him for he is a Christian. / But more for that in low simplicity / He lends out money gratis, and brings down / The rate of usance here with us in Venice. / If I can catch him once upon the hip, / I will feed fat the ancient grudge I bear him. / He hates our sacred nation, and he rails, / Even there where merchants most do congregate. [I. iii. (42)]

17 The devil can cite Scripture for his purpose. [I. iii. (99)]

18 A goodly apple rotten at the heart. / O, what a goodly outside falsehood hath! [I. iii. (102)]

19 Many a time and oft / In the Rialto you have rated me. [I. iii. (107)]

20 For sufferance is the badge of all our tribe. [I. iii. (111)]

21 You call me misbeliever, cut-throat dog, / And spet upon my Jewish gaberdine. [I. iii. (112)]

22 Shall I bend low, and in a bondsman's key, / With bated breath, and whispering humbleness. [I. iii. (124)]

23 O father Abram! what these Christians are, / Whose own hard dealing teaches them suspect / The thoughts of others! [I. iii. (161)]

24 I like not fair terms and a villain's mind. [I. iii. (180)]

25 Mislike me not for my complexion, / The shadowed livery of the burnished sun. [II. i. 1]

26 O heavens! this is my true-begotten father. [II. ii. (36)]

27 An honest, exceeding poor man. [II. ii. (54)]

28 It is a wise father that knows his own child. [II. ii. (83)]

29 There is some ill a-brewing towards my rest, / For I did dream of money-bags to-night. [II. v. 17]

30 And the vile squealing of the wry-necked fife. [II. v. (30)]

31 But love is blind, and lovers cannot see / The pretty follies that themselves commit. [II. vi. 36]

32 What! must I hold a candle to my shames? [II. vi. 41]

1 My daughter! O my ducats! O my daughter! / Fled with a Christian! O my Christian ducats! [II. viii. 15]

2 Hanging and wiving goes by destiny. [II. ix. 83]

3 Let him look on his bond. [III. i. (51, 52, 54)]

4 Hath not a Jew eyes? hath not a Jew hands, organs, dimensions, senses, affections, passions? [III. i. (63)]

5 If you prick us, do we not bleed? if you tickle us, do we not laugh? if you poison us, do we not die? and if you wrong us, shall we not revenge? [III. i. (69)]

6 The villany you teach me I will execute, and it shall go hard but I will better the instruction. [III. i. (76)]

7 I would not have given it for a wilderness of monkeys. [III. i. (130)]

8 He makes a swan-like end, / Fading in music. [III. ii. 44]

9 Tell me where is fancy bred, / Or in the heart or in the head? / How begot, how nourishèd? [III. ii. 63]

10 The world is still deceived with ornament. / In law, what plea so tainted and corrupt / But, being seasoned with a gracious voice, / Obscures the show of evil? [III. ii. 74]

11 Thus ornament is but the guilèd shore / To a most dangerous sea; the beauteous scarf / Veiling an Indian beauty; in a word, / The seeming truth which cunning times put on / To entrap the wisest. [III. ii. 97]

12 An unlessoned girl, unschooled, unpractised; / Happy in this, she is not yet so old / But she may learn. [III. ii. 160]

13 Here are a few of the unpleasant'st words / That ever blotted paper! [III. ii. 252]

14 I'll not answer that: / But say it is my humour. [IV. i. 42]

15 A harmless necessary cat. [IV. i. 55]

16 I am a tainted wether of the flock, / Meetest for death: the weakest kind of fruit / Drops earliest to the ground. [IV. i. 114]

17 The quality of mercy is not strained, / It droppeth as the gentle rain from heaven / Upon the place beneath: it is twice blessed; / It blesseth him that gives and him that takes: / 'Tis mightiest in the mightiest; it becomes / The thronèd monarch better than his crown; / His sceptre shows the force of temporal power, / The attribute to awe and majesty, / Wherein doth sit the dread and fear of kings; / But mercy is above the sceptred sway, / It is enthronèd in the hearts of kings, / It is an attribute of God himself, / And earthly power doth then show likest God's / When mercy seasons justice. Therefore, Jew, / Though justice be thy plea, consider this, / That in the course of justice none of us / Should see salvation: we do pray for mercy, / And that same prayer doth teach us all to render / The deeds of mercy. [IV. i. (184)]

18 Wrest once the law to your authority: / To do a great right, do a little wrong. [IV. i. (215)]

19 A Daniel come to judgement! yea! a Daniel! / O wise young judge, how I do honour thee! [IV. i. (223)]

20 'Tis not in the bond. [IV. i. (263)]

21 For, as thou urgest justice, be assured / Thou shalt have justice, more than thou desir'st. [IV. i. (316)]

22 A second Daniel, a Daniel, Jew! / Now, infidel, I have thee on the hip. [IV. i. (334)]

23 I thank thee, Jew, for teaching me that word. [IV. i. (342)]

24 You take my house when you do take the prop / That doth sustain my house; you take my life / When you do take the means whereby I live. [IV. i. (376)]

25 He is well paid that is well satisfied. [IV. i. (416)]

26 LORENZO: In such a night / Troilus methinks mounted the Troyan walls, / And sighed his soul toward the Grecian tents, / Where Cressid lay that night.
JESSICA: In such a night / Did Thisbe fearfully o'ertrip the dew, / And saw the lion's shadow ere himself, / And ran dismayed away.
LORENZO: In such a night / Stood Dido with a willow in her hand / Upon the wild sea-banks, and waft her love / To come again to Carthage.
JESSICA: In such a night / Medea gathered the enchanted herbs / That did renew old Aeson. [V. i. 3]

27 How sweet the moonlight sleeps upon this bank! / Here will we sit, and let the

sounds of music / Creep in our ears: soft stillness and the night / Become the touches of sweet harmony. [V. i. 54]

1 Look how the floor of heaven / Is thick inlaid with patines of bright gold: / There's not the smallest orb which thou behold'st / But in his motion like an angel sings. / Still quiring to the young-eyed cherubins; / Such harmony is in immortal souls; / But, whilst this muddy vesture of decay / Doth grossly close it in, we cannot hear it. [V. i. 58]

2 I am never merry when I hear sweet music. [V. i. 69]

3 The man that hath not music in himself, / Nor is not moved with concord of sweet sounds, / Is fit for treasons, stratagems, and spoils; / The motions of his spirit are dull as night, / And his affections dark as Erebus: / Let no such man be trusted. [V. i. 83]

4 How far that little candle throws his beams! / So shines a good deed in a naughty world. [V. i. 90]

5 How many things by season seasoned are / To their right praise and true perfection! [V. i. 107]

6 For a light wife doth make a heavy husband. [V. i. 130]

The Merry Wives of Windsor

7 I will make a Star-chamber matter of it. [I. i. 1]

8 She has brown hair, and speaks small like a woman. [I. i. (48)]

9 Seven hundred pounds and possibilities is goot gifts. [I. i. (63)]

10 I had rather than forty shillings I had my Book of Songs and Sonnets here. [I. i. (205)]

11 'Convey' the wise it call. 'Steal!' foh! a fico for the phrase. [I. iii. (30)]

12 Here will be an old abusing of God's patience and the king's English. [I. iv. (5)]

13 We burn daylight. [II. i. (54)]

14 Faith, thou hast some crotchets in thy head. [II. i. (158)]

15 Why then the world's mine oyster, / Which I with sword will open. [II. ii. 2]

16 O sweet Anne Page! [III. i. (72)]

17 I cannot tell what the dickens his name is [III. ii. 19]

18 O what a world of vile ill-favoured faults / Looks handsome in three hundred pounds a year! [III. iv. (32)]

19 I have a kind of alacrity in sinking. [III. v. (13)]

20 As good luck would have it. [III. v. (86)]

21 The rankest compound of villanous smell that ever offended nostrils. [III. v. (95)]

22 A man of my kidney. [III. v. (119)]

23 There is a divinity in odd numbers, either in nativity, chance or death. [V. i. (3)]

A Midsummer Night's Dream

24 To live a barren sister all your life, / Chanting faint hymns to the cold fruitless moon. [I. i. 72]

25 But earthlier happy is the rose distilled, / Than that which withering on the virgin thorn, / Grows, lives, and dies, in single blessedness. [I. i. 76]

26 And she, sweet lady, dotes, / Devoutly dotes, dotes in idolatry. [I. i. 108]

27 For aught that ever I could read, / Could ever hear by tale or history, / The course of true love never did run smooth. [I. i. 123]

28 Swift as a shadow, short as any dream, / Brief as the lightning in the collied night, / That, in a spleen, unfolds both heaven and earth, / And ere a man hath power to say, 'Behold!' / The jaws of darkness do devour it up: / So quick bright things come to confusion. [I. i. 144]

29 Love looks not with the eyes, but with the mind, / And therefore is winged Cupid painted blind. [I. i. 234]

30 The most lamentable comedy, and most cruel death of Pyramus and Thisby. [I. ii. 11)]

31 Masters, spread yourselves. [I. ii. (16)]

32 A part to tear a cat in, to make all split. [I. ii. (32)]

33 This is Ercles' vein. [I. ii. (43)]

34 I'll speak in a monstrous little voice. [I. ii. (55)]

35 I am slow of study. [I. ii. (70)]

1 I will aggravate my voice so that I will roar you as gently as any sucking dove; I will roar you as 'twere any nightingale. [I. ii. (84)]

2 A proper man, as one shall see in a summer's day. [I. ii. (89)]

3 Over hill, over dale, / Thorough bush, thorough brier, / Over park, over pale, / Thorough flood, thorough fire. [II. i. 2]

4 I must go seek some dew-drops here, / And hang a pearl in every cowslip's ear. [II. i. 14]

5 Ill met by moonlight, proud Titania. [II. i. 60]

6 Thorough this distemperature we see / The seasons alter: hoary headed frosts / Fall in the fresh lap of the crimson rose. [II. i. 106]

7 Since once I sat upon a promontory, / And heard a mermaid on a dolphin's back, / Uttering such dulcet and harmonious breath, / That the rude sea grew civil at her song, / And certain stars shot madly from their spheres, / To hear the sea-maid's music. [II. i. 149]

8 And the imperial votaress passed on, / In maiden meditation, fancy-free. / Yet marked I where the bolt of Cupid fell; / It fell upon a little western flower, / Before milk-white, now purple with love's wound, / And maidens call it Love-in-idleness. [II. i. 163]

9 I'll put a girdle round about the earth / In forty minutes. [II. i. 175]

10 I know a bank whereon the wild thyme blows, / Where oxlips and the nodding violet grows / Quite over-canopied with luscious woodbine, / With sweet musk-roses, and with eglantine. [II. i. 249]

11 You spotted snakes with double tongue, / Thorny hedge-hogs, be not seen. [II. ii. 9]

12 God shield us! – a lion among ladies, is a most dreadful thing; for there is not a more fearful wild-fowl than your lion living. [III. i. (32)]

13 Look in the almanack, find out moonshine. [III. i. (55)]

14 What hempen homespuns have we swaggering here? [III. i. (82)]

15 Bless thee, Bottom! bless thee! thou art translated. [III. i. (124)]

16 Lord, what fools these mortals be! [III. ii. 115]

17 So we grew together, / Like to a double cherry, seeming parted, / But yet an union in partition; / Two lovely berries moulded on one stem. [III. ii. 208]

18 She was a vixen when she went to school: / And though she be but little, she is fierce. [III. ii. 324]

19 Jack shall have Jill; / Nought shall go ill; / The man shall have his mare again, / And all shall be well. [III. ii. 461]

20 I have a reasonable good ear in music: let us have the tongs and bones. [IV. i. (32)]

21 I have an exposition of sleep come upon me. [IV. i. (44)]

22 My hounds are bred out of the Spartan kind, / So flewed, so sanded; and their heads are hung / With ears that sweep away the morning dew; / Crook-kneed, and dew-lapped like Thessalian bulls; / Slow in pursuit, but matched in mouth like bells. [IV. i. (125)]

23 The eye of man hath not heard, the ear of man hath not seen, man's hand is not able to taste, his tongue to conceive, nor his heart to report, what my dream was. [IV. i. (218)]

24 It shall be called Bottom's Dream, because it hath no bottom. [IV. i. (222)]

25 The lunatic, the lover, and the poet, / Are of imagination all compact. [V. i. 7]

26 The lover, all as frantic, / Sees Helen's beauty in a brow of Egypt: / The poet's eye, in a fine frenzy rolling, / Doth glance from heaven to earth, from earth to heaven; / And, as imagination bodies forth / The forms of things unknown, the poet's pen / Turns them to shapes, and gives to airy nothing / A local habitation and a name. [V. i. 10]

27 Or in the night, imagining some fear, / How easy is a bush supposed a bear! [V. i. 21]

28 Very tragical mirth. [V. i. 57]

29 That is the true beginning of our end. [V. i. 111]

30 Whereat, with blade, with bloody blameful blade, / He bravely broached his boiling bloody breast. [V. i. (148)]

31 The best in this kind are but shadows, and the worst are no worse, if imagination amend them. [V. i. (215)]

1 The iron tongue of midnight hath told twelve; / Lovers to bed; 'tis almost fairy time. [V. i. (372)]

Much Ado About Nothing

2 He hath indeed better bettered expectation than you must expect of me to tell you how. [I. i. (15)]

3 He is a very valiant trencherman. [I. i. (52)]

4 I see, lady, the gentleman is not in your books. [I. i. (79)]

5 BEATRICE: I wonder that you will still be talking, Signior Benedick: nobody marks you.
BENEDICK: What! my dear Lady Disdain, are you yet living? [I. i. (121)]

6 Shall I never see a bachelor of three-score again? [I. i. (209)]

7 In time the savage bull doth bear the yoke. [I. i. (271)]

8 Benedick the married man. [I. i. (278)]

9 I could not endure a husband with a beard on his face: I had rather lie in the woollen. [II. i. (31)]

10 I have a good eye, uncle: I can see a church by daylight. [II. i. (86)]

11 Speak low, if you speak love. [II. i. (104)]

12 Friendship is constant in all other things / Save in the office and affairs of love. [II. i. (184)]

13 Silence is the perfectest herald of joy: I were but little happy if I could say how much. [II. i. (319)]

14 D. PEDRO: Will you have me, lady?
BEATRICE: No, my lord, unless I might have another for working days: your Grace is too costly to wear every day. [II. i. (341)]

15 There was a star danced, and under that was I born. [II. i. (351)]

16 Is it not strange that sheep's guts should hale souls out of men's bodies? [II. iii. (62)]

17 Sigh no more, ladies, sigh no more, / Men were deceivers ever; / One foot in sea, and one on shore, / To one thing constant never. [II. iii. (65)]

18 Sits the wind in that corner? [II. iii. (108)]

19 These paper bullets of the brain awe a man from the career of his humour. [II. iii. (261)]

20 The world must be peopled. When I said I would die a bachelor, I did not think I should live till I were married. [II. iii. (262)]

21 He hath a heart as sound as a bell, and his tongue the clapper; for what his heart thinks his tongue speaks. [III. ii. (12)]

22 Well, every one can master a grief but he that has it. [III. ii. (28)]

23 Are you good men and true? [III. iii. 1]

24 To be a well-favoured man is the gift of fortune; but to write and read comes by nature. [III. iii. (14)]

25 You are thought here to be the most senseless and fit man for the constable of the watch. [III. iii. (22)]

26 2ND WATCH: How if a' will not stand?
DOGBERRY: Why, then, take no note of him, but let him go; and presently call the rest of the watch together, and thank God you are rid of a knave. [III. iii. (28)]

27 For the watch to babble and to talk is most tolerable and not to be endured. [III. iii. (36)]

28 The most peaceable way for you, if you do take a thief, is to let him show himself what he is and steal out of your company. [III. iii. (61)]

29 I am as honest as any man living that is an old man and no honester than I. [III. v. (15)]

30 Comparisons are odorous. [III. v. (18)]

31 If I were as tedious as a king, I could find in my heart to bestow it all of your worship. [III. v. (23)]

32 A good old man, sir; he will be talking; as they say, 'when the age is in, the wit is out'. [III. v. (36)]

33 Our watch, sir, hath indeed comprehended two aspicious persons. [III. v. (49)]

34 O! what men dare do! what men may do! what men daily do, not knowing what they do! [IV. i. (19)]

35 For it so falls out / That what we have we prize not to the worth / Whiles we enjoy it, but being lacked and lost, / Why then we rack the value. [IV. i. (219)]

1 It is proved already that you are little better than false knaves, and it will go near to be thought so shortly. [IV. ii. (23)]

2 Yea, marry, that's the eftest way. [IV. ii. (39)]

3 Flat burglary as ever was committed. [IV. ii. (54)]

4 Thou wilt be condemned into everlasting redemption for this. [IV. ii. (60)]

5 O that he were here to write me down an ass! [IV. ii. (80)]

6 A fellow that hath had losses; and one that hath two gowns, and everything handsome about him. [IV. ii. (90)]

7 Patch grief with proverbs. [V. i. 17]

8 For there was never yet philosopher / That could endure the toothache patiently. [V. i. 35]

9 They have committed false report; moreover, they have spoken untruths; secondarily, they are slanders; sixth and lastly, they have belied a lady; thirdly, they have verified unjust things; and to conclude, they are lying knaves. [V. i. (224)]

10 No, I was not born under a rhyming planet. [V. ii. (40)]

11 Done to death by slanderous tongues. [V. iii. 3]

12 The wolves have preyed; and look, the gentle day, / Before the wheels of Phoebus, round about / Dapples the drowsy east with spots of grey. [V. iii. 25]

Othello

13 A fellow almost damned in a fair wife. [I. i. 21]

14 The bookish theoric. [I. i. 24]

15 We cannot all be masters. [I. i. 43]

16 In following him, I follow but myself. [I. i. 58]

17 But I will wear my heart upon my sleeve / For daws to peck at. [I. i. 64]

18 An old black ram / Is tupping your white ewe. [I. i. 88]

19 You are one of those that will not serve God if the devil bid you. [I. i. 108]

20 Your daughter and the Moor are now making the beast with two backs. [I. i. (117)]

21 Fathers, from hence trust not your daughter's minds / By what you see them act. [I. i. (171)]

22 Keep up your bright swords, for the dew will rust them. [I. ii. 59]

23 The wealthy curlèd darlings of our nation. [I. ii. 68]

24 Most potent, grave, and reverend signiors / My very noble and approved good masters. [I. iii. 76]

25 The very head and front of my offending / Hath this extent, no more. [I. iii. 80]

26 Rude am I in my speech, / And little blessed with the soft phrase of peace, / For since these arms of mine had seven years' pith, / Till now some nine moons wasted, they have used / Their dearest action in the tented field. [I. iii. 81]

27 I will a round unvarnished tale deliver / Of my whole course of love. [I. iii. 90]

28 A maiden never bold; / Of spirit so still and quiet, that her motion / Blushed at herself. [I. iii. 94]

29 Wherein I spake of most disastrous chances, / Of moving accidents by flood and field, / Of hair-breadth 'scapes i' the imminent deadly breach. [I. iii. 134]

30 Antres vast and desarts idle, / Rough quarries, rocks, and hills whose heads touch heaven. [I. iii. 140]

31 The Cannibals that each other eat, / The Anthropophagi, and men whose heads / Do grow beneath their shoulders. [I. iii. 143]

32 My story being done, / She gave me for my pains a world of sighs: / She swore, in faith, 'twas strange, 'twas passing strange; / 'Twas pitiful, 'twas wondrous pitiful: / She wished she had not heard it, yet she wished / That heaven had made her such a man; she thanked me, / And bade me, if I had a friend that loved her, / I should but teach him how to tell my story, / And that would woo her. Upon this hint I spake: / She loved me for the dangers I had passed, / And I loved her that she did pity them. / This only is the witchcraft I have used. [I. iii. 158]

33 To mourn a mischief that is past and gone, / Is the next way to draw new mischief on. [I. iii. 204]

34 The robbed that smiles steals something from the thief. [I. iii. 208]

1 Virtue! a fig! 'tis in ourselves that we are thus, or thus. [I. iii. (323)]

2 Put money in thy purse. [I. iii. (345)]

3 The food that to him now is as luscious as locusts shall be to him shortly as bitter as coloquintida. [I. iii. (354)]

4 Framed to make women false. [I. iii. (404)]

5 Do not put me to 't, / For I am nothing if not critical. [II. i. 118]

6 She never yet was foolish that was fair. [II. i. 136]

7 To suckle fools and chronicle small beer. [II. i. 160]

8 O most lame and impotent conclusion! [II. i. 161]

9 Egregiously an ass. [II. i. (321)]

10 I have very poor and unhappy brains for drinking. [II. iii. (34)]

11 Potations pottle-deep. [II. iii. (57)]

12 And let me the canakin clink: / A soldier's a man; / A life's but a span; / Why then let a soldier drink. [II. iii. (73)]

13 Silence the dreadful bell! it frights the isle / From her propriety. [II. iii. (177)]

14 But men are men; the best sometimes forget. [II. iii. (243)]

15 Thy honesty and love doth mince this matter. [II. iii. (249)]

16 Cassio, I love thee; / But never more be officer of mine. [II. iii. (250)]

17 Reputation, reputation, reputation! O! I have lost my reputation, I have lost the immortal part of myself, and what remains is bestial. [II. iii. (264)]

18 O God! that men should put an enemy in their mouths to steal away their brains. [II. iii. (293)]

19 Good wine is a good familiar creature if it be well used. [II. iii. (315)]

20 How poor are they that have not patience! / What wound did ever heal but by degrees? [III. ii. (379)]

21 Excellent wretch! Perdition catch my soul / But I do love thee! and when I love thee not, / Chaos is come again. [III. iii. 90]

22 Men should be what they seem. [III. iii. 126]

23 Good name in man and woman, dear my lord, / Is the immediate jewel of their souls; / Who steals my purse, steals trash; 'tis something, nothing; / 'Twas mine, 'tis his and has been slave to thousands; / But he that filches from me my good name / Robs me of that which not enriches him, / And makes me poor indeed. [III. iii. 153]

24 O! beware, my lord, of jealousy; / It is the green-eyed monster which doth mock / The meat it feeds on. [III. iii. 165]

25 If I do prove her haggard, / Though that her jesses were my dear heart-strings, / I'd whistle her off and let her down the wind, / To prey at fortune. [III. iii. 260]

26 For I am declined / Into the vale of years. [III. iii. 265]

27 O curse of marriage! / That we can call these delicate creatures ours, / And not their appetities. I had rather be a toad, / And live upon the vapour of a dungeon, / Than keep a corner in the thing I love / For others' uses. [III. iii. 268]

28 Trifles light as air / Are to the jealous confirmations strong / As proofs of holy writ. [III. iii. 323]

29 Not poppy, nor mandragora, / Nor all the drowsy syrups of the world, / Shall ever medicine thee to that sweet sleep / Which thou owedst yesterday. [III. iii. 331]

30 He that is robbed, not wanting what is stolen, / Let him not know't and he's not robbed at all. [III. iii. 343]

31 O! now for ever / Farewell the tranquil mind; farewell content! / Farewell the plumèd troop and the big wars / That make ambition virtue! O farewell! / Farewell the neighing steed and the shrill trump, / The spirit-stirring drum, the ear-piercing fife, / The royal banner, and all quality, / Pride, pomp, and circumstance of glorious war! [III. iii. 348]

32 Be sure of it; give me the ocular proof. [III. iii. 361]

33 On horror's head horrors accumulate. [III. iii. 371]

34 Take note, take note, O world! / To be direct and honest is not safe. [III. iii. 378]

35 But this denoted a foregone conclusion. [III. iii. 429]

36 Like to the Pontic sea, / Whose icy current and compulsive course / Ne'er feels

retiring ebb, but keeps due on / To the Propontic and the Hellespont, / Even so my bloody thoughts, with violent pace, / Shall ne'er look back, ne'er ebb to humble love, / Till that a capable and wide revenge / Swallow them up. [III. iii. 454]

1 They are not ever jealous for the cause, / But jealous for they are jealous. [III. iv. (159)]

2 I would have him nine years a-killing. (IV. i. (186))

3 But yet the pity of it. Iago! [IV. i. (205)]

4 Alas! to make me / The fixèd figure for the time of scorn / To point his slow and moving finger at. [IV. ii. 52]

5 O thou weed! / Who art so lovely fair and smell'st so sweet / That the sense aches at thee, would thou hadst ne'er been born. [IV. ii. 66]

6 O heaven! that such companions thou'dst unfold, / And put in every honest hand a whip / To lash the rascals naked through the world! [IV. ii. 141]

7 The poor soul sat sighing by a sycamore tree, / Sing all a green willow; / Her hand on her bosom, her head on her knee, / Sing willow, willow, willow. [IV. iii. (41)]

8 'Tis neither here nor there. [IV. iii. (59)]

9 He hath a daily beauty in his life / That makes me ugly. [V. i. 19]

10 This is the night / That either makes me or fordoes me quite. [V. i. 128]

11 It is the cause, it is the cause, my soul; / Let me not name it to you, you chaste stars! / It is the cause. Yet I'll not shed her blood, / Nor scar that whiter skin of hers than snow, / And smooth as monumental alabaster. [V. ii. 1]

12 Put out the light and then put out the light. / If I quench thee, thou flaming minister, / I can again thy former light restore, / Should I repent me; but once put out thy light, / Thou cunning'st pattern of excelling nature, / I know not where is that Promethean heat / That can thy light relume. [V. ii. 7]

13 Curse his better angel from his side, / And fall to reprobation. [V. ii. 206]

14 Here is my journey's end, here is my butt, / And very sea-mark of my utmost sail. [V. ii. 266]

15 O ill-starred wench! / Pale as thy smock! when we shall meet at compt, / This look of thine will hurl my soul from heaven, / And fiends will snatch at it. [V. ii. 271]

16 Soft you; a word or two before you go. / I have done the state some service and they know't; / No more of that: I pray you, in your letters, / When you shall these unlucky deeds relate, / Speak of me as I am; nothing extenuate, / Nor set down aught in malice: then must you speak / Of one that loved not wisely but too well; Of one not easily jealous, but, being wrought, / Perplexed in the extreme; of one whose hand, / Like the base Indian, threw a pearl away / Richer than all his tribe; of one whose subdued eyes / Albeit unusèd to the melting mood, / Drop tears as fast as the Arabian trees / Their med'cinable gum. Set you down this; / And say besides, that in Aleppo once, / Where a malignant and a turbaned Turk / Beat a Venetian and traduced the state, / I took by the throat the circumcisèd dog, / And smote him thus. [V. ii. 337]

17 I kissed thee ere I killed thee. [V. ii. 357]

Pericles

18 See, where she comes apparelled like the spring. [I. i. 12]

19 Few love to hear the sins they love to act. [I. i. 92]

20 3RD FISHERMAN: I marvel how the fishes live in the sea.
1ST FISHERMAN: Why, as men do a-land; the great ones eat up the little ones. [II. i. (29)]

21 A man whom both the waters and the wind, / In that vast tennis-court, have made the ball / For them to play upon. [II. i. (64)]

22 This world to me is like a lasting storm, / Whirring me from my friends. [IV. i. 19]

Richard II

23 Old John of Gaunt, time-honoured Lancaster. [I. i. 1]

24 A jewel in a ten-times-barred-up chest / Is a bold spirit in a loyal breast. / Mine honour is my life; both grow in one; / Take honour from me, and my life is done. [I. i. 180]

25 We were not born to sue, but to command. [I. i. 196]

1 The daintiest last to make the end most sweet. [I. iii. 68]

2 This must my comfort be, / That sun that warms you here shall shine on me. [I. iii. 144]

3 How long a time lies in one little word! [I. iii. 213]

4 Things sweet to taste prove in digestion sour. [I. iii. 236]

5 All places that the eye of heaven visits / Are to a wise man ports and happy havens. / Teach thy necessity to reason thus; / There is no virtue like necessity. [I. iii. 275]

6 O! who can hold a fire in his hand / By thinking on the frosty Caucasus? / Or cloy the hungry edge of appetite / By bare imagination of a feast? / Or wallow naked in December snow / By thinking on fantastic summer's heat? / O, no! the apprehension of the good / Gives but the greater feeling to the worse. [I. iii. 294]

7 Methinks I am a prophet new inspired, / And thus expiring to foretell of him: / His rash fierce blaze of riot cannot last, / For violent fires soon burn out themselves; / Small showers last long, but sudden storms are short; / He tires betimes that spurs too fast betimes. [II. i. 31]

8 This royal throne of kings, this sceptered isle, / This earth of majesty, this seat of Mars, / This other Eden, demi-paradise, / This fortress built by Nature for herself / Against infection and the hand of war, / This happy breed of men, this little world, / This precious stone set in the silver sea, / Which serves it in the office of a wall, / Or as a moat defensive to a house, / Against the envy of less happier lands, / This blessed plot, this earth, this realm, this England, / This nurse, this teeming womb of royal kings, / Feared by their breed and famous by their birth, / Renownèd for their deeds as far from home, – / For Christian service and true chivalry, – / As is the sepulchre in stubborn Jewry / Of the world's ransom, blessed Mary's Son: / This land of such dear souls, this dear, dear land. [II. i. 40]

9 England, bound in with the triumphant sea, / Whose rocky shore beats back the envious siege / Of watery Neptune, is now bound in with shame, / With inky blots, and rotten parchment bonds: / That England, that was wont to conquer others, / Hath made a shameful conquest of itself. [II. i. 61]

10 Can sick men play so nicely with their names? [II. i. 84]

11 I am a stranger here in Gloucestershire: / These high wild hills and rough uneven ways / Draw out our miles and make them wearisome. [II. iii. 3]

12 I count myself in nothing else so happy / As in a soul remembering my good friends. [II. iii. 46]

13 Evermore thanks, the exchequer of the poor. [II. iii. 65]

14 Grace me no grace, nor uncle me no uncle. [II. iii. 87]

15 The caterpillars of the commonwealth. [II. iii. 166]

16 Things past redress are now with me past care. [II. iii. 171]

17 Eating the bitter bread of banishment. [III. i. 21]

18 Not all the water in the rough rude sea / Can wash the balm from an anointed king; / The breath of worldly men cannot dispose / The deputy elected by the Lord. [III. ii. 54]

19 O! call back yesterday, bid time return. [III. ii. 69]

20 The worst is death, and death will have his day. [III. ii. 103]

21 Let's talk of graves, of worms and epitaphs; / Make dust our paper, and with rainy eyes / Write sorrow on the bosom of the earth; / Let's choose executors and talk of wills. [III. ii. 145]

22 For God's sake, let us sit upon the ground / And tell sad stories of the death of kings: / How some have been deposed, some slain in war, / Some haunted by the ghosts they have deposed; / Some poisoned by their wives, some sleeping killed; / All murdered: for within the hollow crown / That rounds the mortal temples of a king / Keeps Death his court, and there the antick sits, / Scoffing his state and grinning at his pomp; / Allowing him a breath, a little scene, / To monarchize, be feared, and killed with looks, / Infusing him with self and vain conceit / As if this flesh which walls about our life / Were brass impregnable; and humoured

thus / Comes at the last, and with a little pin / Bores through his castle-wall, and farewell king! [III. ii. 155]

1 The purple testament of bleeding war. [III. iii. 94]

2 What must the king do now? Must he submit? / The king shall do it: must he be deposed? / The king shall be contented: must he lose / The name of king? o' God's name, let it go: / I'll give my jewels for a set of beads, / My gorgeous palace for a hermitage, / My gay apparel for an almsman's gown, / My figured goblets for a dish of wood, / My sceptre for a palmer's walking staff, / My subjects for a pair of carvèd saints, / And my large kingdom for a little grave, / A little little grave, an obscure grave. [III. iii. 143]

3 Some pretty match with shedding tears? / As thus; to drop them still upon one place / Till they have fretted us a pair of graves. [III. iii. 165]

4 Go, bind thou up yon dangling apricocks. [III. iv. 29]

5 If I dare eat, or drink, or breathe, or live, / I dare meet Surrey in a wilderness, / And spit upon him, whilst I say he lies, / And lies, and lies. [IV. i. 73]

6 Gave / His body to that pleasant country's earth, / And his pure soul unto his captain Christ. [IV. i. 97]

7 Peace shall go sleep with Turks and infidels. [IV. i. 139]

8 God save the king! Will no man say, amen? [IV. i. 172]

9 You may my glories and my state depose, / But not my griefs; still am I king of those. [IV. i. 192]

10 With mine own tears I wash away my balm, / With mine own hands I give away my crown. [IV. i. 207]

11 A mockery king of snow. [IV. i. 260]

12 Julius Caesar's ill-erected tower. [V. i. 2]

13 I am sworn brother, sweet, / To grim Necessity, and he and I / Will keep a league till death. [V. i. 20]

14 As in a theatre, the eyes of men, / After a well-graced actor leaves the stage, / Are idly bent on him that enters next, / Thinking his prattle to be tedious. [V. ii. 23]

15 I have been studying how I may compare / The prison where I live unto the world. [V. v. 1]

16 How sour sweet music is / When time is broke and no proportion kept! / So is it in the music of men's lives. [V. v. 42]

17 Mount, mount, my soul! thy seat is up on high, / Whilst my gross flesh sinks downward, here to die. [V. v. 112]

Richard III

18 Now is the winter of our discontent / Made glorious summer by this sun of York. [I. i. 1]

19 Our stern alarums changed to merry meetings; / Our dreadful marches to delightful measures. [I. i. 7]

20 He capers nimbly to a lady's chamber / To the lascivious pleasing of a lute. [I. i. 12]

21 Deformed, unfinished, sent before my time / Into this breathing world, scarce half made up, / And that so lamely and unfashionable / That dogs bark at me as I halt by them. [I. i. 20]

22 In this weak piping time of peace. [I. i. 24]

23 I am determinèd to prove a villain. [I. i. 30]

24 No beast so fierce but knows some touch of pity. [I. ii. 71]

25 Was ever woman in this humour wooed? / Was ever woman in this humour won? [I. ii. 229]

26 Since every Jack became a gentleman / There's many a gentle person made a Jack. [I. iii. 72]

27 And thus I clothe my naked villany / With odd old ends stol'n forth of holy writ, / And seem a saint when most I play the devil. [I. iii. 336]

28 O, I have passed a miserable night, / So full of ugly sights, of ghastly dreams, / That, as I am a Christian faithful man, / I would not spend another such a night, / Though 'twere to buy a world of happy days, / So full of dismal terror was the time! [I. iv. 2]

29 Lord, Lord! methought what pain it was to drown: / What dreadful noise of water in mine ears! / What sights of ugly death within mine eyes! Methought

I saw a thousand fearful wracks; / A thousand men that fishes gnawed upon; / Wedges of gold, great anchors, heaps of pearl, / Inestimable stones, unvalued jewels, / All scattered in the bottom of the sea. / Some lay in dead men's skulls, and in those holes / Where eyes did once inhabit, there were crept, / As 'twere in scorn of eyes, reflecting gems, / That wooed the slimy bottom of the deep, / And mocked the dead bones that lay scattered by. [I. iv. 21]

1 I do not know that Englishman alive / With whom my soul is any jot at odds / More than the infant that is born tonight: / I thank my God for my humility. [II. i. 70]

2 So wise so young, they say, do never live long. [III. i. 79]

3 My Lord of Ely, when I was last in Holborn, / I saw good strawberries in your garden there. [III. iv. 31]

4 Thou art a traitor: / Off with his head! [III. iv. 74]

5 Cousin, thou wast not wont to be so dull: / Shall I be plain? I wish the bastards dead. [IV. ii. 17]

6 High-reaching Buckingham grows circumspect. [IV. ii. 31]

7 I am not in the giving vein today. [IV. ii. 115]

8 Their lips were four red roses on a stalk, / Which in their summer beauty kissed each other. [IV. iii. 12]

9 The sons of Edward sleep in Abraham's bosom. [IV. iii. 38]

10 Let not the heavens hear these tell-tale women / Rail on the Lord's anointed. [IV. iv. 150]

11 An honest tale speeds best being plainly told. [IV. iv. 359]

12 Harp not on that string. [IV. iv. 365]

13 Is the chair empty? is the sword unswayed? / Is the king dead? the empire unpossessed? [IV. iv. 470]

14 True hope is swift, and flies with swallow's wings; / Kings it makes gods, and meaner creatures kings. [V. ii. 23]

15 The king's name is a tower of strength. [V. iii. 12]

16 I have not that alacrity of spirit, / Nor cheer of mind, that I was wont to have. [V. iii. 73]

17 Give me another horse! bind up my wounds! / Have mercy, Jesu! Soft! I did but dream. / O coward conscience, how dost thou afflict me! [V. iii. 178]

18 My conscience hath a thousand several tongues, / And every tongue brings in a several tale, / And every tale condemns me for a villain. [V. iii. 194]

19 A horse! a horse! my kingdom for a horse! [V. iv. 7]

Romeo and Juliet

20 A pair of star-crossed lovers. [Prologue, 6]

21 The two hours' traffic of our stage. [Ib. 12]

22 No, sir, I do not bite my thumb at you, sir; but I bite my thumb, sir. [I. i. (56)]

23 Remember thy swashing blow. [I. i. (68)]

24 Saint-seducing gold. [I. i. (220)]

25 When well-apparelled April on the heel / Of limping Winter treads. [I. ii. 27]

26 Pretty fool, it stinted and said 'Ay'. [I. iii. 48]

27 Thou wilt fall backward when thou comest to age. [I. iii. 56]

28 I am proverbed with a grandsire phrase. [I. iv. 37]

29 O! then, I see, Queen Mab hath been with you. . . . / She is the fairies' midwife, and she comes / In shape no bigger than an agate-stone / On the fore-finger of an alderman, / Drawn with a team of little atomies / Athwart men's noses as they lie asleep: / Her waggon-spokes made of long spinners' legs; / The cover, of the wings of grasshoppers; / The traces, of the smallest spider's web; / The collars, of the moonshine's watery beams; / Her whip, of cricket's bone; the lash, of film; / Her waggoner, a small grey-coated gnat, / Not half so big as a round little worm / Pricked from the lazy finger of a maid; / Her chariot is an empty hazel-nut, / Made by the joiner squirrel or old grub, / Time out o' mind the fairies' coach-makers, / And in this state she gallops night by night / Through lovers' brains, and then they dream of love; / O'er courtiers' knees, that dream on curtsies straight; / O'er lawyers' fingers, who straight dream on fees; / O'er ladies lips, who straight on kisses dream. [I. iv. 53]

1 Sometimes she gallops o'er a courtier's nose, / And then dreams he of smelling out a suit; / And sometimes comes she with a tithe-pig's tail, / Tickling a parson's nose as a' lies asleep, / Then dreams he of another benefice; / Sometimes she driveth o'er a soldier's neck, / And then dreams he of cutting foreign throats. [I. iv. 78]

2 This is that very Mab / That plats the manes of horses in the night; / And bakes the elf-locks in foul sluttish hairs, / Which once untangled much misfortune bodes. [I. iv. 89]

3 For you and I are past our dancing days. [I. v. (35)]

4 O! she doth teach the torches to burn bright. / It seems she hangs upon the cheek of night / Like a rich jewel in an Ethiop's ear. [I. v. (48)]

5 We have a trifling foolish banquet towards. [I. v. (126)]

6 My only love sprung from my only hate! [I. v. (142)]

7 Young Adam Cupid, he that shot so trim /When King Cophetua loved the beggar-maid. [II. i. 13]

8 He jests at scars, that never felt a wound. /But, soft! what light through yonder window breaks? / It is the east, and Juliet is the sun. [II. ii. 1]

9 See! how she leans her cheek upon her hand: / O! that I were a glove upon that hand, / That I might touch that cheek. [II. ii. 23]

10 O Romeo, Romeo! wherefore art thou Romeo? [II. ii. 33]

11 What's in a name? that which we call a rose / By any other name would smell as sweet. [II. ii. 43]

12 For stony limits cannot hold love out. [II. ii. 67]

13 At lovers' perjuries, / They say, Jove laughs. [II. ii. 92]

14 I'll prove more true / Than those that have more cunning to be strange. [II. ii. 100]

15 O! swear not by the moon, the inconstant moon, / That monthly changes in her circled orb, / Lest that thy love prove likewise variable. [II. ii. 109]

16 The God of my idolatry. [II. ii. 114]

17 It is too rash, too unadvised, too sudden; / Too like the lightning, which doth cease to be / Ere one can say it lightens. [II. ii. 118]

18 Love goes toward love, as schoolboys from their books; / But love from love, toward school with heavy looks. [II. ii. 156]

19 How silver-sweet sound lovers' tongues by night, / Like softest music to attending ears! [II. ii. 165]

20 I would have thee gone; / And yet no further than a wanton's bird, / Who lets it hop a little from her hand, / Like a poor prisoner in his twisted gyves, / And with a silk thread plucks it back again, / So loving-jealous of his liberty. [II. ii. 176]

21 Good-night, good-night! parting is such sweet sorrow / That I shall say good-night till it be morrow. [II. ii. 184]

22 Virtue itself turns vice, being misapplied; / And vice sometime's by action dignified. [II. iii. 21]

23 Wisely and slow; they stumble that run fast. [II. iii, 94]

24 O flesh, flesh, how art thou fishified! [II. iv. (41)]

25 I am the very pink of courtesy. [II. iv. (63)]

26 A gentleman, nurse, that loves to hear himself talk, and will speak more in a minute than he will stand to in a month. [II. iv. (156)]

27 These violent delights have violent ends. [II. vi. 9]

28 Too swift arrives as tardy as too slow. [II. vi. 15]

29 O! so light of foot / Will ne'er wear out the everlasting flint. [II. vi. 16]

30 Thy head is as full of quarrels as an egg is full of meat. [III. i. (23)]

31 A word and a blow. [III. i. (43)]

32 No, 'tis not so deep as a well, nor so wide as a church door; but 'tis enough, 'twill serve. [III. i. (101)]

33 A plague o' both your houses! / They have made worms' meat of me. [III. i. (112)]

34 O! I am Fortune's fool. [III. i. (142)]

35 Gallop apace, you fiery-footed steeds, / Towards Phoebus' lodging. [III. ii. 1]

1 Come, civil night, / Thou sober-suited matron, all in black. [III. ii. 10]

2 When he shall die, / Take him and cut him out in little stars, / And he will make the face of heaven so fine / That all the world will be in love with night, / And pay no worship to the garish sun. [III. ii. 21]

3 Thou art wedded to calamity. [III. iii. 3]

4 Adversity's sweet milk, philosophy. [III. iii. 54]

5 It was the nightingale, and not the lark, / That pierced the fearful hollow of thine ear; / Nightly she sings on yon pomegranate tree. [III. v. 2]

6 Night's candles are burnt out, and jocund day / Stands tiptoe on the misty mountain tops. [III. v. 9]

7 Villain and he be many miles asunder. [III. v. 82]

8 'Tis an ill cook that cannot lick his own fingers. [IV. ii. (6)]

9 My poverty, but not my will, consents. [V. i. 75]

10 The time and my intents are savage-wild, / More fierce and more inexorable far / Than empty tigers or the roaring sea. [V. iii. 37]

11 Tempt not a desperate man. [V. iii. 59]

12 How oft when men are at the point of death / Have they been merry! [V. iii. 88]

13 Beauty's ensign yet / Is crimson in thy lips and in thy cheeks, / And death's pale flag is not advancèd there. [V. iii. 94]

14 O! here / Will I set up my everlasting rest, / And shake the yoke of inauspicious stars / From this world-wearied flesh. Eyes look your last! / Arms, take your last embrace! [V. iii. 109]

The Taming of the Shrew

15 Look in the chronicles; we came in with Richard Conqueror. [Induction, i. (4)]

16 Twenty more such names and men as these, / Which never were, nor no man ever saw. [Ib. ii. (97)]

17 No profit grows where is no pleasure ta'en; / In brief, sir, study what you most affect. [I. i. 39]

18 There's small choice in rotten apples. [I. i. (137)]

19 Love in idleness. [I. i. (155)]

20 Nothing comes amiss, so money comes withal. [I. ii. (82)]

21 I must dance bare-foot on her wedding day, / And, for your love to her, lead apes in hell. [II. i. 33]

22 Kiss me, Kate. [II. i. 318]

23 This is the way to kill a wife with kindness. [IV. i. (211)]

24 And as the sun breaks through the darkest clouds, / So honour peereth in the meanest habit. [IV. iii. (175)]

25 O vile, / Intolerable, not to be endured! [V. ii. 93]

26 A woman moved is like a fountain troubled, / Muddy, ill-seeming, thick, bereft of beauty. [V. ii. 143]

27 Such duty as the subject owes the prince, / Even such a woman oweth to her husband. [V. ii. 156]

The Tempest

28 He hath no drowning mark upon him; his complexion is perfect gallows. [I. i. (33)]

29 What seest thou else / In the dark backward and abysm of time? [I. ii. 49]

30 Your tale, sir, would cure deafness. [I. ii. 106]

31 My library / Was dukedom large enough. [I. ii. 109]

32 A rotten carcass of a boat, not rigged, / Nor tackle, sail, nor mast; the very rats / Instinctively have quit it. [I. ii. 146]

33 Knowing I loved my books, he furnished me, / From mine own library with volumes that / I prize above my dukedom. [I. ii. 166]

34 From the still-vexed Bermoothes. [I. ii. 229]

35 I will be correspondent to command, / And do my spiriting gently. [I. ii. 297]

36 You taught me language; and my profit on't / Is, I know how to curse; the red plague rid you, / For learning me your language! [I. ii. 363]

37 Come unto these yellow sands, / And then take hands; / Curtsied when you have, and kissed, – / The wild waves whist. [I. ii. 375]

1 Full fathom five thy father lies; / Of his bones are coral made: / Those are pearls that were his eyes: / Nothing of him that doth fade, / But doth suffer a sea-change / Into something rich and strange. [I. ii. 394]

2 The fringèd curtains of thine eye advance, / And say what thou seest yond. [I. ii. 405]

3 He receives comfort like cold porridge. [II. i. (10)]

4 They'll take suggestion as a cat laps milk. [II. i. (296)]

5 Open-eyed conspiracy / His time doth take. [II. i. (309)]

6 A very ancient and fish-like smell. [II. ii. (27)]

7 Misery acquaints a man with strange bedfellows. [II. ii. (42)]

8 Well, here's my comfort. (*Drinks.*) [II. ii. (48)]

9 The master, the swabber, the boatswain and I, / The gunner and his mate, / Loved Mall, Meg and Marian and Margery, / But none of us cared for Kate; / For she had a tongue with a tang, / Would cry to a sailor 'Go hang!' [II. ii. (49)]

10 'Ban, 'Ban, Ca-Caliban, / Has a new master – Get a new man. [II. ii. (197)]

11 For several virtues / Have I liked several women. [III. i. 42]

12 FERDINAND: Here's my hand.
MIRANDA: And mine with my heart in't. [III. i. 89]

13 Thou deboshed fish thou. [III. ii. (30)]

14 Flout 'em, and scout 'em; and scout 'em, and flout 'em; / Thought is free. [III. ii. (133)]

15 He that dies pays all debts. [III. ii. (143)]

16 Be not afeard: the isle is full of noises, / Sounds and sweet airs, that give delight and hurt not. [III. ii. (147)]

17 You sun-burned sicklemen, of August weary. [IV. i. 134]

18 Our revels now are ended. These our actors, / As I foretold you, were all spirits and / Are melted into air, into thin air: / And, like the baseless fabric of this vision, / The cloud-capped towers, the gorgeous palaces, / The solemn temples, the great globe itself, / Yea, all which it inherit, shall dissolve / And, like this insubstantial pageant faded, / Leave not a rack behind. We are such stuff / As dreams are made on, and our little life / Is rounded with a sleep. [IV. i. 148]

19 I do begin to have bloody thoughts. [IV. i. (221)]

20 With foreheads villanous low. [IV. i. (252)]

21 Now does my object gather to a head. [V. i. 1]

22 The rarer action is / In virtue than in vengeance. [V. i. 27]

23 Ye elves of hills, brooks, standing lakes and groves; / And ye, that on the sands with printless foot / Do chase the ebbing Neptune and do fly him / When he comes back. [V. i. 33]

24 I'll break my staff, / Bury it certain fathoms in the earth, / And, deeper than did ever plummet sound, / I'll drown my book. [V. i. 54]

25 Where the bee sucks, there suck I: / In a cowslip's bell I lie; / There I couch when owls do cry. / On the bat's back I do fly / After summer merrily: / Merrily, merrily shall I live now / Under the blossom that hangs on the bough. [V. i. 88]

26 How beauteous mankind is! O brave new world, / That has such people in't! [V. i. 183]

27 How camest thou in this pickle? [V. i. (281)]

28 Retire me to my Milan, where / Every third thought shall be my grave. [V. i. (310)]

Timon of Athens

29 Our poesy is as a gum, which oozes / From whence 'tis nourished. [I. i. 21]

30 'Tis not enough to help the feeble up, / But to support him after. [I. i. 108]

31 I wonder men dare trust themselves with men. [I. ii. (45)]

32 Men shut their doors against a setting sun. [I. ii. (152)]

33 We have seen better days. [IV. ii. 27]

34 Timon hath made his everlasting mansion / Upon the beachèd verge of the salt flood, / Who once a day with his embossèd froth / The turbulent surge shall cover. [V. i. (220)]

Titus Andronicus

1 He lives in fame that died in virtue's cause. [I. i. 390]

2 She is a woman, therefore may be wooed; / She is a woman, therefore may be won, / She is Lavinia, therefore must be loved. / What, man! more water glideth by the mill / Than wots the miller of; and easy it is / Of a cut loaf to steal a shive, we know. [II. i. 82]

3 Come, and take choice of all my library, / And so beguile thy sorrow. [IV. i. 34]

4 The eagle suffers little birds to sing, / And is not careful what they mean thereby. [IV. iv. (82)]

5 If one good deed in all my life I did, / I do repent it from my very soul. [V. iii. 189]

Troilus and Cressida

6 I have had my labour for my travail. [I. i. (73)]

7 She's a merry Greek indeed. [I. ii. (116)]

8 Women are angels, wooing: / Things won are done; joy's soul lies in the doing: / That she beloved knows nought that knows not this: / Men prize the thing ungained more than it is. [I. ii. (310)]

9 The heavens themselves, the planets, and this centre / Observe degree, priority, and place, / Insisture, course, proportion, season, form, / Office, and custom, in all line of order. [I. iii. 85]

10 Take but degree away, untune that string / And hark what discord follows; each, thing meets / In mere oppugnancy. [I. iii. 109]

11 An envious fever / Of pale and bloodless emulation. [I. iii. 133]

12 To hear the wooden dialogue. [I. iii. 155]

13 The baby figure of the giant mass / Of things to come at large. [I. iii. 345]

14 'Tis mad idolatry / To make the service greater than the god. [II. ii. 56]

15 Thus to persist / In doing wrong extenuates not wrong, / But makes it much more heavy. [II. ii. 186]

16 That little little less than little wit. [II. iii. (14)]

17 I am giddy, expectation whirls me round. / The imaginary relish is so sweet / That it enchants my sense. [III. ii. (17)]

18 This is the monstruosity in love, lady, that the will is infinite and the execution confined. [III. ii. (85)]

19 To be wise, and love, / Exceeds man's might. [III. ii. (163)]

20 Let all pitiful goers-between be called to the world's end after my name; call them all Pandars. [III. ii. (208)]

21 Time hath, my lord, a wallet at his back, / Wherein he puts alms for oblivion, / A great-sized monster of ingratitudes: / Those scraps are good deeds past: which are devoured / As fast as they are made, forgot as soon / As done. [III. iii. 145]

22 Perseverance, dear my lord, / Keeps honour bright: to have done, is to hang / Quite out of fashion, like a rusty mail / In monumental mockery. [III. iii. 150]

23 Time is like a fashionable host / That slightly shakes his parting guest by the hand, / And with his arms outstretched, as he would fly, / Grasps in the comer: welcome ever smiles, / And farewell goes out sighing. [III. iii. 165]

24 Envious and calumniating time. [III. iii. 174]

25 One touch of nature makes the whole world kin. [III. iii. 175]

26 And give to dust that is a little gilt / More laud than gilt o'er-dusted. [III. iii. 178]

27 My mind is troubled, like a fountain stirred; / And I myself see not the bottom of it. [III. iii. (314)]

28 There's language in her eye, her cheek, her lip, / Nay, her foot speaks, her wanton spirits look out / At every joint and motive of her body. [IV. v. 55]

29 The end crowns all, / And that old common arbitrator, Time, / Will one day end it. [IV. v. 223]

30 Lechery, lechery; still, wars and lechery; nothing else holds fashion. [V. ii. (192)]

31 Words, words, mere words, no matter from the heart. [V. iii. (109)]

Twelfth Night

32 If music be the food of love, play on; / Give me excess of it, that, surfeiting, / The appetite may sicken, and so die. / That strain again! it had a dying fall: / O! it came o'er my ear like the sweet

sound / That breathes upon a bank of violets, / Stealing and giving odour! [I. i. 1]

1 O spirit of love! how quick and fresh art thou, / That notwithstanding thy capacity / Receiveth as the sea, nought enters there, / Of what validity and pitch soe'er, / But falls into abatement and low price, / Even in a minute: so full of shapes is fancy, / That it alone is high fantastical. [I. i. 9]

2 I am sure care's an enemy to life. [I. iii. (2)]

3 Speaks three or four languages word for word without book. [I. iii. (28)]

4 Methinks sometimes I have no more wit than a Christian or an ordinary man has; but I am a great eater of beef, and I believe that does harm to my wit. [I. iii. (90)]

5 Wherefore are these things hid? [I. iii. (135)]

6 Is it a world to hide virtues in? [I. iii. (142)]

7 Many a good hanging prevents a bad marriage. [I. v. (20)]

8 Good my mouse of virtue, answer me. [I. v. (68)]

9 A plague o' these pickle herring! [I. v. (127)]

10 One would think his mother's milk were scarce out of him. [I. v. (171)]

11 Lady, you are the cruell'st she alive. [I. v. (260)]

12 *Item*, Two lips, indifferent red; *Item*, Two grey eyes with lids to them; *Item*, One neck, one chin, and so forth. [I. v. (268)]

13 Make me a willow cabin at your gate, / And call upon my soul within the house; / Write loyal cantons of contemnèd love, / And sing them loud even in the dead of night; / Holla your name to the reverberate hills, / And make the babbling gossip of the air / Cry out, 'Olivia'. [I. v. (289)]

14 Farewell, fair cruelty. [I. v. (309)]

15 Not to be a-bed after midnight is to be up betimes. [II. iii. 1]

16 O mistress mine! where are you roaming? / O! stay and hear; your true love's coming, / That can sing both high and low. / Trip no further, pretty sweeting; /

Journeys end in lovers meeting, / Every wise man's son doth know. [II. iii. (42)]

17 In delay there lies no plenty; / Then come kiss me, sweet and twenty, / Youth's a stuff will not endure. [II. iii. (53)]

18 He does it with a better grace, but I do it more natural. [II. iii. (91)]

19 Is there no respect of place, persons, nor time in you? [II. iii. (100)]

20 SIR TOBY: Dost thou think, because thou art virtuous, there shall be no more cakes and ale? CLOWN: Yes by Saint Anne; and ginger shall be hot i' the mouth too. [II. iii. (124)]

21 My purpose is, indeed, a horse of that colour. [II. iii. (184)]

22 I was adored once too. [II. iii. (200)]

23 It gives a very echo to the seat / Where Love is throned. [II. iv. 21]

24 Let still the woman take / An elder than herself, so wears she to him, / So sways she level in her husband's heart: / For, boy, however we do praise ourselves, / Our fancies are more giddy and unfirm, / More longing, wavering, sooner lost and worn, / Than women's are. [II. iv. 29]

25 Then let thy love be younger than thyself, / Or thy affection cannot hold the bent. [II. iv. 36]

26 The spinsters and the knitters in the sun, / And the free maids that weave their thread with bones, / Do use to chant it: it is silly sooth, / And dallies with the innocence of love, / Like the old age. [II. iv. 44]

27 Come away, come away, death, / And in sad cypress let me be laid; / Fly away, fly away, breath: / I am slain by a fair cruel maid. / My shroud of white, stuck all with yew, / O! prepare it: / My part of death, no one so true / Did share it. [II. iv. 51]

28 DUKE: And what's her history? VIOLA: A blank, my lord. She never told her love, / But let concealment like a worm i' the bud, / Feed on her damask cheek: she pined in thought, / And with a green and yellow melancholy, / She sat like Patience on a monument, / Smiling at grief. [II. iv. (111)]

29 I am all the daughters of my father's house, / And all the brothers too. [II. iv. (122)]

1 Be not afraid of greatness: some men are born great, some achieve greatness, and some have greatness thrust upon them. [II. v. (158)]

2 Remember who commended thy yellow stockings, and wished to see thee ever cross-gartered. [II. v. (168)]

3 O world! how apt the poor are to be proud. [III. i. (141)]

4 O! what a deal of scorn looks beautiful / In the contempt and anger of his lip. [III. i. (159)]

5 Love sought is good, but giv'n unsought is better. [III. i. (170)]

6 You will hang like an icicle on a Dutchman's beard. [III. ii. (30)]

7 Let there be gall enough in thy ink, though thou write with a goose-pen, no matter. [III. ii. (54)]

8 I think we do know the sweet Roman hand. [III. iv. (31)]

9 Why this is very midsummer madness. [III. iv. (62)]

10 If this were played upon a stage now, / I could condemn it as an improbable fiction. [III. iv. (142)]

11 More matter for a May morning. [III. iv. (158)]

12 Still you keep o' the windy side of the law. [III. iv. (183)]

13 Out of my lean and low ability I'll lend you something. [III. iv. (380)]

14 I hate ingratitude more in a man / Than lying, vainness, babbling drunkenness, / Or any taint of vice whose strong corruption / Inhabits our frail blood. [III. iv. (390)]

15 CLOWN: What is the opinion of Pythagoras concerning wild fowl? MALVOLIO: That the soul of our grandam might haply inhabit a bird. [IV. ii. (55)]

16 Leave thy vain bibble-babble. [IV. ii. (106)]

17 And thus the whirligig of time brings in his revenges. [V. i. (388)]

18 When that I was and a little tiny boy, / With hey, ho, the wind and the rain; / A foolish thing was but a toy, / For the rain it raineth every day. [V. i. (401)]

19 A great while ago the world begun, / With hey, ho, the wind and the rain; /

But that's all one, our play is done, / And we'll strive to please you every day. [V. i. (417)]

The Two Gentlemen of Verona

20 Home-keeping youth have ever homely wits. [I. i. 2]

21 I have no other but a woman's reason: / I think him so, because I think him so. [I. ii. 23]

22 How wayward is this foolish love / That, like a testy babe, will scratch the nurse / And presently all humbled kiss the rod! [I. ii. 55]

23 O! how this spring of love resembleth / The uncertain glory of an April day. [I. iii. 84]

24 He makes sweet music with th' enamelled stones, / Giving a gentle kiss to every sedge / He overtaketh in his pilgrimage. [II. vii. 28]

25 Except I be by Silvia in the night, / There is no music in the nightingale; / Unless I look on Silvia in the day, / There is no day for me to look upon. [III. i. 178]

26 Much is the force of heaven-bred poesy. [III. ii. 72]

27 Who is Silvia? What is she, / That all our swains commend her? [IV. ii. (40)]

28 How use doth breed a habit in a man! [V. iv. 1]

29 O heaven! were man / But constant, he were perfect. [V, iv. 110]

The Winter's Tale

30 Two lads that thought there was no more behind / But such a day tomorrow as today, / And to be boy eternal. [I. ii. 63]

31 We were as twinned lambs that did frisk i' the sun, / And bleat the one at the other: what we changed / Was innocence for innocence: we knew not / The doctrine of ill-doing, no, nor dreamed / That any did. [I. ii. 67]

32 Paddling palms and pinching fingers. [I. ii. 116]

33 A sad tale's best for winter. / I have one of sprites and goblins. [II. i. 24]

34 The silence often of pure innocence / Persuades when speaking fails. [II. ii. 41]

35 I am a feather for each wind that blows. [II. iii. 153]

1 What's gone and what's past help /
Should be past grief. [III. ii. (223)]

2 *Exit, pursued by a bear.* [III. iii. 57, stage
direction]

3 I would there were no age between ten and
three-and-twenty, or that youth would sleep
out the rest; for there is nothing in the
between but getting wenches with child,
wronging the ancientry, stealing, fighting.
[III. iii. 58]

4 This is fairy gold. [III. iii. (127)]

5 When daffodils begin to peer, / With
heigh! the doxy, over the dale, / Why, then
comes in the sweet o' the year; / For the
red blood reigns in the winter's pale. [IV.
ii. 1]

6 Set my pugging tooth on edge; / For a
quart of ale is a dish for a king. [IV. ii. 7]

7 Summer songs for me and my aunts, /
While we lie tumbling in the hay. [IV. ii.
11]

8 A snapper-up of unconsidered trifles. [IV.
ii. (26)]

9 For the life to come, I sleep out the
thought of it. [IV. ii. (30)]

10 Jog on, jog on, the foot-path way, / And
merrily hent the stile-a: / A merry heart
goes all the day, / Your sad tires in a
mile-a. [IV. ii. (133)]

11 For you there's rosemary and rue, these
keep / Seeming and savour all the winter
long. [IV. iii. 74]

12 Here's flowers for you; / Hot lavender,
mints, savory, marjoram; / The marigold,
that goes to bed wi' the sun, / And with
him rises weeping. [IV. iii. 103]

13 O Proserpina! / For the flowers now
that frighted thou let'st fall / From Dis's
waggon! daffodils, / That come before
the swallow dares, and take / The winds
of March with beauty; violets dim, / But
sweeter than the lids of Juno's eyes / Or
Cytherea's breath; pale primroses, / That
die unmarried ere they can behold /
Bright Phoebus in his strength – a malady
/ Most incident to maids; bold oxlips
and / The crown imperial; lilies of all
kinds, / The flower-de-luce being one.
[IV. iii. 116]

14 What you do / Still betters what is done.
When you speak sweet, / I'd have you do
it ever: when you sing, / I'd have you
buy and sell so; so give alms; / Pray so;

and, for the ordering your affairs, / To
sing them too: when you do dance I wish
you / A wave o' the sea; that you might
ever do / Nothing but that; move still,
still so, / And own no other function.
[IV. iii. 136]

15 Good sooth, she is / The queen of curds
and cream. [IV. iii. 160]

16 Lawn as white as driven snow. [IV. iii.
(220)]

17 The self-same sun that shines upon his
court / Hides not his visage from our
cottage, but / Looks on alike. [IV. iii.
(457)]

18 I'll queen it no inch further, / But milk
my ewes and weep. [IV. iii. (462)]

19 Though I am not naturally honest, / I am
so sometimes by chance. [IV. iii. (734)]

20 Let me have no lying: it becomes none
but tradesmen. [IV. iii. (747)]

Poems

21 Crabbed age and youth cannot live
together: / Youth is full of pleasance,
age is full of care. [*The Passionate Pilgrim,*
xii]

22 Age, I do abhor thee, youth, I do adore
thee. [*Ib.*]

23 Beauty itself doth of itself persuade / The
eyes of men without an orator. [*The Rape
of Lucrece,* 29]

24 For greatest scandal waits on greatest
state. [*Ib.* 1006]

25 Cloud-kissing Ilion. [*Ib.* 1370]

26 And now this pale swan in her watery
nest / Begins the sad dirge of her certain
ending. [*Ib.* 1611]

27 To the only begetter of these insuing
sonnets. [*Sonnets,* Dedication]

28 From fairest creatures we desire increase,
/ That thereby beauty's rose might never
die. [*Ib.* 1]

29 When forty winters shall besiege thy
brow, / And dig deep trenches in thy
beauty's field. [*Ib.* 2]

30 Thou art thy mother's glass, and she in
thee / Calls back the lovely April of her
prime. [*Ib.* 3]

31 When I do count the clock that tells the
time, / I see the brave day sunk in
hideous night; / When I behold the violet

past prime, / And sable curls all silvered o'er with white; / When lofty trees I see barren of leaves, / Which erst from heat did canopy the herd, / And summer's green all girded up in sheaves, / Borne on the bier with white and bristly beard. [*Sonnets*, 12]

1 If I could write the beauty of your eyes / And in fresh numbers number all your graces. [*Ib.* 17]

2 And stretchèd metre of an antique song. [*Ib.*]

3 Shall I compare thee to a summer's day? / Thou art more lovely and more temperate: / Rough winds do shake the darling buds of May, / And summer's lease hath all too short a date. / Sometimes too hot the eye of heaven shines, / And often is his gold complexion dimmed; / And every fair from fair sometimes declines. [*Ib.* 18]

4 But thy eternal summer shall not fade. [*Ib.*]

5 O let my books be then the eloquence / And dumb presagers of my speaking breast. [*Ib.* 23]

6 The painful warrior famousèd for fight, / After a thousand victories once foiled, / Is from the book of honour razèd quite, / And all the rest forgot for which he toiled. [*Ib.* 25]

7 Weary with toil I haste me to my bed. [*Ib.* 27]

8 When in disgrace with fortune and men's eyes / I all alone beweep my outcast state. [*Ib.* 29]

9 Haply I think on thee – and then my state, / Like to the lark at break of day arising / From sullen earth, sings hymns at heaven's gate; / For the sweet love remembered such wealth brings / That then I scorn to change my state with kings. [*Ib.*]

10 When to the sessions of sweet silent thought / I summon up remembrance of things past, / I sigh the lack of many a thing I sought, / And with old woes new wail my dear time's waste: / Then can I drown an eye, unused to flow, / For precious friends hid in death's dateless night, / And weep afresh love's long since cancelled woe, / And moan the expense of many a vanished sight. [*Ib.* 30]

11 But if the while I think on thee, dear friend, / All losses are restored and sorrows end. [*Sonnets*, 30]

12 But since he died, and poets better prove, / Theirs for their style I'll read, his for his love. [*Ib.* 32]

13 Full many a glorious morning have I seen / Flatter the mountain tops with sovereign eye, / Kissing with golden face the meadows green, / Gilding pale streams with heavenly alchemy. [*Ib.* 33]

14 Ah! but those tears are pearl which thy love sheds. / And they are rich and ransom all ill deeds. [*Ib.* 34]

15 Roses have thorns, and silver fountains mud; / Clouds and eclipses stain both moon and sun. [*Ib.* 35]

16 Not marble, nor the gilded monuments / Of princes shall outlive this powerful rhyme. [*Ib.* 55]

17 Being your slave, what should I do but tend / Upon the hours and times of your desire? [*Ib.* 57]

18 So true a fool is love that in your will / Though you do anything, he thinks no ill. [*Ib.*]

19 Like as the waves make towards the pebbled shore, / So do our minutes hasten to their end. [*Ib.* 60]

20 Time doth transfix the flourish set on youth / And delves the parallels in beauty's brow. [*Ib.*]

21 When I have seen by Time's fell hand defaced / The rich-proud cost of outworn buried age. [*Ib.* 64]

22 When I have seen the hungry ocean gain / Advantage on the kingdom of the shore. [*Ib.*]

23 Since brass, nor stone, nor earth, nor boundless sea, / But sad mortality o'ersways their power, / How with this rage shall beauty hold a plea, / Whose action is no stronger than a flower? [*Ib.* 65]

24 Tired with all these, for restful death I cry. [*Ib.* 66]

25 And art made tongue-tied by authority. [*Ib.*]

26 And simple truth miscalled simplicity, / And captive good attending captain ill. [*Ib.*]

27 No longer mourn for me when I am dead / Than you shall hear the surly sullen bell

/ Give warning to the world that I am fled / From this vile world, with vilest worms to dwell. [*Sonnets*, 71]

1 O! if, – I say, you look upon this verse, / When I perhaps compounded am with clay, / Do not so much as my poor name rehearse, / But let your love even with my life decay. [*Ib.*]

2 That time of year thou mayst in me behold / When yellow leaves, or none, or few, do hang / Upon those boughs which shake against the cold, / Bare ruined choirs, where late the sweet birds sang. [*Ib.* 73]

3 Your monument shall be my gentle verse, / Which eyes not yet created shall o'er-read; / And tongues to be, your being shall rehearse, / When all the breathers of this world are dead. [*Ib.* 81]

4 Was it the proud full sail of this great verse, / Bound for the prize of all too precious you? [*Ib.* 86]

5 That affable familiar ghost / Which nightly gulls him with intelligence. [*Ib.*]

6 Farewell! thou art too dear for my possessing, / And like enough thou know'st thy estimate. [*Ib.* 87]

7 Thus have I had thee, as a dream doth flatter, / In sleep a king, but, waking, no such matter. [*Ib.*]

8 Ah! do not, when my heart hath 'scaped this sorrow, / Come in the rearward of a conquered woe; / Give not a windy night a rainy morrow, / To linger out a purposed overthrow. [*Ib.* 90]

9 They that have power to hurt and will do none, / That do not do the thing they most do show, / Who, moving others, are themselves as stone, / Unmovèd, cold, and to temptation slow. [*Ib.* 94]

10 The summer's flower is to the summer sweet, / Though to itself it only live and die. [*Ib.*]

11 For sweetest things turn sourest by their deeds; / Lilies that fester smell far worse than weeds. [*Ib.*]

12 From you have I been absent in the spring, / When proud-pied April, dressed in all his trim, / Hath put a spirit of youth in every thing. [*Ib.* 98]

13 To me, fair friend, you never can be old, / For as you were when first your eye I eyed, / Such seems your beauty still. [*Ib.* 104]

14 Ah! yet doth beauty, like a dial-hand, / Steal from his figure and no pace perceived. [*Sonnets*, 104]

15 Hear this thou age unbred: / Ere you were born was beauty's summer dead. [*Ib.*]

16 When in the chronicle of wasted time / I see descriptions of the fairest wights, / And beauty making beautiful old rhyme, / In praise of ladies dead and lovely knights. [*Ib.* 106]

17 For we, which now behold these present days, / Have eyes to wonder, but lack tongues to praise. [*Ib.*]

18 Not mine own fears, nor the prophetic soul / Of the wide world dreaming on things to come. [*Ib.* 107]

19 And peace proclaims olives of endless age. [*Ib.*]

20 And thou in this shalt find thy monument, / When tyrants' crests and tombs of brass are spent. [*Ib.*]

21 O! never say that I was false of heart, / Though absence seemed my flame to qualify. [*Ib.* 109]

22 Alas! 'tis true I have gone here and there, / And made myself a motley to the view. [*Ib.* 110]

23 My nature is subdued / To what it works in, like the dyer's hand. [*Ib.* 111]

24 Let me not to the marriage of true minds / Admit impediments. Love is not love / Which alters when it alteration finds, / Or tends with the remover to remove: / O, no! it is an ever-fixèd mark. [*Ib.* 116]

25 Love's not Time's fool, though rosy lips and cheeks / Within his bending sickle's compass come. [*Ib.*]

26 If this be error, and upon me proved, / I never writ, nor no man ever loved. [*Ib.*]

27 'Tis better to be vile than vile esteemed, / When not to be receives reproach of being. [*Ib.* 121]

28 The expense of spirit in a waste of shame / Is lust in action; and till action, lust / Is perjured, murderous, bloody, full of blame, / Savage, extreme, rude, cruel, not to trust. [*Ib.* 129]

29 Mad in pursuit and in possession so; / Had, having, and in quest to have, extreme; / A bliss in proof, – and proved, a very woe; / Before, a joy proposed;

behind, a dream. / All this the world well knows; yet none knows well / To shun the heaven that leads men to this hell. [*Sonnets*, 129]

1 My mistress' eyes are nothing like the sun. [*Ib.* 130]

2 Two loves I have of comfort and despair, / Which like two spirits do suggest me still: / The better angel is a man right fair, / The worser spirit a woman coloured ill. [*Ib.* 144]

3 Poor soul, the centre of my sinful earth, / Fooled by these rebel powers that thee array, / Why dost thou pine within and suffer dearth, / Painting thy outward walls so costly gay? [*Ib.* 146]

4 So shalt thou feed on Death, that feeds on men, / And Death once dead, there's no more dying then. [*Ib.*]

5 Hunting he loved, but love he laughed to scorn. [*Venus and Adonis*, 4]

6 Bid me discourse, I will enchant thine ear, / Or like a fairy, trip upon the green, / Or like a nymph, with long dishevelled hair, / Dance on the sands, and yet no footing seen: / Love is a spirit all compact of fire, / Not gross to sink, but light, and will aspire. [*Ib.* 145]

7 Good friend, for Jesu's sake forbear / To dig the dust enclosèd here. / Blest be the man that spares these stones, / And curst be he that moves my bones. [His epitaph]

8 *Item*, I give unto my wife my second best bed. [Will]

G. BERNARD SHAW   1856–1950

9 Breakages, Limited, the biggest industrial corporation in the country. [*The Apple Cart*, I]

10 What use are cartridges in battle? I always carry chocolate instead. [*Arms and the Man*, I]

11 You are a very poor soldier: a chocolate cream soldier! [*Ib.*]

12 I never apologize! [*Ib.* III]

13 You're not a man, you're a machine. [*Ib.*]

14 We have no more right to consume happiness without producing it than to consume wealth without producing it. [*Candida*, I]

15 It is easy – terribly easy – to shake a man's faith in himself. To take advantage of

that to break a man's spirit is devil's work. [*Candida*, I]

16 I'm only a beer teetotaller, not a champagne teetotaller. [*Ib.* III]

17 The worst sin towards our fellow creatures is not to hate them, but to be indifferent to them: that's the essence of inhumanity. [*The Devil's Disciple*, II]

18 I never expect a soldier to think. [*Ib.* III]

19 The British soldier can stand up to anything except the British War Office. [*Ib.*]

20 Stimulate the phagocytes. Drugs are a delusion. [*The Doctor's Dilemma*, I]

21 All professions are conspiracies against the laity. [*Ib.*]

22 Has he attained the seventh degree of concentration? [*Heartbreak House*, I]

23 When our relatives are at home, we have to think of all their good points or it would be impossible to endure them. But when they are away, we console ourselves for their absence by dwelling on their vices. [*Ib.*]

24 She married a numskull. [*Ib.*]

25 There are only two qualities in the world: efficiency and inefficiency; and only two sorts of people: the efficient and the inefficient. [*John Bull's Other Island*, IV]

26 I am a Millionaire. That is my religion. [*Major Barbara*, II]

27 Wot prawce Selvytion nah? [*Ib.*]

28 He never does a proper thing without giving an improper reason for it. [*Ib.* III]

29 He knows nothing; and he thinks he knows everything. That points clearly to a political career. [*Ib.*]

30 Nothing is ever done in this world until men are prepared to kill one another if it is not done. [*Ib.* IV]

31 A lifetime of happiness! No man alive could bear it: it would be hell on earth. [*Man and Superman*, I]

32 The true artist will let his wife starve, his children go barefoot, his mother drudge for his living at seventy, sooner than work at anything but his art. [*Ib.*]

33 It is a woman's business to get married as soon as possible, and a man's to keep unmarried as long as he can. [*Ib.* II]

34 Marry Ann; and at the end of a week you'll find no more inspiration in her than in a plate of muffins. [*Ib.*]

1 Hell is full of musical amateurs: music is the brandy of the damned. [*Man and Superman*, III]

2 An Englishman thinks he is moral when he is only uncomfortable. [*Ib.*]

3 There are two tragedies in life. One is to lose your heart's desire. The other is to gain it. [*Ib.* IV]

4 Do not do unto others as you would they should do unto you. Their tastes may not be the same. [*Ib.* 'Maxims for Revolutionists']

5 The golden rule is that there are no golden rules. [*Ib.*]

6 Democracy substitutes election by the incompetent many for appointment by the corrupt few. [*Ib.*]

7 He who can, does. He who cannot, teaches. [*Ib.*]

8 Marriage is popular because it combines the maximum of temptation with the maximum of opportunity. [*Ib.*]

9 If you strike a child, take care that you strike it in anger, even at the risk of maiming it for life. A blow in cold blood neither can nor should be forgiven. [*Ib.*]

10 The reasonable man adapts himself to the world; the unreasonable one persists in trying to adapt the world to himself. Therefore all progress depends on the unreasonable man. [*Ib.*]

11 Home is the girl's prison and the woman's workhouse. [*Ib.*]

12 Every man over forty is a scoundrel. [*Ib.*]

13 A great devotee of the Gospel of Getting On. [*Mrs Warren's Profession*, IV]

14 The fickleness of the women I love is only equalled by the infernal constancy of the women who love me. [*The Philanderer*, II]

15 He's a gentleman: look at his boots. [*Pygmalion*, 1]

16 PICKERING: Have you no morals, man? DOOLITTLE: Can't afford them, Governor. Neither could you if you was as poor as me. [*Ib.* II]

17 My aunt died of influenza: so they said. ... But it's my belief they done the old woman in. [*Ib.* III]

18 Drank! my word! Something chronic. [*Ib.*]

19 Not bloody likely. [*Ib.*]

20 West wind, wanton wind, wilful wind, womanish wind, false wind from over the water, will you never blow again? [*St Joan*, iii]

21 How can what an Englishman believes be heresy? It is a contradiction in terms. [*Ib.* iv]

22 With the single exception of Homer, there is no eminent writer, not even Sir Walter Scott, whom I can despise so entirely as I despise Shakespeare when I measure my mind against his. ... It would positively be a relief to me to dig him up and throw stones at him. [*Dramatic Opinions and Essays*, Vol. 2. p. 52]

23 There is only one religion though there are a hundred versions of it. [*Plays Pleasant*, Preface]

HENRY WHEELER SHAW
[JOSH BILLINGS]   1818–1885

24 Thrice is he armed that hath his quarrel just, / But four times he who gets his blow in fust. [*Josh Billings, his Sayings*]

25 It is better to know nothing than to know what ain't so. [*Proverb*]

RICHARD SHEALE   16 Cent.

26 For when his legs were smitten off, / He fought upon his stumps. [*Ballad of Chevy Chase*, Pt II. 10]

A. F. SHELDON   1868–1935

27 He profits most who serves best. [*Motto for International Rotary*]

P. B. SHELLEY   1792–1822

28 The cemetery is an open space among the ruins, covered in winter with violets and daisies. It might make one in love with death, to think that one should be buried in so sweet a place. [*Adonais*, Preface]

29 I weep for Adonais – he is dead! / O, weep for Adonais! though our tears / Thaw not the frost that binds so dear a head! [*Ib.* 1]

30 He went, unterrified, / Into the gulf of death; but his clear sprite / Yet reigns o'er earth; the third among the sons of light. [*Ib.* 34]

1 To that high capital, where kingly Death / Keeps his pale court in beauty and decay, / He came. [*Adonais*, 55]

2 He will awake no more, oh, never more! [*Ib*. 64]

3 She faded, like a cloud which had outwept its rain. [*Ib*. 90]

4 Winter is come and gone, / But grief returns with the revolving year. [*Ib*. 154]

5 Alas! that all we loved of him should be, / But for our grief, as if it had not been, / And grief itself be mortal! [*Ib*. 181]

6 The pilgrim of eternity, whose fame / Over his living head like Heaven is bent, / An early, but enduring monument. [*Ib*. 264]

7 It is a dying lamp, a falling shower, / A breaking billow: – even whilst we speak / Is it not broken? [*Ib*. 284]

8 Thou canst not soar where he is sitting now. – / Dust to the dust! but the pure spirit shall flow / Back to the burning fountain whence it came, / A portion of the eternal. [*Ib*. 337]

9 He hath awakened from the dream of life – / 'Tis we, who lost in stormy visions, keep / With phantoms an unprofitable strife, / And in mad trance, strike with our spirit's knife / Invulnerable nothings. [*Ib*. 344]

10 He has outsoared the shadow of our night; / Envy and calumny and hate and pain, / And that unrest which men miscall delight, / Can touch him not and torture not again; / From the contagion of the world's slow stain / He is secure. [*Ib*. 352]

11 He is made one with Nature: there is heard / His voice in all her music. [*Ib*. 370]

12 He is a portion of the loveliness / Which once he made more lovely. [*Ib*. 379]

13 The one remains, the many change and pass; / Heaven's light forever shines, earth's shadows fly; / Life, like a dome of many-coloured glass, / Stains the white radiance of eternity. [*Ib*. 460]

14 The soul of Adonais, like a star, / Beacons from the abode where the eternal are. [*Ib*. 494]

15 At length upon the lone Chorasmian shore / He paused, a wide and melancholy waste / Of putrid marshes. [*Alastor*, 272]

16 Arethusa arose / From her couch of snows / In the Acroceraunian mountains. [*Arethusa*]

17 A widow bird sate mourning for her love / Upon a wintry bough; / The frozen wind crept on above, / The freezing stream below.

There was no leaf upon the forest bare, / No flower upon the ground, / And little motion in the air / Except the mill-wheel's sound. [*Charles I*, III. v]

18 I bring fresh showers for the thirsting flowers, / From the seas and the streams. [*The Cloud*, 1]

19 I wield the flail of the lashing hail, / And whiten the green plains under, / And then again I dissolve it in rain, / And laugh as I pass in thunder. [*Ib*. 9]

20 Sublime on the towers of my skiey bowers, / Lightning my pilot sits; / In a cavern under is fettered the thunder, / It struggles and howls at fits. [*Ib*. 17]

21 I am the daughter of Earth and Water, / And the nursling of the Sky; / I pass through the pores of the ocean and shores; / I change but I cannot die. [*Ib*. 73]

22 Like a child from the womb, like a ghost from the tomb, / I arise and unbuild it again. [*Ib*. 82]

23 How wonderful is Death, / Death and his brother Sleep! [*The Daemon of the World*, i. 1]

24 Yet both so passing strange and wonderful! [*Ib*. i. 8]

25 Wail, for the world's wrong! [*A Dirge*]

26 Tell them that they are dull, / And bid them own that thou art beautiful. [*Epipsychidion*, Advertisement]

27 The spirit of the worm beneath the sod / In love and worship, blends itself with God. [*Ib*. 128]

28 We – are we not formed, as notes of music are, / For one another, though dissimilar? [*Ib*. 142]

29 I never was attached to that great sect, / Whose doctrine is, that each one should select / Out of the crowd a mistress or a friend, / And all the rest, though fair and wise, commend / To cold oblivion. [*Ib*. 149]

1 Those poor slaves ... / Who travel to their home among the dead / By the broad highway of the world, and so / With one chained friend, perhaps a jealous foe, / The dreariest and the longest journey go. [*Epipsychidion*, 155]

2 A ship is floating in the harbour now, / A wind is hovering o'er the mountain's brow; / There is a path on the sea's azure floor, / No keel has ever ploughed that path before; / The halcyons brood around the foamless isles; / The treacherous ocean has forsworn its wiles; / The merry mariners are bold and free:/ Say, my heart's sister, wilt thou sail with me? [*Ib.* 408]

3 Earth and Ocean seem / To sleep in one another's arms, and dream / Of waves, flowers, clouds, woods, rocks, and all that we / Read in their smiles, and call reality. [*Ib.* 509]

4 Chameleons feed on light and air: / Poets' food is love and fame. [*An Exhortation*]

5 Time's printless torrent grew / A scroll of crystal, blazoning the name / Of Adonais! [*Fragment on Keats*]

6 A hater he came and sat by a ditch, / And he took an old cracked lute; / And he sang a song that was more of a screech / 'Gainst a woman that was a brute. [*A Hate-Song*]

7 The world's great age begins anew, / The golden years return, / The earth doth like a snake renew / Her winter weeds outworn: / Heaven smiles, and faiths and empires gleam, / Like wrecks of a dissolving dream. [*Hellas*, 1060]

8 A loftier Argo cleaves the main, / Fraught with a later prize; / Another Orpheus sings again, / And loves, and weeps, and dies. / A new Ulysses leaves once more / Calypso for his native shore. [*Ib.* 1072]

9 Oh, write no more the tale of Troy. [*Ib.* 1078]

10 Although a subtler sphinx renew / Riddles of death Thebes never knew. [*Ib.* 1082]

11 Another Athens shall arise, / And to remoter time / Bequeath, like sunset to the skies, / The splendour of its prime. [*Ib.* 1084]

12 Saturn and Love their long repose / Shall burst, more bright and good /

Than all who fell, than One who rose, / Tan many unsubdued. [*Hellas*, 1090]

13 Oh, cease! must hate and death return? / Cease! must men kill and die? / Cease! drain not to the dregs the urn / Of bitter prophecy. / The world is weary of the past, / Oh, might it die or rest at last! [*Ib.* 1096]

14 Singing how down the vale of Maenalus / I pursued a maiden and clasped a reed. / Gods and men, we are all deluded thus! / It breaks in our bosom and then we bleed. [*Hymn of Pan*]

15 With fearful steps pursuing / Hopes of high talk with the departed dead. [*Hymn to Intellectual Beauty* 51]

16 I arise from dreams of thee / In the first sweet sleep of night. / When the winds are breathing low, / And the stars are shining bright. [*The Indian Serenade*]

17 The nightingale's complaint, / It dies upon her heart. [*Ib.*]

18 Oh lift me from the grass! / I die! I faint! I fail! / Let thy love and kisses rain / On my lips and eyelids pale. / My cheek is cold and white, alas! / My heart beats loud and fast; – / Oh! press it to thine own again, / Where it will break at last. [*Ib.*]

19 Thou Paradise of exiles, Italy! [*Julian and Maddalo*, 57]

20 Most wretched men / Are cradled into poetry by wrong, / They learn in suffering what they teach in song. [*Ib.* 544]

21 O world! O life! O time! / On whose last steps I climb, / Trembling at that where I had stood before; / When will return the glory of your prime? / No more – Oh, never more! [*A Lament*]

22 We watched the ocean and the sky together, / Under the roof of blue Italian weather. [*Letter to Maria Gisborne*, 146]

23 You will see Coleridge – he who sits obscure / In the exceeding lustre and the pure / Intense irradiation of a mind, / Which, with its own internal lightning blind, / Flags wearily through darkness and despair – / A cloud-encircled meteor of the air, / A hooded eagle among blinking owls. / You will see Hunt – one of those happy souls / Which are the salt of the earth, and without whom / This world would smell like what it is – a tomb. [*Ib.* 202]

1 His [Peacock's] fine wit / Makes such a wound, the knife is lost in it. [*Letter to Maria Gisborne*, 240]

2 We'll have fires out of the Grand Duke's wood, / To thaw the six weeks' winter in our blood. / And then we'll talk. [*Ib.* 308]

3 When the lamp is shattered / The light in the dust lies dead – / When the cloud is scattered / The rainbow's glory is shed. / When the lute is broken, / Sweet tones are remembered not; / When the lips have spoken, / Loved accents are soon forgot. [Lines, *When the Lamp is shattered*]

4 O Love! who bewailest / The frailty of all things here, / Why choose you the frailest / For your cradle, your home, and your bier? [*Ib.*]

5 Many a green isle needs must be / In the deep wide sea of Misery. [*Lines written among the Euganean Hills*, 1]

6 Underneath Day's azure eyes / Ocean's nursling, Venice lies, / A peopled labyrinth of walls. [*Ib.* 94]

7 Sun-girt City, thou hast been / Ocean's child, and then his queen; / Now is come a darker day, / And thou soon must be his prey. [*Ib.* 115]

8 The mind which feeds this verse, / Peopling the lone universe. [*Ib.* 318]

9 The fountains mingle with the river / And the rivers with the ocean, / The winds of heaven mix for ever / With a sweet emotion; / Nothing in the world is single; / All things by a law divine / In one spirit meet and mingle. / Why not I with thine? [*Love's Philosophy*]

10 I met Murder on the way – / He had a mask like Castlereagh. [*The Mask of Anarchy*, 5]

11 Rise like lions after slumber / In unvanquishable number, / Shake your chains to earth like dew / Which in sleep had fallen on you – / Ye are many – they are few. [*Ib.* 151]

12 Man's yesterday may ne'er be like his morrow; / Nought may endure but Mutability. [*Mutability*]

13 O wild West Wind, thou breath of Autumn's being, / Thou, from whose unseen presence the leaves dead / Are driven, like ghosts from an enchanter fleeing,

Yellow, and black, and pale, and hectic red, / Pestilence-stricken multitudes: O thou, / Who chariotest to their dark wintry bed

The wingèd seeds, where they lie cold and low, / Each like a corpse within its grave, until / Thine azure sister of the Spring shall blow

Her clarion o'er the dreaming earth. [*Ode to the West Wind*, 1]

14 Wild Spirit, which art moving everywhere; / Destroyer and preserver; hear, oh, hear! [*Ib.* 13]

15 Thou dirge

Of the dying year, to which this closing night / Will be the dome of a vast sepulchre. [*Ib.* 23]

16 Thou who didst waken from his summer dreams / The blue Mediterranean, where he lay, / Lulled by the coil of his crystalline streams,

Beside a pumice isle in Baiae's bay, / And saw in sleep old palaces and towers / Quivering within the wave's intenser day. [*Ib.* 29]

17 If I were a dead leaf thou mightest bear; / If I were a swift cloud to fly with thee. [*Ib.* 43]

18 If even / I were as in my boyhood, and could be

The comrade of thy wanderings over heaven. [*Ib.* 47]

19 Oh, lift me as a wave, a leaf, a cloud! / I fall upon the thorns of life! I bleed!

A heavy weight of hours has chained and bowed / One too like thee: tameless, and swift, and proud. [*Ib.* 53]

20 Make me thy lyre, even as the forest is: / What if my leaves are falling like its own! [*Ib.* 57]

21 Scatter, as from an unextinguished hearth / Ashes and sparks, my words among mankind! / Be through my lips to unawakened earth

The trumpet of a prophecy! O, Wind, / If Winter comes, can Spring be far behind? [*Ib.* 66]

22 I met a traveller from an antique land / Who said: Two vast and trunkless legs of stone / Stand in the desert. [*Ozymandias*]

23 Whose frown / And wrinkled lip, and sneer of cold command, / Tell that its sculptor well those passions read / Which

361

yet survive, stamped on these lifeless things. [*Ozymandias*,]

1 My name is Ozymandias, king of kings: / Look on my works, ye mighty, and despair! [*Ib.*]

2 Sometimes / The Devil is a gentleman. [*Peter Bell the Third*, 81]

3 Hell is a city much like London – / A populous and a smoky city. [*Ib.* 147]

4 Teas, / Where small talk dies in agonies. [*Ib.* 204]

5 'Twas Peter's drift / To be a kind of moral eunuch. [*Ib.* 313]

6 Whether he talked, wrote, or rehearsed – / Still with this dullness was he cursed – / Dull – beyond all conception – dull. [*Ib.* 705]

7 Monarch of gods and daemons, and all spirits / But one, who throng those bright and rolling worlds. [*Prometheus Unbound*, I. 1]

8 The crawling glaciers pierce me with the spears / Of their moon-freezing crystals, the bright chains / Eat with their burning cold into my bones. [*Ib.* I. 31]

9 The wingless, crawling hours, one among whom / – As some dark priest hales the reluctant victim, / Shall drag thee, cruel king, to kiss the blood / From these pale feet. [*Ib.* I. 48]

10 Ere Babylon was dust, / The Magus Zoroaster, my dead child, / Met his own image, walking in the garden. [*Ib.* I. 191]

11 Grief for a while is blind, and so was mine. / I wish no living thing to suffer pain. [*Ib.* I. 304]

12 The good want power, but to weep barren tears. / The powerful goodness want: worse need for them. / The wise want love; and those who love want wisdom; / And all best things are thus confused with ill. [*Ib.* I. 625]

13 Thy words are like a cloud of wingèd snakes; / And yet I pity those they torture not. [*Ib.* I. 632]

14 Peace is in the grave. / The grave hides all things beautiful and good: / I am a God and cannot find it there. [*Ib.* I. 638]

15 From the dust of creeds outworn. [*Ib.* I. 697]

16 On a poet's lips I slept / Dreaming like a love-adept. [*Ib.* I. 737]

17 Feeds on the aëreal kisses / Of shapes that haunt thought's wildernesses. [*Prometheus Unbound*, I. 741]

18 Create he can / Forms more real than living man, / Nurslings of immortality! [*Ib.* I. 747]

19 Leaves this peopled earth a solitude / When it returns no more. [*Ib.* II. iv. 17]

20 To know nor faith, nor love, nor law; to be / Omnipotent but friendless is to reign. [*Ib.* II. iv. 47]

21 He gave man speech, and speech created thought, / Which is the measure of the universe. [*Ib.* II. iv. 72]

22 All spirits are enslaved that serve things evil. [*Ib.* II. iv. 110]

23 All love is sweet, / Given or returned. Common as light is love, / And its familiar voice wearies not ever. [*Ib.* II. v. 39]

24 Life of Life! thy lips enkindle / With their love the breath between them; / And thy smiles before they dwindle / Make the cold air fire; then screen them / In those looks, where whoso gazes / Faints, entangled in their mazes. [*Ib.* II. v. 48]

25 My soul is an enchanted boat, / Which, like a sleeping swan, doth float / Upon the silver waves of thy sweet singing. [*Ib.* II. v. 72]

26 We have passed age's icy caves, / And manhood's dark and tossing waves, / And youth's smooth ocean, smiling to betray: / Beyond the glassy gulfs we flee / Of shadow-peopled infancy, / Through death and birth, to a diviner day. [*Ib.* II. v. 98]

27 Death is the veil which those who live call life: / They sleep, and it is lifted. [*Ib.* III. iii. 113]

28 The loathsome mask has fallen, the man remains / Sceptreless, free, uncircumscribed, but man / Equal, unclassed, tribeless and nationless. [*Ib.* III. iv. 193]

29 Nor yet exempt, though ruling them like slaves, / From chance, and death, and mutability, / The clogs of that which else might oversoar / The loftiest star of unascended heaven, / Pinnacled dim in the intense inane. [*Ib.* III. iv. 200]

30 Familiar acts are beautiful through love. [*Ib.* IV. 403]

31 Man, who wert once a despot and a slave; / A dupe and a deceiver; a decay; / A

traveller from the cradle to the grave /
Through the dim light of this immortal
day. [*Prometheus Unbound*, IV. 549]

1 To suffer woes which hope thinks infinite; / To forgive wrongs darker than
death or night; / To defy power, which
seems omnipotent; / To love, and bear;
to hope till hope creates / From its own
wreck the thing it contemplates; /
Neither to change, nor falter, nor repent;
/ This, like thy glory, Titan, is to be /
Good, great and joyous, beautiful and
free; / This is alone life, joy, empire, and
victory. [*Ib.* IV. 570]

2 I dreamed that, as I wandered by the way, /
Bare winter suddenly was changed to
spring. [*The Question*]

3 There grew pied wind-flowers and violets,
/ Daisies, those pearled Arcturi of the
earth, / The constellated flower that
never sets; / Faint oxslips; tender blue-
bells, at whose birth / The sod scarce
heaved. [*Ib.*]

4 I hastened to the spot whence I had come,
/ That I might there present it! – Oh! to
whom? [*Ib.*]

5 With hue like that when some great
painter dips / His pencil in the gloom of
earthquake and eclipse. [*The Revolt of
Islam*, V. 1925]

6 A sensitive plant in a garden grew, / And
the young winds fed it with silver dew.
[*The Sensitive Plant*, I. 1]

7 It is a modest creed, and yet / Pleasant if
one considers it, / To own that death
itself must be, / Like all the rest, a
mockery. [*Ib.* III. 126]

8 Rarely, rarely, comest thou, / Spirit of
Delight! [Song: *Rarely, Rarely, Comest
Thou*]

9 Let me set my mournful ditty / To a
merry measure; / Thou wilt never come
for pity, / Thou wilt come for pleasure.
[*Ib.*]

10 Men of England, wherefore plough / For
the lords who lay ye low? [*Song to the
Men of England*]

11 The seed ye sow, another reaps; / The
wealth ye find, another keeps. [*Ib.*]

12 An old, mad, blind, despised, and dying
king. [Sonnet: *England in 1819*]

13 Lift not the painted veil which those who
live / Call life. [*Ib. Lift not the Painted
Veil*]

14 Through the unheeding many he did
move, / A splendour among shadows, a
bright blot / Upon this gloomy scene, a
spirit that strove / For truth, and like the
preacher found it not. [Sonnet: *Lift not
the Painted Veil*]

15 Away! the moor is dark beneath the
moon, / Rapid clouds have drunk the
last pale beam of even: / Away! the
gathering winds will call the darkness
soon, / And profoundest midnight
shroud the serene lights of heaven.
[*Stanzas – April 1814*

16 Duty and dereliction guide thee back to
solitude. [*Ib.*]

17 That content surpassing wealth / The
sage in meditation found / And walked
with inward glory crowned. [*Stanzas
written in Dejection*]

18 Yet now despair itself is mild, / Even as
the winds and waters are; / I could lie
down like a tired child, / And weep
away the life of care / Which I have borne
and yet must bear. [*Ib.*]

19 I fear thy kisses, gentle maiden, / Thou
needest not fear mine. [*To —, I fear thy
Kisses*]

20 Music when soft voices die, / Vibrates
in the memory – / Odours, when sweet
violets sicken, / Live within the sense
they quicken.
Rose-leaves, when the rose is dead, /
Are heaped for the belovèd's bed; / And
so thy thoughts, when thou art gone, /
Love itself shall slumber on. [*To —,
Music, When Soft Voices Die*]

21 One word is too often profaned / For me
to profane it, / One feeling too falsely
disdained / For thee to disdain it. [*To —,
One Word is Too Often Profaned*]

22 The worship the heart lifts above / And
the Heavens reject not, – / The desire of
the moth for the star, / Of the night for
the morrow, / The devotion to something
afar / From the sphere of our sorrow.
[*Ib.*]

23 Best and brightest, come away! [*To Jane:
The Invitation*]

24 I am gone into the fields / To take what
this sweet hour yields; – / Reflection,
you may come to-morrow, / Sit by the
fireside with Sorrow. [*Ib.*]

25 Art thou pale for weariness / Of climbing heaven and gazing on the earth, /
Wandering companionless / Among the

stars that have a different birth, – / And
ever changing, like a joyless eye / That
finds no object worth its constancy? [*To
the Moon*]

1 Swiftly walk o'er the western wave, /
Spirit of Night! / Out of the misty
eastern cave, / Where, all the long and
lone daylight, / Thou wovest dreams of
joy and fear. [*To Night*]

2 Kiss her until she be wearied out, /
Then wander o'er city, and sea, and land,
/ Touching all with thine opiate wand – /
Come, long-sought! [*Ib.*]

3 When I arose and saw the dawn, / I
sighed for thee. [*Ib.*]

4 Thy brother Death came, and cried, /
Wouldst thou me? / Thy sweet child
Sleep, the filmy-eyed, / Murmured like
a noontide bee, / Shall I nestle near thy
side? [*Ib.*]

5 I ask of thee, belovèd Night – / Swift be
thine approaching flight, / Come soon,
soon! [*Ib.*]

6 Hail to thee, blithe spirit! / Bird thou
never wert, / That from heaven, or near
it, / Pourest thy full heart / In profuse
strains of unpremeditated art. [*To a Skylark*, 1]

7 And singing still dost soar, and soaring
ever singest. [*Ib.* 10]

8 Like a star of Heaven, / In the broad
daylight / Thou art unseen, but yet I
hear thy shrill delight. [*Ib.* 18]

9 Like a poet hidden / In the light of
thought, / Singing hymns unbidden, /
Till the world is wrought / To sympathy
with hopes and fears it heeded not. [*Ib.*
36]

10 We look before and after, / And pine
for what is not: / Our sincerest laughter /
With some pain is fraught; / Our
sweetest songs are those that tell of saddest thought. [*Ib.* 86]

11 Such harmonious madness / From my
lips would flow / The world should listen
then – as I am listening now. [*Ib.* 103]

12 Then, what is life? I cried. [*The Triumph
of Life*, 544]

13 And like a dying lady, lean and pale, /
Who totters forth, wrapped in a gauzy
veil, / Out of her chamber, led by the
insane / And feeble wanderings of her
fading brain, / The moon arose up in the
murky east, / A white and shapeless
mass – [*The Waning Moon*]

14 For she was beautiful – her beauty made /
The bright world dim, and everything
beside / Seemed like the fleeting image of
a shade. [*The Witch of Atlas*, 137]

15 The rapid, blind / And fleeting generations of mankind. [*Ib.* 615]

16 Ariel to Miranda: – Take / This slave of
music, for the sake / Of him who is the
slave of thee. [*With a Guitar, to Jane*]

17 The rich have become richer, and the
poor have become poorer. [*A Defence of
Poetry*]

18 Poetry is the record of the best and happiest moments of the happiest and best
minds. [*Ib.*]

19 Poets are the unacknowledged legislators
of the world. [*Ib.*]

WILLIAM SHENSTONE
1714–1763

20 Whoe'er has travelled life's dull round, /
Where'er his stages may have been, /
May sigh to think he still has found /
The warmest welcome, at an inn. [*At an
Inn at Henley*]

PHILIP H. SHERIDAN 1831–1888

21 The only good Indian is a dead Indian.
[Attr., at Fort Cobb, 1869]

R. B. SHERIDAN 1751–1816

22 I was afterwards twice tapped for a
dropsy, which declined into a very
profitable consumption! [*The Critic*, I. ii]

23 Yes, sir, puffing is of various sorts: the
principal are, the puff direct – the puff
preliminary – the puff collateral – the
puff collusive, and the puff oblique, or
puff by implication. [*Ib.*]

24 No scandal about Queen Elizabeth, I
hope? [*Ib.* II. i]

25 The Spanish fleet thou canst not see –
because / – It is not yet in sight! [*Ib.* II.
ii]

26 I must – I will – I can – I ought – I do.
[*Ib.*]

27 All that can be said is, that two people
happened to hit on the same thought –

and Shakespeare made use of it first, that's all. [*The Critic*, III. i]

1 I wish sir, you would practise this without me. I can't stay dying here all night. [*Ib.*]

2 *Enter Tilburina stark mad in white satin, and her confidant stark mad in white linen.* [*Ib.* stage direction]

3 The wind whistles – the moon rises – see, / They have killed my squirrel in his cage! / Is this a grasshopper! Ha! no, it is my / Whiskerandos . . . [*Ib.*]

4 An oyster may be crossed in love. [*Ib.*]

5 I loved him for himself alone. [*The Duenna*, I. iii, song]

6 I was struck all on a heap. [*Ib.* II. ii]

7 I don't know any business you have to think at all. Thought does not become a young woman. [*The Rivals*, I. ii]

8 Illiterate him, I say, quite from your memory. [*Ib.*]

9 'Tis safest in matrimony to begin with a little aversion. [*Ib.*]

10 There's a little intricate hussy for you! [*Ib.*]

11 A circulating library in a town is as an ever-green tree of diabolical knowledge! It blossoms through the year! [*Ib.*]

12 A progeny of learning. [*Ib.*]

13 You gentlemen's gentlemen are so hasty. [*Ib.* II. ii]

14 He is the very pineapple of politeness! [*Ib.* III. iii]

15 It gives me the hydrostatics to such a degree. [*Ib.*]

16 The old weather-beaten she-dragon who guards you. [(Of Mrs Malaprop] *Ib.*]

17 An aspersion upon my parts of speech! was ever such a brute! Sure, if I reprehend anything in this world, it is the use of my oracular tongue, and a nice derangement of epitaphs! [*Ib.*]

18 She's as headstrong as an allegory on the banks of the Nile. [*Ib.*]

19 That's too civil by half. [*Ib.* III. iv]

20 No caparisons, miss, if you please. Caparisons don't become a young woman. [*Ib.* IV. ii]

21 You are not like Cerberus, three gentlemen at once, are you? [*Ib.*]

22 My valour is certainly going! – it is sneaking off! – I feel it oozing out as it were at the palms of my hands! [*The Rivals*, V. iii]

23 I own the soft impeachment. [*Ib.*]

24 You shall see them on a beautiful quarto page, where a neat rivulet of text shall meander through a meadow of margin. [*The School for Scandal*, I. i]

25 Here is the whole set! a character dead at every word. [*Ib.* II. ii]

26 I leave my character behind me. [*Ib.*]

27 Here's to the maiden of bashful fifteen; / Here's to the widow of fifty; / Here's to the flaunting extravagant quean, / And here's to the housewife that's thrifty. / Let the toast pass, – / Drink to the lass, / I'll warrant she'll prove an excuse for the glass. [*Ib.* III. iii]

28 An unforgiving eye and a damned disinheriting countenance! [*Ib.* IV. i]

29 You write with ease, to show your breeding, / But easy writing's curst hard reading. [*Clio's Protest*]

30 The Right Honourable gentleman is indebted to his memory for his jests, and to his imagination for his facts. [Speech in reply to Mr Dundas]

GENERAL SHERMAN 1820–1891

31 I am tired and sick of war. Its glory is all moonshine. . . . War is hell. [Attr. words in Address at Michigan Military Academy, 19 June 1879]

JAMES SHIRLEY 1596–1666

32 The glories of our blood and state / Are shadows, not substantial things; / There is no armour against fate; / Death lays his icy hand on kings, / Sceptre and crown / Must tumble down, / And in the dust be equal made / With the poor crooked scythe and spade. [*The Contention of Ajax and Ulysses*, iii]

33 The garlands wither on your brow, / Then boast no more your mighty deeds, / Upon death's purple altar now, / See where the victor-victim bleeds, / Your heads must come, / To the cold tomb; / Only the actions of the just / Smell sweet, and blossom in their dust. [*Ib.*]

THE SHORTER CATECHISM

1 What is the chief end of man?
  To glorify God and to enjoy him for ever.

J. H. SHORTHOUSE   1834–1903

2 'The Church of England', I said ... 'is no doubt a compromise.' [*John Inglesant*, Ch. 39]

ALGERNON SIDNEY   1622–1683

3 Liars ought to have good memories. [*Discourses on Government*, Ch. 2, xv]

SIR PHILIP SIDNEY   1554–1586

4 My true love hath my heart and I have his, / By just exchange one for another given. [*Arcadia*, Bk 3]

5 'Fool,' said my Muse to me, 'look in thy heart and write.' [*Astrophel and Stella*, Sonnet 1]

6 With how sad steps, O Moon, thou climb'st the skies! / How silently, and with how wan a face! / What! may it be that even in heavenly place / That busy archer his sharp arrows tries? [*Ib.* 31]

7 Do they above love to be loved, and yet / Those lovers scorn whom that love doth possess? / Do they call virtue there ungratefulness? [*Ib.*]

8 Come sleep! O sleep, the certain knot of peace, / The baiting place of wit, the balm of woe, / The poor man's wealth, the prisoner's release, / Th' indifferent judge between the high and low. [*Ib.* 39]

9 That sweet enemy, France. [*Ib.* 41]

10 Highway, since you my chief Parnassus be, / And that my Muse, to some ears not unsweet, / Tempers her words to trampling horses' feet / More oft than to a chamber-melody, / Now, blessed you, bear onward blessed me / To her, where I my heart, safe left, shall meet. [*Ib.* 84]

11 Leave me, O Love, which reachest but to dust; / And thou, my mind, aspire to higher things; / Grow rich in that which never taketh rust; / Whatever fades, but fading pleasure brings. [*Ib.* 110]

12 'Who is it that this dark night / Underneath my window plaineth?' / It is one who from thy sight, / Being, ah! exiled, disdaineth / Every other vulgar light. [*Astrophel and Stella*, Song 11]

13 There have been many most excellent poets that have never versified, and now swarm many versifiers that need never answer to the name of poets. [*The Defence of Poesy*]

14 With a tale, forsooth, he cometh unto you; with a tale which holdeth children from play, and old men from the chimney corner. [*Ib.*]

15 Certainly, I must confess mine own barbarousness, I never heard the old song of Percy and Douglas, that I found not my heart moved more than with a trumpet. [*Ib.*]

16 Our erected wit maketh us to know what perfection is. [*Ib.*]

17 To be rhymed to death as is said to be done in Ireland. [*Ib.*]

18 Thy necessity is yet greater than mine. [On giving his water-bottle to a dying soldier on the battlefield of Zutphen]

ABBÉ SIEYÈS   1748–1836

19 *La mort, sans phrases.* – Death, and no phrases. [On voting for the death of Louis XVI. (He himself denied having spoken the qualification)]

20 *J'ai vécu.* – I lived. [Reply when asked what he had done during the Terror]

EMPEROR SIGISMUND   1361–1437

21 I am the Roman Emperor, and am above grammar. [Reply to prelate who had criticized his Latin]

SIMONIDES   c. 556–468 B.C.

22 Go, tell the Spartans, thou who passest by, / That here obedient to their laws we lie. [On the Spartan dead at Thermopylae, transl. Mackail]

GEORGE R. SIMS   1847–1922

23 It is Christmas Day in the workhouse. [*Dragonet Ballads*, 'In the Workhouse: Christmas Day']

EDITH SITWELL   1887–1964

1 Jane, Jane, / Tall as a crane, / The morning light creaks down again. [*Aubade*]

2 Don Pasquito / Hid where the leaves drip with sweet ... / But a word stung him like a mosquito ... / For what they hear, they repeat! [*Façade*. I do like to be beside the Seaside']

3 'See me dance the polka' / Said Mr Wagg like a bear. [*Ib.* 'Polka']

4 Lily O'Grady, / Silly and shady, / Longing to be / A lazy lady. [*Ib.* 'Popular Song']

5 When / Sir / Beelzebub called for his syllabub in the hotel in Hell / Where Proserpine first fell. [*Ib.* 'When Sir Beelzebub']

6 Though the world has slipped and gone, / Sounds my loud discordant cry / Like the steel birds' song on high: / 'Still one thing is left – the Bone!' / Then out danced the Babioun. [*Lullaby*]

7 The Pterodactyl made its nest / And laid a steel egg in her breast. [*Ib.*]

8 Under great yellow flags and banners of the ancient Cold / Began the huge migrations / From some primeval disaster in the heart of Man. [*The Shadow of Cain*]

9 Who dreamed that Christ has died in vain? / He walks again on the Seas of Blood, He comes in the terrible Rain. [*Ib.*]

10 Still falls the Rain – / Dark as the world of man, black as our loss – / Blind as the nineteen hundred and forty nails / Upon the Cross. [*Still Falls the Rain*]

SIR OSBERT SITWELL
         1892–1969

11 Do you remember Mr Goodbeare, the carpenter, / Godfearing and bearded Mr Goodbeare, / Who worked all day / At his carpenter's tray? [*Elegy for Mr Goodbeare*]

12 And Mrs Kinfoot longed to give a dinner / 'To meet the Judge upon the Judgment Day!' [*Malgré lui*]

13 She did not recognise her enemy, / She thought him Dust: / But what is Dust, / Save Time's most lethal weapon, / Her

faithful ally and our sneaking foe? [*Mrs Southern's Enemy*]

JOHN SKELTON   c. 1460–1529

14 With lullay, lullay, like a child, / Thou sleep'st too long, thou art beguiled. [*Lullay, Lullay like a Child*, ed. Henderson, p. 67]

15 Vengeance I ask and cry, / By way of exclamation, / On the whole nation / Of cattes wild and tame: / God send them sorrow and shame! [*Philip Sparrow*, p. 67]

16 O cat of churlish kind, / The fiend was in thy mind / When thou my bird untwined! [*Ib.*]

17 And robin readbreast, / He shall be the priest / The requiem mass to sing, / softly warbeling. [*Ib.* 71]

18 Merry Margaret, / As midsummer flower, / Gentle as falcon / Or hawk of the tower. [*To Mistress Margaret Hussey*, p. 430]

19 With solace and gladness, / Much mirth and no madness, / All good and no badness; / So joyously, / So maidenly, / So womanly, / Her demeaning. [*Ib.*]

CHRISTOPHER SMART
         1722–1771

20 I will consider my Cat Jeoffry. / For he is the servant of the Living God, duly and daily serving him. [*Jubilate Agno*, XIX. 51]

21 For adoration all the ranks / Of angels yield eternal thanks, / And David in the midst. [*Song to David*, 51]

22 Strong is the lion – like a coal / His eyeball – like a bastion's mole / His chest against the foes. [*Ib.* 76]

23 Glorious the northern lights astream; / Glorious the song, when God's the theme; / Glorious the thunder's roar. [*Ib.* 85]

24 And now the matchless deed's achieved, / Determined, dared, and done. [*Ib.* 86]

F. E. SMEDLEY   1818–1864

25 You are looking as fresh as paint. [*Frank Fairleigh*, Ch. 41]

SAMUEL SMILES   1812–1904

1 We often discover what *will* do, by finding out what will not do; and probably he who never made a mistake never made a discovery. [*Self-Help*, Ch. 11]

2 A place for everything, and everything in its place. [*Thrift*, Ch. 5]

ADAM SMITH   1723–1790

3 To found a great empire for the sole purpose of raising up a people of customers, may at first sight appear a project fit only for a nation of shopkeepers. It is, however, a project altogether unfit for a nation of shopkeepers; but extremely fit for a nation that is governed by shopkeepers. [*The Wealth of Nations*, Vol. II. Bk iv. Ch. 7. Pt iii]

ALEXANDER SMITH   1830–1867

4 In winter, when the dismal rain / Came down in slanting lines, / And Wind, that grand old harper, smote / His thunderharp of pines. [*A Life Drama*, ii]

EDGAR SMITH   1857–1938

5 You may tempt the upper classes / With your villainous demi-tasses, / But Heaven will protect the Working Girl. [*Heaven will Protect the Working Girl*]

JAMES and HORACE SMITH
    1775–1839 and 1779–1849

6 What stately vision mocks my waking sense? / Hence, dear delusion, sweet enchantment, hence! [*Rejected Addresses*, 'An Address without a Phoenix']

7 I saw them go: one horse was blind, / The tails of both hung down behind, / Their shoes were on their feet. [*Ib.* 'The Baby's Début']

8 Sated with home, of wife, of children tired, / The restless soul is driven abroad to roam; / Sated abroad, all seen and all admired, / The restless soul is driven to ramble home. [*Ib.* '*Cui Bono?*']

9 In the name of the Prophet – figs! [*Ib.* 'Johnson's Ghost']

10 Hail, glorious edifice, stupendous work! / God bless the Regent and the Duke of York! [*Rejected Addresses*, 'Loyal Effusion']

11 Who makes the quartern loaf and Luddites rise? / Who fills the butchers' shops with large blue flies? [*Ib.*]

12 God bless the Army, bless their coats of scarlet, / God bless the Navy, bless the Princess Charlotte. [*Ib.*]

13 And when that donkey looked me in the face, / His face was sad! and you are sad, my Public! [*Ib.* 'Playhouse Musings']

14 I am a blessed Glendoveer: / 'Tis mine to speak, and yours to hear. [*Ib.* 'The Rebuilding']

15 'You, Clutterbuck, come, stir your stumps, / Why are you in such doleful dumps? / A fireman and afraid of bumps! – / What are they feared on? fools! 'od rot 'em!' / Were the last words of Higginbottom. [*Ib.* 'A Tale of Drury Lane, The Burning']

16 John Richard William Alexander Dwyer / Was footman to Justinian Stubbs, Esquire. [*Ib.* 'The Theatre', 76]

LOGAN PEARSALL SMITH
    1865–1946

17 There are two things to aim at in life: first, to get what you want; and, after that, to enjoy it. Only the wisest of mankind achieve the second. [*Afterthoughts*, 1]

18 There are few sorrows, however poignant, in which a good income is of no avail. [*Ib.*]

19 People say that life is the thing, but I prefer reading. [*Ib.* 6]

20 Thank heaven, the sun has gone in, and I don't have to go out and enjoy it. [Last words]

REV. SAMUEL F. SMITH
    1808–1895

21 My country, 'tis of thee, / Sweet land of liberty, / Of thee I sing. [*America*]

REV. SYDNEY SMITH   1771–1845

22 We cultivate literature on a little oatmeal. [(Proposed motto for the *Edinburgh Review*) *Works*, Vol. 1, Preface]

1 I do not mean to be disrespectful, but the attempt of the Lords to stop the progress of Reform reminds me very forcibly of the great storm at Sidmouth, and of the conduct of the excellent Mrs Partington on that occasion. [Speech at Taunton, Oct. 1831]

2 Poverty is no disgrace to a man, but it is confoundedly inconvenient. [*His Wit and Wisdom*]

3 I look upon Switzerland as an inferior sort of Scotland. [Letter to Lord Holland, 1815]

4 I am convinced digestion is the great secret of life. [Letter to Arthur Kinglake, 30 Sept. 1837]

5 I have no relish for the country; it is a kind of healthy grave. [Letter to Miss G. Harcourt, 1838]

6 It requires a surgical operation to get a joke well into a Scotch understanding. [Lady Holland, *Memoir*, Vol. I. Ch. 2]

7 I heard him [Jeffrey] speak disrespectfully of the Equator! [*Ib.*]

8 Looked as if she had walked straight out of the Ark. [*Ib.* I. 7]

9 No furniture so charming as books. [*Ib.* I. 9]

10 How can a bishop marry? How can he flirt? The most he can say is, 'I will see you in the vestry after service.' [*Ib.*]

11 I have, alas, only one illusion left, and that is the Archbishop of Canterbury. [*Ib.*]

12 Don't you know, as the French say, there are three sexes – men, women, and clergymen? [*Ib.*]

13 Heat, ma'am! It was so dreadful here that I found there was nothing left for it but to take off my flesh and sit in my bones. [*Ib.*]

14 Live always in the best company when you read. [*Ib.* I. 10]

15 He [Macaulay] has occasional flashes of silence that make his conversation perfectly delightful. [*Ib.* I. 11]

16 Let onion atoms lurk within the bowl, / And, scarce-suspected, animate the whole. [*Ib.* 'Recipe for Salad']

17 Serenely full, the epicure would say, / Fate cannot harm me, I have dined to-day. [*Ib.*]

18 Deserves to be preached to death by wild curates. [Lady Holland, *Memoir*, I. 11]

19 What you don't know would make a great book. [*Ib.*]

20 I never read a book before reviewing it, it prejudices a man so. [H. Pearson, *The Smith of Smiths*, Ch. 3]

21 It is a place with only one post a day. . . . In the country I always fear that creation will expire before tea-time. [*Ib.* 5]

22 —'s idea of heaven is, eating *pâtés de foie gras* to the sound of trumpets. [*Ib.* 10]

23 'Whewell's forte is science,' said someone. 'Yes, and his foible is omni-science,' added Sydney. [*Ib.* 11]

24 What two ideas are more inseparable than Beer and Britannia? [*Ib.*]

25 I am just going to pray for you at St Paul's, but with no very lively hope of success. [*Ib.* 13]

TOBIAS SMOLLETT   1721–1771

26 Hark ye, Clinker, you are a most notorious offender. You stand convicted of sickness, hunger, wretchedness, and want. [*Humphrey Clinker*, Letter to Sir Watkin Phillips, 24 May]

27 He was formed for the ruin of our sex. [*Roderick Random*, Ch. 22]

28 That great Cham of literature, Samuel Johnson. [Letter to John Wilkes, 16 Mar. 1759, quoted in Boswell's *Johnson*]

SOCRATES   469–399 B.C.

29 Death is one of two things. Either it is annihilation, and the dead have no consciousness of anything; or, as we are told, it is really a change: a migration of the soul from this place to another. [Plato, *Apology*, 41]

30 Nothing can harm a good man, either in life or after death. [*Ib.* 42]

31 I am a citizen, not of Athens or Greece, but of the world. [Plutarch, *De Exilio*, v]

32 Bad men live to eat and drink, whereas good men eat and drink in order to live. [Plutarch, *Moralia*, 'How a Young Man Ought to Hear Poems', 4]

33 Crito, we ought to offer a cock to Asclepius. See to it, and don't forget. [Last words. Plato, *Phaedo*, 118]

SOLON   c. 640–c. 558 B.C.

1 Call no man happy till he dies, he is at best fortunate. [Herodotus, *Histories*, I. 32]

2 But I grow old always learning many things. [Plutarch, *Solon*, xxxi]

WILLIAM SOMERVILLE
1675–1742

3 The chase, the sport of kings; / Image of war, without its guilt. [*The Chase*, I. 13]

SOPHOCLES   495–406 B.C.

4 Wonders are many, and none is more wonderful than man. [*Antigone*, 322]

5 I depict men as they ought to be, but Euripides portrays them as they are. [Aristotle, *Poetics*, 25]

J. B. L. SOULE   1815–1891

6 Go west, young man. [Article in the *Terre Haute* (Indiana) *Express*, 1851]

ROBERT SOUTHEY   1774–1843

7 It was a summer evening, / Old Kaspar's work was done, / And he before his cottage door / Was sitting in the sun, / And by him sported on the green / His little grandchild Wilhelmine. [*The Battle of Blenheim*]

8 He came to ask what he had found, / That was so large, and smooth, and round. [*Ib.*]

9 But what they fought each other for, / I could not well make out. [*Ib.*]

10 'And everybody praised the Duke, / Who this great fight did win.' / 'But what good came of it at last?' / Quoth little Peterkin. / 'Why, that I cannot tell,' said he, / 'But 'twas a famous victory.' [*Ib.*]

11 How does the water / Come down at Lodore? [*The Cataract of Lodore*]

12 Curses are like young chickens, they always come home to roost. [*The Curse of Kehama*, Motto]

13 From his brimstone bed, at break of day / A walking the Devil is gone, / To look at his little snug farm of the World, / And see how his stock went on. [*The Devil's Walk* (a poem written in collaboration with Coleridge)]

14 How was the Devil dressed? / O, he was in his Sunday best; / His coat was red, and his breeches were blue, / And there was a hole where his tail came through. [*Ib.*]

15 He passed a cottage with a double coach-house, / A cottage of gentility! / And he owned with a grin / That his favourite sin / Is pride that apes humility. [*Ib.*]

16 No stir in the air, no stir in the sea, / The ship was still as she could be. [*The Inchcape Rock*]

17 Till the vessel strikes with a shivering shock, – / 'O Christ, it is the Inchcape Rock!' [*Ib.*]

18 Sir Ralph the Rover tore his hair; / He curst himself in his despair. [*Ib.*]

19 And last of all an Admiral came, / A terrible man with a terrible name, – / A name which you all know by sight very well, / But which no one can speak, and no one can spell. [*The March to Moscow*, 8]

20 My days among the dead are past; / Around me I behold, / Where'er these casual eyes are cast, / The mighty minds of old. [*My Days among the Dead*]

21 Yet leaving here a name, I trust, / That will not perish in the dust. [*Ib.*]

22 You are old, Father William, the young man cried, / And pleasures with youth pass away, / And yet you lament not the days that are gone, / Now tell me the reason, I pray. [*The Old Man's Comforts*]

23 In the days of my youth I remembered my God! / And He hath not forgotten my age. [*Ib.*]

24 How beautiful is night! / A dewy freshness fills the silent air; / No mist obscures, nor cloud, nor speck, nor stain, / Breaks the serene of heaven. [*Thalaba the Destroyer*, I. i]

25 The arts babblative and scribblative. [*Colloquies on the Progress and Prospects of Society*, X. Pt 2]

26 The march of intellect. [*Ib.* XIV]

27 The school that they have set up may properly be called the Satanic School. [*A Vision of Judgment*, Preface]

ROBERT SOUTHWELL
1561?–1595

1 As I in hoary winter's night stood shivering in the snow, / Surprised I was with sudden heat which made my heart to glow; / And lifting up a fearful eye to view what fire was near, / A pretty Babe all burning bright did in the air appear. [*The Burning Babe*]

2 With this he vanished out of sight and swiftly shrunk away, / And straight I callèd unto mind that it was Christmas Day. [*Ib.*]

3 Behold, a silly tender Babe / In freezing winter night. [*New Prince, New Pomp*]

4 Times go by turns, and chances change by course, / From foul to fair, from better hap to worse. [*Times go by Turns*]

HERBERT SPENCER   1820–1903

5 Time: That which man is always trying to kill, but which ends in killing him. [*Definitions*]

6 Science is organized knowledge. [*Education*, Ch. 2]

7 This survival of the fittest. [*Principles of Biology*, III. Ch. 12, 'Indirect Equilibrium', 165]

8 Progress, therefore, is not an accident, but a necessity. . . . It is a part of nature. [*Social Statics*, I. Ch. 2. 4]

9 Education has for its object the formation of character. [*Ib.* II. xvii. 4]

10 No one can be perfectly free till all are free; no one can be perfectly moral till all are moral; no one can be perfectly happy till all are happy. [*Ib.* IV. 30. 16]

11 It was remarked to me . . . that to play billiards was the sign of an ill-spent youth. [Duncan, *Life and Letters of Spencer*, Ch. 20]

STEPHEN SPENDER   1909–

12 After the first powerful manifesto / The black statement of pistons, without more fuss / But gliding like a queen, she leaves the station. [*The Express*]

13 I think continually of those who were truly great. / Who, from the womb, remembered the soul's history / Through corridors of light. [*I think continually of those*]

14 My parents kept me from children who were rough / And who threw words like stones and who wore torn clothes. [*My parents kept me from children who were rough*]

EDMUND SPENSER   1552?–1599

15 The merry cuckoo, messenger of spring, / His trumpet shrill hath thrice already sounded. [*Amoretti*, 19]

16 Fresh spring the herald of love's mighty king. [*Ib.* 70]

17 One day I wrote her name upon the strand, / But came the waves and washèd it away: / Again, I wrote it with a second hand: / But came the tide, and made my pains his prey. / Vain man, said she, that dost in vain assay, / A mortal thing so to immortalize. [*Ib.* 75]

18 Our life shall live, and later life renew. [*Ib.*]

19 Triton blowing loud his wreathèd horn. [*Colin Clout's Come Home Again*, 245]

20 The woods shall to me answer and my echo ring. [*Epithalamion*, 18]

21 Pour out the wine without restraint or stay, / Pour not by cups, but by the bellyful, / Pour out to all that wull. [*Ib.* 250]

22 Ah! when will this long weary day have end, / And lend me leave to come unto my love? [*Ib.* 278]

23 Now welcome, night, thou night so long expected, / That long day's labour dost at last defray. [*Ib.* 315]

24 A gentle knight was pricking on the plain. [*The Faerie Queene*, Bk I. Canto i. Stanza 1]

25 And on his breast a bloody cross he bore, / The dear remembrance of his dying Lord. [*Ib.* I. i. 2]

26 A bold bad man! that dared to call by name / Great Gorgon, prince of darkness and dead night. [*Ib.* I. i. 37]

27 Her angel's face, / As the great eye of heaven, shinèd bright, / And made a sunshine in the shady place. [*Ib.* I. iii. 6]

28 Still, as he fled, his eye was backward cast, / As if his fear still followed him behind. [*Ib.* I. ix. 21]

1 Sleep after toil, port after stormy seas, / Ease after war, death after life, does greatly please. [*The Faerie Queene*, I. ix. 40]

2 And all for love, and nothing for reward. [*Ib.* II. viii. 2]

3 Gather therefore the rose, whilst yet is prime, / For soon comes age, that will her pride deflower. [*Ib.* II. xii. 75]

4 Call me the Squire of Dames. [*Ib.* III. vii. 51]

5 And as she looked about, she did behold, / How over that same door was likewise writ, / Be bold, be bold, and everywhere, Be bold. [*Ib.* III. xi. 54]

6 Dan Chaucer, well of English undefiled, / On Fame's eternal beadroll worthy to be filed. [*Ib.* IV. ii. 32]

7 A monster, which the Blatant Beast men call, / A dreadful fiend, of gods and men ydrad. [*Ib.* V. xii. 37]

8 The gentle mind by gentle deeds is known: / For a man by nothing is so well bewrayed, / As by his manners. [*Ib.* VI. iii. 1]

9 It is the mind that maketh good or ill, / That maketh wretch or happy, rich or poor. [*Ib.* VI. ix. 30]

10 I was promised on a time, / To have reason for my rhyme; / From that time unto this season, / I received nor rhyme nor reason. [*Lines on his promised Pension* (traditional)]

11 Full little knowest thou that hast not tried, / What hell it is, in suing long to bide: / To lose good days, that might be better spent; / To waste long nights in pensive discontent; / To speed today, to be put back tomorrow; / To feed on hope, to pine with fear and sorrow. [*Mother Hubberd's Tale*, 895]

12 To eat thy heart through comfortless despairs: / To fawn, to crouch, to wait, to ride, to run, / To spend, to give, to want, to be undone. [*Ib.* 904]

13 Calm was the day, and through the trembling air / Sweet-breathing Zephyrus did softly play. [*Prothalamion*, 1]

14 Against the bridal day, which is not long: / Sweet Thames! run softly, till I end my song. [*Ib.* 17]

15 With that, I saw two swans of goodly hue / Come softly swimming down along the lee; / Two fairer birds I yet did never see. [*Ib.* 37]

16 At length they all to merry London came, / To merry London, my most kindly nurse, / That to me gave this life's first native source: / Though from another place I take my name, / An house of ancient fame. [*Prothalamion*, 127]

BENEDICT SPINOZA   1632–1677

17 Nature abhors a vacuum. [*Ethics*, Pt I. 15, note]

18 Man is a social animal. [*Ib.* IV. 35, note]

19 We feel and know that we are eternal. [*Ib.* V. 23, note]

REV. W. A. SPOONER   1844–1930

20 Kinquering Congs their titles take. [Announcing the hymn in New College Chapel, 1879]

21 I remember your name perfectly, but I just can't think of your face. [Attr.]

22 Let us drink to the queer old Dean. [Attr.]

23 Sir, you have tasted two whole worms; you have hissed all my mystery lectures and been caught fighting a liar in the quad; you will leave Oxford by the next town drain. [Attr.]

SIR CECIL SPRING-RICE   1859–1918

24 I vow to thee, my country – all earthly things above – / Entire and whole and perfect the service of my love. [*I vow to thee, my Country*]

25 And her ways are ways of gentleness, and all her paths are peace. [*Ib.*]

26 I am the Dean of Christ Church, Sir: / There's my wife; look well at her. / She's the Broad and I'm the High; / We are the University. [*The Masque of Balliol*]

SIR JOHN SQUIRE   1884–1958

27 It did not last: the Devil howling, 'Ho! / Let Einstein be!' restored the status quo. [*Answer to Pope's Epitaph on Sir Isaac Newton*]

28 But I'm not so think as you drunk I am. [*Ballade of Soporific Absorption*]

1 At last incapable of further harm, / The lewd forefathers of the village sleep. [*If Gray had had to write his Elegy in the Cemetery of Spoon River*]

MME DE STAËL   1766–1817

2 *Tout comprendre c'est tout purdonner.* – To understand all is to forgive all. [Common misquotation of *Corinne*, XVIII. Ch. 5]

JOSEPH STALIN   1879–1953

3 How many divisions has the Pope ? [Attr.]

SIR H. M. STANLEY   1841–1904

4 Dr Livingstone, I presume. [*How I found Livingstone*, Ch. 11]

FRANK L. STANTON   1857–1927

5 Sweetes' li'l' feller, / Everybody knows; / Dunno what to call 'im, / But he's mighty lak' a rose! [*Sweetes' Li'l' Feller*]

JOHN STARK   1728–1822

6 We beat them to-day or Molly Stark's a widow. [Before the battle of Bennington, 16 Aug. 1777]

SIR RICHARD STEELE
     1672–1729

7 There are so few who can grow old with a good grace. [*The Spectator*, 263]

8 Will Honeycomb calls these over-offended ladies the outrageously virtuous. [*Ib.* 266]

9 It is to be noted that when any part of this paper appears dull, there is a design in it. [*The Tatler*, 38]

10 Though her mien carries much more invitation than command, to behold her is an immediate check to loose behaviour; to love her is a liberal education. [*Ib.* 49]

11 The insupportable labour of doing nothing. [*Ib.* 54]

12 Reading is to the mind what exercise is to the body. [*Ib.* 147]

13 A little in drink, but at all times yr faithful husband. [Letter to his wife, 27 Sept. 1708]

GERTRUDE STEIN   1874–1946

14 Rose is a rose is a rose is a rose. [*Sacred Emily*]

HENRI BEYLE called
STENDHAL   1783–1842

15 Almost all our misfortunes in life come from the wrong notions we have about the things that happen to us. To know men thoroughly, to judge events sanely is, therefore, a great step towards happiness. [*Journal*, 10 Dec. 1801]

16 Romanticism is the art of presenting people with the literary works which are capable of affording them the greatest possible pleasure, in the present state of their customs and beliefs.
     Classicism, on the other hand, presents them with the literature that gave the greatest possible pleasure to their great-grandfathers. [*Racine et Shakespeare*, Ch. 3]

17 A novel is a mirror walking along a main road. [*Le Rouge et le noir*, Ch. 49]

J. K. STEPHEN   1859–1892

18 Birthdays? yes, in a general way; / For the most if not for the best of men: / You were born (I suppose) on a certain day: / So was 1: or perhaps in the night: what then ? [*Sincere Flattery of R.B.*]

19 An old half-witted sheep / Which bleats articulate monotony, / And indicates that two and one are three. [*Sonnet* (in parody of Wordsworth)]

20 When the Rudyards cease from Kipling / And the Haggards ride no more. [*To R.K.*]

JAMES STEPHENS   1882–1950

21 I heard a bird at dawn / Singing sweetly on a tree, / That the dew was on the lawn, / And the wind was on the lea; / But I didn't listen to him, / For he didn't sing to me. [*The Rivals*]

1 I heard a sudden cry of pain! / There is a rabbit in a snare. [*The Snare*]

LAURENCE STERNE 1713–1768

2 They order, said I, this matter better in France. [*A Sentimental Journey*, opening]

3 I had had an affair with the moon, in which there was neither sin nor shame. [*Ib.* 'The Monk, Calais']

4 As an Englishman does not travel to see Englishmen, I retired to my room. [*Ib.* 'Preface, In the Desobligeant']

5 The learned Smelfungus. [*Ib.* 'Calais, In the Street', 3]

6 I pity the man who can travel from Dan to Beersheba, and cry, 'Tis all barren. [*Ib.*]

7 There are worse occupations in this world than feeling a woman's pulse. [*Ib.* 'The Pulse. Paris']

8 But in Paris, as none kiss each other but the men, I did what amounted to the same thing –
– I bid God bless her. [*Ib.* 'The Fille de Chambre, Paris']

9 I am positive I have a soul; nor can all the books with which materialists have pestered the world ever convince me of the contrary. [*Ib.* 'Maria, Moulines']

10 God tempers the wind, said Maria, to the shorn lamb. [*Ib.* 'Maria']

11 So that when I stretched out my hand, I caught hold of the fille de chambre's – [*Ib.* conclusion]

12 'Pray, my dear,' quoth my mother, 'have you not forgot to wind up the clock? –' 'Good G—!' cried my father, making an exclamation, but taking care to moderate his voice at the same time, – 'Did ever woman, since the creation of the world, interrupt a man with such a silly question?' [*Tristram Shandy*, Vol. I. Ch. 1]

13 So long as a man rides his hobby-horse peaceably and quietly along the king's highway, and neither compels you or me to get up behind him, – pray, Sir, what have either you or I to do with it? [*Ib.* I. 7]

14 'Tis known by the name of perseverance in a good cause, – and of obstinacy in a bad one. [*Ib.* I. 17]

15 My uncle Toby would never offer to answer this by any other kind of argument than that of whistling half a dozen bars of Lillabulero. [*Tristram Shandy*, I. 21]

16 Writing, when properly managed, (as you may be sure I think mine is) is but a different name for conversation. [*Ib.* II. 11]

17 'I'll not hurt a hair of thy head : – Go,' says he, lifting up the sash and opening his hand as he spoke, to let it [a fly] escape, – 'go poor devil, get thee gone, why should I hurt thee? – This world surely is wide enough to hold both thee and me.' [*Ib.* II. 12]

18 That's another story, replied my father. [*Ib.* II. 17]

19 'I wish', quoth my uncle Toby, 'you had seen what prodigious armies we had in Flanders.' [*Ib.* II. 18]

20 'Our armies swore terribly in Flanders,' cried my uncle Toby, 'but nothing to this.' [*Ib.* III. 11]

21 Of all the cants which are canted in this canting world, – though the cant of hypocrites may be the worst, – the cant of criticism is the most tormenting! [*Ib.* III. 12]

22 The nonsense of the old women (of both sexes). [*Ib.* V. 16]

23 There is a North-west passage to the intellectual world. [*Ib.* V. 42]

24 You forget the great Lipsius, quoth Yorick, who composed a work the day he was born; – they should have wiped it up, said my uncle Toby, and said no more about it. [*Ib.* VI. 2]

25 'He shall not die, by G—,' cried my uncle Toby. – The Accusing Spirit which flew up to heaven's chancery, blushed as he gave it in; – and the Recording Angel, as he wrote it down, dropped a tear upon the word, and blotted it out for ever. [*Ib.* VI. 8]

26 A man should know something of his own country, too, before he goes abroad. [*Ib.* VII. 2]

27 'L—d!' said my mother, 'what is all this story about?' – 'A Cock and a Bull,' said Yorick. [*Ib.* IX. 33]

28 This sad vicissitude of things. [Sermon: *The Character of Shimei*]

ROBERT LOUIS STEVENSON
1850–1894

1 Every one lives by selling something. [*Across the Plains*, 9, 'Beggars']

2 Politics is perhaps the only profession for which no preparation is thought necessary. [*Familiar Studies of Men and Books*, 'Yoshida-Torajiro']

3 Am I no a bonny fighter? [*Kidnapped*, Ch. 10]

4 I've a grand memory for forgetting, David. [*Ib.* Ch. 18]

5 I have thus played the sedulous ape to Hazlitt, to Lamb, to Wordsworth, to Sir Thomas Browne, to Defoe, to Hawthorne, to Montaigne, to Baudelaire and to Obermann. [*Memories and Portraits*, Ch. 4]

6 I regard you with an indifference closely bordering on aversion. [*New Arabian Nights*, 'Story of the Bandbox']

7 For my part, I travel not to go anywhere, but to go. I travel for travel's sake. The great affair is to move. [*Travels with a Donkey*, 'Cheylard and Luc']

8 If landscapes were sold like the sheets of characters of my boyhood, one penny plain and twopence coloured, I should go the length of twopence every day of my life. [*Ib.* 'Father Apollinaris']

9 Fifteen men on the dead man's chest – / Yo-ho-ho, and a bottle of rum! / Drink and the devil had done for the rest – [*Treasure Island*, Ch. 1]

10 Tip me the black spot. [*Ib.* 3]

11 Pieces of eight! [*Ib.* 10]

12 Many's the long night I've dreamed of cheese – toasted, mostly. [*Ib.* 15]

13 In marriage, a man becomes slack and selfish, and undergoes a fatty degeneration of his moral being. [*Virginibus Puerisque*, I. 1]

14 Marriage is like life in this – that it is a field of battle, and not a bed of roses. [*Ib.*]

15 To marry is to domesticate the Recording Angel. Once you are married, there is nothing left for you, not even suicide, but to be good. [*Ib.* I. 2]

16 The cruellest lies are often told in silence. [*Ib.* I. 4, 'Truth of Intercourse']

17 Old and young, we are all on our last cruise. [*Virginibus Puerisque*, 'Crabbed Age and Youth']

18 Give me the young man who has brains enough to make a fool of himself! [*Ib.*]

19 Books are good enough in their own way, but they are a mighty bloodless substitute for life. [*Ib.* 'An Apology for Idlers']

20 Extreme *busyness*, whether at school or college, kirk or market, is a symptom of deficient vitality. [*Ib.*]

21 There is no duty we so much underrate as the duty of being happy. [*Ib.*]

22 To travel hopefully is a better thing than to arrive, and the true success is to labour. [*Ib.* 'El Dorado']

23 Though we are mighty fine fellows nowadays, we cannot write like Hazlitt. [*Ib.* 'Walking Tours']

24 It's deadly commonplace, but, after all, the commonplaces are the great poetic truths. [*Weir of Hermiston*, Ch. 6]

25 Nothing like a little judicious levity. [*The Wrong Box*, Ch. 7]

26 I believe in an ultimate decency of things. [Letter, 23 Aug. 1893]

27 In winter I get up at night / And dress by yellow candle-light. / In summer quite the other way, / I have to go to bed by day. [*A Child's Garden of Verses*, i, 'Bed in Summer']

28 A child should always say what's true / And speak when he is spoken to, / And behave mannerly at table: / At least as far as he is able. [*Ib.* v, 'Whole Duty of Children']

29 When I am grown to man's estate / I shall be very proud and great, / And tell the other girls and boys / Not to meddle with my toys. [*Ib.* xii, 'Looking Forward']

30 The pleasant land of counterpane. [*Ib.* xvi, 'The Land of Counterpane']

31 I have a little shadow that goes in and out with me, / And what can be the use of him is more than I can see. [*Ib.* xviii, 'My Shadow']

32 The child that is not clean and neat, / With lots of toys and things to eat, / He is a naughty child, I'm sure – / Or else his dear papa is poor. [*Ib.* xix, 'System']

33 The friendly cow, all red and white, / I love with all my heart: / She gives me

cream with all her might, / To eat with apple-tart. [*A Child's Garden of Verses*, xxiii, 'The Cow']

1 The world is so full of a number of things, / I'm sure we should all be as happy as kings. [*Ib.* xxiv, 'Happy Thought']

2 Children, you are very little, / And your bones are very brittle. [*Ib.* xxvii, 'Good and Bad Children']

3 Must we to bed indeed? Well then, / Let us arise and go like men, / And face with an undaunted tread / The long black passage up to bed. [*Ib.* xli, 'North-West Passage, 1, Good-Night']

4 Give to me the life I love, / Let the lave go by me, / Give the jolly heaven above / And the byway nigh me. [*Songs of Travel*, i, 'The Vagabond']

5 Wealth I ask not, hope nor love, / Nor a friend to know me; / All I seek, the heaven above / And the road below me. [*Ib.*]

6 I will make you brooches and toys for your delight / Of bird-song at morning and star-shine at night. [*Ib.* xi]

7 In the highlands, in the country places, / Where the old plain men have rosy faces. [*Ib.* xvi]

8 Sing me a song of a lad that is gone, / Say, could that lad be I? / Merry of soul he sailed on a day / Over the sea to Skye. [*Ib.* xlii]

9 Blows the wind today, and the sun and the rain are flying, / Blows the wind on the moors today and now, / Where about the graves of the martyrs the whaups are crying, / My heart remembers how! [*Ib.* xlv, 'To S. R. Crockett']

10 Be it granted me to behold you again in dying, / Hills of home! [*Ib.*]

11 Go, little book, and wish to all / Flowers in the garden, meat in the hall, / A bin of wine, a spice of wit, / A house with lawns enclosing it, / A living river by the door, / A nightingale in the sycamore! [*Underwoods*, ·I. i, 'Envoy']

12 There's nothing under Heaven so blue / That's fairly worth the travelling to. [*Ib.* I. ii, 'A Song of the Road']

13 Under the wide and starry sky, / Dig the grave and let me lie. / Glad did I live and gladly die, / And I laid me down with a will. / This be the verse you grave for me: / 'Here he lies where he longed to be; / Home is the sailor, home from sea, / And the hunter home from the hill.' [*Underwoods*, I. xxi, 'Requiem']

14 I am a kind of farthing dip, / Unfriendly to the nose and eyes; / A blue-behinded ape, I skip / Upon the trees of Paradise. [*Ib.* I. xxx, 'A Portrait']

WILLIAM STEVENSON
1546?–1575

15 I can not eat but little meat, / My stomach is not good; / But sure I think, that I can drink / With him that wears a hood. / Though I go bare, take ye no care, / I am nothing a-cold: / I stuff my skin, so full within, / Of jolly good ale and old. [*Gammer Gurton's Needle*, II, song (the authorship is disputed)]

SAMUEL J. STONE 1839–1901

16 The Church's one foundation / Is Jesus Christ her Lord; / She is His new creation / By water and the Word. [Hymn]

HARRIET BEECHER STOWE
1811–1896

17 'Who was your mother?' 'Never had none,' said the child, with another grin. 'Never had any mother? What do you mean? Where were you born?' 'Never was born,' persisted Topsy: 'never had no father, nor mother, nor nothin'. I was raised by a speculator.' [*Uncle Tom's Cabin*, Ch. 20]

18 'Do you know who made you?' 'Nobody as I knows on,' said the child, with a short laugh. . . . 'I 'spect I growed.' [*Ib.*]

19 I's wicked – I is. I's mighty wicked, anyhow. I can't help it. [*Ib.*]

LYTTON STRACHEY 1880–1932

20 'Before she came', said a soldier, 'there was cussin' and swearin', but after that it was as 'oly as a church.' The most cherished privilege of the fighting man was abandoned for the sake of Miss Nightingale. [*Eminent Victorians*, 'Florence Nightingale']

1 Yet her conception of God was certainly not orthodox. She felt towards Him as she might have felt towards a glorified sanitary engineer; and in some of her speculations she seems hardly to distinguish between the Deity and the Drains. [*Eminent Victorians*, 'Florence Nightingale']

2 It should not merely be useful and ornamental; it should preach a high moral lesson. [(On the Prince Consort's plans for the Great Exhibition) *Queen Victoria*, Ch. 4. vii]

3 Albert was merely a young foreigner, who suffered from having no vices, and whose only claim to distinction was that he had happened to marry the Queen of England. [*Ib.* 5. i]

4 Mr Gladstone was in his shirt-sleeves at Hawarden, cutting down a tree, when the royal message was brought to him. 'Very significant,' he remarked, when he had read the letter, and went on cutting down his tree. [*Ib.* 8. i]

5 The Faery [Queen Victoria], he determined, should henceforth wave her wand for him [Disraeli] alone. [*Ib.* 8. iii]

BISHOP WILLIAM STUBBS
1825–1901

6 Froude believes Kingsley a divine. / And Kingsley goes to Froude for history. [Letter to J. R. Green, 17 Dec. 1871]

SIR JOHN SUCKLING 1609–1642

7 Why so pale and wan, fond lover? / Prithee, why so pale? / Will, when looking well can't move her, / Looking ill prevail? / Prithee, why so pale? [*Aglaura*, IV. i, song]

8 If of herself she will not love, / Nothing can make her: / The devil take her! [*Ib.*]

9 Her feet beneath her petticoat, / Like little mice, stole in and out. / As if they feared the light. [*Ballad Upon a Wedding*]

10 Her lips were red, and one was thin, / Compared to that was next her chin / (Some bee had stung it newly). [*Ib.*]

11 Out upon it, I have loved / Three whole days together; / And am like to love three more, / If it prove fair weather.

Time shall moult away his wings, / Ere he shall discover / In the whole wide world again / Such a constant lover. [*A Poem with the Answer*]

SUETONIUS   c. 70–c. 140

12 *Festina lente.* – Hasten slowly. [*Augustus*, 25]

13 *Urbem ... excoluit adeo, ut iure sit gloriatus marmoream se relinquere. quam latericiam accepisset.* – He so improved the city that he justly boasted he had found it brick and left it marble. [*Ib.* 28]

14 *Ave, Imperator, morituri te salutant.* – Hail, Emperor, those about to die salute you. [*Claudius*, 21]

MAXIMILIAN, DUC DE SULLY
1559–1641

15 The English take their pleasures sadly after the fashion of their country. [*Memoirs*]

HENRY HOWARD,
EARL OF SURREY   1517?–1547

16 My friend, the things that do attain / The happy life be these, I find: / The riches left, not got with pain; / The fruitful ground, the quiet mind. [*Martial's Quiet Life*]

17 The soote season, that bud and bloom forth brings, / With green hath clad the hill and eke the vale. [*Spring*]

R. S. SURTEES   1803–1864

18 The only infallible rule we know is, that the man who is always talking about being a gentleman never is one. [*Ask Mamma*, Ch. 1]

19 I'll fill hup the chinks wi' cheese. [*Handley Cross*, Ch. 15]

20 Full o' beans and benevolence. [*Ib.* 27]

21 Hellish dark, and smells of cheese! [*Ib.* 50]

22 Three things I never lends – my 'oss, my wife, and my name. [*Hillingdon Hall*, Ch. 33]

23 Champagne certainly gives one werry gentlemanly ideas, but for a continuance, I don't know but I should prefer mild

hale. [*Jorrock's Jaunts and Jollities*, No. 9]

1 Better be killed than frightened to death. [*Mr Facey Romford's Hounds*, Ch. 32]

2 The young ladies entered the drawing-room in the full fervour of sisterly animosity. [*Mr Sponge's Sporting Tour*, Ch. 17]

3 Women never look so well as when one comes in wet and dirty from hunting. [*Ib.* 21]

4 He was a gentleman who was generally spoken of as having nothing a-year, paid quarterly. [*Ib.* 24]

5 There is no secret so close as that between a rider and his horse. [*Ib.* 31]

6 When at length they rose to go to bed, it struck each man as he followed his neighbour upstairs that the one before him walked very crookedly. [*Ib.* 35]

JONATHAN SWIFT 1667–1745

7 'Tis an old maxim in the schools, / That flattery's the food of fools; / Yet now and then your men of wit, / Will condescend to take a bit. [*Cadenus and Vanessa*, 758]

8 How haughtily he cocks his nose, / To tell what every schoolboy knows. [*The Country Life*, 81]

9 A coming shower your shooting corns presage. [*A Description of a City Shower*, 9]

10 I often wished that I had clear, / For life, six hundred pounds a-year, / A handsome house to lodge a friend; / A river at my garden's end, / A terrace walk, and half a rood / Of land set out to plant a wood. [*Imitation of Horace*, II. vi. 1]

11 Convey a libel in a frown, / And wink a reputation down. [*Journal of a Modern Lady*, 192]

12 Hail fellow, well met, / All dirty and wet: / Find out, if you can, / Who's master, who's man. [*My Lady's Lamentation*, 171]

13 Philosophy, the lumber of the schools. [*Ode to Sir W. Temple*, ii]

14 Some great misfortune to portend, / No enemy can match a friend. [*On the Death of Dr Swift*, 119]

15 The rest will give a shrug, and cry, / 'I'm sorry – but we all must die!' [*Ib.* 211]

16 Yet malice never was his aim; / He lashed the vice, but spared the name; / No individual could resent, / Where thousands equally were meant. [*On the Death of Dr Swift*, 512]

17 As learned commentators view / In Homer more than Homer knew. [*On Poetry*, 103]

18 Read all the prefaces of Dryden, / For these our critics much confide in; / (Tho' merely writ at first for filling, / To raise the volume's price a shilling). [*Ib.* 251]

19 Hobbes clearly proves that every creature / Lives in a state of war by nature. [*Ib.* 319]

20 So, naturalists observe, a flea / Hath smaller fleas that on him prey; / And these have smaller fleas to bite 'em, / And so proceed *ad infinitum*. [*Ib.* 337]

21 Hated by fools, and fools to hate / Be that my motto and my fate. [*To Dr Delaney, On the Libels*, 171]

22 A beggarly people! / A church and no steeple! [(Of a Dublin church) Attr. by Malone]

23 Satire is a sort of glass, wherein beholders do generally discover everybody's face but their own. [*The Battle of the Books*, Preface]

24 Instead of dirt and poison we have rather chosen to fill our hives with honey and wax; thus furnishing mankind with the two noblest of things, which are sweetness and light. [*Ib.*]

25 I have heard of a man who had a mind to sell his house, and therefore carried a piece of brick in his pocket, which he showed as a pattern to encourage purchasers. [*The Drapier's Letters*, No. 2]

26 He [the emperor] is taller by almost the breadth of my nail than any of his court; which alone is enough to strike an awe into the beholders. [*Gulliver's Travels*, 'Voyage to Lilliput', Ch. 2]

27 Big-endians and small-endians. [*Ib.* 4]

28 He could not forbear taking me up in his right hand, and stroking me gently with the other, after an hearty fit of laughing, asked me whether I were a Whig or a Tory. [*Ib.* 'Voyage to Brobdingnag', Ch. 3]

29 I cannot but conclude the bulk of your natives to be the most pernicious race of

little odious vermin that nature ever suffered to crawl upon the surface of the earth. [*Gulliver's Travels*, 'Voyage to Brobdingnag', 6]

1 He was amazed how so impotent and grovelling an insect as I (these were his expressions) could entertain such inhuman ideas. [*Ib.* 7]

2 He gave it for his opinion, that whoever could make two ears of corn or two blades of grass to grow upon a spot of ground where only one grew before, would deserve better of mankind, and do more essential service to his country than the whole race of politicians put together. [*Ib.*]

3 He had been eight years upon a project for extracting sunbeams out of cucumbers, which were to be put into phials hermetically sealed, and let out to warm the air in raw inclement summers. [*Ib.* 'Voyage to Laputa', Ch. 5]

4 I said the thing which was not. [*Ib.* 'Voyage to the Houyhnhnms', Ch. 3]

5 I told him . . . that we ate when we were not hungry, and drank without the provocation of thirst. [*Ib.* 6]

6 My horses understand me tolerably well; I converse with them at least four hours every day. They are strangers to bridle or saddle; they live in great amity with me, and friendship to each other. [*Ib.* 11]

7 With my own fair hands. [*Journal to Stella*, 4 Jan. 1711]

8 We are so fond of one another, because our ailments are the same. [*Ib.* 1 Feb. 1711]

9 I love good creditable acquaintance; I love to be the worst of the company. [*Ib.* 17 May 1711]

10 Monday is parson's holiday. [*Ib.* 3 Mar. 1712]

11 I have been assured by a very knowing American of my acquaintance in London, that a young healthy child well nursed is at a year old a most delicious, nourishing, and wholesome food, whether stewed, roasted, baked, or boiled, and I make no doubt that it will equally serve in a fricassee, or a ragout. [*A Modest Proposal*]

12 Promises and pie-crust are made to be broken. [*Polite Conversation*, Dialogue 1]

13 Bachelor's fare; bread and cheese, and kisses. [*Ib.*]

14 Like an owl in an ivy-bush. [*Polite Conversation*, Dialogue 1]

15 Why every one as they like; as the good woman said when she kissed her cow. [*Ib.*]

16 She wears her clothes, as if they were thrown on her with a pitchfork [*Ib.*]

17 Faith, that's as well said as if I had said it myself. [*Ib.* 2]

18 I always love to begin a journey on Sundays, because I shall have the prayers of the church, to preserve all that travel by land, or by water. [*Ib.*]

19 'Tis happy for him, that his father was before him. [*Ib.* 3]

20 What though his head be empty, provided his commonplace book be full. [*A Tale of a Tub*, Sect. VII]

21 I never saw, heard, nor read, that the clergy were beloved in any nation where Christianity was the religion of the country. Nothing can render them popular but some degree of persecution. [*Thoughts on Religion*]

22 We have just enough religion to make us hate, but not enough to make us love one another. [*Thoughts on Various Subjects*]

23 The reason why so few marriages are happy is because young ladies spend their time in making nets, not in making cages. [*Ib.*]

24 A nice man is a man of nasty ideas. [*Ib.*]

25 Party is the madness of many, for the gain of a few. [*Ib.*]

26 Proper words in proper places, make the true definition of style. [*Letter to a Young Clergyman*, 9 Jan. 1720]

27 If Heaven had looked upon riches to be a valuable thing, it would not have given them to such a scoundrel. [Letter to Miss Vanhomrigh, 12 Aug. 1720]

28 Principally I hate and detest that animal called man; although I heartily love John, Peter, Thomas, and so forth. [Letter to Pope, 29 Sept. 1725]

29 Not die here in a rage, like a poisoned rat in a hole. [Letter to Bolingbroke, 21 Mar. 1729]

30 I shall be like that tree, I shall die at the top. [Attr.]

31 Good God! What a genius I had when I wrote that book. [(Of *The Tale of A Tub*) Attr.]

1 Ah, a German and a genius! a prodigy, admit him! [Last words, when Handel was announced. Attr.]

2 *Ubi saeva indignatio ulterius cor lacerare nequit.* – Where fierce indignation can no longer tear his heart. [Swift's epitaph]

A. C. SWINBURNE   1837–1909

3 Maiden, and mistress of the months and stars / Now folded in the flowerless fields of heaven. [*Atalanta in Calydon*, opening]

4 When the hounds of spring are on winter's traces, / The mother of months in meadow or plain / Fills the shadows and windy places / With lisp of leaves and ripple of rain; / And the brown bright nightingale amorous / Is half assuaged for Itylus, / For the Thracian ships and the foreign faces, / The tongueless vigil and all the pain. [*Ib.* Chorus, 'When the Hounds of Spring', i]

5 Bind on thy sandals, O thou most fleet, / Over the splendour and speed of thy feet; / For the faint east quickens, the wan west shivers, / Round the feet of the day and the feet of the night. [*Ib.* ii]

6 For winter's rains and ruins are over, / And all the season of snows and sins; / The days dividing lover and lover, / The light that loses, the night that wins. [*Ib.* iv]

7 And in green underwood and cover / Blossom by blossom the spring begins. [*Ib.*]

8 Before the beginning of years / There came to the making of man / Time with a gift of tears, / Grief with a glass that ran. [*Ib.* Chorus, 'Before the Beginning of Years']

9 For a day and a night and a morrow, / That his strength might endure for a span / With travail and heavy sorrow, / The holy spirit of man. [*Ib.*]

10 And beauty and length of days, / And night, and sleep in the night. [*Ib.*]

11 He weaves, and is clothed with derision; / Sows, and he shall not reap; / His life is a watch or a vision / Between a sleep and a sleep. [*Ib.*]

12 Shall I strew on thee rose or rue or laurel, / Brother, on this that was the veil of thee? / Or quiet sea-flower moulded by the sea, / Or simplest growth of meadow-sweet or sorrel? [*Ave atque Vale*, i]

13 For whom all winds are quiet as the sun, / All waters as the shore. [*Ave atque Vale*, xviii]

14 Change in a trice ! The lilies and languors of virtue / For the raptures and roses of vice. [*Dolores*, ix]

15 O sanguine and subtle Dolores, / Our Lady of Pain. [*Ib.* xiii]

16 Time turns the old days to derision, / Our loves into corpses or wives. [*Ib.* xx]

17 Come down and redeem us from virtue, / Our Lady of Pain. [*Ib.* xxxv]

18 I shall remember while the light lives yet / And in the night time I shall not forget. [*Erotion*]

19 In a coign of the cliff between lowland and highland, / At the sea-down's edge between windward and lee, / Walled round with rocks as an inland island, / The ghost of a garden fronts the sea. [*A Forsaken Garden*, i]

20 The thorns he spares when the rose is taken; / The rocks are left when he wastes the plain. / The wind that wanders, the weeds wind-shaken, / These remain. [*Ib.* iii]

21 As a god self-slain on his own strange altar, / Death lies dead. [*Ib.* x]

22 I am tired of tears and laughter, / And men that laugh and weep; / Of what may come hereafter / For men that sow and reap. [*The Garden of Proserpine*, ii]

23 Pale, beyond porch and portal, / Crowned with calm leaves, she stands, / Who gathers all things mortal / With cold immortal hands. [*Ib.* vii]

24 We are not sure of sorrow, / And joy was never sure. [*Ib.* x]

25 We thank with brief thanksgiving / Whatever gods may be / That no man lives forever, / That dead men rise up never; / That even the weariest river / Winds somewhere safe to sea. [*Ib.* xi]

26 I am that which began: / Out of me the years roll; / Out of me God and man; / I am equal and whole; / God changes, and man, and the form of them bodily; / I am the soul. [*Hertha*, i]

27 A creed is a rod, / And a crown is of night: / But this thing is God: / To be man with thy might, / To grow straight in the strength of thy sprit, and live out thy life as the light. [*Ib.* xiv]

1 Hope thou not much, and fear thou not at all. [*Hope and Fear*]

2 Glory to Man in the highest! for Man is the master of things. [*Hymn of Man*, last line]

3 I have lived long enough, having seen one thing, that love hath an end; / Goddess and maiden and queen, be near me now and befriend. [*Hymn to Proserpine*]

4 Yea, is not even Apollo, with hair and harpstring of gold, / A bitter God to follow, a beautiful God to behold? [*Ib.*]

5 Thou hast conquered, O pale Galilean; the world has grown grey from thy breath; / We have drunken of things Lethean, and fed on the fullness of death. [*Ib.*]

6 O ghastly glories of saints, dead limbs of gibbeted Gods! [*Ib.*]

7 A little soul for a little bears up this corpse which is man. [*Ib.*]

8 I remember the way we parted, / The day and the way we met; / You hoped we were both broken-hearted, / And knew we should both forget. [*An Interlude*]

9 And the best and the worst of this is / That neither is most to blame, / If you have forgotten my kisses / And I have forgotten your name. [*Ib.*]

10 Swallow, my sister, O sister swallow, / How can thine heart be full of the spring? / A thousand summers are over and dead. / What hast thou found in the spring to follow? / What hast thou found in thine heart to sing? / What wilt thou do when the summer is shed? [*Itylus*, i]

11 Till life forget and death remember, / Till thou remember and I forget. [*Ib.* v]

12 Let us go hence, my songs; she will not hear. [*A Leave-Taking*, i]

13 While three men hold together, / The kingdoms are less by three. [*A Song in Time of Order*, iv]

14 I will go back to the great sweet mother, / Mother and lover of men, the sea. [*The Triumph of Time*, xxxiii]

15 There lived a singer in France of old / By the tideless dolorous midland sea. / In a land of sand and ruin and gold / There shone one woman, and none but she. [*Ib.* xli]

16 Mr Whitman's Venus is a Hottentot wench under the influence of cantharides and adulterated rum. [*Whitmania: Studies in Prose and Poetry*]

ARTHUR SYMONS   1865–1945

17 As a perfume doth remain / In the folds where it hath lain, / So the thought of you, remaining / Deeply folded in my brain, / Will not leave me: all things leave me: / You remain. [*Memory*]

J. M. SYNGE   1871–1909

18 When I was writing 'The Shadow of the Glen' I got more aid than any learning would have given me from a chink in the floor of the old Wicklow house where I was staying, that let me hear what was being said by the servant girls in the kitchen. [*The Playboy of the Western World*, Preface]

19 They're cheering a young lad, the champion playboy of the Western World. [*Ib.* III]

20 I'd know his way of spitting, and he astride the moon. [*Ib.*]

PUBLILIUS SYRUS   1 Cent. B.C.

21 *Bis dat qui cito dat.* – He gives twice who gives promptly. [Attr.]

22 *Necessitas non habet legem.* – Necessity knows no law. [Attr.]

JOSEPH TABRAR   1857–1931

23 In over a year and a half / I've only sung it once, / And I don't suppose I shall sing it again / For months and months and months. [*For Months and Months and Months*]

TACITUS   c. 55–c. 117

24 Everything unknown is taken as marvellous; but now the limits of Britain are laid bare. [*Agricola*, 30]

25 Where they make a desert they call it peace. [*Ib.*]

26 It is a characteristic of the human mind to hate the man one has injured. [*Ib.* 45]

1 *Elegantiae arbiter.* – Arbiter of taste. [(Of Petronius) *Annals*, xvi. 18]

HIPPOLYTE TAINE   1828–1893

2 Vice and virtues are products like sulphuric acid and sugar. [*Histoire de la littérature anglaise*, Introduction, iii]

CHARLES-MAURICE DE TALLEYRAND   1754–1838

3 It is the beginning of the end. [Remark on Napoleon's Russian campaign, 1812]

4 *Défiez-vous des premiers mouvements; ils sont presque toujours bons.* – Mistrust first impulses; they are nearly always good. [Also attr. to Count Montrond]

5 *Pas trop de zèle.* – Not too much zeal. [Attr.]

6 Speech was given to man to disguise his thoughts. [Also attr. to many others]

7 War is much too serious a thing to be left to military men. [Attr. Quoted by Briand to Lloyd George]

NAHUM TATE and   1652–1715
NICHOLAS BRADY   1659–1726

8 As pants the hart for cooling streams, / When heated in the chase. [Version of Psalm 42]

9 Through all the changing scenes of life. [Hymn]

10 While shepherds watched their flocks by night / All seated on the ground, / The angel of the Lord came down / And glory shone around.

   'Fear not,' said he; for mighty dread / Had seized their troubled mind; / 'Glad tidings of great joy I bring / To you and all mankind.' [Christmas hymn]

ANN and JANE TAYLOR   1782–1866 and 1783–1827

11 I thank the goodness and the grace / Which on my birth have smiled, / And made me, in these Christian days, / A happy English child. [*A Child's Hymn of Praise*]

12 Thank you, pretty cow, that made / Pleasant milk to soak my bread. [*The Cow* (by Ann Taylor)]

13 Twinkle, twinkle, little star, / How I wonder what you are! / Up above the world so high, / Like a diamond in the sky! [*The Star* (by Jane Taylor)]

BAYARD TAYLOR   1825–1878

14 Till the sun grows cold, / And the stars are old, / And the leaves of the Judgment Book unfold. [*Bedouin Song*]

BISHOP JEREMY TAYLOR   1613–1667

15 Desperate by too quick a sense of constant infelicity. [*Holy Dying*, i. 5]

16 Every school-boy knows it. [*On the Real Presence*, V. §1]

17 The union of hands and hearts. [*Sermons*, 'The Marriage Ring', Pt 1]

18 He that loves not his wife and children, feeds a lioness at home and broods a nest of sorrows. [*Ib.* 'Married Love']

JOHN TAYLOR   1580–1653

19 'Tis a mad world, my masters. [*Western Voyage*, 1]

SIR WILLIAM TEMPLE   1628–1699

20 When all is done, human life is, at the greatest and the best, but like a froward child, that must be played with and humoured a little to keep it quiet till it falls asleep, and then the care is over. [*Essay on Poetry*]

ALFRED, LORD TENNYSON   1809–1892

21 Cleave ever to the sunnier side of doubt. [*The Ancient Sage*, 68]

22 A pasty costly made, / Where quail and pigeon, lark and leveret lay, / Like fossils of the rock, with golden yolks / Imbedded and injellied. [*Audley Court*, 22]

1 Dust are our frames; and, gilded dust, our pride / Looks only for a moment whole and sound. [*Aylmer's Field*, 1]

2 Bare-footed came the beggar maid / Before the king Cophetua. [*The Beggar Maid*]

3 A happy bridesmaid makes a happy bride. [*The Bridesmaid*]

4 I come from haunts of coot and hern, / I make a sudden sally, / And sparkle out among the fern, / To bicker down a valley. [*The Brook*, song]

5 For men may come and men may go, / But I go on for ever. [*Ib.*]

6 I wind about, and in and out, / With here a blossom sailing, / And here and there a lusty trout, / And here and there a grayling. [*Ib.*]

7 Claspt hands and that petitionary grace / Of sweet seventeen subdued me as she spoke. [*Ib.* 112]

8 Half a league, half a league, / Half a league onward. / All in the valley of Death / Rode the six hundred. [*The Charge of the Light Brigade*]

9 'Forward the Light Brigade!' / Was there a man dismayed? [*Ib.*]

10 Someone had blundered: / Theirs not to make reply, / Theirs not to reason why, / Theirs but to do and die. [*Ib.*]

11 Cannon to right of them, / Cannon to left of them, / Cannon in front of them / Volleyed and thundered. [*Ib.*]

12 Into the jaws of Death, / Into the mouth of Hell. [*Ib.*]

13 Where Claribel low-lieth / The breezes pause and die. [*Claribel*]

14 May there be no moaning of the bar, / When I put out to sea. [*Crossing the Bar*]

15 When that which drew from out the boundless deep / Turns again home. [*Ib.*]

16 Twilight and evening bell, / And after that the dark! / And may there be no sadness of farewell, / When I embark;

For tho' from out our bourne of Time and Place / The flood may bear me far, / I hope to see my Pilot face to face / When I have crost the bar. [*Ib.*]

17 O love, what hours were thine and mine, / In lands of palm and southern pine. [*The Daisy*, 1]

18 I climbed the roofs at break of day; / Sun-smitten Alps before me lay. / I stood among the silent statues, / And statued pinnacles, mute as they. [*The Daisy*, 61]

19 The bitter east, the misty summer / And gray metropolis of the North. [(Edinburgh) *Ib.* 103]

20 This proverb flashes thro' his head, / 'The many fail, the one succeeds'. [*The Day-Dream*, 'The Arrival', 15]

21 And is there any moral shut / Within the bosom of the rose? [*Ib.* 'Moral', 7]

22 Dan Chaucer, the first warbler, whose sweet breath / Preluded those melodious bursts that fill / The spacious times of great Elizabeth. [*A Dream of Fair Women*, 5]

23 A daughter of the gods, divinely tall, / And most divinely fair. [*Ib.* 87]

24 Ringed with the azure world, he stands. / The wrinkled sea beneath him crawls; / He watches from his mountain walls, / And like a thunderbolt he falls. [*The Eagle*]

25 Edward Bull / The curate; he was fatter than his cure. [*Edwin Morris*, 14]

26 God made the woman for the man, / And for the good and increase of the world. [*Ib.* 43]

27 And when they buried him the little port / Had seldom seen a costlier funeral. [*Enoch Arden*, last lines]

28 Barbarous experiment, barbarous hexameters. [*Experiments in Quantity*, 'On Translations of Homer']

29 O mighty-mouthed inventor of harmonies, / O skilled to sing of Time or Eternity, / God-gifted organ voice of England, / Milton, a name to resound for ages. [*Ib.* 'Milton, Alcaics']

30 O you chorus of indolent reviewers. [*Ib.* 'Milton, Hendecasyllabics']

31 News from the humming city comes to it / In sound of funeral or of marriage bells. [*The Gardener's Daughter*, 35]

32 Half light, half shade, / She stood, a sight to make an old man young. [*Ib.* 139]

33 Then she rode forth, clothed on with chastity. [*Godiva*, 53]

34 Light shall spread, and man be liker man / Thro' all the season of the golden year. [*The Golden Year*, 35]

1 Pray God our greatness may not fail /
Thro' craven fears of being great. [*Hands
all Round*]

2 Dreams are true while they last, and do
we not live in dreams? [*The Higher
Pantheism*]

3 Closer is He than breathing, and nearer
than hands and feet. [*Ib.*]

4 Wearing the white flower of a blameless
life. [*Idylls of the King*, Dedication, 24]

5 From the great deep to the great deep he
goes. [*Ib.* 'The Coming of Arthur', 410]

6 Live pure, speak true, right wrong,
follow the King – / Else, wherefore born?
[*Ib.* 'Gareth and Lynette', 117]

7 Lead and I follow. [*Ib.* 726]

8 No, no, too late! ye cannot enter now.
[*Ib.* 'Guinevere', 168]

9 To reverence the King, as if he were /
Their conscience, and their conscience as
their King, / To break the heathen and
uphold the Christ, / To ride abroad
redressing human wrongs, / To speak no
slander, no, nor listen to it, / To honour
his own word as if his God's. [*Ib.* 465]

10 To love one maiden only, cleave to her, /
And worship her by years of noble deeds,
/ Until they won her. [*Ib.* 472]

11 Our fair father Christ. [*Ib.* 559]

12 We needs must love the highest when we
see it. [*Ib.* 655]

13 For good ye are and bad, and like to
coins, / Some true, some light, but every
one of you / Stamped with the image of
the King. [*Ib.* 'The Holy Grail', 25]

14 God make thee good as thou art beautiful. [*Ib.* 136]

15 His honour rooted in dishonour stood, /
And faith unfaithful kept him falsely
true. [*Ib.* 'Lancelot and Elaine', 871]

16 He makes no friend who never made a
foe. [*Ib.* 1082]

17 Our hoard is little, but our hearts are
great. [*Ib.* 'The Marriage of Geraint',
352]

18 For man is man and master of his fate.
[*Ib.* 355]

19 It is the little rift within the lute, / That
by and by will make the music mute. [*Ib.*
'Merlin and Vivien', 388]

20 Some black wether of St Satan's fold.
[*Idylls of the King*, 'Merlin and Vivien',
748]

21 For men at most differ as Heaven and
Earth, / But women, worst and best, as
Heaven and Hell. [*Ib.* 812]

22 O great and sane and simple race of
brutes / That own no lust because they
have no law! [*Ib.* 'Pelleas and Ettarre',
471]

23 I found Him in the shining of the stars, /
I marked Him in the flowering of His
fields, / But in His ways with men I find
Him not. [*Ib.* 'The Passing of Arthur', 9]

24 So all day long the noise of battle rolled /
Among the mountains by the winter sea.
[*Ib.* 170]

25 On one side lay the Ocean, and on one /
Lay a great water, and the moon was full.
[*Ib.* 179]

26 The sequel of to-day unsolders all / The
goodliest fellowship of famous knights /
Whereof this world holds record. [*Ib.* 182]

27 An arm / Rose up from out the bosom
of the lake, / Clothed in white samite,
mystic, wonderful. [*Ib.* 197]

28 This way and that dividing the swift mind.
[*Ib.* 227]

29 I heard the water lapping on the crag, /
And the long ripple washing in the reeds.
[*Ib.* 284]

30 Authority forgets a dying king. [*Ib.* 289]

31 For now I see the true old times are dead,
/ When every morning brought a noble
chance, / And every chance brought out
a noble knight. [*Ib.* 397]

32 The days darken round me and the years,
/ Among new men, strange faces, other
minds. [*Ib.* 405]

33 The old order changeth, yielding place to
new, / And God fulfils Himself in many
ways, / Lest one good custom should
corrupt the world. [*Ib.* 408]

34 Pray for my soul. More things are
wrought by prayer / Than this world
dreams of. [*Ib.* 415]

35 For what are men better than sheep or
goats / That nourish a blind life within
the brain, / If, knowing God, they lift not
hands of prayer / Both for themselves
and those who call them friend? / For so
the whole round earth is every way /
Bound by gold chains about the feet of
God. [*Ib.* 418]

1 Where falls not hail, or rain, or any snow, / Nor ever wind blows loudly. [*Idylls of the King*, 'The Passing of Arthur', 428]

2 Shadows of three dead men and thou wast one of the three. [*In the Garden at Swainston*]

3 Believing where we cannot prove. [*In Memoriam*, Prologue]

4 Thou madest Death: and lo, thy foot / Is on the skull which thou hast made. [*Ib.*]

5 Thou madest man, he knows not why. [*Ib.*]

6 Our little systems have their day; / They have their day and cease to be: / They are but broken lights of thee, / And thou, O Lord, art more than they. [*Ib.*]

7 I held it truth with him who sings / To one clear harp in divers tones, / That men may rise on stepping stones / Of their dead selves to higher things. [*Ib.* i]

8 Dark house, by which once more I stand / Here in the long unlovely street. [*Ib.* vii]

9 On the bald street breaks the blank day. [*Ib.*]

10 Or where the kneeling hamlet drains / The chalice of the grapes of God. [*Ib.* x]

11 To-night the winds begin to rise / And roar from yonder dropping day: / The last red leaf is whirled away, / The rooks are blown about the skies. [*Ib.* xv]

12 I do but sing because I must, / And pipe but as the linnets sing. [*Ib.* xxi]

13 The linnet born within the cage, / That never knew the summer woods. [*Ib.* xxvii]

14 I hold it true, whate'er befall; / I feel it when I sorrow most; / 'Tis better to have loved and lost / Than never to have loved at all. [*Ib.*]

15 The time draws near the birth of Christ. [*Ib.* xxviii]

16 Behold a man raised up by Christ! [*Ib.* xxxi]

17 Her eyes are homes of silent prayer. [*Ib.* xxxii]

18 'Twere best at once to sink to peace, / Like birds the charming serpent draws, / To drop head-foremost in the jaws / Of vacant darkness and to cease. [*Ib.* xxxiv]

19 And so the Word had breath, and wrought / With human hands the creed of creeds / In loveliness of perfect deeds, / More strong than all poetic thought. [*In Memoriam*, xxxvi]

20 How fares it with the happy dead? [*Ib.* xliv]

21 Be near me when my light is low, / When the blood creeps, and the nerves prick / And tingle; and the heart is sick, / And all the wheels of Being slow. [*Ib.* l]

22 Time, a maniac scattering dust, / And Life, a Fury slinging flame. [*Ib.*]

23 Do we indeed desire the dead / Should still be near us at our side? / Is there no baseness we would hide? / No inner vileness that we dread? [*Ib.* li]

24 Hold thou the good: define it well: / For fear divine philosophy / Should push beyond her mark and be / Procuress to the Lords of Hell. [*Ib.* liii]

25 Oh yet we trust that somehow good / Will be the final goal of ill. [*Ib.* liv]

26 But what am I? / An infant crying in the night: / An infant crying for the light: / And with no language but a cry. [*Ib.*]

27 So careful of the type she seems, / So careless of the single life. [*Ib.* lv]

28 Nature, red in tooth and claw. [*Ib.* lvi]

29 What hope of answer or redress? / Behind the veil, behind the veil. [*Ib.*]

30 Peace; come away: we do him wrong / To sing so wildly: let us go. [*Ib.* lvii]

31 O Sorrow, wilt thou live with me / No casual mistress, but a wife. [*Ib.* lix]

32 Sleep, Death's twin-brother, knows not Death, / Nor can I dream of thee as dead. [*Ib.* lxviii]

33 I dreamed there would be Spring no more, / That Nature's ancient power was lost. [*Ib.* lxix]

34 So many worlds, so much to do, / So little done, such things to be. [*Ib.* lxxiii]

35 Round thee with the breeze of song / To stir a little praise of dust. [*Ib.* lxxv]

36 God's finger touched him, and he slept. [*Ib.* lxxxv]

37 Fresh from brawling courts / And dusty purlieus of the law. [*Ib.* lxxxix]

38 There lives more faith in honest doubt, / Believe me, than in half the creeds. [*Ib.* xcvi]

1 He seems so near and yet so far. [*In Memoriam*, xcvii]

2 Ring out, wild bells, to the wild sky. [*Ib.* cvi]

3 Ring out the old, ring in the new, / Ring, happy bells, across the snow: / The year is going, let him go; / Ring out the false, ring in the true. [*Ib.*]

4 Ring out the feud of rich and poor, / Ring in redress to all mankind. [*Ib.*]

5 Ring out a slowly dying cause, / And ancient forms of party strife; / Ring in the nobler modes of life, / With sweeter manners, purer laws. [*Ib.*]

6 Ring out the want, the care, the sin, / The faithless coldness of the times. [*Ib.*]

7 Ring out false pride in blood and place, / The civic slander and the spite. [*Ib.*]

8 Ring out the thousand wars of old, / Ring in the thousand years of peace. [*Ib.*]

9 Not the schoolboy heat, / The blind hysterics of the Celt. [*Ib.* cix]

10 The grand old name of gentleman. [*Ib.* cxi]

11 'Tis held that sorrow makes us wise. [*Ib.* cxiii]

12 Now fades the long last streak of snow, / Now burgeons every maze of quick / About the flowering squares, and thick / By ashen roots the violets grow. [*Ib.* cxv]

13 The lark becomes a sightless song. [*Ib.*]

14 My regret / Becomes an April violet, / And buds and blossoms like the rest. [*Ib.*]

15 Trust that those we call the dead / Are breathers of an ampler day. [*Ib.* cxviii]

16 But I was *born* to other things. [*Ib.* cxx]

17 There rolls the deep where grew the tree. [*Ib.* cxxiii]

18 Even tho' thrice again / The red fool-fury of the Seine / Should pile her barricades with dead. [*Ib.* cxxvii]

19 Thy voice is on the rolling air; / I hear thee where the waters run; / Thou standest in the rising sun, / And in the setting thou art fair. [*Ib.* cxxx]

20 Wearing all that weight / Of learning lightly like a flower. [*Ib.* Conclusion]

21 That God, which ever lives and loves, / One God, one law, one element, / And one far-off divine event, / To which the whole creation moves. [*Ib.*]

22 All along the valley, stream that flashest white. [*In the Valley of the Cauteretz*]

23 The voice of the dead was a living voice to me. [*Ib.*]

24 Lady Clara Vere de Vere, / Of me you shall not win renown: / You thought to break a country heart / For pastime, ere you went to town. [*Lady Clara Vere de Vere*]

25 A simple maiden in her flower / Is worth a hundred coats-of-arms. [*Ib.*]

26 The lion on your old stone gates / Is not more cold to you than I. [*Ib.*]

27 The gardener Adam and his wife / Smile at the claims of long descent. [*Ib.*]

28 'Tis only noble to be good. / Kind hearts are more than coronets, / And simple faith than Norman blood. [*Ib.*]

29 On either side the river lie / Long fields of barley and of rye, / That clothe the wold and meet the sky; / And thro' the field the road runs by / To many-towered Camelot. [*The Lady of Shalott*, i]

30 Willows whiten, aspens quiver, / Little breezes dusk and shiver / Thro' the wave that runs for ever / By the island in the river. [*Ib.*]

31 Only reapers, reaping early / In among the bearded barley. [*Ib.*]

32 She has heard a whisper say, / A curse is on her if she stay / To look down to Camelot. [*Ib.* ii]

33 Or when the moon was overhead, / Came two young lovers lately wed; / 'I am half sick of shadows,' said / The Lady of Shalott. [*Ib.*]

34 A bow-shot from her bower-eaves, / He rode between the barley-sheaves, / The sun came dazzling thro' the leaves, / And flamed upon the brazen greaves / Of bold Sir Lancelot. [*Ib.* iii]

35 'Tirra lirra', by the river / Sang Sir Lancelot. [*Ib.*]

36 She left the web, she left the loom, / She made three paces thro' the room, / She saw the water-lily bloom, / She saw the helmet and the plume, / She looked down to Camelot. / Out flew the web and floated wide; / The mirror cracked from side to side; / 'The curse is come upon me,' cried / The Lady of Shalott. [*Ib.*]

1 He said, 'She has a lovely face; / God in his mercy lend her grace, / The Lady of Shalott.' [*The Lady of Shalott*, iv]

2 Ah God! the petty fools of rhyme / That shriek and sweat in pigmy wars. [*Literary Squabbles*]

3 The noblest answer unto such, / Is kindly silence when they brawl. [(Altered in later version to 'perfect silence') *Ib.*]

4 Nourishing a youth sublime / With the fairy tales of science, and the long result of Time. [*Locksley Hall*, 11]

5 In the spring a young man's fancy lightly turns to thoughts of love. [*Ib.* 20]

6 As the husband is, the wife is: thou art mated with a clown. [*Ib.* 47]

7 He will hold thee, when his passion shall have spent its novel force, / Something better than his dog, a little dearer than his horse. [*Ib.* 49]

8 Cursed be the gold that gilds the straitened forehead of a fool! [*Ib.* 62]

9 As the many-wintered crow that leads the clanging rookery home. [*Ib.* 68]

10 Such a one do I remember, whom to look at was to love. [*Ib.* 72]

11 Like a dog, he hunts in dreams, and thou art staring at the wall, / Where the dying night-lamp flickers, and the shadows rise and fall. [*Ib.* 79]

12 Thou shalt hear the 'Never, never', whispered by the phantom years. [*Ib.* 83]

13 With a little hoard of maxims preaching down a daughter's heart. [*Ib.* 94]

14 But the jingling of the guinea helps the hurt that Honour feels. [*Ib.* 105]

15 Men, my brothers, men the workers, ever reaping something new: / That which they have done but earnest of the things that they shall do. [*Ib.* 117]

16 Heard the heavens fill with shouting, and there rained a ghastly dew / From the nations' airy navies grappling in the central blue. [*Ib.* 123]

17 Till the war-drum throbbed no longer, and the battle-flags were furled / In the Parliament of man, the Federation of the world. [*Ib.* 127]

18 The kindly earth shall slumber, lapt in universal law. [*Ib.* 130]

19 So I triumphed ere my passion, sweeping thro' me, left me dry, / Left me with the palsied heart, and left me with the jaundiced eye. [*Locksley Hall*, 131]

20 Yet I doubt not thro' the ages one increasing purpose runs, / And the thoughts of men are widened with the process of the suns. [*Ib.* 137]

21 Knowledge comes, but wisdom lingers. [*Ib.* 143]

22 I am shamed thro' all my nature to have loved so slight a thing. [*Ib.* 148]

23 I will take some savage woman, she shall rear my savage race. [*Ib.* 168]

24 Not with blinded eyesight poring over miserable books. [*Ib.* 172]

25 I the heir of all the ages, in the foremost files of time. [*Ib.* 178]

26 Let the great world spin for ever down the ringing grooves of change. [*Ib.* 182]

27 Better fifty years of Europe than a cycle of Cathay. [*Ib.* 184]

28 He is but a landscape-painter, / And a village maiden she. [*The Lord of Burleigh*, 7]

29 'Courage!' he said, and pointed toward the land, / 'This mounting wave will roll us shorewards soon.' / In the afternoon they came unto a land / In which it seemèd always afternoon. [*The Lotos-Eaters*, 1]

30 A land of streams! some, like a downward smoke, / Slow-dropping veils of thinnest lawn, did go. [*Ib.* 10]

31 Our island home / Is far beyond the wave; we will no longer roam. [*Ib.* 44]

32 Music that gentlier on the spirit lies, / Than tired eyelids upon tired eyes. [*Ib.* 'Choric Song', i]

33 All things have rest: why should we toil alone, / We only toil, who are the first of things. [*Ib.* ii]

34 There is no joy but calm! [*Ib.*]

35 Ah, why / Should life all labour be? [*Ib.* iv]

36 Time driveth onward fast, / And in a little while our lips are dumb. / Let us alone. What is it that will last? / All things are taken from us, and become / Portions and parcels of the dreadful Past. [*Ib.*]

387

1 Is there any peace / In ever climbing up the climbing wave? [*The Lotos-Eaters*, 'Choric Song', iv]

2 Round and round the spicy downs the yellow Lotos-dust is blown. [*Ib.* viii]

3 Live and lie reclined / On the hills like Gods together, careless of mankind. [*Ib.*]

4 The clouds are lightly curled / Round their golden houses, girdled with the gleaming world. [*Ib.*]

5 Surely, surely, slumber is more sweet than toil, the shore / Than labour in the deep mid-ocean, wind and wave and oar; / Oh rest ye, brother mariners, we will not wander more. [*Ib.*]

6 The rise / And long roll of the Hexameter. [*Lucretius*, 10]

7 I saw the flying atom-streams / And torrents of her myriad universe, / Ruining along the illimitable inane. [*Ib.* 38]

8 Weeded and worn the ancient thatch / Upon the lonely moated grange. [*Mariana*]

9 She only said, 'My life is dreary, / He cometh not,' she said; / She said, 'I am aweary, aweary, / I would that I were dead.' [*Ib.*]

10 Her tears fell with the dews at even; / Her tears fell ere the dews were dried. [*Ib.*]

11 Upon the middle of the night, / Waking she heard the night-fowl crow. [*Ib.*]

12 The blue fly sung in the pane; the mouse / Behind the mouldering wainscot shrieked. [*Ib.*]

13 Faultily faultless, icily regular, splendidly null, / Dead perfection, no more. [*Maud*, Pt 1. II]

14 One still strong man in a blatant land, / Whatever they call him, what care I, / Aristocrat, democrat, autocrat – one / Who can rule and dare not lie. [*Ib.* 1. X. v]

15 But ah for a man to arise in me, / That the man I am may cease to be! [*Ib.* 1. X. vi]

16 Birds in the high Hall-garden / When twilight was falling, / Maud, Maud, Maud, Maud, / They were crying and calling. [*Ib.* 1. XII. i]

17 Gorgonised me from head to foot / With a stony British stare. [*Ib.* 1. XIII. ii]

18 Go not, happy day, / From the shining fields, / Go not, happy day, / Till the maiden yields. [*Maud*, 1, XVII]

19 Come into the garden, Maud, / For the black bat, night, has flown, / Come into the garden, Maud, / I am here at the gate alone; / And the woodbine spices are wafted abroad, / And the musk of the rose is blown.

For a breeze of morning moves, / And the planet of Love is on high, / Beginning to faint in the light that she loves / On a bed of daffodil sky. [*Ib.* 1. XXII. i]

20 All night have the roses heard / The flute, violin, bassoon; / All night has the casement jessamine stirred / To the dancers dancing in tune; / Till a silence fell with the waking bird, / And a hush with the setting moon. [*Ib.* 1. XXII. iii]

21 The rose was awake all night for your sake, / Knowing your promise to me; / The lilies and roses were all awake, / They sighed for the dawn and thee. [*Ib.* 1. XXII. viii]

22 Queen rose of the rosebud garden of girls. [*Ib.* 1. XXII. ix]

23 There has fallen a splendid tear / From the passion-flower at the gate. / She is coming, my dove, my dear; / She is coming, my life, my fate, / The red rose cries, 'She is near, she is near': / And the white rose weeps, 'She is late'. [*Ib.* 1. XXII. x]

24 O that 'twere possible / After long grief and pain / To find the arms of my true love / Round me once again! [*Ib.* 2. IV. i.]

25 I embrace the purpose of God and the doom assigned. [*Ib.* 3. VI. v]

26 You must wake and call me early, call me early, mother dear; / To-morrow 'ill be the happiest time of all the glad New-year; / Of all the glad New-year, mother, the maddest merriest day; / For I'm to be Queen o' the May, mother, I'm to be Queen o' the May. [*The May Queen*]

27 After it, follow it, / Follow The Gleam. [*Merlin and the Gleam*]

28 After-dinner talk / Across the walnuts and the wine. [*The Miller's Daughter*, 31]

29 What, it's you, / The padded man – that wears the stays. [*The New Timon and the Poets*]

1 Dosn't thou 'ear my 'erse's legs, as they canters awaäy? / Proputty, proputty, proputty – that's what I 'ears 'em saäy. [*Northern Farmer. New Style*, i]

2 Doänt thou marry for munny, but goä wheer munny is! [*Ib.* v]

3 Maäybe she warn't a beauty: – I niver giv it a thowt. [*Ib.* vi]

4 Taäke my word for it, Sammy, the poor in a loomp is bad. [*Ib.* xii]

5 Bury the Great Duke / With an empire's lamentation. [*Ode on the Death of the Duke of Wellington*, i]

6 The last great Englishman is low. [*Ib.* iii]

7 O friends, our chief state-oracle is mute. [*Ib.* iv]

8 Great in council and great in war, / Foremost captain of his time. [*Ib.*]

9 O fall'n at length that tower of strength / Which stood four-square to all the winds that blew! [*Ib.*]

10 This is England's greatest son, / He that gained a hundred fights, / Nor ever lost an English gun. [*Ib.* vi]

11 In that world-earthquake, Waterloo! [*Ib.*]

12 Our loyal passion for our temperate kings. [*Ib.* vii]

13 Who never sold the truth to serve the hour, / Nor paltered with eternal God for power. [*Ib.*]

14 Truth-teller was our England's Alfred named. [*Ib.*]

15 Not once or twice in our rough island-story, / The path of duty was the way to glory. [*Ib.* viii]

16 The toppling crags of Duty scaled / Are close upon the shining table-lands / To which our God Himself is moon and sun. [*Ib.*]

17 There lies a vale in Ida, lovelier / Than all the valleys of Ionian hills. [*Oenone*, 1]

18 O mother Ida, many-fountained Ida, / Dear mother Ida, harken ere I die. [*Ib.* 22]

19 I built my soul a lordly pleasure-house, / Wherein at ease for aye to dwell. [*The Palace of Art*, i]

20 An English home – gray twilight poured / On dewy pastures, dewy trees, / Softer than sleep – all things in order stored, / A haunt of ancient Peace. [*Ib.* xxii]

21 Two godlike faces gazed below; / Plato the wise and large-browed Verulam, / The first of those who know. [*The Palace of Art*, xlii]

22 'Make me a cottage in the vale,' she said, / 'Where I may mourn and pray.' [*Ib.* lxxiii]

23 Our Playwright may show / In some fifth Act what this wild drama means. [*The Play*]

24 Dowered with the hate of hate, the scorn of scorn, / The love of love. [*The Poet*]

25 Then the maiden Aunt / Took this fair day for text, and from it preached / An universal culture for the crowd. [*The Princess*, Prologue, 107]

26 I seemed to move among a world of ghosts, / And feel myself the shadow of a dream. [*Ib.* I. 17]

27 As thro' the land at eve we went, / And plucked the ripened ears, / We fell out, my wife and I, / O we fell out I know not why, / And kissed again with tears. [*Ib.* II, song]

28 O hard, when love and duty clash! [*Ib.* II. 273]

29 Jewels five-words long / That on the stretched forefinger of all Time / Sparkle for ever. [*Ib.* II. 355]

30 Sweet and low, sweet and low, / Wind of the western sea. [*Ib.* III, song]

31 Sleep, my little one, sleep, my pretty one, sleep. [*Ib.*]

32 The splendour falls on castle walls / And snowy summits old in story: / The long light shakes across the lakes, / And the wild cataract leaps in glory. / Blow, bugle, blow, set the wild echoes flying, / Blow, bugle; answer, echoes, dying, dying, dying. [*Ib.* IV, song]

33 O sweet and far from cliff and scar / The horns of Elfland faintly blowing! [*Ib.*]

34 Our echoes roll from soul to soul, / And grow for ever and for ever. [*Ib.*]

35 Tears, idle tears, I know not what they mean, / Tears from the depth of some divine despair. [*Ib.* IV, second song]

36 Looking on the happy Autumn-fields, / And thinking of the days that are no more. [*Ib.*]

37 Dear as remembered kisses after death. [*Ib.*]

1 O Swallow, Swallow, flying, flying South, / Fly to her, and fall upon her gilded eaves, / And tell her, tell her, what I tell to thee. [*The Princess*, IV, third song]

2 Bright and fierce and fickle is the South, / And dark and true and tender is the North. [*Ib.*]

3 O tell her, brief is life but love is long. [*Ib.*]

4 Thy voice is heard thro' rolling drums, / That beat to battle where he stands. [*Ib.* IV, fourth song]

5 Man is the hunter; woman is his game: / The sleek and shining creatures of the chase, / We hunt them for the beauty of their skins. [*Ib.* V. 147]

6 Man for the field and woman for the hearth: / Man for the sword and for the needle she: / Man with the head and woman with the heart: / Man to command and woman to obey; / All else confusion. [*Ib.* V. 427]

7 Home they brought her warrior dead: / She nor swooned, nor uttered cry: / All her maidens, watching, said, / 'She must weep or she will die.' [*Ib.* VI, song]

8 The woman is so hard / Upon the woman. [*Ib.* VI. 205]

9 Ask me no more: thy fate and mine are sealed: / I strove against the stream and all in vain: / Let the great river take me to the main: / No more, dear love, for at a touch I yield; / Ask me no more. [*Ib.* VII, song]

10 Now sleeps the crimson petal, now the white; / Nor waves the cypress in the palace walk; / Nor winks the gold fin in the porphyry font: / The fire-fly wakens: waken thou with me. [*Ib.* VII, second song]

11 Now lies the Earth all Danaë to the stars. [*Ib.*]

12 Now slides the silent meteor on, and leaves / A shining furrow, as thy thoughts in me. [*Ib.*]

13 Come down, O maid, from yonder mountain height: / What pleasure lives in height (the shepherd sang)? [*Ib.* VII, third song]

14 Love is of the valley, come thou down / And find him. [*Ib.*]

15 The moan of doves in immemorial elms, / And murmuring of innumerable bees. [*The Princess*, VII. 206]

16 The woman's cause is man's: they rise or sink / Together. [*Ib.* VII. 243]

17 Happy he / With such a mother! faith in womankind / Beats with his blood. [*Ib.* VII. 308]

18 Revolts, republics, revolutions, most / No graver than a schoolboys' barring out. [*Ib.* Conclusion, 65]

19 No little lily-handed Baronet he, / A great broad-shouldered genial Englishman, / A lord of fat prize-oxen and of sheep, / A raiser of huge melons and of pine, / A patron of some thirty charities. [*Ib.* 84]

20 For it was in the golden prime / Of good Haroun Alraschid. [*Recollections of the Arabian Nights*, 11]

21 At Flores in the Azores Sir Richard Grenville lay. [*The Revenge*, i]

22 I should count myself the coward if I left them, my Lord Howard, / To these Inquisition dogs and the devildoms of Spain. [*Ib.* ii]

23 And they blest him in their pain, that they were not left to Spain, / To the thumbscrew and the stake, for the glory of the Lord. [*Ib.* iii]

24 Shall we fight or shall we fly? / Good Sir Richard, tell us now, / For to fight is but to die! / There'll be little of us left by the time this sun is set. [*Ib.* iv]

25 We be all good Englishmen. / Let us bang these dogs of Seville, the children of the devil, / For I never turned my back upon Don or devil yet. [*Ib.*]

26 And a dozen times we shook 'em off as a dog that shakes his ears / When he leaps from the water to the land. [*Ib.* viii]

27 And the sun went down, and the stars came out far over the summer sea, / But never a moment ceased the fight of the one and the fifty-three. [*Ib.* ix]

28 God of battles, was ever a battle like this in the world before? [*Ib.*]

29 A day less or more / At sea or ashore, / We die – does it matter when? [*Ib.* xi]

30 Sink me the ship, Master Gunner – sink her, split her in twain! / Fall into the hands of God, not into the hands of Spain! [*Ib.*]

1 We have children, we have wives, / And the Lord hath spared our lives. / We will make the Spaniard promise, if we yield, to let us go; / We shall live to fight again and to strike another blow. [*The Revenge*, xii]

2 They praised him to his face with their courtly foreign grace. [*Ib.* xiii]

3 I have fought for Queen and Faith like a valiant man and true; / I have only done my duty as a man is bound to do. [*Ib.*]

4 Riflemen, Riflemen, Riflemen form! [*Riflemen Form!*]

5 Deep on the convent-roof the snows / Are sparkling to the moon: / My breath to heaven like vapour goes: / May my soul follow soon! [*St Agnes' Eve*]

6 Make Thou my spirit pure and clear / As are the frosty skies. [*Ib.*]

7 The Sabbaths of Eternity, / One Sabbath deep and wide – / A light upon the shining sea – / The Bridegroom with his bride! [*Ib.*]

8 Battering the gates of heaven with storms of prayer. [*St Simeon Stylites*, 7]

9 A city clerk, but gently born and bred. [*Sea Dreams*, 1]

10 What does little birdie say / In her nest at peep of day? [*Ib.* song]

11 Baby, sleep a little longer, / Till the little limbs are stronger. [*Ib.*]

12 My strength is as the strength of ten, / Because my heart is pure. [*Sir Galahad*, i]

13 How sweet are looks that ladies bend / On whom their favours fall! [*Ib.* ii]

14 A maiden knight – to me is given / Such hope, I know not fear. [*Ib.* vi]

15 All armed I ride, whate'er betide, / Until I find the holy Grail. [*Ib.* vii]

16 We were two daughters of one race. [*The Sisters*]

17 When cats run home and light is come, / And dew is cold upon the ground. [Song: *The Owl*]

18 Alone and warming his five wits, / The white owl in the belfry sits. [*Ib.*]

19 Oh teach me yet / Somewhat before the heavy clod / Weighs on me, and the busy fret / Of that sharp-headed worm begins / In the gross blackness underneath. [*Supposed Confessions of a Second-rate Sensitive Mind*, conclusion]

20 The woods decay, the woods decay and fall, / The vapours weep their burden to the ground, / Man comes and tills the field and lies beneath, / And after many a summer dies the swan. [*Tithonus*, 1]

21 Here at the quiet limit of the world, / A white-haired shadow roaming like a dream / The ever-silent spaces of the East. [*Ib.* 7]

22 The Gods themselves cannot recall their gifts. [*Ib.* 49]

23 The steam / Floats up from those dim fields about the homes / Of happy men that have the power to die, / And grassy barrows of the happier dead. [*Ib.* 68]

24 A life that moves to gracious ends / Thro' troops of unrecording friends, / A deedful life, a silent voice. [*To —, after reading a Life and Letters*]

25 Betray the trust: / Keep nothing sacred: 'tis but just / The many-headed beast should know. [*Ib.*]

26 Wielder of the stateliest measure ever moulded by the lips of man. [*To Virgil*]

27 A still small voice spake unto me, / 'Thou art so full of misery, / Were it not better not to be?' [*The Two Voices*, i]

28 This truth within thy mind rehearse, / That in a boundless universe / Is boundless better, boundless worse. [*Ib.* ix]

29 I wept. 'Tho' I should die, I know / That all about the thorn will blow / In tufts of rosy-tinted snow.' [*Ib.* xx]

30 Then comes the check, the change, the fall, / Pain rises up, old pleasures pall. / There is one remedy for all. [*Ib.* lv]

31 'Consider well,' the voice replied, / 'His face, that two hours since hath died; / Wilt thou find passion, pain or pride?' [*Ib.* lxxxi]

32 Whatever crazy sorrow saith, / No life that breathes with human breath / Has ever truly longed for death. [*Ib.* cxxxii]

33 It little profits that an idle king, / By this still hearth, among these barren crags, / Matched with an aged wife, I mete and dole / Unequal laws unto a savage race. [*Ulysses*, 1]

34 I will drink / Life to the lees. [*Ib.* 6]

35 Thro' scudding drifts the rainy Hyades / Vext the dim sea. [*Ib.* 10]

1 Much have I seen and known; cities of men / And manners, climates, counciis, governments, / Myself not least, but honoured of them all; / And drunk delight of battle with my peers, / Far on the ringing plains of windy Troy. [*Ulysses*, 13]

2 All experience is an arch wherethro' / Gleams that untravelled world, whose margin fades / For ever and for ever when I move. [*Ib.* 19]

3 To rust unburnished, not to shine in use. [*Ib.* 23]

4 This gray spirit yearning in desire / To follow knowledge like a sinking star, / Beyond the utmost bound of human thought. [*Ib.* 30]

5 This is my son, mine own Telemachus. [*Ib.* 33]

6 Death closes all: but something ere the end, / Some work of noble note, may yet be done, / Not unbecoming men that strove with Gods. [*Ib.* 51]

7 The long day wanes: the slow moon climbs: the deep / Moans round with many voices. [*Ib.* 55]

8 My purpose holds / To sail beyond the sunset, and the baths / Of all the western stars, until I die. / It may be that the gulfs will wash us down; / It may be we shall touch the Happy Isles, / And see the great Achilles. [*Ib.* 59]

9 Tho' / We are not now that strength that in old days / Moved earth and heaven: that which we are we are; / One equal temper of heroic hearts, / Made weak by time and fate, but strong in will / To strive, to seek, to find, and not to yield. [*Ib.* 65]

10 An' I thowt 'twur the will o' the Lord, but Miss Annie she said it wur draäins. [*The Village Wife*, ii]

11 God made Himself an awful rose of dawn. [*The Vision of Sin*, iii: also last line]

12 Let us hob-and-nob with Death. [*Ib.* iv]

13 Every moment dies a man, / Every moment one is born. [*Ib.*]

14 Drink to lofty hopes that cool – / Visions of a perfect State. [*Ib.*]

15 Sea-king's daughter from over the sea, Alexandra! [*A Welcome to Alexandra*]

16 O plump head-waiter at The Cock, / To which I most resort / How goes the time? 'Tis five o'clock. / Go fetch a pint of port. [*Will Waterproof's Lyrical Monologue*, i]

17 Softly, thro' a vinous mist, / My college friendships glimmer. [*Ib.* v]

18 That eternal want of pence / Which vexes public men. [*Ib.* vi]

19 As on this whirligig of Time / We circle with the seasons. [*Ib.* viii]

20 High above roaring Temple-bar, / And set in Heaven's third story, / I look at all things as they are, / But thro' a kind of glory. [*Ib.* ix]

21 Carved cross-pipes, and, underneath, / A pint-pot neatly graven. [*Ib.* last lines]

22 A land of settled government, / A land of just and old renown, / Where Freedom slowly broadens down / From precedent to precedent. [*You ask me why*]

23 A louse in the locks of literature. [Said of Churton Collins. Charteris, *Life and Letters of Sir Edmund Gosse*]

TERENCE   c. 195–159 B.C.

24 *Hinc illae lacrimae.* – Hence these tears. [*Andria*, 126]

25 *Amantium irae amoris integratio est.* – Lover's quarrels are the renewal of love. [*Ib.* 555]

26 *Homo sum; humani nil a me alienum puto.* – I am a man, and reckon nothing human alien to me. [*Heauton Timoroumenos*, 25]

27 *Fortis fortuna adiuvat.* – Fortune favours the brave. [*Phormio*, 203]

28 *Quot homines tot sententiae: suo quoque mos.* – As many opinions as there are men; each a law to himself. [*Ib.* 454]

TERTULLIAN   c. 160–c. 220

29 *O testimonium animae naturaliter Christianae.* – O witness of the soul Christian by nature. [*Apologeticus*, xvii]

30 See how these Christians love one another. [*Ib.* xxxix]

31 The blood of the martyrs is the seed of the Church. [*Ib.* 1]

32 *Credo quia impossibile.* – I believe because it is impossible. ((Usual adapt. of '*Certum est quia impossibile est.*' – 'It is certain . . .') *De Carne Christi*, v]

EDWARD TESCHEMACHER
19 Cent.

1 Where my caravan has rested, / Flowers I leave you on the grass. [*Where my Caravan has Rested*]

W. M. THACKERAY   1811–1863

2 It is impossible, in our condition of society, not to be sometimes a snob. [*The Book of Snobs*, Ch. 3]

3 'Tis strange what a man may do, and a woman yet think him an angel. [*Henry Esmond*, Bk I. Ch. 7]

4 We love being in love, that's the truth on't. [*Ib.* II. 15]

5 Why do they always put mud into coffee on board steamers? Why does the tea generally taste of boiled boots? [*The Kickleburys on the Rhine*]

6 Kind, cheerful, merry Dr Brighton. [*The Newcomes*, Ch. 9]

7 What money is better bestowed than that of a schoolboy's tip? [*Ib.* 16]

8 As the last bell struck, a peculiar sweet smile shone over his face, and he lifted up his head a little, and quickly said, 'Adsum!' and fell back. It was the word we used at school, when names were called; and lo, he, whose heart was as that of a little child, had answered to his name, and stood in the presence of The Master. [*Ib.* 80]

9 Yes, I am a fatal man, Madame Fribsbi. To inspire hopeless passion is my destiny. [(Mirobolant) *Pendennis*, Ch. 23]

10 Remember, it is as easy to marry a rich woman as a poor woman. [*Ib.* 28]

11 For a slashing article, sir, there's nobody like the Capting. [*Ib.* 32]

12 The *Pall Mall Gazette* is written by gentlemen for gentlemen. [*Ib.*]

13 Runs not a river by my palace wall? Have I not sacks to sew up wives withal? [*The Rose and the Ring*, Ch. 9]

14 'No business before breakfast, Glum!' says the King. 'Breakfast first, business next.' [*Ib.* 11]

15 There are some meannesses which are too mean even for man – woman, lovely woman alone, can venture to commit them. [*A Shabby-Genteel Story*, Ch. 3]

16 This I set down as a positive truth. A woman with fair opportunities and without a positive hump, may marry whom she likes. [*Vanity Fair*, Ch. 4]

17 Whenever he met a great man he grovelled before him, and my-lorded him as only a free-born Briton can do. [*Ib.* 13]

18 Them's my sentiments. [(Fred Bullock) *Ib.* 21]

19 Darkness came down on the field and city: and Amelia was praying for George, who was lying on his face, dead, with a bullet through his heart. [*Ib.* 32]

20 Nothing like blood, sir, in hosses, dawgs, and men. [(James Crawley) *Ib.* 35]

21 I think I could be a good woman if I had five thousand a year. [(Becky Sharp) *Ib.* 36]

22 Come, children, let us shut up the box and the puppets, for our play is played out. [*Ib.* 67]

23 There's no sweeter tobacco comes from Virginia, and no better brand than the Three Castles. [*The Virginians*, Ch. 1]

24 Fashnable fax and polite annygoats. [*The Yellowplush Papers*, Pt 1, title]

25 There were three sailors of Bristol City / Who took a boat and went to sea. [*Little Billee*]

26 There was gorging Jack and guzzling Jimmy, / And the youngest he was little Billee. [*Ib.*]

27 Little we fear / Weather without, / Sheltered about / The Mahogany Tree. [*The Mahogany Tree*]

28 Werther had a love for Charlotte, / Such as words could never utter; / Would you know how first he met her? / She was cutting bread and butter. [*The Sorrows of Werther*]

W. M. THAYER   1820–1898

29 Log-cabin to White House. [Title of biography of President Garfield]

ADOLPHE THIERS   1797–1877

30 *Il faut tout prendre au sérieux, mais rien au tragique.* – Everything must be taken seriously, nothing tragically. [Speech in National Assembly, 24 May 1873]

BRANDON THOMAS   1857–1914

1   I am Charley's aunt from Brazil, where the nuts come from. [*Charley's Aunt*, I]

DYLAN THOMAS   1914–1953

2   Where blew a flower may a flower no more / Lift its head to the blows of the rain; / Though they be mad and dead as nails, / Heads of the characters hammer through daisies; / Break in the sun till the sun breaks down, / And death shall have no dominion. [*And Death shall Have no Dominion*]

3   Oh as I was young and easy in the mercy of his means, / Time held me green and dying / Though I sang in my chains like the sea. [*Fern Hill*]

4   The force that through the green fuse drives the flower / Drives my green age. [*The Force that through the green Fuse*]

5   The hand that signed the treaty bred a fever, / And famine grew, and locusts came; / Great is the hand that holds dominion over / Man by a scribbled name. [*The Hand that Signed the Paper*]

6   Light breaks where no sun shines; / Where no sea runs, the waters of the heart / Push in their tides. [*Light Breaks where no Sun Shines*]

7   My birthday began with the water- / Birds and the birds of the winged trees flying my name. [*Poem in October*]

8   And I must enter again the round / Zion of the water bead / And the synagogue of the ear of corn. [*A Refusal to Mourn the Death, by Fire, of a Child in London*]

9   Shall gods be said to thump the clouds / When clouds are cursed by thunder? [*Shall Gods be said to Thump the Clouds?*]

10   This bread I break was once the oat, / This wine upon a foreign tree / Plunged in its fruit; / Man in the day or wind at night / Laid the crops low, broke the grape's joy. [*This Bread I Break*]

11   It is a winter's tale / That the snow blind twilight ferries over the lakes / And floating fields from the farm in the cup of the vales. [*A Winter's Tale*]

12   It is spring, moonless night in the small town, starless and bible-black. [*Under Milk Wood*]

13   The boys are dreaming wicked or of the bucking ranches of the night and the jollyrodgered sea. [*Under Milk Wood*]

14   Sleeping as quiet as death, side by wrinkled side, toothless, salt and brown, like two old kippers in a box. [*Ib.*]

15   Straightfaced in his cunning sleep he pulls the legs of his dreams. [*Ib.*]

16   Here's your arsenic, dear. / And your weedkiller biscuit. / I've throttled your parakeet. / I've spat in the vases. / I've put cheese in the mouseholes. Here's your ... / ... nice tea, dear. [*Ib.*]

17   Nothing grows in our garden, only washing. And babies. [*Ib.*]

18   The ship's clock in the bar says half past eleven. Half past eleven is opening time. The hands of the clock have stayed still at half past eleven for fifty years. It is always opening time in the Sailors Arms. [*Ib.*]

19   Which of their gandering hubbies moaned in Milk Wood for your naughty mothering arms and body like a wardrobe, love? [*Ib.*]

20   I see you got a mermaid in your lap he said and he lifted his hat. He is a proper Christian. [*Ib.*]

21   Mr Pugh reads, as he forks the shroud meat in, from *Lives of the Great Poisoners*. [*Ib.*]

22   And when you think of all those babies she's got, then all I can say is she'd better give up bird nesting ... it isn't the right kind of hobby at all for a woman that can't say no even to midgets. [*Ib.*]

23   Johann Sebastian mighty Bach. Oh Bach fach. [*Ib.*]

24   He was sitting straight up in bed and rocking from side to side as though the bed were on a rough road; the knotted edges of the counterpane were his reins; his invisible horses stood in a shadow beyond the bedside candle. Over a white flannel nightshirt he was wearing a red waistcoat with walnut-sized brass buttons. [*Portrait of the Artist as a Young Dog*, 'A Visit to Grandpa's']

25   'Look at Little Cough,' said Brazell. 'Isn't he extraordinary? He's growing out of the sand. Little Cough hasn't got any legs.' [*Ib.* 'Extraordinary Little Cough']

EDWARD THOMAS 1878–1917

1 Yes. I remember Adlestrop – / The name, because one afternoon / Of heat the express-train drew up there / Unwontedly. It was late June. [*Adlestrop*]

2 I have come to the borders of sleep, / The unfathomable deep / Forest where all must lose / Their way. [*Lights Out*]

3 Out in the dark over the snow / The fallow fawns invisible go / With the fallow doe; / And the winds blow / Fast as the stars are slow. [*Out in the Dark*]

4 The new moon hangs like an ivory bugle / In the naked frosty blue. [*The Penny Whistle*]

5 I love roads: / The goddesses that dwell / Far along them invisible / Are my favourite gods. [*Roads*]

6 Open your eyes to the air / That has washed the eyes of the stars / Through all the dewy night: / Up with the light, / To the old wars: / Arise, arise. [*The Trumpet*]

7 When these woods were young / The thrushes' ancestors / As sweetly sung / In the old years. [*Under the Woods*]

8 Out of us all / That make rhymes, / Will you choose / Sometimes – / As the winds use / A crack in a wall / Or a drain, / Their joy or their pain / To whistle through – / Choose me, / You English words? [*Words*]

R. S. THOMAS 1913–

9 We will listen instead to the wind's text / Blown through the roof, or the thrush's song / In the thick bush that proved him wrong, / Wrong from the start, for nature's truth / Is primary and her changing seasons / Correct out of a vaster reason / The vague errors of the flesh. [*Song at the Year's Turning*, 'The Minister', end]

10 We were a people taut for war; the hills / Were no harder, the thin grass / Clothed them more warmly than the coarse / Shirts our small bones. [*Welsh History*]

DOUGLAS THOMPSON 19 Cent.

11 And fearful the death of the diver must be, / Sleeping alone, sleeping alone, sleeping alone in the depths of the sea! [Song: *The Diver*]

FRANCIS THOMPSON 1859–1907

12 And I look through my tears on a soundless-clapping host / As the run-stealers flicker to and fro, / To and fro: – / O my Hornby and my Barlow long ago! [*At Lord's*]

13 Nothing begins, and nothing ends, / That is not paid with moan; / For we are born in other's pain, / And perish in our own. [*Daisy*]

14 I fled Him, down the nights and down the days; / I fled Him, down the arches of the years; / I fled him, down the labyrinthine ways / Of my own mind; and in the midst of tears / I hid from Him, and under running laughter. [*The Hound of Heaven*, 1]

15 But with unhurrying chase, / And unperturbèd pace, / Deliberate speed, majestic instancy, / They beat – and a Voice beat / More instant than the Feet – / 'All things betray thee, who betrayest Me.' [*Ib.* 10]

16 I said to Dawn: Be sudden – to Eve: Be soon. [*Ib.* 30]

17 My days have crackled and gone up in smoke, / Have puffed and burst as sun-starts on a stream. / Yea, faileth now even dream / The dreamer, and the lute the lutanist. [*Ib.* 122]

18 I dimly guess what Time in mists confounds; / Yet ever and anon a trumpet sounds / From the hid battlements of Eternity. [*Ib.* 143]

19 O world invisible, we view thee, / O world intangible, we touch thee, / O world unknowable, we know thee. [*The Kingdom of God*]

20 Not where the wheeling systems darken, / And our benumbed conceiving soars! – / The drift of pinions, would we hearken, / Beats at our own clay-shuttered doors. / The angels keep their ancient places; – / Turn but a stone, and start a wing! [*Ib.*]

21 Shall shine the traffic of Jacob's ladder / Pitched between Heaven and Charing Cross. [*Ib.*]

22 Secret was the garden; / Set i' the pathless awe / Where no star its breath can

draw. / Life, that is its warden, / Sat behind the fosse of death. Mine eyes saw not, and I saw. [*The Mistress of Vision*, 1]

1 When thy seeing blindeth thee / To what thy fellow-mortals see; / When thy sight to thee is sightless; / Their living, death; their light, most lightless; / Search no more – / Pass the gates of Luthany, tread the region Elenore. [*Ib*. 20]

2 When to the new eyes of thee / All things by immortal power, / Near or far, / Hiddenly / To each other linkèd are, / That thou canst not stir a flower / Without troubling of a star. [*Ib*. 22]

3 Summer set lip to earth's bosom bare, / And left the flushed print in a poppy there. [*The Poppy*]

4 I hang 'mid men my needless head, / And my fruit is dreams, as theirs is bread: / The goodly men and the sun-hazed sleeper / Time shall reap, but after the reaper / The world shall glean of me, me the sleeper. [*Ib*.]

5 What heart could have thought you? – / Past our devisal / (O filigree petal) / Fashioned so purely? [*To a Snowflake*]

6 His hammer of wind, / And His graver of frost. [*Ib*.]

7 Look for me in the nurseries of Heaven. [*To my Godchild*]

W. H. THOMPSON   1810–1886

8 We're none of us infallible – not even the youngest among us. [Remark to a junior fellow, when Master of Trinity]

JAMES THOMSON   1700–1748

9 When Britain first, at heaven's command, / Arose from out the azure main, / This was the charter of the land, / And guardian angels sung this strain: / 'Rule, Britannia, rule the waves: / Britons never will be slaves.' [*Alfred: a Masque*, II. v]

10 Delightful task! to rear the tender thought, / To teach the young idea how to shoot. [*The Seasons*, 'Spring', 1152]

11 An elegant sufficiency, content, / Retirement, rural quiet, friendship, books, / Ease and alternate labour, useful life, / Progressive virtue, and approving Heaven! [*Ib*. 1161]

12 The meek-eyed Morn appears, mother of dews. [*The Seasons*, 'Summer', 47]

13 Falsely luxurious! will not man awake? [*Ib*. 67]

14 Or sighed and looked unutterable things. [*Ib*. 1188]

15 While listening senates hang upon thy tongue. [*Ib*. 'Autumn', 15]

16 For loveliness / Needs not the foreign aid of ornament, / But is, when unadorned, adorned the most. [*Ib*. 204]

17 Welcome, kindred glooms! / Congenial horrors, hail! [*Ib*. 'Winter', 5]

18 There studious let me sit, / And hold high converse with the mighty dead. [*Ib*. 431]

19 Oh! Sophonisba! Sophonisba! Oh! [*Sophonisba*, III. ii]

JAMES THOMSON   1834–1882

20 The City is of Night; perchance of Death, / But certainly of Night. [*The City of Dreadful Night*, i]

21 For life is but a dream whose shapes return, / Some frequently, some seldom, some by night / And some by day. [*Ib*.]

22 The chambers of the mansion of my heart, / In every one whereof thine image dwells, / Are black with grief eternal for thy sake. [*Ib*. x]

23 I find no hint throughout the universe / Of good or ill, of blessing or of curse: / I find alone Necessity Supreme. [*Ib*. xiv]

24 As we rush, as we rush in the train, / The trees and the houses go wheeling back, / But the starry heavens above the plain / Come flying on our track. [*Sunday at Hampstead*, x]

25 A little straw hat with the streaming blue ribbons / Is soon to come dancing over the bridge. [*Sunday up the River*, i]

26 Give a man a horse he can ride, / Give a man a boat he can sail. [*Ib*. xv]

H. D. THOREAU   1817–1862

27 The mass of men lead lives of quiet desperation. [*Walden*, 'Economy']

28 I have lived some thirty years on this planet, and I have yet to hear the first

syllable of valuable or even earnest advice from my seniors. [*Walden*, 'Economy']

1 As if you could kill time without injuring eternity. [*Ib.*]

2 Beware of all enterprises that require new clothes. [*Ib.*]

3 Our life is frittered away by detail. .... Simplify, simplify. [*Ib.* 'Where I Lived, and What I Lived For']

4 Time is but the stream I go a-fishing in. [*Ib.*]

5 I never found the companion that was so companionable as solitude. [*Ib.* 'Solitude']

6 I had three chairs in my house; one for solitude, two for friendship, three for society. [*Ib.* 'Visitors']

7 I frequently tramped eight or ten miles through the deepest snow to keep an appointment with a beech-tree, or a yellow birch, or an old acquaintance among the pines. [*Ib.* 'Winter Visitors']

8 It takes two to speak the truth, – one to speak, and another to hear. [*A Week on the Concord and Merrimack Rivers*, 'Wednesday']

9 Some circumstantial evidence is very strong, as when you find a trout in the milk. [*Miscellanies*]

ROSE H. THORPE   1850–1939

10 As she climbed the dusty ladder on which fell no ray of light, – / Up and up, her white lips saying, 'Curfew shall not ring tonight.' [*Curfew Must not Ring Tonight*]

REV. GODFREY THRING
1823–1903

11 Fierce raged the tempest o'er the deep. [Hymn]

THUCYDIDES   *c.* 471–*c.* 400 B.C.

12 To famous men all the earth is a sepulchre. [*History*, II. 43. iii]

13 It is great glory in a woman to show no more weakness than is natural to her sex, and not be talked of, either for good or evil by men. [*Ib.* II. 45. ii]

14 That war is an evil is something that we all know, and it would be pointless to go on cataloguing all the disadvantages involved in it. No one is forced into war by ignorance, nor, if he thinks he will gain from it, is he kept out of it by fear. The fact is that one side thinks that the profits to be won outweigh the risks to be incurred, and the other side is ready to face danger rather than accept an immediate loss. [*History*, IV. 4]

JAMES THURBER   1894–1961

15 It's a Naïve Domestic Burgundy without Any Breeding, But I Think You'll be Amused by its Presumption. [*Men, Women and Dogs*, title of cartoon]

16 Well, if I Called the Wrong Number, Why Did You Answer the Phone? [*Ib.*]

17 I suppose that the high-water mark of my youth in Columbus, Ohio, was the night the bed fell on my father. [*My Life and Hard Times*, Ch. 1]

18 Her own mother lived the latter years of her life in the horrible suspicion that electricity was dripping invisibly all over the house. [*Ib.* 2]

19 When the dam broke, or, to be more exact, when everybody in town *thought* that the dam broke. [*Ib.* 3]

20 The ghost that got into our house on the night of November 17, 1915, raised such a hullabaloo of misunderstandings that I am sorry I didn't just let it keep on walking, and go to bed. [*Ib.* 4]

21 Then, with that faint fleeting smile playing about his lips, he faced the firing squad; erect and motionless, proud and disdainful, Walter Mitty, the undefeated, inscrutable to the last. [*My World and Welcome to It*, 'The Secret Life of Walter Mitty']

22 The War between Men and Women. [Series of cartoons]

EDWARD, FIRST BARON
THURLOW   1731–1806

23 When I forget my sovereign, may God forget me! [Speech in House of Lords, 15 Dec. 1778]

1 As guardian of His Majesty's conscience. [Speech in House of Lords, 1779]

2 Did you ever expect a corporation to have a conscience, when it has no soul to be damned, and no body to be kicked? [Attr.]

PAUL W. TIBBET 20 Cent.

3 A mushroom of boiling dust up to 20,000 feet. [Description of atomic bomb explosion]

TIBULLUS 54?–18? B.C.

4 *Te spectem, suprema mihi cum venerit hora, / Te teneam moriens deficiente manu.* – May I see you when my last hour comes, and hold you with my dying hand. [I. i. 59]

5 *Nile pater, quanam possim te dicere causa / Aut quibus in terris occuluisse caput? / Te propter nullos tellus tua postulat imbres, / Arida nec pluvio supplicat herba Iovi.* – Father Nile, why or in what lands can I say you have hidden your head? On your account your Egypt never sues for showers, nor does the dry grass bow to Jupiter the Rain-bringer. [I. vii. 23]

THOMAS TICKELL 1686–1740

6 I hear a voice you cannot hear, / Which says I must not stay; / I see a hand you cannot see, / Which beckons me away. [*Colin and Lucy*]

7 There taught us how to live; and (oh! too high / The price for knowledge) taught us how to die. [*On the Death of Mr Addison*, 81]

JOHN TILLOTSON 1630–1694

8 If God were not a necessary Being of himself, He might almost seem to be made for the use and benefit of mankind. [*Sermon* 93]

HARRY TILZER [ALBERT VON TILZER] 1878–1956

9 Come, Come, Come and have a drink with me / Down at the old 'Bull and Bush'. [Song]

MATTHEW TINDAL 1657–1733

10 Matters of fact, which as Mr Budgell somewhere observes, are very stubborn things. [*Will of Matthew Tindal*]

TITUS VESPASIANUS 40 or 41–81

11 Friends, I have lost a day. [Suetonius, *Titus*, 8]

JOHN TOBIN 1770–1804

12 The man that lays his hand upon a woman, / Save in the way of kindness, is a wretch / Whom 'twere gross flattery to name a coward. [*The Honeymoon*, II. i]

JACOPONE DA TODI ?–1306

13 *Stabat mater dolorosa / Iuxta crucem lacrimosa.* – At the cross her station keeping / Stood the mournful mother weeping. [*Stabat mater* (*English Hymnal* translation)]

LEO TOLSTOY 1828–1910

14 All happy families resemble one another, each unhappy family is unhappy in its own way. [*Anna Karenina*, I. Ch. 1]

15 This new feeling has not changed me, has not made me happy and enlightened all of a sudden, as I dreamed it would. ... Be it faith or not – I don't know what it is – through suffering this feeling has crept just as imperceptibly into my heart and has lodged itself firmly there. [*Ib.* VII. 19]

16 But my life now, my whole life, independently of anything that can happen to me, every minute of it is no longer meaningless as it was before, but has a positive meaning of goodness with which I have the power to invest it. [*Ib.*]

17 I am always with myself, and it is I who am my tormentor. [*Memoirs of a Madman*]

18 The highest wisdom has but one science – the science of the whole – the science explaining the whole creation and man's place in it. [*War and Peace*, V. Ch. 2]

19 The chief attraction of military service has consisted and will consist in this

compulsory and irreproachable idleness. [*War and Peace*, VII. 1]

1 All, everything that I understand, I understand only because I love. [*Ib.* VII. 16]

2 Love is God, and to die means that I, a particle of love, shall return to the general and eternal source. [*Ib.*]

3 Pure and complete sorrow is as impossible as pure and complete joy. [*Ib.* XV. 1]

4 The most powerful weapon of ignorance – the diffusion of printed material. [*Ib.* Epilogue, Pt II. Ch. 8]

A. M. TOPLADY   1740–1778

5 Rock of ages, cleft for me, / Let me hide myself in Thee. [Hymn]

CYRIL TOURNEUR   1575?–1626

6 Were't not for gold and women, there would be no damnation. [*The Revenger's Tragedy*, II. i]

7 Does the silk-worm expend her yellow labours / For thee? For thee does she undo herself? / Are lordships sold to maintain ladyships, / For the poor benefit of a bewildering minute? [*Ib.* III. iv]

THOMAS TRAHERNE 1637?–1674

8 You never enjoy the world aright, till the sea itself floweth in your veins, till you are clothed with the heavens, and crowned with the stars. [*Centuries of Meditations*, i. 29]

9 The corn was orient and immortal wheat, which never should be reaped, nor was ever sown. I thought it had stood from everlasting to everlasting. [*Ib.* iii. 3]

10 The Men! O what venerable and reverend creatures did the aged seem! Immortal Cherubims! And young men glittering and sparkling angels, and maids strange seraphic pieces of life and beauty! Boys and girls tumbling in the street, and playing, were moving jewels. [*Ib.*]

H. D. TRAILL   1842–1900

11 Why do you wear your hair like a man, / Sister Helen? [*After Dilettante Concetti* (a parody of D. G. Rossetti)]

12 Look in my face. My name is Used-to-was; / I am also called Played-out and Done-to-death, / And It-will-wash-no-more. [*After Dilettante Concetti*]

REV. JOSEPH TRAPP   1679–1747

13 The King, observing with judicious eyes / The state of both his universities, / To Oxford sent a troop of horse, and why? / That learned body wanted loyalty; / To Cambridge books, as very well discerning / How much that loyal body wanted learning. [On George I's donation of a library to Cambridge. (For reply see Sir William Browne)]

HERBERT TRENCH   1865–1923

14 O dreamy, gloomy, friendly trees. [*O Dreamy, Gloomy, Friendly Trees*]

15 Come, let us make love deathless, thou and I. [*To Arolilia*, ii]

ARCHBISHOP R. V. TRENCH
1807–1886

16 England, we love thee better than we know. [*Gibraltar*]

G. M. TREVELYAN   1876–1962

17 Education . . . has produced a vast population able to read but unable to distinguish what is worth reading. [*English Social History*, Ch. 18]

ANTHONY TROLLOPE 1815–1882

18 He must have known me if he had seen me as he was wont to see me, for he was in the habit of flogging me constantly. Perhaps he did not recognize me by my face. [*Autobiography*, Ch. 1]

19 Three hours a day will produce as much as a man ought to write. [*Ib.* 15]

20 Among these Mr Quiverful, the rector of Puddingdale, whose wife still continued to present him from year to year with fresh pledges of her love. [*Barchester Towers*, Ch. 7]

21 The blood of Tiberius flows in her veins. She is the last of the Neros! [*Ib.* 11]

1 Not only humble but umble, which I look upon to be the comparative, or, indeed, superlative degree. [*Doctor Thorne*, Ch. 4]

2 In these days a man is nobody unless his biography is kept so far posted up that it may be ready for the national breakfast-table on the morning after his demise. [*Ib.* 25]

3 It's dogged as does it. It ain't thinking about it. [*Last Chronicle of Barset*, Ch. 61]

4 Those who offend us are generally punished for the offence they give; but we so frequently miss the satisfaction of knowing that we are avenged! [*The Small House at Allington*, Ch. 50]

5 The tenth Muse, who now governs the periodical press. [*The Warden*, Ch. 14]

ST VINCENT TROUBRIDGE 1895–1963

6 There is an iron curtain across Europe. [*Sunday Empire News*, 21 Oct. 1945]

JOHN TRUMBULL 1750–1831

7 But optics sharp it needs, I ween, / To see what is not to be seen. [*McFingal*, Canto i. 67]

A. W. TUER 1838–1900

8 English as she is Spoke. [Title of Portuguese-English conversational guide]

MARTIN TUPPER 1810–1889

9 A good book is the best of friends, the same today and for ever. [*Proverbial Philosophy*, Series I, 'Of Reading']

10 It is well to lie fallow for a while. [*Ib.* 'Of Recreation']

MARSHAL TURENNE 1611–1675

11 *Dieu est toujours pour les gros bataillons.* – God is always on the side of the big battalions [Attr.]

IVAN TURGENEV 1818–1883

12 I agree with no man's opinion. I have some of my own. [*Fathers and Sons*, Ch. 13]

13 The temerity to believe in nothing. [*Fathers and Sons*, 14]

14 Go and try to disprove death. Death will disprove you, and that's all! [*Ib.* 27]

15 Whatever a man prays for, he prays for a miracle. Every prayer reduces itself to this: 'Great God, grant that twice two be not four.' [*Prayer*]

16 Diary of a Superfluous Man. [Title of story (the phrase was taken from Pushkin's *Eugene Onegin*)]

W. J. TURNER 1889–1946

17 When I was but thirteen or so / I went into a golden land, / Chimborazo, Cotopaxi / Took me by the hand. [*Romance*]

THOMAS TUSSER 1524?–1580

18 At Christmas play and make good cheer, / For Christmas comes but once a year. [*Five Hundred Points of Good Husbandry*, 'The Farmer's Daily Diet']

19 Yet true it is, as cow chaws cud, / And trees at spring do yield forth bud, / Except wind stands as never it stood, / It is an ill wind turns none to good. [*Ib.* 'A Description of the Properties of Winds']

20 'Tis merry in hall / When beards wag all. [*Ib.* 'August's Abstract']

21 Who goeth a borrowing / Goeth a sorrowing. / Few lend (but fools) / Their working tools. [*Ib.* 'September's Abstract']

22 In doing of either, let wit bear a stroke, / For buying or selling of pig in a poke. [*Ib.* 'September's Husbandry']

23 February, fill the dyke / With what thou dost like. [*Ib.* 'February's Husbandry']

24 Sweet April showers / Do spring May flowers. [*Ib.* 'April's Husbandry']

25 Some respite to husbands the weather may send, / But housewives' affairs have never an end. [*Ib.* 'Preface to the Book of Housewifery']

26 Seek home for rest, / For home is best. [*Ib.* 'Instructions to Housewifery']

27 The stone that is rolling can gather no moss; / For master and servant oft changing is loss. [*Ib.* 'Housewifely Admonitions']

MARK TWAIN
[S. L. CLEMENS] 1835–1910

1 There was things which he stretched, but mainly he told the truth. [*The Adventures of Huckleberry Finn*, Ch. 1]

2 *Pilgrim's Progress*, about a man who left his family, it didn't say why. The statements was interesting, but tough. [*Ib.* 17]

3 All kings is mostly rapscallions. [*Ib.* 23]

4 If there was two birds sitting on a fence, he would bet you which one would fly first. [*The Celebrated Jumping Frog*]

5 Soap and education are not as sudden as a massacre, but they are more deadly in the long run. [*The Facts concerning the Recent Resignation*]

6 I admire him [Cecil Rhodes], I frankly confess it; and when his time comes I shall buy a piece of the rope for a keepsake. [*Following the Equator*]

7 They spell it Vinci and pronounce it Vinchy; foreigners always spell better than they pronounce. [*Innocents Abroad*, Ch. 19]

8 Guides cannot master the subtleties of the American joke. [*Ib.*]

9 Are you going to hang him *anyhow* – and try him afterward? [*Innocents at Home*, Ch. 5]

10 When I'm playful I use the meridians and parallels of latitude for a seine, and drag the Atlantic Ocean for whales! I scratch my head with the lightning and purr myself to sleep with the thunder! [*Life on the Mississippi*, Ch. 3]

11 All the modern inconveniences. [*Ib.* 43]

12 At bottom he [Carlyle] was probably fond of them [the Americans], but he was always able to conceal it. [*My First Lie*]

13 An experienced, industrious, ambitious, and often quite picturesque liar. [*Private History of a Campaign that Failed*]

14 Cauliflower is nothing but cabbage with a college education. [*Pudd'nhead Wilson's Calendar*]

15 It is difference of opinion that makes horse races. [*Ib.*]

16 All say, 'How hard it is to die'–a strange complaint to come from the mouths of people who have had to live. [*Ib.*]

17 They make a mouth at you and say thank you 'most to death, but there ain't-a-going to be no core. [*Tom Sawyer Abroad*, Ch. 1]

18 The cross of the Legion of Honour has been conferred upon me. However, few escape that distinction. [*A Tramp Abroad*, Ch. 8]

19 Some of his words were not Sunday-school words. [*Ib.* 20]

20 This poor little one-horse town. [*The Undertaker's Chat*]

21 There was worlds of reputation in it, but no money. [*A Yankee at the Court of King Arthur*, Ch. 9]

22 A classic is something that everybody wants to have read and nobody wants to read. [Speech: *The Disappearance of Literature*]

23 The report of my death was an exaggeration. [Cable from Europe to the Associated Press]

EDWARD SMITH UFFORD
1851–1928

24 Throw out the life-line, throw out the life-line, / Someone is sinking today. [Revivalist hymn]

LUDWIG UHLAND 1787–1862

25 *In gleichem Schritt und Tritt.* – Alike in step and tread. [*Ich hatt' einen Kameraden*]

UMBERTO I 1844–1900

26 It is one of the incidents of the profession. [After an attempt on his life]

UPANISHADS 7 Cent. B.C.

27 This earth is the honey of all beings; all beings the honey of this earth. [*Famous Debates in the Forest*, V]

28 Death said: 'The good is one thing, the pleasant another; these two, having different objects, chain a man. It is well with him who clings to the good; he who chooses the pleasant misses his end.' [*Katha Upanishad*, ii]

1 I am this world and I eat this world. Who knows this, knows. [*Taittireeya Upanishad*, III. 10]

RALPH R. UPTON   Late 19 Cent.

2 Stop; look; listen. [Notice devised in 1912 for American railway crossings]

W. UPTON   18 Cent.

3 The lass so neat, with smile so sweet, / Has won my right good will, / I'd crowns resign to call thee mine, / Sweet lass of Richmond Hill. [*The Lass of Richmond Hill*]

VALERIUS MAXIMUS
fl. c. A.D. 15

4 I appeal from Philip drunk to Philip sober. [*Facta et Dicta Memorabilia*, VI. ii]

SIR JOHN VANBRUGH
1664–1726

5 The want of a thing is perplexing enough, but the possession of it is intolerable. [*The Confederacy*, I. ii]

6 As if a woman of education bought things because she wanted 'em. [*Ib.* II. i]

7 Much of a muchness. [*The Provoked Husband*, I. i]

8 BELINDA: Ay, but you know we must return good for evil.
LADY BRUTE: That may be a mistake in the translation. [*The Provoked Wife*, I. i]

W. H. VANDERBILT   1821–1885

9 The public be damned! [(Reply to a question whether the public should be consulted about luxury trains) A. W. Cole's *Letter, New York Times*, 25 Aug. 1918]

C. J. VAUGHAN   1816–1897

10 Must you go? Can't you stay? [(Method of breaking up awkward schoolboy breakfast parties, often quoted as: 'Can't you go? Must you stay?') G. W. E.

Russell's *Collections and Recollections*, Ch. 24]

HENRY VAUGHAN   1622–1695

11 I cannot reach it; and my striving eye / Dazzles at it, as at eternity. [*Childhood*]

12 Man is the shuttle, to whose winding quest / And passage through these looms / God ordered motion, but ordained no rest. [*Man*]

13 Men might look and live as glow-worms shine, / And face the moon: / Wise Nicodemus saw such light / As made him know his God by night. [*The Night*]

14 Dear night! this world's defeat; / The stop to busy fools; care's check and curb. [*Ib.*]

15 There is in God (some say) / A deep but dazzling darkness; as men here / Say it is late and dusky, because they / See not all clear; / O for that night! where I in him / Might live invisible and dim. [*Ib.*]

16 My soul, there is a country / Far beyond the stars, / Where stands a wingèd sentry / All skilful in the wars: / There, above noise and danger, / Sweet peace sits crowned with smiles, / And one born in a manger / Commands the beauteous files. [*Peace*]

17 For none can thee secure, / But one, who never changes, / Thy God, thy life, thy cure. [*Ib.*]

18 But life is, what none can express, / A quickness, which my God hath kissed. [*Quickness*]

19 Happy those early days! when I / Shined in my angel-infancy / Before I understood this place / Appointed for my second race, / Or taught my soul to fancy aught / But a white celestial thought. [*The Retreat*]

20 And in those weaker glories spy / Some shadows of eternity. [*Ib.*]

21 But felt through all this fleshly dress / Bright shoots of everlastingness. [*Ib.*]

22 O how I long to travel back, / And tread again that ancient track! / That I might once more reach that plain, / Where first I left my glorious train; / From whence th' enlightened spirit sees / That shady city of palm-trees. [*Ib.*]

23 Some men a forward motion love, / But I by backward steps would move, / And

when this dust falls to the urn, / In that state I came, return. [*The Retreat*]

1 Search well another world; who studies this, / Travels in clouds, seeks manna, where none is. [*The Search*, last lines]

2 They are all gone into the world of light! / And I alone sit lingering here; / Their very memory is fair and bright, / And my sad thoughts doth clear. [*They Are All Gone*]

3 I see them walking in an air of glory, / Whose light doth trample on my days; / My days which are at best but dull and hoary, / Mere glimmering and decays. [*Ib.*]

4 Dear, beauteous death! the jewel of the just, / Shining no where, but in the dark. [*Ib.*]

5 Remove me hence unto that hill, / Where I shall need no glass. [*Ib.*]

6 I saw Eternity the other night / Like a great ring of pure and endless light, / All calm. as it was bright, / And round beneath it, Time in hours, days, years, / Driv'n by the spheres / Like a vast shadow moved; in which the world / And all her train were hurled. [*The World*]

7 This ring the Bride-groom did for none provide / But for his bride [*Ib.*]

MARQUIS DE VAUVENARGUES 1715–1747

8 Great thoughts come from the heart. [*Réflexions et maximes*, 127]

9 In order to carry out great enterprises, one must live as if one will never have to die. [*Ib.* 142]

THOMAS, LORD VAUX 1510–1556

10 For Age, with stealing steps, / Hath clawed me with his clutch. [*The Aged Lover Renounceth Love*]

VEGETIUS 4 Cent. A.D.

11 *Qui desiderat pacem, praeparet bellum.* – Let him who desires peace prepare for war. [*De re mil.* 3, Prologue]

PIERRE VERGNIAUD 1753–1793

12 There was reason to fear that, like Saturn, the Revolution might devour each of its children in turn. [Lamartine, *Histoire des Girondins*, Bk xxxviii. Ch. 20]

PAUL VERLAINE 1844–1896

13 *De la musique avant toute chose, / Et pour cela préfère l'Impair, / Plus vague et plus soluble dans l'air, / Sans rien en lui qui pèse ou qui pose.* – Music before all else, and for that choose the irregular, which is vaguer and melts better into the air, having nothing in it that is heavy or emphatic. [*L'Art poétique*, 1]

14 *Prends l'éloquence et tords-lui son cou!* – Take eloquence and wring its neck. [*Ib.* 21]

15 *Et tout le reste est littérature.* – And everything else is just literature. [*Ib.* 36]

16 *Les sanglots longs / Des violons / De l'automne / Blessent mon cœur / D'une langueur / Monotone.* – The long sobs of the autumn violins infect my heart with a monotonous languor. [*Chanson d'automne*]

17 *Son regard est pareil au regard des statues, / Et pour sa voix, lointaine, et calme, et grave, elle a / L'inflexion des voix chères qui se sont tues.* – Her gaze is like the gaze of statues, and her voice, far-away, calm and grave, speaks with the accent of those who were dear and are now silent. [*Mon Rêve familier*]

18 *Il pleure dans mon cœur / Comme il pleut sur la ville.* – Tears fall in my heart like the rain on the town. [*Romances sans paroles*, iii]

QUEEN VICTORIA 1819–1901

19 I will be good. [(Resolution on ascending the throne) Martin, *The Prince Consort*]

20 He [Gladstone] speaks to Me as if I was a public meeting. [G. W. E. Russell, *Collections and Recollections*, Ch. 14]

21 We are not interested in the possibilities of defeat. [To A. J. Balfour, Dec. 1899]

22 We are not amused. [*Notebooks of a Spinster Lady*, 2 Jan. 1900]

ALFRED DE VIGNY   1797–1863

1 *Le vrai Dieu, le Dieu fort, est le Dieu des idées.* – The true God, the mighty God, is the God of ideas. [*La Bouteille à la mer*]

2 *La femme, enfant malade et douze fois impur.* – Woman, a sick child and twelve times unclean. [*La Colère de Samson*]

3 *J'aime le son du cor, le soir, au fond des bois.* – I love the sound of the horn, at evening, from the depths of the woods. [*Le Cor*]

4 *J'aime la majesté des souffrances humaines.* – I love the majesty of human sufferings. [*La Maison du berger*]

5 *Hélas je suis, Seigneur, puissant et solitaire, / Laissez-moi m'endormir du sommeil de la terre!* – Alas, Lord, I am powerful but alone. Let me sleep the sleep of the earth. [*Moïse*]

6 *Seul le silence est grand; tout le reste est faiblesse.* – Only silence is great; all else is weakness. [*La Mort du loup*]

7 *Fais énergiquement ta longue et lourde tâche / Dans la voie où le sort a voulu t'appeler, / Puis, après, comme moi, souffre et meurs sans parler.* – Perform your long and heavy task with energy, treading the path to which Fate has been pleased to call you. Then, afterwards, like me, suffer and die without a word. [*Ib.*]

8 An army is a nation within a nation; it is one of the vices of our age. [*Servitude et grandeur militaire*, 1. Ch. 2]

GEORGE VILLIERS *see under* BUCKINGHAM, 2ND DUKE OF

VILLIERS DE L'ISLE ADAM
                  1838–1889

9 *Vivre? les serviteurs feront cela pour nous.* – Live? Our servants will do that for us. [*Axel*, IV. ii]

FRANÇOIS VILLON   1431–1465?

10 *Mais où sont les neiges d'antan?* – Where are last year's snows? [*Ballade des dames du temps jadis*]

ST VINCENT OF LERINS
                      5 Cent.

11 *Quod semper, quod ubique, quod ab omnibus creditum est.* – What has been believed always, everywhere, and by everyone. [*Commonitorium*, ii]

VIRGIL   70–19 B.C.

12 *Arma virumque cano, Troiae qui primus ab oris / Italiam fato profugus Lavinaque venit / Litora.* – I sing of arms and of the hero who first came from the shores of Troy, exiled by Fate, to Italy and its Lavinian shore. [*Aeneid*, I. 1]

13 *Tantae molis erat Romanam condere gentem.* – Such a struggle was it to found the Roman race. [*Ib.* I. 33]

14 *Furor arma ministrat.* – Anger supplies the arms. [*Ib.* I. 150]

15 *O passi graviora, dabit deus his quoque finem.* – You have endured worse things, God will grant an end even to these. [*Ib.* I. 199]

16 *Forsan et haec olim meminisse iuvabit.* – Perhaps one day this too will be pleasant to remember. [*Ib.* I. 203]

17 *Durate, et vosmet rebus servate secundis.* – Endure, and preserve yourselves for better things. [*Ib.* I. 207]

18 *Sunt lacrimae rerum et mentem mortalia tangunt.* – Human deeds have their tears, and mortality touches the heart. [*Ib.* I. 462]

19 *Mens sibi conscia recti.* – A mind conscious of the right. [*Ib.* I. 604]

20 *Conticuere omnes intentique ora tenebant.* – All were silent and kept their gaze fixed upon him. [*Ib.* II. 1]

21 *Quaeque ipse miserrima vidi / Et quorum pars magna fui.* – I have myself seen these sad events, and played no small part in them. [*Ib.* II. 5]

22 *Timeo Danaos et dona ferentes.* – I fear the Greeks, even though they offer gifts. [*Ib.* II. 49]

23 *In utrumque paratus, / Seu versare dolos seu certae occumbere morti.* – Prepared for either event, to set his traps or to meet with certain death. [*Ib.* II. 61]

24 *Horresco referens.* – I shudder at the word. [*Ib.* II. 204]

1 *Tacitae per amica silentia lunae.* – Through the friendly silence of the quiet moon. [*Aeneid*, II. 255]

2 *Quantum mutatus ab illo / Hectore qui redit exuvias indutus Achilli.* – How changed from that Hector who returned, clad in the spoils of Achilles. [*Ib.* II. 274]

3 *Fuimus Troes, fuit Ilium et ingens / Gloria Teucrorum.* – We are Trojans no more, Ilium is destroyed, and the great glory of the Trojans has passed. [*Ib.* II. 325]

4 *Una salus victis nullam sperare salutem.* – There is but one safe thing for the vanquished: not to hope for safety. [*Ib.* II. 354]

5 *Dis aliter visum.* – The gods thought otherwise. [*Ib.* II. 428]

6 *Quid non mortalia pectora cogis, / Auri sacra fames!* – To what cannot you compel the hearts of men, O cursed lust for gold! [*Ib.* III. 56]

7 *Agnosco veteris vestigia flammae.* – I feel again a spark of that ancient flame. [*Ib.* IV. 23]

8 *O luce magis dilecta sorore.* – O you, dearer than the light to your sister. [*Ib.* IV. 31]

9 *Nec me meminisse pigebit Elissae / Dum memor ipse mei, dum spiritus hos regit artus.* – Nor will the thought of Dido be bitter to me so long as I have memory and breath controls these limbs. [*Ib.* IV. 335]

10 *Varium et mutabile semper / Femina.* – Woman is always fickle and changing. [*Ib.* IV. 569]

11 *Hos successus alit: possunt, quia posse videntur.* – Success nourished them; they seemed to be able, and so they were able. [*Ib.* V. 231]

12 *Facilis descensus Averni: / Noctes atque dies patet atri ianua Ditis; / Sed revocare gradum superasque evadere ad auras, / Hoc opus, hic labor est.* – The way down to hell is easy. The gates of black Dis stand open night and day. But to retrace one's steps and escape to the upper air – that is toil, that is labour. [*Ib.* VI. 126]

13 *Procul, o procul este, profani.* – Hence, away, uninitiated ones. [*Ib.* VI. 258]

14 *Tendebantque manus ripae ulterioris amore.* – Their hands outstretched in yearning for the other shore. [*Ib.* VI. 314]

15 *Spiritus intus alit, totamque infusa per artus / Mens agitat molem et magno se corpore miscet.* – The spirit within nourishes, and the mind, diffused through all the members, sways the mass and mingles with the whole frame. [(Of the Universe) *Aeneid*, VI. 726]

16 *Tu regere imperio populos, Romane, memento / (Hae tibi erunt artes), pacisque imponere morem, / Parcere subiectis et debellare superbos.* – O Romans, be it your care to rule the nations with imperial sway; these shall be your arts: to impose the rule of peace, to spare the humbled and to crush the proud. [*Ib.* VI. 851]

17 *Sunt geminae Somni portae, quarum altera fertur / Cornea, qua veris facilis datur exitus umbris, / Altera candenti perfecta nitens elephanto, / Sed falsa ad caelum mittunt insomnia manes.* – There are two gates of Sleep, whereof one is said to be of horn, through which the spirits of truth find an easy passage, the other made of gleaming white ivory, through which the gods send up false dreams to the upper world. [*Ib.* VI. 893]

18 *Geniumque loci . . . precatur.* – Prayed to the Genius of the place. [*Ib.* VII. 13]

19 *Flectere si nequeo superos, Acheronta movebo.* – If I cannot bend the gods, I will let hell loose. [*Ib.* VII. 312]

20 *Pedibus timor addidit alas.* – Fear lent wings to his feet. [*Ib.* VIII. 224]

21 *Nox ruit et fuscis tellurem amplectitur alis.* – Night came down and wrapped the earth in its dusky wings. [*Ib.* VIII. 369]

22 *Me, me, adsum qui feci, in me convertite ferrum.* – Here am I who did the deed. Turn your sword on me. [*Ib.* IX. 427]

23 *Sic itur ad astra.* – Thus shall you go to the stars. [*Ib.* IX. 641]

24 *Experto credite.* – Trust one who has proved it. [*Ib.* XI. 283]

25 *Formosam resonare doces Amaryllida silvas.* – You teach the woods to echo back the charms of Amaryllis. [*Eclogue* I. 5]

26 *Deus nobis haec otia fecit.* – A god gave us this leisure. [*Ib.* I. 6]

27 *Non equidem invideo, miror magis.* – Indeed I am not envious, rather I am amazed. [*Ib.* I. 11]

1 *Et penitus toto divisos orbe Britannos.* –
And the Britons completely isolated from
the whole world. [*Eclogue*, I. 66]

2 *Quem fugis, a, demens? Habitarunt di
quoque silvas.* – Whom do you flee, madman? Even gods have lived in the woods.
[*Ib.* II. 60]

3 *Latet anguis in herba.* – A snake lurks in
the grass. [*Ib.* III. 93]

4 *Magnus ab integro saeclorum nascitur
ordo. / Iam redit et virgo, redeunt Saturnia
regna / Iam nova progenies caelo demittitur alto.* – The great march of the centuries begins anew. Now the maiden
returns, now Saturn is king again, and a
new race descends from on high. [*Ib.* IV.
5]

5 *Incipe, parve puer: qui non risere parenti, /
Nec deus hunc mensa, dea nec dignata
cubili est.* – Begin then, little boy, no one
who has not given his mother a smile has
ever been thought worthy of his table by
a god, or by a goddess of her bed. [*Ib.* IV.
62]

6 *Arcades ambo, / Et cantare pares et
respondere parati.* – Arcadians both, and
each as ready as the other to lead off with
a song, or to give an apt response. [*Ib.*
VII. 4]

7 *Nunc scio quid sit Amor.* – At last I know
what Love is really like. [*Ib.* VIII. 43]

8 *Non omnia possumus omnes.* – We are not
all capable of everything. [*Ib.* VIII. 63]

9 *Sunt et mihi carmina, me quoque dicunt /
Vatem pastores; sed non ego credulus illis.
/ Nam neque adhuc Vario videor nec
dicere Cinna / Digna, sed argutos inter
strepere anser olores.* – I too have written
songs. I too have heard the shepherds call
me bard. But I am incredulous of them:
I have the feeling that I cannot yet compare with Varius or Cinna, but cackle like
a goose among melodious swans. [*Ib.* IX.
33]

10 *Omnia vincit Amor: et nos cedamus
Amori.* – Love carries all before him: we
too must yield to Love. [*Ib.* X. 69]

11 *Ultima Thule.* – Farthest Thule. [*Georgics*,
I. 30]

12 *Labor omnia vicit / Improbus et duris
urgens in rebus egestas.* – Persistent work
triumphed, and the stress of need in a
hard life. [*Ib.* I. 145]

13 *Imponere Pelio Ossam / Scilicet, atque
Ossae frondosum involvere Olympum.* –
Indeed, to pile Ossa on Pelion, and to roll
leafy Olympus upon Ossa. [*Georgies*, I.
281]

14 *O fortunatos nimium, sua si bona norint, /
Agricolas! Quibus ipsa procul discordibus
armis / Fundit humo facilem victum
iustissima tellus.* – How blest beyond all
blessings are farmers, if they but knew
their happiness! Far from the clash of
arms, the most just earth brings forth
from the soil an easy living for them. [*Ib.*
II. 458]

15 *Felix qui potuit rerum cognoscere causas.* –
Happy is he who has been able to learn
the causes of things. [*Ib.* II. 490]

16 *Fortunatus et ille deos qui novit agrestis.* –
Happy is he who knows the country gods.
[*Ib.* II. 493]

17 *Sed fugit interea, fugit inreparabile tempus.* – Meanwhile time is flying – flying
never to return. [*Ib.* III. 284]

18 *Agmine facto / Ignavum fucos pecus a
praesepibus arcent.* – They form a line,
and drive out the idle bands of drones
from the hives. [*Ib.* IV. 167]

19 *Si parva licet componere magnis.* – If one
may measure small things by great. [*Ib.*
IV. 176]

20 *At genus immortale manet, multosque per
annos / Stat fortuna domus, et avi numer-
antur avorum.* – But the race remains
immortal, the star of their house is constant through many years, and the grandfather's grandfathers are numbered in the
roll. [*Ib.* IV. 208]

FRANÇOIS-MARIE AROUET,
   called VOLTAIRE   1694–1778

21 *Si Dieu n'existait pas, il faudrait l'in-
venter.* – If God did not exist, it would be
necessary to invent Him. [*À l'Auteur du
livre des Trois Imposteurs*]

22 *Sachez que le secret des arts / Est de
corriger la nature.* – The secret of the arts
is to correct nature. [*À M. de Verrière*]

23 *Tous les genres sont bons, hors le genre
ennuyeux.* – All styles are good except the
tiresome sort. [*L'Enfant prodigue*, Preface to edition of 1738]

24 *Le superflu, chose très nécessaire.* – The
superfluous, a very necessary thing. [*Le
Mondain*, 22]

1 *Dans ce meilleur des mondes possibles.* –
In this best of all possible worlds. [*Candide*, Ch. i and *passim*]

2 *Ceux qui ont avancé que tout est bien ont dit une sottise: il fallait dire que tout est au mieux.* – Those who maintain that all is right talk nonsense; they ought to say that all is for the best. [*Ib.* Ch. i]

3 *Cunégonde ... vit entre les broussailles le docteur Pangloss qui donnait une leçon de physique expérimentale à la femme de chambre de sa mère, petite brune très jolie et très docile.* – Cunégonde ... saw Dr Pangloss behind some bushes giving a lesson in experimental philosophy to her mother's waiting-woman, a little brunette who seemed eminently teachable. [*Ib.*]

4 *Dans ce pays-ci il est bon de tuer de temps en temps un amiral pour encourager les autres.* – In this country we find it pays to shoot an admiral from time to time to encourage the others. [*Ib.* xxiii]

5 *Le travail éloigne de nous trois grands maux: l'ennui, le vice et le besoin.* – Work banishes those three great evils, boredom, vice, and poverty. [*Ib.* xxx]

6 *Cela est bien dit, répondit Candide, mais il faut cultiver notre jardin.* – That's true enough, said Candide, but we must go and work in the garden. [*Ib.*]

7 *Ils ne se servent de la pensée que pour autoriser leurs injustices, et n'emploient les paroles que pour déguiser leurs pensées.* – [Men] use thought only to justify their wrong-doings, and words only to conceal their thoughts. [*Dialogue du Chapon et de la Poularde*]

8 *Le mieux est l'ennemi du bien.* – The best is the enemy of the good. [*Dictionnaire philosophique*, 'Art dramatique']

9 *Ce corps qui s'appelait et qui s'appelle encore le saint empire romain n'était en aucune manière ni saint, ni romain, ni empire.* – This agglomeration which was called and still calls itself the Holy Roman Empire was neither holy, nor Roman, nor an empire in any way. [*Essai sur les mœurs et l'esprit des nations*, lxx]

10 *L'histoire n'est que le tableau des crimes et des malheurs.* – History is just the portrayal of crimes and misfortunes. [*L'Ingénu*, Ch. x]

11 *Toutes les histoires anciennes, comme le disait un de nos beaux esprits, ne sont que des fables convenues.* – All our ancient history, as one of our wits remarked, is no more than accepted fiction. [*Jeannot et Colin*]

12 *On doit des égards aux vivants; on ne doit aux morts que la vérité.* – One owes respect to the living; but to the dead one owes nothing but the truth. [*Lettres sur Œdipe*, i, note]

13 *Si Dieu nous a fait à son image, nous le lui avons bien rendu.* – If God made us in His image, we have certainly returned the compliment. [*Le Sottisier*, xxxii]

14 *N'ayant jamais pu réussir dans le monde, il se vengeait par en médire.* – Never having been able to succeed in the world, he took his revenge by speaking ill of it. [*Zadig*, Ch. iv]

15 *On presse l'orange, et on jette l'écorce.* – They squeeze the orange and throw away the skin. [Letter to Mme Denis, about his quarrel with Frederick the Great, 2 Sept. 1751]

16 *Quoi que vous fassiez, écrasez* l'infâme, *et aimez qui vous aime.* – Whatever you do crush that infamous thing [superstition], and love those who love you. [Letter to M. d'Alembert, 28 Nov. 1762]

17 *Quand la populace se mêle de raisonner, tout est perdu.* – Once the people begin to reason, all is lost. [Letter to Damilaville, 1 Apr. 1766]

18 *On dit que Dieu est toujours pour les gros bataillons.* – It is said that God is always on the side of the big battalions. [Letter to M. le Riche, 6 Feb. 1770 (cf. under Marshal Turenne)]

19 I disapprove of what you say, but I will defend to the death your right to say it. [Attr. to Voltaire in S. G. Tallentyre, *The Friends of Voltaire*, 1907]

RICHARD WAGNER   1813–1883

20 Now you have seen what we can do. Now want it! and if you do, we will achieve an art. [Speech after performance of *Die Götterdämmerung*]

W. S. WALKER   1795–1846

21 Too solemn for day, too sweet for night, / Come not in darkness, come not in light; / But come in some twilight interim, /

When the gloom is soft, and the light is dim. [*Too solemn for Day*]

HENRY WALLACE 1888–1965

1 The century on which we are entering can be and must be the century of the common man. [Address, 8 May 1942]

W. R. WALLACE ?–1881

2 The hand that rocks the cradle / Is the hand that rules the world. [*John o' London's Treasure Trove*]

GRAHAM WALLAS 1858–1932

3 The little girl had the makings of a poet in her who, being told to be sure of her meaning before she spoke, said: 'How can I know what I think till I see what I say?' [*The Art of Thought*]

EDMUND WALLER 1606–1687

4 Poets that lasting marble seek / Must carve in Latin or in Greek. [*Of English Verse*]

5 The seas are quiet, when the winds give o'er; / So calm are we, when passions are no more. [*Of the Last Verses in the Book*]

6 The soul's dark cottage, battered and decayed, / Lets in new light thro' chinks that time has made. / Stronger by weakness, wiser men become / As they draw near to their eternal home: / Leaving the old, both worlds at once they view, / That stand upon the threshold of the new. [*Ib.*]

7 That which her slender waist confined / Shall now my joyful temples bind; / No monarch but would give his crown / His arms might do what this has done. [*On a Girdle*]

8 A narrow compass, and yet there / Dwells all that's good, and all that's fair: / Give me but what this ribbon tied, / Take all the sun goes round beside. [*Ib.*]

9 Go, lovely rose, / Tell her that wastes her time and me, / That now she knows, / When I resemble her to thee, / How sweet and fair she seems to be. [*Song*]

10 How small a part of time they share, / That are so wondrous sweet and fair. [*Song*, contd.]

11 Why came I so untimely forth / Into a world which, wanting thee, / Could entertain us with no worth / Or shadow of felicity? [*To a very young Lady*]

HORACE WALPOLE, 4TH EARL OF ORFORD 1717–1797

12 Our supreme governors, the mob. [Letter to Horace Mann, 7 Sept. 1743]

13 Every drop of ink in my pen ran cold. [Letter to George Montagu, 3 July 1752]

14 It is charming to totter into vogue. [Letter to G. A. Selwyn, 2 Dec. 1765]

15 The next Augustan age will dawn on the other side of the Atlantic. ... At last some curious traveller from Lima will visit England, and give a description of the ruins of St Paul's, like the editions of Balbec and Palmyra. [Letter to Mann, 24 Nov. 1774]

16 The world is a comedy to those that think, a tragedy to those that feel. [Letter to the Countess of Upper Ossory, 16 Aug. 1776]

SIR ROBERT WALPOLE 1676–1745

17 Madam, there are fifty thousand men slain this year in Europe, and not one Englishman. [Remark to Queen Caroline, 1734]

18 They now *ring* the bells, but they will soon *wring* their hands. [Remark on the declaration of war with Spain. 1739]

19 The balance of power. [Speech in House of Commons, 13 Feb. 1741]

20 Sir Robert Walpole's definition of the gratitude of place-expectants, 'That it is a lively sense of *future* · favours'. [W. Hazlitt, *Lectures on the English Comic Writers*, 'Wit and Humour']

21 Anything but history, for history must be false. [Remark to his son, who offered to read to him. *Walpoliana*, Vol. i. p. 60]

22 All those men have their price. [(Reference to pretended patriots) *Ib.* i. 88]

WILLIAM WALSH 1663–1708

1 In love alone we hate to find / Companions of our woe. [Song: *Of all the Torments*]

2 I can endure my own despair, / But not another's hope. [*Ib.*]

IZAAK WALTON 1593–1683

3 As no man is born an artist, so no man is born an angler. [*Compleat Angler*, 'Epistle to the Reader']

4 I am, Sir, a Brother of the Angle. [*Ib.* Pt I. Ch. 1]

5 I remember that a wise friend of mine did usually say, 'that which is everybody's business is nobody's business'. [*Ib.* I. 2]

6 An excellent angler, and now with God. [*Ib.* I. 4]

7 I love such mirth as does not make friends ashamed to look upon one another next morning. [*Ib.* I. 5]

8 No man can lose what he never had. [*Ib.*]

9 Use him [your frog] as though you loved him. [*Ib.* I. 8]

10 This dish of meat is too good for any but anglers, or very honest men. [*Ib.*]

11 I love any discourse of rivers, and fish and fishing. [*Ib.* I. 18]

12 Look to your health; and if you have it, praise God, and value it next to a good conscience; for health is the second blessing that we mortals are capable of; a blessing that money cannot buy. [*Ib.* I. 21]

13 The great Secretary of Nature and all learning, Sir Francis Bacon. [*Life o Herbert*]

14 Of this blest man, let his just praise be given, / Heaven was in him before he was in heaven. [Written in Dr Richard Sibbes' *Returning Backslider*]

BISHOP WILLIAM WARBURTON 1698–1779

15 Orthodoxy is my doxy; heterodoxy is another man's doxy. [Remark to Lord Sandwich]

ARTEMUS WARD [CHARLES FARRAR BROWN] 1834–1867

16 I now bid you a welcome adoo. [*Artemus Ward His Book*, 'The Shakers']

17 I wish thar was winders to my Sole, sed I, so that you could see some of my feelins. [*Ib.* 'The Showman's Courtship']

18 If you mean gettin hitched, I'M IN! [*Ib.*]

19 My pollertics, like my religion, being of an exceedin accommodatin character. [*Ib.* 'The Crisis']

20 Shall we sell our birthrite for a mess of potash? [*Ib.*]

21 N.B. This is rote Sarcasticul. [*Ib.* 'A Visit to Brigham Young']

22 I girdid up my Lions & fled the Seen. [*Ib.*]

23 Did you ever hav the measels, and if so how many? [*Ib.* 'The Census']

24 'Fair youth, do you know what I'd do with you if you was my sun?' 'No,' sez he. 'Wall,' sez I, 'I'd appint your funeral tomorrow arternoon & the *korps should be ready*! You're too smart to live on this yearth.' [*Ib.* 'Edwin Forrest as Othello']

25 Before he retired to his virtuous couch. [*Ib.*]

26 The female woman is one of the greatest institooshuns of which this land can boste. [*Ib.* 'Woman's Rights']

27 Do me eyes deceive me earsight? Is it some dreams? [*Ib.* 'Moses, the Sassy']

28 I'm not a politician and my other habits are good. [*Ib.* 'Fourth of July Oration']

29 The ground flew up and hit me in the hed. [*Ib.* 'Thrilling Scenes in Dixie']

30 I presunted myself at Betty's bedside late at nite, with considerbul licker koncealed about my persun. [*Ib.* 'Betsy-Jain Reorgunised']

31 Why these weeps? [*Artemus Ward's Lecture*]

32 I prefer temperance hotels – although they sell worse liquor than any other kind of hotels. [*Ib.*]

33 He [Brigham Young] is dreadfully married. He's the most married man I ever saw in my life. [*Ib.*]

34 Why is this thus? What is the reason of this thusness? [*Ib.*]

1 Let us be happy and live within our means, even if we have to borrer the money to do it with. [*Science and Natural History*]

THOMAS WARD   1577–1639

2 Where to elect there is but one, / 'Tis Hobson's choice, – take that or none. [*England's Reformation*, Ch. iv. p. 326]

E. F. WARE   1841–1911

3 O Dewey was the morning / Upon the first of May, / And Dewey was the Admiral / Down in Manila Bay; / And Dewey were the Regent's eyes, / Them orbs of royal blue! / And Dewey feel discouraged? / I Dew not think we Dew. [*Manila*]

SUSAN WARNER   1819–1885

4 Jesus loves me – this I know, / For the Bible tells me so. [*The Love of Jesus*]

SAMUEL WARREN   1807–1877

5 There is probably no man living, though ever so great a fool, that cannot do *something* or other well. [*Ten Thousand a Year*, xxviii]

H. S. WASHBURN   1813–1903

6 We shall meet, but we shall miss him, / There will be one vacant chair. [*The Vacant Chair*]

GEORGE WASHINGTON
               1732–1799

7 Father, I cannot tell a lie. I did it with my little hatchet. [Attr.]

8 We must consult Brother Jonathan. [(Jonathan Trumble, Governor of Connecticut) Frequent remark during American Revolution]

9 It is our true policy to steer clear of permanent alliance with any portion of the foreign world. [Farewell Address, 17 Sept. 1796]

ROWLAND WATKYNS   17 Cent.

10 I love him not, but show no reason can / Wherefore, but this, I *do not love* the man. [*Flamma sine Fumo*, 'Antipathy']

SIR WILLIAM WATSON 1858–1936

11 April, April, / Laugh thy girlish laughter; / Then, the moment after, / Weep thy girlish tears! [*April*]

12 The staid, conservative, / Came-over-with-the-Conqueror type of mind. [*A Study in Contrasts*, I. i. 42]

ISAAC WATTS   1674–1748

13 Whene'er I take my walks abroad, / How many poor I see! / What shall I render to my God / For all his gifts to me? [*Divine Songs for Children*, iv, 'Praise for Mercies']

14 While others early learn to swear, / And curse and lie and steal. [*Ib.*]

15 Lord, I ascribe it to Thy grace, / And not to chance, as others do, / That I was born of Christian race, / And not a Heathen or a Jew. [*Ib.* vi, 'Praise for the Gospel']

16 There is a dreadful Hell, / And everlasting pains; / There sinners must with devils dwell / In darkness, fire, and chains. [*Ib.* xi, 'Heaven and Hell']

17 Let dogs delight to bark and bite, / For God has made them so, / Let bears and lions growl and fight, / For 'tis their nature to.

But, children, you should never let / Such angry passions rise; / Your little hands were never made / To tear each other's eyes. [*Ib.* xvi, 'Against Quarrelling and Fighting']

18 Birds in their little nests agree; / And 'tis a shameful sight, / When children of one family / Fall out, and chide, and fight. [*Ib.* xvii, 'Love between Brothers and Sisters']

19 How doth the little busy bee / Improve each shining hour, / And gather honey all the day / From every opening flower!

How skilfully she builds her cell! / How neat she spreads the wax; / And labours hard to store it well / With the sweet food she makes. [*Ib.* xx, 'Against Idleness and Mischief']

1 For Satan finds some mischief still / For idle hands to do. [*Divine Songs for Children*, xx, 'Against Idleness and Mischief']

2 The tulip and the butterfly / Appear in gayer coats than I: / Let me be dressed fine as I will, / Flies, worms, and flowers exceed me still. [*Ib.* xxii, 'Against Pride in Clothes']

3 Hush! my dear, lie still and slumber, / Holy angels guard thy bed! [*Ib.* xxxv, 'Cradle Hymn']

4 Hark! from the tombs a doleful sound. [Hymn]

5 There is a land of pure delight / Where saints immortal reign; / Infinite day excludes the night, / And pleasures banish pain. [Hymn]

6 Could we but climb where Moses stood, / And view the landskip o'er, / Nor Jordan's stream, nor death's cold flood, / Should fright us from the shore. [*Ib.*]

7 When I can read my title clear / To mansions in the skies, / I bid farewell to every fear, / And wipe my weeping eyes. [Hymn]

8 When I survey the wondrous Cross, / On which the Prince of Glory died, / My richest gain I count but loss / And pour contempt on all my pride. [Hymn]

9 Were the whole realm of nature mine, / That were a present far too small; / Love so amazing, so divine / Demands my soul, my life, my all. [*Ib.*]

10 'Tis the voice of the sluggard: I heard him complain, / 'You have waked me too soon, I must slumber again.' [*Moral Songs*, i, 'The Sluggard']

11 Our God, our help in ages past, / Our hope for years to come, / Our shelter from the stormy blast, / And our eternal home.

Beneath the shadow of Thy Throne / Thy saints have dwelt secure; / Sufficient is Thine Arm alone, / And our defence is sure.

Before the hills in order stood, / Or earth received her frame, / From everlasting Thou art God, / To endless years the same.

A thousand ages in Thy sight / Are like an evening gone; / Short as the watch that ends the night / Before the rising sun.

Time like an ever-rolling stream / Bears all its sons away; / They fly forgotten as a dream / Dies at the opening day. [*Psalms*, xc. First line altered by John Wesley to 'O God . . .']

EVELYN WAUGH   1903–1966

12 We schoolmasters must temper discretion with deceit. [*Decline and Fall*, Ch. 2]

13 Very hard for a man with a wig to keep order. [*Ib.* 3]

14 That's the public-school system all over. They may kick you out, but they never let you down. [*Ib.*]

15 I'm one of the blind alleys off the main road of procreation. [*Ib.* 12]

16 The Happier Hunting Ground assumes all responsibility. [*The Loved One*]

17 What did your Loved One pass on from? [*Ib.*]

18 Creative Endeavour lost her wings, Mrs Ape. [*Vile Bodies*, Ch. 1]

19 Particularly against books the Home Secretary is. If we can't stamp out literature in the country, we can at least stop it being brought in from outside. [*Ib.* 2]

20 I feel my full income when that young man is mentioned. [*Ib.* 6]

F. E. WEATHERLY   1848–1929

21 Where are the boys of the Old Brigade? [*The Old Brigade*]

22 Roses are flowering in Picardy, / But there's never a rose like you. [*Roses of Picardy*]

SIDNEY WEBB, LORD PASSFIELD   1859–1947

23 The inevitability of gradualness. [Presidential Address to the Labour Party Conference, 1920]

DANIEL WEBSTER   1782–1852

24 There is always room at the top. [When advised not to become a lawyer, since the profession was overcrowded]

25 The past, at least, is secure. [Second speech on Foot's Resolution, 26 Jan. 1830]

1 He touched the dead corpse of the Public Credit, and it sprang upon its feet. [Speech in praise of Alexander Hamilton, made in New York, 10 Mar. 1831]

2 Fearful concatenation of circumstances. [*Argument on the Murder of Captain White*]

JOHN WEBSTER   1580?–1625?

3 Glories like glow-worms, afar off shine bright, / But looked to near, have neither heat nor light. [*The Duchess of Malfi*, IV. ii. 148]

4 I know death hath ten thousand several doors / For men to take their exits. [*Ib.* IV. ii. 222]

5 Cover her face; mine eyes dazzle: she died young. [*Ib.* IV. ii. 267]

6 We are merely the stars' tennis-balls, struck and bandied / Which way please them. [*Ib.* V. iv. 52]

7 When I look into the fish-ponds in my garden, / Methinks I see a thing armed with a rake, / That seems to strike at me. [*Ib.* V. v. 5]

8 Is not old wine wholesomest, old pippins toothsomest, old wood burn brightest, old linen wash whitest? Old soldiers, sweethearts, are surest, and old lovers are soundest. [*Westward Hoe*, II. ii]

9 'Tis just like a summer bird-cage in a garden; the birds that are without despair to get in, and the birds that are within despair and are in a consumption for fear they shall never get out. [*The White Devil*, I. ii. 47]

10 Call for the robin redbreast and the wren, / Since o'er shady groves they hover, / And with leaves and flowers do cover / The friendless bodies of unburied men. [*Ib.* V. iv. 100]

11 But keep the wolf far thence, that's foe to men, / For with his nails he'll dig them up again. [*Ib.* V. iv. 108]

12 My soul, like to a ship in a black storm, / Is driven, I know not whither. [*Ib.* V. vi. 248]

13 I have caught / An everlasting cold; I have lost my voice / Most irrecoverably. [*Ib.* V. vi. 270]

JOSIAH WEDGWOOD   1730–1795

14 Am I not a man and a brother? [Inscription on a medal, afterwards the motto of the Anti-Slavery Society]

ARTHUR WELLESLEY, DUKE OF WELLINGTON
1769–1852

15 All the business of war, and indeed all the business of life, is to endeavour to find out what you don't know from what you do; that's what I called 'guessing what was at the other side of the hill'. [*Croker Papers*, Vol. iii]

16 I used to say of him [Napoleon] that his presence on the field made the difference of forty thousand men. [Stanhope, *Notes on Conversations with the Duke of Wellington*, 2 Nov. 1831]

17 Ours [our army] is composed of the scum of the earth. [*Ib.* 4 Nov. 1831]

18 There is no mistake; there has been no mistake; and there shall be no mistake. [*Wellingtoniana*, 1852]

19 Possible? Is anything impossible? Read the newspapers. [Quoted in *Words of Wellington*]

20 I don't know what effect these men will have upon the enemy, but, by God, they terrify me. [On a draft sent out to him in Spain, 1809]

21 Nothing except a battle lost can be half so melancholy as a battle won. [Dispatch from the field of Waterloo]

22 A battle of giants. [Referring in conversation with Samuel Rogers to the battle of Waterloo]

23 Don't quote Latin; say what you have to say, and then sit down. [Advice to a new M.P.]

24 I never saw so many shocking bad hats in my life. [On seeing the first Reformed Parliament]

25 The battle of Waterloo was won on the playing fields of Eton. [Attr. by Montalembert, *De l'avenir politique de l'Angleterre*]

26 Educate men without religion and you make them but clever devils. [Attr.]

27 I don't care a twopenny damn what becomes of the ashes of Napoleon Bonaparte. [Attr.]

1 Publish and be damned. [Attr.]

2 Sparrowhawks, Ma'am. [Alleged answer to Queen Victoria's question as to how the sparrows could be got out of the trees that were to be enclosed in Paxton's glass pavilion for the 1851 Exhibition]

3 Up Guards and at them again! [Attr. words at Waterloo. He himself said that his words probably were 'Stand up, Guards!' and that he then gave the order to attack]

H. G. WELLS   1866–1946

4 Roöötten Beëëastly Silly Hole! [*The History of Mr Polly*, Ch. I. 2]

5 And then came the glorious revelation of that great Frenchman whom Mr Polly called Raboo-loose. [*Ib.*]

6 'Sesquippledan,' he would say. 'Sesquippledan verboojuice.' [*Ib*. I. 5]

7 I'll make a gory mess of you. I'll cut bits orf you. [*Ib*. IX. 6]

8 'I'm a Norfan, both sides,' he would explain, with the air of one who had seen trouble. [*Kipps*, Bk I. Ch. vi. 1]

9 You can't have money like that and not swell out. [*Ib*. II. iv. 2]

10 I was thinking jest what a Rum Go everything is. [*Ib*. III. iii. 8]

11 Human history becomes more and more a race between education and catastrophe. [*The Outline of History*, Ch. 15]

12 The Shape of Things to Come. [Title of book, 1933]

CHARLES WESLEY   1707–1788

13 Gentle Jesus, meek and mild, / Look upon a little child, / Pity my simplicity, / Suffer me to come to thee. [Hymn]

14 Hark how all the welkin rings, / 'Glory to the King of Kings, / Peace on earth, and mercy mild, / God and sinners reconciled.' [Christmas hymn. First two lines altered by George Whitfield to: 'Hark! the herald-angels sing / Glory to the new-born king']

15 Jesu, lover of my soul, / Let me to thy bosom fly, / While the nearer waters roll, / While the tempest still is high; / Hide me, O my Saviour, hide, / Till the storm

of life is past: / Safe into the haven guide, / O receive my soul at last. [Hymn]

16 Other refuge have I none, / Hangs my helpless soul on Thee. [*Ib*.]

17 Cover my defenceless head / With the shadow of thy wing. [*Ib*.]

18 Lo! He comes with clouds descending, / Once for favoured sinners slain. [Hymn]

JOHN WESLEY   1703–1791

19 I look upon all the world as my parish. [*Journal*, 11 June 1739]

20 If justice and truth take place, if he is rewarded according to his desert, his name will stink to all generations. [(Of Lord Chesterfield) *Diary*, 11 Oct. 1775]

21 Though I am always in haste, I am never in a hurry. [Letter to a member of the Society, 10 Dec. 1777]

22 Let it be observed, that slovenliness is no part of religion; that neither this nor any text of Scripture, condemns neatness of apparel. Certainly this is a duty, not a sin. 'Cleanliness is, indeed, next to godliness.'* [*Sermon* xciii, 'On Dress'. *This phrase is probably Hebrew in origin]

REV. SAMUEL WESLEY
1662–1735

23 Style is the dress of thought; a modest dress, / Neat, but not gaudy, will true critics please. [*An Epistle to a Friend concerning Poetry*]

MAE WEST   1893–1980

24 Come up and see me some time. [*Diamond Lil* (film, 1932)]

LORD WESTBURY   1800–1873

25 Then, sir, you will turn it over once more in what you are pleased to call your mind. [T. A. Nash, *Life of Lord Westbury*, II. 292]

ARCHBISHOP WHATELY OF
DUBLIN   1787–1863

26 Happiness is no laughing matter. [*Apothegms*]

413

J. A. McNEILL WHISTLER
1834–1903

1 I am not arguing with you – I am telling you. [*The Gentle Art of Making Enemies*]

2 'I only know of two painters in the world,' said a newly introduced feminine enthusiast to Whistler, 'yourself and Velazquez.' 'Why,' answered Whistler in dulcet tones, 'why drag in Velazquez?' [D. C. Seitz, *Whistler Stories*]

3 Yes, madam, Nature is creeping up. [(Answer to a lady who said that a certain landscape reminded her of his pictures) *Ib.*]

4 No, I ask it for the knowledge of a lifetime. [(Answer to counsel in his case against Ruskin, who had asked, 'For two days' labour you ask two hundred guineas?') *Ib.*]

5 I'm lonesome. They are all dying. I have hardly a warm personal enemy left. [*Ib.*]

6 OSCAR WILDE: I wish I had said that. WHISTLER: You will Oscar, you will. [L. C. Ingleby, *Oscar Wilde*]

E. B. WHITE
1899–

7 Commuter – one who spends his life / In riding to and from his wife; / A man who shaves and takes a train, / And then rides back to shave again. [*The Commuter*]

HENRY KIRKE WHITE 1785–1806

8 Much in sorrow, oft in woe, / Onward, Christians, onward go. [Hymn. Altered by Dr W. B. Collyer to 'Oft in danger, oft in woe']

JOSEPH BLANCO WHITE
1775–1841

9 Mysterious Night! when our first parent knew / Thee from report divine, and heard thy name, / Did he not tremble for this lovely frame, / This glorious canopy of light and blue? [*To Night*]

T. H. WHITE 1906–1964

10 Seventeen years ago, come Michaelmas, and been after the Questing Beast ever since. Boring, very. [*The Sword in the Stone*, Ch. 2]

11 Train all the Pellinores with that ideah in mind. Limited eddication, rather. Fewmets, and all that. [*Ib.*]

12 But I unfortunately was born at the wrong end of time, and I have to live *backwards* from in front. [*Ib.* 3]

WILLIAM ALLEN WHITE
1868–1944

13 All dressed up, with nowhere to go. [On the Progressive Party in 1916, after Theodore Roosevelt retired from the Presidential campaign]

W. L. WHITE 1900–1973

14 They Were Expendable. [Title of book, 1942]

GEORGE WHITEFIELD
1714–1770

15 I had rather wear out than rust out. [Attr. by Robert Southey]

A. N. WHITEHEAD 1861–1947

16 The deliberate aim at Peace very easily passes into its bastard substitute, Anaesthesia. [*Adventures of Ideas*, Ch. 20]

17 An instant of time, without duration, is an imaginative logical construction. Also each duration of time mirrors in itself all temporal durations. [*Science and the Modern World*, Ch. iv]

WILLIAM WHITEHEAD
1715–1785

18 Yes, I'm in love, I feel it now, / And Caelia has undone me; / And yet I'll swear I can't tell how / The pleasing plague stole on me. [*The Je ne sçay quoi*, song]

19 Say, can you listen to the artless woes / Of an old tale, which every schoolboy knows. [*The Roman Father*, Prologue]

WILLIAM WHITING 1825–1878

20 O hear us when we cry to Thee / For those in peril on the sea. [Hymn: *Eternal Father, Strong to Save*]

WALT WHITMAN   1819–1892

1 I hear it was charged against me that I sought to destroy institutions, / But really I am neither for nor against institutions. [*I Hear It was Charged against Me*]

2 If any thing is sacred the human body is sacred. [*I Sing the Body Electric*, 125]

3 O Captain! my Captain! our fearful trip is done, / The ship has weathered every rack, the prize we sought is won, / The port is near, the bells I hear, the people all exulting. [*O Captain! my Captain!*]

4 But O heart! heart! heart! / O the bleeding drops of red, / Where on the deck my Captain lies, / Fallen cold and dead. [*Ib.*]

5 Out of the cradle endlessly rocking, / Out of the mocking-bird's throat, the musical shuttle. [*Out of the Cradle endlessly Rocking*]

6 Have you your pistols? have you your sharp-edged axes? / Pioneers! O pioneers! [*Pioneers! O Pioneers!*]

7 Camerado, this is no book, / Who touches this touches a man. [*So Long!* 53]

8 A great city is that which has the greatest men and women. [*Song of the Broad-Axe*, 108]

9 Where the populace rise at once against the never-ending audacity of elected persons. [*Ib.* 121]

10 I celebrate myself, and sing myself. [*Song of Myself*, 1. 1]

11 I loafe and invite my soul. [*Ib.* 1. 4]

12 Always the procreant urge of the world. [*Ib.* 3. 45]

13 I believe a leaf of grass is no less than the journey-work of the stars. [*Ib.* 31. 663]

14 I think I could turn and live with animals, they're so placid and self-contained, / I stand and look at them long and long. / They do not sweat and whine about their condition, / They do not lie awake in the dark and weep for their sins, / They do not make me sick discussing their duty to God, / Not one is dissatisfied, not one is demented with the mania of owning things, / Not one kneels to another, nor to his kind that lived thousands of years ago, / Not one is respectable or unhappy over the whole earth. [*Ib.* 32. 684]

15 Behold, I do not give lectures or a little charity, / When I give I give myself. [*Song of Myself*, 40. 994]

16 Do I contradict myself? / Very well then I contradict myself, / (I am large, I contain multitudes). [*Ib.* 51. 1324]

17 I sound my barbaric yawp over the roofs of the world. [*Ib.* 52. 1333]

18 Afoot and light-hearted I take to the open road, / Healthy, free, the world before me. [*Song of the Open Road*, 1. 1]

19 When lilacs last in the dooryard bloomed, / And the great star early drooped in the western sky in the night, / I mourned, and yet shall mourn with ever-returning spring. [*When Lilacs last in the Dooryard Bloomed*, 1. 1]

JOHN GREENLEAF WHITTIER   1807–1892

20 'Shoot, if you must, this old gray head, / But spare your country's flag,' she said. [*Barbara Frietchie*, 35]

21 For all sad words of tongue or pen, / The saddest are these: 'It might have been!' [*Maud Muller*, 105]

22 The Indian Summer of the heart. [*Memories*, ix]

23 Dinna ye hear it? – Dinna ye hear it? / The pipes o' Havelock sound. [*The Pipes at Lucknow*, iv]

REV. CORNELIUS WHUR   1782–1853

24 But lasting joys the man attend / Who has a polished female friend! [*The Accomplished Female Friend*]

G. J. WHYTE-MELVILLE   1821–1878

25 Then drink, puppy, drink, and let every puppy drink. [*Drink, Puppy, Drink*]

26 The swallows are making them ready to fly, / Wheeling out on a windy sky: / Goodbye, Summer, goodbye, goodbye. [*Goodbye, Summer*]

27 Wrap me up in my tarpaulin jacket, / And say a poor buffer lies low, / And six stalwart lancers shall carry me / With steps solemn, mournful, and slow. [*The Tarpaulin Jacket*]

BISHOP SAMUEL
WILBERFORCE   1805–1873

1 If I were a cassowary / On the plains of Timbuctoo, / I would eat a missionary, / Cassock, bands, and hymn-book too. [Impromptu verse]

ELLA WHEELER WILCOX
1855–1919

2 No question is ever settled / Until it is settled right. [*Settle the Question Right*]

3 Laugh and the world laughs with you; / Weep, and you weep alone; / For the sad old earth must borrow its mirth, / But has trouble enough of its own. [*Solitude*]

4 So many gods, so many creeds, / So many paths that wind and wind, / While just the art of being kind / Is all the sad world needs. [*The World's Need*]

OSCAR WILDE   1854–1900

5 I never saw a man who looked / With such a wistful eye / Upon that little tent of blue / Which prisoners call the sky. [*The Ballad of Reading Gaol*, Pt I. iii]

6 Yet each man kills the thing he loves, / By each let this be heard, / Some do it with a bitter look, / Some with a flattering word. / The coward does it with a kiss, / The brave man with a sword! [*Ib.* I. vii]

7 I know not whether Laws be right, / Or whether Laws be wrong; / All that we know who lie in gaol / Is that the wall is strong; / And that each day is like a year, / A year whose days are long. [*Ib.* V. i]

8 The vilest deeds like poison-weeds / Bloom well in prison-air; / It is only what is good in Man / That wastes and withers there: / Pale Anguish keeps the heavy gate / And the warder is Despair. [*Ib.* V. v]

9 Down the long and silent street, / The dawn, with silver-sandalled feet, / Crept like a frightened girl. [*The Harlot's House*]

10 Tread lightly, she is near / Under the snow, / Speak gently, she can hear / The daisies grow. [*Requiescat*]

11 And yet, and yet, / These Christs that die upon the barricades, / God knows it I am with them, in some ways. [*Sonnet to Liberty*]

12 Other people are quite dreadful. The only possible society is oneself. [*An Ideal Husband*, III]

13 Really, if the lower orders don't set us a good example, what on earth is the use of them? [*The Importance of Being Earnest*, I]

14 Truth is rarely pure, and never simple. [*Ib.*]

15 I have invented an invaluable permanent invalid called Bunbury, in order that I may be able to go down into the country whenever I choose. [*Ib.*]

16 The amount of women in London who flirt with their own husbands is perfectly scandalous. It looks so bad. It is simply washing one's clean linen in public. [*Ib.*]

17 In married life three is company and two is none. [*Ib.*]

18 LANE: There were no cucumbers in the market this morning, sir. I went down twice.
ALGERNON: No cucumbers!
LANE: No, Sir. Not even for ready money. [*Ib.*]

19 Rise, sir, from this semi-recumbent posture. [*Ib.*]

20 To lose one parent, Mr Worthing, may be regarded as a misfortune; to lose both looks like carelessness. [(Abbreviated in some editions) *Ib.*]

21 All women become like their mothers. That is their tragedy. No man does. That's his. [*Ib.*]

22 The old-fashioned respect for the young is fast dying out. [*Ib.*]

23 The good ended happily, and the bad unhappily. That is what Fiction means. [*Ib.* II]

24 Charity, dear Miss Prism, charity! None of us are perfect. I myself am peculiarly susceptible to draughts. [*Ib.*]

25 I never travel without my diary. One should always have something sensational to read in the train. [*Ib.*]

26 On an occasion of this kind it becomes more than a moral duty to speak one's mind. It becomes a pleasure. [*Ib.*]

27 CECILY: When I see a spade I call it a spade.
GWENDOLEN: I am glad to say I have never seen a spade. It is obvious that our

social spheres have been widely different. [*The Importance of Being Earnest*, II]

1 Your friend Bunbury is quite exploded. [*Ib.*]

2 In matters of grave importance, style, not sincerity, is the vital thing. [*Ib.* III]

3 Three addresses always inspire confidence, even in tradesmen. [*Ib.*]

4 Never speak disrespectfully of Society, Algernon. Only people who can't get into it do that. [*Ib.*]

5 No woman should ever be quite accurate about her age. It looks so calculating. [*Ib.*]

6 Prism! Where is that baby? [*Ib.*]

7 This suspense is terrible. I hope it will last. [*Ib.*]

8 It is a terrible thing for a man to find out suddenly that all his life he has been speaking nothing but the truth. [*Ib.*]

9 I can resist everything except temptation. [*Lady Windermere's Fan*, I]

10 I am the only person in the world I should like to know thoroughly. [*Ib.* II]

11 A man who knows the price of everything and the value of nothing. [(Definition of a cynic) *Ib.* III]

12 Experience is the name every one gives to their mistakes. [*Ib.*]

13 The English country gentleman galloping after a fox – the unspeakable in full pursuit of the uneatable. [*A Woman of No Importance*, I]

14 One should never trust a woman who tells one her real age. A woman who would tell one that would tell one anything. [*Ib.*]

15 LORD ILLINGWORTH: The Book of Life begins with a man and a woman in a garden.
MRS ALLONBY: It ends with Revelations. [*Ib.*]

16 Children begin by loving their parents. After a time they judge them. Rarely, if ever, do they forgive them. [*Ib.* II]

17 GERALD: I suppose society is wonderfully delightful!
LORD ILLINGWORTH: To be in it is merely a bore. But to be out of it simply a tragedy. [*Ib.* III]

18 You should study the Peerage, Gerald. ... It is the best thing in fiction the English have ever done. [*A Woman of No Importance*, III]

19 There is no such thing as a moral or an immoral book. Books are well written, or badly written. [*The Portrait of Dorian Gray*, Preface]

20 All art is quite useless. [*Ib.*]

21 There is only one thing in the world worse than being talked about, and that is not being talked about. [*Ib.* Ch. 1]

22 A man cannot be too careful in the choice of his enemies. [*Ib.*]

23 It is only shallow people who do not judge by appearances. [*Ib.* 2]

24 When good Americans die they go to Paris. [*Ib.* 3]

25 I can sympathize with everything, except suffering. [*Ib.*]

26 Women represent the triumph of matter over mind, just as men represent the triumph of mind over morals. [*Ib.* 4]

27 Meredith is a prose Browning, and so is Browning. [*The Critic as Artist*, Pt i, 'Intentions']

28 A little sincerity is a dangerous thing, and a great deal of it is absolutely fatal. [*Ib.* ii]

29 Ah! don't say you agree with me. When people agree with me I always feel that I must be wrong. [*Ib.*]

30 As long as war is regarded as wicked, it will always have its fascination. When it is looked upon as vulgar, it will cease to be popular. [*Ib.*]

31 There is no sin except stupidity. [*Ib.*]

32 Art never expresses anything but itself. [*The Decay of Lying*]

33 Please do not shoot the pianist. He is doing his best. [*Impressions of America*, 'Leadville']

34 As for the virtuous poor, one can pity them, of course, but one cannot possibly admire them. [*The Soul of Man under Socialism*]

35 With our James vulgarity begins at home, and should be allowed to stay there. [Letter to the *World*, on the subject of Whistler]

36 The man who can dominate a London dinner-table can dominate the world.

[Quoted by R. Aldington in his edition of Wilde]

1 The gods bestowed on Max the gift of perpetual old age. [(Max Beerbohm) *Ib.*]

2 I have nothing to declare except my genius. [(At the New York Customs House) F. Harris, *Oscar Wilde*]

3 He [Bernard Shaw] hasn't an enemy in the world, and none of his friends like him. [Shaw, *Sixteen Self Sketches*, Ch. 17]

4 'Ah, well then,' said Oscar, 'I suppose that I shall have to die beyond my means.' [(When asked a very large sum for an operation) Sherard, *Life of Wilde*]

EMPEROR WILHELM I
1797–1888

5 I haven't got time to be tired. [Answer during his last illness]

JOHN WILKES   1727–1797

6 The chapter of accidents is the longest chapter in the book. [Attr. by Southey, in *The Doctor*, Vol. iv. p. 166]

WILLIAM III   1650–1702

7 There is one certain means by which I can be sure never to see my country's ruin: I will die in the last ditch. [Quoted in Hume's *History of England*]

8 He [Professor Dodwell] has set his heart on being a martyr, and I have set mine on disappointing him. [Attr. remark on a Jacobite]

9 Every bullet has its billet. [John Wesley, *Journal*, 6 June 1765]

HARRY WILLIAMS   1874–1924
and JACK JUDGE   1878–1938

10 Good-bye Piccadilly, Farewell Leicester Square; / It's a long, long way to Tipperary, but my heart's right there! [*It's a Long Way to Tipperary*]

11 I'm Afraid to Go Home in the Dark. [Title of song]

12 In the Shade of the Old Apple Tree. [Title of song]

N. P. WILLIS   1806–1867

13 At present there is no distinction among the upper ten thousand of the city. [*The Necessity for a Promenade Drive*]

WENDELL WILLKIE   1892–1944

14 There exists in the world today a gigantic reservoir of good will toward us, the American people. [*One World*, Ch. 10]

W. G. WILLS   1828–1891

15 I'll sing thee songs of Araby, / And tales of fair Cashmere. [*Lalla Rookh*]

D. EARDLEY WILMOT   19 Cent.

16 But with love brooding there, why, no place can compare / With my little grey home in the west. [*My Little Grey Home*]

HARRIETTE WILSON   1789–1846

17 I shall not say why and how I became, at the age of fifteen, the mistress of the Earl of Craven. [*Memoirs*, first sentence]

JOHN WILSON   1785–1854
see NORTH, CHRISTOPHER

JOHN WILSON   ?–1889

18 O for a book and a shady nook, / Either in door or out; / With the green leaves whispering overhead, / Or the street cries all about, / Where I may read all at my ease, / Both of the new and old; / For a jolly good book whereon to look, / Is better to me than gold. [Motto to second-hand book catalogue, quoted in Lubbock, *Pleasures of Life*]

SANDY WILSON   1924–

19 But it's nicer, much nicer in Nice. [*The Boy Friend*, II]

T. WOODROW WILSON
1856–1924

20 There is such a thing as a man being too proud to fight. [Address at Philadelphia, 10 May 1915]

1 Armed neutrality. [Message to Congress, 26 Feb. 1917]

2 The world must be made safe for democracy. [Address to Congress, 2 Apr. 1917]

ARTHUR WIMPERIS   1874–1953

3 Gilbert the Filbert, / The Colonel of the Knuts. [*Gilbert the Filbert*]

4 I've gotter motter – / Always merry and bright! ['My Motter', from *The Arcadians* III]

5 Cheer up, cully, you'll soon be dead! / A short life and a gay one! [*Ib.*]

ANNE FINCH, COUNTESS OF WINCHILSEA   1661–1720

6 We faint beneath the aromatic pain. [*The Spleen*]

WILLIAM WINDHAM   1750–1810

7 Those entrusted with arms ... should be persons of some substance and stake in the country. [Speech in the House of Commons, 22 July 1807]

GEORGE WITHER   1588–1667

8 I loved a lass, a fair one, / As fair as e'er was seen; / She was indeed a rare one, / Another Sheba queen. [*A Love Sonnet*]

9 'Twas I that beat the bush, / The bird to others flew, / For she, alas, hath left me, / Falero, lero, loo. [*Ib.*]

10 Shall I, wasting in despair, / Die because a woman's fair? [*Sonnet*]

11 For, if she be not for me, / What care I how fair she be. [*Ib.*]

P. G. WODEHOUSE   1881–1975

12 He spoke with a certain what-is-it in his voice, and I could see that, if not actually disgruntled, he was far from being gruntled. [*The Code of the Woosters*]

13 Donning the soup-and-fish in preparation for the evening meal. [*Jeeves and the Impending Doom*]

14 There was another ring at the front door. Jeeves shimmered out and came back with a telegram. [*Jeeves Takes Charge*]

JOHN WOLCOT *see* **PINDAR, PETER**

CHARLES WOLFE   1791–1823

15 Not a drum was heard, not a funeral note, / As his corse to the rampart we hurried. [*The Burial of Sir John Moore*, i]

16 We buried him darkly at dead of night, / The sods with our bayonets turning. [*Ib.* ii]

17 But he lay like a warrior taking his rest, / With his martial cloak around him. [*Ib.* iii]

18 We carved not a line, and we raised not a stone – / But we left him alone with his glory. [*Ib.* viii]

JAMES WOLFE   1727–1759

19 I would rather have written those lines [Gray's *Elegy*] than take Quebec. [On the night before the storming of Quebec.]

20 Now God be praised, I will die in peace. [Dying words]

CARDINAL WOLSEY   1475?–1530

21 Had I but served God as diligently as I have served the King, he would not have given me over in my gray hairs. [To Sir William Kingston]

22 Father abbot, I am come to lay my weary bones among you. [Said to the Abbot of Leicester Abbey, 26 Nov. 1529]

MRS HENRY WOOD   1814–1887

23 Dead! and ... never called me mother. [*East Lynne* (dramatized version)]

J. T. WOOD   19 Cent.

24 Wait till the clouds roll by, Jenny, / Wait till the clouds roll by. [Song: *Wait Till the Clouds Roll By*]

VIRGINIA WOOLF   1882–1941

25 Those comfortably padded lunatic asylums which are known euphemistically as the stately homes of England. [*The Common Reader*, 'Lady Dorothy Nevill']

1 A Room of One's Own. [Title of book]

ALEXANDER WOOLLCOTT
1887–1943

2 I must get out of these wet clothes and into a dry Martini. [Quoted in *Reader's Digest*]

ELIZABETH WORDSWORTH
1840–1932

3 If all the good people were clever, / And all clever people were good, / The world would be nicer than ever / We thought that it possibly could.

But somehow, 'tis seldom or never / The two hit it off as they should; / The good are so harsh to the clever, / The clever so rude to the good! [*Good and Clever*]

WILLIAM WORDSWORTH
1770–1850

4 Where art thou, worse to me than dead? [*The Affliction of Margaret*]

5 My apprehensions come in crowds; / I dread the rustling of the grass; / The very shadows of the clouds / Have power to shake me as they pass. [*Ib.*]

6 Three times to the child I said, / 'Why, Edward, tell me why?' [*Anecdote for Fathers*]

7 Action is transitory – a step, a blow. / The motion of a muscle – this way or that – / 'Tis done, and in the after-vacancy / We wonder at ourselves like men betrayed: / Suffering is permanent, obscure and dark, / And shares the nature of infinity. [*The Borderers*, III. 1539]

8 Who is the happy warrior? Who is he / That every man in arms should wish to be? [*Character of the Happy Warrior*]

9 Who doomed to go in company with pain, / And fear, and bloodshed, miserable train! / Turns his necessity to glorious gain. [*Ib.*]

10 More skilful in self-knowledge, even more pure, / As tempted more; more able to endure, / As more exposed to suffering and distress. [*Ib.*]

11 From low to high doth dissolution climb. [*Ecclesiastical Sonnets*, III. 34, 'Mutability']

12 Tax not the royal Saint with vain expense. [*Ecclesiastical Sonnets*, III. 43, 'Inside of King's College Chapel, Cambridge']

13 Give all thou canst; high Heaven rejects the lore / Of nicely-calculated less or more. [*Ib.*]

14 The light that never was, on sea or land, / The consecration, and the poet's dream. [*Elegiac Stanzas, suggested by a Picture of Peele Castle*]

15 I have submitted to a new control: / A power is gone, which nothing can restore; / A deep distress hath humanised my soul. [*Ib.*]

16 Farewell, farewell the heart that lives alone, / Housed in a dream, at distance from the kind! [*Ib.*]

17 Not without hope we suffer and we mourn. [*Ib.*]

18 Oh! many are the poets that are sown / By Nature; men endowed with highest gifts, / The vision and the faculty divine; / Yet wanting the accomplishment of verse. [*The Excursion*, I. 77]

19 Strongest minds / Are often those of whom the noisy world / Hears least. [*Ib.* I. 91]

20 Rapt into still communion that transcends / The imperfect offices of prayer and praise. [*Ib.* I. 215]

21 The good die first, / And they whose hearts are dry as summer dust / Burn to the socket. [*Ib.* I. 500]

22 Thus was I reconverted to the world; / Society became my glittering bride, / And airy hopes my children. [*Ib.* III. 734]

23 One in whom persuasion and belief / Had ripened into faith, and faith become / A passionate intuition. [*Ib.* IV. 1293]

24 Spires whose 'silent fingers point to heaven'. [*Ib.* VI. 19 (echoing Coleridge's *The Friend*, No. 14)]

25 A man of hope and forward-looking mind / Even to the last! [*Ib.* VII. 276]

26 Nor less I deem that there are powers / Which of themselves our minds impress; / That we can feed this mind of ours / In a wise passiveness. [*Expostulation and Reply*]

27 Think you, 'mid all this mighty sum / Of things forever speaking, / That nothing of itself will come, / But we must still be seeking? [*Ib.*]

1 The rapt one, of the godlike forehead, / The heaven-eyed creature sleeps in earth: / And Lamb, the frolic and the gentle, / Has vanished from his lonely hearth. [*Extempore Effusion upon the Death of James Hogg*]

2 How fast has brother followed brother, / From sunshine to the sunless land! [*Ib.*]

3 I travelled among unknown men, / In lands beyond the sea: / Nor, England! did I know till then / What love I bore to thee. [*I travelled among unknown Men*]

4 I wandered lonely as a cloud / That floats on high o'er vales and hills, / When all at once I saw a crowd, / A host, of golden daffodils. [*I wandered lonely as a Cloud*]

5 Continuous as the stars that shine / And twinkle on the milky way. [*Ib.*]

6 Ten thousand saw I at a glance, / Tossing their heads in sprightly dance. [*Ib.*]

7 The waves beside them danced; but they / Out-did the sparkling waves in glee: / A poet could not but be gay, / In such a jocund company. [*Ib.*]

8 They flash upon that inward eye / Which is the bliss of solitude. [*Ib.*]

9 Him whom she loves, her Idiot Boy. [*The Idiot Boy*, 41]

10 The gods approve / The depth, and not the tumult, of the soul. [*Laodamia*, 74]

11 He spake of love, such love as spirits feel / In worlds whose course is equable and pure; / No fears to beat away – no strife to heal, – / The past unsighed for, and the future sure. [*Ib.* 97]

12 More pellucid streams, / An ampler ether, a diviner air, / And fields invested with purpureal gleams. [*Ib.* 104]

13 These waters, rolling from their mountain-springs / With a soft inland murmur. [*Lines composed a few miles above Tintern Abbey*, 3]

14 That best portion of a good man's life, / His little, nameless, unremembered acts / Of kindness and of love. [*Ib.* 33]

15 That blessed mood, / In which the burthen of the mystery, / In which the heavy and the weary weight, / Of all this unintelligible world, / Is lightened. [*Ib.* 37]

16 We are laid asleep / In body, and become a living soul: / While with an eye made quiet by the power / Of harmony, and the deep power of joy, / We see into the life of things. [*Lines composed a few miles above Tintern Abbey*, 45]

17 More like a man / Flying from something that he dreads than one / Who sought the thing he loved. [*Ib.* 70]

18 For Nature then ... / To me was all in all. [*Ib.* 72]

19 The sounding cataract / Haunted me like a passion: the tall rock, / The mountain, and the deep and gloomy wood, / Their colours and their forms, were then to me / An appetite. [*Ib.* 76]

20 I have learned / To look on nature, not as in the hour / Of thoughtless youth; but hearing oftentimes / The still, sad music of humanity. [*Ib.* 88]

21 I have felt / A presence that disturbs me with the joy / Of elevated thoughts; a sense sublime / Of something far more deeply interfused, / Whose dwelling is the light of setting suns, / And the round ocean and the living air, / And the blue sky, and in the mind of man. [*Ib.* 93]

22 All the mighty world / Of eye, and ear, – both what they half create, / And what perceive. [*Ib.* 105]

23 Nature never did betray / The heart that loved her. [*Ib.* 122]

24 Nor greetings where no kindness is, nor all / The dreary intercourse of daily life, / Shall e'er prevail against us, or disturb / Our cheerful faith, that all which we behold / Is full of blessings. [*Ib.* 130]

25 I heard a thousand blended notes, / While in a grove I sate reclined, / In that sweet mood when pleasant thoughts / Bring sad thoughts to the mind. [*Lines written in Early Spring*]

26 If this belief from heaven be sent, / If such be Nature's holy plan, / Have I not reason to lament / What man has made of man? [*Ib.*]

27 The sweetest thing that ever grew / Beside a human door! [*Lucy Gray*]

28 O'er rough and smooth she trips along, / And never looks behind; / And sings a solitary song / That whistles in the wind. [*Ib.*]

29 The cottage which was named the Evening Star / Is gone. [*Michael*, 476]

30 Nuns fret not at their convent's narrow room; / And hermits are contented with their cells. [*Miscellaneous Sonnets*, I. 1]

1 'Twas pastime to be bound / Within the sonnet's scanty plot of ground; / Pleased if some souls (for such there needs must be) / Who have felt the weight of too much liberty, / Should find brief solace there, as I have found. [*Miscellaneous Sonnets*, I. 1]

2 A flock of sheep that leisurely pass by, / One after one; the sound of rain, and bees / Murmuring; the fall of rivers, winds and seas, / Smooth fields, white sheets of water, and pure sky; / I have thought of all by turns, and yet do lie / Sleepless! [*Ib.* I. 14, 'To Sleep']

3 The first cuckoo's melancholy cry. [*Ib.*]

4 Blessed barrier between day and day. [*Ib.*]

5 Surprised by joy – impatient as the wind / I turned to share the transport. [*Ib.* I. 27]

6 The holy time is quiet as a nun / Breathless with adoration. [*Ib.* I. 30]

7 Where lies the land to which yon ship must go? [*Ib.* I. 31]

8 The world is too much with us; late and soon, / Getting and spending, we lay waste our powers: / Little we see in Nature that is ours; / We have given our hearts away, a sordid boon! / The sea that bares her bosom to the moon; / The winds that will be howling at all hours, / And are up-gathered now like sleeping flowers; / For this, for everything, we are out of tune. [*Ib.* I. 33]

9 Great God! I'd rather be / A pagan suckled in a creed outworn; / So might I, standing on this pleasant lea, / Have glimpses that would make me less forlorn; / Have sight of Proteus rising from the sea; / Or hear old Triton blow his wreathèd horn. [*Ib.*]

10 Scorn not the Sonnet; Critic, you have frowned, / Mindless of its just honours; with this key / Shakspeare unlocked his heart. [*Ib.* II. 1]

11 When a damp / Fell round the path of Milton, in his hand / The thing became a trumpet; whence he blew / Soul-animating strains – alas, too few! [*Ib.*]

12 Earth has not anything to show more fair: / Dull would be he of soul who could pass by / A sight so touching in its majesty: / This city now doth, like a garment, wear / The beauty of the morning; silent, bare, / Ships, towers, domes, theatres, and temples lie / Open

unto the fields, and to the sky; / All bright and glittering in the smokeless air. [*Miscellaneous Sonnets*, II. 36, 'Upon Westminster Bridge']

13 Ne'er saw I, never felt, a calm so deep! / The river glideth at his own sweet will: / Dear God! the very houses seem asleep; / And all that mighty heart is lying still! [*Ib.*]

14 Why art thou silent! Is thy love a plant / Of such weak fibre that the treacherous air / Of absence withers what was once so fair? [*Ib.* III. 25]

15 *A Poet!* – He hath put his heart to school. [*Ib.* III. 27]

16 My heart leaps up when I behold / A rainbow in the sky. [*My heart leaps up*]

17 The child is father of the man; / And I could wish my days to be / Bound each to each by natural piety. [*Ib.*]

18 Once did she hold the gorgeous east in fee; / And was the safeguard of the west. [*National Independence and Liberty*, I. 6, 'On the Extinction of the Venetian Republic']

19 Venice, the eldest child of Liberty. [*Ib.*]

20 When she took unto herself a mate, / She must espouse the everlasting sea. [*Ib.*]

21 Men are we, and must grieve when even the shade / Of that which once was great is passed away. [*Ib.*]

22 Thou hast great allies; / Thy friends are exultations, agonies, / And love, and man's unconquerable mind. [*Ib.* I. 8, 'To Toussaint l'Ouverture']

23 Two voices are there; one is of the sea, / One of the mountains; each a mighty voice: / In both from age to age thou didst rejoice, / They were thy chosen music, Liberty! [*Ib.* I. 12, 'On the Subjugation of Switzerland']

24 Plain living and high thinking are no more. [*Ib.* I. 13, 'Written in London, Sept. 1802']

25 Milton! thou shouldst be living at this hour: / England hath need of thee: she is a fen / Of stagnant waters. [*Ib.* I. 14, 'London, 1802']

26 Thy soul was like a star, and dwelt apart. [*Ib.*]

27 We must be free or die, who speak the tongue / That Shakspeare spake; the faith and morals hold / Which Milton held. [*Ib.* I. 16]

1 Another year! – another deadly blow! /
Another mighty empire overthrown! /
And we are left, or shall be left, alone.
[*National Independence and Liberty*, I. 27,
'Nov. 1806']

2 With gentle hand / Touch – for there is a
spirit in the woods. [*Nutting*]

3 O Nightingale, thou surely art / A
creature of a 'fiery heart'. [*O Nightingale*]

4 That was the song – the song for me! [*Ib.*]

5 There was a time when meadow, grove,
and stream, / The earth, and every common sight, / To me did seem / Apparelled
in celestial light, / .The glory and the
freshness of a dream. / It is not now as it
hath been of yore: – / Turn wheresoe'er
I may, / By night or day, / The things
which I have seen I now can see no more.
[*Ode, Intimations of Immortality*, i]

6 The rainbow comes and goes, / And
lovely is the rose, / The moon doth with
delight / Look round her when the heavens are bare, / Waters on a starry night
/ Are beautiful and fair; / The sunshine
is a glorious birth; / But yet I know,
where'er I go. / That there hath past
away a glory from the earth. [*Ib.* ii]

7 While the young lambs bound / As to the
tabor's sound. [*Ib.* iii]

8 A timely utterance gave that thought
relief, / And I again am strong. [*Ib.*]

9 The winds come to me from the fields of
sleep. [*Ib.*]

10 The babe leaps up on his mother's arm.
[*Ib.* iv]

11 Whither is fled the visionary gleam? /
Where is it now, the glory and the dream?
[*Ib.*]

12 Our birth is but a sleep and a forgetting: /
The soul that rises with us, our life's star,
/ Hath had elsewhere its setting, / And
cometh from afar: / Not in entire forget-
fulness, / And not in utter nakedness, /
But trailing clouds of glory do we come /
From God who is our home: / Heaven
lies around us in our infancy! / Shades
of the prison-house begin to close /
Upon the growing boy. [*Ib.* v]

13 The youth who daily farther from the
east / Must travel, still is Nature's priest, /
And by the vision splendid / Is on his
way attended; / At length the man per-
ceives it die away, / And fade into the
light of common day. [*Ib.*]

14 Earth fills her lap with pleasures of her
own: / Yearnings she hath in her own
natural kind. [*Ode, Intimations of Immortality*, vi]

15 Behold the child among his new-born
blisses, / A six-years' darling of a pigmy
size! [*Ib.* vii]

16 Thou best philosopher, who yet dost
keep / Thy heritage, thou eye among the
blind. [*Ib.* viii]

17 Provoke / The years to bring the inevitable yoke. [*Ib.*]

18 O joy! that in our embers / Is something
that doth live, / That nature yet remembers / What was so fugitive! / The
thought of our past years in me doth
breed / Perpetual benediction. [*Ib.* ix]

19 Those obstinate questionings / Of sense
and outward things, / Fallings from us,
vanishings; / Blank misgivings of a
Creature / Moving about in worlds not
realised, / High instincts before which
our mortal nature / Did tremble like a
guilty thing surprised. [*Ib.*]

20 Hence in a season of calm weather /
Though inland far we be, / Our souls
have sight of that immortal sea / Which
brought us hither, / Can in a moment
travel thither, / And see the children
sport upon the shore, / And hear the
mighty waters rolling evermore. [*Ib.*]

21 Though nothing can bring back the hour
/ Of splendour in the grass, of glory in the
flower. [*Ib.* x]

22 In the faith that looks through death, /
In years that bring the philosophic mind.
[*Ib.*]

23 And O, ye fountains, meadows, hills and
groves, / Forebode not any severing of
our loves! / Yet in my heart of hearts I
feel your might. [*Ib.* xi]

24 The clouds that gather round the setting
sun / Do take a sober colouring from an
eye / That hath kept watch o'er man's
mortality. [*Ib.*]

25 To me the meanest flower that blows can
give / Thoughts that do often lie too
deep for tears. [*Ib.*]

26 Stern Daughter of the Voice of God! /
O Duty! if that name thou love / Who
art a light to guide, a rod / To check the
erring and reprove. [*Ode to Duty*]

27 Me this unchartered freedom tires; / I
feel the weight of chance-desires: / My

423

hopes no more must change their name, /
I long for a repose that ever is the same.
[*Ode to Duty*]

1 Thou dost preserve the stars from wrong.
[*Ib.*]

2 Give unto me, made lowly wise, / The
spirit of self-sacrifice. [*Ib.*]

3 The dew was falling fast, the stars began
to blink; / I heard a voice; it said,
'Drink, pretty creature, drink!' [*The Pet-
Lamb*]

4 There's something in a flying horse, /
There's something in a huge balloon; /
But through the clouds I'll never float /
Until I have a little boat, / Shaped like
the crescent-moon. [*Peter Bell*, Pro-
logue, 1]

5 A primrose by a river's brim / A yellow
primrose was to him, / And it was nothing more. [*Ib.* I. 248]

6 Some sipping punch, some sipping tea, /
But, as you by their faces see, / All silent and all damned! [*Ib.* I. 518 (later
omitted)]

7 After ten months' melancholy, / Became
a good and honest man. [*Ib.* III. 1134]

8 One that would peep and botanize /
Upon his mother's grave. [*A Poet's
Epitaph*]

9 A reasoning, self-sufficing thing, / An
intellectual all-in-all! [*Ib.*]

10 You must love him, ere to you / He will
seem worthy of your love. [*Ib.*]

11 The harvest of a quiet eye, / That broods
and sleeps on his own heart. [*Ib.*]

12 Dust as we are, the immortal spirit grows
/ Like harmony in music; there is a dark
/ Inscrutable workmanship that reconciles
/ Discordant elements. [*The Prelude*, I.
340]

13 Small circles glittering idly in the moon, /
Until they melted all into one track / Of
sparkling light. [*Ib.* I. 365]

14 A huge peak, black and huge, / As if with
voluntary power instinct / Upreared its
head. [*Ib.* I. 378]

15 The grim shape / Towered up between
me and the stars, and still, / For so it
seemed, with purpose of its own / And
measured motion like a living thing, /
Strode after me. [*Ib.* I. 381]

16 My brain / Worked with a dim and undetermined sense / Of unknown modes of
being. [*The Prelude*, I. 391]

17 Huge and mighty forms, that do not live /
Like living men, moved slowly through
the mind / By day, and were a trouble to
my dreams. [*Ib.* I. 398]

18 The leafless trees and every icy crag /
Tinkled like iron. [*Ib.* I. 441]

19 Science appears as what in truth she is, /
Not as our glory and our absolute boast,
/ But as a succedaneum, and a prop / To
our infirmity. [*Ib.* II. 212]

20 Where the statue stood / Of Newton with
his prism and silent face, / The marble
index of a mind for ever / Voyaging
through strange seas of thought, alone.
[*Ib.* III. 60]

21 I made no vows, but vows / Were then
made for me; bond unknown to me /
Was given, that I should be, else sinning
greatly, / A dedicated spirit. [*Ib.* IV. 334]

22 When from our better selves we have too
long / Been parted by the hurrying
world, and droop, / Sick of its business,
of its pleasures tired, / How gracious,
how benign, is solitude. [*Ib.* IV. 354]

23 Spirits overwrought / Were making night
do penance for a day / Spent in a round
of strenuous idleness. [*Ib.* IV. 376]

24 There was a boy: ye knew him well, ye
cliffs / And islands of Winander! [*Ib.* V.
364 (cf. *There Was a Boy*)]

25 When the earliest stars began / To move
along the edges of the hills. [*Ib.* V. 366
(cf. as above)]

26 A gentle shock of mild surprise / Has
carried far into his heart the voice / Of
mountain torrents. [*Ib.* V. 382 (cf. as
above)]

27 Visionary power / Attends the motions
of the viewless winds, / Embodied in the
mystery of words. [*Ib.* V. 595]

28 Through the turnings intricate of verse, /
Present themselves as objects recognised,
/ In flashes, and with glory not their own.
[*Ib.* V. 603]

29 Whether we be young or old, / Our
destiny, our being's heart and home, /
Is with infinitude, and only there; / With
hope it is, hope that can never die, /
Effort, and expectation, and desire, /
And something evermore about to be.
[*Ib.* VI. 603]

1 The brook and road / Were fellow-travellers in this gloomy strait. [*The Prelude*, VI. 621 (cf. *The Simplon Pass*)]

2 The immeasurable height / Of woods decaying, never to be decayed, / The stationary blasts of waterfalls. [*Ib*. VI. 624 (cf. as above)]

3 Characters of the great Apocalypse, / The types and symbols of Eternity, / Of first, and last, and midst, and without end. [*Ib*. VI. 638 (cf. as above)]

4 Brothers all / In honour, as in one community, / Scholars and gentlemen. [*Ib*. IX. 227]

5 Bliss was it in that dawn to be alive, / But to be young was very heaven! [*Ib*. XI. 108 (cf. *French Revolution*)]

6 That which sets / ... The budding rose above the rose full blown. [*Ib*. XI. 118 (cf. as above)]

7 Not in Utopia, – subterranean fields, – / Or some secreted island, Heaven knows where! / But in the very world, which is the world / Of all of us, – the place where, in the end, / We find our happiness, or not at all! [*Ib*. XI. 140 (cf. as above)]

8 There is / One great society alone on earth: / The noble living and the noble dead. [*Ib*. XI. 393]

9 The pious bird with the scarlet breast, / Our little English robin. [*The Redbreast chasing the Butterfly*]

10 There was a roaring in the wind all night; / The rain came heavily and fell in floods. [*Resolution and Independence*, i]

11 Fears and fancies thick upon me came. [*Ib*. iv]

12 I thought of Chatterton, the marvellous boy, / The sleepless soul that perished in his pride. [*Ib*. vii]

13 By our own spirits are we deified: / We poets in our youth begin in gladness; / But thereof come in the end despondency and madness. [*Ib*.]

14 The oldest man he seemed that ever wore grey hairs. [*Ib*. viii]

15 As an old stone is sometimes seen to lie / Couched on the bald top of an eminence. [*Ib*. ix]

16 Like a sea-beast crawled forth, that on a shelf / Of rock or sand reposeth, there to sun itself. [*Ib*.]

17 Upon the margin of that moorish flood / Motionless as a cloud the old man stood, / That heareth not the loud winds when they call; / And moveth all together, if it move at all. [*Resolution and Independence*, xi]

18 Mighty poets in their misery dead. [*Ib*. xvii]

19 Still glides the stream, and shall for ever glide; / The form remains, the function never dies. [*The River Dvddon*, 34, 'After-Thought']

20 Enough, if something from our hands have power / To live, and act, and serve the future hour; / And if, as toward the silent tomb we go, / Through love, through hope, and faith's transcendent dower, / We feel that we are greater than we know. [*Ib*.]

21 The good old rule / Sufficeth them, the simple plan, / That they should take, who have the power, / And they should keep who can. [*Rob Roy's Grave*, 37]

22 A youth to whom was given / So much of earth – so much of heaven, / And such impetuous blood. [*Ruth*, 124]

23 She dwelt among the untrodden ways / Beside the springs of Dove, / A maid whom there were none to praise / And very few to love:

A violet by a mossy stone / Half hidden from the eye! / – Fair as a star, when only one / Is shining in the sky.

She lived alone, and few could know / When Lucy ceased to be; / But she is in her grave, and, oh, / The difference to me! [*She Dwelt among the untrodden Ways*]

24 She was a phantom of delight / When first she gleamed upon my sight; / A lovely apparition, sent / To be a moment's ornament. [*She Was a Phantom of Delight*]

25 I saw her upon nearer view, / A spirit, yet a woman too! / Her household motions light and free, / And steps of virgin-liberty. [*Ib*.]

26 And now I see with eye serene / The very pulse of the machine; / A being breathing thoughtful breath, / A traveller between life and death. [*Ib*.]

27 A perfect woman, nobly planned, / To warn, to comfort, and command. [*Ib*.]

28 For still, the more he works, the more / Do his weak ankles swell. [*Simon Lee*, 59]

1 A slumber did my spirit seal; / I had no human fears: / She seemed a thing that could not feel / The touch of earthly years.

No motion has she now, no force; / She neither hears nor sees; / Rolled round in earth's diurnal course, / With rocks, and stones, and trees. [*A Slumber did my Spirit Seal*]

2 To be a prodigal's favourite – then, worse truth, / A miser's pensioner – behold our lot! / O man, that from thy fair and shining youth / Age might but take the things youth needed not! [*The Small Celandine*]

3 Behold her, single in the field, / Yon solitary Highland lass! [*The Solitary Reaper*]

4 A voice so thrilling ne'er was heard / In spring-time from the cuckoo-bird, / Breaking the silence of the seas / Among the farthest Hebrides. [*Ib.*]

5 Will no one tell me what she sings? – / Perhaps the plaintive numbers flow / For old, unhappy, far-off things / And battles long ago. [*Ib.*]

6 The silence that is in the starry sky, / The sleep that is among the lonely hills. [*Song at the Feast of Brougham Castle, 163*]

7 Degenerate Douglas! oh, the unworthy lord! [*Sonnet, composed at — Castle*]

8 Stepping westward seemed to be / A kind of *heavenly* destiny. [*Stepping Westward*]

9 Strange fits of passion have I known: / And I will dare to tell, / But in the lover's ear alone, / What once to me befell. [*Strange Fits of Passion*]

10 What fond and wayward thoughts will slide / Into a lover's head! / 'O mercy!' to myself I cried, / 'If Lucy should be dead!' [*Ib.*]

11 One impulse from a vernal wood / May teach you more of man, / Of moral evil and of good, / Than all the sages can. [*The Tables Turned*]

12 I've measured it from side to side: / 'Tis three feet long, and two feet wide. [*The Thorn* (early version)]

13 Three years she grew in sun and shower, / Then Nature said, 'A lovelier flower / On earth was never sown; / This child

14 I to myself will take; / She shall be mine, and I will make / A Lady of my own. [*Three Years she Grew*]

14 The stars of midnight shall be dear / To her; and she shall lean her ear / In many a secret place. [*Ib.*]

15 'Tis said that some have died for love. [*'Tis Said that some have Died*]

16 Sweet childish days, that were as long / As twenty days are now. [*To a Butterfly, I've Watched you now*]

17 Small service is true service, while it lasts. [*To a Child, Written in her Album*]

18 O blithe new-comer! I have heard, / I hear thee and rejoice. / O cuckoo, shall I call thee bird, / Or but a wandering voice? [*To the Cuckoo*]

19 Thrice welcome, darling of the spring! / Even yet thou art to me / No bird, but an invisible thing, / A voice, a mystery. [*Ib.*]

20 Still longed for, never seen. [*Ib.*]

21 Thou unassuming common-place / Of Nature. [*To the Daisy, 'With little here to do'*]

22 Oft on the dappled turf at ease / I sit, and play with similes, / Loose types of things through all degrees. [*Ib.*]

23 Ethereal minstrel! pilgrim of the sky! / Dost thou despise the earth where cares abound? [*To a Skylark, 'Ethereal Minstrel!'*]

24 Type of the wise who soar, but never roam; / True to the kindred points of heaven and home! [*Ib.*]

25 Up with me! up with me into the clouds! [*To a Skylark, 'Up with me!'*]

26 Pleasures newly found are sweet / When they lie about our feet. [*To the Small Celandine, 'Pleasures newly Found'*]

27 – A simple child, / That lightly draws its breath, / And feels its life in every limb, / What should it know of death? [*We Are Seven*]

28 Still / The little maid would have her will, / And said, 'Nay, we are seven!' [*Ib.*]

29 Like an army defeated / The snow hath retreated. [*Written in March*]

30 There's not a nook within this solemn pass / But were an apt confessional for one / Taught by his summer spent, his autumn gone, / That life is but a tale of

morning grass / Withered at eve.
[*Yarrow Revisited*, 6, 'The Trossachs']

1 Let ... / The swan on still St Mary's
Lake / Float double, swan and shadow!
[*Yarrow Unvisited*]

2 Like – but oh, how different! [*Yes, it
was the mountain Echo*]

3 There neither is, nor can be, any *essential*
difference between the language of prose
and metrical composition. [*Preface to the
Lyrical Ballads*]

4 Poetry is the breath and finer spirit of all
knowledge; it is the impassioned expression which is in the countenance of all
Science. [*Ib.*]

5 Poetry is the spontaneous overflow of
powerful feelings: it takes its origin from
emotion recollected in tranquillity. [*Ib.*]

6 Every great and original writer, in proportion as he is great and original, must
himself create the taste by which he is to
be relished. [*Ib.*]

H. C. WORK   1832–1884

7 Father, dear father, come home with me
now, / The clock in the steeple strikes
one. [*Come Home, Father* (Temperance
song)]

8 My grandfather's clock was too large for
the shelf. / So it stood ninety years on the
floor. [*Grandfather's Clock*]

9 But it stopped short – never to go again – /
When the old man died. [*Ib.*]

10 It mus' be now de kingdom coming, /
An' de year ob Jubilo! [*Kingdom Coming*]

11 'Hurrah! hurrah! we bring the Jubilee! /
Hurrah! hurrah! the flag that makes you
free!' / So we sang the chorus from
Atlanta to the sea / As we were marching
through Georgia. [*Marching Through
Georgia*]

12 There's a good time coming, it's almost
here, / 'Twas a long, long time on the way.
[*Wake Nicodemus*]

SIR HENRY WOTTON   1568–1639

13 How happy is he born and taught, /
That serveth not another's will; / Whose
armour is his honest thought, / And

simple truth his utmost skill! [*The
Character of a Happy Life*]

14 And entertains the harmless day / With
a religious book, or friend. [*Ib.*]

15 Lord of himself, though not of lands, /
And having nothing, yet hath all. [*Ib.*]

16 He first deceased; she for a little tried /
To live without him: liked it not, and
died. [*Upon the Death of Sir Albert
Morton's Wife*]

17 You meaner beauties of the night, / That
poorly satisfy our eyes, / More by your
number than your light; / You common
people of the skies, / What are you when
the sun shall rise? [*Upon his Mistress, the
Queen of Bohemia*]

18 Virtue is the roughest way, / But proves
at night a bed of down. [*Upon the sudden
Restraint of the Earl of Somerset*]

19 An ambassador is an honest man sent to
lie abroad for the good of his country.
[Written in a friend's album]

SIR CHRISTOPHER WREN
1632–1723

20 *Si monumentum requiris, circumspice.*– If
you seek his monument, look round.
[Inscription in St Paul's (written by his
son)]

SIR THOMAS WYATT
1503?–1542

21 And wilt thou leave me thus? / Say nay,
say nay, for shame! [*And wilt thou leave
me thus?*]

22 Forget not yet the tried intent / Of such
a truth as I have meant, / My great
travail so gladly spent / Forget not yet.
[*Forget not yet*]

23 They flee from me that sometime did me
seek / With naked foot stalking in my
chamber. [*They flee from me*]

24 Whoso list to hunt, I know where is an
hind, / But as for me, alas, I may no
more. [*Whoso list to hunt*]

25 There is written her fair neck round
about: / *Noli me tangere*, for Caesar's I
am; / And wild for to hold, though I seem
tame. [*Ib.*]

WILLIAM WYCHERLEY
1640?–1716

1 Go to your business, I say, pleasure, whilst I go to my pleasure, business. [*The Country Wife*, II]

2 I have been toiling and moiling for the prettiest piece of china, my dear. [*Ib*. IV. iii]

3 Well, a widow, I see, is a kind of sinecure. [*The Plain Dealer*, V. iii]

JOHN WYCLIFFE   ?–1471

4 I believe that in the end the truth will conquer. [To the Duke of Lancaster, 1381, quoted in J. R. Green's *Short History of the English People*]

P. WYNDHAM LEWIS   1884–1957

5 The root of the comic is to be sought in the sensations resulting from the observations of a thing behaving like a person. But from that point of view all men are necessarily comic; for they are all things, or physical bodies, behaving as persons. [*The Wild Body*]

XENOPHON   c. 430–c. 359 B.C.

6 The sea! The sea! [*Anabasis*, IV. vii]

W. B. YEATS   1865–1939

7 I said, 'A line will take us hours maybe; / Yet if it does not seem a moment's thought, / Our stitching and unstitching has been naught.' [*Adam's Curse*]

8 Better go down upon your marrow-bones / And scrub a kitchen pavement, or break stones / Like an old pauper, in all kinds of weather; / For to articulate sweet sounds together / Is to work harder than all these. [*Ib.*]

9 His element is so fine / Being sharpened by his death, / To drink from the wine-breath / While our gross palates drink from the whole wine. [*All Souls' Night*]

10 When I was young, / I had not given a penny for a song / Did not the poet sing it with such airs / That one believed he had a sword upstairs. [*All Things can Tempt me*]

11 O body swayed to music, O brightening glance, / How can we know the dancer from the dance? [*Among School Children*, viii]

12 Now that my ladder's gone, / I must lie down where all the ladders start, / In the foul rag-and-bone shop of the heart. [*The Circus Animals' Desertion*]

13 There's more enterprise / In walking naked. [*A Coat*]

14 The years like great black oxen tread the world, / And God the herdsman goads them on behind, / And I am broken by their passing feet. [*The Countess Cathleen*, IV]

15 Down by the salley gardens my love and I did meet; / She passed the salley gardens with little snow-white feet. / She bid me take love easy, as the leaves grow on the tree; / But I, being young and foolish, with her would not agree. [*Down by the Salley Gardens*]

16 I have met them at close of day / Coming with vivid faces / From counter or desk among grey / Eighteenth-century houses. / I have passed with a nod of the head / Or polite meaningless words. [*Easter 1916*]

17 All changed, changed utterly: / A terrible beauty is born. [*Ib.*]

18 One that is ever kind said yesterday: / 'Your well-belovèd's hair has threads of grey, / And little shadows come about her eyes.' [*The Folly of Being Comforted*]

19 Time can but make her beauty over again. [*Ib.*]

20 O heart! O heart! if she'd but turn her head, / You'd know the folly of being comforted. [*Ib.*]

21 The little fox he murmured, / 'O what of the world's bane?' / The sun was laughing sweetly, / The moon plucked at my rein; / But the little red fox murmured, / 'O do not pluck at his rein, / He is riding to the townland / That is the world's bane.' [*The Happy Townland*]

22 I have spread my dreams under your feet; / Tread softly because you tread on my dreams. [*He wishes for the Cloths of Heaven*]

23 Out-worn heart, in a time out-worn, / Come clear of the nets of wrong and right. [*Into the Twilight*]

1 Nor law, nor duty bade me fight, / Nor public men, nor cheering crowds, / A lonely impulse of delight / Drove to this tumult in the clouds. [*An Irish Airman Foresees his Death*]

2 I will arise and go now, and go to Innisfree, / And a small cabin build there, of clay and wattles made: / Nine bean-rows will I have there, a hive for the honey-bee, / And live alone in the bee-loud glade. [*The Lake Isle of Innisfree*]

3 And I shall have some peace there, for peace comes dropping slow, / Dropping from the veils of the morning to where the cricket sings. [*Ib.*]

4 And evening full of the linnet's wings. [*Ib.*]

5 The wind blows out of the gates of the day, / The wind blows over the lonely of heart, / And the lonely of heart is withered away. [*The Land of Heart's Desire*]

6 The land of faery, / Where nobody gets old and godly and grave, / Where nobody gets old and crafty and wise, / Where nobody gets old and bitter of tongue. [*Ib.*]

7 All things uncomely and broken, all things worn out and old, / The cry of a child by the roadway, the creak of a lumbering cart, / The heavy steps of the ploughman, splashing the wintry mould, / Are wronging your image that blossoms a rose in the deeps of my heart. [*The Lover tells of the Rose in his Heart*]

8 Time drops in decay, / Like a candle burnt out. [*The Moods*]

9 Why, what could she have done, being what she is? / Was there another Troy for her to burn? [*No Second Troy*]

10 A pity beyond all telling / Is hid in the heart of love. [*The Pity of Love*]

11 Rose of all Roses, Rose of all the World! [*The Rose of Battle*]

12 Who dreamed that beauty passes like a dream? [*The Rose of the World*]

13 Under the passing stars, foam of the sky, / Lives on this lonely face. [*Ib.*]

14 Turning and turning in the widening gyre / The falcon cannot hear the falconer; / Things fall apart; the centre cannot hold; / Mere anarchy is loosed upon the world, / The blood-dimmed tide is loosed, and everywhere / The ceremony of innocence

is drowned; / The best lack all conviction, while the worst / Are full of passionate intensity. [*The Second Coming*]

15 And what rough beast, its hour come round at last, / Slouches towards Bethlehem to be born? [*Ib.*]

16 Far-off, most secret and inviolate Rose, / Enfold me in my hour of hours. [*The Secret Rose*]

17 A woman of so shining loveliness / That men threshed corn at midnight by a tress, / A little stolen tress. [*Ib.*]

18 When shall the stars be blown about the sky, / Like the sparks blown out of a smithy, and die? [*Ib.*]

19 Romantic Ireland's dead and gone, / It's with O'Leary in the grave. [*September 1913*]

20 And pluck till time and times are done / The silver apples of the moon, / The golden apples of the sun. [*The Song of Wandering Aengus*]

21 The brawling of a sparrow in the eaves, / The brilliant moon and all the milky sky, / And all that famous harmony of leaves, / Had blotted out man's image and his cry. [*The Sorrow of Love*]

22 Civilisation is hooped together, brought / Under a rule, under the semblance of peace / By manifold illusion. [*Supernatural Songs*, 'Meru']

23 What shall I do with this absurdity – / O heart, O troubled heart – this caricature, / Decrepit age that has been tied to me / As to a dog's tail? [*The Tower*, i]

24 Death and life were not / Till man made up the whole, / Made lock, stock and barrel / Out of his bitter soul. [*Ib.* iii]

25 When you are old and grey and full of sleep, / And nodding by the fire, take down this book. [*When you are old*]

26 But one man loved the pilgrim soul in you, / And loved the sorrows of your changing face. [*Ib.*]

27 Love fled / And paced upon the mountains overhead / And hid his face amid a crowd of stars. [*Ib.*]

FREDERICK AUGUSTUS, DUKE OF YORK   1763–1827

28 Then the little man [Walpole] wears a shocking bad hat. [Attr. remark at Newmarket]

ANDREW YOUNG   1807–1889

1 There is a happy land, / Far, far away, / Where saints in glory stand, / Bright, bright as day. [Hymn]

EDWARD YOUNG   1683–1765

2 Some, for renown, on scraps of learning dote, / And think they grow immortal as they quote. [*Love of Fame*, Satire I. 89]

3 Be wise with speed; / A fool at forty is a fool indeed. [*Ib.* II. 281]

4 With skill she vibrates her eternal tongue, / For ever most divinely in the wrong. [*Ib.* VI. 105]

5 One to destroy, is murder by the law; / And gibbets keep the lifted hand in awe; / To murder thousands, takes a specious name, / War's glorious art, and gives immortal fame. [*Ib.* VII. 55]

6 How commentators each dark passage shun, / And hold their farthing candle to the sun. [*Ib.* VII. 97]

7 Tired Nature's sweet restorer, balmy sleep! / He, like the world, his ready visit pays / Where fortune smiles; the wretched he forsakes. [*Night Thoughts*, 'Night I', 1]

8 Night, sable goddess! from her ebon throne, / In rayless majesty, now stretches forth / Her leaden sceptre o'er a slumb'ring world. [*Ib.* 18]

9 Creation sleeps. 'Tis as the general pulse / Of life stood still, and Nature made a pause; / An awful pause! prophetic of her end. [*Ib.* 23]

10 The bell strikes one. We take no note of time / But from its loss. [*Ib.* 55]

11 Be wise today; 'tis madness to defer. [*Ib.* 390]

12 Procrastination is the thief of time. [*Ib.* 393]

13 Time flies, death urges, knells call, heaven invites, / Hell threatens. [*Night Thoughts*, 'Night 2', 292]

14 Man wants but little, nor that little long. [*Ib.* 'Night 4', 118]

15 A God all mercy is a God unjust. [*Ib.* 233]

16 By night an atheist half believes a God. [*Ib.* 'Night 5', 176]

G. W. YOUNG   late 19 Cent.

17 Though in silence, with blighted affection, I pine, / Yet the lips that touch liquor must never touch mine! [*The Lips That Touch Liquor*]

JAN ZAMOYSKI   1541–1605

18 The king reigns, but does not govern. [Speech in Polish Parliament, 1605]

ISRAEL ZANGWILL   1864–1926

19 Scratch the Christian and you find the pagan – spoiled. [*Children of the Ghetto*, II. Ch. 6]

ÉMILE ZOLA   1840–1902

20 *Une œuvre d'art est un coin de la création vu à travers un tempérament.* – A work of art is a corner of creation seen through a temperament. [*Mes Haines*, 'M. H. Taine, Artiste']

21 *La vérité est en marche; rien ne peut plus l'arrêter.* – Truth is on the march; nothing can stop it now. [Article on the Dreyfus case]

22 *Les documents humains.* – Human documents. [Title of an article]

23 *J'accuse.* – I accuse. [Title of an open letter to the French President concerning the Dreyfus case]

INDEX

References are given thus: '173:3', which means 'page 173, quotation 3'.

Plurals, and the third person singular of verbs, where these take only an 's', are indexed with the singular or nominative; for example, 'hate' and 'hates' are indexed together, 'hate' being abbreviated to 'h.', and 'hates' to 'h.s'. Where the plural or third person form has '-es' or '-ies' (e.g. 'misses', 'hurries'), these are indexed separately.

This index includes foreign as well as English words. The former are printed in italics.

Irregular, archaic, and dialect spellings are indexed under the normal modern spelling of the word, unless the former spelling is likely to be well known. Some words are indexed under both forms.

A

A: A was an apple-pie 271:21
   'A,' whispered C, '... I'm going' 231:19
   first write a crowned A 106:23
A: A noir, E blanc 297:2
Abased: exalt himself shall be a. 49:14
Abate: a., – Cardinal, – Christ 77:4
Abatement: a. and low price 352:1
Abbot: slumber a.s, purple 284:20
Abdiel: seraph A., faithful found 258:2
A-bed: a-b. after midnight 352:15
Aberdour: half owre to A. 21:13
Abhorrence: my heart's a.! 77:14
Abide: a. with me! 240:8
   a. with me from morn to eve 220:1
   and nowhere did a. 115:1
   something in him we cannot a. 308:3
Abiit: a., excessit, evasit 112:6
Abilities: from each according to his a. 247:17
   have but moderate a. 296:9
Ability: lean and low a. 353:13
   studies serve ... for a. 18:38
Able: seemed to be a. 405:11
Ablution: priestlike task of pure a. 217:16
Abode: a. where the eternal are 359:14
Abomination: a. of desolation 49:19
Abora: singing of Mount A. 116:5
Abou: A. Ben Adhem 201:13
About: a. it and a. 159:2
Abra: though I called another, A. came 292:36
Abraham: sleep in A.'s bosom 347:9
Abram: O father A.! 337:23
Abridgement: a. of all that was pleasant 173:3
Abroad: before he goes a. 374:26
   for the good of my country ... a. 156:22
   no more; I will a. 187:23
Absalom: A., my son 33:9
Absence: a. from whom we love 122:21
   a. makes the heart grow fonder 6:19 25:5
   a. seemed my flame to qualify 356:21
   a. withers what was once so fair 422:14
   conspicuous ... by its a. 302:17

Absence – *contd*
   cry of A., A., in the heart 296:1
   dote on his very a. 337:14
   in a fit of a. of mind 307:26
   we console ourselves for their a. 357:23
Absent: a. are always in the wrong 133:2
   a. in body 53:27
   been a. in the spring 356:12
   presents ... endear a.s 228:14
   though you be a. here 121:20
   when we are a. one from another 31:18
Absent: a.s ont toujours tort 133:2
Absolute: how a. the knave is! 319:16
   so a. she seems 258:13
Absolutism: a. moderated by assassination 6:15
   a. tempered by assassination 267:9
Abstain: you shall a. 171:6
Abstinence: lean and sallow a. 253:9
Abstract: a.s and brief chronicles 316:21
Absurd: nothing so a. 111:27
Absurdity: do with this a. 429:23
Abundance: shall have a. 49:23
Abuse: more dangerous the a. 80:24
   suffered from a. of lechery 144:19
Abused: by himself a. 286:29
Abyssinian: A. maid 116:5
Academe: arts, the a.s 331:23
   olive-grove of A. 259:2
Academi: inter silvas A. 196:22
Academus: groves of A. 196:22
Accent: loved a.s are soon forgot 361:3
Acceptable: a. in thy sight 35:2
Accident: a.s will occur 134:30
   chapter of a.s 109:10 418:6
   have it found out by a. 229:20
   many a happy a. 250:32
   moving a.s by flood and field 342:29
   runs into a.s 246:5
Accipe: a. fraterno multum manantia fletu 103:18
Accommodant: plus a.s ... plus habiles 227:13
Accommodement: avec lui des a.s 262:15
Accomplishment: a. of verse 420:18

431

Account: but sent to my a. 315:20
   give a. .... in the day of judgement 48:10
   making up the main a. 76:10
Accursed: think themselves a. 324:26
Accuse: j'a. 430:23
Accused: apology before you be a. 106:4
Acheronta: A. movebo 405:19
Achieve: a. of, the mastery of the thing! 195:14
   to a. that I have done 244:6
Achieving: still a., still pursuing 237:4
Achilles: A.' wrath, to Greece 289:20
   clad in the spoils of A. 405:2
   see the great A. 392:8
   stood upon A.' tomb 91:18
   what name A. assumed 69:15
Achilli: qui redit exuvias indutus A. 405:2
Achitophel: false A. was first 146:19
Acid: drank prussic a. 23:7
Acquaintance: a.s are all very commonplace 185:19
   good creditable a. 379:9
   good friend, but bad a. 91:2
   hope our a. may be a long 'un 138:14
   if a man does not make new a. 207:16
   should auld a. be forgot 82:21
   what! old a.! 322:6
Acquiesce: will ... soberly a. 70:14
Acquist: new a. of true experience 259:27
Acre: few paternal a.s bound 288:6
   three a.s and a cow 117:6
Acroceraunian: snows in the A. mountains 359:16
Act: a. upon it, if you can! 168:17
   and sleep an a. or two 326:15
   both a. and know 247:5
   every a. ... as if it were the last 14:22
   familiar a.s are beautiful 362:30
   four first a.s already past 29:17
   his a.s being seven ages 311:14
   last a. crowns the play 294:2
   may show in some fifth A. 389:23
   thoughts ... packed into a narrow a. 76:11
   through the A. of Settlement 296:14
   unproportioned thought his a. 314:32
   unremembered a.s of kindness 421:14
   value ... in ... every a. 14:27
   within the meaning of the A. 6:18
Acte: a. gratuite 167:22
Acting: a. of a dreadful thing 327:6
   a. ... the lowest of the arts 264:16
   when he was off, he was a. 173:5
Action: a. is transitory 420:7
   a. will furnish belief 113:3
   by a. dignified 348:22
   complete a. of some magnitude 10:1
   dearest a. in the tented field 342:26
   do a good a. by stealth 229:20
   in a. faithful 288:5
   in a. how like an angel! 316:13
   lose the name of a. 316:29
   my a.s are my ministers' 106:7
   single complete a. 63:2
   spheres of a. 175:18
   suit the a. to the word 317:12
   that and th' a. fine 187:29
Actor: a.s ... were all spirits 350:18
   assembled like amateur a.s 153:13
   best a.s in the world 316:17

Actor – *contd*
   fault and not the a. of it 336:11
   well-graced a. leaves the stage 346:14
Adam: A. lay I-bowndyn 5:1
   A. the goodliest man 257:15
   as in A. all die 54:12
   create again that A. 92:6
   gardener A. and his wife 386:27
   grave man, nicknamed A. 113:5
   offending A. out of him 323:23
   old A. in this Child 291:35
   old A., the carrion crow 26:21
   son of A. and of Eve 292:29
   when A. delved 20:1
Adazzle: a., dim 195:5
Added: all these things shall be a. 47:18
Adder: bright day that brings forth the a. 327:4
   deaf a. that stoppeth her ear 36:11
Addresses: a. always inspire confidence 417:3
   a. ... to conceal our whereabouts 303:5
Adieu: a., a., kind friends 8:13
   a. for evermore 83:29
   a.! she cries 166:21
   bid you a welcome a. 409:16
Adieu: a. veau, vache, cochon 227:14
Adlestrop: I remember A. 395:1
Admiral: a.s all 269:25
   shoot an a. 407:4
Admiralty: price of a. 224:14
Admiration: as great in a. 326:14
   from a. to love 15:18
   season your a. 314:22
Admire: not to a. is all the art 91:25 289:25
   one cannot possibly a. them 417:34
Admired: all who understood a. 290:16
Admit: labour to a. you 143:9
Admittance: no a. till the week after next 102:5
Ado: much a. there was 65:10
Adonais: blazoning the name of A.! 360:5
   soul of A., like a star 359:14
   weep for A. 358:29
Adonis: this A. in loveliness 201:20
Adoption: their a. tried 314:32
Adoration: all a., duty 312:18
   breathless with a. 422:6
   for a. all the ranks 367:21
Adore: as you too shall a. 238:14
   positively I a. Miss Dombey 135:5
Adored: I was a. once 352:22
Adorn: touched nothing ... he did not a. 209:15
Adorned: unadorned, a. the most 396:16
Adsum: 'A.!' and fell back 393:8
Adullam: political Cave of A. 66:12
Adultery: gods [call] a. 90:15
   who never committed a. 248:16
Advance: retrograde if it does not a. 167:19
Advantage: a. of my honest endeavours 68:24
   nailed for our a. 320:7
   take a. that get a. 151:4
Adventure: awfully big a. 24:2
   most beautiful a. in life 163:8
   narrates the a.s of his mind 162:10
Adversary: agree with thine a. quickly 47:3
   mine a. had written a book 34:11
   never sallies out and sees her a. 260:15
Adversity: a. .... blessing of the New 17:8
   a. doth best discover virtue 17:10

Angel – *contd*
a. – borne ... on my bosom 74:32
a. dropped down from the clouds 321:31
a. girt with golden wings 252:26
a. of death has been abroad 66:9
A. of Death spread his wings 93:1
a. of the Lord came down 382:10
a. of the Lord came upon them 50:11
a. of this life 76:16
A. that presided o'er my birth 59:9
a. whom thou still hast served 335:29
a.s affect us oft 142:2
a.s all were singing out of tune 93:25
a.s and ministers of grace 315:6
a.s are all Tories 94:1
a.s are bright still 335:5
a.s are painted fair 276:4
a.s fear to tread 286:17
a.s keep their ancient places 395:20
a.s may be familiar 279:1
a.s, nor principalities, nor powers 53:3
a.s on the walls of heaven 245:24
a.s tremble while they gaze 178:21
a.s yield eternal thanks 367:21
a.s' visits, short and bright 271:12
as far as a.s' ken 255:20
beautiful and ineffectual a. 12:11
better a. is a man 357:2
blow your trumpets, A.s 143:1
by that sin fell the a.s 326:3
curse his better a. 344:13
domesticate the Recording A. 375:15
drive an a. from your door 60:25
entertained a.s unawares 56:2
fault of a.s and of gods 284:28
flights of a.s sing thee 320:5
forget-me-nots of the a.s 236:17
four a.s to my bed 2:22
give his a.s charge over thee 37:13
glorious a.s ever stand 269:2
her a.'s face 371:27
holy a.s guard thy bed! 411:3
if an a. out of heaven 110:7
in comparison ... I am a A. 135:9
let a.s prostrate fall 281:13
like an a. sings 339:1
like a.s trumpet-tongued 333:4
little lower than the a.s 34:29
make the a.s weep 336:16
man did eat a.s' food 36:32
ministering a. 306:18 319:23
not Angles but a.s 179:5
on the side of the a.s 140:17
praise him, A.s in the height! 220:11
Recording A., as he wrote it down 374:25
she drew an a. down 147:26
sorrow for a.s 74:3
unto the world, and to a.s 53:26
walking, like two a.s white 65:22
which a. voices tell 251:15
wrote like an a. 165:2
young men glittering ... a.s 399:10
Angel-duck: a.-d., winged and silly 228:5
Angeli: non Angli sed A. 179:5
Angelicam: a. habent faciem 179:5
Angel-infancy: I shined in my a.-i. 402:19
Angel-visit: a.-v.s, few and far between 96:21

Anger: a. is a brief madness 196:12
a. is one of the sinews of the soul 164:8
a. makes dull men witty 16:19
care that you strike it in a. 358:9
holy a. and pious grief 22:12
monstrous a. of the guns 276:16
more in sorrow than in a. 314:25
Angle: Brother of the A. 409:4
themselves in every a. greet 246:21
Angler: a.s or very honest men 409:10
excellent a., and now with God 409:6
no man is born an a. 409:3
Angleterre: perfide A. 64:2
Angli: quod A vocarentur 179:5
Anglo-Saxon: A.-S. attitudes 101:30
Angry: a. and poor and happy 110:4
a. with my friend 60:14
A. Young Man 279:17
be ye a. and sin not 54:46
Anguis: latet a. in herba 406:3
Anguish: A. keeps the heavy gate 416:8
drinking deep of that divinest a. 66:24
Angusta: res a. domi 213:20
Animae: testimonium a. Christianae 392:29
Animal: all a.s are equal 275:8
a.s are such agreeable friends 151:14
a.s went in one by one 6:20
anything but that vain a. 298:5
climbed down from this a. 240:17
could turn and live with a.s 415:14
distinguish us from the other a.s 25:16
man ... a political a. 10:4
man ... a religious a. 81:14
man is a gaming a. 228:25
man is a social a. 372:18
man is a tool-making a. 162:21
man is a tool-using a. 99:16
monstrous a. a husband and wife 158:5
noble a., splendid in ashes 69:18
poor, bare, forked a. 330:7
we are vertebrate a.s 249:4
Animal: a. est très méchant 9:7
Animosity: fervour of sisterly a. 378:2
Animula: a. vagula blandula 180:8
Animus: a. si te non deficit aequus 196:16
Anither: and never made a. 82:25
Ankle: his weak a.s swell 425:28
Ann: A., A.! come! quick 131:7
Anna: here thou, great A.! 288:22
Annabel: I and my A. Lee 283:8
Annal: a.s are blank in history books 98:26
if you have writ your a.s true 313:11
short and simple a.s 177:4
war's a.s will cloud into night 182:10
Anne: Queen A.'s dead 117:24
sister A., can you see nothing 281:12
Anni: a. praedantur euntes 196:23
Annie: for bonnie A. Laurie 144:21
Annihilating: a. all that's made 246:26
Annihilation: Moment in A.'s waste 159:7
Anno domini: a. d. ... most fatal complaint 189:22
shall taste my *A.D.* 156:18
Annoy: only does it to a. 100:14
Annuity: a. is a very serious business 16:2
buy an a. cheap 136:2
Annulus: consumitur a. usu 276:8

Anointed: rail on the Lord's a. 347:10
   touch the Lord's A. 7:18
Anser: inter strepere a. olores 406:9
Answer: a. came there none 101:25 305:11
   dusty a. gets the soul 250:3
   fishes' a. was 'We cannot 101:28
   for lack of a. the eagerer 194:12
   give me your a., do! 128:14
   ne'er a.s till a husband cools 287:26
   sent an a. back to me 101:28
   silver a. rang 70:4
   soft a. turneth away wrath 39:28
   what hope of a. 385:29
   would not stay for an a. 16:26
Ant: go to the a. 39:8
Antagonist: a. is our helper 81:18
Antelope: deer and the a. play 189:19
Anthem: grand old Puritan a. 236:12
   here followeth the a. 291:5
   hollaing, and singing of a.s 322:17
   loud your a.s raise 23:11
   pealing a. swells 177:6
   plaintive a. fades 217:6
Anthropophagi: A. and men whose heads 342:31
Antic: a. disposition on 315:28
Antick: there the a. sits 345:22
Antidote: a. to desire 119:13
   sweet oblivious a. 335:18
Antipathies: violent a. ... suspicious 185:18
Antipathy: a. of good to bad 289:15
   sympathetic a. 221:3
Antipodes: A. in shoes 247:15
Antiquity: I will write for A.! 229:18
   little skill in a. 164:6
Antithesis: one vile a. 285:16
Antre: a.s vast and desarts idle 342:30
Anvil: must ... be the a. or the hammer 171:13
Anybody: then no one's a. 168:19
Anything: wot's the good of a.? 110:15
Apart: and dwelt a. 422:26
Ape: a.s, though clothed in scarlet 211:29
   blue-behinded a., I skip 376:14
   is man an a. 140:17
   ivory, and a.s and peacocks 247:25
   lead a.s in hell 349:21
   leave Now for dogs and a.s! 73:5
   like an angry a. 336:16
   played the sedulous a. 375:5
Aphrodisiac: a. divinely subsidized 164:1
Apocalypse: characters of the great A. 425: 3
Apollo: after the songs of A. 332:3
   A., with hair and harpstring 381:4
   bards in fealty to A. 218:3
   burnèd is A.'s laurel-bough 245:13
   musical as is A.'s lute 252:35
   not here, O A. 10:17
   Phoebus A. turned fasting friar 250:13
   'tis A. comes leading 10:18
Apollyon: A. straddled quite over 79:18
Apologize: I never a.! 357:12
Apostate: characteristic of a.s 241:25
Apostle: A.s would have done as they 90:16
Apparel: a. for an almsman's gown 346:2
   a. oft proclaims the man 314:33
   every true man's a. 336:28
Apparition: lovely a. 425:24
Appeal: I a. unto Caesar 52:34

Appear: no sooner ... a. than it is swept away 14:29
Appearance: judge not according to the a. 51:34
   not judge by a.s 417:23
Appeased: wilt be a. or no? 73:24
Appeasement: political a. 237:24
Appelation: my low-class a. 65:1
Appendage: proud of such an a. 301:11
Appendice: je m'enorgueillis d'un pareil a. 301:11
Appétit: a. vient en mangeant 294:7
Appetite: a. comes with eating 294:7
   a. may sicken and so die 351:32
   hungry edge of a. 345:6
   increase of a. had grown 314:13
   other women cloy the a.s 309:29
   subdue your a.s 136:17
   were then to me an a. 421:19
Applaud: should a. again 335:20
Applause: a.! delight! the wonder 212:13
   a. of listening senates 177:12
   attentive to his own a. 285:12
Apple: all was for an a. 5:1
   a. rotten at the heart 337:18
   a. trees will never get across 163:11
   a.s, cherries, hops and women 138:1
   a.s on the Dead Sea's shore 89:4
   a.s were gathered and stored 153:17
   as the a. of his eye 32:12
   choice in rotten a.s 349:18
   comfort me with a.s 42:7
   moon-washed a.s of wonder 146:9
   putting a.s wondrous ripe 75:14
   silver a.s of the moon 429:20
   where the a. reddens 78:8
Apple-dumpling: who refuses a.-d.s 228:17
Appliance: a.s and means to boot 323:2
   by desperate a. are relieved 318:23
Application: lays in the a. on it 135:3
Appointment: a. with a beech-tree 397:7
Apprehension: a. of the good 345:6
   a.s come in crowds 420:5
   death is most in a. 336:21
   in a. how like a god! 316:13
Appris: et n'ont rien a. 149:28
Approbation: a. from Sir Hubert Stanley 266:20
Apricock: yon dangling a.s 346:4
April: A., A., laugh thy girlish laughter 410:11
   A. is the cruellest month 152:23
   A., May, of June, and July-flowers 188:16
   lovely A. of her prime 354:30
   now that A.'s there 73:12
   proud-pied A. dressed 356:12
   sweet A. showers 400:24
   'twas A., as the bumpkins say 122:18
   uncertain glory of an A. day 353:23
   well-apparelled A. 347:25
April-fool: one of love's A.-f.s 118:21
Aprille: A. with his shoures sote 106:17
Aqua: scribere oportet a. 103:13
Aquarius: how is your trade, A. 176:10
Aquitaine: prince d'A. à la tour abolie 269:21
Arab: A.'s Farewell to his Steed 271:16
Arabia: A. breathes from yonder box 288:15
   far are the shades of A. 131:11
Arabian: in the A. woods 259:23
Araby: A. the blest 257:8
   sing thee songs of A. 418:15
Aral: shine upon the A. Sea 11:21

Babies: bit the b. in the cradles 75:10
  only washing. And b. 394:17
Bab-lock-hithe: stripling Thames at B.-l.-h. 11:9
Baby: b. at my breast 310:13
  B., sleep a little longer 391:11
  bye, b. bunting 272:1
  down comes the b. 58:16
  hush thee, my b. 306:6
  hush-a-bye, b. 272:18
  mother cried, b. lept 179:2
  rock-a-bye b. 58:16
  they found a bachelor's b. 13:21
  when the first b. laughed 23:28
  where did you come from, b. 242:18
  where is that b.? 417:6
Babylon: B. is fallen 57:10
  by the rivers of B. 38:24
  ere B. was dust 362:10
  how many miles to B.? 272:16
  I was a King in B. 186:21
  London is a modern B. 141:8
Bacchus: B. ever fair 147:16
  B. ... from out the purple grape 252:20
  charioted by B. and his pards 217:2
'Baccy: 'b. for the Clerk 224:12
Bach: if B. wriggles 87:11
  Johann Sebastian mighty B. 394:23
Bachelor: b., a solicitor, a Freemason 145:15
  b. of three-score again 341:6
  b.'s fare; bread and cheese 379:13
  I would die a b. 341:20
  two old b.s were living 233:3
Back: at my b. I always hear 247:12
  he hath borne me on his b. 319:17
  never turned his b. but marched 72:23
  one glance at the lettered b. 76:14
  our b.s is easy ris 136:9
  will ye no come b. again? 191:26
Backgammon: only athletic sport ... was b. 205:7
Backing: call you that b. 321:3
Backward: thou wilt fall b. 347:27
Backwards: live *b.* from in front 414:12
Bacon: b. where there's not ... a hook 104:16
  great Secretary ... Sir Francis B. 409:13
  think how B. shined 287:8
Bad: altogether irreclaimably b. 99:15
  and the b. unhappily 416:23
  b. affright, afflict the best 177: 20
  b. die late 130:18
  b.'s the best of us 25:21
  being a little b. 337:1
  good compensate b. in man 77:2
  much b. in the best of us 190:14
  was b. she was horrid 237:16
  when b. men combine 81:23
Bade: he that b. thee cometh 50:29
Badly: worth doing b. 110:12
Badness: b. of her b., when she's bad 24:3
Baffled: b. to fight better 72:23
  b., get up and begin again 73:32
  though b. oft 92:31
Bag: b. and baggage ... clear out 170:23
  not with b. and baggage 311:23
  steal the b.s to hold the crumbs 5:11
  three b.s full 271:23
  what did *you* take out of the b. 293:21
Baggage: believe the b. loves me 118:20

Bag-piper: like parrots at a b.-p. 337:3
Bah: sing 'B. to you 169:36
Bailey: remember poor Miss B. 118:2
Baize: gave the thick red b. 30:1
Baker: b. rhymes for his pursuit 77:13
Baker Street: B.S. irregulars 145:18
Balance: b. of power 408:19
  in nice b. 283:28
  redress the b. of the Old 97:19
Bald: b. as the bare mountain tops 12:17
  go up, thou b. head 33:23
Baldheaded: go into it b. 238:25
Bale: undid his corded b.s 11:15
Ball: b. for them to play upon 344:21
  B. no question makes 159:10
  elliptical billiard b.s 169:22
  on a round b. 144:6
  only wind it into a b. 59:15
  urge the flying b. 178:9
  vanished, after the b. 183:13
Ballad: old b. of Sir Patrick Spence 115:20
  permitted to make all the b.s 160:19
  with a woeful b. 311:14
Ballad-monger: metre b.-m.s 321:19
Ballast: b. is old wine 280:7
Ballet: b. dance of bloodless categories 64:13
Ball-floor: dance on this b.-f. thin 62:13
Balloon: something in a huge b. 424:4
Ballot: b. is stronger than the bullet 234:21
Balm: b. from an anointed king 345:18
  b. of hurt minds 333:23
  I wash away my b. 346:10
  is there no b. in Gilead? 44:18
Banbury: to B. Cross 273:22
Band: b. of glorious angels 269:2
  brake their b.s in sunder 37:26
  drew them ... with b.s of love 45:2
  strong as iron b.s 237:17
  when the b. begins to play 224:19
Bandersnatch: frumious B. 101:8
Bandusiae: O fons B. 198:5
Bane: b.s, when they are bare 21:20
  deserve the precious b. 256:11
  here lie Willie Michie's b.s 83:17
  O what of the world's b.? 428:21
Bang: if the big b. does come 275:27
  not with a b. but a whimper 152:9
Banish: b. all the world 321:14
  I b. you 313:5
Banishment: bitter bread of b. 345:17
Banjo: wid my b. on my knee 162:2
Bank: as I sat on a sunny b. 6:21
  b.s and braes o' bonnie Doon 85:3
  cashiers of the Musical B.s 86:32
  from the B. to Mandalay 223:30
  I know a b. 340:10
  moonlight sleeps upon this b. 338:27
  pregnant b. swelled up 142:17
  upon a b. of violets 351:32
  waly up the b. 21:23
Banker: saw a b.'s clerk 102:14
Bankrupt: b. of life 146:21
Banner: b., torn, but flying 89:17
  b. with the strange device 236:19
  hang out the b.s 335:21
  Munich! all thy b.s wave 96:11
  royal b., and all quality 343:31

Beauty – *contd*

makest his b. to consume 35:25
much the most affecting b. 81:3
near your b. with my nails 325:10
no spring, nor summer b. 142:9
none of B.'s daughters 93:21
parallels in b.'s brow 355:20
perhaps some b. lies 254:7
poetic truth and poetic b. 12:15
she walks in b. 93:4
such b. as a woman's eye 331:20
such seems your b. still 356:13
terrible b. is born 428:17
thick, bereft of b. 349:26
thing of b. is a joy for ever 214:25
this is that Lady B. 301:3
thy b.'s silent music 97:2
'tisn't b., so to speak 225:20
trenches in thy b.'s field 354:29
unmask her b. to the moon 314:30
veiling an Indian b. 338:11
was b.'s summer dead 356:15
whose b. is past change 195:5
Bed: ample make this b. 139:14
and so to b. 280:17
b. be blest 2:22
b. by night 172:20
b.s for all who come 300:19
creep into thy narrow b. 10:27
each within our narrow b. 102:21
go to b. by day 375:27
grief ... lies in his b. 328:32
his b. the hard, cold ground 144:11
I in my b. again 5:2
made his pendent b. 331:1
make my b. soon 20:24
must we to b. indeed? 376:3
my second best b. 357:8
nicer to stay in b. 231:5
night the b. fell on my father 397:17
proves at night a b. of down 427:18
remember thee upon my b. 36:17
rose to go to b. 378:6
rouse them from their lowly b. 177:3
sing aloud upon their b.s 38:33
spare b. for my friends 281:5
take up thy b., and walk 51:30
this b. thy centre is 144:1
thought worthy ... of her b. 406:5
welcome to your gory b. 84:10
Bedchamber: curse not the rich in thy b. 41:26
Beddes: at his b. heed 107:6
Bedecked: so b., ornate, and gay 259:19
Bedeuten: ich weiss nicht, was soll es b. 186:2
Bed-fellow: strange b.-f.s 350:7
Bedonebyasyoudid: Mrs B. 222:2
Bedside: presunted myself at Betty's b. 409:30
Bed-staff: twinkling of a b.-s. 308:28
Bed-time: I would it were b.-t. 321:37
Bee: b., doth suck his sweet 235:23
b. has quit the clover 223:22
b. with honied thigh 253:29
brisk as a b. in conversation 206:33
busy b. improve each shining hour 410:19
horribly bored by a b. 232:3
murmured like a noontide b. 364:4
murmuring of innumerable b.s 390:15

Bee – *contd*

some b. had stung it newly 377:10
star that bringest home the b. 96:23
where the b. sucks 350:25
Beech-tree: b.-t. single on the greensward 249:15
Beef: great eater of b. 352:4
roast b. of England 157:19
stole a piece of b. 273:29
Beefsteak: as English ... as a b. 184:13
Beelzebub: B. called for his syllabub 367:5
Beer: all b. and skittles 95:15
B. and Britannia 369:24
B.! O Hodgson, Guinness 95:4
chronicle small b. 343:7
come, my lad, and drink some b. 210:27
felony to drink small b. 325:13
goned afay mit de lager b. 233:25
Beer-sheba: from Dan to B. 32:31
Beethoven: B.'s Fifth Symphony 161:18
Beetle: b., that we tread upon 336:21
b. wheels his droning flight 176:22
God to a black b. 249:4
shard-borne b. 334:14
where the b. winds 117:12
Before: all be as b., Love 78:7
gone b. to that unknown ... shore 228:4
I have been here b. 301:7
Befriend: be near me now and b. 381:3
Beg: better ... to die than to b. 46:23
to b. I am ashamed 50:38
Began: I am that which b. 380:26
Begetter: only b. 354:27
Beggar: absent-minded b. 222:8
bare-footed came the b. maid 383:2
be not made a b. by ... borrowing 46:9
b. that I am 316:12
stiff-necked Glasgow b.! 224:2
when b.s die 327:13
whiles I am a b., I will rail 328:28
Beggared: b. all description 309:27
Beggar-maid: Cophetua loved a b.-m. 348:7
Beggary: b. in the love 309:14
no vice but b. 328:28
Beginning: as it was in the b. 290:24
before the b. of years 380:8
begin at the b. 101:4
b., a middle and an end 10:1
b. of a feast 321:35
from small b.s grow 147:28
homes and first b.s 28:7
I am ... the b. and the end 57:25
in my b. is my end 151:28
in the b. God created 30:9
nothing so difficult as a b. 91:13
perhaps, the end of the b. 111:15
told you from the b. 43:27
true b. of our end 340:29
Begot: how b., how nourished? 338:9
Begotten: B. not made 291:31
Begriffe: wo B. fehlen 171:8
Beguiled: sleep'st too long, thou art b. 367:14
Begun: b., continued, and ended in thee 291:34
b. has half done 196:11
Behave: b. yourself! 135:11
Behaviour: can never prompt b. 297:27
check to loose b. 373:10
put himself upon his good b. 91:22

Blind – *contd*
  if the b. lead the b. 48:22
  maimed, and the halt, and the b. 50:31
  right to be b. sometimes 269:16
Blinded: b. ere yet a-wing 181:16
Bliss: b. in our brows 309:19
  b. was it in that dawn 425:5
  farewell earth's b. 268:29
  it excels all other b. 150:8
  sum of earthly b. 258:12
  what is b., and which the way? 210:27
  wingèd hours of b. 96:21
Bloater: if you were queen of b.s 193:22
Block: old b. itself 82:1
Blockhead: bookful b. 286:16
  I call thee b. 61:10
Blood: b. and iron 58:4
  b. and judgement are ... co-mingled 317:15
  b. and soil 129:12
  b. clean from my hand 333:25
  b. is nipped 332:1
  b. is their argument 324:17
  b. more stirs to rouse 320:22
  b. of patriots and tyrants 204:16
  b. of the martyrs is the seed 392:31
  b.'s a rover 199:13
  b., toil, tears and sweat 111:7
  cant all be of the B. royal 13:8
  freeze thy young b. 315:12
  good enough to shed his b. 299:14
  had so much b. in him 335:11
  here's the smell of the b. 335:13
  his b. be on us 49:33
  His b. upon the rose 283:7
  I am innocent of the b. 49:32
  I'll not shed her b. 344:11
  I ..mell the b. of a British man 330:12
  in b. stepped in so far 334:31
  inhabits our frail b. 353:14
  kiss the b. from these pale feet 362:9
  man whose b. is warm 337:5
  [more] than Norman b. 386:28
  nothing like b., sir 393:20
  nothing to offer but b. 111:7
  pure and eloquent b. 143:24
  red b. reigns 354:5
  smell the b. of an Englishman 272:8
  still the b. is strong 307:13
  summon up the b. 324:10
  that sheds his b. with me 324:26
  thicks man's b. with cold 114:25
  thy brother's b. crieth unto me 30:30
  to shed innocent b. 44:7
  washed in the b. of the Lamb 191:3
  welt'ring in his b. 147:20
  when the b. creeps 385:21
  white in the b. of the Lamb 57:3
  whose b. is fet 324:11
  whose b. is very snow-broth 336:6
  whoso sheddeth man's b. 31:9
  write ... in the b. that she has spilt 121:27
  young b. must have its course 221:18
Bloody: b., bold, and resolute 334:37
  come out, thou b. man 33:8
  not b. likely 358:19
  what b. man is that? 332:6
Bloom: b. is gone 11:26

– *contd*
  [charm] a sort of b. on a woman 24:5
  how can ye b. sae fresh 85:3
  its b. is shed 84:18
  snatched away in beauty's b. 93:3
  then b.s each thing 268:31
  vernal b., or summer's rose 256:37
  will it b. this year? 152:30
Blossom: b. that hangs on the bough 350:25
  it b.s through the year 365:11
  love's perfect b. 279:1
  with b. and with briddes roune 4:23
Blot: b. upon this gloomy scene 363:14
  does the sun and moon b. out 59:3
  greatest art, the art to b. 289:11
Blotted: b. it out for ever 374:25
  would he had b. a thousand 212:19
Blow: b., bugle, b. 389:32
  b. hot and cold 2:29
  b. in cold blood 358:9
  b. in the teeth of a wrong 248:2
  b. on whom I please 311:11
  b.s a man up like a bladder 321:11
  b.s and buffets of the world 334:9
  first b. is half the battle 173:39
  gets his b. in fust 358:24
  hand that gave the b. 149:14
  themselves must strike the b. 88:23
  this b. migh. be the be-all 333:2
  thy swashing b. 347:23
  word and a b. 79:20 348:31
Blow-pipe: like the b.-p. flame 195:11
Blowy: Snowy, Flowy, B. 154:5
Blubbered: Cloe, how b. 292:24
Blude: b. that's shed on the earth 21:16
  they waded through red b. 21:16
Blue: deeply, beautifully b. 91:19
  drink till all look b. 161:13
  floating in the B.! 252:5
  grappling in the central b. 387:16
  little boy b., come blow 272:28
  Presbyterian true b. 86:9
Blue Beard: B. B.'s domestic chaplain 138:9
Bluebell: tender b.s, at whose birth 363:3
Blume: du bist wie eine B. 186:3
Blunder: frae mony a b. free us 84:25
  one of Nature's agreeable b.s 121:25
  wonder at so grotesque a b. 29:12
  worse than a crime, it's a b. 64:5
Blunderbuss: b. against religion 207:12
Blundered: someone had b. 383:10
Blush: beautiful as woman's b. 229:24
  bring a b. into the cheek 137:26
  with a b. retire 135:7
Blut: B. und Boden 129:12
Board: I struck the b. 187:23
Boast: glory and our absolute b. 424:19
  such is the patriot's b. 173:13
Boasteth: then he b. 39:43
Boasting: b.s as the Gentiles use 224:11
Boat: beautiful pea-green b. 232:16
  b. shaped like the crescent-moon 424:4
  give a man a b. 396:26
  going towards my b. 130:16
  if men are together in a b. 180:13
  leathern b. begin to hoist 247:15
  messing about in b.s 175:9

C

Care – *contd*
  past my help is past my c. 26:1
  ravelled sleave of c. 333:23
  sae weary fu' o' c. 85:3
  so wan with c. 320:6
  then the c. is over 382:20
  to c. and not to c. 151:19
  void of c.s and strife 281:21
  weep away the life of c. 363:18
  what I am none c.s 112:14
  wherefore to-night so full of c. 65:12
Cared: c. for none of these things 52:28
  c. not to be at all 256:17
Career: bright and brief c. is o'er 306:3
  nothing which might damage his c. 24:7
  suspend your mad c. 124:23
Careful: not c. what they mean 351:4
Careless: c. ... with artful care 119:15
Carelessness: lose both looks like c. 416:20
Cargo: c. of ivory 247:25
Caricature: c., decrepit age 429:23
Carlyle: C. Tennyson, Browning 293:25
Carmina: c. non prius audita 197:22
  nec vivere c. possunt 196:21
  sunt et mihi c. 406:9
Carnage: c. and his conquests cease 88:14
Carnally: to be c. minded 52:53
Carol: c. of a bird 93:14
Caroling: so little cause for c.s 181:18
Carpe: c. diem 197:10
Carpenter: C. said nothing 101:23
  c. who has made you a bad table 207:23
  'I doubt it,' said the C. 101:9
  Walrus and the C. 101:19
Carpet: c.s rose along the dusty floor 215:13
  toast ... dropped on ... c. 204:20
Carriage: c.s blocking ... the Cromwell Road 224:1
  very small second-class c. 169:8
Carrière: c. ouverte aux talents 98:22 268:14
Carry: meeter to c. off the latter 280:4
Cart: C. and a pound of Rice 232:15
  creak of a lumbering c. 429:7
Carthage: come again to C. 338:26
  to C. I came 14:13
Carthago: delenda est C. 102:24
Cartridge: what use are c.s 357:10
Case: c. ... caused by a woman 214:1
  nothing to do with the c. 169:26
  only heard one side of the c. 87:16
  only his own side of the c. 251:7
Casement: c. ope at night 217:10
  magic c.s, opening on the foam 217:5
  on this c. shone the wintry moon 215:10
Casey: C. Jones, he mounted 6:27
Cash: ah, take the C. 158:22
  c. payment ... the sole nexus 98:13
Cashmere: tales of fair C. 418:15
Casket: hushèd C. of my Soul 218:10
Casque: c.s that did affright 323:22
Cassia: heap c., sandal-buds 75:3
Cassio: C., I love thee 343:16
Cassock: c., bands, and hymn-book 416:1
Cassowary: if I were a c. 416:1
Cast: c. me off discourteously 7:9
Castilian: old C. poor noble 94:3
Castle: Doubting C. 79:24

Castle – *contd*
  no better brand than the Three C.s 393:23
  this c. hath a pleasant seat 332:30
Castlereagh: mask like C. 361:10
Castum: c. esse decet pium poetam 103:5
  c. esse ... versiculos nihil necesse est 103:5
Casualty: crass C. obstructs the sun 182:4
Cat: as a c. laps milk 350:4
  black c. with bright green eyes 262:20
  c. and the fiddle 272:13
  C. He walked by himself 225:5
  c. will mew 319:28
  c.s and monkeys, monkeys and c.s 204:6
  c.s may have had their goose 95.23
  Cheshire C 100:15
  consider my C. Jeoffry 367:20
  do c.s eat bats? 100:6
  don't want to swing a c. 134:32
  fought the dogs and killed the c.s 75:10
  hanging of his c. on Monday 65:6
  harmless necessary c. 338:15
  How C.s Spend their Time 22:5
  I'll bell the c. 144:18
  made a c. laugh 282:18
  melodious c.s under the moon 202:7
  more ways of killing a c. 222:5
  O c. of churlish kind 367:16
  part to tear a c. in 339:32
  poor c. in the adage 333:7
  runcible c. with crimson whiskers 233:1
  to see how the c. jumps 307:12
  what c.'s averse to fish? 178:3
  when c.s run home 391:17
  when I play with my c. 263:17
Catalogue: c. was so large 118:26
Cataract: c. leaps in glory 389:32
  sounding c. haunted me 421:19
Catastrophe: c. of the old comedy 329:19
  I'll tickle your c. 322:22
Catch: c. as c. can 161:5
Catechism: so ends my c. 322:1
Categories: ballet dance of bloodless c. 64:13
Caterpillar: c. on the leaf 58:24
  c.s of the commonwealth 345:15
Cathay: cycle of C. 387:27
Catholic: myself a C. will be 121:19
Cato: like C., give his little senate laws 285:12
Catoni: sed victa C. 239:7
Cattes: nation of c. wild and tame 367:15
Cattle: and also much c. 45:10
  c. upon a thousand hills 36:4
  go and call the c. home 221:16
  troublesome c. to deal with 238:18
Caucasus: thinking on the frosty C. 345:6
Cauldron: c. bubble 334:32
  sang around my ears a c. 14:13
Cauliflower: c. is nothing but cabbage 401:14
Causas: rerum cognoscere c. 406:15
Cause: able to learn the c.s of things 406:15
  any of you know c. 292:1
  aren't any good brave c.s 275:27
  believing in the justice of our c. 180:10
  c. above renown 269:26
  c. that perishes with them 113:4
  c. which I knew not 34:10
  c.s why and wherefore 325:1
  foretell for what high c. 247:8

Chaucer – *contd*
 Dan C., well of English 372:6
 more nigh to learned C. 24:10
 not lodge thee by C. 212:13
 since C. was alive and hale 230:8
Chavender: c. or chub 302:22
Cheapside: as if C. were mad 122:26
Cheat: an' c. you yet 82:14
 never be deterred from detecting ... a c. 209:2
 sweet c. gone 131:17
Cheated: c. into some fine passages 219:12
Cheating: without actually C. 290:1
Check: comes the c., the change 391:30
 dreadful is the c. 66:22
Checkmate: cheating c. by painting 176:3
Cheek: blood spoke in her c.s 143:24
 c. is cold and white, alas! 360:18
 c. that doth not fade 215:16
 c. upon her hand 348:9
 c.s of sorry grain 253:12
 coined my c. to smiles 89:10
 feed on her damask c. 352:28
 give this c. a little red 287:18
 he that loves a rosy c. 97:21
 I might touch that c. 348:9
 pale grew thy c. 94:6
 resting ... a warm wet c. 230:5
 ruddy c.s Augustus had 191:5
 smite thee on thy right c. 47:5
Cheer: be of good c. 48:18
 C.! Boys, c.! 242:22
 c. of mind that I was wont 347:16
 c. up, cully 419:5
 c. up, the worst is yet to come 205:11
 come c. up, my lads! 165:1
 cups, that c. 125:11
 don't c., boys 281:19
 play and make good c. 400:18
 scarce forbear to c. 241:10
Cheerfulness: c. was always breaking in 151:1
Cheerly: c., c., she loves me dearly 215:3
Cheese: ate the c.s out of the vats 75:10
 dreamed of c. – toasted 375:12
 eggs and a pound of c. 95:2
 I've put c. in the mouseholes 394:16
 smells of c. 377:21
Chef-d'œuvre: son âme au milieu des c.s-d'œ.
 162:10
Chemist: c., fiddler, statesman 147:1
Cheque: political blank c. 174:29
Chequer-board: C.-b. of Nights and Days 159:9
Cherries: c. grow that none can buy 3:19
 c. grow which none may buy 97:7
 c., hops and women 138:1
Cherry: c. ripe, ripe, ripe, I cry 188:18
 c. was as red 217:15
 double c., seeming parted 340:17
 loveliest of trees, the c. 199:11
 O ruddier than the c. 165:18
Cherry orchard: before the c. o. was sold 108:18
Cherry-isle: land, or c.-i. 188:18
Cherry-ripe: c.-r. themselves do cry 3:19 97:7
Cherry-stone: c. carve heads upon c.-s.s 210:8
Cherry-tree: bow down, good c.-t. 20:8
Cherubim: c. and seraphim falling down 185:28
 c. does cease to sing 58:21
 heaven's c. 333:4

Cherubin: young-eyed c.s 339:1
Chess: devil played at c. 68:24
 life's too short for c. 94:14
Chess-board: called the c.-b. white 71:5
Chest: c. of drawers by day 172:20
 like a bastion's mole his c. 367:22
 on the dead man's c. 375:9
Chester: charge, C., charge! 306:19
Chesterton: dared attack my C. 28:16
Chestnut: spreading c. tree 237:17
Chevalier: darling, the young C. 268:1
Chevalier: c. sans peur et sans reproche 25:3
Cheviot: mountains of C. 20:9
Chewed: few to be c. and digested 19:2
Chicken: all my pretty c.s 335:8
 c. in his pot every Sunday 186:22
 count their c.s 86:25
 don't count your c.s 3:1
 some c.; some neck! 111:14
Chid: you'll never be c. 150:15
Chief: C. who in triumph advances 305:17
 I'm the c. of Ulva's isle 96:14
 whosoever will be c. among you 49:4
Child: as soon as he reflects, he [Byron] is a c.
 171:24
 because I'm nobody's c. 102:18
 cease towards the c. she bare 123:14
 c. among his new-born blisses 423:15
 c., by nature's kindly law 287:3
 c. I to myself will take 426:13
 c. imposes on the man 148:7
 c. is afraid of being whipped 206:29
 C. is father of the Man 422:17
 c. is known by his doings 39:42
 c. of a day, thou knowest not 229:25
 c.'s a plaything for an hour 229:21
 c. that is not clean and neat 375:32
 c., that must be played with 378:20
 cry of a c. by the roadway 429:7
 dead c. some weeks before 16:5
 devoured the infant c. 198:23
 every c. may joy to hear 60:20
 for the mother's sake the c. 116:11
 half devil and half c. 224:28
 happy English c. 382:11
 he became a little c. 61:2
 healthy c. well nursed 379:11
 here a little c. I stand 189:12
 I heard one calling, 'C.' 187:24
 I was a c. and she was a c. 283:8
 if you strike a c. 358:9
 is it well with the c.? 33:24
 lie down like a tired c. 363:18
 little c. shall lead them 43:1
 look upon a little c. 413:13
 nicest c. I ever knew 27:21
 on a cloud I saw a c. 60:18
 simple C., that lightly draws 426:27
 sometimes say, Poor C.! 279:12
 spoil the c. 86:20
 train up a c. 40:4
 Tuesday's c. is full of grace 273:6
 unto us a c. is born 42:32
 waters wild went o'er his c. 96:16
 when I was a c., I spake as a c. 54:5
 where is my c.? 88:15
 while the Heav'n-born c. 255:6

Creator – *contd*
  law of our C. 80:23
  remember now thy C. 41:32
Creature: all c.s great and small 3:11
  call these delicate c.s ours 343:27
  c., formed of joy and mirth 59:9
  c. in whom excelled 258:23
  c. lives in a state of war 378:19
  c. native and indued 319:12
  c. of a 'fiery heart' 423:3
  c.s carried by, by constables 280:24
  c.s that by a rule ... teach 323:26
  every c. of God is good 55:23
  every c. shall be purified 245:5
  from fairest c.s 354:28
  lone lorn c. 134:11
  meaner c.s kings 347:14
  most perverse c.s in the world   2:6
  only c. that consumes 275:6
  ravished this fair c. 157:21
  reasonable c.s of God 69:4
  served the c. 52:41
  shining c.s of the chase 390:5
Credat: c. Iudaeus Apella 198:18
Credit: corpse of the Public C. 412:1
  greatly to his c. 168:29
  let the C. go 158:22
  some c. in being jolly 135:30
  stories ... not to thy c. 95:20
  there an't much c. in that 135:29
Creditor: not everyone who wishes makes c.s
    294:15
Creditum: quod ab omnibus c. est 404:11
Credo: c. quia impossibile 392:32
Credulity: craving c. 140:15
  c. is the man's weakness 229:3
Credulus: non ego c. illis 406:9
Creed: c. is a rod 380:27
  dust of c.s outworn 362:15
  have a comfortable c. 90:25
  modest c., and yet pleasant 363:7
  suckled in a c. outworn 422:9
  than in half the c.s 385:38
  vain are the thousand c.s 66:20
  we have a Calvinistic c. 282:10
  with human hands the c. of c.s 385:19
Creep: 'Ay!' said C. 131:26
  c., and let no more be said 10:27
Crescent: blunt their c.s 147:27
Crescent-moon: shaped like the c.-m. 424:4
Cressid: C. lay that night 338:26
Crest: c.s and tombs of brass 356:20
Crew: c. of the captain's gig 168:8
  set the c. laughing 160:12
  we were a ghastly c. 115:4
Crewe: taken me on to C. 235:15
Cricket: c. on the hearth 253:24
Cried: out of the depths have I c. 38:20
  suddenly c. and turned away 67:6
Crier: c. of green sauce 294:13
  when the c. cried, 'O Yes' 23:3
Cries: c. like dead letters 194:23
  on me she c. 20:20
Crime: c. of being a young man 282:8
  c.s are committed in your name 298:24
  greatest c. is to have been born 94:26
  let the punishment fit the c. 169:20

Crime – *contd*
  more ... commonplace a c. is 145:4
  Napoleon of c. 145:14
  now madden to c. 88:12
  one virtue and a thousand c.s 90:8
  register of the c.s ... of mankind 167:11
Crime: c. a ses degrés 293:4
  pire qu'un c. 64:5
Criminal: punishment of a c. 226:15
Criminel: ami du c. 24:15
Crisp: deep and c. 269:7
Crispian: feast of C. 324:24
  rouse him at the name of C. 324:24
Crispin: upon Saint C.'s Day 145:24 324:26
Critic: before you trust in c.s 92:15
  c. ... narrates the adventures of his mind
    162:10
  C., you have frowned 422:10
  c.s all are ready made 92:14
  c.s much confide in 378:18
  first attribute of a good c. 239:3
  nor in the c. let the man be lost 286:11
  therefore they turn c.s 116:26
Critical: calm and ... c. 137:9
  nothing if not c. 343:5
Criticism: blown about by every wind of c. 210:11
  cant of c. is the most tormenting! 374:21
  c. is applied only to what 204:8
  c. of life 12:15
  father of English c. 206:11
  most penetrating of c.s 202:10
  my own definition of c. 12:8
  people ask you for c. 248:22
  Stealthy School of C. 301:9
  they pass no c.s 151:14
Criticizing: pleasure of c. 226:13
Critique: c. est celui qui raconte 162:10
Crocodile: doth the little c. 100:8
  what manner o' thing is your c.? 309:33
  wisdom of the c.s 18:16
Cromwell: C., damned to everlasting fame 287:8
  C. guiltless of his country's blood 177:11
  C. knocked about a bit 235:14
Crony: trusty, drouthy c. 84:16
Crooked: c. be made straight 153:16
  c. shall be made straight 43:22
  straight minds grown c. 267:4
  strive to set the c. straight 266:5
  there was a c. man 274:1
Crop: a-watering the last year's c. 151:2
  who said, 'C.s are ripe'? 131:28
Cross: at the c. her station 398:13
  c. be uncrossed 153:16
  C. of Jesus going on before 23:10
  I survey the wondrous C. 411:8
  no c., no crown 280:15
  on his breast a bloody c. 371:25
  on the bitter c. 320:7
  sparkling c. she wore 288:17
  take up his c., and follow 48:28
Crossed: c. in love 15:26
Crosses: clinging to their c. 109:16
  c. from his sov'reign hand 189:13
  c., row on row 242:17
Cross-gartered: ever c.-g. 353:2
Cross-patch: c.-p., draw the latch 272:4
Crotchet: c.s in thy head 339:14

Crow: c. makes wing 334:17
  many wintered c. 387:9
  risen to hear him c. 151:5
  there is an upstart c. 179:4
Crowd: c. flowed over London Bridge 152:29
  c. is not company 18:22
  c.s without company 167:7
  far from the madding c.'s 177:14
  if you can talk with c.s 223:8
  not feel the c. 125:12
  'twas in a c. 25:11
  uninitiated c. 197:22
  vain the ardour of the c. 178:15
Crown: casting down their golden c.s 185:28
  c. imperial 354:13
  c. is of night 380:27
  c. of twelve stars 57:7
  c.s resign to call thee mine 402:3
  fell down, and broke his c. 272:23
  from the c. to the toe top full 332:25
  give thee a c. of life 56:33
  go forth and conquer a c. 275:29
  hairy great c. on 'er 'ead 225:1
  head that wears the c. 323:3
  I give away my c. 346:10
  monarch better than his c. 338:17
  never thought of hath worn the c. 46:5
  not the king's c. 336:12
  power of the C. has increased 13:2
  to obtain a corruptible c. 53:34
  walked earth with c. and palm 76:24
  within the hollow c. 345:22
Crowned: c., and again discrowned 205:8
Crow-toe: tufted c.-t. 254:33
Crucem: iuxta c. lacrimosa 398:13
Crucified: c., dead, and buried 290:31
Crucify: wouldn't even c. him 99:29
Cruel: c. as she's fair 128:19
  c., not unnatural 318:6
  c. only to be kind 318:20
Cruelty: C. has a human heart 61:9
  farewell, fair c. 352:14
  top full of direst c. 332:25
Cruise: our last c. 375:17
Crumb: c.s ... from the rich man's table 50:42
  c.s ... from their masters' table 48:24
  picker-up of learning's c.s 72:25
  who craved no c. 170:19
Crumbling: c. beneath the fingers 243:8
Crumpet: Hot Muffin and C. ... Company 136:14
Cruse: small c. best fits my little wine 189:2
Crushed: together c. and bruised 289:19
Crusoe: wished longer ... *Robinson C.* 211:5
Crust: all the upper c. 180:12
Crutch: shouldered his c. 172:11
Cry: c. is still they come 335:21
  don't you c. for me 162:2
  hear us when we c. 414:20
  heard a sudden c. of pain 374:1
  I c. in the day-time 35:5
  or to any loud c. 102:7
  with no language but a c. 385:26
Crying: voice of one c. 46:32
Cubili: dea nec dignitata c. 406:5
Cubit: c. unto his stature 47:16
Cuckold: great year for c.s 294:16
Cuckoo: as the c. is in June 321:25

Cuckoo – *contd*
  c., jug-jug, pu-we 268:31
  c.: O word of fear 331:30
  c. then, on every tree 331:30
  first c.'s melancholy cry 422:3
  lhude sing c. 4:25
  merry c., messenger of Spring 371:15
  O C., shall I call thee bird 426:18
  rainbow and a c.'s song 130:5
  responsive to the c.'s note 178:14
  who can hedge in the c. 104:16
Cuckoo-bird: from the c.-b. 426:4
Cuckoo-bud: c.-b.s of yellow hue 331:30
Cucumber: c. should be well sliced 210:20
  no c.s in the market 416:18
  sunbeams out of c.s 379:3
Cue: c. is villanous melancholy 329:19
  with a twisted c. 169:22
Culpa: O felix c. 260:25
Culture: as a man of c. rare 169:31
  c. ... passion for sweetness and light 12:19
  c. ... pursuit of our·total perfection 11:34
  c., the acquainting ourselves 12:18
  hear any one talk of C. 171:2
  highest possible stage in moral c. 129:13
  universal c. for the crowd 389:25
Cumnor: walls of C. Hall 250:29
Cunning: c. ... Heaven has given to the saints 221:22
  c. men pass for wise 18:13
  forget her c. 38:25
  more c. to be strange 348:14
Cup: ah, fill the C. 159:6
  awake ... and fill the C. 158:14
  come, fill the C. 158:17
  come fill up my c. 305:9
  c.s, that cheer 125:11
  his c. the bare of his palm 144:11
  in the hand ... there is a c. 36:30
  in their flowing c.s ... remembered 324:25
  kiss but in the c. 212:12
  let this c. pass 49:29
  tak a c. o' kindness 82:22
Cupboard: c. was bare 273:11
  her c.s opened 182:28
  Hons' c., which was always stifling 261:3
  she went to the c. 132:13
Cupid: bolt of C. fell 340:8
  C. and my Campaspe played 240:4
  C.'s darts do not feel 6:2
  giant-dwarf, Dan C. 331:18
  note which C. strikes 69:9
  winged C. painted blind 339:29
  young Adam C. 348:7
Cupidinum: mater saeva C. 198:10
Cur: as c.s mouth a bone 110:24
  common cry of c.s 313:5
  curtail the already c.-tail'd c. 95:9
  half lurcher and half c. 125:21
  round the ears of the old c. 86:17
Cura: post equitem sedet atra C. 197:23
Curate: c. ... fatter than his cure 383:25
  c.s, long dust, will come 67:8
  I was a pale young c. 170:12
  mildest c. going 168:6
  preached to death by wild c.s 369:18
Curd: eating her c.s and whey 272:30

Curd – *contd*
  mere white c. of ass's milk 285:14
Cure: death is the c. of all diseases 69:10
  God, thy life, thy c. 402:17
  grand c. of all the maladies 99:13
  labour against our own c. 69:10
  no c. for birth and death 304:2
Curfew: c. shall not ring tonight 397:10
  c. tolls the knell 176:21
  far-off c. sound 253:23
Curiosity: full of 'satiable c. 225:6
Curious: not c. in unnecessary matters 45:34
Curiouser: c. and c. 100:7
Curl: sable c.s all silvered o'er 354:31
  who had a little c. 237:16
Currency: debasing the moral c. 151:15
Current: beauty ... must be c. 253:10
  icy c. and compulsive course 343:36
  their c.s turn awry 316:29
Curse: c. be ended 153:16
  c. God and die 33:36
  c. is come upon me 386:36
  c. is on her if she stay 386:32
  c. of hell frae me 20:14
  c.s are like young chickens 370:12
  c.s not loud but deep 335:17
  I know how to c. 349:36
  never was heard such a terrible c. 22:13
  rigged with c.s dark 254:28
Cursed: c. him in sleeping 22:12
  he ... c. that rascally thief 22:12
Cursing: c. and swearin' 376:20
Curtain: all the neat c.s 262:20
  c.s, never meant to draw 288:3
  iron c. across Europe 400:6
  iron c. has descended 111:17
  let fall the c.s 125:11
  lets the c. fall 284:22
  ring down the c. 294:26
Curtiosity: full of 'satiable c. 225:6
Curtsey: c. while you're thinking 101:11
Curtsies: dream on c. straight 347:29
Cusha: 'C.! C.! C.!' calling 203:16
Cushes: c. on his thighs 321:31
Cushion: cannon off the c.! 108:17
  sit on a c. and sew 272:5
Custodes: quis custodiet ipsos c.? 214:2
Custom: c. ... is the great guide 201:9
  c. more honoured in the breach 315:5
  c. reconciles us 81:4
  C., that is before all law 129:4
  c., that unwritten law 129:19
  c. to whom c. [is due] 53:14
  c.s curtsey to great kings 325:4
  lest one good c. should corrupt 384:33
  ne'er quite understand the c.s 279:3
Customer: raising up a people of c.s 368:3
  tough c. in argeyment 133:14
Cut: c. off out of the land 44:1
  it is soon c. off 37:9
  most unkindest c. of all 327:33
  takes the short c. to everything 210:16
  who c. and come again 126:16
Cut-purse: and the c.-p. sworn 5:4
  c.-p. of the empire 318:15
Cycno: nigroque simillima c. 213:23
Cymbal: tinkling c. 54:1

Cymbal – *contd*
  upon the loud c.s 39:1
Cynicism: c. is intellectual dandyism 250:15
Cynosure: c. of neighbouring eyes 254:7
Cypress: c. in the palace walk 390:10
  in sad c. let me be laid 352:27
  nor shady c. tree 300:16
Cythère: C. ... un pays fameux 25:1
Cytherea: sweeter than ... C.'s breath 354:13

D

D: use a big, big D. 168:22
Dad: called my brother's father d. 328:25
Daddy: Ask D., He Won't Know 268:18
  D.'s gone a-hunting 272:1
Daffadillies: d. fill their cups 254:33
Daffadowndilly: Diaphenia, like the d. 110:14
Daffodil: d.s, that come before the swallow 354:13
  fair d.s, we weep to see 189:5
  host of golden d.s 421:4
  when d.s begin to peer 354:5
Daffy-down-dilly: D.-d.-d. is new come 272:6
Dagger: air-drawn d. 336:23
  but a d. of the mind 333:16
  give me the d.s 333:24
  is this a d. 333:16
  speak d.s to her but use none 318:6
Daggers-drawing: always been at d.-d. 86:22
Daily Telegraph: young lions of the *D.T.* 12:6
Dainties: not fed of the d. 331:19
Daisies: d. pied and violets blue 331:30
  d. smell-less, yet most quaint 26:12
  she can hear the d. grow 416:10
Daisy: D., D., give me your answer 128:14
Dalhousy: D., the great God of War 283:26
Dalliance: d. in the wardrobe lies 323:28
  primrose path of d. 314:31
Dam: give a singel d. 160:16
  when the d. broke 397:19
Dame: d. has lost her shoe 272:2
  struts his d.s before 254:4
  sulky sullen d. 84:13
Dame: belle d. sans merci 215:12 216:7
Damn: d. with faint praise 285:12
  I don't care a twopenny d. 412:27
  man who said, 'D.! 183:9
  stealthily, like a parson's d. 182:25
Damnation: d.'s a good girl 163:18
  deep d. of his taking-off 333:4
  distilled d. 181:2
  I dare d. 319:4
  there would be no d. 399:6
  twenty-nine distinct d.s 77:16
Damned: all silent and all d.! 424:6
  d. be him that first cries 336:3
  d. from here to Eternity 223:2
  d. if you do ... d. if you don't 144:22
  d. like an ill-roasted egg 311:20
  d. than mentioned not at all! 282:5
  I will see thee d. first 97:12
  one d. thing after another 200:18
  thou must be d. perpetually 245:8
Damozel: blessed d. leaned out 300:20
Damp: d.s there drip 181:14

Damsel: d. lay deploring 166:22
   d. with a dulcimer 116:5
   d.s met in forest wide 258:34
   d.s playing with timbrels 36:26
   to every man a d. or two 32:24
Dan: Dangerous D. McGrew 308:22
   from D. even to Beer-sheba 32:31
   from D. to Beersheba 374:6
Danaë: all D. to the stars 390:11
Danaos: timeo D. et dona ferentes 404:22
Dance: best d. e'er cam 83:9
   but come and join the d. 101:2
   d.s as often as d. it can 115:16
   each d. the other would 131:25
   I must d. bare-foot 349:21
   on with the d.! 88:27
   riot, feast and d. 258:29
   who have learned to d. 286:7
   will you join the d. 101:1
Dancer: d.s are all gone 151:30
   d.s dancing in tune 388:20
   it was a d. that got it 25:17
   know the d. from the dance 428:11
Dancing: past our d. days 348:3
Dancing-master: manners of a d.-m. 207:11
Dane-geld: once you have paid him the D.-g. 222:23
Danger: d. on the deep 25:9
   d.s ... despised grow great 80:25
   face d. rather than ... loss 397:14
   loved me for the d.s 342:32
   oft in d., oft in woe 414:8
   pleased with the d. 146:20
   run into any kind of d. 291:4
   security is the mother of d. 164:13
   she feared no d. 147:34
   think on the d.s of the seas 277:21
   this nettle, d. 320:29
   those who brave its d.s 237:8
   till d.'s troubled night depart 96:27
   what d.s thou canst make us scorn! 84:20
   with d.s compassed round 258:5
Dangerous: d. to know 228:2
   little learning is a d. thing 285:24
Daniel: D. come to judgement! 338:19
   second D., a D., Jew! 338:22
Danseur: d. qui l'obtint 25:17
Dansez: d. maintenant 226:19
Dante: D. of the dread Inferno 74:32
   D., who loved well because he hated 74:30
Dappled: glory be to God for d. things 195:3
Dare: I d. do all that may become 333:8
   I d. eat, or drink 346:5
   'I d. not' wait upon 'I would' 333:7
   O! what men d. do! 341:34
   what man d., I d. 334:26
Darien: silent, upon a peak in D. 218:4
Dark: after that the d. 383:16
   at one stride comes the d. 114:27
   awake in the d. 269:22
   between the d. and the daylight 236:11
   children fear to go in the d. 17:2
   colours will agree in the d. 17:5
   damned long, d., boggy ... way 173:37
   d. with excessive bright 257:2
   don't want to go home in the d. 187:9
   fell of d., not day 194:22

Dark – *contd*
   hellish d., and smells 377:21
   I'm Afraid to Go Home in the D. 418:11
   is as good i' th' d. 188:25
   no where, but in the d. 403:4
   O d., d., d., ... irrecoverably d. 259:10
   out in the d. over the snow 395:3
   we are for the d. 310:8
   what in me is d. illumine 255:18
   with darkness ridged the riven d. 163:3
Darkling: d. I listen 217:5
Darkness: awful d. and silence reign 232:9
   between his D. and his Brightness 94:2
   blackness of d. for ever 56:28
   brought them out of d. 37:26
   cast him into outer d. 49:9
   cast out into outer d. 47:31
   come not in d. 407:21
   d. again and a silence 237:15
   d. came down on the field 393:19
   d. comprehended it not 51:16
   d. deepens 240:8
   d. hide it from my face 300:18
   d. more clear than noonday 300:13
   d. silvers away 65:11
   d. visible served only 255:21
   d. was upon the face of the deep 30:9
   d. which may be felt 31:38
   deep but dazzling d. 402:15
   deep into the d. peering 283:17
   detract from the ... idea of d. 208:16
   encounter d. as a bride 336:22
   in d. and in the shadow of death 50:9
   in d., fire, and chains 410:16
   instruments of d. 332:14
   jaws of d. do devour 339:28
   jaws of d. vacant 385:18
   lighten our d. 291:8
   loved d. rather than light 51:27
   people that walked in d. 42:31
   rear of d. thin 254:4
   universal d. buries all 284:22
   what of the D.? 233:14
   world to d. and to me 176:21
   year of now done d. 194:14
Darling: d. of a pigmy size 423:15
   d. of the Gods was born 247:8
   d. of the Spring! 426:19
   oh, my d. Clementine! 264:10
   she is the d. of my heart 98:7
   was Nature's d. laid 178:19
   wealthy curlèd d.s of our nation 342:23
Dart: d. of longing love 112:25
   shook a dreadful d. 256:30
   time shall throw a d. at thee 69:19
Dat: bis d. qui cito d. 381:21
Date: all too short a d. 355:3
Dative: observe the d.? 95:13
Daughter: attorney's elderly ugly d. 170:13
   bailiff's d. of Islington 20:2
   d. am I in my mother's house 224:5
   d. of Earth and Water 359:21
   d. of Jove, relentless power 177:20
   d. of the gods, divinely tall 383:23
   d.s of men, that they were fair 31:3
   d.s of my father's house 352:29
   fairer d. of a fair mother 197:11

Daughter – *contd*
king's d. o' Noroway 21:10
like a Duke-and-a-Duchess's d. 23:7
my d.! O my ducats! 338:1
stern D. of the Voice of God! 423:26
sweet her artless d.s 218:1
this Lord Ullin's d. 96:14
trust not your d.s' minds 342:21
two d.s of one race 391:16
undaunted d. of desires 126:22
wash your dirty d. 8:16
will ever rear a d. 165:21
Dauphin: kingdom of daylight's d. 195:13
David: D. his ten thousands 32:41
D. in the midst 367:21
D.'s world with Sibyl's blending 105:3
in royal D.'s city 3:14
King D. and King Solomon 269:1
Daw: for d.s to peck at 342:17
Dawn: arose and saw the d. 364:3
dappled d. doth rise 254:3
d. comes up like thunder 223:28
D. with her rose-tinted hands 192:30
d., with silver-sandalled feet 416:9
D.'s Left Hand was in the Sky 138:14
grey d. breaking 248:5
grey d. is breaking 127:11
I said to D.: Be sudden 395:16
sighed for the d. and thee 388:21
such as creation's d. beheld 89:29
Dawning: somebody in the d. passing through 182:21
Day: and enjoy bright d. 252:32
and the d. but one 64:7
as it fell upon a d. 23:19
as long as twenty d.s are now 426:16
because the d.s are evil 55:1
benight our happiest d. 142:16
breaks the blank d. 385:9
breathers of an ampler d. 386:15
bright d. is done 310:8
calm was the d. 372:13
chilly d. for Willie 5:20
compare thee to a summer's d. 355:3
courts of everlasting d. 255:5
d. be never so longe 184:8
d. be time enough to mourn 128:20
d. begins to droop 66:6
d. breaks not, it is my heart 142:5
d. brought back my night 260:3
d. has put on his jacket 192:6
d. is at hand 53:12
d. less or more 390:29
d. may be the last 269:15
d. of wrath and doom 104:3
d. of wrath, that dreadful d. 306:2
d. returns too soon 93:17
d.'s at the morn 75:16
d. shall gentle his condition 324:26
d., so cool, so calm, so bright 188:9
d. stands tiptoe 349:6
d. sunk in hideous night 354:31
d. unto d. uttereth speech 34:39
d.'s garish eye 253:29
d.'s labour dost at last defray 371:23
d.s among the dead are past 370:20
d.s and moments quickly flying 102:21

Day – *contd*
d.s darken round me 384:32
d.s dividing lover and lover 380:6
d.s ... mere glimmering 403:3
d.s ... swifter than a weaver's shuttle 33:41
d.s that are no more 389:36
d.s, that might be better spent 372:11
d.s will finish up the year 325:17
dearly love but one d. 98:8
each d. dies with sleep 195:2
each d. is like a year 416:7
entertains the harmless d. 427:14
everything is only for a d. 14:28
find it after many d.s 41:27
first, last, everlasting d. 142:3
flee ... to a diviner d. 362:26
fogs prevail upon the d. 148:11
former d.s were better 41:13
friends, I have lost a d. 398:11
full of sweet d.s and roses 188:10
go not, happy d. 388:18
good morning to the d. 212:2
good things of d. 334:17
happy those early d.s! 402:19
have their d. and cease to be 385:6
he that outlives this d. 324:24
his d.s are as grass 37:21
I loved the garish d. 270:12
in the brave d.s of old 241:8
in the cool of the d. 151:20
infinite d. excludes the night 411:5
it was Thy d., sweet! 126:24
lament not the d.s that are gone 370:22
left alone with our d. 14:9
life is but a d. 217:11
live laborious d.s 254:26
live this d. as if 'twere thy last 220:13
Lochiel! beware of the d. 96:12
long d. wanes 392:7
long weary d. have end 371:2
looked on better d.s 311:132
maddest merriest d. 388:26
met them at close of d. 428:16
my d.s have crackled and gone up 395:17
no d. for me to look upon 353:25
not a d. without a line 283:5
not in the length of d.s 263:10
not to me returns d. 256:37
now the d. is over 23:8
one d., about noon 130:16
precincts of the cheerful d. 177:16
ride ten thousand d.s 143:27
runs through the roughest d. 332:18
seemed to have known a better d. 305:20
shall stand at the latter d. 34:7
sing in the summer d. 190:20
so foul and fair a d. 332:9
spend a single d. really well 220:10
spent ere half my d.s 259:32
such a d. tomorrow 353:30
take the whole long d.? 300:17
tender eye of pitiful d. 334:16
their fallen d. about her 278:19
think ... every d. is your last 196:13
think warm d.s will never cease 218:18
Thou wast up by break of d. 187:27
though fall'n on evil d.s 258:5

474

Death – *contd*

d. is still working like a mole 187:31
d. is the cure of all diseases 69:10
d. is the veil 362:27
d. itself awakes 323:1
d. itself must be ... a mockery 363:7
d. lays his icy hand on kings 365:32
D. lies dead 380:21
d. makes equal 189:14
d. ... nourished during his whole life 296:18
d. of each day's life 333:23
d. of the most noblest knights 244:11
d. opens unknown doors 248:3
d. or life ... be the sweeter 336:19
d. shall be no more 143:5
d. shall have no dominion 394:2
d. ... the least of all evils 16:24
d., thou shalt die 143:5
d. whene'er he call 170:17
d., which happened in his berth 193:9
D. who comes at last 306:9
d. will disprove you 400:14
D. will find me long before I tire 67:20
d. will have his day 345:20
d. will take us in tow 133:5
d.'s pale flag 349:13
dens, and shades of d. 256:28
die the d. of the righteous 32:5
direful d. indeed they had 160:16
dull cold ear of d. 177:7
either it [d.] is annihilation 369:29
eloquent, just, and mighty D.! 295:11
fear and danger of violent d. 190:10
fear d.? 75:26
fed on the fullness of d. 381:5
first day of our jubilee is d. 69:1
for restful d. I cry 355:24
for that which is born d. is certain 30:8
from d. to life ... recover 146:7
gone to her d. 193:4
half in love with easeful D. 217:5
half-dead, a living d. 259:12
has ever truly longed for d. 391:32
hear his d., ye blockheads! 205:21
heavens themselves blaze forth the d. 327:13
hob-and-nob with D. 392:12
how wonderful is D. 359:23
I could not stop for D. 139:15
if ought but d. part thee and me 32:34
in d.'s dateless night 355:10
in that sleep of d. 316:29
in the hour of d. 291:15
in their d. they were not divided 33:1
influence hath allotted d. and hell 245:10
into the jaws of D. 383:12
keeps D. his court 345:22
king my father's d. 153:1
kingly D. keeps his pale court 359:1
knocking at D.'s door 144:12
land of the shadow of d. 42:31
last enemy ... is d. 54:13
lead him to d. 298:7
live ever – or else swoon to d. 217:17
look on d. itself! 334:1
love thee better after d. 70:8
make one in love with d. 358:28
meetest for d. 338:16

Death – *contd*

men fear d. 17:2
murder, and from sudden d. 291:14
my d. was an exaggeration 401:23
neither d., nor life, nor angels 53:3
none blessed before his d. 46:6
not D., but Love 70:4
not d., for I stood up 139:16
now boast thee, d. 310:14
O d., where is thy sting? 54:20 284:24
of d. no one so true 352:27
often thought upon d. 16:24
out of ... the shadow of d. 37:26
pale D. knocks 197:4
parting ... an image of d. 151:13
parting gives a foretaste of d. 305:3
person appearing after d. 209:19
points of d. in a waste 153:17
quiet us in a d. so noble 259:24
Reaper whose name is D. 237:5
remedy for everything except d. 105:5
revenge triumphs over d. 17:3
river of d. has brimmed 270:6
sleep is a d. 69:13
sleep is good, d. is better 186:5
sleep ... knows not D. 385:32
so many years of fearing d. 327:18
so shalt thou feed on D. 357:4
stories of the d. of kings 345:22
studied in his d. 332:19
taste brought d. into the world 255:16
that sat on him was D. 57:1
there is d. in the pot 33:25
there's d. in the cup 83:27
there shall be no more d. 57:20
this fell sergeant, d. 320:1
this is d., and the sole d. 72:14
thou madest D. 385:4
thy brother D. came 364:4
till d. us do part 292:7
'tis d. to us 234:10
to be carnally minded is d. 52:53
to build the house of d. 263:8
to muddy d. 319:12
two luxuries ... the hour of my d. 219:16
under the ribs of D. 253:4
valley of the shadow of d. 35:10
vasty hall of d. 11:3
wages of sin is d. 52:50
way to dusty d. 335:23
we are in d. 292:17
we owe God a d. 323:7
Webster was much possessed by d. 153:8
what should it know of d.? 426:27
what sights of ugly d. 346:29
what we fear of d. 336:24
when d. to either shall come 66:5
whom d. could not daunt 21:2
why fear d.? 163:8
worse than d. 122:21
worst friend and enemy is but D. 67:14
worst is d. 345:20
you'll burn to d. 191:12
Death-pale: d.-p. were they all 216:7
Debellare: d. *superbos* 405:16
Debt: d. which cancels all others 118:6
double d. to pay 172:20

Debt – *contd*
  forgive us our d.s 47:10
  paid the d. of nature 156:12
Debtor: not everyone is a d. 294:15
Decay: d. doth grossly close 339:1
Decayed: decaying, never to be d. 425:2
Deceased: he first d. 427:16
Deceit: prophesy d.s 43:9
  temper discretion with d. 411:12
  these d.s are strong almost as life 267:5
  we hug the dear d. 120:21
Deceive: let no man d. you 54:47
  oh, don't d. me 7:2
  when first we practise to d. 306:17
  with intent to d. 184:3
Deceived: be not d. 54:40
  why ... should we desire to be d.? 86:1
  world, which wishes to be d. 65:5
Deceiver: dupe and a d. 362:31
  I'm a gay d. 118:1
  men were d.s ever 341:17
  thou fond d. 173:8
December: drear-nighted D. 218:15
Decency: ultimate d. of things 375:26
  want of d. is want of sense 299:21
Decently: d. and in order 54:8
Decide: who shall d. 287:29
Decision: valley of d. 45:6
Deck: d. put on its leaves 160:13
  on a tilting d. sings 130:10
  stood on the burning d. 186:10
Decline: D.-and-Fall-Off-the-Rooshan-Empire
    137:22
  professionally he d.s and falls 137:21
  Son of Morn in weary Night's d. 59:7
Decoration: deserves some sort of d. 275:22
Decorum: cant about d. 83:32
Decorum: *dulce et d. est* 197:24
Decree: by a changeless d. 175:13
Dee: across the sands of D. 221:16
  lay me doun and d. 144:21
  lived on the river D. 57:27
Deed: because their d.s were evil 51:27
  blow the horrid d. 333:4
  boast no more your mighty d.s 365:33
  by gentle d.s is known 372:8
  d. of dreadful note 336:15
  d. that my own soul has ... decreed 217:12
  d. whereat valour will weep 313:12
  d. without a name 334:36
  d.s ... for fellowship's sake 266:18
  excused his devilish d.s 257:16
  free from all dishonest d.s 97:3
  if doughty d.s my lady please 128:9
  in loveliness of perfect d.s 385:19
  live in d.s, not years 19:19
  looks quite through the d.s 326:26
  makes ill d.s done 329:7
  matchless d.'s achieved 367:24
  one good d. in all my life 351:5
  renownèd for their d.s 345:8
  rich and ransom all ill d.s 355:14
  right d. for the wrong reason 153:18
  scraps are good d.s past 351:21
  so shines a good d. 339:4
  these d.s must not be thought 333:22
  these unlucky d.s relate 344:16

Deed – *contd*
  thrice-noble d.s 240:19
  time the d. took place 152:19
  vilest d.s like poison-weeds 416:8
Deep: d. calleth unto d. 35:29
  d. moans round with many voices 392:7
  d., still threatening to devour 257:6
  dive into the bottom of the d. 320:23
  drew from out the boundless d. 383:15
  fountains of the great d. 31:6
  from the great d. to the great d. 384:5
  home on the rolling d. 304:4
  maketh the d. to boil 34:18
  not so d. as a well 348:32
  rocked in the cradle of the d. 251:12
  slimy bottom of the d. 346:29
  there rolls the d. 386:17
  though d., yet clear 131:33
  very singularly d. young man 169:33
Deer: 'poor d.,' quoth he 310:28
  running of the d. 7:14
  stricken d. 125:2
  stricken d. go weep 317:26
  Time's d. is slain 267:6
Deeth: d. is an ende 107:26
Défaut: d.s de leurs qualités 21:25
  sa moindre d. 226:18
Defeat: not interested in ... d. 403:21
Defect: d.s of their qualities 21:25
Defence: he is my d. 36:15
  never make a d. ... before you be accused 106:4
  our d. is sure 411:11
Defend: d. to the death your right 407:19
Défend: il se d. 9:7
Defended: what God abandoned, these d. 199:8
Defender: I mean the Faith's D. 88:5
Defiled: d. with their own works 37:25
Defileth: d. a man 48:21
Deformed: d. unfinished 346:21
Degenerate: everything d.s in the hands 301:16
Degeneration: undergoes a fatty d. 375:13
Degree: d., priority, and place 351:9
  scorning the base d.s 327:5
  take but d. away 351:10
  y-fallen out of heigh d. 107:28
Deified: by our own spirits are we d. 425:13
  one day more I am d. 73:27
De'il: clever d.s he'll mak them 83:17
  D.'s awa' wi' the Exciseman 83:9
Deities: d. of his own invention 282:19
  never found the d. so kindly 294:14
Deity: D. and Drains 377:1
Delay: d.s have dangerous ends 325:7
  reproved each dull d. 172:13
  sweet reluctant amorous d. 257:14
Delectable: D. Mountains 79:25
Delectando: lectorem d. pariterque monendo 196:2
Deliberation: d. sat and public care 256:24
Delicately: Agag came unto him d. 32:40
Délice: savourer les rapides d.s 227:20
Delicta: d. maiorum ... lues 198:3
Delight: all d.s are vain 331:9
  d. in simple things 222:18
  d. ... in the ... pains of others 81:1
  d. that fathers thought 195:11
  drunk d. of battle with my peers 392:1
  from ... d. rises ... bitterness 239:19

Doubter: am the d. and the doubt 154:9
Doubting: D. Castle 79:24
Douglas: degenerate D.! 426:7
  doughty D. bound him 20:4
  D. in his hall 306:15
  D., 'tender and true 126:20 191:30
  heard the song of Percy and D. 366:15
  like D. conquer 192:23
  maugre of doughty D. 20:9
Dove: came in a d. 244:5
  d. descending breaks the air 152:5
  d. found no rest 31:7
  gently as any sucking d. 340:1
  had I the wings of a d. 126:6
  harmless as d.s 47:40
  hawk at eagles with a d. 188:7
  I had wings like a d. 36:7
  moan of d.s in ... elms 390:15
Dover: milestones on the D. Road! 135:24
  think of the chalk cliffs of D. 19:22
Dowel: D., Dobet and Dobest 230:19
Dower: d. of lights and fires 126:22
  faith's transcendent d. 425:20
Down: all in the D.s 166:19
  d. and away below 10:20
  d., Sir! Put it d.! 27:27
  he that is d. 79:29
  let it come d. 334:19
  round and round the spicy d.s 388:2
  soon came d. again 122:27
  when they were d., they were d. 6:4
  with d. upon your feet 149:1
Downhearted: are we d.? 225:24
Doxy: d., over the dale 354:5
Drachenfels: castle crag of D. 89:5
Dragon: battell on the d. blak 150:3
  habitation of d.s 43:14
  laid hold on the d. 57:16
  see the old D. 141:28
Dragonflies: d. dráw fláme 194:11
Dragon-fly: d.-f. hangs like a blue thread 301:1
Dragon-green: d.-g., the luminous 160:5
Drain: between the Deity and the D.s 377:1
  by the next town d. 372:23
  pale owing to the d.s 13:5
  she said it wur d.s 392:10
Drake: D. he's in his hammock 270:1
Drama: close the d. with the day 29:17
  d.'s laws, the d.'s patrons give 205:18
  what this wild d. means 389:23
Draught: d.s of intellectual day 126:22
  peculiarly susceptible to d.s 416:24
  shallow d.s intoxicate the brain 285:24
Draw: d.s him, yet she follows 237:12
  let me try and d. you 75:21
Drawer: d.s of water 32:17
Drawling: taught us D. 100:26
Drayhorse: great grey d. 194:16
Dread: close your eyes with holy d. 116:6
  d. and fear of kings 338:17
  d. had seized their troubled mind 382:10
  d. is a sympathetic antipathy 221:3
  d. of something after death 316:29
  flying from something that he d.s 421:17
Dream: arise from d.s of thee 360:16
  as a d. doth flatter 356:7
  as d.s are made on 350:18

Dream — contd
  awakened from the d. of life 359:9
  behold it was a d. 79:27
  broke this happy d. 142:7
  consecration, and the poet's d. 420:14
  do noble things, not d. them 221:13
  d. all night without a stir 215:22
  d. of fighting fields no more 305:16
  d. of perfect bliss 25:26
  d. of those that wake 292:37
  dreamed a dreary d. 20:3
  d.s are true while they last 384:2
  d.s he of smelling 348:1
  d.s no mortal ever dared to d. 283:17
  d.s ... ought to serve 18:31
  d.s out of the ivory gate 68:16
  faileth now even d. 395:17
  fly forgotten as a d. 411:11
  glory and the d. 423:11
  glory and the freshness of a d. 423:5
  gods send up false d.s 405:17
  housed in a d. 420:16
  I d. when I am awake 94:27
  I have bad d.s 316:11
  if there were d.s to sell 26:22
  in a long immortal d. 216:8
  insane d. we take for waking 72:19
  into the land of my d.s 221:11
  is but a d. within a d. 283:12
  is it some d.s? 409:27
  Land of D.s is better far 59:19
  latest d. I ever dreamed 216:6
  less than nothing, and d.s 228:15
  life is but a d. 396:21
  life is but an empty d. 236:30
  my d. thou brok'st not 142:7
  old men shall d. d.s 45:5
  old men's d.! 146:26
  one man with a d. 275:29
  our d.s are tales 131:9
  perceived they had dreamed a d. 77:28
  real are the d.s of Gods 216:8
  shall be called Bottom's D. 340:24
  short as any d. 339:28
  silently as a d. 125:22
  soft! I did but d. 347:17
  some possible d. ... is uncurling 14:1
  spread my d.s under your feet 428:22
  to d. of, not to tell! 115:18
  to keep a d. or grave apart 70:10
  ugly sights, of ghastly d.s 346:28
  waken from his summer d.s 361:16
  what d.s may come 316:29
  what my d. was 340:23
  wovest d.s of joy and fear 364:1
  you tread on my d.s 428:22
Dreamer: behold, this d. cometh 31:21
  d. of dreams 266:5
  if there arise ... a d. of dreams 32:8
  we are the d.s of dreams 275:28
Dreaming: boys are d. wicked 394:13
  d. on things to come 356:18
Dreamt: d. that I dwelt in marble halls 79:8
Dress: all this fleshly d. 402:21
  always d. aright 102:16
  be plain in d. 263:3
  make their d. a principal part 185:1

Dress – *contd*
  modest d., neat, but not gaudy 413:23
Dressed: all d. up and no place 85:6
  d. up, with nowhere to go 414:13
  good temper when he's well d. 135:29
Dresses: d. are made in Paris 303:14
Drink: another little d. 179:16
  d., and leave the world unseen 216:26
  d. deep, or taste not 285:24
  d. ... had done for the rest 375:9
  d., pretty creature, d.! 424:3
  d. to me only 212:12
  d. with me, and d. as I 275:1
  d.s, and gapes for d. 121:9
  every creature d. but I 121:10
  five reasons we should d. 3:9
  his d., the running stream 144:11
  I d. for the thirst to come 294:6
  little in d. 373:13
  long time between d.s 265:22
  never to refuse a d. after dark 249:13
  rise alone and still d. more 280:3
  strong d. is raging 39:40
  taste for d., combined with gout 168:12
  thirsty and ye gave me d. 59:25
  thou shalt d. it with pleasure 46:4
  wants but little d. below 192:13
  what should we do for d. 5:6
  willing to taste any d. once 94:16
Drinking: comes next to d. 132:10
  d. is the soldier's pleasure 147:17
  d. largely sobers us 285:24
  not the d. that is to be blamed 308:2
  now is the time for d. 197:14
  there's nothing like d. 133:7
  with constant d. fresh and fair 121:9
Dripping: constant d. hollows 239:15
Driven: all d. into the same fold 197:17
Driving: d. is like the d. of Jehu 33:28
  d. rapidly *from* something 209:10
Drone: drive out the ... d.s 406:18
  lazy yawning d. 323:26
Dronkenesse: d. is verray sepulture 107:30
Droop: begin to d. and drowse 334:17
Drop: as a d. of a bucket 43:26
  better to d. thy friends 95:25
  few small d.s of rain 21:21
  like kindred d.s 124:31
  merrily did we d. 114:16
  nor any d. to drink 114:23
  one d. would save my soul 245:9
  people whom one should like ... to d. 210:2
  ruddy d.s that warm my heart 176:14
Dropping: d. in a very rainy day 40:21
Droppy: Hoppy, Croppy, D. 154:5
Dropsy: twice tapped for a d. 364:22
Dross: can separate thy d. 88:22
Drown: what pain it was to d. 346:29
Drowned: better ... d. in the depth 48:32
  but he'll be d. 271:7
Drowning: to d. no mark upon him 349:28
Drudge: *Lexicographer* ... harmless d. 206:1
Drug: d.s are a delusion 357:20
  most powerful d. used by mankind 225:21
Drum: *bang-whang-whang* goes the d. 78:4
  dumb as a d. 138:13
  en de bangin' er de d.s 183:26

Drum – *contd*
  heard thro' rolling d.s 390:4
  my pulse like a soft d. 221:10
  not a d. was heard 419:15
  rumble of a distant D. 158:22
  spirit-stirring d. 343:31
  take my d. to England 269:28
Drunk: all learned and all d.! 125:18
  as you d. I am 372:28
  d. is he, who prostrate lies 280:3
  d. to bed 309:18
  gloriously d., obey 125:19
  hasten to be d. 147:30
  man ... must get d. 90:28
  never happy ... but when he is d. 209:10
  this meeting is d. 138:25
Drunkard: rolling English d. 109:30
Drunken: and got more d. 289:30
  d., but not with wine 43:7
  stagger like a d. man 37:29
Drunkenness: branch of the sin of d. 203:25
Dry: friend, or being d. 3:9
  oh! I am so d. 156:15
  what shall be done in the d.? 51:11
Dryad: light winged D. of the trees 216:25
Dryden: all the prefaces of D. 378:18
  copious D. wanted 289:11
  D. calls the fairy way 2:7
  D. taught to join 289:10
  poetry of D., Pope 12:14
  to read D. ... you need only count 116:25
Dublin: in D.'s fair city 7:16
Ducat: O my Christian d.s! 338:1
Duchess: D.! Oh my dear paws! 100:10
  D. said in a hoarse growl 100:13
Duck: D. and the Kangaroo 232:12
  four d.s on a pond 4:4
  wild d. Stick at the bottom 203:8
  your precious 'lame d.s'! 164:24
Duckling: Ugly D. 4:10
Dudgeon: civil d. first grew high 86:3
Due: render ... to all their d.s 53:14
Duke: bury the Great D. 389:5
  d.s were three a penny 168:18
  everybody praised the D. 370:10
  knows enough who knows a d. 125:33
Dukedom: prize above my d. 349:33
Dulce: d. est desipere in loco 198:13
  d. et decorum est 197:24
  d. ridentem Lalagen 197:13
Dulcimer: damsel with a d. 116:5
Dull: d. – beyond all conception 362:6
  d. without a single absurdity 174:4
  d. would he be of soul 422:12
  not wont to be so d. 347:5
  Sherry is d., naturally d. 208:5
  so smoothly d. 284:12
  tell them that they are d. 359:26
  though gentle, yet not d. 131:33
  venerably d. 110:26
Dullard: d.'s envy of brilliant men 27:12
Dullness: cause of d. in others 161:7
  d. ever loves a joke 284:8
  with this d. was he cursed 362:6
Dumb: d. as a drum 138:13
Dummheit: mit der D. kämpfen Götter selbst 304:17

485

East – *contd*
  E. is E., and West is West 222:12
  ebbing to the ... e. 231:14
  ever-silent spaces of the E. 391:21
  from the e. must travel 423:13
  hold the gorgeous e. in fee 422:18
  in the chambers of the E. 61:12
  it is the e. 348:8
  look E., where ... thousands are 78:6
  man with his back to the E. 114:12
  rise not from the E. 126:24
  there is neither E. nor West 222:12
  tried to hustle the E. 224:4
  when the wind is blowing in the E. 133:21
Easy: I was young and e. 394:3
Eat: e. and drink in order to live 369:32
  e. exceedingly, and prophesy 211.17
  e., or drink, or whatsoever ye do 53:41
  I did sit and e. 188:3
  I e. and e., I swear 325:2
  I e. the air promise-crammed 317:18
  I e. this world 402:1
  let us e. and drink 54:14
  man is what he e.s 157:11
  neither should he e. 55:19
  some hae meat and canna e. 84:12
  tell me what you e. 66:16
  to e., and to drink, and to be merry 41:19
Eaten: e. me out of house 322:23
  they'd e. every one 101:25
Eater: e. came forth meat 32:26
Eating: appetite comes with e. 294:7
  e. and drinking 49:21
  not the e. ... that is to be blamed 308:2
  not to know what he is e. 228:16
Eau: '*l'e.*,' replied Nicholas 136:26
Eave: fall upon her gilded e.s 390:1
Eave-drop: e.-d.s fall heard only 115:29
Eccentricities: e. of genius 138:17
Eccentricity: e., heresy, anomalies 304:1
Ech: e. man for him-self 107:21
Echo: and my e. ring 371:20
  applaud thee to the very e 335:20
  e. caught faintly the sound 156:14
  e. is not faint at last 230:11
  every bosom returns an e. 206:12
  in worship of an e. 89:10
  very e. to the seat 352:23
Echoes: e. roll from soul to soul 389:34
  wild e. flying 389:32
Eclipse: built in th' e. 254:28
  E. first, the rest nowhere 274:24
  gloom of earthquake and e. 363:5
  late e.s in the sun and moon 329:16
  total e. without all hope 259:10
Economic: bottom of the e. pyramid 299:4
Economist: sophisters, e.s, and calculators 81:8
Economy: e. is going without something 194:2
Ecstasy: blasted with e. 317:8
  maintain this e., is success 278:21
  not e. but it was comfort 135:25
Eden: lest we lose our E.s 78:8
  make this earth an E. 100:3
  on the east of E. 31:2
  other E., demi-paradise 345:8
  some flow'rets of E. 265:12
  voice that breathed o'er E. 220:3

Eden – *contd*
  wandering steps and slow through E. 258:31
  with E. didst devise the Snake 159:15
  with loss of E. 255:16
Eden-sweet: E.-s. the ray 250:6
Edge: vast e.s drear 10:14
Edifice: hail, glorious e. 368:10
Edition: new e. of human nature 184:20
Edmonton: wife should dine at E. 123:4
Educated: e. man's 77:3
Education: and a liberal e. 187:3
  by e. most have been misled 148:7
  e. forms the common mind 287:16
  e. has for its object 371:9
  e. is a little too pedantic 118:16
  e. makes a people easy to lead 68:5
  e. ... population able to read 399:17
  is a liberal e. 373:10
  limited e., rather 414:11
  race between e. and catastrophe 413:11
  travel ... part of e. 18:8
Edward: sons of E. sleep 347:9
  why E. tell me why? 420:6
  your ain mither dear, E., E. 20:14
Edwardian: E. Wilderness 275:26
Edwin: always call you E. 157:4
Ee: drumlie grew his e. 20:11
Eel: as e.s are to be flayed 91:20
Effect: dire e.s from civil discord 1:15
  little e. after much labour 16:7
Efficacy: purest e. and extraction 260:12
Efficiency: e. and inefficiency 357:25
Effort: e. very nearly killed her 28:2
Égard: *on doit des é.s aux vivants* 407:12
Egestas: *duris urgens in rebus e.* 406:12
Egg: boil e.s in your shoes 233:4
  but to roast their e.s 18:15
  damned like an ill-roasted e. 311:20
  e. boiled very soft 15:3
  e. is full of meat 348:30
  fatal e. by Pleasure laid 124:10
  hairless as an e. 189:1
  laid a steel e. 367:7
  lays e.s inside a paper bag 5:11
  learned roast an e. 289:13
  like an e. without salt 104:2
  like eating an e. without salt 225:14
  radish and an e. 125:14
  see it when the e.s are fried 104:21
  to cook himself a couple of e.s 105:19
  you've got a bad e. 293:26
Eglantine: musk-roses, and with e. 340:10
Ego: too much E. in your Cosmos 225:7
Ego: *E. et Rex meus* 325:29
Egypt: all the first-born of E. 311:3
  E., when we sat by the flesh-pots 31:41
  I am dying, E. 310:4
Egyptian: E.s worshipped an insect 141:15
  spoiled the E.s 31:40
Eight: pieces of e.! 375:11
Eighty: fourscore was as e. 217:15
Einstein: let E. be! 372:27
Elbow: knees and e.s ... glued together 59:21
Eld: palsied e. 336:20
Elder: e. man not at all 17:18
  miss not the discourse of the e.s 46:12
Elderly: e. man of 42 13:3

Endeavour – *contd*
  disinterested e. to learn 12:8
Ending: bread-sauce of the happy e. 204:9
  never e., still beginning 147:21
Endow: e. a college, or a cat 287:30
  I thee e. 292:9
Endurance: patient e. is godlike 236:18
Endure: e., and preserve yourselves 404:17
  for thy peace, she shall e. 302:14
  more able to e., as more exposed 420:10
Endured: much is to be e. 206:25
Endureth: e. to the end shall be saved 47:41
Enemies: choice of his e. 417:22
  his e. shall lick the dust 36:28
  his e. 'Toasted-cheese' 102:8
  let his e. be scattered 36:22
  love your e. 47:6
  make e. of nations 124:31
  mortal e. ever since 234:4
  naked to mine e. 326:5
  one of my most intimate e. 300:24
Enemy: bridge is for a flying e. 90:9
  do be my e. 61:11
  e. faints not, nor faileth 113:19
  e. hath done this 48:15
  found me, O mine e. 33:20
  hasn't an e. in the world 418:3
  how goes the e.? 296:8
  last e. that shall be destroyed 54:13
  my vision's greatest e. 59:1
  no e. can match a friend 378:14
  our friends the e. 29:16
  put an e. in their mouths 343:18
  shall he see no e. 310:38
  sweet e., France 366:9
  these men will have upon the e. 412:20
  warm personal e. left 414:5
Energy: e. is eternal delight 61:18
  march, and e. divine 289:10
Enfant: allons, e.s de la patrie 301:13
  e. terrible of literature 87:14
  e.s terribles 165:15
  lorsque l'e. paraît 201:1
Engagement: loose from every honourable e. 81:24
Engine: e. that moves in predestinate 183:9
  e.s to play a little on our own 81:5
  that two-handed e. 254:32
Engineer: glorified sanitary e. 377:1
England: be E. what she will 110:20
  done for you, E., my E. 186:16
  E.! awake! awake! 59:16
  E., bound in with the triumphant sea 345:9
  E. expects every man 269:17
  E. has saved herself 282:14
  E. hath need of thee 422:25
  E., home and beauty 12:27 64:15
  E. is a nation of shopkeepers 268:13
  E. is a paradise for women 85:23
  E. is the mother of Parliaments 66:11
  E. is the paradise of individuality 304:1
  E. is the paradise of women 160:24
  E. keep my bones 329:8
  E. mourns for her dead 57:31
  E. never did, nor never shall 329:11
  E.'s far and honour a name 270:6
  E.'s the one land, I know 67:9
  E. that was wont to conquer 345:9

England – *contd*
  E. ... the workshop of the world 140:7
  E. to itself do rest but true 329:11
  E. was merry E. 306:14
  E., we love thee 399:16
  E. will have her neck wrung 111:14
  E., with all thy faults, I love thee 124:33
  E.'s greatest son 389:10
  further off from E. 101:2
  gentlemen in E. now a-bed 324:26
  happy is E. 218:1
  here did E. help me 73:17.
  in E. ... given to horses 206:2
  in this realm of E. 292:22
  lost the last of E. 28:25
  men of E., wherefore plough 363:10
  occurred nowhere but in E. 119:23
  oh, to be in E. 73:12
  perfidious E. 64:2
  poorest he that is in E. 295:7
  slaves cannot breathe in E. 124:32
  ten thousand of those men in E. 324:21
  that is for ever E. 67:16
  there'll always be an E. 277:23
  this earth, this realm, this E. 345:8
  thoughts by E. given 67:17
  we are the people of E. 110:1
  what should they know of E. 222:25
  who dies if E. live? 222:29
  you gentlemen of E. 277:21
  youth of E. are on fire 323:28
England: Gott strafe E.! 164:17
English: Allah created the E. mad 223:16
  and the king's E. 339:12
  cool, and quite E. 92:1
  E. ... a foul-mouthed nation 185:3
  E. as she is Spoke 400:8
  E. is what you speak 102:11
  E. ... least a nation of ... philosophers 19:18
  E. take their pleasures sadly 377:15
  E. that of the sea 296:16
  E. ... the *nicest* people 231:13
  enters at the E. gate 199:25
  especially if he went among the E. 24:6
  on, on you noblest E. 324:11
  rooted in the E. character 86:34
  trick of our E. nation 322:18
  well of E. undefiled 372:6
  wut's good's all E. 238:29
  with our E. dead 324:10
Englishman: as thorough an E. 222:1
  broad-shouldered genial E. 390:19
  E., being flattered, is a lamb 105:23
  E. does not travel to see 374:4
  E. thinks he is moral 358:2
  he is an E.! 168:29
  know that E. alive 347:1
  last great E. is low 389:6
  not one E. [slain] 408:17
  smell the blood of an E. 272:8
  to be an E. is to belong 268:21
  what an E. believes be heresy 358:21
Englishmen: absurd nature of E. 280:20
  first to His E. 260:17
  mad dogs and E. 121:5
  we be all good E. 390:25
  when two E. meet 206:4

Eternity – *contd*
hid battlements of E. 395:18
image of e. 90:2
intimates e. to man 1:14
lovers' hours be full e. 143:14
make the mighty ages of e. 100:2
nothing of a god but e. 313:10
prepared for you from all e. 15:2
some shadows of e. 402:20
tease us ... as doth e. 216:18
through nature to e. 314:8
types and symbols of E. 425:3
without injuring e. 397:1
Ether: ampler e. 421:12
Ethics: good are the E. 113:7
Ethiop: in an E.'s ear 348:4
Ethiopian: E. change his skin 44:20
Étoile: du fond de l'Océan des é.s nouvelles 188:15
Eton: playing fields of E. 412:25
Eunuch: but strain, time's e. 195:10
kind of moral e. 362:5
Eureka: e.l 9:18
Euripides: chorus-ending from E. 71:3
E. portrays them as they are 370:5
our E., the human 70:11
Europe: better fifty years of E. 387:27
E., Afrique and an Asia 144:6
save E. by her example 282:14
wisest woman in E. 152:27
Eurydice: half-regained E. 254:16
Evade: excede, – e.–, – erump! 192:18
Eve: and E. span 20:1
bathed in e.'s loveliness 131:29
chaste E. 117:11
child of our grandmother E. 331:12
close at the ear of E. 257:24
fairest of her daughters E. 257:15
fallen sons of E. 110:5
said ... to E.: Be soon 395:16
vanquished e., as night prevails 199:25
Eve-jar: spins the brown e.-j. 249:17
Even: grey-hooded E. 252:24
last pale beam of e. 363:15
sweet approach of e. 256:37
would God it were e. 32:11
Evening: coming on of grateful e. 257:21
e. full of the linnet's wings 429:4
e. is spread out against the sky 152:11
in the e. it is cut down 37:8
like an e. gone 411:11
note, when e. shuts 76:8
quiet-coloured end of e. 74:8
it was a summer e. 370:7
welcome peaceful e. in 125:11
winter e. settles down 152:21
Event: e. has happened 80:22
experience from this great e. 259:27
greatest e. ... that ever happened 162:7
not to have controlled e.s 234:19
one e. happeneth to them all 41:2
one far-off divine e. 386:21
three e.s in a man's life 226:8
Eventide: fast falls the e. 240:8
Ever: for e. and for e. when I move 392:2
I go on for e. 383:5
it may be for e. 127:12
yesterday, and to day, and for e. 56:3

Everlasting: E. had not fixed 314:11
from e. thou art God 411:11
from e. to e. thou art God 37:5
had stood from e. to e. 399:9
Everlastingness: shoots of e. 402:21
Evermore: e. about to be 424:29
Everyone: e. soon or late 76:22
e. suddenly burst out singing 304:7
when e. is somebodee 168:19
Everything: e., and nothing thoroughly 263:12
e. in its place 368:2
sans taste, sans e. 311:14
smattering of e. 139:9
Everywhere: out of the e. 242:18
Evidence: circumstantial e. 397:9
e. of things not seen 55:38
it's not e. 138:28
shall call rebutting e. 213:2
Evil: be not overcome of e. 53:11
call e. good, and good e. 42:24
death ... the least of all e.s 16:24
deliver us from e. 47:11
do e. that good may come 52:44
enslaved that serve things e. 362:22
eschew e. and do good 35:21
e. be thou my Good 257:7
e. that men do lives after them 327:26
e. which I would not, that I do 52:51
e.s, monstrous either one 296:1
e.s which never arrived 154:14
feared God and eschewed e. 33:32
feet run to e. 44:7
few and e. ... the years of my life 31:28
good men made e. wrangling 267:4
government ... a necessary e. 277:6
I will fear no e. 35:10
is thine eye e. 49:3
it is an unruly e. 56:10
less grievous of two e.s 305:1
make imaginary e.s 173:28
maketh his sun rise on the e. 47:7
may look e. in theory 80:21
money is the root of all e.s 55:28 87:2
must expect new e.s 18:17
no man is justified in doing e. 299:17
obscures the show of e. 338:10
partial e., universal good 286:27
resist not e. 47:5
still to find means of e. 255:25
sufficient unto the day is the e. 47:19
they are necessary e.s 206:20
what all the blessed e.'s for 71:7
Ewe: e.s breed not 23:21
save one little e. lamb 33:6
tupping your white e. 342:18
Ewigkeit: afay in the e.! 233:25
Ewig-Weibliche: das E.-W. zieht uns hinan
171:12
Exactitude: l'e. est la politesse 238:7
Exactness: with e. grinds He 237:6
Exaggeration: report ... was an e. 401:23
Exalted: humble himself shall be e. 49:14
Examination: e.s are formidable 118:5
Example: e. is always more efficacious 206:27
e. is the school of mankind 81:36
lower orders don't set us a good e. 416:13
take e. by your father 138:8

Excel: thou shalt not e. 31:29
'tis useless to e. 240:11
Excellence: e.s carried to an excess 116:27
Excellent: yet be in practice e. 80:21
Excelsior: strange device, E.1 236:19
Excess: best things carried to e. 111:1
give me e. of it 351:32
not the eating ... but the e. 308:2
nothing to e. 8:23
road of e. leads to .. wisdom 61:22
wasteful and ridiculous e. 329:4
Exchange: by just e. 366:4
Exciseman: De'il's awa' wi' the E. 83:9
Exciting: found it less e. 168:9
too e. to be pleasant 138:6
Exclamation: breathed a sort of e. 182:25
Excrucior: fieri sentio et e. 103:17
Excuse: e. every man will plead 308:5
fault the worse by the e. 329:5
Execution: e. confined 351:18
some are daily led to e. 295:12
Executioner: mine own E. 144:7
proves its own e. 161:10
Executor: choose e.s and talk of wills 345:21
delivering o'er to e.s 323:26
Exercise: for cure, on e. depend 147:31
talk ... 'tis their e. 26:7
Exertion: e. is too much for me 280:6
saved herself by her e.s 282:14
Exhalation: like a bright e. 325:30
rose like an e. 256:12
Exile: kiss long as my e. 313:8
Exiled: from thy sight, being, ah! e. 366:12
Existed: I have never e. before 30:6
Existence: ages before we have e. 228:15
every e. would exist in Thee 66:21
e. or when hope is gone 15:15
e. saw him spurn 205:17
he put out of e. 137:25
let us contemplate ... 135:34
more about it than its bare e. 86:33
struggle for e. 129:16
'tis woman's whole e. 90:21
Exit: e., pursued by a bear 354:2
men to take their e.s 412:4
they have their e.s 311:14
Expect: blessed is the man who e.s nothing 289:28
I e. less of [mankind] 210:6
Expectation: better bettered e. 341:2
e. whirls me round 351:17
now sits E. in the air 323:28
Expediency: evil on the ground of e. 299:17
Expedient: all things are not e. 53:39
to pursue the e. 173:2
Expendable: They Were E. 414:14
Expenditure: e. nineteen nineteen six 134:19
Expensive: more e. but is more durable 231:22
Experience: all e. is an arch 392:2
encounter ... the reality of e. 212:28
e. is ... their mistakes 417:12
expert beyond e. 153:9
insight ... worth a life's e. 192:19
old age, and e., hand in hand 298:7
old e. do attain 253:31
than e. to make me sad 312:9
travel ... a part of e. 18:8
triumph of hope over e. 208:23

Experience – contd
what e. and history teach 185:29
Experientia: e. does it 134:16
Experiment: desist from the e. 228:19
Expert: e. ... knows more and more 86:2
Experto: e. credite 405:24
Explanation: explain his e. 90:10
I do loathe e.s 23:27
Expletive: e.s their feeble aid 286:5
Exploit: honour is flashed off e. 195:6
Exploitation: e. ... of man by man 155:25
Exposed: more e. to suffering 420:10
Exposition: e. of sleep 340:21
Exposure: unseemly e. of the mind 185:4
Expressed: ne'er so well e. 285:27
Expression: e. ... called bald 12:17
indirect e.s before a Caledonian 228:20
vulgar e. of the passion 118:7
Extensive: e. and peculiar 138:7
Extenuate: nothing e. 344:16
Extinct: purpose of becoming e. 128:10
Extinguished: nature ... seldom e. 18:32
Extol: how shall we e. thee 29:6
Extreme: e.s meet 193:21 249:14
Extrème: e.s se touchent 249:14
Exuberance: e. of his own verbosity 140:23
Exultation: friends are e.s, agonies 422:22
Eye: as the apple of his e. 32:12
as 'twere in scorn of e.s 346:29
beam that is in thine own e. 47:21
bright e.s rain influence 254:12
but from Thine e.s 126:24
changing, like a joyless e. 363:25
close your e.s with holy dread 116:6
closed his e.s in endless night 178:21
courtier's, soldier's, scholar's e. 317:7
day's azure e.s 361:6
drink to me only with thine e.s 212:12
drops the closing e. requires 177:17
dry one's e.s and laugh 73:32
ever more peep through their e.s 337:3
e. begins to see 66:22
e. for e., tooth for tooth 31:42
e. is not satisfied with seeing 40:36
e. is on fire 79:3
e. of heaven, shinèd bright 371:27
e. of heaven to garnish 329:4
e. of man hath not heard 340:23
e. unused to flow 355:10
e. was backward cast 371:28
e.s are nothing like the sun 357:1
e.s deceive me earsight 409:27
e.s have they, but they see not 38:3
e.s, like stars, start from 315:12
e.s look your last! 349:14
e.s looked love to e.s 88:26
e.s not yet created 356:3
e.s of men ... are idly bent 346:14
e.s of most unholy blue! 264:20
e.s that shone, now dimmed 265:13
e.s too expressive to be blue 10:19
e.s upraised as one inspired 117:19
e.s were as a flame of fire 56:29
e.s were deeper than the depth 300:20
e.s were with his heart 89:23
flash upon that inward e. 421:8
fringèd curtains of thine e. 350:2

Eye – *contd*

from women's e.s this doctrine 331:23
gasp and stretch one's e.s 28:2
get thee glass e.s 330:28
happiness through another man's e.s 312:16
have e.s to wonder 356:17
he had but one e. 136:16
he that formed the e. 37:17
heaven in her e. 258:10
his e.s through the helmet-slit 266:8
his flashing e. 116:6
holds him with his glittering e. 114:15
I have a good e., uncle 341:10
I have a pair of e.s 138:29
I turn my ravished e.s 1:16
I was e.s to the blind 34:10
I will lift up mine e. 38:10
if thine e. offend thee 48:34
in her aspect and her e.s 93:4
in the optics of these e.s 69:1
Item, Two grey e.s with lids 352:12
keep me as the apple of the e. 34:37
kindling her undazzled e.s 260:18
left me with the jaundiced e. 387:19
lifting up a fearful e. 371:1
light, that lies in woman's e.s 265:6
lockt up from mortal e. 127:7
looks ... with a threatening e. 329:2
love-darting e.s 253:12
man a microscopic e. 286:23
mine e. seeth thee 34:19
mine e.s arede the myster wight 284:13
mine e.s dazzle 412:5
mine e.s have seen the glory 200:9
mine e.s saw not, and I saw 395:22
mine e.s smell onions 309:12
my e.s were blind with stars 191:1
my gushing e.s o'erflow 284:32
no e.s, but fountains 226:1
no longer blinded by our e.s 67:19
no more assail mine e.s 131:14
one auspicious and one dropping e. 314:4
one whose subdued e.s 344:16
ope their golden e.s 313:16
open your e.s to the air 395:6
our gloom pleased e.s 218:9
painted to the e.s 141:22
pair of sparkling e.s 168:16
Paradys stood formed in hir e.s 108:11
pearls that were his e.s 350:1
poorly satisfy our e.s 427:17
purges the e.s 92:26
sail, with unshut e. 10:22
see the whites of their e.s 293:28
see them wink the other e. 167:27
see with, not thro', the e. 59:4
send home my long strayed e.s 143:18
shall see e. to e. 43:36
still-soliciting e. 329:14
strike mine e.s, but not my heart 211:25
striving e. dazzles at it 402:11
swellin' ... before my wery e.s 138:24
tempts your wandering e.s 178:5
there's language in her e. 351:28
those e.s, the break of day 336:27
thou e. among the blind 423:16
thy dying e.s were closed 284:29

Eye – *contd*

tongue is in his e.s 160:23
two lovely black e.s 113:24
unforgiving e. 365:28
vacant heart and hand, and e. 306:25
when first your e. I eyed 356:13
when with eagle e.s he stared 218:4
where did you get your e.s 242:18
where e.s did once inhabit 346:29
where you turn your e.s 288:9
while I have e.s to see 189:4
who sees with equal e. 286:20
wipe my weeping e.s 411:7
with e.s severe 311:14
with his half-shut e.s 288:27
with his keener e. 247:4
with its soft black e. 265:10
with lack-lustre e. 311:6
with my little e. 274:16
with such a wistful e. 416:5
yellow to the jaundiced e. 286:14
your quaint enamelled e.s 254:33
Eyeball: e. owns the mystic rod 77:23
like a coal his e.-b. 367:22
my e.-b.s roll 285:2
Eyelid: tinged the e.s and the hands 278:19
tired e.s upon tired eyes 387:32
wilt weigh my e.s down 322:30
with e.s heavy and red 193:20

F

Fable: neither give heed to f.s 55:20
profane and old wives' f.s 55:24
Fable: des f.s convenues 407:11
Fabric: like the baseless f. 350:18
out of the earth a f. 256:12
silently ... the f. rose 125:22
Fabrum: f. ... suae ... fortunae 9:14
Fabula: de te f. narratur 198:14
Face: before I knew thy f. 142:2
bid them wash their f.s 312:31
blubbered is that pretty f. 292:24
born with a different f. 61:15
coming with vivid f.s 428:16
cover her f. 412:5
did not recognize me by my f. 399:18
everybody's f. but their own 378:23
f. made up, out of no other shop 127:8
F. of Man is blackened 159:15
f. one would meet in every place 215:17
f. that launched a thousand ships 245:6
f. that two hours since hath died 391:31
f.s are but a gallery 18:22
familiar with her f. 287:2
fyr-reed cherubinnes f. 107:16
garden in her f. 97:7
God hath given you one f. 317:5
grind the f.s of the poor 42:22
hawk-like foreign f.s 243:6
he seems to hide his f. 259:26
hid his f. amid a crowd 429:27
hides a smiling f. 123:18
human f. divine 256:37
I am the family f. 182:6

Face – *contd*

I know the f.s I shall see 301:4
in nice clean f.s 22:10
just can't think of your f. 372:21
kissing with golden f. 355:13
lives on this lonely f. 429:13
look on her f. 288:18
Lord make his f. shine 32:2
my f. – I don't mind it 156:2
my f. is my fortune 274:13
never f. so pleased 161:16
oil to make his f. to shine 37:22
old familiar f.s 228:6
painting a f. and not washing it 164:4
pardoned all except her .. 91:26
plain men have rosy f.s 376:7
praised him to his f. 391:2
sea of upturned f.s 307:4
seen in one autumnal f. 142:9
she has a lovely f. 387:1
shining morning f. 311:14
so many millions of f.s 69:5
sorrows of your changing f. 429:26
strange f.s, other minds 384:32
their innocent f.s clean 60:24
them that will f. me 321:3
then f. to f. 54:5
these f.s in the crowd 290:11
those angel f.s smile 270:13
transmitter of a foolish f. 304:9
turneth his f. to the wall 87:30
two godlike f.s 289:21
visit her f. too roughly 314:12
white f.s like town children 201:6
wish I loved its silly f. 295:16
with a caricature of a f. 169:27
with how wan a f. 366:6
with twain he covered his f. 42:26
your f., my thane, is as a book 332:28
your honest sonsie f. 84:24

Fact: beyond the obvious f.s 145:15
f. the whole world knows 233:2
F.s are chiels that winna ding 83:10
f.s are sacred 305:6
f.s when you come to brass tacks 152:22
fashnable f.s and polite annygoats 393:24
in one f. we all agree 113:13
matters of f. ... are very stubborn 398:10
what I want is F.s 135:16

Faction: heat of religious f. 167:16
to die for f. is a common evil 147:12

Faculty: how infinite in f.! 316:13

Fade: f. away into the forest 216:26
f. far away, dissolve 216:26
nothing of him that doth f. 350:1
she cannot f. 216:14
they only f. away 8:4

Fading: fair things are f. away 25:4

Faenore: solutus omni f. 197:1

Faery: beautiful, a f.'s child 216:2
F. ... wave her wand for him alone 377:5
land of f. 429:6

Faiblesse: le reste est f. 404:6

Fail: I die! I faint! I f.! 360:18
I would sooner f. 219:8
if we should f. 333:10
many f., the one succeeds 383:20

Fail – *contd*

no such word as – *f.* 240:14
some night you'll f. us 75:21

Failing: every f. but their own 92:32
f.s leaned to Virtue's side 172:12
sifted her and separated her f.s 118:26

Failure: half the f.s in life 183:7

Faint: f. yet pursuing 32:25

Fainted: utterly have f. 35:14

Fainting: F. in coils 100:26

Fair: all so excellently f. 115:23
ambition – to be f. 240:10
and all that's f. 408:8
anything to show more f. 422:12
brave deserves the f. 147:14
f. and softly, John he cried 122:29
f. and yet not fond 277:2
f. as is the rose in May 108:4
f. is foul, and foul is f. 332:5
f. is too foul an epithet 245:22
from f. sometimes declines 355:3
good as she was f. 298:19
lovely f. and smell'st so sweet 344:5
not f. to outward view 114:10
she f., divinely f. 258:20
what care I how f. she be 419:11
what's right and f. 200:19
wilt thou love and she be f. 216:14

Fairer: can't say no f. than that 134:35
comes up f. 198:11

Fairest: O f. of creation! 258:23

Fairies: f. at the bottom of our garden 164:20
f. break their dances 199:6
f. were of the old profession 120:5
farewell rewards and f. 120:4
I don't believe in f. 24:1
since the f. left off dancing 308:8
that was the beginning of f. 23:28

Fairing: thou'll get thy f. 84:22

Fairy: and like a f. 264:11
f. tales of science 387:4
f., trip upon the green 357:6
f. way of writing 2:7
little f. ... falls down dead 24:1
'tis almost f. time 341:1

Fais: f. ce que voudras 294:11

Fait: un seul f. accompli 63:2

Faith: abideth f., hope and charity 54:6
alter in my f. of him 211:22
be it f. or not 398:15
belief had ripened into f. 420:23
constitutes poetic f. 116:19
easy to shake a man's f. 357:15
f. and fire within us 182:12
f. as a grain of mustard seed 48:30
f. before the world confessed 200:7
F. is kneeling by his bed 146:7
f. is the substance of things 55:38
f. let graceless zealots fight 287:4
f. shines equal 66:19
f. that looks through death 423:22
f. that stands on authority 155:2
f. unfaithful kept him ... true 384:15
f. without works is dead 56:8
f.'s defying 23:21
him that is weak in the f. 53:17
his f. perhaps ... might be wrong 121:18

Flies – *contd*
  shops with large blue f. 368:11
  small f. were caught 16:22
  unfading moths, immortal f. 67:4
Flight: above the vulgar f. 267.10
  alarms of struggle and f. 10:15
  attained by sudden f. 236:25
  beetle wheels his droning f. 176:22
  his f. was madness 335:3
  in what fond f. 301:3
  winged his roving f. 289:5
Flim-flam: pretty f.-f. 26:3
Flinders: little Polly F. 273:1
Flint: wear out the everlasting f. 348:29
Flip: world in motion with a f. 278:12
Float: f.s on high o'er vales 421:4
Flock: feed his f. like a shepherd 43:25
  in fleecy f.s of light 66:2
  my f.s feed not 23:21
  not armies ... but f.s of sheep 104:10
  shepherd that leaveth the f. 45:16
  silent was the f. in woolly fold 215:6
  summer's rose, or f.s, or herds 256:37
  watched their f.s by night 382:10
  where f.s have took delight 61:6
Flock-bed: on once a f.-b. 288:3
Flogging: f. me constantly 399:18
Flood: bathe in fiery f.s 336:23
  beachèd verge of the salt f. 350:34
  f. did, and fire shall o'erthrow 143:2
  giant race before the f. 147:32
  let the f.s clap their hands 37:19
  love you ten years before the f. 247:11
  nor can the f.s drown it 42:16
  nor death's cold f. 411:6
  thorough f., thorough fire 340:3
Floor: curled up on the f. 184:6
  fell upon the sandy f. 279:18
  f. lay paved with broken hearts 238:9
  f.s of plaster 288:3
  nicely sanded f. 172:20
  ninety years on the f. 427:8
  not drunk is he who from the f. 280:3
Flora: tasting of F. 216:26
Florence: F. blossoming in stone 236:23
Flores: at F. in the Azores 390:21
Floribus: in ipsis f. angat 239:19
Flos: ut f. in saeptis secretus nascitur hortis 103:12
Floures: f. whyte and rede 108:3
Flourish: and all things f. 288:9
  peculiar f. of his right arm 137:25
Flourisheth: f. and groweth up 37:8
Flourishing: f. like a green bay tree 35:23
  shall be fat and f. 37:16
Flout: f. 'em, and scout 'em 350:14
Flow: dark as winter was the f. 96:10
  O could I f. like thee 131:33
  what need you f. 8:18
Flower: as a f. of the field 37:21
  as the f. of the field 43:23
  blushing f.s shall rise 288:9
  bunch of other men's f.s 263:25
  constellated f. that never sets 363:3
  ensnared with f.s 246:25
  ev'ry f. is united 165:25
  fairest f., no sooner blown 255:3
  f. in his hand when he awoke 116:16

Flower – *contd*
  f. is born to blush unseen 177:10
  f. of kings and knights 244:12
  f. springs up secretly 103:12
  F. that once has blown 159:1
  f. that sad embroidery wears 254:33
  f.s appear on the earth 42:8
  f.s as gay as ever 121:20
  f.s, as in their causes, sleep 98:1
  f.s I leave you on the grass 393:1
  f.s in the garden 376:11
  f.s now that frighted thou let'st 354:13
  f.s o' the forest are a' wede away 154:4
  f.s of all hue 257:11
  f.s of the forest are withered 113:25
  f.s soon will be asleep 23:9
  f.s that bloom in the spring 169:26
  f.s that grow between 237:5
  f.s to strew Thy way 187:27
  gather the f.s 247:9
  gathered f.s are dead, Yasmin 160:9
  grass withereth, the f. fadeth 43:24
  ground with vernal f.s 254:33
  He paints the wayside f. 96:3
  Heaven in a wild f. 58:18
  here's f.s for you 354:12
  lack the f. that's like thy face 313:23
  later f.s for the bee 218:18
  lightly like a f. 386:20
  look like the innocent f. 332:29
  lovelier f. ... was never sown 426:13
  may a f. no more lift its head 394:2
  meanest f. that blows 423:25
  no f. upon the ground 359:17
  no stronger than a f. 355:23
  same f. that smiles to-day 189:9
  say it with f.s 274:20
  see what f.s are at my feet 217:3
  sweet will be the f. 123:19
  thou canst not stir a f. 396:2
  up-gathered now like sleeping f.s 422:8
  upon a little western f. 340:8
  wee modest crimson-tippèd f. 84:26
  white f. of a blameless life 384:4
  with the f.s she comes 233:13
  you seize the f. 84:18
Flower-de-luce: f.-d.-l. being one 354:13
Floweret: meanest f. of the vale 178:13
Flower-pot: water your damned f.-p.s 77:14
Fluffy: f., with no brains 187:13
Flummoxed: reg'larly f. 138:23
Flute: blows out his brains upon the f. 77:13
  f., harp, sackbut 44:32
  soft complaining f. 148:19
Flux: all is f. 187:10
Fly: above the world you f. 100:18
  blue f. sung in the pane 388:12
  busy, curious, thirsty f. 275:1
  f. ... may sting a stately horse 207:9
  f. sat upon the axle-tree 19:7
  f. that sips treacle 166:6
  for the noise of a f. 144:10
  I cannot f. 335:26
  I, said the F. 274:15
  is you cannot f. 155:22
  man is not a f. 286:23
  then f. betimes 98:2

Fool – *contd*
  resolved to live a f. 25:19
  shoal of f.s for tenders 118:29
  smarts so little as a f. 285:7
  so is the laughter of a f. 41:11
  stop to busy f.s 402:14
  straitened forehead of a f. 387:8
  suffer f.s gladly 54:31
  thirty millions, mostly f.s 99:33
  though ever so great a f. 410:5
  to suckle f.s 343:7
  twenty-seven millions mostly f.s 99:7
  very clever woman to manage a f. 225:11
  what f.s these mortals be! 340:16
  whoever shall say, Thou f. 47:2
  wise ... is made a f. 154:21
  wisest f. in Christendom 186:24
  words ... are the money of f.s 190:8
  you will always be f.s! 158:11
Foolery: hateful form of f. 74:20
Foolish : chosen the f. things 53:22
  never said a f. thing 298:3
  never yet was f. that was fair 343:6
  not even know your own f. business 109:13
Foolishness: f. with God 53:25
  will not his f. depart from him 40:23
Foonf: F. speaking 214:18
Foot: always one f. on the ground 294:19
  and the Forty-second F. 193:7
  dash thy f. against a stone 37:13
  f. is on my native heath 307:7
  hand for hand, f. for f. 31:42
  nay, her f. speaks 351:28
  one f. in sea 341:17
  print of a man's naked f. 130:16
  squeeze a right-hand f. 102:4
  suffer thy f. to be moved 38:11
  with shining F. shall pass 159:23
  words a f. and a half long 195:22
Footfall: f.s echo in the memory 151:25
Foot-in-the-grave: f.-i.-t.-g. young man 169:39
Footman: f. to Justinian Stubbs 368:16
  I have seen the eternal F. 152:16
Footprint: f.s on the sands of time 237:3
  frightened by the f.s 196:9
  looking for a man's f. 27:11
Footstep: distant f.s echo 236:14
  plants his f.s in the sea 123:17
Footstool: thine enemies thy f. 37:30
Fop: six-foot column of f. 193:14
Foppery: excellent f. of the world 329:17
For: neither f.s nor against institutions 415:1
Forbearance: f. ceases to be a virtue 80:26
Force: achieve more than our f. 81:19
  ev'ry member of the f. 298:12
  f. alone is but temporary 80:9
  f. is not a remedy 66:14
  f. that through the green fuse 394:4
  living f. ... be dried up 144:14
  one of the f.s of nature 250:28
  surprised by unjust f. 253:6
  who overcomes by f. 256:10
Force: plus que f. ni que rage 227:2
Forced: king so rudely f. 152:32
Ford: our F. 202:5
Fordoes: or f. me quite 344:10
Forefather: lewd f.s of the village 373:1

Forefather – *contd*
  rude f.s of the hamlet 177:2
  think of your f.s 1:6
Forefinger: f. of all Time 389:29
Forehead: f.s villanous low 350:20
  in the middle of her f. 237:16
  seal of God in their f.s 57:5
Foreigner: f.s always spell better 401:7
Fore-mast: f.-m. wi' his knee 20:13
Forest: f. primeval 236:16
  f. where all must lose their way 395:2
  f.s ancient as the hills 115:31
  when f.s are rended 306:21
Foretell: expiring do f. of him 345:7
Forever: man has F. 73:5
  that no man lives f. 380:25
Forge: behold, in the quick f. 324:28
Forget: f. not yet 427:22
  if thou wilt, f. 300:16
  in the night time I shall not f. 380:18
  knew we should both f. 381:8
  lest we f. – lest we f. 224:10
  pass us; but do not quite f. 110:1
  pray you now, f. and forgive 330:33
  till thou remember and I f. 381:11
  we f. because we must 10:12
  you should f. and smile 300:12
Forgetfulness: not in entire f. 423:12
  steep my senses in f. 322:30
  to dumb f. a prey 177:16
Forgetting: grand memory for f. 375:4
  if f. could be willed 249:17
  sleep and a f. 423:12
Forgive: father, f. them 51:12
  f. them that trespass 290:22
  God f. you, but I never can 153:25
  they never can f. 8:6
  to f., divine 286:12
  to understand all is to f. all 373:2
Forgiveness: F. give – and take 159:15
  F. of sins 291:1
  f. to the injured does belong 149:6
  mutual F. of each vice 59:6
Forgot: f. as soon as done 351:21
  f. for which he toiled 355:6
  proposed as things f. 286:15
Forgotten: f. man at the bottom 299:4
  f. nothing and learnt nothing 149:28
  f. what I have done for him 238:2
  I am clean f. 35:17
Fork: dashed the bold f. 95:24
  hunt it with f.s and hope 102:10
Forlorn: make me less f. 422:9
  perilous seas, in faery lands f. 217:5
Form: all things ... are of like f.s 14:24
  f. had not yet lost 256:6
  f. remains 425:19
  f.s more real than living man 362:18
  f.s of things unknown 340:26
  f.s, that do not live like living 424:17
  from outward f.s to win 115:24
  in f., in moving, how express 316:13
  mould of f. 317:7
  on his listless f. and face 182:13
  silent f., dost tease us out of thought 216:18
  take thy f. from off my door! 283:19
  vents in mangled f.s 311:10

France – *contd*
nearer is to F. 101:2
order ... this matter better in F. 374:2
sweet enemy, F. 366:9
vasty fields of F. 323:22
France: F., *mère des arts* 149:22
Francesca: F. di Rimini, miminy-piminy 169:37
Frankfort: to F., and got drunk 289:30
Frankie: F. and Johnny were lovers 7:6
Fraternité: Liberté! Égalité! F.! 9:10
Fratrum: par nobile f. 198:19
Fray: fought was this noble f. 145:24
Freckled: fickle, f. (who knows how?) 195:5
Fred: here lies F. 5:14
Frederick: here is cruel F. 191:7
Free: die to make men f. 200:11
  f. as nature first made man 149:5
  1 ... never shall be f. 143:10
  I only ask to be f. 133:22
  man was born f. 301:15
  men everywhere could be f. 234:18
  Mother of the F. 29:6
  must be f. or die 422:27
  no one can be perfectly f. 371:10
  none the less f. than you were before 15:1
  o'er the land of the f. 220:22
  so f. as the sons of the waves 165:1
  so f. we seem 70:17
  that moment they are f. 124:32
  thou art f. 11:16
Freedom: assure f. to the free 234:23
  battle for f. and truth 202:25
  Cause of F. is the cause of God 64:10
  four essential f.s 299:10
  F. and Whisky gang thegither 82:24
  f. is a noble thing 22:6
  F. is Slavery 275:12
  F. shall awhile repair 117:17
  F. shrieked – as Kosciusko fell! 96:19
  F. slowly broadens down 392:22
  F.'s battle once begun 92:31
  F.'s home or Glory's grave 92:30
  new birth of f. 235:1
  none can love f. heartily 260:22
  regained my f. with a sigh 93:15
  service is perfect f. 291:3
  this uncharted f. tires 423:27
  what stands if F. fall? 222:29
  yet, F.! yet thy banner 89:17
Freely: f. ye have received, f. give 47:38
Freeman: F. butters Stubbs 298:14
Freemason: F., and an asthmatic 145:15
Freezy: Breezy, Sneezy, F. 154:5
French: F. are wiser than they seem 18:20
  F. are with equal advantage content 97:9
  F. cook; we open tins 164:25
  F. the empire of the land 296:16
  F., whose verse 178:25
  hate the F. because ... slaves 173:23
  he's gone to fight the F. 212:25
  I speak ... F. to men 106:12
  some are fond of F. 247:24
  something fishy about the F. 121:3
  what's the water in F., sir? 136:26
Frenchies: F. seek him everywhere 275:3
Frenchman: hate a F. as ... the devil 269:12
  truth the brilliant F. never knew 126:4

Frenchmen: fifty million F. 180:2
  ten thousand F. sent below 279:15
Frensh: F. of Paris was to hir 106:22
  F. she spak ful faire 106:22
Frenzy: f., moping melancholy 258:26
  in a fine f. rolling 340:26
  never loved the f. of the sun 220:23
Fresh: f. as a bridegroom 320:19
  f. as is the month of May 106:21
  quick and f. art thou 352:1
Freshness: f. fills the silent air 370:24
Fret: f. of that sharp-headed worm 391:19
  weariness, the fever, and the f. 216:26
Freude: F., *schöner Götterfunken* 304:11
Friar: cannot all be f.s 105:4
  f. I will be 201:18
  f.s white, black, and grey 257:3
  turned fasting f. 250:13
Friday: my man F. 130:17
Friend: all their f.s could say 232:13
  believe the aged f. 72:13
  best of f.s must part 8:12
  enter on my list of f.s 125:31
  faithful are the wounds of a f. 40:20
  faithful f. is the medicine of life 46:1
  falling out of faithful f.s 150:20
  few f.s and many books 121:23
  forsake not an old f. 46:4
  found ... in the heart of a f. 236:6
  f. ... closer than a brother 39:39
  f., go up higher 50:29
  f. should bear his f.'s infirmities 328:10
  F. who never changes 251:3
  f. ... with whom I may be sincere 154:23
  f.s are lapped in lead 23:20
  f.s ashamed to look upon 409:7
  f.s called him 'Candle-ends' 102:8
  f.s, Romans, countrymen 327:26
  f.s the merest keep much 74:6
  f.s were very good to him 27:26
  f.s who set forth at our side 11:5
  gained from Heaven ... a f. 177:19
  golden f.s I had 199:31
  good f., but bad acquaintance 91:2
  hard to part when f.s are dear 22:4
  How to Win F.s 100:1
  I lose a f. 304:5
  I'm his f., I won't wrong him 118:27
  I was angry with my f. 60:14
  if I had a f. that loved her 342:32
  in every mess I find a f. 133:6
  knolling a departed f. 322:12
  laughter and the love of f.s 28:7
  make to yourselves f.s 50:40
  Maker, Defender, Redeemer and F. 175:14
  makes no f. who never made a foe 384:16
  mere f.s are we 74:6
  merely comes to meet one's f.s 82:8
  mine own familiar f. 35:27
  never want a f. in need 134:38
  no enemy can match a f. 378:14
  none of his f.s like him 418:3
  nor a f. to know me 376:5
  of f.s, of hope, of all bereft 122:1
  old f.s are best 308:1
  one had need be very much his f. 122:19
  only a f. in name 46:18

Friend – *contd*
save me, from the candid f. 97:15
say, 'Welcome, f.!' 127:9
separateth very f.s 39:34
shameful to distrust one's f.s 297:15
sharpeneth the countenance of his f. 40:22
their sad f.s do say 144:4
those f.s thou hast 314:32
thy f.s are exultations 422:22
to his f.s and his relations 170:15
troops of f.s 335:17
troops of unrecording f.s 391:24
truest f. to thy lover 244:14
want of f.s, and empty purse 65:8
way to have a f. is to be one 154:24
whirring me from my f.s 344:22
who lost no f. 288:5
who's your fat f.? 78:13
with a religious book, or f. 427:14
with one chained f. 360:1
wounded in the house of my f.s 45:17
Friendly: social, f., honest man 83:13
Friendship: elegance of female f. 206:28
f. hardly ever does 15:10
f. is a disinterested commerce 173:27
f. is constant in all other things 341:12
f. is Love without his wings! 93:6
f. . . . may grow into love 94:11
f.'s laws are by this rule 289:24
keep his f. *in constant repair* 207:16
little f. in the world 18:37
most f. is feigning 311:16
my college f.s glimmer 392:17
pious f.s of the female sex! 118:28
that is indeed true f. 303:18
thy f. . . . made my heart to ache 61:11
two for f. 397:6
wing of f. never moults 137:6
Fright: wake in a f. 22:12
Frightened: killed than f. to death 378:1
Frisson: vous créez un f. nouveau 201:5
Fritter: or 'F. my wig!' 102:7
Frog: expiring f. 138:4
f. he would a wooing go 272:9
f.s and snails and puppy-dogs' 274:11
public, like a f. 139:17
toe of f. 334:33
Fromage: vaut bien un f. 226:21
Front: deep on his f. engraven 256:24
large f. and eye sublime 257:13
Frontier-grave: f.-g. is far away 269:27
Frost: f. is over and done 76:17
F. performs its secret ministry 115:27
f. that binds so dear a head 358:29
His graver of f. 396:6
hoary headed f.s fall 340:6
secret ministry of f. 115:29
third day comes a f. 325:31
Froth: with his embossèd f. 350:34
Froude: goes to F. for history 377:6
Frown: convey a libel in a f. 378:11
f. and wrinkled lip and sneer 361:23
f. of the great 313:25
her very f.s are fairer far 114:11
Phyllis, without f. or smile 307:24
Frugal: she had a f. mind 122:25
Fruit: all pleasant f.s do flow 97:7

Fruit – *contd*
bring forth f. in old age 37:16
by their f.s ye shall know them 47:29
f. for their songs 2:15
f. of that forbidden tree 255:16
f., when it is expensive 282:7
kindly f.s of the earth 291:17
like Dead Sea f.s 265:11
like f., my soul 313:28
my f. is dreams 396:4
weakest kind of f. 338:16
Fruitful: be f. and multiply 30:13
Fry: such as 'F. me!' 102:7
Frye: I made him f. 107:35
Fucos: f. . . . a praesepibus arcent 406:18
Fudge: two-fifths sheer f. 239:2
Fuel: adding f. to the flame 259:21
f. to maintain his fires 97:21
Fugaces: eheu f., Postume 197:20
Fugitive: what was so f.! 423:18
Full: f. man and a fasting 307:2
without o'er-flowing f. 131:33
Fulmen: brutum f. 282:25
Fulness: and the f. thereof 35:11 53:40
Fun: come and spoil the f. 101:17
f. grew fast and furious 84:21
I thought *What Jolly F.!* 295:16
missed all the f. 22:8
no reference to f. in any Act 187:17
such f. I do not understand 191:21
Function: F. never dies 425:19
own no other f. 354:14
Fundament: frigid upon the f. 268:27
Funeral: appint your f. tomorrow 409:24
f. baked meats 314:19
misbehaved once at a f. 229:15
not a f. note 419:15
seldom seen a costlier f. 383:27
to see my own f. 150:14
with mirth in f. 314:4
Funny: f. peculiar, or f. ha-ha? 184:15
write as f. as I can 192:7
Fur: make the f. fly 86:17
oh my f. and whiskers 100:10
with the f. side inside 5:9
Furies: fierce as ten f. 256:30
see the F. arise! 147:23
Furiously: he driveth f. 33:28
Furnace: burning fiery f. 44:33
heat not a f. 325:22
Furniture: no f. so charming as books 369:9
piece of mere church f. 125:34
Furor: f. arma ministrat 404:14
Furrow: f. followed free 114:21
I must plough my f. 300:3
leaves a shining f. 390:12
on a half-reaped f. 218:19
Further: shalt thou go and no f. 278:1
Fury: comes the blind F. 254:26
f., like a woman scorned 118:18
f. of a patient man 147:9
said cunning old F. 100:9
Furze: f. unprofitably gay 172:16
Fuse: through the green f. 394:4
Fust: to f. in us unused 318:26
Fustian: f.'s so sublimely bad 285:11
Fustilarian: you f.! 322:22

Future: cannot fight against the f. 170:22
f. contained in time past 151:24
f. sure 421:11
I mean a F. Life 85:28
looked down another f. 13:24
never plan the f. by the past 81:27
no F., howe'er pleasant! 237:2
Fuzzy-Wuzzy: 'ere's to you, F.-W. 222:30

G

Gaberdine: spet upon my Jewish g. 337:21
Gael: great G.s of Ireland 109:20
Gai: toujours g., archy. toujours g. 246:6
Gaierty: drive us to the G. Hotel 13:12
Gain: God bless all our g.s 69:25
man's loss comes ... from his g. 72:14
richest g. I count but loss 411:8
sacerdotal g., but general loss 88:22
what things were g. for me 55:6
Gaiter: all is gas and g.s! 137:2
Galatians: great text in G. 77:16
Gale: g.s shall fan the glade 288:9
note that swells the g. 178:13
Galère: dans cette g. 261:14
mer immense où fuyalent des g.s 188:14
vogue la g. 294:21
Galilaee: vicisti, G. 213:4
Galilean: conquered, O pale G. 381:5
Gall: g. enough in thy ink 353:7
g. for my meat 36:27
I am g., I am heartburn 194:24
no g., no glory 280:15
Gallant: he was a braw g. 20:7
Gallantry: what men call g. 90:15
Galleon: like a Spanish great g. 164:16
Gallery: faces are but a g. 18:22
Galley: taken by a Spanish g. 20:18
up to in that g. 261:14
Galloped: Dircæ g., we g. all three 73:19
Gallows: complexion is perfect g. 349:28
g. in my garden 109:23
Galumphing: went g. back 101:9
Gamaliel: at the feet of G. 52:32
Gambit: simple g. of Jonah's 290:2
Game: g. beyond the prize 269:26
g. is done 114:26
g. ... never lost till won 126:19
g. on these lone heaths 185:8
g.'s afoot 324:13
how you played the g. 296:13
more than a g. 200:20
play up! and play the g.! 270:5
plenty of time to win this g. 145:21
rigour of the game 228:21
Winning G.s without ... Cheating 290:1
Gamesmanship: G. or, The Art of Winning 290:1
Gammon: world of g. and spinnage 134:26
Gamut: g. of her emotions 277:20
Gang: old g. 111:2
Ganglia: protect the lumbar g. 202:2

Gaol: who lie in g. 416:7
Gap: made a g. in nature 309:28
sleep out this great g. 309:22
Garde: G. ... ne se rend pas 95:29
Garden: come into the g., Maud 388:19
G. by the Water blows 158:16
g. in her face 3:18
g. is a lovesome thing 68:10
g.s bright with sinuous rills 115:31
ghost of a g. fronts the sea 380:19
go and work in the g. 407:6
God Almighty first planted a g. 18:36
God the first g. made 121:12
God walking in the g. 30:22
how does your g. grow? 273:5
I know a little g. close 266:9
man and a woman in a g. 417:15
nearer God's Heart in a g. 180:6
secret was the g. 395:22
see the g. and God there 73:3
small house, and large g. have 121:23
through his g. walketh God 77:23
through this same G. 159:22
'tis an unweeded g. 314:11
Touraine ... the g. of France 294:12
who loves a g. 125:9
Gardener: g. of the untoward 76:28
g. Robin, day by day 123:30
G., Time 141:21
will come the G. in white 160:9
Garland: g. is to be run for 260:15
g.s wither on your brow 365:33
silken flanks with g.s drest 216:17
whose g.s dead 265:14
withered is the g. 310:5
Garment: doth, like a g., wear 422:12
down to the skirts of his g.s 38:22
g.s heavy with their drink 319:12
had not on a wedding g. 49:8
stuffs out his vacant g.s 328:32
they part my g.s among them 35:8
twitch the Nymph's last g. off 71:13
Garnished: empty, swept, and g. 48:12
Garret: and living in a g. 161:2
Garter: take away the star and g. 16:9
Gas: all is g. and gaiters! 137:2
g. smells awful 277:17
Gasp: at the last g. 46:29
Gast: trüber G. auf der dunklen Erde 171:16
Gate: after we pass the g. 145:3
against the eastern g. 254:5
at heaven's g. sings 313:16
at one g. to make defence 259:17
at the g. alone 388:19
battering the g.s of heaven 391:8
g.s of hell shall not prevail 48:26
iron g. ground its teeth 77:12
lead you in at Heaven's g. 59:15
lift up your heads, O ye g.s 35:12
matters not how strait the g. 186:19
no latch ter de golden g. 183:26
out of the g.s of the day 429:5
remarkable wrought-iron g.s 30:2
sat by the celestial g. 93:24
strait is the g. 47:27
wide is the g. 47:26
Gath: tell it not in G. 32:42

508

Glen: down the rushy g. 4:3
Glendoveer: I am a blessed G. 368:14
Glimmering: mere g. and decays 403:3
Glimpse: nor g. divine 284:22
  their g. was gone 148:2
Gloaming: in the g., O my darling! 275:5
  late, late in the g. 191:28
Gloat: hear me g.! 225:17
Globe: great g. itself 350:18
  in this distracted g. 315:23
  wears the turning g. 199:5
Globule: primordial atomic g. 169:12
Gloire: g. en gros sous 201:4
  jour de g. est arrivé 301:13
Gloom: in the g. of earthquake 363:5
  inspissated g. 208:16
  welcome, kindred g.s! 396:17
  when the g. is soft 407:21
Gloria: fuit ... g. Teucrorum 405:3
  militavi non sine g. 198:7
  sic transit g. mundi 220:6
Glories: g. and my state depose 346:9
  g. like glow-worms, afar off 412:3
  g. of our blood and state 365:32
  in those weaker g. spy 402:20
  see Heaven's g. shine 66:19
Glorious: but Tam was g. 84:17
  g. the northern lights 367:23
  g. things of thee are spoken 270:16
  more g. as more hacked 284:16
  'tis a g. thing, I ween 168:15
Glory: be thine the g. 148:2
  calls the g. from the grey 76:8
  do all to the g. of God 53:41
  duty was the way to g. 389:15
  excess of g. obscured 256:6
  face ... hath its ancient g. 229:16
  filled with the g. of God 3:6
  for the hope of g. 291:21
  Freedom's home or G.'s grave 92:30
  full meridian of my g. 325:30
  g. and the freshness of a dream 423:5
  g. and the good of Art 77:5
  g. be to God for dappled things 195:3
  g. dropped from their youth 77:28
  g. in the flower 423:21
  g. is all moonshine 365:31
  g. is departed from Israel 32:37
  g., jest, and riddle 286:29
  g. of Europe is extinguished 81:8
  g. of the coming of the Lord 200:9
  g. of the Lord shone round about 50:11
  g. of the Trojans has passed 405:3
  g. of the world passes away 220:6
  g., spare my aching sight 176:19
  g. to Man in the highest! 381:2
  g. to the King of Kings 413:14
  heavens declare the g. of God 34:39
  hoary head is a crown of g. 39:33
  in a sea of g. 325:31
  is crowned with g. now 220:4
  King of g. shall come in 35:12
  left him alone with his g. 419:18
  past away a g. 423:6
  paths of g. lead 177:5
  pomp and g. of this world 326:1
  sudden g. is the passion 190:9

Glory – contd
  thro' a kind of g. 392:20
  'tis to g. we steer 165:1
  uncertain g. of an April day 353:23
  walked with inward g. crowned 363:17
  walking in an air of g. 403:3
  whose g. is in their shame 55:7
  why in the name of G. 215:29
  with a g. in his bosom 200:11
  with g. not their own 424:28
Gloss: set so fine a g. 74:22
Gloucestershire: here in G. 345:11
Glove: he played at the g. 20:7
  my g.s on my hand 183:11
  that I were a g. 348:9
  walk through the fields in g.s 120:14
Glowered: Tammie g., amaz'd, and curious 84:21
Glow-worm: g.-w. in the grass 93:10
  g.-w. shows the matin to be near 315:22
  her eyes the g.-w. lend thee 188:24
  live as g.-w.s shine 402:13
Gnashing: weeping and g. of teeth 47:31 49:9
Gnat: g. that dances in thy ray 279:14
  small g.s mourn 218:21
  small grey-coated g. 347:29
  strain at a g. 49:15
Go: as often as from thee I g. 143:14
  g., and do thou likewise 50:22
  how you do g. it! 68:8
  I have a g., lady, don't I? 275:18
  I will not let thee g. 31:19 65:17
  must you g.? 402:10
  no necessity for [the soul] to g. anywhere 62:18
  one to come, and one to g. 101:31
  to 'g. it' a bit 94:13
  whither thou goest, I will g. 32:33
Goad: words ... are as g.s 42:1
Goal: stands up to keep the g. 199:24
Goat: lust of the g. is the bounty 61:29
  paddling with hoofs of a g. 70:1
  sheep from the g.s 49:24
Goblet: g.s for a dish of wood 346:2
  upon a parcel-gilt g. 322:24
Goblin: g.s 'll git you 296:17
  hag and hungry g. 5:3
  spirit of health or g. 315:6
God: a' should not think of G. 324:7
  abode of G. ... in the earth and sea 239:11
  about the best thing G. invents 73:1
  afraid of ... his nagging g.s 220:23
  am a G. and cannot find it 362:14
  and G. the soul 286:26
  assumes the g. 147:15
  attribute of G. himself 338:17
  beautiful G. to behold 381:4
  before the g.s that made the g.s 109:18
  bitter G. to follow 381:4
  blends itself with G. 359:27
  by searching find out G. 34:2
  by that G. we both adore 283:18
  by the nine g.s he swore 241:4
  Cabots talk only to G. 64:1
  cannot serve G. and mammon 47:15
  charged with the grandeur of G. 194:17
  coming down from G. 57:19
  conspired against our G. 245:3
  dear G. who loveth us 115:13

God – *contd*

do not know much about g.s 151:35
doubtless G. never did 87:31
ef you want to take in G. 238:19
either a beast or a g. 10:5
either a wild beast or a g. 18:21
every g. did seem to set 318:12
every man, with him, was G. 147:2
fall into the hands of G. 390:30
fear first in the world made g.s 212:1
fear G., and keep his commandments 42:3
fear G. Honour the King 56:17
feeble G. has stabbed me 165:16
further from G. 4:11
glorify G. and to enjoy him 366:1
G. all mercy is a G. unjust 430:15
G. Almighty's gentlemen 147:6
G. and angels to be lookers-on 16:14
G. at first made man 188:4
G. be thanked who has matched us 67:13
G. bless us every one! 134:9
G. changes, and man 380:26
G. created man in his own image 30:12
G. created the heaven and the earth 30:9
G. doth not need 260:1
G. exact day-labour 260:1
G. fulfils Himself in many ways 384:33
G. has not said a word 75:25
G. has written all the books 87:16
G. hath spoken once 36:16
G. Himself is moon and sun 389:16
G. himself scarce seemèd there 115:11
G. in the whizzing of ... wind 280:9
G. is a righteous Judge 34:27
G. is faithful 53:38
G. is in heaven, and thou upon earth 41:7
G. is love 56:25
G. is Love – I dare say 87:17
G. is not mocked 54:40
G. is the perfect poet 75:2
G. is thy law 257:19
G. is working his purpose 3:6
G. made him 337:12
G. made Himself an awful rose 392:11
G. must be glad 75:17
g. of my idolatry 348:16
G. of our fathers 224:9
g. of the golden bow 215:18
G. of things as they are 224:27
G. ... planted a garden 18:36
G.'s in his heaven 75:16
G. saw everything that he had made 30:14
g. self-slain 380:21
G. so commanded 258:21
G. stooping shows sufficient 76:26
G., take the gentle path 187:25
G. the All-terrible! 110:18
G. the Father turns a school-divine 289:7
G. to a black beetle 249:4
G. to aggrándise 194:12
G. who best taught song 76:20
G. who is our home 423:12
g.s arrive 154:10
g.s be said to thump the clouds 394:9
g.s themselves cannot recall 391:22
g.s themselves throw incense 331:1
g.s thought otherwise 405:5

God – *contd*

good G. prepare me 281:10
had I but served my G. 326:5
has G. then forgotten 238:2
he for G. only 257:13
he wants nothing of a g. 313:10
honest G. is the noblest work 87:21 203:18
how can he love G. 56:27
I bid G. bless her 374:8
I but served G. 419:21
I'll leap up to my G.! 245:9
I neglect G. 144:10
if G. be for us 53:2
if G. did not exist 406:21
if G. made us in His image 407:13
if G. were not a necessary Being 398:8
if I cannot bend the g.s 405:19
inclines to think there is a G. 113:12
into the hands of the living G. 55:37
just are the ways of G. 259:16
justify the ways of G. 255:18
kills the image of G. 260:13
know his G. by night 402:13
leads – G. knows where 91:28
let G. arise 36:22
let G. be true 52:43
'Let us worship G.!' he says 83:5
limbs of gibbeted G.s 381:6
Little Tin G.s on Wheels 224:8
live with the g.s 14:31
maketh that there were no G. 18:5
man be more just than G. 33:39
man ... the breath of G. 69:8
many are afraid of G. 235:21
mills of G. grind slowly 237:6
my G., I love Thee 102:22
my G., why hast thou forsaken me? 49:35
nature is the art of G. 68:23
next to of course g. 128:3
no more use for G. 278:12
no opinion of G. 18:6
none deny there is a G. 18:5
nor no G. could please 146:17
not G. that I don't accept 144:16
not serve G. if the devil bid you 342:19
not three G.s: but one G. 291:10
now G. alone knows 225:23
on the hills like G.s together 388:3
one G. created us 45:18
one G., one law, one element 386:21
one, on G.'s side 281:24
one that feared G. 33:32
plainly say, 'My G. my King' 188:1
please G. to call me 291:41
power doth then show likest G.'s 338:17
presume not G. to scan 286:28
pretence that G. put it there 226:4
prompting of what I call G. 76:29
said in his heart, There is no G. 34:34
see G. made and eaten 71:15
service greater than the g. 351:14
service ranks the same with G. 75:20
she for G. in him 257:13
sing My G. and King 187:18
so many g.s, so many creeds 416:4
spittle wiped off from the face of G.! 76:23
teach me, my G. and King 187:28

God – *contd*

thank G. I have done with him 207:13
thank whatever g.s may be 186:17
there is in G. (some say) 402:15
they said, G. forbid 51:8
they shall see G. 46:39
thou shalt have one G. only 113:15
three personed G. 143:8
through his garden walketh G. 77:23
thy G. [shall be] my G. 32:33
thy G., thy life, thy cure 402:17
thy G.'s and truth's 326:4
to the Unknown G. 52:25
tribunal now, higher than G.'s 77:3
turn to G. to praise and pray 73:17
unto G. the things that are G.'s 49:11
Very G. of Very G. 291:31
vindicate the ways of G. 286:19
were I Lord G. 242:20
what G. abandoned 199:8
whatever g.s may be 380:25
when I reflect that G. is just 204:17
who think not G. at all 259:16
whom the g.s love 91:16
with G. all things are possible 48:42
with G. be the rest 75:30
with G. he passed the days 278:3
wrestling with (my G.!) my G. 194:14
ye shall be as G.s 30:20
Goddamn: sing: G. 290:7
Goddess: G., allow this aged man 280:13
g. and maiden and queen 381:3
g., excellently bright 211:21
heavenly g. sing! 289:20
she moves a g. 289:21
Goddesses: g. that dwell far along 395:5
God-intoxicated: G.-i. man 271:19
Goer-between: pitiful g.s-b. be called ... Pandars 351:20
Goest: whither g. thou? 52:1
Goethe: open thy G. 99:23
Gog: G., the land of Magog 44:30
Going: g. out with the tide 134:31
g. to and fro in the earth 33:33
shall preserve thy g. out 38:13
softly she was g. up 115:1
Gold: all the g. that the goose 2:25
and next my g.! 212:2
better to me than g. 418:18
city was pure g. 57:23
crucify mankind upon a cross of g. 78:14
from the red g. keep thy finger 306:25
g.? a transient, shining trouble 175:11
g. and silver becks me 328:31
g. by bronze heard 213:1
g. is the touchstone 164:12
g. that gilds the ... forehead 387:8
g. with plenty of looking glasses 13:7
if g. ruste 107:14
litel g. in cofre 107:6
more to be desired ... than g. 35:1
nor all that glisters, g. 178:5
O cursed lust for g.! 405:6
O delvèd g., the wailers heap 70:2
panaceas, potable g. 85:19
patines of bright g. 339:1
provoketh fools sooner than g. 310:24

Gold – *contd*

purest g., by tortures tried 285:21
saint-seducing g. 347:24
scarfs, garters, g. 287:3
silver and g. have I none 52:14
so pale, is yet of g. 126:13
this is fairy g. 354:4
to gild refinèd g. 91:4 329:4
to ... g. most things are penetrable 98:28
travelled in the realms of g. 218:3
true worship's g. 88:22
wedges of g., great anchors 346:29
were't not for g. 399:6
what survives is g. 76:7
what's become of all the g. 77:32
Golden: God of the g. bow 215:18
g. opes 254:29
g. round 332:23
Gold-fish: g.-f. in a glass bowl 303:9
Goldsmith: G., poet, naturalist 209:15
Gondola: g. of London 141:2
Gone: I would have thee g. 348:20
now thou art g. 254:21
thou art g., and for'ever 305:18
Gong: strong g.s groaning 109:28
Good: all g. and no badness 367:19
all g. to me is lost 257:7
all that's g. and ... fair 408:8
be g., sweet maid 221:13
behold it was very g. 30:14
beneath the g. how far 178:22
call a man *a g. man*, upon easier 210:6
call evil g., and g. evil 42:24
care not whether a man is g. or evil 59:18
doing g. to base fellows 104:15
every creature ... is g. 55:23
evil because I am g.? 49:3
evil that g. may come 52:44
g. absolute, not for me, though 113:7
g. and ill together 309:9
g. and increase of the world 383:26
g. and market of his time 318:26
g. are so harsh to the clever 420:3
g. as thou art beautiful 384:14
g. attending captain ill 355:26
g., but not religious g. 183:3
g. compensate bad in man 77:2
g. deed is not wasted 94:28
g. die early 130:18
g. die first 420:21
g. ended happily 416:23
g. for that man ... not been born 49:27
g. in everything 310:26
g. is oft interrèd with their bones 327:26
g. is one ... pleasant another 401:28
g. must associate 81:23
g. people were clever 420:3
g. that I would I do not 52:51
g. to the poor, to kindred dear 97:23
g. want power, but to weep 362:12
g. we oft might win 336:7
g. when it leaves the Creator's 301:16
g. will be the final goal 385:25
greatest g. that mortals know 1:17
he wos wery g. to me 133:25
highest g. 112:3
hold thou the g. 385:24

513

Grace – *contd*
ye are fallen from g. 54:39
your G. is too costly to wear 341:14
Graceless: G. . . . and Aimless waited their turn 167:21
Gracing: either other sweetly g. 97:2
Gracious: g. and courteous to strangers 17:33
Lord . . . be g. unto thee 32:2
Gradualness: inevitability of g. 411:23
Graeca: exemplaria G. nocturna versate manu 195:26
Graeculus: omnia novit G. esuriens 213:18
Grail: until I find the holy G. 391:15
Grain: bearded g. at a breath 237:5
say which g. will grow 332:10
warmth to swell the g. 96:2
Grais: G. ingenium . . . dedit . . . Musa 196:1
Gramina: redeunt iam g. campis 198:12
Grammaire: g. qui sait régenter 261:10
Grammar: heedless of g. 22:14
I . . . am above g. 366:21
what sairs your g.s 83:11
Grammarian: g.s dispute 195:21
Gramophone: puts a record on the g. 153:4
Grampian: on the G. hills 192:21
Grand: baith g. and comfortable 23:26
it *would* be g.! 101:19
Grandeur: baldness full of g. 12:17
charged with the g. of God 194:17
g. hear with a disdainful smile 177:4
g. is a dream 125:6
Grandfather: g.s' g.s are numbered 406:20
Grandmother: not marry his G. 292:23
Grandsire: g. cut in alabaster 337:5
Grange: at the moated g. 336:26
lonely moated g. 388:8
Grape: burst Joy's g. 216:23
G. that can . . . Sects confute 159:8
g.s of the wine-press 240:22
g.s of wrath are stored 200:9
have eaten sour g.s 44:24
sour g.s and ashes without you 13:13
sure the g.s are sour 2:24
Grapeshot: whiff of g. 98:29
Grass: be the green g. above me 300:16
g. below – above the vaulted sky 112:15
g. beyond the door 301:7
g. grows all up and down 281:1
g. withereth, the flower fadeth 43:24
his days are as g. 37:21
I am the g.; I cover all 303:22
I fall on g. 246:25
kissed the lovely g. 67:5
leaf of g. is no less than . . . stars 415:13
lift me from the g. 360:18
like g. that groweth up 37:8
morning g. withered at eve 426:30
presage the g.'s fall 247:6
quivered through the g. 139:21
thin g. clothed them 395:10
two blades of g. to grow 379:2
Grass-bank: g.-b. beyond 4:4
Grasshopper: cover, of the wings of g.s 347:29
g. shall be a burden 41:34
half-a-dozen g.s under a fern 81:12
Gratitude: g. of place-expectants 408:20
Grave: a-mouldering in the g. 180:16

Grave – *contd*
dig the g. and let me lie 376:13
digs my g. at each remove 187:31
dread the g. as little as my bed 220:14
fretted us a pair of g.s 346:3
g. hides all things beautiful 362:14
g. is not its goal 236:30
g.'s a fine and private place 247:12
g. with rising flow'rs be dressed 284:30
g.s are severed, far and wide 186:12
g.s have yawned 327:12
g.s stood tenantless 313:34
in cold g. she was lain 21:21
in his colde g. allone 107:25
in the g. whither thou goest 41:21
kind of healthy g. 369:5
lead but to the g. 177:5
learned the secrets of the g. 278:19
let's talk of g.s 345:21
little, little g., an obscure g. 346:2
my g. is broke up again 143:22
my love, sits on your g. 21:22
O g., where is thy victory? 54:20 284:24
on his g., with shining eyes 11:1
on my g., as now my bed 69:13
pompous in the g. 69:18
rush to glory, or the g. 96:11
see myself go into my g. 281:10
she is in her g. 425:23
sitting crowned upon the g. 190:11
strewed thy g. 319:25
that ayont the g., man 84:30
thy humble g. adorned 284:29
to find ourselves dishonourable g.s 326:23
without a governorship . . . to the g. 105:1
without a g., unknelled 89:28
Graver: g. had a strife 212:9
Graviora: O passi g. 404:15
Gray: G., a born poet 12:13
Robin G. was gudeman to 23:15
Grayling: here and there a g. 383:6
Great: but far above the g. 178:22
craven fears of being g. 384:1
g. in council and g. in war 389:8
g. man helped the poor 241:7
g. men are almost always bad men 1:2
g. ones that ebb and flow 330:35
g. seemed to him little 242:2
how indigent the g.! 178:15
Lord hath done g. things 38:15
no g. man lives in vain 99:2
nor its g. scholars g. men 192:17
rightly to be g. 318:22
some men are born g. 353:1
those who were truly g. 371:13
to be g. is to be misunderstood 155:6
Greater: are g. than we know 425:20
g. prey upon the less 178:28
Greatest: city which has the g. men 415:8
fail than not be among the g. 219:8
g. man you had ever seen 211:4
Great-grandfather: g.-g. was but a waterman 79:22
Great-heart: one G.-h. 79:28
Greatness: all the far-stretched g. 295:11
be not afraid of g. 353:1
farewell, to all my g.! 325:31
g. he could not want 212:23

516

H

Hall: I dwelt in marble h.s 79:8
   in h. among ladies 244:14
   vasty h. of death 11:3
Hallow: Christ ... and all his h.s 195:8
Halt: how long h. ye 33:15
Halter: come and cut the h. 164:11
   h.s in the hanged man's house 104:18
Halves: I'll go h. with him 294:20
Ham: case when there's h. 137:24
Hame: gae h., my mither dear: 20:22
   h., h., h. to my ain countree! 128:6
   thou must bring her h. 21:10
Hamelin: H. Town's in Brunswick 75:9
Hamlet: forefathers of the h. 177:2
   H. ... the Prince ... being left out 307:8
   h.s brown and dim-discovered spires 117:13
   I am not Prince H. 152:17
   saw H. Prince of Denmark played 156:6
   where the kneeling h. drains 385:10
Hammer: h., h., h. 293:15
Hampden: some village H. 177:11
Hand: about to kiss your h. 168:20
   and then take h.s 349:37
   as an old Parliamentary h. 170:26
   bear thee up in their h.s 37:13
   before rude h.s have touched it 212:5
   bite the h. that fed them 81:21
   by foreign h.s thy dying eyes 284:29
   caught the world's great h.s 201:17
   cloud ... like a man's h. 33:17
   come, knit h.s 252:23
   cursed be the h. 20:21
   dying, bless the h. 149:14
   fasten their h.s upon their hearts 199:2
   fortress, and a dubious h. 205:22
   go into his h. and pierce it 43:17
   great is the h. that holds dominion 394:5
   hair with automatic h. 153:4
   h. for h., foot for foot 31:42
   h. in h., on the edge of the sand 232:19
   h. is ever at his lips 216:21
   h. is not able to taste 340:23
   h. is unworthy your acceptance 15:22
   h. of little employment 319:15
   h. that made us is divine 2:12
   h. that rocks the cradle 408:2
   h. that signed the treaty 394:5
   h., the head, and the heart 302:11
   h. to execute 112:18 167:17 213:11
   h. you cannot see 398:6
   h.s are the h.s of Esau 31:17
   h.s outstretched in yearning 405:14
   h.s that the rod of empire 177:8
   h.s were never made to tear 410:17
   hat was in his h. 205:16
   hath not a Jew h.s 338:4
   hath shook h.s with time 161:11
   her h. on her bosom 344:7
   her prentice h. she tried on man 83:22
   here's my h. 350:12
   hidden h. is ... at its old game 213:2
   his h. will be against every man 31:13
   his red right h. 256:21
   hold your h. but as long as all may 74:7
   I fear thy skinny h.! 114:29
   if you want to win her h. 64:16
   into thy h.s I commend 35:16

Hand – contd
   keep my h.s from picking 291:40
   keep the lifted h. in awe 430:5
   laid our groping h.s away 67:19
   lays his icy h. on kings 365:32
   lend thy guiding h. 259:8
   let not man have the upper h. 34:32
   let not thy left h. know 47:8
   letters in a big round h. 168:25
   lift my h.s, and eyes 89:20
   lift not thy h.s to It 159:12
   lifting distressful h.s 276:21
   long h.s slowly twining 134:22
   Love, we are in God's h. 70:17
   mischief still for idle h.s 411:1
   my own fair h.s 379:7
   oozing out ... at the palms of my h.s 365:22
   pale h.s I loved 194:10
   right h. forget her cunning 38:25
   saw the air ... with your h. 317:9
   shake h.s for ever 146:6
   shall thy h. lead me 38:26
   signed it wi' his h. 21:9
   spirit-small h. propping it 71:19
   sweeten this little h. 335:13
   taking me up in his right h. 378:28
   their h.s are blue 232:14
   there's a h. 82:23
   they gied him my h. 23:15
   they pierced my h.s and my feet 35:8
   this h. hath offended 126:21
   violent h.s upon themselves 292:15
   washed his h.s before the multitude 49:32
   waved her lily h. 166:21
   were h. and glove 124:22
   what coarse h.s he has! 135:10
   whatsoever thy h. findeth to do 41:21
   will these h.s ne'er be clean? 335:12
   with cold immortal h.s 380:23
   with large and sinewy h.s 237:17
Handel: compared to H. 88:1
Handiwork: firmament sheweth his h. 34:39
   not-incurious in God's h. 72:25
Handkerchief: drenches h.s like towels 92:26
   moral pocket h.s 138:15
   no little h. to wipe his little nose 23:1
Handle: h. toward my hand 333:16
   polished up that h. so successfullee 168:24
   taste not; h. not 55:12
Handsome: everything h. about him 342:6
   h. in three hundred pounds 339:18
Handwork: pronounced on the rest of his h. 77:9
Handy-dandy: change places; and h.-d. 330:26
Hang: going to h. him anyhow 401:9
   h. a man first 262:10
   h. themselves, in hope 164:11
   she would h. on him 314:13
   something in them to h. him 296:15
   we must ... all h. together 162:20
   we will h. you, never fear 170:5
   will not h. myself today 109:24
Hanged: in the h. man's house 104:18
   not h. for stealing horses 180:15
   to be h. in a fortnight 209:17
Hanging: h. and marriage ... go by Destiny 157:3
   h. and wiving goes by destiny 338:2
   h. is too good for him 79:21

Hanging – *contd*
  h. prevents a bad marriage 352:7
Hangman: with these h.'s hands 333:20
Hanner: lost our little H. 2:20
Hanyfink: wot's the good of H.? 110:15
Hap: better h. to worse 371:4
Happen: everything ... h.s as it should 14:25
Happier: h. than I know 258:9
Happiest: called 'the h. of men' 92:6
  h. if ye seek no happier state 257:23
  h. women, like the h. nations 151:11
Happiness: and the pursuit of h. 204:12
  boring about somebody else's h. 202:8
  consume h., without producing it 357:14
  find our h., or not at all 425:7
  greatest h. for the greatest numbers 202:1
  greatest h. of the greatest number 29:7
  h.: a good bank account 301:17
  h. is no laughing matter 413:26
  h. of the common man 30:5
  h.! our being's end 287:5
  h. too swiftly flies 178:12
  lifetime of h. ... hell on earth 357:31
  look into h. through another 312:16
  makes the h. she does not find 205:27
  no h. within this circle of flesh 69:1
  nothing ... by which so much h. 209:9
  recall ... h. when in misery 129:8
  result h. 134:19
  sight of them is necessary to h. 206:22
  take his h. away, too 203:9
Happy: all be as h. as kings 376:1
  angry and poor and h. 110:4
  ask yourself whether you are h. 251:5
  call no man h. 370:1
  duty of being h. 375:21
  h. could I be with either 166:8
  h. if I could say how much 341:13
  h. the man, and h. he alone 148:25
  h. the man who, far from business 197:1
  he who has once been h. 62:15
  how h. is he born 427:13
  in nothing else so h. 345:12
  misery is to have been h. 62:17
  never h. ... but when he is drunk 209:10
  no lot ... h. 197:21
  only one thing to make me h. 184:23
  perfectly h. till all are h. 371:10
  to make men h. 289:25
  who so h., – O who 232:12
  won't be h. till he gets it 4:14
Harangue: tu feras après ta h. 226:25
Harbinger: amber scent ... her h. 259:19
  evening star, Love's h. 258:28
  merry Spring-time's h. 26:12
  morning star, day's h. 259:28
Hard: and it shall go h. 338:6
  'h.' replied the Dodger 137:14
  h. to catch and conquer 249:16
Hard-boiled: h.-b. as a picnic egg 277:15
Harder: borne a yet h. thing 192:32
Hardship: suffered many h.s 192:29
Hardy: H. ... village atheist 110:11
  kiss me, H. 269:19
Hare: as thou woldest finde an h. 107:34
  h. came, hop, hop, hop 191:20
  h. limped trembling 215:6

Hare – *contd*
  h. sits snug in leaves 191:19
  I like the hunting of the h. 62:16
  lion than to start a h. 320:22
  March H. went on 100:16
Harebell: among the heath and h.s 67:1
  h., like thy veins 313:23
Harlot: every h. was a virgin once 59:7
  h.'s cry from street to street 58:30
Harm: do not h. nor question 142:22
  incapable of further h. 373:1
  nothing can h. a good man 369:30
  she'll do me no h. 272:20
  to win us to our h. 332:14
  wouldn't do us any h. 179:16
Harmony: from heavenly h. 148:16
  h. in discord 196:17
  h. is in immortal souls 339:1
  heaven drowsy with the h. 331:22
  hidden soul of h. 254:15
  made quiet by the power of h. 421:16
  music where ever there is h. 69:9
  sentimentally I am disposed to h. 228:13
  touches of sweet h. 338:27
Harness: between the joints of the h. 33:22
  die with h. on our back 335:25
  lay dead in his h. 46:30
Haroun: prime of good H. Alraschid 390:20
Harp: hanged our h.s 38:24
  h. not on that string 347:12
  h. slung behind him 265:1
  h. that once through Tara's halls 264:22
  my h. on a weeping willow 8:13
  sings to one clear h. 385:7
  to high-born Hoel's h. 176:13
Harping: still h. on my daughter 316:5
Harry: breed again such a King H. 145:24
  but H., H. 323:17
  cry 'God for H.!' 324:13
  H. the King, Bedford and Exeter 324:25
  H. with his beaver on 321:31
Harshness: no h. gives offence 286:7
Hart: as the h. panteth 35:28
  h. ungallèd play 317:26
  pants the h. for cooling streams 382:8
Hart: sentant la h. 246:4
Harumfrodite: kind of a giddy h. 224:13
Harvest: h. is passed 44:17
  h. of a quiet eye 424:11
  h. truly is plenteous 47:37
  in h. teach 61:21
  my h.. what I reap 75:7
  she laughs with a h. 205:4
  white already to h. 51:29
Has: one of the h. beens 193:2
Haste: h. ... ingratitude 297:23
  h. still pays h. 336:31
  make what h. I can to be gone 127:24
  then why such h.? 166:14
  this sweaty h. 313:33
  though I am always in h. 413:21
Hasten: h. slowly 377:12
Hastened: h. to the spot whence I had come 363:4
Hasty: thou need na start awa sae h. 84:27
Hat: away went h. and wig 122:30
  black h. – which is not there 64:9
  forbade me to put off my h. 162:9

Heart – *contd*

kind h.s are more than coronets 386:28
King of H.s ... hasn't a moustache 94:17
left me with the palsied h. 387:19
look in thy h. and write 366:5
love gushed from my h. 115:2
lusty h. beginneth to blossom 244:7
made my h. to glow 371:1
makes the h. grow fonder 6:19 25:5
maketh glad the h. of man 37:22
maketh the h. sick 39:21
man after his own h. 32:39
many a h. is aching 183:13
men with Splendid H.s may go 67:9
merry h. ... cheerful countenance 39:29
merry h. goes all the day 354:10
mighty h. is lying still 422:13
mine eyes, but not my h. 211:25
mine h. will not serve now to see 244:12
mine with my h. in't 350:12
more knowledge of the h. 208:26
much against my h. 279:13
my h. aches 216:24
my h. did leap for joy 162:8
my h. is at rest 61:7
my h. is inditing a great matter 35:30
my h. leaps up 422:16
my h. remembers how! 376:9
my h.'s in the Highlands 84:3 307:9
my h'.s right there! 418:10
my h., safe-left, shall meet 366:10
my h. was in the sea 23:15
natural language of the h. 308:26
nearer to the H.'s desire 159:21
no matter from the h. 351:31
nor his h. to report 340:23
not ... to steal away your h.s 328:2
now cracks a noble h. 320:5
O h., O troubled h. 429:23
open my h. and you will see 72:11
open not thine h. to every man 46:3
our h. is not quiet 14:12
our h.s are great 384:17
out-worn h., in a time out-worn 428:23
paved with broken h.s 238:9
poor h. would fain deny 335:17
pourest thy full h. 364:6
preaching down a daughter's h. 387:13
put his h. to school 422:15
Queen of H.s she made some tarts 273:20
rag-and-bone shop of the h. 428:12
return, my roving h. 141:27
rose in the deeps of my h. 429:7
said to H., 'How goes it?' 28:9
set not your h. on [riches] 36:16
shall command my h. and me 127:7
she wants a h. 287:23
sink h. and voice opprest 269:10
sleeps on his own h. 424:11
so the h. be right 295:15
stronger breast-plate than a h. 325:12
tears the h. out of it 225:25
their h. is in their boots 109:29
there will your h. be also 47:13
this h., all evil shed away 67:17
thou hast my h. 292:26
thou voice of my h. 127:12

Heart – *contd*

thousand h.s beat happily 88:26
to break a country h. 386:24
true love hath my h. 366:4
two h.s beating each to each 74:13
two h.s that beat as one 238:15
vacant h. and hand and eye 306:25
Ward has no h. 298:16
warm h. within 122:15
watched my foolish h. expand 72:1
wear my h. upon my sleeve 342:17
what h. could have thought you? 396:5
where's the man could ease a h. 277:18
which weighs upon the h. 335:18
while your h.s are yearning 161:15
whispers the o'erfraught h. 335:7
wind blows over the lonely of h. 429:5
with rue my h. is laden 199:31
woman with the h. 390:6
wound a h. that's broken 306:4
wound themselves about this h. 126:3
Heart-ache: say we end the h.-a 316:29
Heartburn: I am gall, I am h. 194:24
Heart-easing: simply tell the most h.-e. things 217:14
Hearth: though they sweep their h.s 120:4
Heat: burden and h. of the day 49:2
h. of the sun 313:25
I in pyjamas for the h. 231:11
I was with sudden h. 371:1
neither h. nor light 412:3
not without dust and h. 260:15
thinking on fantastic summer's h. 345:6
that Promethean h. 344:12
Heath: foot is on my native h. 307:7
game on these lone h.s 185:8
Heathen: break the h. 384:9
counsel of the h. to nought 35:20
h. in his blindness 185:25
h. in 'is blindness 222:24
not a H. or a Jew 410:15
pore benighted h. 222:30
why do the h. rage 34:22
Heather: how the h. looks 139:24
Heaven: airs from h. 315:6
all of h. we have 1:17
all places are distant from h. 85:18
all that h. allows 298:4
all this and h. too 187:4
all we know of h. 139:20
and all to h. 211:13
approving H. 396:11
as near to h. by sea as by land 168:1
as nigh h. as my own 265:20
at peace, under an English h. 67:18
between H. and Charing Cross 395:21
builds a H. in Hell's despair 60:8
by that h. that bends above us 283:18
call it the road to h. 21:17
can make a h. of hell 255:27
candidate of h. 148:23
day when h. was falling 199:8
earth was nigher h. 75:18
even from the gates of h. 79:26
eye of h. shines 355:3
face of h. so fine 349:2
fair and open face of h. 218:8

Heaven – *contd*
gentle rain from h. 338:17
glance from h. to earth 340:26
God created the h. and the earth 30:9
have treasure in h. 48:39
h. and earth are not ruthful 230:23
h. be in these lips 245:6
h. commences ere the world be past! 172:7
H. did a recon.pense 177:19
H. had looked upon riches 379:27
H. held his hand 122:6
H. in a wild flower 58:18
h. invites, hell threatens 430:13
h. itself, that points out 1:14
h. itself would stoop 253:14
h. lies around us 423:12
h. on earth 257:10
h. to throne in 313:10
H. views it with delight 246:22
h. was in him before 409:14
h.s declare the glory of God 34:39
h.s fill with shouting 387:16
h.s look bright, my dear 265:8
h.s themselves, the planets 351:9
hell I suffer seems a h. 257:6
hung be the h.s with black 325:5
husbandry in h. 333:13
I create new h.s 44:13
I hope for h. thereby 102:22
I'll quit the port o' H. 269:28
if the h.s fell 294:8
in that h. of all their wish 67:4
in the blue h.'s height 250:26
in the nurseries of H. 396:7
infinite meadows of h. 236:17
is he in h.? – Is he in hell? 275:3
it is a h. on earth 17:1
it's h. for climate 23:25
jolly h. above 376:4
kingdom of h. suffereth violence 48:5
learned on earth ... practise in h. 74:27
leave her to h. 315:21
leave to H. the measure 205:26
let not the h.s hear 347:10
light from H. 85:1
look how the floor of h. 339:1
love is h. and h. is love 305:24
more things in h. and earth 315:27
new h. and a new earth 57:18
not scorned in H. 124:2
nothing under H. so blue 376:12
of such is the kingdom of h. 202:12
serene lights of h. 363:15
serve in h. 255:28
shun the h. that leads 356:29
so much of h. 425:22
spark from h. to fall 11:10
starry cope of h. 257:28
starry h.s above me 214:12
starry h.s above the plain 396:24
steep and thorny way to h. 314:31
thank h., fasting 312:7
theirs is the kingdom of h. 46:38
there may be h. 77:30
there's h. above 73:29
these the gems of h. 257:21
till you are clothed with the h.s 399:8

Heaven – *contd*
today, between Hell and H. 301:6
tricks before high h. 336:16
unfolds both h. and earth 339:28
way to h. ... as ready by water 154:7
what's a h. for? 70:18
when h. and earth shall pass away 306:2
whispered in h. 156:14
ye h.s adore Him 220:11
yon are the hills of h. 20:12
Heaviness: h. foreruns the good event 323:9
take no h. to heart 46:20
Heavy: h., but no less divine 91:12
makes it much more h. 351:15
Hebraism: H., strictness of conscience 12:4
Hebrew: I said it in H. 102:11
Hebrides: amongst the farthest H. 426:4
colder than the H. 160:4
in dreams behold the H.! 307:13
Hectore: mutatus ab illo H. 405:2
Hecuba: what's H. to him 316:24
Hedge: unkempt about those h.s blows 67:7
Hedge-hog: h.-h.s, be not seen 340:11
Heed: h.s what we have taught 165:21
take h. lest we fall 53:37
Heeded: heard it, but he h. not 89:23
Heel: lifted up his h. 35:27
ran out at the h.s of their boots 161:5
Heffalump: to catch a H. 252:7
Heifer: had not plowed with my h. 32:27
lead'st thou that h. lowing 216:17
Height: h.s by great men reached 236:25
immeasurable h. of woods 425:2
nor h., nor depth, nor ... creature 53:3
what pleasure lives in h. 390:13
Heimatlos: wie des Windes Sausen, h. 304:18
Heine: H. for songs 72:17
Heir: creation's h. 173:12
h. as great in admiration 326:14
h. of all the ages 387:25
Heiresses: all h. are beautiful 149:9
Helen: blithe H., and the rest 97:8
burd H. dropped 20:21
dust hath closed H.'s eye 268:30
H., make me immortal 245:6
H., thy beauty is to me 283:20
H.'s beauty in a brow of Egypt 340:26
I were where H. lies 20:20
like another H. 147:24
Helena: dross that is not H. 245:6
Helican: how the h. 250:23
Helicon: H. breaks down in cliff 10:17
watered our horses in H. 106:1
Hell: all h. broke loose 257:27
all we need of h. 139:20
and begin raising h. 233:6
and that's his h. 85:13
better to reign in h. 255:28
characters of h. to trace 176:15
down, down to h. 325:21
entrance leads to H. 253:1
for where we are is h. 245:4
gates of h. shall not prevail 48:26
go through h. to get it 246:7
go to h. like lambs 109:29
heaven invites, h. threatens 430:13
heav'n of h., a h. of heav'n 255:27

Hoarse: h. with having little else 93:25
Hoary: h. head is a crown 39:33
Hob-and-nob: h.-a.-n. with death 392:12
Hobbes: H. clearly proves 378:19
Hobbies: h., and humours 304:1
Hobby: isn't the ... h. for a woman 394:22
Hobby-horse: rides his h.-h. peaceably 374:13
Hobson: 'tis H.'s choice 410:2
Hoe: tickle her with a h. 205:4
  with outstretched h. I slew 122:7
Hog: eat h. a solid hower 250:10
  fattest h. in Epicurus' sty 248:10
  liken his Grace to an acorned h. 73:10
Holborn: when I was last in H. 347:3
Hold: first cries 'H., enough!' 336:3
  h. fast that which is good 55:18
Hold-fast: h.-f. is the only dog 324:9
Hole: h. where his tail came 370:14
  knows of a better h. 19:20
  might stop a h. 319:21
  Roöötten Beëëastly Silly H.! 413:4
Holiday: job of work's her h. 105:3
  to make a Roman h. 89:23
  year were playing h.s 320:18
Holily: wouldst thou h. 332:22
Holiness: h. of the heart's affections 218:24
  put off h. 59:18
Hollow: h. voice is all I have 193:10
  Providence fashioned us h. 238:21
Holly: heigh-ho! the h.! 311:16
  h. bears the crown 7:14
  h. branch shone on the old oak wall 25:7
Holocaust: lay ere while a h. 259:23
Holy: as you came from the h. land 295:8
  blasphemy against the H. Ghost 48:9
  died to make men h. 200:11
  everything that lives is h. 58:17
  h., divine, good, amiable 258:23
  h., h., h., Lord God Almighty! 185:27
  it was as h. as a church 376:20
  neither h., nor Roman, nor an empire 407:9
Homage: h. paid by vice to virtue 297:22
  no h. unto the sun 69:12
Home: any more at h. like you 181:1
  at h., I was in a better place 310:33
  best country ever is at h. 173:13
  comin' for to carry me h. 8:10
  draw near to their eternal h. 408:6
  driven to ramble h. 368:8
  England, h. and beauty 12:27 64:15
  English h. 389:20
  farewell h.! 127:2
  father, come h. with me now 427:7
  filled one h. with glee 186:12
  Go H. in the Dark 418:11
  go the Same Way H. 267:12
  her h. is on the deep 96:26
  his floating h. 122:1
  h. art gone 313:25
  h. is best 400:26
  h. is the girl's prison 358:11
  h. life ceases to be free 202:21
  h. to his mother's house 259:6
  h. where the buffalo roam 189:19
  hunter h. from the hill 376:13
  little grey h. in the west 418:16
  man goeth to his long h. 41:34

Home – *contd*
  man who thinks to found a h. 144:20
  our island h. 387:31
  quiet h.s and first beginnings 28:7
  return h. and rest on the couch 103:7
  shall never more go h. 241:2
  stately h.s of England 121:4 186:14 419:25
  there's no place like h. 279:19
  travel to their h. among the dead 360:1
  turns again h. 383:15
  what's the good of a h. 179:13
  who live at h. at ease 277:21
  won't go h. till morning 78:23
Homer: H. ... nods 196:3
  H. will be all the books you need 78:20
  in H. more than H. knew 378:17
  our poets steal from H. 85:9
  seven cities warred for H. 189:16
  sound thy H.'s ... name 126:1
  you must not call it H. 29:14
Homerus: bonus dormitat H. 196:3
Homespun: h.s have we swaggering 340:14
Homines: non h., non di 196:5
  quidquid agunt h. 213:15
  quot h. tot sententiae 392:28
Homme: h. est ... un méchant animal 262:17
  je n'en suis pas moins h.! 262:14
  pauvre h.! 262:12
Homo: ecce h. 52:6
  h. sum; humani nil a me alienum 392:26
Hon: concentrate in the H.s' cupboard 261:3
Honest: good to be h. and true 7:21
  h. as any man living 341:29
  h. God is the noblest work 87:21 203:18
  h. man's the noblest work 83:6 287:7
  h. men are better than numbers 127:15
  I am not naturally h. 354:19
  lines written by the most h. man 296:15
  made h. by an act of parliament 211:22
  though I be poor, I'm h. 250:33
  to be direct and h. is not safe 343:34
  to be h., as this world goes 316:4
  whatsoever things are h. 55:10
Honester: old man and no h. 341:29
Honesty: h. is praised and starves 213:14
  h., manhood, nor good fellowship 320:15
  I am armed so strong in h. 328:9
  wins not more than h. 326:4
Honey: earth is the h. 401:27
  flowing with milk and h. 31:33
  gather h. all the day 410:19
  h., and plenty of money 232:16
  is there h. still for tea? 67:12
  locusts and wild h. 46:33
  sweeter ... than h. and the honeycomb 35:1
  Tiggers don't like h. 252:3
  with milk and h. blest 269:10
Honey-bee: so work the h.-b.s 323:26
Honey-dew: on h.-d. hath fed 116:6
Honneur: tout est perdu fors l'h. 162:11
Honour: all is lost save h. 162:11
  and h. a name 270:6
  blushing h.s thick upon him 325:31
  bright h. from the pale-faced moon 320:23
  can h. set to a leg? 322:1
  can h.'s voice provoke 177:7
  decliner of h.s and titles 156:5

Joy – *contd*
    j. shall be in heaven 50:34
    j.! that in our embers 423:18
    j. was never sure 380:24
    J., whose hand is ever at his lips 216:23
    j.'s soul lies in the doing 351:8
    j.s are but fantastical 142:10
    j.s of parents are secret 17:12
    j.s to this are folly 85:7
    kisses the J. as it flies 59:10
    lasting j.s the man attend 415:24
    let j. be unconfined 88:27
    not a j. the world can give 93:22
    perfectest herald of j. 341:13
    Phyllis is my only j. 307:23
    pledges of Heav'n's j. 252:16
    season made for j.s 166:4
    snatch a fearful j. 178:10
    sons of God shouted for j. 34:14
    stern j. which warriors feel 305:19
    such present j.s therein 150:8
    surprised by j. 422:5
    thing of beauty is a j. 214:25
    thy bed of crimson j. 60:15
    to former j.s recurring 173:8
    wild j.s of living 77:6
    writhed not at passing j. 218:16
Joyously: so j., so maidenly 367:19
Jubilee: day of our j. is death 69:1
    we bring the J. 427:11
Jubilo: year of J. 427:10
Jubjub: beware the J. bird 101:8
Judas: he's J. to a tittle 72:31
Juden: die J., die es verdient 162:22
Judge: and were j.s of fact 293:10
    but j. you as you are 336:13
    cause is to be decided by the j. 210:12
    fool with j.s, amongst fools a j. 122:13
    God is a righteous J. 34:27
    God is the j. 36:29
    I'll be j., I'll be jury 100:9
    J., and a good J. too 170:16
    j. between the high and low 366:8
    j. not, that ye be not judged 47:20
    j. not the play 130:4
    j. of the widows 36:23
    j.s all ranged 166:10
    j.s soon the sentence sign 288:24
    O wise young j. 338:19
    shall not the J. ... do right 31:14
    sole j. of truth 286:29
    to meet the J. 367:12
Judgement: account ... in the day of j. 48:10
    Daniel come to j. 338:19
    dice of j. 294:18
    He which is the top of j. 336:13
    I expect a j. 133:19
    if he had any j. in the world 118:27
    in the day of j. 291:15
    j.! thou art fled to brutish beasts 327:29
    leaves of the J. Book unfold 382:14
    legal j. of his equals 243:11
    no one complains of his j. 297:16
    reserve thy j. 314:33
    say a j. falls on a man 308:3
    'tis with our j.s as our watches 285:22
    vulgarize the day of j. 205:3

Judgement – *contd*
    wait till j. break 139:14
    waits upon the j. 318:14
    would not give his j. rashly 2:4
    your representative owes you ... his j. 80:17
Jug: git loose from de j. 183:25
    j., j., j., j., tereu 240:5
    j. j. to dirty ears 152:33
    little brown j. 7:10
    one old j. without a handle 232:8
Juggler: j., and a fortune-teller 312:26
Juliet: and J. is the sun 348:8
Julius: ere the mightiest J. fell 313:34
    ye towers of J. 176:18
July: winter – ending in J. 92:2
July-flower: June, and J.-f.s 188:16
Jumblies: lands where the J. live 232:14
Jump: efery dime she gife a j. 233:22
June: leafy month of J. 115:5
    newly sprung in J. 84:4
Jungle: cutting through the j. 235:6
Juno: lids of J.'s eyes 354:13
    she's J. when she walks 212:6
Jupiter: J. the Rain-bringer 398:5
Jurisprudence: gladsome light of J. 114:3
Jury: I'll be judge, I'll be j. 100:9
    j., passing on the prisoner's life 336:8
    trial by j. ... will be a delusion 132:1
Just: be j., and fear not 326:4
    blood of this j. person 49:32
    it raineth on the j. 64:8
    jewel of the j. 403:4
    j. men made perfect 56:1
    j. shall live by faith 52:40
    man ... more j. than God 33:39
    only the actions of the j. 365:33
    rain on the j. and on the unjust 47:7
    what I plead is j. 195:9
    whatsoever things are j. 55:10
Juster: not, Celia, that I j. am 307:21
Justice: and then the j. 311:14
    as thou urgest j. 338:21
    Chief J. was rich 241:22
    even-handed j. 333:3
    has no sense of j. 305:4
    I'll do him j. 118:27
    in the course of j. 338:17
    j. is a hallowed place 19:8
    j. is such a fine thing 234:3
    j. of my quarrel 245:17
    j. or injustice of the cause 210:12
    'j.' was done 183:2
    let j. be done 157:9
    love of j. in most men 297:14
    loved j. and hated iniquity 179:6
    mercy seasons j. 338:17
    poetic J., with her lifted scale 283:28
    revenge is a kind of wild j. 17:6
    sad-eyed j., with his surly hum 323:26
    see how yond j. rails 330:26
    temper so j. with mercy 258:25
    thou shalt have j. 338:21
    though j. be thy plea 338:17
    Thwackum was for doing j. 158:1
Justifiable: j. to men 259:16
Justification: j. in every line 119:22
Justly: do j., and to love mercy 45:12

King – *contd*
k. has written a braid letter 21:9
k. himself has followed her 172:27
k. is a thing men have made 308:4
k. is dead 9:12
k. lived long ago 75:18
k. never dies 58:7
k. of infinite space 316:11
k. of shreds and patches 318:16
k. of the castle 272:22
k. over the water 6:16
k. reigns, but does not govern 430:18
k. shall be contented 346:2
k. sits in Dunfermline 21:8
K. that ruled, as he thought fit 97:22
k. was in his counting-house 273:27
k.'s name is a tower 347:15
k.s and rulers ... become philosophers 282:21
k.s crept out again 69:23
k.s have sat upon the ground 46:5
k.s is mostly rapscallions 401:3
k.s it makes gods 347:14
k.s may be blest 84:17
k.s that fear their subjects' 325:17
k.s when the world begun 75:19
k.s will be tyrants from policy 81:11
lad that's born to be k. 64:6
little profits that an idle k. 391:33
lose the name of k. 346:2
mirror of all Christian k.s 323:28
mockery k. of snow 346:11
more royalist than the k. 9:8
my God and K. 187:18
O worship the K. 175:12
of cabbages -- and k.s 101:21
or walk with k.s 223:8
our sovereign lord the k. 298:3
Ozymandias, k. of k.s 362:1
part ... k.s can cause or cure 173:16
passing brave to be a k. 245:21
passion for our temperate k.s 389:12
people ... no k. could govern 146:17
plainly say, 'My God my K.' 188:1
plots ... ruin k.s 146:18
reverence the K. 384:9
rightwise k. ... of all England 243:18
ruin seize thee, ruthless K.! 176:12
saddest of all K.s 205:8
setter up and puller down of k.s 325:19
shall be accounted poet k.s 217:14
sing, Long live the K. 123:6
so excellent a k. 314:12
stamped with the image of the K. 384:13
subject's duty is the k.'s 324:18
than k. of all these dead 192:31
think the k. sees thee still 187:22
this hath not offended the k. 265:18
three k.s into the east 83:31
till the K. enjoys his own again 277:22
what have k.s 324:19
what must the k. do now? 346:2
whatsoever K. shall reign 7:18
while k.s are arming 306:25
whilst thus I sing, I am a K. 111:21
who is this K. of glory? 35:12
whom the k. delighteth to honour 33:31
worse k. never left a realm undone 93:26

538

Kingdom: children ... into the k. of heaven 48:31
children of the k. shall be cast out 47:31
existence of an unseen k. 86:33
in this k. by the sea 283:8
k. for a little grave 346:2
k. for it was too small 322:5
k. of God is within you 51:2
k.s are clay 309:15
k.s are less by three 381:13
my k. for a horse! 347:19
now de k. coming 427:10
of such is the k. of heaven 50:5
order to a peopled k. 323:26
rich man ... into the k. of heaven 48:41
seek ye first the k. of God 47:18
shewed unto him all the k.s 50:15
state of man, like to a little k. 327:6
thy k. is divided 44:36
trample a k. down 275:29
we have kissed away k.s 309:36
Kingfisher: as k.s catch fire 194:11
Kingsley: believes K. a divine 377:6
Kinship: any k. with the stars 249:21
Kinsmen: k. according to the flesh 53:4
Kipling: Rudyards cease from K. 373:20
Kipper: sleeping ... like two old k.s 394:14
Kirkconnell: on fair K. lea 20:20
Kirtle: kilted her green k. 21:14
Kiss: ae fond k. 82:18
bee's k. now! 73:23
break off this last lamenting k. 142:16
come let us k. and part 146:5
coward does it with a k. 416:6
gentle k. to every sedge 353:24
I crave one k. 21:22
I dare not ask a k. 189:6
I saw you take his k.! 279:2
kingdom of that final k. 126:23
k. her until she be wearied 364:2
k. long as my exile 313:8
k. me, and be quiet 263:3
k. me, sweet and twenty 352:17
k. my lord before I die 245:25
k. till the cow come home 26:10
k. without a moustache 104:2
leave a k. but in the cup 212:12
moth's k., first! 73:22
none k. each other but the men 374:8
nothing wrong in a connubial k. 90:31
only to k. the air 189:7
part at last without a k. 266:7
without a single k. 73:22
you must not k. and tell 118:11
Kissed: I wist, before I k. 21:24
k. for forty years 301:21
k. likewise the maid 126:9
k. thee ere I killed thee 344:17
might have toyed and k. 165:22
Kisses: at cards for k. 240:4
a-wastin' Christian k. 223:29
bread and cheese, and k. 379:13
but my k. bring again 336:27
fear thy k., gentle maiden 363:19
feeds on the aëreal k. 362:17
give me a thousand k. 103:3
I understand thy k. 321:22
kiss me with the k. of his mouth 42:4

Lait: l. tombe: adieu 227:14
Laity: conspiracies against the l. 357:21
Lake: its worst to vex the l. 75:23
  l. that was a fair water 244:3
  scalped ... by the Great L.s 241:13
Lalagen: dulce ridentem L. 197:13
Lamb: as a l. to the slaughter 43:40
  behold the bleeding L. of God 141:25
  gather the l.s with his arm 43:25
  in the blood of the L. 57:3
  l. or an ox ... to the slaughter 44:19
  L., the frolic and the gentle 421:1
  l. was sure to go 180:11 273:4
  l.s could not forgive 136:12
  l.s that did frisk i' the sun 353:31
  little L., who made thee? 61:1
  London's towers receive the L. 59:17
  Mary had a little l. 180:11 273:4
  pipe a song about a L. 60:19
  who made the L. make thee? 60:17
  young l.s bound 423:7
Lamely: so l. and unfashionable 346:21
Lament: l. is cries countless 194:23
  nought other to l. 279:7
Lamentation: with an empire's l. 389:5
Lamenting: he was left l. 96:16
Lammas: it fell about the L. tide 20:4
Lamp: bright, like golden l.s 246:18
  it is a dying l. 359:7
  l. unto my feet 38:7
  l.s are going out 179:12
  l.s shone o'er fair women 88:26
  old l.s for new 9:16
  unlit l. and the ungirt loin 77:29
  when the l. is shattered 361:3
Lampada: vitai l. tradunt 239:17
Lancaster: time-honoured L. 344:23
Lancelot: bold Sir L. 386:34
  L. or Pelleas, or Pellenore 258:34
Lancer: six stalwart l.s 415:27
Land: away into the silent l. 300:11
  between a splendid and a happy l. 172:23
  cast the water of my l. 335:20
  England's green and pleasant l. 59:20
  French the empire of the l. 296:16
  house and l. are gone 161:6
  ill fares the l. 172:4
  in l.s beyond the sea 421:3
  know ye the l. 88:12
  l. become brown sharp points 153:17
  l. flowing with milk and honey 31:33
  l. of Hope and Glory 29:6
  l. of lost content 199:28
  l. of my sires! 306:1
  l. of settled government 392:22
  l. of such dear souls 345:8
  l. of the mountain and the flood 306:1
  l. self-interest groans 88:8
  l. to which the ship would go 113:21
  leaps from the water to the l. 390:26
  lord of himself, though not of l.s 427:15
  marching to the Promised L. 23:12
  mire of the last l. 67:20
  my own, my native l.! 305:28
  native L. – Good Night 88:18
  no more l., say fish 67:4
  pass, like night, from l. to l. 115:10

Land – *contd*
  plot of l. not too large 198:20
  pointed toward the l. 387:29
  rood of l. set out 378:10
  search the l. of living men 306:8
  she is far from the l. 265:5
  sing ... in a strange l. 38:25
  their l.s after their own names 36:3
  there is a l. of pure delight 411:5
  think there is no l. 16:13
  this dear, dear l. 345:8
  there is a happy l. 430:1
  to spy out the l. 32:3
  to the l. o' the leal 268:4
  thro' the l. at eve 389:27
  under the l. you used to plough 199:23
  where lies the l. 422:7
  woman led him to the promised l. 150:7
Land: kennst du das L. 171:22
Landlady: l. ... is a parallelogram 231:20
Landmark: l. is a kopje-crest 182:1
  remove not the ancient l. 40:5
Land-rat: l.-r.s and water-rats 337:15
Landscape: fades the glimmering l. 176:22
  l. ... a condition of the spirit 4:6
  l. tire the view 150:10
Landscape-painter: is but an l.-p. 387:28
Land-thieves: l.-t. and water-thieves 337:15
Lane: ghost will walk . . in an English l. 72:9
  there's a country l. 277:23
Language: ancient l.s ... a luxury 66:8
  and my l. is plain 184:1
  dear l. which I spake 241:1
  decent obscurity of a learned l. 167:8
  don't think anything of that l. 136:26
  everything else in our l. ... perish 242:13
  fancies that broke through l. 76:11
  for learning me your l. 349:36
  great feast of l.s 331:25
  in l. strange she said 216:4
  in the best chosen l. 15:12
  instructed in all l.s 136:15
  l. all nations understand 27:18
  l. is fossil poetry 155:3
  l. of the age is never ... poetry 178:25
  l. that would make your hair curl 170:8
  l. was not powerful enough 136:27
  l.s are the pedigree 210:17
  my l. fails 28:1
  no l., but the l. of the heart 285:18
  poetical l. ... current l. heightened 195:17
  sorry when any l. is lost 210:17
  speaks three or four l.s 352:3
  that those lips had l.! 123:25
  use any l. you choose 169:7
  wit in all l.s 149:16
  you taught me l. 349:36
Languid: art thou l. 269:3
Languish: relieve my l. 128:20
Laodameia: L. died; Helen died 230:10
Lap: dropt in her L. 158:26
  fills her l. with pleasures 423:14
  tumbling into some men's l.s 16:17
Lap-dog: l.-d.s breathe their last 288:29
  l.-d.s give themselves the rousing 288:12
  l.-d.s, parrots, perish all! 289:1
  pianoforte, a l.-d., and a parrot 98:10

Leave – *contd*
  often took l., but was loath 293:1
Leaven: little l. leaveneth 53:28
Leaves: as the l. grow 428:15
  crowned with calm l. 380:23
  famous harmony of l. 429:21
  green l. whispering overhead 418:18
  half with green l. 240:16
  l. are falling like its own 361:20
  l. could turn with care 146:13
  l. dead are driven, like ghosts 361:13
  l. in the glassy stream 319:11
  L. of Life keep falling 158:18
  l. they were withering and sere 283:22
  like the l. of the trees 192:27
  poetry comes . . . as the l. to a tree 219:2
  shatter your l. 254:17
  silent l. are still 93:10
  thick as autumnal l. 255:29
  time for the burning of the l. 57:30
  with l. and flowers do cover 412:10
  yellow l., or none 356:2
Leben: ein ruheloser Marsch war unser L. 304:18
  unnütz L. ist ein früher Tod 171:14
Lechery: still, wars and l. 351:30
Lecteur: hypocrite l.! 24:13
Lecture: Caudle's Curtain L.s 205:2
  I do not give l.s 415:15
Leda: L., the beloved of Jupiter 230:10
  L., was the mother of Helen 278:19
Lee: between windward and l. 380:19
  down along the l. 372:15
Leek: by this l., I will . . . revenge 325:2
Leer: assent with civil l. 285:12
Lees: drink life to the l. 391:34
  mere l. is left 334:2
Left: l. a lot of little things 222:8
  she, alas, hath l. me 419:9
  to the l. you are sure to be right 155:26
Leg: Being, erect upon two l.s 138:26
  cannon-ball took off his l.s 193:6
  four l.s good, two l.s bad 275:7
  he has a l. 250:12
  he pulls the l.s of his dreams 394:15
  honest woman and a broken l. 105:3
  I leave my second l. 193:7
  if you could see my l.s 135:6
  kiss my Julia's dainty l. 189:1
  l.s of iron 44:31
  l.s without the man 125:20
  literary man – *with* a wooden l. 137:20
  pleasure in the l.s of a man 38:32
  sylph . . . could stand upon one l. 136:28
  which l. goes after which? 127:10
Legem: vel per l. terrae 243:11
Leges: silent enim l. inter arma 112:9
Legion: give me back my l.s 94:19
  l. of the lost ones 223:1
  L. that never was 'listed 223:25
  my name is L. 49:40
Legiones: l. redde 94:19
Legislative: l. . . . nominated by the executive 167:10
Legislator: unacknowledged l.s 364:19
Legunt: sed ista l. 246:14
Leicester: farewell L. Square 418:10
Leiden: l. oder triumphieren 171:13

Leisure: God gave us this l. 405:26
  l. answers l. 336:31
  l. to be good 177:21
Lemon: squeeze out of a l. 166:23
Lemon-tree: land where the l.-t.s flower 171:22
Lend: few l. (but fools) 400:21
  I'll l. you something 353:13
  men who l. 228:17
  three things I never l.s 377:22
Lender: borrower nor a l. be 314:34
Lene: l. . . . as is a rake 107:5
Length: drags its slow l. along 286:6
  l. and breadth enough 21:7
Lenten: l. ys come with love 4:23
Leonard: L., Rafael, Agnolo and me 70:19
Leopard: l. shall lie down 43:1
  l.s sat under a juniper tree 151:20
  or the l. his spots 44:20
Lerne: gladly wolde he l. 107:7
Lesley: O saw ye bonnie L. 82:25
Less: l., and what worlds away! 71:22
  nicely-calculated l. or more 420:13
  rather than be l. 256:17
Lessen: l. from day to day 100:27
Lesson: had an Imperial l. 223:20
  preach a high moral l. 377:2
  reason they're called l.s 100:27
  this is that other l. 249:11
Lethe: in ease on L. wharf 315:15
  no, no, go not to L. 216:21
  upon the tedious shores of L. 228:15
Lethean: drunken of things L. 381:5
Letter: art o' l. writing 138:21
  cries like dead l.s 194:23
  I copied all the l.s 168:25
  king has written a braid l. 21:9
  last, till you write your l. 143:28
  l. killeth 54:24
  O ay, l.s – I had l.s 118:30
  pause awhile from l.s 205:20
  republic of l.s 1:18
  sayings . . . like women's l.s 184:18
  thou unnecessary l.! 329:24
  was a l. from his wife 102:13
  when he wrote a l. 18:12
Lettres: nought the l. space 108:13
Level: one dead l. ev'ry mind 284:19
Leveller: l.s wish to level *down* 208:4
Levelling: cannot bear l. *up* 208:4
Leven: across yon lilly l. 21:17
Levi: jump, as Mr L. did 23:2
Leviathan: draw out L. 34:17
Levity: little judicious l. 375:25
Lex: salus populi suprema est l. 112:1
Lexicographer: L. . . . harmless drudge 206:1
Liar: all men are l.s 38:4
  but every man a l. 52:43
  fighting a l. 372:23
  I am the club L. 303:6
  l., and the father of it 51:38
  l. of the first magnitude 118:9
  l.s ought to have good memories 366:3
  love of a lie, l.s find ready-made 74:19
  often quite picturesque l. 401:13
  only answered 'Little l.!' 28:4
Libel: l. in a frown 378:11
Liberal: either a little L. 169:5

Lilac: l.s last in the dooryard 415:19
　　l.s out of the dead land 152:23
Lilac-time: down to Kew in l.-t. 271:20
Lilies: and a few l. blow 194:20
　　breaking the golden l. afloat 70:1
　　consider the l. of the field 47:17
　　had three l. in her hand 300:20
　　in the beauty of the l. 200:11 ·
　　l. of all kinds 354:13
　　l. that fester smell 356:11
　　l. without, roses within 247:7
Lillabulero: half a dozen bars of L. 374:15
Lilting: heard them l. 154:4
Lily: as the l. among thorns 42:6
　　fair as the l. 110:14
　　I see a l. on thy brow 216:2
　　paint the l. 91:4　329:4
　　seen but a bright l. grow 212:5
　　set thick with l. 266:9
Lily-livered: thou l.-l. boy 335:16
Lily-seed: wanderest the l.-s. to find 266:17
Limb: both of wind and l. 86:15
　　consent to have a l. amputated 208:12
　　if these poor l.s die, safest 67:15
　　l.s were made in England 324:12
　　thy decent l.s composed 284:29
　　till the little l.s are stronger 391:11
　　well compensated in l.s 10:7
Limbo: into a L. large and broad 257:4
Lime-tree: l.-t. bower my prison! 116:13
Limit: l.s cannot hold love out 348:12
　　quiet l. of the world 391:21
　　there is ... a l. 80:26
　　wide the l.s stand 172:23
Lincoln: back o' merry L. 20:22
　　when Abraham L. was shovelled 303:20
Linden: on L., when the sun was low 96:10
Line: cadence of a rugged l. 148:22
　　cancel half a l. 159:11
　　creep in one dull l. 286:5
　　fight it out on this l. 175:15
　　in my lagging l.s you miss 195:12
　　l. upon l., l. upon l. 43:6
　　l. will take us hours dumb 428:7
　　l.s and liife are free 187:23
　　l.s are fallen unto me 34:36
　　lives along the l. 286:25
　　never blotted out a l. 212:19
　　own the happy l.s 286:9
　　rather have written those l.s 419:19
　　silken l.s, and silver hooks 142:4
　　sorrows of thy l.! 141:20
　　thin red l. tipped with steel 302:19
　　town-crier spoke my l.s 317:9
　　verse, the full-resounding l. 289:10
　　we carved not a l. 419:18
　　will the l. stretch out 335:1
Lineament: moulded the changing l.s 278:19
Linen: did not love clean l. 207:22
　　l. often changed, the sweeter 160:21
　　old l. wash whitest 412:8
　　purple and fine l. 50:41
　　washing one's clean l. 416:16
Liner: L. she's a lady 223:21
Lingering: something l. 169:24
Lining: silver l. on the night 252:27
　　there's a silver l. 161:15

548

Linked: to each other l. are 396:2
Linnet: as the l.s sing 385:12
　　I heard a l. 65:16
　　l. born within the cage 385:13
Linsey-woolsey: l.-w. brothers 284:10
Linsy-woolsy: lawless l.-w. brother 86:18
Lion: beard the l. in his den 306:15
　　better than a dead l. 41:20
　　devil as a roaring l. 56:21
　　hear the l. roar 123:16
　　I girdid up my L.s 409:22
　　lamb; threatened, a l. 105:23
　　like l.s after slumber 361:11
　　l. among ladies 340:12
　　L. and the Lizard keep 158:25
　　l. and the unicorn were fighting 272:26
　　l. on your old stone gates 386:26
　　l.'s shadow ere himself 338:26
　　l.s roar after their prey 37:23
　　mated by the l. 309:3
　　old l. is dead 278:5
　　righteous are bold as a l. 40:24
　　strong is the l. 367:22
　　there is a l. in the way 40:16
　　thou wear a l.'s hide! 328:30
　　wrath of the l. ... wisdom of God 61:29
　　young l. and the fatling together 43:1
　　young l.s of the *Daily Telegraph* 12:6
Lioness: feeds a l. at home 382:18
　　l. hath whelpèd in the streets 327:12
Lip: crimson in thy l.s 349:13
　　dear red curve of her l.s 247:23
　　her l.s suck forth my soul 245:6
　　I saw their starved l.s 216:7
　　item, Two l.s 352:12
　　keep a stiff upper l. 102:17
　　keep the door of my l.s 38:28
　　kiss of your clay-cold l.s 21:22
　　let me put my l.s to it 136:3
　　l.s cannot fail of taking their plie 80:5
　　l.s that touch liquor 430:17
　　l.s were four red roses 347:8
　　l.s were red, and one was thin 377:10
　　little while our l.s are dumb 387:36
　　Lord, open thou our l.s 290:23
　　moisten poor Jim's l.s 146:15
　　on a poet's l.s 362:16
　　or a coral l. admires 97:21
　　red l.s are not so red 276:20
　　red was on your l., Mary 58:12
　　see my l.s tremble 285:2
　　smily round the l.s 238:27
　　take those l.s away 336:27
　　that those l.s had language! 123:25
　　what need a vermeil-tinctured l. 253:12
　　when I ope my l.s 337:7
　　where my Julia's l.s do smile 188:18
　　whispering, with white l.s 89:2
Lippo: poor brother L. 72:29
Lipsius: forget the great L. 374:24
Liquefaction: l. of her clothes 189:11
Liquor: but l. is quicker 268:25
　　claret is the l. for boys 209:25
　　good l., I stoutly maintain 173:36
　　lips that touch l. 430:17
　　l. koncealed about my persun 409:30
　　l. talks mighty loud 183:25

Love – *contd*

l. and murder will out 118:8
l. and scandal are the best sweeteners 157:28
l. and to cherish 292:7
l. bade me welcome 188:2
l. be younger than thyself 352:25
l. being in l. 393:4
l. but her and l. for ever 82:19
l. but her for ever 82:25
l. but only her 89:25
L. carries all before him 406:10
l. ceases to be a pleasure 27:14
l., cherish and to obey 292:8
l. did make thee run into 310:34
l. even with my life decay 356:1
l. ... fate of leisured societies 268:17
l. ... giv'n unsought is better 353:5
l. goes toward l. 348:18
l. had been sae ill 21:24
L., half angel and half bird 76:19
l. hath an end 381:3
l. he bore to learning 172:17
l. he laughed to scorn 357:5
l. I gave thee, with myself to l. 72:27
l. in a hut ... is ... cinders, ashes, dust 216:9
L. in her sunny eyes does ... play 121:11
l. in her train stood ready 65:14
l. in idleness 340:8 349:19
l., in my bosom, like a bee 235:23
l. is a sickness full of woes 128:17
l. is a spirit all compact 357:6
l. is best 74:9
l. is dying 23:21
l. is enough 266:10
l. is God 399:2
l. is heaven, and heaven is l. 305:24
l. is like linen 160:21
l. is like the measles 204:23
l. is long 390:3
l. is not l. which alters 356:24
l. is of the valley 390:14
l. is strong as death 42:15
l. is swift of foot 187:26
l. is the fulfilling of the law 53:15
l. is the wisdom of the fool 211:9
l. is then our duty 166:4
l. itself have rest 93:17
l. lies beyond the tomb 112:16
l. likes stratagem and subterfuge 76:18
l. looks not with the eyes 339:29
l. me little, so you l. me long 188:23
l. me no more 146:3
l. never subsides into friendship 94:11
l. ... no season knows 143:30
l. o' life's young day 266:22
l. of l. 389:24
l. prove likewise variable 348:15
l. rules the court, the camp, the grove 305:24
l.'s a man of war 187:26
l.'s but the frailty of the mind 119:3
l.'s like the measles 205:6
l.'s not Time's fool 356:25
l.'s the noblest frailty 149:8
l. scene on a bearskin 202:4
L. seeketh not itself to please 60:8
l. sleeping in the shade 249:15
l. slights it [death] 17:3

Love – *contd*

l. so amazing, so divine 411:9
l. sought is good 353:5
l. sprung from my only hate! 348:6
l. still has something of the sea 307:20
l. that can be reckoned 309:14
l. that makes the world go round 7:22
l. that moves the sun 129:10
l. that so desires 249:18
l. that time was not as ... nowadays 244:8
l. that was more than l. 283:8
l. that we have loved together 244:11
l. thee better after death 70:8
l. thyself last 326:4
l. to hatred turned 118:18
l. we swore would last 130:11
L., which reachest but to dust 366:11
l. which us doth bind 246:21
l. will make a dog howl 26:9
l. ... without dissimulation 53:7
L. without his wings 93:6
l. without the help of anything 59:9
l. wol nat ben constreyned 107:18
l. ... would at once be dried up 114:14
l.'s young dream 264:23
loved and still l.s 298:18
make us l. one another 379:22
man's l. is of man's life 90:21
may he l. who never loved 9:1
me and my true l. 8:2
men l. in haste 91:39
met you not with my true l. 295:8
mie l. ys dedde 106:15
mischievous devil l. is 87:17
monstruosity in l. 351:18
more l. or more disdain 97:24
more of l. than matrimony 174:13
my dear and only l., I pray 264:7
my l. climbed up to me! 221:12
my l. and I did meet 428:15
my l. is of a birth as rare 246:20
my L.'s like a red red rose 84:4
my l.! ye do me wrong 7:9
my true l. hath my heart 366:4
ne'er ebb to humble l. 343:36
never doubt I l. 316:2
new every morning is the l. 219:21
no l. lost between us 174:3
no man dies for l. 149:11
not Death, but L. 70:4
nuptial l. maketh mankind 17:21
O my l. is slain 142:12
O spirit of l.! 352:1
off with the old l. 7:21
office and affairs of l. 341:12
oh to l. so, be so loved 72:22
one that l.s his fellow-men 201:14
our l. hath no decay 142:3
pangs of disprized l. 316:29
passing the l. of women 33:3
perfect l. casteth out fear 56:26
prize o' learning l. 72:13
prove ... the sports of l. 212:3
put aside a long-standing l. 103:15
quarrels are the renewal of l. 392:25
red, l.'s proper hue 258:15
regain l. once possessed 259:20

Love – *contd*
renewing is of l. 150:20
right to dissemble your l. 220:5
right true end of l. 142:13
sad and heavy was the l. 20:10
see now l. perfect too 76:4
seem worthy of your l. 424:10
separate us from the l. of God. 53:3
she bid me take l. easy 428:15
she never told her l. 352:28
sighed for the l. of a ladye 170:19
sit down, says L. 188:3
so faithful in l. 306:11
so is my l. among the daughters 42:6
so true a fool is l. 355:18
some have died for l 426:15
speak low, if you speak l. 341:11
spring of l. gushed 115:2
such ever was l.'s way 72:12
such l. as spirits feel 421:11
sweet l. remembered 355:9
sweetest l. I do not go 143:25
tale deliver of whole course of l. 342:27
ten men l. what I hate 76:9
thank heaven ... for a good man's l. 312:7
that ye l. one another 51:44
then O, my true l. said 280:10
then they dream of l. 347:29
they above l. to be loved 366:7
this spring of l. resembleth 353:23
those who l. want wisdom 362:12
thou shalt l. thy neighbour 32:1 48:38
though last, not least in l. 327:22
thy l. is better than wine 42:4
to be wise, and l. 351:19
to let the warm L. in 217:10
to look at was to l. 387:10
to Mercy, Pity, Peace and L. all pray 60:23
to tell thy l., l. that never told can be 60:2
true l. never did run smooth 339:27
true l.'s gift 305:27
true l. sits him down 8:11
trust thou thy L. 302:14
turns to thoughts of l. 387:5
two l.s I have 357:2
use him as though you l. him 62:13
waft her l. to come 338:26
wanton l. corrupteth 17:21
wayward is this foolish l. 353:22
we must l. one another or die 14:5
what l. I bore to thee 421:3
when I was in l. with you 199:17
when l. and duty clash! 389:28
when l. begins to sicken and decay 328:5
when l. once pleads admission 1:12
when L. speaks, the voice 331:22
where L. is throned 352:23
whoever l.s, if he do not 142:13
whose l. will never die 251:3
whose l.s I prize 313:5
with all their quantity of l. 319:26
with all thy faults I l. thee 124:33
with l. brooding there 418:16
you cannot call it l. 318:14
you made me l. you 242:15
your true l.'s coming 352:16
Love-adept: dreaming like a l.-a. 362:16

Loved: better l. ye canna be 267:20
better l. you'll never be 191:26
better to have l. and lost 87:28
for I l. the man 212:20
I l. him for himself alone 365:5
I l. him not; and yet 230:3
l. her that she did pity them 342:32
l. long since, and lost 270:13
l. needs only to be seen 148:1
l. not wisely but too well 344:16
l. so long and sees no more 298:18
never l. sae kindly 82:20
never to have l. at all 385:14
no man ever l. 356:26
no sooner l. but they sighed 312:15
out upon it, I have l. 377:11
place and the l. one all together 74:26
say why I l. him 263:13
she who has never l. 166:11
sought the thing he l. 421:17
sour to them that l. 326:11
that l. not at first sight 245:28
this man l. *me*! 230:5
thou hast not l. 310:34
to have l., to have thought 10:16
what did your L. One pass on from? 411:17
Love-in-idleness: maidens call it L.-i.-i. 340:8
Love-light: l.-l. in your eye 58:12
Loveliness: her l. I never knew 114:10
its l. increases 214:25
of so shining l. 429:17
portion of the l. 359:12
to brood over ... your l. 219:16
Lovely: l. and a fearful thing 90:29
l., and gentle, and beautiful 133:27
l. and pleasant in their lives 33:1
l. that are not beloved 279:6
more l. and more temperate 355:3
once he made more l. 359:12
thy last on all things l. 131:15
whatsoever things are l. 55:10
Love-match: l.-m. was the only thing 150:13
Lover: all mankind love a l. 154:26
and then the l. 311:14
came two young l.s lately wed 386:33
it was a l. 312:19
l. all as frantic 340:26
l. of my life, O soldier-saint 76:25
l.'s ear will hear 331:21
l.'s eyes will gaze 331:21
l.s are round her 265:5
l.s cannot see the pretty follies 337:31
l.s find their peace at last 160:7
l.s, just at twelve, awake 288:12
l.s lying two by two 199:15
l.s scorn whom that love do possess 366:7
l.s were all untrue 149:12
l.s' seasons run 143:29
lunatic, the l., and the poet 340:25
make two l.s happy 283:25
my fause l. stole my rose 85:4
old l.s are soundest 412:8
pair of star-crossed l.s 347:20
run into't as to a l.'s bed 310:3
sighed as a l. 167:6
such a constant l. 377:11
sweet l.s love the spring 312:19

M

Man – *contd*

as the m. overtook me 79:20
as you know me all, a plain, blunt m. 328:2
away, slight m.! 328:8
became a good and honest m. 424:7
behold the m. 52:5
best good m. 298:2
breathes there the m. 305:28
but m., proud m. 336:16
but not the m. 306:32
came to the making of m. 380:8
child imposes on the m. 148:7
childhood shows the m. 258:36
created m. in his own image 30:12
diapason closing full in M. 148:16
dispute it like a m. 335:9
every m.'s hand against him 31:13
father of the M. 422:17
for a m. to find out suddenly 417:8
from m. to pig, and from pig to m. 275:9
get a new m. 350:10
God at first made m. 188:4
grand old m., the Prime Minister 271:15
grew within this learned m. 245:13
happiness of the common m. 30:5
he thinks, good easy m. 325:31
he was a m. 314:21
he was her m. 7:6
heaven had made her such a m. 342:32
held to the last m. 180:10
honest, exceeding poor m. 337:27
how can m. die better 241:5
how poor a thing is m. 129:2
I know thee not, old m. 323:20
inner m. 54:43 292:13
is the old m. agreeable? 137:5
is the substantial M. 68:11
kindest m. that ever struck 244:14
large-hearted m. 70:9
let him pass for a m. 337:12
let not m. have the upper hand 34:32
let the end try the m. 322:25
live a m. forbid 332:8
living-dead m. 312:26
love not m. the less 89:26
m. ... a being born to believe 140:16
m. ... a political animal 10:4
m. ... a religious animal 81:14
m. ... abideth not 36:3
m. after his own heart 32:39
m. ... always to be blessed 286:21
m. and bird and beast 115:12
m. appears on earth for a little 26:23
m. be gracious and courteous 17:33
m. be liker m. 383:34
m. be more pure than his maker 33:39
m. became a living soul 30:15
m. bites a dog that is news 128:15
m. by whom the offence cometh 48:33
m. can die but once 323:7
m. cannot choose but pay 278:23
m. comes and tills the field 391:20
m. delights not me 316:13
m., equal, unclassed, tribeless 362:28
m. for the field 390:6
m. has his will 192:14
m., in ignorance sedate 205:25

m. is a gaming animal 228:25
m. is a noble animal 69:18
m. is a piece of the Continent 144:8
m. is a social animal 372:18
m. is a tool-making animal 162:21
m. is a tool-using animal 99:16
m. is as old as he's feeling 117:7
m. is born unto trouble 33:40
m. is m. and master 384:18
m. is Nature's sole mistake 170:6
m. is nobody unless 400:2
m. is not m. as yet 75:4
m. ... is *so* in the way 165:9
m. is the hunter 390:5
M. is the master of things 381:2
m. is the measure 293:6
m. is the shuttle 402:12
m. is the whole world 69:8
m. is ... to be surpassed 270:20
m. ... laid the crops low 394:10
m. marks the earth with ruin 89:27
m. may fish with the worm 318:25
M. may not marry his Grandmother 292:23
m. more sinned against than sinning 330:3
M. of baser Earth didst make 159:15
m. ... plays many parts 311:14
m. recovered of the bite 174:18
m. remains sceptreless, free 362:28
m.'s a m. for a' that! 83:18
m.'s a ribald – M.'s a rake 170:6
m.'s worth something 71:8
m. sent from God 51:17
m. shall have his mare again 340:19
m., so faint, so spiritless 322:11
m. so various that he seemed to be 147:1
m. that hath not music 339:3
m. that is born of a woman 34:4 292:16
m. wants but little 174:10 430:14
m. was formed for society 58:6
m. was made to mourn 84:1
m. who knows the price 417:11
m. who used to notice such things 181:13
m. whom the king delighteth 33:31
m. will go down into the pit 19:24
m. with all his noble qualities 129:14
m. with his back to the East 114:12
m. with the head 390:6
m.'s desire is for the woman 117:2
m.'s inhumanity to m. 84:2
m.'s nature runs 18:33
meekest m. and the gentlest 244:14
met a m. who wasn't there 249:5
miscreate, m. redeemed 76:23
more wonderful than m. 370:4
much one m. can do 247:5
my handsome young m. 20:24
Nature made thee to temper m. 276:4
new m. may be raised up 291:35
nice unparticular m. 182:24
no m. can justly censure 69:6
no m. does. That's his 416:21
no m. in this world hath lived better 244:6
no m. is an island 144:8
no m. see me more 325:30
no such m. be trusted 339:3
nobody ... call me a fussy m. 251:25

Man – *contd*

not a m., you're a machine 357:13
not good that the m. should be alone 30:16
nothing great but m. 181:5
nothing so becomes a m. 324:10
O good old m.! 310:32
old m. broken with storms 326:6
Old M. in a tree 232:3
Old M. who said, 'Hush!' 232:4
Old M. with a beard 232:5
old m. with an old soul 93:29
oldest m. he seemed 425:14
one discovers a m. 278:9
one m. among a thousand 41:16
one m. picked out of ten thousand 316:4
only m. is vile 185:25
outward semblance of a m. 138:26
padded m. 388:29
people arose as one m. 32:32
play is the tragedy 'M.' 283:11
poor, infirm, weak and despised old m. 329:33
rib and crooked piece of m. 69:8
save to one m. 205:10
scarce be a m. before thy mother 26:4
scenes where m. has never trod 112:15
see the green m. pass 191:19
she knows her m. 148:29
she tried on m. 83:22
should a m. whose blood 337:5
smiling, destructive m. 233:11
strange what a m. may do 393:3
strong m. in a blatant land 388:14
strong m. must go 75:27
such is the race of M. 178:16
tempt not a desperate m. 349:11
that animal called m. 379:28
that m. again 214:20
that the m. I am may cease 388:15
think that m. was I 20:9
this bold bad m. 325:25
this m. is now become a god 326:21
this was a m.! 328:20
thou art the m. 33:7
thou madest m. 385:5
to be m. with thy might 380:27
to m. alone beneath the heaven 305:27
twelfth part of m. for woman 69:8
very foolish, fond old m. 330:32
was the mildest mannered m. 91:1
way of a m. with a maid 40:30
well favoured m. is the gift 341:24
went mad and bit the m. 174:17
what a piece of work is a m.! 316:13
what m. has made of m. 421:26
whoso would be a m. 155:4
will not m. awake? 396:13
you was a good m. 183:6
you'll be a M., my son! 223:9
Man-at-arms: m.-a.-a. must now serve 280:12
Mandalay: on the road to M. 223:28
Mandragora: give me to drink m. 309:21
not poppy, nor m. 343:29
Mandrake: get with child a m. 143:26
Mane: plats the m.s of horses 348:2
Manger: m. for His bed 3:14
one born in a m. 402:16
wrapt in the rude m. 255:6

Manges: dis-moi ce que tu m. 66:16
Mangle: immense pecuniary M. 139:10
Mangler: m. in a million million 137:30
Manhood: hold their m.s cheap 324:26
M. a struggle 140:27
m., long misled 148:2
reserves for a bright m. 240:14
Manifest: work shall be made m. 53:24
Manifesto: first powerful m. 371:12
Mankind: and ride m. 154:12
as I know more of m. 210:6
brightest, meanest of m. 287:8
careless of m. 388:3
crucify m. upon a cross of gold 78:14
deserve better of m. 379:2
fleeting generations of m. 364:15
how beauteous m. is 350:26
I am involved in M. 144:9
lost m., dreading to find 13:20
made ... for the ... benefit of m. 398:8
m. are the asses 92:25
m. from China to Peru 205:19
mass of m. understand it [Monarchy] 19:17
study of m. is man 286:28
to fly from ... m. 89:6
when m. is dead, and the world cold 64:3
willing to love all m. 209:21
Manliness: silent m. of grief 172:25
Man-milliner: architectural m.-m. 302:2
Mann: kleiner M., was nun? 156:13
Manna: seeks m., where none is 403:1
Manner: bewrayed as by his m.s 372:8
cease to think about the m. 185:17
corrupt good m.s 54:15
evil m.s live in brass 326:10
for m.s' sake 46:15
ice of her Ladyship's m.s 290:14
m.s can be known to few 206:17
m.s living as they rise 286:19
noble m.s veil defect 279:1
their tricks and their m.s 137:27
to the m. born 315:5
Mansion: are many m.s 51:45
before the starry threshold ... my m. 252:17
build thee more stately m.s 192:15
built the splendid m. which 27:22
large m. of many apartments 219:5
Timon hath made his everlasting m. 350:34
to m.s in the skies 411:7
Mansionry: his loved m. 333:1
Mantle: cast his m. upon him 33:19
in scarlet m. warm 123:30
twitched his m. blue 255:2
Mantuan: pretty i' the M.! 95:13
Manu: te teneam ... deficiente m. 398:4
Manure: it is its natural m. 204:16
Manus: tendebanque m. 405:14
Manuscript: brown Greek m.s 71:14
Many: because we are too m. 182:26
for we are m. 49:40
m. men, m. women, and m. children 207:20
m. still must labour 90:5
mutable, rank-scented m. 313:2
ye are m. – they are few 361:11
Map: roll up that m. 282:15
Mar: Lieutenant-Colonel to the Earl of M. 283:26
striving to better, oft we m. 329:21

Marathon: M. looks on the sea 91:7
Marble: but this in m. 26:8
  cold m. leapt to life 251:19
  found it brick and left it m. 377:13
  made up of m. and mud 184:10
  m. to retain 88:10
  not m., nor the gilded monuments 355:16
Marbre: vers, m., onyx, émail 165:13
March: day's m. nearer home 264:5
  droghte of M. 106:17
  her m. is o'er the mountain waves 96:26
  in the mad M. days 248:1
  life was but a battle and a m. 304:18
  majestic m., and energy divine 289:10
  m. of a nation 278:1
  m. of the human mind 80:13
  m. of the retreating world 276:23
  take the winds of M. 354:13
Märchen: ein M. aus alten Zeiten 186:2
Marches: m. to delightful measures 346:19
Marching: our God is m. on 200:10
Mare: lend me your grey m. 8:14
Margaret: clerk Saunders and May M. 20:10
  M. as midsummer flower 367:18
Margin: meander through a meadow of m. 365:24
  upon the m. of that moorish flood 425:17
Marian: M.'s nose looks red 332:2
Mariana: this dejected M. 336:26
Marie: M. Carmichael, and me 21:5
  M. Seaton, and M. Beaton 21:5
  Queen had four M.s 21:5
Marigold: m., that goes to bed 354:12
Marin: combien de m.s 201:2
Mariner: I fear thee, ancient M.! 114:29
  it is an ancient m. 114:13
  merry m.s are bold and free 360:2
  rest ye, brother m.s 388:5
  we be three poor m.s 296:2
  ye M.s of England 96:24
Marjoram: mints, savory, m. 54:12
Mark: ever fixèd m. 356:24
  God save the m.! 320:21
  m. the archer little meant! 306:4
  may none these m.s efface 93:20
  no m., nor likelihood 321:24
  nobody m.s you 341:5
  set a m. upon Cain 31:1
Market: m.s by the sea shut fast 160:7
Marlborough: from M.'s eyes 205:24
Marlowe: M.'s mighty line 212:14
Marmalade: m.-downwards-incidence 204:20
Marmoream: sit gloriatus m. se relinquere 377:13
Marred: man that's m. 309:8
Marriage: far from being natural ... to live in a state
  of m. 208:25
  few m.s are happy 379:23
  furnish forth the m. tables 314:19
  hanging prevents a bad m. 352:7
  in m., a man becomes slack 375:13
  it won't be a stylish m. 128:14
  m. ... go by Destiny 157:3
  m. has been made in Heaven 303:14
  m. has many pains 206:26
  m. ... is a field of battle 375:14
  [m.] is like a cage 263:22
  m. is nothing but a civil contract 308:7
  m. is popular 358:8

Marriage – *contd*
  m. of true minds 356:24
  marrying and giving in m. 49:21
  no more m.s 317:6
  not against hasty m.s 117:8
  O curse of m.! 343:27
  rob a lady ... by way of m. 158:4
  very unhappy in m. 208:23
  with dirge in m. 314:4
Married: Benedick the m. man 341:8
  delight we m. people have 281:2
  Happy Though M. 181:12
  honest man who m. 174:5
  if they're not m. it's impossible 248:18
  live till I were m. 341:20
  m., and wooed and a'. 300:6
  m. past redemption 149:10
  m. to a single life 127:3
  mocks m. men 331:30
  most m. man I ever saw 409:33
  never m., and that's his hell 85:13
  next to being m. 15:26
  O let us be m.! 232:17
  reader, I m. him 66:18
  unpleasing to a m. ear 331:30
  was m., charming, chaste 90:13
  woman's business to get m. 357:33
  young man m. is ... marred 224:16 309:8
Marries: signify whom one m. 298:21
Marrow: busk ye, my winsome m. 181:4
Marrow-bone: go down upon your m.-b.s 428:8
Marry: advise no man to m. 211:3
  better to m. than to burn 53:30
  come back and m. me 271:24
  doänt thou m. for munny 389:2
  every man should m. 141:4
  if I m., Sir Sampson 118:13
  m. come up! – you m., Ma'am 193:10
  m. ... the Recording Angel 375:15
  m. thee, purely to be rid of thee 118:23
  neither m. nor are given in marriage 49:12
  persuade him to m. one 234:13
  then I can't m. you 274:14
  they that m. ancient people 164:11
  they'd never m. 187:6
  to persons about to m. 293:11
  when a man should m.? 17:18
Mars: eye like M. 318:12
  this seat of M. 345:8
Marshal: baton of a m. of France 268:11
Marshonging: allonging and m. 135:17
Martini: into a dry M. 420:2
Martlet: temple-haunting m. 333:1
Martyr: about the graves of the m.s 376:9
  I am the M. of the People 106:5
  noble army of M.s 290:26
  set his heart on being a m. 418:8
Martyrdom: for the Moors, and m. 127:2
Marvel: match me such m. 80:4
Mary: born of the Virgin M. 290:31
  everywhere that M. went 180:11 273:4
  M. had a little lamb 180:11 273:4
  M. hath chosen that good part 50:23
  M.! I want a lyre 124:20
  M., M., quite contrary 273:5
  M. was that Mother mild 3:14
  my M.! 126:2

Milk – *contd*
m. of human kindness 81:29
m. to soak my bread 382:12
m. were scarce out of him 352:10
putting m. into babies 111:16
take my m. for gall 332:27
Milking: going a m.. sir 274:12
Mill: among these dark Satanic m.s 59:20
at the m. with slaves 259:9
m.s of God grind slowly 237:6
Milldam: bonnie m.s o' Binnorie 20:5
Miller: m. sees not all the water 85:24
than wots the m. of 351:2
there was a jolly m. 57:27
Million: mortal m.s live *alone* 11:29
Millionaire: hat on a Bradford m. 153:3
he must be a m. 167:27
M. That is my religion 357:26
Millionen: seid umschlungen, M.! 304:13
Mill-race: love ... drove her into the m.-r. 203:7
Millstone: m. were hanged about his neck 48:32
Milton: Chinese Wall of M. 153:19
England's M. equals both in fame 126:1
fell round the path of M. 422:11
M., a name to resound for ages 383:29
M. ... could cut a Colossus 210:8
M.'s the prince of poets 91:12
M.! thou shouldst be living 422:25
M. was for us 74:2
morals hold which M. held 422:27
more than M. can to justify 200:1
read not M. 95:27
reason M. wrote in fetters 61:20
some mute inglorious M. 177:11
Miminy-piminy: Francesca di Rimini, m.-p.
169:37
Min: is the old m. agreeable? 137:5
Mince: m. and slices of quince 232:19
Mind: affect little m.s 141:5
art to find the m.'s construction 332:20
as the m. is pitched 125:27
beauty ... exists in the m. 201:8
body filled and vacant m. 324:20
bring the philosophic m. 423:22
change your m. .... is to be ... free 15:1
clear your *m.* of cant 210:5
clothed and in his right m. 49:41
concentrates his m. wonderfully 209:17
dividing the swift m. 384:28
duty to speak one's m. 416:26
extend thy m. o'er all the world 258:36
farewell the tranquil m. 343:31
fate of all great m.s 305:1
fruitful ground, the quiet m. 377:16
gentle m. by gentle deeds 372:8
hath a maimed m. 164:8
his m. is open 64:14
hobgoblin of little m.s 155:5
I am not in my perfect m. 330:32
I callèd unto m. 371:2
I should not m. anything at all 15:25
in my m., of all mankind 21:3
in my m.'s eye 314:20
in the m. of man 421:21
infirmity of noble m. 254:26
let us with a gladsome m. 259:7
lose myself in other men's m.s 229:5

Mind – *contd*
man cannot have a pure m. 228:17
man's m. to move in charity 17:1
man's unconquerable m. 422:22
many sorts of m. as moss 287:14
march of the human m. 80:13
mighty m.s of old 370:20
m. a mother of immortal song 195:11
m. as narrow as the neck of a vinegar cruet
210:19
m., aspire to higher things 366:11
m. at peace with all 93:5
m. conscious of the right 404:19
m. deep in its fountain 89:6
m. forever voyaging 424:20
m. has mountains 195:1
m. is here o'erthrown 317:7
m. is its own place 255:27
m. not to be changed by place 255:27
m. quite vacant is a m. distressed 124:16
m. sees God in clouds 286:22
m. ... sways the mass 405:15
m. that maketh good or ill 372:9
m., that ocean 246:26
m., that very fiery particle 91:36
m. to me a kingdom is 150:8
m.s are not ever craving 126:12
m.s innocent and quiet 238:12
m.s like mine at least 77:5
minister to a m. diseased 335:18
moved slowly through the m. 424:17
my m. is troubled 351:27
never brought to m. 82:21
not with the eyes, but with the m. 339:29
nothing great but m. 181:5
of ... beauty is the m. diseased 89:19
persuaded in his own m. 53:18
pity the state of his m. 209:11
purest and most thoughtful m.s 302:10
refuge of weak m.s 109:6
robs the m. of all its powers 81:2
serve thee with a quiet m. 291:27
that spoke the vacant m. 172:8
those they have no m. to 86:12
to keep an even m. 197:16
to make up one's m. about nothing 219:17
triumph of m. over morals 417:26
unbent her m. .... over a book 228:24
unseemly exposure of the m. 185:4
uttereth all his m. 40:26
weak m.s led captive 258:33
yet is thy m. perplexed? 131:1
you are pleased to call your m. 413:25
Mindfulness: right m., right contemplation 79:1
Mine: deep in unfathomable m.s 123:17
excavating for a m. 264:10
love's undiscovered m.s 69:20
never can be m. 279:5
what's m. is yours 337:2
would she were m.! 236:2
Miner: dwelt a m., forty-niner 264:10
Minerva: M. when she talks 212:6
Mingle: m., you that m. may! 251:2
Minion: this morning morning's m. 195:13
Minister: m.s of grace defend us 315:6
one fair spirit for my m. 89:25
stickit m. 306:28

Morrow – *contd*
good-night till it be m 348:21
m. shall take thought for ... itself 47:19
ne'er be like his m. 361:12
there is a budding m. in midnight 218:7
trust as you can in the m. 197:10
windy night a rainy m. 356:8
Mors: pallida M. aequo pulsat pede 197:4
Morsel: as a sweet m. 187:2
m., cold upon dead Caesar's trencher 309:37
m. for a monarch 309:24
Mort: il n'y a pas de m.s 243:10
m., sans phrases 366:19
Ô M., vieux capitaine 24:19
Mortal: fools these m.s be! 340:16
gathers all things m. 380:23
like the early race of m.s 197:1
m. man be more just than God 33:39
m. thing so to immortalize 371:17
m.s, that would follow me 253:14
m.s, whose pleasures 124:11
no m. can bear 166:9
raised a m. to the skies 147:26
we m.s are capable of 409:12
we m.s cross the ocean 71:2
Mortalia: mentem m. tangunt 404:18
Mortality: it smells of m. 330:25
kept a watch o'er man's m. 423:24
m., behold and fear! 25:20
m. o'ersways their power 355:23
m.'s too weak to bear 271:12
m. weighs heavily on me 218:6
nothing serious in m. 334:2
old m. 69:14
to frail m. shall trust 19:13
Mortalium: ut prisca gens m. 197:1
Morti: certae occumbere m. 404:23
Morwe: seyn, of a ful misty m. 108:7
Mos: suo quoque m. 392:28
Moscow: go back to M. 108:22
Moses: climb where M. stood 411:6
Hand of M. on the Bough 158:15
Mosquito: word stung him like a m. 367:2
Most: he who did m., shall bear m. 77:11
make the m. on 'em 139:8
m. may err as grossly 147:8
Mot: m., c'est le Verbe 200:21
Mote: m. that is in thy brother's eye 47:21
thikke as m.s in the sonne-beem 107:38
Moth: but the m.s get into it 231:22
desire of the m. for the star 363:22
like ... a m. fretting a garment 35:25
m. and rust doth corrupt 47:12
m.s fluttering among the heath 67:1
unfading m.s, immortal flies 67:4
Mother: art thy m.'s glass 354:30
back to the great sweet m. 381:14
dearer was the m. for the child 116:11
disclaim her for a m. 167:4
does your m. know 23:5
don't tell my m. 187:12
from whence his m. rose 307:20
great care of his M. 251:22
happy he with such a m.! 390:17
his M., who was patient 279:9
I arose a m. in Israel 32:19
leave to your ain m. dear 20:14

Mother – *contd*
m. a lady, ... lovely and bright 306:6
m. cried, baby lept 179:2
m. drudge for his living at seventy 357:32
m. of all living 30:28
m. of months in meadow 380:4
m., wi' her needle and her shears 83:3
m. will never see you again 15:23
my m. didna speak 23:15
my m. groaned 60:12
never called me m. 419:23
never had any m. 376:17
O M., Mary M. 301:6
one whom his m. comforteth 44:14
stood the mournful m. 398:13
ten times our m. 317:27
was ever found a m. 166:12
women become like their m.s 416:21
you was a woman and a m. 137:30
Motion: between the m. and the act 152:8
God ordered m. 402:12
household m.s light and free 425:25
in his m. like an angel 339:1
little m. in the air 359:17
measured m. like a living thing 424:15
men a forward m. love 402:23
m. blushed at herself 342:28
m.s of his spirit are dull 339:3
no m. has she now 426:1
this sensible warm m. 336:23
two weeping m.s 127:5
with a mazy m. 116:2
Motley: m.'s the only wear 311:9
myself a m. to the view 356:22
Motto: I've gotten m. 419:4
my m. and my fate 378:21
Mould: and then broke the m. 9:21
m. yourself as you would wish 220:8
splashing the wintry m. 429:7
Mouldy: m. from over-keeping 104:9
Moulting: m. they're pretty revolting 268:19
Mount: I m.! I fly! 284:24
now he m.s above me 148:32
Mountain: beautiful must be the m.s 65:23
before the m.s were brought forth 37:5
flatter the m. tops 355:13
from Greenland's icy m.s 185:24
high m.s are a feeling 89:7
how the snowy m.s 8:18
if I never see another m. 229:11
misty m. tops 349:6
m. and hill shall be made low 43:22
m. in labour 227:10
m. leave to feed 318:13
m. tops that freeze 325:28
m.s are the beginning 302:5
m.s by the winter sea 384:24
m.s divide us and the waste 307:13
m.s interposed make enemies 124:31
m.s look on Marathon 91:7
m.s skipped like rams 38:2
m.s will be in labour 195:23
paced upon the m.s overhead 429:27
robes the m. in its azure hue 96:17
say unto this m., Remove 48:30
steepy m. yields 246:1
to the Delectable M.s 79:25

Nature – *contd*
N. wears one universal grin 158:6
n. yet remembers 423:18
N.'s ancient power was lost 385:33
n.'s copy's not eterne 334:13
n.'s handmaid, art 147:28
N.'s infinite book of secrecy 309:16
N.'s laws lay hid in night 285:19
N.'s soft nurse 322:30
n.'s truth is primary 395:9
n.'s white hand sets ope 127:8
n.'s works to me expunged 257:1
noble n. poetically gifted 12:26
observer of human n. 137:35
o'erstep not the modesty of n. 317:12
one touch of n. 351:25
opinion of their position in n. 248:25
representations of general n. 206:17
rest on N. fix 114:7
so priketh hem n. 106:18
them which is of other n.s 136:4
things rank and gross in n. 314:11
those which n. hath built 164:14
through n. to eternity 314:8
through n. up to n.'s God 287:9
'tis N.'s fault alone 110:28
'tis their n. to 410:17
to correct n. 406:22
to hold ... the mirror up to n. 317:13
voice of N. cries 177:17
wait on n.'s mischief 332:27
was N.'s darling laid 178:19
write and read comes by n. 341:24
you've conquered human n. 136:17
Nature: de corriger la n. 406:22
n. est un temple 24:14
Naught: it is n., saith the buyer 39:43
let it be for n. 70:5
maimed and set at n. 87:30
Navarre: helmet of N. 240:23
Nave: n. to the chaps 332:7
Navee: Ruler of the Queen's N.! 168:24
Navies: nation's airy n. 387:16
when n. are stranded! 306:21
Navy: God bless the N. 368:12
Nay: let ... your n. [be] n. 56:13
say n., say n., for shame! 427:21
Nazarene: restored ... by a N. physician 72:26
Nazareth: any good thing out of N. 51:22
Neaera: tangles of N.'s hair 254:25
Near: so n. and yet so far 386:1
while he is n. 44:3
Nearer: n., my God, to Thee 1:8
n. than hands and feet 384:3
Neat: n., but not gaudy 413:23
n., not gaudy 229:13
still to be n. 211:23
Neatness: condemns n. of apparel 413:22
Necessaries: provided with all n. 136:15
Necessary: action ... objectively n. 214:13
wondrous n. man 250:30
Nécessité: Je n'en vois pas la n. 9:20
Necessities: dispense with its n. 267:2
feigned n., imaginary n. 127:23
marked by its disregard for the n. 248:20
Necessity: find alone N. Supreme 396:23
n. hath no law 127:23

Necessity – *contd*
n. is the plea 282:13
n. knows no law 381:22
n., the tyrant's plea 257:16
n.'s sharp pinch 329:29
sworn brother ... to grim N. 346:13
teach thy n. to reason 345:5
thy n. is yet greater than mine 366:18
turns his n. to glorious gain 420:9
Necht: braw brecht moonlecht n. 231:3
Neck: Gilpin, n or naught 122:30
n. God made for other use 199:14
one n., one chin and so forth 352:12
people had only one n. 95:1
they had a lith in their n. 13:18
Nectarine: n., and curious peach 246:25
Ned: no more work for poor old N. 162:6
Need: n. of a world of men 75:5
n. to talk is a primary impulse 104:20
search of what he n.s 264:15
stress of n. in a hard life 406:12
to each according to his n.s 247:17
Needle: go through the eye of a n. 48:41
plying her n. and thread 193:20
true as the n. to the pole 63:16
wi' her n. and her shears 83:3
Needy: lifteth the n. 38:1
Negation: n. of God 170:28
Neglect: little n. may breed 162:16
sweet n. more taketh me 211:25
wise and salutary n. 80:8
Neglected: to have his all n. 207:6
Negligent: admired than by the n. 309:35
Negroes: n. in the West Indies 138:15
n. more philosophy displayed 91:20
Neige: n.s d'antan 404:10
Neighbour: after his n.'s wife 44:15
as ever coveted his n.'s goods 222:1
good fences make good n.s 163:11
hate your n. 242:11
love thy n. as thyself 32:1 48:38
n. whom he had promised to defend 241:13
our n. and our work farewell 219:22
our n.'s house is on fire 81:5
policy of the good n. 299:7
your n.'s wall is on fire 196:20
Neighed: n. after his neighbour's 44:15
Nell: pretty, witty N. 280:25
Nelly: let not poor N. starve 106:9
Nelson: good Lord N. 150:7
N. touch 269:11
of N. and the North 96:5
of N. only a touch 74:25
Neptune: chase the ebbing N. 350:23
flatter N. for his trident 313:4
great N.'s ocean 333:25
N.'s empire stands 313:35
siege of watery N. 345:9
Nero: last of the N.s! 399:21
Nerve: he ... strengthens our n.s 81:18
is weakness to expredge my n.s 136:13
n.s are bad to-night 152:34
nobody feels for my poor n.s 15:24
Nest: n. is in a watered shoot 300:7
n. of singing birds 206:31
their n.s in my beard! 232:5
Nesting: better give up bird n. 394:22

Nestor: though N. swear the jest 337:3
Net: fain would fling the n. 249:18
  fall into their own n.s 38:29
  in vain the n. is set 39:3
  n.s of wrong and right 428:23
Nettle: stroke a n. 189:20
Neutrality: armed n. 419:1
  just for a word, – 'n.' 29:19
Never: 'N., n.,' whispered 387:12
  n. to come there no more 122:7
  n. were, nor no man ever saw 349:16
  no more, oh, n. more! 359:2
  what n.? no, n.! 168:22
Nevermore: quoth the Raven, 'N.' 283:19
New: by whom the n. are tried 286:3
  I make all things n. 57:21
  n. things are made familiar 206:13
  no n. thing under the sun 40:36
  on with the n. 7:21
  ring in the n. 386:3
  something n. out of Africa 283:2
  to tell or to hear some n. thing 52:24
New South Wales: govern N. S. W. 28:1
New World: called the N. W. into existence 97:19
New York: little old N. Y. 187:5
New Zealand: some traveller from N. Z. 241:20
New-comer: O blithe n.-c.! 426:18
New-found-land: my n.-f.-l. 142:14
Newgate: condemned cells of N. 87:22
New-nothing-very-much-thank-you: just be the
  Brave N.-n.-v.-m.-t.-y. 275:27
News: brought me bitter n. 120:16
  everyone has ... a piece of good n. 30:3
  for evil n. rides post 259:22
  good n. from a far country 40:10
  good n. yet to hear 109:32
  man bites a dog that is n. 128:15
  master-passion is the love of n. 126:14
  nearly time for the n. 153:14
  never good to bring bad n. 309:32
  n. from all nations 125:10
  n. from the humming city 383:31
  n. much older than their ale 172:19
  n. that's fit to print 274:19
  n. value 295:17
  while good n. baits 259:22
Newspaper: men and morning n.s 281:23
  n.s always excite curiosity 229:6
  read the n.s 412:19
Newspeak: N. was the official language 275:13
Newstatesmanship: *people to mention* in N. 290:5
Newt: eye of n. 334:33
Newton: God said, 'Let N. be!' 285:19
  souls of five hundred ... N.s 117:5
  statue stood of N. 424:20
New-year: of all the glad N.-y. 388:26
Nexus: payment ... the sole n. 98:13
Nez: énorme, mon n.! 301:11
  pas plus loin que son n. 227:5
Niagara: wouldn't *live* under N. 99:31
Nice: much nicer in N. 418:19
  n. man ... of nasty ideas 379:24
  spice and all things n. 274:11
Nicest: n. people in the world 231:13
Nick: Satan, N., or Clootie 82:13
Nickie-ben: fare you weel, auld N.-b.! 82:15
Nickname: n. is the heaviest stone 185:15

Nicodemus: N. saw such light 402:13
Niger: left bank of the N. 133:20
Nigger: don't agree with n.s 238:22
  whar de good n.s go 162:6
Nigh: shall not come n. thee 37:12
Night: as darker grows the n. 173:24
  black it stood as n. 256:30
  borrower of the n. 334:6
  City is of N. 396:20
  come, civil n. 349:1
  come, seeling n. 334:16
  dead vast and middle of the n. 314:23
  even in the dead of n. 352:13
  every n. and alle 21:1
  few hours from the n. 265:8
  fled the shades of n. 257:29
  foul womb of n. 324:16
  God makes sech n.s 238:26
  hangs upon the cheek of n. 348:4
  hath n. to do with sleep 252:21
  how beautiful is n.! 370:24
  I cry ... in the n. season 35:5
  I in hoary winter's n. 371:1
  in beauty, like the n. 93:4
  in love with n. 349:2
  in such a n. 338:26
  in the dead of n. 322:11
  in the forests of the n. 60:16
  it was mirk, mirk n. 21:16
  it was the middle of the n. 101:16
  it will not last the n. 251:13
  lamps in a green n. 246:18
  lightning in the collied n. 339:28
  making n. do penance 424:23
  making n. hideous 315:8
  many a watchful n.! 323:13
  moon walks the n. 131:27
  mysterious N.! 414:9
  naughty n. to swim in 330:8
  n., and sleep in the n. 380:10
  n. darkens the streets 256:2
  N., eldest of things 256:32
  n. has a thousand eyes 64:7
  n. ... in its dusky wings 405:21
  n. is beginning to lower 236:11
  n. is dark, and I am far from home 270:11
  n. is drawing nigh 23:8
  n. is far spent 53:16
  n. is fine, the walrus said 101:22
  n. joint-labourer with the day 313:33
  n. long we have not stirred 75:25
  n. of time far surpasseth the day 69:17
  N., sable goddess! 430:8
  n. ... starless and bible-black 394:12
  n. that either makes me 344:10
  n. that first we met 25:10
  n.! this world's defeat 402:14
  n., thou n. so long expected 371:23
  n. unto n. sheweth knowledge 34:39
  n. was made for loving 93:17
  n. ... when no man can work 51:39
  n., where I in him might live 402:15
  n. with her train of stars 186:20
  n. with this her solemn bird 257:21
  n.'s black agents 334:17
  n.'s candles are burnt out 349:6
  n.s and feasts of the gods! 198:21

Ocean – *contd*

purposeless, glad o. comes 279:10
smooth o., smiling to betray 362:26
thou deep and dark blue o. 89:27
unfathomed caves of o. 177:10
upon a painted o. 114:22

O'clock: it is ten o'c. 311:6

October: golden O. declined 153:17
night in the lonesome O. 283:22

Octosyllabic: facility of o. verse 90:4

Odd: and this was scarcely o. 101:25
how o. of God 156:8
must find it exceedingly o. 225:27
nothing o. will do long 209:8
o. thing – as o. as can be 131:23
this was o., because it was 101:16

Odds: facing fearful o. 241:5
o. is gone 310:5

Ode: I intended an O. 141:23

Oderint: o., dum metuant 1:1

Odi: o. et amo 103:17

Odium: o. and aversion 119:14

Odour; o.s from the spicy shore 257:8
o.s, when sweet violets sicken 363:20
stealing and giving o.! 351:32

Odyssey: thunder of the O. 230:14

Œuf: pour se faire cuire deux æ.s 105:19

Œuvre: æ. sort plus belle 165:13

Offal: with this slave's o. 316:26

Offence: after o. returning 259:20
dire o. from am'rous causes 288:11
for a rock of o. 42:29
needs be that o.s come 48:33
o. is rank, it smells 318:7
yet detest th' o. 284:34

Offend: o. one of these little ones 48:32
o. us generally punished 400:4

Offended: for him have I o. 327:25

Offender: o.s who might well be underground 169:14

Offending: very head and front of my o. 342:25

Office: bringer ... hath but a losing o. 322:12
by o. boys for o. boys 303:16
clear in his great o. 333:4
imperfect o.s of prayer and praise 420:20
insolence of o. 316:29
o. and affairs of love 341:12
season, form, o. and custom 351:9

Office-boy: o.-b. to an Attorney's firm 168:24

Officer: never more be o. of mine 343:16

Offspring: o. of heav'n first-born 256:34
time's noblest o. is the last 29:17
true source of human o. 257:22

O'Grady: Colonel's Lady and Judy O'G. 223:18
Lily O'G., silly and shady 367:4

Ogre: famous men of old, the O.s 176:6

Oil: anointed with fresh o. 37:14
lamps with everlasting o. 252:25
o. to make his face to shine 37:22
with boiling o. in it, I fancy 169:24
words were softer than o. 36:9

Ointment: better than precious o. 41:10
like the precious o. 38:22

O.K.: O.K.-words 290:5

Old: darling, I am growing o. 296:7
friend, you never can be o. 356:13
good o. man, sir 341:32

Old – *contd*

grow o. along with me 75:31
grow o. with a good grace 373:7
grown o. before my time 300:15
I grow o. ... I grow o. 152:18
I have been young, and now am o. 35:22
lads that ... will never be o. 199:21
love everything that's o. 173:33
must be very o., Sir Giles 266:11
not o. but mellow 281:22
O. Age a regret 140:27
o. age is woman's hell 233:26
o. man who would not say his prayers 272:11
Public is an o. woman 99:26
ring out the o. 386:3
she is not yet so o. 338:12
some day before I'm o.! 223:12
they shall not grow o. 57:32
thinking of the o. 'un! 134:13
too o. to go again to my travels 106:10
too o. to learn 329:25
very o. are we men 131:9
when the o. man died 427:9
when they get to feeling o. 67:11
when you are o. and grey 429:25
where nobody gets o. 429:6
which should accompany o. age 335:17
woman as o. as she looks 117:7
you are o., Father William 100:11

Old Kent Road: knocked 'em in the O. K. R. 110:17

Oldest: o. hath borne most 331:7

O'Leary: with O'L. in the grave 429:19

Olive: ranged the o. stones 71:9

Olive-branches: o.-b. round thy table 38:19

Olive-leaf: in her mouth was an o.-l. 31:8

Olivia: cry out, 'O.' 352:13

Olores: inter strepere anser o. 406:9

Olympo: Pelion imposuisse O. 198:1

Olympum: frondosum involvere O. 406:13

Olympus: all O.' faded hierarchy 217:7

Ombrifuge: o. (Lord love you!) 95:10

Omen: quod di o. avertant 112:8

Omnes: o. eodem cogimur 197:17

Omnia: non o. possumus omnes 406:8

Omnipotent: to be o. but friendless 362:20

Omniscience: his foible is o. 369:23
his specialism is o. 145:10

One: great o.s eat up the little o.s 344:20
how to be o. up 290:3
more bright ... than O. who rose 360:12
must labour for the o. 90:5
o. and o., with a shadowy third 71:23
o. of us two, Herminius 241:2
O. remains the many change 359:13

One-and-twenty: when I was o.-a.-t. 199:16

One-horse: little o.-h. town 401:20

Onion: o. atoms lurk within the bowl 369:16
you're an o.! 203:3

Onward: little o. lend 259:8
o., the sailors cry 64:6

Open: movement into the o. 62:18
so o. that nothing is retained 64:14

Opening: always o. time 394:18

Operation: requires a surgical o. 369:6

Opes: inter o. inops 198:6

Ophir: from distant O. 247:25

Owl – *contd*

o. in an ivy-bush 379:14

O. looked up to the stars 232:16

o. that shrieked 333:18

o. .... was a-cold 215:6

o.s would have hooted in St Peter's 177:22

sings the staring o. 332:1

they bought an O. 232:15

two o.s and a hen 232:5

when o.s do cry 350:25

white o. in the belfry sits 391:18

Owlet: o. whoops to the wolf 115:8

Owl-song: sadder than o.-s.s 92:5

Own: came unto his o. 51:19

do what I will with mine o. 49:3

I never o. to it before her 134:2

ill-favoured thing, sir, but mine o. 312:20

think and call my o. 148:21

Owning: mania of o. 415:14

Ox: o. goeth to the slaughter 39:11

o. knoweth his owner 42:18

stalled o. and hatred therewith 39:30

thou shalt not muzzle the o. 32:10

Oxen: who drives fat o. 210:9

years like great black o. 428:14

Oxenford: Clerk ther was of O. 107:4

Oxford: clever men at O. 175:10

gently put back at O. 27:1

in O. made an art 148:14

reminds me ... of O. 190:1

to ... O. I acknowledge no obligation 167:4

to O. sent a troop of horse 69:21 399:13

twins of learning ... Ipswich and O! 326:12

Oxlip: bold o.s 354:13

o.s and the nodding violet 340:12

Oxus: shorn and parcelled O. 11:20

Oyster: made an uncommon fine o. 138:11

o. may be crossed in love 365:4

o. shop for mermaids 192:4

poverty and o.s 138:10

who first swallowed an o. 204:2

Oysterman: tall young o. 192:2

Ozymandias: my name is O. 362:1

P

Pace: and unperturbèd p. 395:15

creeps in this petty p. 335:23

divers p.s with divers persons 312:3

made three p.s through the room 386:36

no p. perceived 356:14

p. is too good to inquire 271:7

two p.s of the vilest earth 322:5

Pacem: qui desiderat p. 403:11

Pacific: stared at the P. 218:4

Pacis: p.que imponere morem 405:16

Pack-horse: p.-h. on the down 266:6

Paddington: as London is to P. 97:16

Paddock: cold as p.s though they be 189:12

Padlock: p. – on her mind 292:27

Padre: p. said, whatever have you 168:5

Pagan: p. suckled in a creed outworn 422:9

you find the p. – spoiled 430:19

Page: blotted from life's p. 88:25

hither, p., and stand by me 269:8

Page – *contd*

O sweet Anne P.! 339:16

on a beautiful quarto p. 365:24

Pageant: insubstantial p. faded 350:18

Pagoda: by the old Moulmein P. 223:32

Paid: he is well p. 338:25

we ha' p. in full! 224:14

Pain: after long grief and p. 388:24

calumny and hate and p. 359:10

doomed to go in company with P. 420:9

faint beneath the aromatic p. 419:6

gave p. to the bear 241:26

gentleman ... never inflicts p. 270:10

I believe I gave you some p. 118:32

I love to give p. 118:32

labour ... physics p. 333:28

made my p.s his prey 371:17

no living thing to suffer p. 362:11

no p., dear mother 7:15 156:15

no p. felt she 75:24

no p., no palm 280:15

nothing but the intermission of p. 308:9

of p., darkness and cold 75:29

our Lady of P. 380:15, 380:17

p. and anguish wring the brow 306:18

p. clings cruelly to us 215:1

p. in our little finger 184:16

p. of finite hearts 78:2

p. purchased, doth inherit p. 331:9

p. rises up, old pleasures pall 391:30

p.s to become what we now see 208:5

pleasure in poetic p.s 123:34

relieved their p. 172:10

shall there be any more p. 57:26

stranger yet to p. 178:7

surgeon's idea of p. 14:1

sympathize with people's p.s 202:8

tongueless vigil and all the p. 380:4

we are born in other's p. 395:13

wicked to deserve such p. 71:30

Paint: flinging a pot of p. 302:3

looking as fresh as p. 367:25

p. an inch thick 319:19

p.s men as they should be 226:14

sucked the p. all off 2:21

Painter: great p. dips his pencil 363:5

I hate all ... P.s 166:24

I only know of two p.s 414:2

Painting: difference between p. a face 164:4

I have heard of your p.s 317:5

two styles of portrait p. 136:22

Palace: gorgeous p. for a hermitage 346:2

gorgeous p.s 350:18

p. and a prison on each hand 89:12

spider ... is in the king's p.s 40:31

stately p. before him 79:16

Paladin: sing of knights and p.s 129:1

starry p. 77:21

Pale: in the winter's p. 354:5

p. as thy smock! 344:15

p., beyond porch and portal 380:23

p. kings and princes too 216:7

p. owing to the drains 13:5

prithee, why so p.? 377:7

Palestine: haven in sunny P. 247:25

Paling: piece-bright p. shuts 195:8

Pall: in sceptred p. 253:25

Path – *contd*
  p. of gold for him 75:5
  p. of the just is as the ... light 39:7
  p. on the sea's azure floor 360:2
  side of every p. we tread 125:32
  take the gentle p. 187:25
  thy p. be dark as night 243:1
  thy p.s drop fatness 36:20
Pathetic: that's what it is, p. 252:8
Patience: abusing of God's p. 339:12
  heard of the p. of Job 56:12
  in your p. possess ye 51:9
  like p. on a monument 352:28
  p. and shuffle the cards 105:9
  P. ... neighbour to despair 11:11
  p., to prevent that murmur 260:1
  p. will achieve more 81:19
  pattern of all p. 330:2
  poor are they that have not p.! 343:20
  though p. be a tired mare 324:2
  with p. He stands waiting 237:6
Patience: p. et longueur de temps 227:2
Patient: and kill the p. 18:23
  but not so p. 322:15
  p. etherised upon a table 152:11
Patine: thick inlaid with p.s 339:1
Patria: sed miles, sed pro p. 269:27
Patrick: ballad of Sir P. Spence 115:22
  to Sir P. Spens 21:9
Patrie: j'aimai ma p. 28:26
Patriot: all these country p.s 88:7
  p. of the world alone 97:13
  so to be p.s 81:25
  summer soldier and the sunshine p. 277:5
  true p.s we 24:9
Patriotism: p. is not enough 104:1
  p. ... last refuge of a scoundrel 209:5
Patron: best of all p.s 103:10
  p. and the jail 205:20
  P. Commonly a wretch 206:3
  p. of some thirty charities 390:19
  p. ... who looks with unconcern 207:7
Pattern: p. of excelling nature 344:12
Paunch: his p. grew mutinous 75:12
Pauper: p. in the midst of wealth 198:6
  p., whom nobody owns! 271:11
Paupertas: nil habet ... p. durius in se 213:19
Pause: intervals and happy p.s 19:9
  must give us p. 316:29
  nature made a p. 430:9
Pavement: scrub a kitchen p. 428:8
Pavilion: keep them secretly in a p. 35:18
Paviour: p.s cry, God bless you 156:3
Paw: Duchess! Oh my dear p.s 100:10
Pawn: yielding a p. thought to gain 68:24
Pay: I can't p., why I can owe 189:14
  I scent which p.s the best 238:25
  make me able to p. 280:18
  p. – p. – p.! 222:10
  shorter hours and better p. 5:8
  vow and not p. 41:8
  when will you p. me? 273:14
  wonders what's to p. 199:7
  work, and for what p.? 302:7
  ye must p. for one by one! 224:18
  you ought to p., you know 101:13
Paysage: un p. ... est un état de l'âme 4:6

Peace: all her paths are p. 39:5
  and calls it – p.! 88:14
  and on earth p. 50:12
  and slept in p. 326:7
  and the star of p. return 96:27
  any p. in ever climbing up? 388:1
  at once to sink to p. 385:18
  calm world and a long p. 321:33
  depart in p., according to thy word 50:13
  ease, and peaceful sloth, not p. 256:23
  eternal want of p. 392:18
  for ever hold his p. 292:5
  had Zimri p. 33:29
  hand carry gentle p. 326:4
  haunt of ancient P. 389:20
  I am for p. 38:9
  I see p. to corrupt 258:30
  I shall have some p. there 429:3
  if these should hold their p. 51:7
  in p. there's nothing so becomes 324:10
  inglorious arts of p. 247:3
  let him who desires p. 403:11
  made p. between us 234:4
  never was ... a bad p. 162:14
  no p. ... unto the wicked 43:34
  nor shall this p. sleep with her 326:14
  not p. at any price 205:5
  not to send p., but a sword 48:2
  on all the peaks lies p. 171:18
  our p. betrayed us; we betrayed our p. 267:4
  p. above all earthly dignities 326:2
  p. and consolation hath dismissed 259:27
  p. and rest can never dwell 255:21
  p. ... at any price 112:19
  p. be within thy walls 38:14
  p. comes dropping slow 429:3
  p., commerce, and honest friendship 204:14
  p. for our time ... p. with honour 105:16
  p. hath her victories 260:7
  p. I hope with honour 140:22
  p. in our time, O Lord 290:30
  p. is broken into pieces 193:12
  p. is crowned with smiles 402:16
  p. is in the grave 362:14
  p. is indivisible 235:11
  p. is of the nature of a conquest 323:10
  p. of God 55:9
  p. on earth, and mercy mild 413:14
  p. on the earth 307:18
  P. ... passes into ... Anaesthesia 414:16
  p., p., when there is no p. 44:16
  p. proclaims olives 356:19
  p., retrenchment and reform 66:10
  p. shall go sleep with Turks 346:7
  piping time of p. 346:22
  righteousness and p. have kissed 37:4
  seek p., and ensue it 35:21
  soft phrase of p. 342:26
  that publisheth p. 43:35
  they call it p. 381:25
  thousand years of p. 386:8
  under the semblance of p. 429:22
  what is p.? Is it war 133:27
Peaceable: most p. way for you 341:28
Peacemaker: blessed are the p.s 46:39
Peach: little p. in the orchard 157:12
Peacock: p.s and lilies 302:9

Peacock – *contd*
  pride of the p. 61:29
  who said, 'P. Pie'? 131:28
Peak: huge p., black and huge 424:14
  p. of summer's past 130:11
Peal: night's yawning p. 334:14
  wildest p. for years 190:15
Pear: go round the prickly p. 152:7
Pearl: earth with orient p. 257:30
  for p.s must dive below 148:30
  great anchors, heaps of p. 346:29
  ocean for orient p. 245:2
  p. in every cowslip's ear 340:4
  p. of great price 48:16
  p. ... richer than all his tribe 344:16
  p.s before swine 47:22
  she named the infant P. 184:12
  string of p.s to me 298:15
Peasant: p. sees, or dreams he sees 256:15
  yonder p. who is he? 269:8
Peasantry: p., their country's pride 172:4
Pease-porridge: p.-p. hot, p.-p. cold 273:17
Pebble: chose a p. from the brook 123:10
  not the only p. on the beach 64:16
  on the unnumbered idle p.s chafes 330:20
  smoother p. or a prettier shell 270:14
Pebble-stone: see this p.-s.? 95:9
Peccator: esto p. et pecca fortiter 239:20
Peccavi: p. [I have Scinde] 268:5
Pécher: pas p. que p. en silence 262:16
Pectora: quid non mortalia p. cogis 405:6
Peculiar: extensive and p. 138:7
  secret way p. to himself 135:9
Pecuniary: immense p. Mangle 139:10
Peel: d'ye ken John P. 176:2
  I'm going to p. you 203:3
Peer: being ... all the Twelve P.s 104:6
  fare like my p.s 75:29
  House of P.s, throughout the war 169:6
  in the P.s will take his place 68:3
  rhyming p. 285:5
Peerage: I shall have gained a p. 269:14
  you should study the P. 417:18
Pegasus: wind a fiery P. 321:31
Peine: abolir la p. de mort 214:15
Pelican: p. of the wilderness 37:20
  Ploffskin, Pluffskin, P. 232:20
  wonderful bird is the p. 250:23
Pelio: imponere P. Ossam 406:13
Pelion: P. imposuisse Olympo 198:1
Pellenore: Pelleas, or P. 258:34
Pellinore: train all the P.s 414:11
Pen: clerk ... who p.s a stanza 285:5
  dip their p.s in ... human kindness 81:29
  I'll make thee glorious by my p. 264:9
  made a rural p. 60:20
  my p. ran cold 408:13
  Owl and the Waverley p. 4:17
  p. has gleaned my teaming brain 218:11
  p. in his hand ... becomes a torpedo 206:33
  p. is mightier 240:13
  p. of a ready writer 35:30
  some daemon stole my p. 284:5
  with such acts fill a p. 145:24
  write, p. 331:14
Penalty: abolish the death p. 214:15
Pence: loss of p. ... would trouble 122:28

Pence – *contd*
  take care of the p. 108:28
Pendre: ils commencent ici par faire p. un homme
  262:10
Penetrate: seize and clutch and p. 153:9
Penny: nobody seemed one p. the worse 22:13
  one a p., two a p. 272:15
  p. for a song 428:10
  shall have but a p. a day 273:25
Pensée: fait venir de coupables p.s 262:13
  paroles ... déguiser leurs p.s 407:7
  p. ... pour autoriser leurs injustices 407:7
Pensioner: miser's p. 426:2
Pentameter: p. aye falling in melody 116:9
Pent-house: upon his p.-h. lid 332:8
Penury: p. repressed their noble range 177:9
People: all p. that on earth 220:19
  approaching springtime of the p.s 63:18
  beggarly p.! a church 378:22
  cry of the Little P.s 233:12
  don't dink mooch of p.s 233:19
  from the p. and for the p. 141:9
  God's pampered p. 146:17
  good of the p. is the chief law 112:1
  good p. all, of every sort 174:14
  good p.'s wery scarce 139:8
  hath comforted his p. 43:37
  here are the p. 272:12
  in Scotland supports the p. 206:2
  indictment against a whole p. 80:12
  look after our p. 305:7
  Lord prefers common-looking p. 235:5
  new-caught, sullen p.s 224:28
  no vision, the p. perish 40:27
  of the p., by the p. 235:1
  opponent of the chosen p. 12:9
  other p. are quite dreadful 416:12
  other p. to be ... to your liking 220:8
  peculiar p. 56:16
  p. all exulting 415:3
  p. begin to reason 407:17
  p. imagine a vain thing 34:22
  p. taut for war 395:10
  p. to be very agreeable 16:6
  p. who can't get into it 417:4
  p. who left that station 152:2
  p. whose annals are blank 98:26
  p.'s judgement always true 147:8
  p.'s voice is odd 289:6
  pills for pale p. 4:13
  some of the p. all the time 235:4
  speak not when the p. listens 306:25
  subdue the p. under us 36:1
  thy p. shall be my p. 32:33
  thy p. still are fed 141:26
  two p. ... hit on the same thought 364:27
  voice of the p. 3:8
  what kind of a p. do they think we are? 111:13
  what the p. think so 81:31
  ye are the p. 34:3
  ye beat my p. to pieces 42:22
Pepper: peck of pickled p. 273:18
Peppered: I have p. two of them 321:5
Perception: doors of p. were cleansed 62:4
  prime agent of all human p. 116:17
Percy: P. out of Northumberland 20:9
  song of P. and Douglas 366:15

Philosophy – *contd*
 p. drawn from examples 140:5
 p. inclineth ... to atheism 18:4
 p. is a good horse 173:25
 P. should push beyond her mark 385:24
 p. ... the handmaid to religion 16:16
 p., the lumber of the schools 378:13
 p. to be substantially true 304:3
 p. will clip an angel's wings 216:10
 wisdom all and false p. 256:28
Phoebus: before the wheels of P. 342:12
 bright P. in his strength 354:13
 P., arise 146:12
 P. 'gins arise 313:16
 towards P.' lodging 348:35
 wheels of P.' wain 252:24
Phoenician: drowned P. Sailor 152:28
Phoenix: dies, the maiden p. 326:14
Phone: Why Did You Answer the P.? 397:16
Phrase: p. by which such things are settled 91:31
 p. would be more german 319:33
 sudden, unintelligible p. 279:7
 taffeta p.s 331:27
 with a grandsire p. 347:28
Phyllida: P., my P.! 141:22
Phyllis: neat-handed P. dresses 254:8
Physic: throw p. to the dogs 335:19
Physician: died last night of my p. 292:35
 help of too many p.s 3:10
 honour a p. 46:19
 is there no p. there? 44:18
 p., heal thyself 50:16
 time is the great p. 140:30
 whole need not a p. 47:34
Physique: leçon de p. expérimentale 407:3
Pia mater: never stretched the *p. m.* 68:19
Pianist: do not shoot the p. 417:33
Pianoforte: p., a lap-dog 98:10
Piano-playing: dey had p.-p. 233:21
Picardy: roses are flowering in P. 411:22
Piccadilly: good-bye P. 418:10
Picker-up: p.-u. of learning's crumbs 72:25
Picking: from p. and stealing 291:40
Pickle: camest thou in this p. 350:27
Pickwick: P., the Owl 4:17
Pickwickian: word in its P. sense 137:34
Pictura: ut p. poesis 196:4
Picture: all his p.s faded 60:4
 Earth's last p. is painted 224:26
 exquisite p. of human manners 167:3
 look here upon this p. 318:12
 one ... goes to a p. gallery 249:2
 p. ... a thing and a thought 277:12
 p., placed the busts between 65:7
 p.s for the page atone 284:4
 p.s in our eyes 142:18
 reader, look not on his p. 212:10
 without p.s or conversations 100:5
Pie: Bellamy's veal p.s 282:17
 when the p. was opened 273:27
Piebald: peeled, patched, and p. 284:10
Piece: I took her to p.s 118:26
 old, revived new p. 284:6
 peace is broken into p.s 193:12
 thirty p.s of silver 49:26
Pie-crust: promises and p.-c. 379:12
Piedmontese: P. that rolled mother 260:5

Pieman: Simple Simon met a p. 273:26
Pier: from this here p. 23:3
Pierian: deep of the P. spring 146:2
 taste not the P. spring 285:24
Pietate: reddite mi hoc pro p. mea 103:16
Piety: bound ... by natural p. 422:17
 mistaken and over-zealous p. 80:20
 nor all thy P. nor Wit 159:11
 to p. more prone 3:16
Piffle: as p. before the wind 13:9
Pig: as naturally as p.s squeak 86:4
 dear P. are you willing 232:18
 little p. went to market 274:4
 looked from p. to man 275:9
 selling of p. in a poke 400:22
 stole a p. and away 274:8
 whether p.s have wings 101:21
Piggy: said the P. I will 232:18
Piggy-wig: in a wood a P.-w. stood 232:17
Pigmy-body: fretted the p.-b. 146:20
Pilate: said jesting P. 16:26
 suffered under Pontius P. 290:31
Pile: earn a monumental p. 124:27
Pilgrim: came forth with p. steps 259:5
 forth, p., forth! 106:16
 land of the p.s and so forth 128:3
 longer ... excepting ... *P.'s Progress* 211:5
 onward goes the p. band 23:12
 P. of Eternity 359:6
 p. of the sky! 426:23
 p. soul in you 429:26
 P.'s Progress, about a man 401:2
 p.s passinge to and fro 107:26
 strangers and p.s on the earth 55:39
 tired p.'s limbs affected 97:5
 to be a p. 79:31
Pilgrimage: folk to goon on p.s 106:18
 I'll take my p. 295:10
 inn and quiet p. 97:4
 my p.'s last mile 142:30
 overtaketh in his p. 353:24
 with songs beguile your p. 160:6
Pill: death ... lay in every p. 165:8
 out-lived the doctor's p. 166:5
 P. for curing ... Society 99:10
 p. which none of us can bear 211:1
 p.s ... against an earthquake 2:17
 pink p.s for pale people 4:13
Pillage: p. they with merry march 323:26
Pillar: antique p.s massy proof 253:30
 builded over with p.s of gold 59:13
 triple p. of the world 309:13
Pillicock: P. sat on P.-hill 330:5
Pillow: finds the down p. hard 313:22
 like a p. on a bed 142:17
Pilot: daring p. in extremity 146:20
 P. of the Galilean lake 254:29
 p. of the living God 249:11
 P. that weathered the storm 97:18
 see my P. face to face 383:16
Pimpernel: demmed, elusive P. 275:3
Pimple: p. on her nose 297:5
Pin: have heard a p. drop 298:20
 in merry p. 123:2
 little p. bores through 345:22
 nor heed the crooked p.s 193:22
 pinned it wi' a siller p. 21:24

Plough: p. the wave no more 123:23
  tested his first p. 71:11
  wherefore p. for the lords 363:10
Ploughman: heavy steps of the p. 429:7
  p. homeward plods 176:21
Ploy: one p. of Gattling's 290:4
Pluck: p. it [thine eye] out 48:34
Plum: among the p.s 190:20
  biscuit or confectionary p. 124:1
  pulled out a p. 272:29
  some gave them p. cake 272:26
Plume: see my white p. shine 240:23
Plummet: did ever p. sound 350:24
Plumpskin: P., Ploshskin, Pelican 232:20
Plunder: take your ill-got p. 270:4
  what a place to p. 62:11
Plundered: there he p. snug 284:3
Plunge: p. in a pool's living water 77:6
Plures: abiit ad p. 281:16
Pluto: tears down P.'s cheek 253:26
  won the ear of P. 254:16
Pneumatic: girl. Wonderfully p. 202:6
Poacher: p. a keeper 221:23
Pobble: P. who has no toes 232:21
  p.s are happier without their toes 233:2
Pocket: fill my p.s with change 136:29
  not scruple to pick a p. 132:3
  pot into the middle p. 108:17
  put it in his p. 318:15
  young man feels his p.s 199:7
Pocket-handkerchief: p.-h. before his streaming
  eyes 101:24
Pocket-money: furnished with p.-m. 136:15
Pod: when the p.s went pop 129:21
Poe: comes P., with his raven 239:2
Poem: it is a pretty p., Mr Pope 29:14
  ought himself to be a true p. 260:11
  p. lovely as a tree 221:4
  p. unlimited 316:11
  p.s are made by fools 221:5
  rhyme ... [no] true ornament of p. 255:14
Poesis: ut pictura p. 196:4
Poesy: drainless shower of light is p. 217:13
  force of heaven-bred p. 353:26
  on the viewless wings of P. 217:2
  p. is as a gum 350:29
  that I may overwhelm myself in p. 217:12
Poet: all p.s are mad 85:11
  business of a p. ... is to examine 206:24
  certain also of your own p.s 52:27
  English p.s after my death 219:9
  ever yet a great p. 116:22
  God is the perfect p. 75:2
  Gray, a born p. 12:13
  I hate all p.s 166:24
  like a P. hidden 364:9
  lunatic, the lover, and the p. 340:25
  muse on Nature with a p.'s eye 96:20
  no person can be a p. 242:7
  not deep the P. sees 11:4
  p., and of the Devil's party 61:20
  p. could not but be gay 421:7
  p. is the most unpoetical 219:11
  p.'s made as well as born 212:17
  p. sing it with such airs 428:10
  p. soaring in the high region 260:21
  p. without love 98:11

Poet – *contd*
  p.'s eye in a fine frenzy 340:26
  p.'s pen turns them to shapes 340:26
  p.s better prove 355:12
  p.s ... have ... licence 195:18
  p.s in their misery dead 425:18
  p.s [make men] witty 19:4
  P.s militant below 121:19
  p.s of the proud old lineage 160:6
  p.s painful vigils keep 284:2
  P.s ... sown by Nature 420:18
  p.s that have never versified 366:13
  p.s that lasting marble seek 408:4
  p.s ... unacknowledged legislators 364:19
  p.s' food is love and fame 360:4
  should possess a p.'s brain 146:1
  souls of p.s dead and gone 216:11
  stand still, true p. 75:21
  things that the first p.s had 145:25
  three p.s, in three distant ages 148:9
  to a p. nothing can be useless 206:23
  touchy tribe of p.s 196:24
  when the P. dies ... Nature mourns 305:26
  which only p.s know 124:34
  worst of all p.s 103:10
  you will never be a p. 149:21
Poetaster: hunt a p. down 92:24
Poète: P. ... semblable au prince des nuées 24:12
Poetess: maudlin p. 285:5
Poetical: gods had made thee p. 312:5
  verges on the p. 138:20
Poetis: p. quidlibet audendi semper fuit ... potestas
  195:18
Poetry: as a friend he drops into p. 137:21
  as in painting, so in p. 196:4
  can even enjoy p. 242:7
  cradled into p. by wrong 360:20
  Fleshly School of P. 78:15
  genuine p. is conceived 10:14
  hate p. that has a palpable design 218:29
  if p. comes not as naturally 219:2
  in whining P. 144:2
  language .. never language of p. 178:25
  mincing p. 321:20
  not p., but prose run mad 285:11
  p. a mere mechanic art 124:24
  p. almost necessarily declines 242:6
  p. = the *best* words 117:1
  P. ... finer spirit of all knowledge 427:4
  p. is as exact a science 160:1
  p. is conceived in their wits 12:14
  p. is founded on the hearts of men 64:3
  p. is more philosophical 10:2
  p. is ... more than good sense 117:4
  p. is not the proper antithesis 116:24
  P. is the spontaneous overflow 427:5
  p. ... record of the best ... moments 364:18
  p.'s a mere drug, Sir 157:2
  p.'s unnat'ral; no man ever talked p. 138:19
  p. should be great and unobtrusive 218:29
  p. should surprise by a fine excess 219:1
  p. strays into my memory 200:6
  p., which is in Oxford made 148:14
  p. would be made subsequent 260:20
  religious p. ... by the undevout 200:4
  resuscitate the dead art of p. 290:12
  sir, what is p.? 209:14

Poetry – *contd*
stars ... the p. of heaven! 89:8
when p. has a meaning 200:5
where is p. to be found? 206:14
Point: none of them p. away 196:9
not to put too fine a p. 133:24
p. of the turning world 151:27
p.s of heaven and home! 426:24
think of all their good p.s 357:23
thus I bore my p. 321:5
you've missed the p. 153:10
Poison: bitter p. to others 239:18
coward's weapon, p. 160:22
p. us, do we not die? 338:5
strongest p. ever known 58:28
turning to P. while the bee-mouth 216:23
Poisoner: *Lives of the Great P.s* 394:21
my little sister the p. 27:7
Poker: p.s into true-love knots 116:8
Pole: all sights from p. to p. 11:22
beloved from p. to p.! 115:3
expotition to the North P. 252:12
soldier's p. is fallen 310:5
Police: Thought P. mattered 275:11
Policeman: ask a p.! 298:12
p.'s lot is not a happy one 170:2
Polish: p. it ... and p. it 62:23
Polissez: p.-le sans cesse et le repolissez 62:23
Politely: most p., most p.! 170:5
Politeness: glance of great p. 94:2
very pineapple of p. 365:14
Politesse: p. des rois 238:7
Political: man ... a p. animal 10:4
that points clearly to a p. career 357:29
Politician: I'm not a p. 409:28
like a scurvy p., seem to see 330:28
p. is an arse 128:5
p. is he who says 299:19
p.s neither hope nor hate 146:25
whole race of p.s 379:2
Politics: confound their p. 98:6
continuation of p. by other means 112:20
finality is not the language of p. 140:13
my p., like my religion 409:19
out of the range of practical p. 170:24
p. is no exact science 58:2
p. is ... the only profession 375:2
p. like ours profess 178:28
p. we bar 170:4
Politik: Fortsetzung der P. mit anderen Mitteln 112:20
Polka: see me dance the p. 367:3
Poll: talked like poor P. 165:2
Polly: depends poor P.'s life 165:24
our P. is a sad slut! 165:21
Poltague: to tempt my Lady P. 28:13
Polygamy: before p. was made a sin 146:14
Pomegranate: on yon p. tree 349:5
Pomp: grinning at his p. 345:22
in lowly p. ride on 251:20
p.s and vanity 291:38
puts all the p. to flight 285:1
take physic, p. 330:4
vain p. and glory 326:1
Pompilia: our P., faultless 76:27
P.. will you let 77:4
Pond: mantle like a standing p. 337:6

Pontic: like to the P. sea 343:36
Ponto: 'P.!' he cried 27:27
Poodle: you slawzy p. 163:21
Pooh-Bah: P.-B. (Lord High Everything Else) 169:9
Pool: mantle of the standing p. 330:9
where the p.s are bright and deep 191:27
Poor: anger ... [keeps men] p. 16:19
apt the p. are to be proud 353:3
as for the virtuous p. 417:34
blessed are the p. 46:38
destruction of the p. 39:15
father to the p. 34:10
foundst me p. 172:26
grind the faces of the p. 42:22
hail, the p. man's day 175:6
he that considereth the p. 35:26
how many p. I see! 410:13
I am as p. as Job 322:15
if you was as p. 358:16
inconvenient to be p. 122:5
p. always ye have 51:43
p. and the maimed, and the halt 50:31
p. but honest 309:6
p. but she was honest 8:5
p. have become poorer 364:17
p. in a loomp is bad 389:4
p. man at his gate 3:12
p. man loved the great 241:7
p. what gets the blame 8:8
p., yet hast thou golden slumbers? 131:1
raiseth up the p. out of the dust 38:1
simple annals of the p. 177:4
that plenty should attain the p. 88:8
too p. for a bribe 178:23
Pope: better to err with P. 92:16
Dryden, P., and all their school 12:14
how many divisions has the P.? 373:3
if P. be not a poet 206:14
since I am a man I can become p. 104:23
their Priests, their P.s 72:5
to read ... [P.] you need only count 116:25
washing the hands of the P. 22:11
Popery: antiquity inclines a man to P. 164:6
Poplar: p.s are felled 124:5
Poppet: it's no go, my p. 243:5
Poppies: drowsed with the fume of p. 218:19
p. blow between the crosses 242:17
Poppy: blindly scattereth her p. 69:16
left the flushed print in a p. 396:3
not p., nor mandragora 343:29
Populace: Barbarians, Philistines, and P. 12:1
Popular: nothing can render them p. 379:21
war ... will cease to be p. 417:30
Popularité: p.? ... la gloire en gros sous 201:4
Popularity: p. is a crime 180:14
Population: only talked of p. 174:5
Populi: salus p. suprema est lex 112:1
vox p., vox Dei 3:8
Porcelain: p. clay of humankind 149:7
Pore: p. by the hour 22:16
Porpentine: quills upon the fretful p. 315:12
Porpoise: p. close behind us 100:28
Porridge: receives comfort like cold p. 350:3
Porsena: Lars P. of Clusium 241:4
Port: all dissolved in p. 284:14
ancient tales and p. 28:17

Port – *contd*
  close the five p.s of knowledge 68:13
  go fetch a pint of p. 392:16
  p. after stormy seas 372:1
  p. for men 209:25
  p. is near 415:3
  p.s and happy havens 345:5
Portae: geminae Somni p. 405:17
Portal: P.s are alternate Night and Day 158:24
Portcullis: let the p. fall 306:16
Porte: p. soit ouverte ou fermée 267:17
Porter: mechanic p.s crowding 323:26
  mister p., what shall I do? 235:15
  moon shone bright on Mrs P. 153:2
Portion: p. of a good man's life 421:14
  p. of that around me 89:7
  p.s ... of the dreadful Past 387:36
  they have no p. in us 145:3
  wales a p. with judicious care 83:5
Portrait: always a p. of himself 87:23
  every time I paint a p. 304:5
  P. of the Artist 212:27
Pose: combine a p. imperious 168:20
Posh: two p. papers on a Sunday 275:21
Posies: pocket full of p. 273:23
  thousand fragrant p. 246:3
Position: one p., wrong for years 14:6
Possessed: I have p. 92:33
  limited in order to be p. 81:32
Possessing: too dear for my p. 356:6
  yet p. all things 54:29
Possession: he had great p.s 48:40
  my p.s for a moment of time 153:27
  p. of it is intolerable 402:5
Possibilities: to believe only p. 69:2
Possibility: unconvincing p. 10:3
Possible: O that 'twere p. 388:24
  with God all things are p. 48:42
Possunt: p. quia posse videntur 405:11
Post: place with only one p. 369:21
  p. o'er land and ocean 260:1
Postboy: never ... see a dead p. 139:6
Post-chaise: driving rapidly in a p.-c. 209:10
  in a p.-c. with a pretty woman 209:16
Posterior: p.s of this day 331:26
Posterity: P. doing something for us 2:16
  think of your p. 1:6
  what has p. done? 297:6
Postero: quam minimum credula p. 197:10
Posthumously: some are born p. 271:2
Postscript: all the pith is in the p. 184:18
  most material in a p. 18:12
Postume: fugaces, P., P., labuntur anni 197:20
Posture: same our p.s were 142:19
  this semi-recumbent p. 416:19
Pot: deep to boil like a p. 34:18
  Joan doth keel the p. 332:1
  kettle and the earthen p. 46:8
  may all go to p. 173:18
  there is death in the p. 33:25
  who the P.? 159:16
Potation: forswear thin p.s 323:12
  p.s pottle-deep 343:11
Potato: for a bashful young p. 169:34
Potomac: quiet along the P. 242:16
Potoribus: scribuntur aquae p. 196:21
Pottage: birthright for a mess of p. 31:16

Potter: dash them ... like a p.'s vessel 34:23
  hath not the p. power 53:5
  who *is* the P.? 159:16
Pouch: and p. on side 311:14
Pouched: you've p. the ... money 22:7
Pouncet-box: held a p.-b. 320:19
Pound: draw for a thousand p.s 2:18
  I'll give thee a silver p. 96:13
  passing rich with forty p.s 172:9
  p.s will take care of themselves 108:28
  six-hundred p.s a year 378:10
  'tis for a thousand p.! 122:32
Pour: p. on him all we can 188:4
  p. out to all that wull 371:21
Poverty: crime so shameful as p. 156:20
  in a state of ambitious p. 213:21
  neither p. nor riches 40:28
  p. and oysters 138:10
  p., but not my will 349:9
  p. ... has no harder pang 213:19
  p. is no disgrace 369:2
  p. of goods is easily cured 263:24
  p.'s catching 27:17
  worth by p. depressed 205:14
Powder: food for p. 321:34
  keep your p. dry 58:5
  your p.'s runnin' low 269:28
Power: against principalities, against p.s 55:3
  all p. is a trust 141:9
  defy P., which seems omnipotent 363:1
  does not know you, O heavenly p.s 171:20
  earthly p. doth then show 338:17
  empire is no more than p. 146:28
  fear of some divine ... p.s 85:25
  fooled by these rebel p.s 357:3
  force of temporal p. 338:17
  genius is a mind of large general p s 206:7
  greater the p. 80:24
  I, who saw p. 76:4
  if something from our hands have p. 425:20
  in thy will is my p. to believe 77:10
  nobility is but the act of p. 17:34
  paltered with eternal God for p. 389:13
  pomp of p. 177:5
  p. belongeth unto God 36:16
  p. is gone, which nothing can restore 420:15
  p. tends to corrupt 1:2
  p.s that be 53:13
  P.s which ... our minds impress 420:26
  princedoms, virtues, p.s 257:37
  principalities nor p.s 53:3
  sing his p. and his love! 175:12
  some P. the giftie gie us 84:25
  strange desire to seek p. 17:23
  subject unto the higher p.s 53:12
  to Jesus for the cleansing p. 191:3
  we lay waste our p.s 422:8
  with voluntary p. instinct 424:14
Powerful: p. goodness want 362:12
Practice: my p. is never very absorbing 145:9
  P. drives me mad 6:3
  ruinous in p. 80:21
  without having good p. 210:23
Practise: p. this without me 365:1
Prague: beautiful city of P. 293:9
Praise: all his pleasure p. 278:3
  all things thou wouldst p. 131:16

Praise – *contd*
- alms of thy superfluous p. 146:4
- approbation ... is p. indeed 266:20
- beauty is past change: p. him 195:5
- censure ... is oblique p. 209:22
- dispraised were no small p. 258:35
- high p.s of God 38:33
- however do p. ourselves 352:24
- if there be any p. 55:10
- let his just p. be given 409:14
- let us now p. famous men 224:15
- mouth shall shew forth thy p. 290:23
- our noble England's p. 240:19
- p. him and magnify him 290:28
- p. him upon the loud cymbals 39:1
- p. the Lord! ye heavens 220:11
- some p. at morning 286:10
- stir a little p. of dust 385:35
- swells the note of p. 177:6
- they only want p. 248:22
- thou hast perfected p. 49:6
- to refuse p. 297:20
- to their right p. 339:5
- utter all thy p. 2:8

Praised: more in him to be p. 212:21

Praising: doing one's p. for oneself 87:26
- p. the way things were 195:25
- p. what is lost 309:11

Prattle: thinking his p. to be tedious 346:14

Pray: as lief p. with Kit Smart 207:21
- go away and cannot p. 151:23
- going to p. for you 369:25
- inadequate to p. for my sons 163:20
- live more nearly as we p. 219:24
- one to p. 2:22
- p. all the livelong day 60:13
- p. for us now 151:17
- p. without ceasing 55:17
- remained to p. 172:14
- whatever a man p.s for 400:15
- whene'er he went to p. 174:15
- where I may mourn and p. 389:22

Prayed: he's p. for my soul 224:2
- this was what I p. for 198:20

Prayer: and feed on p.s 280:12
- be called a house of p. 49:5
- better than good men's p.s 104:14
- Christopher Robin is saying his p.s 252:1
- fall to thy p.s 323:20
- for a pretence make long p.s 50:6
- four spend in p. 114:7
- have the p.s of the church 379:18
- homes of silent p. 385:17
- let the p. re-echo 235:8
- lift not hands of p. 384:35
- make mention of you in my p.s 52:39
- more things are wrought by p. 384:34
- O thou that hearest p. 36:19
- people's p. 146:26
- pray but one p. for me 266:14
- p. all his business 278:3
- p. makes ... armour bright 123:15
- p. reduces itself to this 400:15
- p.s in the hall 13:6
- rises from p. a better man 250:19
- same p. doth teach us all 338:17
- so deaf to my p.s 220:5

Prayer – *contd*
- thought ... is the most perfect p. 234:7

Prayer-book: p.-b.s are the toys of age 287:3

Prayeth: p. best, who loveth 115:13
- p. well, who loveth 115:12

Praying: now he is p. 318:8
- p. only acts as an obbligato 163:20

Preach: as never sure to p. again 25:2

Preached: deserves to be p. to death 369:18

Preacher: p.s say, Do as I say 308:11

Preaching: better than any p. 155:7

Precedent: create good p.s 17:24
- from p. to p. 392:22
- p. embalms a principle 140:11 307:16

Precept: by p. and by example 92:17
- example ... more efficacious than p. 206:27
- p. must be upon p. 43:6
- p.s for the teacher's sake 192:11

Precious: p. in the sight of the Lord 38:5
- were most p. to me 335:9

Precise: p. and taciturn 261:2

Precisian: devil turned p.! 248:14

Predecessor: one of my illustrious p.s 157:17

Predestination: p. in ... connectin'-rod 223:26
- with P. round 159:14

Predestinator: Assistant P. 202:4

Prediction: p.s ought to serve 18:31

Prees: flee fro the p. 106:16

Preferment: knocking at P.'s door 11:8
- so I gained p. 7:17

Prejudice: I am ... a bundle of p.s 228:18
- p. runs in favour of two 136:16

Preparation: no p. is thought necessary 375:2

Prepared: p. for either event 404:23

Presager: p.s of my speaking breast 355:5

Presbyter: new P. is but old Priest 260:6

Presbyterian: P. true blue 86:9

Presence: conspicuous by its p. 302:17
- lord of thy p. 328:21
- p. that disturbs me 421:21
- scanter of your maiden p. 315:3

Present: act in the living P.! 237:2
- future, predominate over the p. 206:5
- P. has latched its postern 181:13
- p. in spirit 53:27
- p. it! – Oh! to whom? 363:4
- p.s ... endear absents 228:14
- things p., worst 322:20

Presentation: under the p. of that 312:23

Presentment: counterfeit p. 318:12

Preserver: p.; hear, oh, hear! 361:14

Presided: p. rather than ruled 140:25

President: perpetual p. 99:32

Press: fell dead-born from the p. 201:10
- god of our idolatry, the P. 124:12
- governs the periodical p. 400:5
- I am ... a gentleman of the P. 140:14
- liberty of the P. is the *Palladium* 213:7
- we p. too close in church and mart 70:10

Press-men: so we be named P.-m. 10:10

Presumption: Amused by its P. 397:15

Pretence: p.s to break known rules 127:23

Pretender: no harm in blessing – the P. 38:5

Pretending: p. ... to gifts of the Holy Ghost 85:30

Prêteuse: fourmi n'est pas p. 226:18

Pretio: omnia ... cum p. 213:22

Probability: p. is the very guide 85:29
Probationer: yet a young p. 148:23
Probitas: p. laudatur et alget 213:14
Problem: clearing the world of its ... p.s 137:25
  quite a three-pipe p. 145:8
Proceeding: p.s interested him no more 184:6
Process: p. of the suns 387:20
Procession: their dances were p. 120:5
Proconsul: great P. 241:23
Procrastination: from that to incivility and p. 132:10
  p. is the thief of time 430:12
Procreate: we might p. like trees 69:8
Procreation: for the p. of children 292:4
  main road of p. 411:15
Procul: p. este, severae! 276:6
  qui p. hinc 269:27
Procuress: p. to the lords of Hell 385:24
Prodigal: p. of ease 146:21
Prodigies: what p. surprise 205:24
Prodigious: 'p.!' exclaimed Dominie Sampson 306:30
Prodigy: German ... p., admit him! 380:1
Produce: P.! P.! 99:25
Product: fraction of a p. 99:25
  vice and virtues are p.s 382:2
Production: noblest p. 1:21
Proelia: vivit post p. Magnus 239:9
Profaned: word is too often p. 363:21
Profani: procul este, p. 405:13
Profession: all p.s are conspiracies 357:21
  fairies were of the old p. 120:5
  incidents of the p. 401:26
  most ancient p. in the world 225:16
Professor: learn'd p. Ruhnken 289:30
  p. is one who talks 14:10
  p. of the fact 221:1
  P.s of the Dismal Science 99:6
Profit: he p.s most who serves best 358:27
  in all labour there is p. 39:26
  p. grows where is no pleasure 349:17
  thinks that the p.s ... outweigh 397:14
  what p. hath a man 40:34
  what shall it p. a man 50:2
  who mingles p. with pleasure 196:2
  winds will blow the p. 243:5
Profited: what is a man p. 48:29
Progenies: iam nova p. caelo demittitur 406:4
Progress: history of p. 241:19
  p. depends on the unreasonable man 358:10
  p. is based upon a universal 87:7
  p. ... is not an accident 371:8
  p. is the law of life 75:4
  p. through the world is trouble 237:14
Project: p. for extracting sunbeams 379:3
Prole: p.s are not human 275:16
Prologue: make a long p. 46:28
  p.s to the swelling act 332:15
  witty p. to a very dull play 118:24
Promise: I have p.s to keep 163:13
  ill keeper of p. 17:30
  keep the word of p. 336:1
  p.s ... made to be broken 379:12
  who broke no p. 288:5
  whose p. none relies on 298:3
Promising: you were so p. 163:16
Promontory: I sat upon a p. 340:7

Promontory – *contd*
  set on the p. which I named 72:3
  sterile p. 316:13
Promotion: sweat but for p. 310:32
Proof: bliss in p. 356:29
  dost thou ask p.? 11:29
  give me the ocular p. 343:32
  how I would correct the p.s 112:17
Prooshan: others may be P.s 136:4
Proosian: French, or Turk, or P. 168:30
Prop: little p. best fits 189:2
  succedaneum and a p. 424:19
  when you do take the p. 338:24
Propagation: was all our p. 142:18
Propensities: excite my amorous p. 207:2
Proper: never does a p. thing 357:28
  p. man, as one shall see 340:2
Properly: never did anything p. 233:4
Properties: general p. and large appearances 206:24
Property: coveting other men's p. 303:17
  give me a snug little p. 150:12
  mortgaging of his extensive p. 213:3
  p. has its duties 146:10
  p. is theft 293:7
  p. owns them 203:20
Prophecies: p., they shall fail 54:3
Prophesy: eat exceedingly, and p. 211:17
  never p. – onless ye know 238:28
  p. unto the wind 44:29
  sons and daughters shall p. 45:5
  we p. in part 54:4
Prophet: beware of false p.s 47:28
  historian is a p. in reverse 304:19
  if there arise among you a p. 32:8
  in the name of the P. 368:9
  is Saul also among the p.s 32:38
  is the law and the p.s 47:25
  methinks I am a p. 345:7
  p. is not without honour 48:17
  'P.!' said I, 'thing of evil' 283:18
  there is a p. in Israel 33:26
  What-you-may-call-it is his p.! 135:4
Prophetic: p. of her end 430:9
Propontic: P. and the Hellespont 343:36
Proportion: no p. kept! 346:16
  p. to be observed in ... every act 14:27
Propose: Man p.s but God disposes 220:9
  oppose everything, and p. nothing 132:11
  why don't the men p.? 25:13
Propre: par malheur j'y étais p. 25:17
Propriété: p. c'est le vol 293:7
Propriety: employment ... evince its p. 16:3
  sole p. in Paradise 257:22
  study first P. 95:26
Proputty: p., p., p. – that's what I 'ears 389:1
Prose: and nearest p. 148:15
  blank verse and blanker p. 94:4
  differs in nothing from p. 178:25
  I love thee in p. 292:26
  language of p. and metrical 427:3
  never pin up my hair with p. 118:31
  not verse now, only p. 71:18
  p. and verse were much the same 284:5
  p. – words in their best order 117:1
  p. [is opposed to] metre 116:24
  shows that p. is verse 92:17

R

Redemption: condemned into everlasting r. 342:4
Redemptorem: tantum meruit habere R. 260:25
Redire: unde negant r. quemquam 103:1
Redress: r. to all mankind 386:4
  things past r. 345:16
Reed: bring me a hundred r.s 165:17
  bruised r. shall he not break 43:29
  down in the r.s by the river 70:1
  man ... is a thinking r. 278:15
  r. is as the oak 313:25
  r. shaken with the wind 48:4
  staff of this broken r. 43:17
Reek: r. o' the rotten fens 313:5
Reel: they r. to and fro 37:29
  threesome r.s, and foursome r.s 83:9
Reeling: r. and writhing 100:25
Reference: verify your r.s 301:18
Reflection: R., you may come tomorrow 363:24
Reform: peace, retrenchment and r. 66:10
  r. ... will prove unavailing 98:14
  to innovate is not to r. 81:28
Reformation: reforming of the R. itself 260:17
Reformer: r.s are bachelors 264:14
Refuge: eternal God is thy r. 52:15
  God is our r. and strength 35:31
  other r. have I none 413:16
Refugee: guttural sorrow of the r.s 243:6
Refusal: great r. 129:7
  r. ... looks almost like a favour 119:17
Refute: I r. it *thus* 208:10
Regard: son r. est pareil au r. des statues 403:17
Regarder: se r. soi-même un fort long temps 262:8
Regent: all who revelled with the R. 27:2
  God bless the R. 368:10
Reges: quidquid delirant r. 196:10
Regiment: led his r. from behind 168:9
  Monstrous R. of Women 225:26
  r. blind with the dust 270:6
Region: blue r.s of the air 61:12
  reside in thrilling r. 336:23
Regret: r. becomes an April violet 386:14
Regular: brought r. and draw'd mild 136:5
Reign: but friendless is to r. 362:20
  r.s, but does not govern 430:18
Reilly: Mr R. who owns the hotel 7:20
Rein: do not pluck at his r. 428:21
Reiz: fanden darin keinen R. 85:27
Rejected: despised and r. of men 43:38
Rejoice: again I say, R. 55:8
  r. with me 50:33
  r. with them that r. 53:8
Relation: fate chooses your r.s 131:32
  great men have their poor r.s 134:4
  poor r. ... irrelevant 229:7
Relative: set out one day in a r. way 79:6
  when our r.s are at home 357:23
Relaxes: bless r. 62:1
Release: prisoner's r. 366:8
Relent: shall make him once r. 79:31
Reliance: no virtue now in blind r. 220:24
Relic: cold and unhonoured his r.s 265:3
Relief: for this r. much thanks 313:29
  gave that thought r. 423:8
  r. of man's estate 16:12
Religio: tantum r. potuit 239:13
Religion: about again to our r. 164:6
  airy subtleties in r. 68:19

Religion – *contd*
  anything – but live for it [r.] 118:3
  bashfulness in ... r. 2:9
  educate men without r. 412:26
  enough r. to make us hate 379:22
  for r. when in rags 79:23
  her r. ... with her learning did suit 292:31
  men will wrangle for r. 118:3
  Millionaire. That is my r. 357:26
  my r. is to do good 277:8
  not a r. for gentlemen 106:8
  nothing is so fatal to r. 81:33
  one r. ... a hundred versions 358:23
  one r. is as true as another 85:26
  philosophy bringeth ... to r. 18:4
  philosophy ... handmaid to r. 16:16
  pure r. and undefiled 56:7
  really but of one r. 309:1
  r. blushing veils 284:22
  r. but a childish toy 245:15
  r. ... designates the attitude 213:6
  r. for an active faith 68:20
  r. has made an honest woman 163:22
  r. is allowed to invade 249:8
  r. is by no means a proper subject 109:11
  r. is whatever he is most interested in 24:4
  r. justice, counsel 17:36
  r. ... [of] exceedin' accommodatin' character
    409:19
  r. of feeble minds 81:17
  r. of humanity 277:9
  r. ... the opium of the people 247:18
  rum and true r. 90:23
  sensible men are all of the same r. 140:29
  take my r. from the priest 174:21
  to which men are driven by r. 239:13
  true meaning of r. 19:21
  we need r. for r.'s sake 120:23
Religious: to be r. more or less 87:20
Relish: imaginary r. is so sweet 351:17
Remain: all things leave me: you r. 381:17
  be amongst you and r. 291:33
  weeds wind-shaken, these r. 380:20
Remark: made our r.s before us 142:1
  which I wish to r. 184:1
Remarkable: nothing left r. 310:5
Remedies: extreme r. ... for extreme diseases
    190:3
  r. oft in ourselves do lie 309:5
  require desperate r. 157:6
  will not apply new r. 18:17
Remedy: one r. for all 391:30
  r. against this consumption 322:19
  r. for everything except death 105:5
  r. is worse than the disease 18:2
  sharp r., but a sure one 295:14
  suggests no r. 303:13
  they sought the r. 312:15
  things without all r. 334:10
Remember: he'll r. with advantages 324:25
  I r., I r. 193:11
  I r. thee upon my bed 36:17
  if thou wilt, r. 300:16
  in the morning we will r. them 57:32
  r. me when I am gone 300:11
  r. one man saw you 75:21
  r. such things were 335:9

Remember – *contd*
r. while the light lives yet 380:18
that which r.s 14:28
this too will be pleasant to r. 404:16
till thou r. and I forget 381:11
to r. for years 4:4
you should r. and be sad 300:12
Remembered: that which is r. 14:28
would have made myself r. 219:18
Remembrance: poetry ... almost a r. 219:1
r. of his dying Lord 371:25
r. of things past 355:10
Remembren: it r., when it passed is 108:9
Remorse: farewell fear, farewell r. 257:7
loathsome centipede, R. 233:15
R., the fatal egg 124:10
Remove: bends with the remover to r. 356:24
r. hence ... and it shall r. 48:30
Remuneration: r.! O! that's the Latin 331:16
Render: r. unto Caesar 49:11
Rendezvous: I have a r. with Death 307:25
Rendu: le lui avons bien r. 407:13
Renown: men of r. 31:5
r. and grace is dead 334:2
shall forfeit fair r. 305:29
sing the glorious day's r. 96:5
you shall not win r. 386:24
Rent: r. the envious Casca made 327:32
Repartee: cannot think of any r. 29:9
Repay: I will r. 53:10
Repeat: what they hear, they r.! 367:2
Repent: change, nor falter, nor r. 363:1
r. you of your sins 291:30
Repentance: cost his enemies a long r. 91:2
just persons which need no r. 50:34
Winter Garment of R. 158:17
Repine: do not r., my friends 135:33
Reply: theirs not to make r. 383:10
third, 'the r. churlish' 312:21
Report: how he may r. thy words 259:21
ill r. while you live 316:21
r. me and my cause 320:2
they have committed false r. 342:9
whatsoever things are of good r. 55:10
Reporter: gallery in which the r.s sit 241:15
Repose: earned a night's r. 237:19
gives way to in r. 333:14
hushed in grim r. 176:17
long for a r. 423:27
r. is tabooed by anxiety 169:7
seek not yet r. 154:2
tumultuous life and great r. 279:10
Reprehend: r. anything in this world 365:17
Representation: just r.s of general nature 206:17
taxation without r. 276:2
Representative: r. owes you ... his judgement 80:17
Reproach: not to be receives r. of being 356:27
r. of men and despised 35:6
without fear and without r. 25:3
Reprobation: fall to r. 344:13
Reproof: fourth, 'the r. valiant' 312:21
r.s from authority 17:25
Republic: r. of letters 1:18 173:20
Reputation: at ev'ry word a r. dies 288:23
murdered r.s of the week 118:25
R. for a Song 159:18

Reputation – *contd*
r.! O! I have lost my r. 343:17
seeking the bubble r. 311:14
wink a r. down 378:11
worlds of r. in it 401:21
written out of r. 29:15
Requiem: to thy high r. become a sod 217:5
Require: r. it ... to be brought reg'lar 136:5
what doth the Lord r. of thee 45:12
Res: ad eventum festinat et in medias r. 195:24
Researches: no deep r. vex the brain 126:15
Resemblance: its own r. find 246:26
Resemble: when I r. her to thee 408:9
Residence: forted r. 'gainst the tooth 336:30
Resist: I can r. everything 417:9
Resisted: know not what's r. 82:17
Resistentialism: R. is concerned 204:19
Resolution: native hue of r. 316:29
Resource: few people had intellectual r.s 208:24
Respect: each other must r. 279:1
no r. of place, persons 352:19
old-fashioned r. for the young 416:22
one owes r. to the living 407:12
Respectable: not one is r. 415:14
very delectable, highly r. 169:38
Respecter: no r. of persons 52:20
Rest: all things have r. 387:33
and the R. is Lies 159:1
be with them that r. 259:18
crept silently to R. 158:28
far, far better r. 139:13
I will give you r. 48:7
leave the r. to the gods 197:8
long, long ago at r. 120:18
motion, but ordained no r. 402:12
name led all the r. 201:15
now she's at r. 147:33
r. asleep within the tomb 63:14
r. for the people of God 74:28
seek home for r. 400:26
set up my everlasting r. 349:14
sing thee to thy r. 320:5
so may he r. 326:8
talk about the r. of us 190:14
to r., the cushion 288:4
toil and not to seek for r. 239:6
until it r.s in thee 14:12
we'll do the r. 4:20
Reste: j'y suis, j'y r. 243:2
Resting: age 'tis r. merely 72:8
my r. place is found 70:15
Restoration: Church's R. in 1883 29:21
Restored: dead and then r. to life 72:26
Restorer: tired Nature's sweet r. 430:7
Restraint: you praise the firm r. 96:4
Result: r. happiness 134:19
Resumption: only way to r. 106:13
Resurrection: foretaste of the r. 305:3
I am the r. and the life 51:41
in the r. they neither marry 49:12
looking for the r. 292:19
r. of the body 291:1 292:19
R. to eternal life 292:18
Retainer: play the Old R. 27:30
Retire: sign ... to r. from the world 141:3
with a blush r. 135:7
Retirement: r. urges sweet return 258:19

Rottenness – *contd*
pillared firmament is r. 253:7
Rough: among his fellow r.s 145:20
o'er r. and smooth she trips 421:28
r. and ready man 71:6
r. places plain 43:22
Rough-hew: r.-h. them how we will 319:29
Roughness: r. breedeth hate 17:25
Round: go r. about, Peer! 203:1
gone the whole r. of creation 77:9
light fantastic r. 252:23
so large, and smooth, and r. 370:8
travelled life's dull r. 364:20
trivial r. 219:23
when he once attains the upmost r. 327:5
Roundelaie: synge unto mie r. 106:15
Rousseau: gospel according to [R.] 98:30
I shall not ask Jean Jacques R. 124:4
mock on, Voltaire, R. 59:22
Rout: pleasures of having a r. 193:15
where meet a public r. 130:3
Rover: living a r. 25:4
Roving: go no more a r. 93:17
Row: r., brothers, r. 264:17
r. one way and look another 85:10
Rowing: looking one way, and r. 79:22
Rowley: 'Heigh ho!' says R. 272:9
Royal: ay, there's the r. 316:29
Rub: ay, there's the r. 316:29
Rubbish: out of this stony r. 152:25
Rubies: price is far above r. 40:32
wisdom is above r. 34:9
wisdom is better than r. 39:12
Rudder: bowsprit got mixed with the r. 102:9
Rude: it's very r. of him 101:17
Rue: nought shall make us r. 329:11
Ruffian: by the menaces of a r. 209:2
that father r. 321:13
Ruh': mein R. ist hin 171:9
über allen Gipfeln ist R. 171:18
Ruin: I'm one of the r.s 235:14
majestic though in r. 256:24
never to see my country's r. 418:7
r. seize thee, ruthless King! 176:12
r. upon r., rout on rout 256:33
r.s of forgotten times 69:14
seed of r. in himself 10:30
sink with enormous r. down! 141:28
spreading r. and scattering ban 70:1
Ruinae: Impavidum ferient r. 197:26
Rule: can r. and dare not lie 388:14
declared absolute r. 257:13
little r., a little sway 150:11
my gran'ther's r. was safer 238:28
old r. sufficeth them 425:21
r. is that there are no golden r.s 358:5
r. of men entirely great 240:13
R. of three doth puzzle me 6:3
r.s him, never shows she r.s 287:26
simple little r.s and few 28:19
too fond to r. alone 285:12
twelve good r.s 172:21
Ruler: r.s of the darkness 55:3
Rum: cantharides and adulterated r. 381:16
r. and true religion 90:23

Rum – *contd*
what a R. Go everything is 413:10
yo-ho-ho, and a bottle of r.! 375:9
Rumination: by often r. 312:8
Rumour: r. of oppression and deceit 124:30
r.s of wars 49:17
Rum-ti-Foo: balmy isle of R.-t.-F. 168:2
Run: fights and r.s away 5:13
gwine to r. all night! 161:22
he who r.s may read 125:32
may r. that readeth it 45:13
r. at least twice as fast 101:12
running it never r.s from us 142:3
we will make him r. 247:13
Runcible: with a r. spoon 232:19
Running: all the r. *you* can do 101:12
Run-stealer: r.-s.s flicker to and fro 395:12
Rupert: R. of parliamentary discussion 140:8
Rus: r. in urbe 246:16
Ruskin: R. he sticks his tusk in 68:1
Russell: as you did my Lord R. 262:19
Russia: last out a night in R. 336:10
R. has two generals 270:19
Russian: some people … may be R.s 136:4
think of a single R. novel 249:2
Rust: moth and r. doth corrupt 47:12
r. of the whole week 2:3
r. to the harrow 131:28
to r. unburnished 392:3
which never taketh r. 366:11
Rustic: amazed the gazing r.s 172:18
Rustling: dread the r. of the grass 420:5
Ruth: sad heart of R. 217:5
Rye: coming through the r. 83:1
r. reach to the chin 280:10

S

Sabaoth: Lord God of S. 290:25
Sabbath: never broke the S., but for gain 147:4
S. … the poor man's day 175:6
s. was made for man 49:36
S.s of Eternity one S. 391:7
smiled when a S. appeared 126:7
Sable: a s. silvered 314:26
Sabrina: S. fair, listen 253:13
Sack: addict themselves to s. 323:12
s. the lot! 158:12
s.s to sew up wives 393:13
this intolerable deal of s.! 321:15
Sacred: if anything is s. 415:2
Sacrifice: only make a s. to God 289:27
our spotless s.! 141:25
s.s of God are a broken spirit 36:6
stands thine ancient s. 224:10
turn delight into a s. 187:19
unpitied s. in a contemptible struggle 81:23
woman will always s. herself 248:17
Sacrificer: s.s, but not butchers 327:8
Sad: how s. and bad and mad 72:7
s. tires in a mile-a 354:10
thou art absent, I am s. 271:17
Sadder: s. and a wiser man 115:14
Saddled: s. and bridled to be ridden 241:28

Sadness: and the s. of her s. 24:3
  in a most humorous s. 312:8
Saecla: mutantur s. animantum 239:17
Saeclum: solvet s. in favilla 104:3
Safe: I wish him s. at home! 212:25
  one s. thing ... not to hope for safety 405:4
  s. shall be my going 67:15
  see me s. up 265:21
Safely: but to be s. thus 334:7
Safety: in ... counsellors there is s. 39:16
  pluck this flower, s. 320:29
  safe though all s.'s lost 67:15
Sage: hoary s. replied, 'Come, my lad 210:27
  I've read your German s. 113:14
  s.s may pour out their ... treasure 91:3
  sit the sainted s. 177:25
  than all the s.s can 426:11
  without hardness will be s. 10:26
Sage: s. avec sobrieté 262:4
Said: everything has been s. 226:11
  I wish I had s. that 414:6
  no more to be s. 5:14
  s. I to myself, s. I 169:4
  so very little s. 110:25
  that's as well s. 379:17
  that's what I s. 131:29
Sail: fills the white and rustling s. 128:8
  here she comes i' faith full s. 118:29
  s.s filled, and streamers waving 259:19
  s.s filled with a lusty wind 105:24
  s.s o' cramoisy 20:23
  s.s ripped, seams opening 124:3
  sister, wilt thou s. with me? 360:2
  thy white s.s crowding 66:1
  to the white dipping s.s 248:4
  weather-beaten s. more willing 97:5
  white s.'s shaking 248:5
Sailed: s. away for a year 232:17
Sailing: comes this way s. 259:19
Sailor: cry to a s. 'Go hang!' 350:9
  do with a drunken s. 8:21
  home is the s., home from sea 376:13
  lass that loves a s. 133:9
  no man will be a s. 207:17
  s.s but men 337:15
  three s.s of Bristol City 393:25
Sailor-men: odd that S.-m. should wear 23:4
  s. m , 'ave their faults 203:24
Sail-yard: till his s.-y.s tremble 105:24
Saint: able to corrupt a s. 320:12
  all s.s else be defaced 179:8
  all the s.s adore Thee 185:28
  before we *know* he's a s. 178:31
  Communion of S.s 291:1
  don't grow into plaster s.s 224:20
  follow your s. 97:1
  for all the S.s 200:7
  gather with the s.s 303:23
  ghastly glories of s.s 381:6
  great s., to pray to thee 121:19
  heav'n ... the s. sustained 285:21
  I call 's.' what s.s call something else 76:24
  in vain the s. adore 146:3
  little s. best fits a little shrine 189:2
  my late espousèd s. 260:2
  not privileged to see a s. 76:24
  place has with the race of s.s 188:19

Saint – *contd*
  precious ... death of his s.s 38:5
  s. when most I play the devil 346:27
  s.s be joyful in glory 38:33
  s.s must bear with me 76:24
  s.s will aid 115:19
  slaughtered s.s, whose bones 260:4
  tax not the royal S. 420:12
  that I may see my s. 212:2
  their Priests, their Popes, their S.s 72:5
  thy quire of S.s 143:13
  thy s.s have dwelt secure 411:11
  to lose with my lost s.s 70:8
  'twould a s. provoke 287:17
  weakest s. upon his knees 123:15
  well done, S.! 124:8
  where s.s immortal reign 411:5
  where s.s in glory stand 430:1
  would she could make of me a s. 119:18
Saint: ni s., ni romain, ni empire 407:9
St Agnes: S. A.' Eve – Ah, bitter chill 215:6
St Anne: S. A., the mother of Mary 278:19
  yes by S. A. 352:20
St Clement: say the bells of S. C.'s 273:13
St Crispin: upon S. C.'s day 324:26
St George: England and S. G.! 324:13
  from S. G.'s, Hanover Square 87:22
  S. G., that swinged the dragon 328:24
St Hugh: dirge for S. H.'s soul 131:6
St Ives: going to S. I. 271:22
St James: Ladies of S. J.'s! 141:22
St John: awake my S. J.! 286:18
  studied his last chapter of S. J. 71:11
  there S. J. mingles 289:4
St Paul: description of the ruins of S. P.'s
    408:15
  say I am designing S. P.'s 29:13
  sketch the ruins of S. P.'s 241:20
St Peter: S. P. sat by the ... gate 93:24
St Praxed: S. P.'s ... the church for peace 71:12
St Trinian: Terror of S. T.'s 307:17
Sainted: thing enskyed and s. 336:5
Sais: que s.-je? 263:19
Saki: S., you shall pass 159:24
Sal: s. Atticum 283:4
Salad: my s. days 309:25
  wholesome s. from the brook 125:30
Salley: down by the s. gardens 428:15
Sally: make a sudden s. 383:4
  none like pretty S. 98:7
  S. is gone from Ha'nacker Hill 28:14
Salmon-fisher: s.-f.s moist 247:15
Salt: seasoned with s. 55:14
  ye are the s. of the earth 46:40
Saltpetre: s.-p. should be digged 320:21
Salt-spoon: o'er hard-boiled eggs the s.-s. 95:24
Salus: una s. victis 405:4
Salute: those about to die s. you 377:14
Salvation: my bottle of s. 295:10
  my rock and my s. 36:15
  no s. outside the Church 14:17
  none of us should see s. 338:17
  now is the day of s. 54:28
  pleasant methods of s. 286:13
  what prawce S. nah? 357:27
  work out your own s. 55:5
Samarkand: Golden Road to S. 160:10

Same: all the s. a hundred years hence 136:21
  he is much the s. 16:8
Samian: cup with S. wine 91:10
Samite: clothed in white s. 384:27
Samphire: gathers s., dreadful trade! 330:20
Sana: mens s. in corpore sano 214:8
Sand: all 'ot s. an' ginger 222:31
  come unto these yellow s.s 349:37
  little grains of s. 100:2
  on the s.s with printless foot 350:23
  plain to be seen in the s. 130:16
  roll down their golden s. 185:24
  s.s and crystal brooks 142:4
  see such quantities of s. 101:19
  sold lily-vite s. 7:4
  steer too nigh the s.s 146:20
  throw the s., against the wind 59:22
  throws ... s. in their eyes 191:4
  world in a grain of s. 58:18
Sandal: bind on thy s.s 380:5
  bright and battering s.! 194:16
  his s. shoon 318:30.
  s.s were for Clementine 264:11
Sandalwood: s., cedarwood 247:25
Sane: could be held by no s. man 72:4
  fitter being s. than mad 70:22
Sang: he s. as he sat 278:22
Sanglot: d'immortels qui sont de purs s.s 267:16
  s.s longs des violons 403:16
Sap: world's whole s. 143:20
Sapientia: s. prima stultitia caruisse 196:7
Sapphire-blaze: living throne, the s.-b. 178:21
Sappho: S. loved and sung 91:6
Sarcasm: s. ... language of the devil 99:19
Sarcastical: this is rote S. 409:21
Sashes: one of his nice new s. 175:5
Sat: where we s. side by side 58:11
Satan: get thee behind me, S. 48:27
  S. exalted sat 256:16
  S. finds some mischief 411:1
  S. met his ancient friend 94:3
  S., thou art but a dunce 59:7
  S. trembles when he sees 123:15
  which is the Devil and S. 57:16
Satanic: called the S. School 370:27
Sated: s. with home 368:8
Satire: let s. be my song 92:12
  s. is a sort of glass 378:23
  s. or sense, alas! 285:14
  s. should, like a polished razor 263:4
Satirist: second English s. 180:18
Satisfaction: miss the s. of knowing 400:4
  s. ... depends on your will 263:10
Satisfied: not be s. unless I produce 242:14
  paid that is well s. 338:25
  s. with what is assigned 14:31
Saturday: betwixt a S. and Monday 98:8
Saturn: gray-haired S., quiet 215:19
  S. and Love 360:12
Saturnia: redeunt S. regna 406:4
Satyr: Hyperion to a s. 314:12
  s.s grazing on the lawns 245:14
Sauce: crier of green s. 294:13
  hunger is the best s. 105:2
  of all the s. 238:29
  only one s. 97:20
Saucer: s. like some full moon 263:1

Saul: is S. also among the prophets? 32:38
  S. hath slain his thousands 32:41
Saule: Christ receive thy s. 21:1
Savage: noble s. ran 149:5
  s. as a bear with a sore head 246:8
  s., extreme, rude, cruel 356:28
  take some s. woman 387:23
Savante: s. afin d'être 261:9
Save: God, make speed to s. us 290:23
  himself he cannot s. 49:34
  you would s. none of me 142:23
Savent: s. tout sans avoir rien appris 262:11
Saviour: then bespoke our S. 20:8
Savoir: belle chose que de s. quelquechose 261:6
Savour: salt hath lost its s. 46:40
  s. as all the spicery 244:5
  send forth a stinking s. 41:23
Saw: full of wise s.s 311:14
Say: let us not always s. 76:5
  s. what you have to s. 412:23
  s.s little, thinks less 156:19
  till I see what I s. 408:3
  want to know what it s.s 134:37
  what I could s. if I chose 100:23
  you're thinking what to s. 101:11
  you should s. what you mean 100:16
Saying: as I was s. the other day 234:2
  keep on s. it long enough 29:5
Scab: make yourself s.s 312:27
Scale: by geometric s. 86:6
  in equal s. weighing 314:4
  on every golden s. 100:8
  would not sink i' the s. 76:3
Scallop: s. shell of quiet 295:10
Scandal: love and s. are the best 157:28
  no s. about Queen Elizabeth 364:24
  s. waits on greatest state 354:24
Scandale: s. du monde 262:16
Scapegoat: let him go for a s. 31:46
Scar: he jests at s.s 348:8
Scarf: beauteous s. veiling 338:11
Scarlet: bless their coats of s. 368:12
  love that loves a s. coat 193:8
  purple and s. colour 57:15
Scattered: Israel is upon the hills 33:21
Scene: changing s.s of life 382:9
  come no more behind your s.s 207:2
  every day speaks a new s. 294:2
  from s.s like these old Scotia's 83:6
  gay gilded s.s 1:16
  girdid up my Lions & fled the S. 409:22
  last s. of all 311:14
  live o'er each s. 288:10
  o'er all this s. of man 286:18
  our lofty s. be acted o'er 327:19
  proud s. was o'er 284:1
  s. individable 316:17
  upon that memorable s. 247:4
Scenery: end of all natural s. 302:5
  s. is fine 219:3
Scepticism: wise s. 239:3
Sceptre: s. and crown must tumble down 365:32
  s. for a palmer's walking staff 346:2
  s., learning, physic must 313:25
  s. o'er a slumb'ring world 430:8
  s. shows the force 338:17
Scheme: best laid s.s o' mice an' men 84:28

Seed – *contd*
  in s. time learn 61:21
  robs not one light s. 215:20
  scatter the good s. on the land 96:2
  s. fell by the wayside 48:14
  s. in their loins were hostile 13:24
  s. ye sow, another reaps 363:11
  wingèd s.s, where they lie cold 361:13
Seeing: Giant's Causeway worth s.? 209:26
  only one way of *s.* them 302:12
  precious s. to the eye 331:21
  s. many things 43:30
  when thy s. blindeth thee 396:1
Seek: s. and ye shall find 47:23
  s. him here, we s. him there 275:3
  s. ye the Lord while he may be found 44:3
  that is all I s. 21:22
  that sometime did me s. 427:23
  what you s. is here 196:16
  you shall s. all the day 337:8
Seeking: must still be s. 420:27
  would not be s. Me 278:17
Seem: I know not 's.s' 314:9
  men should be what they s. 343:22
  s.s, madam! Nay, it is 314:9
  things are not what they s. 236:30
  things are seldom what they s. 168:27
Seemed: all s. but were not all 258:1
Seeming: keep s. and savour 354:11
Seemly: s. so to do 220:20
Seen: because thou art not s. 311:15
  for to be s. of men 49:13
See-saw: s.-s., Margery Daw 273:25
Sein: couvrez ce s. 262:13
Seine: red fool-fury of the S. 386:18
Seismic: s. with laughter 23:14
Selection: by the term of Natural S. 129:15
Self: arch-flatterer ... is a man's s. 17:20
  concentred all in s. 305:29
  each one a murdered s. 301:4
  enlarges ... a man's s. to himself 229:4
Self-honoured: s.-h., self-secure 11:19
Self-indulgence: favourite form of s.-i. 248:17
Self-knowledge: more skilful in s.-k. 420:10
Self-limitation: in s.-l. ... a master ... shows himself 171:17
Self-love: s.-l. and social are the same 287:12
Self-lover: nature of extreme s.-l.s 18:15
Self-sacrifice: spirit of s.-s. 424:2
Self-schooled: s.-s., self-scanned 11:17
Self-slaughter: canon 'gainst s.-s. 314:11
Self-sufficient: know how to be s.-s. 263:14
Selima: pensive S. reclined 178:2
Selling: lives by s. something 375:1
Selves: as I am mine, their sweating s. 194:25
  from our better s. ... parted 424:22
  stepping stones of their dead s. 385:7
Semblance: all the outward s. of a man 138:26
  outface it with their s.s 310:25
Seminary: come from a ladies' s. 169:17
Semper: quod s., quod ubique 404:11
Senate: listening s.s hang 396:15
Senator: green-robed s.s of ... woods 215:22
Senior: earnest advice from my s.s 396:28
Senior-junior: s.-j., giant-dwarf 331:18
Sens: bon s. est la chose 132:14
  bon s. s'accorde avec la rime 62:19

608

Sens – *contd*
  donner un s. plus pur 243:17
Sensation: but s. is s. 210:13
  life of s.s rather than of thoughts! 218:26
Sensational: always have something s. 416:25
Sense: batteries of alluring s. 246:22
  betrayed me into common s. 284:5
  between a man of s. and his books 109:5
  devoid of s. and motion 256:20
  dim and undetermined s. 424:16
  echo to the s. 286:7
  five S.s, the chief inlets 61:17
  fountain of good s. 149:19
  hath the daintier s. 319:15
  heart and the soul and the s.s 77:7
  in its Pickwickian s. 137:34
  it enchants my s. 351:17
  man of s. only trifles 109:4
  men of s. approve 286:8
  men of s. ... of one religion 309:1
  much fruit of s. 286:1
  no substitute for s. 153:9
  palter ... in a double s. 336:1
  poetry ... must be good s. 117:4
  purer s. to the language 243:17
  s. aches at thee 344:5
  s. may reach and apprehend 142:21
  s. sublime of something ... interfused 421:21
  s.s, affections, passions 338:4
  s.s would have cooled 335:22
  stings and motions of the s. 336:6
  take care of the s. 100:22
  through s. and nonsense 147:10
  unto our gentle s.s 332:30
  with s. and feeling beneath it 113:5
  withdraws us from the power of our s.s 206:5
Senseless: most s. and fit man 341:25
Sensibility: dissociation of s. 153:21
  it modified his s. 153:20
  wanting s. 125:31
Sensible: s. men are all of the same religion 140:29
Sensuous: simple, s. and passionate 260:20
Sentence: he mouths a s. 110:24
  s. first – verdict afterwards 101:6
  s. is for open war 256:18
  speak after s. 205:9
Sentiment: s. is what I am not acquainted with 160:18
  s. that rubs you up the wrong way 249:3
  s.s to which every bosom returns 206:12
  them's my s.s 393:18
Sentiment: premiers s. ... les plus naturels 238:6
Sentimentality: s. is only sentiment 249:3
Sentinel: s. on Whitehall gate 240:20
Sentry: where stands a wingèd s. 402:16
Separate: s. them one from another 49:24
Separation: prepare for a s. 294:5
  restraints ... to prevent s. 208:25
September: thirty days hath S. 6:9
Sepulchre: dome of a vast s. 361:15
  like whited s.s 49:16
  s. in stubborn Jewry 345:8
Sequel: s. of to-day unsolders all 384:26
Seraglio: rounded S. Point 250:8
Seraph: where S.s might despair 88:16
Seraphim: above it stood the s.s 42:26

Shower – *contd*
  dying lamp, a falling s. 359:7
  s. your shooting corns presage 378:9
  small s.s last long 345:7
  suck the honied s.s 254:33
  this is our finest s.! 275:20
Showery: S., Flowery, Bowery 154:5
Showing: men of little s. 224:15
Shred: thing of s.s and patches 169:10
Shriek: s.s to pitying heav'n are cast 288:29
Shrieking: s. and squeaking 75:11
Shrimp: but a s. of an author 178:26
Shrine: honour the s. where you alone 179:8
Shriving-time: not s.-t. allowed 319:31
Shroud: land-breeze shook the s.s 123:21
  s. of white, stuck all with yew 352:27
  who ever comes to s. me 142:22
Shrug: rest will give a s. 378:15
Shudder: I s. at the word 404:24
Shuddering: shall I with s. fall 250:4
Shun: I thought he would s. me 25:11
  ten men ... s. what I follow 76:9
Shutter: close the s.s fast 125:11
Shuttle: each throwing his s. 74:11
  swifter than a weaver's s. 33:41
Shuttlecock: vhen you an't the s. 138:6
Sick: but they that are s. 47:34
  created s., commanded to be sound 179:11
  hired to watch the s. 124:26
  I am s. at heart 313:29
  I am s. of love 42:7
  more than a little s. 222:17
  nothing but to make him s. 142:13
  seriously s. man on our hands 270:18
  s. in soul and body both 190:16
  they are as s. that surfeit 337:9
Sickle: bending s.'s compass 356:25
  s. in his hand 237:9
  with his s. keen he reaps 237:5
Sicklemen: s. of August weary 350:17
Sickness: he hath the falling s. 326:28
  in s. and in health 292:7
  s. enlarges the dimensions 229:4
  s. full of woes 128:17
  stand convicted of s. 369:26
Side: all on one s. 311:20
  hear the other s. 14:18
  passed by on the other s. 50:21
  pierce my s. 143:6
  said on both s.s 2:4
  to go by thy s. 4:21
Sidera: sublimi feriam s. vertice 197:2
Sidmouth: great storm at S. 369:1
Sidney: S.'s self, the starry paladin 77:21
Siege: did march to the s. 21:2
  laugh a s. to scorn 335:21
Sieve: in a s. they went to sea 232:13
Sigh: beadle to a humorous s. 331:17
  for my pains a world of s.s 342:32
  I ever s. and pine 187:23
  made of s.s and tears 312:17
  on the Bridge of S.s 89:12
  over the Bridge of S.s 221:2
  passing tribute of a s. 177:15
  prompts th' eternal s. 287:5
  s. is the sword of an angel king 59:14
  s. no more, ladies 341:17

Sigh – *contd*
  s.s are the natural language 308:26
  s.s for ever on her pensive bed 288:30
  sovereign of s.s and groans 331:18
  took her with a s. 60:3
  'twill cost a s., a tear 22:4
  waft a s. from Indus 284:33
Sighed: I s. for thee 364:3
  no sooner s. but they asked 312:15
  s. and looked, and s. 147:22
  s. and looked unutterable things 396:14
Sighing: plague of s. and grief! 321:11
  s. like furnace 311:14
  sorrow and s. shall flee 43:16
Sight: all s.s from pole to pole 11:22
  by faith, not by s. 54:26
  earth, and every common s. 423:5
  expense of many a vanished s. 355:10
  few more impressive s.s in the world 24:8
  he vanished out of s. 371:2
  hide them from my aching s. 16:9
  it is not yet in s.! 364:25
  lost to s., to mem'ry dear 235:9
  never admit them in your s. 16:1
  preposterous s.! 125:20
  s. so touching in its majesty 422:12
  s. to dream of, not to tell! 115:18
  s. to make an old man young 383:32
  so brave a s. 246:2
  so full of ugly s.s 346:28
  spare my aching s. 176:19
  thy s. to thee is sightless 396:1
  triple s. in blindness keen 218:7
Sign: discern the s.s of the times 48:25
  never s. a walentine 138:22
  only a s. shown 237:15
  outward and visible s. 291:42
  seeketh after a s. 48:11
  s.s and my wonders 31:37
  without changing the s. 231:18
Signal: really do not see the s.! 269:16
Signal-elm: s.-e. that looks on Ilsley 11:23
Significant: 'Very s.,' he remarked 377:4
Signior: potent, grave, and reverend s.s 342:24
Signo: in hoc s. vinces 119:25
Silence: breaking the s. of the seas 426:4
  elected s., sing to me 194:18
  friendly s. of the quiet moon 405:1
  frosty s. in the gardens 153:5
  God strikes a s. through you all 70:2
  in the s. of the sleep-time 72:21
  its military s. 14:1
  kindly s. when they brawl 387:3
  like s., listening to s. 193:18
  my gracious s., hail! 312:29
  occasional flashes of s. 369:15
  rang through the s. of the shrine 82:12
  rest is s. 320:4
  s. and sleep like fields 131:10
  s. augmenteth grief 179:9
  s. fell with the waking bird 388:20
  s. ... his mother tongue 173:31
  s. is deep as Eternity 98:21
  s. is the perfectest herald 341:13
  s. is wonderful to listen to 183:5
  s., like a poultice, comes 192:9
  s. more musical than any song 300:13

Silence – *contd*
s. often of pure innocence 353:34
s. resumes her reign 70:14
s. sank like music 115:7
s. sounds no worse than cheers 199:18
s. surged softly backward 131:22
s. that is in the starry sky 426:6
small change of s. 250:21
talent for s. 201:21
there was s. deep as death 96:6
there was s. in heaven 57:4
'tis visible s. 301:1
with s. and tears 94:8
Silence: seul le s. est grand 404:6
Silent: all s. and all damned! 424:6
and am not s. 35:5
be for ever s. 248:12
impossible to be s. 80:22
s. and kept their gaze fixed upon him 404:20
s. in seven languages 304:21
talents ... of the more s. class 91:29
Silentia: per amica s. lunae 405:1
Silk: soft as s. remains 189:20
when as in s.s my Julia goes 189:11
Silk-worm: s.-w. expend her yellow labours 399:7
Silly: it is s. sooth 352:26
Siloam: cool S.'s shady rill 185:23
Silvas: habitarunt di quoque s. 406:2
resonare doces Amaryllida s. 405:25
Silver: for a handful of s. he left us 74:1
s. and gold have I none 52:14
thirty pieces of s. 49:26
Silvia: except I be by S. 353:25
unless I look on S. 353:25
who is S.? 353:27
Simile: s., that solitary shines 289:9
sit, and play with s.s 426:22
Similitude: I have ... used s.s 45:3
Simon: real S. Pure 104:4
simple S. met a pieman 273:26
Simple: compounded of many s. 312:8
levels ... the s. with the wise 105:11
never pure, and rarely s. 416:14
Simplicitas: O sancta s.! 201:23
Simplicity: in low s. he lends 337:16
pity my s. 413:13
s. a child 285:20
with s. or with severity 12:26
Simplification: s. of language 228:28
Simplify: s., s. 397:3
Sin: all my s.s remembered 317:1
bare the s. of many 44:2
by that s. fell the angels 326:3
careless of the damning s. 122:17
commit the oldest s.s 323:15
confess our manifold s.s 290:18
cover the multitude of s.s 56:20
deal not with us after our s.s 291:18
expiate your father's s.s 198:3
for she knew no s. 147:34
from expensive s.s refrain 174:4
guilty of dust and s. 188:2
he that is without s. 51:35
his favourite s. is pride 370:15
his s.s were scarlet 28:12
I'm living in s. 187:12
if we say that we have no s. 56:23

Sin – *contd*
in the blossoms of my s. 315:20
is the root of all s.s 203:25
lie awake ... and weep for their s.s 415:14
no s. except stupidity 417:31
no s. for a man to labour 320:14
present a more dreadful record of s. 145:7
remember not the s.s of my youth 35:13
season of snows and s.s 380:6
s. I impute to each frustrate ghost 77:29
s. is behovely 213:5
s. to covet honour 324:23
s. ye do by two and two 224:18
s.s they are inclined to 86:12
s.s they love to act 344:19
some are thinkin' on their s.s 83:25
some rise by s. 336:9
sometimes s.'s a pleasure 90:20
stand in awe and s. not 34:24
there was neither s. nor shame 374:3
though your s.s be as scarlet 42:20
waive the quantum o' the s. 83:16
where s. abounded 52:48
which is my s. 143:12
wilt thou forgive that s. 143:12
world's as ugly, ay, as s. 235:20
worst s. towards our fellow creatures 357:17
your s. will find you out 32:6
Sincerity: s. is a dangerous thing 417:28
s., is the vital thing 417:2
Sinew: stiffen the s.s 324:10
Sinful: ma says it's s. 136:25
Sing: and I not s.? 92:11
can s. both high and low 352:16
charmingly sweet you s.! 232:17
he didn't s. to me 373:21
he knew himself to s. 254:18
persons die before they s. 115:26
s. because I must 385:12
s.; for I know ye s. 26:14
s. me your song O! 170:18
s. that extremely lovely thing 168:7
so zestfully canst thou s.? 181:16
suppose I shall s. it again 381:23
tell me what she s.s 426:5
themselves when he did s. 325:28
when ... not worth saying, they s. it 25:14
who s. to find your hearts 160:6
will s. like birds i' the cage 330:35
Singe: that it do s. yourself 325:22
Singer: German s.! I should as soon 163:2
idle s. of an empty day 266:4
lived a s. in France 381:15
none hear beside the s. 230:7
s.s went before 36:26
Singest: soaring ever s. 364:7
Singing: suddenly burst out s. 304:7
there is delight in s. 230:7
ye have a s. face 26:14
Singing-boy: six little s.-b.s 22:10
Single: nothing in the world is s. 361:9
s. in the field 426:3
s. man in possession of a good fortune 15:16
Singularity: s. is ... a clue 145:4
Sink: pour them down the s. 110:7
Sinking: someone is s. today 401:24
strange alacrity in s. 144:13

Slave – *contd*
must suckle s.s 91:11
rogue and peasant s. 316:23
s.s cannot breathe in England 124:32
S.s of the Lamp 10:10
s.s . . . preached him and Christ 72:4
soundly as the wretched s. 324:20
very s. of circumstance 93:16
you were a Christian s. 186:21
Slavery: s. they can have anywhere 80:15
Slay: does not s., nor is it slain 30:7
Slayer: red s. thinks he slays 154:8
who considers this is a s. 30:7
Sleep: awaked as one out of s. 36:33
between a s. and a s. 380:11
care-charmer S. 128:20
care-charming S. 26:13
Death and his brother S.! 359:23
dovecot doors of s. 250:25
each day dies with s. 195:2
first sweet s. of night 360:16
give their readers s. 284:2
giveth his beloved s. 38:17 70:2
God bless the inventor of s. 105:11
great gift of s. 186:20
here I lay me down to s. 6:5
I have come to the borders of s. 395:2
I s., but my heart waketh 42:12
in s. a king 356:7
let them s., Lord 143:3
life is rounded with a s. 350:18
Macbeth does murder s. 333:23
medicine thee to that sweet s. 343:29
no s. till morn 88:27
O s.! O gentle s.! 322:30
old and grey and full of s. 429:25
one short s. past 143:5
quiet s. and a sweet dream 248:7
rock you to s. and guard you 203:5
sang themselves to s. 190:18
six hours in s. 114:7
s. after toil 372:1
s. as I in childhood . . . slept 112:15
s. before you fight 10:8
s., death's counterfeit 334:1
s., Death's twin-brother 385:32
s. is a death 69:13
s. is good, death is better 186:5
s.! it is a gentle thing 115:3
s. like double-gentlemen 137:10
s., my boy, my dearest boy! 203:5
s., my little one, s. 389:31
s. of a labouring man 41:9
s. shall neither night nor day 332:8
s. that is among the lonely hills 426:6
s. that knits up 333:23
S., the certain knot of peace 366:8
s. the s. of death 59:16
s. the s. that knows not breaking 305:16
s. to wake 72:23
sooner to s. 221:20
sweet child S., the filmy-eyed 364:4
sweet restorer, balmy s.! 430:7
talks in someone else's s. 14:10
then, s., dear, s. 26:20
there are two gates of S. 405:17
threatened, not in vain, with s. 286:6

Sleep – *contd*
thy deep and dreamless s. 67:21
till tired he s.s 287:3
time enough for s. 199:13
to s.: perchance to dream 316:29
unseasonable and immoderate s. 206:15
voice cry 's. no more! 333:23
what hath night to do with s.? 252:21
when we s. we are awake 263:18
where s.s she now? 131:29
while some must s. 317:26
will not let you s. 21:22
yet a little s. 39:9
Sleeper: goodly men and the sun-hazed s. 396:4
in the seven s.s' den 142:24
s.s in that quiet earth 67:1
Sleepeth: not dead but s. 47:36
peradventure he s. 33:16
Sleeping: s. alone in the depths 395:11
wakened us from s. 67:13
Sleepless: yet do lie s.! 422:2
Sleepy-head: let's to bed, says S.-h. 272:3
Slepen: that s. i ne mai 4:24
Slept: he s. with his fathers 33:14
we thought her dying when she s. 193:5
Slide: s.s . . . will now be shown 213:3
Slimy: s. things did crawl 114:24
Sling: s.s and arrows 316:29
Slip: since he gave us all the s. 78:5
Slipper: same old s.s, same old rice 229:23
walks in his golden s.s 79:23
Slop-kettle: coffee and other s.-k. 113:22
Sloth: much time in studies is s. 18:39
resty s. 313:22
shake off dull s. 220:12
Slough: s. was Despond 79:12
Slovenliness: s. is not part of religion 413:22
Slow: but ain't it s.? 187:14
s. and steady wins the race 235:16
s. of speech, and of a s. tongue 31:35
tardy as too s. 348:28
tarry a while, says S. 272:3
Slug: s.s that come crawling out 22:16
Sluggard: foul s.'s comfort 98:15
s. is wiser in his own conceit 40:17
'tis the voice of the s. 411:10
Slug-horn: s.-h. to my lips I set 71:32
Slumber: equal quantity of s. 137:10
hast thou golden s.s? 131:1
he . . . will not s. 38:11
imagine unquiet s.s 67:1
lie still and s. 411:3
like infant's s.s, pure and light 220:2
little sleep, a little s. 39:9
ports of s. open wide 323:13
s. did my spirit seal 426:1
s. is more sweet than toil 388:5
S.'s chain has bound me 265:13
s.s kiss your eyes 131:4
to soothing s. seven 211:13
Slut: I am not a s. 312:6
now foul s.s in dairies 120:4
Sly: tough . . . and devilish s.! 134:36
Small: contemneth s. things 46:10
day of s. things 45:14
grind exceeding s. 237:6
they said, is it s.? 232:4

Small-Clothes: Gumbril's Patent S.-C. 202:2
Smart: as lief pray with Kit S. 207:21
  s. to live on this yearth 409:24
  surety ... shall s. for it 39:17
Smartness: s. of an attorney's clerk 141:19
Smattering: s. of everything 139:9
Smelfungus: learned S. 374:5
Smell: ancient and fish-like s. 350:6
  and s. so sweet 320:21
  compound of villanous s. 339:21
  sweet keen s. 301:7
Smile: eternal s.s his emptiness betray 285:15
  fleeting s. playing about his lips 397:21
  good gigantic s. 73:25
  I dare not beg a s. 189:6
  one vast substantial s. 134:8
  one who has not given his mother a s. 406:5
  seldom he s.s, and s.s in such a sort 326:27
  share the good man's s. 172:15
  s., and be a villain 315:24
  s. at us, pay us, pass us 110:1
  s. on the face of the tiger 6:7
  s., s., s. 13:1
  s. that glowed celestial 258:15
  s. that was childlike and bland 184:2
  s. we would aspire to 326:1
  s.s awake you 131:4
  s.s before they dwindle 362:24
  s.s, the tears, of boyhood's years 265:13
  smiled a kind of sickly s. 184:6
  teeth in way of s. 337:3
  vain tribute of a s. 305:25
  with a s. on her lips 306:12
  with s.s and soap 102:10
Smiled: Never S. Again 186:13
  until she s. on me 114:10
Smilest: thou s. and art still 11:16
Smiling: it was s. in my face 333:9
  s. through her tears 192:28
Smirk: serious and the s. 136:22
Smite: stands ready to s. once 254:32
  up and s. them 269:5
Smith: bless you, Wicked Captain S. 118:2
  chuck it, S.! 109:17
  s. a mighty man is he 237:17
  s. was the first murderer's son 125:25
Smithy: village s. stands 237:17
Smitten: one be s. against the other 46:8
Smok: whan she cast of hir s. 107:37
Smoke: above the s. and stir 252:18
  as s. is driven away 36:22
  corrupted by this stinking s. 204:1
  little s., in pallid moonshine, died 215:9
  streams ... like a downward s. 387:30
Smooth: s. as monumental alabaster 344:11
  speak unto us s. things 43:9
Smote: and s. him thus 344:17
  s. him under the fifth rib 33:4
  s. him with the edge of the sword 32:4
  s. them hip and thigh 32:28
Smyler: s. with the knyf 107:23
Snaffle: use the s. and the bit 96:4
Snail: creeping like s. 311:14
  like s.s did creep 189:10
  said a whiting to a s. 100:28
  s.'s on the thorn 75:16
  turn not pale, beloved s. 101:2

616

Snake: didst devise the S. 159:15
  doth like a s. renew 360:7
  like a wounded s., drags 286:6
  scotched the s. 334:11
  s. came to my water-trough 231:11
  s. is living yet 28:19
  s. lurks in the grass 406:3
  spotted s.s with double tongue 340:11
Snapper-up: s.-u. of unconsidered trifles 354:8
Snare: deliver thee from the s. 37:11
  delusion, a mockery, and a s. 132:1
Snark: s. was a Boojum 102:12
Snatches: s. of old tunes 319:12
Sneer: s. of cold command 361:23
  teach the rest to s. 285:12
  who can refute a s.? 277:11
Sneering: I was born s. 169:12
Sneeze: beat him when he s.s 100:14
Sneezed: not to be s. at 117:25
Snewed: it s. ... of mete and drinke 107:9
Snickersnee: I drew my s.! 169:23
Snip: S.! snap! s.! they go 191:17
Snob: not to be sometimes a S. 393:2
Snoring: whom, s., she disturbs 124:26
Snow: bloodless lay the untrodden s. 96:10
  but the fall o' the s. 212:5
  by the frost from purest s. 313:9
  deep s. piled above thee 66:23
  fare-wel al the s. 108:12
  garment was white as s. 44:37
  go through sleet and s. 182:7
  half-buried in the s. 236:22
  hath melted like s. 93:2
  He sends the s. in winter 96:2
  I shall be whiter than s. 36:5
  ivy-tod is heavy with s. 115:8
  last year's s.s 404:10
  lawn as white as driven s. 354:16
  long last streak of s. 386:12
  naked in December s. 345:6
  she is near under the s. 416:10
  s. came flying in ... flakes 65:18
  s. falls in the river 84:18
  s. had fallen many nights 64:4
  s. had fallen, s. on s. 300:10
  s. hath retreated 426:29
  s. lay dinted 269:9
  s. lay round about 269:7
  s. on the bare branch 115:23
  s. upon the Desert's dusty face 158:23
  s.s are sparkling to the moon 391:5
  s.s have fled 198:12
  stood shivering in the s. 371:1
  they shall be as white as s. 42:20
  we shall have s. 273:7
  wish a snow in May 331:11
Snowy: S., Flowy, Blowy 154:5
Snuff: only took s. 173:6
  you abuse s.! 116:30
Snuff-box: of amber s.-b. justly vain 289:2
Snug: s. as a bug 162:13
So: if I said s., it was s. 173:22
Soap: nice cake of s. 22:11
  s. and education 401:5
  used your s. two years ago 293:23
  washing his hands with invisible s. 193:13
  what! no s.? 161:3

Straw: find quarrel in a s. 318:28
  s. to make brick 31:36
  take a s. and throw it up 308:6
  tickled with a s. 287:3
Strawberries: feed upon s., sugar and cream 272:5
  good s. in your garden 347:3
  s. swimming in the cream 280:10
  two or three great s. 16:21
Stray: you'll fondly s. 166:1
Stream: as the s.s in the south 38:15
  freezing S. below 359:17
  land of s.s! 387:30
  lapse of murmuring s.s 258:8
  large s.s from little fountains 156:7
  make my s. my great example 131:33
  more pellucid s.s 421:12
  shallow s.s run dimpling all the way 285:15
  sitting by desolate s.s 275:28
  still glides the s. 425:19
  s. I go a-fishing in 397:4
  s. runs fast 264:17
  s. that flashest white 386:22
  s.s, wherefrom ye learn your song 65:23
  strove against the s. 390:9
  swap horses ... crossing a s. 235:2
  when meadow, grove and s. 423:5
Streamer: s.s waving in the wind 166:19
Strebt: irrt der Mensch, so lang er s. 171:3
Street: down the long and silent s. 416:9
  gibber in the Roman s.s 313:34
  in the long unlovely s. 385:8
  jumping the London s.s 243:7
  on the bald s. 385:9
  s. cries all about 418:18
  s. ... was pure gold 57:23
  s. which is called Straight 52:18
  through s.s broad and narrow 7:16
Strength: as thy days, so shall thy s. be 32:14
  excellent to have a giant's s. 336:15
  God is our refuge and s. 35:31
  God would give him s. 212:23
  in the s. of the horse 38:32
  is a tower of s. 347:15
  my s. is as the s. of ten 391:12
  my s. is made perfect 54:34
  s. might endure for a span 380:9
  s. that in old days moved earth 392:9
  s. the more is 79:32
  s. through joy 234:14
  their s. is to sit still 43:8
  they go from s. to s. 37:2
  to try the soul's s. on 73:21
Stress: storm and s. 225:22
Stretched: things which he s. 401:1
Strife: ancient forms of party s. 386:5
  keep ... an unprofitable s. 359:9
  none was worth my s. 230:2
  or a double s. 19:14
  revolving hopeless s. 65:12
  s. is o'er, the battle done 289:32
Strike: end of the envoy, I shall s. 301:12
  fine [passage], s. it out 208:29
  that seems to s. at me 412:7
String: chewing little bits of s. 27:24
  end of a golden s. 59:15
  harp not on that s. 347:12
  nothing of my own but the s. 263:25

String – *contd*
  s.s ... in the human heart 133:16
  untune that s. 351:10
  warbled to the s. 253:26
Stripling: sword nor spear the s. took 123:10
Strive: errs so long as he s.s 171:3
Stroke: till I received thy s. 123:11
Strong: be s. and quit yourselves 32:36
  I again am s. 423:8
  like men be s. 54:21
  only the S. shall thrive 308:21
  out of the s. came forth sweetness 32:26
  s. in will to strive 392:9
  s. man armed keepeth his palace 50:24
  s. man must go 75:27
  s. men shall bow themselves 41:33
  s. without rage 131:33
  suffer and be s. 236:26
  two s. men stand face to face 222:12
  wants that little s. 192:13
  we then that are s. 53:21
Stronger: s. by weakness 408:6
Strongest: s. man upon earth 202:26
  s. shall stand the most weak 77:11
Stronghold: safe s. our God is still 239:22
  turn you to the s. 45:15
Strove: I s., made head 76:5
  I s. with none 230:2
  little still she s. 90:17
Struck: collected ... its strength and s. 199:4
Structure: s. in a winding stair 187:32
Struggle: gaze ... on another's s.s 239:16
  perpetual s. for room and food 244:15
  say not the s. naught availeth 113:19
Strumpet: s.'s fool 309:13
Strut: s.s and frets his hour 335:23
Stubble: earth's base built on s. 253:7
Stubbs: S. butters Freeman 298:14
Stud: thrust out ... from the devil's s. 71:29
Student: s. to the end of my days 108:16
Studie: s. was but litel on the bible 107:11
Studies: s. serve for delight 18:38
  too much time in s. 18:39
Studious: s. let me sit 396:18
Study: I am slow of s. 339:35
  in some brown s. 240:7
  not s. to live 19:10
  result of previous s. 15:20
  s. is a weariness of the flesh 42:2
  s. is like the heaven's glorious sun 331:10
  s. what you most affect 349:17
Studying: s. how I may compare 346:15
Stuff: listen all day to such s. 100:12
  of that perilous s. 335:18
  s. of life to knit me 199:27
  was there ever ... such s. 166:28
  we are such s. 350:18
Stultitiam: misce s. consiliis brevem 198:13
Stumble: brother, do not s. 243:1
  s. that run fast 348:23
Stumbling: for a stone of s. 42:29
Stumbling-block: let no man put a s.-b. 53:20
Stump: he fought upon his s.s 358:26
Stupid: came of entirely s. people 99:14
Stupidity: against s. the gods 304:17
  no sin except s. 417:31
  such ... s., Sir, is not in Nature 208:5

Talking – *contd*
you will still be t. 341:5
Tall : new and neat and adequately t. 109:23
t. he almost touched the sky 191:13
Taller : t. by almost the breadth of my nail 378:26
Tambourine : play the t. on her other knee 136:28
Tamburlaine : T., the scourge of God 245:27
Tame : t. when once it is within thee 187:20
wild ... though I seem t. 427:25
Tameless : like thee : t., and swift 361:19
Tamer : t. of the human breast 177:20
Tane : t. unto the tither did say 21:19
Tangere : noli me t. 52:11
Tankard : unfailing remedy – the T. 95:5
Tannenbaum : O T., O T. 304:23
Tanqueray : *Second Mrs. T.* 28:5
Tap : t. at the pane 74:13
Taper : at the t. of conwiviality 137:6
glimmering t.s to the sun 126:15
hold up to the sun my little t. 91:37
out went the t. as she hurried in 215:9
Tapestry : wrong side of a Turkish t. 200:12
Tapping : suddenly there came a t. 283:16
Tapster : folks of a surly T. tell 159:17
Tara : mute as T.'s walls 264:22
Taradiddle : for telling t.s 233:16
Ta-ra-ra-boom-de-ay : T.! 304:10
Tar-Baby : contrapshun what he called a T.-B. 183:17
T.-B. ain't sayin' 183:18
Tarde : cinco en punto de la t. 237:23
Tarried : too long we have t. 232:17
Tarsus : stately ship of T. 259:19
Tart : Knave of Hearts he stole the t.s 273:20
rice and a cranberry t. 232:15
Tartar : you will find the T. 243:13
Task : common t. would furnish 219:23
gets his t., and there's an end 206:29
long day's t. is done 310:2
sore t. does not divide 313:32
thy worldly t. hast done 313:25
what he reads as a t. 207:25
what is our t.? 235:17
Task-master : my great T.-M.'s eye 259:30
Tasmanian : T.s ... are now extinct 248:16
Tassie : fill it in a silver t. 83:19
Taste : arbiter of t. 382:1
create the t. by which he is to be relished 427:6
depends upon the t. and fancy 138:27
disliked the killibeate t. 138:32
let me t. the whole 75:29
never t. who always drink 293:3
sans eyes, sans t. 311:14
suspect his t. in higher matters 228:16
t. not; handle not 55:12
t.s may not be the same 358:4
things sweet to t. 345:4
various are the t.s of men 3:7
whose mortal t. brought death 255:16
Taught : as if you t. them not 286:15
Taughte : afterward he t. 107:13
Tavern : happiness ... by a good t. 209:9
opened a t. for his friends 144:20
sat in t.s while the tempest hurled 198:26
there is a t. in the town 8:11
within the T. caught 159:13
Tavernes : he knew the t. wel 107:3

Taxation : t. without representation 276:2
Taxes : all t. ... fall upon agriculture 167:14
as true as t. 134:25
except death and t. 162:15
Tea : best sweeteners of t. 157:28
here's your nice ... t., dear 394:16
if this is t., then I wish for coffee 293:27
slavery of the t. and coffee 113:22
t., although an Oriental 110:8
t. ... taste of boiled boots 393:5
when the t. is brought 262:20
Teach : t. me, my God and King 187:28
Teachable : eminently t. 407:3
Teaches : he who cannot, t. 358:7
Team : is my t. ploughing 199:22
Tear : and a t. in her eye 306:12
big round t.s coursed 310:27
bitter t.s to shed 120:16
bread of t.s 37:1
drew iron t.s 253:26
drop, drop, slow t.s 160:20
drop t.s as fast 344:17
droppe the brynie t. wythe mee 106:15
dropped a t. upon the word 374:25
every t. from every eye 58:26
far too freely moved to t.s 27:29
God shall wipe away all t.s 57:20
hence these t.s 392:24
his droppings of warm t.s 70:11
human deeds have their t.s 404:18
if you have t.s 327:31
keep time with my salt t.s 211:20
kissed again with t.s 389:27
lie too deep for t.s 423:25
meed of some melodious t. 254:19
never ate his bread with t.s 171:20
parted in silence and t.s 94:6
rained many a t. 319:5
shed a bitter t. 101:19
shed one English t. 241:1
some natural t.s they dropped 258:31
son of these t.s should perish 14:14
source of sympathetic t.s 178:20
splendid t. from the passion-flower 388:23
t. is an intellectual thing 59:14
t.s are in the falling rain 233:13
t.s fell with the dews 388:10
t.s, idle t.s 389:35
t.s such as angels weep 256:9
t.s that overflow thy urn 229:25
T.s wash out a Word of it 159:11
t.s when they would devour 18:16
those t.s are pearl 355:14
'twill cost a sigh, a t. 22:4
watered heaven with their t.s 60:17
weep thy girlish t.s 410:11
Tease : because he knows it t.s 100:14
ye thus t. me together 166:8
Tea-shop : looking ... in the low-class t.-s.s 65:2
Tea-tray : like a t.-t. in the sky 100:18
Teche : and gladly t. 107:7
Teddy bear : what are you thinking about, T. B.? 202:9
Tedious : returning were as t. 334:31
were as t. as a king 341:31
Teeth : escaped with the skin of my t. 34:6
keep their t. clean 312:31

Thorn – *contd*
  withering on the virgin t. 339:25
Thoroughfare: mind ... a t. for all thoughts 219:17
Thought: armour is his honest t. 427:13
  best that is known and t. 10:8
  best which has been t. and said 11:34
  between a thing and a t. 277:12
  bloody t.s with violent pace 343:36
  device for avoiding t. 186:8
  every third t. ... my grave 350:28
  familiar to my slaughterous t.s 335:22
  forge and working-house of t. 324:28
  give thy t.s no tongue 314:32
  great t.s come from the heart 403:8
  have bloody t.s 350:19
  he t. I t. he t. I slept 279:2
  heart that t. the t. 20:21
  hidden in the light of t. 364:9
  I shun the t. that lurks 250:26
  in loftiness of t. surpassed 148:9
  joy of elevated t. 421:21
  more strong than all poetic t. 385:19
  my sad t.s doth clear 403:2
  my t.s are not your t.s 44:4
  my t.s remain below 318:9
  near to be t. so shortly 342:1
  not for thy t.s but mine 89:16
  not seem a moment's t. 428:7
  nought is worth a t. 290:13
  one t., one grace, one wonder 245:23
  pale cast of t. 316:29
  perish the t.! 111:26
  pleasant t.s bring sad t.s 421:25
  poetry ... wording of his own highest t.s 219:1
  pure in t. as angels 298:19
  rear the tender t. 396:10
  restrain in me the cursed t.s 333:14
  second and sober t.s 187:1
  she pined in t. 352:28
  speech created t. 362:21
  strange seas of t., alone 424:20
  sweet silent t. 355:10
  take no t. for the morrow 47:19
  taking t. can add one cubit 47:16
  then feed on t.s 256:36
  they do not feel their t. 153:20
  thou pleasing, dreadful t.! 1:14
  t. does not become a young woman 365:7
  t. is free 350:14
  t. raised to heaven is the most perfect prayer
    234:7
  t. of all by turns 422:2
  t. of thee puts all the pomp 285:1
  t. of you remaining deeply folded 381:17
  t.'s the slave of life 322:4
  t. to Donne was an experience 153:20
  t. would destroy their paradise 178:12
  t.s, all passions, all delights 116:7
  t.s are often new 206:9
  t.s hardly to be packed 76:11
  t.s his only friends 97:4
  t.s of youth are long 236:28
  t.s pay no duty 240:1
  t.s that wander through eternity 256:20
  t.s to memory dear 306:22
  t.s ... too deep for tears 423:25
  t.s which were not their t.s 89:11

Thought – *contd*
  to a green t. 246:26
  to conceal their t.s 407: 7
  to disguise his t.s 382:6
  to have common t. 287:22
  trouble himself with any such t.s 324:7
  two souls with but a single t. 238:15
  unmeaning thing they call a t. 286:6
  wad ye tak a t. an' men'! 82:15
  wayward t.s will slide 426:10
  we ought to control our t.s 129:13
  we t. so still 232:20
  what oft was t. 285:27
  what our t.s make it 14:25
  white celestial t. 402:19
  wish was father ... to that t. 323:14
Thousand: difference of forty t. 412:16
  draw for a t. pounds 2:18
  fifty t. men slain 408:17
  from the t.s He hath freed 105:22
  if I had five t. a year 393:21
  one ten t. of those men 324:21
  slain his t.s, and David his ten t.s 32:41
  ten t. saw I at a glance 421:6
  t. shall fail at thy side 37:12
  t. shall flee at the rebuke 43:11
  t.s at his bidding speed 260:1
  t.s equally were meant 378:16
Thraldom: but single t. 19:14
Thread: feels at each t. 286:25
  silver t.s among the gold 296:7
  spinning the t. of your being 15:2
  this line of scarlet t. 32:16
  with a silk t. plucks 348:20
Threadneedle: Old Lady of T. Street 170:20
Threat: no terror, Cassius, in your t.s 328:9
  t.s of pain and ruin 177:12
Threatening: breathing out t.s 52:16
Three: ever T. and ever One 269:6
  grant but t. 91:9
  night she'll hae but t. 21:5
  simplicity of the t. per cents 307:14
  thou wast one of the t. 385:2
  though he was only t. 251:22
  t. is company 416:17
Threepenny: t.-bus young man 169:38
Threescore: of my t. years and ten 199:12
  t. s. [miles] and ten 272:16
Thresh: t. of the deep-sea rain 223:23
Threshold: stand upon the t. of the new 408:6
Thrift: t., t., Horatio! 314:19
  with due respective t. 278:23
Throat: cutting foreign t.s 348:1
  down the t. of Old Time 135:8
  scuttled ship or cut a t. 91:1
  sore t.s are always worse 15:14
Throne: beneath the shadow of Thy T. 411:11
  burnished t. glowed 152:31
  first by the t. 74:4
  flows by the t. of God 303:23
  from her ebon t. 430:8
  guiding the fiery-wheeled t. 253:20
  here is my t. 328:29
  living t., the sapphire-blaze 178:21
  this royal t. of kings 345:8
  t. of human felicity 211:7
  t.s, dominations, princedoms 257:37

W

Walk – *contd*
  whene'er I take my w.s abroad 410:13
  where'er you w. 288:9
  will you w. a little faster? 100:28
Walked: he w. by himself 225:5
  neighbour ... w. very crookedly 378:6
  when she has w. before 172:27
Walking: craves wary w. 327:4
  I nauseate w. 119:6
  I was w. all alane 21:19
  sorry I did not let it keep on w. 397:20
  w. up and down in it 33:33
Wall: backs to the w. 180:10
  beyond the fiery w.s of the world 239:12
  Chinese W. of Milton 153:19
  four great w.s ... to cover 70:19
  in the office of a w. 345:8
  on the outward w.s 335:21
  or close the w. up 324:10
  outward w.s so costly gay 357:3
  pin bores through his castle-w. 345:22
  stone w.s do not a prison make 238:12
  that doesn't love a w. 163:10
  that the w. is strong 416:7
  these w.s thy sphere 144:1
  thou art staring at the w. 387:11
  w.s of dung 288:3
  watch the w., my darling 224:12
  white-washed w. 172:20
  with w.s and towers was girdled 115:31
  without a city w. 3:15
  wooden w.s are the best w.s 121:1
Wallace: wha hae wi' W. bled 84:10
Waller: W. was smooth 289:10
Walnut: across the w.s and the wine 388:28
  w. tree with two dun cows 303:12
Walrus: suppose, the w. said 101:19
  w. and the carpenter 101:19
Walsinghame: holy land of W. 295:8
Waltz: band swoons to a w. 202:13
Waly: w. w. up the bank 21:23
Wan: why so pale and w. 377:7
Wand: with thine opiate w. 364:2
Wander: not forced him w. 112:23
  would w., if I might 266:9
Wandered: I've w. east, I've w. west 266:22
Wanderer: foiled circuitous w. 11:20
  w. from the narrow way 124:9
  w. is man from birth 10:24
Wandering: chid their w.s 172:10
  have one with me w. 266:9
Want: convicted of ... wretchedness, and w. 369:26
  everything that he w.s 200:19
  I didn't w. to do it 242:15
  I shall not w. 35:9
  people don't know what they w. 246:7
  ring out the w., the care 386:6
  third is freedom from w. 299:10
  to provide for human w.s 81:7
  w. of a thing is perplexing 402:5
  w. of money is so 87:2
  w. something you probably won't w. 194:2
  you can do what you w. 203:12
Wanted: bought things because she w, 'em 402:6
Wanting: art found w. 44:35
  w. that have wanted everything 184:23

Wanton: sleep, pretty w.s 131:4
  w. smiled, father wept 179:2
  weep not, my w. 179:1
Wantonness: kindles in clothes a w. 188:20
Wapping: parted at W. Old Stairs 281:11
War: all skilful in the w.s 402:16
  all their w.s are merry 109:20
  blast of w. blows 324:10
  brazen throat of w. 258:29
  but it is not w. 63:26
  desires peace, prepare for w. 403:11
  disciplines of w.s 324:15
  do in the Great W., daddy? 4:18
  except the British W. Office 357:19
  forced into w. by ignorance 397:14
  galleon, and an English man of w. 164:16
  guarantee success in w. 111:18
  has to maintain itself by w. 264:1
  hath all this w. been wrought 244:11
  he maketh w.s to cease 35:32
  he that first invented w. 245:20
  Horses and Power and W. 222:13
  I am tired and sick of w. 365:31
  image of w., without its guilt 370:3
  in w., moral considerations account 268:7
  laws are dumb in time of w. 112:9
  little of the w. as he will 18:26
  marching as to w. 23:10
  money the sinews of w. 18:25
  neither shall they learn w. 42:21
  never was a good w. 162:14
  no less renowned than w. 260:7
  no less than w. to waste 258:30
  no w. nor prince's funeral 247:6
  nor w. nor battle's sound 255:7
  sentence is for open w. 256:18
  so dauntless in w. 306:11
  state of w. by nature 378:19
  still, w.s and lechery 351:30
  sweat in pigmy w.s 387:2
  testament of bleeding w. 346:1
  that w. is an evil 397:14
  they are for w. 38:9
  they came forth to w. 243:9
  thousand w.s of old 386:8
  to the old w.s: arise 395:6
  to w. and arms I fly 238:13
  unsuccessful or successful w. 124:30
  voices prophesying w.! 116:3
  W., and the pity of W. 276:24
  W. between Men and Women 397:22
  w. ... continuation of politics 112:20
  w., dearth, age, agues 143:2
  w. he sung, is toil 147:21
  w., is hell 365:31
  w. is much too serious 382:7
  W. is Peace 275:12
  w. is regarded as wicked 417:30
  w. of everyone against everyone 190:7
  w.'s a game 125:24
  w. to the knife 277:10
  w. waged without monetary reserves 294:9
  w., w. is still the cry 88:19
  w. was in his heart 36:9
  w.'s glorious art 430:5
  w.s and rumours of w.s 49:17
  w.s brought nothing about 149:12

Wave – *contd*
lift me as a w., a leaf 361:19
light-hearted masters of the w.s 11:14
longed-for dash of w.s 11:20
mounting w. will roll us shorewards 387:29
out-did the sparkling w.s in glee 421:7
silver w.s of thy sweet singing 362:25
sunk beneath the w. 123:20
thro' the w. that runs for ever 386:30
upon an orient w. 255:11
walk o'er the western w. 364:1
w. hangs that shall cut off their sun 130:10
w.s beside them danced 421:7
w.s make towards the pebbled shore 355:19
w.s wanne 244:10
what are the wild w.s saying 100:4
when the w.s went high 146:20
wild w.s whist 349:37
with w. and whirlwind wrestle 236:9
Wax: as w. melteth before the fire 36:22
how neat she spreads the w. 410:19
mysterious virtue of w. and parchment 80:11
w. to receive 88:10
Wax-work: if you think we're w.-w.s 101:13
Way: and w.s be foul 332:1
as I wandered by the w. 363:2
broad is the w. 48:26
catch the nearest w. 332:21
consider her w.s 39:8
dirty, dangerous w. 173:37
dwelt among the untrodden w.s 425:23
fall not out by the w. 31:27
find out his uncouth w. 256:25
fled him down the labyrinthine w.s 395:14
flowers to strew Thy w. 187:27
from the cheerful w.s of men 257:1
heav'n's wide pathless w. 253:22
her w.s are w.s of pleasantness 39:5
I am already on the w. 221:9
I am the w., the truth, and the life 51:46
in His w.s with men I find Him not 384:23
let me count the w.s 70:7
long is the w. and hard 256:26
many are the w.s ... to heaven 105:4
mony a weary w. 266:22
narrow is the w. 48:27
neither are your w.s my w.s 44:4
newest kind of w.s 323:15
nine and sixty w.s 223:10
plods his weary w. 176:21
prepare ye the w. of the Lord 43:21
rough uneven w.s 345:11
scorning parochial w.s 182:14
solar w. or milky w. 286:22
that's the eftest w. 342:2
this is the w. 43:13
to justify God's w.s to man 200:1
took their solitary w. 258:31
twinkle on the milky w. 421:5
W. is like an empty vessel 230:22
w. of an eagle in the air 40:30
w. up is the w. down 187:11
w. was long, the wind was cold 305:20
w.s are w.s of gentleness 372:25
w.s I keep, and pass, and turn 154:8
whole breadth of the w. 79:18
wonderful w. wid you 175:19

Way – *contd*
work its w. with the women 139:2
your great and gracious w.s 279:7
We: on horseback after w. 122:24
people like us, are W. 224:25
they're not w., w. are 142:20
w., w. only, are left 11:5
Weak: concessions of the w. 80:7
delicately w. 287:21
surely the W. shall perish 308:21
to be w. is miserable 255:24
w. alone repent 90:6
Weakness: all else is w. 404:6
amiable w. 158:3
made perfect in w. 54:34
no more w. than is natural 397:13
no w., no contempt, dispraise 259:24
Weal: come w., come woe 307:3
Wealth: all that w. e'er gave 177:5
as their w. increaseth 245:16
consume w. without producing it 357:14
if our w. commands us 81:35
if we command our w. 81:35
pauper in the midst of w. 198:6
poor man's w. 366:8
rich man's w. is his ... city 39:15
squandering w. was his peculiar art 147:3
w. and commerce, laws 244:18
w. I ask not 376:5
w. ye find, another keeps 363:11
where w. accumulates 172:4
Weaned: were we not w. till then? 142:24
Weapon: w. which heaven has given 221:22
Wear: better to w. out 128:2
costly to w. every day 341:14
rather w. out than rust 414:15
so w.s she to him 352:24
Weariness: pale for w. of climbing heaven 363:25
study is a w. of the flesh 42:2
w. can snore 313:22
w. may toss him 188:5
w., the fever, and the fret 216:26
Weary: art thou w.? 269:3
w. be at rest 33:37
w. let him sit 187:30
w. se'nnights 332:8
w., stale, flat, and unprofitable 314:11
Weasel: pop goes the w.! 244:16
w. sucks eggs 311:1
Weather: come wind, come w. 79:30
dreadful hot w. 16:4
first talk is of the w. 206:4
good ... in itself, but not in fine w. 113:7
if it prove fair w. 377:11
it was gorgeous w. 95:18
little we fear w. without 393:27
season of calm w. 423:20
through pleasant and through cloudy w. 22:4
under the roof of blue Italian w. 360:22
w. the cuckoo likes 182:19
Weather-wise: some are w.-w. 162:17
Web: O, what a tangled w. we weave 306:17
out flew the w. 386:36
trafficked for strange w.s 278:19
Webster: W. was much possessed by death 153:8
Wed: December when they w. 312:11
Wedding: bought her w. clothes 2:13

Wheel – *contd*

I cannot mind my w. 230:4
round went the w.s 122:26
shee the w.s go round 180:7
turn thy w.! 329:26
w. broken at the cistern 41:35
w. ... in the midst of a w. 44:23
w. is come full circle 331:3
w.'s kick and the wind's song 248:5
why tarry the w.s of his chariots 32:25
your w. is out of order 97:10
Wheelbarrow: as she wheeled her w. 7:16
When: What and Why and W. 223:13
Where: echo answers – 'W.?' 88:15
go we know not w. 336:23
have they fixed the w. and when? 184:9
Wherefore: he had a w. 86:7
mind the why and w. 168:28
Wherewithal: had not always w. 292:34
Whig: caught the W.s bathing 140:9
first W. was the Devil 209:23
he hated a W. 210:29
I do not like much to see a W. 210:18
Tory men and W. measures 140:26
we have dished the W.s 132:12
whether I were a W. 378:28
W. to pretend to be honest 210:22
W.s admit no force but argument 69:21
Whimper: with a bang but a w. 152:9
Whimsies: they have my w. 292:26
Whinger: out with your w. 22:7
Whip: hath chastised you with w.s 33:12
in every honest hand a w. 344:6
smack went the w. 122:26
w. for a horse 40:11
w. maketh marks in the flesh 46:13
w., of cricket's bone 347:29
Whipped: for false quantities, was w. 148:28
Whipping: who would 'scape w.? 316:22
Whirligig: on this w. of Time 392:19
Whirlwind: rides in the w. 1:9
shall reap the w. 44:38
sweeping w.'s sway 176:17
Whisker: dye one's w.s green 102:3
Whiskies: extent of two w. 263:6
Whisky: freedom and w. gang thegither 82:24
Whisper: busy w., circling round 172:17
there's a w. down the field 223:22
w. who dares! 252:1
Whispering: it keeps eternal w.s 218:5
Whist: loved a good game at w. 228:21
Whistle: again the Cousin's w. 70:20
as clear as a w. 88:3
joly w. wel y-wet 107:33
let it w. as it will 306:13
pay too much for your w. 162:19
quoth she, and w.s thrice 114:26
w., and I'll come to you 85:2
Whistling: w. aloud 58:14
w. half a dozen bars 374:15
w. to keep myself 149:4
White: change from black to w. 191:14
nor w. so very w. 97:14
O! my soul is w. 61:4
O so w.! O so soft! 212:5
their w. it stays for ever 141:22
too w. for hell 148:4

White – *contd*

w. already to harvest 51:29
w., clear w. inside 223:4
w. in a single night 93:13
W. Man's burden 224:29
w. shall not neutralize the black 77:2
w. – then melts for ever 84:18
Whitehall: sentinel on W. gate 240:20
up and down W. H. Court 281:1
Whitest: regard him as the w. man 213:3
Whitethroat: w. builds, and all the swallows 73:14
Whitewash: whiter than the w. 8:16
Whither: I know not *W.* 159:4
Whiting: 'extremes meet', as the w. said 193:21
said a w. to a snail 100:28
Who: How and Where and W. 223:13
w. or why, or which or *what*? 232:7
Whole: I am equal and w. 380:26
parts of one stupendous w. 286:26
seeing the w. of them 302:12
till thou inspire the w. 117:15
who saith, 'a W. I planned 75:31
w. has been surveyed 206:21
w. need not a physician 48:34
Whooping: out of all w.! 311:24
Whore: all the w.s were burnt alive 292:33
judgement of the great w. 57:14
more like a w.'s than a man's 223:33
teach the morals of a w. 207:11
woman's a w. 209:1
Whoring: w. with their own inventions 37:25
Why: for every w. 86:7
mind the w. and wherefore 168:28
not to reason w. 383:10
they knew not w. 86:3
w., Edward, tell me w.? 420:6
'w.' is plain as way 311:12
W. not knowing 159:4
Wicked: half so w. as Lord George Hell 27:2
heart is ... desperately w. 44:21
I's mighty w. 376:19
let the w. fall 38:29
let the w. perish 36:22
little better than one of the w. 320:13
no peace ... unto the w. 43:34
something w. this way comes 334:34
w. cease from troubling 33:37
w. flee when no man pursueth 40:24
Wickedness: little to the w. of a woman 46:12
manifold sins and w. 290:18
path of w. 21:17
spiritual w. in high places 55:3
w. is always easier 210:16
ye have plowed w. 45:1
Wicket-gate: I see yonder w.-g. 79:11
Widdicombe: go to W. Fair 8:14
Wide: w. as a church-door 348:32
world too w. 311:14
Widow: and she was a w. 50:18
be wery careful o' w.s 138:8
came a certain poor w. 50:7
devour w.s' houses 50:6
do like other w.s 166:7
'eard o' the W. at Windsor 225:1
here's to the w. of fifty 365:27
judge of the w.s 36:23
or Molly Stark's a w. 373:6

Women – *contd*
  passing the love of w. 33:3
  punishment that w. bear 312:25
  souls of w. are so small 86:30
  these tell-tale w. rail 347:10
  though w. are angels 93:7
  W. and Horses and Power 222:13
  w. and wine should life 166:2
  w. are a sex by themselves 27:5
  w. are angels, wooing 351:8
  w. are much more like each other 109 : 7
  w. are not so young 26:26
  w. are strongest 45:21
  w are ... troublesome cattle 238:18
  w. become like their mothers 416:21
  w. cloy the appetites 309:29
  w. come and go 152:12
  w. [differ] ... as Heaven and Hell 384:21
  w. have no characters 287:20
  w. I cannot but give way to 281:3
  w. in London who flirt 416:16
  w. keep silence 54:7
  w. must be half-workers 313:17
  w. never look so well 378:3
  w. pardoned all 91:26
  w. represent the triumph 417:26
  w. require both 87:29
  w. run to extremes 226:7
  w. should talk an hour after supper 26:7
  w. ... styled but the shadows 212:11
Womman: worthy w. al hir lyve 107:12
Wommen: w. desyren to have sovereyntee 108:1
Won: I've w., I've w.! 114:26
  melancholy as a battle w. 412:21
  not unsought be w. 258:11
  things w. are done 351:8
  what you w. or lost 296:13
  where you will never w. 20:12
  woman in this humour w. 346:25
  woman, therefore may be w. 351:2
  woman, therefore to be w. 325:9
Wonder: all a w. and a wild desire 76:19
  common w. of all men 69:5
  his w.s in the deep 37:28
  his w.s to perform 123:17
  how I w. what you are! 382:13
  I w. by my troth 142:24
  I w. what you're at 100:18
  lost the w. of our age 179:9
  signs and my w.s 31:37
  still the w. grew 172:18
  transcendent w. 99:1
  without our special w. 334:28
  w.s are many 370:4
  w.s we seek without us 68:22
Wondered: stood in his shoes and he w. 217:15
Wonderful: name shall be called W. 42:32
  w., w., and most w.! 311:24
Wonderfully: fearfully and w. made 38:27
Woo: April when they w. 312:11
  why ... do I w.? 279:4
Wood: bows down to w. and stone 222:24
  dark impenetrable w. 306:20
  enter these enchanted w.s 250:7
  for the w.s against the world 62:12
  gods have lived in the w.s 406:2
  green w.s laugh 61:3

Wood – *contd*
  heap on more w.! 306:13
  impulse from a vernal w. 426:11
  never knew the summer w.s 385:13
  old w. burn brightest 412:8
  out of the Grand Duke's w. 361:2
  set out to plant a w. 378:10
  springth the w. nu 4:25
  to fresh w.s, and pastures new 255:2
  to the rooky w. 334:17
  to the sleeping w.s all night 115:5
  when all the w.s are still 260:9
  when these w.s were young 395:7
  w.s are lovely, dark and deep 163:13
  w.s decay and fall 391:20
  w.s have no voice 266:10
  w.s shall to me answer 371:20
  w.s that wave o'er Delphi's steep 178:18
  w.s to echo ... charms of Amaryllis 405:25
Woodbine: over-canopied with luscious w. 340:10
  well-attired w. 254:33
Woodcock: springes to catch w.s 315:2
Woodman: spare, w., spare 96:8
Wood-note: his native w.-n.s wild 254:13
Woodshed: something nasty in the w. 167:20
Wooed: kindness of w. and wooer 276:20
  that would be w. and not unsought 258:11
  therefore may be w. 351 : 2
  therefore to be w. 325 : 9
  woman in this humour w. 346:25
  w., and married, and a' 300:6
Woof: weave the warp, and weave the w. 176:15
Wool: came for w. ... went home shorn 74:18
  go for w. and come back shorn 104:7
  have you any w.? 271:23
  place where de w. ought to grow 162:5
  to tease the housewife's w. 253:12
Woollen: odious! in w.! 287:17
  rather lie in the w. 341:9
Worching: w. and wandring 230:18
Word: be not the slave of W.s 99:17
  best w.s in the best order 117:1
  bethumped with w.s 328:25
  by water and the W. 376:16
  can man preach thy eternal w.? 188:12
  choose me, you English w.s 395:8
  darkeneth ... by w.s without knowledge 34:12
  discover the time of each w. 116:25
  every w. that proceedeth out of the mouth 32:7
  few of the unpleasantest w.s 338:13
  fierce and wild at every w. 187:24
  fine w.s butter no parsnips 307:1
  for teaching me that w. 338:23
  grief ... repeats his w.s 328:32
  have heard the Holy W. 60:6
  hear what comfortable w.s 291:32
  honour his own w. 384:9
  I said – I didn't mince my w.s 152:35
  idle w. that men shall speak 48:10
  in his mouth as household w.s 324:25
  in the beginning was the W. 51:15
  in the captain's but a choleric w. 336:17
  in the midst of the w. 102:12
  in two w.s 174:25
  in w. mightier than they 258:3
  intolerable wrestle with w.s 151:29
  is heard a discouraging w. 189:19

Word – *contd*

let thy w.s be few 41:7
long w.s Bother Me 252:6
many w.s to prove it wrong 206:19
matter decocted into a few w.s 164:15
much in few w.s 46:16
my w.s are my own 106:7
my w.s fly up 318:9
name is a dirty w. 275:23
one w. is too often profaned 363:21
one w. to me over the corn 266:15
perhaps we have not the w. 12:10
polite meaningless w.s 428:16
proper w.s in proper places 379:26
proud w. you never spoke 230:5
sad w.s of tongue or pen 415:21
scatter ... my w.s among mankind! 361:21
sincere milk of the w. 56:15
some with a flattering w. 416:6
spareth his w.s 39:37
speak that once familiar w. 25:8
suit ... the w. to the action 317:12
ten, low w.s oft creep 286:5
that I kept my w.', he said 131:21
threw w.s like stones 371:14
thy uncreating w. 284:22
thy w. is a lamp 38:7
time for such a w. 335:23
time lies in one little w.! 345:3
to neither a w. 166:8
torture one poor w. 148:12
very good w.s for the lips 135:26
wasn't the w.s 6:8
what is that w., honour? 322:1
wild and whirling w.s 315:26
winged w.s 192:25
w. and a blow 79:20 348:31
w., at random spoken 306:4
w. ... cannot be recalled 196:19
w. for w. without book 352:3
W. had breath, and wrought 385:19
w. of God is quick and powerful 55:36
w. or two before you go 344:16
w. spoken in due season 39:31
w. that teems with hidden meaning 170:10
w. ... to save the situation 171:8
w. wad ane o' them speak 20:16
w. which should never come out of a lady's lips 160:17
w.s a foot and a half long 195:22
w.s are like leaves 286:1
w.s are ... the most powerful drug 225:21
w.s are the W., and the W. is God 200:21
w.s are wise men's counters 190:8
w.s but wind 86:23
w.s could never utter 393:28
w.s may be false and full of art 308:26
w.s no virtue can digest 245:23
w.s of learned length 172:18
w.s of love then spoken 265:13
w.s of my mouth ... be acceptable 35:2
w.s of the wise are as goads 42:1
w.s only to conceal their thoughts 407:7
w.s ... smoother than butter 36:9
w.s ... so full of subtle flame 25:19
w.s without thoughts never to heaven go 318:9
w.s, w.s, mere w.s 351:31

Word – *contd*

w.s, w.s, w.s 316:6
young man hears the w.s I speak 135:9
you've spoken the foremost w. 20:17
Wordsworth: let simple W. chime 92:23
Work: all our w.s, begun 291:34
all their w.s ... to be seen 49:13
all ye W.s of the Lord 290:28
at her flowery w. 253:29
at his dirty w. again 285:8
breed one w. that wakes 195:10
devil and all his w.s 291:36
do no w. today 324:21
do the w. that's nearest 221:14
every man's w. ... manifest 53:24
faints the cold w. 117:15
for their w. continueth 224:15
full of good w.s 52:19
[God's] ordinary w.s convince it 18:3
hard and dirty w. for the rest 302:7
has plenty of w. to do 204:22
his w.s ... like a new edition 184:20
I like w. 204:25
I want w. 320:32
if any would not w. 55:19
it is warm w. 269:15
last and best of all God's w.s! 258:23
look on my w.s, ye mighty 362:1
man goeth forth to his w. 37:24
man's w. or his own gifts 260:1
no w., nor device ... in the grave 41:21
noblest w. of God 83:6 287:7
noblest w. of man 87:21 203:18
noblest w.s and foundations 17:14
nothing to do but w. 221:6
persistent w. triumphed 406:12
reward him according to his w.s 55:34
rich in good w.s 55:30
shall thy w. decay? 142:28
some w. of noble note 392:6
strive on to finish the w. 235:3
there's bread and w. for all 58:13
these are thy glorious w.s 257:33
these see the w.s of the Lord 37:28
when no man can w. 51:39
who first invented w. 228:8
who has found his w. 99:11
w. ... a portrait of himself 87:23
w. banishes ... three great evils 407:5
w. is the grand cure 99:13
w. of faith and labour of love 55:15
w. the day he was born 374:24
w.s of supererogation 292:20
Worker: men the w.s 387:15
w.s of the world, unite 247:16
Working: every man and woman will be w. 108:21
have another for w. days 341:14
Heaven will protect the W. Girl 368:5
Workman: w. that hath copies by 144:6
Workmanship: dark inscrutable w. 424:12
Workshop: art can only be learned in the w. 87:1
England ... w. of the world 140:7
World: about the pendant w. 336:23
all's right with the w. 75:16
all the sad w. needs 416:4
all the uses of this w. 314:11
all the w. is queer 276:15

World – *contd*
all the w.'s a stage 311:14
all this unintelligible w. 421:15
allured to brighter w.s 172:13
and yet abide the w.! 139:22
any way to perpetuate the w. 69:8
as much of life as the w. 210:21
being ere the w. was made 298:10
best of all possible w.s 94:18 407:1
bestride the narrow w. 326:23
better the w. with a blow 248:2
better w. than this 310:22
both w.s at once they view 408:6
brought nothing into this w. 55:27
by the w. forgot 284:35
Caesar might have stood against the w. 327:30
can dominate the w. 417:36
daffed the w. aside 321:30
dark as the w. of man 367:10
do to spite the w. 334:9
estate of the w. 335:24
esteems that busy w. an idler 125:8
exhausted w.s, and then imagined new 205:17
fair volume which we w. do name 146:13
fled from this vile w. 355:27
for whom the outside w. exists 165:14
force of the wicked w. 221:22
free, the w. before me 415:18
freedom ... everywhere in the w. 299:10
get the start of the majestic w. 326:22
girdled with the gleaming w. 388:4
God so loved the w. 51:26
half of the w. cannot understand 15:4
hand that rules the w. 408:2
have a w. to gain 247:16
have not loved the w. 89:10
heard the w. around 255:7
hold the w. but as the w. 337:4
hope the w. can show 143:25
how the w. wags 311:6
I am a little w. 142:29
I am this w., and I eat this w. 402:1
if all the w. were paper 5:6
if he shall gain the whole w. 48:29 50:2
in a w. I never made 199:3
in faith and hope the w. 287:4
in the morning of the w. 75:18
in this harsh w. 320:3
in w.s not realised 423:19
into the dangerous w. 60:12
into this breathing w. 346:21
it's a jolly strange w. 29:3
laid the w. away 67:2
leaves the w. to darkness 176:21
let loose upon the w. with £300 24:6
let the great w. spin for ever 387:26
let the w. go its own way 139:25
let the w. sink 188:13
let the w. slide 189:14
look round the habitable w.! 148:26
mad w., my masters 65:9 382:19
make a hell of this w. 26:17
makes the whole w. kin 351:25
makes the w. go round 7:22
man adapts himself to the w. 358:10
mighty w. of eye, and ear 421:22
more w.s than I can lose 148:31

World – *contd*
my credit in this w. 159:18
never enjoy the w. aright 399:8
no w. but mass of public wrongs 226:1
noisy w. hears least 420:19
O brave new w. 350:26
O w. invisible, we view thee 395:19
O w.! O life! O time 360:21
on the passing w. to turn 205:20
one loves His w. so much 75:17
one to face the w. with 74:31
other w.s, and other seas 246:26
pass through this w. but once 179:7
places to learn the w. in 108:26
pleased with ... the w. at large 202:11
point of the turning w. 151:27
reconverted to the w. 420:22
ringed with the azure w. 383:24
roll of the w. eastward 182:23
same the whole w. over 8:8
search well another w. 403:1
seek the empty w. again 66:24
service of the antique w. 310:32
shakers of the w. forever 275:28
shines a good deed in a naughty w. 339:4
so long as the w. contains us both 73:31
so many w.s, so much to do 385:34
so runs the w. away 317:26
some say the w. will end in fire 163:9
take note, take note, O w.! 343:34
ten to the w. allot 211:13
there never was a merry w. 308:8
they did in the golden w. 310:15
they only saved the w. 28:8
this dark w. and wide 259:32
this fals w. is but transitory 150:1
this little w. 345:8
this the w. well knows 356:29
this working day w. 310:23
this w. passeth away 53:31
this w. surely is wide enough 374:17
this w. uncertain is 268:29
though the w. be a-waning 266:10
three corners of the w. in arms 329:11
throughout the sensual w. 265:16
to become fit for this w. 218:23
turn your back upon the w. 236:27
untravelled w. whose margin fades 392:2
upon the rack of this tough w. 331:6
vanity of this wicked w. 291:38
verdict of the w. is final 14:16
voice of the w. 69:7
wandering between two w.s 10:25
way the w. ends 152:9
we, who are men of the w. 139:2
what is this w.? what asketh men 107:25
when all the w. dissolves 245:5
when all the w. is young 221:18
where in this small-talking w. 163:23
while ago the w. begun 353:19
whole w. in the face 237:18
whole w. turn to coal 188:11
wilderness of this w. 79:10
with how little wisdom the w. 277:1
w. ... a large prison 295:12
w. ... a school of inquiry 263:23
w. and all her train 403:6

Wrath – *contd*
I fly infinite w. 257:6
nursing her w. 84:13
slow to speak, slow to w. 56:6
sun go down upon your w. 54:46
throw away thy w. 187:25
told my w., my w. did end 60:14
Wreath: subtle w. of hair 142:22
Wreck: king my brother's w. 153:1
with sunken w. 323:25
w.s of a dissolving dream 360:7
Wren: hurt the little w. 58:23
I bore this w. 148:32
robin redbreast and the w. 412:10
Sir Christopher W. said, 'I am going to dine 29:13
w. goes to't, and the small gilded fly 330:23
Wrestle: he that w.s with us 81:18
intolerable w. with words 151:29
w. not against flesh and blood 55:3
Wrestling: I wretch lay w. 194:14
Wretch: excellent w.! 343:21
hailed the w. who won 89:22
hollow-eyed, sharp-looking w. 312:26
maketh w. or happy, rich or poor 372:9
pulled the poor w. 319:12
such a destined w. as I 122:1
w. who supports with insolence 206:3
Wretched: skilled to raise the w. 172:10
w. he forsakes 430:7
Wring: soon w. their hands 408:18
Wrinkle: no w. on thine azure brow 89:29
stamps the w. deeper 88:25
which w.s will devour 268:30
Writ: old ends stol'n forth of holy w. 346:27
Write: able neither to read nor w. 185:11
contrive to w. so even 15:19
enraged I w. I know not how 179:9
look in thy heart and w. 366:5
man may w. at any time 207:3
much as a man ought to w. 399:19
only a little more I have to w. 188:22
w. and read comes by nature 341:24
w. apace, read somewhat seldomer 71:6
w. well hereafter in laudable things 260:11
you w. with ease 365:29
Writer: original w. is not one who imitates nobody 106:14
talent alone cannot make a w. 155:10
w.s become more numerous 173:19
Writhe: ghastly w. from the waist 134:22
Writhing: reeling and w., of course 100:25
Writing: incurable itch for w. 214:3
this or that in his w. 87:10
true ease in w. 286:7
way of w. without thinking 144:13
w. . . . a different name for conversation 374:16
w. an exact man 19:3
w. increaseth rage 179:9
w. on what pleased me best 184:23
Written: what I have w. I have w. 52:7
w. out of reputation 29:15
Wroghte: first he w. 107:13
Wrong: all his life . . . in the w. 298:7
always in the w. 147:1
but he done her w. 7:6
called them by w. names 71:10

Wrong – *contd*
cuts the w. man's head off 138:12
divinely in the w. 430:4
do a little w. 338:18
endless labour to be w. 210:26
feel that I must be w. 417:29
feel that something has gone w. 290:3
kings to govern w. 284:17
mass of public w.s 226:1
my love, ye do me w. 7:9
never dreamed . . . w. would triumph 72:23
no sense of w.s can rouse 97:12
not that you do w. by design 213:9
one idea, and that is a w. one 208:22
one w. more to man 74:3
oppressor's w. 316:29
redressing human w.s 384:9
right w., follow the King 384:6
should suffer w. no more 241:4
telling a man he was w. 113:24
wail, for the world's w.! 359:25
where is the w. I did them? 74:18
who have done the w. 149:6
w. extenuates not w. 351:15
w. from the start 290:12
w. left unredressed on earth 222:6
w. to sing so wildly 385:30
w. us, shall we not revenge? 338:5
w.s darker than death or night 363:1
Wrote: ever w. except for money 209:12
sorry now I w. it 80:3
Wroth: w. with one we love 115:20
Wynken: W., Blynken and Nod 157:14

X

Xanadu: in X. did Kubla Khan 115:31

Y

Yale: Y. College and my Harvard 249:12
Yankee: Y. Doodle came to town 22:2
Yard: y. was as long 217:15
Yarn: of a mingled y. 309:9
y. from a laughing fellow-rover 248:7
Yasmin: toward thy bed, Y. 160:8
Yawp: I sound my barbaric y. 415:17
Yë: slepen at the nyght with open y. 106:18
Yea: everlasting Y. 99:21
in russet y.s 331:28
let your y. be y. 56:13
Year: ah! happy y.s 88:21
all the season of the golden y. 383:34
another y.! – another deadly blow! 423:1
before the mellowing y. 254:17
crownest the y. with thy goodness 36:20
cuts off twenty y.s of life 327:18
declined into the vale of y.s 343:26
ever the knightly y.s were gone 186:21
few more y.s shall roll 63:14
fourteen hundred y.s ago 320:7
gave up the y.s to be 67:2